COLLINS

SPANISH★ENGLISH
ENGLISH★SPANISH
DICTIONARY

MIKE GONZALEZ

BERKLEY BOOKS, NEW YORK

General Editor
R. H. Thomas

The text of this dictionary has been
adapted from the Collins Gem
Spanish-English, English-Spanish
Dictionary

First published in this edition 1982

Contributors
Margaret Tejerizo, John Forry,
Carmen Billinghurst, Liam Kane, Pat Freehan

Editorial Staff
Irene Lakhani

This Berkley book contains the complete
text of the original edition.
It has been completely reset in a typeface
designed for easy reading and was printed
from new film.

COLLINS SPANISH/ENGLISH · ENGLISH/SPANISH
DICTIONARY

A Berkley Book / published by arrangement with
Collins Publishers

PRINTING HISTORY
Collins Gem edition published 1982
Berkley edition / August 1982

ISBN: 0-425-08008-0

A BERKLEY BOOK ® TM 757,375
Berkley Books are published by The Berkley Publishing Group,
200 Madison Avenue, New York, NY 10016.
The name "BERKLEY" and the "B" logo
are trademarks belonging to Berkley Publishing Corporation.

PRINTED IN THE UNITED STATES OF AMERICA

20 19 18

INTRODUCCIÓN

INTRODUCTION

Quien desee leer y entender el inglés encontrará en este diccionario un extenso léxico moderno que abarca una amplia gama de locuciones de uso corriente. Igualmente encontrará, en su debido orden alfabético, las abreviaturas, las siglas, los nombres geográficos más conocidos y, además, las principales formas de verbo irregulares, donde se le referirá a las respectivas formas de base, hallándose allí la traducción.

Quien aspire comunicarse y expresarse en lengua extranjera, hallará aquí una clara y detallada explicación de las palabras básicas, empleándose un sistema de indicadores que le remitirán a la traducción más apta y le señalarán su correcto uso.

The user whose aim is to read and understand Spanish will find a comprehensive and up-to-date wordlist including numerous phrases in current use. He will also find listed alphabetically the main irregular forms with a cross-reference to the basic form where a translation is given, as well as some of the most common abbreviations, acronyms and geographical names.

The user who wishes to communicate and to express himself in the foreign language will find clear and detailed treatment of all the basic words, with numerous indicators pointing to the appropriate translation, and helping him to use it correctly.

ABREVIATURAS		ABBREVIATIONS
adjetivo, locución adjetivo	a	adjective, adjectival phrase
abreviatura	ab(b)r	abbreviation
adverbio, locución adverbial	ad	adverb, adverbial phrase
administración, lengua administrativa	ADMIN	administration
agricultura	AGR	agriculture
América Latina	AM	Latin America
anatomía	ANAT	anatomy
arquitectura	ARQ, ARCH	architecture
astrología, astronomía	ASTRO	astrology, astronomy
el automóvil	AUT(O)	the motor car and motoring
aviación, viajes aéreos	AVIAT	flying, air travel
biología	BIO(L)	biology
botánica, flores	BOT	botany
inglés británico	Brit	British English
química	CHEM	chemistry
conjunción	conj	conjunction
lengua familiar	col	colloquial usage
comercio, finanzas, banca	COM(M)	commerce, finance, banking
construcción	CONSTR	building
compuesto	cpd	compound element
cocina	CULIN	cookery
determinante, articulo	det	determiner, article
economía	ECON	economics
electricidad, electrónica	ELEC	electricity, electronics
enseñanza, sistema escolar y universitario	ESCOL	schooling, schools and universities
especialmente	esp	especially
exclamación, interjección	excl	exclamation, interjection
feminino	f	feminine
lengua familiar	fam	colloquial usage
ferrocarril	FERRO	railways
uso figurado	fig	figurative use
fotografia	FOTO	photography
(verbo inglés) del cual la particula es inseparable	fus	(phrasal verb) where the particle is inseparable
generalmente	gen	generally
geografía, geología	GEO	geography, geology
geometría	GEOM	geometry
invariable	inv	invariable
irregular	irg	irregular
lo jurídico	JUR	law
gramática, lingüística	LING	grammar, linguistics
masculino	m	masculine

matemáticas	MAT(H)	mathematics
medicina	MED	medical term, medicine
masculino/feminino	m/f	masculine/feminine
lo militar, ejército	MIL	military matters
música	MUS	music
sustantivo, nombre	n	noun
navegación, náutica	NAUT	sailing, navigation
sustantivo numérico	num	numeral noun
complemento	obj	(grammatical) object
	o.s.	oneself
peyorativo	pey, pej	derogatory, pejorative
fotografía	PHOT	photography
fisiología	PHYSIOL	physiology
plural	pl	plural
política	POL	politics
participio de pasado	pp	past participle
prefijo	pref	prefix
preposición	prep	preposition
pronombre	pron	pronoun
psicología, psiquiatría	PSICO, PSYCH	psychology, psychiatry
tiempo pasado	pt	past tense
sustantivo no empleado en el plural	q	collective (uncountable) noun, not used in plural
ferrocarril	RAIL	railways
religión, lo eclesiástico	REL	religion, church service
	sb	somebody
escolar, universitario	SCOL	schools, universities
singular	sg	singular
	sth	something
sujeto	su(b)j	(grammatical) subject
sufijo	suff	suffix
tauromaquia	TAUR	bullfighting
técnica, tecnología	TEC(H)	technical term, technology
telecomunicaciones	TELEC, TEL	telecommunications
televisión	TV	television
imprenta, tipografía	TYP	typography, printing
inglés norteamericano	US	American English
verbo	vb	verb
verbo intransitivo	vi	intransitive verb
verbo pronominal	vr	reflexive verb
verbo transitivo	vt	transitive verb
zoología, animales	ZOOL	zoology
marca registrada	®	registered trademark
indica un equivalente cultural	≈	introduces a cultural equivalent

SPANISH PRONUNCIATION

Consonants

c	[k]	caja	c before *a*, *o* or *u* is pronounced as in *c*at
ce, ci	[θe, θi]	cero cielo	c before *e* or *i* is pronounced as in *th*in
ch	[tʃ]	chiste	ch is pronounced as *ch* in *ch*air
d	[d, ð]	danés ciudad	at the beginning of a phrase or after *l* or *n*, d is pronounced as in English. In any other position it is pronounced like *th* in *th*e
g	[g, ɤ]	gafas paga	g before *a*, *o* or *u* is pronounced as in *g*ap, if at the beginning of a phrase or after *n*. In other positions the sound is softened
ge, gi	[xe, xi]	gente girar	g before *e* or *i* is pronounced similar to *ch* in Scottish lo*ch*
h		haber	h is always silent in Spanish
j	[x]	jugar	j is pronounced similar to *ch* in Scottish lo*ch*
ll	[ʎ]	talle	ll is pronounced like the *lli* in mi*lli*on
ñ	[ɲ]	niño	ñ is pronounced like the *ni* in o*ni*on
q	[k]	que	q is pronounced as *k* in *k*ing
r, rr	[r, rr]	quitar garra	r is always pronounced in Spanish, unlike the silent *r* in dance*r*. rr is trilled, like a Scottish *r*
s	[s]	quizás isla	s is usually pronounced as in pa*s*s, but before *b*, *d*, *g*, *l*, *m* or *n* it is pronounced as in ro*s*e
v	[b, ß]	vía dividir	v is pronounced something like *b*. At the beginning of a phrase or after *m* or *n* it is pronounced as *b* in *b*oy. In any other position the sound is softened
z	[θ]	tenaz	z is pronounced as *th* in *th*in

b, f, k, l, m, n, p, t and x are pronounced as in English.

Vowels

[a]	p*a*ta	not as long as *a* in f*a*r. When followed by a consonant in the same syllable (i.e. in a closed syllable), as in am*a*nte, the *a* is short, as in b*a*t
[e]	m*e*	like *e* in th*ey*. In a closed syllable, as in g*e*nte, the *e* is short as in p*e*t
[i:]	p*i*no	as in m*ea*n or mach*i*ne
[o]	l*o*	as in l*o*cal. In a closed syllable, as in c*o*ntrol, the *o* is short as in c*o*t
[u:]	l*u*nes	as in r*u*le. It is silent after *q*, and in *gue*, *gui*, unless marked *güe*, *güi* e.g. antig*üe*dad

Diphthongs

ai, ay	b*ai*le	as *i* in r*i*de
au	*au*to	as *ou* in sh*ou*t
ei, ey	bu*ey*	as *ey* in gr*ey*
eu	d*eu*da	both elements pronounced independently [e] + [u:]
oi, oy	h*oy*	as *oy* in t*oy*

Stress

The rules of stress in Spanish are as follows:
(a) when a word ends in a vowel or in *n* or *s*, the second last syllable is stressed: pat*a*ta, pat*a*tas, c*o*me, c*o*men
(b) when a word ends in a consonant other than *n* or *s*, the stress falls on the last syllable: par*e*d, habl*a*r
(c) when the rules set out in a and b are not applied, an acute accent appears over the stressed vowel: com*ú*n, geograf*í*a, ingl*é*s

In the phonetic transcription, the symbol ['] precedes the syllable on which the stress falls.

PRONUNCIACIÓN INGLESA

Vocales y diptongos

	Ejemplo inglés	*Ejemplo español/explicación*
ɑ:	f*a*ther	Entre *a* de p*a*dre y *o* de n*o*che
ʌ	b*u*t, c*o*me	*a* muy breve
æ	m*a*n, c*a*t	Se mantienen los labios en la posición de *e* en p*e*na y luego se pronuncia el sonido *a*
ə	f*a*ther, *a*go	Sonido indistinto parecido a una *e* u *o* casi mudas
ɔ:	b*i*rd, h*ea*rd	Entre *e* abierta, y *o* cerrada, sonido alargado
ɛ	g*e*t, b*e*d	como en p*e*rro
ɪ	*i*t, b*i*g	Más breve que en s*i*
i:	t*ea*, s*ee*	Como en f*i*no
ɔ	h*o*t, w*a*sh	Como en t*o*rre
ɔ:	s*a*w, *a*ll	Como en p*o*r
u	p*u*t, b*oo*k	Sonido breve, más cerrado que en b*u*rro
u:	t*oo*, y*ou*	Sonido largo, como en *u*no
aɪ	fl*y*, h*i*gh	Como en fr*ai*le
au	h*ow*, h*ou*se	Como en p*au*sa
ɛə	th*ere*, b*ear*	Casi como en v*ea*, pero el sonido *a* se mezcla con el indistinto [ə]
eɪ	d*ay*, ob*ey*	*e* cerrada seguida por una *i* débil
ɪə	h*ere*, h*ear*	Como en man*ía*, mezclándose el sonido *a* con el indistinto [ə]
əu	g*o*, n*o*te	[ə] seguido por una breve *u*
ɔɪ	b*oy*, *oi*l	Como en v*oy*
uə	p*oor*, s*ure*	*u* bastante larga más el sonido indistinto [ə]

Consonantes

	Ejemplo inglés	Ejemplo español/explicación
d	mended	Como en conde, andar
g	go, get, big	Como en grande, gol
dʒ	gin, judge	Como en la ll andaluza y en Generalitat (catalán)
ŋ	sing	Como en vínculo
h	house, he	Como la jota hispanoamericana
j	young, yes	Como en ya
k	come, mock	Como en caña, Escocia
r	red, tread	Se pronuncia con la punta de la lengua hacia atrás y sin hacerla vibrar
s	sand, yes	Como en casa, sesión
z	rose, zebra	Como en desde, mismo
ʃ	she, machine	Como en chambre (francés), roxo (portugués)
tʃ	chin, rich	Como en chocolate
v	valley	Como en f, pero se retiran los dientes superiores vibrándolos contra el labio inferior
w	water, which	Como en la u de huevo, puede
ʒ	vision	Como en journal (francés)
θ	think, myth	Como en receta, zapato
ð	this, the	Como en la d de hablado, verdad

b, p, f, m, n, l, t iguales que en español

El signo * indica que la r final escrita apenas se pronuncia en inglés británico cuando la palabra siguiente empieza con vocal. El signo ['] indica la sílaba acentuada.

ESPAÑOL - INGLÉS
SPANISH - ENGLISH

A

a [a] *prep* (*a + el = al*) (*lugar*) at, in, on; (*dirección*) to; (*destino*) to, towards; (*tiempo*) at; ~ **la derecha/ izquierda** on the right/left; **al lado de** beside, at the side of; **subir** ~ **un avión/tren** to get on or board a plane/train; **hablar** ~ **larga distancia** to speak long distance; ~ **las cuatro** at four o'clock; ¿~ **qué hora?** at what time?; ~ **los 30 años** at 30 years of age; **al día siguiente** the next day; ~ **eso de las cuatro** at about four o'clock; **al poco tiempo** a short time later; **al verlo yo** when I saw it; (*manera*): **hacerlo** ~ **la fuerza** to do it by force; **ir** ~ **caballo/pie** to go on horseback/foot; (*evaluación*): **poco** ~ **poco** little by little; **de dos** ~ **tres** from two to three; **ocho horas al día** eight hours a or per day; ~ **50 ptas el kilo** 50 pesetas a kilo; (*con verbo*): **empezó** ~ **llover** it started raining; **enseñar** ~ **leer** to teach to read; **voy** ~ **llevarlo** I am going to carry it; (*complemento de objeto*): **quiero** ~ **mis padres** (*not translated*) I love my parents; (*complemento circunstancial*): **cercano** ~ near (to); **por miedo** ~ out of fear of; (*frases elípticas*): ~ **comer!** let's eat!; ¿~ **qué viene eso?** what's the meaning of this?; ~ **ver** let's see.

abacero, a [aβa'θero, a] *nm/f* grocer.

abad, esa [a'βað, 'θesa] *nm/f* abbot/abbess; ~**ía** *nf* abbey.

abajo [a'βaxo] *ad* (*situación*) down, below, underneath; (*en casa*) downstairs; (*dirección*) down, downwards; ~ **de** *prep* below, under; **el piso de** ~ the downstairs flat; **la parte de** ~ the lower part; ¡~ **el gobierno!** down with the government!; **cuesta/río** ~ downhill/downstream; **de arriba** ~ from top to bottom; **el** ~ **firmante** the undersigned; **más** ~ lower or further down; **echar** ~ to bring down.

abalanzar [aβalan'θar] *vt* to weigh; (*equilibrar*) to balance; (*arrojar*) to hurl; ~**se** *vr*: ~**se sobre** o **contra** to throw o.s. at.

abandonado, a [aβando'naðo, a] *a* derelict; (*desatendido*) abandoned; (*desierto*) deserted; (*descuidado*) neglected.

abandonar [aβando'nar] *vt* (*dejar*) to leave, abandon, desert; (*descuidar*) to neglect; (*ceder, dejar de*) to give up; ~**se** *vr*: ~**se a** to abandon o.s. to.

abandono [aβan'dono] *nm* (*acto*) desertion, abandonment; (*estado*)

abandon, neglect; (*renuncia*) withdrawal, retirement; **perdió por** ~ he lost by default.

abanicar [aβani'kar] *vt* to fan; **abanico** *nm* fan; (*NAUT*) derrick.

abaratar [aβara'tar] *vt* to lower (the price of) // *vi*, ~**se** *vr* to go or come down in price.

abarcar [aβar'kar] *vt* to include, embrace; (*AM*) to monopolize.

abarrotar [aβarro'tar] *vt* to bar; (*NAUT*) to stow; (*fig*) to overstock.

abarrote [aβa'rrote] *nm* packing; ~**s** *nmpl* (*AM*) groceries, provisions; ~**ro, a** *nm/f* (*AM*) grocer.

abastecer [aβaste'θer] *vt* to supply; **abastecimiento** *nm* supply; (*suministrar*) supplying.

abasto [a'βasto] *nm* supply; (*abundancia*) abundance; **dar** ~ **con** to manage to finish.

abatido, a [aβa'tiðo, a] *a* dejected, downcast.

abatimiento [aβati'mjento] *nm* (*acto*) demolition; (*moral*) dejection, depression.

abatir [aβa'tir] *vt* (*muro*) to demolish; (*pájaro*) to shoot, bring down; (*fig*) to depress; (*humillar*) to humiliate // *vi* to go off course; ~**se** *vr* to be depressed; ~**se sobre** to swoop or pounce on.

abdicación [aβðika'θjon] *nf* abdication; **abdicar** *vi* to abdicate.

abdomen [aβ'ðomen] *nm* abdomen.

abecedario [aβeθe'ðarjo] *nm* alphabet; (*libro*) spelling book.

abedul [aβe'ðul] *nm* birch.

abeja [a'βexa] *nf* bee.

aberración [aβerra'θjon] *nf* aberration.

abertura [aβer'tura] *nf* opening, gap; (*fig*) openness.

abeto [a'βeto] *nm* fir.

abierto, a [a'βjerto, a] *pp de* **abrir** // *a* open; (*AM*) generous.

abigarrado, a [aβiɣa'rraðo, a] *a* multi-coloured.

abismar [aβis'mar] *vt* to humble, cast down; ~**se** *vr* to sink; ~**se en** (*fig*) to be plunged into.

abismo [a'βismo] *nm* abyss.

abjurar [aβxu'rar] *vt*, *vi* to abjure, forswear.

ablandar [aβlan'dar] *vt* to soften up; (*AUTO*) to run in // *vi*, ~**se** *vr* to grow softer.

ablución [aβlu'θjon] *nf* ablution.

abnegación [aβneɣa'θjon] *nf* self-denial; **abnegarse** *vr* to act unselfishly.

abobado, a [aβo'βaðo, a] *a* silly.

abobar [aβo'βar] *vt* to daze.

abocar [aβo'kar] *vt* to seize in one's mouth; ~**se** *vr* to approach.

abochornar [aβotʃor'nar] *vt* to embarrass; ~**se** *vr* to get flustered; (*BOT*) to wilt.

abofetear [aβofete'ar] *vt* to slap (in the face).

abogacía [aβoɣa'θia] *nf* legal profession; (*ejercicio*) practice of the law; **abogado** *nm* lawyer.

abogar [aβo'ɣar] *vi*: ~ **por** to plead for; (*fig*) to advocate.

abolengo [aβo'lengo] *nm* ancestry, lineage.

abolición [aβoli'θjon] *nf* abolition.

abolir [aβo'lir] *vt* to abolish; (*cancelar*) to cancel.

abolladura [aβoʎa'ðura] *nf* dent; (*chichón, choque*) bump; **abollar** *vt* to dent; to raise a bump on.

abominación [aβomina'θjon] *nf* abomination.

abonado, a [aβo'naðo, a] *a* (*deuda*) paid // *nm/f* subscriber.

abonar [aβo'nar] *vt* (*deuda*) to settle; (*terreno*) to fertilize; (*idea*) to endorse; ~**se** *vr* to subscribe; **abono** *nm* payment; fertilizer; subscription.

abordar [aβor'ðar] *vt* to board; (*fig*) to broach.

aborigen [aβo'rixen] *nm* aborigine.

aborrecer [aβorre'θer] *vt* to hate, loathe; **aborrecible** *a* hateful, loathsome.

abortar [aβor'tar] *vi* (*malparir*) to have a miscarriage; (*deliberadamente*) to have an abortion; **hacerse** ~ to have an abortion; **aborto** *nm* miscarriage; abortion.

abotonar [aβoto'nar] *vt* to button (up), do up // *vi* to bud.

abovedado, a [aβoβe'ðaðo, a] *a* vaulted, domed.

abrasar [aβra'sar] *vt* to burn (up); (*AGR*) to dry up, parch.

abrazar [aβra'θar] *vt* to embrace.

abrazo [a'βraθo] *nm* embrace, hug; **un** ~ (*en carta*) with best wishes.

abrelatas [aβre'latas] *nm inv* tin opener.

abreviar [aβre'βjar] *vt* to abbreviate; (*texto*) to abridge; (*plazo*) to reduce; **abreviatura** *nf* abbreviation.

abrigar [aβri'ɣar] *vt* (*proteger*) to shelter; (*suj: ropa*) to keep warm; (*fig*) to cherish; **abrigo** *nm* shelter; (*apoyo*) support; (*prenda*) coat, overcoat.

abril [a'βril] *nm* April.

abrir [a'βrir] *vt* to open (up) // *vi* to open; ~**se** *vr* to open (up); (*extenderse*) to open out; (*cielo*) to clear; ~**se paso** to find *or* force a way through.

abrochar [aβro'tʃar] *vt* (*vestido*) to button (up); (*AM*) to staple; (*zapato*) to buckle; (*atar*) to lace up.

abrumar [aβru'mar] *vt* to overwhelm; (*sobrecargar*) to weigh down; (*agotar*) to wear out; ~ **se** *vr* to become foggy.

abrupto, a [a'βrupto, a] *a* abrupt; (*empinado*) steep.

absceso [aβs'θeso] *nm* abscess.

absolución [aβsolu'θjon] *nf* (*REL*) absolution; (*JUR*) pardon; (: *de acusado*) acquittal.

absoluto, a [aβso'luto, a] *a* absolute; **en** ~ *ad* in no way, not at all.

absolver [aβsol'βer] *vt* to absolve; (*JUR*) to pardon; (: *acusado*) to acquit.

absorber [aβsor'βer] *vt* to absorb; (*embeber*) to soak up.

absorción [aβsor'θjon] *nf* absorption.

absorto, a [aβ'sorto, a] *pp de* **absorber** // *a* absorbed, engrossed.

abstemio, a [aβs'temjo, a] *a* teetotal.

abstención [aβsten'θjon] *nf* abstention; **abstenerse** *vr*: **abstenerse de** to abstain *or* refrain from.

abstinencia [aβsti'nenθja] *nf* abstinence; (*ayuno*) fasting.

abstracción [aβstrak'θjon] *nf* abstraction; (*despiste*) absent-mindedness; ~ **hecha de** leaving aside.

abstraer [aβstra'er] *vt* to abstract // *vi*: ~ **de** to leave aside; ~**se** *vr* to be/become absorbed.

abstraído, a [aβstra'iðo, a] *a* preoccupied; (*despistado*) absent-minded.

absuelto [aβ'swelto] *pp de* **absolver**.

absurdo, a [aβ'surðo, a] *a* absurd.

abuelo, a [a'βwelo, a] *nm/f* grandfather/mother.

abulia [a'βulja] *nf* spinelessness, weakness.

abultado, a [aβul'taðo, a] *a* bulky.

abultar [aβul'tar] *vt* to enlarge; (*aumentar*) to increase; (*fig*) to exaggerate // *vi* to be bulky.

abundancia [aβun'danθja] *nf* abundance, plenty; **abundante** *a* abundant, plentiful; **abundar** *vi* to abound, be plentiful.

aburrido, a [aβu'rriðo, a] *a* (*hastiado*) bored; (*que aburre*) boring; **aburrimiento** *nm* boredom, tedium; **aburrir** *vt* to bore; **aburrirse** *vr* to be bored, get bored.

abusar [aβu'sar] *vi* to go too far; ~ **de** to abuse; **abuso** *nm* imposition; abuse.

abyecto, a [aβ'jekto, a] *a* wretched, abject.

A.C. *abr de* **Año de Cristo** A.D. (Anno Domini).

a/c *abr de* al **cuidado de** c/o (care of).

acá [a'ka] *ad* (*lugar*) here; (*tiempo*) now.

acabado, a [aka'βaðo, a] *a* finished, complete; (*perfecto*) perfect; (*agotado*) worn out; (*fig*) masterly // *nm* finish.

acabar [aka'βar] *vt* (*llevar a su fin*) to finish, complete; (*llegar al final de*) to finish, conclude; (*perfeccionar*) to complete; (*consumir*) to use up; (*rematar*) to finish off // *vi* to finish, end, come to an end; ~ **con** to put an end to; ~ **de llegar** to have just arrived; ~ **por** to end (up) by; ~**se** *vr* to finish, stop; (*terminarse*) to be over; (*agotarse*) to run out; **¡se acabó!** that's enough!; it's all over!

academia [aka'ðemja] *nf* academy; **académico, a** *a* academic.

acaecer [akae'θer] *vi* to happen, occur; **acaecimiento** *nm* occurrence, happening.

acalorar [akalo'rar] *vt* to heat; (*fig*) to inflame; ~**se** *vr* (*fig*) to get heated.

acampar [akam'par] *vi* to camp.

acanalar [akana'lar] *vt* to groove; (*ondular*) to corrugate.

acantilado, a [akanti'laðo, a] *a* steep sheer // *nm* cliff.

acaparar [akapa'rar] *vt* to monopolize; (*acumular*) to hoard.

acariciar [akari'θjar] *vt* to caress; (*fig*) to cherish.

acarrear [akarre'ar] *vt* to transport; (*fig*) to cause, result in; **acarreo** *nm* transport, haulage; (*precio*) carriage.

acaso [a'kaso] *ad* perhaps, maybe // *nm* chance; **por si** ~ just in case; **si** ~ **n** case; **al** ~ at random.

acatamiento [akata'mjento] *nm* respect; (*reverencia*) reverence; (*deferencia*) deference; **acatar** *vt* to respect; to revere; (*obedecer*) to obey.

acatarrarse [akata'rrarse] *vr* to catch a cold.

acaudalado, a [akauða'laðo, a] *a* well-off; **acaudalar** *vt* to accumulate.

acaudillar [akauði'ʎar] *vt* to lead, command.

acceder [akθe'ðer] *vi* to accede, agree.

accesible [akθe'siβle] *a* accessible.

acceso [ak'θeso] *nm* access, entry; (*camino*) access road; (*MED*) attack, fit.

accesorio, a [akθe'sorjo, a] *a, nm* accessory.

accidentado, a [akθiðen'taðo, a] *a* uneven; (*áspero*) rough; (*montañoso*) hilly; (*azaroso*) eventful // *nm/f* injured person.

accidental [akθiðen'tal] *a* accidental; **accidentarse** *vr* to have an accident.

accidente [akθi'ðente] *nm* accident; (*MED*) faint; ~**s** *nmpl* unevenness *sg*, roughness *sg*.

acción [ak'θjon] *nf* action; (*acto*) action, act, deed; (*COM*) share; (*JUR*) action, lawsuit; ~ **ordinaria/preferente** ordinary/preference share; **accionar** *vt* to work, operate // *vi* to gesticulate.

accionista [akθjo'nista] *nm/f* shareholder.

acebo [a'θeβo] *nm* holly; (*árbol*) holly tree.

acechanza [aθe'tʃanθa] *nf* = **acecho**.

acechar [aθe'tʃar] *vt* to spy on; (*aguardar*) to lie in wait for; **acecho** *nm* spying, watching; ambush.

acedía [aθe'ðia] *nf* acidity; (*MED*) heartburn; (*fig*) sourness.

aceitar [aθei'tar] *vt* to oil, lubricate; **aceite** *nm* oil; (*de oliva*) olive oil; **aceitera** *nf* oilcan; **aceitoso, a** *a* oily.

aceituna [aθei'tuna] *nf* olive.

acelerar [aθele'rar] *vt* to accelerate.

acento [a'θento] *nm* accent; (*acentuación*) stress; **acentuar** *vt* to accent; to stress; (*fig*) to accentuate.

acepción [aθep'θjon] *nf* meaning; (*preferencia*) preference.

acepillar [aθepi'ʎar] *vt* to brush; (*alisar*) to plane.

aceptación [aθepta'θjon] *nf* acceptance; (*aprobación*) approval; **aceptar** *vt* to accept; to approve.

acequia [a'θekja] *nf* irrigation ditch.

acera [a'θera] *nf* pavement.

acerado, a [aθe'raðo, a] *a* steel; (*afilado*) sharp, (*fig: duro*) steely; (*mordaz*) biting.

acerbo, a [a'θerβo, a] *a* bitter; (*fig*) harsh.

acerca [a'θerka] ~ **de** *ad* about, concerning.

acercar [aθer'kar] *vt* to bring *or* move nearer; ~**se** *vr* to approach, come near.

acero [a'θero] *nm* steel.

acérrimo, a [a'θerrimo, a] *a* out-and-out, staunch.

acertado, a [aθer'taðo, a] *a* correct; (*apropiado*) apt; (*sensato*) sensible.

acertar [aθer'tar] *vt* (*dar en: el blanco*) to hit; (*llegar a encontrar*) to get right; (*adivinar*) to guess; (*alcanzar*) to achieve // *vi* to get it right, be right; ~ **a** to manage to; ~ **con** to happen on.

acertijo [aθer'tixo] *nm* riddle, puzzle.

acervo [a'θerβo] *nm* heap; ~ **común** undivided estate.

acicalar [aθika'lar] *vt* to polish; (*adornar*) to bedeck; ~**se** *vr* to smarten o.s. up.

acicate [aθi'kate] *nm* spur.

acidez [aθi'ðeθ] *nf* acidity

ácido, a [a'θiðo, a] *a* sour, acid // *nm* acid.

acierto [a'θjerto] *nm* success; (*buen paso*) wise move; (*solución*) solution; (*habilidad*) skill, ability.

aclamación [aklama'θjon] *nf* acclamation; (*aplausos*) applause; **aclamar** *vt* to acclaim; to applaud.

aclaración [aklara'θjon] *nf* rinsing, rinse; (*clasificación*) classification.

aclarar [akla'rar] *vt* to clarify, explain; (*ropa*) to rinse // *vi* to clear up; ~**se** *vr* ~ **se la garganta** to clear one's throat.

aclimatación [aklimata'θjon] *nf* acclimatization; **aclimatar** *vt* to acclimatize; **aclimatarse** *vr* to become acclimatized.

acobardar [akoβar'ðar] *vt* to daunt, intimidate.

acodarse [ako'ðarse] *vr*: ~ **en** to lean on.

acogedor, a [akoxe'ðor, a] *a* welcoming; (*hospitalario*) hospitable; **acoger** *vt* to welcome; (*abrigar*) to shelter; **acogerse** *vr* to take refuge; **acogida** *nf* reception; refuge.

acolchar [akol'tʃar] *vt* to pad; (*enpizar*) to upholster; (*fig*) to cushion.

acometer [akome'ter] *vt* to attack; (*emprender*) to undertake; **acometida** *nf* attack, assault.

acomodadizo, a [akomoða'ðiθo, a] *a* obliging, acquiescent.

acomodado, a [akomo'ðaðo, a] *a* suitable; (*precio*) moderate; (*persona*) well-to-do.

acomodador, a [akomoða'ðor, a] *nm/f* usher/ette.

acomodar [akomo'ðar] *vt* to adjust; (*alojar*) to accommodate; (*convenir*) to suit; (*reparar*) to repair; (*reconciliar*) to reconcile // *vi* to suit, be suitable; ~**se** *vr* to conform; (*instalarse*) to install o.s.; (*adaptarse*) to adapt o.s.

acomodo [ako'moðo] *nm* arrangement; (*puesto*) post.

acompañar [akompa'ɲar] *vt* to accompany; (*documentos*) to enclose.

acondicionar [akondiθjo'nar] *vt* to arrange, prepare; (*determinar*) to condition.

acongojar [akongo'xar] *vt* to distress, grieve.

aconsejar [akonse'xar] *vt* to advise, counsel; ~**se** *vr*: ~**se con** to consult.

acontecer [akonte'θer] *vi* to happen, occur; **acontecimiento** *nm* event.

acopio [a'kopjo] *nm* store, stock; (*asamblea*) gathering.

acoplamiento [akopla'mjento] *nm* coupling, joint; **acoplar** *vt* to fit, couple; (*unir*) to connect.

acorazado, a [akora'θaðo, a] *a* armour-plated, armoured // *nm* battleship.

acordar [akor'ðar] *vt* (*resolver*) to agree, resolve; (*recordar*) to remind; (*MUS*) to tune; ~**se** *vr* to agree; ~**se (de)** to remember; **acorde** *a* in agreement; (*MUS*) harmonious // *nm* chord.

acordeón [akorðe'on] *nm* accordion.

acordonado, a [akorðo'naðo, a] *a* cordoned-off.

acorralar [akorra'lar] *vt* to round up, corral.

acortar [akor'tar] *vt* to shorten; (*duración*) to cut short; (*cantidad*) to reduce; ~**se** *vr* to become shorter.

acosar [ako'sar] *vt* to pursue relentlessly; (*fig*) to hound, pester.

acostar [akos'tar] *vt* (*en cama*) to put to bed; (*en suelo*) to lay down; (*barco*) to bring alongside; ~**se** *vr* to go to bed; to lie down.

acostumbrar [akostum'brar] *vt*: ~ **a uno a** to accustom sb to // *vi*: ~ **a** to be used to; ~**se** *vr*: ~**se a** to get used to.

acotación [akota'θjon] *nf* marginal note; (*GEO*) elevation mark; (*de límite*) boundary mark; (*TEATRO*) stage direction.

acre ['akre] *a* sharp, bitter; (*fig*) biting // *nm* acre.

acrecentar [akreθen'tar] *vt* to increase, augment.

acreditar [akreði'tar] *vt* (*garantizar*) to vouch for, guarantee; (*autorizar*) to authorize; (*dar prueba de*) to prove; (*COM: abonar*) to credit; (*embajador*) to accredit; ~**se** *vr* to become famous.

acreedor, a [akree'ðor, a] *a*: ~ **a** worthy of // *nm/f* creditor.

acribillar [akriβi'ʎar] *vt*: ~ **a balazos** to riddle with bullets.

acrimonia [akri'monja], **acritud** [akri'tuð] *nf* acrimony.

acta ['akta] *nf* certificate; (*de comisión*) minutes *pl*, record; ~ **de nacimiento/matrimonial** birth/marriage certificate; ~ **notarial** affidavit.

actitud [akti'tuð] *nf* attitude; (*postura*) posture.

activar [akti'βar] *vt* to activate; (*acelerar*) to expedite.

actividad [aktiβi'ðað] *nf* activity.

activo, a [ak'tiβo, a] *a* active; (*vivo*) lively // *nm* assets *pl*.

acto ['akto] *nm* act, action; (*ceremonia*) ceremony; (*TEATRO*) act; **en el** ~ immediately.

actor [ak'tor] *nm* actor; (*JUR*) plaintiff.

actora [ak'tora] *a*: **parte** ~ prosecution; (*demandante*) plaintiff.

actriz [ak'triθ] *nf* actress.

actuación [aktwa'θjon] *nf* action; (*comportamiento*) conduct, behaviour; (*JUR*) proceedings *pl*; (*desempeño*) performance.

actual [ak'twal] *a* present(-day), current; ~**idad** *nf* present, present time; ~**idades** *nfpl* news *sg*; (*película, nodo*) newsreel *sg*; **en la** ~**idad** nowadays, at the present time.

actualizar [aktwali'θar] *vt* to update, modernize.

actualmente [aktwal'mente] *ad* now, nowadays, at present.

actuar [ak'twar] *vi* (*obrar*) to work, operate; (*actor*) to act, perform // *vt* to work, operate; ~ **de** to act as.

actuario [ak'twarjo] *nm* clerk; (*COM*) actuary.

acuarela [akwa'rela] *nf* watercolour.

acuario [a'kwarjo] *nm* aquarium; **A~** (*ASTRO*) Aquarius.

acuático, a [a'kwatiko, a] *a* aquatic.

acuciar [aku'θjar] *vt* to urge on.

acuclillarse [akukli'ʎarse] *vr* to crouch down.

acudir [aku'ðir] *vi* to come along, turn up; ~ **a** to turn to; ~ **en ayuda de** to go to the aid of.

acuerdo *etc vb ver* **acordar** // [a'kwerðo] *nm* agreement; **¡de** ~**!** agreed!; **de** ~ **con** (*persona*) in agreement with; (*acción, documento*) in accordance with.

acumulador [akumula'ðor] *nm* storage battery; **acumular** *vt* to accumulate, collect.

acuñar [aku'ɲar] *vt* (*moneda*) to coin, mint; (*poner cuñas*) to wedge.

acuoso, a [a'kwoso, a] *a* watery.

acurrucarse [akurru'karse] *vr* to crouch; (*ovillarse*) to curl up.

acusación [akusa'θjon] *nf* accusation; **acusar** *vt* to accuse; (*revelar*) to reveal; (*denunciar*) to denounce.

acuse [a'kuse] *nm*: ~ **de recibo**

acknowledgement of receipt.
acústico, a [a'kustiko, a] a acoustic // nm hearing aid.
achacar [atʃa'kar] vt to attribute.
achacoso, a [atʃa'koso, a] a sickly.
achaque [a'tʃake] nm ailment.
achicar [atʃi'kar] vt to reduce; (humillar) to humiliate; (NAUT) to bale out.
achicoria [atʃi'korja] nf chicory.
achicharrar [atʃitʃa'rrar] vt to scorch, burn.
adagio [a'ðaxjo] nm adage; (MUS) adagio.
adaptación [aðapta'θjon] nf adaptation; **adaptar** vt to adapt; (acomodar) to fit.
a. de C. abr = **a. de J.C.**
A. de C. abr = **A.C.**
adecuado, a [aðe'kwaðo, a] a adequate; (apto) suitable; (oportuno) appropriate; **adecuar** vt to adapt; to make suitable.
a. de J.C. abr de antes de Jesucristo B.C. (before Christ).
adelantado, a [aðelan'taðo a] a advanced; (reloj) fast; **pagar por ~** to pay in advance; **adelantamiento** nm advance, advancement; (AUTO) overtaking; (progreso) progress.
adelantar [aðelan'tar] vt to move forward; (avanzar) to advance; (acelerar) to speed up // vi, **~se** vr to go forward, advance; (AUTO) to overtake.
adelante [aðe'lante] ad forward(s), onward(s), ahead // excl come in!; **de hoy en ~** from now on; **más ~** later on; (más allá) further on.
adelanto [aðe'lanto] nm advance; (mejora) improvement; (progreso) progress.
adelgazar [aðelxa'θar] vt to thin (down); (afilar) to taper // vi, **~se** vr to grow thin.
ademán [aðe'man] nm gesture; **ademanes** nmpl manners; **en ~ de** as if to.
además [aðe'mas] ad besides; (por otra parte) moreover; (también) also; **~ de** besides, in addition to.
adentro [a'ðentro] ad inside, in; **mar ~** out at sea; **tierra ~** inland.
adepto, a [a'ðepto, a] nm/f supporter.
aderezar [aðere'θar] vt to prepare; (persona, ensalada) to dress; (comida) to season; **~se** vr to dress up; **aderezo** nm preparation; dressing; seasoning.
adeudar [aðeu'ðar] vt to owe // vi to become related by marriage; **~se** vr to run into debt.
adherirse [aðe'rirse] vr: **~ a** to adhere to.
adhesión [aðe'sjon] nf adhesion; (fig) adherence.
adición [aði'θjon] nf addition.
adicionar [aðiθjo'nar] vt to add.
adicto, a [a'ðikto, a] a: **~ a** given to; (dedicado) devoted to // nm/f supporter, follower.
adiestrar [aðjes'trar] vt to train, teach; (conducir) to guide, lead; **~se** vr to practise; (enseñarse) to train o.s.

adinerado, a [aðine'raðo, a] a wealthy.
adiós [a'ðjos] excl (para despedirse) goodbye!, cheerio!; (para saludar) hello!
aditivo [aði'tiβo] nm additive.
adivinanza [aðiβi'nanθa] nf riddle; **adivinar** vt to prophesy; (conjeturar) to guess; **adivino, a** nm/f fortune-teller.
adj a abr de adjunto encl. (enclosed)
adjetivo [aðxe'tiβo] nm adjective.
adjudicación [aðxuðika'θjon] nf award; **adjudicar** vt to award; **adjudicarse** vr: **adjudicarse algo** to appropriate sth.
adjuntar [aðxun'tar] vt to attach, enclose; **adjunto, a** a attached, enclosed // nm/f assistant.
administración [aðministra'θjon] nf administration; (dirección) management; **administrador, a** nm/f administrator; manager/ess.
administrar [aðminis'trar] vt to administer; **administrativo, a** a administrative.
admirable [aðmi'raβle] a admirable; **admiración** nf admiration; (asombro) wonder; (LING) exclamation mark; **admirar** vt to admire; (extrañar) to surprise; **admirarse** vr to be surprised.
admisible [aðmi'siβle] a admissible.
admitir [aðmi'tir] vt to admit; (aceptar) to accept.
admonición [aðmoni'θjon] nf warning.
adobe [a'ðoβe] nm adobe, sun-dried brick.
adolecer [aðole'θer] vi to be ill, fall ill, **~ de** to suffer from.
adolescente [aðoles'θente] nm/f adolescent.
adonde [a'ðonðe] conj (to) where.
adónde [a'ðonðe] ad = **dónde.**
adopción [aðop'θjon] nf adoption.
adoptar [aðop'tar] vt to adopt.
adoquín [aðo'kin] nm paving stone.
adorar [aðo'rar] vt to adore.
adormecer [aðorme'θer] vt to put to sleep; **~se** vr to become sleepy, fall asleep.
adornar [aðor'nar] vt to adorn.
adorno [a'ðorno] nm adornment; (decoración) decoration.
adquiero etc vb ver **adquirir.**
adquirir [aðki'rir] vt to acquire, obtain.
adquisición [aðkisi'θjon] nf acquisition.
adrede [a'ðreðe] ad on purpose.
adscribir [aðskri'βir] vt to appoint.
aduana [a'ðwana] nf customs pl.
aduanero, a [aðwa'nero, a] a customs cpd // nm/f customs officer.
aducir [aðu'θir] vt to adduce; (dar como prueba) to offer as proof.
adueñarse [aðwe'narse] vr: **~ de** to take possession of.
adulación [aðula'θjon] nf flattery.
adular [aðu'lar] vt to flatter.
adulterar [aðulte'rar] vt to adulterate // vi to commit adultery.
adulterio [aðul'terjo] nm adultery.
adulto, a [a'ðulto, a] a, nm/f adult.

adusto, a [a'ðusto, a] *a* stern; (*austero*) austere.

advenedizo, a [aðßene'ðiθo, a] *nm/f* upstart.

advenimiento [aðßeni'mjento] *nm* arrival; (*al trono*) accession.

adverbio [að'ßerßjo] *nm* adverb.

adversario, a [aðßer'sarjo, a] *nm/f* adversary.

adversidad [aðßersi'ðað] *nf* adversity; (*contratiempo*) setback.

adverso, a [að'ßerso, a] *a* adverse; (*opuesto*) opposite.

advertencia [aðßer'tenθja] *nf* warning; (*prefacio*) preface, foreword.

advertir [aðßer'tir] *vt* to notice; (*avisar*) to warn // *vi:* ~ **en** to notice.

Adviento [að'ßjento] *nm* Advent.

adyacente [aðja'θente] *a* adjacent.

aéreo, a [a'ereo, a] *a* aerial.

aerodeslizador [aeroðesliθa'ðor], **aerodeslizante** [aeroðesli'θante] *nm* hovercraft.

aeronáutica [aero'nautika] *nf* aeronautics *sg.*

aeropuerto [aero'pwerto] *nm* airport.

afabilidad [afaßili'ðað] *nf* friendliness; **afable** *a* affable.

afán [a'fan] *nm* hard work; (*deseo*) desire.

afanar [afa'nar] *vt* to harass; ~**se** *vr:* ~**se por** to strive to; **afanoso, a** *a* hard; (*trabajador*) industrious.

afear [afe'ar] *vt* to make ugly; (*mutilar*) to deface.

afección [afek'θjon] *nf* affection; (*MED*) disease.

afectación [afekta'θjon] *nf* affectation; **afectado, a** *a* affected; **afectar** *vt* to affect.

afectísimo, a [afek'tisimo, a] *a* affectionate; ~ **suyo** yours truly.

afecto, a [a'fekto, a] *a* affectionate // *nm* affection; ~ **a** fond of.

afectuoso, a [afek'twoso, a] *a* affectionate.

afeitar [afei'tar] *vt* to shave; ~**se** *vr* to shave.

afeminado, a [afemi'naðo, a] *a* effeminate.

aferrado, a [afe'rraðo, a] *a* stubborn.

aferrar [afe'rrar] *vt* to moor; (*fig*) to grasp // *vi* to moor.

afianzamiento [afjanθa'mjento] *nm* strengthening; guarantee; (*COM*) security; **afianzar** *vt* to strengthen; to guarantee; to secure; **afianzarse** *vr* to become established.

afición [afi'θjon] *nf* fondness, liking; **la** ~ the fans *pl;* **pinto por** ~ I paint as a hobby; **aficionado, a** *a* keen, enthusiastic; amateur // *nm/f* enthusiast, fan; amateur.

aficionar [afiθjo'nar] *vt:* ~ **a uno a algo** to make sb like sth; ~**se** *vr:* ~**se a algo** to grow fond of sth.

afilado, a [afi'laðo, a] *a* sharp.

afilar [afi'lar] *vt* to sharpen.

afiliarse [afi'ljarse] *vr* to become affiliated to.

afín [a'fin] *a* bordering, adjacent; (*parecido*) similar; (*conexo*) related.

afinar [afi'nar] *vt* (*TEC*) to refine; (*MUS*) to tune // *vi* to play/sing in tune.

afinidad [afini'ðað] *nf* affinity; (*parentesco*) relationship; **por** ~ **by** marriage.

afirmación [afirma'θjon] *nf* affirmation; **afirmar** *vt* to affirm, state; (*sostener*) to strengthen; **afirmativo, a** *a* affirmative.

aflicción [aflik'θjon] *nf* affliction; (*dolor*) grief.

afligir [afli'xir] *vt* to afflict; (*apenar*) to distress; ~**se** *vr* to grieve.

aflojar [aflo'xar] *vt* to slacken; (*desatar*) to loosen, undo; (*relajar*) to relax // *vi* to drop; (*bajar*) to go down; ~**se** *vr* to relax.

afluente [aflu'ente] *a* flowing; (*elocuente*) eloquent // *nm* tributary.

afluir [aflu'ir] *vi* to flow.

afmo, a *abr de* **afectísimo(a) suyo(a)**.

afónico, a [a'foniko, a] *a* (*ronco*) hoarse; (*sin voz*) voiceless.

afortunado, a [afortu'naðo, a] *a* fortunate, lucky.

afrancesado, a [afranθe'saðo, a] *a* francophile; (*pey*) frenchified.

afrenta [a'frenta] *nf* affront, insult; (*deshonra*) dishonour, shame; **afrentar** *vt* to affront; to dishonour; **afrentarse** *vr* to be ashamed; **afrentoso, a** *a* insulting.

Africa ['afrika] *nf* Africa; ~ **del Sur** South Africa; **africano, a** *a, nm/f* African.

afrontar [afron'tar] *vt* to confront; (*poner cara a cara*) to bring face to face.

afuera [a'fwera] *ad* out, outside; ~**s** *nfpl* outskirts, suburbs.

agachar [aɣa'tʃar] *vt* to bend, bow; ~**se** *vr* to stoop, bend.

agalla [a'ɣaʎa] *nf* (*ZOOL*) gill; ~**s** *nfpl* (*MED*) tonsillitis *sg;* (*ANAT*) tonsils.

agarradera [aɣarra'ðera] *nf* (*AM*), **agarradero** [aɣarra'ðero] *nm* handle; ~**s** *npl* pull *sg,* influence *sg.*

agarrado, a [aɣa'rraðo, a] *a* mean, stingy.

agarrar [aɣa'rrar] *vt* to grasp, grab; (*AM*) to take, catch // *vi* (*planta*) to take root; ~**se** *vr* to hold on (tightly).

agarrotar [aɣarro'tar] *vt* (*lío*) to tie tightly; (*persona*) to squeeze tightly; (*reo*) to garrotte; ~**se** *vr* (*motor*) to seize up; (*MED*) to stiffen.

agasajar [aɣasa'xar] *vt* to treat well, fête; **agasajo** *nm* lavish hospitality.

agencia [a'xenθja] *nf* agency; ~ **de viajes/inmobiliaria** travel/estate agency.

agenda [a'xenda] *nf* diary.

agente [a'xente] *nm* agent; (*de policía*) policeman; ~ **femenino** policewoman.

ágil ['axil] *a* agile, nimble; **agilidad** *nf* agility, nimbleness.

agio ['axjo] *nm* speculation.

agiotista [axjo'tista] *nm* (stock)jobber; (*especulador*) speculator.

agitación [axita'θjon] nf shaking, waving, stirring; (del mar) roughness; (fig) agitation.

agitar [axi'tar] vt to wave, shake, stir; (fig) to stir up, excite; ~se vr to get excited.

aglomerar [axlome'rar] vt, ~se vr to agglomerate, crowd together.

agnóstico, a [ax'nostiko, a] a, nm/f agnostic.

agobiar [axo'βjar] vt to weigh down; (oprimir) to oppress; (cargar) to burden.

agolparse [axol'parse] vr to crowd together.

agonía [axo'nia] nf agony, anguish.

agonizante [axoni'θante] a dying.

agonizar [axoni'θar] vi (también estar agonizando) to be dying.

agosto [a'yosto] nm August.

agotado, a [axo'taðo, a] a exhausted; (libros) out of print; (acabado) finished; (mercancías) sold out; **agotamiento** nm exhaustion.

agotar [axo'tar] vt to exhaust; (consumir) to drain; (recursos) to use up, deplete; ~se vr to be exhausted; (acabarse) to run out; (libro) to go out of print.

agraciar [axra'θjar] vt (JUR) to pardon; (con premio) to reward.

agradable [axra'ðaßle] a pleasing, pleasant, nice.

agradar [axra'ðar] vt, vi to please.

agradecer [axraðe'θer] vt to thank; (favor etc) to be grateful for; **agradecimiento** nm thanks pl; gratitude.

agrado [a'xraðo] nm affability; (gusto) liking.

agrandar [axran'dar] vt to enlarge; (fig) to exaggerate; ~se vr to get bigger.

agrario, a [a'xrarjo, a] a agrarian.

agravar [axra'βar] vt to make heavier; (irritar) to aggravate; (oprimir) to oppress; ~se vr to worsen, get worse.

agraviar [axra'βjar] vt to offend; (ser injusto con) to wrong; ~se vr to take offence; **agravio** nm offence; wrong; (ofensa) grievance.

agregado [axre'xaðo] nm aggregate; (persona) attaché.

agregar [axre'xar] vt to gather; (añadir) to add; (persona) to appoint.

agresión [axre'sjon] nf aggression; **agresivo, a** a aggressive.

agriar [a'xrjar] vt to (turn) sour; ~se vr to turn sour.

agricultor, a [axrikul'tor, a] nm/f farmer; **agricultura** nf agriculture, farming.

agridulce [axri'ðulθe] a bittersweet.

agrietarse [axrje'tarse] vr to crack; (la piel) to chap.

agrio, a [a'xrjo, a] a bitter.

agronomía [axrono'mia] nf agronomy, agriculture.

agrupación [axrupa'θjon] nf group; (acto) grouping.

agrupar [axru'par] vt to group.

agua ['axwa] nf water; (lluvia) rain; (NAUT) wake; (ARQ) slope of a roof; ~s nfpl (de piedra) water sg, sparkle sg; (MED) water sg, urine sg; (NAUT) waters; ~s abajo/arriba downstream/upstream; ~ bendita/destilada/potable holy/distilled/drinking water; ~ corriente running water; ~ de colonia eau de cologne; ~s jurisdiccionales territorial waters; ~s mayores excrement sg.

aguacate [axwa'kate] nm avocado pear.

aguacero [axwa'θero] nm (heavy) shower.

aguado, a [a'xwaðo, a] a watery, watered down // nf (AGR) watering place; (NAUT) water supply; (ARTE) water-colour.

aguafiestas [axwa'fjestas] nm/f inv spoilsport.

aguafuerte [axwa'fwerte] nf etching.

aguamar [axwa'mar] nm jellyfish.

aguantable [axwan'taßle] a bearable; **aguantar** vt to bear, put up with; (contener) to hold; (sostener) to hold up // vi to last; **aguantarse** vr to restrain o.s.

aguar [a'xwar] vt to water down.

aguardar [axwar'ðar] vt to wait for.

aguardiente [axwar ðjente] nm brandy.

aguarrás [axwa'rras] nm turpentine.

agudeza [axu'ðeθa] nf sharpness; (ingenio) wit; **agudo, a** a sharp; (voz) high-pitched, piercing; (dolor, enfermedad) acute.

agüero [a'xwero] nm omen; (pronóstico) prediction.

aguijar [axi'xar] vt to goad; (incitar) to urge on // vi to hurry along.

aguijón [axi'xon] nm sting; (BOT) spine; (estímulo, fig) spur; **aguijonear** vt = aguijar.

águila ['axila] nf eagle; (fig) genius.

aguileño, a [axi'leɲo, a] a aquiline; (facciones) sharp-featured.

aguinaldo [axi'naldo] nm Christmas box.

aguja [a'xuxa] nf needle; (de reloj) hand; (ARQ) spire; (TEC) firing-pin; ~s nfpl (ZOOL) ribs; (FERRO) points.

agujerear [axuxere'ar] vt to make holes in; **agujero** nm hole.

agujetas [axu'xetas] nfpl stitch sg; (rigidez) stiffness sg.

aguzar [axu'θar] vt to sharpen; (fig) to incite.

ahí [a'i] ad there; de ~ que so that, with the result that; ~ llega here he comes; por ~ that way; (allá) over there.

ahijado, a [ai'xaðo, a] nm/f godson/daughter.

ahínco [a'inko] nm earnestness.

ahitar [ai'tar] vt to surfeit; ~se vr to stuff o.s.

ahíto, a [a'ito, a] a: estoy ~ I have indigestion // nm indigestion.

ahogar [ao'xar] vt to drown; (asfixiar) to suffocate, smother; (fuego) to put out; ~se vr (en el agua) to drown; (asfixia) to drown o.s.; (por asfixia) to suffocate.

ahogo [a'oxo] nm shortness of breath; (fig) financial difficulty.

ahondar [aon'dar] vt to deepen, make

deeper; (*fig*) to go deeply into // vi: ~ **en** to go deeply into.

ahora [a'ora] *ad* now; (*poco tiempo ha*) a moment ago, just now; (*dentro de poco*) in a moment // *conj* now; ~ **voy** I'm coming; ~ **mismo** right now; ~ **bien** now then; **por** ~ for the present.

ahorcar [aor'kar] *vt* to hang; ~**se** *vr* to hang o.s.

ahorita [ao'rita] *ad* (*fam*) right now.

ahorrar [ao'rrar] *vt* (*dinero*) to save; (*esfuerzos*) to save, avoid; **ahorro** *nm* economy, saving; (*frugalidad*) thrift; **ahorros** *nmpl* savings.

ahuecar [awe'kar] *vt* to hollow (out); (*voz*) to deepen; ~**se** *vr* to give o.s. airs.

ahumar [au'mar] *vt* to smoke, cure; (*llenar de humo*) to fill with smoke // *vi* to smoke; ~**se** *vr* to fill with smoke.

ahuyentar [aujen'tar] *vt* to drive off, frighten off; (*fig*) to dispel; ~ **se** *vr* to run away.

airado, a [ai'raðo, a] *a* angry; **airar** *vt* to anger; **airarse** *vr* to get angry.

aire ['aire] *nm* air; (*viento*) wind; (*corriente*) draught; (*MUS*) tune; ~**s** *nmpl*: **darse** ~**s** to give o.s. airs; **al** ~ **libre** in the open air; ~ **acondicionado** air conditioning; **airoso, a** *a* windy; draughty; (*fig*) graceful.

aislador [aisla'ðor] *nm* insulator; **aislar** *vt* to isolate; (*ELEC*) to insulate.

ajar [a'xar] *vt* to spoil; (*fig*) to abuse.

ajedrez [axe'ðreθ] *nm* chess.

ajeno, a [a'xeno, a] *a* (*que pertenece a otro*) somebody else's; (*impropio*) inappropriate; (*extraño*) alien, foreign; ~ **a** foreign to; ~ **de** free from, devoid of.

ajetreo [axe'treo] *nm* bustle.

ají [a'xi] *nm* chili, red pepper; (*salsa*) chili sauce.

ajo ['axo] *nm* garlic; ~ **porro** o **puerro** leek.

ajorca [a'xorka] *nf* bracelet.

ajuar [a'xwar] *nm* household furnishings *pl*; (*de novia*) trousseau; (*de niño*) layette.

ajustado, a [axus'taðo, a] *a* (*tornillo*) tight; (*cálculo*) right; (*ropa*) tight-fitting; (*DEPORTE: resultado*) close.

ajustar [axus'tar] *vt* (*adaptar*) to adjust; (*encajar*) to fit; (*TEC*) to engage; (*contratar*) to hire; (*IMPRENTA*) to make up; (*apretar*) to tighten; (*concertar*) to agree (on); (*reconciliar*) to reconcile; (*cuenta*) to settle // *vi* to fit; ~**se** *vr* to come to an agreement.

ajuste [a'xuste] *nm* adjustment; (*TEC costura*) fitting; (*acuerdo*) compromise; (*de cuenta*) settlement.

al [al] = **a** + **el**, *ver* **a**.

ala ['ala] *nf* wing; (*de sombrero*) brim; (*futbolista*) winger.

alabanza [ala'ßanθa] *nf* praise.

alabar [ala'ßar] *vt* to praise; ~ **se** *vr*: ~**se de** to boast of (being).

alabear [alaße'ar] *vt*, ~**se** *vr* to warp.

alacena [ala'θena] *nf* cupboard.

alacrán [ala'kran] *nm* scorpion.

alambicado, a [alambi'kaðo, a] *a* distilled; (*fig*) affected.

alambicar [alambi'kar] *vt* to distil.

alambique [alam'bike] *nm* still.

alambrado [alam'braðo] *nm* wire fence; (*red*) wire netting; **alambre** *nm* wire; **alambre de púas** barbed wire; **alambrista** *nm/f* tightrope walker.

alameda [ala'meða] *nf* (*plantío*) poplar grove; (*lugar de paseo*) avenue, tree-lined walk.

álamo ['alamo] *nm* poplar; ~ **temblón** aspen.

alano [a'lano] *nm* mastiff.

alar [a'lar] *nm* eaves *pl*.

alarde [a'larðe] *nm* (*MIL*) review; (*ostentación*) show, display; **hacer** ~ **de** to boast of.

alargar [alar'xar] *vt* to lengthen, extend; (*paso*) to hasten; (*brazo*) to stretch out; (*cuerda*) to pay out; (*conversación*) to spin out; ~**se** *vr* to get longer; ~**se en** to enlarge upon; (*pey*) to drag out.

alarido [ala'riðo] *nm* shriek.

alarma [a'larma] *nf* alarm.

alazán [ala'θan] *nm* sorrel.

alba ['alßa] *nf* dawn.

albacea [alßa'θea] *nm/f* executor/trix.

Albania [al'ßanja] *nf* Albania.

albañal [alßa'ɲal] *nm* drain, sewer.

albañil [alßa'ɲil] *nm* bricklayer; (*cantero*) mason.

albaricoque [alßari koke] *nm* apricot.

albedrío [alße'ðrio] *nm*: **libre** ~ free will.

alberca [al'ßerka] *nf* reservoir.

albergar [alßer'xar] *vt*, ~**se** *vr* to shelter.

albergue [al'ßerxe] *nm* shelter, refuge; ~ **de juventud** youth hostel.

albóndiga [al'ßondiɣa] *nf* meatball.

albor [al'ßor] *nm* whiteness; (*amanecer*) dawn; ~**ada** *nf* dawn; (*diana*) reveille; ~**ear** *vi* to dawn.

albornoz [alßor'noθ] *nm* (*de los árabes*) burnous; (*para el baño*) bathrobe.

alborotar [alßoro'tar] *vi* to make a row // *vt* to agitate, stir up; ~**se** *vr* to get excited; (*mar*) to get rough; **alboroto** *nm* row, uproar.

alborozar [alßoro'θar] *vt* to gladden; ~**se** *vr* to rejoice.

alborozo [alßo'roθo] *nm* joy.

albricias [al'ßriθjas] *nfpl* reward *sg* // *excl* good news!

álbum ['alßum] *nm* album.

albumen [al'ßumen] *nm* egg white.

alcachofa [alka'tʃofa] *nf* artichoke.

alcalde [al'kalde] *nm* mayor.

alcaldía [alkal'dia] *nf* mayoralty; (*lugar*) mayor's office.

alcance [al'kanθe] *nm* reach; (*COM*) adverse balance; (*de periódico*) stop-press (news); **de pocos** ~**s** not very clever; ~ **de última hora** late postal collection.

alcancía [alkan'θia] *nf* money box.

alcantarilla [alkanta'riʎa] *nf* (*de aguas*

cloacales) sewer; (en la calle) gutter.

alcanzar [alkan'θar] vt (algo: con la mano, el pie) to reach; (alguien en el camino) to catch up with; (autobús) to catch; (suj: bala) to hit, strike // vi: ~ a hacer to manage to do.

alcatraz [alka'traθ] nm gannet.

alcázar [al'kaθar] nm fortress; (palacio) royal palace; (NAUT) quarter-deck.

alcoba [al'koβa] nf bedroom.

alcohol [al'kol] nm alcohol; **alcohólico, a** a alcoholic; ~ **ismo** nm alcoholism.

alcornoque [alkor'noke] nm cork tree.

aldaba [al'daβa] nf (door) knocker.

aldea [al'dea] nf village; ~ **no, a** a village cpd // nm/f villager.

aleación [alea'θjon] nf alloy.

aleccionar [alekθjo'nar] vt to instruct; (adiestrar) to train.

alegación [aleɣa'θjon] nf allegation; **alegar** vt to allege; (JUR) to plead; (AM) to dispute, argue.

alegato [ale'ɣato] nm (JUR) allegation; (AM) argument.

alegoría [aleɣo'ria] nf allegory.

alegrar [ale'ɣrar] vt (causar alegría) to cheer up; (fuego) to poke; (fiesta) to liven up; ~**se** vr to get merry or tight; ~**se de** to be glad about.

alegre [a'leɣre] a happy, cheerful; (fam) merry, tight; (licencioso) risqué, blue; **alegría** nf happiness; merriment.

alejamiento [alexa'mjento] nm removal; (distancia) remoteness.

alejar [ale'xar] vt to remove; (fig) to estrange; ~**se** vr to move away.

aleluya [ale'luja] nm (canto) hallelujah; (Pascuas) Easter time // nf Easter print.

alemán, ana [ale'man, ana] a, nm/f German // nm (lengua) German.

Alemania [ale'manja] nf: ~ **Federal/Oriental** West/East Germany.

alentado, a [alen'taðo, a] pp de **alentar** // a brave; (orgulloso) proud; (fuerte) strong.

alentador, a [alenta'ðor, a] a encouraging.

alentar [alen'tar] vt to encourage; ~**se** vr to cheer up.

alerce [a'lerθe] nm larch.

alergia [a'lerxja] nf allergy.

alero [a'lero] nm (de tejado) eaves pl; (de carruaje) mudguard.

alerta [a'lerta] a, nm alert.

aleta [a'leta] nf (de pez) fin; (de ave) wing; (de coche) mudguard.

aletargar [aletar'ɣar] vt to make drowsy; (entumecer) to make numb; ~**se** vr to grow drowsy; to become numb.

aletazo [ale'taθo] nm wingbeat, flap of the wing.

aletear [alete'ar] vi to flutter.

aleve [a'leβe] a treacherous.

alevosía [aleβo'sia] nf treachery.

alfabeto [alfa'βeto] nm alphabet.

alfarería [alfare'ria] nf pottery; (tienda) pottery shop; **alfarero** nm potter.

alférez [al'fereθ] nm (MIL) second lieutenant; (NAUT) ensign.

alfiler [alfi'ler] nm pin; (broche) clip; ~ **de seguridad** safety pin.

alfombra [al'fombra] nf carpet; (más pequeña) rug; **alfombrar** vt to carpet; **alfombrilla** nf rug, mat; (MED) German measles.

alforja [al'forxa] nf saddlebag.

alforza [al'forθa] nf pleat.

alga ['alɣa] nf seaweed, alga.

algarabía [alɣara'βia] nf (fam) gibberish; (BOT) cornflower.

algarrobo [alɣa'rroβo] nm carob tree.

algazara [alɣa'θara] nf din, uproar.

álgebra ['alxeβra] nf algebra.

algo ['alɣo] pron something; anything // ad somewhat, rather; **por** ~ **será** there must be some reason for it.

algodón [alɣo'ðon] nm cotton; (planta) cotton plant; (dulce) candy floss; ~ **hidrófilo** cotton wool.

algodonero, a [alɣoðo'nero, a] a cotton cpd // nm/f cotton grower // nm cotton plant.

alguacil [alɣwa'θil] nm bailiff; (TAUR) mounted official.

alguien ['alxjen] pron someone, somebody, anybody.

alguno, a [al'ɣuno, a] **algún** [al'ɣun] a some, any // pron some; one; someone, somebody; ~ **que otro libro** some book or other; **algún día iré** I'll go one or some day; **sin interés** ~ without the slightest interest; ~ **que otro** an occasional one; ~**s piensan** some (people) think.

alhaja [a'laxa] nf jewel; (tesoro) precious object, treasure; (pey) rogue.

aliado, a [a'ljaðo, a] a allied.

alianza [a'ljanθa] nf alliance.

aliar [a'ljar] vt to ally; ~**se** vr to form an alliance.

alias ['aljas] ad alias.

alicantino, a [alikan'tino, a] a of or from Alicante.

alicates [ali'kates] nmpl: ~ **de uñas** nail clippers.

aliciente [ali'θjente] nm incentive; (atracción) attraction.

alienación [aljena'θjon] nf alienation.

aliento [a'ljento] nm breath; (respiración) breathing; **sin** ~ breathless.

aligerar [alixe'rar] vt to lighten; (reducir) to shorten; (aliviar) to alleviate; (mitigar) to ease.

alimaña [ali'maɲa] nf pest.

alimentación [alimenta'θjon] nf (comida) food; (acción) feeding; (tienda) grocer's (shop); **alimentar** vt to feed; (nutrir) to nourish; **alimentarse** vr to feed.

alimenticio, a [alimen'tiθjo, a] a nourishing.

alimento [ali'mento] nm food; (nutrición) nourishment; ~**s** nmpl (JUR) alimony sg.

alinear [aline'ar] vt to align; ~**se** vr: ~**se en** to fall in with.

aliñar [ali'nar] *vt* to adorn; (*preparar*) to prepare; (*CULIN*) to season; **aliño** *nm* decoration; (*esmero*) neatness; (*CULIN*) dressing.

alisar [ali'sar] *vt* to smooth; (*pulir*) to polish.

aliso [a'liso] *nm* alder.

alistamiento [alista'mjento] *nm* recruitment; **alistar** *vt* to recruit; (*inscribir*) to enrol; **alistarse** *vr* to enlist; to enrol.

aliviar [ali'βjar] *vt* (*carga*) to lighten; (*persona*) to relieve; (*dolor*) to alleviate; ~ **se** *vr*: ~ **se de** to unburden o.s. of.

alivio [a'liβjo] *nm* alleviation, relief.

aljibe [al'xiβe] *nm* cistern; (*AUTO*) oil tanker.

aljofaina [alxo'faina] *nf* = **jofaina**.

alma ['alma] *nf* soul; (*persona*) person; (*que anima*) life and soul; (*TEC*) core.

almacén [alma'θen] *nm* (*depósito*) warehouse, store; (*MIL*) magazine; (*AM*) shop; **almacenes** *nmpl* department store *sg*; **almacenaje** *nm* storage.

almacenar [almaθe'nar] *vt* to store, put in storage; (*proveerse*) to stock up (with); **almacenero** *nm* warehouseman.

almanaque [alma'nake] *nm* almanac.

almeja [al'mexa] *nf* shellfish, clam.

almendra [al'mendra] *nf* almond; **almendro** *nm* almond tree.

almiar [al'mjar] *nm* hayrick.

almíbar [al'miβar] *nm* syrup; **almibarado, a** *a* syrupy.

almidón [almi'ðon] *nm* starch; **almidonar** *vt* to starch.

almirantazgo [almiran'taθxo] *nm* admiralty; **almirante** *nm* admiral.

almohada [almo'aða] *nf* pillow; (*funda*) pillowcase; **almohadilla** *nf* cushion; (*TEC*) pad; (*AM*) pincushion.

almoneda [almo'neða] *nf* auction; (*liquidación*) clearance sale.

almorranas [almo'rranas] *nfpl* piles, haemorrhoids.

almorzar [almor'θar] *vt*: ~ **una tortilla** to have an omelette for lunch // *vi* to (have) lunch.

almuerzo [al'mwerθo] *nm* lunch.

alnado, a [al'naðo, a] *nm/f* stepson/daughter.

alocado, a [alo'kaðo, a] *a* crazy.

alojamiento [aloxa'mjento] *nf* lodging(s) (*pl*); (*viviendas*) housing.

alojar [alo'xar] *vt* to lodge; ~ **se** *vr* to lodge, stay.

alondra [a'londra] *nf* lark, skylark.

alpargata [alpar'xata] *nf* rope-soled sandal; (*de lona*) canvass shoe.

Alpes ['alpes] *nmpl*: **los** ~ **the Alps.**

alpinismo [alpi'nismo] *nm* mountaineering, climbing; **alpinista** *nm/f* mountaineer, climber.

alquería [alke'ria] *nf* farmhouse.

alquilar [alki'lar] *vt* to rent (out), let, hire (out); (*de inquilino*) to rent, hire; **se**

alquilan casas houses to let.

alquiler [alki'ler] *nm* renting, letting, hiring; (*arriendo*) rent, hire charge; **de ~ for hire.**

alquimia [al'kimja] *nf* alchemy.

alquitrán [alki'tran] *nm* tar.

alrededor [alreðe'ðor] *ad* around, about; ~ **es** *nmpl* surroundings; ~ **de** *prep* around, about; **mirar a su** ~ to look (round) about one.

alta ['alta] *nf ver* **alto.**

altanería [altane'ria] *nf* haughtiness, arrogance; **altanero, a** *a* arrogant, haughty.

altar [al'tar] *nm* altar.

altavoz [alta'βoθ] *nm* loudspeaker; (*amplificador*) amplifier.

alteración [altera'θjon] *nf* alteration; (*alboroto*) disturbance; (*discusión*) quarrel; **alterar** *vt* to alter; to disturb; **alterarse** *vr* (*alimento etc*) to go bad or off; (*voz*) to falter; (*persona*) to get upset.

altercado [alter'kaðo] *nm* argument.

alternar [alter'nar] *vi* to alternate // *vi*, ~ **se** *vr* to alternate; (*turnar*) to take turns; ~ **con** to mix with; **alternativo, a** *a* alternative; (*alterno*) alternating // *nf* alternative; (*elección*) choice; **alternativas** *nfpl* ups and downs.

alteza [al'teθa] *nf* (*tratamiento*) highness; (*altura*) height.

altibajos [alti'βaxos] *nmpl* ups and downs.

altiplanicie [altipla'niθje] *nf*, **altiplano** [alti'plano] *nm* high plateau.

altisonante [altiso'nante] *a* high-flown.

altitud [alti'tuð] *nf* altitude.

altivez [alti'βeθ] *nf* haughtiness, arrogance; **altivo, a** *a* haughty, arrogant.

alto, a ['alto, a] *a* high; (*de tamaño*) tall; (*precio, importante*) high; (*sonido*) high, sharp; (*noble*) high, lofty // *nm* halt; (*MUS*) alto; (*GEO*) hill; (*AM*) pile // *ad* (*de sitio*) high; (*de sonido*) loud, loudly // *nf* (certificate of) discharge // *excl* halt!; **tiene 2 metros de** ~ he is 2 metres tall; **en** ~ **a mar** on the high seas; **en voz** ~ **a** in a loud voice; **las** ~ **as horas de la noche** the small hours; **en lo** ~ **de** at the top of; **pasar por** ~ to overlook; **dar de** ~ **a** to discharge.

altoparlante [altopar'lante] *nm* (*AM*) loudspeaker.

altura [al'tura] *nf* height; (*NAUT*) depth; (*GEO*) latitude; **tiene 1.80 de** ~ he is 1 metre 80cm tall; **a esta** ~ **del año** at this time of the year.

alubia [a'luβja] *nf* French bean, kidney bean.

alucinación [aluθina'θjon] *nf* hallucination; **alucinar** *vi* to hallucinate // *vt* to deceive; (*fascinar*) to fascinate.

alud [a'luð] *nm* avalanche.

aludir [alu'ðir] *vi*: ~ **a** to allude to; **darse por** ~ to take the hint.

alumbrado [alum'braðo] *nm* lighting; **alumbramiento** *nm* lighting; (*MED*) childbirth, delivery.

alumbrar [alum'brar] vt to light (up); (ciego) to restore the sight of // vi to give birth.

aluminio [alu'minjo] nm aluminium.

alumno, a [a'lumno, a] nm/f pupil, student.

alunizar [aluni'θar] vi to land on the moon.

alusión [alu'sjon] nf allusion.

alusivo, a [alu'siβo, a] a allusive.

aluvión [alu'βjon] nm alluvium; (fig) flood.

alza ['alθa] nf rise; ~ s nfpl sights.

alzada [al'θaða] nf (de caballos) height; (JUR) appeal.

alzamiento [alθa'mjento] nm (aumento) rise, increase; (acción) lifting, raising; (mejor postura) higher bid; (rebelión) rising; (COM) fraudulent bankruptcy.

alzar [al'θar] vt to lift (up); (precio, muro) to raise; (cuello de abrigo) to turn up; (AGR) to gather in; (IMPRENTA) to gather; ~se vr to get up, rise; (rebelarse) to revolt; (COM) to go fraudulently bankrupt; (JUR) to appeal.

allá [a'ʎa] ad (lugar) there; (por ahí) over there; (tiempo) then; ~ **abajo** down there; **más** ~ further on; **más** ~ **de** beyond; ¡~ **tu!** that's your problem!

allanar [aʎa'nar] vt to flatten, level (out); (igualar) to smooth (out); (fig) to subdue; (JUR) to burgle, break into; ~se vr to fall down; ~se a to submit to, accept.

allegado, a [aʎe'xaðo, a] a near, close // nm/f relation.

allegar [aʎe'xar] vt to gather (together); (añadir) to add; ~ se vr to approach.

allí [a'ʎi] ad there; ~ **mismo** right there; **por** ~ over there; (por ese camino) that way.

ama ['ama] nf lady of the house; (dueña) owner; (institutriz) governess; (madre adoptiva) foster mother; ~ **de cría o de leche** wet-nurse; ~ **de llaves** housekeeper.

amabilidad [amaβili'ðað] nf kindness; (simpatía) niceness; **amable** a kind, nice.

amado, a [a'maðo, a] nm/f beloved, sweetheart.

amaestrar [amaes'trar] vt to train; (preparar) to coach.

amagar [ama'xar] vt, vi to threaten; **amago** nm threat; (gesto) threatening gesture; (MED) symptom.

amalgama [amal'xama] nf amalgam; **amalgamar** vt to amalgamate; (combinar) to combine, mix.

amamantar [amaman'tar] vt to suckle, nurse.

amanecer [amane'θer] vi to dawn // nm dawn; **el niño amaneció afiebrado** the child woke up with a fever.

amanerado, a [amane'raðo, a] a affected.

amansar [aman'sar] vt to tame; (templar) to subdue.

amante [a'mante] a: ~ **de** fond of // nm/f lover.

amapola [ama'pola] nf poppy.

amar [a'mar] vt to love.

amargado, a [amar'xaðo, a] a bitter; **amargar** vt to make bitter; (fig) to embitter; **amargarse** vr to get bitter.

amargo, a [a'marxo, a] a bitter; **amargura** nf bitterness.

amarillento, a [amari'ʎento, a] a yellowish; (tez) sallow; **amarillo, a** a, nm yellow.

amarrar [ama'rrar] vt to moor; (sujetar) to tie up.

amartelar [amarte'lar] vt to make jealous; (enamorar) to win the heart of; ~se vr: ~se **de** to fall in love with.

amartillar [amarti'ʎar] vt = martillar.

amasar [ama'sar] vt to knead; (mezclar) to mix, prepare; (MED) to massage; (confeccionar) to concoct; **amasijo** nm kneading; mixing; (masa) dough; (pasta) paste; (fig) hotchpotch.

amateur ['amatur] nm/f amateur.

amatista [ama'tista] nf amethyst.

amazona [ama'θona] nf horsewoman; **A~s** nm: **el A~s** the Amazon.

ambages [am'baxes] nmpl: **sin** ~ in plain language.

ámbar ['ambar] nm amber.

ambición [ambi'θjon] nf ambition; **ambicionar** vt to aspire to; **ambicioso, a** a ambitious.

ambidextro, a [ambi'ðekstro, a] a ambidextrous.

ambiente [am'bjente] nm atmosphere; (medio) environment.

ambigüedad [ambixwe'ðað] nf ambiguity; **ambiguo, a** a ambiguous.

ámbito ['ambito] nm compass; (campo) field; (límite) boundary; (fig) scope.

ambos, as ['ambos, as] apl, pron pl both.

ambulancia [ambu'lanθja] nf ambulance.

ambulante [ambu'lante] a walking cpd, itinerant.

ambulatorio [ambula'torjo] nm national health clinic.

amedrentar [ameðren'tar] vt to scare.

amén [a'men] excl amen ~ **de** except for.

amenaza [ame'naθa] nf threat; **amenazar** vt, vi to threaten.

amenguar [amen'xwar] vt to diminish; (fig) to dishonour.

amenidad [ameni'ðað] nf pleasantness.

ameno, a [a'meno, a] a pleasant.

América [a'merika] nf America; ~ **del Norte/del Sur** North/South America; ~ **Central/Latina** Central/Latin America; **americano, a** a, nm/f American // nf coat, jacket.

ametralladora [ametraʎa'ðora] nf machine gun.

amigable [ami'xaβle] a friendly.

amígdala [a'mixðala] nf tonsil; **amigdalitis** nf tonsillitis.

amigo, a [a'mixo, a] a friendly // nm/f friend.

amilanar [amila'nar] vt to scare.

aminorar [amino'rar] *vt* to diminish; (*reducir*) to reduce.
amistad [amis'tað] *nf* friendship; ~**es** *nfpl* friends; **amistoso, a** *a* friendly.
amnesia [am'nesja] *nf* amnesia.
amnistía [amnis'tia] *nf* amnesty.
amo ['amo] *nm* owner; (*dueño*) boss; ~ **de casa** householder.
amodorrarse [amoðo'rrarse] *vr* to get sleepy.
amolar [amo'lar] *vt* to sharpen; (*fig*) to bore.
amoldar [amol'dar] *vt* to mould; (*adaptar*) to adapt.
amonestación [amonesta'θjon] *nf* warning; **amonestaciones** *nfpl* marriage banns; **amonestar** *vt* to warn; to publish the banns of.
amontonar [amonto'nar] *vt* to collect, pile up; ~**se** *vr* to crowd together; (*acumularse*) to pile up.
amor [a'mor] *nm* love; (*amante*) lover; **hacer el** ~ to make love; (*cortejar*) to court.
amoratado, a [amora'taðo, a] *a* purple, blue with cold.
amordazar [amorða'θar] *vt* to muzzle; (*fig*) to gag.
amorío [amo'rio] *nm* (*fam*) love affair.
amoroso, a [amo'roso, a] *a* affectionate, loving.
amortajar [amorta'xar] *vt* to shroud.
amortiguador [amortigwa'ðor] *nm* shock absorber; (*parachoques*) bumper; (*silenciador*) silencer; **amortiguar** *vt* to deaden; (*ruido*) to muffle; (*color*) to soften.
amortización [amortiθa'θjon] *nf* redemption, repayment.
amotinar [amoti'nar] *vt* to stir up, incite (to riot); ~**se** *vr* to mutiny.
amparar [ampa'rar] *vt* to protect; ~**se** *vr* to seek protection; (*abrigar*) to shelter; **amparo** *nm* help, protection.
ampliación [amplja'θjon] *nf* enlargement; (*extensión*) extension; **ampliar** *vt* to enlarge; to extend.
amplificación [amplifika'θjon] *nf* enlargement; **amplificador** *nm* amplifier; **amplificar** *vt* to amplify.
amplio, a ['ampljo, a] *a* spacious; (*de falda etc*) full; (*extenso*) extensive; (*ancho*) wide; **amplitud** *nf* spaciousness; extent; (*fig*) amplitude.
ampolla [am'poʎa] *nf* blister; (*MED*) ampoule.
amputar [ampu'tar] *vt* to cut off, amputate.
amueblar [amwe'βlar] *vt* to furnish.
amurallar [amura'ʎar] *vt* to wall up/in.
anacronismo [anakro'nismo] *nm* anachronism.
ánade [a'naðe] *nm* duck.
anadear [anaðe'ar] *vi* to waddle.
anales [a'nales] *nmpl* annals.
analfabetismo [analfaβe'tismo] *nm* illiteracy; **analfabeto, a** *a* illiterate.

análisis [a'nalisis] *nm* analysis.
analizar [anali'θar] *vt* to analyse.
analogía [analo'xia] *nf* analogy.
ananá(s) [ana'na(s)] *nm* pineapple.
anaquel [ana'kel] *nm* shelf.
anarquía [anar'kia] *nf* anarchy; **anarquismo** *nm* anarchism; **anarquista** *nm/f* anarchist.
anatomía [anato'mia] *nf* anatomy.
anciano, a [an'θjano, a] ε old, aged // *nm/f* old man/woman // *nm* elder.
ancla ['ankla] *nf* anchor; ~**dero** *nm* anchorage; **anclar** *vi* to (drop) anchor.
ancho, a ['antʃo, a] *a* wide; (*falda*) full; (*fig*) liberal // *nm* width; (*FERRO*) gauge; **ponerse** ~ to get conceited; **estar a sus** ~**as** to be at one's ease.
anchoa [an'tʃoa] *nf* anchovy.
anchura [an'tʃura] *nf* width; (*extensión*) wideness; (*fig*) freedom.
andaderas [anda'ðeras] *nfpl* baby walker *sg*.
andadura [anda'ðura] *nf* gait, pace.
Andalucía [andalu'θia] *nf* Andalusia; **andaluz, a** *a, nm/f* Andalusian.
andamio [an'damjo], **andamiaje** [anda-'mjaxe] *nm* scaffold.
andar [an'dar] *vt* to go cover, travel // *vi* to go, walk, travel; (*funcionar*) to go, work; (*estar*) to be // *nm* walk, gait, pace; ~**se** *vr* to go away; ~ **a pie/a caballo/en bicicleta** to go on foot/on horseback/by bicycle; **¡anda!, ¡andando!** go on!; (*vamos*) come on!; (*bien*) well!, **anda en los 40** he's about 40.
andariego, a [anda'rjexo, a] *a* fond of travelling.
andén [an'den] *nm* (*FERRO*) platform; (*NAUT*) quayside; (*AUTO*) hard shoulder.
Andes ['andes] *nmpl*: **los** ~ the Andes.
Andorra [an'dorra] *nf* Andorra.
andrajo [an'draxo] *nm* rag; ~**so, a** *a* ragged.
andurriales [andu'rrjales] *nmpl* out-of-the-way place *sg*.
anduve *etc vb ver* **andar**.
anécdota [a'nekðota] *nf* anecdote, story.
anegar [ane'xar] *vt* to flood; (*ahogar*) to drown; ~**se** *vr* to drown; (*hundirse*) to sink.
anemia [a'nemja] *nf* anaemia.
anestésico [anes'tesiko] *nm* anaesthetic.
anexar [anek'sar] *vt* to annex; (*documento*) to attach; **anexo, a** *a* attached // *nm* annexe.
anfibio, a [an'fiβjo, a] *a* amphibious // *nm* amphibian.
anfiteatro [anfite'atro] *nm* amphitheatre; (*TEATRO*) dress circle.
anfitrión, ona [anfi'trjon, ona] *nm/f* host.
ángel ['anxel] *nm* angel; **angélico, a, angélical** *a* angelic(al).
angina [an'xina] *nf* (*MED*) inflammation of the throat; ~ **de pecho** angina (pectoris).
anglicano, a [angli'kano, a] *a, nm/f* Anglican.

angosto, a [an'gosto, a] a narrow.

angostura [angos'tura] nf narrowness; (paso) narrow passage.

anguila [an'gila] nf eel; ~s nfpl slipway sg.

ángulo ['angulo] nm angle; (esquina) corner; (curva) bend.

angustia [an'gustja] nf anguish; **angustiar** vt to distress, grieve.

anhelante [ane'lante] a eager; (deseoso) longing; **anhelar** vt to be eager for; to long for, desire // vi to pant, gasp; **anhelo** nm eagerness; desire.

anidar [ani'ðar] vi to nest.

anillo [a'niλo] nm ring; ~ de boda wedding ring.

ánima ['anima] nf soul; las ~s the Angelus (bell) sg.

animación [anima'θjon] nf liveliness; (vitalidad) life; (actividad) bustle; **animado, a** a lively; (vivaz) animated.

animadversión [animaðßer'sjon] nf illwill, antagonism.

animal [ani'mal] a animal; (fig) stupid // nm animal; (fig) fool; (bestia) brute.

animar [ani'mar] vt (BIO) to animate, give life to; (fig) to liven up, brighten up, cheer up; (estimular) to stimulate; ~se vr to cheer up, feel encouraged; (decidirse) to make up one's mind.

ánimo ['animo] nm soul, mind; (valentía) courage // excl cheer up!

animosidad [animosi'ðað] nf animosity.

animoso, a [ani'moso, a] a brave; (vivo) lively.

aniquilar [aniki'lar] vt to annihilate, destroy; ~se vr to be wiped out, disappear; (empeorarse) to deteriorate.

anís [a'nis] nm aniseed.

aniversario [anißer'sarjo] nm anniversary.

anoche [a'notʃe] ad last night; **antes de** ~ the night before last.

anochecer [anotʃe'θer] vi to get dark // nm nightfall, dark.

anomalía [anoma'lia] nf anomaly.

anonadamiento [anonaða'mjento] nm annihilation; (desaliento) discouragement; **anonadar** vt to annihilate; to discourage; **anonadarse** vr to get discouraged.

anónimo, a [a'nonimo, a] a anonymous; (com) limited // nm anonymity.

anormal [anor'mal] a abnormal.

anotación [anota'θjon] nf note.

anotar [ano'tar] vt to note down; (comentar) to annotate.

ansia ['ansja] nf anxiety; (añoranza) yearning; **ansiar** vt to long for.

ansiedad [ansje'ðað] nf anxiety.

ansioso, a [an'sjoso, a] a anxious; (anhelante) eager.

antagónico, a [anta'voniko, a] a antagonistic; (opuesto) contrasting; **antagonista** nm/f antagonist.

antaño [an'taɲo] ad long ago.

Antártico [an'tartiko] nm: el ~ the Antarctic.

ante ['ante] prep before, in the presence of; (encarado con) faced with // nm suede, buckskin; ~ todo above all.

anteanoche [antea'notʃe] ad the night before last.

anteayer [antea'jer] ad the day before yesterday.

antebrazo [ante'ßraθo] nm forearm.

antecedente [anteθe'ðente] a previous // nm antecedente: ~s nmpl record sg, background sg.

anteceder [anteθe'ðer] vt to precede, go before.

antecesor, a [anteθe'sor, a] nm/f predecessor; (antepasado) ancestor.

antedicho, a [ante'ðitʃo, a] a aforementioned.

antelación [antela'θjon] nf: con ~ in advance.

antemano [ante'mano]: de ~ ad beforehand, in advance.

antena [an'tena] nf antenna; (de televisión etc) aerial.

anteojo [ante'oxo] nm eyeglass; ~s nmpl spectacles, glasses.

antepasados [antepa'saðos] nmpl ancestors.

antepecho [ante'petʃo] nm guardrail, parapet; (repisa) ledge, sill.

anteponer [antepo'ner] vt to place in front; (fig) to prefer; ~se vr: ~se a to overcome.

anteproyecto [antepro'jekto] nm preliminary sketch; (fig) blueprint.

anterior [ante'rjor] a preceding, previous; ~idad nf: con ~idad a prior to, before.

antes ['antes] ad sooner; (primero) first; (con prioridad) before; (hace tiempo) previously, once; (más bien) rather // prep: ~ de before /; conj: ~ (de) que before; ~ bien (on) rather; dos días ~ two days before or previously; ~ muerto que esclavo better dead than enslaved; tomo el avión ~ que el barco I take the plane rather than the boat; cuanto ~, lo ~ posible as soon as possible.

antesala [ante'sala] nf anteroom.

antibiótico [anti'ßjotiko] nm antibiotic.

anticipación [antiθipa'θjon] nf anticipation; (com) advance; con 10 minutos de ~ 10 minutes early; **anticipado, a** a (in) advance.

anticipar [antiθi'par] vt to anticipate; (adelantar) to bring forward; (com) to advance; ~se vr: ~se a su época to be ahead of one's time.

anticipo [anti'θipo] nm = anticipación.

anticonceptivo, a [antikonθep'tißo, a] a nm contraceptive.

anticongelante [antikonxe'lante] nm antifreeze.

anticuado, a [anti'kwaðo, a] a out-of-date, old-fashioned; (desusado) obsolete.

anticuario [anti'kwarjo] nm antique dealer.

antídoto [an'tiðoto] *nm* antidote.

antifaz [anti'faθ] *nm* mask; (*velo*) veil.

antigualla [anti·'ʋwaʎa] *nf* antique; (*reliquia*) relic.

antiguamente [antiχwa'mente] *ad* formerly; (*hace mucho tiempo*) long ago.

antigüedad [antiχwe'ðað] *nf* antiquity; (*artículo*) antique; (*rango*) seniority; **antiguo, a** *a* old, ancient; (*que fue*) former.

antílope [an'tilope] *nm* antelope.

antillano, a [anti'ʎano, a] *a, nm/f* West Indian.

Antillas [an'tiʎas] *nfpl*: **las** ~ the West Indies.

antipara [anti'para] *nf* screen.

antipatía [antipa'tia] *nf* antipathy, dislike; **antipático, a** *a* disagreeable, unpleasant.

antisemita [antise'mita] *nm/f* antisemite.

antítesis [an'titesis] *nf* antithesis.

antojadizo, a [antoxa'ðiθo, a] *a* capricious.

antojarse [anto'xarse] *vr* (*desear*): **se me antoja comprarlo** I have a mind to buy it; (*pensar*): **se me antoja que** I have a feeling that.

antojo [an'toxo] *nm* caprice, whim; (*rosa*) birthmark; (*lunar*) mole.

antología [antolo'xia] *nf* anthology.

antorcha [an'tortʃa] *nf* torch.

antro ['antro] *nm* cavern.

antropófago, a [antro'pofaxo, a] *a, nm/f* cannibal.

antropología [antropolo'xia] *nf* anthropology.

anual [a'nwal] *a* annual.

anualidad [anwali'ðað] *nf* annuity.

anuario [a'nwarjo] *nm* yearbook.

anublar [anu'βlar] *vt* to cloud; (*oscurecer*) to darken; ~**se** *vr* to become cloudy, cloud over; (*bot*) to wither.

anudar [anu'ðar] *vt* to knot, tie; (*unir*) to join; ~**se** *vr* to get tied up.

anulación [anula'θjon] *nf* annulment; (*cancelación*) cancellation; **anular** *vt* to annul; to cancel; (*revocar*) to revoke, repeal // *nm* ring finger.

anunciación [anunθja'θjon] *nf* announcement; **anunciar** *vt* to announce; (*proclamar*) to proclaim; (*com*) to advertise.

anuncio [a'nunθjo] *nm* announcement; (*señal*) sign; (*com*) advertisement; (*cartel*) poster.

anzuelo [an'θwelo] *nm* hook; (*para pescar*) fish hook.

añadidura [aɲaði'ðura] *nf* addition, extra; **por** ~ besides, in addition.

añadir [aɲa'ðir] *vt* to add.

añejo, a [a'ɲexo, a] *a* old.

añicos [a'ɲikos] *nmpl*: **hacer** ~ to smash, shatter.

año ['aɲo] *nm* year; **¡Feliz A**~ **Nuevo!** Happy New Year!; **tener 15** ~**s** to be 15 (years old); **los** ~**s 60** the sixties; ~ **bisiesto/escolar** leap/school year.

añoranza [aɲo'ranθa] *nf* nostalgia; (*anhelo*) longing.

apacentar [apaθen'tar] *vt* to pasture, graze.

apacible [apa'θiβle] *a* gentle, mild.

apaciguar [apaθi'ʋwar] *vt* to pacify, calm (down).

apadrinar [apaðri'nar] *vt* to sponsor, support; (*rel*) to act as godfather to.

apagado, a [apa'xaðo, a] *a* out; (*volcán*) extinct; (*cal*) slaked; (*color*) dull; (*voz*) quiet, timid; (*sonido*) muted, muffled; (*apático*) listless.

apagar [apa'xar] *vt* to put out; (*sonido*) to silence, muffle; (*sed*) to quench; (*fig*) to kill.

apagón [apa'xon] *nm* blackout, power cut.

apalabrar [apala'βrar] *vt* to agree to; (*obrero*) to engage.

apalear [apale'ar] *vt* to beat, thrash; (*agr*) to winnow.

apañar [apa'ɲar] *vt* to pick up; (*asir*) to take hold of, grasp; (*vestir*) to dress up; (*reparar*) to mend, patch up; ~**se** *vr* to manage, get along.

aparador [apara'ðor] *nm* sideboard; (*escaparate*) shop window.

aparato [apa'rato] *nm* apparatus; (*máquina*) machine; (*doméstico*) appliance; (*boato*) ostentation; ~**so, a** *a* showy, ostentatious.

aparcamiento [aparka'mjento] *nm* car park.

aparcar [apar'kar] *vt, vi* to park.

aparecer [apare'θer] *vi*, ~**se** *vr* to appear.

aparejado, a [apare'xaðo, a] *a* fit, suitable.

aparejar [apare'xar] *vt* to prepare; (*caballo*) to saddle, harness; (*naut*) to fit out, rig out; **aparejo** *nm* preparation; harness; rigging; (*de poleas*) block and tackle.

aparentar [aparen'tar] *vt* to feign; (*parecer*) to look, seem (to be).

aparente [apa'rente] *a* apparent; (*adecuado*) suitable.

aparición [apari'θjon] *nf* appearance; (*de libro*) publication.

apariencia [apa'rjenθja] *nf* (outward) appearance; **en** ~ outwardly, seemingly.

apartado, a [apar'taðo, a] *a* separate; (*lejano*) remote /; *nm* post office box; (*tipográfico*) paragraph.

apartamento [aparta'mento] *nm* apartment, flat.

apartamiento [aparta'mjento] *nm* separation; (*aislamiento*) remoteness; (*am*) apartment, flat.

apartar [apar'tar] *vt* to separate; (*quitar*) to remove; (*mineralogía*) to extract; ~**se** *vr* to separate, part; (*irse*) to move away, keep away; **aparte** *ad* (*separadamente*) separately; (*además*) besides // *nm* aside; (*tipográfico*) new paragraph.

apasionado, a [apasjo'naðo, a] *a* passionate; biassed, prejudiced.

apasionar [apasjo'nar] vt to arouse passion in; ~**se** vr to get excited.

apatía [apa'tia] nf apathy.

apático, a [a'patiko, a] a apathetic.

apdo nm abr de **apartado (de correos)**.

apeadero [apea'ðero] nm halt, wayside station.

apearse [ape'arse] vr to dismount; (bajarse) to get down/out.

apedrear [apeðre'ar] vt to stone.

apegarse [ape'xarse] vr: ~**se a** to become attached to; **apego** nm attachment, fondness.

apelación [apela'θjon] nf appeal.

apelante [ape'lante] nm/f appellant.

apelar [ape'lar] vi to appeal; ~ **a** to resort to.

apellidar [apeʎi'ðar] vt to call, name; ~**se** vr to be called; **apellido** nm surname, name.

apenar [ape'nar] vt to grieve, trouble ~**se** vr to grieve.

apenas [a'penas] ad scarcely, hardly // conj as soon as, no sooner.

apéndice [a'pendiθe] nm appendix; **apendicitis** nf appendicitis.

apercibir [aperθi'βir] vt to prepare; (avisar) to warn; (JUR) to summon; (AM) to notice, see; ~**se** vr to get ready.

aperitivo [aperi'tiβo] nm aperitif.

apertura [aper'tura] n ing.

apesadumbrar [apes...n'brar] vt to grieve, sadden; ~**se** vr to distress o.s.

apestar [apes'tar] vt to infect // vi to stink.

apetecer [apete'θer] vt: ¿te apetece una tortilla? do you fancy an omelette?; **apetecible** a desirable; (llamativo) attractive.

apetito [ape'tito] nm appetite; ~**so, a** a appetizing; (fig) tempting.

apiadarse [apja'ðarse] vr: ~ **de** to take pity on.

ápice ['apiθe] nm apex; (fig) whit, iota.

apio ['apjo] nm celery.

aplacar [apla'kar] vt to placate; ~**se** vr to calm down.

aplanamiento [aplana'mjento] nm smoothing, levelling.

aplanar [apla'nar] vt to smooth, level; (allanar) to roll flat, flatten.

aplastar [aplas'tar] vt to squash (flat); (fig) to crush.

aplaudir [aplau'ðir] vt to applaud.

aplauso [a'plauso] nm applause; (fig) approval, acclaim.

aplazamiento [aplaθa'mjento] nm postponement, adjournment; **aplazar** vt to postpone, defer.

aplicación [aplika'θjon] nf application; (esfuerzo) effort.

aplicado, a [apli'kaðo, a] a diligent, hard-working.

aplicar [apli'kar] vt (ejecutar) to apply; ~**se** vr to apply o.s.

aplomo [a'plomo] nm aplomb, self-assurance.

apocado, a [apo'kaðo, a] a timid.

apocamiento [apoka'mjento] nm timidity; (depresión) depression.

apocar [apo'kar] vt to reduce; ~**se** vr to feel small, feel humiliated.

apodar [apo'ðar] vt to nickname.

apoderado [apoðe'raðo] nm agent, representative; **apoderar** vt to authorize, empower; (JUR) to grant (a) power of attorney to; **apoderarse** vr: apoderarse de to take possession of.

apodo [a'poðo] nm nickname.

apogeo [apo'xeo] nm peak, summit.

apología [apolo'xia] nf eulogy; (defensa) defence.

apoplejía [apople'xia] nf apoplexy, stroke.

aporrear [aporre'ar] vt to beat (up); **aporreo** nm beating.

aportar [apor'tar] vt to contribute // vi to reach port; ~**se** vr (AM) to arrive, come.

aposentar [aposen'tar] vt to lodge, put up; **aposento** nm lodging; (habitación) room.

apostar [apos'tar] vt to bet, stake; (destinar) to station, post // vi to bet.

apostilla [apos'tiʎa] nf note, comment.

apóstol [a'postol] nm apostle.

apóstrofe [a'postrofe] nm insult; (reprimenda) reprimand.

apóstrofo [a'postrofo] nm apostrophe.

apostura [apos'tura] nf neatness, elegance.

apoyar [apo'jar] vt to lean, rest; (fig) to support, back; ~**se** vr: ~**se en** to lean on; **apoyo** nm support, backing; (sostén) prop.

apreciable [apre'θjaβle] a considerable; (fig) esteemed.

apreciación [apreθja'θjon] nf appreciation; (COM) valuation; **apreciar** vt to evaluate, assess; (COM) to appreciate, value.

aprecio [a'preθjo] nm valuation, estimate; (fig) appreciation.

aprehender [apreen'der] vt to apprehend, seize; **aprehensión** nf detention, capture.

apremiante [apre'mjante] a urgent, pressing; **apremiar** vt to compel, force // vi to be urgent, press; **apremio** nm compulsion; urgency.

aprender [apren'der] vt, vi to learn.

aprendiz, a [apren'diθ, a] nm/f apprentice; (principiante) learner; ~**aje** nm apprenticeship.

aprensión [apren'sjon] nm apprehension, fear; (delicadeza) squeamishness; **aprensivo, a** a apprehensive; (nervioso) nervous, timid.

apresar [apre'sar] vt to seize; (capturar) to capture.

aprestar [apres'tar] vt to prepare, get ready; (TEC) to prime, size; ~**se** vr to get ready.

apresurado, a [apresu'raðo, a] a hurried,

hasty; **apresuramiento** nm hurry, haste.
apresurar [apresu'rar] vt to hurry, accelerate; ~**se** vr to hurry, make haste.
apretado, a [apre'taðo, a] a tight; (escritura) cramped; (difícil) difficult; (fam) stingy.
apretar [apre'tar] vt to squeeze, press; (TEC) to tighten; (presionar) to press together, pack // vi to be too tight; (insistir) to insist.
apretón [apre'ton] nm squeeze; (abrazo) hug; (aglomeración) crush; (dificultad) difficulty, jam; (carrera) dash, sprint; ~ **de manos** handshake; **apretura** nf squeeze; hug; crush; difficulty, jam; (escasez) scarcity.
aprieto [a'prjeto] nm squeeze, press; (dificultad) difficulty, jam.
aprisionar [aprisjo'nar] vt to imprison.
aprobación [aproßa'θjon] nf approval; (de examen) pass; (nota) pass mark; **aprobar** vt to approve (of); to pass // vi to pass.
apropiación [apropja'θjon] nf appropriation.
apropiado, a [apro'pjaðo, a] a appropriate.
apropiar [apro'pjar] vt to adapt, make fit; ~**se** vr: ~**se de** to appropriate.
aprovechado, a [aproße'tʃaðo, a] a diligent, hardworking; (económico) thrifty; (pey) unscrupulous, grasping; **aprovechamiento** nm use, exploitation.
aprovechar [aproße'tʃar] vt to use, exploit, profit from; (sacar partido de) to take advantage of // vi to progress, improve; ~**se** vr: ~**se de** to make use of, take advantage of, ¡**que aproveche!** enjoy your meal!
aproximación [aproksima'θjon] nf approximation; (cercanía) nearness; (de lotería) consolation prize; **aproximado, a** a approximate; **aproximar** vt to bring nearer; **aproximarse** vr to come near, approach.
aptitud [apti'tuð] nf aptitude; (idoneidad) suitability.
apto, a ['apto, a] a suitable.
apuesto, a [a'pwesto, a] a neat, elegant // nf bet, wager.
apuntador [apunta'ðor] nm prompter.
apuntalar [apunta'lar] vt to prop up.
apuntar [apun'tar] vt (con arma) to aim at; (con dedo) to point at or to; (anotar) to note (down); (TEATRO) to prompt; (dinero) to stake; ~**se** vr to score a point.
apunte [a'punte] nm note.
apuñalar [apuɲa'lar] vt to stab.
apurado, a [apu'raðo, a] a needy; (difícil) difficult, dangerous; (agotado) exhausted; (AM) hurried, rushed.
apurar [apu'rar] vt (purificar) to purify; (agotar) to drain; (recursos) to use up; (molestar) to annoy; ~**se** vr to worry; (AM) to hurry.
apuro [a'puro] nm (aprieto) fix, jam; (escasez) want, hardship; (aflicción) distress; (AM) haste, urgency.

aquejar [ake'xar] vt to distress, grieve; (MED) to afflict.
aquel, aquella, aquellos, as [a'kel, a'keʎa, a'keʎos, as] det that, (pl) those.
aquél, aquélla, aquéllos, as [a'kel, a'keʎa, a'keʎos, as] pron that (one); (pl) those (ones).
aquello [a'keʎo] pron that, that business.
aquí [a'ki] ad (lugar) here; (tiempo) now; ~ **arriba** up here; ~ **mismo** right here; ~ **yace** here lies; **de** ~ **a siete días** a week from now.
aquietar [akje'tar] vt to quieten (down), calm (down).
árabe ['araße] a Arab, Arabian, Arabic // nm/f Arab // nm (lengua) Arabic.
Arabia Saudita [araßjasau'ðita] nf Saudi Arabia.
arado [a'raðo] nm plough.
aragonés, esa [arayo'nes, esa] a, nm/f Aragonese.
arancel [aran'θel] nm tariff, duty; ~ **de aduanas** customs duty.
araña [a'raɲa] nf (ZOOL) spider; (de luces) chandelier.
arañar [ara'ɲar] vt to scratch.
arañazo [ara'ɲaθo] nm scratch.
arar [a'rar] vt to plough, till.
arbitrador, a [arßitra'ðor, a] nm/f arbiter.
arbitraje [arßi'traxe] nm arbitration.
arbitrar [arßi'trar] vt to arbitrate in; (DEPORTE) to referee // vi to arbitrate.
arbitrariedad [arßitrarje'ðað] nf arbitrariness; (acto) arbitrary act; **arbitrario, a** a arbitrary.
arbitrio [ar'ßitrjo] nm free will; (JUR) adjudication, decision.
árbitro ['arßitro] nm arbitrator; (DEPORTE) referee; (TENIS) umpire.
árbol ['arßol] nm (BOT) tree; (NAUT) mast; (TEC) axle, shaft; **arbolado, a** a wooded, tree-lined // nm woodland.
arboladura [arßola'ðura] nf rigging; **arbolar** vt to hoist, raise; **arbolarse** vr to rear up.
arboleda [arßo'leða] nf grove, plantation.
arbusto [ar'ßusto] nm bush, shrub.
arca ['arka] nf chest, box; (caja fuerte) strongbox.
arcada [ar'kaða] nf arcade; (de puente) arch, span; ~**s** nfpl retching sg.
arcaduz [arka'ðuθ] nm pipe, conduit.
arcaico, a [ar'kaiko, a] a archaic.
arce ['arθe] nm maple tree.
arcediano [arθe'ðjano] nm archdeacon.
arcilla [ar'θiʎa] nf clay.
arco ['arko] nm arch; (MAT) arc; (MIL, MUS) bow; ~ **iris** rainbow.
archipiélago [artʃi'pjelaxo] nm archipelago.
archivar [artʃi'ßar] vt to file (away); **archivo** nm archive(s) (pl).
arder [ar'ðer] vi, vt to burn.
ardid [ar'ðið] nm ruse.

ardiente [ar'ðjente] *a* **burning**; (*apasionado*) ardent.

ardilla [ar'ðiʎa] *nf* squirrel.

ardor [ar'ðor] *nm* (*calor*) heat, warmth; (*fig*) ardour; ~ **de estómago** heartburn; ~**oso**, **a** *a* = **ardiente**.

arduo, a [ar'ðwo, a] *a* arduous.

área ['area] *nf* area; (*DEPORTE*) penalty area.

arena [a'rena] *nf* sand; (*de una lucha*) arena; (*MED*) stone.

arenal [are'nal] *nm* sandy ground; (*arena movediza*) quicksand.

arengar [aren'gar] *vt* to harangue.

arenisco, a [are'nisko, a] *a* sandy // *nf* sandstone; (*cascajo*) grit.

arenoso, a [are'noso, a] *a* sandy.

arenque [a'renke] *nm* herring.

arete [a'rete] *nm* earring.

argamasa [arɣa'masa] *nf* mortar, plaster.

argamasar *vt* to mortar, plaster.

Argel [ar'xel] *n* Algiers; ~**ia** *nf* Algeria **argelino, a** *a*, *nm/f* Algerian.

argentino, a [arxen'tino, a] *a* Argentinian; (*de plata*) silvery // *nm/f* Argentinian // *nf*: A~**a** Argentina.

argolla [ar'xoʎa] *nf* (large) ring; (*juego*) croquet.

argot [ar'xo] *nm* slang.

argucia [ar'xuθja] *nf* subtlety, sophistry.

argüir [ar'xwir] *vt* to deduce; (*discutir*) to argue; (*indicar*) to indicate, imply; (*censurar*) to reproach // *vi* to argue.

argumentación [arxumenta'θjon] *nf* (line of) argument; **argumentar** *vt*, *vi* to argue.

argumento [arxu'mento] *nm* argument; (*de obra*) plot.

aria ['arja] *nf* aria.

aridez [ari'ðeθ] *nf* aridity, dryness.

árido, a ['ariðo, a] *a* arid, dry; ~**s** *nmpl* dry goods.

Aries ['arjes] *nm* Aries.

ariete [a'rjete] *nm* battering ram.

ario, a [a'rjo, a] *a* Aryan.

arisco, a [a'risko, a] *a* surly; (*insociable*) unsociable.

aristócrata [aris'tokrata] *nm/f* aristocrat.

aritmética [arit'metika] *nf* arithmetic.

arma ['arma] *nf* arm; ~**s** *nfpl* arms; ~ **blanca** blade, knife; (*espada*) sword; ~ **de fuego** firearm; ~**s cortas** small arms.

armadillo [arma'ðiʎo] *nm* armadillo.

armado, a [ar'maðo, a] *a* armed; (*TEC*) reinforced // *nf* armada; (*flota*) fleet.

armadura [arma'ðura] *nf* (*MIL*) armour; (*TEC*) framework; (*ZOOL*) skeleton; (*FÍSICA*) armature.

armamento [arma'mento] *nm* armament; (*NAUT*) fitting-out.

armar [ar'mar] *vt* (*soldado*) to arm; (*máquina*) to assemble; (*navío*) to fit out; ~**la**, ~ **un lío** to start a row.

armario [ar'marjo] *nm* wardrobe.

armatoste [arma'toste] *nm* large useless object, contraption.

armazón [arma'θon] *nf* body, chassis; (*de mueble etc*) frame; (*ARQ*) skeleton.

armería [arme'ria] *nf* (*museo*) military museum; (*tienda*) gunsmith's.

armiño [ar'miɲo] *nm* stoat; (*piel*) ermine.

armisticio [armis'tiθjo] *nm* armistice.

armonía [armo'ria] *nf* harmony.

armónica [ar'monika] *nf* harmonica.

armonioso, a [armo'njoso, a] *a* harmonious.

arnés [ar'nes] *nm* armour; **arneses** *nmpl* harness *sg*.

aro ['aro] *nm* ring; (*tejo*) quoit; (*pendiente*) earring.

aroma [a'roma] *nm* aroma.

aromático, a [aro'matiko, a] *a* aromatic.

arpa ['arpa] *nf* harp.

arpía [ar'pia] *nf* shrew.

arpista [ar'pista] *nm/f* harpist.

arpón [ar'pon] *nm* harpoon.

arquear [arke'ar] *vt* to arch, bend; ~**se** *vr* to arch, bend; **arqueo** *nm* (*gen*) arching, curve; (*de navío*) tonnage.

arqueología [arkeolo'xia] *nf* archaeology; **arqueólogo, a** *nm/f* archaeologist.

arquero [ar'kero] *nm* archer, bowman.

arquetipo [arke'tipo] *nm* archetype.

arquitecto [arki'tekto] *nm* architect; **arquitectura** *nf* architecture.

arrabal [arra'βal] *nm* suburb; (*AM*) slum.

arraigado, a [arrai'xaðo, a] *a* deep-rooted; (*fig*) established.

arraigar [arrai'xar] *vt* to establish // *vi*, ~**se** *vr* to take root.

arrancar [arran'kar] *vt* (*sacar*) to pull up, extract, pull out; (*separar*) to snatch (away), wrest; (*fig*) to extract // *vi* to start, pull out.

arranque [a'rranke] *nm* sudden start; (*AUTO*) start; (*fig*) fit, outburst.

arras ['arras] *nfpl* pledge *sg* security *sg*.

arrasar [arra'sar] *vt* (*aplanar*) to level, flatten; (*destruir*) to demolish; (*llenar*) to fill up // *vi* to clear.

arrastrado, a [arras'traðo, a] *a* poor, wretched; (*AM*) servile.

arrastrar [arras'trar] *vt* to drag (along); (*fig*) to drag down, degrade; (*suj*: *agua*, *viento*) to carry away // *vi* to drag, trail on the ground; ~**se** *vr* to crawl; (*fig*) to grovel; **llevar algo arrastrado** to drag sth along.

arrastre [a'rrastre] *nm* drag, dragging; (*DEPORTE*) crawl.

arrayán [arra'jan] *nm* myrtle.

arrear [arre'ar] *vt* to drive, urge on; (*enganchar*) to harness // *vi* to hurry along; **¡arre(a)!** get up!, gee up!

arrebatado, a [arreβa'taðo, a] *a* rash, impetuous; (*repentino*) sudden, hasty.

arrebatar [arreβa'tar] *vt* to snatch (away), seize; (*fig*) to captivate; ~**se** *vr* to get carried away, get excited.

arrebato [arre'βato] *nm* fit of rage, fury; (*éxtasis*) rapture.

arreglado, a [arre'xlaðo, a] *a* (*ordenado*)

neat, orderly; (*moderado*) moderate, reasonable.

arreglar [arre'xlar] *vt* (*poner orden*) to tidy up; (*algo roto*) to fix, repair; (*problema*) to solve; (*MUS*) to arrange; ~se *vr* to reach an understanding; **arreglárselas** (*fam*) to get by, manage.

arreglo [a'rrexlo] *nm* settlement; (*orden*) order; (*acuerdo*) agreement; (*MUS*) arrangement, setting.

arremangar [arreman'gar] *vt* to roll up, turn up; ~se *vr* to roll up one's sleeves.

arremeter [arreme'ter] *vt* to attack, assault.

arrendador, a [arrenda'ðor, a] *nm/f* landlord/lady; (*inquilino*) tenant.

arrendamiento [arrenda'mjento] *nm* letting; (*alquilar*) hiring; (*contrato*) lease; (*alquiler*) rent; **arrendar** *vt* to let, lease; to rent; **arrendatario,** a *nm/f* tenant.

arreo [a'rreo] *nm* adornment; ~s *nmpl* harness *sg*, trappings.

arrepentimiento [arrepenti'mjento] *nm* regret, repentance.

arrepentirse [arrepen'tirse] *vr*: ~ de to regret, repent of.

arrestar [arres'tar] *vt* to arrest; (*encarcelar*) to imprison; **arresto** *nm* arrest; (*MIL*) detention; (*audacia*) boldness, daring; **arresto domiciliario** house arrest.

arriar [a'rrjar] *vt* (*velas, bandera*) to lower, strike; (*un cable*) to pay out; ~se *vr* to flood.

arriba [a'rriβa] *ad* (*posición*) above, overhead, on top; (*en casa*) upstairs; (*dirección*) up, upwards; ~ de above, higher (up) than; ~ **del todo** at the very top; **el piso de** ~ the flat upstairs; **de** ~ **abajo** from top to bottom; **calle** ~ up the street; **lo** ~ **mencionado** the aforementioned; ~ **de 20 pesetas** more than 20 pesetas; ¡~ **las manos!** hands up!

arribar [arri'βar] *vi* to put into port; (*llegar*) to arrive.

arribista [arri'βista] *nm/f* parvenu/e, upstart.

arriendo [a'rrjendo] *nm* = **arrendamiento**.

arriero [a'rrjero] *nm* muleteer.

arriesgado, a [arrjes'xaðo, a] *a* (*peligroso*) risky; (*audaz*) bold, daring; **arriesgar** *vt* to risk; (*poner en peligro*) to endanger; **arriesgarse** *vr* to take a risk.

arrimar [arri'mar] *vt* (*acercar*) to bring close; (*poner de lado*) to set aside; ~se *vr* to come close or closer; ~se a to lean on; **arrimo** *nm* approach; (*fig*) support.

arrinconado, a [arrinko'naðo, a] *a* forgotten, neglected; **arrinconar** *vt* to put in a corner; (*fig*) to put on one side; (*abandonar*) to push aside; **arrinconarse** *vr* to withdraw from the world.

arrodillarse [arroði'ʎarse] *vr* to kneel, kneel down.

arrogancia [arro'xanθja] *nf* arrogance; **arrogante** *a* arrogant.

arrojar [arro'xar] *vt* to throw, hurl; (*humo*) to emit, give out; (*COM*) to yield, produce; ~se *vr* to throw or hurl o.s.

arrojo [a'rroxo] *nm* daring.

arrollador, a [arroʎa'ðor, a] *a* crushing, overwhelming.

arropar [arro'par] *vt* to cover, wrap up; ~se *vr* to wrap o.s. up.

arrope [a'rrope] *nm* syrup.

arrostrar [arros'trar] *vt* to face (up to); ~se *vr* to rush into the fight.

arroyo [a'rrojo] *nm* stream; (*de la calle*) gutter.

arroz [a'rroθ] *nm* rice; ~ **con leche** rice pudding.

arruga [a'rruxa] *nf* fold; (*de cara*) wrinkle; (*de vestido*) crease; **arrugar** *vt* to fold; to wrinkle; to crease; **arrugarse** *vr* to get creased.

arruinar [arrwi'nar] *vt* to ruin, wreck; ~se *vr* to be ruined.

arrullar [arru'ʎar] *vi* to coo // *vt* to lull to sleep.

arsenal [arse'nal] *nm* naval dockyard; (*MIL*) arsenal.

arsénico [ar'seniko] *nm* arsenic.

arte ['arte] *nm* (*gen m en sg y siempre f en pl*) art; (*maña*) skill, guile; ~s *nfpl* arts.

artefacto [arte'fakto] *nm* appliance; (*ARQUEOLOGÍA*) artefact.

artejo [ar'texo] *nm* knuckle.

arteria [ar'terja] *nf* artery.

artesanía [artesa'nia] *nf* craftsmanship; (*artículos*) handicrafts *pl*; **artesano** *nm* artisan, craftsman.

ártico, a ['artiko, a] *a* Arctic // *nm*: **el Á**~ the Arctic.

articulación [artikula'θjon] *nf* articulation; (*MED, TEC*) joint; **articulado, a** *a* articulated; jointed; **articular** *vt* to articulate; to join together.

artículo [ar'tikulo] *nm* article; (*cosa*) thing, article; ~s *nmpl* goods.

artífice [ar'tifiθe] *nm* artist, craftsman; (*fig*) architect.

artificial [artifi'θjal] *a* artificial.

artificio [arti'fiθjo] *nm* art, skill; (*artesanía*) craftsmanship; (*astucia*) cunning; ~so, a *a* skilful, clever; cunning.

artillería [artiʎe'ria] *nf* artillery.

artillero [arti'ʎero] *nm* artilleryman, gunner.

artimaña [arti'maɲa] *nf* trap, snare; (*astucia*) cunning.

artista [ar'tista] *nm/f* (*pintor*) artist, painter; (*TEATRO*) artist, artiste; **artístico, a** *a* artistic.

artritis [ar'tritis] *nf* arthritis.

arzobispo [arθo'βispo] *nm* archbishop.

as [as] *nm* ace.

asa ['asa] *nf* handle; (*fig*) lever.

asado [a'saðo] *nm* roast (meat).

asador [asa'ðor] *nm* spit.

asalariado, a [asala'rjaðo, a] *a* paid, wage-earning // *nm/f* wage earner.

asaltabancos [asalta'bankos] *nm inv* bank robber.

asaltador, a [asalta'ðor, a], **asaltante** [asal'tante] *nm/f* assailant; **asaltar** *vt* to attack, assault; (*fig*) to assail; **asalto** *nm* attack, assault; (*DEPORTE*) round.

asamblea [asam'blea] *nf* assembly; (*reunión*) meeting.

asar [a'sar] *vt* to roast.

asbesto [as'βesto] *nm* asbestos.

ascendencia [asθen'denθja] *nf* ancestry; (*AM*) ascendancy.

ascender [asθen'der] *vi* (*subir*) to ascend, rise; (*ser promovido*) to gain promotion // *vt* to promote; ~ **a** to amount to; **ascendiente** *nm* ascendency, influence // *nm/f* ancestor.

ascensión [asθen'sjon] *nf* ascent; **la A~** the Ascension.

ascensionista [asθensjo'nista] *nm/f* balloonist.

ascenso [as'θenso] *nm* ascent; (*promoción*) promotion.

ascensor [asθen'sor] *nm* lift, elevator.

ascético, a [as'θetiko, a] *a* ascetic.

asco ['asko] *nm* loathing, disgust; (*cosa*) loathsome thing; **el ajo me da** ~ I hate or loathe garlic.

ascua ['askwa] *nf* ember.

aseado, a [ase'aðo, a] *a* clean; (*arreglado*) tidy; (*pulcro*) smart; **asear** *vt* to clean, wash; to tidy (up); (*adornar*) to adorn.

asediar [ase'ðjar] *vt* to besiege, lay siege to; (*fig*) to chase, pester; **asedio** *nm* siege; (*COM*) run.

asegurado, a [aseɣu'raðo, a] *a* insured; **asegurador, a** *nm/f* insurer; underwriter.

asegurar [aseɣu'rar] *vt* (*consolidar*) to secure, fasten; (*dar garantía de*) to guarantee; (*preservar*) to safeguard; (*afirmar, dar por cierto*) to assure, affirm; (*tranquilizar*) to reassure; (*tomar un seguro*) to insure; ~ **se** *vr* to assure o.s., make sure.

asemejarse [aseme'xarse] *vr* to be alike; ~ **a** to be like, resemble.

asentado, a [asen'taðo, a] *a* established, settled.

asentar [asen'tar] *vt* (*sentar*) to seat, sit down; (*poner*) to place, establish; (*alisar*) to level, smooth down or out; (*anotar*) to note down; (*afirmar*) to affirm, assent; (*afinar*) to sharpen, hone // *vi* to be suitable, suit.

asentir [asen'tir] *vi* to assent, agree.

aseo [a'seo] *nm* cleanliness; ~ **s** *nmpl* toilet *sg*, cloakroom *sg*.

asequible [ase'kiβle] *a* attainable, available.

aserradero [aserra'ðero] *nm* sawmill; **aserrar** *vt* to saw.

aserrín [ase'rrin] *nm* sawdust.

asesinar [asesi'nar] *vt* to murder; (*POL*) to assassinate; (*fig*) to pester; **asesinato** *nm* murder; assassination.

asesino, a [ase'sino, a] *nm/f* murderer, killer; (*POL*) assassin.

asesor, a [ase'sor, a] *nm/f* adviser, consultant.

asfalto [as'falto] *nm* asphalt.

asfixia [as'fiksja] *nf* suffocation.

asfixiar [asfik'sjar] *vt*, ~ **se** *vr* to asphyxiate, suffocate.

asgo *etc vb ver* **asir**.

así [a'si] *ad* (*de esta manera*) so, in this way, like this, thus; (*aunque*) although; (*tan luego como*) as soon as; ~ **que** so, therefore; ~ **como** as well as; ~ **y todo** even so; **¿no es** ~? isn't it?, didn't you? *etc*.

Asia ['asja] *nf* Asia; **asiático, a** *a* Asiatic, Asian.

asidero [asi'ðero] *nm* handle.

asiduidad [asiðwi'ðað] *nf* assiduousness; **asiduo, a** *a* assiduous; (*frecuente*) frequent // *nm/f* regular (customer).

asiento [a'sjento] *nm* (*mueble*) seat, chair; (*de coche, en tribunal etc*) seat; (*localidad*) seat, place; (*fundamento*) site; (*colocación*) establishment; (*depósito*) sediment; (*cordura*) good sense; ~ **delantero/trasero** front/back seat.

asignación [asiɣna'θjon] *nf* (*atribución*) assignment; (*reparto*) allocation; (*cita*) appointment; (*sueldo*) salary; **asignar** *vt* to assign, allocate.

asignatura [asiɣna'tura] *nf* subject.

asilo [a'silo] *nm* (*refugio*) asylum, refuge; (*establecimiento*) home, institution.

asimilación [asimila'θjon] *nf* assimilation.

asimilar [asimi'lar] *vt* to assimilate; ~ **se** *vr*: ~ **se a** to resemble; (*incorporarse*) to become assimilated to.

asimismo [asi'mismo] *ad* in the same way, likewise.

asir [a'sir] *vt* to seize, grasp.

asistencia [asis'tenθja] *nf* audience; (*MED*) attendance; (*ayuda*) assistance; **asistir** *vt* to assist // *vi* to attend, be present.

asma ['asma] *nf* asthma.

asno ['asno] *nm* donkey; (*fig*) ass.

asociación [asoθja'θjon] *nf* association; (*COM*) partnership; ~ **aduanera** customs union; **asociado, a** *a* associate // *nm/f* associate; partner.

asociar [aso'θjar] *vt* to combine.

asolear [asole'ar] *vt* to put in the sun; ~ **se** *vr* to sunbathe.

asomar [aso'mar] *vt* to show, stick out // *vi* to appear; ~ **se** *vr* to appear, show up; ~ **la cabeza por la ventana** to put one's head out of the window.

asombrar [asom'brar] *vt* (*causar admiración, sorpresa*) to amaze, astonish; (*asustar*) to frighten; (*dar sombra a*) to shade; ~ **se** *vr* to be amazed; to be frightened; **asombro** *nm* amazement, astonishment; fright; **asombroso, a** *a* astonishing, amazing.

asomo [a'somo] *nm* hint, sign; (*apariencia*) appearance.

aspa ['aspa] *nf* (*cruz*) cross; (*de molino*) sail.

aspar [as'par] *vt* to reel, wind; (*fig*) to vex, annoy.

aspaviento [aspa'ßjento] *nm* exaggerated display of feeling; (*fam*) fuss.

aspecto [as'pekto] *nm* (*apariencia*) look, appearance; (*fig*) aspect.

aspereza [aspe're θa] *nf* roughness; (*agrura*) sourness; (*severidad*) harshness, surliness; **áspero, a** *a* rough; bitter, sour; harsh.

aspersión [asper'sjon] *nf* sprinkling.

áspid ['aspið] *nm* asp.

aspiración [aspira'θjon] *nf* breath, inhalation; (*MUS*) short pause; **aspiraciones** *nfpl* (*AM*) aspirations.

aspiradora [aspira'ðora] *nf* vacuum cleaner.

aspirar [aspi'rar] *vt* to breathe in // *vi*: ~ a to aspire to.

aspirina [aspi'rina] *nf* aspirin.

asquear [aske'ar] *vt* to sicken // *vi* to be sickening; ~**se** *vr* to feel disgusted; **asqueroso, a** *a* disgusting, sickening.

asta ['asta] *nf* lance; (*arpón*) spear; (*mango*) shaft, handle; (*ZOOL*) horn; a **media** ~ at half mast.

astilla [as'tiʎa] *nf* splinter; (*pedacito*) chip; ~**s** *nfpl* firewood *sg*.

astillero [asti'ʎero] *nm* shipyard.

astringente [astrin'xente] *a, nm* astringent.

astringir [astrin'xir] *vt* to bind.

astro ['astro] *nm* star.

astrología [astrolo'xia] *nf* astrology; **astrólogo, a** *nm/f* astrologer.

astronauta [astro'nauta] *nm/f* astronaut.

astronomía [astrono'mia] *nf* astronomy; **astrónomo** *nm* astronomer.

astucia [as'tuθja] *nf* astuteness; (*destreza*) clever trick; **astuto, a** *a* astute; (*taimado*) cunning.

asueto [a'sweto] *nm* holiday; (*tiempo libre*) time off *q*.

asumir [asu'mir] *vt* to assume.

asunción [asun'θjon] *nf* assumption.

asunto [a'sunto] *nm* (*tema*) matter, subject; (*negocio*) business.

asustar [asus'tar] *vt* to frighten; ~**se** *vr* to be/become frightened.

atacar [ata'kar] *vt* to attack.

atadura [ata'ðura] *nf* bond, tie.

atajo [a'taxo] *nm* short cut; (*DEPORTE*) tackle.

ataque [a'take] *nm* attack; ~ **cardíaco** heart attack.

atar [a'tar] *vt* to tie, tie up; ~**se** *vr* (*fig*) to be *or* get embarrassed.

atardecer [atarðe'θer] *vi* to get dark // *nm* evening; (*crepúsculo*) dusk.

atareado, a [atare'aðo, a] *a* busy.

atarear [atare'ar] *vt* to give a job to; ~**se** *vr* to be busy, keep busy.

atascamiento [ataska'mjento] *nm* = **atasco.**

atascar [atas'kar] *vt* to clog up; (*obstruir*) to jam; (*fig*) to hinder; ~**se** *vr* to stall;

(*cañería*) to get clogged up; **atasco** *nm* obstruction; (*AUTO*) traffic jam.

ataúd [ata'uð] *nm* coffin.

ataviar [ata'ßjar] *vt* to deck, array; ~**se** *vr* to dress up.

atavío [ata'ßio] *nm* attire, dress; ~**s** *nmpl* finery *sg*.

atemorizar [atemori'θar] *vt* to frighten, scare; ~**se** *vr* to get scared.

Atenas [a'tenas] *n* Athens.

atención [aten'θjon] *nf* attention; (*bondad*) kindness; (*cortesía*) civility // *excl* (be) careful!, look out!

atender [aten'der] *vt* to attend to, look after // *vi* to pay attention.

atenerse [ate'nerse] *vr*: ~ a to abide by, adhere to.

atentado [aten'taðo] *nm* crime, illegal act; (*asalto*) assault; (*contra la vida de uno*) attempt on sb's life.

atentar [aten'tar] *vi*: ~ a *o* contra to commit an outrage against.

atento, a [a'tento, a] *a* attentive, observant; (*cortés*) polite, thoughtful.

atenuación [atenwa'θjon] *nf* attenuation, lessening; **atenuante** *a* attenuating, extenuating; **atenuar** *vt* to attenuate; (*disminuir*) to lessen, minimize.

ateo, a [a'teo, a] *a* atheistic // *nm/f* atheist.

aterrador, a [aterra'ðor, a] *a* frightening.

aterrar [ate'rrar] *vt* to pull down, demolish; (*AGR*) to cover with earth; (*espantar*) to frighten; ~**se** *vr* to be frightened.

aterrizar [aterri'θar] *vi* to land.

aterrorizar [aterrori'θar] *vt* to terrify; (*MIL, POL*) to terrorize.

atesorar [ateso'rar] *vt* to hoard, store up.

atestar [ates'tar] *vt* to pack, stuff; (*JUR*) to attest, testify to.

atestiguar [atesti'ɣwar] *vt* to testify to, bear witness to.

atiborrar [atiβo'rrar] *vt* to fill, stuff; ~**se** *vr* to stuff o.s.

ático ['atiko] *nm* attic.

atildar [atil'dar] *vt* to criticize; ~**se** *vr* to spruce o.s. up.

atisbar [atis'ßar] *vt* to spy on; (*echar ojeada*) to peep at.

atizar [ati'θar] *vt* to poke; (*horno etc*) to stoke; (*fig*) to stir up, rouse.

atlántico, a [at'lantiko, a] *a* Atlantic // *nm*: **el (océano) A~** the Atlantic (Ocean).

atlas ['atlas] *nm* atlas.

atleta [at'leta] *nm* athlete; **atlético, a** *a* athletic; **atletismo** *nm* athletics *sg*.

atmósfera [at'mosfera] *nf* atmosphere.

atolondramiento [atolondra'mjento] *nm* bewilderment; (*insensatez*) silliness.

atollar [ato'ʎar] *vi*, ~**se** *vr* to get stuck; (*fig*) to get into a jam.

atómico, a [a'tomiko, a] *a* atomic.

atomizador [atomiθa'ðor] *nm* atomizer.

átomo ['atomo] *nm* atom.

atónito, a [a'tonito, a] *a* astonished, amazed.

atontado, a [aton'taðo, a] *a* stunned; (*bobo*) silly, daft.

atontar [aton'tar] *vt* to stun; ~**se** *vr* to become bewildered.

atormentar [atormen'tar] *vt* to torture; (*molestar*) to torment; (*acosar*) to plague harass.

atornillar [atorni'Aar] *vt* to screw on or down.

atracar [atra'kar] *vt* (NAUT) to moor; (*robar*) to hold up, rob; (*fam*) to stuff (with food) // *vi* to moor.

atracción [atrak'θjon] *nf* attraction.

atraco [a'trako] *nm* holdup, robbery.

atractivo, a [atrak'tißo, a] *a* attractive // *nm* attraction; (*belleza*) attractiveness.

atraer [atra'er] *vt* to attract.

atrancar [atran'kar] *vt* (*con tranca, barra*) to bar, bolt.

atrapar [atra'par] *vt* to trap; (*fig*) to take in, deceive.

atrás [a'tras] *ad* (*movimiento*) back, backwards; (*lugar*) behind; (*tiempo*) previously; **ir hacia** ~ to go back or backwards; to go to the rear; **estar** ~ to be behind or at the back.

atrasado, a [atra'saðo, a] *a* slow; (*pago*) overdue, late; (*país*) backward.

atrasar [atra'sar] *vi* to be slow; ~**se** *vr* to remain behind; (*llegar tarde*) to arrive late; **atraso** *nm* slowness, lateness, delay; (*de país*) backwardness; **atrasos** *nmpl* arrears.

atravesar [atraße'sar] *vt* (*cruzar*) to cross (over); (*traspasar*) to pierce, go through; (*poner al través*) to lay or put across; ~**se** *vr* to come in between; (*intervenir*) to interfere.

atrayente [atra'jente] *a* attractive.

atreverse [atre'ßerse] *vr* to dare; (*insolentarse*) to be insolent; **atrevido, a** *a* daring; insolent; **atrevimiento** *nm* daring insolence.

atribuir [atrißu'ir] *vt* to attribute; (*funciones*) to confer.

atribular [atrißu'lar] *vt* to afflict, distress; ~**se** *vr* to grieve, be distressed.

atributo [atri'ßuto] *nm* attribute.

atrocidad [atroθi'ðað] *nf* atrocity, outrage.

atropellar [atrope'Aar] *vt* (*derribar*) to knock over, knock down; (*empujar*) to push (aside); (*pasar por encima de*) to run over, run down; (*agraviar*) to insult; ~**se** *vr* to act hastily; **atropello** *nm* accident; push; insult; (*agravio*) wrong; (*atrocidad*) outrage.

atroz [a'troθ] *a* atrocious, awful.

atto, a *abr de* **atento**.

atuendo [a'twendo] *nm* dress.

atún [a'tun] *nm* tuna, tunny.

aturdir [atur'ðir] *vt* to stun; (*de ruido*) to deafen; (*fig*) to dumbfound, bewilder.

audacia [au'ðaθja] *nf* boldness, audacity; **audaz** *a* bold, audacious; (*descarado*) cheeky, impudent.

audible [au'ðißle] *a* audible.

audición [auð'θjon] *nf* hearing; (TEATRO) audition.

audiencia [au'ðjenθja] *nf* audience; (JUR) high court.

auditor [auði'tor] *nm* (JUR) judge-advocate; (COM) auditor.

auditorio [auði'torjo] *nm* audience; (*sala*) auditorium.

auge ['auxe] *nm* boom; (*clímax*) climax.

augurar [auxu'rar] *vt* to predict; (*presagiar*) to portend; **augurio** *nm* omen; **augurios** *nmpl* good wishes.

aula ['aula] *nf* classroom.

aullar [au'Aar] *vi* to howl, yell.

aullido [au'Aiðo] *nm* howl, yell.

aumentar [aumen'tar] *vt* (*precios, sueldo*) to raise; (*producción*) to increase; (*con microscopio, anteojos*) to magnify // *vi*, ~**se** *vr* to increase (*subirse*) to rise; (*multiplicarse*) to multiply; **aumento** *nm* increase; rise.

aun [a'un] *ad* even.

aún [a'un] *ad* still, yet.

aunque [a'unke] *conj* though, although, even though, even if.

aura ['aura] *nf* gentle breeze; (*fig*) popularity.

aureola [aure'ola] *nf* halo.

auricular [auriku'lar] *nm* (*dedo*) little finger; (*del teléfono*) earpiece, receiver; ~**es** *nmpl* headphones.

ausencia [au'senθja] *nf* absence.

ausentarse [ausen'tarse] *vr* to go/stay away, absent o.s.

ausente [au'sente] *a* absent.

auspicios [aus'piθjos] *nmpl* auspices; (*protección*) protection *sg*.

austeridad [austeri'ðað] *nf* austerity; **austero, a** *a* austere.

austral [aus'tral] *a* southern.

Australia [aus'tralja] *nf* Australia; **australiano, a** *a, nm/f* Australian.

Austria ['austrja] *nf* Austria; **austríaco, a** *a, nm/f* Austrian.

autenticar [autenti'kar] *vt* to authenticate, **auténtico, a** *a* authentic.

auto ['auto] *nm* (JUR) edict, decree (: *order*) writ; (*fam*) car; ~**s** *nmpl* (JUR) proceedings; (: *acta*) court record *sg*.

autobiografía [autoßjoxra'fia] *nf* autobiography.

autobús [auto'ßus] *nm* bus.

autocar [auto'kar] *nm* coach.

autócrata [au'tokrata] *nm/f* autocrat.

autóctono, a [au'toktono, a] *a* native, indigenous.

autodefensa [autoðe'fensa] *nf* self-defence.

autodeterminación [autoðeter'mina-θjon] *nf* self-determination.

autoescuela [autoes'kwela] *nf* driving school.

autógrafo [au'toxrafo] *nm* autograph.

autómata [au'tomata] *nm* automaton.

automático, a [auto'matiko, a] *a* automatic.

automotor, triz [automo'tor, 'triz] *a* self-propelled // *nm* Diesel train.

automóvil [auto'moβil] *nm* (motor) car, automobile; **automovilístico, a** *a* driving *cpd*, motoring *cpd*.

autonomía [autono'mia] *nf* autonomy; **autónomo, a** *a* autonomous.

autopista [auto'pista] *nf* motorway.

autopsia [au'topsja] *nf* autopsy.

autor, a [au'tor, a] *nm/f* author.

autoridad [autori'ðað] *nf* authority; **autoritario, a** *a* authoritarian.

autorización [autoriθa'θjon] *nf* authorization; **autorizado, a** *a* authorized; (*aprobado*) approved; **autorizar** *vt* to authorize; to approve.

autorretrato [autorre'trato] *nm* self-portrait.

autoservicio [autoser'βiθjo] *nm* self-service restaurant.

autostop [auto'stop] *nm* hitch-hiking; **hacer el ~** to hitch-hike; **~ista** *nm/f* hitch-hiker.

autosuficiencia [autosufi'θjenθja] *nf* self-sufficiency.

auxiliar [auksi'ljar] *vt* to help // *nm/f* assistant; **auxilio** *nm* assistance, help; **primeros auxilios** first aid *sg*.

Av *abr de* Avenida.

aval [a'βal] *nm* guarantee; (*persona*) guarantor.

avalancha [aβa'lantʃa] *nf* avalanche.

avaluar [aβa'iwar] *vt* to value, appraise.

avance [a'βanθe] *nm* advance; (*pago*) advance payment.

avanzar [aβan'θar] *vt, vi*, **~se** *vr* to advance.

avaricia [aβa'riθja] *nf* avarice, greed; **avariento, a** *a* avaricious, greedy.

avaro, a [a'βaro, a] *a* miserly, mean // *nm/f* miser.

avasallar [aβasa'ʎar] *vt* to subdue, subjugate; **~se** *vr* to submit.

Avda *abr de* Avenida.

ave ['aβe] *nf* bird; **~ de rapiña** bird of prey.

avellana [aβe'ʎana] *nf* hazelnut; **avellano** *nm* hazel tree.

avemaría [aβema'ria] *nf* Hail Mary, Ave Maria.

avena [a'βena] *nf* oats *pl*.

avenencia [aβe'nenθja] *nf* agreement; (*COM*) bargain.

avenida [aβe'niða] *nf* (*calle*) avenue; (*de río*) flood, spate.

avenir [aβe'nir] *vt* to reconcile; **~se** *vr* to come to an agreement, reach a compromise.

aventajado, a [aβenta'xaðo, a] *a* outstanding; **aventajar** *vt* (*sobrepasar*) to surpass, outstrip; (*preferir*) to prefer; **aventajarse** *vr* to surpass or excel o.s.

aventar [aβen'tar] *vt* to fan, blow;

(*esparcir*) to scatter; (*grano*) to winnow; **~se** *vr* to fill with air.

aventura [aβen'tura] *nf* adventure; (*casualidad*) chance; **aventurado, a** *a* risky; **aventurero, a** *a* adventurous.

avergonzar [aβerxon'θar] *vt* to shame; (*desconcertar*) to embarrass; **~se** *vr* to be ashamed; to be embarrassed.

avería [aβe'ria] *nf* damage; (*TEC*) breakdown, fault.

averiguación [aβerixwa'θjon] *nf* investigation; (*determinación*) ascertainment; **averiguar** *vt* to investigate; to find out, ascertain.

aversión [aβer'sjon] *nf* aversion, dislike.

avestruz [aβes'truθ] *nm* ostrich.

avezarse [aβe'θarse] *vr*: **~se a algo** to grow used to sth.

aviación [aβja'θjon] *nf* aviation *q*; (*fuerzas aéreas*) air force.

aviador, a [aβja'ðor, a] *nm/f* aviator, airman/woman.

avicultura [aβikul'tura] *nf* poultry farming.

avidez [aβi'ðeθ] *nf* avidity, eagerness; **ávido, a** *a* avid, eager.

avinagrado, a [aβina'xraðo, a] *a* sour, acid; **avinagrarse** *vr* to turn sour.

avío [a'βio] *nm* preparation; **~s** *nmpl* gear *sg*, kit *sg*.

avión [a'βjon] *nm* aeroplane; (*ave*) martin; **~ de reacción** jet plane.

avisar [aβi'sar] *vt* (*advertir*) to warn, notify; (*informar*) to tell; (*aconsejar*) to advise, counsel; **aviso** *nm* warning; (*noticia*) notice; (*prudencia*) caution, discretion.

avispa [a'βispa] *nf* wasp.

avispado, a [a'βispaðo, a] *a* sharp, clever.

avispar [aβis'par] *vt* to spur (on); **~se** *vr* to fret, worry.

avispero [aβis'pero] *nm* wasp's nest.

avispón [aβis'pon] *nm* hornet.

avistar [aβis'tar] *vt* to sight, spot; **~se** *vr* to have an interview.

avituallar [aβitwa'ʎar] *vt* to supply with food.

avivar [aβi'βar] *vt* to strengthen, intensify; **~se** *vr* to revive, acquire new life.

avizorar [aβiθo'rar] *vt* to spy on.

axila [ak'sila] *nf* armpit.

axioma [ak'sjoma] *nm* axiom.

ay [ai] *excl* (*dolor*) ow!, ouch!; (*aflicción*) oh!, oh dear!; **¡~ de mí!** poor me!; **¡~ del que!** pity help or woe betide whoever!

aya ['aja] *nf* governess; (*niñera*) children's nurse.

ayer [a'jer] *ad, nm* yesterday; **antes de ~** the day before yesterday.

ayo ['ajo] *nm* tutor.

ayuda [a'juða] *nf* help, assistance; (*MED*) enema; (*AM*) laxative // *nm* page; **ayudante, a** *nm/f* assistant, helper; (*ESCOL*) assistant; (*MIL*) adjutant; **ayudar** *vt* to help, assist.

ayunar [aju'nar] *vi* to fast; **ayunas** *nfpl*: **estar en ayunas** (*no haber comido*) to be fasting; (*ignorante*) to be in the dark; **ayuno** *nm* fasting; ignorance.

ayuntamiento [ajunta'mjento] *nm* (*consejo*) council; (*edificio*) town hall; (*cópula*) sexual intercourse.

azabache [aθa'βatʃe] *nm* jet.

azada [a'θaða] *nf* hoe.

azafata [aθa'fata] *nf* air hostess.

azafrán [aθa'fran] *nm* saffron.

azahar [aθa'ar] *nm* orange/lemon blossom.

azar [a'θar] *nm* (*casualidad*) chance, fate; (*desgracia*) misfortune, accident; **por ~** by chance; **al ~** at random.

azararse [aθare'arse] *vr* = **azorarse**.

azogue [a'θoxe] *nm* mercury.

azoramiento [aθora'mjento] *nm* alarm; (*confusión*) confusion.

azorar [aθo'rar] *vt* to alarm; **~se** *vr* to get alarmed.

Azores [a'θores] *nmpl*: **los ~** the Azores.

azotar [aθo'tar] *vt* to whip, beat; (*pegar*) to spank; **azote** *nm* (*látigo*) whip; (*latigazo*) lash, stroke; (*en las nalgas*) spank; (*calamidad*) calamity.

azotea [aθo'tea] *nf* terrace roof.

azteca [aθ'teka] *a, nm/f* Aztec.

azúcar [a'θukar] *nm* sugar; **azucarado, a** a sugary, sweet.

azucarero, a [aθuka'rero, a] *a* sugar *cpd* // *nm* sugar bowl.

azucena [aθu'θena] *nf* white lily.

azufre [a'θufre] *nm* sulphur.

azul [a'θul] *a, nm* blue.

azulejo [aθu'lexo] *nm* glazed tile.

azuzar [aθu'θar] *vt* to incite, egg on.

B

B.A. *abr de* **Buenos Aires.**

baba ['baβa] *nf* spittle, saliva; **babear** *vi* to drool, slaver.

babel [ba'βel] *nm o f* bedlam.

babero [ba'βero] *nm* bib.

babor [ba'βor] *nm* port (side).

babucha [ba'βutʃa] *nf* slipper.

bacalao [baka'lao] *nm* cod(fish).

bacía [ba'θia] *nf* basin, bowl.

bacín [ba'θin] *nm* chamber pot.

bacteria [bak'terja] *nf* bacterium, germ.

báculo ['bakulo] *nm* stick, staff.

bache ['batʃe] *nm* pothole, rut; (*fig*) bad patch.

bachillerato [batʃiʎe'rato] *nm* (*ESCOL*) school-leaving examination.

bagaje [ba'vaxe] *nm* baggage.

bagatela [baxa'tela] *nf* trinket, trifle.

bahía [ba'ia] *nf* bay.

bailar [bai'lar] *vt, vi* to dance; **~ín, ina** *nm/f* (*ballet*) dancer; **baile** *nm* dance; (*formal*) ball.

baja ['baxa] *nf ver* **bajo.**

bajada [ba'xaða] *nf* descent; (*camino*) slope; (*de aguas*) ebb.

bajamar [baxa'mar] *nf* low tide.

bajar [ba'xar] *vi* to go/come down; (*temperatura, precios*) to drop, fall; (*de coche*) to get out; (*de autobús*) to get off // *vt* (*cabeza*) to bow, bend; (*escalera*) to go/come down; (*precio, voz*) to lower; (*llevar abajo*) to take down; **~se** *vr* to bend down; to get out of; to get off; (*fig*) to humble o.s.

bajeza [ba'xeθa] *nf* baseness *q*; (*una ~*) vile deed.

bajío [ba'xio] *nm* shoal, sandbank; (*AM*) lowlands *pl*.

bajo, a ['baxo, a] *a* (*terreno*) low(-lying); (*mueble, número, precio*) low; (*piso*) ground; (*de estatura*) small, short; (*color*) pale; (*sonido*) faint, soft, low; (*voz: en tono*) deep; (*metal*) base; (*humilde*) low, humble // *ad* (*hablar*) low, quietly; (*volar*) low // *prep* under, below, underneath // *nm* (*mus*) bass // *nf* drop, fall; (*mil*) casualty; **~ la lluvia** in the rain; **dar de ~a** (*soldado*) to discharge; (*empleado*) to dismiss, sack.

bajón [ba'xon] *nm* (*mus*) bassoon; (*baja*) decline, fall, drop.

bajorrelieve [baxorre'ljeβe] *nm* bas-relief.

bala ['bala] *nf* bullet.

baladí [bala'ði] *a* trivial.

baladrón, ona [bala'ðron, ona] *a* boastful.

bálago ['balaxo] *nm* thatch.

balance [ba'lanθe] *nm* (*balanceo*) oscillation, rocking; (*NAUT*) roll; (*COM*) balance; (: *libro*) balance sheet; (: *cuenta general*) stocktaking; **~ar** *vt* to balance // *vi*, **~arse** *vr* to swing (to and fro); (*vacilar*) to hesitate; **balanceo** *nm* swinging.

balanza [ba'lanθa] *nf* balance, scales *pl*; **~ comercial** balance of trade; **~ de pagos** balance of payments; (*ASTRO*) **B~** = **Libra.**

balar [ba'lar] *vi* to bleat.

balazo [ba'laθo] *nm* (*golpe*) shot; (*herida*) bullet wound.

balbucear [balβuθe'ar] *vi, vt* to stammer, stutter; **balbuceo** *nm* stammering, stuttering.

balbucir [balβu'θir] *vi, vt* to stammer, stutter.

balcón [bal'kon] *nm* balcony.

baldaquín [balda'kin], **baldaquino** [balda'kino] *nm* canopy.

baldar [bal'dar] *vt* to cripple.

balde ['balde] *nm* bucket, pail; **de ~** *ad* (for) free, for nothing; **en ~** *ad* in vain.

baldío, a [bal'dio, a] *a* uncultivated // *nm* waste land.

baldón [bal'don] *nm* (*injuria*) insult.

baldosa [bal'dosa] *nf* paving stone.

Baleares [bale'ares] *nfpl*: **las (Islas) ~** the Balearic Islands.

balido [ba'liðo] *nm* bleat, bleating.

balística [ba'listika] *nf* ballistics *pl*.

baliza [ba'liθa] *nf* (*AVIAT*) beacon; (*NAUT*) buoy.

balneario, a [balne'arjo, a] *a:* **estación**
~**a** bathing resort // *nm* spa, health
resort.

balón [ba'lon] *nm* ball.

baloncesto [balon'θesto] *nm* basketball.

balsa ['balsa] *nf* raft; (*BOT*) balsa wood.

bálsamo ['balsamo] *nm* balsam, balm.

baluarte [ba'lwarte] *nm* bastion, bulwark.

ballena [ba'ʎena] *nf* whale.

ballesta [ba'ʎesta] *nf* crossbow; (*AUTO*)
spring.

ballet [ba'le] *nm* ballet.

bambolear [bambole'ar] *vi,* ~**se** *vr* to
swing, sway; (*silla*) to wobble; **bamboleo**
nm swinging, swaying; wobbling.

bambú [bam'bu] *nm* bamboo.

banca ['banka] *nf* (*asiento*) bench; (*COM*)
banking; ~**da** *nf* (*banco*) stone bench;
(*TEC*) bench.

bancario, a [ban'karjo, a] *a* banking *cpd,*
bank *cpd.*

bancarrota [banka'rrota] *nf* (*esp*
fraudulent) bankruptcy.

banco ['banko] *nm* bench; (*ESCOL*) desk;
(*COM*) bank; (*GEO*) stratum; ~ **de
crédito/de ahorros** credit/ savings
bank; ~ **de arena** sandbank; ~ **de hielo**
iceberg.

banda ['banda] *nf* band; (*pandilla*) gang;
(*NAUT*) side, edge; **la B**~ **Oriental**
Uruguay; ~ **sonora** soundtrack.

bandada [ban'daða] *nf* (*de pájaros*) flock;
(*de peces*) shoal.

bandeja [ban'dexa] *nf* tray.

bandera [ban'dera] *nf* (*de tela*) flag;
(*estandarte*) banner.

banderilla [bande'riʎa] *nf* banderilla.

banderola [bande'rola] *nf* banderole,
pennant.

bandidaje [bandi'ðaxe] *nm* banditry;
bandido *nm* bandit.

bando ['bando] *nm* (*edicto*) edict,
proclamation; (*facción*) faction; **los** ~**s**
the banns.

bandolero [bando'lero] *nm* bandit,
brigand.

banquero [ban'kero] *nm* banker.

banqueta [ban'keta] *nf* (*asiento*) bench;
(*escabel*) stool.

banquete [ban'kete] *nm* banquet; (*para
convidados*) formal dinner.

banquillo [ban'kiʎo] *nm* (*JUR*) dock,
prisoner's bench; (*banco*) bench; (*para los
pies*) footstool.

bañador [baɲa'ðor] *nm* swimming
costume.

bañar [ba'ɲar] *vt* (*niño*) to bath, bathe;
(*objeto*) to dip; (*de barniz*) to coat; ~**se** *vr*
(*en el mar*) to bathe, swim; (*en la bañera*)
to bath, have a bath.

bañera [ba'ɲera] *nf* bath(tub).

bañero [ba'ɲero] *nm* lifeguard.

bañista [ba'ɲista] *nm/f* bather.

baño ['baɲo] *nm* (*en bañera*) bath; (*en río*)
dip, swim; (*cuarto*) bathroom; (*bañera*)
bath(tub); (*capa*) coating.

baptista [bap'tista] *nm/f* baptist.

baqueta [ba'keta] *nf* (*MUS*) drumstick.

bar [bar] *nm* bar.

barahúnda [bara'unda] *nf* uproar,
hubbub.

baraja [ba'raxa] *nf* pack (of cards);
barajar *vt* (*naipes*) to shuffle; (*fig*) to
jumble up.

baranda [ba'randa] *nf* rail, railing.

barandilla [baran'diʎa] *nf* rail, railing.

baratija [bara'tixa] *nf* trinket.

baratillo [bara'tiʎo] *nm* (*tienda*) junkshop;
(*subasta*) bargain sale; (*conjunto de cosas*)
secondhand goods *pl.*

barato, a [ba'rato, a] *a* cheap // *nm*
bargain sale // *ad* cheap, cheaply;
baratura *nf* cheapness.

baraúnda [bara'unda] *nf* = **barahúnda.**

barba ['barβa] *nf* (*ANAT*) chin; (*pelo*) beard,
whiskers *pl.*

barbacoa [barβa'koa] *nf* (*parrilla*)
barbecue; (*carne*) barbecued meat.

barbado, a [bar'βaðo, a] *a* bearded // *nm*
seedling.

barbaridad [barβari'ðað] *nf* barbarity;
(*acto*) barbarism; (*atrocidad*) outrage; **una**
~ (*fam*) a huge amount; **¡qué** ~**!** (*fam*)
how awful!

barbarie [bar'βarje] *nf,* **barbarismo**
[barβa'rismo] *nm* barbarism; (*crueldad*)
barbarity.

bárbaro, a ['barβaro, a] *a* barbarous,
cruel; (*grosero*) rough, uncouth // *nm/f*
barbarian // *ad:* **lo pasamos** ~ (*fam*) we
had a tremendous time; **¡qué** ~**!** (*fam*)
how marvellous!; **un éxito** ~ (*fam*) a
terrific success; **es un tipo** ~ (*fam*) he's
a splendid chap.

barbear [barβe'ar] *vt* (*AM*) to shave.

barbecho [bar'βetʃo] *nm* fallow land.

barbero [bar'βero] *nm* barber,
hairdresser.

barbilampiño [barβilam'piɲo] *a* smooth-
faced; (*fig*) inexperienced.

barbilla [bar'βiʎa] *nf* chin, tip of the chin.

barbotar [barβo'tar], **barbotear**
[barβote'ar] *vt, vi* to mutter, mumble.

barbudo, a [bar'βuðo, a] *a* bearded.

barca ['barka] *nf* (small) boat; ~ **de
pesca** fishing boat; ~ **de pasaje** ferry;
~**za** *nf* barge; ~**za de desembarco**
landing craft.

barcelonés, esa [barθelo'nes, esa] *a* of *or*
from Barcelona.

barco ['barko] *nm* boat; (*buque*) ship; ~
de carga cargo boat.

bardar [bar'ðar] *vt* to thatch.

baritono [ba'ritono] *nm* baritone.

barman ['barman] *nm* barman.

Barna *abr de* **Barcelona.**

barniz [bar'niθ] *nm* varnish; (*en la loza*)
glaze; (*fig*) veneer; ~ **para las uñas** nail
varnish; ~**ar** *vt* to varnish; (*loza*) to glaze.

barómetro [ba'rometro] *nm* barometer.

barquero [bar'kero] *nm* boatman.

barquillo [bar'kiʎo] *nm* cone, cornet.

barra ['barra] nf bar, rod; (de un bar, café) bar; (de pan) small loaf; (palanca) lever; ~ de carmín o de labios lipstick.
barraca [ba'rraka] nf hut, cabin.
barranca [ba'rranka] nf ravine, gully; **barranco** nm ravine; (fig) difficulty
barrena [ba'rrena] nf drill; **barrenar** vt to drill (through), bore; **barreno** nm large drill, borer.
barrer [ba'rrer] vt to sweep; (quitar) to sweep away.
barrera [ba'rrera] nf barrier.
barriada [ba'rrjaða] nf quarter, district.
barricada [barri'kaða] nf barricade.
barrido [ba'rriðo] nm, **barrida** [ba'rriða] nf sweep, sweeping.
barriga [ba'rriɣa] nf belly; (panza) paunch; **barrigón, ona**, **barrigudo, a** a fat, potbellied.
barril [ba'rril] nm barrel, cask.
barrio ['barrjo] nm (en el pueblo) district, quarter; (fuera del pueblo) suburb.
barro ['barro] nm (lodo) mud; (objetos) earthenware; (MED) pimple.
barroco, a [ba'rroko, a] a, nm baroque.
barroso, a [ba'rroso, a] a (lodoso) muddy; (MED) pimply.
barruntar [barrun'tar] vt (conjeturar) to guess; (presentir) to suspect; **barrunto** nm guess; suspicion.
bartola [bar'tola]: a la ~ ad: tirarse a la ~ to take it easy, do nothing.
bártulos ['bartulos] nmpl things, belongings.
barullo [ba'ruʎo] nm row, uproar.
basa ['basa] nf base; (fig) basis; ~mento nm base, plinth.
basar [ba'sar] vt to base; ~se vr: ~se en to be based on.
basca ['baska] nf nausea.
báscula ['baskula] nf (platform) scales pl.
base ['base] nf base; a ~ de on the basis of.
básico, a ['basiko, a] a basic.
basílica [ba'silika] nf basilica.
bastante [bas'tante] a (suficiente) enough, sufficient; (no poco(s)) quite a lot of // ad (suficientemente) enough, sufficiently; (muy) quite, rather.
bastar [bas'tar] vi to be enough or sufficient; ~se vr to be self-sufficient; ~ para to be enough to; ¡basta! (that's) enough!
bastardilla [bastar'ðiʎa] nf italics pl.
bastardo, a [bas'tarðo, a] a, nm/f bastard.
bastidor [basti'ðor] nm frame; (de coche) chassis.
basto, a ['basto, a] a coarse, rough; ~s nmpl (NAIPES) clubs.
bastón [bas'ton] nm (gen) stick, staff; (para el paseo) walking stick.
basura [ba'sura] nf rubbish, refuse.
basurero [basu'rero] nm (hombre) dustman; (lugar) rubbish dump; (cubo) (rubbish) bin.
bata ['bata] nf (salto de cama) dressing

gown, housecoat; (de alumno etc) smock, overall.
batalla [ba'taʎa] nf battle; de ~ everyday, for everyday use.
batallar [bata'ʎar] vi to fight.
batallón [bata'ʎon] nm battalion.
bate ['bate] nm bat; ~ador nm batter, batsman.
batería [bate'ria] nf battery; (MUS) drums pl; ~ de cocina kitchen utensils pl.
batido, a [ba'tiðo, a] a (camino) beaten, well-trodden // nm (CULIN) batter; ~ de leche milk shake.
batidora [bati'ðora] nf beater, mixer.
batir [ba'tir] vt to beat, strike; (vencer) to beat, defeat; (revolver) to beat, mix; (acuñar) to strike, mint; (pelo) to comb; ~se vr to fight; ~ palmas to clap, applaud.
batuta [ba'tuta] nf baton.
baúl [ba'ul] nm trunk; (AUTO) boot.
bautismo [bau'tismo] nm baptism, christening.
bautizar [bauti'θar] vt to baptize, christen; (fam) to water down; **bautizo** nm baptism, christening.
bayo, a ['bajo, a] a bay // nf berry.
bayoneta [bajo'neta] nf bayonet.
baza ['baθa] nf trick.
bazar [ba'θar] nm bazaar.
bazofia [ba'θofja] nf left-overs pl.
beato, a [be'ato, a] a blessed; (piadoso) pious // nm/f lay brother/sister.
bebé [be'βe] nm baby.
bebedero, a [beβe'ðero, a] a drinkable // nm (para animales) drinking trough; (de vasija) spout.
bebedizo, a [beβe'ðiθo, a] a drinkable // nm potion.
bebedor, a [beβe'ðor, a] a hard-drinking.
beber [be'βer] vt, vi to drink.
bebida [be'βiða] nf drink.
beca ['beka] nf grant, scholarship.
befa ['befa] nf ver **befo**.
befar [be'far] vt to scoff at.
befo, a ['befo, a] a thick-lipped // nm lip // nf: hacer ~a de to jeer, mock.
beldad [bel'dað] nf beauty.
belfo, a ['belfo, a] = **befo**.
belga ['belɣa] a, nm/f Belgian.
Bélgica ['belxika] nf Belgium.
bélico, a ['beliko, a] a warlike, martial; **belicoso, a** a (guerrero) warlike; (agresivo) aggressive, bellicose.
beligerante [belixe'rante] a belligerent.
bellaco, a [be'ʎako, a] a sly, cunning // nm villain, rogue; **bellaquería** nf (acción) dirty trick; (calidad) wickedness.
belleza [be'ʎeθa] nf beauty.
bello, a [be'ʎo, a] a beautiful, lovely; ~as artes fine arts.
bellota [be'ʎota] nf acorn.
bemol [be'mol] nm (MUS) flat; esto tiene ~es (fam) this is a real problem.
bendecir [bende'θir] vt to bless.
bendición [bendi'θjon] nf blessing.

bendito, a [ben'dito, a] *pp de* **bendecir** // *a* holy; (*afortunado*) lucky; (*feliz*) happy; (*sencillo*) simple // *nm/f* simple soul.

benedictino, a [beneðik'tino, a] *a, nm* Benedictine.

beneficencia [benefi'θenθja] *nf* charity.

beneficiar [benefi'θjar] *vt* (*hacer bien a*) to benefit, be of benefit to; (*tierra*) to cultivate; (*mina*) to exploit; (*mineral*) to process, treat; **~se** *vr* to benefit, profit; **~io, a** *nm/f* beneficiary.

beneficio [bene'fiθjo] *nm* (*bien*) benefit, advantage; (*ganancia*) profit, gain; (AGR) cultivation; **~so, a** *a* beneficial.

benéfico, a [be'nefiko, a] *a* beneficent, charitable.

beneplácito [bene'plaθito] *nm* approval, consent.

benevolencia [beneßo'lenθja] *nf* benevolence, kindness; **benévolo, a** *a* benevolent, kind.

benignidad [beniɣni'ðað] *nf* (*afabilidad*) kindness; (*suavidad*) mildness; **benigno, a** *a* kind; mild.

beodo, a [be'oðo, a] *a* drunk.

berenjena [beren'xena] *nf* aubergine, eggplant.

Berlín [ber'lin] *n* Berlin; **berlinés, esa** *a* of or from Berlin // *nm/f* Berliner.

bermejo, a [ber'mexo, a] *a* red.

Berna ['berna] *n* Berne.

berrear [berre'ar] *vi* to bellow, low.

berrido [be'rriðo] *nm* bellow, bellowing.

berrinche [be'rrintʃe] *nm* (*fam*) temper, tantrum.

berro ['berro] *nm* watercress.

berza [ˈberθa] *nf* cabbage.

besar [be'sar] *vt* to kiss; (*fig*) to graze; **~se** *vr* to kiss (one another); **beso** *nm* kiss.

bestia ['bestja] *nf* beast, animal; (*fig*) idiot; **~ de carga** beast of burden.

bestial [bes'tjal] *a* bestial; (*fam*) terrific; **~idad** *nf* bestiality; (*fam*) stupidity.

besuquear [besuke'ar] *vt* to cover with kisses; **~se** *vr* to kiss and cuddle.

betún [be'tun] *nm* bitumen, asphalt; (*para calzado*) shoe polish.

biberón [biße'ron] *nm* feeding bottle.

Biblia ['bißlja] *nf* Bible.

bíblico, a ['bißliko, a] *a* biblical.

bibliografía [bißljoɣra'fia] *nf* bibliography.

biblioteca [bißljo'teka] *nf* library; (*mueble*) bookshelves *pl*; **~ de consulta** reference library; **~rio, a** *nm/f* librarian.

B.I.C. *nf abr de* **Brigada de Investigación Criminal** CID (Criminal Investigation Department); FBI (Federal Bureau of Investigation) (*US*).

bicarbonato [bikar'ßo'nato] *nm* bicarbonate.

bicicleta [biθi'kleta] *nf* bicycle, bike.

bicho ['bitʃo] *nm* (*animal*) small animal; (*sabandija*) bug, insect; (TAUR) bull.

bidé [bi'ðe] *nm* bidet.

bien [bjen] *nm* good; (*interés*) advantage, benefit // *ad* well; (*correctamente*) properly, right; (*oler*) nice; (*muy*) very; **más ~** rather // *excl*: ¡(**muy**) **~!** well done! // *conj*: **no ~ llovió, bajó la temperatura** no sooner had it rained than the temperature dropped; **~ que** although; **~es inmuebles/muebles** real estate *sg*/personal property *sg*; **~es de consumo** consumer goods; **~es raíces** real estate *sg*.

bienal [bje'nal] *a* biennial.

bienandanza [bjenan'danθa] *nf* happiness.

bienaventurado, a [bjenaßentu'raðo, a] *a* (*feliz*) happy, fortunate; (*sencillo*) simple, naïve.

bienestar [bjenes'tar] *nm* well-being.

bienhechor, a [bjene'tʃor, a] *a* beneficent.

bienvenida [bjenße'niða] *nf* welcome; **bienvenido** *excl* welcome!

biftec [bif'tek] *nm* (beef)steak.

bifurcación [bifurka'θjon] *nf* fork.

bigamia [bi'xamja] *nf* bigamy; **bígamo, a** *a* bigamous // *nm/f* bigamist.

bigote [bi'xote] *nm* moustache; **bigotudo, a** *a* moustached.

bilbaíno, a [bilßa'ino, a] *a* of or from Bilbao.

bilingüe [bi'lingwe] *a* bilingual.

billar [bi'ʎar] *nm* billiards *sg*; (*lugar*) billiard hall.

billete [bi'ʎete] *nm* ticket; (*de banco*) banknote; (*carta*) note; **~ simple** single (ticket); **~ de ida y vuelta** return (ticket); **~ kilométrico** runabout ticket.

billetera [biʎe'tera] *nf*, **billetero** [biʎe'tero] *nm* wallet.

billón [bi'ʎon] *nm* billion.

bimensual [bimen'swal] *a* twice monthly.

bimotor [bimo'tor] *a* twin-engined // *nm* twin-engined plane.

binóculo [bi'nokulo] *nm* pince-nez.

biografía [bjoɣra'fia] *nf* biography; **biógrafo, a** *nm/f* biographer.

biología [bjolo'xia] *nf* biology; **biológico, a** *a* biological; **biólogo, a** *nm/f* biologist.

biombo ['bjombo] *nm* (folding) screen.

biopsia [bi'opsja] *nf* biopsy.

biplano [bi'plano] *nm* biplane.

birlar [bir'lar] *vt* (*derribar*) to knock down; (*matar*) to kill; (*fam*) to pinch.

bis [bis] *excl* encore! // *ad*: **viven en el 27 ~** they live at 27a.

bisabuelo, a [bisa'ßwelo, a] *nm/f* great-grandfather/mother.

bisagra [bi'saɣra] *nf* hinge.

bisbisar [bisßi'sar], **bisbisear** [bisßise'ar] *vt* to mutter, mumble.

bisexual [bisek'swal] *a* bisexual.

bisiesto [bi'sjesto] *a*: **año ~** leap year.

bisnieto, a [bis'njeto, a] *nm/f* great-grandson/daughter.

bisonte [bi'sonte] *nm* bison.

bisoño, a [bi'soɲo, a] *a* green, inexperienced.

bistec [bis'tek], **bisté** [bis'te] *nm* steak.
bisturí [bistu'ri] *nm* scalpel.
bisutería [bisute'ria] *nf* imitation or costume jewellery.
bizarría [biθa'rria] *nf* (*valor*) bravery; (*generosidad*) generosity; **bizarro, a** *a* brave; generous.
bizcar [biθ'kar] *vi* to squint, **bizco, a** *a* cross-eyed.
bizcocho [biθ'kotʃo] *nm* (*CULIN*) sponge cake.
bizquear [biθke'ar] *vi* to squint.
blanco, a ['blanko, a] *a* white // *nm/f* white man/woman, white // *nm* (*color*) white; (*intervalo*) space, interval; (*en texto*) blank; (*MIL, fig*) target // *vi* (*MUS*) minim; **en ~** blank; **noche en ~** sleepless night; **estar sin ~** to be broke
blancura [blan'kura] *nf* whiteness.
blandir [blan'dir] *vt* to brandish.
blando, a ['blando, a] *a* soft; (*tierno*) tender, gentle; (*carácter*) mild; (*fam*) cowardly; **blandura** *nf* softness; tenderness; mildness.
blanquear [blanke'ar] *vt* to whiten; (*fachada*) to whitewash; (*paño*) to bleach // *vi* to turn white, **blanquecino, a** *a* whitish; **blanqueo** *nm* whitewashing; bleaching.
blanquillo, a [blan'kiʎo, a] *a* white.
blasfemar [blasfe'mar] *vi* to blaspheme, curse; **blasfemia** *nf* blasphemy.
blasón [bla'son] *nm* coat of arms; (*fig*) honour; **blasonar** *vt* to emblazon // *vi* to boast, brag.
bledo ['bleðo] *nm*: **(no) me importa un ~** I don't care two hoots.
blindaje [blin'daxe] *nm* armour, armour-plating; **blindar** *vt* to armour, armour-plate.
bloc [blok] *nm* writing pad.
bloque ['bloke] *nm* block; (*POL*) bloc; **~ de cilindros** cylinder block.
bloquear [bloke'ar] *vt* to blockade; **bloqueo** *nm* blockade; (*COM*) freezing, blocking.
bluejean ['bludʒin] *nm inv* jeans *pl*.
blusa ['blusa] *nf* (*de alumno*) smock; (*de mujer*) blouse.
boardilla [boar'ðiʎa] *nf* = **buhardilla**.
boato [bo'ato] *nm* show, ostentation.
bobada [bo'βaða], **bobería** [boβe'ria] *nf* foolish action/ statement.
bobina [bo'βina] *nf* (*TEC*) bobbin; (*FOTO*) spool; (*ELEC*) coil; **bobinar** *vt* to wind.
bobo, a ['boβo, a] *a* (*tonto*) daft, silly; (*cándido*) naïve // *nm* (*TEATRO*) clown, funny man, fool.
boca ['boka] *nf* mouth; (*de crustáceo*) pincer; (*de cañón*) muzzle; (*de vino*) flavour, taste; (*entrada*) mouth, entrance; **~s** *nfpl* (*de río*) mouth *sg*; **~ abajo/arriba** face down/up; **a ~ de jarro** point-blank; **se me hace la ~ agua** my mouth is watering.
bocacalle [boka'kaʎe] *nf* entrance to a street.

bocadillo [boka'ðiʎo] *nm* (*emparedado*) sandwich; (*comida ligera*) snack.
bocado [bo'kaða] *nm* mouthful, bite; (*de caballo*) bridle; **~ de Adán** Adam's apple.
bocanada [boka'naða] *nf* (*de vino*) mouthful, swallow; (*de aire*) gust, puff.
boceto [bo'θeto] *nm* sketch, outline.
bocina [bo'θina] *nf* (*MUS*) trumpet; (*AUTO*) horn; (*para hablar*) megaphone; (*para sordos*) ear trumpet.
bocha ['botʃa] *nf* bowl; **~s** *nfpl* bowls.
bochinche [bo'tʃintʃe] *nm* (*fam*) uproar.
bochorno [bo'tʃorno] *nm* (*calor*) sultry weather; (*vergüenza*) embarrassment; **~so, a** *a* sultry; embarrassing; (*sofocante*) stuffy.
boda ['boða] *nf* (*también* **~s** *nfpl*) wedding, marriage; (*fiesta*) wedding reception; **~s de plata/de oro** silver/golden wedding.
bodega [bo'ðexa] *nf* (*de vino*) (wine) cellar; (*depósito*) storeroom; (*de barco*) hold.
bodegón [boðe'xon] *nm* cheap restaurant; (*ARTE*) still life.
bofe ['bofe] *nm* (*también* **~s** *nmpl*) lung.
bofetada [bofe'taða] *nf* slap (in the face).
bofetón [bofe'ton] *nm* punch (in the face).
boga ['boxa] *nf* (*NAUT*) rowing; (*fig*) vogue, fashion // *nm/f* rower; **en ~** in vogue; **bogar** *vi* (*remar*) to row; (*navegar*) to sail.
Bogotá [boxo'ta] *n* Bogota; **bogotano, a** *a* of or from Bogota.
bohardilla [boar'ðiʎa] *nf* = **buhardilla**.
bohemio, a [bo'emjo, a] *a, nm/f* Bohemian.
boicot [boi'kot] *nm* boycott; **~ear** *vt* to boycott; **~eo** *nm* boycott.
boina ['boina] *nf* beret.
bola ['bola] *nf* (*gen*) ball; (*canica*) marble; (*NAIPES*) (grand) slam; (*betún*) shoe polish; **~ de billar** billiard ball; **~ de nieve** snowball.
bolchevique [boltʃe'βike] *nm/f* Bolshevik.
boleadoras [bolea'ðoras] *nfpl* (*LAM*) bolas.
bolera [bo'lera] *nf* skittle alley.
boleta [bo'leta] *nf* (*billete*) ticket; (*permiso*) pass, permit.
boletín [bole'tin] *nm* bulletin; (*periódico*) journal, review; (*billete*) ticket; **~ escolar** school report; **~ de noticias** news bulletin; **~ de pedido** application form; **~ de precios** price list; **~ de prensa** press release.
boleto [bo'leto] *nm* ticket.
boliche [bo'litʃe] *nm* (*bola*) jack; (*juego*) bowls *sg*; (*lugar*) bowling alley.
bolígrafo [bo'lixrafo] *nm* ball-point pen.
bolívar [bo'liβar] *nm* monetary unit of Venezuela.
Bolivia [bo'liβja] *nf* Bolivia; **boliviano, a** *a, nm/f* Bolivian.
bolo ['bolo] *nm* skittle; (*píldora*) (large) pill; (*juego de*) **~s** *nmpl* skittles *sg*.
bolsa ['bolsa] *nf* (*cartera*) purse; (*saco*) bag; (*ANAT*) cavity, sac; (*COM*) stock exchange; (*MINERÍA*) pocket; **~ de agua**

caliente hot water bottle; ~ **de aire** air pocket; ~ **de papel** paper bag.

bolsillo [bol'siʎo] nm pocket; (cartera) purse; **de** ~ pocket(-size).

bolsista [bol'sista] nm/f stockbroker.

bolso ['bolso] nm (bolsa) bag; (de mujer) handbag.

bollo ['boʎo] nm (pan) roll; (bulto) bump, lump; (abolladura) dent.

bomba ['bomba] nf (MIL) bomb; (TEC) pump // a (fam): **noticia** ~ shattering piece of news // ad (fam): **pasarlo** ~ to have a great time; ~ **atómica/de humo/de retardo** atomic/smoke/ time bomb; ~ **de gasolina** petrol pump; ~ **de mano** grenade; ~ **lacrimógena** tear gas bomb.

bombardear [bombarðe'ar] vt to bombard; (MIL) to bomb; **bombardeo** nm bombardment; bombing.

bombardero [bombar'ðero] nm bomber.

bombear [bombe'ar] vt (agua) to pump (out or up); (MIL) to bomb; ~**se** vr to warp.

bombero [bom'bero] nm fireman.

bombilla [bom'biʎa] nf bulb.

bombín [bom'bin] nm bowler hat.

bombo ['bombo] nm (MUS) bass drum; (TEC) drum.

bombón [bom'bon] nm chocolate.

bonachón, ona [bona'tʃon, ona] a good-natured, easy-going.

bonaerense [bonae'rense] a of or from Buenos Aires.

bonancible [bonan'θiβle] a (tiempo) fair, calm.

bonanza [bo'nanθa] nf (NAUT) fair weather; (fig) bonanza; (MINERÍA) rich pocket or vein.

bondad [bon'dað] nf goodness, kindness; **tenga la** ~ **de** (please) be good enough to; ~**oso, a** a good, kind.

bonito, a [bo'nito, a] a (lindo) pretty; (agradable) nice.

bono ['bono] nm voucher; (FIN) bond.

boquear [boke'ar] vi to gasp.

boquerón [boke'ron] nm (anchoa) anchovy; (agujero) large hole.

boquete [bo'kete] nm gap, hole.

boquiabierto, a [bokia'βjerto, a] a open-mouthed (in astonishment).

boquilla [bo'kiʎa] nf (para riego) nozzle; (para cigarro) cigarette holder; (MUS) mouthpiece.

borbollar [borβo'ʎar], **borbollear** [borβoʎe'ar], **borbotar** [borβo'tar] vi to bubble.

borbotón [borβo'ton] nm bubbling.

bordado [bor'ðaðo] nm embroidery.

bordar [bor'ðar] vt to embroider.

borde ['borðe] nm edge, border; (de camino etc) side; (en la costura) hem; **al** ~ **de** (fig) on the verge or brink of; ~**ar** vt to border.

bordo ['borðo] nm (NAUT) side; **a** ~ **on** board.

Borinquén [borin'ken] nm Puerto Rico;

borinqueño, a a a, nm/f Puerto Rican.

borra ['borra] nf (pelusa) fluff; (sedimento) sediment.

borrachera [borra'tʃera] nf (ebriedad) drunkenness; (orgía) spree, binge.

borracho, a [bo'rratʃo, a] a drunk // nm/f (que bebe mucho) drunkard, drunk; (temporalmente) drunk, drunk man/woman.

borrador [borra'ðor] nm (escritura) first draft, rough sketch; (cuaderno) scribbling pad; (goma) rubber, eraser.

borrajear [borraxe'ar] vt, vi to scribble.

borrar [bo'rrar] vt to erase, rub out.

borrascoso, a [borras'koso, a] a stormy.

borrica [bo'rrika] nf she-donkey; (fig) stupid woman; ~**da** nf foolish action/statement.

borrico [bo'rriko] nm donkey; (fig) stupid man.

borrón [bo'rron] nm (mancha) stain; (proyecto) rough draft; (de cuadro) sketch.

borroso, a [bo'rroso, a] a vague, unclear; (escritura) illegible.

bosque ['boske] nm wood, forest.

bosquejar [boske'xar] vt to sketch; **bosquejo** nm sketch.

bosta ['bosta] nf dung, manure.

bostezar [boste'θar] vi to yawn; **bostezo** nm yawn.

bota ['bota] nf (saco) leather wine bottle; (calzado) boot.

botadura [bota'ðura] nf launching.

botánico, a [bo'taniko, a] nm/f botanist // nf botany.

botar [bo'tar] vt to throw, hurl; (NAUT) to launch; (fam) to throw out // vi to bounce.

bote ['bote] nm (salto) bounce; (golpe) thrust; (vasija) tin, can; (embarcación) boat; **de** ~ **en** ~ packed, jammed full; ~ **salvavidas** lifeboat.

botella [bo'teʎa] nf bottle.

botica [bo'tika] nf chemist's (shop), pharmacy; ~**rio**, a nm/f chemist, pharmacist.

botija [bo'tixa] nf (earthenware) jug; **botijo** nm (earthenware) jug; (tren) excursion train.

botín [bo'tin] nm (calzado) half boot; (polaina) spat; (MIL) booty.

botiquín [boti'kin] nm (armario) medicine cabinet; (portátil) first-aid kit.

botón [bo'ton] nm button; (BOT) bud; (de florete) tip; ~ **de oro** buttercup.

botones [bo'tones] nm buttons sg, bellboy.

bóveda ['boβeða] nf (ARQ) vault.

boxeador [boksea'ðor] nm boxer.

boxeo [bok'seo] nm boxing.

boya ['boja] nf (NAUT) buoy; (flotador) float.

bozal [bo'θal] a (novato) raw, green; (tonto) stupid; (salvaje) wild // nm (de caballo) halter; (de perro) muzzle.

bracear [braθe'ar] vi (agitar los brazos) to wave one's arms; (nadar) to swim (the crawl).

bracero [bra'θero] nm labourer; (en el campo) farmhand.

bracete [bra'θete]: **de ~** ad arm in arm.

braga ['braɣa] nf (cuerda) sling, rope; (de bebé) nappy; **~s** nfpl (de mujer) panties.

bragueta [bra'ɣeta] nf fly, flies pl.

braille [breil] nm braille.

bramar [bra'mar] vi to bellow, roar; **bramido** nm bellow, roar.

brasa ['brasa] nf live coal.

brasero [bra'sero] nm brazier.

Brasil [bra'sil] nm: **el ~ Brazil**; **brasileño, a** a, nm/f Brazilian.

bravata [bra'ßata] nf boast.

braveza [bra'ßeθa] nf (valor) bravery; (ferocidad) ferocity.

bravío, a [bra'ßio, a] a wild; (feroz) fierce.

bravo, a ['braßo, a] a (valiente) brave; (bueno) fine, splendid; (feroz) ferocious; (salvaje) wild // excl bravo!; **bravura** nf bravery; ferocity; (pey) boast.

braza ['braθa] nf fathom; **nadar a la ~** to swim the breast-stroke.

brazada [bra'θaða] nf stroke.

brazado [bra'θaðo] nm armful.

brazalete [braθa'lete] nm (pulsera) bracelet; (banda) armband.

brazo ['braθo] nm arm; (ZOOL) foreleg; (BOT) limb, branch; **a ~ partido** hand-to-hand; **del ~** arm in arm.

brea ['brea] nf pitch, tar.

brebaje [bre'ßaxe] nm potion.

brecha ['bretʃa] nf breach, gap, opening.

brega ['breɣa] nf (lucha) struggle; (trabajo) hard work.

breve ['breße] a short, brief // nf breve; **~dad** nf brevity, shortness.

brezal [bre'θal] nm moor(land), heath; **brezo** nm heather.

bribón, ona [bri'ßon, ona] a idle, lazy // nm/f (vagabundo) vagabond; (pícaro) rascal, rogue.

bricolaje [briko'laxe] nm do-it-yourself, DIY.

brida ['briða] nf bridle, rein; (TEC) clamp; a **toda ~** at top speed.

bridge [britʃ] nm bridge.

brigada [bri'ɣaða] nf (unidad) brigade; (trabajadores) squad, gang // nm ≈ staff-sergeant, sergeant-major.

brillante [bri'ʎante] a brilliant // nm diamond; **brillar** vi to shine.

brillo ['briʎo] nm shine; (brillantez) brilliance; (fig) splendour; **sacar ~ a** to polish.

brincar [brin'kar] vi to skip about, hop about, jump about; **está que brinca** he's hopping mad.

brinco ['brinko] nm hop, skip, jump.

brindar [brin'dar] vi: **~ a o por** to drink (a toast) to // vt to offer, present.

brindis ['brindis] nm toast; (TAUR) (ceremony of) dedicating the bull.

brío ['brio] nm spirit, dash; **brioso, a** a spirited, dashing.

brisa ['brisa] nf breeze.

británico, a [bri'taniko, a] a British // nm/f Briton, British person.

brocal [bro'kal] nm rim.

brocha ['brotʃa] nf brush.

broche ['brotʃe] nm brooch; **~ para papeles** (AM) paper clip.

broma ['broma] nf (bulla) fun; (chanza) joke; **en ~** in fun, as a joke; **bromear** vi to joke.

bromista [bro'mista] a fond of joking // nm/f joker, wag.

bronca ['bronka] nf row.

bronce ['bronθe] nm bronze; **~ado, a** a bronze; (por el sol) tanned // nm (sun)tan; (TEC) bronzing.

broncearse [bronθe'arse] vr to get a suntan.

bronco, a ['bronko, a] a (superficie) rough; (manera) rude, surly; (voz) harsh.

bronquitis [bron'kitis] nf bronchitis.

brotar [bro'tar] vi (BOT) to sprout; (aguas) to gush (forth), flow; (MED) to break out; **brote** nm (BOT) shoot; (MED, fig) outbreak.

bruces ['bruθes]: **de ~** ad: caer o dar de **~** to fall headlong, fall flat; **estar de ~** to lie face downwards.

bruja ['bruxa] nf witch; (lechuza) owl; **brujería** nf witchcraft.

brujo ['bruxo] nm wizard, magician.

brújula ['bruxula] nf compass.

bruma ['bruma] nf mist; **brumoso, a** a misty.

bruñido [bru'ñiðo] nm polish; **bruñir** vt to polish.

brusco, a ['brusko, a] a (súbito) sudden; (áspero) brusque.

Bruselas [bru'selas] n Brussels.

brutal [bru'tal] a brutal; (fig) sudden; **~idad** nf brutality.

bruto, a ['bruto, a] a (idiota) stupid; (bestial) brutish; (peso) gross; (diamante etc) raw, uncut; **en ~** raw, unworked.

Bs.As. abr de **Buenos Aires.**

buba ['bußa] nf tumour.

bucal [bu'kal] a: **por ~ ~** by or through the mouth, orally.

bucear [buθe'ar] vi to dive // vt to explore; **buceo** nm diving; (fig) investigation.

bucle ['bukle] nm curl.

budismo [bu'ðismo] nm Buddhism.

buenamente [bwena'mente] ad (fácilmente) easily; (voluntariamente) willingly.

buenaventura [bwenaßen'tura] nf (suerte) good luck; (adivinación) fortune.

bueno, a ['bweno, a] a buen [bwen] a (amable) kind; (MED) well; (guapo) attractive; **¡~as! hello; buen día, ~as días** good morning!; good afternoon!; hello!; **~as tardes** good afternoon!; good evening!; **~as noches** good night!; **¡buen sinvergüenza resultó!** a fine rascal he turned out to be // excl right!, all right!; **~, ¿y qué?** well, so what?

buey [bwei] nm ox.

búfalo ['bufalo] nm buffalo.

bufanda [bu'fanda] nf scarf, muffler.

bufar [bu'far] vi to snort.

bufete [bu'fete] *nm* (*mesa*) desk; (*de abogado*) lawyer's office.

bufo, a ['bufo, a] *a* comic.

bufón, ona [bu'fon, ona] *a* funny // *nm* clown.

buhardilla [buar'ðiʎa] *nf* (*ventana*) skylight; (*desván*) attic.

búho ['buo] *nm* owl; (*fig*) hermit, recluse.

buhonero [buo'nero] *nm* pedlar.

buitre ['bwitre] *nm* vulture.

bujía [bu'xia] *nf* (*vela*) candle; (*ELEC*) candle (power); (*AUTO*) spark plug.

bula ['bula] *nf* (*papal*) bull.

bulbo ['bulβo] *nm* bulb.

búlgaro, a ['bulxaro, a] *a, nm/f* Bulgarian.

bulto ['bulto] *nm* (*paquete*) package; (*fardo*) bundle; (*tamaño*) size, bulkiness; (*MED*) swelling, lump; (*silueta*) vague shape; (*estatua*) bust, statue; **de mucho/poco ~** important/unimportant.

bulla ['buʎa] *nf* (*ruido*) uproar; (*de gente*) crowd.

bullicio [bu'ʎiθjo] *nm* (*ruido*) uproar; (*movimiento*) bustle.

bullir [bu'ʎir] *vi* (*hervir*) to boil; (*burbujear*) to bubble; (*mover*) to move, stir.

buñuelo [bu'nwelo] *nm* fritter.

buque ['buke] *nm* ship, vessel.

burbuja [bur'βuxa] *nf* bubble; **burbujear** *vi* to bubble.

burdel [bur'ðel] *nm* brothel.

burdo, a ['burðo, a] *a* coarse, rough.

burgués, esa [bur'xes, esa] *a* middle-class, bourgeois; **burguesía** *nf* middle class, bourgeoisie.

burla ['burla] *nf* (*mofa*) gibe; (*broma*) joke; (*engaño*) trick.

burladero [burla'ðero] *nm* (*bullfighter's*) refuge.

burlador, a [burla'ðor, a] *a* mocking // *nm* (*bromista*) joker; (*libertino*) seducer.

burlar [bur'lar] *vt* (*engañar*) to deceive; (*seducir*) to seduce // *vi*, **~se vr** to joke; **~se de** to make fun of.

burlesco, a [bur'lesko, a] *a* burlesque.

burlón, ona [bur'lon, ona] *a* mocking.

burocracia [buro'kraθja] *nf* civil service; (*pey*) bureaucracy.

burócrata [bu'rokrata] *nm/f* civil servant; (*pey*) bureaucrat.

burra ['burra] *nf* (she-)donkey; (*fig*) stupid woman.

burro ['burro] *nm* donkey; (*fig*) ass, idiot.

bursátil [bur'satil] *a* stock-exchange *cpd*.

busca ['buska] *nf* search, hunt; **en ~ de** in search of.

buscapleitos [buska'pleitos] *nm/f inv* troublemaker.

buscar [bus'kar] *vt* to look for, search for, seek // *vi* to look, search, seek; **se busca empleado** employee wanted.

buscón, ona [bus'kon, ona] *a* thieving // *nm* petty thief // *nf* whore.

busilis [bu'silis] *nm* (*fam*) snag.

busque *etc vb ver* **buscar.**

búsqueda ['buskeða] *nf* = **busca.**

busto ['busto] *nm* bust.

butaca [bu'taka] *nf* armchair; (*de cine, teatro*) stall, seat.

butano [bu'tano] *nm* butane.

buzo ['buθo] *nm* diver.

buzón [bu'θon] *nm* letter box; (*en la calle*) pillar box.

C

c. *abr de* **capítulo.**

C. *abr de* **centígrado; compañía.**

C/ *abr de* **calle.**

c.a. *abr de* **corriente alterna.**

cabal [ka'βal] *a* (*exacto*) exact; (*correcto*) right, proper; (*acabado*) finished, complete; **~es** *nmpl*: **estar en sus ~es** to be in one's right mind.

cabalgadura [kaβalxa'ðura] *nf* mount, horse.

cabalgar [kaβal'xar] *vt, vi* to ride.

caballa [ka'βaʎa] *nf* mackerel.

caballeresco, a [kaβaʎe'resko, a] *a* noble, chivalrous.

caballería [kaβaʎe'ria] *nf* mount; (*MIL*) cavalry.

caballeriza [kaβaʎe'riθa] *nf* stable; **caballerizo** *nm* groom, stableman.

caballero [kaβa'ʎero] *nm* rider, horseman; (*hombre galante*) gentleman; (*de la orden de caballería*) knight; (*hidalgo*) noble(man); (*señor, término de cortesía*) sir.

caballerosidad [kaβaʎerosi'ðað] *nf* chivalry.

caballo [ka'βaʎo] *nm* horse; (*AJEDREZ*) knight; (*NAIPES*) queen; **~ de vapor** *o* **de fuerza** horsepower.

cabaña [ka'βaɲa] *nf* (*casita*) hut, cabin; (*rebaño*) flock.

cabaré, cabaret (*pl* **cabarets**) [kaβa're] *nm* cabaret.

cabás [ka'βas] *nm* satchel.

cabecear [kaβeθe'ar] *vt* to head // *vi* to nod; (*negar*) to shake one's head.

cabecera [kaβe'θera] *nf* (*gen*) head; (*de distrito*) chief town; (*IMPRENTA*) headline.

cabecilla [kaβe'θiʎa] *nm/f* ringleader; (*fig: fam*) hothead.

cabellera [kaβe'ʎera] *nf* hair; (*de cometa*) tail.

cabello [ka'βeʎo] *nm* (*también* **~s** *nmpl*) hair *sg*; **cabelludo, a** *a* hairy.

caber [ka'βer] *vi* (*entrar*) to fit, go; (*tener lugar*) to have enough room; **caben 3 más** there's room for 3 more.

cabestrillo [kaβes'triʎo] *nm* sling.

cabestro [ka'βestro] *nm* halter.

cabeza [ka'βeθa] *nf* head; (*POL*) chief, leader; **~da** *nf* (*golpe*) butt; (*al dormirse*) nod.

cabezudo, a [kaβe'θuðo, a] *a* bigheaded; (*fig*) pigheaded.

cabida [ka'βiða] *nf* space.

cabildo [ka'βildo] *nm* (*de iglesia*) chapter; (*POL*) town council.

cabina [ka'ßina] *nf* booth; (*de camión*) cabin.

cabizbajo, a [kaßiθ'ßaxo, a] *a* crestfallen, dejected.

cable [ka'ßle] *nm* cable; ~**grama** *nm* cablegram.

cabo ['kaßo] *nm* (*de objeto*) end, extremity; (*de tiempo, proceso*) end; (*persona*) head, chief; (*MIL*) corporal; (*NAUT*) rope, cable; (*GEO*) cape; **al** ~ **de 3 días** after 3 days; **al fin y al** ~ in the end.

cabra ['kaßra] *nf* (she-)goat, nanny goat.

cabré *etc vb ver* **caber.**

cabria ['kaßrja] *nf* hoist, derrick.

cabrío, a [ka'ßrio, a] *a* goatish; **macho** ~ (he-)goat, billy goat.

cabriola [ka'ßrjola] *nf* caper.

cabritilla [kaßri'tiʎa] *nf* kid, kidskin.

cabrito [ka'ßrito] *nm* kid.

cabrón [ka'ßron] *nm* cuckold; (*fig: fam*) bastard (*fam!*).

cacahuete [kaka'wete] *nm* peanut, monkey nut.

cacao [ka'kao] *nm* cocoa; (*BOT*) cacao.

cacarear [kakare'ar] *vi* (*persona*) to boast; (*gallo*) to cackle.

cacería [kaθe'ria] *nf* hunting, shooting.

cacerola [kaθe'rola] *nf* pan, saucepan.

cacique [ka'θike] *nm* chief, local ruler; (*POL*) local boss; **caciquismo** *nm* (system of) dominance by the local boss.

caco ['kako] *nm* pickpocket.

cacto ['kakto], **cactus** ['kaktus] *nm* cactus.

cacumen [ka'kumen] *nm* (*fig: fam*) acumen.

cachar [ka'tʃar] *vt* to smash, break.

cacharro [ka'tʃarro] *nm* earthenware pot.

cachear [katʃe'ar] *vt* to search, frisk.

cachemira [katʃe'mira] *nf* cashmere.

cacheo [ka'tʃeo] *nm* searching, frisking.

cachimba [ka'tʃimba] *nf*, **cachimbo** [ka-'tʃimbo] *nm* pipe.

cachiporra [katʃi'porra] *nf* truncheon.

cachivache [katʃi'ßatʃe] *nm* pot; (*utensilio*) utensil; (*persona*) good-for-nothing.

cacho, a ['katʃo, a] *a* bent, crooked // *nm* (small) bit.

cachondeo [katʃon'ðeo] *nm* (*fam*) farce, joke.

cachondo, a [ka'tʃondo, a] *a* (*ZOOL*) on heat; (*vulg*) randy, sexy; (*gracioso*) funny.

cachorro, a [ka'tʃorro, a] *nm/f* (*perro*) pup, puppy; (*león*) cub.

cada ['kaða] *a inv* each; (*antes de número*) every; ~ **día** each day, every day; ~ **uno/a** each one, every one; ~ **vez más** more and more; **uno de** ~ **diez** one out of every ten.

cadalso [ka'ðalso] *nm* scaffold.

cadáver [ka'ðaßer] *nm* (dead) body, corpse.

cadena [ka'ðena] *nf* chain; (*TV*) channel; **trabajo en** ~ assembly line work.

cadencia [ka'ðenθja] *nf* cadence, rhythm.

cadera [ka'ðera] *nf* hip.

cadete [ka'ðete] *nm* cadet.

caducar [kaðu'kar] *vi* (*permiso, ley*) to lapse, expire; (*persona*) to become senile; **caduco, a** *a* expired; (*persona*) very old.

C.A.E. *abr de* **cobrese al entregar** COD (cash on delivery).

caer [ka'er] *vi*, ~**se** *vr* to fall (down); ~ **bien/mal** to make a good/bad impression; **el pago cae mañana** the payment is due tomorrow; ~ **en la cuenta** to catch on.

café [ka'fe] (*pl* ~**s**) *nm* (*bebida, planta*) coffee; (*lugar*) café // *a* (*color*) brown; **cafetal** *nm* coffee plantation.

cafetero, a [kafe'tero, a] *a* coffee *cpd* // *nf* coffee pot.

cáfila ['kafila] *nf* (*de personas*) group; (*de ovejas*) flock.

caída [ka'iða] *nf* (*gen*) fall; (*declive*) slope; (*disminución*) fall, drop.

caigo *etc vb ver* **caer.**

caimán [kai'man] *nm* alligator.

caimiento [kai'mjento] *nm* fall, falling.

caja ['kaxa] *nf* box; (*para reloj*) case; (*de ascensor*) shaft; (*CCM*) cashbox; (*donde se hacen los pagos*) cashdesk; ~ **de ahorros** savings bank; ~ **de cambios** gearbox; ~ **fuerte,** ~ **de caudales** safe, strongbox.

cajero, a [ka'xero, a] *nm/f* cashier.

cajetilla [kaxe'tiʎa] *nf* small box; (*de cigarrillos*) packet.

cajón [ka'xon] *nm* big box; (*de mueble*) drawer.

cal [kal] *nf* lime.

cala ['kala] *nf* (*GEO*) cove, inlet; (*de barco*) hold; (*MED*) suppository.

calabaza [kala'ßaθa] *nf* (*BOT*) pumpkin.

calabozo [kala'ßoθo] *nm* prison (cell).

calamar [kala'mar] *nm* squid.

calambre [ka'lambre] *nm* cramp.

calamidad [kalami'ðað] *nf* calamity, disaster.

calamina [kala'mina] *nf* calamine.

calaña [ka'laɲa] *nf* model, pattern.

calar [ka'lar] *vt* to soak, drench; (*penetrar*) to pierce, penetrate; (*comprender*) to see through; (*vela, red*) to lower; ~**se las gafas** to stick one's glasses on.

calavera [kala'ßera] *nf* skull.

calcañar [kalka'ɲar], **calcañal** [kalka-'ɲal], **calcaño** [kal'kaɲo] *nm* heel.

calcar [kal'kar] *vt* (*reproducir*) to trace; (*imitar*) to copy.

calceta [kal'θeta] *nf* (knee-length) stocking; **hacer** ~ to knit; **calcetín** *nm* sock.

calcina [kal'θina] *nf* concrete.

calcinar [kalθi'nar] *vt* to burn, blacken.

calcio ['kalθjo] *nm* calcium.

calco ['kalko] *nm* tracing.

calcomanía [kalkoma'nia] *nf* transfer.

calculadora [kalkula'ðora] *nf* calculator; ~ **de bolsillo** pocket calculator.

calcular [kalku'lar] *vt* (*MAT*) to calculate, compute; (*suponer, creer*) to reckon, expect; **cálculo** *nm* calculation; reckoning.

caldear [kalde'ar] *vt* to warm (up), heat (up); (*los metales*) to weld.

caldera [kal'dera] *nf* boiler.

calderilla [kalde'riʎa] *nf* (REL) vessel for holy water; (*moneda*) small change.

caldero [kal'dero] *nm* small boiler.

calderón [kalde'ron] *nm* cauldron.

caldo ['kaldo] *nm* stock; (*consomé*) consommé; (*para la ensalada*) dressing.

calefacción [kalefak'θjon] *nf* heating.

calendario [kalen'darjo] *nm* calendar.

calentador [kalenta'ðor] *nm* heater.

calentar [kalen'tar] *vt* to heat (up); ~**se** *vr* to heat up, warm up; (*fig*) to get heated.

calentura [kalen'tura] *nf* (MED) fever, (high) temperature; **calenturiento, a** *a* feverish.

calero, a [ka'lero, a] *a* lime *cpd*.

calibrar [kali'βrar] *vt* to gauge, measure; **calibre** *nm* (*de cañón*) calibre, bore; (*diámetro*) diameter; (*fig*) calibre.

calidad [kali'ðað] *nf* quality; **en ~ de** in the capacity of.

cálido, a ['kaliðo, a] *a* hot; (*fig*) warm.

caliente [ka'ljente] *a* hot; (*sin exceso*) warm; (*fig*) fiery; (*disputa*) heated.

calificación [kalifika'θjon] *nf* qualification; (*de alumno*) grade, mark.

calificado, a [kalifi'kaðo, a] *a* qualified, competent; (*trabajador*) skilled.

calificar [kalifi'kar] *vt* to qualify; (*enaltecer*) to distinguish; (*alumno*) to grade, mark; (*determinar*) to describe.

calma ['kalma] *nf* calm; (*pachorra*) slowness.

calmante [kal'mante] *nm* sedative, tranquillizer.

calmar [kal'mar] *vt* to calm, calm down // *vi* (*tempestad*) to abate; (*mente etc*) to become calm.

calmoso, a [kal'moso, a], **calmudo, a** [kal'muðo, a] *a* calm, quiet.

calofrío [kalo'frio] *nm* = **escalofrío**.

calor [ka'lor] *nm* heat; (~ *agradable*) warmth.

caloría [kalo'ria] *nf* calorie.

calorífero, a [kalo'rifero, a] *a* heat-producing, heat-giving // *nm* heating system.

calumnia [ka'lumnja] *nf* calumny, slander; **calumnioso, a** *a* slanderous.

caluroso, a [kalu'roso, a] *a* hot; (*sin exceso*) warm; (*fig*) enthusiastic.

calva ['kalβa] *nf* bald patch; (*en bosque*) clearing.

calvario [kal'βarjo] *nm* stations *pl* of the cross.

calvicie [kal'βiθje] *nf* baldness.

calvo, a ['kalβo, a] *a* bald; (*terreno*) bare, barren; (*tejido*) threadbare.

calza ['kalθa] *nf* wedge, chock.

calzado, a [kal'θaðo, a] *a* shod // *nm* footwear // *nf* roadway, highway.

calzador [kalθa'ðor] *nm* shoehorn.

calzar [kal'θar] *vt* to put on; (*un mueble*) to put a wedge under; ~**se** *vr*: ~**se los zapatos** to put on one's shoes; **¿qué (número) calza?** what size do you wear or take?

calzón [kal'θon] *nm* (*también* **calzones** *nmpl*) shorts *pl*.

calzoncillos [kalθon'θiʎos] *nmpl* underpants.

callado, a [ka'ʎaðo, a] *a* quiet.

callar [ka'ʎar] *vt* to keep quiet about, say nothing about // *vi*, ~**se** *vr* to keep quiet, be silent.

calle ['kaʎe] *nf* street; (DEPORTE) lane; ~ **arriba/abajo** up/down the street; ~ **de un solo sentido** one-way street.

calleja [ka'ʎexa] *nf* alley, narrow street; **callejear** *vi* to wander about the streets; **callejero, a** a street *cpd*.

callejón [kaʎe'xon] *nm* alley, passage; ~ **sin salida** one-way street.

callejuela [kaʎe'xwela] *nf* side-street, alley.

callista [ka'ʎista] *nm/f* chiropodist.

callo ['kaʎo] *nm* callus; (*en el pie*) corn; ~**s** *nmpl* tripe *sg*; ~**so, a** a horny, rough.

cama ['kama] *nf* bed; (GEO) stratum; ~ **de matrimonio** double bed.

camada [ka'maða] *nf* litter; (*de personas*) gang, band.

camafeo [kama'feo] *nm* cameo.

camandulear [kamandule'ar] *vi* to be a hypocrite.

cámara ['kamara] *nf* (*gen*) chamber; (*habitación*) room; (*sala*) hall; (CINE) cine camera; (*fotográfica*) camera; ~ **de aire** inner tube.

camarada [kama'raða] *nm* comrade, companion.

camarera [kama'rera] *nf* (*en restaurante*) waitress; (*en casa, hotel*) maid.

camarero [kama'rero] *nm* waiter.

camarilla [kama'riʎa] *nf* (*clan*) clique; (POL) lobby.

camarín [kama'rin] *nm* dressing room.

camarón [kama'ron] *nm* shrimp.

camarote [kama'rote] *nm* cabin.

cambiable [kam'bjaβle] *a* (*variable*) changeable, variable; (*intercambiable*) interchangeable.

cambiante [kam'bjante] *a* variable // *nm* moneychanger.

cambiar [kam'bjar] *vt* (*gen*) to change; (*de moneda*) to change; (*dinero*) to exchange // *vi* (*gen*) to change; ~**se** *vr* (*mudarse*) to move; (*de ropa*) to change; ~**(se) de...** to change one's ... .

cambio ['kambjo] *nm* change; (*trueque*) exchange; (COM) rate of exchange; (*oficina*) (foreign) exchange office; (*dinero menudo*) small change; **en ~** on the other hand; (*en lugar de eso*) instead; ~ **de velocidades** gear lever; ~ **de vía** points *pl*.

cambista [kam'bista] *nm* (COM) exchange broker; (FERRO) switchman.

camelar [kame'lar] vt (*galantear*) to flirt with; (*engañar*) to cajole.

camello [ka'meʎo] nm camel.

camilla [ka'miʎa] nf (*cama*) cot; (*MED*) stretcher.

caminante [kami'nante] nm/f traveller.

caminar [kami'nar] vi (*marchar*) to walk, go; (*viajar*) to travel, journey // vt (*recorrer*) to cover, travel.

caminata [kami'nata] nf long walk.

camino [ka'mino] nm (*gen*) way, road; (*senda*) track; **a medio ~** halfway (there); **en el ~** on the way, en route.

camión [ka'mjon] nm lorry, truck.

camisa [ka'misa] nf shirt; (*BOT*) skin; **~ de dormir** nightdress; **~ de fuerza** straitjacket; **camisería** nf outfitter's (shop).

camiseta [kami'seta] nf (*prenda*) vest; (*de deportista*) singlet.

camisón [kami'son] nm nightdress, nightgown.

campamento [kampa'mento] nm camp.

campana [kam'pana] nf bell; **~da** nf peal; **~rio** nm belfry.

campanilla [kampa'niʎa] nf (*campana*) small bell; (*burbuja*) bubble.

campaña [kam'paɲa] nf (*MIL, POL*) campaign; (*campo*) countryside.

campar [kam'par] vi to camp; (*sobresalir*) to excel, stand out.

campeón, ona [kampe'on, ona] nm/f champion; **campeonato** nm championship.

campesino, a [kampe'sino, a] a country cpd, rural // nm/f countryman/woman; (*agricultor*) farmer.

campestre [kam'pestre] a country cpd, rural.

camping ['kampin] nm camping; (*lugar*) campsite; **hacer ~** to go camping.

campiña [kam'piɲa] nf countryside.

campo ['kampo] nm (*fuera de la ciudad*) country, countryside; (*AGR, ELEC*) field; (*de fútbol*) ground, pitch; (*de golf*) course; (*de tenis*) court; (*MIL*) camp.

camposanto [kampo'santo] nm cemetery.

camuflaje [kamu'flaxe] nm camouflage.

Canadá [kana'ða] nm Canada; **canadiense** a, nm/f Canadian // nf fur-lined jacket.

canal [ka'nal] nm canal; (*GEO*) channel, strait; (*de televisión*) channel; (*de tejado*) gutter; **~izar** vt to channel.

canalón [kana'lon] nm (*conducto vertical*) drainpipe; (*del tejado*) gutter.

canalla [ka'naʎa] nf rabble, mob // nm swine, rotter.

canapé [kana'pe] (pl **~s**) nm sofa, settee; (*CULIN*) canapé.

canario, a [ka'narjo, a] a, nm/f (native) of the Canary Isles // nm canary.

canasta [ka'nasta] nf (round) basket; **canasto** nm large basket.

cancelación [kanθela'θjon] nf cancellation.

cancelar [kanθe'lar] vt to cancel; (*una deuda*) to write off.

cáncer ['kanθer] nm (*MED*) cancer; **C~** (*ASTRO*) Cancer.

canciller [kanθi'ʎer] nm chancellor.

canción [kan'θjon] nf song; **~ de cuna** lullaby; **cancionero** nm song book.

candado [kan'daðo] nm padlock.

candela [kan'dela] nf candle.

candelero [kande'lero] nm (*para vela*) candlestick; (*de aceite*) oil lamp.

candente [kan'dente] a red-hot; (*fig*) burning.

candidato [kandi'ðato] nm/f candidate.

candidez [kandi'ðeθ] nf (*sencillez*) simplicity; (*simpleza*) naiveté; **cándido, a** a simple; naive.

candil [kan'dil] nm oil lamp; **~eja** nf small oil lamp.

candor [kan'dor] nm (*sinceridad*) frankness; (*inocencia*) innocence.

canela [ka'nela] nf cinnamon.

canelón [kane'lon] nm (*canal*) drainpipe; (*carámbano*) icicle.

cangrejo [kan'grexo] nm crab.

canguro [kan'guro] nm kangaroo.

caníbal [ka'niβal] a, nm/f cannibal.

canica [ka'nika] nf marble.

canijo, a [ka'nixo, a] a frail, sickly.

canino, a [ka'nino, a] a canine // nm canine (tooth).

canjear [kanxe'ar] vt to exchange.

cano, a ['kano, a] a grey-haired, white-haired.

canoa [ka'noa] nf canoe.

canon ['kanon] nm canon; (*pensión*) rent; (*COM*) tax.

canónigo [ka'noniɣo] nm canon.

canonizar [kanoni'θar] vt to canonize.

canoro, a [ka'noro, a] a melodious.

cansado, a [kan'saðo, a] a tired, weary; (*tedioso*) tedious, boring.

cansancio [kan'sanθjo] nm tiredness, fatigue.

cansar [kan'sar] vt (*fatigar*) to tire, tire out, weary; (*aburrir*) to bore; (*fastidiar*) to bother; **~se** vr to tire, get tired; (*aburrirse*) to get bored.

cantante [kan'tante] a singing // nm/f singer.

cantar [kan'tar] vt to sing // vi (*gen*) to sing; (*insecto*) to chirp; (*rechinar*) to squeak // nm (*acción*) singing; (*canción*) song; (*poema*) poem.

cántara ['kantara] nf large pitcher.

cántaro ['kantaro] nm pitcher, jug.

cantatriz [kanta'triθ] nf singer.

cante ['kante] nm: **~ jondo** flamenco singing.

cantera [kan'tera] nf quarry.

cantidad [kanti'ðað] nf quantity, amount.

cantilena [kanti'lena] nf = **cantinela**.

cantimplora [kantim'plora] nf (*frasco*) water bottle, canteen; (*sifón*) syphon.

cantina [kan'tina] nf canteen; (*de estación*) buffet; (*sótano*) wine cellar.

cantinela [kanti'nela] *nf* ballad, song.

canto ['kanto] *nm* (*gen*) singing; (*canción*) song; (*borde*) edge, rim; (*de un cuchillo*) back; ~ **rodado** boulder.

cantor, a [kan'tor, a] *nm/f* singer.

canturrear [kanturre'ar], **canturriar** [kantu'rrjar] *vi* to sing softly.

caña ['kaɲa] *nf* (*BOT: tallo*) stem, stalk; (*carrizo*) reed; (*de cerveza*) glass; (*ANAT: del brazo*) long bone; (: *de la pierna*) shinbone; (*MINERÍA*) gallery; ~ **de azúcar** sugar cane.

cañada [ka'ɲaða] *nf* (*entre dos montañas*) gully, ravine; (*camino*) cattle track.

caño ['kaɲo] *nm* (*tubo*) tube, pipe; (*de aguas servidas*) sewer; (*MUS*) pipe; (*NAUT*) navigation channel; (*de fuente*) jet.

cañón [ka'ɲon] *nm* tube, pipe; (*MIL*) cannon; (*de fusil*) barrel; (*GEO*) canyon, gorge.

cañonero [kaɲo'nero] *nm* gunboat.

caoba [ka'oβa] *nf* mahogany.

caos ['kaos] *nm* chaos.

cap. *abr de* **capítulo.**

capa ['kapa] *nf* cloak, cape; (*GEO*) layer, stratum; (*pretexto*) pretence.

capacidad [kapaθi'ðað] *nf* (*medida*) capacity; (*aptitud*) capacity, ability.

capacitación [kapaθita'θjon] *nf* training.

capar [ka'par] *vt* to castrate, geld.

caparazón [kapara'θon] *nm* shell.

capataz [kapa'taθ] *nm* foreman.

capaz [ka'paθ] *a* able, capable; (*amplio*) capacious, roomy.

capcioso, a [kap'θjoso, a] *a* wily, deceitful.

capellán [kape'ʎan] *nm* chaplain; (*sacerdote*) priest.

caperuza [kape'ruθa] *nf* hood; **caperucita** *nf*: **Caperucita Roja** Little Red Riding Hood.

capilla [ka'piʎa] *nf* chapel; (*capucha*) hood, cowl.

capital [kapi'tal] *a* capital // *nm* (*COM*) capital // *nf* capital; ~ **social** share capital.

capitalismo [kapita'lismo] *nm* capitalism; **capitalista** *a, nm/f* capitalist.

capitalizar [kapitali'θar] *vt* to capitalize.

capitán [kapi'tan] *nm* captain.

capitana [kapi'tana] *nf* flagship.

capitanear [kapitane'ar] *vt* to captain.

capitolio [kapi'toljo] *nm* capitol.

capitoné [kapito'ne] *nm* removal van.

capitulación [kapitula'θjon] *nf* (*rendición*) capitulation, surrender; (*acuerdo*) agreement, pact.

capitular [kapitu'lar] *vi* to come to terms, make an agreement // *a* chapter *cpd*.

capítulo [ka'pitulo] *nm* chapter; ~s *nmpl*: ~s **matrimoniales** marriage contract *sg*.

capó [ka'po] *nm* bonnet.

caporal [kapo'ral] *nm* chief, leader.

capota [ka'pota] *nf* (*de mujer*) bonnet; (*de coche*) hood, roof.

capote [ka'pote] *nm* (*abrigo, de militar*)

greatcoat; (*de torero*) cloak; (*NAIPES*) slam.

Capricornio [kapri'kornjo] *nm* Capricorn.

capricho [ka'pritʃo] *nm* whim, caprice; ~**so, a** *a* capricious.

cápsula ['kapsula] *nf* capsule; (*de botella*) cap.

captar [kap'tar] *vt* to win (over).

captura [kap'tura] *nf* capture; (*JUR*) arrest; **capturar** *vt* to capture; to arrest.

capucha [ka'putʃa] *nf* hood, cowl.

cara ['kara] *nf* face; (*aspecto*) appearance; (*de moneda*) face; (*de disco*) side; (*fig*) boldness; ~ **a** *ad* facing; **de** ~ **opposite**, facing; **dar la** ~ to face the consequences; ¿ ~ **o cruz?** heads or tails?

carabina [kara'βina] *nf* carbine, rifle.

caracol [kara'kol] *nm* (*ZOOL*) snail; (*concha*) shell.

caracolear [karakole'ar] *vi* to prance about.

carácter [ka'rakter] (*pl* **caracteres**) *nm* character.

característico, a [karakte'ristiko, a] *a* characteristic // *nf* characteristic.

caracterizar [karakteri'θar] *vt* (*distinguir*) to characterize, typify; (*honrar*) to confer (a) distinction on.

caramba [ka'ramba] *excl* well!, good gracious!

carámbano [ka'rambano] *nm* icicle.

caramelo [kara'melo] *nm* (*dulce*) sweet; (*dulce de* ~) toffee; (*azúcar fundida*) caramel.

caramillo [kara'miʎo] *nm* (*flauta*) recorder; (*montón*) untidy heap; (*chisme, enredo*) bit of gossip.

carapacho [kara'patʃo] *nm* shell, carapace.

caraqueño, a [kara'keɲo, a] *a, nm/f* (native) of Caracas.

carátula [ka'ratula] *nf* (*careta, máscara*) mask; (*TEATRO*): **la** ~ the stage.

caravana [kara'βana] *nf* caravan; (*fig*) group; (*sucesión de autos*) stream; (*embotellamiento*) traffic jam.

carbón [kar'βon] *nm* coal; **papel** ~ carbon paper; **carbonero** *nm/f* coal merchant; **carbonilla** *nf* coal dust.

carbonizar [karβoni'θar] *vt* to carbonize; (*quemar*) to char.

carbono [kar'βono] *nm* carbon.

carburador [karβura'ðor] *nm* carburettor.

carcajada [karka'xaða] *nf* (loud) laugh, guffaw.

cárcel ['karθel] *nf* prison, jail; (*TEC*) clamp; **carcelero, a** *a* prison *cpd* // *nm/f* warder.

carcomer [karko'mer] *vt* to bore into, eat into; (*fig*) to undermine; ~**se** *vr* to become worm-eaten; (*fig*) to decay.

carcomido, a [karko'miðo, a] *a* worm-eaten; (*fig*) rotten.

cardenal [karðe'nal] *nm* (*REL*) cardinal; (*equimosis*) bruise.

cárdeno, a ['karðeno, a] *a* purple; (*lívido*) livid.

cardíaco, a [kar'ðiako, a] a cardiac, heart cpd.

cardinal [karði'nal] a cardinal.

cardo ['karðo] nm thistle.

cardumen [kar'ðumen] nm shoal.

carear [kare'ar] vt to bring face to face; (comparar) to compare; ~**se** vr to come face to face, meet.

carecer [kare'θer] vi: ~ **de** to lack, be in need of.

carencia [ka'renθja] nf lack; (escasez) shortage; (MED) deficiency.

carente [ka'rente] a: ~ **de** lacking, devoid of.

carestía [kares'tia] nf (escasez) scarcity, shortage; (COM) high cost.

careta [ka'reta] nf mask.

carga ['karɣa] nf (peso, ELEC) load; (de barco) cargo, freight; (MIL) charge; (obligación, responsabilidad) duty, obligation.

cargadero [karɣa'ðero] nm goods platform, loading bay.

cargado, a [kar'ɣaðo, a] a loaded; (ELEC) live; (café, te) strong; (el cielo) overcast.

cargamento [karɣa'mento] nm (acción) loading; (mercancías) load, cargo.

cargar [kar'ɣar] vt (barco, arma) to load; (ELEC) to charge; (COM: algo en cuenta) to charge, debit; (MIL: enemigo) to charge // vi to load (up); (inclinarse) to lean; ~ **con** to pick up, carry away.

cargo ['karɣo] nm (puesto) post, office; (responsabilidad) duty, obligation; (fig) weight, burden; (JUR) charge; **hacerse ~ del gobierno** to take charge of the government.

carguero [kar'ɣero] nm freighter, cargo boat; (avión) freight plane.

caribe [ka'riße] a, nm/f (native) of the Caribbean.

Caribe [ka'riße] nm: **el ~** the Caribbean.

caricatura [karika'tura] nf caricature.

caricia [ka'riθja] nf caress.

caridad [kari'ðað] nf charity.

cariño [ka'riɲo] nm affection, love; (caricia) caress; (en carta) love...; ~**so, a** a affectionate.

caritativo, a [karita'tißo, a] a charitable.

carmesí [karme'si] a, nm crimson.

carnal [kar'nal] a carnal; **primo ~** first cousin.

carnaval [karna'ßal] nm carnival.

carne ['karne] nf flesh; (CULIN) meat; **echar ~s** to put on weight.

carnero [kar'nero] nm sheep; ram; (carne) mutton.

carnet [kar'ne] nm: ~ **de conducir** driving licence.

carnicería [karniθe'ria] nf butcher's (shop); (mercado) meat market.

carnicero, a [karni'θero, a] a carnivorous // nm/f butcher // nm carnivore.

carnívoro, a [kar'nißoro, a] a carnivorous.

carnoso, a [kar'noso, a] a beefy, fat.

caro, a ['karo, a] a dear; (COM) dear, expensive // ad dear, dearly.

carpeta [kar'peta] nf table cover; (para documentos) folder, file.

carpintería [karpinte'ria] nf carpentry, joinery; **carpintero** nm carpenter.

carraspera [karras'pera] nf hoarseness.

carrera [ka'rrera] nf (DEPORTE) running; (espacio recorrido) run; (certamen) race; (trayecto) course; (profesión) career; (ESCOL) course.

carreta [ka'rreta] nf wagon, cart.

carrete [ka'rrete] nm reel, spool; (TEC) coil.

carretel [karre'tel] nm reel, spool.

carretera [karre'tera] nf (main) road, highway.

carretilla [karre'tiʎa] nf trolley; (AGR) (wheel)barrow.

carril [ka'rril] nm furrow; (de autopista) lane; (FERRO) rail.

carrillo [ka'rriʎo] nm (ANAT) cheek; (TEC) pulley.

carrizo [ka'rriθo] nm reed.

carro ['karro] nm cart, wagon; (MIL) tank; (AM: coche) car.

carrocería [karroθe'ria] nf bodywork, coachwork.

carta ['karta] nf letter (CULIN) menu; (naipe) card; (mapa) map; (JUR) document; ~ **de crédito** credit card; ~ **certificada** registered letter.

cartel [kar'tel] nm (anuncio) poster, placard; (alfabeto) wall chart; (COM) cartel.

cartera [kar'tera] nf (de bolsillo) wallet; (de colegial, cobrador) satchel; (de señora) handbag; (para documentos) briefcase; (COM, POL) portfolio.

cartero [kar'tero] nm postman.

cartón [kar'ton] nm cardboard; (ARTE) cartoon.

cartucho [kar'tutʃo] nm (MIL) cartridge.

casa ['kasa] nf house; (hogar) home; (edificio) building; (COM) firm, company; (de tablero de ajedrez) square; ~ **consistorial** town hall; ~ **de huéspedes** boarding house, ~ **de socorro** first aid post; ~ **editorial** publishing house.

casamiento [kasa'mjento] nm marriage, wedding.

casar [ka'sar] vt to marry; (JUR) to quash, annul // nm hamlet; ~**se** vr to marry, get married.

cascada [kas'kaða] nf waterfall.

cascar [kas'kar] vt, ~**se** vr to crack, split, break (open).

cáscara ['kaskara] nf (de huevo, fruta seca) shell; (de fruta) skin; (de limón) peel.

casco ['kasko] nm (de bombero, soldado) helmet; (cráneo) skull; (de botella, obús) fragment; (BOT: de cebolla) skin; (tonel) cask, barrel; (NAUT: de barco) hull; (zool: de caballo) hoof; (botella) empty bottle.

caserío [kase'rio] nm hamlet; (casa) country house.

casero, a [ka'sero, a] a domestic, household cpd // nm/f (propietario) landlord/lady; (*portero*) caretaker; (*COM*) house agent.

caseta [ka'seta] *nf* hut; (*para bañista*) cubicle; (*de feriantes*) stall.

casi ['kasi] *ad* almost; ~ **te caes** you almost fell.

casilla [ka'siʎa] *nf* (*casita*) hut, cabin; (*TEATRO*) box office; (*de ajedrez*) square.

casino [ka'sino] *nm* club.

caso ['kaso] *nm* case; **en ~ de...** in case of...; **el ~ es que** the fact is that; **hacer ~ a** to pay attention to; **hacer** o **venir al ~** to be relevant.

caspa ['kaspa] *nf* dandruff.

cassette [ka'set] *nf* cassette.

casta ['kasta] *nf* caste; (*raza*) breed; (*linaje*) lineage.

castaña [kas'taɲa] *nf* chestnut.

castaño, a [kas'taɲo, a] *a* chestnut-brown // *nm* chestnut tree.

castañuela [kasta'ɲwela] *nf* castanet.

castellano, a [kaste'ʎano, a] *a* Castilian // *nm* (*lengua*) Castilian, Spanish.

castidad [kasti'ðað] *nf* chastity, purity.

castigar [kasti'xar] *vt* to punish; (*DEPORTE*) to penalize; (*afligir*) to afflict; **castigo** *nm* punishment; (*DEPORTE*) penalty.

castillo [kas'tiʎo] *nm* castle.

castizo, a [kas'tiθo, a] *a* (*LING*) pure; (*de buena casta*) purebred, pedigree.

casto, a ['kasto, a] *a* chaste, pure.

castor [kas'tor] *nm* beaver.

castrar [kas'trar] *vt* to castrate.

casual [ka'swal] *a* fortuitous, accidental; ~**idad** *nf* chance, accident; (*combinación de circunstancias*) coincidence.

cataclismo [kata'klismo] *nm* cataclysm.

catalán, ana [kata'lan, ana] *a, nm/f* Catalan, Catalonian.

catalizador [kataliθa'ðor] *nm* catalyst.

catálogo [ka'taloxo] *nm* catalogue.

Cataluña [kata'luɲa] *nf* Catalonia.

cataplasma [kata'plasma] *nf* poultice.

catar [ka'tar] *vt* to taste, sample.

catarata [kata'rata] *nf* (*GEO*) waterfall, falls *pl*; (*MED*) cataract.

catarro [ka'tarro] *nm* catarrh; (*constipado*) cold.

catástrofe [ka'tastrofe] *nf* catastrophe.

catedral [kate'ðral] *nf* cathedral.

catedrático, a [kate'ðratiko, a] *nm/f* professor.

categoría [katexo'ria] *nf* category; (*rango*) rank, standing; (*calidad*) quality.

categórico, a [kate'xoriko, a] *a* categorical.

catolicismo [katoli'θismo] *nm* Catholicism.

católico, a [ka'toliko, a] *a, nm/f* Catholic.

catorce [ka'torθe] *num* fourteen.

caución [kau'θjon] *nf* bail; **caucionar** *vt* to prevent, guard against; (*JUR*) to bail, go bail for.

caucho ['kautʃo] *nm* rubber.

caudal [kau'ðal] *nm* (*de río*) volume, flow;

(*fortuna*) wealth; (*abundancia*) abundance; ~**oso, a** *a* (*río*) large; (*aguas*) copious; (*persona*) wealthy, rich.

caudillo [kau'ðiʎo] *nm* leader, chief.

causa ['kausa] *nf* cause; (*razón*) reason; (*JUR*) lawsuit, case; **causar** *vt* to cause.

cáustico, a ['kaustiko, a] *a* caustic.

cautela [kau'tela] *nf* caution, cautiousness; **cauteloso, a** *a* cautious, wary, careful.

cautivar [kauti'ßar] *vt* to capture; (*fig*) to captivate.

cautiverio [kauti'ßerjo] *nm*, **cautividad** [kautißi'ðað] *nf* captivity.

cautivo, a [kau'tißo, a] *a, nm/f* captive.

cauto, a ['kauto, a] *a* cautious, careful.

cavar [ka'ßar] *vt* to dig.

caverna [ka'ßerna] *nf* cave, cavern.

cavidad [kaßi'ðað] *nf* cavity.

cavilar [kaßi'lar] *vt* to ponder.

cayado [ka'jaðo] *nm* (*de pastor*) staff, crook; (*de obispo*) crozier.

cayó *etc vb ver* **caer.**

caza ['kaθa] *nf* (*gen*) hunting, shooting; (*una* ~) hunt, chase; (*animales*) game // *nm* (*AVIAT*) fighter.

cazador [kaθa'ðor] *nm* hunter.

cazar [ka'θar] *vt* to hunt; (*perseguir*) to chase; (*coger*) to catch.

cazo ['kaθo] *nm* saucepan.

cazuela [ka'θwela] *nf* pan; (*guisado*) casserole.

cebada [θe'ßaða] *nf* barley.

cebar [θe'ßar] *vt* (*animal*) to fatten (up); (*anzuelo*) to bait; (*MIL, TEC*) to prime; (*pasión*) to nourish; (*ira*) to inflame.

cebo ['θeßo] *nm* (*para animales*) feed, food; (*para peces, fig*) bait; (*de arma*) charge.

cebolla [θe'ßoʎa] *nf* onion.

cebra ['θeßra] *nf* zebra.

cecear [θeθe'ar] *vi* to lisp; **ceceo** *nm* lisp.

cedazo [θe'ðaθo] *nm* sieve.

ceder [θe'ðer] *vt* to hand over, give up, part with // *vi* (*renunciar*) to give in, yield; (*disminuir*) to diminish, decline; (*romperse*) to give way.

cedro ['θeðro] *nm* cedar.

cédula ['θeðula] *nf* certificate, document; ~ **de aduana** customs permit.

C.E.E. *nf abr de* **Comunidad Económica Europea** E.E.C. (European Economic Community).

cegar [θe'xar] *vt* to blind; (*fig: pozo*) to block up, fill up // *vi* to go blind; ~**se** *vr* to be blinded (*de* by).

ceguedad [θexe'ðað], **ceguera** [θe'xera] *nf* blindness.

ceja ['θexa] *nf* eyebrow.

cejar [θe'xar] *vi* to move back, go back; (*fig*) to back down.

cejijunto, a [θexi'xunto, a] *a* with bushy eyebrows; (*fig*) scowling.

celada [θe'laða] *nf* ambush, trap.

celador, a [θela'ðor, a] *nm/f* (*de edificio*) watchman; (*de museo etc*) attendant.

celar [θe'lar] *vt* (*vigilar*) to watch over; (*encubrir*) to conceal, hide.

celda ['θelda] *nf* cell.
celebración [θeleβra'θjon] *nf* celebration.
celebrar [θele'βrar] *vt* to celebrate; (*alabar*) to praise // *vi* to be glad; ~se *vr* to occur, take place.
célebre ['θelebre] *a* famous; (*chistoso*) witty, funny.
celebridad [θeleβri'ðað] *nf* (*gen*) fame; (*persona*) celebrity; (*festividad*) celebration(s) (*pl*).
celeste [θe'leste] *a* celestial, heavenly.
celestial [θeles'tjal] *a* celestial, heavenly.
celibato [θeli'βato] *nm* celibacy.
célibe ['θeliβe] *a* celibate // *nm/f* unmarried person.
celo ['θelo] *nm* zeal; (*REL*) fervour; (*pey*) envy; (*de animales*) rut, heat; ~s *nmpl* jealousy *sg*.
celofán [θelo'fan] *nm* cellophane.
celoso, a [θe'loso, a] *a* (*envidioso*) jealous; (*trabajo*) zealous; (*desconfiado*) suspicious.
celta ['θelta] *nm/f* Celt.
célula ['θelula] *nf* cell.
cementar [θemen'tar] *vt* to cement.
cementerio [θemen'terjo] *nm* cemetery, graveyard.
cemento [θe'mento] *nm* cement; (*hormigón*) concrete.
cena ['θena] *nf* evening meal.
cenagal [θena'xal] *nm* bog, quagmire.
cenar [θe'nar] *vt* to have for supper // *vi* to dine.
cenicero [θeni'θero] *nm* ashtray.
cenit [θe'nit] *nm* zenith.
ceniza [θe'niθa] *nf* ash, ashes *pl*.
censo ['θenso] *nm* (*empadronamiento*) census; (*JUR*) tax; (*renta*) rent; (*carga sobre una casa*) mortgage.
censor [θen'sor] *nm* censor.
censura [θen'sura] *nf* (*POL*) censorship; (*moral*) censure, criticism.
censurar [θensu'rar] *vt* (*idea*) to censure; (*cortar: película*) to censor.
centella [θen'teʎa] *nf* spark.
centellar [θenteʎar], **centellear** [θenteʎe'ar] *vi* (*metal*) to gleam; (*estrella*) to twinkle; (*fig*) to sparkle; **centelleo** *nm* gleam(ing); twinkling; sparkling.
centenar [θente'nar] *nm* hundred.
centenario, a [θente'narjo, a] *a* centenary.
centésimo, a [θen'tesimo, a] *a* hundredth.
centígrado, a [θen'tixraðo, a] *a* centigrade.
centímetro [θen'timetro] *nm* centimetre.
céntimo, a ['θentimo, a] *a* hundredth // *nm* cent.
centinela [θenti'nela] *nm* sentry, guard.
central [θen'tral] *a* central // *nf* head office; (*TEC*) plant; (*TELEC*) exchange.
centralización [θentraliθa'θjon] *nf* centralization.
centralizar [θentrali'θar] *vt* to centralize.
centrar [θen'trar] *vt* to centre.
céntrico, a ['θentriko, a] *a* centre.
centro ['θentro] *nm* centre.

centroamericano, a [θentroameri'kano, a] *a, nm/f* Central American.
ceñidor [θeni'ðor] *nm* sash.
ceñir [θe'nir] *vt* (*rodear*) to encircle, surround; (*ajustar*) to fit (tightly), (*apretar*) to tighten.
ceño ['θeno] *nm* frown, scowl; **fruncir el** ~ to frown, knit one's brow.
cepillar [θepi'ʎar] *vt* to brush; (*madera*) to plane (down); **cepillo** *nm* (*gen*) brush; (*TEC*) plane.
cera ['θera] *nf* wax.
cerámico, a [θe'ramiko, a] *a* ceramic // *nf* ceramics *sg*.
cerca ['θerka] *nf* fence // *ad* near, nearby, close; ~s *nmpl* foreground *sg*; ~ **de** *prep* near, close to.
cercanía [θerka'nia] *nf* nearness, closeness; ~s *nfpl* outskirts.
cercano, a [θer'kano, a] *a* close, near.
cercar [θer'kar] *vt* to fence in; (*rodear*) to surround.
cerciorar [θerθjo'rar] *vt* (*informar*) to inform; (*asegurar*) to assure; ~se *vr* (*descubrir*) to find out; (*asegurarse*) to make sure.
cerco ['θerko] *nm* (*AGR*) enclosure; (*AM*) fence; (*MIL*) siege.
cerdo ['θerðo] *nm* pig.
cereal [θere'al] *nm* cereal.
cerebro [θe'reβro] *nm* brain; (*fig*) brains *pl*.
ceremonia [θere'monja] *nf* ceremony; **ceremonial** *a, nm* ceremonial; **ceremonioso, a** *a* ceremonious; (*cumplido*) formal.
cereza [θe'reθa] *nf* cherry.
cerilla [θe'riʎa] *nf* (*fósforo*) match.
cerner [θer'ner] *vt* to sift, sieve; (*fig*) to scan, watch // *vi* to blossom; (*lloviznar*) to drizzle; ~se *vr* to hover.
cernidor [θerni'ðor] *nm* sieve
cero ['θero] *nm* nothing, zero.
cerrado, a [θe'rraðo, a] *a* closed, shut; (*con llave*) locked; (*tiempo*) cloudy, overcast; (*curva*) sharp; (*acento*) thick, broad.
cerradura [θerra'ðura] *nf* (*acción*) closing; (*mecanismo*) lock.
cerraja [θe'rraxa] *nf* lock.
cerrar [θe'rrar] *vt* to close, shut; (*paso, carretera*) to close; (*grifo*) to turn off; (*trato, cuenta, negocio*) to close, ~ **con llave** to lock // *vi* to close, shut; (**la noche**) to come down; ~se *vr* to close, shut.
cerro ['θerro] *nm* hill.
cerrojo [θe'rroxo] *nm* (*herramienta*) bolt; (*de puerta*) latch.
certamen [θer'tamen] *nm* competition, contest.
certero, a [θer'tero, a] *a* accurate; (*cierto*) sure, certain.
certeza [θer'teθa] **certidumbre** [θerti'ðumbre] *nf* certainty.
certificado [θertifi'kaðo] *nm* certificate.
certificar [θertifi'kar] *vt* (*asegurar*,

atestar) to certify; (carta) to register.
cervato [θer'βato] nm fawn.
cervecería [θerβeθe'ria] nf (fábrica)
brewery; (tienda) public house.
cerveza [θer'βeθa] nf beer.
cesación [θesa'θjon] nf cessation;
(suspensión) suspension.
cesante [θe'sante] a out of a job.
cesar [θe'sar] vi to cease, stop.
cese ['θese] nm (de trabajo) dismissal; (de
pago) suspension.
césped ['θespeð] nm grass, lawn.
cesta ['θesta] nf basket; **cesto** nm (large)
basket, hamper.
ch... ver bajo la letra CH, después de C.
Cía abr de **compañía**.
cianuro [θja'nuro] nm cyanide.
ciar [θjar] vi to go backwards.
cicatriz [θika'triθ] nf scar.
ciclismo [θi'klismo] nm cycling.
ciclo ['θiklo] nm cycle.
ciclón [θi'klon] nm cyclone.
ciego, a ['θjeɣo, a] a blind // nm/f blind
man/woman.
cielo ['θjelo] nm sky; (REL) heaven; ¡~s!
good heavens!
ciempiés [θjem'pjes] nm centipede.
cien [θjen] num ver **ciento**.
ciénaga ['θjenaɣa] nf marsh, swamp.
ciencia ['θjenθja] nf science; ~-ficción nf
science fiction.
cieno ['θjeno] nm mud, mire.
científico, a [θjen'tifiko, a] a scientific //
nm/f scientist.
ciento ['θjento], **cien** num hundred; **pagar
al 10 por** ~ to pay at 10 per cent.
cierne ['θjerne] nm: **en** ~ in blossom.
cierre ['θjerre] nm closing, shutting; (con
llave) locking; ~ **a cremallera** zip
fastener.
cierro etc vb ver **cerrar.**
cierto, a ['θjerto, a] a sure, certain; (un tal)
a certain; (correcto) right, correct; ~
hombre a certain man; **sí, es** ~ yes,
that's correct.
ciervo ['θjerβo] nm (especie) deer;
(macho) stag.
cierzo ['θjerθo] nm north wind.
cifra ['θifra] nf number, numeral;
(cantidad) number, quantity; (secreta)
code; (siglas) abbreviation.
cifrar [θi'frar] vt to code, write in code;
(resumir) to abridge.
cigarra [θi'ɣarra] nf cicada.
cigarrera [θiɣa'rrera] nf cigar case.
cigarrillo [θiɣa'rriʎo] nm cigarette.
cigarro [θi'ɣarro] nm cigarette; (puro)
cigar.
cigüeña [θi'ɣweɲa] nf stork.
cilíndrico, a [θi'lindriko, a] a cylindrical.
cilindro [θi'lindro] nm cylinder; (rodillo)
roller.
cima ['θima] nf (de montaña) top, peak; (de
árbol) top; (fig) summit, height.
címbalo ['θimbalo] nm cymbal.
cimbrar [θim'brar], **cimbrear** [θimbre-

'ar] vt to brandish; ~**se** vr (al viento) to
sway.
cimentar [θimen'tar] vt to lay the
foundations of.
cimiento [θi'mjento] nm foundation.
cinc [θink] nm zinc.
cincel [θin'θel] nm chisel; ~**ar** vt to chisel.
cinco ['θinko] num five.
cincuenta [θin'kwenta] num fifty.
cincho ['θintʃo] nm sash, belt.
cine ['θine] nm cinema.
cinematográfico, a [θinemato'ɣrafiko,
a] a cine-, film cpd.
cínico, a ['θiniko, a] a cynical // nm/f
cynic.
cinismo [θi'nismo] nm cynicism.
cinta ['θinta] nf band, strip; (de seda, lana,
algodón) ribbon, tape; (película) reel; (de
máquina de escribir) ribbon; (métrica) tape
measure; (magnetofónica) tape; (adhesiva)
adhesive tape.
cinto ['θinto] nm belt, girdle.
cintura [θin'tura] nf waist.
cinturón [θintu'ron] nm belt; ~ **de
seguridad** safety belt.
ciprés [θi'pres] nm cypress (tree).
circo ['θirko] nm circus.
circuito [θir'kwito] nm circuit.
circulación [θirkula'θjon] nf circulation;
(AUTO) traffic.
circular [θirku'lar] a, nf circular // vi, vt
to circulate.
círculo ['θirkulo] nm circle.
circuncidar [θirkunθi'dar] vt to
circumcise; **circuncisión** nf circumcision;
circunciso, a pp de **circuncidar** // a
circumcised.
circundar [θirkun'dar] vt to surround.
circunferencia [θirkunfe'renθja] nf
circumference.
circunlocución [θirkunloku'θjon] nf,
circunloquio [θirkun'lokjo] nm
circumlocution.
circunscribir [θirkunskri'βir] vt to
circumscribe; ~**se** vr to be limited.
circunscripción [θirkunskrip'θjon] nf
division; (POL) constituency.
circunspección [θirkunspek'θjon] nf
circumspection.
circunspecto, a [θirkuns'pekto, a] a
circumspect, cautious.
circunstancia [θirkuns'tanθja] nf
circumstance.
circunstante [θirkuns'tante] nm/f
onlooker, bystander.
cirio ['θirjo] nm (wax) candle.
ciruela [θi'rwela] nf plum; ~ **pasa** prune.
cirugía [θiru'xia] nf surgery; ~ **estética**
plastic surgery.
cirujano [θiru'xano] nm surgeon.
cisne ['θisne] nm swan.
cisterna [θis'terna] nf cistern.
cita ['θita] nf appointment, engagement;
(de novios) date; (referencia) quotation.
citación [θita'θjon] nf (JUR) summons sg;
(referencia) quotation.

citar [θi'tar] vt (gen) to make an appointment with; (JUR) to summons; (un autor, texto) to quote.

citrón [θi'tron] nm lemon.

ciudad [θju'ðað] nf town; (capital de país etc) city; ~**ano**, **a** nm/f citizen; ~**ela** nf citadel, fortress.

cívico, a ['θiβiko, a] a civic.

civil [θi'βil] a civil // nm (guardia) policeman; ~**idad** nf civility, courtesy.

civilización [θiβiliθa'θjon] nf civilization.

civilizar [θiβili'θar] vt to civilize.

civismo [θi'βismo] nm public spirit.

cizaña [θi'θaɲa] nf discord.

clamar [kla'mar] vt to clamour for // vi to cry out, clamour.

clamor [kla'mor] nm (grito) cry, shout; (gemido) whine; (de campana) knell; (fig) clamour, protest.

clamorear [klamore'ar] vt to clamour for // vi (campana) to toll; **clamoreo** nm clamour(ing).

clandestino, a [klandes'tino, a] a clandestine; (POL) underground.

clara ['klara] nf (de huevo) white of an egg; (del día) bright interval.

claraboya [klara'βoja] nf skylight.

clarear [klare'ar] vi (el día) to dawn; (el cielo) to clear up, brighten up; ~**se** vr to be transparent.

claridad [klari'ðað] nf (del día) brightness; (de estilo) clarity.

clarificar [klarifi'kar] vt to clarify.

clarín [kla'rin] nm bugle.

clarinete [klari'nete] nm clarinet.

clarividencia [klariβi'ðenθja] nf clairvoyance; (fig) far-sightedness.

claro, a ['klaro, a] a (gen) clear; (luminoso) bright; (poco subido) light; (evidente) clear, evident; (ralo) sparse; (poco espeso) thin // nm (en escritura) space; (en bosque) clearing // ad clearly // excl of course!

clase ['klase] nf class; ~ **alta/media/obrera** upper/middle/ working class.

clásico, a ['klasiko, a] a classical; (fig) classic.

clasificación [klasifika'θjon] nf classification; (DEPORTE) league.

clasificar [klasifi'kar] vt to classify.

claudicar [klauði'kar] vi to limp; (fig) to back down.

claustro ['klaustro] nm cloister.

cláusula ['klausula] nf clause.

clausura [klau'sura] nf closing, closure.

clavar [kla'βar] vt (clavo) to knock in, drive in; (cuchillo, tenedor) to stick, thrust; (mirada) to fix.

clave ['klaβe] nf key; (MUS) clef.

clavel [kla'βel] nm carnation.

clavícula [kla'βikula] nf collar bone.

clavija [kla'βixa] nf peg, dowel, pin; (ELEC) plug.

clavo ['klaβo] nm (de metal) nail; (BOT) clove; (callo) corn.

claxon ['klakson] nm horn.

clemencia [kle'menθja] nf mercy, clemency; **clemente** a merciful, clement.

cleptómano, a [klep'tomano, a] nm/f kleptomaniac.

clerical [kleri'kal] a clerical // nm clergyman.

clérigo ['klerixo] nm clergyman.

clero ['klero] nm clergy.

cliente ['kljente] nm/f client, customer.

clientela [kljen'tela] nf clientele, customers pl.

clima ['klima] nm climate.

clínica ['klinika] nf clinic; (particular) private hospital.

clip [klip] nm paper clip.

clorhídrico, a [klo'ridriko, a] a hydrochloric.

cloroformo [kloro'formo] nm chloroform.

club [klub] (pl ~s o ~es) nm club.

C.N.T. abr de **Confederación Nacional de Trabajo.**

coacción [koak'θjon] nf coercion, compulsion.

coalición [koali'θjon] nf coalition.

coartar [koar'tar] vt to limit, restrict.

cobarde [ko'βarðe] a cowardly // nm coward; **cobardía** nf cowardice.

cobertizo [koβer'tiθo] nm shelter.

cobertor [koβer'tor] nm bedspread.

cobertura [koβer'tura] nf cover.

cobija [ko'βixa] nf roof; **cobijar** vt (cubrir) to cover; (abrigar) to shelter.

cobra ['koβra] nf cobra.

cobrador [koβra'ðor] nm (de autobús) conductor; (de impuestos, gas) collector.

cobrar [ko'βrar] vt (cheque) to cash; (sueldo) to collect, draw; (objeto) to recover; (precio) to charge; (deuda) to collect // vi to draw one's pay; ~**se** vr to recover, get well; **cóbrese al entregar** cash on delivery (COD).

cobre ['koβre] nm copper; ~**s** nmpl brass instruments.

cobro ['koβro] nm recovery; (paga) payment.

cocaína [koka'ina] nf cocaine.

cocción [kok'θjon] nf cooking.

cocear [koθe'ar] vi to kick.

cocer [ko'θer] vt, vi to cook; (en agua) to boil; (en horno) to bake; ~**se** to suffer intensely.

cocido [ko'θiðo] nm stew.

cocina [ko'θina] nf kitchen; (aparato) cooker, stove; (acto) cookery; **cocinar** vt, vi to cook.

cocinero, a [koθi'nero, a] nm/f cook.

coco ['koko] nm (árbol) coconut palm; (fruto) coconut.

cocodrilo [koko'ðrilo] nm crocodile.

coche ['kotʃe] nm car, motorcar; (de tren, de caballos) coach, carriage; (fúnebre) hearse; (para niños) pram; ~ **celular** Black Maria, prison van.

coche-cama [kotʃe'kama] (pl **coches-camas**) nm sleeping car, sleeper.

cochera [ko'tʃera] nf garage.

cochero [ko'tʃero] nm coachman.

cochino, a [ko'tʃino, a] a filthy, dirty // nm pig.

codazo [ko'ðaθo] nm jab, poke (with the elbow).

codear [koðe'ar] vi to elbow, jostle; ~se vr: ~se con to rub shoulders with.

códice ['koðiθe] nm manuscript, codex.

codicia [ko'ðiθja] nf greed; (fig) lust; **codiciar** vt to covet; **codicioso, a** a covetous.

código ['koðiɣo] nm code; ~ **civil** common law.

codillo [ko'ðiʎo] nm (ZOOL) knee; (TEC) elbow (joint).

codo ['koðo] nm (ANAT, de tubo) elbow; (ZOOL) knee.

codorniz [koðor'niθ] nf quail.

coerción [koer'θjon] nf coercion.

coetáneo, a [koe'taneo, a] a contemporary.

coexistencia [koeksis'tenθja] nf coexistence; **coexistir** vi to coexist.

cofradía [kofra'ðia] nf brotherhood, fraternity.

cofre ['kofre] nm chest.

coger [ko'xer] vt (gen) to take (hold of); (objeto caído) to pick up; (frutas) to pick, harvest; (resfriado, ladrón, pelota) to catch // vi: ~ **por el buen camino** to take the right road; ~se vr to catch; (robar) to steal.

cogida [ko'xiða] nf gathering, harvesting; (de peces) catch.

cogote [ko'xote] nm back or nape of the neck.

cohabitar [koaβi'tar] vi to live together, cohabit.

cohechar [koe'tʃar] vt to bribe; **cohecho** nm (acción) bribery; (soborno) bribe.

coherente [koe'rente] a coherent.

cohesión [koe'sjon] nm cohesion.

cohete [ko'ete] nm rocket.

cohibición [koiβi'θjon] nf restraint, restriction.

cohibir [koi'βir] vt to restrain, restrict.

coincidencia [koinθi'ðenθja] nf coincidence; (acuerdo) agreement.

coincidir [koinθi'ðir] vi (en idea) to coincide, agree; (en lugar) to coincide.

coito ['koito] nm intercourse, coitus.

cojear [koxe'ar] vi (persona) to limp, hobble; (mueble) to wobble, rock.

cojera [ko'xera] nf lameness; (andar cojo) limp.

cojín [ko'xin] nm cushion; **cojinete** nm small cushion, pad; (TEC) ball bearing.

cojo, a ['koxo, a] a (que no puede andar) lame; (manco) crippled; (mueble) shaky // nm/f lame person; cripple.

col [kol] nf cabbage; ~ **de Bruselas** Brussels sprouts.

cola ['kola] nf (gen) tail; (de gente) queue; (lugar) end, last place; (para pegar) glue, gum; **hacer la** ~ to queue (up).

colaborador, a [kolaβora'ðor, a] nm/f collaborator.

colaborar [kolaβo'rar] vi to collaborate.

coladera [kola'ðera] nf strainer.

coladura [kola'ðura] nf (filtración) straining; (residuo) grounds pl, dregs pl.

colapso [ko'lapso] nm collapse; ~ **nervioso** nervous breakdown.

colar [ko'lar] vt (líquido) to strain off; (ropa) to bleach; (metal) to cast // vi to ooze, seep (through); ~se vr to slip in or past.

colateral [kolate'ral] nm collateral.

colcha ['koltʃa] nf bedspread.

colchón [kol'tʃon] nm mattress.

colear [kole'ar] vi to wag its tail.

colección [kolek'θjon] nf collection; **coleccionista** nm/f collector.

colecta [ko'lekta] nf collection.

colectar [kolek'tar] vt to collect.

colectivo, a [kolek'tiβo, a] a collective, joint.

colector [kolek'tor] nm collector; (sumidero) sewer.

colega [ko'lexa] nm/f colleague.

colegio [ko'lexjo] nm (gen) college; (escuela) (private) school; (de abogados etc) association.

colegir [kole'xir] vt (juntar, reunir) to collect, gather; (deducir) to infer, conclude.

cólera ['kolera] nf (ira) anger; (MED) cholera.

colérico, a [ko'leriko, a] a angry, furious.

coleta [ko'leta] nf pigtail.

colgadero [kolxa'ðero] nm (gancho) hook; (percha) hanger.

colgadura [kolxa'ðura] nf hangings pl, drapery.

colgante [kol'xante] a hanging // nm drop earring.

colgar [kol'xar] vt to hang (up); (ropa) to hang (out); (teléfono) to hang up // vi to hang.

coliflor [koli'flor] nf cauliflower.

colilla [ko'liʎa] nf fag end, butt.

colina [ko'lina] nf hill.

colindante [kolin'dante] a adjacent, neighbouring.

colindar [kolin'dar] vi to adjoin, be adjacent.

colisión [koli'sjon] nf collision; (choque) crash.

colmado, a [kol'maðo, a] a abundant, copious; (cuchara etc) heaped.

colmar [kol'mar] vt to fill to the brim; (fig) to fulfil, realize.

colmena [kol'mena] nf beehive.

colmillo [kol'miʎo] nm (diente) eye tooth; (de elefante) tusk; (de perro) fang.

colmo ['kolmo] nm height, summit.

colocación [koloka'θjon] nf placing; (empleo) job, position; (de mueble) place, position.

colocar [kolo'kar] vt to place, put,

position; (*poner en empleo*) to find a job for.

Colombia [ko'lombja] *nf* Colombia; **colombiano,** a a, *nm/f* Colombian.

colon ['kolon] *nm* colon.

colonia [ko'lonja] *nf* colony; (*de casas*) housing estate; (*agua de* ∼) cologne.

colonización [koloniθa'θjon] *nf* colonization.

colonizador, a [koloniθa'ðor, a] a colonizing // *nm/f* colonist, settler.

colonizar [koloni'θar] *vt* to colonize.

coloquio [ko'lokjo] *nm* conversation; (*congreso*) conference.

color [ko'lor] *nm* colour.

colorado, a [kolo'raðo, a] a (*que tiene color*) coloured; (*rojo*) red.

colorar [kolo'rar] *vt* to colour; (*teñir*) to dye.

colorear [kolore'ar] *vt* to colour // *vi* to redden.

colorido [kolo'riðo] *nm* colouring.

colosal [kolo'sal] a colossal.

columbrar [kolum'brar] *vt* to glimpse, spy.

columna [ko'lumna] *nf* column; (*pilar*) pillar; (*apoyo*) support.

columpiar [kolum'pjar] *vt*, ∼se *vr* to swing; **columpio** *nm* swing.

collar [ko'ʎar] *nm* necklace; (*de perro*) collar.

coma ['koma] *nf* comma // *nm* coma.

comadre [ko'maðre] *nf* (*partera*) midwife; (*madrina*) godmother; (*vecina*) neighbour; ∼ar *vi* to gossip.

comandancia [koman'danθja] *nf* command.

comandante [koman'dante] *nm* commandant.

comandar [koman'dar] *vt* to command.

comarca [ko'marka] *nf* region.

comarcar [komar'kar] *vi*: ∼ con to border on, be adjacent to.

combar [kom'bar] *vt* to bend, curve.

combate [kom'bate] *nm* fight; (*fig*) battle; **combatiente** *nm* combatant.

combatir [komba'tir] *vt* to fight, combat.

combinación [kombina'θjon] *nf* combination; (*QUÍMICA*) compound; (*bebida*) cocktail; (*plan*) scheme, setup.

combinar [kombi'nar] *vt* to combine.

combustible [kombus'tiβle] *nm* fuel.

combustión [kombus'tjon] *nf* combustion.

comedia [ko'meðja] *nf* comedy; (*TEATRO*) play, drama.

comediante [kome'ðjante] *nm/f* (comic) actor/actress.

comedido, a [kome'ðiðo, a] a moderate; (*cortés*) courteous.

comedirse [kome'ðirse] *vr* to behave moderately; (*ser cortés*) to be courteous.

comedor, a [kome'ðor, a] *nm/f* (*persona*) glutton // *nm* (*habitación*) dining room; (*restaurante*) restaurant; (*cantina*) canteen.

comentador, a [komenta'ðor, a] *nm/f* = **comentarista**.

comentar [komen'tar] *vt* to comment on; (*fam*) to discuss.

comentario [komen'tarjo] *nm* comment, remark; (*literario*) commentary; ∼s *nmpl* gossip *sg*.

comentarista [komenta'rista] *nm/f* commentator.

comento [ko'mento] *nm* = **comentario**.

comenzar [komen'θar] *vt*, *vi* to begin, start, commence.

comer [ko'mer] *vt* (*gen*) to eat; (*DAMAS, AJEDREZ*) to take, capture // *vi* to eat; (*almorzar*) to have lunch; ∼se *vr* to eat up.

comercial [komer'θjal] a commercial; (*relativo al negocio*) business *cpd*.

comerciante [komer'θjante] *nm/f* trader, merchant.

comerciar [komer'θjar] *vi* to trade, do business.

comercio [ko'merθjo] *nm* commerce; (*tráfico*) trade; (*negocio*) business; (*fig*) dealings *pl*.

comestible [komes'tiβle] a eatable, edible // *nm* foodstuff.

cometa [ko'meta] *nm* comet // *nf* kite.

cometer [kome'ter] *vt* to commit.

cometido [kome'tiðo] *nm* (*misión*) task, assignment; (*deber*) commitment.

comezón [kome'θon] *nf* itch, itching.

cómico, a ['komiko, a] a comic(al) // *nm/f* comedian; (*de teatro*) (comic) actor/actress.

comida [ko'miða] *nf* (*alimento*) food; (*almuerzo, cena*) meal; (*de mediodía*) lunch.

comienzo [ko'mjenθo] *nm* beginning, start.

comillas [ko'miʎas] *nfpl* inverted commas.

comisario [komi'sarjo] *nm* commissary; (*POL*) commissar.

comisión [komi'sjon] *nf* commission.

comité [komi'te] *nm* committee.

como ['komo] ad as; (*tal* ∼) like; (*aproximadamente*) about, approximately // *conj* (*ya que, puesto que*) as, since; (*en seguida que*) as soon as; ¡∼ no! of course!; ∼ no lo haga hoy unless he does it today; ∼ si as if; es tan alto ∼ ancho it is as high as it is wide.

cómo ['komo] ad how?, why? // *excl* what?, I beg your pardon? // *nm*: el ∼ y el porqué the whys and wherefores.

comodidad [komoði'ðað] *nf* comfort; venga a su ∼ come at your convenience.

comodín [komo'ðin] *nm* joker.

cómodo, a ['komoðo, a] a comfortable; (*práctico, de fácil uso*) convenient.

compacto, a [kom'pakto, a] a compact.

compadecer [kompaðe'θer] *vt* to pity, be sorry for; ∼se *vr*: ∼se de to pity, be sorry for.

compadre [kom'paðre] *nm* (*padrino*) godfather; (*amigo*) friend, pal.

compañero, a [kompa'ɲero, a] nm/f companion; ~ **de clase** classmate.

compañía [kompa'ɲia] nf company.

comparación [kompara'θjon] nf comparison; **en** ~ **con** in comparison with.

comparar [kompa'rar] vt to compare.

comparativo, a [kompara'tiβo, a] a comparative.

comparecer [kompare'θer] vi to appear (in court).

compartimiento [komparti'mjento] nm division; (distribución) distribution; (FERRO) compartment.

compartir [kompar'tir] vt to divide (up), share (out).

compás [kom'pas] nm (MUS) beat, rhythm; (MAT) compasses pl; (NAUT) compass.

compasión [kompa'sjon] nf compassion, pity.

compasivo, a [kompa'siβo, a] a compassionate.

compatibilidad [kompatiβili'ðað] nf compatibility.

compatible [kompa'tiβle] a compatible.

compatriota [kompa'trjota] nm/f compatriot.

compeler [kompe'ler] vt to compel.

compendiar [kompen'djar] vt to summarize; (libro) to abridge; **compendio** nm summary; abridgement.

compensación [kompensa'θjon] nf compensation.

compensar [kompen'sar] vt to compensate.

competencia [kompe'tenθja] nf (incumbencia) domain, field; (aptitud, idoneidad) competence; (rivalidad) competition.

competente [kompe'tente] a (persona, jurado, tribunal) competent; (conveniente) fit, suitable.

competición [kompeti'θjon] nf competition.

competir [kompe'tir] vi to compete.

compilar [kompi'lar] vt to compile.

complacencia [kompla'θenθja] nf (placer) pleasure; (satisfacción) satisfaction; (buena voluntad) willingness.

complacer [kompla'θer] vt to please; ~ **se** vr to be pleased.

complaciente [kompla'θjente] a kind, obliging, helpful.

complejo, a [kom'plexo, a] a, nm complex.

complementario, a [komplemen'tarjo, a] a complementary.

completar [komple'tar] vt to complete.

completo, a [kom'pleto, a] a complete; (perfecto) perfect; (lleno) full // nm full complement.

complicar [kompli'kar] vt to complicate.

cómplice ['kompliθe] nm/f accomplice.

complot [kom'plot] nm plot; (conspiración) conspiracy.

componenda [kompo'nenda] nf compromise; (pey) shady deal.

componer [kompo'ner] vt to make up, put together; (MUS, LITERATURA, IMPRENTA) to compose; (algo roto) to mend, repair; (adornar) to adorn; (arreglar) to arrange; (reconciliar) to reconcile; ~ **se** vr: ~ **se de** to consist of.

comportamiento [komporta'mjento] nm behaviour, conduct.

comportarse [kompor'tarse] vr to behave.

composición [komposi'θjon] nf composition.

compositor, a [komposi'tor, a] nm/f composer.

compostura [kompos'tura] nf (reparación) mending, repair; (arreglo) arrangement; (acuerdo) agreement; (actitud) composure.

compra ['kompra] nf purchase; ~ **s** nfpl purchases, shopping sg.

comprador, a [kompra'ðor, a] nm/f buyer, purchaser.

comprar [kom'prar] vt to buy, purchase.

comprender [kompren'der] vt to understand; (incluir) to comprise, include.

comprensión [kompren'sjon] nf understanding; (totalidad) comprehensiveness.

comprensivo, a [kompren'siβo, a] a comprehensive; (actitud) understanding.

compresión [kompre'sjon] nf compression.

comprimir [kompri'mir] vt to compress; (fig) to control.

comprobante [kompro'βante] a verifying, supporting // nm proof.

comprobar [kompro'βar] vt to check; (probar) to prove; (TEC) to check, test.

comprometer [komprome'ter] vt to compromise; (exponer) to endanger; ~ **se** vr to compromise o.s.; (involucrarse) to get involved.

compromiso [kompro'miso] nm (obligación) obligation; (cometido) commitment; (convenio) agreement; (dificultad) awkward situation.

compuesto, a [kom'pwesto, a] a: ~ **de** composed of, made up of // nm compound.

compulsión [kompul'sjon] nf compulsion.

compunción [kompun'θjon] nf compunction, regret.

computador [komputa'ðor] nm, **computadora** [komputa'ðora] nf computer.

comulgar [komul'xar] vi to receive communion.

común [ko'mun] a common // nm: **el** ~ the community.

comunicación [komunika'θjon] nf communication; (ponencia) report.

comunicar [komuni'kar] vt, vi, ~ **se** vr to communicate; **comunicativo, a** a communicative.

comunidad [komuni'ðað] nf community.

comunión [komu'njon] nf communion.

comunismo [komu'nismo] nm

communism; **comunista** a, nm/f communist.

con [kon] prep with; (a pesar de) in spite of; ~ **que** so, and so; ~ **apretar el botón** by pressing the button.

concebir [konθe'βir] vt, vi to conceive.

conceder [konθe'ðer] vt to concede.

concejo [kon'θexo] nm council.

concentración [konθentra'θjon] nf concentration.

concentrar [konθen'trar] vt, ~**se** vr to concentrate.

concepción [konθep'θjon] nf conception.

concepto [kon'θepto] nm concept.

concertar [konθer'tar] vt (MUS) to harmonize; (acordar: precio) to agree; (: tratado) to conclude; (trato) to arrange, fix up; (combinar: esfuerzos) to coordinate; (reconciliar: personas) to reconcile // vi to harmonize, be in tune.

concesión [konθe'sjon] nf concession.

conciencia [kon'θjenθja] nf conscience.

concienzudo, a [konθjen'θuðo, a] a conscientious.

concierto [kon'θjerto] nm concert; (obra) concerto.

conciliar [konθi'ljar] vt to reconcile.

concilio [kon'θiljo] nm council.

conciso, a [kon'θiso, a] a concise.

concluir [konklu'ir] vt, vi, ~**se** vr to conclude.

conclusión [konklu'sjon] nf conclusion.

concordar [konkor'ðar] vt to reconcile // vi to agree, tally; **concordia** nf concord, harmony.

concretar [konkre'tar] vt to make concrete, make more specific; ~**se** vr to become more definite.

concreto, a [kon'kreto, a] a, nm (AM) concrete; **en** ~ (en resumen) to sum up; (especificamente) specifically; **no hay nada en** ~ there's nothing definite.

concurrir [konku'rrir] vi (juntarse: ríos) to meet, come together; (: personas) to gather, meet; (ponerse de acuerdo, coincidir) to concur; (competir) to compete; (contribuir) to contribute.

concurso [kon'kurso] nm (de público) crowd; (ESCOL, DEPORTE, competencia) competition; (coincidencia) coincidence; (ayuda) help, cooperation.

concusión [konku'sjon] nf concussion.

concha ['kontʃa] nf shell.

conde ['konde] nm count.

condecorar [kondeko'rar] vt to decorate.

condena [kon'dena] nf sentence.

condenación [kondena'θjon] nf (gen) condemnation; (condena) sentence; (REL) damnation.

condenar [konde'nar] vt to condemn; (JUR) to convict; ~**se** vr (JUR) to confess (one's guilt); (REL) to be damned.

condensar [konden'sar] vt to condense.

condescender [kondesθen'der] vi to acquiesce, comply.

condición [kondi'θjon] nf condition;

condicionado, a a conditioned.

condicional [kondiθjo'nal] a conditional.

condimento [kondi'mento] nm seasoning.

condolerse [kondo'lerse] vr to sympathize.

conducir [kondu'θir] vt to take, convey; (AUTO) to drive // vi to drive; (fig) to lead; ~**se** vr to behave.

conducta [kon'dukta] nf conduct, behaviour.

conducto [kon'dukto] nm pipe, tube; (fig) channel.

conductor, a [konduk'tor, a] a leading, guiding // nm (FISICA) conductor; (de vehículo) driver.

conduje etc vb ver **conducir**.

conduzco etc vb ver **conducir**.

conectar [konek'tar] vt to connect (up), plug in.

conejo [ko'nexo] nm rabbit.

conexión [konek'sjon] nf connection.

confeccionar [konfekθjo'nar] vt to make (up).

confederación [konfeðera'θjon] nf confederation.

conferencia [konfe'renθja] nf conference; (lección) lecture; (TELEC) call.

conferir [konfe'rir] vt to award.

confesar [konfe'sar] vt to confess, admit.

confesión [konfe'sjon] nf confession.

confesionario [konfesjo'narjo] nm confesional.

confiado, a [kon'fjaðo, a] a (crédulo) trusting; (presumido) confident; (pey) conceited, vain.

confianza [kon'fjanθa] nf trust (aliento, confidencia) confidence; (familiaridad) intimacy, familiarity; (pey) vanity, conceit.

confiar [kon'fjar] vt to entrust // vi to trust.

confidencia [konfi'ðenθja] nf confidence.

confidencial [konfiðen'θjal] a confidencial.

confidente [konfi'ðente] nm/f confidante; (policial) informer.

configurar [konfiɣu'rar] vt to shape, form.

confín [kon'fin] nm limit; ~**es** nmpl edges.

confinar [konfi'nar] vi to confine; (desterrar) to banish.

confirmar [konfir'mar] vt to confirm.

confiscar [konfis'kar] vt to confiscate.

confitería [konfite'ria] nf confectionery; (tienda) confectioner's (shop).

confitura [konfi'tura] nf jam.

conflicto [kon'flikto] nm conflict; (fig) clash.

conformar [konfor'mar] vt to shape, fashion // vi to agree; ~**se** vr to conform; (resignarse) to resign o.s.

conforme [kon'forme] a (gen) alike, similar; (de acuerdo) agreed, in agreement; (resignado) resigned // ad as // excl agreed! // nm agreement // prep: ~ **a** in accordance with.

conformidad [konformi'ðað] *nf*
(*semejanza*) similarity; (*acuerdo*)
agreement; (*resignación*) resignation.
confortable [konfor'taβle] *a* comfortable.
confortar [konfor'tar] *vt* to comfort.
confrontar [konfron'tar] *vt* to confront;
(*dos personas*) to bring face to face;
(*cotejar*) to compare // *vi* to border.
confundir [konfun'dir] *vt* to blur;
(*equivocar*) to mistake, confuse; (*mezclar*)
to mix; (*turbar*) to confuse; ~**se** *vr* to
become blurred; (*turbarse*) to get
confused; (*equivocarse*) to make a
mistake; (*mezclarse*) to mix.
confusión [konfu'sjon] *nf* confusion.
confuso, a [kon'fuso, a] *a* confused.
congelar [konxe'lar] *vt* to freeze; ~**se** *vr*
(*sangre, grasa*) to congeal.
congeniar [konxe'njar] *vi* to get on (well).
conglomeración [konglomera'θjon] *nf*
conglomeration.
congoja [kon'goxa] *nf* distress, grief.
congratular [kongratu'lar] *vt* to
congratulate.
congregación [kongreγa'θjon] *nf*
congregation.
congresista [kongre'sista] *nm/f* delegate,
congressman/woman.
congreso [kon'greso] *nm* congress.
conjetura [konxe'tura] *nf* guess;
conjeturar *vt* to guess.
conjugar [konxu'γar] *vt* to combine, fit
together; (*un verbo*) to conjugate.
conjunción [konxun'θjon] *nf* conjunction.
conjunto, a [kon'xunto, a] *a* joint, united
// *nm* whole; (*MUS*) group; **en** ~ **as a**
whole.
conmemoración [konmemora'θjon] *nf*
commemoration.
conmemorar [konmemo'rar] *vt* to
commemorate.
conmigo [kon'miγo] *pron* with me; with
myself.
conminar [konmi'nar] *vt* to threaten.
conmiseración [konmisera'θjon] *nf* pity,
commiseration.
conmoción [konmo'θjon] *nf* shock; (*MED*)
concussion; (*fig*) upheaval.
conmovedor, a [konmoβe'ðor, a] *a*
touching, moving; (*impresionante*)
exciting.
conmover [konmo'βer] *vt* to shake,
disturb; (*fig*) to move.
conmutador [konmuta'ðor] *nm* switch.
conocedor, a [konoθe'ðor, a] *a* expert,
knowledgeable // *nm/f* expert.
conocer [kono'θer] *vt* (*gen*) to know; (*por
primera vez*) to meet, get to know;
(*entender*) to know about; (*reconocer*) to
know, recognize; ~**se** *vr* (*una persona*) to
know o.s.; (*dos personas*) to (get to) know
each other.
conocido, a [kono'θiðo, a] *a* (well-)known
// *nm/f* acquaintance.
conocimiento [konoθi'mjento] *nm*
knowledge; (*MED*) consciousness; ~**s** *nmpl*

(*personas*) acquaintances; (*ciencia*)
knowledge *sg*.
conozco *etc vb ver* **conocer.**
conque ['konke] *conj* and so, so then.
conquista [kon'kista] *nf* conquest.
conquistador, a [konkista'ðor, a] *a*
conquering // *nm* conqueror.
conquistar [konkis'tar] *vt* to conquer.
consagrar [konsa'xrar] *vt* (*REL*) to
consecrate; (*fig*) to devote.
consciente [kons'θjente] *a* conscious.
consecución [konseku'θjon] *nf*
acquisition; (*de fin*) attainment.
consecuencia [konse'kwenθja] *nf*
consequence, outcome; (*firmeza*)
consistency.
consecuente [konse'kwente] *a* consistent.
consecutivo, a [konseku'tiβo, a] *a*
consecutive.
conseguir [konse'xir] *vt* to get, obtain;
(*sus fines*) to attain.
consejero, a [konse'xero, a] *nm/f* adviser,
consultant; (*POL*) councillor.
consejo [kon'sexo] *nm* advice; (*POL*)
council.
consenso [kon'senso] *nm* consensus.
consentimiento [konsenti'mjento] *nm*
consent.
consentir [konsen'tir] *vt* (*permitir, tolerar*)
to consent to; (*mimar*) to pamper, spoil;
(*admitir*) to admit // *vi* to agree, consent.
conserje [kon'serxe] *nm* caretaker;
(*portero*) porter.
conserva [kon'serβa] *nf* (*acción*)
preserving; (*alimento*) preserved food.
conservación [konserβa'θjon] *nf*
conservation; (*de alimentos, vida*)
preservation.
conservador, a [konserβa'ðor, a] *a*
preservative; (*POL*) conservative // *nm/f*
conservative; (*de museo*) keeper.
conservar [konser'βar] *vt* to conserve,
keep; (*alimentos, vida*) to preserve; ~**se** *vr*
to survive.
considerable [konsiðe'raβle] *a*
considerable.
consideración [konsiðera'θjon] *nf*
consideration; (*estimación*) respect.
considerado, a [konsiðe'raðo, a] *a*
(*prudente, reflexivo*) considerate;
(*respetado*) respected.
considerar [konsiðe'rar] *vt* to consider.
consigna [kon'sixna] *nf* (*orden*) order,
instruction; (*para equipajes*) left-luggage
office.
consigo [kon'sixo] *pron* (*m*) with him; (*f*)
with her; (*Vd.*) with you; (*reflexivo*) with
o.s.
consiguiente [konsi'xjente] *a* consequent;
por ~ **and so, therefore, consequently.**
consistente [konsis'tente] *a* consistent;
(*sólido*) solid, firm; (*válido*) sound.
consistir [konsis'tir] *vi*: ~ **en**
(*componerse de*) to consist of; (*ser
resultado de*) to be due to.
consolación [konsola'θjon] *nf* consolation.

consolar [konso'lar] *vt* to console.
consolidar [konsoli'ðar] *vt* to consolidate.
consomé [konso'me] *nm* consommé, clear soup.
consonante [konso'nante] a consonant, harmonious // *nf* consonant.
conspicuo, a [kons'pikwo, a] a conspicuous.
conspiración [konspira'θjon] *nf* conspiracy.
conspirador, a [konspira'ðor, a] *nm/f* conspirator.
conspirar [konspi'rar] *vi* to conspire.
constante [kons'tante] a constant.
constar [kons'tar] *vi* (*evidenciarse*) to be clear *or* evident; ~ **de** to consist of.
consternación [konsterna'θjon] *nf* consternation.
constipación [konstipa'θjon] *nf* = **constipado.**
constipado, a [konsti'paðo, a] a: **estar** ~ to have a cold // *nm* cold.
constitución [konstitu'θjon] *nf* constitution; **constitucional** a constitutional.
constituir [konstitu'ir] *vt* (*formar, componer*) to constitute, make up; (*fundar, erigir, ordenar*) to constitute, establish.
constitutivo, a [konstitu'tißo, a] a constitutive, constituent.
constituyente [konstitu'jente] a constituent.
constreñir [konstre'nir] *vt* (*obligar*) to compel, oblige; (*restringir*) to restrict.
construcción [konstruk'θjon] *nf* construction, building.
constructor, a [konstruk'tor, a] *nm/f* builder.
construir [konstru'ir] *vt* to build, construct.
consuelo [kon'swelo] *nm* consolation, solace.
cónsul ['konsul] *nm* consul; **consulado** *nm* consulate.
consulta [kon'sulta] *nf* consultation.
consultar [konsul'tar] *vt* to consult.
consultorio [konsul'torjo] *nm* information bureau; (*MED*) surgery.
consumar [konsu'mar] *vt* to complete, carry out; (*crimen*) to commit; (*matrimonio*) to consummate.
consumición [konsumi'θjon] *nf* consumption; (*bebida*) drink; (*en restaurante*) meal.
consumidor, a [konsumi'ðor, a] *nm/f* consumer.
consumir [konsu'mir] *vt* to consume; ~ **se** *vr* to be consumed; (*persona*) to waste away.
consumo [kon'sumo] *nm*, **consunción** [konsun'θjon] *nf* consumption.
contabilidad [kontaßili'ðað] *nf* accounting, book-keeping; (*profesión*) accountancy.
contacto [kon'takto] *nm* contact.
contado, a [kon'taðo, a] a: ~ **s** (*escasos*)

numbered, scarce, few // *nm*: **al** ~ for cash.
contador [konta'ðor] *nm* (*aparato*) meter; (*COM*) accountant; (*de café*) counter.
contagiar [konta'xjar] *vt* (*enfermedad*) to pass on, transmit; (*persona*) to infect; ~ **se** *vr* to become infected.
contagio [kon'taxjo] *nm* infection.
contagioso, a [konta'xjoso, a] a infectious; (*fig*) catching.
contaminación [kontamina'θjon] *nf* contamination.
contaminar [kontami'nar] *vt* to contaminate.
contar [kon'tar] *vt* (*páginas, dinero*) to count; (*anécdota*) to tell // *vi* to count; ~ **con** to rely on, count on.
contemplación [kontempla'θjon] *nf* contemplation.
contemplar [kontem'plar] *vt* to contemplate; (*mirar*) to look at.
contemporáneo, a [kontempo'raneo, a] a, *nm/f* contemporary.
contender [konten'der] *vi* (*gen*) to contend; (*en un concurso*) to compete.
contener [konte'ner] *vt* to contain, hold; (*retener*) to hold back, contain.
contenido, a [konte'niðo, a] a (*moderado*) restrained; (*reprimido*) suppressed // *nm* contents *pl*, content.
contentar [konten'tar] *vt* (*satisfacer*) to satisfy; (*complacer*) to please; ~ **se** *vr* to be satisfied.
contento, a [kon'tento, a] a contented, content; (*alegre*) pleased; (*feliz*) happy // *nm* contentment; (*felicidad*) happiness.
contestación [kontesta'θjon] *nf* answer, reply.
contestar [kontes'tar] *vt* to answer, reply; (*JUR*) to corroborate, confirm.
contigo [kon'tivo] *pron* with you.
contiguo, a [kon'tivwo, a] a (*de al lado*) next; (*vecino*) adjacent, adjoining.
continental [konti'nen'tal] a continental.
continente [konti'nen'e] a, *nm* continent.
contingencia [kontin'xenθja] *nf* contingency; (*riesgo*) risk; **contingente** a, *nm* contingent.
continuación [kontinwa'θjon] *nf* continuation; **a** ~ then, next.
continuar [konti'nwar] *vt* to continue, go on with // *vi* to continue, go on.
continuidad [kontinwi'ðað] *nf* continuity.
continuo, a [kon'tinwo, a] a (*sin interrupción*) continuous; (*acción perseverante*) continual.
contorno [kon'torno] *nm* outline; (*GEO*) contour; ~ **s** *nmpl* neighbourhood *sg*, environs.
contorsión [kontor'sjon] *nf* contortion.
contra ['kontra] *prep*, *ad* against // *nm* con.
contraataque [kontraa'take] *nm* counter-attack.
contrabajo [kontra'ßaxo] *nm* double bass.

contrabandista [kontraßan'dista] *nm/f* smuggler.

contrabando [kontra'ßando] *nm* (*acción*) smuggling; (*mercancías*) contraband.

contracción [kontrak'θjon] *nf* contraction; (*encogimiento*) shrinkage.

contracepción [kontraθep'θjon] *nf* contraception.

contraceptivo [kontraθep'tißo] *nm* contraceptive.

contradecir [kontraðe'θir] *vt* to contradict.

contradicción [kontraðik'θjon] *nf* contradiction.

contradictorio, a [kontraðik'torjo, a] *a* contradictory.

contraer [kontra'er] *vt* to contract; (*encoger*) to shrink; (*limitar*) to restrict; ~**se** *vr* to contract; to shrink; (*limitarse*) to limit o.s.

contragolpe [kontra'xolpe] *nm* backlash.

contrahacer [kontraa'θer] *vt* to copy, imitate; (*falsificar*) to forge.

contramaestre [kontrama'estre] *nm* foreman.

contrapelo [kontra'pelo]: **a** ~ *ad* the wrong way.

contrapesar [kontrape'sar] *vt* to counterbalance; (*fig*) to offset.

contrariar [kontra'rjar] *vt* (*oponerse*) to oppose; (*poner obstáculo*) to impede; (*enfadar*) to vex.

contrariedad [kontrarje'ðað] *nf* (*oposición*) opposition; (*obstáculo*) obstacle, setback; (*disgusto*) vexation, annoyance.

contrario, a [kon'trarjo, a] *a* contrary; (*de persona*) opposed; (*sentido, lado*) opposite // *nm/f* enemy, adversary; (*DEPORTE*) opponent; **de lo** ~ otherwise.

contrarrestar [kontrarres'tar] *vt* to counteract; (*pelota*) to return.

contrastar [kontras'tar] *vt* to resist // *vi* to contrast.

contraste [kon'traste] *nm* contrast.

contratante [kontra'tante] *nm/f* contractor.

contratar [kontra'tar] *vt* (*firmar un acuerdo para*) to contract for; (*empleados, obreros*) to hire, engage; ~**se** *vr* to sign on.

contratiempo [kontra'tjempo] *nm* setback.

contratista [kontra'tista] *nm/f* contractor.

contrato [kon'trato] *nm* contract.

contravención [kontraßen'θjon] *nf* contravention, violation.

contravenir [kontraße'nir] *vi*: ~ **a** to contravene, violate.

contraventana [kontraßen'tana] *nf* shutter.

contribución [kontrißu'θjon] *nf* (*municipal etc*) tax; (*ayuda*) contribution.

contribuir [kontrißu'ir] *vt*, *vi* to contribute; (*COM*) to pay (in taxes).

contribuyente [kontrißu'jente] *nm/f* (*COM*) taxpayer; (*que ayuda*) contributor.

control [kon'trol] *nm* control; (*inspección*) inspection, check; ~**ar** *vt* to control; to inspect, check.

controversia [kontro'ßersja] *nf* controversy.

convalecencia [konßale'θenθja] *nf* convalescence.

convalecer [konßale'θer] *vi* to convalesce, get better.

convaleciente [konßale'θjente] *a*, *nm/f* convalescent.

convencer [konßen'θer] *vt* to convince; (*persuadir*) to persuade.

convencimiento [konßenθi'mjento] *nm* convincing; (*persuasióa*) persuasion; (*certidumbre*) conviction.

convención [konßen'θjon] *nf* convention.

convencional [konßenθjo'nal] *a* conventional.

convenido, a [konße'niðo, a] *a* agreed.

conveniencia [konße'njenθja] *nf* suitability; (*conformidad*) agreement; (*utilidad, provecho*) usefulness; ~**s** *nfpl* conventions; (*COM*) property *sg*.

conveniente [konße'njente] *a* suitable; (*útil*) useful.

convenio [kon'ßenjo] *nm* agreement, treaty.

convenir [konße'nir] *vi* (*estar de acuerdo*) to agree; (*ser conveniente*) to suit, be suitable; ~**se** *vr* to agree.

convento [kon'ßento] *nm* monastery; (*de monjas*) convent.

converger [konßer'xer], **convergir** [konßer'xir] *vi* to converge.

conversación [konßersa'θjon] *nf* conversation.

conversar [konßer'sar] *vi* to talk, converse.

conversión [konßer'sjon] *nf* conversion.

convertir [konßer'tir] *vt* to convert.

convicción [konßik'θon] *nf* conviction.

convicto, a [kon'ßikto, a] *a* convicted, found guilty; (*condenaðo*) condemned.

convidado, a [konßi'ðaðo, a] *nm/f* guest.

convidar [konßi'ðar] *vt* to invite.

convincente [konßir'ßente] *a* convincing.

convite [kon'ßite] *nm* invitation; (*banquete*) banquet.

convivencia [konßi'ßenθja] *nf* coexistence, living together.

convocar [konßo'kar] *vt* to summon, call (together).

convulsión [konßul'sjon] *nf* convulsion.

conyugal [konju'xal] *a* conjugal.

coñac [ko'nak] *nm* cognac, brandy.

cooperación [koopera'θjon] *nf* cooperation.

cooperar [koope'rar] *vi* to cooperate.

cooperativo, a [koopera'tißo, a] *a* cooperative // *nf* cooperative.

coordinación [koorðina'θjon] *nf* coordination.

coordinar [koorði'nar] *vt* to coordinate.

copa [ˈkopa] *nf* cup; (*vaso*) glass; (*de árbol*) top; (*de sombrero*) crown; ~s *nfpl* (*NAIPES*) ≈ hearts.

copia [ˈkopja] *nf* copy; **copiar** *vt* to copy.

copioso, a [koˈpjoso, a] *a* copious, plentiful.

copita [koˈpita] *nf* (small) glass; (*GOLF*) tee.

copla [ˈkopla] *nf* verse; (*canción*) (*popular*) song.

coqueta [koˈketa] *a* flirtatious, coquettish; **coquetear** *vi* to flirt.

coraje [koˈraxe] *nm* courage; (*ánimo*) spirit; (*ira*) anger.

coral [koˈral] *a* choral // *nf* choir.

corazón [koraˈθon] *nm* heart.

corazonada [koraθoˈnaða] *nf* impulse; (*presentimiento*) presentiment, hunch.

corbata [korˈβata] *nf* tie.

corcovado, a [korkoˈβaðo, a] *a* hunchbacked.

corchete [korˈtʃete] *nm* catch, clasp.

corcho [ˈkortʃo] *nm* cork; (*PESCA*) float

cordel [korˈðel] *nm* cord, line.

cordero [korˈðero] *nm* lamb.

cordial [korˈðjal] *a* cordial; ~**idad** *nf* warmth, cordiality.

cordillera [korðiˈʎera] *nf* range, chain (of mountains).

Córdoba [ˈkorðoβa] *n* Cordoba; **cordobés, esa** *a* of *or* from Cordoba.

cordón [korˈðon] *nm* (*cuerda*) cord, string; (*de zapatos*) lace; (*policía*) cordon.

corneta [korˈneta] *nf* bugle.

coro [ˈkoro] *nm* chorus; (*conjunto de cantores*) choir.

corolario [koroˈlarjo] *nm* corollary.

corona [koˈrona] *nf* crown; (*de flores*) garland; ~**ción** *nf* coronation; **coronar** *vt* to crown.

coronel [koroˈnel] *nm* colonel.

coronilla [koroˈniʎa] *nf* crown (of the head).

corporación [korporaˈθjon] *nf* corporation.

corporal [korpoˈral] *a* corporal.

corpulento, a [korpuˈlento] *a* (*árbol*) stout; (*persona*) well-built.

corral [koˈral] *nm* farmyard; ~**illo** *nm* playpen.

correa [koˈrea] *nf* strap; (*cinturón*) belt.

corrección [korekˈθjon] *nf* correction; (*reprensión*) rebuke; **correccional** *nm* reformatory.

correcto, a [koˈrekto, a] *a* correct; (*persona*) well-mannered.

corredor, a [koreˈðor, a] *a* running; (*rápido*) fast // *nm* (*COM*) agent, broker; (*pasillo*) corridor, passage; (*DEPORTE*) runner.

corregir [koreˈxir] *vt* (*error*) to correct; (*amonestar, reprender*) to rebuke, reprimand; ~**se** *vr* to reform.

correo [koˈreo] *nm* post, mail; (*persona*) courier; (*cartero*) postman; **C**~ Post Office; ~ **aéreo** airmail.

correr [koˈrer] *vt* to run; (*viajar*) to cover, travel; (*cortinas*) to draw; (*cerrojo*) to shoot // *vi* to run; (*líquido*) to run, flow; (*moneda*) to pass, be valid; ~**se** *vr* to slide, move; (*colores*) to run.

correspondencia [korespon'denθja] *nf* correspondence; (*FERRO*) connection.

corresponder [korespon'der] *vi* to correspond; (*convenir*) to be suitable; (*pertenecer*) to belong; (*tocar*) to concern; ~**se** *vr* (*por escrito*) to correspond; (*amarse*) to have mutual affection.

correspondiente [korespon'djente] *a* corresponding // *nm* correspondent.

corrido, a [ko'rriðo, a] *a* (*avergonzado*) abashed; (*fluido*) fluent // *nf* run, dash; (*de toros*) bullfight; **3 noches** ~**as** 3 nights running; **un kilo** ~ **a** good kilo.

corriente [ko'rrjente] *a* (*agua*) running; (*fig*) flowing; (*dinero etc*) current; (*común*) ordinary, normal // *nf* current // *nm* current month.

corrillo [ko'rriʎo] *nm* huddle; (*fig*) clique.

corro [ˈkorro] *nm* ring, circle (of people).

corroborar [korroβo'rar] *vt* to corroborate.

corroer [korro'er] *vt* to corrode; (*GEO*) to erode.

corromper [korrom'per] *vt* (*madera*) to rot; (*alimento*) to turn bad; (*fig*) to corrupt.

corrosivo, a [korro'siβo, a] *a* corrosive.

corrupción [korrup'θjon] *nf* rot, decay; (*fig*) corruption.

corsé [kor'se] *nm* corset.

cortado, a [kor'taðo, a] *a* (*con cuchillo*) cut; (*leche*) sour; (*confuso*) confused; (*disconcertado*) embarrassed; (*estilo*) abrupt // *nm* white coffee (with just a little milk).

cortador, a [korta'ðor, a] *a* cutting // *nf* cutter, slicer.

cortadura [korta'ðura] *nf* cut.

cortar [kor'tar] *vt* to cut; (*el agua*) to cut off; (*un pasaje*) to cut out // *vi* to cut; ~**se** *vr* (*turbarse*) to become embarrassed; (*leche*) to turn, curdle; ~**se el pelo** to have one's hair cut.

corte [ˈkorte] *nm* cut, cutting; (*filo*) edge; (*de tela*) piece, length; **las C**~**s** the Spanish Parliament.

cortedad [korte'ðað] *nf* shortness; (*fig*) bashfulness, timidity.

cortejar [korte'xar] *vt* to court.

cortejo [kor'texo] *nm* entourage; ~ **fúnebre** funeral procession.

cortés [kor'tes] *a* courteous, polite.

cortesía [korte'sia] *nf* courtesy.

corteza [kor'teθa] *nf* (*de árbol*) bark; (*de pan*) crust.

cortina [kor'tina] *nf* curtain.

corto, a [ˈkorto, a] *a* (*breve*) short; (*tímido*) bashful; (*poco inteligente*) not very clever; ~ **de vista** short-sighted; **estar** ~ **de fondos** to be short of funds.

corvo, a [ˈkorβo, a] *a* curved.

cosa [ˈkosa] *nf* thing; (*asunto*) affair; ~ **de** about; **eso es** ~ **mía** that's my affair.

cosecha [ko'setʃa] *nf* (*AGR*) harvest; (*de vino*) vintage.
cosechar [kose'tʃar] *vt* to harvest, gather (in).
coser [ko'ser] *vt* to sew.
cosmético, a [kos'metiko, a] *a, nm* cosmetic.
cosquillas [kos'kiʎas] *nfpl:* **hacer ~** to tickle; **tener ~** to be ticklish.
cosquilloso, a [koski'ʎoso, a] *a* ticklish; (*fig*) touchy.
costa ['kosta] *nf* (*gasto*) cost; (*GEO*) coast.
costado [kos'taðo] *nm* side.
costal [kos'tal] *nm* sack.
costar [kos'tar] *vt* (*valer*) to cost; (*necesitar*) to require, need; **me cuesta hacer** I find it hard to do.
Costa Rica [kosta'rika] *nf* Costa Rica; **costarricense, costarriqueño, a** *a, nm/f* Costa Rican.
coste ['koste] *nm* = **costo**.
costilla [kos'tiʎa] *nf* rib; (*CULIN*) chop.
costo ['kosto] *nm* cost, price; **~ de la vida** cost of living; **~so, a** *a* costly, expensive.
costra ['kostra] *nf* crust; (*MED*) scab.
costumbre [kos'tumbre] *nf* custom, habit.
costura [kos'tura] *nf* sewing, needlework; (*de medias*) seam.
costurera [kostu'rera] *nf* dressmaker.
costurero [kostu'rero] *nm* sewing box *or* case.
cotejar [kote'xar] *vt* to compare.
cotejo [ko'texo] *nm* comparison.
cotidiano, a [koti'ðjano, a] *a* daily, day to day.
cotización [kotiθa'θjon] *nf* (*COM*) quotation, price; (*cuota*) dues *pl*.
cotizar [koti'θar] *vt* (*COM*) to quote, price; **~se** *vr:* **~se a** to sell at, fetch.
coto ['koto] *nm* (*terreno cercado*) enclosure; (*de caza*) reserve.
coyote [ko'jote] *nm* coyote, prairie wolf.
coyuntura [kojun'tura] *nf* (*ANAT*) joint; (*oportunidad*) opportunity.
cráneo ['kraneo] *nm* skull, cranium.
cráter ['krater] *nm* crater.
creación [krea'θjon] *nf* creation.
creador, a [krea'ðor, a] *a* creative // *nm/f* creator.
crear [kre'ar] *vt* to create, make.
crecer [kre'θer] *vi* (*niño*) to grow; (*precio*) to rise; (*días*) to get longer; (*mar*) to swell.
crecido, a [kre'θiðo, a] *a* (*persona, planta*) full-grown; (*cantidad*) large; (*fig*) conceited.
creciente [kre'θjente] *a* (*persona*) growing; (*cantidad*) increasing; (*luna*) crescent // *nm* crescent // *nf* flood.
crecimiento [kreθi'mjento] *nm* growth; (*aumento*) increase.
credenciales [kreðen'θjales] *nfpl* credentials.
crédito ['kreðito] *nm* credit.
credo ['kreðo] *nm* creed.
crédulo, a ['kreðulo, a] *a* credulous.
creencia [kre'enθja] *nf* belief.

creer [kre'er] *vt, vi* to think, believe; **~se** *vr* to believe o.s. (to be); **¡ya lo creo!** I should think so!
creíble [kre'iβle] *a* credible, believable.
crema ['krema] *nf* cream; (*de huevo*) custard.
cremallera [krema'ʎera] *nf* zip (fastener).
crepúsculo [kre'puskulo] *nm* twilight, dusk.
crespón [kres'pon] *nm* crêpe.
creta ['kreta] *nf* chalk.
creyente [kre'jente] *nm/f* believer.
creyó *etc vb ver* **creer.**
cría ['kria] *nf* (*de animales*) rearing, breeding; (*animal*) baby animal; (*niño*) child.
criadero [kria'ðero] *nm* nursery; (*ZOOL*) breeding place.
criado, a [kri'aðo, a] *a* bred, reared // *nm* servant // *nf* servant, maid; **mal/bien ~** badly/well brought up.
criador [kria'ðor] *nm* breeder.
crianza [kri'anθa] *nf* rearing, breeding; (*fig*) breeding.
criar [kri'ar] *vt* to suckle, feed; (*educar*) to bring up; (*producir*) to grow, produce; (*animales*) to breed.
criatura [kria'tura] *nf* creature; (*niño*) baby, (*small*) child.
criba ['kriβa] *nf* sieve; **cribar** *vt* to sieve.
crimen ['krimen] *nm* crime.
criminal [krimi'nal] *a, nm/f* criminal.
crin [krin] *nf* (*también* **~es** *nfpl*) mane.
crisis ['krisis] *nf inv* crisis.
crispar [kris'par] *vt* (*músculo*) to make contract; (*nervios*) to set on edge.
cristal [kris'tal] *nm* crystal; (*de ventana*) glass, pane; (*lente*) lens; **~ino, a** *a* crystalline; (*fig*) clear // *nm* lens of the eye; **~izar** *vt, vi* to crystallize.
cristiandad [kristjar'ðað] *nf* Christianity.
cristianismo [kristja'nismo] *nm* Christianity.
cristiano, a [kris'tjano, a] *a, nm/f* Christian.
Cristo ['kristo] *nm* (*dios*) Christ; (*crucifijo*) crucifix.
criterio [kri'terjo] *nm* criterion; (*juicio*) judgement.
criticar [kriti'kar] *vt* to criticize.
crítico, a ['kritiko, a] *a* critical // *nm* critic // *nf* criticism.
cromo ['kromo] *nm* chrome.
crónico, a ['kroniko, a] *a* chronic // *nf* chronicle, account.
cronista [kro'nista] *nm/f* chronicler.
cruce ['kruθe] *nm* crossing; (*de carreteras*) crossroads.
crucificar [kruθifi'kar] *vt* to crucify.
crucifijo [kruθi'fixo] *nm* crucifix.
crucigrama [kruθi'ɣrama] *nm* crossword (puzzle).
crudo, a ['kruðo, a] *a* raw; (*no maduro*) unripe; (*petróleo*) crude; (*rudo, cruel*) cruel.

cruel [krwel] a cruel.
crueldad [krwel'ðað] nf cruelty.
crujido [kru'xiðo] nm creak.
crujir [kru'xir] vi (madera) to creak; (dedos) to crack; (dientes) to grind; (nieve, arena) to crunch.
cruz [kruθ] nf cross; (de moneda) tails sg.
cruzado, a [kru'θaðo, a] a crossed // nm crusader // nf crusade.
cruzar [kru'θar] vt to cross; ~se vr to cross; (personas) to pass each other.
cuaderno [kwa'ðerno] nm notebook; (de escuela) exercise book; (NAUT) logbook.
cuadra [kwa'ðra] nf (caballeriza) stable; (gran sala) hall.
cuadrado, a [kwa'ðraðo, a] a square // nm (MAT) square; (regla) ruler.
cuadrar [kwa'ðrar] vt to square // vi: ~ con to square with, tally with; ~se vr (soldado) to stand to attention.
cuadrilla [kwa'ðriʎa] nf party, group.
cuadro ['kwaðro] nm square; (de vidrio) frame; (PINTURA) painting; (TEATRO) scene.
cuádruplo, a ['kwaðruplo, a], **cuádruple** ['kwaðruple] a quadruple.
cuajar [kwa'xar] vt to thicken; (leche) to curdle; (sangre) to congeal; (adornar) to adorn; ~se vr to curdle; to congeal; (llenarse) to fill up.
cual [kwal] ad like, as // pron: el ~ etc which; (persona: sujeto) who; (: objeto) whom // a such as; **cada** ~ each one; ~ **más**, ~ **menos** some more, some less; **tal** ~ just as it is.
cuál [kwal] pron interr which (one).
cualesquier(a) [kwales'kjer(a)] pl de **cualquier(a)**.
cualidad [kwali'ðað] nf quality.
cualquiera [kwal'kjera], **cualquier** [kwal'kjer] a any // pron anybody, anyone; (quienquiera) whoever; **en cualquier parte** anywhere; ~ **que sea** whichever it is; (persona) whoever it is.
cuando ['kwando] ad when; (aún si) if, even if // conj (puesto que) since // prep: **yo,** ~ **niño...** when I was a child...; ~ **no sea así** even if it is not so; ~ **más** the more; ~ **menos** the less; ~ **no** if not, otherwise; **de** ~ **en** ~ from time to time.
cuándo ['kwando] ad when; ¿**desde** ~?, ¿**de** ~ **acá**? since when?
cuanto, a ['kwanto, a] a all that, as much as // pron all that (which), as much as; **llévate todo** ~ **quieras** take as much as you like; **en** ~ (en seguida que) as soon as; (ya que) since, inasmuch as; **en** ~ **profesor** as a teacher; **en** ~ **a** as for; ~ **más difícil sea** the more difficult it is; ~ **más hace (tanto) menos avanza** the more he does, the less he progresses; ~ **antes** as soon as possible; **unos** ~**s libros** a few books.
cuánto, a ['kwanto, a] a what a lot of; (interr: sg) how much?; (: pl) how many? // pron, ad how much?; (interr: sg) how much?; (: pl) how many?; ¡~ **a gente!** what a lot of people!; ¿~ **cuesta?** how much does it

cost?; ¿~**s estamos?** what's the date?; **Señor no sé** ~**s** Mr. So-and-So.
cuarenta [kwa'renta] num forty.
cuarentena [kwaren'tena] nf quarantine.
cuartear [kwarte'ar] vt to quarter; (dividir) to divide up; ~**se** vr to crack, split.
cuartel [kwar'tel] nm (de ciudad) quarter, district; (MIL) barracks pl; ~ **general** headquarters pl.
cuarteto [kwar'teto] nm quartet.
cuarto, a ['kwarto, a] a fourth // nm (MAT) quarter, fourth; (habitación) room // nf (MAT) quarter, fourth; (palmo) span; ~ **de baño** bathroom; ~ **de hora** quarter (of an) hour.
cuatro ['kwatro] num four.
cuba ['kuβa] nf cask, barrel; (fig) drunkard.
Cuba ['kuβa] nf Cuba; **cubano, a** a, nm/f Cuban.
cúbico, a ['kuβiko, a] a cubic.
cubierto, a [ku'βjerto, a] pp de **cubrir** // a covered // nm cover; (en la mesa) place; ~**s** nmpl cutlery sg // nf cover, covering; (neumático) tyre; (NAUT) deck; **a** ~ **de** covered with or from.
cubo ['kuβo] nm cube; (de madera) bucket, tub; (TEC) drum.
cubrir [ku'βrir] vt to cover; ~**se** vr (cielo) to become overcast.
cucaracha [kuka'ratʃa] nf cockroach.
cuchara [ku'tʃara] nf spoon; (TEC) scoop; ~**da** nf spoonful; ~**dita** nf teaspoonful.
cucharita [kutʃa'rita] nf teaspoon.
cucharón [kutʃa'ron] nm ladle.
cuchichear [kutʃitʃe'ar] vi to whisper.
cuchilla [ku'tʃiʎa] nf (large) knife; (de arma blanca) blade.
cuchillo [ku'tʃiʎo] nm knife.
cuello ['kweʎo] nm (ANAT) neck; (de vestido, camisa) collar.
cuenca ['kwenka] nf (escudilla) hollow; (ANAT) eye socket; (GEO) bowl, deep valley.
cuenta ['kwenta] nf (cálculo) count, counting; (en café, restaurante) bill; (COM) account; (de collar) bead; (fig) account; **a fin de** ~**s** in the end; **caer en la** ~ to catch on; **darse** ~ **de** to realize; **tener en** ~ to bear in mind; **echar** ~**s** to take stock; ~ **corriente/de ahorros** current/savings account.
cuento etc vb ver **contar** // ['kwento] nm story.
cuerdo, a ['kwerðo, a] a sane; (prudente) wise, sensible // nf (MAT) rope; (hilo) string; (de reloj) spring; **dar** ~ **a un reloj** to wind up a clock.
cuerno ['kwerno] nm horn.
cuero ['kwero] nm (ZOOL) skin, hide; (TEC) leather; **en** ~**s** stark naked; ~ **cabelludo** scalp.
cuerpo ['kwerpo] nm body.
cuesta ['kwesta] nf slope; (en camino etc) hill; ~ **arriba/abajo** uphill/downhill; **a** ~**s** on one's back.
cuestión [kwes'tjon] nf matter, question,

issue; (riña) quarrel, dispute.
cuesto etc vb ver **costar.**
cueva ['kweßa] nf cave; (bodega) cellar.
cuidado [kwi'ðaðo] nm care, carefulness; (preocupación) care, worry; excl careful!, look out!
cuidadoso, a [kwiða'ðoso, a] a careful; (preocupado) anxious.
cuidar [kwi'ðar] vt (MED) to care for; (ocuparse de) to take care of, look after // vi: ~ de to take care of, look after; ~se vr to look after o.s.; ~se de hacer algo to take care not to do something.
culebra [ku'leßra] nf snake.
culebrear [kuleßre'ar] vi to wriggle along; (río) to meander.
culinario, a [kuli'narjo, a] a culinary, cooking cpd.
culminación [kulmina'θjon] nf culmination.
culo ['kulo] nm bottom, backside.
culpa ['kulpa] nf fault; (JUR) guilt; **tener la ~ (de)** to be to blame (for).
culpabilidad [kulpaßili'ðað] nf guilt.
culpable [kul'paßle] a guilty // nm/f culprit.
culpar [kul'par] vt to blame; (acusar) to accuse.
cultivador, a [kultißa'ðor, a] nm/f farmer // nf cultivator.
cultivar [kulti'ßar] vt to cultivate.
cultivo [kul'tißo] nm cultivation; (plantas) crop.
culto, a ['kulto, a] a (cultivado) cultivated; (que tiene cultura) cultured // nm (homenaje) worship; (religión) cult.
cultura [kul'tura] nf culture.
cumbre ['kumbre] nf summit, top.
cumpleaños [kumple'aɲos] nm birthday.
cumplido, a [kum'pliðo, a] a complete, perfect; (abundante) plentiful; (cortés) courteous // nm compliment; (cortesía) courtesy.
cumplimentar [kumplimen'tar] vt to congratulate.
cumplimiento [kumpli'mjento] nm (de un deber) fulfilment; (acabamiento) completion; (cumplido) compliment.
cumplir [kum'plir] vt (orden) to carry out, obey; (promesa) to carry out, fulfil; (condena) to serve; (años) to reach, attain // vi: ~ con (deberes) to carry out, fulfil; ~se vr (plazo) to expire.
cuna ['kuna] nf cradle, cot.
cuñado, a [ku'ɲaðo, a] nm/f brother/sister-in-law.
cuota ['kwota] nf (parte proporcional) share; (cotización) fee, dues pl.
cupe etc vb ver **caber.**
cura ['kura] nf (curación) cure; (método curativo) treatment // nm priest.
curación [kura'θjon] nf cure; (acción) curing.
curar [ku'rar] vt (herida) to treat, dress; (enfermo) to cure; (carne, pescado) to cure,

salt; (cuero) to tan // vi, ~se vr to get well, recover.
curiosear [kurjose'ar] vt to glance at, look over // vi to look round, wander round.
curiosidad [kurjosi'ðað] nf curiosity.
curioso, a [ku'rjoso, a] a curious // nm/f bystander, onlooker.
cursi ['kursi] a (fam) in bad taste, vulgar.
cursivo, a [kur'sißo, a] a italic // nf italics pl.
curso ['kurso] nm course; **en ~ (año)** current; (proceso) going on, under way.
curvo, a ['kurßo, a] a (gen) curved; (torcido) bent // nf (gen) curve, bend.
custodia [kus'toðja] nf care, safekeeping, custody.
custodiar [kusto'ðjar] vt (guardar) to keep, take care of; (vigilar) to guard, watch over.
custodio [kus'toðjo] nm guardian, keeper.
cutis ['kutis] nm skin, complexion.
cuyo, a ['kujo, a] pron (de quien) whose, of whom; (de que) of which.

CH

chabacano, a [tʃaßa'kano, a] a vulgar, coarse.
chacal [tʃa'kal] nm jackal.
chacota [tʃa'kota] nf fun (and games).
chal [tʃal] nm shawl.
chalán [tʃa'lan] nm (pey) shady dealer.
chaleco [tʃa'leko] nm waistcoat, vest (US); ~ **salvavidas** life jacket.
chalupa [tʃa'lupa] nf launch, boat.
champán [tʃam'pan] nm, **champaña** [tʃam'paɲa] nf champagne.
champiñón [tʃampi'ɲon] nm mushroom.
champú [tʃam'pu] nm shampoo.
chamuscar [tʃamus'kar] vt to scorch, sear, singe.
chantaje [tʃan'taxe] nm blackmail.
chapa ['tʃapa] nf (de metal) plate, sheet; (de madera) board, panel.
chaparrón [tʃapa'rron] nm downpour, cloudburst.
chapotear [tʃapote'ar] vt to sponge down // vi (fam) to splash about.
chapucero, a [tʃapu'θero, a] a rough, crude // nm/f bungler.
chapurrar [tʃapu'rrar], **chapurrear** [tʃapurre'ar] vt (idioma) to speak badly; (bebidas) to mix.
chapuzar [tʃapu'θar] vi to duck.
chaqueta [tʃa'keta] nf jacket.
charca ['tʃarka] nf pond, pool.
charco ['tʃarko] nm pool, puddle.
charla ['tʃarla] nf talk, chat; (conferencia) lecture.
charlar [tʃar'lar] vi to talk, chat.
charlatán, ana [tʃarla'tan, ana] nm/f chatterbox; (embaidor) trickster; (curandero) charlatan.
charol [tʃa'rol] nm varnish; (cuero) patent leather.

chascarrillo [tʃaska'rriʎo] nm (fam) funny story.

chasco ['tʃasko] nm (broma) trick, joke; (desengaño) disappointment.

chasquear [tʃaske'ar] vt (engañar) to disappoint; (bromear) to play a trick on; (látigo) to crack; (lengua) to click.

chasquido [tʃas'kiðo] nm (de lengua) click; (de látigo) crack.

chato, a ['tʃato, a] a flat // excl hey handsome/beautiful!

chaval, a [tʃa'ßal, a] nm/f lad/girl.

checo(e)slovaco, a [tʃeko(e)slo'ßako, a] a, nm/f Czech, Czechoslovak.

Checo(e)slovaquia [tʃeko(e)slo'ßakja] nf Czechoslovakia.

cheque ['tʃeke] nm cheque.

chequeo [tʃe'keo] nm (MED) check-up; (AUTO) service.

chequera [tʃe'kera] nf cheque-book.

chico, a ['tʃiko, a] a small, little // nm/f (niño, niña) child; (muchacho, muchacha) boy/girl.

chicharrón [tʃitʃa'rron] nm crackling.

chichón [tʃi'tʃon] nm bump, hump.

chiflado, a [tʃi'flaðo, a] a daft, barmy.

chiflar [tʃi'flar] vt to hiss, boo; ~se vr: ~se por to be/go crazy about.

chile ['tʃile] nm chilli, red pepper.

Chile ['tʃile] nm Chile; chileno, a a, nm/f Chilean.

chillar [tʃi'ʎar] vi (persona) to yell, scream; (animal salvaje) to howl; (cerdo) to squeal; (puerta) to creak.

chillido [tʃi'ʎiðo] nm (de persona) yell, scream; (de animal) howl; (de frenos) screech(ing).

chillón, ona [tʃi'ʎon, ona] a (niño) noisy; (color) loud, gaudy.

chimenea [tʃime'nea] nf chimney; (hogar) fireplace.

China ['tʃina] nf: la ~ China.

chinche ['tʃintʃe] nf bug; (TEC) drawing pin // nm/f nuisance, pest.

chino, a ['tʃino, a] a, nm/f Chinese // nm (lengua) Chinese.

Chipre ['tʃipre] nf Cyprus; chipriota, chipriote a, nm/f Cypriot.

chiquito, a [tʃi'kito, a] a very small, tiny // nm/f kid.

chirle ['tʃirle] a watery, wishy-washy.

chirriar [tʃi'rrjar] vi (goznes) to creak, squeak; (pájaros) to chirp, sing.

chirrido [tʃi'rriðo] nm creak(ing), squeak(ing); (de pájaro) chirp(ing).

chis [tʃis] excl sh!

chisme ['tʃisme] nm (habladurías) piece of gossip; (fam: objeto) thing, thingummyjig.

chismoso, a [tʃis'moso, a] a gossiping // nm/f gossip.

chispa ['tʃispa] nf spark; (fig) sparkle; (ingenio) wit; (fam) drunkenness.

chispeante [tʃispe'ante] a sparkling, scintillating.

chispear [tʃispe'ar] vi to spark; (lloviznar) to drizzle.

chisporrotear [tʃisporrote'ar] vi (fuego) to throw out sparks; (leña) to crackle; (aceite) to hiss, splutter.

chiste ['tʃiste] nm joke, funny story.

chistoso, a [tʃis'toso, a] a (gracioso) funny, amusing; (bromista) witty.

chivo, a ['tʃißo, a] nm/f (billy/nanny-)goat.

chocante [tʃo'kante] a startling; (extraño) odd; (ofensivo) shocking; (antipático) annoying.

chocar [tʃo'kar] vi (coches, trenes) to collide, crash // vt to shock; (sorprender) to startle; ~ con to collide with; (fig) to run into or up against; ¡chócala! put it there!

chocolate [tʃoko'late] a, nm chocolate.

chochear [tʃotʃe'ar] vi to dodder, be senile.

chocho, a ['tʃotʃo, a] a doddering, senile; (fig) soft, doting.

chollo ['tʃoʎo] nm (fam) bargain, snip.

choque ['tʃoke] nm (impacto) impact; (golpe) jolt; (AUTO) crash; (ELEC, MED) shock; (MIL) clash; (fig) conflict.

chorizo [tʃo'riθo] nm hard pork sausage, salami.

chorrear [tʃorre'ar] vi to gush, spout (out); (gotear) to drip, trickle.

chorro ['tʃorro] nm jet; (fig) stream.

choza ['tʃoθa] nf hut, shack.

chuleta [tʃu'leta] nf chop, cutlet.

chulo ['tʃulo] nm (pícaro) rascal; (fam: joven lindo) dandy.

chupado, a [tʃu'paðo, a] a (delgado) skinny, gaunt; (ajustado) tight.

chupar [tʃu'par] vt to suck; (absorber) to absorb; ~se vr to grow thin.

churro, a ['tʃurro, a] a coarse // nm fritter.

chuscada [tʃus'kaða] nf funny remark, joke.

chusco, a ['tʃusko, a] a funny; (persona) coarse but amusing.

chusma ['tʃusma] nf rabble, mob.

D

D. abr de Don.

Da. abr de Doña.

dactilógrafo, a [dakti'loɣrafo, a] nm/f typist.

dádiva ['daðißa] nf (donación) donation; (regalo) gift.

dado, a ['daðo, a] pp de dar // nm die; ~s nmpl dice; ~ que conj given that.

dador, a [da'ðor, a] nm/f (gen) giver.

dama ['dama] nf (gea) lady; (AJEDREZ) queen; ~s nfpl draughts.

damasco [da'masko] nm (tela) damask.

damnificar [damnifi'kar] vt (gen) to harm; (persona) to injure.

danés, esa [da'nes, esa] a Danish // nm/f Dane.

danzar [dan'θar] vt, vi to dance.

dañar [da'nar] vt (objeto) to damage;

(*persona*) to hurt; ~**se** *vr* to get hurt.
dañino, a [da'ɲino, a] *a* harmful.
daño ['daɲo] *nm* (*a un objeto*) damage; (*a una persona*) harm, injury; ~**s y perjuicios** (*JUR*) damages; **hacer** ~ **a** to damage; to harm, injure.
dar [dar] *vt* (*gen*) to give; (*TEATRO*) to perform, put on; (*película*) to show; (*intereses*) to yield; (*naipes*) to deal; (*la hora*): ~ **las 3** to strike 3 // *vi*: ~ **a** to look out on(to), overlook; ~ **con** (*persona etc*) to meet, run into; (*idea*) to hit on; ~ **contra** to knock against, bang into; ~ **de cabeza** to fall on one's head; ~ **en** (*objeto*) to strike, hit; (*broma*) to catch on to; ~ **de sí** to give, stretch; ~**se** *vr* (*pasar*) to happen; (*presentarse*) to occur; ~**se a** to be given to; ~**se por** to consider o.s.; **dárselas de** to pose as; ~ **de comer/beber a uno** to give sb sth to eat/drink; **da lo mismo** *o* **qué más da** it's all the same; ~ **en el blanco** to hit the mark; **me da pena** it saddens me; ~**se prisa** to hurry (up).
dardo ['darðo] *nm* dart.
dársena ['darsena] *nf* dock.
datar [da'tar] *vi*: ~ **de** to date from.
dátil ['datil] *nm* date.
dato ['dato] *nm* fact, piece of information.
d. de J. C. *abr de* **después de Jesucristo** A.D. (Anno Domini).
de [de] *prep* of; from; **libro** ~ **cocina** cookery book; **el hombre** ~ **largos cabellos** the man with long hair; **guantes** ~ **cuero** leather gloves; **fue a Londres** ~ **profesor** he went to London as a teacher; **una** ~ **dos** one or the other; ~ **mañana** in the morning; **vestido** ~ **negro** dressed in black; **más/menos** ~ more/less than; ~ **cabeza** on one's head; ~ **cara a** facing.
deambular [deambu'lar] *vi* to stroll, wander.
debajo [de'ßaxo] *ad* underneath; ~ **de** below, under; **por** ~ **de** beneath.
debate [de'ßate] *nm* debate; **debatir** *vt* to debate.
deber [de'ßer] *nm* duty // *vt* to owe // *vi*: **debe (de)** it must, it should; **debo hacerlo** I must do it; **debe de ir** he should go; ~**se** *vr*: ~**se a** to be owing *or* due to.
debido, a [de'ßiðo, a] *a* proper, just; ~ **a** due to, because of.
débil [de'ßil] *a* (*persona, carácter*) weak; (*luz*) dim; **debilidad** *nf* weakness; dimness; **debilidad senil** senility.
debilitar [deßili'tar] *vt* to weaken; ~**se** *vr* to grow weak.
débito ['deßito] *nm* debit.
década ['dekaða] *nf* decade.
decadencia [deka'ðenθja] *nf* decadence.
decaer [deka'er] *vi* (*declinar*) to decline; (*debilitarse*) to weaken.
decaimiento [dekai'mjento] *nm* (*declinación*) decline; (*desaliento*) discouragement; (*MED: empeoramiento*) weakening; (: *estado débil*) weakness.

decano, a [de'kano, a] *nm/f* dean.
decapitar [dekapi'tar] *vt* to behead.
decena [de'θena] *nf*: **una** ~ ten (or so).
decencia [de'θenθja] *nf* (*modestia*) modesty; (*honestidad*) respectability.
decente [de'θente] *a* (*correcto*) seemly, proper; (*honesto*) respectable.
decepción [deθep'θjon] *nf* disappointment; **decepcionar** *vt* to disappoint.
decidir [deθi'ðir] *vt* (*persuadir*) to convince, persuade; (*resolver*) to decide // *vi* to decide; ~**se** *vr*: ~**se a** to make up one's mind to.
décimo, a ['deθimo, a] *a* tenth // *nm* tenth.
decir [de'θir] *vt* (*expresar*) to say; (*contar*) to tell; (*hablar*) to speak // *nm* saying; ~**se** *vr*: **se dice que** it is said that; ~ **para/entre sí** to say to o.s.; **querer** ~ to mean.
decisión [deθi'sjon] *nf* (*resolución*) decision; (*firmeza*) decisiveness.
decisivo, a [deθi'sißo, a] *a* decisive.
declamar [dekla'mar] *vt, vi* to declaim.
declaración [deklara'θjon] *nf* (*manifestación*) statement; (*explicación*) explanation; **declarar** *vt* to declare, state; to explain // *vi* to declare; (*JUR*) to testify; **declararse** *vr* to propose.
declinar [dekli'nar] *vt* (*gen*) to decline; (*JUR*) to reject // *vi* (*el día*) to draw to a close; (*salud*) to deteriorate.
declive [de'kliße] *nm* (*cuesta*) slope; (*inclinación*) incline.
decolorarse [dekolo'rarse] *vr* to become discoloured.
decoración [dekora'θjon] *nf* decoration.
decorado [deko'raðo] *nm* scenery, set.
decorar [deko'rar] *vt* to decorate; **decorativo, a** *a* ornamental, decorative.
decoro [de'koro] *nm* (*respeto*) respect; (*dignidad*) decency; (*recato*) decorum, propriety; ~**so, a** *a* (*decente*) decent; (*modesto*) modest; (*digno*) proper.
decrecer [dekre'θer] *vi* to decrease, diminish.
decrépito, a [de'krepito, a] *a* decrepit.
decretar [dekre'tar] *vt* to decree; **decreto** *nm* decree.
dedal [de'ðal] *nm* thimble.
dedicación [deðika'θjon] *nf* dedication; **dedicar** *vt* (*libro*) to dedicate; (*tiempo, dinero*) to devote; (*palabras: decir, consagrar*) to dedicate, devote; **dedicatoria** *nf* (*de libro*) dedication.
dedo ['deðo] *nm* finger; ~ (**del pie**) toe; ~ **pulgar** thumb; ~ **índice** index finger; ~ **mayor** *o* **cordial** middle finger; ~ **anular** ring finger; ~ **meñique** little finger.
deducción [deðuk'θjon] *nf* deduction.
deducir [deðu'θir] *vt* (*concluir*) to deduce, infer; (*COM*) to deduct.
defecto [de'fekto] *nm* defect, flaw; (*ELEC*) fault; **defectuoso, a** *a* defective, faulty.
defender [defen'der] *vt* to defend.
defensa [de'fensa] *nf* defence; (*DEPORTE*)

back; **defensivo, a** a defensive // nf: **a la defensiva** on the defensive.

defensor, a [defen'sor, a] a defending //
nm/f (abogado) defending counsel;
(protector) protector.

deficiencia [defi'θjenθja] nf deficiency;
deficiente a (defectuoso) defective,
(imperfecto) deficient, wanting.

déficit ['defiθit] nm deficit.

definición [defini'θjon] nf definition.

definir [defi'nir] vt (determinar) to
determine, establish; (decidir) to define;
(aclarar) to clarify; **definitivo, a** a
definitive; **en definitiva** definitively.

deformación [deforma'θjon] nf
(alteración) deformation; (distorsión)
distortion.

deformar [defor'mar] vt (gen) to deform;
~se vr to become deformed; **deforme** a
(informe) deformed; (feo) ugly; (mal
hecho) misshapen.

defraudar [defrau'ðar] vt (decepcionar) to
disappoint; (estafar) to cheat, defraud;
(engañar) to deceive.

defunción [defun'θjon] nf decease,
demise.

degeneración [dexenera'θjon] nf (de las
células) degeneration; (moral)
degeneracy; **degenerar** vi to degenerate.

degollar [dexo'ʎar] vt (animal) to
slaughter; (decapitar) to behead,
decapitate.

degradar [dexra'ðar] vt to debase,
degrade; ~se vr to demean o.s.

degüello [de'xweʎo] nm: **entrar a ~** to
slaughter, put to the sword.

degustación [dexusta'θjon] nf sampling,
tasting.

deidad [dei'ðað] nf deity, divinity.

deificar [deifi'kar] vt (persona) to deify.

dejación [dexa'θjon] nf (abandono)
abandonment.

dejadez [dexa'ðeθ] nf (negligencia)
neglect; (descuido) untidiness, carelessness; **dejado, a** a (negligente) careless;
(indolente) lazy.

dejar [de'xar] vt (gen) to leave; (permitir)
to allow, let; (abandonar) to abandon,
forsake; (beneficios) to produce, yield //
vi: ~ **de** (parar) to stop; (no hacer) to fail
to; ~ **a un lado** to leave or set aside.

dejo ['dexo] nm (LING) accent; (sabor
fuerte) tang; (sabor que queda) aftertaste.

del [del] = **de** + **el**, ver **de**.

delantal [delan'tal] nm apron.

delante [de'lante] ad in front; (enfrente)
opposite; (adelante) ahead; ~ **de** in front
of, before.

delantero, a [delan'tero, a] a front // nm
(DEPORTE) forward // nf (de vestido, casa)
front part; (DEPORTE) forward line; **llevar
la ~ a a uno** to be ahead of sb.

delatar [dela'tar] vt to inform on or
against, betray; **delator, a** nm/f informer.

delegación [delexa'θjon] nf delegation;
(COM) office, branch; ~ **de policía** police
station; ~ **municipal** local government

office; **delegado, a** nm/f delegate; (COM)
agent; **delegar** vt to delegate.

deleitar [delei'tar] vt to delight; ~se vr:
~se con o en to delight in, take pleasure
in; **deleite** am delight, pleasure.

deletrear [deletre'ar] vi to spell (out);
(fig) to interpret, decipher; **deletreo** nm
spelling; interpretation, decipherment.

deleznable [deleθ'naβle] a inv (frágil)
fragile; (resbaloso) slippery; (fugaz)
fleeting.

delfín [del'fin] nm dolphin.

delgadez [delxa'ðeθ] nf thinness, slimness;
delgado, a a (gen) thin; (persona) slim,
tain; (tierra) poor; (tela etc) light, delicate.

deliberación [deliβera'θjon] nf
deliberation; **deliberar** vt to debate,
discuss.

delicadeza [delika'ðeθa] nf (gen)
delicacy; (refinamiento, sutileza)
refinement.

delicado, a [deli'kaðo, a] a (gen) delicate;
(sensible) sensitive; (quisquilloso) touchy.

delicia [de'liθja] nf delight.

delicioso, a [deli'θjoso, a] a (gracioso)
delightful; (agreeable; (placentero)
pleasant; (exquisito) delicious.

delincuencia [delin'kwenθja] nf
delinquency; **delincuente** nm/f
delinquent, criminal.

delinquir [delin'kir] vi to commit an
offence.

delirante [deli'rante] a delirious; **delirar**
vi to be delirious, rave.

delirio [de'lirjo] nm (MED) delirium;
(palabras insensatas) wanderings pl,
ravings pl.

delito [de'lito] nm (infracción) offence;
(crimen) crime; ~ **político/común**
political/common crime.

demagogo [dema'voxo] nm demagogue.

demanda [de'manda] nf (pedido, COM)
demand; (petición) request; (JUR) action,
lawsuit; **demandante** nm/f claimant.

demandar [deman'dar] vt (gen) to
demand, (JUR) to sue.

demarcación [demarka'θjon] nf (de
terreno) demarcation; **demarcar** vt to
demarcate.

demás [de'mas] a: los ~ **niños** the other
children, the remaining children // proa:
los/las ~ the others, the rest (of them);
lo ~ the rest (of it) // ad besides.

demasía [dema'sia] nf (exceso) excess,
surplus; (atrevimiento) boldness; (insolencia) outrage; **comer en** ~ to eat to
excess.

demasiado, a [dema'sjaðo, a] a too, too
much; ~s too many // ad too, too much;
¡es ~! it's too much!

demencia [de'menθja] nf (locura)
madness; **demente** nm/f lunatic // a mad,
insane.

democracia [demo'kraθja] nf democracy.

demócrata [de'mokrata] nm/f democrat;
democrático, a a democratic.

demoler [demo'ler] vt to demolish; **demolición** nf demolition.

demonio [de'monjo] nm devil, demon; ¡~s! hell!, confound it!; ¿cómo ~s? how the hell?

demora [de'mora] nf delay; **demorar** vt (retardar) to delay, hold back; (dilatar) to hold up // vi to linger, stay on.

demostración [demostra'θjon] nf (de teorema) demonstration; (de afecto) show, display.

demostrar [demos'trar] vt (probar) to prove; (mostrar) to show; (manifestar) to demonstrate; **demostrativo, a** a demonstrative.

denegar [dene'ɣar] vt (rechazar) to refuse; (JUR) to reject.

denigrar [deni'ɣrar] vt (desacreditar, infamar) to denigrate; (injuriar) to insult.

denominación [denomina'θjon] nf (nombramiento) designation; (clase) denomination.

denotar [deno'tar] vt (indicar) to indicate; (significar) to denote.

densidad [densi'ðað] nf (FÍSICA) density; (fig) thickness.

denso, a ['denso, a] a (apretado) solid; (espeso, pastoso) thick; (fig) heavy.

dentadura [denta'ðura] nf (set of) teeth pl; ~ postiza false teeth pl.

dentera [den'tera] nf (sensación desagradable) the shivers pl, the shudders pl; (envidia) envy, jealousy; (deseo) desire.

dentista [den'tista] nm/f dentist.

dentro ['dentro] ad inside // prep: ~ de in, inside, within; **vayamos a** ~ let's go inside; **mirar por** ~ to look inside; ~ **de tres meses** within three months.

denuedo [de'nweðo] nm boldness, daring.

denuncia [de'nunθja] nf (delación) denunciation; (acusación) accusation; (de accidente) report; **denunciar** vt to report; (delatar) to inform on or against.

departamento [departa'mento] nm (sección administrativa) department, section; (de caja, tren) compartment; (AM: piso) apartment, flat.

dependencia [depen'denθja] nf dependence; (POL) dependency; (COM) office, section.

depender [depen'der] vi: ~ de to depend on.

dependienta [depen'djenta] nf saleswoman, shop assistant; **dependiente** a dependent // nm salesman.

deplorable [deplo'raβle] a deplorable; **deplorar** vt to deplore.

deponer [depo'ner] vt to lay down // vi (JUR) to give evidence; (declarar) to testify.

deportar [depor'tar] vt to deport.

deporte [de'porte] nm sport; **deportista** a sports cpd // nm/f sportsman/woman.

depositante [deposi'tante], **depositador, a** [deposita'ðor, a] nm/f depositor.

depositar [deposi'tar] vt (dinero) to deposit; (mercaderías) to put away, store;

(AM: persona) to confide; ~se vr to settle; ~io, a nm/f trustee.

depósito [de'posito] nm (gen) deposit; (de mercaderías) warehouse, store; (de agua, gasolina etc) tank; ~ de equipajes cloakroom.

depravar [depra'βar] vt to deprave; ~se vr to become depraved.

depreciar [depre'θjar] vt to depreciate, reduce the value of; ~se vr to depreciate, lose value.

depredación [depreða'θjon] nf (saqueo, pillaje) pillage; (malversación) depredation.

depresión [depre'sjon] nf depression.

deprimido, a [depri'miðo, a] a depressed.

deprimir [depri'mir] vt to depress; ~se vr (persona) to become depressed.

depuración [depura'θjon] nf purification; (POL) purge; **depurar** vt to purify; (purgar) to purge.

derecha [de'retʃa] nf right(-hand) side; (POL) right.

derechamente [deretʃa'mente] ad (dirección) straight.

derecho, a [de'retʃo, a] a right, right-hand // nm (privilegio) right; (lado) right(-hand) side; (leyes) law // ad straight, directly; ~s nmpl (de aduana) duty sg; (de autor) royalties; **tener** ~ **a** to have a right to.

deriva [de'riβa] nf: **ir** o **estar a la** ~ to drift, be adrift.

derivación [deriβa'θjon] nf derivation.

derivar [deri'βar] vt (gen) to derive; (desviar) to drift; ~se vr to derive, be derived; to drift.

derramamiento [derrama'mjento] nm (de sangre) shedding; (dispersión) spilling.

derramar [derra'mar] vt to spill; (echar) to pour out; (cispersar) to scatter; ~se vr to pour out; ~ lágrimas to weep.

derrame [de'rrame] nm (de líquido) spilling; (de sangre) shedding; (de tubo etc) overflow; (perdida) loss, leakage; (MED) discharge; (declive) slope.

derredor [derre'ðor] ad: **al** o **en** ~ **de** around, about.

derretido, a [derre'tiðo, a] a melted, molten.

derretir [derre'tir] vt (gen) to melt; (nieve) to thaw; (fig) to squander; ~se vr to melt.

derribar [derri'βar] vt to knock down; (construcción) to demolish; (persona, gobierno, político) to bring down; ~se vr to fall down.

derrocar [derro'kar] vt (despeñar) to demolish, knock down; (gobierno) to bring down, overthrow.

derrochar [derro'tʃar] vt to squander; **derroche** nm (despilfarro) waste, squandering.

derrota [de'rrota] nf (camino, vereda) road, route; (NAUT) course; (MIL) defeat, rout; (fig) disaster; **derrotar** vt (gen) to defeat; (destruir) to ruin; **derrotero** nm (rumbo) course.

derrumbar [derrum'bar] vt to throw down; ~se vr (despeñarse) to collapse; (precipitarse) to throw o.s. down.

desabotonar [desaβoto'nar] vt to unbutton, undo // vi to open out; ~se vr to come undone.

desabrido, a [desa'βriðo, a] a (insípido, soso) insipid, tasteless; (persona) rude, surly; (respuesta) sharp.

desabrochar [desaβro'tʃar] vt (botones, broches) to undo, unfasten; (fig) to expose; ~se vr to confide, unburden o.s.

desacato [desa'kato] nm (falta de respeto) disrespect; (irreverencia) insulting behaviour; (JUR) contempt.

desacertado, a [desaθer'taðo, a] a (equivocado) mistaken; (inoportuno) unwise.

desacertar [desaθer'tar] vi (errar) to be mistaken; (desatinar) to act unwisely.

desacierto [desa'θjerto] nm mistake, error.

desacomodar [desakomo'ðar] vt (molestar) to put out, inconvenience; **desacomodo** nm (incomodidad) inconvenience; (molestia) trouble.

desaconsejado, a [desakonse'xaðo, a] a ill-advised; **desaconsejar** vt to dissuade, advise against.

desacordarse [desakor'ðarse] vr (MUS) to get out of tune; **desacorde** a inv discordant.

desacreditar [desakreði'tar] vt (desprestigiar) to discredit, bring into disrepute; (denigrar) to run down.

desacuerdo [desa'kwerðo] nm (conflicto) discord, disagreement; (error) error, blunder.

desafecto, a [desa'fekto, a] a (opuesto) disaffected // nm (hostilidad) disaffection.

desafiar [desa'fjar] vt (retar) to challenge; (enfrentarse a) to defy.

desafilar [desafi'lar] vt to blunt; ~se vr to become blunt.

desafinado, a [desafi'naðo] a: estar ~ to be out of tune; **desafinarse** vr (MUS) to go out of tune.

desafío [desa'fio] nm (reto) challenge; (combate) duel; (resistencia) defiance; (competencia) competition.

desafortunado, a [desafortu'naðo, a] a (desgraciado) unfortunate, unlucky.

desagradable [desaγra'ðaβle] a (fastidioso, enojoso) unpleasant; (irritante) disagreeable.

desagradar [desaγra'ðar] vi (disgustar) to displease; (molestar) to bother; **desagradecido, a** a ungrateful.

desagrado [desa'γraðo] nm (disgusto) displeasure; (contrariedad) dissatisfaction.

desagraviar [desaγra'βjar] vt to make amends to; **desagravio** nm (recompensa) amends; (: en efectivo) compensation.

desaguadero [desaγwa'ðero] nm drain.

desagüe [des'aγwe] nm (de un líquido) drainage; (cañería) drainpipe.

desaguisado, a [desaγi'saðo, a] a illegal /" nm outrage.

desahogado, a [desao'γaðo, a] a (descarado) brazen, impudent; (holgado) comfortable; (espacioso) roomy.

desahogar [desao'γar] vt (consolar) to console; (aliviar) to ease, relieve; (ira) to vent; ~se vr (extenderse) to take it easy; (desfogarse) to let off steam.

desahogo [desa'oγo] nm (alivio) relief; (comodidad) comfort, ease; (descaro) impudence.

desahuciar [desau'θjar] vt (enfermo) to give up hope for; (inquilino) to evict; **desahucio** nm eviction.

desairado, a [desai'raðo, a] a (menospreciado) disregarded; (desgarbado) shabby.

desairar [desai'rar] vt (menospreciar) to slight, snub; (ultrajar) to dishonour.

desaire [des'aire] nm (afrenta) rebuff; (menosprecio) slight (falta de garbo) unattractiveness, lack of charm.

desajustar [desaxus'tar] vt (desarreglar) to disarrange; (descencertar) to throw off balance; ~se vr to get out of order; (cintura) to loosen.

desajuste [desa'xuste] nm (de máquina) disorder; (situación) imbalance.

desalentador, a [desalenta'ðor, a] a disheartening; **desalentar** vt (desanimar) to discourage; **desalentar** a uno to make sb breathless.

desaliento [desa'ljento] nm discouragement.

desalinear [desaline'ar] vt to throw out of the straight; ~se vr to go off the straight.

desaliño [desa'liŋo] nm (negligencia) slovenliness.

desalmado, a [desal'maðo, a] a (cruel) cruel, heartless.

desalojamiento [desaloxa'mjento] nm ousting; (cambio de residencia) removal; (: forzado) eviction.

desalojar [desalo'xar] vt (expulsar, echar) to eject; (abandonar) to abandon, evacuate // vi to move out.

desamarrar [desama'rrar] vt to untie; (NAUT) to cast off.

desamor [desa'mor] nm (frialdad) indifference; (odio) dislike; (enemistad) enmity.

desamparado, a [desampa'raðo, a] a (persona) helpless (lugar: expuesto) exposed, (desierto) deserted.

desamparar [desampa'rar] vt (abandonar) to desert, abandon (JUR) to leave defenceless; (barco) to abandon.

desandar [desan'dar] vt: ~ lo andado o el camino to retrace one's steps.

desanimado, a [desani'naðo, a] a (persona) downhearted; (espectáculo, fiesta) dull; **desanimar** vt (desalentar) to discourage; (deprimir) to depress.

desapacible [desapa'θiβle] a (gen) unpleasant; (carácter) disagreeable (voz) harsh.

desaparecer [desapare'θer] vt (gen) to hide // vi (gen) to disappear; (el sol, la luz) to vanish; **desaparición** nf disappearance.

desapego [desa'pexo] nm (frialdad) coolness; (distancia) detachment.

desapercibido, a [desaperθi'βiðo, a] a (desprevenido) unprepared; **pasar** ~ to go unnoticed.

desaplicación [desaplika'θjon] nf (negligencia) slackness; (ocio) laziness; **desaplicado, a** a slack; lazy.

desaprensivo, a [desapren'siβo, a] a unscrupulous.

desaprobar [desapro'βar] vt (reprobar) to disapprove of; (condenar) to condemn; (no consentir) to reject.

desaprovechado, a [desaproβe'tʃaðo, a] a (improductivo) unproductive; (atrasado) backward; **desaprovechar** vt to waste.

desarmar [desar'mar] vt (MIL, fig) to disarm; (TEC) to take apart, dismantle; **desarme** nm disarmament.

desarraigar [desarrai'xar] vt to uproot; **desarraigo** nm uprooting.

desarreglado, a [desarre'xlaðo, a] a (TEC) out of order; (desordenado) disorderly, untidy.

desarreglar [desarre'xlar] vt (desordenar) to disarrange; (mecánica) to put out of order; (trastocar) to upset, disturb.

desarreglo [desa'rrexlo] nm (de casa, persona) untidiness; (desorden) disorder.

desarrollar [desarro'ʎar] vt (gen) to develop; (extender) to unfold; ~se vr to develop; (extenderse) to open (out); (film) to develop; **desarrollo** nm development.

desarticular [desartiku'lar] vt (hueso) to put out; (objeto) to take apart; (fig) to break up.

desaseo [desa'seo] nm (suciedad) slovenliness; (desarreglo) untidiness.

desasir [desa'sir] vt to loosen; ~se vr to extricate o.s.; ~se de to let go, give up.

desasosegar [desasose'xar] vt (inquietar) to disturb; (afligir) to make uneasy; ~se vr to become uneasy.

desasosiego [desaso'sjexo] nm (intranquilidad) uneasiness; (aflicción) restlessness; (ansiedad) anxiety.

desastrado, a [desas'traðo, a] a (desaliñado) shabby; (sucio) dirty; (desgraciado, adverso) wretched.

desastre [des'astre] nm disaster; **desastroso, a** a disastrous.

desatado, a [desa'taðo, a] a (desligado) untied; (violento) violent, wild.

desatar [desa'tar] vt (nudo) to untie; (paquete) to undo; (separar) to detach; ~se vr (zapatos) to come untied; (tormenta) to break.

desatender [desaten'der] vt (no prestar atención a) to disregard; (abandonar) to neglect; (invitado) to slight.

desatento, a [desa'tento, a] a (distraído) inattentive; (descortés) discourteous.

desatinado, a [desati'naðo, a] a (disparatado) wild, reckless; (absurdo) foolish, silly; **desatinar** vi (desvariar) to behave foolishly; **desatino** nm (idiotez) foolishness, folly; (error) blunder.

desautorizado, a [desautor'iθaðo, a] a unauthorized; **desautorizar** vt (oficial) to deprive of authority; (informe) to deny.

desavenencia [desaβe'nenθja] nf (desacuerdo) disagreement; (discrepancia) rift, quarrel.

desaventajado, a [desaβenta'xaðo, a] a (inferior) inferior; (poco ventajoso) disadvantageous.

desayunar [desaju'nar] vi to have breakfast // vt to have for breakfast; **desayuno** nm breakfast.

desazón [desa'θon] nf (insipidez) tastelessness; (angustia) anxiety; (fig) annoyance.

desazonar [desaθo'nar] vt to make tasteless; (fig) to annoy, upset; ~se vr (enojarse) to be annoyed; (preocuparse) to worry, be anxious; (MED) to be off colour.

desbandarse [desβan'darse] vr (MIL) to disband; (fig) to flee in disorder.

desbarajuste [desβara'xuste] nm confusion, disorder.

desbaratar [desβara'tar] vt (deshacer, destruir) to ruin; (malgastar) to squander; (mecánica) to take apart.

desbordar [desβor'ðar] vt (exceder) to exceed // vi, ~se vr (río) to overflow; (entusiasmo) to erupt; (persona) to express one's feelings freely.

descabalgar [deskaβal'xar] vi to dismount.

descabellado, a [deskaβe'ʎaðo, a] a (disparatado) wild, crazy; (insensato) ridiculous.

descabellar [deskaβe'ʎar] vt to ruffle; (TAUR: toro) to give the coup de grace to.

descabezar [deskaβe'θar] vt (persona) to behead; (árbol) to lop; ~se vr (AGR) to shed the grain; (fig) to rack one's brains.

descafeinado [deskafei'naðo] nm decaffeinated coffee.

descalabro [deska'laβro] nm blow; (desgracia) misfortune.

descalzar [deskal'θar] vt (zapato) to take off; **descalzo, a** a barefoot(ed); (fig) destitute.

descaminado, a [deskami'naðo, a] a (equivocado) on the wrong road; (fig) misguided.

descaminar [deskami'nar] vt (alguien) to misdirect; (fig) to lead astray; ~se vr (en la ruta) to go the wrong way; (fig) to go astray.

descansado, a [deskan'saðo, a] a (gen) rested; (que tranquiliza) restful; **descansar** vt (gen) to rest // vi to rest, have a rest; (echarse) to lie down.

descanso [des'kanso] nm (reposo) rest; (alivio) relief; (pausa) break; (DEPORTE) interval, half time.

descarado, a [deska'raðo, a] a (sin

vergüenza) shameless; (*insolente*) cheeky.
descararse *vr* to be insolent *or* cheeky.

descarga [des'karɣa] *nf* (ARQ. ELEC. MIL)
discharge; (NAUT) unloading.

descargadero [deskarɣa'ðero] *nm* wharf.

descargar [deskar'ɣar] *vt* to unload;
(*golpe*) to let fly; ~**se** *vr* to unburden o.s.;
descargo *nm* unloading; (COM) receipt;
(JUR) evidence.

descarnado, a [deskar'naðo, a] *a*
scrawny; (*fig*) bare.

descaro [des'karo] *nm* (*atrevimiento*)
shamelessness, nerve; (*insolencia*) cheek.

descarriar [deska'rrjar] *vt* (*descaminar*)
to misdirect; (*fig*) to lead astray; ~**se** *vr*
(*perderse*) to lose one's way; (*separarse*) to
stray; (*pervertirse*) to err, go astray.

descarrilamiento [deskarrila'mjento]
nm (*de tren*) derailment.

descartar [deskar'tar] *vt* (*rechazar*) to
reject; (*poner a un lado*) to set aside;
(*eliminar*) to rule out; ~**se** *vr* (NAIPES) to
discard; ~**se de** to shirk; **descartado, a** *a*
rejected; set aside, eliminated.

descendencia [desθen'denθja] *nf* (*origen*)
origin, descent; (*hijos*) offspring.

descender [desθen'der] *vt* (*bajar-
escalera*) to go down; (: *equipajes*) to take
down // *vi* to descend; (*temperatura, nivel*)
to fall, drop; ~ **de** to be descended from.

descendiente [desθen'djente] *nm/f*
descendant.

descenso [des'θenso] *nm* descent; (*de
temperatura*) drop.

descifrar [desθi'frar] *vt* to decipher.

descolgar [deskol'ɣar] *vt* (*bajar*) to take
down; (*teléfono*) to pick up; ~**se** *vr* to let
o.s. down.

descolorir [deskolo'rir], **descolorar**
[deskolo'rar] *vt* = **decolorar**.

descomedido, a [deskome'ðiðo, a] *a*
(*descortés*) rude; (*excesivo*) excessive.

descompaginar [deskompaxi'nar] *vt*
(*desordenar*) to disarrange, mess up.

descompasado, a [deskompa'saðo, a] *a*
(*sin proporción*) out of all proportion; (*excesivo*) excessive.

descomponer [deskompo'ner] *vt*
(*desordenar*) to disarrange, disturb; (TEC)
to put out of order; (*dividir*) to break down
(into parts); (*fig*) to provoke; ~**se** *vr*
(*corromperse*) to rot, decompose; (*el
tiempo*) to change (for the worse); (TEC) to
break down; (*irritarse*) to lose one's
temper.

descomposición [deskomposi'θjon] *nf*
(*gen*) breakdown; (*de fruta etc*)
decomposition.

descompostura [deskompos'tura] *nf*
(TEC) breakdown; (*desorganización*)
disorganization; (*desorden*) untidiness.

descompuesto, a [deskom'pwesto, a] *a*
(*corrompido*) decomposed; (*roto*) broken;
(*descarado*) brazen; (*furioso*) angry.

desconcertado, a [deskonθer'taðo, a] *a*
disconcerted, bewildered.

desconcertar [deskonθer'tar] *vt*

(*confundir*) to baffle; (*incomodar*) to upset,
put out; (TEC) to put out of order; (ANAT) to
dislocate; ~**se** *vr* (*turbarse*) to be upset.

desconcierto [deskon'θjerto] *nm* (*gen*)
disorder; (*dar*) damage; (*desorientación*)
uncertainty; (*inquietud*) uneasiness.

desconectar [deskonek'tar] *vt* to
disconnect.

desconfianza [deskon'fjanθa] *nf* distrust;
desconfiar *vi* to be distrustful;
desconfiar de to distrust, suspect.

desconocer [deskono'θer] *vt* (*alguien*) to
ignore; (*ignorar*) not to know, be ignorant
of; (*no recordar*) to fail to remember; (*no
aceptar*) to deny; (*repudiar*) to disown.

desconocimiento [deskonoθi'mjento] *nm*
(*falta de conocimientos*) ignorance;
(*repudio*) disregard; (*ingratitud*)
ingratitude.

desconsiderado, a [deskonsiðe'raðo, a] *a*
(*descuidado*) inconsiderate; (*insensible*)
thoughtless.

desconsolar [deskonso'lar] *vt* to distress;
~**se** *vr* to despair.

desconsuelo [deskon'swelo] *nm* (*tristeza*)
distress; (*desesperación*) despair.

descontar [deskon'tar] *vt* (*deducir*) to
take away, deduct; (*rebajar*) to discount;
(*predecir, dar por cierto*) to take for
granted.

descontento, a [deskon'tento, a] *a*
dissatisfied // *nm* dissatisfaction,
discontent.

descorazonar [deskoraθo'nar] *vt* to
discourage, dishearten.

descorchar [deskor'tʃar] *vt* to uncork.

descortés [deskor'tes] *a* (*mal educado*)
discourteous; (*grosero*) rude.

descoser [desko'ser] *vt* to unstitch; ~**se**
vr to come apart (at the seams).

descosido, a [desko'siðo, a] *a* (*costura*)
unstitched; (*indiscreto*) indiscreet; (*desordenado*) disjointed.

descoyuntar [deskojun'tar] *vt* (ANAT) to
dislocate.

descrédito [des'kreðito] *nm* discredit.

descreído, a [deskre'iðo, a] *a* (*incrédulo*)
incredulous; (*falto de fe*) unbelieving.

describir [deskri'βir] *vt* to describe.

descripción [deskrip'θjon] *nf* description.

descrito [des'krito] *pp* de **describir**.

descuajar [deskwa'xar] *vt* (*disolver*) to
melt; (*planta*) to pull out by the roots.

descubierto, a [desku'βjerto, a] *pp* de
descubrir // *a* uncovered, bare; (*persona*)
bareheaded; al ~ in the open.

descubrimiento [deskuβri'mjento] *nm*
(*hallazgo*) discovery; (*revelación*)
revelation.

descubrir [desku'βrir] *vt* to discover, find;
(*inaugurar*) to unveil; (*vislumbrar*) to
detect; (*revelar*) to reveal, show (*quitar la
tapa*) to uncover; ~**se** *vr* to reveal o.s.;
(*quitarse sombrero*) to take off one's hat;
(*confesar*) to confess.

descuento [des'kwento] *nm* discount; ~
jubilatorio retirement pension.

descuidado, a [deskwi'ðaðo, a] *a* (*sin cuidado*) careless; (*desordenado*) untidy; (*olvidadizo*) forgetful; (*dejado*) neglected; (*desprevenido*) unprepared.

descuidar [deskwi'ðar] *vt* (*dejar*) to neglect; (*olvidar*) to overlook // *vi*, ~**se** *vr* (*distraerse*) to be careless; (*estar desaliñado*) to let o.s. go; (*desprevenirse*) to drop one's guard; **¡descuida!** don't worry!; **descuido** *nm* (*dejadez*) carelessness; (*olvido*) negligence.

desde ['desðe] *ad* from; ~ **que** *conj* since; ~ **lejos** from afar; ~ **ahora en adelante** from now onwards; ~ **hace 3 días** for 3 days now; ~ **luego** of course.

desdecirse [desðe'θirse] *vr* (*de promesa*) to go back on one's word.

desdén [des'ðen] *nm* scorn.

desdeñar [desðe'ɲar] *vt* (*despreciar*) to scorn.

desdicha [des'ðitʃa] *nf* (*desgracia*) misfortune; (*infelicidad*) unhappiness; **desdichado, a** *a* (*sin suerte*) unlucky; (*infeliz*) unhappy.

desdoblar [desðo'ßlar] *vt* (*extender*) to spread out; (*desplegar*) to unfold; (*separar en dos*) to split.

desear [dese'ar] *vt* to want, desire, wish for.

desecar [dese'kar] *vt*, ~**se** *vr* to dry up.

desechar [dese'tʃar] *vt* (*basura*) to throw out *or* away; (*ideas*) to reject, discard; **desechos** *nmpl* rubbish *sg*, waste *sg*.

desembalar [desemba'lar] *vt* to unpack.

desembarazado, a [desembara'θaðo, a] *a* (*libre*) clear, free; (*desenvuelto*) free and easy.

desembarazar [desembara'θar] *vt* (*desocupar*) to clear; (*desenredar*) to free; ~**se** *vr*: ~**se de** to free o.s. of, get rid of.

desembarcar [desembar'kar] *vt*, *vi*, ~**se** *vr* to land.

desembocadura [desemboka'ðura] *nf* (*de río*) mouth; (*de calle*) opening.

desembocar [desembo'kar] *vi* to flow into; (*fig*) to result in.

desembolso [desem'bolso] *nm* payment; ~**s** *nmpl* expenses; ~ **inicial** deposit, down payment.

desemejante [deseme'xante] *a* dissimilar, unlike; **desemejanza** *nf* dissimilarity.

desempeñar [desempe'ɲar] *vt* (*cargo*) to hold; (*papel*) to perform; (*lo empeñado*) to redeem; ~**se** *vr* to get out of debt; ~ **un papel** (*fig*) to play (a role).

desempeño [desem'peɲo] *nm* redeeming; (*de cargo*) occupation; (*TEATRO, fig*) performance.

desempleado, a [desemple'aðo, a] *nm/f* unemployed person; **desempleo** *nm* unemployment.

desencadenar [desenkaðe'nar] *vt* to unchain; (*ira*) to unleash; ~**se** *vr* to break loose; (*tormenta*) to burst.

desencajar [desenka'xar] *vt* (*hueso*) to put out of joint; (*mandíbula*) to dislocate;

(*mecanismo, pieza*) to disconnect, disengage.

desencanto [desen'kanto] *nm* disillusionment.

desenfadado, a [desenfa'ðaðo, a] *a* (*desenvuelto*) uninhibited; (*descarado*) forward; **desenfado** *nm* (*libertad*) freedom; (*comportamiento*) free and easy manner; (*descaro*) forwardness.

desenfrenado, a [desenfre'naðo, a] *a* (*descontrolado*) uncontrolled; (*inmoderado*) unbridled; **desenfreno** *nm* (*vicio*) wildness; (*de las pasiones*) lack of self-control.

desengañar [desenga'ɲar] *vt* to disillusion; ~**se** *vr* to become disillusioned; **desengaño** *nm* disillusionment; (*decepción*) disappointment.

desenlace [desen'laθe] *nm* outcome.

desenmarañar [desenmara'ɲar] *vt* (*desenredar*) to disentangle; (*fig*) to unravel.

desenredar [desenre'ðar] *vt* to resolve; (*intriga*) to unravel; ~**se** *vr* to extricate o.s.

desentenderse [desenten'derse] *vr*: ~ **de** to pretend to be ignorant about; (*apartarse*) to have nothing to do with.

desenterrar [desente'rrar] *vt* to exhume; (*tesoro, fig*) to unearth, dig up.

desentrañar [desentra'ɲar] *vt* to disembowel; (*misteric*) to unravel.

desentumecer [desentume'θer] *vt* (*pierna etc*) to stretch; (*DEPORTE*) to loosen up.

desenvoltura [desenßol'tura] *nf* (*libertad, gracia*) ease; (*descaro*) free and easy manner; (*desvergüenza*) forwardness.

desenvolver [desenßol'ßer] *vt* (*paquete*) to unwrap; (*madeja*) to disentangle; (*fig*) to develop; ~**se** *vr* (*desarrollarse*) to unfold, develop; (*arreglárselas*) to extricate o.s.

deseo [de'seo] *nm* desire, wish; ~**so, a** *a*: **estar** ~**so de** to be anxious to.

desequilibrado, a [desekili'ßraðo, a] *a* unbalanced.

desertar [deser'tar] *vi* to desert.

desesperación [desespera'θjon] *nf* (*impaciencia*) desperation, despair; (*irritación*) fury.

desesperar [desespe'rar] *vt* to drive to despair; (*exasperar*) to drive to distraction // *vi*: ~ **de** to despair of; ~**se** *vr* to despair, lose hope.

desestimar [desesti'mar] *vt* (*menospreciar*) to have a low opinion of; (*rechazar*) to reject.

desfachatez [desfatʃa'teθ] *nf* (*insolencia*) impudence; (*descaro*) cheek.

desfalco [des'falko] *nm* embezzlement.

desfallecer [desfaʎe'θer] *vi* (*perder las fuerzas*) to become weak; (*desvanecerse*) to faint.

desfavorable [desfaßo'raßle] *a* unfavourable.

desfigurar [desfiɣu'rar] *vt* (*cara*) to disfigure; (*cuerpo*) to deform.

desfilar [desfi'lar] *vi* to parade; **desfile** *nm* procession.

desgaire [des'xaire] *nm* (*desaliño, desgano*) slovenliness; (*menosprecio*) disdain.

desgajar [desxa'xar] *vt* (*arrancar*) to tear off; (*romper*) to break off; ~**se** *vr* to come off.

desgana [des'xana] *nf* (*falta de apetito*) loss of appetite; (*renuencia*) unwillingness; **desganarse** *vr* to lose one's appetite; (*cansarse*) to become bored.

desgarrar [desxa'rrar] *vt* to tear (up); (*fig*) to shatter; **desgarro** *nm* (*muscular*) tear; (*aflicción*) grief; (*descaro*) impudence.

desgastar [desxas'tar] *vt* (*deteriorar*) to wear away *or* down; (*estropear*) to spoil; ~**se** *vr* to get worn out; **desgaste** *nm* wear (and tear); (*MED*) weakening, decline.

desgracia [des'xraθja] *nf* misfortune; (*accidente*) accident; (*vergüenza*) disgrace; (*contratiempo*) setback; **por** ~ unfortunately.

desgraciado, a [desxra'θjaðo, a] *a* (*infortunado*) unlucky, unfortunate; (*miserable*) wretched; (*infeliz*) miserable; (*feo*) ugly; (*desagradable*) unpleasant.

desgreñado, a [desxre'naðo, a] *a* dishevelled.

deshacer [desa'θer] *vt* (*casa*) to break up; (*dañar*) to damage; (*TEC*) to take apart; (*enemigo*) to defeat; (*diluir*) to melt; (*contrato*) to break; (*intriga*) to solve; ~**se** *vr* (*disolverse*) to melt; (*despedazarse*) to come apart *or* undone; ~**se de** to get rid of; ~**se en lágrimas** to burst into tears.

deshecho, a [des'etʃo, a] *a* undone.

deshelar [dese'lar] *vt* (*cañería*) to thaw; (*heladera*) to defrost.

desheredar [desere'ðar] *vt* to disinherit.

deshielo [des'jelo] *nm* (*de cañería*) thaw; (*de heladera*) defrosting.

deshilar [desi'lar] *vt* (*tela*) to unravel.

deshonesto, a [deso'nesto, a] *a* indecent.

deshonra [des'onra] *nf* (*deshonor*) dishonour; (*vergüenza*) shame; **deshonrar** *vt* to dishonour; (*insultar*) to insult.

deshora [des'ora]: **a** ~ *ad* at the wrong time.

desierto, a [de'sjerto, a] *a* (*casa, calle, negocio*) deserted // *nm* desert.

designar [desiɣ'nar] *vt* (*nombrar*) to designate; (*indicar*) to fix.

designio [de'sixnjo] *nm* (*proyecto*) plan; (*destino*) fate.

desigual [desi'xwal] *a* (*terreno*) uneven; (*lucha etc*) unequal.

desilusión [desilu'sjon] *nf* disappointment, disillusionment; **desilusionar** *vt* to disappoint; **desilusionarse** *vr* to become disillusioned.

desinfectar [desinfek'tar] *vt* to disinfect.

desinflar [desin'flar] *vt* to deflate.

desintegración [desinteɣra'θjon] *nf* disintegration

desinterés [desinte'res] *nm* (*objetividad*) disinterestedness; (*altruismo*) unselfishness.

desistir [desis'tir] *vi* (*renunciar*) to stop, desist.

desleal [desle'al] *a* (*infiel*) disloyal; ~**tad** *nf* disloyalty.

deslenguado, a [deslen'gwaðo, a] *a* (*grosero*) foul-mouthed.

desligar [desli'ɣar] *vt* (*desatar*) to untie, undo; (*separar*) to separate; ~**se** *vr* (*dos personas*) to break up, separate; (*de un compromiso*) to extricate o.s.

desliz [des'liθ] *nm* (*de coche*) skid; (*de persona*) slip, slide; (*fig*) lapse; ~**ar** *vt* to slip, slide; ~**arse** *vr* (*escurrirse: persona*) to slip, slide; (*coche*) to skid; (*aguas mansas*) to flow gently; (*error*) to slip in.

deslucido, a [deslu'θiðo, a] *a* (*gen*) dull; (*torpe*) awkward, graceless; (*marchitado*) tarnished.

deslumbrar [deslum'brar] *vt* to dazzle.

desmán [des'man] *nm* (*exceso*) outrage; (*abuso de poder*) abuse.

desmandarse [desman'darse] *vr* (*abusarse*) to behave badly; (*excederse*) to get out of hand; (*caballo*) to bolt.

desmantelar [desmante'lar] *vt* (*deshacer*) to dismantle; (*casa*) to strip.

desmayado, a [desma'jaðo, a] *a* (*sin sentido*) unconscious; (*carácter*) dull; (*débil*) faint, weak.

desmayar [desma'jar] *vi* to lose heart; ~**se** *vr* (*MED*) to faint; **desmayo** *nm* (*desvanecimiento*) faint; (*sin conciencia*) unconsciousness; (*depresión*) dejection.

desmedido, a [desme'ðiðo, a] *a* excessive; **desmedirse** *vr* to go too far, forget o.s.

desmejorar [desmexo'rar] *vt* (*dañar*) to impair, spoil; (*MED*) to weaken.

desmembrar [desmem'brar] *vt* (*MED*) to dismember; (*fig*) to separate.

desmentir [desmen'tir] *vt* (*contradecir*) to contradict; (*refutar*) to deny // *vi*: ~ **de** to refute; ~**se** *vr* to contradict o.s.

desmenuzar [desmenu'θar] *vt* (*deshacer*) to crumble; (*examinar*) to examine closely.

desmerecer [desmere'θer] *vt* to be unworthy of // *vi* (*deteriorarse*) to deteriorate.

desmesurado, a [desmesu'raðo, a] *a* disproportionate.

desmontar [desmon'tar] *vt* (*deshacer*) to dismantle; (*tierra*) to level // *vi* to dismount.

desmoralizar [desmorali'θar] *vt* to demoralize.

desmoronar [desmoro'nar] *vi* to wear away, erode; ~**se** *vr* (*edificio, dique*) to fall into disrepair; (*sociedad*) to decay; (*economía*) to decline.

desnivel [desni'βel] *nm* (*de terreno*) unevenness; **paso a** ~ (*AUTO*) flyover)

desnudar [desnu'ðar] *vt* (*desvestir*) to

undress; (despojar) to strip; ~se vr (des-
vestirse) to get undressed; **desnudo, a** a
naked // nm/f nude; **desnudo de** devoid
or bereft of.

desobedecer [desoβeðe'θer] vt, vi to
disobey; **desobediencia** nf disobedience.

desocupación [desokupa'θjon] nf (ocio)
leisure; (desempleo) unemployment;
desocupado, a a at leisure; unemployed;
(deshabitado) empty, vacant; **desocupar**
vt to vacate.

desodorante [desoðo'rante] nm
deodorant.

desolación [desola'θjon] nf (lugar)
desolation; (fig) grief; **desolar** vt to ruin,
lay waste; **desolarse** vr to grieve.

desorden [des'orðen] nm confusion;
(político) disorder.

desorganizar [desorvani'θar] vt
(desordenar) to disorganize; (deshacer) to
disrupt.

desorientar [desorjen'tar] vt (extraviar)
to mislead; (confundir, desconcertar) to
confuse; ~se vr (perderse) to lose one's
way.

despabilado, a [despaβi'laðo, a] a
(despierto) wide-awake; (fig) alert, sharp.

despabilar [despaβi'lar] vt (vela) to snuff;
(el ingenio) to sharpen; (fortuna, negocio)
to squander // vi, ~se vr to wake up.

despacio [des'paθjo] ad slowly.

despachar [despa'tʃar] vt (negocio) to do,
complete; (enviar) to send, dispatch;
(vender) to sell, deal in; (billete) to issue;
(mandar ir) to send away.

despacho [des'patʃo] nm (oficina) office;
(de paquetes) dispatch; (venta) sale;
(comunicación) message; (eficacia)
efficiency; (rapidez) promptness.

desparramar [desparra'mar] vt
(esparcir) to scatter; (noticia) to spread;
(dinero, fortuna) to squander; (líquido) to
spill.

despavorido, a [despaβo'riðo, a] a
terrified.

despectivo, a [despek'tiβo, a] a
(despreciativo) derogatory; (LING)
pejorative.

despecho [des'petʃo] nm spite; a ~ de in
spite of.

despedazar [despeða'θar] vt to tear to
pieces.

despedida [despe'ðiða] nf (adios)
farewell; (de obrero) sacking.

despedir [despe'ðir] vt (visita) to see off,
show out; (licenciar: empleado) to
discharge; (inquilino) to evict; (objeto) to
hurl; (flecha) to fire; (olor etc) to give out
or off; ~se vr: ~se de to say goodbye to.

despegar [despe'var] vt to unstick // vi to
take off; ~se vr to come loose, come
unstuck; **despego** nm detachment.

despegue [des'peve] nm takeoff.

despeinado, a [despei'naðo, a] a
dishevelled, unkempt.

despejado, a [despe'xaðo, a] a (lugar)

clear, free; (cielo) cloudless, clear; (persona) wide-awake.

despejar [despe'xar] vt (gen) to clear;
(misterio) to clarify, clear up // vi (el
tiempo) to clear; ~se vr (tiempo, cielo) to
clear (up); (misterio) to become clearer;
(persona) to relax.

despejo [des'pexo] nm (de casa, calle etc)
brightness; (desenvoltura) self-confidence;
(talento, ingenio) alertness.

despensa [des'pensa] nf larder.

despeñadero [despeɲa'ðero] nm (GEO)
cliff, precipice.

desperdicio [desper'ðiθjo] nm
(despilfarro) squandering; (residuo) waste.

desperezarse [despere'θarse] vr to
stretch (o.s.).

desperfecto [desper'fekto] nm (deterioro)
slight damage; (defecto) flaw,
imperfection.

despertador [desperta'ðor] nm alarm
clock.

despertar [desper'tar] vt (persona) to
wake up; (vocación) to awaken;
(recuerdos) to revive; (apetito) to arouse
// vi, ~se vr to awaken, wake up // nm
awakening.

despido [des'piðo] nm dismissal, sacking.

despierto etc vb ver **despertar.**

despierto, a [des'pjerto, a] a awake; (fig)
sharp, alert.

despilfarro [despil'farro] nm (derroche)
squandering; (lujo desmedido) extravagance.

despistar [despis'tar] vt to throw off the
track or scent; (fig) to mislead, confuse;
~se vr to take the wrong road; (fig) to
become confused.

desplazamiento [desplaθa'mjento] nm
displacement; ~ de tierras landslip.

desplegar [desple'var] vt (tela, papel) to
unfold, open out; (bandera) to unfurl.

despoblar [despo'βlar] vt (de gente) to
depopulate.

despojar [despo'xar] vt (alguien: de sus bienes) to divest of, deprive of; (casa) to strip,
leave bare; (alguien: de su cargo) to strip
of; **despojo** nm (acto) plundering; (objetos)
plunder, loot; **despojos** nmpl waste sg;
(rocas, ladrillos) debris sg.

desposado, a [despo'saðo, a] a, nm/f
newly-wed.

desposeer [despose'er] vt (despojar) to
dispossess.

déspota ['despota] nm despot.

despreciar [despre'θjar] vt (desdeñar) to
despise, scorn; (afrentar) to slight;
desprecio nm scorn, contempt; slight.

desprender [despren'der] vt (separar) to
separate; (desatar) to unfasten; (olor) to
give off; ~se vr (botón: caerse) to fall off;
(: abrirse) to unfasten; (olor, perfume) to be
given off; ~se de to follow from; **se**
desprende que it transpires that.

desprendimiento [desprendi'mjento] nm
(gen) loosening; (de botón que se cae)
detachment; (de botón que se abre)

unfastening; (generosidad) disinterestedness; (indiferencia) detachment; (de gas) release; (de tierra, rocas) landslide.

despreocupado, a [despreoku'paðo, a] a (sin preocupación) unworried, nonchalant; (desprejuiciado) impartial; (negligente) careless; **despreocuparse** vr to be carefree; **despreocuparse de** to have no interest in.

desprevenido, a [despreβe'niðo, a] a (no preparado) unprepared, unready.

desproporción [despropor'θjon] nf disproportion, lack of proportion.

después [des'pwes] ad afterwards, later; (próximo paso) next; ~ **de comer** after lunch; **un año** ~ a year later; ~ **se debatió el tema** next the matter was discussed; ~ **de corregido el texto** after the text had been corrected; ~ **de todo** after all.

desquite [des'kite] nm (satisfacción) satisfaction; (venganza) revenge.

destacar [desta'kar] vt to emphasize, point up; (MIL) to detach, detail // vi, ~ **se** vr (resaltarse) to stand out; (persona) to be outstanding or exceptional.

destajo [des'taxo] nm: **trabajar a** ~ to do piecework.

destapar [desta'par] vt (gen) to open; (cacerola) to take the lid off, uncover; ~ **se** vr (revelarse) to reveal one's true character.

destartalado, a [destarta'laðo, a] a (desordenado) untidy; (ruinoso) tumbledown.

destello [des'teʎo] nm (de estrella) twinkle; (de faro) signal light.

destemplado, a [destem'plaðo, a] a (MUS) out of tune; (voz) harsh; (MED) out of sorts, indisposed.

desteñir [deste'ɲir] vt to fade // vi, ~ **se** vr (color) to fade; **esta tela no destiñe** this fabric will not run.

desterrar [deste'rrar] vt (exilar) to exile (fig) to banish, dismiss.

destierro [des'tjerro] nm exile.

destilación [destila'θjon] nf distillation; **destilar** vt to distil; **destilería** nf distillery.

destinar [desti'nar] vt to destine; (funcionario) to appoint, assign; (fondos) to set aside (a for); ~ **se** vr to be destined.

destinatario, a [destina'tarjo, a] nm/f addressee.

destino [des'tino] nm (suerte) destiny; (de viajero) destination; (función) use.

destituir [destitu'ir] vt to dismiss.

destornillador [destorniʎa'ðor] nm screwdriver; **destornillar** vt, **destornillarse** vr (tornillo) to unscrew.

destreza [des'treθa] nf (habilidad) skill; (maña) dexterity; (facilidad) handiness.

destrozar [destro'θar] vt (romper) to smash, break (up); (estropear) to ruin; (deshacer) to shatter; (el corazón) to break.

destrozo [des'troθo] nm (acción)

destruction; (desastre) smashing; ~**s** nmpl (pedazos) pieces; (daños) havoc sg.

destrucción [destruk'θjon] nf destruction.

destruir [destru'ir] vt to destroy.

desunir [desu'nir] vt to separate; (TEC) to disconnect; (fig) to cause a quarrel or rift between.

desusado, a [desu'saðo, a] a (anticuado) obsolete.

desvalido, a [desβa'liðo, a] a (desprotegido) destitute; (POL) underprivilegec; (sin fuerzas) helpless.

desván [des'βan] nm attic.

desvanecer [desβane'θer] vt (disipar) to dispel; (borrar) to blur; ~ **se** vr (humo) to vanish, disappear; (color) to fade; (recuerdo) to fade away.

desvanecimiento [desβaneθi'mjento] nm (desaparición) disappearance; (de colores) fading; (evaporación) evaporation; (MED) fainting fit.

desvariar [desβa'rjar] vi (enfermo) to be delirious; **desvarío** nm delirium.

desvelar [desβe'lar] vt to keep awake; ~ **se** vr to stay awake; (fig) to be vigilant or watchful; **desvelo** nm lack of sleep; (insomnio) sleeplessness; (fig) vigilance.

desventaja [desβen'taxa] nf disadvantage.

desventura [desβen'tura] nf misfortune.

desvergonzado, a [desβerɣon'θaðo, a] a shameless.

desvergüenza [desβer'ɣwenθa] nf (descaro) shamelessness; (insolencia) impudence; (mala conducta) effrontery.

desviación [desβja'θjon] nf deviation.

desviar [des'βjar] vt to turn aside; (río) to alter the course of; (navío) to divert, reroute; (conversación) to sidetrack; ~ **se** vr (apartarse del camino) to turn aside, deviate; (: barco) to go off course.

desvío [des'βio] nm (desviación) detour, diversion; (fig) indifference.

desvirtuar [desβir'twar] vt, ~ **se** vr to spoil.

desvivirse [desβi'βirse] vr: ~ **por** to long for, crave for.

detallar [deta'ʎar] vt to detail; (COM) to sell retail.

detalle [de'taʎe] nm detail; (fig) gesture, token; **al** ~ in detail.

detallista [deta'ʎista] nm/f retailer.

detener [dete'ner] vt (tren, persona) to stop (JUR) to arrest; (objeto) to keep; ~ **se** vr to stop; (demorarse) ~ **se en** to delay over, linger over.

detenido, a [dete'niðo, a] a (preso) arrested, under arrest; (minucioso) detailed; (tímido) timid // nm/f person under arrest, prisoner.

detergente [deter'xente] nm detergent.

deteriorar [deterjo'rar] vt to spoil, damage; ~ **se** vr to deteriorate; (relaciones) to become damaged; **deterioro** nm deterioration.

determinación [determina'θjon] nf (empeño) determination; (decisión) decision; **determinar** vt (*plazo*) to fix; (*precio*) to settle; **determinarse** vr to decide.

detestar [detes'tar] vt to detest.

detonar [deto'nar] vi to detonate.

detrás [de'tras] ad behind; (*atrás*) at the back; ~ **de** behind.

detrimento [detri'mento] nm harm, damage; **en** ~ **de** to the detriment of.

deuda ['deuða] nf (*condición*) indebtedness, debt; (*cantidad*) debt.

deudor, a [deu'ðor, a] a: **saldo** ~ debit balance // nm/f debtor.

devaluación [deßalwa'θjon] nf devaluation.

devastar [deßas'tar] vt (*destruir*) to devastate.

devoción [deßo'θjon] nf devotion.

devolución [deßolu'θjon] nf devolution; (*reenvío*) return, sending back; (*reembolso*) repayment.

devolver [deßol'ßer] vt (*gen*) to return; (*carta al correo*) to send back; (*COM*) to repay, refund; (*visita, la palabra*) to return.

devorar [deßo'rar] vt to devour.

devoto, a [de'ßoto, a] a devout // nm/f admirer.

di vb ver **dar; decir**.

día ['dia] nm day; ¿**qué** ~ **es?** what's the date?; **estar/poner al** ~ to be/keep up to date; **el** ~ **de hoy/de mañana** today/tomorrow; **al** ~ **siguiente** on the following day; **vivir al** ~ to live from hand to mouth; **de** ~ by day, in daylight; **en pleno** ~ in full daylight.

diablo ['djaßlo] nm devil; **diablura** nf prank; **diabluras** nfpl mischief sg.

diabólico, a [dja'ßoliko, a] a diabolical.

diafragma [dja'fraxma] nm diaphragm.

diagnosis [djax'nosis] nf, **diagnóstico** [djax'nostiko] nm diagnosis.

dialecto [dja'lekto] nm dialect.

diálogo ['djaloxo] nm dialogue.

diamante [dja'mante] nm diamond.

diapositiva [djaposi'tißa] nf (*FOTO*) slide, transparency.

diario, a ['djarjo, a] a daily // nm newspaper.

diarrea [dja'rrea] nf diarrhoea.

dibujar [dißu'xar] vt to draw, sketch; **dibujo** nm drawing; **dibujos animados** cartoons.

diccionario [dikθjo'narjo] nm dictionary.

dice etc vb ver **decir**.

diciembre [di'θjembre] nm December.

dictado [dik'taðo] nm dictation.

dictador [dikta'ðor] nm dictator; **dictadura** nf dictatorship.

dictamen [dik'tamen] nm (*opinión*) opinion; (*juicio*) judgment.

dicho, a ['ditʃo, a] pp de **decir** // a: **en** ~**s países** in the aforementioned countries // nm saying // nf happiness.

diente ['djente] nm (*ANAT, TEC*) tooth; (*ZOOL*) fang; (: *de elefante*) tusk; (*de ajo*) clove; **da** ~ **con** ~ his teeth are

chattering; **hablar entre** ~**s** to mutter, mumble.

dieron vb ver **dar**.

diesel ['disel] a: **motor** ~ diesel engine.

dieta ['djeta] nf diet.

diez [djeθ] num ten.

diferencia [dife'renθja] nf difference; **diferenciar** vt to differentiate between // vi to differ; **diferenciarse** vr to differ, be different; (*distinguirse*) to distinguish o.s.

diferente [dife'rente] a different.

difícil [di'fiθil] a difficult.

dificultad [difikul'taθ] nf difficulty; (*problema*) trouble.

dificultar [difikul'tar] vt (*complicar*) to complicate, make difficult; (*estorbar*) to obstruct.

difundir [difun'dir] vt (*esparcir*) to spread, diffuse; (*divulgar*) to divulge; ~**se** vr to spread (out).

difunto, a [di'funto, a] a dead, deceased // nm/f deceased (person).

digerir [dixe'rir] vt to digest; (*fig*) to absorb.

digital [dixi'tal] a digital.

dignarse [dix'narse] vr to deign to.

dignidad [dixni'ðað] nf dignity; (*honra*) honour.

digno, a ['dixno, a] a worthy.

digo etc vb ver **decir**.

dije etc vb ver **decir**.

dilatación [dilata'θjon] nf (*expansión*) dilation.

dilatado, a [dila'taðo, a] a dilated; (*ancho*) widened; (*largo*) long drawn-out; (*extenso*) extensive.

dilatar [dila'tar] vt (*cuerpo*) to dilate; (*prolongar*) to stretch; (*en el tiempo*) to prolong.

dilema [di'lema] nm dilemma.

diligencia [dili'xenθja] nf diligence; (*ocupación*) errand, job; ~**s** nfpl (*JUR*) formalities; **diligente** a diligent.

diluir [dilu'ir] vt to dilute.

diluvio [di'lußjo] nm deluge, flood.

dimensión [dimen'sjon] nf dimension.

diminuto, a [dimi'nuto, a] a tiny.

dimitir [dimi'tir] vi to resign.

dimos vb ver **dar**.

Dinamarca [dina'marka] nf Denmark; **dinamarqués, esa** a Danish // nm/f Dane.

dinámico, a [di'namiko, a] a dynamic.

dinamita [dina'mita] nf dynamite.

dínamo ['dinamo] nf dynamo.

dineral [dine'ral] nm large sum of money, fortune.

dinero [di'nero] nm money; ~ **efectivo** cash, ready cash.

dio vb ver **dar**.

dios [djos] nm god.

diosa ['djosa] nf goddess.

diplomacia [diplo'maθja] nf diplomacy; (*fig*) tact; **diplomático, a** a diplomatic // nm/f diplomat.

diputado, a [dipu'taðo, a] *nm/f* delegate; (*Cortes*) deputy.

diré *etc vb ver* **decir.**

dirección [direk'θjon] *nf* direction; (*señas*) address; (*AUTO*) steering; (*gerencia*) management; (*POL*) leadership; ~ **única** *o* **obligatoria** *o* **prohibida** one-way.

directo, a [di'rekto, a] *a* direct; **transmitir en** ~ to broadcast live.

director, a [direk'tor, a] *a* leading // *nm/f* director; ~ **de cine/de escena** producer/stage manager.

dirigir [diri'xir] *vt* to direct; (*carta*) to address; (*obra de teatro, film*) to produce, direct; (*coche, barco*) to steer; (*avión*) to fly; (*MUS*) to conduct; (*comercio*) to manage; ~**se a** vr: ~**se a** to go towards, make one's way towards; (*fig*) to speak to.

discernir [disθer'nir] *vt* (*distinguir, discriminar*) to discern.

disciplina [disθi'plina] *nf* discipline; **disciplinar** *vt* to discipline.

discípulo, a [dis'θipulo, a] *nm/f* disciple.

disco ['disko] *nm* disc; (*DEPORTE*) discus; (*TELEC*) dial; (*AUTO*) signal; (*fam*) boring affair; ~ **de larga duración/de duración extendida** long-playing record (L.P.)/extended play record (E.P.); ~ **de freno** brake disc.

discordia [dis'korðja] *nf* discord.

discoteca [disko'teka] *nf* discotheque.

discreción [diskre'θjon] *nf* discretion; (*reserva*) prudence; (*secreto*) secrecy; **comer a** ~ to eat as much as one wishes; **discrecional** *a* (*facultativo*) discretionary.

discrepancia [diskre'panθja] *nf* (*diferencia*) discrepancy; (*desacuerdo*) disagreement.

discreto, a [dis'kreto, a] *a* (*diplomático*) discreet; (*sensato*) sensible; (*listo*) shrewd; (*reservado*) quiet; (*sobrio*) sober; (*retraído*) unobtrusive; (*razonable*) reasonable.

discriminación [diskrimina'θjon] *nf* discrimination.

disculpa [dis'kulpa] *nf* excuse; (*pedir perdón*) apology; **disculpar** *vt* to excuse, pardon; **disculparse** *vr* to excuse o.s.; to apologize.

discurrir [disku'rrir] *vt* to invent // *vi* (*pensar, reflexionar*) to think, meditate; (*recorrer*) to roam, wander; (*el tiempo*) to pass, flow by.

discurso [dis'kurso] *nm* speech; (*razonamiento*) reasoning power.

discutir [disku'tir] *vt* (*debatir*) to discuss; (*pelear*) to argue about; (*contradecir*) to contradict.

diseminar [disemi'nar] *vt* to disseminate, spread.

diseño [di'seɲo] *nm* (*dibujo*) design.

disfraz [dis'fraθ] *nm* (*máscara*) disguise; (*excusa*) pretext; ~**ar** *vt* to disguise; ~**arse** *vr*: ~**arse de** to disguise o.s. as.

disfrutar [disfru'tar] *vt* to enjoy // *vi* to enjoy o.s.; ~ **de** to enjoy, possess.

disgustar [disɣus'tar] *vt* (*no gustar*) to displease; (*contrariar, enojar*) to annoy,

upset; ~**se** *vr* to be annoyed; (*dos personas*) to fall out.

disgusto [dis'ɣusto] *nm* (*repugnancia*) disgust; (*contrariedad*) annoyance; (*tristeza*) grief; (*riña*) quarrel; (*avería*) misfortune.

disidente [disi'ðente] *nm* dissident.

disimular [disimu'lar] *vt* (*ocultar*) to hide, conceal; (*perdonar*) to excuse // *vi* to dissemble.

disipar [disi'par] *vt* to dispel; (*fortuna*) to squander; ~**se** *vr* (*nubes*) to vanish; (*indisciplinarse*) to dissipate.

disminución [disminu'θjon] *nf* diminution.

disminuir [disminu'ir] *vt* (*acortar*) to decrease; (*achicar*) to diminish; (*estrechar*) to lessen.

disoluto, a [diso'luto, a] *a* dissolute.

disolver [disol'βer] *vt* (*gen*) to dissolve; ~**se** *vr* to be dissolved.

disparar [dispa'rar] *vt*, *vi* to shoot, fire.

disparate [dispa'rate] *nm* (*tontería*) foolish remark; (*error*) blunder.

disparo [dis'paro] *nm* shot.

dispensar [dispen'sar] *vt* to dispense; (*disculpar*) to excuse.

dispersar [disper'sar] *vt* to disperse; ~**se** *vr* to scatter.

disponer [dispo'ner] *vt* (*arreglar*) to arrange; (*ordenar*) to put in order; (*preparar*) to prepare, get ready // *vi*: ~ **de** to have, own; ~**se** *vr*: ~**se para** to prepare to, prepare for.

disponible [dispo'niβle] *a* available.

disposición [disposi'θjon] *nf* arrangement, disposition; (*aptitud*) aptitude; **a la** ~ **de** at the disposal of.

dispuesto, a [dis'pwesto, a] *pp de* **disponer** // *a* (*arreglado*) arranged; (*preparado*) disposed.

disputar [dispu'tar] *vt* (*discutir*) to dispute, question; (*contender*) to contend for // *vi* to argue.

distanciar [distan'θjar] *vt* to space out; ~**se** *vr* to become estranged.

distante [dis'tante] *a* distant.

diste, disteis *vb ver* **dar.**

distinción [distin'θjon] *nf* (*gen*) distinction; (*claridad*) clarity; (*elegancia*) elegance; (*honor*) honour.

distinguir [distin'ɡir] *vt* to distinguish; (*escoger*) to single out; ~**se** *vr* to be distinguished.

distinto, a [dis'tinto, a] *a* different; (*claro*) clear.

distracción [distrak'θjon] *nf* (*pasatiempo*) hobby, pastime; (*olvido*) absent-mindedness, distraction.

distraer [distra'er] *vt* (*entretener*) to entertain; (*divertir*) to amuse; (*fondos*) to embezzle; ~**se** *vr* (*entretenerse*) to amuse o.s.; (*perder la concentración*) to allow one's attention to wander.

distraído, a [distra'iðo, a] *a* (*gen*) absent-minded; (*entretenido*) amusing.

distribuir [distriβu'ir] *vt* to distribute.

distrito [dis'trito] *nm* (*sector, territorio*) region; (*barrio*) district.
disturbio [dis'turβjo] *nm* disturbance.
disuadir [diswa'ðir] *vt* to dissuade.
disuelto [di'swelto] *pp de* **disolver.**
divagar [diβa'xar] *vi* (*desviarse*) to digress; (*errar*) to wander.
diván [di'βan] *nm* divan.
divergencia [diβer'xenθja] *nf* divergence.
diversidad [diβersi'ðað] *nf* diversity, variety.
diversificar [diβersifi'kar] *vt* to diversify.
diversión [diβer'sjon] *nf* (*gen*) entertainment; (*actividad*) hobby, pastime.
diverso, a [di'βerso, a] *a* diverse; ~s sundry.
divertir [diβer'tir] *vt* (*entretener, recrear*) to amuse, entertain; (*apartar, distraer*) to divert; ~se *vr* (*pasarlo bien*) to have a good time; (*distraerse*) to amuse o.s.
dividir [diβi'ðir] *vt* (*gen*) to divide; (*separar*) to separate; (*distribuir*) to distribute, share out.
divino, a [di'βino, a] *a* divine.
divisa [di'βisa] *nf* (*emblema, moneda*) emblem, badge; ~s *nfpl* currency *sg.*
división [diβi'sjon] *nf* (*gen*) division; (*de partido*) split; (*de país*) partition; (*LING*) hyphen; (*divergencia*) divergence.
divorciar [diβor'θjar] *vt* to divorce; ~se *vr* to get divorced; **divorcio** *nm* divorce.
divulgar [diβul'xar] *vt* (*desparramar*) to spread; (*hacer circular*) to divulge, circulate; ~se *vr* to leak out.
doblar [do'βlar] *vt* (*gen*) to double; (*papel*) to fold; (*caño*) to bend; (*la esquina*) to turn, go round; (*film*) to dub // *vi* to turn; (*campana*) to toll; ~se *vr* (*plegarse*) to fold (up), crease; (*encorvarse*) to bend; ~se de risa/dolor to be doubled up with laughter/pain.
doble ['doβle] *a* (*gen*) double; (*de dos aspectos*) dual; (*fig*) two-faced // *nm* double; (*campana*) toll(ing); ~s *nmpl* (*DEPORTE*) doubles *sg* // *nm/f* (*TEATRO*) double, stand-in; con ~ sentido with a double meaning.
doce ['doθe] *num* twelve.
docena [do'θena] *nf* dozen.
dócil ['doθil] *a* (*pasivo*) docile; (*obediente*) obedient.
doctor, a [dok'tor, a] *nm/f* doctor.
doctrina [dok'trina] *nf* doctrine, teaching.
documentación [dokumenta'θjon] *nf* documentation, papers *pl.*
documento [doku'mento] *nm* (*certificado*) document.
dólar ['dolar] *nm* dollar.
doler [do'ler] *vt, vi* to hurt; (*fig*) to grieve; ~se *vr* (*de su situación*) to grieve, feel sorry; (*de las desgracias ajenas*) to sympathize; me duele el brazo my arm hurts.
dolor [do'lor] *nm* pain; (*fig*) grief, sorrow.

domar [do'mar], **domesticar** [domesti-'kar] *vt* to tame.
domicilio [domi'θiljo] *nm* home; ~ particular private residence; ~ social head office.
dominante [domi'nante] *a* dominant; (*person*) domineering.
dominar [domi'nar] *vt* (*gen*) to dominate; (*idiomas etc*) to have a command of // *vi* to dominate, prevail; ~se *vr* to control o.s.
domingo [do'mingo] *nm* Sunday.
dominio [do'minjo] *nm* (*tierras*) domain; (*autoridad*) power, authority; (*de las pasiones*) grip, hold; (*de varios idiomas*) command.
don [don] *nm* (*talento*) gift; ~ Juan Gómez Mr Juan Gomez *or* Juan Gomez Esq.
donaire [do'naire] *nm* charm.
doncella [don'θeʎa] *nf* (*criada*) maid; (*muchacha*) girl.
donde ['donde] *ad* where // *prep*: el coche está allí ~ el farol the car is over there by the lamppost *or* where the lamppost is; por ~ through which; en ~ where, in which.
dónde ['donde] *ad interr* where?; ¿a ~ vas? where are you going (to)?; ¿de ~ vienes? where have you come from?; ¿por ~? where?, whereabouts?
dondequiera [donde'kjera] *ad* anywhere; por ~ everywhere, all over the place // *conj*: ~ que wherever.
doña ['doɲa] *nf* título de mujer que no se traduce.
dorado, a [do'raðo, a] *a* (*color*) golden; (*TEC*) gilt.
dormir [dor'mir] *vt*: ~ la siesta por la tarde to have an afternoon nap // *vi* to sleep; ~se *vr* to go to sleep.
dormitar [dormi'tar] *vi* to doze.
dormitorio [dormi'torjo] *nm* bedroom; ~ común dormitory.
dos [dos] *num* two.
dosis ['dosis] *nf inv* dose, dosage.
dotado, a [do'taðo, a] *a* (*gifted*) gifted; ~ de endowed with.
dotar [do'tar] *vt* to endow; dote *nf* dowry; dotes *nfpl* gifts.
doy *vb ver* **dar.**
drama ['drama] *nm* drama.
dramaturgo [drama'turxo] *nm* dramatist, playwright.
droga ['droxa] *nf* drug.
drogadicto, a [droxa'ðikto, a] *nm/f* drug addict.
ducha ['dutʃa] *nf* (*baño*) shower; (*MED*) douche; **ducharse** *vr* to take a shower.
duda ['duða] *nf* doubt.
dudoso, a [du'ðoso, a] *a* (*incierto*) hesitant; (*sospechoso*) doubtful.
duelo ['dwelo] *nm* (*combate*) duel; (*luto*) mourning.
duende ['dwende] *nm* imp, goblin.
dueño, a ['dweɲo, a] *nm/f* (*propietario*)

owner; *(de casa)* landlord/lady; *(empresario)* employer.

duermo *etc vb ver* **dormir.**

dulce ['dulθe] *a* sweet // *ad* gently, softly // *nm* sweet.

dulzura [dul'θura] *nf* sweetness; *(ternura)* gentleness.

duplicar [dupli'kar] *vt (hacer el doble de)* to duplicate; ~**se** *vr* to double.

duque ['duke] *nm* duke.

duquesa [du'kesa] *nf* duchess.

duración [dura'θjon] *nf* duration.

duradero, a [dura'ðero, a] *a* lasting.

durante [du'rante] *ad* during.

durar [du'rar] *vi (permanecer)* to last; *(recuerdo)* to remain.

dureza [du're θa] *nf (calidad)* hardness.

durmí *etc vb ver* **dormir.**

durmiente [dur'mjente] *nm/f* sleeper.

duro, a ['duro, a] *a (gen)* hard; *(carácter)* tough // *ad* hard // *nm (moneda)* five peseta coin/note.

E

e [e] *conj* and.

E *abr de* **este.**

ebanista [eβa'nista] *nm* cabinetmaker.

ébano ['eβano] *nm* ebony.

ebrio, a ['eβrjo, a] *a* drunk.

ebullición [eβuʎi'θjon] *nf* boiling; *(fig)* ferment.

eclesiástico, a [ekle'sjastiko, a] *a* ecclesiastical.

eclipse [e'klipse] *nm* eclipse.

eco ['eko] *nm* echo; **tener** ~ to catch on.

ecología [ekolo'xia] *nf* ecology.

economato [ekono'mato] *nm* cooperative store.

economía [ekono'mia] *nf (sistema)* economy; *(cualidad)* thrift.

económico, a [eko'nomiko, a] *a (barato)* cheap, economical; *(persona)* thrifty; *(COM. plan)* financial; *(: situación)* economic.

economista [ekono'mista] *nm/f* economist.

ecuador [ekwa'ðor] *nm* equator; **el E**~ Ecuador.

ecuánime [e'kwanime] *a (carácter)* level-headed; *(estado)* calm.

ecuestre [e'kwestre] *a* equestrian.

echar [e'tʃar] *vt* to throw; *(agua, vino)* to pour (out); *(empleado: despedir)* to fire, sack; *(bigotes)* to grow; *(hojas)* to sprout; *(cartas)* to post; *(humo)* to emit, give out // *vi*: ~ **a correr/llorar** to break into a run/burst into tears; ~**se** *vr* to lie down; ~ **llave a** to lock (up); ~ **abajo** *(gobierno)* to overthrow; *(edificio)* to demolish; ~ **mano a** to lay hands on.

edad [e'ðað] *nf* age; ¿**qué** ~ **tienes?** how old are you?; **tiene ocho años de** ~ he is eight (years old); **de** ~ **mediana/avanzada** middle-aged/ advanced in years; **la E**~ **Media** the Middle Ages.

edición [eði'θjon] *nf (acto)* publication; *(ejemplar)* edition.

edicto [e'ðikto] *nm* edict, proclamation.

edificio [eði'fiθjo] *nm* building; *(fig)* edifice, structure.

editar [eði'tar] *vt (publicar)* to publish; *(preparar textos)* to edit.

editor, a [eði'tor, a] *nm/f (que publica)* publisher; *(de periódico etc)* editor // *a*: **casa** ~**a** publishing house; ~**ial** *a* editorial // *nm* leading article, editorial; **casa** ~**ial** publishing house.

educación [eðuka'θjon] *nf* education; *(crianza)* upbringing; *(modales)* (good) manners *pl.*

educar [eðu'kar] *vt* to educate; *(criar)* to bring up; *(voz)* to train.

EE. UU. *nmpl abr de* **Estados Unidos** USA (United States of America).

efectivo, a [efek'tiβo, a] *a* effective; *(real)* actual, real // *nm*: **pagar en** ~ to pay (in) cash; **hacer** ~ **un cheque** to cash a cheque.

efecto [e'fekto] *nm* effect, result; ~**s** *nmpl* goods; *(COM)* assets; **en** ~ in fact; *(respuesta)* exactly, indeed.

efectuar [efek'twar] *vt* to carry out; *(viaje)* to make.

eficacia [efi'kaθja] *nf (de persona)* efficiency; *(de medicamento)* effectiveness.

eficaz [efi'kaθ] *a (persona)* efficient; *(acción)* effective.

egipcio, a [e'xipθjo, a] *a, nm/f* Egyptian.

Egipto [e'xipto] *nm* Egypt.

egoísmo [exo'ismo] *nm* egoism.

egoísta [exo'ista] *a* egoistical, selfish // *nm/f* egoist.

egregio, a [e'xrexjo, a] *a* eminent, distinguished.

Eire ['eire] *nm* Eire.

ej. *abr de* **ejemplo.**

eje ['exe] *nm (GEO, MAT)* axis; *(de rueda)* axle; *(de máquina)* shaft, spindle; **la idea** ~ the central idea.

ejecución [exeku'θjon] *nf (gen.)* execution; *(cumplimiento)* fulfilment; *(actuación)* performance; *(JUR: embargo de deudor)* attachment, distraint.

ejecutar [exeku'tar] *vt (gen)* to execute, carry out; *(matar)* to execute *(cumplir)* to fulfil; *(MUS)* to perform; *(JUR: embargar)* to attach, distrain (on).

ejecutivo, a [exeku'tiβo, a] *a* executive; **el poder** ~ the Executive (Power).

ejemplar [exem'plar] *a* exemplary // *nm* example; *(ZOOL)* specimen; *(de libro)* copy; *(de periódico)* number, issue.

ejemplo [e'xemplo] *nm* example; **por** ~ for example.

ejercer [exer'θer] *vt* to exercise; *(influencia)* to exert; *(un oficio)* to practise // *vi (practicar)* to practise *(de así)*; *(tener oficio)* to hold office.

ejercicio [exer'θiθjo] *nm* exercise; *(período)* tenure; ~ **comercial** financial year.

ejército [e'xerθito] *nm* army; **entrar en**

el ~ to join the army, join up.
el [el] *det* the.
él [el] *pron* (*persona*) he; (*cosa*) it; (*después de prep*: *persona*) him; (: *cosa*) it.
elaborar [elaβo'rar] *vt* to elaborate; (*hacer*) to make; (*preparar*) to prepare; (*trabajar*) to work; (*calcular*) to work out.
elasticidad [elastiθi'ðað] *nf* elasticity; **elástico, a** *a* elastic; (*flexible*) flexible // *nm* elastic.
elección [elek'θjon] *nf* election; (*selección*) choice, selection.
electorado [elekto'raðo] *nm* electorate, voters *pl*.
electricidad [elektriθi'ðað] *nf* electricity.
electricista [elektri'θista] *nm/f* electrician.
eléctrico, a [e'lektriko, a] *a* electric // *nm* electric train.
electrizar [elektri'θar] *vt* to electrify.
electro... [elektro] *pref* electro...; **~cardiógrafo** *nm* electrocardiograph; **~cución** *nf* electrocution; **~cutar** *vt* to electrocute; **~chapado, a** *a* electroplated; **electrodo** *nm* electrode; **~domésticos** *nmpl* (electrical) household appliances; **~imán** *nm* electromagnet; **~magnético, a** *a* electromagnetic; **~motor** *nm* electric motor.
electrónico, a [elek'troniko, a] *a* electronic // *nf* electronics *sg*.
electrotecnia [elektro'teknja] *nf* electrical engineering; **electrotécnico, a** *nm/f* electrical engineer.
electrotermo [elektro'termo] *nm* immersion heater.
elefante [ele'fante] *nm* elephant; **~ marino** elephant seal.
elegancia [ele'ɣanθja] *nf* (*gracia*) elegance, grace; (*estilo*) stylishness; **elegante** *a* elegant, graceful; stylish, fashionable.
elegía [ele'xia] *nf* elegy.
elegir [ele'xir] *vt* (*escoger*) to choose, select; (*optar*) to opt for; (*presidente*) to elect.
elemental [elemen'tal] *a* (*claro, obvio*) elementary; (*fundamental*) elemental, fundamental.
elemento [ele'mento] *nm* element; (*fig*) ingredient; **~s** *nmpl* elements, rudiments.
elevación [eleβa'θjon] *nf* elevation; (*acto*) raising, lifting; (*de precios*) rise; (GEO *etc*) height, altitude; (*de persona*) loftiness; (*pey*) conceit, pride.
elevar [ele'βar] *vt* to raise, lift (up); (*precio*) to put up; **~se** *vr* (*edificio*) to rise; (*precios*) to go up; (*transportarse, enajenarse*) to get carried away; (*engreírse*) to become conceited.
eliminar [elimi'nar] *vt* to eliminate, remove.
eliminatoria [elimina'torja] *nf* heat, preliminary (round).
elite [e'lite] *nf* elite.
elocuencia [elo'kwenθja] *nf* eloquence.
elogiar [elo'xjar] *vt* to praise, eulogize; **elogio** *nm* praise; (*tributo*) tribute.
eludir [elu'ðir] *vt* (*evitar*) to avoid, evade; (*escapar*) to escape, elude.
ella ['eʎa] *pron* (*persona*) she; (*cosa*) it; (*después de prep*: *persona*) her; (: *cosa*) it.
ellas ['eʎas] *pron* (*personas y cosas*) they; (*después de prep*) them.
ello ['eʎo] *pron* it.
ellos ['eʎos] *pron* they; (*después de prep*) them.
emanar [ema'nar] *vi*: **~ de** to emanate from, come from; (*derivar de*) to originate in.
emancipar [emanθi'par] *vt* to emancipate; **~se** *vr* to become emancipated, free o.s.
embadurnar [embaður'nar] *vt* to smear.
embajada [emba'xaða] *nf* embassy; (*mensaje*) message, errand.
embajador, a [embaxa'ðor, a] *nm/f* ambassador/ambassadress.
embalar [emba'lar] *vt* (*envolver*) to parcel, wrap (up); (*envasar*) to package // *vi* to sprint.
embarazada [embara'θaða] *a* pregnant // *nf* pregnant woman.
embarazar [embara'θar] *vt* to obstruct, hamper; (*a una mujer*) to make pregnant; **~se** *vr* (*aturdirse*) to become embarrassed; (*confundirse*) to get into a muddle; (*mujer*) to become pregnant.
embarazo [emba'raθo] *nm* (*de mujer*) pregnancy; (*impedimento*) obstacle, obstruction; (*timidez*) embarrassment.
embarcación [embarka'θjon] *nf* (*barco*) boat, craft; (*acto*) embarkation.
embarcadero [embarka'ðero] *nm* pier, landing stage.
embarcar [embar'kar] *vt* (*cargamento*) to ship, stow; (*persona*) to embark, put on board; **~se** *vr* to embark, go on board.
embargar [embar'ɣar] *vt* (*impedir*) to impede, hinder; (JUR) to seize, impound.
embarque [em'barke] *nm* shipment, loading.
embaular [embau'lar] *vt* to pack (into a trunk); (*fig*) to stuff o.s. with.
embebecerse [embeβe'θerse] *vr* (*extasiarse*) to be lost in wonder, be amazed.
embeber [embe'βer] *vt* (*absorber*) to absorb, soak up; (*empapar*) to saturate // *vi* to shrink; **~se** *vr*: **~se en la lectura** to be engrossed *or* absorbed in a book.
embellecer [embeʎe'θer] *vt* to embellish, beautify.
embestida [embes'tiða] *nf* attack, onslaught; (*carga*) charge; **embestir** *vt* to attack assault; to charge, attack // *vi* to attack.
emblema [em'blema] *nm* emblem.
embobado, a [embo'βaðo, a] *a* (*atontado*) stunned, bewildered.
embocadura [emboka'ðura] *nf* narrow entrance; (*de río*) mouth; (MUS) mouthpiece.
émbolo ['embolo] *nm* (AUTO) piston.

embolsar [embol'sar] vt to pocket, put in one's pocket.

emborrachar [emborra'tʃar] vt to intoxicate, make drunk; ~**se** vr to get drunk.

emboscada [embos'kaða] nf (celada) ambush.

embotar [embo'tar] vt to blunt, dull; ~**se** vr (adormecerse) to go numb.

embotellar [embote'ʎar] vt to bottle; ~**se** vr (circulación) to get into a jam.

embozar [embo'θar] vt to muffle (up).

embragar [embra'var] vi to let in the clutch.

embrague [em'braxe] nm (también **pedal de** ~) clutch.

embravecer [embraβe'θer] vt to enrage, infuriate; ~**se** vr to become furious; (el mar) to get rough; (tormenta) to rage.

embriagado, a [embrja'vaðo, a] a (emborrachado) intoxicated, drunk.

embriagar [embrja'var] vt (emborrachar) to intoxicate, make drunk; (alegrar) to delight; ~**se** vr (emborracharse) to get drunk.

embriaguez [embrja'veθ] nf (borrachera) drunkenness; (fig) rapture, delight.

embrollar [embro'ʎar] vt (el asunto) to confuse, complicate; (persona) to involve, embroil; ~**se** vr (confundirse) to get into a muddle or mess; ~**se con uno** to get into an argument with sb.

embrollo [em'broʎo] nm (enredo) muddle, confusion; (aprieto) fix, jam; (pey: engaño) fraud; (: trampa) trick.

embromar [embro'mar] vt (burlarse de) to tease, make fun of.

embrutecer [embrute'θer] vt (brutalizar) to brutalize; (depravar) to deprave; (atontar) to stupefy; ~**se** vr to become brutal; to become depraved.

embudo [em'buðo] nm funnel; (fig: engaño) fraud; (: trampa) trick.

embuste [em'buste] nm trick; (impostura) imposture; (mentira) lie; (hum) fib; ~**ro, a** a lying, deceitful // nm/f (tramposo) cheat; (impostor) impostor; (mentiroso) liar; (hum) fibber.

embutido [embu'tiðo] nm (CULIN) sausage; (TEC) inlay.

embutir [embu'tir] vt (TEC) to inlay; (llenar) to pack tight, cram, stuff.

emergencia [emer'xenθja] nf emergency; (surgimiento) emergence.

emerger [emer'ver] vi to emerge, appear.

emigración [emivra'θjon] nf (éxodo) migration; (destierro) emigration.

emigrar [emi'vrar] vi (pájaros) to migrate; (personas) to emigrate.

eminencia [emi'nenθja] nf eminence; **eminente** a eminent, distinguished; (GEO) high.

emisario [emi'sarjo] nm emissary.

emisión [emi'sjon] nf (acto) emission; (COM etc) issue; (RADIO, TV: acto) broadcasting; (: programa) broadcast, programme.

emisora [emi'sora] nf (de onda corta) shortwave radio station; (aparato) broadcasting station.

emitir [emi'tir] vt (olor etc) to emit, give off; (moneda etc) to issue; (opinión) to express; (RADIO) to broadcast.

emoción [emo'θjon] nf emotion; (excitación) excitement; (turbación) worry, anxiety.

emocionante [emoθjo'nante] a (excitante) exciting; thrilling; (conmovedor) moving, touching; (impresionante) striking, impressive.

emocionar [emoθjo'nar] vt (excitar) to excite, thrill; (conmover) to move, touch; (impresionar) to impress.

empacho [em'patʃo] nm (MED) indigestion; (fig) embarrassment.

empalagoso, a [empala'voso, a] a cloying; (fig) tiresome.

empalmar [empal'mar] vt to join, connect // vi (dos caminos) to meet, join; **empalme** nm joint, connection; junction; (de trenes) connection.

empanada [empa'naða] nf pie, patty.

empantanarse [empanta'narse] vr to get swamped; (fig) to get bogged down.

empañar [empa'ɲar] vt (niño) to swaddle, wrap up; ~**se** vr (nublarse) to get misty, steam up.

empapar [empa'par] vt (mojar) to soak, saturate; (absorber) to soak up, absorb; ~**se** vr: ~**se de** to soak up.

empapelar [empape'lar] vt (paredes) to paper; (envolver con papel) to wrap (up) in paper.

empaquetar [empake'tar] vt to pack, parcel up.

empastar [empas'tar] vt (embadurnar) to paste; (diente) to fill.

empatar [empa'tar] vi to draw, tie; **empate** nm draw, tie.

empedernido, a [empeðer'niðo, a] a hard, heartless; (fijado) hardened, inveterate.

empedrar [empeðer'nir] vt to harden.

empedrado, a [empe'ðraðo, a] a paved // nm paving; **empedrar** vt to pave.

empeñado, a [empe'ɲaðo, a] a (objeto) pawned; (persona) determined.

empeñar [empe'ɲar] vt (objeto) to pawn, pledge; (persona) to compel; ~**se** vr (obligarse) to bind o.s., pledge o.s.; (endeudarse) to get into debt; ~**se en** to be set on, be determined to.

empeorar [empeo'rar] vt to make worse, worsen // vi to get worse, deteriorate.

empequeñecer [empekeɲe'θer] vt to dwarf; (fig) to belittle.

emperador [empera'ðor] nm emperor.

emperatriz [empera'triθ] nf empress.

empezar [empe'θar] vt, vi to begin, start.

empiezo etc vb ver **empezar**.

empinar [empi'nar] *vt* to raise (up) // *vi* (*fam*) to drink, booze (*fam*); ~**se** *vr* (*persona*) to stand on tiptoe; (*animal*) to rear up; (*camino*) to climb steeply; (*edificio*) to tower.

empírico, a [em'piriko, a] *a* empirical.

emplasto [em'plasto], **emplaste** [em-'plaste] *nm* (*MED*) plaster; (: *cataplasma*) poultice; (*componenda*) compromise.

emplazamiento [empla0a'mjento] *nm* site, location; (*JUR*) summons sg.

emplazar [empla'0ar] *vt* (*ubicar*) to site, place, locate; (*JUR*) to summons; (*convocar*) to summon.

empleado, a [emple'aðo, a] *nm/f* (*gen*) employee; (*de banco etc*) clerk.

emplear [emple'ar] *vt* (*usar*) to use, employ; (*dar trabajo a*) to employ; ~**se** *vr* (*conseguir trabajo*) to be employed; (*ocuparse*) to occupy o.s.

empleo [em'pleo] *nm* (*puesto*) job; (*puestos: colectivamente*) employment; (*uso*) use, employment.

empobrecer [empoßre'0er] *vt* to impoverish; ~**se** *vr* to become poor or impoverished; **empobrecimiento** *nm* impoverishment.

emporio [em'porjo] *nm* emporium, trading centre; (*gran almacén*) department store.

emprender [empren'der] *vt* (*empezar*) to begin, embark on; (*acometer*) to tackle, take on.

empreñar [empre'nar] *vt* to make pregnant; ~**se** *vr* to become pregnant.

empresa [em'presa] *nf* enterprise.

empréstito [em'prestito] *nm* (public) loan.

empujar [empu'xar] *vt* to push, shove; **empuje** *nm* thrust; (*presión*) pressure; (*fig*) vigour, drive.

empujón [empu'xon] *nm* push, shove.

empuñar [empu'nar] *vt* (*asir*) to grasp, take (firm) hold of.

emular [emu'lar] *vt* to emulate; (*rivalizar*) to rival.

émulo, a ['emulo, a] *nm/f* rival, competitor.

en [en] *prep* (*gen*) in; (*sobre*) on, upon; **meter** ~ **el bolsillo** to put in *or* into one's pocket; (*lugar*): **vivir** ~ **Toledo** to live in Toledo; ~ **casa** at home; (*tiempo*): **lo terminó** ~ **6 días** he finished it in 6 days; ~ **el mes de enero** in the month of January; ~ **aquel momento/aquella época** at that moment/that time; ~ **aquel día/aquella ocasión** on that day/that occasion; ~ **serio** seriously; ~ **fin** well, well then; **ir de puerta** ~ **puerta** to go from door to door; ~ **tren** by train.

enajenación [enaxena'0jon] *nf*, **enajenamiento** [enaxena'mjento] *nm* alienation; (*fig: distracción*) absent-mindedness; (: *embelesamiento*) rapture, trance; (*extrañamiento*) estrangement.

enajenar [enaxe'nar] *vt* to alienate; (*fig*)

to carry away; ~**se** *vr* (*de un bien*) to deprive o.s.; (*amigos*) to become estranged, fall out.

enamorado, a [enamo'raðo, a] *a* in love; **enamorar** *vt* to inspire love; **enamorarse** *vr* to fall in love.

enano, a [e'nano, a] *a* tiny // *nm/f* dwarf.

enardecer [enarðe'0er] *vt* (*pasiones*) to fire, inflame; (*persona*) to fill with enthusiasm; (: *llenar de ira*) to fill with anger; ~**se** *vr* to get excited; (*entusiasmarse*) to get enthusiastic (*por* about); (*de cólera*) to blaze.

encabezamiento [enkaße0a'mjento] *nm* (*de carta*) heading; (*de periódico*) headline; (*preámbulo*) foreword, preface; (*registro*) roll, register.

encabezar [enkaße'0ar] *vt* (*manifestación*) to lead, head; (*lista*) to be at the top of; (*carta*) to put a heading to; (*libro*) to entitle; (*empadronar*) to register.

encadenar [enkaðe'nar] *vt* to chain (together); (*poner grilletes a*) to shackle.

encajar [enka'xar] *vt* (*ajustar*) to fit (into); (*golpe*) to give, deal, (*entrometer*) to insert // *vi* to fit (well); (*fig: corresponder a*) to match; ~**se** *vr* to intrude; ~**se en un sillón** to squeeze into a chair.

encaje [en'kaxe] *nm* (*labor*) lace; (*inserción*) insertion; (*ajuste*) fitting.

encajonar [enkaxo'nar] *vt* to box (up), put in a box.

encaminar [enkami'nar] *vt* to direct, send; ~**se** *vr*: ~**se a** to set out for.

encandilar [enkandi'lar] *vt* to dazzle; (*fuego*) to poke.

encantador, a [enkanta'ðor, a] *a* charming, lovely // *nm/f* magician, enchanter/tress.

encantar [enkan'tar] *vt* to charm, delight; (*hechizar*) to bewitch, cast a spell on; **encanto** *nm* (*magia*) spell, charm; (*fig*) charm, delight.

encarcelar [enkarθe'lar] *vt* to imprison, jail.

encarecer [enkare'0er] *vt* to put up the price of; (*pedir*) to recommend, urge // *vi*, ~**se** *vr* to get dearer.

encarecimiento [enkareθi'mjento] *nm* price increase; (*pedido insistente*) urging.

encargado, a [enkar'xaðo, a] *a* in charge // *nm/f* agent, representative; (*responsable*) person in charge; ~ **de negocios** chargé d'affaires.

encargar [enkar'xar] *vt* to entrust; (*recomendar*) to urge, recommend; ~**se** *vr*: ~**se de** to look after, take charge of.

encargo [en'karxo] *nm* (*pedido*) assignment, job; (*responsabilidad*) responsibility; (*recomendación*) recommendation; (*COM*) order.

encarnación [enkarna'0jon] *nf* incarnation, embodiment.

encarrilar [enkarri'lar] *vt* to correct, put on the right track; (*tren*) to put back on the rails.

encausar [enkau'sar] *vt* to prosecute, sue.

encauzar [enkau'θar] vt to channel.

enceguecer [enθexe'θer] vt to blind // vi, ~se vr to go blind.

encendedor [enθende'dor] nm lighter.

encender [enθen'der] vt (con fuego) to light; (incendiar) to set fire to; (luz, radio) to put on, switch on; (inflarse) to inflame; ~se vr to catch fire; (excitarse) to get excited; (de cólera) to flare up; (el rostro) to blush.

encendido [enθen'diðo] nm ignition.

encerrar [enθe'rrar] vt (confinar) to shut in, shut up; (comprender, incluir) to include, contain.

encía [en'θia] nf gum.

encierro [en'θierro] nm shutting in, shutting up; (calabozo) prison.

encima [en'θima] ad (sobre) above, over; (además) besides; ~ de (en) on, on top of; (sobre) above, over; (además de) besides, on top of; por ~ de over; ¿llevas dinero ~? have you any money on you?; se me vino ~ it got on top of me.

encinta [en'θinta] a pregnant.

enclavar [enkla'βar] vt (clavar) to nail; (atravesar) to pierce; (sitio) to set; (fig: fam) to swindle.

encoger [enko'xer] vt (gen) to shrink, contract; (fig: asustar) to scare; (: desanimar) to discourage; ~se vr to shrink, contract; (fig) to cringe; ~se de hombros to shrug one's shoulders.

encojar [enko'xar] vt to lame; (tullir) to cripple; ~se vr to go lame; to become crippled.

encolar [enko'lar] vt (engomar) to glue, paste; (pegar) to stick down.

encolerizar [enkoleri'θar] vt to anger, provoke; ~se vr to get angry.

encomendar [enkomen'dar] vt to entrust, commend; ~se vr: ~se a to put one's trust in.

encomiar [enko'mjar] vt to praise, pay tribute to.

encomienda [enko'mjenda] nf (encargo) charge, commission; (precio) price; (elogio) tribute; ~ postal (AM) parcel post.

encomio [en'komjo] nm praise, tribute.

enconado, a [enko'naðo, a] a (MED) inflamed; (: dolorido) sore; (fig) angry.

enconar [enko'nar] vt (MED) to inflame; (fig) to anger, irritate; ~se vr (MED) to become inflamed; (fig) to get angry or irritated.

encono [en'kono] nm (rencor) rancour, spite; (odio) ill-feeling.

encontrado, a [enkon'traðo, a] a (contrario) contrary, conflicting; (hostil) hostile.

encontrar [enkon'trar] vt (hallar) to find; (inesperadamente) to meet, run into; ~se vr to meet (each other); (situarse) to be (situated); (entrar en conflicto) to crash, collide; ~se con to meet (with); ~se bien de salud to feel well.

encorvar [enkor'βar] vt to curve; (inclinar) to bend (down); ~se vr to bend down, bend over, stoop.

encrespar [enkres'par] vt (cabellos) to curl; (agua) to ripple; (fig) to anger, irritate; ~se vr (el mar) to get rough; (fig) to get annoyed, irritated.

encrucijada [enkruθi'xaða] nf crossroads sg; (empalme) junction.

encuadernación [enkwaðerna'θjon] nf binding.

encuadernador, a [enkwaðerna'ðor, a] nm/f bookbinder.

encuadrar [enkwa'ðrar] vt (retrato) to frame; (ajustar) to fit, insert; (encerrar) to contain.

encubrir [enku'βrir] vt (ocultar) to hide, conceal; (criminal) to harbour, shelter.

encuentro etc vb ver **encontrar** // [en'kwentro] nm (de personas) meeting; (de trenes) collision, crash; (DEPORTE) match, game; (MIL) encounter.

encuesta [en'kwesta] nf inquiry, investigation; ~ judicial post mortem.

encumbrado, a [enkum'braðo, a] a (edificio) lofty, towering; (persona) eminent, distinguished.

encumbrar [enkum'brar] vt (edificio) to raise; (elevar) to elevate; (persona) to exalt; ~se vr to rise, tower; (fig) to become conceited.

encharcado, a [entʃar'kaðo, a] a still; (estancado) stagnant.

enchufar [entʃu'far] vt (ELEC) to plug in; (TEC) to connect, fit together; **enchufe** nm (ELEC: clavija) plug; (: toma) plug, socket; (de dos tubos) joint, connection; (fam: influencia) contact, connection; (: puesto) cushy job.

endemoniado, a [endemo'njaðo, a] a possessed (of the devil), (endiabolado) devilish; (furioso) furious, wild.

endentar [enden'tar] vt, vi to engage, mesh.

enderezar [endere'θar] vt (poner derecho) to straighten (out); (: verticalmente) to set upright; (carta) to address; (fig) to straighten or sort out; (dirigir) to direct; ~se vr (persona sentado) to stand up; (fig) to correct one's ways.

endeudarse [endeu'ðarse] vr to get into debt.

endiablado, a [endja'βlaðo, a] a devilish, diabolical; (hum) mischievous; (fig) furious, angry.

endomingarse [endomin'garse] vr to dress up, put on one's best clothes.

endosar [endo'sar] vt (cheque etc) to endorse.

endulzar [endul'θar] vt to sweeten; (fig) to soften.

endurecer [endure'θer] vt to harden; (fig) to harden, toughen; ~se vr to harden, grow hard.

endurecido, a [endure'θiðo, a] a (duro) hard; (fig) hardy, tough; **estar** ~ **a algo** to be hardened or used to sth.

endurecimiento [endureθi'mjento] nm

(*acto*) hardening; (*tenacidad*) toughness; (*crueldad*) cruelty; (*insensibilidad*) callousness.

enemigo, a [ene'miɣo, a] *a* enemy, hostile // *nm/f* enemy // *nf* enmity, hostility.

enemistad [enemis'tað] *nf* enmity.

enemistar [enemis'tar] *vt* to make enemies of, cause a rift between; ~**se** *vr* to become enemies; (*amigos*) to fall out.

energía [ener'xia] *nf* (*vigor*) energy, drive; (*TEC, ELEC*) energy, power.

enérgico, a [e'nerxiko, a] *a* (*gen*) energetic; (*voz, modales*) forceful.

enero [e'nero] *nm* January.

enfadar [enfa'ðar] *vt* to anger, annoy; ~**se** *vr* to get angry or annoyed.

enfado [en'faðo] *nm* (*enojo*) anger, annoyance; (*disgusto*) trouble, bother; ~**so, a** *a* annoying; (*aburrido*) tedious.

énfasis ['enfasis] *nm* emphasis, stress.

enfático, a [en'fatiko, a] *a* emphatic; (*afectado*) pompous.

enfermar [enfer'mar] *vt* to make ill // *vi* to fall ill, be taken ill.

enfermedad [enferme'ðað] *nf* illness; ~ **venérea** venereal disease.

enfermería [enferme'ria] *nf* infirmary; (*de colegio etc*) sick bay.

enfermero, a [enfer'mero, a] *nm/f* male nurse/nurse.

enfermizo, a [enfer'miθo, a] *a* (*persona*) sickly, unhealthy; (*lugar*) unhealthy.

enfermo, a [en'fermo, a] *a* ill, sick // *nm/f* invalid, sick person; (*en hospital*) patient.

enflaquecer [enflake'θer] *vt* (*adelgazar*) to make thin; (*debilitar*) to weaken; ~**se** *vr* (*adelgazarse*) to become thin, lose weight; (*debilitarse*) to grow weak; (*fig*) to lose heart.

enfocar [enfo'kar] *vt* (*foto etc*) to focus; (*problema etc*) to approach, look at.

enfoque [en'foke] *nm* focus.

enfrentar [enfren'tar] *vt* (*peligro*) to face (up to), confront; (*oponer, carear*) to put face to face; ~**se** *vr* (*dos personas*) to face or confront each other; (*dos equipos*) to meet; ~**se a** *o* **con** to face up to, confront.

enfrente [en'frente] *ad* opposite; ~ **de** *prep* opposite, facing; **la casa de** ~ the house opposite, the house across the street.

enfriamiento [enfria'mjento] *nm* chilling, refrigeration; (*MED*) cold, chill.

enfriar [enfri'ar] *vt* (*alimentos*) to cool, chill; (*algo caliente*) to cool down; (*habitación*) to air, freshen; ~**se** *vr* to cool down; (*MED*) to catch a chill; (*amistad*) to cool.

enfurecer [enfure'θer] *vt* to enrage, madden; ~**se** *vr* to become furious, fly into a rage; (*mar*) to get rough.

engalanar [engala'nar] *vt* (*adornar*) to adorn; (*ciudad*) to decorate; ~**se** *vr* to get dressed up.

enganchar [engan'tʃar] *vt* (*gen*) to hook; (*ropa*) to hang up; (*dos vagones*) to hitch up; (*TEC*) to couple, connect; (*MIL*) to

recruit; (*fig: fam: persona*) to rope into; ~**se** *vr* (*MIL*) to enlist, join up

enganche [en'gantʃe] *nm* hook; (*TEC*) coupling, connection; (*acto*) hooking (up); (: *ropa*) hanging up; (*MIL*) recruitment, enlistment.

engañar [enga'nar] *vt* to deceive; (*trampear*) to cheat, swindle; ~**se** *vr* (*equivocarse*) to be wrong; (*disimular la verdad*) to deceive or kid o.s.

engaño [en'gano] *nm* deceit; (*trampa*) trick, swindle; (*error*) mistake, misunderstanding; (*ilusión*) delusion; ~**so, a** *a* (*tramposo*) crooked; (*mentiroso*) dishonest, deceitful; (*aspecto*) deceptive; (*consejo*) misleading, wrong.

engarzar [engar'θar] *vt* (*joya*) to set, mount; (*fig*) to link, connect.

engatusar [engatu'sar] *vt* (*fam*) to coax.

engendrar [enxen'drar] *vt* to breed; (*procrear*) to beget; (*fig*) to cause, produce; **engendro** *nm* (*BIO*) foetus; (*fig*) monstrosity; (*idea*) brainchild.

engolfarse [engol'farse] *vr*: ~ **en** to bury o.s in, become deeply involved in.

engomar [engo'mar] *vt* to gum, glue, stick.

engordar [engor'ðar] *vt* to fatten // *vi* to get fat, put on weight.

engranaje [engra'naxe] *nm* gear.

engranar [engra'nar] *vt* to put into gear // *vi* to interlock.

engrandecer [engrande'θer] *vt* to enlarge, magnify; (*alabar*) to praise, speak highly of; (*exagerar*) to exaggerate.

engrasar [engra'sar] *vt* (*TEC: poner grasa*) to grease; (: *lubricar*) to lubricate, oil; (*manchar*) to make greasy; (*animal*) to fatten.

engreído, a [engre'iðo, a] *a* vain, conceited; **engreírse** *vr* to become conceited.

engrosar [engro'sar] *vt* (*ensanchar*) to enlarge; (*aumentar*) to increase; (*hinchar*) to swell // *vi* to get fat; ~**se** *vr* to increase; to swell.

enhebrar [ene'βrar] *vt* to thread.

enhorabuena [enora'βwena] *nf* congratulations *pl* // *ad* well and good.

enigma [e'niɣma] *nm* enigma; (*problema*) puzzle; (*misterio*) mystery.

enjabonar [enxaβo'nar] *vt* to soap; (*fam: adular*) to soft-soap; (: *regañar*) to scold.

enjambre [en'xambre] *nm* swarm.

enjaular [enxau'lar] *vt* to put in a cage; (*fam*) to jail, lock up.

enjuagar [enxwa'ɣar] *vt* (*ropa*) to rinse (out).

enjugar [enxu'ɣar] *vt* to wipe (off); (*lágrimas*) to dry; (*déficit*) to wipe out.

enjuiciar [enxwi'θjar] *vt* (*JUR: procesar*) to prosecute, try; (*fig*) to judge.

enjuto, a [en'xuto, a] *a* dry, dried up; (*fig*) lean, skinny

enlace [en'laθe] *nm* link, connection; (*relación*) relationship; (*casamiento*) marriage; (*de carretera, trenes*) connection; **agente**

de ~ broker; ~ **sindical** shop steward.

enlazar [enla'θar] vt (atar) to tie; (conectar) to link, connect; (AM) to lasso; ~se vr (novios) to get married; (dos familias) to become related by marriage; (conectarse) to link (up), be linked.

enlodar [enlo'ðar], **enlodazar** [enloða-'θar] vt to muddy, cover in mud; (fig: manchar) to stain; (: rebajar) to debase.

enloquecer [enloke'θer] vi to drive mad // vi, ~se vr to go mad.

enlutar [enlu'tar] vt to dress in mourning; ~se vr to go into mourning.

enmarañar [enmara'ɲar] vt (enredar) to tangle (up), entangle; (complicar) to complicate; (confundir) to confuse; ~se vr (enredarse) to become entangled; (confundirse) to get confused; (nublarse) to cloud over.

enmascarar [enmaska'rar] vt to mask; ~se vr to put on a mask; ~se de to masquerade as.

enmendar [enmen'dar] vt to emend, correct; (constitución etc) to amend; (compensar) to make good; (comportamiento) to reform; ~se vr to reform, mend one's ways; **enmienda** nf correction; amendment; reform; (compensación) compensation, indemnity.

enmohecerse [enmoe'θerse] vr (metal) to rust, go rusty; (muro, plantas) to get mouldy.

enmudecer [enmuðe'θer] vt to silence // vi, ~se vr (perder el habla) to go silent; (guardar silencio) to keep quiet.

ennegrecer [ennexre'θer] vt (poner negro) to blacken; (oscurecer) to darken; ~se vr to turn black; (oscurecerse) to get dark.

ennoblecer [ennoβle'θer] vt to ennoble; (fig) to embellish, adorn.

enojadizo, a [enoxa'ðiθo, a] a irritable, short-tempered.

enojar [eno'xar] vt (encolerizar) to anger; (disgustar) to annoy, upset; ~se vr to get angry; to get annoyed.

enojo [e'noxo] nm (cólera) anger; (disgusto) annoyance; ~s nmpl trials, problems; ~so, a a annoying.

enorgullecerse [enorɣuʎe'θerse] vr to be proud; ~ de to pride o.s. on, be proud of.

enorme [e'norme] a enormous, huge; (fig) monstrous; **enormidad** nf hugeness, immensity; (despropósito) absurdity, piece of nonsense; (perversidad) monstrosity.

enraizar [enrai'θar] vi to take root.

enredadera [enreða'ðera] nf (BOT) creeper, climbing plant.

enredar [enre'ðar] vt (ovillo) to tangle (up), entangle; (peces) to net; (situación) to complicate, confuse; (meter cizaña) to sow discord among or between; (implicar) to embroil, implicate; ~se vr to get entangled, get tangled (up); (situación) to get complicated; (persona) to get embroiled; (AM: fam) to meddle.

enredo [en'reðo] nm (maraña) tangle;

(confusión) mix-up, confusion; (intriga) intrigue.

enrevesado, a [enreβe'saðo, a] a unruly, uncontrollable; (enredado) complicated, involved.

enriquecer [enrike'θer] vt to make rich, enrich; ~se vr to get rich.

enrojecer [enrxe'θer] vt to redden // vi, ~se vr (meterse) to become red hot; (persona) to blush.

enrollar [enro'ʎar] vt to roll (up), wind (up).

enroscar [enros'kar] vt (torcer, doblar) to coil (round), wind; (tornillo, rosca) to screw in; ~se vr to coil, wind.

ensalada [ensa'laða] nf salad; **ensaladilla** nf Russian salad.

ensalzar [ensal'θar] vt (alabar) to praise, extol; (exaltar) to exalt.

ensambladura [ensambla'ðura] nf, **ensamblaje** [ensam'blaxe] nm assembly; (TEC) joint; **ensamblar** vt to assemble.

ensanchar [ensan'tʃar] vt (hacer más ancho) to widen; (agrandar) to enlarge, expand; ~se vr to get wider, expand; (pey) to give o.s. airs; **ensanche** nm (de vestido, calle) widening; (de negocio) expansion.

ensangrentar [ensanɡren'tar] vt to stain with blood; ~se vr (fig) to get angry.

ensañar [ensa'ɲar] vt to enrage; ~se vr: ~se con to delight in tormenting.

ensartar [ensar'tar] vt (gen) to string (together) (aguja) to thread.

ensayar [ensa'jar] vt to test, try (out); (TEATRO) to rehearse.

ensayista [ensa'jista] nm/f essayist.

ensayo [en'sajo] nm test, trial; (QUIMICA) experiment; (TEATRO) rehearsal; (DEPORTE) try; (obra literaria) essay.

ensenada [ense'naða] nf inlet, cove.

enseñanza [ense'ɲanθa] nf (educación) education; (acción) teaching; (doctrina) teaching, doctrine.

enseñar [ense'ɲar] vt (educar) to teach; (instruir) to teach, instruct; (mostrar, señalar) to show.

enseres [en'seres] nmpl goods and chattels, things.

ensimismarse [ensimis'marse] vr (abstraerse) to become lost in thought; (estar absorto) to be lost in thought; (AM) to become conceited.

ensoberbecerse [ensoβerβe'θerse] vr to become proud; (hacerse arrogante) to become arrogant; (mar) to get rough.

ensordecer [ensorðe'θer] vt to deafen // vi to go deaf.

ensortijar [ensorti'xar] vt, ~se vr (cabellos) to curl.

ensuciar [ensu'θjar] vt (manchar) to dirty, soil; (fig) to defile; ~se vr (mancharse) to get dirty; (fig) to dirty/wet o.s.

ensueño [en'sweɲo] nm (sueño) dream, fantasy; (ilusión) illusion; (soñando despierto) reverie.

entablado [enta'βlaðo] nm (piso)

floorboards pl; (armazón) boarding.

entablar [enta'βlar] vt (recubrir) to board (up); (AJEDREZ, DAMAS) to set up; (conversación) to strike up; (JUR) to file // vi to draw.

entallar [enta'ʎar] vt (piedra) to sculpt; (madera) to carve; (grabar) to engrave; (traje) to tailor // vi: **el traje entalla bien** the suit fits well.

entender [enten'der] vt (comprender) to understand; (darse cuenta) to realize; (creer, pensar) to think, believe; (querer decir) to mean // vi: ~ **de** to know all about; ~ **en** to deal with, have to do with; ~**se** vr (comprenderse) to be understood; (ponerse de acuerdo) to understand one another, have an understanding; (aliarse) to agree, reach an agreement; (fam) to have an affair; **me entiendo con la mecánica** I'm (quite) good at mechanics.

entendido, a [enten'diðo, a] a (comprendido) skilled; (inteligente) knowledgeable // nm/f (experto) expert; (docto) knowledgeable person // excl agreed!; **entendimiento** nm (comprensión) understanding; (facultad intelectual) the mind, intellect; (juicio) judgement.

enterado, a [ente'raðo, a] a well-informed; **estar** ~ **de** to know about, be aware of.

enteramente [entera'mente] ad entirely, completely.

enterar [ente'rar] vt (informar) to inform, tell; ~**se** vr to find out, get to know.

entereza [ente'reθa] nf (totalidad) entirety; (fig: energía) strength of mind; (honradez) integrity; (severidad) strictness, severity.

enternecer [enterne'θer] vt (ablandar) to soften; (apiadar) to touch, move; ~**se** vr to be touched, be moved.

entero, a [en'tero, a] a (total) whole, entire; (fig: recto) honest; (: firme) firm, resolute // nm (COM: punto) point; (AM: pago) payment.

enterrador [enterra'ðor] nm gravedigger.

enterrar [ente'rrar] vt to bury.

entibiar [enti'βjar] vt to cool; (fig) to cool (down).

entidad [enti'ðað] nf (empresa) firm, company; (organismo) body; (sociedad) society; (FILOSOFÍA) entity.

entiendo etc vb ver **entender**.

entierro [en'tjerro] nm (acción) burial; (funeral) funeral.

entomología [entomolo'xia] nf entomology.

entonación [entona'θjon] nf (LING) intonation; (fig) conceit.

entonado, a [ento'naðo, a] a (MUS) in tune; (fig) conceited.

entonar [ento'nar] vt (canción) to intone; (colores) to tone; (MED) to tone up // vi to be in tune; ~**se** vr (engreírse) to give o.s. airs.

entonces [en'tonθes] ad then, at that time;

desde ~ since then; **en aquel** ~ at that time; **(pues)** ~ and so.

entornar [entor'nar] vt (puerta, ventana) to half close, leave ajar; (los ojos) to screw up.

entorpecer [entorpe'θer] vt (adormecer los sentidos) to dull, benumb; (impedir) to obstruct, hinder; (: tránsito) to slow down, delay; **entorpecimiento** nm numbness; slowing-down, delay; (letargia) lethargy.

entrado, a [en'traðo, a] ε: ~ **en años** elderly; **una vez** ~ **el verano** in the summer(time), when summer comes // nf (acción) entry, access; (sitio) entrance, way in; (COM) receipts pl, takings pl; (CULIN) entree; (DEPORTE) innings sg; (TEATRO) house, audience; (para el cine etc) ticket; (COM): ~**as y salidas** income and expenditure; (TEC): ~**a de aire** air intake or inlet.

entrante [en'trante] a next, coming // nm inlet; **ser** ~ **en una casa** to have the run of a house.

entraña [en'trana] nf (fig: centro) heart, core; (raíz) root; ~**s** nfpl (ANAT) entrails; **entrañable** a close, intimate.

entrar [en'trar] vt (introducir) to bring in // vi (meterse) to go/come in, enter; (comenzar): ~ **diciendo** to begin by saying; **no me entra** I can't get the hang of it; **el año que entra** next year.

entre ['entre] prep (dos) between; (más de dos) among(st); **pensaba** ~ **mí** I thought to myself.

entreabrir [entrea'βrir] vt to half-open, open halfway.

entrecejo [entre'θexo] nm: **fruncir el** ~ to frown.

entredicho [entre'ðitʃo] nm prohibition, ban; (JUR) injunction.

entrega [en'treχa] nf (de mercancías) delivery; (rendición) surrender; **novela por** ~**s** serial, novel in instalments.

entregar [entre'χar] vt (dar) to hand (over), deliver; (ceder) to give up; ~**se** vr (rendirse) to surrender, give in, submit; (dedicarse) to devote o.s.

entrelazar [entrela'θar] vt to entwine.

entremés [entre mes] nm (CULIN) side-dish; **entremeses** nmpl hors d'œuvres.

entremeter [entreme'ter] vt to insert, put in; ~**se** vr to meddle, interfere; **entremetido, a** a meddling, interfering.

entremezclar [entremeθ'klar] vt, ~**se** vr to intermingle.

entrenador [entrena'ðor] nm trainer, coach; **entrenarse** vr to train.

entreoír [entreo'ir] vt to half hear.

entresacar [entresa'kar] vt to pick out, select.

entresuelo [entre'swelo] nm (sótano) basement.

entretanto [entre'tanto] ad meanwhile, meantime; **en el** ~ in the meantime.

entretejer [entrete'xer] vt to interweave.

entretener [entrete'ner] vt (divertir) to entertain, amuse; (detener) to hold up,

delay; (*cuidar*) to maintain; ~se *vr*
(*divertirse*) to amuse o.s.; (*retrasarse*) to
delay, linger; **entretenido, a** *a*
entertaining, amusing; **entretenimiento**
nm entertainment, amusement; (*cuidado*)
upkeep, maintenance.

entrever [entre'ßer] *vt* to glimpse, catch
a glimpse of.

entreverar [entreße'rar] *vt* to mix (up).

entrevista [entre'ßista] *nf* interview;
entrevistar *vt* to interview;
entrevistarse *vr* to have an interview.

entristecer [entriste'θer] *vt* to sadden,
grieve; ~se *vr* to grow sad.

entrometer [entrome'ter] *etc* =
entremeter *etc*.

entroncar [entron'kar] *vi* to be connected
or related.

entronque [en'tronke] *nm* connection,
link.

entuerto [en'twerto] *nm* wrong, injustice.

entumecer [entume'θer] *vt* to numb,
benumb; ~se *vr* (*por el frío*) to go or
become numb; **entumecido, a** *a* numb,
stiff.

enturbiar [entur'ßjar] *vt* (*el agua*) to
disturb, make cloudy; (*fig*) to fog, confuse;
~se *vr* (*oscurecerse*) to become cloudy;
(*fig*) to get confused, become obscure.

entusiasmar [entusjas'mar] *vt* to excite,
fill with enthusiasm; (*gustar mucho*) to
delight; ~se *vr*: ~se con *o* por to get
enthusiastic or excited about.

entusiasmo [entu'sjasmo] *nm*
enthusiasm; (*deleite*) delight; (*excitación*)
excitement.

entusiasta [entu'sjasta] *a* enthusiastic //
nm/f enthusiast.

enumerar [enume'rar] *vt* to enumerate.

enunciación [enunθja'θjon] *nf*,
enunciado [enun'θjaðo] *nm* enunciation;
(*declaración*) declaration, statement;
enunciar *vt* to enunciate; to declare,
state.

envainar [enßai'nar] *vt* to sheathe.

envalentonar [enßalento'nar] *vt* to give
courage to; ~se *vr* to take courage,
become bolder; (*pey: jactarse*) to boast,
brag.

envanecer [enßane'θer] *vt* to make
conceited; ~se *vr* to grow vain or
conceited.

envasar [enßa'sar] *vt* (*empaquetar*) to
pack, wrap; (*enfrascar*) to bottle; (*enlatar*)
to tin; (*embolsar*) to pocket // *vi* (*fig: fam:
vino*) to knock back; **envase** *nm* packing,
wrapping; bottling; tinning, canning;
pocketing; (*recipiente*) container;
(*paquete*) package; (*botella*) bottle; (*lata*)
tin, can.

envejecer [enßexe'θer] *vt* to make old,
age // *vi*, ~se *vr* (*volverse viejo*) to grow
old; (*fig*) to become old-fashioned.

envenenar [enßene'nar] *vt* to poison; (*fig*)
to embitter.

envergadura [enßerɣa'ðura] *nf* (*fig*)
scope, compass.

envés [en'ßes] *nm* (*de tela*) back, wrong
side.

enviar [en'ßjar] *vt* to send.

envidia [en'ßiðja] *nf* (*deseo ferviente*)
envy; (*celos*) jealousy; **envidiar** *vt*
(*desear*) to envy; (*tener celos de*) to be
jealous of.

envilecer [enßile'θer] *vt* to debase,
degrade; ~se *vr* to lower o.s.

envío [en'ßio] *nm* (*acción*) sending; (*de
mercancías*) consignment; (*com*)
remittance.

enviudar [enßju'ðar] *vi* to be widowed.

envoltura [enßol'tura] *nf* (*cobertura*)
cover; (*embalaje*) wrapper, wrapping; (*funda*) case.

envolver [enßol'ßer] *vt* to wrap (up);
(*cubrir*) to cover; (*enemigo*) to surround;
(*implicar*) to involve, implicate; ~se *vr*
(*cubrirse*) to wrap o.s. up; (*implicarse*) to
become involved.

envuelto [en'ßwelto] *pp de* **envolver**.

enzarzar [enθar'θar] *vt* (*fig*) to involve (in
a dispute).

épico, a ['epiko, a] *a* epic // *nf* epic.

epidemia [epi'ðemja] *nf* epidemic;
epidémico, a *a* epidemic.

epifanía [epifa'nia] *nf* Epiphany.

epilepsia [epi'lepsja] *nf* epilepsy.

epílogo [e'piloxo] *nm* epilogue.

episodio [epi'soðjo] *nm* episode.

epístola [e'pistola] *nf* epistle; (*fam*) letter.

epitafio [epi'tafjo] *nm* epitaph.

época ['epoka] *nf* period, time; (*historia*)
age, epoch; **hacer** ~ to be epoch-making.

equidad [eki'ðað] *nf* equity.

equilibrar [ekili'ßrar] *vt* to balance;
equilibrio *nm* balance, equilibrium; **equi-
librista** *nm/f* (*funámbulo*) tightrope
walker; (*acróbata*) acrobat.

equipaje [eki'paxe] *nm* luggage; (*equipo*)
equipment, kit; (*naut: tripulación*) crew;
~ **de mano** hand luggage.

equipar [eki'par] *vt* (*proveer*) to equip.

equipararse [ekipa'rarse] *vr*: ~ **con** to
be on a level with.

equipo [e'kipo] *nm* (*materiales*)
equipment; (*grupo*) team; (: *de obreros*)
shift.

equis [ekis] *nf* (the letter) X.

equitación [ekita'θjon] *nf* (*acto*) riding;
(*arte*) horsemanship.

equitativo, a [ekita'tißo, a] *a* equitable,
fair.

equivalente [ekißa'lente] *a*, *nm*
equivalent; **equivaler** *vi* to be equivalent
or equal.

equivocación [ekißoka'θjon] *nf* mistake,
error; **equivocarse** *vr* to be wrong, make
a mistake; **equivocarse de camino** to
take the wrong road; **equívoco, a** *a* (*dudoso*) suspect; (*ambiguo*) ambiguous // *nm*
ambiguity; (*juego de palabras*) play on
words.

era *vb ver* **ser** // ['era] *nf* era, age.

erais *vb ver* **ser**.

éramos *vb ver* **ser.**

eran *vb ver* **ser.**

erario [e'rarjo] *nm* exchequer, treasury.

eras *vb ver* **ser.**

eres *vb ver* **ser.**

erguir [er'xir] *vt* to raise, lift; (*poner derecho*) to straighten; ~**se** *vr* to straighten up; (*fig*) to swell with pride.

erigir [eri'xir] *vt* to erect, build; ~**se** *vr*: ~**se en** to set o.s. up as.

erizado, a [eri'θaðo, a] *a* bristly.

erizarse [eri'θarse] *vr* to stand on end.

erizo [e'riθo] *nm* hedgehog; (~ **de mar**) sea-urchin.

ermitaño, a [ermi'taɲo, a] *nm/f* hermit.

erótico, a [e'rotiko, a] *a* erotic; **erotismo** *nm* eroticism.

erradicar [erraði'kar] *vt* to eradicate.

errado, a [e'rraðo, a] *a* mistaken, wrong.

errante [e'rrante] *a* wandering, errant.

errar [e'rrar] *vi* (*vagar*) to wander, roam; (*equivocarse*) to err, make a mistake // *vt*: ~ **el camino** to take the wrong road; ~ **el tiro** to miss.

erróneo, a [e'rroneo, a] *a* (*equivocado*) wrong, mistaken; (*falso*) false, untrue.

error [e'rror] *nm* error, mistake; ~ **de imprenta** misprint.

eructar [eruk'tar] *vt* to belch.

erudición [eruði'θjon] *nf* erudition, learning.

erudito, a [eru'ðito, a] *a* erudite, learned.

erupción [erup'θjon] *nf* eruption; (*MED*) rash.

es *vb ver* **ser.**

esa, esas *det ver* **ese.**

ésa, ésas *pron ver* **ése.**

esbelto, a [es'βelto, a] *a* slim, slender.

esbozo [es'βoθo] *nm* sketch, outline.

escabeche [eska'βetʃe] *nm* brine; (*de aceitunas etc*) pickle; **pescado en** ~ pickled fish.

escabel [eska'βel] *nm* (low) stool.

escabroso, a [eska'βroso, a] *a* (*accidentado*) rough, uneven; (*fig*) tough, difficult; (: *atrevido*) risqué.

escabullirse [eskaβu'ʎirse] *vr* to slip away; (*irse*) to clear out.

escala [es'kala] *nf* (*proporción, MUS*) scale; (*de mano*) ladder; (*AVIAT*) stopover; **hacer** ~ **en** to stop or call in at; ~ **de colores** range of colours.

escalafón [eskala'fon] *nm* (*escala de salarios*) salary scale, wage scale; (*lista etc*) list; (*registro*) register.

escalar [eska'lar] *vt* (*montaña etc*) to climb, scale; (*casa*) to burgle, break into.

escalera [eska'lera] *nf* stairs *pl*, staircase; (*escala*) ladder; (*NAIPES*) run; ~ **mecánica** escalator; ~ **de caracol** spiral staircase.

escalinata [eskali'nata] *nf* outside staircase.

escalofrío [eskalo'frio] *nm* chill; ~**s** *nmpl* (*fig*) shivers; **escalofriante** *a* chilling.

escalón [eska'lon] *nm* step, stair; (*de escalera*) rung.

escama [es'kama] *nf* (*de pez, serpiente*) scale; (*de jabón*) flake; (*fig*) resentment.

escamado, a [eska'maðo, a] *a* wary, cautious.

escamotar [eskamo'tar], **escamotear** [eskamote'ar] *vt* (*quitar*) to lift, swipe (*fam*); (*hacer desaparecer*) to make disappear.

escampar [eskam'par] *vt impersonal* to stop raining; (*del cielo*) to clear (up).

escandalizar [eskandali'θar] *vt* to scandalize, shock; ~**se** *vr* to be shocked; (*ofenderse*) to be offended.

escándalo [es'kandalo] *nm* scandal; (*alboroto, tumulto*) row, uproar; **escandaloso, a** *a* scandalous, shocking.

escandinavo, a [eskandi'naβo, a] *a*, *nm/f* Scandinavian.

escaño [es'kaɲo] *nm* bench; (*POL*) seat.

escapar [eska'par] *vi* (*gen*) to escape, run away; (*DEPORTE*) to break away; ~**se** *vr* to escape, get away; (*gas*) to leak (out).

escaparate [eskapa'rate] *nm* shop window; (*AM*) wardrobe.

escape [es'kape] *nm* (*de gas*) leak; (*de motor*) exhaust; (*de persona*) escape.

escarabajo [eskara'βaxo] *nm* beetle; ~**s** *nmpl* (*fam*) scribble *sg*.

escaramuza [eskara'muθa] *nf* skirmish; (*fig*) brush.

escarbar [eskar'βar] *vt* (*gallina*) to scratch; (*dientes*) to pick; (*orejas*) to clean; (*fig*) to inquire into, investigate.

escarcha [es'kartʃa] *nf* frost.

escarlata [eskar'lata] *a inv* scarlet; **escarlatina** *nf* scarlet fever.

escarmentar [eskarmen'tar] *vt* to punish severely // *vi* to learn one's lesson; **escarmiento** *nm* (*ejemplo*) lesson, example; (*castigo*) punishment.

escarnecer [eskarne'θer] *vt* to mock, ridicule; **escarnio, escarnecimiento** *nm* mockery; (*injuria*) insult.

escarpado, a [eskar'paðo, a] *a* (*abrupto*) sheer; (*inclinado*) steep; (*accidentado*) craggy.

escasear [eskase'ar] *vt* to skimp (on) // *vi* to be scarce.

escasez [eska'seθ] *nf* (*falta*) shortage, scarcity; (*pobreza*) poverty; (*mezquindad*) meanness.

escaso, a [es'kaso, a] *a* (*poco*) scarce; (*raro*) rare; (*ralo*) thin, sparse; (*limitado*) limited.

escatimar [eskati'mar] *vt* (*limitar*) to skimp (on); (*reducir*) to curtail, cut down.

escena [es'θena] *nf* scene.

escenario [esθe'narjo] *nm* (*TEATRO*) stage; (*CINE*) set; (*fig*) scene.

escepticismo [esθepti'θismo] *nm* scepticism; **escéptico, a** *a* sceptical // *nm/f* sceptic.

esclarecer [esklare'θer] *vt* (*iluminar*) to light up, illuminate; (*misterio, problema*) to shed light on; (*ennoblecer*) to ennoble.

esclavitud [esklaβi'tuð] *nf* slavery
esclavizar [esklaβi'θar] *vt* to enslave.
esclavo, a [es'klaβo, a] *nm/f* slave.
escoba [es'koβa] *nf* broom.
escocer [esko'θer] *vt* to annoy // *vi* to burn, sting; ~**se** *vr* to chafe, get chafed.
escocés, esa [esko'θes, esa] *a* Scottish // *nm/f* Scotsman/woman, Scot.
Escocia [es'koθja] *nf* Scotland.
escoger [esko'xer] *vt* to choose, pick, select; **escogido, a** *a* chosen, selected; (*calidad*) choice, select; **escogimiento** *nm* choice.
escolar [esko'lar] *a* school *cpd* // *nm/f* schoolboy/girl, pupil.
escolta [es'kolta] *nf* escort; **escoltar** *vt* to escort.
escombro [es'kombro] *nm* mackerel; ~**s** *nmpl* (*basura*) rubbish *sg*; (*restos*) debris *sg*.
esconder [eskon'der] *vt* to hide, conceal; ~**se** *vr* to hide; **escondite** *nm* hiding place; (*juego*) hide-and-seek.
escondrijo [eskon'drixo] *nm* hiding-place, hideout.
escopeta [esko'peta] *nf* shotgun.
escoplo [es'koplo] *nm* chisel.
Escorpio [es'korpjo] *nm* Scorpio.
escorpión [eskor'pjon] *nm* scorpion.
escote [es'kote] *nm* (*de vestido*) low neck; (*parte*) share; **pagar a** ~ to share the expenses.
escotillón [eskoti'ʎon] *nm* trapdoor.
escozor [esko'θor] *nm* (*dolor*) sting(ing); (*fig*) grief, heartache.
escribano, a [eskri'βano, a], **escribiente** [eskri'βjente] *nm/f* clerk.
escribir [eskri'βir] *vt, vi* to write; ~ **a máquina** to type; **¿cómo se escribe?** how do you spell it?
escrito, a [es'krito, a] *pp de* **escribir** // *nm* (*documento*) document; (*manuscrito*) text, manuscript; **por** ~ in writing.
escritor, a [eskri'tor, a] *nm/f* writer.
escritorio [eskri'torjo] *nm* desk; (*oficina*) office.
escritura [eskri'tura] *nf* (*acción*) writing; (*caligrafía*) (hand)writing; (*JUR*: *documento*) deed.
escrúpulo [es'krupulo] *nm* scruple; (*minuciosidad*) scrupulousness; **escrupuloso, a** *a* scrupulous.
escrutar [eskru'tar] *vt* to scrutinize, examine; (*votos*) to count.
escrutinio [eskru'tinjo] *nm* (*examen atento*) scrutiny; (*recuento de votos*) poll; (*resultado de elección*) voting, ballot.
escuadra [es'kwaðra] *nf* (*MIL etc*) squad; (*NAUT*) squadron; (*de coches etc*) fleet; **escuadrilla** *nf* (*de aviones*) squadron; (*AM: de obreros*) gang.
escuadrón [eskwa'ðron] *nm* squadron.
escuálido, a [es'kwaliðo, a] *a* (*flaco, maciento*) pale, wan; (*sucio*) squalid.
escuchar [esku'tʃar] *vt* to listen to // *vi* to listen.

escudilla [esku'ðiʎa] *nf* bowl, basin.
escudo [es'kuðo] *nm* shield.
escudriñar [eskuðri'ɲar] *vt* (*examinar*) to investigate, examine closely; (*mirar de lejos*) to scan.
escuela [es'kwela] *nf* school.
escueto, a [es'kweto, a] *a* plain, unadorned.
esculpir [eskul'pir] *vt* to sculpt; (*grabar*) to engrave; (*tallar*) to carve; **escultor, a** *nm/f* sculptor/-ress; **escultura** *nf* sculpture.
escupidora [eskupi'ðora], **escupidera** [eskupi'ðera] *nf* spittoon; (*orinal*) bedpan.
escupir [esku'pir] *vt, vi* to spit (out).
escurridero [eskurri'ðero] *nm* draining-board.
escurridizo, a [eskurri'ðiθo, a] *a* slippery.
escurrir [esku'rrir] *vt* (*ropa*) to wring out; (*verduras*) to strain; (*platos*) to drain // *vi* (*los líquidos*) to drip; (*resbalarse*) to slip, slide; ~**se** *vr* (*gotear*) to drip; (*secarse*) to drain; (*resbalarse*) to slip, slide; (*escaparse*) to slip away.
ese, esa, esos, esas ['ese, 'esa, 'esos, 'esas] *det* (*sg*) that; (*pl*) those.
ése, ésa, ésos, ésas ['ese, 'esa, 'esos, 'esas] *pron* (*sg*) that (one); (*pl*) those (ones...; ~... **éste...** the former... the latter...; **¡no me vengas con** ~**as** don't give me any more of that nonsense.
esencia [e'senθja] *nf* essence; **esencial** *a* essential.
esfera [es'fera] *nf* sphere; (*de reloj*) face; **esférico, a** *a* spherical.
esforzado, a [esfor'θaðo, a] *a* (*enérgico*) energetic, vigorous; (*valiente*) brave.
esforzar [esfor'θar] *vt* (*fortalecer*) to strengthen; (*alentar*) to encourage; ~**se** *vr* to exert o.s., make an effort.
esfuerzo [es'fwerθo] *nm* effort; (*TEC*) stress; (*valer*) courage, spirit.
esfumarse [esfu'marse] *vr* to fade away.
esgrima [es'xrima] *nf* fencing.
esguince [es'xinθe] *nm* (*MED*) sprain; (*ademán*) swerve, dodge; (*ceño*) scowl, frown.
eslabón [esla'βon] *nm* link, **eslabonar** *vt* to link, connect.
esmaltar [esmal'tar] *vt* to enamel; (*las uñas*) to paint, varnish; **esmalte** *nm* enamel; **esmalte de uñas** nail varnish, nail polish.
esmerado, a [esme'raðo, a] *a* careful, neat.
esmeralda [esme'ralda] *nf* emerald.
esmerarse [esme'rarse] *vr* (*aplicarse*) to take great pains, exercise great care; (*brillar*) to shine, do well.
esmero [es'mero] *nm* (great) care.
esnob [es'nob] *a inv* (*persona*) snobbish; (*coche etc*) posh // *nm/f* snob; ~**ismo** *nm* snobbery.
eso ['eso] *pron* that that thing *or* matter; ~ **de su coche** all that about his car, ~ **de ir al cine** all that about going to the cinema, **the idea of going to the cinema** a ~ **de las cinco** at about five o'clock; **en**

~ thereupon, at that point; ~ es that's it; ¡~ sí que es vida! now this is really living!; por ~ te lo dije that's why I told you.

esos ['esos] det ver ése.

ésos ['esos] pron ver ése.

espabilar [espaßi'lar] vt (vela) to snuff; ~se vr (despertarse) to wake up; (animarse) to liven up, look lively.

espacial [espa'θjal] a inv (del espacio) space cpd.

espaciar [espa'θjar] vt to space (out); (divulgar) to spread; ~se vr: ~se en un tema to enlarge on a subject.

espacio [es'paθjo] nm space; (MUS) interval; (emisión) (short) programme, spot; el ~ space; ~so, a a spacious, roomy; (lento) slow.

espada [es'paða] nf sword; ~s nfpl (NAIPES) spades.

espaguetis [espa'vetis] nmpl spaghetti sg.

espalda [es'palda] nf (gen) back; ~s nfpl (hombros) shoulders; a ~s de uno behind sb's back; cargado de ~s round-shouldered; tenderse de ~s to lie (down) on one's back; volver la ~ a alguien to give sb the cold shoulder.

espaldar [espal'dar] nm (de asiento) back.

espaldilla [espal'ðiʎa] nf shoulder-blade.

espantadizo, a [espanta'ðiθo, a] a timid, easily frightened.

espantajo [espan'taxo] nm, espanta-pájaros [espanta'paxaros] nmpl scarecrow sg.

espantar [espan'tar] vt (asustar) to frighten, scare; (ahuyentar) to frighten off; (asombrar) to horrify, appal; ~se vr to get frightened or scared; to be appalled.

espanto [es'panto] nm (susto) fright; (terror) terror; (fantasma) ghost; (asombro) astonishment; ~so, a a frightening; terrifying; astonishing.

España [es'paɲa] nf Spain; español, a a Spanish // nm/f Spaniard // nm (lengua) Spanish.

esparadrapo [espara'ðrapo] nm sticking plaster.

esparcido, a [espar'θiðo, a] a scattered; (fig) jolly, cheerful.

esparcimiento [esparθi'mjento] nm (de líquido) spilling; (dispersión) spreading; (derramamiento) scattering; (fig) cheerfulness.

esparcir [espar'θir] vt to spread; (derramar) to scatter; (líquido) to spill; ~se vr to spread (out); to scatter; to spill; (divertirse) to enjoy o.s.

espárrago [es'parraxo] nm asparagus.

espasmo [es'pasmo] nm spasm.

especia [es'peθja] nf spice.

especial [espe'θjal] a special; ~idad nf speciality.

especie [es'peθje] nf (BIO) species; (clase) kind, sort; (asunto) matter; (comentario) remark, comment; en ~ in kind.

especificar [espeθifi'kar] vt to specify; específico, a a specific.

espécimen [es'peθimen] (pl especímenes) nm specimen.

especioso, a [espe'θjoso, a] a (perfecto) perfect; (fig) deceitful.

espectáculo [espek'takulo] nm (gen) spectacle; (TEATRO etc) show.

espectador, a [espekta'ðor, a] nm/f spectator.

espectro [es'pektro] nm ghost; (fig) spectre.

especular [espeku'lar] vt, vi to speculate; especulativo, a a speculative.

espejismo [espe'xismo] nm mirage.

espejo [es'pexo] nm mirror; (fig) model; ~ de retrovisión rear-view mirror.

espeluznante [espeluθ'nante] a inv horrifying, hair-raising.

espera [es'pera] nf (pausa, intervalo) wait, period of waiting; (JUR. plazo) respite; en ~ de waiting for; (con expectativa) expecting.

esperanza [espe'ranθa] nf (confianza) hope; (expectativa) expectation; (perspectiva) prospect; esperanzar vt to give hope to.

esperar [espe'rar] vt (aguardar) to wait for; (tener expectativa de) to expect; (desear) to hope for // vi to wait; to expect; to hope.

esperma [es'perma] nf sperm.

espesar [espe'sar] vt to thicken; ~se vr to thicken, get thicker.

espeso, a [es'peso, a] a thick; espesor nm thickness.

espetar [espe'tar] vt (pollo) to put on a spit or skewer; (pregunta) to pop; (dar: reto, sermón) to give.

espetón [espe'ton] nm (asador) spit, skewer; (aguja) large pin; (empujón) jab, poke.

espía [es'pia] nm/f spy; espiar vt (observar) to spy on; (acechar) to watch out for.

espina [es'pina] nf thorn; (de madera, astilla) splinter; (de pez) bone; ~ dorsal spine.

espinaca [espi'naka] nf spinach.

espinar [espi'nar] vt (herir) to prick; (fig) to sting, hurt.

espinazo [espi'naθo] nm spine, backbone.

espino [es'pino] nm hawthorn.

espinoso, a [espi'noso, a] a (planta) thorny, prickly; (fig) bony.

espionaje [espjo'naxe] nm spying, espionage.

espiral [espi'ral] a, nf spiral.

espirar [espi'rar] vt to breathe out, exhale.

espiritista [espiri'tista] a, nm/f spiritualist.

espíritu [es'piritu] nm spirit; espiritual a spiritual.

espita [es'pita] nf tap; (fig: fam) drunkard.

esplendidez [esplendi'ðeθ] nf (abundancia) lavishness; (magnificencia) splendour.

esplendor [esplen'dor] nm splendour.

espolear [espole'ar] *vt* to spur on.

espolvorear [espolßore'ar] *vt* (*echar polvos*) to dust; (*esparcir*) to dust, sprinkle.

esponja [es'ponxa] *nf* sponge; (*fig*) sponger.

esponjarse [espon'xarse] *vr* (*fam: hincharse*) to swell with pride; (: *de salud*) to glow with health.

esponjoso, a [espon'xoso, a] *a* spongy, porous.

espontaneidad [espontanei'ðað] *nf* spontaneity; **espontáneo, a** *a* spontaneous.

esposa [es'posa] *nf* wife; **~s** *nfpl* handcuffs; **esposar** *vt* to handcuff.

esposo [es'poso] *nm* husband.

espuela [es'pwela] *nf* spur.

espuma [es'puma] *nf* foam; (*de cerveza*) froth, head; (*de jabón*) lather; **espumoso, a** *a* frothy, foamy; (*vino*) sparkling.

esqueleto [eske'leto] *nm* skeleton.

esquema [es'kema] *nm* (*diagrama*) diagram; (*dibujo*) plan; (*plan*) scheme; (FILOSOFIA) schema.

esquí [es'ki] (*pl* **esquís**) *nm* (*objeto*) ski; (*deporte*) skiing.

esquilar [eski'lar] *vt* to shear.

esquilmar [eskil'mar] *vt* (*cosechar*) to harvest; (*empobrecer: suelo*) to exhaust; (*fig*) to skin.

esquimal [eski'mal] *a, nm/f* Eskimo.

esquina [es'kina] *nf* corner.

esquirol [eski'rol] *nm* (*fam*) blackleg.

esquivar [eski'ßar] *vt* to avoid; (*evadir*) to dodge, elude; **~ se** *vr* to withdraw.

esquivez [eski'ßeθ] *nf* (*altanería*) aloofness; (*desdeño*) scorn, disdain; **esquivo, a** *a* (*altanero*) aloof; (*desdeñoso*) scornful, disdainful.

esta ['esta] *det ver* **este**.

ésta ['esta] *pron ver* **éste**.

está *vb ver* **estar**.

estabilidad [estaßili'ðað] *nf* stability; **estable** *a* stable.

establecer [estaßle'θer] *vt* to establish; **~ se** *vr* to establish o.s.; (*echar raíces*) to settle; **establecimiento** *nm* establishment.

estaca [es'taka] *nf* stake, post; (*para tiendas*) peg.

estacada [esta'kaða] *nf* (*cerca*) fence, fencing; (*palenque*) stockade.

estación [esta'θjon] *nf* station; (*del año*) season; **~ de autobuses** bus station.

estacionamiento [estaθjona'mjento] *nm* (AUTO) parking; (MIL) stationing; (*colocación*) placing.

estacionar [estaθjo'nar] *vt* (AUTO) to park; (MIL) to station; (*colocar*) to place; **~ lo, a** *a* stationary; (COM: *mercado*) slack.

estadio [es'taðjo] *nm* (*fase*) stage, phase; (DEPORTE) stadium.

estadista [esta'ðista] *nm* (POL) statesman; (ESTADÍSTICA) statistician.

estadística [esta'ðistika] *nf* (*una ~*) figure, statistic; (*ciencia*) statistics *sg.*

estado [es'taðo] *nm* (POL: *condición*) state; (*social*) status; **~ de las cuentas** statement of accounts; **~ mayor** staff; **E~s Unidos** (**EE. UU.**) United States (USA).

estafa [es'tafa] *nf* swindle, trick; **estafar** *vt* to swindle, defraud.

estafeta [esta'feta] *nf* (*correo*) post; (*oficina de correos*) post office; **~ diplomática** diplomatic bag.

estallar [esta'ʎar] *vi* to burst; (*explotar*) to explode; (*epidemia, rebelión*) to break out; **~ en llanto** to burst into tears; **estallido** *nm* explosion; (*fig*) outbreak.

estampa [es'tampa] *nf* (*imagen*) image; (*impresión, imprenta*) print, engraving; (*imagen, figura: de persona*) appearance; (*fig: huella*) footprint.

estampado, a [estam'paðo, a] *a* printed // *nm* (*impresión: acción*) printing; (: *efecto*) print; (*marca*) stamping.

estampar [estam'par] *vt* (*imprimir*) to print; (*marcar*) to stamp; (*metal*) to engrave; (*poner sello en*) to stamp; (*fig*) to stamp, imprint.

estampida [estam'piða] *nf* stampede; (*estampido*) bang, report.

estampido [estam'piðo] *nm* bang, report.

estampilla [estam'piʎa] *nf* stamp.

están *vb ver* **estar**.

estancar [estan'kar] *vt* (*aguas*) to hold up, hold back; (COM) to monopolize; (*fig*) to block, hold up; **~ se** *vr* to stagnate.

estancia [es'tanθja] *nf* (*permanencia*) stay; (*sala*) living-room; (AM) farm, ranch; **estanciero** *nm* farmer, rancher.

estanco, a [es'tanko, a] *a* watertight // *nm* (*monopolio*) state monopoly; (*tienda*) tobacconist's (shop).

estandarizar [estandari'θar] *vt* to standardize.

estandarte [estan'darte] *nm* banner, standard.

estanque [es'tanke] *nm* (*lago*) pool, pond; (AGR) reservoir.

estanquero, a [estan'kero, a], **estanquillero, a** [estanki'ʎero, a] *nm/f* tobacconist.

estante [es'tante] *nm* (*armario*) rack, stand; (*biblioteca*) bookcase; (*anaquel*) shelf; (AM) prop; **estantería** *nf* shelving, shelves *pl.*

estantigua [estan'tixwa] *nf* (*fantasma*) apparition.

estaño [es'taɲo] *nm* tin.

estar [es'tar] *vi* (*gen*) to be; (*en casa*) to be in; (*ubicarse*) to be found; (*presente*) to be present; **estamos a 2 de mayo** it is the 2nd May; **¿cómo está Ud?** how are you?; **~ enfermo** to be ill; **~ viejo/joven** (*parecerse*) to seem old/young; (*seguido de una preposición*) **¿a cuánto estamos de Madrid?** how far are we from Madrid?; **~ de fiesta o vacaciones** to be on holiday; **las uvas están a 5 pesetas** grapes are at 5 pesetas; **María no está** Maria isn't in; **~ por** (. *moción*) to be in favour of; (: *persona*) to support, back; **está por hacer** it remains to be done; **¿estamos?** are we agreed?

estas ['estas] *det ver* **este**.

éstas ['estas] *pron ver* **éste**.

estás *vb ver* **estar**.

estatal [esta'tal] *a inv* state cpd.

estático, a [es'tatiko, a] *a* static.

estatificar [estatifi'kar] *vt* to nationalize.

estatua [es'tatwa] *nf* statue.

estatuir [estatu'ir] *vt* (*establecer*) to establish; (*determinar*) to prove.

estatura [esta'tura] *nf* stature, height.

estatuto [esta'tuto] *nm* (*JUR*) statute; (*de ciudad*) bye-law; (*de comité*) rule.

este ['este] *nm* east.

este, esta, estos, estas ['este, 'esta, 'estos, 'estas] *det* (*sg*) this; (*pl*) these.

éste, ésta, éstos, éstas ['este, 'esta, 'estos, 'estas] *pron* (*sg*) this (one); (*pl*) these (ones); ~... **ése**... the latter... the former... .

esté *etc vb ver* **estar**.

estela [es'tela] *nf* wake, wash; (*fig*) trail.

estenografía [estenoɣra'fia] *nf* shorthand, stenography.

estepa [es'tepa] *nf* (*GEO*) steppe.

estera [es'tera] *nf* mat(ting).

estereo... [estereo] *pref* stereo...; ~**fónico, a** *a* stereophonic; ~**tipar** *vt* to stereotype; ~**tipo** *nm* stereotype.

estéril [es'teril] *a* sterile, barren; (*fig*) vain, futile.

esterlina [ester'lina] *a*: **libra** ~ pound sterling.

estético, a [es'tetiko, a] *a* aesthetic // *nf* aesthetics *sg*.

estiércol [es'tjerkol] *nm* dung, manure.

estigma [es'tiɣma] *nm* stigma.

estilar [esti'lar] *vi*, ~**se** *vr* to be in fashion, be used, be worn.

estilo [es'tilo] *nm* style; (*TEC*) stylus; (*DEPORTE*) stroke; **algo por el** ~ something of the sort.

estima [es'tima] *nf* esteem, respect.

estimación [estima'θjon] *nf* (*evaluación*) estimation; (*aprecio*, *afecto*) esteem, regard.

estimar [esti'mar] *vt* (*evaluar*) to estimate; (*valorar*) to value; (*apreciar*) to esteem, respect; (*pensar*, *considerar*) to think, reckon; **¡se estima!** thanks very much!

estimulante [estimu'lante] *a* stimulating // *nm* stimulant; **estimular** *vt* to stimulate; (*excitar*) to excite; (*animar*) to encourage; **estímulo** *nm* stimulus; (*ánimo*) encouragement.

estío [es'tio] *nm* summer.

estipulación [estipula'θjon] *nf* stipulation, condition; **estipular** *vt* to stipulate.

estirado, a [esti'raðo, a] *a* (*tenso*) (stretched *or* drawn) tight; (*fig*) stiff, pompous.

estirar [esti'rar] *vt* to stretch; (*conversa-*

ción, *presupuesto*) to stretch out; ~**se** *vr* to stretch.

estirón [esti'ron] *nm* pull, tug; (*crecimiento*) spurt, sudden growth **dar un** ~ to shoot up.

estirpe [es'tirpe] *nf* stock, lineage.

estival [esti'βal] *a* summer cpd.

esto ['esto] *pron* this, this thing *or* matter; ~ **de la boda** this business about the wedding.

estofa [es'tofa] *nf* (*tela*) quilting; (*calidad*, *clase*) quality, class.

estofado, a [esto'faðo, a] *a* (*CULIN*) stewed; (*bordado*) quilted // *nm* stew.

estofar [esto'far] *vt* (*bordar*) to quilt; (*CULIN*) to stew.

estoico, a [es'toiko, a] *a* (*FILOSOFÍA*) stoic(al); (*fig*) cold, indifferent.

estólido, a [es'toliðo, a] *a* stupid.

estómago [es'tomaɣo] *nm* stomach; **tener** ~ to be thick-skinned.

estorbar [estor'βar] *vt* to hinder, obstruct; (*fig*) to bother, disturb // *vi* to be in the way; **estorbo** *nm* (*molestia*) bother, nuisance; (*obstáculo*) hindrance, obstacle.

estornudar [estornu'ðar] *vi* to sneeze.

estos ['estos] *det ver* **este**.

éstos ['estos] *pron ver* **éste**.

estoy *vb ver* **estar**.

estrafalario, a [estrafa'larjo, a] *a* odd, eccentric; (*desarreglado*) slovenly, sloppy.

estragar [estra'xar] *vt* to deprave, corrupt; (*deteriorar*) to ruin; **estrago** *nm* ruin, destrucion; **hacer estragos en** to wreak havoc among.

estragón [estra'xon] *nm* (*CULIN*) tarragon.

estrangul [estran'gul] *nm* mouthpiece.

estrangulación [estrangula'θjon] *nf* strangulation.

estrangulador, a [estrangula'ðor, a] *nm/f* strangler // *nm* (*TEC*) throttle; (*AUTO*) choke.

estrangulamiento [estrangula'mjento] *nm* (*AUTO*) bottleneck.

estrangular [estrangu'lar] *vt* (*persona*) to strangle; (*MED*) to strangulate.

estraperlo [estra'perlo] *nm* black market.

estratagema [estrata'xema] *nf* (*MIL*) stratagem; (*astucia*) cunning.

estrategia [estra'texja] *nf* strategy; **estratégico, a** *a* strategic.

estratificar [estratifi'kar] *vt* to stratify.

estrato [es'trato] *nm* stratum, layer.

estrechar [estre'tʃar] *vt* (*reducir*) to narrow; (*vestido*) to take in; (*persona*) to hug, embrace; ~**se** *vr* (*reducirse*) to narrow, grow narrow; (*apretarse*) to embrace; (*reducir los gastos*) to economize; ~ **la mano** to shake hands; ~ **amistad con alguien** to become very friendly with sb.

estrechez [estre'tʃeθ] *nf* narrowness; (*de ropa*) tightness; (*intimidad*) intimacy; (*COM*) want *or* shortage of money; **estrecheces** *nfpl* financial difficulties; ~ **de conciencia** small-mindedness; ~ **de miras** narrow-mindedness.

estrecho, a [es'tretʃo, a] a narrow; *(apretado)* tight; *(íntimo)* close, intimate; *(miserable)* mean // nm strait.

estregar [estre'xar] vt *(sobar)* to rub (hard); *(rascar)* to scrape.

estrella [es'treʎa] nf star; ~ **de mar** starfish.

estrellar [estre'ʎar] vt *(hacer añicos)* to smash (to pieces); *(huevos)* to fry; ~**se** vr to smash; *(chocarse)* to crash; *(fracasar)* to be smashed to pieces.

estremecer [estreme'θer] vt to shake; ~**se** vr to shake, tremble; **estremecimiento** nm *(conmoción)* tremor; *(sobresalto)* shock; *(temblor)* trembling, shaking.

estrenar [estre'nar] vt *(vestido)* to wear for the first time; *(casa)* to move into; *(película, obra de teatro)* to present for the first time; ~**se** vr *(persona)* to make one's début; **estreno** nm *(primer uso)* first use; *(en un empleo)* début, first appearance; *(CINE etc)* première.

estreñir [estre'nir] vt to constipate; ~**se** vr to become constipated.

estrépito [es'trepito] nm noise, racket; *(fig)* fuss; **estrepitoso, a** a noisy; *(fiesta)* rowdy, boisterous.

estría [es'tria] nf groove.

estribar [estri'βar] vi: ~ **en** to rest on, be supported by.

estribo [es'triβo] nm *(de jinete)* stirrup; *(de coche, tren)* step; *(de puente)* support; *(fig)* basis, foundation; *(GEO)* spur.

estribor [estri'βor] nm starboard.

estricnina [estrik'nina] nf strychnine.

estricto, a [es'trikto, a] a *(riguroso)* strict; *(severo)* severe.

estro ['estro] nm inspiration.

estropajo [estro'paxo] nm scourer.

estropear [estrope'ar] vt *(arruinar)* to spoil; *(dañar)* to damage; *(lisiar)* to maim; *(tullir)* to cripple; ~**se** vr *(objeto)* to get damaged; *(persona)* to be crippled.

estructura [estruk'tura] nf structure.

estruendo [es'trwendo] nm *(ruido)* racket, din; *(fig: alboroto)* uproar, turmoil; *(pompa)* pomp.

estrujar [estru'xar] vt *(apretar)* to squeeze; *(aplastar)* to crush; *(magullar)* to bruise; *(fig)* to drain, bleed.

estuario [es'twarjo] nm estuary.

estuche [es'tutʃe] nm box, case.

estudiante [estu'ðjante] nm/f student; **estudiantil** a inv student cpd.

estudiantina [estuðjan'tina] nf student music group.

estudiar [estu'ðjar] vt to study.

estudio [es'tuðjo] nm study; *(CINE, ARTE, RADIO)* studio; ~**s** nmpl studies; *(erudición)* learning sg; ~**so, a** a studious.

estufa [es'tufa] nf heater, fire.

estulticia [estul'tiθja] nf foolishness.

estupefacto, a [estupe'fakto, a] a speechless, thunderstruck.

estupendo, a [estu'pendo, a] a wonderful,

terrific; *(fam)* great; ¡~! that's great!, fantastic!

estupidez [estupi'ðeθ] nf *(torpeza)* stupidity; *(tontería)* piece of nonsense.

estúpido, a [es tupiðo, a] a stupid, silly.

estupor [estu por] nm stupor; *(fig)* astonishment, amazement.

estupro [es'tupro] nm rape.

estuve etc vb ver **estar.**

etapa [e'tapa] nf stage; *(DEPORTE)* leg; *(parada)* stopping place; *(fig)* stage, phase.

eternidad [eterni'ðaθ] nf eternity; **eterno, a** a eternal, everlasting.

ético, a ['etiko, a] a ethical // nf ethics pl.

etíope [e'tiope] a, nm/f Ethiopian.

Etiopía [etjo'pia] nf Etiopia.

etiqueta [eti'keta] nf *(modales)* etiquette; *(papel)* label, tag.

eucalipto [euka'lipto] nm eucalyptus.

Eucaristía [eukaris'tia] nf Eucharist.

eufemismo [eufe'mismo] nm euphemism.

euforia [eu'forja] nf euphoria.

eugenesia [euxe'nesja] nf, **eugenismo** [euxe'nismo] nm eugenics sg.

eunuco [eu'nuko] nm eunuco.

Europa [eu'ropa] nf Europe; **europeo, a** a, nm/f European.

éuscaro, a ['euskaro, a] a Basque // nm *(lengua)* Basque.

Euskadi [eus'kaði] nm the Basque Provinces pl.

eutanasia [euta'nasja] nf euthanasia.

evacuación [eβakwa'θjon] nf evacuation; **evacuar** vt to evacuate.

evadir [eβa'ðir] vt to evade, avoid; ~**se** vr to escape.

evaluar [eβa'lwar] vt to evaluate.

evangélico, a [eβan'xeliko a] a evangelic(al)

evangelio [eβan'xeljo] nm gospel.

evaporación [eβapora'θjon] nf evaporation.

evaporar [eβapo'rar] vt to evaporate; ~**se** vr to vanish.

evasión [eβa'sjon] nf escape, flight; *(fig)* evasion.

evasivo, a [eβa'siβo, a] a evasive non-committal.

evento [e'βento] nm unforeseen event; *(eventualidad)* eventuality; **a cualquier** ~ in any event.

eventual [eβen'twal] a possible, conditional *(upon circumstances)*; *(trabajador)* casual, temporary.

evidencia [eβi'ðenθja] nf *(certidumbre)* evidence, proof; **evidenciar** vt *(hacer patente)* to make evident; *(probar)* to prove, show; **evidenciarse** vr to be evident.

evidente [eβi'ðente] a obvious, clear, evident.

evitar [eβi'tar] vt *(evadir)* to avoid; *(impedir)* to prevent.

evocar [eβo'kar] vt to evoke, call forth.

evolución [eβolu'θjon] nf *(desarrollo)* evolution, development; *(cambio)* change;

(MIL) manoeuvre; **evolucionar** vi to evolve; (MIL, AVIAT) to manoeuvre.

ex [eks] a ex-; **el ~ ministro** the former minister, the ex-minister.

exacerbar [eksaθer'βar] vt to irritate, annoy; (agravar) to aggravate.

exactitud [eksakti'tuδ] nf exactness; (precisión) accuracy; (puntualidad) punctuality; **exacto, a** a exact; accurate; punctual; **¡exacto!** exactly!

exageración [eksaxera'θjon] nf exaggeration; **exagerar** vt, vi to exaggerate.

exaltado, a [eksal'taδo, a] a (apasionado) over-excited, worked-up; (exagerado) extreme; (excitado) elated.

exaltar [eksal'tar] vt to exalt, glorify; ~**se** vr (excitarse) to get excited or worked-up; (arrebatarse) to get carried away.

examen [ek'samen] nm examination.

examinar [eksami'nar] vt to examine; ~**se** vr to be examined, sit an examination.

exangüe [ek'sangwe] a (desangrado) bloodless; (sin fuerzas) weak.

exasperar [eksaspe'rar] vt to exasperate; ~**se** vr to get exasperated, lose patience.

Exca. abr de **Excelencia.**

excedente [eksθe'δente] a, nm excess, surplus.

exceder [eksθe'δer] vt to exceed, surpass; ~**se** vr (extralimitarse) to go too far; (sobrepasarse) to excel o.s.

excelencia [eksθe'lenθja] nf excellence; **E~** Excellency; **excelente** a excellent.

exceso, a [eks'θelso, a] a lofty, sublime.

excentricidad [eksθentriθi'δaδ] nf eccentricity; **excéntrico, a** a, nm/f eccentric.

excepción [eksθep'θjon] nf exception; **excepcional** a exceptional.

excepto [eks'θepto] ad excepting, except (for).

exceptuar [eksθep'twar] vt to except, exclude.

excesivo, a [eksθe'siβo, a] a excessive.

exceso [eks'θeso] nm (gen) excess; (COM) surplus.

excitación [eksθita'θjon] nf (sensación) excitement; (acción) excitation.

excitado, a [eksθi'taδo, a] a excited; (emociones) aroused; **excitar** vt to excite; (incitar) to urge; **excitarse** vr to get excited.

exclamación [eksklama'θjon] nf exclamation; **exclamar** vi to exclaim.

excluir [eksklu'ir] vt to exclude; (dejar fuera) to shut out; (descartar) to reject; **exclusión** nf exclusion; (descarte) rejection; **con exclusión de** excluding.

exclusiva [eksklu'siβa], **exclusividad** [eksklusiβi'δaδ] nf exclusiveness; (PRENSA) exclusive; (COM) sole right or agency.

exclusivo, a [eksklu'siβo, a] a exclusive; (único) sole.

Excmo. abr de **excelentísmo.**

excomulgar [ekskomul'xar] vt (REL) to excommunicate; (excluir) to ban, banish.

excomunión [eksko̩mu'njon] nf excommunication.

excoriar [eksko'rjar] vt to flay, skin.

excursión [ekskur'sjon] nf excursion, outing; **excursionismo** nm sightseeing.

excusa [eks'kusa] nf excuse; (disculpa) apology.

excusado, a [eksku'saδo, a] a unnecessary; (disculpado) excused, forgiven // nm lavatory, toilet.

excusar [eksku'sar] vt to excuse; (evitar) to avoid; (impedir) to prevent; ~**se** vr (rehusarse) to decline a request; (disculparse) to apologize.

execrar [ekse'krar] vt to loathe.

exención [eksen'θjon] nf exemption.

exento, a [ek'sento, a] pp de **eximir** // a exempt; ~ **de derechos** tax-free.

exequias [ek'sekjas] nfpl funeral rites, obsequies.

exhalación [eksala'θjon] nf (del aire) exhalation; (vapor) fumes pl, vapour; (rayo) shooting star.

exhalar [eksa'lar] vt to exhale, breathe out; (olor etc) to give off; (suspiro) to breathe, heave.

exhausto, a [ek'sausto, a] a exhausted.

exhibición [eksiβi'θjon] nf exhibition, display, show.

exhibir [eksi'βir] vt to exhibit, display, show.

exhortación [eksorta'θjon] nf exhortation; **exhortar** vt: **exhortar a** to exhort to.

exigencia [eksi'xenθja] nf demand, requirement; **exigente** a demanding.

exigir [eks'xir] vt (gen) to demand, require; (pago) to exact.

exilio [ek'siljo] nm exile.

eximio, a [ek'simjo, a] a (excelente) choice, select; (eminente) distinguished, eminent.

eximir [eksi'mir] vt to exempt.

existencia [eksis'tenθja] nf existence; ~**s** nfpl stock(s) (pl).

existir [eksis'tir] vi to exist, be.

éxito [eksito] nm (resultado) result, outcome; (triunfo) success; **tener ~** to be successful.

exonerar [eksone'rar] vt to exonerate; ~ **de una obligación** to free from an obligación.

exorcizar [eksorθi'θar] vt to exorcize.

exótico, a [ek'sotiko, a] a exotic.

expandir [ekspan'dir] vt to expand.

expansión [ekspan'sjon] nf expansion.

expatriarse [ekspa'trjarse] vr to emigrate; (POL) to go into exile.

expectativa [ekspekta'tiβa] nf (espera) expectation; (perspectiva) prospect.

expedición [ekspeδi'θjon] nf (excursión) expedition; (envío) shipment; (rapidez) speed.

expediente [ekspe'δjente] nm expedient; (JUR: procedimento) action, proceedings pl; (: papeles) dossier, file, record.

expedir [ekspe'ðir] vt (despachar) to send, forward; (libreta cívica, pasaporte) to issue; (fig) to deal with.

expedito, a [ekspe'ðito, a] a (libre) clear, free; (pronto) prompt, speedy.

expendedor, a [ekspende'ðor, a] nm/f (vendedor) dealer; (aparato) (vending) machine; ~ **de cigarrillos** cigarette machine.

expendeduría [ekspendeðu'ria] nf shop; (estanco) tobacconist's (shop).

expensas [eks'pensas] nfpl expenses; **a ~ de** at the expense of.

experiencia [ekspe'rjenθja] nf experience; (científica) experiment.

experimentado, a [eksperimen'taðo, a] a experienced.

experimentar [eksperimen'tar] vt (en laboratorio) to experiment with; (probar) to test, try out; (notar, observar) to experience; (sufrir) to suffer; **experimento** nm experiment.

experto, a [eks'perto, a] a (práctico) expert; (diestro) skilled, experienced // nm/f expert.

expiar [ekspi'ar] vt to atone for.

expirar [ekspi'rar] vi to expire.

explayar [ekspla'jar] vt to extend, expand; ~**se** vr to extend, spread; ~**se con uno** to confide in sb.

explicación [eksplika'θjon] nf explanation; **explicar** vt to explain; **explicarse** vr to explain (o.s.).

explícito, a [eks'pliθito, a] a explicit.

explorador, a [eksplora'ðor, a] nm/f (pionero) explorer; (MIL) scout // nm (MED) probe; (TEC) (radar) scanner; **los E~es** the Scouts.

explorar [eksplo'rar] vt to explore; (MED) to probe; (radar) to scan.

explosión [eksplo'sjon] nf explosion; **explosivo, a** a explosive.

explotación [eksplota'θjon] nf exploitation; (de planta etc) running, operation; **explotar** vt to exploit; to run, operate // vi to explode.

exponer [ekspo'ner] vt to expose; (cuadro) to display; (vida) to risk; (idea) to explain; ~**se** vr to expose o.s., leave o.s. open.

exportación [eksporta'θjon] nf (acción) export; (mercancías) exports pl; **exportar** vt to export.

exposición [eksposi'θjon] nf (gen) exposure; (de arte) show, exhibition; (petición) petition; (explicación) explanation; (narración) account, statement.

exposímetro [ekspo'simetro] nm (FOTO) exposure meter.

exprés [eks'pres] nm (AM) express (train).

expresar [ekspre'sar] vt to express; **expresión** nf expression; **expresiones** nfpl regards.

expreso, a [eks'preso, a] pp de **expresar** // a (claro) specific, clear; (rápido) fast // nm: **mandar por ~** to send by express (delivery).

exprimir [ekspri'mir] vt (fruta) to squeeze (out); (ropa) to wring out; (fig) to express emphatically.

expropiar [ekspro'pjar] vt to expropriate.

expuesto, a [eks'pwesto] a exposed; (cuadro etc) on show, on display.

expugnar [ekspuɣ'nar] vt to take by storm.

expulsar [ekspul'sar] vt (echar) to eject; (arrojar) to throw out; (expeler) to expel; (desalojar) to drive out; (despedir) to sack, fire; (a un futbolista) to send off; **expulsión** nf expulsion; sending-off.

expurgar [ekspur'ɣar] vt to expurgate.

exquisito, a [ekski'sito, a] a exquisite; (agradable) delightful.

éxtasis ['ekstasis] nm ecstasy.

extender [eksten'der] vt (gen) to extend; (los brazos) to stretch out, hold out; (mapa) to spread (out), open (out); (mantequilla) to spread; (certificado) to issue; (cheque, recibo) to make out; (documento) to draw up; ~**se** vr (gen) to extend (en el suelo) to stretch out; (epidemia) to spread; **extendido, a** a (abierto) spread out, open; (brazos) outstretched; (prevaleciente) widespread; **extensión** nf (de país) expanse, stretch; (de libro) extent; (de tiempo) length, duration; (AM) extension; **en toda la extensión de la palabra** in every sense of the word; **extenso, a** a extensive; (prevaleciente) widespread.

extenuar [ekste'nwar] vi (agotar) to exhaust; (debilitar) to weaken.

exterior [ekste'rjor] a (de fuera) external; (afuera) outside, exterior; (apariencia) outward; (comercio) foreign // nm (gen) exterior, outside; (aspecto) outward appearance; (DEPORTE) wing(er); **el ~** foreign parts pl; **al ~** outwardly, on the surface.

exterminar [ekstermi'nar] vt to exterminate; **exterminio** nm extermination.

externo, a [eks'terno, a] a (exterior) external, outside; (superficial) outward // nm/f day pupil.

extinguir [ekstin'gir] vt (fuego) to extinguish, put out; (raza, población) to wipe out; ~**se** vr (fuego) to go out; (ICO) to die out, become extinct.

extinto, a [eks'tinto, a] a extinct.

extintor [ekstin'tor] nm (fire) extinguisher.

extra ['ekstra] a, nm/f extra // nm extra; (bono) bonus.

extracción [ekstrak'θjon] nf extraction; (en lotería) draw.

extracto [eks'trakto] nm extract.

extraer [ekstra'er] vt to extract, take out.

extralimitarse [ekstralimi'tarse] vr to go too far.

extranjero, a [ekstran'xero, a] a foreign // nm/f foreigner // nm foreign lands pl; **en el ~** abroad.

extrañar [ekstra'ɲar] vt (desterrar) to exile; (sorprender) to find strange or odd;

(AM) to miss; ~se vr (sorprenderse) to be amazed, be surprised; (distanciarse) to become estranged, grow apart.

extrañeza [ekstra'neθa] nf (rareza) strangeness, oddness; (asombro) amazement, surprise.

extraño, a [eks'trano, a] a (extranjero) foreign; (raro, sorprendente) strange, odd.

extraordinario, a [ekstraorði'narjo, a] a extraordinary; (edición, número) special // nm (plato) special dish; (de periódico) special edition; **horas ~as** overtime sg.

extravagancia [ekstraßa'xanθja] nf extravagance; **extravagante** a extravagant; (extraño) strange, odd; (excéntrico) eccentric; (estrafalario) outlandish.

extraviado, a [ekstra'ßjaðo, a] a lost, missing.

extraviar [ekstra'ßjar] vt (desviar) to mislead; (perder) to lose, misplace; ~se vr to lose one's way, get lost.

extravío [ekstra'ßio] nm loss; (fig) deviation.

extremar [ekstre'mar] vt to carry to extremes; ~se vr to do one's utmost, make every effort.

extremaunción [ekstremaun'θjon] nf extreme unction.

extremeño, a [ekstre'meno, a] a, nm/f Extremaduran.

extremidad [ekstremi'ðað] nf (punta) extremity; (fila) edge; ~es nfpl (ANAT) extremities.

extremo, a [eks'tremo, a] a extreme; (último) last // nm end; (límite, grado sumo) extreme; **en último** ~ as a last resort; ~ **derecho/izquierdo** outside-right/ outside-left.

extrínseco, a [eks'trinseko, a] a extrinsic.

extrovertido, a [ekstroßer'tiðo, a] a, nm/f extrovert.

exuberancia [eksuße'ranθja] nf exuberance; **exuberante** a exuberant; (fig) luxuriant, lush.

exvoto [eks'ßoto] nm votive offering.

eyacular [ejaku'lar] vt, vi to ejaculate.

F

f.a.b. abr de **franco a bordo** f.o.b. (free on board).

fábrica ['faßrika] nf factory; **marca de** ~ trademark; **precio de** ~ factory price.

fabricación [faßrika'θjon] nf (manufactura) manufacture; (producción) production; **de** ~ **casera** home-made; ~ **en serie** mass production.

fabricante [faßri'kante] nm/f manufacturer.

fabricar [faßri'kar] vt (hacer) to manufacture, make; (construir) to build; (elaborar) to fabricate, devise.

fabril [fa'ßril] a: **industria** ~ manufacturing industry.

fábula ['faßula] nf (cuento) fable; (chisme) rumour.

facción [fak'θjon] nf (POL) faction; (del rostro) feature.

fácil ['faθil] a (simple) easy; (probable) likely.

facilidad [faθili'ðað] nf (capacidad) ease; (sencillez) simplicity; (de palabra) fluency; ~es nfpl facilities.

facilitar [faθili'tar] v: (hacer fácil) to make easy; (proporcionar) to provide; (hacer posible) to arrange; (hacer más fácil) to facilitate.

fácilmente ['faθilmente] ad easily.

factible [fak'tißle] a feasible.

factor [fak'tor] nm factor.

factura [fak'tura] nf (cuenta) bill; (hechura) manufacture; **facturar** vt (COM) to invoice, charge for.

facultad [fakul'tað] nf (aptitud, ESCOL etc) faculty; (poder) power.

facha ['fatʃa] nf (fam: aspecto) look; (: desagradable) unpleasant sight.

fachada [fa'tʃaða] nf (ARQ) façade, front.

faena [fa'ena] nf (trabajo) work; (quehacer) task, job; ~s **de la casa** housework sg.

fagot [fa'got] nm (MUS) bassoon.

faisán [fai'san] nm pheasant.

faja ['faxa] nf (para la cintura) sash; (de mujer) corset; (de tierra) strip; (venda) bandage.

falange [fa'lanxe] nf (POL) Falange.

falda ['falda] nf (prenda de vestir) skirt.

falibilidad [falißili'ðað] nf fallibility.

fálico, a ['faliko, a] a phallic.

falo ['falo] nm phallus.

falsedad [false'ðað] nf (hipocresía) falseness; (mentira) falsehood.

falsificar [falsifi'kar] vt (firma etc) to forge; (voto etc) to rig; (moneda) to counterfeit.

falso, a ['falso, a] a (gen) false; (erróneo) mistaken; (moneda etc) fake; **en** ~ falsely.

falta ['falta] nf (defecto) fault, flaw; (privación) lack, want; (ausencia) absence; (carencia) shortage; (equivocación) mistake; (DEPORTE) foul; **hacer** ~ to be missing or lacking.

faltar [fal'tar] vi (escasear) to be lacking, be wanting; (ausentarse) to be absent, be missing; (fallar: mecanismo) to go wrong, break down; **faltan 2 horas para llegar** there are 2 hours to go till arrival; ~ **el respeto a alguien** to be disrespectful to sb; **echar a** ~ **a alguien** to miss sb; **¡no faltaba más!** that's the last straw!

falto, a ['falto, a] a (desposeído) deficient, lacking; (necesitado) poor, wretched.

falla ['faʎa] nf (defecto) fault, flaw; (fracaso) failure.

fallar [fa'ʎar] vt (JUR) to pronounce sentence on // vi (memoria) to fail; (motor) to miss.

fallecer [faʎe'θer] vi to pass away, die; **fallecimiento** nm decease, demise.

fallo ['faʎo] nm (JUR) verdict, ruling; (fracaso) failure.

fama ['fama] *nf* (*renombre*) fame; (*reputación*) reputation.

familia [fa'milja] *nf* family.

familiar [fami'ljar] *a* (*relativo a la familia*) family *cpd*; (*conocido, informal*) familiar // *nm* relative; **~idad** *nf* (*gen*) familiarity; (*informalidad*) homeliness; **~izarse** *vr* to familiarize o.s. with.

famoso, a [fa'moso, a] *a* (*renombrado*) famous; (*fam: fabuloso*) great.

fanático, a [fa'natiko, a] *a* fanatical // *nm/f* (*gen*) fanatic; (*CINE etc*) fan; (*de deportes*) supporter; **fanatismo** *nm* fanaticism.

fanfarrón, ona [fanfa'rron, ona] *a* boastful; (*pey*) showy.

fango ['fango] *nm* mud; **~so, a** *a* muddy.

fantasía [fanta'sia] *nf* fantasy, imagination; (*fam*) conceit, vanity; **joyas de ~** imitation jewellery *sg*.

fantasma [fan'tasma] *nm* (*espectro*) ghost, apparition.

fantástico, a [fan'tastiko, a] *a* fantastic.

farmacéutico, a [farma'θeutiko, a] *a* pharmaceutical // *nm/f* chemist, pharmacist.

farmacia [far'maθja] *nf* chemist's (shop), pharmacy; **~ de turno** all-night chemist.

faro ['faro] *nm* (*NAUT: torre*) lighthouse; (*AUTO*) headlamp; **~s laterales** sidelights; **~s traseros** rear lights.

farol [fa'rol] *nm* (*luz*) lantern, lamp; (*de calle*) streetlamp.

farsa ['farsa] *nf* (*gen*) farce.

farsante [far'sante] *nm/f* fraud, fake.

fascinar [fasθi'nar] *vt* (*deslumbrar*) to fascinate.

fascismo [fas'θismo] *nm* fascism; **fascista** *a, nm/f* fascist.

fase ['fase] *nf* phase.

fastidiar [fasti'ðjar] *vt* (*disgustar*) to annoy, bother; (*estropear*) to spoil; (*aburrir*) to bore; **~se** *vr* (*dañarse*) to harm o.s.; (*disgustarse*) to get annoyed *or* cross.

fastidio [fas'tiðjo] *nm* (*disgusto*) annoyance; (*tedio*) boredom; **~so, a** *a* (*molesto*) annoying; (*aburrido*) tedious.

fatal [fa'tal] *a* (*gen*) fatal; (*inevitable*) unavoidable; (*desgraciado*) ill-fated; (*fam: malo, pésimo*) awful; **~idad** *nf* (*destino*) fate; (*mala suerte*) misfortune.

fatiga [fa'tixa] *nf* (*cansancio*) fatigue, weariness; **fatigar** *vt* to tire, weary; **fatigarse** *vr* to get tired; **fatigoso, a** *a* (*cansador*) tiring; (*aburrido*) tiresome.

fatuo, a [fa'tuo, a] *a* (*vano*) fatuous; (*presuntuoso*) conceited.

fauces ['fauθes] *nfpl* jaws, mouth *sg*.

favor [fa'βor] *nm* favour; **entrada de ~** complimentary ticket; **haga el ~ de...** would you be so good as to..., kindly...; **por ~** please; **~able** *a* favourable.

favorecer [faβore'θer] *vt* (*gen*) to favour; (*vestido etc*) to become, flatter; **este peinado le favorece** this hairstyle suits her.

favorito, a [faβo'rito, a] *a, nm/f* favourite.

faz [faθ] *nf*: **la ~ de la tierra** the face of the earth.

fe [fe] *nf* (*REL*) faith; (*confianza*) belief; (*documento*) certificate; (*lealtad*) fidelity, loyalty; **prestar ~ a** to believe, credit; **actuar con buena/mala ~** to act in good/bad faith; **dar ~ de** to bear witness to.

fealdad [feal'daθ] *nf* ugliness.

febrero [fe'βrero] *nm* February.

febril [fe'βril] *a* feverish.

fecundar [fekun'dar] *vt* (*generar*) to fertilize, make fertile; **fecundo, a** *a* (*fértil*) fertile; (*prolífico*) prolific; (*fructífero*) fruitful; (*abundante*) abundant; (*productivo*) productive.

fecha ['fetʃa] *nf* date; **en ~ próxima** soon; **hasta la ~** to date, so far; **poner ~** to date; **con ~ adelantada** post-dated.

federación [federa'θjon] *nf* federation.

federal [fede'ral] *a* federal; **~ismo** *nm* federalism.

felicidad [feliθi'ðað] *nf* (*satisfacción, contento*) happiness; (*suerte feliz*) (good) luck; **~es** *nfpl* best wishes, congratulations.

felicitación [feliθita'θjon] *nf* congratulation; **felicitar** *vt* to congratulate.

feligrés, esa [feli'xres, esa] *nm/f* parishioner.

feliz [fe'liθ] *a* (*contento*) happy; (*afortunado*) lucky.

felonía [felo'nia] *nf* felony, crime.

felpudo [fel'puðo] *nm* doormat.

femenino, a [feme'nino, a] *a, nm* feminine.

feminista [femi'nista] *nf* feminist.

fénix ['feniks] *nm* (*ave*) phoenix.

fenómeno [fe'nomeno] *nm* phenomenon; (*fig*) freak, accident // *a inv* great // *excl* smashing!, marvellous!

feo, a ['feo, a] *a* (*gen*) ugly; (*desagradable*) bad, nasty.

féretro ['feretro] *nm* (*ataúd*) coffin; (*sarcófago*) bier.

feria ['ferja] *nf* (*gen*) fair; (*AM*) village market; (*día de asueto*) holiday, rest day.

fermentar [fermen'tar] *vi* to ferment.

ferocidad [feroθi'ðað] *nf* fierceness, ferocity.

feroz [fe'roθ] *a* (*cruel*) cruel; (*salvaje*) fierce.

férreo, a ['ferreo, a] *a* iron.

ferretería [ferrete'ria], **ferrería** [ferre'ria] *nf* (*trastes*) ironmongery; (*tienda*) ironmonger's (shop), hardware store.

ferrocarril [ferroka'rril] *nm* railway; **~ de cremallera** rack railway.

fértil ['fertil] *a* (*productivo*) fertile; (*rico*) rich; **fertilidad** *nf* (*gea*) fertility; (*productividad*) fruitfulness; **fertilizar** *vt* to fertilize.

fervor [fer'βor] *nm* fervour; **~oso, a** *a* fervent.

festejar [feste'xar] *vt* (*agasajar*) to

entertain lavishly; (*galantear*) to court; (*su cumpleaños*) to celebrate; **festejo** *nm* (*diversión*) entertainment; (*galanteo*) courtship; (*fiesta*) celebration.

festividad [festiβi'ðað] *nf* festivity.

festivo, a [fes'tiβo, a] *a* (*de fiesta*) festive; (*fig*) witty; (*CINE, LITERATURA*) humorous.

fétido, a ['fetiðo, a] *a* (*hediondo*) foul-smelling; (*podrido*) rotten.

fiado [fi'aðo] *nm*: **comprar al** ~ to buy on credit.

fiador, a [fia'ðor, a] *nm/f* (*JUR*) surety, guarantor; (*COM*) backer // *nm* (*de arma*) safety catch; (*cerrojo*) tumbler; **salir ~ por alguien** to go bail for sb.

fiambre ['fjambre] *nm* cold meat.

fianza ['fjanθa] *nf* surety; (*JUR*): **libertad bajo** ~ release on bail.

fiar [fi'ar] *vt* (*salir garante de*) to guarantee; (*vender a crédito*) to sell on credit // *vi* to trust; ~**se** *vr* to trust (in), rely on; ~**se de uno** to rely on sb.

fiasco ['fjasko] *nm* fiasco.

fibra ['fiβra] *nf* fibre.

ficción [fik'θjon] *nf* fiction.

ficticio, a [fik'tiθjo, a] *a* (*imaginario*) fictitious; (*falso*) fabricated.

ficha ['fitʃa] *nf* (*en juegos*) token, counter; (*tarjeta*) (index) card; (*ELEC*) plug; **fichar** *vt* (*archivar*) to file, index; **estar fichado** to have a record; **fichero** *nm* card index.

fidelidad [fiðeli'ðað] *nf* (*lealtad*) fidelity, loyalty; **alta** ~ high fidelity, hi-fi.

fideos [fi'ðeos] *nmpl* noodles.

fiebre ['fjeβre] *nf* (*MED*) fever; (*fig*) feverish excitement; ~ **amarilla/del heno** yellow/hay fever; ~ **palúdica** malaria; **tener** ~ to have a temperature.

fiel [fjel] *a* (*leal*) faithful, loyal; (*fiable*) reliable; (*exacto*) accurate, exact // *nm* inspector; (*aguja*) needle, pointer; **los** ~**es** the faithful.

fieltro ['fjeltro] *nm* felt.

fiereza [fje'reθa] *nf* (*bravura*) fierceness; (*lealdad*) ugliness.

fiero, a ['fjero, a] *a* (*cruel*) cruel; (*feroz*) fierce; (*duro*) harsh // *nf* (*animal feroz*) wild animal or beast.

fiesta ['fjesta] *nf* party; (*de pueblo*) festival; ~**s** *nfpl* (*caricias*) endearments; (*vacaciones*) holiday *sg*; (*broma*) jokes; (*juerga*) fun and games; (*REL*): ~ **de guardar** day of obligation.

figura [fi'ɣura] *nf* (*gen*) figure; (*forma, imagen*) shape, form; (*cara*) face; (*TEATRO*) marionette; (*NAIPES*) face card.

figurar [fiɣu'rar] *vt* (*representar*) to represent; (*fingir*) to figure // *vi* to figure; ~**se** *vr* (*imaginarse*) to imagine; (*suponer*) to suppose.

fijar [fi'xar] *vt* (*gen*) to fix; (*estampilla*) to affix, stick (on); (*fig*) to settle (on), decide; ~ **con hilos** to sew on; ~**se** *vr*: ~**se en** to notice.

fijo, a ['fixo, a] *a* (*gen*) fixed; (*firme*) firm; (*permanente*) permanent // *ad*: **mirar** ~ to stare.

fila ['fila] *nf* row; (*cola, columna*) queue; (*cadena*) line; **ponerse en** ~ to line up, get into line.

filántropo [fi'lantropo] *nm* philanthropist.

filatelia [fila'telja] *nf* philately.

filete [fi'lete] *nm* (*carne*) steak; (*pescado*) fillet.

filial [fi'ljal] *a* filial // *nf* subsidiary.

Filipinas [fili'pinas] *nfpl*: **las** ~ the Philippines.

filmar [fil'mar] *vt* to film, shoot.

filo ['filo] *nm* (*gen*) edge; **sacar** ~ **a** to sharpen; **al** ~ **del mediodía** at about midday; **de doble** ~ double-edged.

filosofía [filoso'fia] *nf* philosophy; **filósofo** *nm* philosopher.

filtrar [fil'trar] *vt, vi* to filter, strain; ~**se** *vr* to filter; (*fig*) to dwindle; **filtro** *nm* (*TEC, utensilio*) filter; (*CULIN*) strainer.

fin [fin] *nm* (*gen*) end; (*objetivo*) aim, purpose; **al** ~ **y al cabo** when all's said and done; **a** ~ **de** in order to; **por** ~ finally; **en** ~ in short; ~ **de semana** weekend; ~**al** **a** final // *nm* end, conclusion // *nf* final; ~**alista** *nm/f* finalist; ~**alizar** *vt* to end, finish // *vi*, ~**alizarse** *vr* to end, come to an end.

financiar [finan'θjar] *vt* to finance; **financiero, a** *a* financial.

finca ['finka] *nf* country estate; (*casa*) country house.

fingir [fin'xir] *vt* (*simular*) to simulate; (*pretextar*) to sham, fake // *vi* (*aparentar*) to pretend, feign; ~**se** *vr* to pretend to be.

finlandés, esa [finlan'des, esa] *a* Finnish // *nm/f* Finn // *nm* (*lengua*) Finnish.

Finlandia [fin'landja] *nf* Finland.

fino, a ['fino, a] *a* (*gen*) fine; (*delgado*) slender; (*puro*) pure; (*de buenas maneras*) polite, refined; (*inteligente*) shrewd.

firma ['firma] *nf* signature; (*COM*) firm, company; **firmar** *vt* to sign.

firme ['firme] *a* (*gen*) firm; (*estable*) stable; (*sólido*) solid; (*compacto*) compact; (*constante*) steady; (*decidido*) resolute // *nm* road (surface); ~**mente** *ad* firmly; ~**za** *nf* firmness; (*constancia*) steadiness; (*solidez*) solidity.

fiscal [fis'kal] *a* fiscal // *nm* Public Prosecutor.

fisgar [fis'xar] *vt* to pry into; (*pescar*) to spear, harpoon.

físico, a ['fisiko, a] *a* physical // *nm* physique // *nm/f* physicist // *nf* physics *sg*.

flaco, a ['flako, a] *a* (*muy delgado*) skinny, lean; (*débil*) weak, feeble.

flagrante [fla'xrante] *a* flagrant.

flamante [fla'mante] *a* brilliant; (*nuevo*) brand-new.

flamenco, a [fla'menko, a] *a* (*de Flandes*) Flemish; (*agitanado*) gipsy // *nm* (*canto y baile*) flamenco.

flan [flan] *nm* creme caramel.

flaqueza [fla'keθa] *nf* (*delgadez*) leanness; (*fig*) weakness.

flash [flaʃ] *nm* (*FOTO*) flash.

flauta ['flauta] *nf* flute.

fleco ['fleko] *nm* fringe.

flecha ['fletʃa] *nf* arrow.

flema ['flema] *nm* phlegm.

flequillo [fle'kiʎo] *nm* (*pelo*) fringe.

flete ['flete] *nm* (*carga*) freight; (*alquiler*) charter; (*precio*) freightage.

flexible [flek'siβle] *a* flexible.

flojo, a ['floxo, a] *a* (*gen*) loose; *sin fuerzas*) limp; (*débil*) weak.

flor [flor] *nf* flower; (*piropo*) compliment; a ~ **de** on the surface of; **~ecer** *vi* (BOT) to flower; (*fig*) to flourish; **~eciente** *a* (BOT) in flower, flowering; (*fig*) thriving.

flota ['flota] *nf* fleet.

flotar [flo'tar] *vi* (*gen*) to float; (*colgar*) to hang; **flote** *nm*: **a flote** afloat; **sacar a flote** (*fig*) to get back on one's feet.

fluctuar [fluk'twar] *vi* (*oscilar*) to fluctuate; (*vacilar*) to waver.

fluidez [flui'ðeθ] *nf* fluidity; (*fig*) fluency.

fluido, a ['fluiðo, a] *a, nm* fluid.

fluir [flu'ir] *vi* to flow.

flujo ['fluxo] *nm* flow; ~ **y reflujo** ebb and flow; ~ **de sangre** (MED) loss of blood.

foca ['foka] *nf* seal.

foco ['foko] *nm* focus; (ELEC) floodlight.

fogón [fo'xon] *nm* (*de cocina*) stove.

fogoso, a [fo'xoso, a] *a* spirited.

follaje [fo'ʎaxe] *nm* foliage.

folleto [fo'ʎeto] *nm* pamphlet.

fomentar [fomen'tar] *vt* (MED) to foment; **fomento** *nm* (MED) fomentation; (*promoción*) promotion; **Ministerio de Fomento** Ministry of Public Works.

fonda ['fonda] *nf* inn; (*restaurante*) buffet.

fondo ['fondo] *nm* (*de mar*) bottom; (*cuarto*) back; (ARTE *etc*) background; (*reserva*) fund; **~s** *nmpl* (COM) funds, resources; **una investigación a ~ a** a thorough investigation; **en el ~ a** at bottom, deep down.

fontanería [fontane'ria] *nf* plumbing; **fontanero** *nm* plumber.

forastero, a [foras'tero, a] *a* (*extraño*) alien, strange // *nm/f* stranger.

forcejear [forθexe'ar] *vi* (*luchar*) to struggle; (*esforzarse*) to make violent efforts.

forjar [for'xar] *vt* to forge.

forma ['forma] *nf* (*figura*) form, shape; (*molde*) mould, pattern; (MED) fitness; (*método*) way, means; **las ~s** the conventions.

formación [forma'θjon] *nf* (*gen*) formation; (*educación*) education.

formal [for'mal] *a* (*gen*) formal; (*fig: persona*) serious; **~idad** *nf* formality; seriousness.

formar [for'mar] *vt* (*componer*) to form, shape; (*constituir*) to make up, constitute; (ESCOL) to train, educate; **~se** *vr* (*cobrar forma*) to form, take form; (*hacer línea*) to form up; (*desarrollarse*) to develop.

formidable [formi'ðaβle] *a* (*temible*) formidable; (*asombroso*) tremendous.

formulario [formu'larjo] *nm* form.

fornido, a [for'niðo, a] *a* strapping, well-built.

foro ['foro] *nm* (*gen*) forum; (JUR) court.

forrar [fo'rrar] *vt* (*abrigo*) to line; (*libro*) to cover; **forro** *nm* (*de cuaderno*) cover; (*costura*) lining; (*de sillón*) upholstery; **forro de freno** brake lining.

fortalecer [fortale'θer] *vt* to strengthen.

fortaleza [forta'leθa] *nf* (*gen*) strength; (*determinación*) resolution.

fortuito, a [for'twito, a] *a* accidental.

fortuna [for'tuna] *nf* (*suerte*) fortune, (*good*) luck; (*riqueza, caudal*) fortune, wealth.

forzar [for'θar] *vt* (*puerta*) to force (open); (*casa*) to break into; (*compeler*) to compel.

forzoso, a [for'θoso, a] *a* necessary.

fosa ['fosa] *nf* (*sepultura*) grave; (*en tierra*) pit, (MED) cavity.

fósforo ['fosforo] *nm* (*metaloide*) phosphorus; (AM) match.

foso ['foso] *nm* ditch; (TEATRO) pit; (AUTO): ~ **de reconocimiento** inspection pit.

foto ['foto] *nf* photo, snap(shot); **~copia** *nf* photocopy; **~copiador** *nm* photocopier; **~copiar** *vt* to photocopy.

fotografía [fotora'fia] *nf* (*gen*) photography; (*una ~*) photograph; **fotografiar** *vt* to photograph.

fotógrafo, a [fo'toxrafo, a] *nm/f* photographer.

fracaso [fra'kaso] *nm* (*desgracia, revés*) failure; **fracasar** *vi* (*gen*) to fail.

fracción [frak'θjon] *nf* fraction; (POL) faction; **fraccionar** *vt* to divide, break up.

fractura [frak'tura] *nf* fracture, break.

fragancia [fra'xanθja] *nf* (*olor*) fragrance; (*perfume*) perfume.

frágil ['fraxil] *a* (*débil*) fragile; (*quebradizo*) breakable; **fragilidad** *nf* fragility; (*de persona*) frailty.

fragmento [frax'mento] *nm* (*pedazo*) fragment.

fragor [fra'xor] *nm* (*ruido intenso*) din; (*de gente*) uproar.

fragua ['fraxwa] *nf* forge; **fraguar** *vt* to forge; (*fig*) to concoct // *vi* to harden.

fraile ['fraile] *nm* (REL) friar; (: *monje*) monk.

frambuesa [fram'bwesa] *nf* raspberry.

francés, esa [fran'θes, esa] *a* French // *nm/f* Frenchman/woman // *nm* (*lengua*) French.

Francia ['franθja] *nf* France.

franco, a ['franko, a] *a* (*leal, abierto*) frank, open; (*generoso, liberal*) generous, liberal; (COM: *exento*) free // *nm* franc.

francotirador, a [frankotira'ðor, a] *nm/f* sniper.

franela [fra'nela] *nf* flannel.

franja ['franxa] *nf* fringe.

franquear [franke'ar] *vt* (*camino*) to clear; (*carta, paquete postal*) to stamp; (*obstáculo*) to overcome; **~se** *vr* (*ceder*) to give way; (*confiarse a alguien*) to unburden o.s.

franqueo [fran'keo] nm postage.
franqueza [fran'keθa] nf (candor) frankness; (generosidad) generosity.
frasco ['frasko] nm bottle; (al vacío) (vacuum) flask.
frase ['frase] nf sentence; ~ **hecha** set phrase.
fraude ['frauðe] nm (cualidad) dishonesty; (acto) fraud; **fraudulento, a** a fraudulent.
frecuencia [fre'kwenθja] nf frequency; **con** ~ frequently, often.
fregador [freɣa'ðor] nm sink.
fregar [fre'ɣar] vt (frotar) to scrub; (platos) to wash (up); (AM) to annoy.
freír [fre'ir] vt to fry.
frenar [fre'nar] vt to brake; (fig) to check.
frenesí [frene'si] nm frenzy; **frenético, a** a frantic.
freno ['freno] nm (TEC, AUTO) brake; (de cabalgadura) bit; (fig) check.
frente ['frente] nm (ARQ, POL) front; (de objeto) front part // nf forehead, brow; **en** ~ **de** in front of; (en situación opuesta de) opposite; **chocar de** ~ to crash head-on; **hacer** ~ **a** to face up to.
fresa ['fresa] nf strawberry.
fresco, a ['fresko, a] a (nuevo) fresh; (frío) cool // nm (aire) fresh air; (ARTE) fresco; (fam) shameless person; (persona insolente) impudent person // nf cool part of the day; **tomar el** ~ to get some fresh air; **frescura** nf freshness; (descaro) cheek, nerve; (calma) calmness.
frialdad [frial'dað] nf (gen) coldness; (indiferencia) indifference.
fricción [frik'θjon] nf (gen) friction; (acto) rub(bing); (MED) massage.
frigidez [frixi'ðeθ] nf frigidity.
frigorífico [friɣo'rifiko] nm refrigerator.
frijol [fri'xol] nm kidney bean.
frío, a ['frio, a] a cold // nm cold(ness).
frito, a ['frito, a] a fried; **me trae** ~ **ese hombre** I'm sick and tired of that man.
frívolo, a ['friβolo, a] a frivolous.
frontera [fron'tera] nf frontier; **fronterizo, a** a a frontier cpd; (contiguo) bordering.
frontón [fron'ton] nm (DEPORTE) pelota court.
frotar [fro'tar] vt to rub; ~**se** vr: ~**se las manos** to rub one's hands.
fructífero, a [fruk'tifero, a] a fruitful.
frugal [fru'xal] a frugal.
fruncir [frun'θir] vt to pucker; (costura) to pleat; ~ **el ceño** to knit one's brow.
frustrar [frus'trar] vt to frustrate.
fruta ['fruta] nf fruit; **frutería** nf fruit shop.
fue vb ver **ser, ir.**
fuego ['fweɣo] nm (gen) fire; (MED) rash; **a** ~ **lento** on a low flame or gas; **¿tienes** ~? have you a light?
fuente ['fwente] nf (de una plaza) fountain; (manantial, fig) spring; (origen) source; (plato) large dish.
fuera etc vb ver **ser, ir** // ['fwera] ad

out(side); (en otra parte) away; (excepto, salvo) except, save // prep: ~ **de** outside; (fig) besides; ~ **de sí** beside o.s.
fuerte ['fwerte] a (gen) strong; (golpe) hard; (ruido) loud; (comida) rich; (lluvia) heavy; (dolor) intense // ad strongly; hard; loud(ly).
fuerza ['fwerθa] nf (fortaleza) strength; (TEC, ELEC) power; (coacción) force; (MIL) forces pl; **a** ~ **de** by dint of; **cobrar** ~**s** to recover one's strength; **tener** ~**s para** to have the strength to; **a la** ~, **por** ~ forcibly, by force.
fuga ['fuɣa] nf (huida) flight, escape; (de gas) leak; **fugarse** vr to flee, escape; **fugaz** a fleeting; **fugitivo, a** a, nm/f fugitive.
fui vb ver **ser, ir.**
fulano, a [fu'lano, a] nm/f so-and-so, what's-his-name.
fulgor [ful'xor] nm brilliance.
fumar [fu'mar] vt, vi to smoke; ~**se** vr (disipar) to squander; ~ **en pipa** to smoke a pipe.
funámbulo, a [fu'nambulo, a] nm/f tightrope-walker.
función [fun'θjon] nf function; (de puesto) duties pl; (espectáculo) show; **entrar en funciones** to take up one's duties; **funcionar** vi (gen) to function; (máquina) to work.
funcionario, a [funθjo'narjo, a] nm/f official; (público) civil servant.
funda ['funda] nf (gen) cover; (de almohada) pillowcase.
fundación [funda'θjon] nf foundation.
fundamental [fundamen'tal] a fundamental, basic.
fundamentar [fundamen'tar] vt (poner base) to lay the foundations of; (establecer) to found; (fig) to base; **fundamento** nm (base) foundation.
fundar [fun'dar] vt to found; (dotar de fondos) to endow; ~**se** vr: ~**se en** to be founded on.
fundición [fundi'θjon] nf fusing; (fábrica) foundry.
fundir [fun'dir] vt (gen) to fuse; (metal) to smelt, melt down; (COM) to merge; (estatua) to cast; ~**se** vr (sólido) to merge, blend; (unirse) to fuse together.
fúnebre ['funeβre] a funeral cpd, funereal.
funeral [fune'ral] nm funeral.
furgón [fur'xon] nm wagon.
furia ['furja] nf (ira) fury; (violencia) violence; **furibundo, a** a furious; **furioso, a** a (irecundo) furious; (violento) violent; **furor** nm (cólera) rage.
furtivo, a [fur'tiβo, a] a furtive.
furúnculo [fu'runkulo] nm (MED) boil.
fusible [fu'siβle] nm fuse.
fusil [fu'sil] nm rifle; ~**ar** vt to shoot.
fusión [fu'sjon] nf (gen) melting; (unión) fusion; (COM) merger.
fútbol ['futβol] nm football; **futbolín** nm table football; **futbolista** nm footballer.

fútil ['futil] a trifling; **futilidad, futileza** nf triviality.

futuro, a [fu'turo, a] a, nm future.

G

gabacho, a [ga'ßatʃo, a] a Pyrenean; (fam) frenchified // nm/f Pyrenean villager.

gabán [ga'ßan] nm overcoat.

gabardina [gaßar'ðina] nf raincoat, gabardine.

gabinete [gaßi'nete] nm (POL) cabinet; (estudio) study; (de abogados etc) office.

gaceta [ga' θeta] nf gazette; **gacetilla** nf (en periódico) news in brief; (de personalidades) gossip column.

gacha ['gatʃa] nf mush; **~s** nfpl porridge sg.

gafas ['gafas] nfpl glasses; **~ oscuras** dark glasses.

gaita ['gaita] nf flute; (~ gallega) bagpipes pl.

gajes ['gaxes] nmpl (salario) pay; **los ~ del oficio** occupational hazards.

gajo ['gaxo] nm (gen) bunch; (de árbol) bough; (de naranja) segment.

gala ['gala] nf full dress; (fig: lo mejor) cream, flower; **~s** nfpl finery sg; **estar de ~** to be in one's best clothes; **hacer ~ de** to display, show off.

galán [ga'lan] nm lover, gallant; (hombre atractivo) ladies' man; (TEATRO): **primer ~** leading man.

galano, a [ga'lano, a] a (elegante) elegant; (bien vestido) smart.

galante [ga'lante] a gallant; **galantear** vt (hacer la corte a) to court, woo; **galanteo** nm (coqueteo) flirting; (de pretendiente) wooing; **galantería** nf (caballerosidad) gallantry; (cumplido) politeness; (comentario) compliment.

galaxia [ga'laksja] nf galaxy.

galera [ga'lera] nf (nave) galley; (carro) wagon; (MED) hospital ward; (IMPRENTA) galley.

galería [gale'ria] nf (gen) gallery; (balcón) veranda(h); (de casa) corridor.

Gales ['gales] nm Wales; **galés, esa** a Welsh // nm/f Welshman/woman // nm (lengua) Welsh.

galgo, a ['galɣo, a] nm/f greyhound.

galimatías [galima'tias] nmpl (lenguaje) gibberish sg, nonsense sg.

galón [ga'lon] nm (MIL) stripe; (medida) gallon.

galopar [galo'par] vi to gallop; **galope** nm gallop.

galvanizar [galßani'θar] vt to galvanize.

gallardía [gaʎar'ðia] nf (galantería) dash; (valor) bravery; (elegancia) elegance.

gallego, a [ga'ʎeɣo, a] a, nm/f Galician.

galleta [ga'ʎeta] nf biscuit.

gallina [ga'ʎina] nf hen // nm (fam) coward; **~ ciega** blind man's buff.

gallo ['gaʎo] nm cock, rooster.

gama ['gama] nf (MUS) scale; (fig) range.

gamba ['gamba] nf prawn.

gamberro, a [gam'berro, a] nm/f hooligan, lout.

gamuza [ga'muθa] nf chamois.

gana ['gana] nf (deseo) desire, wish; (apetito) appetite; (voluntad) will; (añoranza) longing; **de buena ~** willingly; **de mala ~** reluctantly; **me da la ~ de** I feel like, I want to; **tener ~s de** to feel like.

ganadería [ganaðe'ria] nf (ganado) livestock; (ganado vacuno) cattle pl; (cría, comercio) cattle raising.

ganado [ga'naðo] nm livestock; **~ lanar** sheep pl; **~ vacuno** cattle pl; **~ porcino** pigs pl.

ganador, a [gana'ðor, a] a winning // nm/f winner.

ganancia [ga'nanθja] nf (lo ganado) gain; (aumento) increase; (beneficio) profit; **~s** nfpl (ingresos) earnings; (beneficios) profit sg, winnings.

ganapán [gana'pan] nm (obrero casual) odd-job man; (individuo tosco) lout.

ganar [ga'nar] vt (obtener) to get, obtain; (sacar ventaja) to gain; (COM) to earn; (DEPORTE, premio) to win; (derrotar a) to beat; (alcanzar) to reach // vi (DEPORTE) to win; **~se** vr: **~se la vida** to earn one's living.

gancho ['gantʃo] nm (gen) hook; (colgador) hanger.

gandul, a [gan'dul, a] a, nm/f good-for-nothing.

ganga ['ganga] nf (cosa buena y barata) bargain; (buena situación) cushy job.

gangrena [gan'grena] nf gangrene.

gansada [gan'saða] nf (fam) stupid thing to do.

ganso, a ['ganso, a] nm/f (ZOOL) gander/goose; (fam) idiot.

ganzúa [gan'θua] nf skeleton key // nm burglar.

gañán [ga'nan] nm farmhand, farm labourer.

garabato [gara'ßato] nm (gancho) hook; (garfio) grappling iron; (escritura) scrawl, scribble; (fam) sex appeal.

garaje [ga'raxe] nm garage.

garante [ga'rante] a responsible // nm/f guarantor.

garantía [garan'tia] nf guarantee.

garantizar [garanti'θar], **garantir** [garan'tir] vt (hacerse responsable de) to vouch for; (asegurar) to guarantee.

garbanzo [gar'ßanθo] nm chickpea.

garbo ['garßo] nm grace, elegance; **~so, a** a graceful, elegant.

garfa ['garfa] nf claw.

garfio ['garfjo] nm grappling iron.

garganta [gar'ɣanta] nf (interna) throat; (externa, de botella) neck; **gargantilla** nf necklace.

gárgara ['garɣara] nf gargle, gargling.

gárgola ['garɣola] nf gargoyle.

garita [ga'rita] nf cabin, hut; (MIL) sentry box; (de camión) cab.

garra ['garra] nf (de gato, TEC) claw; (de ave) talon; (fam) hand, paw (fam).

garrafa [ga'rrafa] nf carafe, decanter.

garrido, a [ga'rriðo, a] a handsome.

garrote [ga'rrote] nm (palo) stick; (porra) cudgel; (suplicio) garrotte; (MED) tourniquet.

garrulería [garrule'ria] nf chatter.

gárrulo, a ['garrulo, a] a (charlatán) talkative; (ave) twittering; (arroyo) murmuring.

garzo, a ['garθo, a] a blue // nf heron.

gas [gas] nm gas.

gasa ['gasa] nf gauze.

gaseoso, a [gase'oso, a] a gassy, fizzy // nf lemonade, fizzy drink; (fam) pop.

gasolina [gaso'lina] nf petrol, gas(oline) (US); **gasolinera** nf petrol station.

gasómetro [ga'sometro] nm gasometer.

gastado, a [gas'taðo, a] a (rendido) spent; (raído) worn, threadbare; (usado: frase etc) trite.

gastar [gas'tar] vt (dinero, tiempo) to spend; (fuerzas) to use up; (desperdiciar) to waste; (llevar) to wear; ~se vr to wear out; (estropearse) to waste; ~ **bromas** to crack jokes.

gasto ['gasto] nm (desembolso) expenditure, spending; (consumo, uso) use; ~s nmpl (desembolsos) expenses; (cargos) charges, costs.

gatear [gate'ar] vi (andar a gatas) to go on all fours; (trepar) to climb // vt to scratch.

gatillo [ga'tiʎo] nm (de arma de fuego) trigger; (de dentista) forceps.

gato, a ['gato, a] nm/f cat // nm (TEC) jack; **andar a** ~**as** to go on all fours.

gatuno, a [ga'tuno, a] a feline.

gaucho ['gautʃo] nm gaucho.

gaveta [ga'ßeta] nf drawer.

gavilla [ga'ßiʎa] nf sheaf.

gaviota [ga'ßjota] nf seagull.

gay [ge] a gay, homosexual.

gayo, a ['gajo, a] a gay, merry.

gazapera [gaθa'pera] nf (conejera) rabbit warren; (de gente) den of thieves; **gazapo** nm young rabbit; (fam) sly fellow.

gazmoño, a [gaθ'moɲo, a], **gazmoñero, a** [gaθmo'ɲero, a] nm/f prude; (pretencioso) prig; (hipócrita) hypocrite.

gazpacho [gaθ'patʃo] nm gazpacho, cold vegetable soup.

gelatina [xela'tina] nf (plato) jelly; (polvos etc) gelatine.

gema ['xema] nf gem.

gemelo, a [xe'melo, a] a, nm/f twin; ~s nmpl (de camisa) cufflinks; **G**~**s** (ASTRO) Gemini sg; ~**s de campo** field glasses.

gemido [xe'miðo] nm (quejido) moan, groan; (aullido) howl.

gemir [xe'mir] vi (quejarse) to moan, groan; (aullar) to howl.

genealogía [xenealo'xia] nf genealogy.

generación [xenera'θjon] nf generation.

generador [xenera'ðor] nm generator.

general [xene'ral] a general // nm general; **por lo o en** ~ in general; ~**idad** nf generality; **G**~**itat** nf Catalan parliament; ~**ización** nf generalization; ~**izar** vt to generalize; ~**izarse** vr to become generalised, spread; ~**mente** ad generally.

generar [xene'rar] vt to generate.

genérico, a [xe'neriko, a] a generic.

género ['xenero] nm (clase) kind, sort; (tipo) type; (BIO) genus; (LING) gender; (COM) material; ~ **humano** human race.

generosidad [xenerosi'ðað] nf generosity; **generoso, a** a generous.

genial [xe'njal] a inspired; (idea) brilliant; (afable) genial.

genio ['xenjo] nm (carácter) nature, disposition; (humor) temper; (facultad creadora) genius; **de mal** ~ bad-tempered.

gente ['xente] nf (personas) people pl; (raza) race; (nación) nation; (parientes) relatives pl.

gentil [xen'til] a (elegante) graceful; (encantador) charming; ~**eza** nf grace; charm; (cortesía) courtesy.

gentío [xen'tio] nm crowd, throng.

genuflexión [xenuflek'sjon] nf genuflexion.

genuino, a [xe'nwino, a] a genuine.

geografía [xeoɣra'fia] nf geography.

geología [xeolo'xia] nf geology.

geometría [xeome'tria] nf geometry.

gerencia [xe'renθja] nf management; **gerente** nm (supervisor) manager; (jefe) director.

germen ['xermen] nm germ.

germinar [xermi'nar] vi to germinate.

gesticulación [xestikula'θjon] nf (ademán) gesticulation; (mueca) grimace.

gestión [xes'tjon] nf management; (diligencia, acción) negotiation; (esfuerzo) effort; **gestionar** vt (lograr) to try to arrange; (llevar) to manage; (discutir) to negotiate.

gesto ['xesto] nm (mueca) grimace; (ademán) gesture.

gestoría [xesto'ria] nf estate agent's.

Gibraltar [xißral'tar] nm Gibraltar.

gigante [xi'xante] a, nm/f giant.

gilipollas [xili'poʎas] excl (fam) bastard! (fam).

gimnasia [xim'nasja] nf gymnastics pl; **gimnasio** nm gymnasium; **gimnasta** nm/f gymnast.

gimotear [ximote'ar] vi to whine, whimper.

ginebra [xi'neßra] nf gin.

ginecólogo, a [xine'koloɣo, a] nm/f gynecologist.

gira ['xira] nf tour, trip.

girar ['xi'rar] vt (dar la vuelta) to turn (around); (: rápidamente) to spin; (COM: cheque) to draw; (comerciar: letra de cambio) to issue // vi to turn (round); (rápido) to spin; (COM) to draw.

girasol [xira'sol] nm sunflower.
giratorio, a [xira'torjo, a] a (gen) revolving; (puente) swing.
giro ['xiro] nm (movimiento) turn, revolution; (LING) expression; (COM) draft; ~ bancario/postal money/ postal order.
gitano, a [xi'tano, a] a, nm/f gypsy.
glacial [gla'θjal] a icy, freezing.
glándula ['glandula] nf gland.
globo ['globo] nm (esfera) globe, sphere; (aerostato, juguete) balloon.
gloria ['glorja] nf glory; gloriarse v to boast.
glorieta [glo'rjeta] nf (de jardín) bower, arbour; (plazoleta) roundabout.
glorificar [glorifi'kar] vt (enaltecer) to glorify, praise; ~se vr: ~se de to boast of.
glorioso, a [glo'rjoso, a] a glorious.
glosa ['glosa] nf comment; glosar v (comentar) to comment on; (fig) to criticize.
glosario [glo'sarjo] nm glossary.
glotón, ona [glo'ton, ona] a gluttonous, greedy; glotonería nf gluttony, greed.
gobernación [goβerna'θjon] nf government, governing; gobernador, a a governing // nm governor; gobernante a governing.
gobernar [goβer'nar] vt (dirigir) to guide, direct; (regir) to rule, govern // vi to govern; (NAUT) to steer.
gobierno [go'βjerno] nm (POL) government; (dirección) guidance, direction; (NAUT) steering.
goce ['goθe] nm enjoyment.
gol [gol] nm goal.
gola ['gola] nf gullet; (garganta) throat.
golf [golf] nm golf.
golfa ['golfa] nf (fam) tart, whore.
golfo ['golfo] nm (GEO) gulf; (fam: niño) urchin; (gamberro) lout.
golondrina [golon'drina] nf swallow.
golosina [golo'sina] nf (gen) titbit; (dulce) sweet; goloso, a a sweet-toothed.
golpe ['golpe] nm (gen) blow; (de puño) punch; (de mano) smack; (de corazón) beat; (de remo) stroke; (fig: choque) clash; no dar ~ to be bone idle; de un ~ with one blow; de ~ suddenly; ~ de estado coup d'état; golpear vt, vi to strike, knock; (asestar) to beat; (de puño) to punch; (golpetear) to tap.
goma ['goma] nf (caucho) rubber; (elástico) elastic; ~ espuma foam rubber; ~ de pegar gum, glue.
gomita [go'mita] nf elastic band.
góndola ['gondola] nf (barco) gondola; (de tren) goods wagon.
gordo, a [gordo, a] a (gen) fat; (persona) plump; (tela) coarse; (fam) enormous; el premio ~ (en lotería) first prize; gordura nf fat; (corpulencia) fatness, stoutness.
gorgojo [gor'xoxo] nm (insecto) grub; (fam) runt.

gorila [go'rila] nm gorilla.
gorjear [gorxe'ar] vi to twitter, chirp; gorjeo nm twittering, chirping.
gorra ['gorra] nf (gen) cap; (de niño) bonnet; (militar) bearskin // nm scrounger.
gorrión [go'rrjon] nm sparrow.
gorro ['gorro] nm (gen) cap; (de niño, mujer) bonnet.
gorrón [go'rron] nm pebble.
gota ['gota] nf (gen) drop; (de sudor) bead; (MED) gout; gotear vi to drip; (lloviznar) to drizzle; gotera nf leak.
gótico, a ['gotiko, a] a Gothic.
gozar [go'θar] vi to enjoy o.s.; ~ de (disfrutar) to enjoy; (poseer) to possess.
gozne ['goθne] nm hinge.
gozo ['goθo] nm (alegría) joy; (placer) pleasure, ~so, a a joyous, joyful.
grabación [graβa'θjon] nf recording.
grabado [gra'βaðo] nm print, engraving; grabador nm engraver.
grabadora [graβa'dora] nf tape-recorder.
grabar [gra'βar] vt to engrave; (discos, cintas) to record.
gracejo [gra'θexo] nm (humor) wit, humour; (elegancia) grace.
gracia ['graθja] nf (encanto) grace, gracefulness; (chiste) joke; (humor) humour, wit; ¡~s! thanks!; ¡muchas ~s! thanks very much!; ~s a thanks to; tener ~ to be funny; (ser divertido) to be enjoyable; no me hace ~ I am not keen; gracioso, a a (divertido) funny, amusing; (cómico) comical // nm (TEATRO) comic character.
grada ['grada] nf (de escalera) step; (de anfiteatro) tier, row.
gradación [graða'θjon] nf gradation.
gradería [graðe'ria] nf (gradas) (flight of) steps pl; (de anfiteatro) tiers pl rows pl; ~ cubierta covered stand.
grado ['graðo] nm degree; (de aceite, vino) grade; (grada) step; (MIL) rank; de buen ~ willingly.
graduación [graðwa'θjon] nf (del alcohol) proof, strength; (ESCOL) graduation.
gradual [gra'ðwal] a gradual.
graduar [gra'ðwar] vt (gen) to graduate; (clasificar) to grade; (MIL) to commission; ~se vr to graduate.
gráfica, a ['grafiko, a] a graphic // nf diagrama // nf graph.
grajo ['graxo] nm rook.
Gral abr de General.
gramática [gra'matika] nf grammar.
gramo ['gramo] nm gramme.
gran [gran] a ver grande.
grana ['grana] nf (BOT) seedling; (ZOOL) cochineal (color, tela) scarlet.
Granada [gra'naða] n Granada.
granada [gra'naða] nf pomegranate; (MIL) grenade; granadino a nf grenadine.
granadino a [grana'ðino, a] a of Granada // nm/f native or inhabitant of Granada.

granado, a [gra'naðo, a] *a* choice, select // *nm* pomegranate tree.

granar [gra'nar] *vi* to seed.

granate [gra'nate] *nm* garnet.

Gran Bretaña [granbre'taɲa] *nf* Great Britain.

grande ['grande], **gran** [gran] *a* (*de tamaño*) big, large; (*alto*) tall; (*distinguido*) great; (*impresionante*) grand // *nm* grandee; **grandeza** *nf* greatness.

grandioso, a [gran'djoso, a] *a* magnificent, grand.

grandor [gran'dor] *nm* size.

granel [gra'nel]: **a ~** *ad* in abundance; (*COM*) in bulk.

granero [gra'nero] *nm* granary, barn.

granito [gra'nito] *nm* (*AGR*) small grain; (*roca*) granite; (*MED*) pimple.

granizado [grani'θaðo] *nm* iced drink; **granizar** *vi* to hail; **granizo** *nm* hail.

granja ['granxa] *nf* (*gen*) farm; (*lechería*) dairy; (*café*) milk bar.

granjear [granxe'ar] *vt* (*cobrar*) to earn; (*ganar*) to win; (*avanzar*) to gain; **granjería** *nf* (*COM*) profit; (*AGR*) farming.

grano ['grano] *nm* grain; (*semilla*) seed; (*baya*) berry; (*MED*) pimple; **~s** *nmpl* cereals.

granoso, a [gra'noso, a] *a* granulated.

granuja [gra'nuxa] *nf* grape seed // *nm* rogue; (*golfillo*) urchin.

grapa ['grapa] *nf* staple; (*TEC*) clamp.

grasa ['grasa] *nf* (*gen*) grease; (*de cocina*) fat, lard; (*sebo*) suet; (*mugre*) filth; (*escoria*) dross; **grasiento, a** *a* greasy; (*de aceite*) oily.

gratificación [gratifika'θjon] *nf* (*propina*) tip; (*bono*) bonus; (*recompensa*) reward; **gratificar** *vt* to tip; to reward.

gratis ['gratis] *ad* free.

gratitud [grati'tuð] *nf* gratitude.

grato, a ['grato, a] *a* (*agradable*) pleasant, agreeable; (*bienvenido*) welcome.

gratuito, a [gra'twito, a] *a* (*gratis*) free; (*sin razón*) gratuitous.

gravamen [gra'βamen] *nm* (*carga*) burden; (*impuesto*) tax.

gravar [gra'βar] *vt* to burden.

grave ['graβe] *a* heavy; (*serio*) grave, serious; **~dad** *nf* gravity.

grávido, a ['graβiðo, a] *a* (*preñada*) pregnant; (*lleno, cargado*) full.

gravitación [graβita'θjon] *nf* gravitation; **gravitar** *vi* to gravitate; **gravitar sobre** to rest on.

gravoso, a [gra'βoso, a] *a* (*pesado*) burdensome; (*costoso*) costly.

graznar [graθ'nar] *vi* (*cuervo*) to squawk; (*pato*) to quack; (*hablar ronco*) to croak; **graznido** *nm* squawk; croak.

Grecia ['greθja] *nf* Greece.

greguería [greɣe'ria] *nf* hubbub.

gremio ['gremjo] *nm* (*sindicato*) trade union; (*asociación*) professional association.

greña ['greɲa] *nf* (*cabellos*) shock of hair;

(*maraña*) tangle; **greñudo, a** *a* (*persona*) dishevelled; (*hair*) tangled.

gresca ['greska] *nf* uproar.

grey [grei] *nf* flock.

griego, a ['grjeɣo, a] *a, nm/f* Greek.

grieta ['grjeta] *nf* crack; **grietarse** *vr* = **agrietarse.**

grifo, a ['grifo, a] *a* curly, kinky // *nm* tap.

grillo ['griʎo] *nm* (*ZOOL*) cricket; (*BOT*) shoot; **~s** *nmpl* shackles, irons.

gripe ['gripe] *nf* flu, influenza.

gris [gris] *a* (*color*) grey.

grita ['grita] *nf* uproar; **gritar** *vt, vi* to shout, yell; **grito** *nm* shout, yell; (*de horror*) scream; **a grito pelado** at the top of one's voice.

grosella [gro'seʎa] *nf* (red)currant; **~ negra** blackcurrant.

grosería [grose'ria] *nf* (*actitud*) rudeness; (*comentario*) vulgar comment; **grosero, a** *a* (*poco cortés*) rude; (*ordinario*) vulgar, crude.

grosor [gro'sor] *nm* thickness.

grotesco, a [gro'tesko, a] *a* grotesque.

grúa ['grua] *nf* (*TEC*) crane; (*de petróleo*) derrick.

grueso, a ['grweso, a] *a* thick; (*voluminoso*) stout // *nm* bulk // *nf* gross; **el ~ de** the bulk of.

grulla ['gruʎa] *nf* crane.

gruñido [gru'niðo] *nm* grunt; (*fig*) grumble; **gruñir** *vi* (*animal*) to growl; (*fam*) to grumble.

grupa ['grupa] *nf* (*ZOOL*) rump.

grupo ['grupo] *nm* group; (*TEC*) unit, set.

gruta ['gruta] *nf* grotto.

guadamecí [gwaðame'θi], **guadamecil** [gwaðame'θil] *nm* embossed leather.

guadaña [gwa'ðaɲa] *nf* scythe; **guadañar** *vt* to scythe, mow.

guano ['gwano] *nm* (*AM*) guano.

guante ['gwante] *nm* glove.

guapo, a ['gwapo, a] *a* good-looking, attractive; (*hombre*) handsome; (*elegante*) smart // *nm* lover, gallant.

guarda ['gwarða] *nm* guard, keeper // *nf* guarding; (*custodia*) custody; **~bosque** *nm* gamekeeper; **~costas** *nm inv* coastguard vessel; **~dor, a** *a* protective // *nm/f* guardian, protector; **~espaldas** *nm/f inv* bodyguard; **~polvo** *nm* dust cover; (*de niño*) smock; (*para el trabajo*) overalls *pl*; **guardar** *vt* (*gen*) to keep; (*vigilar*) to guard, watch over; (*dinero: ahorrar*) to save, put by; **guardarse** *vr* (*preservarse*) to protect o.s.; (*evitar*) to avoid; **guardarropa** *nm* (*armario*) wardrobe; (*en establecimiento público*) cloakroom.

guardería [gwarðe'ria] *nf* (children's) nursery.

guardia ['gwarðja] *nf* (*MIL*) guard; (*cuidado*) care, custody // *nm* (*policía*) policeman; **estar de ~** to be on guard; **montar ~** to mount guard; **G~ Civil** Civil Guard; **G~ Nacional** police; **~ urbano** traffic policeman.

guardián, ana [gwar'ðjan, ana] nm/f (gen) guardian, keeper; (sereno) watchman.

guardilla [gwar'ðiʎa] nf attic.

guarecer [gware'θer] vt (proteger) to protect; (abrigar) to shelter; ~**se** vr to take refuge.

guarida [gwa'riða] nf (de animal) den, lair; (refugio) refuge.

guarismo [gwa'rismo] nm figure, number.

guarnecer [gwarne'θer] vt (equipar) to provide; (adornar) to adorn; (TEC) to reinforce; **guarnición** nf (de vestimenta) trimming; (de piedra) mount; (CULIN) garnish; (arneses) harness; (MIL) garrison.

guarro, a ['gwarro, a] nm/f pig.

guasa ['gwasa] nf joke; **guasón, ona** a witty; (bromista) joking // nm/f wit; joker.

Guatemala [gwate'mala] nf Guatemala.

gubernativo, a [gußerna'tißo, a] a governmental.

guedeja [ge'ðexa] nf long hair; (de león) mane.

guerra ['gerra] nf war; (pelea) struggle; ~ **fría** cold war; **dar** ~ to annoy; **guerrear** vi to wage war; **guerrero, a** a fighting; (carácter) warlike // nm/f warrior.

guerrilla [ge'rriʎa] nf guerrilla warfare; (tropas) guerrilla band or group.

guía ['gia] nm/f guide // nf (libro) guidebook; ~ **de ferrocarriles** railway timetable; ~ **de teléfonos** telephone directory; **guiar** vt to guide, direct; (AUT) to steer; **guiarse** vr: **guiarse por** to be guided by.

guija ['gixa] nf, **guijarro** [gi'xarro] nm pebble; (camino) cobblestone.

guijo ['gixo] nm gravel; (de playa) shingle.

guillotina [giʎo'tina] nf guillotine.

guinda ['ginda] nf morello cherry.

guindar [gin'dar] vt to hoist.

guindilla [gin'diʎa] nf Guinea pepper.

guiñapo [gi'ɲapo] nm (harapo) rag; (persona) reprobate, rogue.

guiñar [gi'ɲar] vi to wink; (parpadear) to blink.

guión [gi'on] nm (conductor) leader; (LING) hyphen, dash; (CINE) script; **guionista** nm/f scriptwriter.

guirnalda [gir'nalda] nf garland.

guisa ['gisa] nf: **a** ~ **de** as, like, in the way of.

guisado [gi'saðo] nm stew.

guisante [gi'sante] nm pea; ~ **de olor** sweet pea.

guisar [gi'sar] vt, vi to cook; **guiso** nm cooked dish.

guita ['gita] nf twine.

guitarra [gi'tarra] nf guitar.

gula ['gula] nf gluttony, greed.

gusano [gu'sano] nm maggot; (lombriz) earthworm; ~ **de luz** glow-worm; ~ **de seda** silk-worm.

gustar [gus'tar] vt to taste, sample // vi to please, be pleasing; ~ **de algo** to like or enjoy sth; **me gustan las uvas** I like grapes.

gusto ['gusto] nm (sentido, sabor) taste; (placer) pleasure; **tiene** ~ **a menta** it tastes of mint; **tener buen** ~ to have good taste; **sentirse a** ~ to feel at ease; **mucho** ~ **en conocerle** pleased to meet you; **el** ~ **es mío** the pleasure is mine; **con** ~ willingly, gladly; ~**so, a** a (sabroso) tasty; (agradable) pleasant.

gutural [gutu'ral] a guttural.

H

ha vb ver **haber.**

haba ['aßa] nf bean.

Habana [a'ßana] nf: **la** ~ Havana.

habano [a'ßano] nm Havana cigar.

haber [a'ßer] vb auxiliar to have; **de** ~**lo sabido** if I had known (it); ~ **de** to have to // vb impersonal: **hay** there is/are; **hay que** it is necessary to, one must; ¿**qué hay?** how's it going? **no hay de qué** don't mention it // nm (ingreso) income; (COM: crédito) credit; ~**es** nmpl assets.

habichuela [aßi'tʃwela] nf kidney bean.

hábil ['aßil] a (listo) clever, smart; (capaz) fit, capable; (experto) expert; **día** ~ working day; **habilidad** nf (gen) skill, ability (inteligencia) cleverness.

habilitación [aßilita'θjon] nf qualification; (colocación de muebles) fitting out; (financiamiento) financing.

habilitar [aßili'tar] vt (capacitar) to enable; (dar instrumentos) to equip; (financiar) to finance.

hábilmente [aßil'mente] ad skilfully, expertly.

habitación [aßita'θjon] nf (cuarto) room; (casa) dwelling, abode; (ZOO: morada) habitat; ~ **sencilla** o particular single room; ~ **doble** o matrimonial double room.

habitante [aßi'tante] nm/f inhabitant.

habitar [aßi'tar] vt (residir en) to inhabit; (ocupar) to occupy // vi to live.

hábito ['aßito] nm habit; **habitual** a habitual.

habituar [aßi'twar] vt to accustom; ~**se** vr: ~**se a** to get used to.

habla ['aßla] nf (capacidad de hablar) speech; (idioma) language (dialecto) dialect; **perder el** ~ to become speechless; **de** ~ **francesa** French-speaking; **estar al** ~ to be in contact; ¡**González al** ~! González speaking!

hablador, a [aßla'ðor, a] a talkative // nm/f chatterbox.

habladuría [aßlaðu'ria] nf rumour; (sarcasmo) sarcastic comment; ~**s** nfpl gossip sg.

hablar [a'ßlar] vt to speak, talk // vi to speak; ~**se** vr to speak to each other; ~ **con** to speak to; ~ **de** to speak of or about; '**se habla inglés**' 'English spoken here'.

hablilla [a'ßliʎa] nf story, rumour.

habré *etc vb ver* **haber.**
hacedero, a [aθe'ðero, a] *a* feasible.
hacedor, a [aθe'ðor, a] *nm/f* maker.
hacendoso, a [aθen'doso, a] *a* industrious.
hacer [a'θer] *vt* (*gen*) to make; (*crear*) to create; (*TEC*) to manufacture; (*preparar*) to prepare; (*ejecutar*) to do, execute; (*obligar*) to force, compel // *vi* (*comportarse*) to act, behave; (*disimular*) to pretend; (*importar*) to be important, matter; (*convenir, ser apto*) to be suitable; ~**se** *vr* (*fabricarse*) to be made, be done; (*volverse*) to become; (*acostumbrarse a*) to get used to; ~ **la maleta** to pack; ~ **una pregunta** to ask a question; ~ **una visita** to visit; ~ **bien/mal** to act rightly/wrongly; **hace frío/calor** it's cold/hot; **hace dos años** two years ago; **hace poco** a little while ago; ~ **el malo** (*TEATRO*) to play (the part of) the villain; ¿**qué** ~? what is to be done?; ~ **como que** *o* **como si** to act as though *or* as if; ~ **de** to act as; **me hice un traje** I had a suit made; ~**se el sordo** to turn a deaf ear; ~**se viejo** to grow old; ~**se con algo** to get hold of sth; ~**se a un lado** to stand aside.
hacia ['aθja] *prep* (*en dirección de*) towards; (*cerca de*) near; ~ **arriba/abajo** up(wards)/down(wards); ~ **mediodía** about noon.
hacienda [a'θjenda] *nf* (*propiedad*) property; (*estancia*) farm, ranch; (*AM*) plantation; ~ **pública** public finance; (**Ministerio de**) **H**~ Treasury, Exchequer.
hacina [a'θina] *nf* pile, stack.
hacha ['atʃa] *nf* axe; (*antorcha*) torch.
hache ['atʃe] *nf* (the letter) H.
hada ['aða] *nf* fairy.
hago *etc vb ver* **hacer.**
Haití [ai'ti] *nm* Haiti.
halagar [ala'xar] *vt* (*mostrar afecto*) to show affection to; (*lisonjear*) to flatter.
halago [a'laxo] *nm* pleasure, delight; (*atractivo*) attraction; (*adulación*) flattery; **halagüeño, a** *a* pleasing; attractive; flattering.
halcón [al'kon] *nm* falcon, hawk.
hálito ['alito] *nm* breath.
hallar [a'ʎar] *vt* (*gen*) to find; (*descubrir*) to discover; (*toparse con*) to run up against; ~**se** *vr* to be (situated); **hallazgo** *nm* discovery; (*cosa*) find.
hamaca [a'maka] *nf* hammock; ~ **plegable** deckchair.
hambre ['ambre] *nf* hunger; (*carencia*) famine; (*fig*) longing; **tener** ~ to be hungry; ~**ar** *vi, vt* to starve; **hambriento, a** *a* hungry, starving.
hamburguesa [ambur'xesa] *nf* hamburger.
hampa ['ampa] *nf* underworld; **hampón** *nm* tough.
han *vb ver* **haber.**
haragán, ana [ara'xan, ana] *a, nm/f* good-for-nothing; **haraganear** *vi* to idle, loaf about.
harapiento, a [ara'pjento, a] *a* tattered, in rags; **harapo** *nm* rag.
haré *etc vb ver* **hacer.**
harina [a'rina] *nf* flour; (*polvo*) powder; **harinero, a** *nm/f* flour merchant; **harinoso, a** *a* floury.
hartar [ar'tar] *vt* to satiate, glut; (*fig*) to tire, sicken; ~**se** *vr* (*de comida*) to fill o.s., gorge o.s.; (*cansarse*) to get fed up (*de* with); **hartazgo** *nm* surfeit, glut; **harto, a** *a* (*lleno*) full; (*cansado*) fed up // *ad* (*bastante*) enough; (*muy*) very; **estar harto de** to be fed up with; **hartura** *nf* (*exceso*) surfeit; (*abundancia*) abundance; (*satisfacción*) satisfaction.
has *vb ver* **haber.**
hasta ['asta] *ad* even // *prep* (*alcanzando a*) as far as, up/down to; (*de tiempo: a tal hora*) till, until; (*antes de*) before // *conj*: ~ **que** until; ~ **luego/la vista** see you soon.
hastiar [as'tjar] *vt* (*gen*) to weary; (*aburrir*) to bore; (*asquear*) to disgust; ~**se** *vr*: ~**se de** to get fed up with; **hastío** *nm* weariness; boredom; disgust.
hato ['ato], **hatillo** [a'tiʎo] *nm* belongings *pl*, kit; (*víveres*) provisions *pl*; (*banda*) gang, group; (*montón*) bundle, heap.
hay *vb ver* **haber.**
Haya ['aja] *nf*: **la** ~ The Hague.
haya *etc vb ver* **haber** // ['aja] *nf* beech tree; **hayal, hayedo** *nm* beech grove.
haz [aθ] *vb ver* **hacer** // *nm* bundle, bunch; (*rayo: de luz*) beam.
hazaña [a'θaɲa] *nf* feat, exploit.
hazmerreír [aθmerre'ir] *nm* laughing stock.
he *vb ver* **haber.**
hebilla [e'βiʎa] *nf* buckle, clasp.
hebra ['eβra] *nf* thread; (*BOT: fibra*) fibre, grain; **tabaco de** ~ loose tobacco.
hebreo, a [e'βreo, a] *a, nm/f* Hebrew // *nm* (*lengua*) Hebrew.
hectárea [ek tarea] *nf* hectare.
hechizar [etʃi'θar] *vt* to cast a spell on, bewitch.
hechizo, a [e'tʃiθo, a] *a* (*gen*) false, artificial; (*removible*) detachable // *nm* witchcraft, magic; (*acto de magia*) spell, charm.
hecho, a ['etʃo, a] *pp de* **hacer** // *a* complete; (*maduro*) mature; (*costura*) ready-to-wear // *nm* deed, act; (*dato*) fact; (*cuestión*) matter; (*suceso*) event // *excl* agreed!, done!; **¡bien** ~**!** well done!; **de** ~ in fact, as a matter of fact.
hechura [e'tʃura] *nf* making, creation; (*producto*) product; (*forma*) form, shape; (*de persona*) build; (*TEC*) craftsmanship; ~**s** *nfpl.* (*COSTURA*) cost of making up *sg.*
heder [e'ðer] *vi* to stink, smell; (*fig*) to be unbearable.
hediondez [eðjon'deθ] *nf* stench, stink; (*cosa*) stinking thing; **hediondo, a** *a*

stinking; (*insoportable*) repulsive, unbearable.

hedor [e'ðor] *nm* stench.

helado, a [e'laðo, a] *a* frozen; (*glacial*) icy; (*fig*) chilly, cold // *nm* ice-cream // *nf* frost.

helar [e'lar] *vt* to freeze, ice (up); (*dejar atónito*) to amaze; (*desalentar*) to discourage // *vi* ~**se** *vr* to freeze.

hélice ['eliθe] *nf* spiral; (*TEC*) propeller.

helicóptero [eli'koptero] *nm* helicopter.

hembra ['embra] *nf* (*BOT, ZOOL*) female; (*mujer*) woman; (*TEC*) nut.

hemorragia [emo'rraxja] *nf* haemorrhage.

hemorroides [emo'rroiðes] *nfpl* haemorrhoids.

hemos *vb ver* **haber.**

henchir [en'tʃir] *vt* to fill, stuff; ~**se** *vr* (*llenarse de comida*) to stuff o.s. (with food); (*inflarse*) to swell (up).

hender [en'der] *vt* to cleave, split; **hendidura** *nf* crack, split; (*GEO*) fissure.

heno ['eno] *nm* hay.

herbicida [erβi'θiða] *nm* weed-killer.

heredad [ere'ðað] *nf* landed property; (*granja*) farm.

heredar [ere'ðar] *vt* to inherit; **heredero, a** *nm/f* heir/heiress.

hereje [e'rexe] *nm/f* heretic; **herejía** *nf* heresy.

herencia [e'renθja] *nf* inheritance.

herido, a [e'riðo, a] *a* injured, wounded // *nm/f* casualty // *nf* wound, injury; (*insulto*) insult.

herir [e'rir] *vt* to wound, injure; (*fig*) to offend.

hermanar [erma'nar] *vt* to match; (*unir*) to join.

hermandad [erman'dað] *nf* brotherhood.

hermano, a [er'mano, a] *nm/f* brother/sister; ~ **gemelo** twin brother; ~ **político** brother-in-law; ~**a política** sister-in-law.

hermético, a [er'metiko, a] *a* hermetic; (*fig*) watertight.

hermoso, a [er'moso, a] *a* beautiful, lovely; (*estupendo*) splendid; (*guapo*) handsome; **hermosura** *nf* beauty.

héroe ['eroe] *nm* hero; **heroico, a** *a* heroic.

heroína [ero'ina] *nf* (*mujer*) heroine; (*droga*) heroin.

heroísmo [ero'ismo] *nm* heroism.

herrador [erra'ðor] *nm* blacksmith; **herradura** *nf*: **curva en herradura** hairpin bend.

herramienta [erra'mjenta] *nf* tool; (*conjunto*) set of tools.

herrería [erre'ria] *nf* smithy; (*TEC*) forge; **herrero** *nm* blacksmith.

herrumbre [e'rrumbre] *nf* rust.

hervidero [erβi'ðero] *nm* (*burbujeo*) boiling, seething; (*fuente*) hot spring.

hervir [er'βir] *vi* (*gen*) to boil; (*burbujear*) to bubble; (*fig*): ~ **de** to teem with; ~ **a**

fuego lento to simmer; **hervor** *nm* boiling; (*fig*) ardour, fervour.

heterogéneo, a [etero'xeneo, a] *a* heterogeneous.

heterosexual [eterosek'swal] *a* heterosexual.

hice *etc vb ver* **hacer.**

hidráulico, a [i'ðrauliko, a] *a* hydraulic // *nf* hydraulics *sg*.

hidro... [iðro] *pref* hydro-..., water-...; ~**ala** *nf* hovercraft; ~**avión** *nm* seaplane; ~**eléctrico, a** *a* hydroelectric; ~**fobia** *nf* hydrophobia, rabies; **hidrófugo, a** *a* camp-proof; **hidrógeno** *nm* hydrogen.

hiedra [ˈjeðra] *nf* ivy.

hiel [jel] *nf* gall, bile; (*fig*) bitterness.

hiela *etc vb ver* **helar.**

hielo ['jelo] *nm* (*gen*) ice; (*escarcha*) frost; (*fig*) coldness, reserve.

hiena ['jena] *nf* hyena.

hierba ['jerβa] *nf* (*BOT*) grass; (*MED*) herb; **mala** ~ weed; (*fig*) evil influence; ~**buena** *nf* mint.

hierro ['jerro] *nm* (*metal*) iron; (*objeto*) iron object; (*herramienta*) tool; ~ **acanalado** corrugated iron; ~ **colado** *o* **fundido** cast iron.

hígado ['iɣaðo] *nm* liver.

higiene [i'xjene] *nf* hygiene; **higiénico, a** *a* hygienic.

higo ['iɣo] *nm* fig; ~ **paso** *o* **seco** dried fig; **higuera** *nf* fig tree.

hijastro, a [i'xastro, a] *nm/f* stepson/daughter.

hijo, a ['ixo, a] *nm/f* son/daughter, child; ~**s** *nmpl* children, sons and daughters; ~ **de papá/mamá** daddy's/mummy's boy; ~ **de puta** bastard, son of a bitch.

hilado, a [i'laðo, a] *a* spun // *nm* yarn.

hilandero, a [ilan'dero, a] *nm/f* spinner.

hilar [i'lar] *vt* to spin; ~ **delgado** to split hairs.

hilera [i'lera] *nf* row, file.

hilo ['ilo] *nm* (*gen*) thread; (*BOT*) fibre; (*metal*) wire; (*de agua*) trickle, thin stream; (*de luz*) beam, ray.

hilvanar [ilβa'nar] *vt* to tack; (*fig*) to do hurriedly.

Himalayas [ima'lajas] *nfpl*: **las** ~ the Himalayas.

himno ['imno] *nm* hymn; ~ **nacional** national anthem.

hincapié [inka'pje] *nm*: **hacer** ~ **en** to emphasize.

hincar [in'kar] *vt* to drive (in), thrust (in); ~**se** *vr*: ~**se de rodillas** to kneel down.

hinchado, a [in'tʃaðo, a] *a* (*gen*) swollen; (*persona*) pompous.

hinchar [in'tʃar] *vt* (*gen*) to swell; (*inflar*) to blow up, inflate; (*fig*) to exaggerate; ~**se** *vr* (*inflarse*) to swell up; (*fam*: *llenarse*) to stuff o.s.; **hinchazón** *nf* (*MED*) swelling; (*altivez*) arrogance.

hinojo [i'noxo] *nm* fennel.

hipar [i'par] *vi* to hiccup; (*perro*) to pant.

hipnotismo [ipno'tismo] *nm* hypnotism;
hipnotizar *vt* to hypnotize.
hipo ['ipo] *nm* hiccups *pl*.
hipocresía [ipokre'sia] *nf* hypocrisy; **hi-pócrita** a hypocritical // *nm/f* hypocrite.
hipódromo [i'poðromo] *nm* racetrack.
hipopótamo [ipo'potamo] *nm* hippopotamus.
hipoteca [ipo'teka] *nf* mortgage.
hipótesis [i'potesis] *nf* hypothesis.
hiriente [i'rjente] *a* offensive, cutting.
hirsuto, a [ir'suto, a] *a* hairy; (*fig*) rough.
hispánico, a [is'paniko, a] *a* Hispanic.
hispano, a [is'pano, a] *a* Hispanic,
Spanish, Hispano-; **H~américa** *nf*
Spanish *or* Latin America; **~americano,
a** *a*, *nm/f* Spanish *or* Latin American.
histeria [is'terja] *nf* hysteria.
historia [is'torja] *nf* (*gen*) history; (*cuento*)
story, tale; **~s** *nfpl* (*chismes*) gossip *sg*;
dejarse de ~s to come to the point;
pasar a la ~ to go down in history;
~dor, a *nm/f* historian; **historiar** *vt* to
chronicle, write the history of; **histórico,
a** *a* historical; (*fig*) historic.
historieta [isto'rjeta] *nf* tale, anecdote;
(*dibujos*) strip cartoon.
hito ['ito] *nm* (*gen*) landmark; (*objetivo*)
goal, target.
hizo *vb ver* **hacer.**
hocico [o'θiko] *nm* snout; (*fig*) grimace;
caer *o* **dar de ~** to fall on one's face.
hockey ['xoki] *nm* hockey; **~ sobre
patines** *o* **hielo** ice hockey.
hogar [o'xar] *nm* fireplace, hearth; (*casa*)
home; (*vida familiar*) home life; **~eño, a** *a*
home; (*persona*) home-loving.
hoguera [o'xera] *nf* (*gen*) bonfire; (*llamas*)
blaze.
hoja ['oxa] *nf* (*gen*) leaf; (*de flor*) petal; (*de
papel*) sheet; (*página*) page; **~ de afeitar**
razor blade; **~ de estaño** tinfoil.
hojalata [oxa'lata] *nf* tin(plate).
hojear [oxe'ar] *vt* to leaf through, turn the
pages of.
hola ['ola] *excl* hello!
Holanda [o'landa] *nf* Holland; **holandés,
esa** *a* Dutch // *nm/f* Dutchman/woman //
nm (*lengua*) Dutch.
holgado, a [ol'xaðo, a] *a* loose, baggy;
(*libre*) free; (*desempleado*) idle; (*rico*) well-
to-do.
holganza [ol'xanθa] *nf* (*ocio*) leisure;
(*pereza*) idleness; (*diversión*) amusement.
holgar [ol'xar] *vi* (*descansar*) to rest;
(*sobrar*) to be superfluous; **~se** *vr* to enjoy
o.s.; **huelga decir que** it goes without
saying that.
holgazán, ana [olxa'θan, ana] *a* idle, lazy
// *nm/f* loafer.
holgura [ol'xura] *nf* looseness, bagginess;
(*TEC*) play, free movement; (*vida*)
comfortable living, luxury.
hollar [o'ʎar] *vt* to tread (on), trample.
hollín [o'ʎin] *nm* soot.
hombradía [ombra'ðia] *nf* manliness.

hombre ['ombre] *nm* (*gen*) man(kind);
(*uno*) man // *excl* (*claro*) of course!; (*para
énfasis*) man, old boy; (*sorpresa*) you don't
say!; **~ de negocios** businessman;
~-rana frogman; **~ de pro** *o* **de
provecho** honest man.
hombrera [om'brera] *nf* shoulder strap.
hombro ['ombro] *nm* shoulder.
hombruno, a [om'bruno, a] *a* mannish.
homenaje [ome'naxe] *nm* (*gen*) homage;
(*lealtad*) allegiance; (*tributo*) tribute.
homicida [omi'θiða] *a* homicidal // *nm/f*
murderer; **homicidio** *nm* murder,
homicide.
homosexual [omosek'swal] *a*, *nm/f*
homosexual.
hondo, a ['ondo, a] *a* deep; (*profundo*) low
// *nm* depth(s) (*pl*), bottom; **~nada** *nf*
hollow, depression; (*cañón*) ravine; (*GEO*)
lowland; **hondura** *nf* depth, profundity.
Honduras [on'duras] *nf* Honduras.
hondureño, a [ondu'reno, a] *a*, *nm/f*
Honduran.
honestidad [onesti'ðað] *nf* purity, chastity;
(*decencia*) decency; **honesto, a** *a* chaste,
decent, honest; (*justo*) just.
hongo ['ongo] *nm* (*BOT: gen*) fungus; (:
comestible) mushroom; (: *venenoso*)
toadstool.
honor [o'nor] *nm* (*gen*) honour; (*gloria*)
glory; **en ~ a la verdad** to be fair;
~able a honourable.
honorario, a [ono'rarjo, a] *a* honorary;
~s *nmpl* fees.
honra ['onra] *nf* (*gen*) honour; (*nombre*)
reputation; (*de persona*) integrity; **~dez** *nf* honesty; (*de persona*)
integrity; **~do, a** *a* honest, upright.
honrar [on'rar] *vt* to honour; **~se** *vr*:
~se con algo/de hacer algo to be
honoured by/to do sth.
honroso, a [on'roso, a] *a* (*honrado*)
honourable; (*respetado*) respectable.
hora ['ora] *nf* (*gen*) time; (*específica*) hour;
¿qué ~ es? what time is it?; **¿a qué ~?**
at what time?; **media ~** half an hour; **a
la ~ de recreo** at playtime; **a primera
~** first thing (in the morning); **a última
~** at the last moment; **en las altas ~s** in
the small hours; **¡a buena ~!** it's high
time!; **dar la ~** to strike the hour; **~s de
oficina/de trabajo** office/working hours;
~s de visita visiting times; **~s extras** *o*
extraordinarias overtime *sg*; **~s punta**
rush hours.
horadar [ora'ðar] *vt* to drill, bore.
horario, a [o'rarjo, a] *a* hourly, hour *cpd*
// *nm* timetable.
horca ['orka] *nf* gallows *sg*.
horcajadas [orka'xaðas]: **a ~** *ad* astride.
horda ['orða] *nf* horde.
horizontal [oriθon'tal] *a* horizontal;
horizonte *nm* horizon.
horma ['orma] *nf* mould.
hormiga [or'mixa] *nf* ant; **~s** *nfpl* (*MED*)
pins and needles.
hormigón [ormi'xon] *nm* concrete; **~**

armado/pretensado reinforced/pre-stressed concrete.

hormigueo [ormi'xeo] nm (comezón) itch; (fig) uneasiness; (amontonamiento) swarming.

hormona [or'mona] nf hormone.

hornillo [or'niʎo] nm small furnace; (cocina) portable stove.

horno ['orno] nm (CULIN) oven; (TEC) furnace; **alto** ~ blast furnace.

horóscopo [o'roskopo] nm horoscope.

horquilla [or'kiʎa] nf hairpin; (AGR) pitchfork.

horrendo, a [o'rrendo, a] a horrendous, frightful.

horrible [o'rriβle] a horrible, dreadful.

horripilante [orripi'lante] a hair-raising; (espeluznante) creepy.

horripilar [orripi'lar] vt: ~ **a uno** to horrify sb; ~**se** vr to be horrified.

horror [o'rror] nm horror, dread; (atrocidad) atrocity; ¡**qué** ~! (fam) oh, my God!; ~**izar** vt to horrify, frighten; ~**izarse** vr to be horrified; ~**oso, a** a horrifying, ghastly.

hortaliza [orta'liθa] nf vegetable.

hortelano, a [orte'lano, a] nm/f (market) gardener.

hosco, a ['osko, a] a dark; (triste, ceñudo) sullen, gloomy.

hospedar [ospe'ðar] vt to put up, lodge; ~**se** vr to stay, lodge.

hospital [ospi'tal] nm hospital.

hospitalario, a [ospita'larjo, a] a hospitable; **hospitalidad** nf hospitality.

hosquedad [oske'ðað] nf sullenness.

hostal [os'tal] nm small hotel.

hostelero, a [oste'lero, a] nm/f innkeeper, landlord/lady.

hostería [oste'ria] nf hostelry.

hostia ['ostja] nf host, consecrated wafer; (fam: golpe) whack, punch // excl: ¡~**s**! damn it!

hostigar [osti'xar] vt to whip; (fig) to harass, pester.

hostil [os'til] a hostile; ~**idad** nf hostility.

hotel [o'tel] nm hotel; ~**ero, a** a hotel cpd // nm/f hotelier.

hoy [oi] ad (este día) today; (el ahora) now(adays) // nm present time; ~ **(en) día** now(adays).

hoya ['oja] nf pit; (sepulcro) grave; (GEO) valley.

hoyo ['ojo] nm hole, pit; **hoyuelo** nm dimple.

hoz [oθ] nf sickle.

hube etc vb ver **haber**.

hucha ['utʃa] nf money box; (fig) nest egg.

hueco, a ['weko, a] a (vacío) hollow, empty; (blanco: papel) blank; (resonante) booming // nm hollow, cavity.

huelga etc vb ver **holgar** // ['welxa] nf strike; **declararse en** ~ to go on strike, come out on strike; ~ **de brazos caídos/de hambre** sit-down/hunger strike; ~ **patronal** lockout.

huelgo etc vb ver **holgar** // ['welxo] nm breath; (espacio) room, space.

huelguista [wel'xista] nm/f striker.

huelo etc vb ver **oler**.

huella ['weʎa] nf (acto de pisar, pisada) tread(ing); (marca del paso) footprint, footstep; (: de animal, máquina) track; ~ **digital** fingerprint; ~ **del sonido** sound track.

huérfano, a ['werfano, a] a orphan(ed) // nm/f orphan.

huerta ['werta] nf market garden; (área de regadío) irrigated region.

huerto ['werto] nm orchard.

hueso ['weso] nm (ANAT) bone; (de fruta) stone.

huésped, a ['wespeð, a] nm/f (invitado) guest; (habitante) resident; (anfitrión) host.

huesudo, a [we'suðo, a] a bony, big-boned.

huevo ['weβo] nm egg; ~ **en cáscara/escalfado/estrellado** o **frito/pasado por agua** boiled/poached/fried/soft-boiled egg; ~**s revueltos** scrambled eggs.

huida [u'iða] nf escape, flight.

huidizo, a [ui'ðiθo, a] a (tímido) shy; (pasajero) fleeting.

huir [u'ir] vt (escapar) to flee, escape (from); (evadir) to avoid; ~**se** vr (escaparse) to escape; (el tiempo) to fly.

hule ['ule] nm (goma) rubber; (encerado) oilskin.

humanidad [umani'ðað] nf (los hombres) mankind); (cualidad) humanity.

humanizar [umani'θar] vt to humanize.

humano, a [u'mano, a] a (gen) human; (humanitario) humane // nm human; **ser** ~ human being.

humareda [uma'reða] nf cloud of smoke.

humear [ume'ar] vi to smoke.

humedad [ume'ðað] nf (del clima) humidity; (de pared etc) dampness; **a prueba de** ~ damp-proof; **humedecer** vt to moisten, wet; **humedecerse** vr to get wet.

húmedo, a ['umeðo, a] a (mojado) damp, wet; (tiempo etc) humid.

humildad [umil'dað] nf humility, humbleness; **humilde** a humble, modest; (pequeño: voz) small.

humillación [umiʎa'θjon] nf humiliation; **humillante** a humiliating; **humillar** vt to humiliate; **humillarse** vr to humble o.s., grovel.

humo ['umo] nm (de fuego) smoke; (gas nocivo) fumes pl; ~**s** nmpl (fig) conceit sg.

humor [u'mor] nm (disposición) mood, temper; (lo que divierte) humour; **de buen/mal** ~ in a good/bad mood; ~**ada** nf witticism; ~**ismo** nm humour; ~**ista** nm/f humorist; ~**ístico, a** a funny, humorous.

hundido, a [un'diðo, a] a (de mejillas) sunken; (de ojos) deep-set.

hundimiento [undi'mjento] nm (gen) sinking; (colapso) collapse.

hundir [un'dir] vt to sink; (edificio, plan) to

ruin, destroy; ~se vr to sink, collapse.

húngaro, a ['ungaro, a] a, nm/f Hungarian.

Hungría [un'gria] nf Hungary.

huracán [ura'kan] nm hurricane.

huraño, a [u'raño, a] a shy; (antisocial) unsociable.

hurgar [ur'xar] vt to poke, jab; (remover) to stir (up).

hurgonear [urxone'ar] vt to poke.

hurón, ona [u'ron, ona] a unsociable // nm (zool) ferret; (persona tímida) shy person; (persona arisca) unsociable person.

hurtadillas [urta'ðiʎas]: **a ~ ad** stealthily, on the sly.

hurtar [ur'tar] vt to steal; ~se vr to hide, withdraw; **hurto** nm theft, stealing.

husmear [usme'ar] vt (oler) to sniff out, scent; (fam) to pry into // vi to smell bad; **husmo** nm strong smell.

huyo etc vb ver **huir.**

I

iba etc vb ver **ir.**

ibérico, a [i'ßeriko, a] a Iberian.

iberoamericano, a [ißeroameri'kano, a] a, nm/f Spanish American.

íbice ['ißiθe] nm ibex.

ibicenco, a [ißi'θenko, a] a Ibizan.

Ibiza [i'ßiθa] nf Ibiza.

ibón [i'ßon] nm lake, tarn.

iceberg ['aisßerx] nm iceberg.

ícono ['ikono] nm ikon, icon.

iconoclasta [ikono'klasta] a iconoclastic // nm/f iconoclast.

ictericia [ikte'riθja] nf jaundice.

ida ['iða] nf going, departure; ~ y vuelta round trip, return.

idea [i'ðea] nf idea; **darse/hacerse una ~ de...** to get an idea of... .

ideal [iðe'al] a, nm ideal; ~ista nm/f idealist; ~izar vt to idealize.

idear [iðe'ar] vt to think up; (aparato) to invent; (viaje) to plan.

ídem ['iðem] pron ditto.

idéntico, a [i'ðentiko, a] a identical.

identidad [iðenti'ðað] nf identity; **carné de ~** identity card.

identificación [iðentifika'θjon] nf identification; **identificar** vt to identify; **identificarse** vr: **identificarse con** to identify o.s. with.

ideología [iðeolo'xia] nf ideology; **ideológico, a** a ideological.

idioma [i'ðjoma] nm (gen) language; (giro) idiom.

idiota [i'ðjota] a idiotic // nm/f idiot; **idiotez** nf idiocy.

idólatra [i'ðolatra] nm/f idolater/tress; **idolatría** nf idolatry.

ídolo ['iðolo] nm idol.

idóneo, a [i'ðoneo, a] a (apto) fit; (conveniente) suitable.

iglesia [i'xlesja] nf church.

ignición [ixni'θjon] nf ignition.

ignominia [ixno'minja] nf ignominy; **ignominioso, a** a ignominious.

ignorado, a [ixno'raðo, a] a unknown; (dato) obscure.

ignorancia [ixno'ranθja] nf ignorance; **ignorante** a ignorant, uninformed // nm/f ignoramus.

ignorar [ixno'rar] vt not to know, be ignorant of.

ignoto, a [ix'noto, a] a unknown.

igual [i'xwal] a (gen) equal; (similar) like, similar; (mismo) (the) same; (constante) constant; (temperatura) even // nm/f equal; **al ~ que** prep, conj like, just like.

igualada [ixwa'laða] nf equaliser.

igualar [ixwa'lar] vt (gen) to equalize, make equal; (allanar, nivelar) to level (off), even (out); ~se vr (platos de balanza) to balance out; (equivaler) to be equal.

igualdad [ixwal'dað] nf equality; (similaridad) sameness; (uniformidad) evenness, uniformity.

igualmente [ixwal'mente] ad equally; (también) also, likewise // excl the same to you.

ikurriña [iku'rriña] nf Basque flag.

ilegal [ile'xal] a illegal.

ilegítimo, a [ile'xitimo, a] a illegitimate.

ileso, a [i'leso, a] a unhurt.

ilícito, a [i'liθito] a illicit.

ilimitado, a [ilimi'taðo, a] a unlimited.

ilógico, a [i'loxiko, a] a illogical.

iluminación [ilumina'θjon] nf (gen) illumination; (alumbrado) lighting.

iluminar [ilumi'nar] vt to illuminate, light (up); (fig) to enlighten.

ilusión [ilu'sjon] nf illusion; (quimera) delusion; (esperanza) hope; **ilusionado, a** a excited.

ilusionista [ilusjo'nista] nm/f conjurer.

iluso, a [i'luso, a] a easily deceived.

ilusorio, a [ilu'sorjo, a] a (de ilusión) illusory, deceptive; (esperanza) vain.

ilustración [ilustra'θjon] nf illustration; (saber) learning, erudition; **la I ~** the Enlightenment; **ilustrado, a** a illustrated; learned.

ilustrar [ilus'trar] vt (gen) to illustrate; (instruir) to instruct; (explicar) to explain, make clear; ~se vr to acquire knowledge.

ilustre [i'lustre] a famous, illustrious.

imagen [i'maxen] nf (gen) image; (dibujo) picture; (semejanza) likeness.

imaginación [imaxina'θjon] nf imagination.

imaginar [imaxi'nar] vt (gen) to imagine; (idear) to think up; (suponer) to suppose; ~se vr to imagine; ~io, a a imaginary; **imaginativo, a** a imaginative.

imán [i'man] nm magnet.

imbécil [im'beθil] nm/f imbecile, idiot; **imbecilidad** nf imbecility.

imbuir [imbu'ir] vi to imbue.

imitación [imita'θjon] nf imitation; **imitar**

vt to imitate; (*parodiar, remedar*) to mimic, ape.

impaciencia [impa'θjenθja] *nf* impatience; **impaciente** *a* impatient; (*nervioso*) anxious.

impacto [im'pakto] *nm* impact.

impar [im'par] *a* odd.

imparcial [impar'θjal] *a* impartial, fair; ~**idad** *nf* impartiality, fairness.

impartir [impar'tir] *vt* to impart, give.

impasible [impa'siβle] *a* impassive.

impavidez [impaβi'ðeθ] *nf* fearlessness, intrepidness; **impávido,** *a* *a* fearless, intrepid.

impecable [impe'kaβle] *a* impeccable.

impedimento [impeði'mento] *am* impediment, obstacle.

impedir [impe'ðir] *vt* (*obstruir*) to impede, obstruct; (*estorbar*) to prevent.

impeler [impe'ler] *vt* to drive, propel; (*fig*) to impel.

impenetrabilidad [impenetraβili'ðað] *nf* impenetrability; **impenetrable** *a* impenetrable; (*fig*) incomprehensible.

impenitente [impeni'tente] *a* unrepentant.

impensado, *a* [impen'saðo, a] *a* unexpected.

imperar [impe'rar] *vi* (*reinar*) to rule, reign; (*fig*) to prevail, reign; (*precio*) to be current.

imperativo, a [impera'tiβo, a] *a* (*persona*) imperious; (*urgente, LING*) imperative.

imperceptible [imperθep'tiβle] *a* imperceptible.

imperdible [imper'ðiβle] *nm* safety pin.

imperdonable [imperðo'naβle] *a* unforgivable, inexcusable.

imperfección [imperfek'θjon] *nf* imperfection.

imperfecto, a [imper'fekto, a] *a* imperfect.

imperial [impe'rjal] *a* imperial; ~**ismo** *nm* imperialism.

impericia [impe'riθja] *nf* (*torpeza*) unskilfulness; (*inexperiencia*) inexperience.

imperio [im'perjo] *nm* empire; (*reino, dominación*) rule, authority; (*fig*) pride, haughtiness; ~**so,** *a* *a* imperious; (*urgente*) urgent; (*imperativo*) imperative.

impermeable [imperme'aβle] *a* impermeable; (*a prueba de agua*) waterproof // *nm* raincoat.

impersonal [imperso'nal] *a* impersonal.

impertérrito, a [imper'territo, a] *a* undaunted.

impertinencia [imperti'nenθja] *nf* (*inoportunidad*) irrelevant; (*insolencia*) impertinence; **impertinente** *a* irrelevant; impertinent.

imperturbable [impertur'βaβle] *a* imperturbable.

ímpetu ['impetu] *nm* (*impulso*) impetus, impulse; (*impetuosidad*) impetuosity; (*violencia*) violence.

impetuosidad [impetwosi'ðað] *nf* impetuousness; (*violencia*) violence; **impetuoso, a** *a* impetuous; (*persona*) headstrong; (*río*) rushing, violent; (*acto*) hasty.

impío, a [im'pio, a] *a* impious, ungodly.

implacable [impla'kaβle] *a* implacable.

implicar [impli'kar] *vt* (*gen*) to implicate, involve; (*entrañar*) to imply.

implícito, a [im'pliθito, a] *a* (*tácito*) implicit; (*sobreentendido*) implied.

implorar [implo'rar] *vt* to beg, implore.

imponente [impo'nente] *a* (*impresionante*) impressive, imposing; (*solemne*) grand // *nm/f* investor.

imponer [impo'ner] *vt* (*gen*) to impose; (*informar*) to inform, instruct; (*exigir*) to exact, command; (*COM*) to invest; ~**se** *vr* to assert o.s.; (*prevalecer*) to prevail.

impopular [impopu'lar] *a* unpopular.

importación [importa'θjon] *nf* (*acto*) importing; (*objetos*) imports *pl*.

importancia [impor'tanθja] *nf* importance; (*valor*) value, significance; (*extensión*) size, magnitude; **importante** *a* important; valuable, significant.

importar [impor'tar] *vt* (*del extranjero*) to import; (*valer*) to amount to, be worth // *vi* to be important, matter; **me importa el rábano** I don't give a damn; **no importa** it doesn't matter.

importe [im'porte] *nm* (*total*) amount; (*valor*) value.

importunar [importu'nar] *vt* to bother, pester.

importuno, a [impor'tuno, a] *a* (*inoportuno, molesto*) inopportune; (*indiscreto*) troublesome.

imposibilidad [imposiβili'ðað] *nf* impossibility; **imposibilitar** *vt* to make impossible, prevent; (*incapacitar*) to disable, cripple.

imposible [impo'siβle] *a* (*gen*) impossible; (*insoportable*) unbearable, intolerable.

imposición [imposi'θjon] *nf* imposition; (*COM*) tax; (*enganche*) deposit.

impostor, a [impos'tor, a] *nm/f* impostor; **impostura** *nf* fraud, imposture.

impotencia [impo'tenθja] *nf* impotence; **impotente** *a* impotent, powerless.

impracticable [imprakti'kaβle] *a* (*irrealizable*) impracticable; (*intransitable*) impassable.

imprecar [impre'kar] *vi* to curse.

impregnar [impreɣ'nar] *vt* to impregnate; ~**se** *vr* to become impregnated.

imprenta [im'prenta] *nf* (*gen*) printing; (*aparato*) press; (*casa*) printer's; (*letra*) print.

imprescindible [impresθin'diβle] *a* essential, indispensable.

impresión [impre'sjon] *nf* (*gen*) impression; (*IMPRENTA*) printing; (*edición*) edition; (*FOTO*) print; (*marca*) imprint; ~ **digital** fingerprint.

impresionable [impresjo'naβle] *a*

(*sensible*) impressionable; (*excitable*) emotional.

impresionante [impresjo'nante] a impressive; (*tremendo*) tremendous; (*maravilloso*) great, marvellous.

impresionar [impresjo'nar] vt (*conmover*) to move; (*afectar*) to impress, strike; (*película fotográfica*) to expose; ~**se** vr to be impressed; (*conmoverse*) to be moved.

impreso, a [im'preso, a] pp de **imprimir** // a printed // nm printed paper/book etc.

impresor [impre'sor] nm printer.

imprevisto, a [impre'βisto, a] a (*gen*) unforeseen; (*inesperado*) unexpected.

imprimir [impri'mir] vt to imprint, impress, stamp; (*textos*) to print.

improbabilidad [improβaβili'ðað] nf (*sin seguridad*) improbability; (*inverosimilitud*) unlikelihood; **improbable** a improbable; unlikely.

improcedente [improθe'ðente] a (*inconveniente*) unsuitable; (*inadecuado*) inappropriate.

improductivo, a [improðuk'tiβo, a] a unproductive.

improperio [impro'perjo] nm insult, taunt.

impropiedad [impropje'ðað] nf impropriety (of language).

impropio, a [im'propjo, a] a improper.

impróvido, a [im'proβiðo, a] a improvident.

improvisación [improβisa'θjon] nf improvisation; **improvisado, a** a improvised; **improvisar** vt to improvise.

improviso, a [impro'βiso, a], **improvisto, a** [impro'βisto, a] a unexpected, unforeseen; **de** ~ unexpectedly, suddenly.

imprudencia [impru'ðenθja] nf imprudence; (*indiscreción*) indiscretion; (*descuido*) carelessness; **imprudente** a imprudent; indiscreet; (*irreflexivo*) unwise.

impúdico, a [im'puðiko, a] a shameless, immodest; (*lujurioso*) lecherous, lewd.

impudor [impu'ðor] nm shamelessness, immodesty; (*lujuria*) lechery, lewdness.

impuesto, a [im'pwesto, a] a imposed; (*informado*) informed // nm tax.

impugnar [impuɣ'nar] vt to oppose, contest; (*refutar*) to refute, impugn.

impulsar [impul'sar] vt = **impeler**.

impulsión [impul'sjon] nf (*TEC*) propulsion; (*fig*) impulse.

impulso [im'pulso] nm impulse; (*fuerza, empuje*) thrust, drive; (*rapto*) urge, impulse.

impune [im'pune] a unpunished; **impunidad** nf impunity.

impureza [impu'reθa] nf impurity; (*fig*) lewdness; **impuro, a** a impure; lewd.

imputación [imputa'θjon] nf imputation.

imputar [impu'tar] vt (*atribuir*) to attribute to; (*cargar*) to impute to.

inacabable [inaka'βaβle] a (*infinito*) endless; (*interminable*) interminable.

inaccesible [inakθe'siβle] a inaccessible.

inacción [inak'θjon] nf (*gen*) inaction; (*desocupación*) inactivity; (*ocio*) idleness.

inaceptable [inaθep'taβle] a inacceptable.

inactividad [inaktiβi'ðað] nf inactivity; (*pereza*) laziness, idleness; (*com*) dullness; **inactivo, a** a inactive.

inadaptación [inaðapta'θjon] nf maladjustment.

inadecuado, a [inaðe'kwaðo, a] a (*insuficiente*) inadequate; (*inapto*) unsuitable.

inadmisible [inaðmi'siβle] a inadmissible.

inadvertencia [inaðβer'tenθja] nf oversight.

inadvertido, a [inaðβer'tiðo, a] a (*distraído*) inattentive; (*no visto*) unnoticed; (*descuidado*) careless.

inagotable [inaɣo'taβle] a inexhaustible.

inaguantable [inaɣwan'taβle] a unbearable.

inalterable [inalte'raβle] a immutable, unchangeable; (*permanente*) permanent.

inanición [inani'θjon] nf starvation.

inanimado, a [inani'maðo, a] a inanimate.

inapto, a [in'apto] a unsuited.

inaudito, a [inau'ðito, a] a unheard-of.

inauguración [inauɣura'θjon] nf inauguration; (*de exposición*) opening; **inaugurar** vt to inaugurate; to open.

I.N.B. abr de **Instituto Nacional de Bachillerato** ≈ secondary school.

inca ['inka] nm/f Inca; ~**ico, a** a Inca.

incalculable [inkalku'laβle] a incalculable.

incandescente [inkandes'θente] a incandescent.

incansable [inkan'saβle] a tireless, untiring.

incapacidad [inkapaθi'ðað] nf incapacity; (*incompetencia*) incompetence; ~ **física/mental** physical/mental incapacity or disability.

incapacitar [inkapaθi'tar] vt (*inhabilitar*) to incapacitate, render unfit; (*descalificar*) to disqualify.

incapaz [inka'paθ] a incapable.

incautación [inkauta'θjon] nf confiscation; **incautarse** vr: **incautarse de** to seize, confiscate.

incauto, a [in'kauto, a] a (*imprudente*) incautious, unwary.

incendiar [inθen'djar] vt to set on fire; (*fig*) to inflame; ~**se** vr to catch fire; ~**io, a** a incendiary; (*fig*) inflammatory.

incendio [in'θendjo] nm fire.

incentivo [inθen'tiβo] nm incentive.

incertidumbre [inθerti'ðumβre] nf (*inseguridad*) uncertainty; (*duda*) doubt.

incesante [inθe'sante], **incesable** [inθe'saβle] a incessant.

incesto [in'θesto] nm incest.

incidencia [inθi'ðenθja] *nf* (*accidente*) incident; (*MAT*) incidence.
incidente [inθi'ðente] *a* incidental *f. nm* incident.
incidir [inθi'ðir] *vi* (*influir*) to influence; (*afectar*) to affect; ~ **en un error** to fall into error.
incienso [in'θjenso] *nm* incense.
incierto, a [in'θjerto, a] *a* uncertain.
incineración [inθinera'θjon] *nf* incineration; (*de cadáveres*) cremation; **incinerar** *vt* to burn; to cremate.
incipiente [inθi'pjente] *a* incipient.
incisión [inθi'sjon] *nf* incision.
incisivo, a [inθi'siβo, a] *a* sharp, cutting; (*fig*) incisive.
incitación [inθita'θjon] *nf* incitement.
incitante [inθi'tante] *a* (*estimulante*) exciting; (*provocativo*) provocative; **incitar** *vt* to incite, rouse.
incivil [inθi'βil] *a* rude, uncivil.
inclemencia [inkle'menθja] *n* (*severidad*) harshness, severity; (*del tiempo*) inclemency; **inclemente** *a* harsh, severe; inclement.
inclinación [inklina'θjon] *nf* (*gen*) inclination; (*de tierras*) slope, incline; (*de cabeza*) nod, bow; (*fig*) leaning, bent.
inclinar [inkli'nar] *vt* to incline; (*cabeza*) to nod, bow; (*tierras*) to slope; (*persuadir*) to persuade; ~**se** *vr* to bow; (*encorvarse*) to stoop; ~**se a** to take after, resemble; ~**se ante** to bow down to; **me inclino a pensar que** I'm inclined to think that.
ínclito, a ['inklito, a] *a* illustrious, renowned.
incluir [inklu'ir] *vt* to include; (*incorporar*) to incorporate; (*meter*) to enclose.
inclusive [inklu'siβe] *ad* inclusive // *prep* including.
incluso, a [in'kluso, a] *a* included // *ad* inclusively; (*hasta*) even.
incógnito, a [in'koɣnito, a] *a* unknown // *nm*: **de** ~ incognito // *nf* unknown factor.
incoherente [inkoe'rente] *a* incoherent.
incoloro, a [inko'loro, a] *a* colourless.
incólume [in'kolume] *a* (*gen*) safe; (*indemne*) unhurt, unharmed.
incomodar [inkomo'ðar] *vt* to inconvenience; (*molestar*) to bother, trouble; (*fastidiar*) to annoy; ~**se** *vr* to put o.s. out; (*fastidiarse*) to get annoyed.
incomodidad [inkomoði'ðað] *nf* inconvenience; (*fastidio, enojo*) annoyance; (*de vivienda*) discomfort.
incómodo, a [in'komoðo, a] *a* (*inconfortable*) uncomfortable; (*molesto*) annoying; (*inconveniente*) inconvenient.
incomparable [inkompa'raβle] *a* incomparable.
incompatible [inkompa'tiβle] *a* incompatible.
incompetencia [inkompe'tenθja] *nf* incompetence; **incompetente** *a* incompetent.
incompleto, a [inkom'pleto, a] *a* incomplete, unfinished.

incomprensible [inkompren'siβle] *a* incomprehensible.
incomunicado, a [inkomuni'kaðo, a] *a* (*aislado*) cut off, isolated; (*confinado*) in solitary confinement.
inconcebible [inkonθe'βiβle] *a* inconceivable.
inconcluso, a [inkon'kluso, a] *a* (*inacabado*) unfinished; (*incompleto*) incomplete.
incondicional [inkondiθjo'nal] *a* unconditional; (*apoyo*) wholehearted; (*partidario*) staunch.
inconexo, a [inko'nekso, a] *a* (*gen*) unconnected; (*desunido*) disconnected.
inconfundible [inkonfun'diβle] *a* unmistakable.
incongruente [inkon'ɣwente] *a* incongruous.
inconmensurable [inkonmensu'raβle] *a* immeasurable, vast.
inconsciencia [inkons'θjenθja] *nf* unconsciousness; (*fig*) thoughtlessness; **inconsciente** *a* unconscious; thoughtless.
inconsecuencia [inkonse'kwenθja] *nf* inconsistency; **inconsecuente** *a* inconsistent.
inconsiderado, a [inkonsiðe'raðo, a] *a* inconsiderate.
inconsistente [inkonsis'tente] *a* weak; (*tela*) flimsy.
inconstancia [inkons'tanθja] *nf* (*inconsecuencia, veleidad*) inconstancy; (*inestabilidad*) unsteadiness; **inconstante** *a* inconstant.
incontestable [inkontes'taβle] *a* unanswerable; (*innegable*) undeniable.
incontinencia [inkonti'nenθja] *nf* incontinence; **incontinente** *a* incontinent.
inconveniencia [inkombe'njenθja] *nf* unsuitability, inappropriateness; (*incorrección*) impoliteness; **inconveniente** *a* unsuitable; impolite // *nm* obstacle; (*desventaja*) disadvantage.
incorporación [inkorpora'θjon] *nf* incorporation; (*del cuerpo*) sitting/standing up; **incorporar** *vt* to incorporate; **incorporarse** *vr* to sit/stand up.
incorrección [inkorrek'θjon] *nf* (*gen*) incorrectness, inaccuracy; (*descortesía*) bad-mannered behaviour; **incorrecto, a** (*gen*) incorrect, wrong; (*facciones*) irregular, odd; (*comportamiento*) bad-mannered.
incorregible [inkorre'xiβle] *a* incorrigible.
incorruptible [inkorrup'tiβle] *a* incorruptible; ~ **a la intemperie** rustproof.
incredulidad [inkreðuli'ðað] *nf* incredulity; (*escepticismo*) scepticism; **incrédulo, a** *a* incredulous, unbelieving; sceptical.
increíble [inkre'iβle] *a* incredible.
incremento [inkre'mento] *nm* increment; (*aumento*) rise, increase.
increpar [inkre'par] *vt* to reprimand.

incruento, a [in'krwento, a] a bloodless.
incrustar [inkrus'tar] vt to incrust; (piedras: en joya) to inlay.
incubar [inku'ßar] vt to incubate; (fig) to hatch.
inculcar [inkul'kar] vt to inculcate.
inculpar [inkul'par] vt (acusar) to accuse; (achacar, atribuir) to charge, blame.
inculto, a [in'kulto, a] a (persona) uneducated, uncultured; (terreno) uncultivated // nm/f ignoramus.
incumplimiento [inkumpli'mjento] nm non-fulfilment; ~ **de contrato** breach of contract.
incurrir [inku'rrir] vi: ~ **en** to incur; (crimen) to commit; ~ **en un error** to fall into error.
indagación [indaɣa'θjon] nf investigation; (búsqueda) search; (JUR) inquest; **indagar** vt to investigate; to search; (averiguar) to ascertain.
indecente [inde'θente] a indecent, improper; (lascivo) obscene.
indecible [inde'θißle] a unspeakable; (indescriptible) indescribable.
indeciso, a [inde'θiso, a] a (por decidir) undecided; (vacilante) hesitant; (resultado) indecisive.
indefectible [indefek'tißle] a unfailing.
indefenso, a [inde'fenso, a] a defenceless.
indefinido, a [indefi'niðo, a] a indefinite; (vago) vague, undefined.
indeleble [inde'leßle] a indelible.
indemnizar [indemni'θar] vt to indemnify; (compensar) to compensate.
independencia [indepen'denθja] nf independence.
independiente [indepen'djente] a (libre) independent; (autónomo) self-sufficient.
indeterminado, a [indetermi'naðo, a] a indefinite; (desconocido) indeterminate.
India ['indja] nf: **la** ~ India.
indicación [indika'θjon] nf indication; (señal) sign; (sugerencia) suggestion, hint; (de termómetro) reading.
indicador [indika'ðor] nm indicator; (TEC) gauge, meter.
indicar [indi'kar] vt (mostrar) to indicate, show; (termómetro etc) to read, register; (señalar) to point to.
índice ['indiθe] nm index; (catálogo) catalogue; (ANAT) index finger, forefinger; (de cuadrante) pointer, needle; (de reloj) hand.
indicio [in'diθjo] nm indication, sign; (huella) trace; (pesquisa) clue.
indiferencia [indife'renθja] nf indifference; (apatía) apathy; **indiferente** a indifferent.
indígena [in'dixena] a indigenous, native; (aborigen) aboriginal // nm/f native; aborigine.
indigencia [indi'xenθja] nf poverty, need.
indigestión [indixes'tjon] nf indigestion.
indigesto, a [indi'xesto, a] a undigested; (indigestible) indigestible; (fig) turgid.

indignación [indiɣna'θjon] nf indignation; **indignado, a** a indignant.
indignar [indiɣ'nar] vt to anger, make indignant; ~**se** vr: ~**se de o por** to get indignant about.
indignidad [indiɣni'ðað] nf (insulto) indignity, insult; (ruindad) vile act; **indigno, a** a (despreciable) low, contemptible; (inmerecido) unworthy.
indio, a ['indjo, a] a, nm/f Indian.
indirecta [indi'rekta] nf insinuation, innuendo; (sugerencia) hint.
indirecto, a [indi'rekto, a] a indirect.
indiscreción [indiskre'θjon] nf (imprudencia) indiscretion; (irreflexión) tactlessness; (acto) gaffe, tactless act.
indiscreto, a [indis'kreto, a] a indiscreet.
indiscutible [indisku'tißle] a indisputable, unquestionable.
indispensable [indispen'saßle] a indispensable.
indisponer [indispo'ner] vt to spoil, upset; (salud) to make ill; ~**se** vr to fall ill; ~**se con uno** to fall out with sb.
indisposición [indisposi'θjon] nf indisposition.
indistinto, a [indis'tinto, a] a indistinct; (vago) vague.
individual [indiβi'ðwal] a individual; (habitación) single // nm (DEPORTE) singles sg.
individuo, a [indi'βiðwo, a] a individual // nm individual; (miembro, socio) member, fellow.
indiviso, a [indi'βiso, a] a undivided.
índole ['indole] nf (naturaleza) nature; (clase) sort, kind.
indolencia [indo'lenθja] nf indolence, laziness.
indomable [indo'maßle] a indomitable; (animal) untameable; (fig) unmanageable.
indómito, a [in'domito, a] a indomitable.
inducir [indu'θir] vt to induce; (inferir) to infer; (persuadir) to persuade.
indudable [indu'ðaßle] a undoubted; (incuestionable) unquestionable.
indulgencia [indul'xenθja] nf indulgence.
indultar [indul'tar] vt (perdonar) to pardon, reprieve; (librar de pago) to exempt; **indulto** nm pardon; exemption.
industria [in'dustrja] nf industry; (habilidad) skill; **industrial** a industrial // nm industrialist.
industrioso, a [indus'trjoso, a] a industrious.
inédito, a [in'eðito, a] a (libro) unpublished; (nuevo) unheard-of.
inefable [ine'faßle] a ineffable, indescribable.
ineficaz [inefi'kaθ] a (inútil) ineffective; (ineficiente) inefficient.
ineludible [inelu'ðißle] a inescapable, unavoidable.
ineptitud [inepti'tuð] nf ineptitude, incompetence; **inepto, a** a inept, incompetent.

inequívoco, a [ine'kiβoko, a] a unequivocal; (*inconfundible*) unmistakable.

inercia [in'erθja] nf inertia; (*fig*) passivity.

inerme [in'erme] a (*sin armas*) unarmed; (*indefenso*) defenceless.

inerte [in'erte] a inert; (*fig*) passive.

inesperado, a [inespe'raðo, a] a unexpected, unforeseen.

inestable [ines'taβle] a unstable.

inevitable [ineβi'taβle] a inevitable.

inexactitud [ineksakti'tuð] nf inaccuracy; **inexacto, a** a inaccurate; (*falso*) untrue.

infamar [infa'mar] vt to dishonour; (*calumniar*) to defame, slander.

infame [in'fame] a infamous // nm/f vile person; **infamia** nf infamy; (*deshonra*) disgrace.

infancia [in'fanθja] nf infancy, childhood.

infante [in'fante] nm (*niño*) infant, child; (*hijo del rey*) prince.

infantería [infante'ria] nf infantry.

infantil [infan'til] a (*pueril, aniñado*) infantile; (*cándido*) childlike; (*literatura*) children's.

infarto [in'farto] nm heart attack.

infatigable [infati'xaβle] a tireless, untiring.

infausto, a [in'fausto, a] a unlucky.

infección [infek'θjon] nf infection **infeccioso, a** a infectious.

infectar [infek'tar] vt to infect; ~**se** vr to become infected.

infelicidad [infeliθi'ðað] nf unhappiness.

infeliz [infe'liθ] a unhappy, wretched // nm/f wretch.

inferior [infe'rjor] a inferior; (*situación*) lower // nm/f inferior, subordinate.

inferir [infe'rir] vt (*deducir*) to infer, deduce; (*causar*) to cause.

infestar [infes'tar] vt (*infectar*) to infect; (*apestar*) to infest; (*fig*) to harass.

inficionar [infiθjo'nar] vt to infect; (*fig*) to corrupt.

infidelidad [infiðeli'ðað] nf (*gen*) infidelity, unfaithfulness; (*REL*) lack of fáith.

infiel [in'fjel] a unfaithful, disloyal; (*falso*) inaccurate // nm/f infidel, unbeliever.

infierno [in'fjerno] nm hell.

ínfimo, a ['infimo, a] a vile, mean.

infinidad [infini'ðað] nf infinity; (*abundancia*) great quantity.

infinito, a [infi'nito, a] a, nm infinite.

inflación [infla'θjon] nf (*hinchazón*) swelling; (*monetaria*) inflation; (*fig*) conceit; **inflacionario, a** a inflationary.

inflamar [infla'mar] vt to set on fire; (*MED*) to inflame; ~**se** vr to catch fire; (*fig*) to become inflamed.

inflar [in'flar] vt (*hinchar*) to inflate, blow up; (*fig*) to exaggerate; ~**se** vr to swell (up); (*fig*) to get conceited.

inflexible [inflek'siβle] a inflexible; (*irrompible*) unbending; (*fig*) strict.

infligir [infli'xir] vt to inflict.

influencia [influ'enθja] nf influence; **influenciar** vt to influence.

influir [influ'ir] vt to influence.

influjo [in'fluxo] nm influence.

influyente [influ'jente] a influential.

información [informa'θjon] nf information; (*noticias*) news sg; (*JUR*) inquiry.

informal [infor'mal] a (*gen*) irregular, incorrect; (*persona*) unreliable; (*poco serio*) frivolous; (*trabajo*) disorganized; (*comportamiento*) unconventional.

informalidad [informali'ðað] nf (*impuntualidad*) unpunctuality; (*incorrección*) bad manners pl; (*ligereza*) frivolity.

informante [infor'mante] am/f informant.

informar [infor'mar] vt (*gen*) to inform; (*revelar*) to reveal, make known // vi (*JUR*) to plead; (*denunciar*) to inform; (*dar cuenta de*) to report on; ~**se** vr to find out; ~**se de** to inquire into.

informe [in'forme] a shapeless // nm report.

infortunio [infor'tunjo] nm misfortune.

infracción [infrak'θjon] nf infraction, infringement; (*transgresión*) transgression.

infranqueable [infranke'aβle] a impassable; (*impracticable*) insurmountable.

infringir [infrin'xir] vt to infringe, contravene.

infructuoso, a [infruk'twoso, a] a fruitless, unsuccessful.

infundado, a [infun'daðo, a] a groundless, unfounded.

infundir [infun'dir] vt to infuse, instil.

ingeniar [inxe'njar] vt to think up, devise; ~**se** vr: ~**se para** to manage to.

ingeniería [inxenje'ria] nf engineering; **ingeniero, a** nm/f engineer; **ingeniero agrónomo/de sonido** agronomist/sound engineer.

ingenio [in'xenjo] nm (*talento*) talent; (*agudeza*) wit; (*habilidad*) ingenuity, inventiveness; (*TEC*): ~ **azucarero** sugar refinery.

ingenioso, a [inxe'njoso, a] a ingenious, clever; (*divertido*) witty.

ingénito, a [in'xenito, a] a innate.

ingenuidad [inxenwi'ðað] nf ingenuousness; (*candor*) candour; **ingenuo, a** a ingenuous.

ingerencia [inxe'renθja] nf = **injerencia**.

ingerir [inxe'rir] vt to ingest; (*tragar*) to swallow; (*consumir*) to consume.

Inglaterra [ingla'terra] nf England.

ingle ['ingle] nf groin.

inglés, esa [in'gles, esa] a English // nm/f Englishman/woman // am (*lengua*) English.

ingratitud [ingrati'tuð] nf ingratitude; **ingrato, a** a (*gen*) ungrateful; (*desagradable*) unpleasant.

ingrediente [ingre'ðjente] nm ingredient.

ingresar [ingre'sar] *vt* (*dinero*) to deposit // *vi* to come in; ~ **en un club** to join a club; ~ **en el hospital** to go into hospital.

ingreso [in'greso] *nm* (*entrada*) entry; (: *en hospital etc*) admission; (*de dinero*) income, takings *pl*.

inhábil [in'aβil] *a* unskilful, clumsy; **día** ~ non-working day.

inhabitable [inaβi'taβle] *a* uninhabitable.

inherente [ine'rente] *a* inherent.

inhibir [ini'βir] *vt* to inhibit; (REL) to restrain.

inhospitalario, a [inospita'larjo, a] *a* inhospitable.

inhumano, a [inu'mano, a] *a* inhuman.

I. N. I. ['ini] *nm abr de* **Instituto Nacional de Industria** = National Enterprise Board.

inicial [ini'θjal] *a, nf* initial.

iniciar [ini'θjar] *vt* (*persona*) to initiate; (*estudios*) to begin, commence; (*conversación*) to start up.

iniciativa [iniθja'tiβa] *nf* initiative; **la** ~ **privada** private enterprise.

inicuo, a [in'ikwo, a] *a* iniquitous.

ininterrumpido, a [ininterrum'piðo, a] *a* uninterrupted.

injerencia [inxe'renθja] *nf* interference.

injertar [inxer'tar] *vt* to graft; (*inyectar*) to inject; **injerto** *nm* graft.

injuria [in'xurja] *nf* (*agravio, ofensa*) offence; (*insulto*) insult; (*daño*) harm; **injuriar** *vt* to insult; to harm; **injurioso, a** *a* offensive; insulting; harmful.

injusticia [inxus'tiθja] *nf* injustice.

injusto, a [in'xusto, a] *a* unjust, unfair.

inmadurez [inmaðu'reθ] *nf* immaturity.

inmarcesible [inmarθe'siβle], **inmarchitable** [inmartʃi'taβle] *a* imperishable.

inmediaciones [inmeðja'θjones] *nfpl* neighbourhood *sg*, environs.

inmediato, a [inme'ðjato, a] *a* immediate; (*contiguo*) adjoining; (*rápido*) prompt; (*próximo*) close, next; **de** ~ immediately.

inmejorable [inmexo'raβle] *a* unsurpassable; (*precio*) unbeatable.

inmenso, a [in'menso, a] *a* immense, huge.

inmerecido, a [inmere'θiðo, a] *a* undeserved.

inmigración [inmixra'θjon] *nf* immigration.

inmiscuirse [inmisku'irse] *vr* to interfere, meddle.

inmobiliario, a [inmoβi'ljarjo, a] *a* real-estate *cpd* // *nf* estate agency.

inmoderado, a [inmoðe'raðo, a] *a* immoderate, excessive.

inmolar [inmo'lar] *vt* to immolate, sacrifice.

inmoral [inmo'ral] *a* immoral.

inmortal [inmor'tal] *a* immortal; ~**izar** *vt* to immortalize.

inmotivado, a [inmoti'βaðo, a] *a* motiveless.

inmóvil [in'moβil] *a* immobile;

(*inamovible*) immovable; (*invariable*) unchanging; (*parado*) still, stationary.

inmueble [in'mweβle] *nm* property.

inmundicia [inmun'diθja] *nf* filth; **inmundo, a** *a* filthy.

inmunidad [inmuni'ðað] *nf* immunity.

inmutar [inmu'tar] *vt* to alter; ~**se** *vr* to turn pale.

innato, a [in'nato, a] *a* innate.

innecesario, a [inneθe'sarjo, a] *a* unnecessary.

innoble [in'noβle] *a* ignoble.

innocuo, a [in'nokwo, a] *a* innocuous.

innovación [innoβa'θjon] *nf* innovation; **innovar** *vt* to introduce.

inocencia [ino'θenθja] *nf* innocence.

inocentada [inoθen'taða] *nf* practical joke.

inocente [ino'θente] *a* (*ingenuo*) naive, simple; (*inculpable*) innocent // *nm/f* simpleton.

inodoro [ino'ðoro] *nm* toilet, lavatory.

inofensivo, a [inofen'siβo, a] *a* inoffensive.

inolvidable [inolβi'ðaβle] *a* unforgettable.

inoperante [inope'rante] *a* unworkable.

inopinado, a [inopi'naðo, a] *a* unexpected.

inoportuno, a [inopor'tuno, a] *a* untimely; (*molesto*) inconvenient.

inoxidable [inoksi'ðaβle] *a*: **acero** ~ stainless steel.

inquebrantable [inkeβran'taβle] *a* unbreakable.

inquietar [inkje'tar] *vt* to worry, trouble, disturb; ~**se** *vr* to worry, get upset; **inquieto, a** *a* anxious, worried; **inquietud** *nf* anxiety, worry.

inquilino, a [inki'lino, a] *nm/f* tenant.

inquirir [inki'rir] *vt* to enquire into, investigate.

insaciable [insa'θjaβle] *a* insatiable.

insalubre [insa'luβre] *a* unhealthy.

inscribir [inskri'βir] *vt* to inscribe; (*lista*) to list; (*censo*) to register; ~**se** *vr* to register; (ESCOL *etc*) to enrol.

inscripción [inskrip'θjon] *nf* inscription; (ESCOL *etc*) enrolment; (*censo*) registration.

insecto [in'sekto] *nm* insect.

inseguridad [inseɣuri'ðað] *nf* insecurity.

inseguro, a [inse'ɣuro, a] *a* insecure; (*inconstante*) unsteady; (*incierto*) uncertain.

insensato, a [insen'sato, a] *a* foolish, stupid.

insensibilidad [insensiβili'ðað] *nf* (*gen*) insensitivity; (*dureza de corazón*) callousness.

insensible [insen'siβle] *a* (*gen*) insensitive; (*duro*) callous; (*movimiento*) imperceptible; (*sin sentido*) numb.

insertar [inser'tar] *vt* to insert.

inservible [inser'βiβle] *a* useless.

insidioso, a [insi'ðjoso, a] *a* insidious.

insignia [in'siɣnja] *nf* (*señal distintivo*)

badge; (*estandarte*) flag; (*condecoración*) decoration.

insignificante [insixnifi'kante] a insignificant.

insinuar [insi'nwar] vt to insinuate, imply; ~se vr: ~se con uno to ingratiate o.s. with sb.

insípido, a [in'sipiðo, a] a insipid

insistencia [insis'tenθja] nf (*obstinación*) insistence; (*porfía*) persistence.

insistir [insis'tir] vi to insist; ~ en algo to stress sth.

insolación [insola'θjon] nf (MED) sunstroke.

insolencia [inso'lenθja] nf insolence; **insolente** a insolent.

insólito, a [in'solito, a] a unusual.

insoluble [inso'luβle] a insoluble.

insolvencia [insol'βenθja] nf insolvency.

insomnio [in'somnjo] nm insomnia.

insondable [inson'daβle] a bottomless.

insoportable [insopor'taβle] a unbearable.

inspección [inspek'θjon] nf inspection, check; **inspeccionar** vt (*examinar*) to inspect, examine; (*controlar*) to check.

inspector, a [inspek'tor, a] nm/f inspector.

inspiración [inspira'θjon] nf inspiration; **inspirar** vt to inspire; (MED) to inhale; **inspirarse** vr: **inspirarse en** to be inspired by.

instalar [insta'lar] vt (*establecer*) to install; (*erguir*) to set up, erect; ~se vr to establish o.s.

instancia [ins'tanθja] nf (JUR) petition; (*ruego*) request; **en última** ~ in the last resort.

instantáneo, a [instan'taneo, a] a instant, instantaneous // nf snap(shot).

instante [ins'tante] nm instant, moment.

instar [ins'tar] vt to press, urge // vi to be ~ pressing or urgent.

instigar [insti'xar] vt to instigate.

instinto [ins'tinto] nm instinct; **por** ~ instinctively.

institución [institu'θjon] nf institution, establishment.

instituir [institu'ir] vt to establish; (*fundar*) to found; **instituto** nm (gen) institute; (*escuela*) high school.

instrucción [instruk'θjon] nf instruction.

instructivo, a [instruk'tiβo, a] a instructive.

instruir [instru'ir] vt (gen) to instruct; (*enseñar*) to teach, educate; (MIL, DEPORTE) to train.

instrumento [instru'mento] nm (gen) instrument; (*herramienta*) tool, implement.

insubordinarse [insuβorði'narse] vr to rebel.

insuficiencia [insufi'θjenθja] nf (*carencia*) lack; (*inadecuación*) inadequacy; **insuficiente** a (gen) insufficient; (*incompetente*) incompetent; (*nota*) inadequate.

insufrible [insu'friβle] a insufferable.

insular [insu'lar] a insular.

insulsez [insul'seθ] nf (*insipidez*) insipidity; (*fig*) dullness.

insultar [insul'tar] vt to insult; **insulto** nm insult.

insuperable [insupe'raβle] a (*excelente*) unsurpassable; (*arduo*) insurmountable.

insurgente [insur'xente] a, nm/f insurgent.

insurrección [insurrek'θjon] nf insurrection, rebellion.

intacto, a [in'takto, a] a intact.

intachable [nta'tʃaβle] a irreproachable.

integral [inte'xral] a: **pan** ~ wholemeal bread.

integrar [inte'xrar] vt to make up, compose; (COM) to repay; (MAT) to integrate.

integridad [intexri'ðað] nf wholeness; (*carácter*) integrity; **íntegro, a** a whole, entire; (*honrado*) honest.

intelectual [intelek'twal] a, nm/f intellectual.

inteligencia [inteli'xenθja] nf intelligence; (*ingenio*) ability; **inteligente** a intelligent.

intemperancia [intempe'ranθja] nf excess, intemperance.

intemperie [intem'perje] nf bad weather; **a la** ~ outdoors, in the open air.

intempestivo, a [intempes'tiβo, a] a untimely.

intención [inten'θjon] nf (gen) intention; (*propósito*) purpose; **con segundas intenciones** maliciously; **de primera** ~ provisionally; **con** ~ deliberately.

intencionado, a [intenθjo'naðo, a] a deliberate; **bien/mal** ~ well-meaning/ill-disposed

intendencia [inten'denθja] nf management, administration.

intenso, a [in'tenso, a] a intense; (*impresión*) vivid; (*sentimiento*) profound, deep.

intentar [inten'tar] vt (*tratar*) to try, attempt; **intento** nm (*intención*) intention, purpose; (*tentativa*) attempt.

intercalar [interka'lar] vt to insert.

intercambio [inter'kambjo] nm exchange, swap.

interceder [interθe'ðer] vi to intercede.

intercesión [interθe'sjon] nf intercession.

interés [inte'res] nm (gen) interest; (*parte*) share, part; (*pey*) self-interest; **intereses creados** vested interests.

interesado, a [intere'saðo, a] a interested; (*prejuiciado*) prejudiced; (*pey*) mercenary, self-seeking.

interesar [intere'sar] vt, vi to interest, be of interest to; ~se vr: ~se en o por to take an interest in.

interferir [interfe'rir] vt to interfere with; (TELEC) to jam // vi to interfere.

interior [inte'rjor] a inner, inside; (COM) domestic, internal // nm interior, inside; (*fig*) soul, mind; **Ministerio del I~** Home Office.

interjección [interxek'θjon] *nf* interjection.

interlocutor, a [interloku'tor] *nm/f* speaker.

intermediario, a [interme'δjarjo, a] *nm/f* intermediary // *nm* middleman.

intermedio, a [inter'meδjo, a] *a* intermediate // *nm* interval.

interminable [intermi'naβle] *a* endless.

intermitente [intermi'tente] *a* intermittent // *nm* indicator.

internacional [internaθjo'nal] *a* international.

internar [inter'nar] *vt* to intern; (*loco*) to commit; ~ **se** *vr* (*en un hospital*) to go into hospital; (*penetrar*) to penetrate.

interno, a [in'terno, a] *a* internal, interior; (*POL etc*) domestic // *nm/f* (*alumno*) boarder.

interpelar [interpe'lar] *vt* (*rogar*) to implore; (*hablar*) to speak to.

interponer [interpo'ner] *vt* to interpose, put in; ~ **se** *vr* to intervene.

interposición [interposi'θjon] *nf* insertion.

interpretación [interpreta'θjon] *nf* interpretation; **interpretar** *vt* to interpret; **interprete** *nm/f* interpreter; (*traductor*) translator; (*músico, TEATRO*) performer, artist(e).

interrogación [interroxa'θjon] *nf* interrogation; (*LING*) question mark; **interrogar** *vt* to interrogate, question.

interrumpir [interrum'pir] *vt* to interrupt; (*ELEC*) to switch off, cut off.

interrupción [interrup'θjon] *nf* interruption.

interruptor [interrup'tor] *nm* (*ELEC*) switch.

intersección [intersek'θjon] *nf* intersection.

interurbano, a [interur'ßano, a] *a*: **llamada** ~ a trunk call.

intervalo [inter'ßalo] *nm* interval; (*descanso*) break; **a** ~ **s** at intervals, every now and then.

intervenir [interße'nir] *vt* (*controlar*) to control, supervise; (*MED*) to operate on // *vi* (*participar*) to take part, participate; (*mediar*) to intervene.

interventor, a [interßen'tor, a] *nm/f* inspector; (*COM*) auditor.

interviú [inter'ßju] *nf* interview.

intestino, a [intes'tino, a] *a* internal; (*doméstico*) domestic // *nm* intestine.

intimar [inti'mar] *vt* to intimate, announce // *vi* to become friendly.

intimidad [intimi'δaδ] *nf* intimacy; (*confianza*) confidence; (*familiaridad*) familiarity; (*vida privada*) private life; (*soledad*) privacy.

íntimo, a ['intimo, a] *a* intimate.

intolerable [intole'raβle] *a* intolerable, unbearable.

intransitable [intransi'taβle] *a* impassable.

intrepidez [intrepi'δeθ] *nf* courage,

bravery; **intrépido, a** *a* intrepid.

intriga [in'trixa] *nf* intrigue; (*plan*) plot; **intrigar** *vt, vi* to intrigue.

intrincado, a [intrin'kaδo, a] *a* intricate.

intrínseco, a [in'trinseko, a] *a* intrinsic.

introducción [introδuk'θjon] *nf* introduction.

introducir [introδu'θir] *vt* (*gen*) to introduce; (*hacer penetrar*) to insert.

intruso, a [in'truso, a] *a* intrusive // *nm/f* intruder.

intuición [intwi'θjon] *nf* intuition.

inundación [inunda'θjon] *nf* flood(ing); **inundar** *vt* to flood; (*fig*) to swamp, inundate.

inusitado, a [inusi'taδo, a] *a* unusual.

inútil [in'util] *a* useless; (*esfuerzo*) vain, fruitless; **inutilidad** *nf* uselessness.

inutilizar [inutili'θar] *vt* to make useless, render useless; ~ **se** *vr* to become useless.

invadir [inßa'δir] *vt* to invade.

inválido, a [in'ßaliδo, a] *a* invalid // *nm/f* invalid.

invariable [inßa'rjaβle] *a* invariable.

invasión [inßa'sjon] *nf* invasion.

invasor, a [inßa'sor, a] *a* invading // *nm/f* invader.

invención [inßen'θjon] *nf* invention.

inventar [inßen'tar] *vt* to invent.

inventario [inßen'tarjo] *nm* inventory.

inventiva [inßen'tißa] *nf* inventiveness.

inventor, a [inßen'tor, a] *nm/f* inventor.

inverosímil [inßero'simil] *a* implausible; (*improbable*) unlikely, improbable.

inversión [inßer'sjon] *nf* (*COM*) investment; (*AUTO*) reversing; **inversionista** *nm/f* investor.

inverso, a [in'ßerso, a] *a* inverse, opposite; **en el orden** ~ in reverse order; **a la** ~ **a** inversely, the other way round.

invertir [inßer'tir] *vt* (*COM*) to invest; (*volcar*) to turn upside down; (*tiempo etc*) to spend; (*AUTO*) to reverse.

investigación [inßestixa'θjon] *nf* investigation; (*estudio*) research; **investigar** *vt* to investigate; (*estudiar*) to do research into.

inveterado, a [inßete'raδo, a] *a* inveterate, confirmed.

invicto, a [in'ßikto, a] *a* unconquered.

invierno [in'ßjerno] *nm* winter.

invitar [inßi'tar] *vt* to invite; (*incitar*) to entice; (*pagar*) to buy, pay for.

invocar [inßo'kar] *vt* to invoke, call on.

inyección [injek'θjon] *nf* injection.

inyectar [injek'tar] *vt* to inject.

ir [ir] *vi* (*gen*) to go; (*viajar*) to travel; (*ropa*) to suit; ~ **caminando** to walk; ~ **en coche/bicicleta/caballo/a pie** to drive/cycle/ride/walk; ¡**voy**! I'm coming!; ~ **de viaje** to travel, go away; **voy para viejo** I'm getting on (in years); ~ **por/a por algo** to go for/go and get sth; ¡**qué va!** (*no diga*) you don't say!; (: ¡*no*!) no way!, rubbish!; ¡**vamos!** come on!; **vaya susto que me has dado** what a fright

you gave me; ~se *vr* to go away, leave;
(*mano etc*) to slip; ¡vete! go away!

ira ['ira] *nf* anger, rage.

iracundo, a [ira'kundo, a] *a* irascible;
(*colérico*) irate.

Irán [i'ran] *nm* Iran; iranés, esa, iraní *a,
nm/f* Iranian.

iris ['iris] *nm* (*arco* ~) rainbow; (ANAT)
iris.

Irlanda [ir'landa] *nf* Ireland; irlandés,
esa *a* Irish // *nm/f* Irishman/woman.

ironía [iro'nia] *nf* irony; irónico, a *a*
ironic(al).

irreal [irre'al] *a* unreal.

irreflexión [irreflek'sjon] *nf*
thoughtlessness.

irremediable [irreme'ðjaßle] *a*
incurable, hopeless.

irresoluto, a [irreso'luto, a] *a* irresolute,
hesitant.

irrespetuoso, a [irrespe'twoso, a] *a*
disrespectful.

irresponsable [irrespon'saßle] *a*
irresponsible.

irrigar [irri'xar] *vt* to irrigate.

irrisorio, a [irri'sorjo, a] *a* derisory,
ridiculous.

irritar [irri'tar] *vt* to irritate, annoy.

irrupción [irrup'θjon] *nf* irruption;
(*invasión*) invasion.

isla ['isla] *nf* island.

islandés, a [islan'des, esa] *a* Icelandic
// *nm/f* Icelander.

Islandia [is'landja] *nf* Iceland.

isleño, a [is'leɲo, a] *a* island *cpd* // *nm/f*
islander.

Israel [isra'el] *nm* Israel; israelí *a, nm/f*
Israeli.

istmo ['istmo] *nm* isthmus.

Italia [i'talja] *nf* Italy; italiano, a *a, nm/f*
Italian.

itinerario [itine'rarjo] *nm* itinerary,
route.

izar [i'θar] *vt* to hoist.

izquierdista [iθkjer'ðista] *nm/f* left-
winger, leftist.

izquierdo, a [iθ'kjerðo, a] *a* left // *nf* left; a
la ~ a on the left.

J

jabalí [xaßa'li] *nm* wild boar.

jabalina [xaßa'lina] *nf* javelin.

jabón [xa'ßon] *nm* soap; jabonar *vt* to
soap.

jaca ['xaka] *nf* pony.

jacinto [xa'θinto] *nm* hyacinth.

jactancia [xak'tanθja] *nf* boasting,
boastfulness.

jactarse [xak'tarse] *vr* to boast, brag.

jadeante [xaðe'ante] *a* panting, gasping;
jadear *vi* to pant, gasp for breath; jadeo
nm panting, gasping.

jaez [xa'eθ] *nm* (*de caballerías*) harness;
(*clase*) kind, sort.

jaguar [xa'ɣwar] *nm* jaguar.

jalar [xa'lar] *vt* to pull, haul.

jalbegue [xal'ßexe] *nm* (*pintura*) whitewash; (*fig*) make-up.

jalea [xa'lea] *nf* jelly.

jaleo [xa'leo] *nm* racket, uproar; (*baile*)
Andalusian popular dance; estar de ~ to
be having a good time; armar un ~ to
kick up a din.

Jamaica [xa'maika] *nf* Jamaica.

jamás [xa'mas] *ad* never; (*sin negación*)
ever.

jamón [xa'mon] *nm* ham.

Japón [xa'pon] *nm*: el ~ Japan; japonés,
esa *a, nm/f* Japanese.

jaque ['xake] *nm* cheque; (*fam*) bully; ~
mate checkmate.

jaqueca [xa'keka] *nf* (*severe*) headache,
migraine.

jarabe [xa'raße] *nm* syrup.

jarcia [xar'θja] *nf* (NAUT) ropes *pl*, rigging;
(*para pescar*) (*fishing*) tackle; (*confusión*,
revoltijo) jumble, mess.

jardín [xar'ðin] *nm* garden; jardinería *nf*
gardening; jardinero, a *nm/f* gardener.

jarra ['xarra] *nf* jar.

jarro ['xarro] *nm* jug.

jaula ['xaula] *nf* cage.

jauría [xau'ria] *nf* pack of hounds.

J. C. *abr de* Jesucristo.

jefatura [xefa'tura] *nf*: ~ de policía
police headquarters *sg*.

jefe ['xefe] *nm* (*gen*) chief, head; (*patrón*)
boss, ~ de camareros head waiter; ~
de cocina chef; ~ de estación station-
master; ~ de estado head of state; ~
supremo commander-in-chief; ser el ~
(*fig*) to be the boss.

jengibre [xen'xißre] *nm* ginger.

jeque ['xeke] *nm* sheik.

jerarquía [xerar'kia] *nf* (*orden*)
hierarchy; (*rango*) rank; jerárquico, a *a*
hierarchic(al).

jerez [xe'reθ] *nm* sherry.

jerga ['xerɣa] *nf* (*tela*) coarse cloth;
(*lenguaje*) jargon, slang.

jerigonza [xeri'xonθa] *nf* (*jerga*) jargon,
slang; (*galimatías*) nonsense, gibberish.

jeringa [xe'ringa] *nf* syringe; (AM)
annoyance, bother; ~ de engrase grease
gun; jeringar *vt* to syringe; (*inyectar*) to
inject; (AM) to annoy, bother.

jeroglífico [xero'xlifiko] *nm* hieroglyphic.

jersé, jersey (*pl* jerseys) [xer'sei] *nm*
jersey, pullover, jumper.

Jerusalén [xerusa'len] *n* Jerusalem.

Jesucristo [xesu'kristo] *n* Jesus Christ.

jesuita [xe'swita] *a, nm* Jesuit.

Jesús [xe'sus] *nm* Jesus; ¡~! good
heavens!; (*al estornudar*) bless you!

jícara ['xikara] *nf* small cup.

jifero [xi'fero, a] *a* (*fam*) filthy // *nm*
butcher's knife; (*matarife*) butcher,
slaughterer.

jinete [xi'nete] *nm* (*horse*)rider.

jipijapa [xipi'xapa] *nm* (AM) straw hat.

jira ['xira] nf (de tela) strip; (excursión) picnic.

jirafa [xi'rafa] nf giraffe.

jirón [xi'ron] nm rag, shred.

jocosidad [xokosi'ðað] nf humour; (chiste) joke.

jocoso, a [xo'koso, a] a humorous, jocular.

jofaina [xo'faina] nf washbasin.

jornada [xor'naða] nf day's journey; (camino o viaje entero) journey; (día de trabajo) working day; (fig) lifetime.

jornal [xor'nal] nm (day's) wage; ~ero nm (day) labourer.

joroba [xo'roßa] nf hump, hunched back; (fam) nuisance; ~do, a a hunchbacked // nm/f hunchback.

jota ['xota] nf letter J; (danza) Aragonese dance; (fam) iota; **no saber** ~ to have no idea.

joven ['xoßen] a young // nm young man, youth // nf young woman, girl.

jovial [xo'ßjal] a cheerful, jovial; ~idad nf cheerfulness, joviality.

joya ['xoja] nf jewel, gem; (fig: persona) gem; **joyería** nf (joyas) jewellery; (tienda) jeweller's (shop); **joyero** nm (persona) jeweller; (caja) jewel case.

juanete [xwa'nete] nm bunion.

jubilación [xußila'θjon] nf (retiro) retirement; (alegría) jubilation.

jubilar [xußi'lar] vt to pension off, retire; (fam) to discard // vi to rejoice; ~se vr to retire.

jubileo [xußi'leo] nm (indulgencia) jubilee; (fam) comings and goings pl.

júbilo ['xußilo] nm joy, jubilation, rejoicing; ~so, a a jubilant.

judaísmo [xuða'ismo] nm Judaism.

judía [xu'ðia] nf Jewess; (CULIN) bean.

judicatura [xuðika'tura] nf (cargo de juez) office of judge; (magistratura) judicature.

judicial [xuði'θjal] a judicial.

judío, a [xu'ðio, a] a Jewish // nm/f Jew/ess.

juego etc vb ver **jugar** // ['xweɣo] nm (gen) play; (pasatiempo, partido) game; (en casino) gambling; (conjunto) set; **fuera de** ~ (persona) offside; (pelota) out of play.

juerga ['xwerɣa] nf good time; (fiesta) party; **ir de** ~ to go out on a spree.

jueves ['xweßes] nm inv Thursday.

juez [xweθ] nm judge; ~ **de línea** linesman; ~ **de salida** starter.

jugada [xu'ɣaða] nf play; **buena** ~ good move/shot/stroke etc.

jugador, a [xuɣa'ðor, a] nm/f player; (en casino) gambler.

jugar [xu'ɣar] vt, vi to play; (en casino) to gamble; ~se vr to gamble (away).

juglar [xu'ɣlar] nm minstrel.

jugo ['xuɣo] nm (BOT) juice; (fig) essence, substance; ~so, a a juicy; (fig) substantial, important.

juguete [xu'ɣete] nm toy; (TEATRO) sketch; ~ar vi to play; ~ría nf toyshop.

juguetón, ona [xuɣe'ton, ona] a playful.

juicio ['xwiθjo] nm judgement; (sana razón) sanity, reason; (opinión) opinion; **estar fuera de** ~ to be out of one's mind; ~**so, a** a wise, sensible.

julio ['xuljo] nm July.

jumento, a [xu'mento, a] nm/f donkey.

junco ['xunko] nm rush, reed.

jungla ['xungla] nf jungle.

junio ['xunjo] nm June.

junta ['xunta] nf ver **junto.**

juntamente [xunta'mente] ad (conjuntamente) together; (al mismo tiempo) together, at the same time.

juntar [xun'tar] vt to join, unite; (maquinaria) to assemble, put together; (dinero) to collect; (puerta) to half-close, leave ajar; ~se vr to join, meet; (reunirse: personas) to meet, assemble; (arrimarse) to approach, draw closer; (continuo, próximo) next, adjacent // ad: **todo** ~ all at once // nf (asamblea) meeting, assembly; (comité, consejo) board, council, committee; (articulación) joint; ~ **a** near (to), next to; ~**s** together.

junto, a ['xunto, a] a (unido) joined, united; (anexo) near, close; to live together; ~**se con uno** to join sb.

juntura [xun'tura] nf (punto de unión) join, junction; (articulación) joint.

jurado [xu'raðo] nm (JUR) juror; (: conjunto de ~s) jury; (de concurso) panel (of judges); (: individuo) member of a panel.

juramentar [xuramen'tar] vt to swear in, administer the oath to; ~se vr to be sworn in, take the oath.

juramento [xura'mento] nm oath; (maldición) oath, curse; **prestar** ~ to take the oath; **tomar** ~ **a** to swear in, administer the oath to.

jurar [xu'rar] vt, vi to swear; ~ **en falso** to commit perjury; **jurárselas a uno** to have it in for sb.

jurídico, a [xu'riðiko, a] a legal.

jurisdicción [xurisðik'θjon] nf (poder, autoridad) jurisdiction; (territorio) district.

jurisprudencia [xurispru'ðenθja] nf jurisprudence.

jurista [xu'rista] nm/f jurist.

justamente [xusta'mente] ad justly, fairly; (precisamente) just, precisely, exactly.

justicia [xus'tiθja] nf justice; (equidad) fairness, justice; **justiciero, a** a just, righteous.

justificación [xustifika'θjon] nf justification; **justificar** vt to justify.

justo, a ['xusto, a] a (equitativo) just, fair, right; (preciso) exact, correct; (ajustado) tight // ad (precisamente) exactly, precisely.

juvenil [xuße'nil] a youthful.

juventud [xußen'tuð] nf (adolescencia) youth; (jóvenes) young people pl.

juzgado [xuθ'ɣaðo] nm tribunal; (JUR) court.

juzgar [xuθ'ɣar] vt to judge; **a** ~ **por...** to judge by..., judging by... .

K

kg *abr de* **kilogramo.**
kilo ['kilo] *nm* kilo // *pref:* ~**gramo** *nm* kilogramme; ~**litro** *nm* kilolitre; ~**metraje** *nm* distance in kilometres; **kilómetro** *nm* kilometre; ~**vatio** *nm* kilowatt.
kiosco ['kjosko] *nm* = **quiosco.**
km *abr de* **kilómetro.**
kv *abr de* **kilovatio.**

L

l *abr de* **litro.**
la [la] *det* the // *pron* her; (*Ud.*) you; (*cosa*) it // *nm* (*MUS*) la; ~ **del sombrero rojo** the girl in the red hat.
laberinto [laβe'rinto] *nm* labyrinth.
labia ['laβja] *nf* fluency; (*pey*) glibness.
labial [la'βjal] *a* labial; **lectura** ~ **l**-reading.
labio ['laβjo] *nm* lip.
labor [la'βor] *nf* labour; (*AGR*) farm work; (*tarea*) job, task; (*costura*) needlework; ~**able** *a* workable; **día** ~**able** working day; ~**ar** *vi* to work; ~**eo** *nm* (*AGR* cultivation; (*de minas*) working; ~**ioso, a** *a* (*persona*) hard-working; (*trabajo*) tough; ~**ista** *a*: **Partido L**~**ista** Labour Party.
labrado, a [la'βraðo, a] *a* worked; (*cincelado*) carved; (*metal*) wrought // *nm* (*AGR*) cultivated field.
labrador, a [laβra'ðor, a] *a* farming // *nm/f* farmer.
labrantío, a [laβran'tio, a] *a* arable.
labranza [la'βranθa] *nf* (*AGR*) cultivation.
labrar [la'βrar] *vt* (*gen*) to work; (*madera etc*) to carve; (*fig*) to cause.
labriego, a [la'βrjexo, a] *nm/f* peasant.
laca ['laka] *nf* lacquer.
lacayo [la'kajo] *nm* lackey.
lacerar [laθe'rar] *vt* to lacerate.
lacio, a ['laθjo, a] *a* (*pelo*) lank; (*movimiento*) limp; (*BOT*) withered.
lacónico, a [la'koniko, a] *a* laconic.
lacrar [la'krar] *vt* (*MED*) to injure the health of; (*dañar*) to harm; (*cerrar*) to seal (*with sealing wax*); ~**se** *vr* to harm o.s.; **lacre** *nm* sealing wax.
lacrimoso, a [lakri'moso, a] *a* tearful.
lactar [lak'tar] *vt*, *vi* to suckle.
ladear [laðe'ar] *vt* to tip, tilt; (*ciudad, colina*) to skirt // *vi* to tilt; ~**se** *vr* to lean.
ladera [la'ðera] *nf* slope.
ladino, a [la'ðino, a] *a* cunning.
lado ['laðo] *nm* (*gen*) side; (*fig*) protection; (*MIL*) flank; **al** ~ **de** beside; **poner de** ~ to put on its side; **poner a un** ~ to put aside; **por todos** ~**s** on all sides, all round.
ladrar [la'ðrar] *vi* to bark; **ladrido** *nm* bark, barking.
ladrillo [la'ðriʎo] *nm* (*gen*) brick; (*azulejo*) tile; (*color*) brick red.

ladrón, ona [la'ðron, ona] *nm/f* thief.
lagar [la'ɣar] *nm* (*wine/oil*) press.
lagarto [la'ɣarto] *nm* (*ZOOL*) lizard; (*fig: fam*) sharp customer; ~ **de Indias** alligator.
lago ['laɣo] *nm* lake.
lágrima ['laɣrima] *nf* tear; **lagrimar** *vi* to weep.
laguna [la'ɣuna] *nf* (*lago*) lagoon; (*hueco*) gap.
laico, a ['laiko, a] *a* lay.
lamentable [lamen'taβle] *a* lamentable, regrettable; (*miserable*) pitiful.
lamentar [lamen'tar] *vt* (*sentir*) to regret; (*deplorar*) to lament; ~**se** *vr* to lament; **lamento** *nm* lament.
lamer [la'mer] *vt* to lick.
lámina ['lamina] *nf* (*plancha delgada*) sheet; (*para estampar, estampa*) plate; **laminar** *vt* (*en libro*) to laminate.
lámpara ['lampara] *nf* lamp; ~ **de alcohol/gas** spirit/gas lamp; ~ **de bolsillo** torch; ~ **de pie** standard lamp.
lampiño [lam'piɲo] *a* clean-shaven.
lana ['lana] *nf* wool.
lance ['lanθe] *nm* (*golpe*) stroke; (*suceso*) event, incident; (*riña*) quarrel; (*tirada*) throw; **libros de** ~ second-hand books.
lancha ['lantʃa] *nf* launch; ~ **automóvil** motorboat; ~ **de pesca** fishing boat; ~ **salvavidas/torpedera** lifeboat/torpedo boat; **lanchero** *nm* boatman.
lanero, a [la'nero, a] *a* woollen.
langosta [lan'ɡosta] *nf* (*insecto*) locust; (*crustáceo*) lobster; (*fig*) plague; **langostín, langostino** *nm* prawn.
languidecer [lanɡiðe'θer] *vi* to languish; **languidez** *nf* langour; **lánguido, a** *a* (*gen*) languid; (*sin energía*) listless.
lanilla [la'niʎa] *nf* nap.
lanudo, a [la'nuðo, a] *a* woolly.
lanza ['lanθa] *nf* (*arma*) lance, spear; (*de vagón*) pole.
lanzadera [lanθa'ðera] *nf* shuttle.
lanzamiento [lanθa'mjento] *nm* (*gen*) throwing; (*NAUT, COM*) launch, launching; ~ **de pesos** putting the shot.
lanzar [lan'θar] *vt* (*gen*) to throw; (*DEPORTE*) to bowl; (*NAUT, COM*) to launch; (*JUR*) to evict; (*MED*) to vomit; ~**se** *vr* to throw o.s.
laña ['laɲa] *nf* clamp.
lapa ['lapa] *nf* limpet.
lapicero [lapi'θero] *nm* propelling pencil.
lápida ['lapiða] *nf* stone; ~ **mortuoria** headstone; ~ **conmemorativa** memorial stone; **lapidar** *vt* to stone; **lapidario, a** *a*, *nm* lapidary.
lápiz ['lapiθ] *nm* pencil; ~ **de color** coloured pencil; ~ **de labios** lipstick.
lapón, ona [la'pon, ona] *nm/f* Laplander, Lapp.
lapso ['lapso] *nm* (*de tiempo*) interval; (*error*) error.
largar [lar'ɣar] *vt* (*soltar*) to release; (*aflojar*) to loosen; (*lanzar*) to launch;

(fam) to let fly; *(pelota)* to throw; *(velas)* to unfurl; *(AM)* to throw; **~se** *vr (fam)* to beat it; *(NAUT)* to set sail; **~se a** *(AM)* to start to.

largo, a ['larvo, a] *a (longitud)* long; *(tiempo)* lengthy; *(persona: alta)* tall; *(fig)* generous // *nm* length; *(MUS)* largo // *ad* widely; **dos años ~s** two long years; **tiene 9 metros de ~** it is 9 metres long; **a lo ~ de** along.

largueza [lar'xeθa] *nf* generosity.

lárice ['lariθe] *nm* larch.

laringe [la'rinxe] *nf* larynx; **laringitis** *nf* laryngitis.

larva ['larβa] *nf* larva.

las [las] *det* the // *pron* them; **~ que cantan** the ones/women/girls who sing.

lascivo, a [las'θiβo, a] *a* lewd.

láser ['laser] *nm* laser.

lasitud [lasi'tuð] *nf* lassitude, weariness.

lástima ['lastima] *nf (pena)* pity; *(queja)* complaint; **dar ~** to be pitiful; **es ~ que** it's a pity that; **¡qué ~!** what a pity!; **ella está hecha una ~** she looks pitiful.

lastimar [lasti'mar] *vt (herir)* to wound; *(ofender)* to offend; *(compadecer)* to pity; **~se** *vr* to hurt o.s.; **~se de** to feel sorry for; **lastimero, a, lastimoso, a** *a* pitiful, pathetic.

lastre ['lastre] *nm (TEC, NAUT)* ballast; *(fig)* dead weight.

lata ['lata] *nf (metal)* tin; *(caja)* tin, can; *(fam)* nuisance; **hoja de ~** tin(plate); **en ~** tinned; **dar (la) ~** to be a nuisance.

latente [la'tente] *a* latent.

lateral [late'ral] *a* side, lateral // *nm (TEATRO)* wings.

latido [la'tiðo] *nm (del corazón)* beat; *(de perro)* yelp.

latifundio [lati'fundjo] *nm* large estate; **latifundista** *nm/f* owner of a large estate.

latigazo [lati'xaθo] *nm (golpe)* lash; *(sonido)* crack; *(fig: regaño)* sharp reproof; *(fam: bebida)* swig.

látigo ['latixo] *nm* whip.

latín [la'tin] *nm* Latin.

latino, a [la'tino, a] *a* Latin; **~americano, a** *a, nm/f* Latin-American.

latir [la'tir] *vi (corazón, pulso)* to beat; *(perro)* to yelp.

latitud [lati'tuð] *nf (GEO)* latitude; *(fig)* breadth.

lato, a ['lato, a] *a* broad.

latón [la'ton] *nm* brass.

latoso, a [la'toso, a] *a (cansado)* annoying; *(aburrido)* boring.

latrocinio [latro'θinjo] *nm* robbery.

laúd [la'uð] *nm* lute.

laudo ['lauðo] *nm (JUR)* decision.

laureado, a [laure'aðo, a] *a* honoured // *nm* laureate.

laurel [lau'rel] *nm (BOT)* laurel; *(CULIN)* bay.

lava ['laβa] *nf* lava.

lavabo [la'βaβo] *nm* washbasin.

lavadero [laβa'ðero] *nm* laundry.

lavado [la'βaðo] *nm* washing; *(de ropa)* laundry; *(ARTE)* wash; **~ de cerebro** brainwashing; **~ en seco** dry cleaning.

lavadora [laβa'ðora] *nf* washing machine.

lavamanos [laβa'manos] *nm inv* washbasin.

lavandería [laβande'ria] *nf* laundry; **~ automática** launderette.

lavaplatos [laβa'platos] *nm o f inv* dishwasher.

lavar [la'βar] *vt* to wash; *(borrar)* to wipe away; **~se** *vr* to wash o.s.; **~se las manos** to wash one's hands; **~ y marcar** *(pelo)* to shampoo and set; **~ en seco** to dry clean.

lavavajillas [laβaβa'xiʎas] *nm inv* dishwasher.

laxante [lak'sante] *nm* laxative.

laya ['laja] *nf* spade; **de la misma ~** *(fig)* of the same sort.

lazada [la'θaða] *nf* bow.

lazo ['laθo] *nm* knot; *(lazada)* bow; *(para animales)* lasso; *(trampa)* snare; *(de camino)* hairpin bend; *(vínculo)* tie.

lb(s) *abr de* **libra(s)**.

le [le] *pron (directo)* him; *(: usted)* you; *(indirecto)* to him; *(: usted)* to you.

leal [le'al] *a* loyal; **~tad** *nf* loyalty.

lebrel [le'βrel] *nm* greyhound.

lección [lek'θjon] *nf* lesson.

lector, a [lek'tor, a] *nm/f* reader.

lectura [lek'tura] *nf* reading.

leche ['letʃe] *nf* milk; **tener mala ~** to be nasty; **~ condensada/en polvo** condensed/powdered milk; **~ desnatada** skimmed milk; **~ de magnesia** milk of magnesia; **~ra** *nf (vendedora)* milkmaid; *(para hervir)* milk pan; *(para servir)* milkjug; *(AM)* cow; **~ría** *nf* dairy.

lecho ['letʃo] *nm (cama)* bed; *(de río)* bottom; *(GEO)* layer.

lechón [le'tʃon] *nm* sucking pig.

lechoso, a [le'tʃoso, a] *a* milky.

lechuga [le'tʃuxa] *nf* lettuce.

lechuza [le'tʃuθa] *nf* owl.

leer [le'er] *vt* to read.

legación [lexa'θjon] *nf* legation.

legado [le'xaðo] *nm (don)* bequest; *(herencia)* legacy; *(enviado)* legate.

legajo [le'xaxo] *nm* file.

legal [le'xal] *a (gen)* legal; *(persona)* trustworthy; **~idad** *nf* legality; **~izar** *vt* to legalize; *(documento)* to authenticate.

légamo ['lexamo] *nm (cieno)* mud, ooze.

legar [le'xar] *vt* to bequeath, leave; **legatario, a** *nm/f* legatee.

legión [le'xjon] *nf* legion; **legionario, a** *a* legionary // *nm* legionnaire.

legislación [lexisla'θjon] *nf* legislation; **legislar** *vt* to legislate.

legitimar [lexiti'mar] *vt* to legitimize; **legítimo, a** *a (genuino)* authentic; *(legal)* legitimate.

lego, a ['lexo, a] *a (REL)* secular; *(ignorante)* ignorant // *nm* layman.

legua ['lexwa] *nf* league.

leguleyo [leɣu'lejo] *nm* (*pey*) petty lawyer.

legumbre [le'ɣumbre] *nf* vegetable.

leido, a [le'iðo, a] *a* well-read.

lejanía [lexa'nia] *nf* distance; **lejano** *a* a far-off; (*en el tiempo*) distant; (*fig*) remote.

lejía [le'xia] *nf* bleach.

lejos ['lexos] *ad* far, far away; **a lo ~** in the distance; **de** *o* **desde ~** from afar **~ de** *prep* far from.

lelo, a ['lelo, a] *a* silly; (*fig*) open-mouthed // *nm/f* idiot.

lema ['lema] *nm* motto; (*POL*) slogan.

lencería [lenθe'ria] *nf* drapery.

lengua ['lengwa] *nf* tongue; **~ moderna** modern language; **morderse la ~** to hold one's tongue.

lenguado [len'gwaðo] *nm* sole.

lenguaje [len'gwaxe] *nm* language.

lenguaraz [lengwa'raθ] *a* talkative; (*pey*) foul-mouthed.

lengüeta [len'gweta] *af* (*ANAT*) epiglottis; (*de balanza, zapatos, MUS*) tongue; (*herramienta*) needle.

lenidad [leni'ðað] *nf* lenience.

lente ['lente] *nm* o *f* lens; (*lupa*) magnifying glass; **~s** *npl* glasses; **~s de contacto** contact lenses.

lenteja [len'texa] *nf* lentil; **lentejuela** *nf* sequin.

lentitud [lenti'tuð] *nf* slowness; **con ~** slowly.

lento, a ['lento, a] *a* slow.

leña ['leɲa] *nf* firewood; **~dor, a, ~tero, a** *nm/f* woodcutter.

leño ['leɲo] *nm* (*trozo de árbol*) log; (*madera*) timber; (*fig*) blockhead.

Leo ['leo] *nm* Leo.

león [le'on] *nm* lion; (*AM*) puma; **~ marino** sea lion; **leonino, a** *a* leonine.

leontina [leon'tina] *nf* watch chain.

leopardo [leo'parðo] *nm* leopard.

lepra ['lepra] *nf* leprosy; **leproso, a** *nm/f* leper.

lerdo, a ['lerðo, a] *a* (*lento*) slow; (*patoso*) clumsy.

les [les] *pron* (*directo*) them; (: *ustedes*) your; (*indirecto*) to them; (: *ustedes*) to you.

lesbiana [les'βjana] *a* nf lesbian.

lesión [le'sjon] *nf* (*daño*) lesion; (*fig*) injury; **lesionado, a** *a* injured // *nm/f* injured person.

letal [le'tal] *a* lethal.

letanía [leta'nia] *nf* litany.

letargo [le'tarɣo] *nm* (*MED*) lethargy.

letra ['letra] *nf* letter; (*escritura*) handwriting; (*MUS*) lyrics *pl*; **~ de cambio** bill of exchange; **~ de imprenta** print; **~do, a** *a* learned; (*fam*) pedantic // *nm* lawyer; **letrero** *nm* (*cartel*) sign; (*etiqueta*) label.

leva ['leβa] *nf* (*NAUT*) weighing anchor; (*MIL*) levy; (*TEC*) lever.

levadizo [leβa'ðiθo] *a*: **puente ~** drawbridge.

levadura [leβa'ðura] *nf* (*para el pan*) yeast; (*de la cerveza*) brewer's yeast.

levantamiento [leβanta'mjento] *nm* raising, lifting; (*rebelión*) revolt, rising; **~ de pesos** weight-lifting.

levantar [leβan'tar] *vt* (*gen*) to raise; (*del suelo*) to pick up, (*hacia arriba*) to lift (up); (*plan*) to make, draw up; (*mesa*) to clear away; (*campamento*) to strike; (*fig*) to cheer up, hearten; **~se** *vr* to get up; (*enderezarse*) to straighten up; (*rebelarse*) to rebel; **~ el ánimo** to cheer up.

levante [le'βante] *nm* east coast; **el L~** the Near East, the Levant.

levar [le'βar] *vt* to weigh anchor; **~se** *vr* to set sail.

leve ['leβe] *a* light; (*fig*) trivial; **~dad** *nf* lightness.

levita [le'βita] *nf* frock coat.

léxico ['leksiko] *am* lexicon, dictionary.

ley [lei] *nf* (*gen*) law; (*fig*) loyalty; (*metal*) standard.

leyenda [le'jenda] *nf* legend.

leyó *etc vb ver* **leer**.

liar [li'ar] *vt* to tie (up); (*unir*) to bind; (*envolver*) to wrap (up); (*enredar*) to confuse; (*cigarrillo*) to roll; **~se** *vr* (*fam*) to get involved; **~se a palos** to get involved in a fight.

Líbano ['liβano] *nm*: **el ~** the Lebanon.

libar [li'βar] *vt* to suck.

libelo [li'βelo] *nm* satire, lampoon; (*JUR*) petition.

libélula [li'βelula] *nf* dragonfly.

liberación [liβera'θjon] *nf* liberation; (*de la cárcel*) release.

liberal [liβe'ral] a, *nm/f* liberal; **~idad** *nf* liberality; (*lujo*) lavishness.

liberar [liβe'rar] *vt* to liberate.

libertad [liβer'tað] *nf* liberty, freedom; **~ de culto/de prensa/de comercio** freedom of worship/the press/of trade; **~ condicional** probation; **~ bajo palabra** parole; **~ bajo fianza** bail.

libertar [liβer'tar] *vt* (*preso*) to set free; (*de una obligación*) to release; (*eximir*) to exempt.

libertino, a [liβer'tino, a] *a* loose-living // *nm/f* libertine.

libra ['liβra] *nf* pound; **L~** (*ASTRO*) Libra; **~ esterlina** pound sterling.

librador, a [liβra'ðor, a] *nm/f* drawer.

libramiento [liβra'mjento] *nm* rescue; (*COM*) delivery.

libranza [li'βranθa] *nf* (*COM*) draft; (*de letra de cambio*) bill of exchange.

librar [li'βrar] *vt* (*de peligro*) to save; (*batalla*) to wage, fight; (*de impuestos*) to exempt; (*secreto*) to reveal; (*mercancías*) to draw (*cheque*) to make out; (*JUR*) to exempt // *vr* to give birth; **~se** *vr* **~se de** to escape from, free o.s. from.

libre ['liβre] *a* (*gen*) free; (*lugar*) unoccupied; (*asiento*) vacant; (*de impuestos*) tax-free; (*de deudas*) free of debts; (*pey*) outspoken; **tiro ~** free kick; **los 100 metros ~** the 100 metres free-style (race); **al aire ~** in the open air.

librería [lißre'ria] nf (biblioteca) library; (comercio) bookshop; **librero, a** nm/f bookseller.

libreta [li'ßreta] nf notebook; ~ **de ahorros** savings book; ~ **de banco** bank book.

libro ['lißro] nm book; ~ **en rústica/en pasta o encuadernado** paperback/hardback; ~ **de bolsillo** paperback; ~ **de caja** cashbook; ~ **de cheques** cheque book; ~ **de inventario** stock-list; ~ **de pedidos** order book; ~ **de texto** textbook.

Lic. abr de **licenciado, a.**

licencia [li'θenθja] nf (gen) licence; (permiso) permission; ~ **por enfermedad/con goce de sueldo** sick leave/paid leave; ~ **de caza/de conductor** game/driving licence; ~ **de derecho/de letras** law/arts degree; ~**do, a** a licensed // nm/f graduate; **licenciar** vt (empleado) to dismiss; (permitir) to permit, allow; (soldado) to discharge; (estudiante) to confer a degree upon; **licenciarse** vr: **licenciarse en letras** to graduate in arts.

licencioso, a [liθen'θjoso, a] a licentious.

liceo [li'θeo] nm (high) school.

licitador [liθita'ðor] nm bidder; (AM) auctioneer; **licitar** vt to bid for; (AM) to sell by auction.

lícito, a ['liθito, a] a (legal) lawful; (justo) fair, just; (permisible) permissible.

licor [li'kor] nm spirits pl; (preparado) liqueur.

licuadora [likwa'ðora] nf food-mixer, liquidizer; **licuar** vt to liquidize.

lid [lið] nf combat; (fig) controversy.

líder ['liðer] nm/f leader; **liderato** nm leadership.

lidia ['liðja] nf bullfight; **toros de** ~ fighting bulls; **lidiar** vt, vi to fight.

liebre ['ljeßre] nf hare.

lienzo ['ljenθo] nm linen; (ARTE) canvas; (pañuelo) handkerchief; (ARQ) wall.

liga ['liɣa] nf (de medias) garter, suspender; (confederación) league; (venda) band; (aleación) alloy; (BOT) mistletoe.

ligadura [liɣa'ðura] nf bond, tie; (MED, MUS) ligature.

ligamento [liɣa'mento] nm (ANAT) ligament; (atadura) tie; (unión) bond.

ligar [li'ɣar] vt (atar) to tie; (unir) to join; (MED) to bind up; (MUS) to slur; (metales) to alloy // vi to mix, blend; (fam) to pick up; (entenderse) to get on (well); ~**se** vr to commit o.s.

ligereza [lixe'reθa] nf lightness; (rapidez) swiftness; (agilidad) agility; (superficialidad) flippancy.

ligero, a [li'xero, a] a (de peso) light; (tela) thin; (rápido) swift, quick; (ágil) agile, nimble; (de importancia) slight; (de carácter) flippant, superficial // ad: **a la** ~ **a** superficially.

lija ['lixa] nf (ZOOL) dogfish; (papel de) ~ sandpaper.

lila ['lila] nf lilac // nm (fam) twit.

lima ['lima] nf file; (BOT) lime; ~ **de carpintero** file; ~ **de uñas** nail-file; **limar** vt to file.

limitación [limita'θjon] nf limitation, limit.

limitar [limi'tar] vt to limit; (reducir) to reduce, cut down // vi: ~ **con** to border on; ~**se** vr: ~**se a** to limit o.s. to.

límite ['limite] nm (gen) limit; (fin) end; (frontera) border; ~ **de velocidad** speed limit.

limítrofe [li'mitrofe] a bordering, neighbouring.

limón [li'mon] nm lemon // a: **amarillo** ~ lemon-yellow; **limonada** nf lemonade; **limonero** nm lemon tree.

limosna [li'mosna] nf alms pl; **vivir de** ~ to live on charity.

limpiabotas [limpja'ßotas] nm inv bootblack, shoeshine boy/girl.

limpiaparabrisas [limpjapara'ßrisas] nm inv windscreen wiper.

limpiar [lim'pjar] vt (gen) to clean; (con trapo) to wipe; (quitar) to wipe away; (zapatos) to shine, polish; (fig) to clean up.

limpieza [lim'rjeθa] nf (estado) cleanliness; (acto) cleaning; (: de las calles) cleansing; (: de zapatos) polishing; (habilidad) skill; (fig) clean-up; (pureza) purity; (MIL): **operación de** ~ mopping-up operation; ~ **en seco** dry cleaning.

limpio, a ['limpjo, a] a clean; (moralmente) pure; (COM) clear, net; (fam) honest // ad: **jugar** ~ to play fair // nm: **pasar en** ~ to make a fair copy.

linaje [li'naxe] nm lineage, family; **linajudo, a** a highborn.

linaza [li'naθa] nf linseed; **aceite de** ~ linseed oil.

lince ['linθe] nm lynx.

linchar [lin'tʃar] vt to lynch.

lindante [lin'dante] a adjoining; ~ **con** bordering on

lindar [lin'dar] vi to adjoin; ~ **con** to border on; **linde** nm o f boundary; **lindero, a** a adjoining // nm boundary.

lindo, a ['lindo, a] a pretty, lovely // ad (AM): **nos divertimos de lo** ~ we had a marvellous time; **canta muy** ~ he/she sings beautifully.

línea ['linea] nf (gen) line; ~ **aérea** airline; ~ **delantera** (DEPORTE) forward line; ~ **de meta** goal line; (de carrera) finishing line; ~ **de saque** service line, base line; ~ **recta** straight line.

lingüista [lin'gwista] nm/f linguist.

linimento [lini'mento] nm liniment.

lino ['lino] nm linen; (BOT) flax.

linóleo [li'noleo] nm lino, linoleum.

linterna [lin'terna] nf lantern, lamp; ~ **eléctrica** o a **pilas** torch.

lío ['lio] nm bundle; (fam) fuss; (desorden) muddle, mess; **armar un** ~ to make a fuss.

liquidación [likiða'θjon] nf liquidation; **venta de** ~ clearance sale.

liquidar [liki'ðar] vt (Ecuar) to liquidize; (eliminar) to liquidate; (mercaderias) to sell off; (pagar) to pay off; (terminar) to wind up; (AM) to ruin; ~se vr to liquefy.

líquido, a ['likiðo, a] a liquid; (ganancia) net; (AM) accurate // nm liquid; ~ **imponible** net taxable income.

lira ['lira] nf (MUS) lyre; (moneda) lira.

lirio ['lirjo] nm (BOT) iris.

Lisboa [lis'ßoa] n Lisbon.

lisiado, a [li'sjaðo, a] a injured // nm/f cripple.

lisiar [li'sjar] vt to maim; ~se vr to injure o.s.

liso, a ['liso, a] a (terreno) flat; (cabello) straight; (superficie) even; (tela) smooth.

lisonja [li'sonxa] nf flattery; **lisonjear** vt to flatter; (fig) to please; **lisonjero, a** a (gen) flattering; (agradable) gratifying, pleasing // nm/f flatterer.

lista ['lista] nf (gen) list; (de alumnos) school register; (de libros) catalogue; (de correos) poste restante; (de platos) menu; (de precios) price list; **pasar** ~ to call the roll; ~ **de espera** waiting list; **tela** ~**s** striped material.

listado, a [lis'taðo, a] a striped.

listo, a ['listo, a] a (perspicaz) smart, clever; (preparado) ready.

listón [lis'ton] nm (tela) ribbon; (de madera, metal) strip.

litera [li'tera] nf (en barco, tren) berth; (en dormitorio) bunk, bunk bed.

literato, a [lite'rato, a] a literary // nm/f writer.

literatura [litera'tura] nf literature.

litigar [liti'xar] vt to fight // vi (JUR) to go to law; (fig) to dispute, argue.

litigio [li'tixjo] nm (JUR) lawsuit; (fig): **en** ~ **con** in dispute with.

litografía [litoxra'fia] nf lithography; (una ~) lithograph.

litoral [lito'ral] a coastal // nm coast, seaboard.

litro ['litro] nm litre.

liviano, a [li'ßjano, a] a (persona) fickle; (cosa, objeto) trivial.

lívido, a ['lißiðo, a] a livid; (AM) pale.

ll... ver bajo la letra LL, después de L.

lo [lo] det neuter del art; ~ **bueno** the good // pron (persona) him; (cosa) it.

loa ['loa] nf praise; **loable** a praiseworthy; **loar** vt to praise.

lobato [lo'ßato] nm wolf cub.

lobo ['loßo] nm wolf; ~ **de mar** sea dog; ~ **marino** seal.

lóbrego, a ['loßrexo, a] a dark; (fig) gloomy.

lóbulo ['loßulo] nm lobe.

locación [loka'θjon] nf lease.

local [lo'kal] a local // nm place, site; (oficinas) premises pl; ~**idad** nf (barrio) locality; (lugar) location; (TEATRO) seat, ticket; ~**izar** vt (ubicar) to locate, find; (restringir) to localize; (situar) to place.

loco, a ['loko, a] a mad // nm/f lunatic, mad person.

locomoción [lokomo'θjon] nf locomotion.

locomotora [lokomo'tora] nf engine.

locuaz [lo'kwaθ] a loquacious.

locución [loku'θjon] nf expression.

locura [lo'kura] nf madness; (acto) crazy act.

lodo ['loðo] nm mud; ~**s** nmpl (MED) mudbath sg.

lógico, a ['loxiko, a] a logical // nf logic.

logística [lo'xistika] nf logistics pl.

lograr [lo'xrar] vt to achieve; (obtener) to get, obtain; ~ **hacer** to manage to do; ~ **que uno venga** to manage to get sb to come.

logro [loxro] nm achievement, success; **prestar a** ~ to lend at a high rate of interest.

loma ['loma] nf hillock.

lombriz [lom'briθ] nf worm; ~ **solitaria** tapeworm.

lomo ['lomo] nm (de animal) back; (de cerdo) pork loin; (de vaca) rib steak; (de libro) spine.

lona ['lona] nf canvas.

Londres ['londres] n London.

longaniza [longa'niθa] nf pork sausage.

longitud [lonxi'tuð] nf length; (GEO) longitude; **tener 3 metros de** ~ to be 3 metres long; ~ **de onda** wavelength.

lonja ['lonxa] nf slice; (de jamón) rasher; ~ **de pescado** fish market.

lontananza [lonta'nanθa] nf background.

loor [lo'or] nm praise.

loro ['loro] nm parrot.

los [los] det the // pron them; (ustedes) you; **mis libros y** ~ **de Ud** my books and yours.

losa ['losa] nf stone; ~ **sepulcral** gravestone.

lote ['lote] nm portion; (COM) lot.

lotería [lote'ria] nf lottery; (juego) lotto.

loza ['loθa] nf crockery.

lozanía [loθa'nia] nf (lujo) luxuriance; (orgullo) pride; **lozano, a** a luxuriant; (animado) lively; (altanero) haughty.

lubricante [lußri'kante] nm lubricant; **lubricar** vt to lubricate.

lucero [lu'θero] nm (ASTRO) bright star; (fig) brilliance.

lucidez [luθi'ðeθ] nf lucidity; **lúcido, a** a lucid.

luciente [lu'θjente] a shining.

luciérnaga [lu'θjernaxa] nf glow-worm.

lucimiento [luθi'mjento] nm (brillo) brilliance; (éxito) success.

lucir [lu'θir] vt to illuminate, light (up); (fig) to show off // vi (brillar) to shine; (tener éxito) to be successful; ~se vr to dress up.

lucrarse [lu'krarse] vr to enrich o.s.

lucro ['lukro] nm profit, gain.

luctuoso, a [luk'twoso, a] a mournful.

lucha ['lutʃa] nf fight, struggle; ~ **de**

clases class struggle; ~ **libre** wrestling; **luchar** *vi* to fight.

ludibrio [lu'ðißrjo] *nm* mockery.

luego ['lweχo] *ad* (*después*) next; (*más tarde*) later, afterwards; (*pronto*) soon; **desde** ~ of course; **tan** ~ **como** as soon as.

lugar [lu'χar] *nm* place; (*sitio*) spot; **en** ~ **de** instead of; **hacer** ~ to make room; **fuera de** ~ out of place; **tener** ~ to take place; ~ **común** commonplace.

lugareño, a [luχa'reɲo, a] *a* village *cpd* // *nm/f* villager.

lúgubre ['luχußre] *a* mournful.

lujo ['luχo] *nm* luxury; (*fig*) profusion, abundance; ~**so, a** a luxurious.

lujuria [lu'χurja] *nf* lust; (*fig*) lewdness.

lumbre ['lumbre] *nf* (*gen*) light.

lumbrera [lum'brera] *nf* luminary; (*en techo*) skylight; (*de barco*) vent, port.

luminoso, a [lumi'noso, a] *a* luminous, shining.

luna ['luna] *nf* moon; (*de un espejo*) glass; (*de gafas*) lens; (*fig*) crescent; ~ **llena/nueva** full/new moon; **estar con** ~ to have one's head in the clouds.

lunar [lu'nar] *a* lunar // *nm* (*ANAT*) mole; **tela a** ~**es** spotted material.

lunes ['lunes] *nm inv* Monday.

luneta [lu'neta] *nf* lens.

lupa ['lupa] *nf* magnifying glass.

lustrar [lus'trar] *vt* (*mueble*) to polish; (*zapatos*) to shine; **lustre** *nm* polish; (*fig*) lustre; **dar lustre a** to polish; **lustroso, a** a shining.

luterano, a [lute'rano, a] *a* Lutheran.

luto ['luto] *nm* mourning; (*congoja*) grief, sorrow; ~**s** *nmpl* mourning clothes; **llevar el** *o* **vestirse de** ~ to be in mourning.

Luxemburgo [luksem'burχo] *nm* Luxembourg.

luz [luθ] (*pl* **luces**) *nf* light; **dar a** ~ **un niño** to give birth to a child; **sacar a** ~ to bring to light; (*ELEC*) **dar** ~ to switch on the light; **prender/apagar la** ~ to put the light on/off; **a todas luces** by any reckoning; **hacer la** ~ **sobre** to understand; **tener pocas luces** to be dim or stupid; ~ **roja/verde** red/green light; (*AUTO*) ~ **de costado** sidelight; ~ **de freno** brake light; ~ **del relámpago** flashlight; **luces de tráfico** traffic lights; **traje de luces** bullfighter's costume.

LL

llaga ['ʎaχa] *nf* wound.

llama ['ʎama] *nf* flame; (*ZOOL*) llama.

llamada [ʎa'maða] *nf* call; ~ **al orden** call to order; **toque de** ~ (*MIL*) call-up; ~ **a pie de página** reference note.

llamamiento [ʎama'mjento] *nm* call.

llamar [ʎa'mar] *vt* to call; (*atención*) to attract // *vi* (*por teléfono*) to telephone; (*a la puerta*) to knock/ring; (*por señas*) to beckon; (*MIL*) to call up; ~**se** *vr* to be

called, be named; ¿**cómo se llama Usted?** what's your name?

llamarada [ʎama'raða] *nf* (*llamas*) blaze; (*rubor*) flush; (*fig*) flare-up.

llamativo, a [ʎama'tiβo, a] a showy; (*color*) loud.

llamear [ʎame'ar] *vi* to blaze.

llaneza [ʎa'neθa] *nf* (*gen*) simplicity; (*honestidad*) straightforwardness, frankness.

llano, a ['ʎano, a] *a* (*superficie*) flat; (*persona*) straightforward; (*estilo*) clear // *nm* plain, flat ground.

llanta ['ʎanta] *nf* (*wheel*) rim; (*AM*): ~ **de goma** tyre.

llanto ['ʎanto] *nm* weeping.

llanura [ʎa'nura] *nf* plain.

llave ['ʎaße] *nf* key; (*del agua*) tap; (*MECÁNICA*) spanner; (*de la luz*) switch; (*MUS*) key; ~ **inglesa** monkey wrench; ~ **de contacto** (*AUTO*) ignition key; **echar** ~ a to lock up; ~**ro** *nm* keyring; **llavín** *nm* latchkey.

llegada [ʎe'χaða] *nf* arrival.

llegar [ʎe'χar] *vi* to arrive; (*alcanzar*) to reach; (*bastar*) to be enough; ~**se** *vr*: ~**se a** to approach; ~ **a** to manage to, succeed in; ~ **a ser** to become; ~ **a las manos de** to come into the hands of.

llenar [ʎe'nar] *vt* (*gen*) to fill; (*espacio*) to cover; (*formulario*) to fill in *or* up; (*deber*) to fulfil; (*fig*) to heap.

lleno, a ['ʎeno, a] *a* full, filled; (*repleto*) full up // *nm* (*abundancia*) abundance; (*ASTRO*) full moon; (*TEATRO*) full house; **dar de** ~ **contra un muro** to hit a wall head-on.

llevadero, a [ʎeßa'ðero, a] a bearable, tolerable.

llevar [ʎe'ßar] *vt* (*gen*) to take; (*ropa*) to wear; (*cargar*) to carry; (*quitar*) to take away; (*conducir a alguien*) to drive; (*cargar hacia*) to transport; (*traer: dinero*) to carry; (*conducir*) to lead; (*MAT*) to carry; ~**se** *vr* to carry off, take away; **llevamos dos días aquí** we have been here for two days; **él me lleva 2 años** he's 2 years older than me; (*COM*): ~ **los libros** to keep the books; ~**se bien** to get on well (together).

llorar [ʎo'rar] *vt*, *vi* to weep; ~ **de risa** to cry with laughter.

lloriquear [ʎorike'ar] *vi* to snivel, whimper.

lloro ['ʎoro] *nm* weeping; **llorón, ona** a tearful // *nm/f* cry-baby; ~**so, a** a (*gen*) weeping, tearful; (*triste*) sad, sorrowful.

llover [ʎo'ßer] *vi* to rain; ~**se** *vr* (*techo*) to leak.

llovizna [ʎo'βiθna] *nf* drizzle; **lloviznar** *vi* to drizzle.

llueve etc *vb ver* **llover**.

lluvia ['ʎuβja] *nf* rain; ~ **radioactiva** radioactive fallout; **lluvioso, a** a rainy.

M

m *abr de* **metro; minuto.**

macarrones [maka'rrones] *nmpl* macaroni *sg.*

macerar [maθe'rar] *vt* to macerate; *(fig)* to mortify; **~se** *vr* to mortify o.s.

maceta [ma'θeta] *nf (de flores)* pot of flowers; *(para plantas)* flowerpot; *(mazo pequeño)* mallet.

macilento, a [maθi'lento, a] *a* wan; *(ojeroso)* haggard.

macis ['maθis] *nf* mace.

macizo, a [ma'θiθo, a] *a* massive; *(puerta)* solid // *nm* mass, chunk; *(de edificios)* block; *(AUTO)* solid tyre.

mácula ['makula] *nf* stain, blemish; *(ANA)* blind spot.

machacar [matʃa'kar] *vt* to crush, pound // *vi* to go on, keep on.

machamartillo [matʃamar'tiʎo]: **a ~ ad: cumplir a ~** to carry out a task to the letter; **eran cristianos a ~** they were totally convinced Christians.

machete [ma'tʃete] *nm (AM)* machete, (large) knife.

macho ['matʃo] *a* male; *(fig)* virile // *nm* male; *(fig)* he-man.

machucar [matʃu'kar] *vt* to pound.

madeja [ma'ðexa] *nf (de lana)* skein, hank; *(de pelo)* mop.

madera [ma'ðera] *nf* wood; *(fig)* nature, character; **una ~** a piece of wood.

madero [ma'ðero] *nm* beam; *(fig)* ship.

madrastra [ma'ðrastra] *nf* stepmother.

madre ['maðre] *a* mother *cpd*; *(AM)* tremendous // *nf* mother; *(ANAT)* womb; *(AGR)* main channel; *(de vino etc)* dregs *pl*; *(de río)* bed; **~ política/soltera** mother-in-law/unmarried mother.

madreperla [maðre'perla] *nf* mother-of-pearl.

madreselva [maðre'selßa] *nf* honeysuckle.

madriguera [maðri'ɣera] *nf* burrow.

madrileño, a [maðri'leɲo, a] *a* of *or* from Madrid // *nm/f* native of Madrid.

madrina [ma'ðrina] *nf (protectora)* godmother; *(ARQ)* prop, shore; *(TEC)* brace; **~ de boda** bridesmaid.

madrugada [maðru'ɣaða] *nf* early morning; *(alba)* dawn, daybreak; **madrugador, a** *a* early-rising; **madrugar** *vi* to get up early; *(fig)* to get ahead.

madurar [maðu'rar] *vt, vi (fruta)* to ripen; *(fig)* to mature; **madurez** *nf* ripeness; maturity; **maduro, a** *a* ripe; mature.

maestra [ma'estra] *nf ver* **maestro.**

maestría [maes'tria] *nf* mastery; *(habilidad)* skill, expertise.

maestro, a [ma'estro, a] *a* masterly; *(perito)* skilled, expert; *(principal)* main; *(educado)* trained // *nm* master/mistress; *(que enseña)* teacher // *nm (autoridad)* authority; *(MUS)* maestro;

(AM) skilled workman; **obra ~a** masterpiece; **~ albañil** master mason.

magia ['maxja] *nf* magic; **mágico, a** *a* magic(al) // *nm/f* magician.

magisterio [maxis'terjo] *nm (enseñanza)* teaching; *(profesión)* teaching profession; *(maestros)* teachers *pl.*

magistrado [mexis'traðo] *nm* magistrate.

magistral [maxis'tral] *a* magisterial; *(fig)* masterly.

magnánimo, a [maɣ'nanimo, a] *a* magnanimous.

magnate [maɣ'nate] *nm* magnate, tycoon.

magnético, a [maɣ'netiko, a] *a* magnetic; **magnetizar** *vt* to magnetize.

magnetofón [maɣneto'fon], **magnetófono** [maɣne'tofono] *nm* tape recorder; **magnetofónico, a** *a*: **cinta magnetofónica** recording tape.

magnífico, a [maɣ'nifiko, a] *a* splendid, magnificent, wonderful.

magnitud [maɣni'tuð] *nf* magnitude.

mago, a ['maxo, a] *nm/f* magician; **los Reyes M~s** the Magi, the Three Wise Men.

magro, a ['maxro, a] *a (persona)* thin, lean; *(carne)* lean.

magullar [maɣu'ʎar] *vt (amoratar)* to bruise; *(dañar)* to damage; *(fam: golpear)* to bash, beat.

mahometano, a [maome'tano, a] *a* Mohammedan.

maíz [ma'iθ] *nm* maize, sweet corn.

majada [ma'xaða] *nf (abrigo)* sheepfold; *(abono)* dung.

majadero, a [maxa'ðero, a] *a* silly, stupid // *nm (TEC)* pestle; *(canilla)* bobbin.

majar [ma'xar] *vt* to crush, grind; *(fig)* to bother, pester.

majestad [maxes'tað] *nf* majesty; **majestuoso, a** *a* majestic.

majo, a ['maxo, a] *a* nice; *(guapo)* attractive, good-looking; *(lujoso)* smart.

mal [mal] *ad* badly; *(equivocadamente)* wrongly; *(con dificultad)* with difficulty // *a* = **malo** // *nm* evil; *(desgracia)* misfortune; *(daño)* harm, hurt; *(MED)* illness; **¡menos ~!** just as well!; **~ que bien** rightly or wrongly.

malabarismo [malaßa'rismo] *nm* juggling; **malabarista** *nm/f* juggler.

malaconsejado, a [malakonse'xaðo, a] *a* ill-advised.

malagueño, a [mala'ɣeɲo, a] *a* of *or* from Málaga.

malaria [ma'larja] *nf* malaria.

malbaratar [malßara'tar] *vt (malgastar)* to squander; *(malvender)* to sell off cheap.

malcontento, a [malkon'tento, a] *a* discontented.

malcriado, a [mal'krjaðo, a] *a (grosero)* rude, bad-mannered; *(consentido)* spoiled.

maldad [mal'dað] *nf* evil, wickedness.

maldecir [malde'θir] *vt* to curse // *vi*: **~ de** to speak ill of.

maldición [maldi'θjon] *nf* curse.

maldito, a [mal'dito, a] *pp de* **maldecir** // *a* (*condenado*) damned; (*perverso*) wicked // *nf*: **soltar la** ~a to talk too much.

maleante [male'ante] *a* wicked // *nm/f* malefactor; **malear** *vt* to spoil; (*fig*) to corrupt.

malecón [male'kon] *nm* pier, jetty.

maledicencia [maleδi'θenθja] *nf* slander, scandal.

maleficiar [malefi'θjar] *vt* to harm, damage; (*hechizar*) to bewitch; **maleficio** *nm* curse, spell.

malestar [males'tar] *nm* (*gen*) discomfort; (*fig*) uneasiness; (*POL*) unrest.

maleta [ma'leta] *nf* case, suitcase; (*AUTO*) boot; **maletín** *nm* small case, bag.

malevolencia [maleßo'lenθja] *nf* malice, spite; **malévolo, a** *a* malicious, spiteful.

maleza [ma'leθa] *nf* (*hierbas malas*) weeds *pl*; (*arbustos*) thicket.

malgastar [malɣas'tar] *vt* (*tiempo, dinero*) to waste; (*salud*) to ruin.

malhechor, a [male'tʃor, a] *nm/f* malefactor; (*criminal*) criminal.

malicia [ma'liθja] *nf* (*maldad*) wickedness; (*astucia*) slyness, guile; (*mala intención*) malice, spite; (*carácter travieso*) mischievousness; ~**s** *nfpl* suspicions; **malicioso, a** *a* wicked, evil; sly, crafty; malicious, spiteful; mischievous.

malignidad [maliɣni'δaδ] *nf* (*MED*) malignancy; (*malicia*) malice.

maligno, a [ma'liɣno, a] *a* evil; (*malévolo*) malicious; (*MED*) malignant.

malo, a ['malo, a] *a* bad; (*falso*) false // *nm/f* villain // *nf* spell of bad luck; **estar** ~ to be ill; **estar de** ~as to be in a bad mood.

malograr [malo'ɣrar] *vt* to spoil; (*plan*) to upset; (*tiempo, ocasión*) to waste; ~**se** *vr* (*plan etc*) to fail, come to grief; (*persona*) to die before one's time; **malogro** *nm* (*fracaso*) failure; (*pérdida*) waste; (*muerte*) early death.

malparado, a [malpa'raδo, a] *a*: **salir** ~ to come off badly.

malparir [malpa'rir] *vi* to have a miscarriage.

malquistar [malkis'tar] *vt* to estrange, cause a rift with/between.

malsano, a [mal'sano, a] *a* unhealthy.

Malta ['malta] *nf* Malta.

maltratar [maltra'tar] *vt* to ill-treat; **maltrato** *nm* ill-treatment; (*ofensa*) abuse, insults *pl*.

maltrecho, a [mal'tretʃo, a] *a* battered, damaged.

malvado, a [mal'ßaδo, a] *a* evil, villainous.

malvavisco [malßa'ßisko] *nm* marshmallow.

malversar [malßer'sar] *vt* to embezzle, misappropriate.

Malvinas [mal'ßinas]: **Islas** ~ *nfpl* Falkland Islands.

malla ['maʎa] *nf* mesh; (*de baño*) bathing costume; ~**s** *nfpl* tights; ~ **de alambre** wire mesh; **hacer** ~ to knit.

Mallorca [ma'ʎorka] *nf* Majorca.

mama ['mama] *nf* (*de animal*) teat; (*de persona*) breast.

mamá [ma'ma] (*pl* ~**s**) *nf* (*fam*) mum, mummy.

mamar [ma'mar] *vt* (*pecho*) to suck; (*fig*) to absorb, assimilate // *vi* to suck.

mamarracho [mama'rratʃo] *nm* sight, mess.

mampara [mam'para] *nf* (*entre habitaciones*) partition; (*biombo*) screen.

mampostería [mamposte'ria] *nf* masonry.

mampuesto [mam'pwesto] *nm* (*piedra*) rough stone; (*muro*) wall, parapet; **de** ~ spare, emergency.

mamut [ma'mut] *nm* mammoth.

manada [ma'naδa] *nf* (*rebaño*) herd; (*de ovejas*) flock; (*de lobos*) pack.

manantial [manan'tjal] *nm* spring; (*fuente*) fountain; (*fig*) source.

manar [ma'nar] *vt* to run with, flow with // *vi* to run, flow; (*abundar*) to abound.

mancebo [man'θeßo] *nm* (*joven*) young man; (*soltero*) bachelor; (*dependiente*) assistant.

mancilla [man'θiʎa] *nf* stain, blemish.

manco, a ['manko, a] *a* one-armed, one-handed; (*fig*) defective, faulty.

mancomún [manko'mun]: **de** ~ *ad* jointly, together; **mancomunar** *vt* to unite, bring together; (*recursos*) to pool; (*JUR*) to make jointly responsible; **mancomunarse** *vr* to unite, merge; **mancomunidad** *nf* union, association; (*POL*) commonwealth; (*JUR*) joint responsibility.

mancha ['mantʃa] *nf* stain, mark; (*boceto*) sketch, outline; **manchar** *vt* (*gen*) to stain, mark; (*ensuciar*) to soil, dirty.

manchego, a [man'tʃeɣo, a] *a* of or from La Mancha.

mandadero [manda'δero] *nm* messenger; (*niño*) errand boy.

mandado [man'daδo] *nm* (*orden*) order; (*comisión*) commission, errand.

mandamiento [manda'mjento] *nm* (*orden*) order, command; (*REL*) commandment; ~ **judicial** warrant.

mandar [man'dar] *vt* (*ordenar*) to order; (*dirigir*) to lead, command; (*enviar*) to send; (*pedir*) to order, ask for // *vi* to be in charge; (*pey*) to be bossy; ~**se** *vr* (*MED*) to get about by o.s.; ¿**mande?** pardon?; ~ **hacer un traje** to have a suit made; ~**se cambiar** to go away, leave.

mandarín [manda'rin] *nm* mandarin // *nf* tangerine, mandarin.

mandatario, a [manda'tarjo, a] *nm/f* (*representante*) agent; (*AM*) leader.

mandato [man'dato] *nm* (*orden*) order; (*POL*) term of office; (: *territorio*) mandate; ~ **judicial** (*search*) warrant.

mandíbula [man'dißula] *nf* jaw.

mandil [man'dil] *nm* (*delantal*) apron; (*vestido*) pinafore dress.

mando ['mando] nm (MIL) command; (de país) rule; (el primer lugar) lead; (POL) term of office; (TEC) control; ~ **a la izquierda** left-hand drive; ~ **remoto** remote control.

mandolina [mando'lina] nf mandolin(e).

mandón, ona [man'don, ona] a bossy, domineering.

manea [ma'nea] nf hobble.

manejable [mane'xaßle] a manageable.

manejar [mane'xar] vt (gen) to manage; (máquina) to work, operate; (idioma, caballo etc) to handle; (casa) to run, manage; (AM) to drive; ~**se** vr (comportarse) to act, behave; (arreglárselas) to manage; (MED) to get about unaided; **manejo** nm management; handling; running; driving; (facilidad de trato) ease, confidence; **manejos** nmpl intrigues.

manera [ma'nera] nf way, manner, fashion; ~**s** nfpl manners; ~ **de ser** way of life; (aire) manner; **de ninguna** ~ no way, by no means; **de otra** ~ otherwise; **de todas** ~**s** at any rate; **no hay** ~ **de persuadirle** there's no way of convincing him.

manga ['manga] nf (de camisa) sleeve; (de riego) hose; (tromba) downpour; (filtro) filter; (NAUT) beam.

mangana [man'gana] nf lasso.

mango ['mango] nm handle; (BOT) mango.

mangonear [mangone'ar] vt to manage, boss about // vi (meterse) to meddle, interfere; (ser mandón) to boss people about.

manguera [man'gera] nf (de riego) hose; (tubo) pipe.

maní [ma'ni] nm (AM) peanut.

manía [ma'nia] nf (MED) mania; (capricho) rage, craze; (disgusto) dislike; (malicia) spite; **maníaco, a** a maniac(al) // nm/f maniac.

maniatar [manja'tar] vt to tie the hands of.

maniático, a [ma'njatiko, a] a maniac(al) // nm/f maniac.

manicomio [mani'komjo] nm asylum, mental hospital.

manifestación [manifesta'θjon] nf (declaración) statement, declaration; (demostración) show, manifestation; (POL) demonstration.

manifestar [manifes'tar] vt to show, manifest; (declarar) to state, declare; **manifiesto, a** a clear, manifest // nm manifesto.

manija [ma'nixa] nf handle.

manilla [ma'niʎa] nf: ~**s de hierro** handcuffs.

maniobra [ma'njoßra] nf manœuvring; (maneja) handling; (fig) manœuvre; (estratagema) stratagem; ~**s** nfpl manœuvres; **maniobrar** vt to manœuvre; (manejar) to handle.

manipulación [manipula'θjon] nf manipulation; **manipular** vt to

manipulate; (manejar) to handle.

maniquí [mani'ki] nm dummy // nf model.

manirroto, a [mani'rroto, a] a lavish, extravagant // nm/f spendthrift.

manivela [mani'ßela] nf crank.

manjar [man'xar] nm (tasty) dish; ~ **blanco** blancmange.

mano ['mano] nf hand; (ZOOL) foot, paw; (de pintura) coat; (serie) lot, series; **a** ~ by hand; **a la** ~ on hand, within reach; **a** ~ **derecha/izquierda** on the right(-hand side)/left(-hand side; **de primera** ~ (at) first hand; **de segunda** ~ (at) second hand; **robo a** ~ **armada** armed robbery; ~ **de obra** labour, manpower; **estrechar la** ~ **a uno** to shake sb's hand.

manojo [ma'noxo] nm handful, bunch; ~ **de llaves** bunch of keys.

manoseado, a [mano'seaðo, a] a well-worn; **manosear** vt (tocar) to handle, touch; (desordenar) to mess up, rumple; (insistir en) to overwork; (AM) to caress, fondle.

manotazo [mano'taθo] nm slap, smack.

mansalva [man'salßa]: **a** ~ ad without risk, without any danger.

mansedumbre [manse'ðumbre] nf gentleness, meekness.

mansión [man'sjon] nf mansion.

manso, a ['manso, a] a gentle, mild, meek; (animal) tame.

manta ['manta] nf blanket; (abrigo) shawl.

manteca [man'teka] nf fat; ~ **de cacahuete/cacao** peanut/cocoa butter; ~ **de cerdo** lard.

mantecado [mante'kaðo] nm ice-cream.

mantel [man'tel] nm tablecloth.

mantener [mante'ner] vt (gen) to support, maintain; (alimentar) to sustain; (conservar) to keep; (TEC) to maintain, service; ~**se** vr (seguir de pie) to be still standing; (no ceder) to hold one's ground; (subsistir) to sustain o.s., keep going; **mantenimiento** nm maintenance; sustenance; (sustento) support.

mantequera [mante'kera] nf (para hacer) churn; (para servir) butter dish.

mantequilla [mante'kiʎa] nf butter.

mantilla [man'tiʎa] nf mantilla; ~**s** nfpl baby clothes.

manto ['manto] nm (capa) cloak; (chal) shawl; (de ceremonia) robe, gown.

mantón [man'ton] nm shawl.

manual [ma'nwal] a manual // nm manual, handbook.

manufactura [manufak'tura] nf manufacture; (fábrica) factory.

manuscrito, a [manus'krito, a] a hand-written // nm manuscript.

manutención [manuten'θjon] nf maintenance; (sustento) support.

manzana [man'θana] nf apple; (ARQ) block.

manzanilla [manθa'niʎa] nf (planta) camomile; (infusión) camomile tea; (vino) manzanilla.

manzano [man'θano] nm apple tree.

maña ['maɲa] nf (gen) skill, dexterity; (pey) guile; (costumbre) habit; (una ~) trick, knack.

mañana [ma'ɲana] ad tomorrow // nm future // nf morning; de o por la ~ in the morning; ¡hasta ~! see you tomorrow!; ~ por la ~ tomorrow morning; **mañanero, a** a early-rising.

mañoso, a [ma'ɲoso, a] a (hábil) skilful; (astuto) smart, clever.

mapa ['mapa] nm map.

maque ['make] nm lacquer.

maqueta [ma'keta] nf (scale) model.

maquillaje [maki'ʎaxe] nm make-up; (acto) making up; **maquillar** vt to make up; **maquillarse** vr to put on (some) make-up.

máquina ['makina] nf machine; (de tren) locomotive, engine; (cámara) camera; (fig) machinery; (: proyecto) plan, project; escrito a ~ typewritten; ~ de afeitar (safety) razor; ~ de escribir typewriter; ~ de coser/lavar sewing/washing machine.

maquinación [makina'θjon] nf machination, scheme, plot.

maquinal [maki'nal] a (fig) mechanical, automatic.

maquinaria [maki'narja] nf (máquinas) machinery; (mecanismo) mechanism, works pl.

maquinista [maki'nista] nm (de tren) engine driver; (TEC) operator; (NAUT) engineer.

mar [mar] nm o f sea; (marea) tide; ~ adentro o afuera out at sea; en alta ~ on the high seas; la ~ de (fam) lots of; el M~ Negro/Báltico the Black/Baltic Sea.

maraña [ma'raɲa] nf (maleza) thicket; (confusión) tangle.

maravilla [mara'βiʎa] nf marvel, wonder; (BOT) marigold; **maravillar** vt to astonish, amaze; **maravillarse** vr to be astonished, be amazed; **maravilloso, a** a wonderful, marvellous.

marca ['marka] nf (gen) mark; (sello) stamp; (COM) make, brand; de ~ excellent, outstanding; ~ de fábrica trademark.

marcado, a [mar'kaðo, a] a marked, strong.

marcar [mar'kar] vt (gen) to mark; (número de teléfono) to dial; (gol) to score; (números) to record, keep a tally of; (el pelo) to set; (fig) to indicate, point to // vi (DEPORTE) to score; (TELEC) to dial; ~se vr (NAUT) to take one's bearings; (fig) to make one's mark, stand out.

marcial [mar'θjal] a martial, military.

marciano, a [mar'θjano, a] a Martian.

marco ['marko] nm frame; (DEPORTE) goal-posts pl; (moneda) mark; (fig) framework; ~ de chimenea mantelpiece.

marcha ['martʃa] nf march; (TEC) running, working; (AUTO) gear; (velocidad) speed; (fig) progress; (dirección) course; **poner en ~** to put into gear; **dar ~ atrás** to reverse, put into reverse; **estar en ~** to be under way, be in motion.

marchante, a [mar'tʃante, a] nm/f dealer, merchant; (AM: cliente) client, customer; (: buhonero) pedlar.

marchar [mar'tʃar] vi to go; (funcionar) to work, go; ~se vr to go (away), leave.

marchitar [martʃi'tar] vt to wither, dry up; ~se vr (BOT) to wither; (fig) to go into a decline; **marchito, a** a withered, faded; (fig) in decline.

marea [ma'rea] nf tide; (llovizna) drizzle.

marear [mare'ar] vt (NAUT) to sail, navigate; (fig) to annoy, upset; (MED): ~ a uno to make sb feel sick; ~se vr (tener náuseas) to feel/be sick; (desvanecerse) to feel faint; (aturdirse) to feel dizzy; (fam: emborracharse) to get a bit drunk.

maremoto [mare'moto] nm tidal wave.

mareo [ma'reo] nm (náusea) sick feeling; (aturdimiento) dizziness; (fam: lata) nuisance.

marfil [mar'fil] nm ivory.

margarina [marɣa'rina] nf margarine.

margarita [marɣa'rita] nf (BOT) daisy; (perla) pearl.

margen ['marxen] nm (borde) edge, border; (fig) margin, space // nf bank; **dar ~ para** to give an opportunity for; **mantenerse al ~** to keep out (of things).

marica [ma'rika] nm magpie; (fam) sissy.

maricón [mari'kon] nm (fam) queer (fam).

marido [ma'riðo] nm husband.

marijuana [mari'xwana] nf marijuana, cannabis.

marina [ma'rina] nf navy; ~ **mercante** merchant navy.

marinero, a [mari'nero, a] a sea cpd; (barco) seaworthy // nm sailor, seaman.

marino, a [ma'rino, a] a sea cpd, marine // nm sailor.

marioneta [marjo'neta] nf puppet.

mariposa [mari'posa] nf butterfly.

mariscos [ma'riskos] nmpl shellfish, seafood sg.

marisma [ma'risma] nf marsh, swamp.

marítimo, a [ma'ritimo, a] a sea cpd, maritime.

marmita [mar'mita] nf pot.

mármol ['marmol] nm marble; **marmóreo, a** a a marble.

marqués, esa [mar'kes, esa] nm/f marquis/marchioness.

marrar [ma'rrar] vi to miss.

marrón [ma'rron] a brown.

marroquí [marro'ki] a Moroccan // nm Morocco (leather).

Marruecos [ma'rrwekos] nm Morocco.

Marsellas [mar'seʎas] n Marseille.

martes ['martes] nm inv Tuesday.

martillar [marti'ʎar] vt to hammer.

martillo [mar'tiʎo] nm hammer; ~

neumático pneumatic drill; ~ **de orejas** claw-hammer.

mártir ['martir] nm/f martyr; **martirio** nm martyrdom; (fig) torture, torment.

marxismo [mark'sismo] nm Marxism; **marxista** nm/f Marxist.

marzo ['marθo] nm March.

mas [mas] conj but.

más [mas] a, ad more; (superlativo) most // conj and, plus; **es ~ de medianoche** it's after midnight; **el libro ~ leído del año** the most-read book of the year; ¡**qué perro ~ feo!** what an ugly dog!; ~ **de, ~ de lo que, ~ que** more than; ~ **bien** rather; ~ **o menos** more or less.

masa ['masa] nf (mezcla) dough; (volumen) volume, mass; (FÍSICA) mass; (ELEC) earth; **en ~ en masse; las ~s** the masses.

masacre [ma'sakre] nf massacre.

masaje [ma'saxe] nm massage.

mascar [mas'kar] vt to chew; (fig) to mumble, mutter.

máscara ['maskara] nf (gen) mask // nm/f masked person; **mascarada** nf masquerade.

masculino, a [masku'lino, a] a masculine; (BIO) male.

mascullar [masku'ʎar] vt to mumble, mutter.

masilla [ma'siʎa] nf putty.

masivo, a [ma'sißo, a] a (enorme) massive; (en masa) mass, en masse.

masón [ma'son] nm (free)mason.

masoquista [maso'kista] nm/f masochist.

masticar [masti'kar] vt to chew; (fig) to ponder.

mástil ['mastil] nm (de navío) mast; (de guitarra) neck; (sostén) post, support.

mastín [mas'tin] nm mastiff; ~ **danés** Great Dane.

masturbación [masturßa'θjon] nf masturbation; **masturbarse** vr to masturbate.

mata ['mata] nf bush, shrub; (de hierbas) tuft; (campo) field; (AM) clump (of trees).

matadero [mata'ðero] nm slaughterhouse, abattoir.

matador, a [mata'ðor, a] a killing // nm/f killer // nm (TAUR) matador, bullfighter.

matanza [ma'tanθa] nf (de personas) killing; (de animales) slaughter(ing).

matar [ma'tar] vt, vi to kill; ~**se** vr (suicidarse) to kill o.s., commit suicide; (por otro) to be killed; ~ **el hambre** to stave off hunger.

mate ['mate] a (sin brillo: color) dull // nm (en ajedrez) (check)mate; (AM: hierba) maté; (: vasija) gourd.

matemáticas [mate'matikas] nfpl mathematics; **matemático, a** a mathematical // nm/f mathematician.

materia [ma'terja] nf (gen) matter; (TEC) material; **en ~ de** on the subject of; ~ **prima** raw material; **material** a material; (dolor) physical // nm material; (TEC) equipment; **materialismo** nm

materialism; **materialista** a materialist(ic); **materialmente** ad materially; (fig) absolutely.

maternal [mater'nal] a motherly, maternal.

maternidad [materni'ðað] nf motherhood, maternity; **materno, a** a motherly, maternal; (lengua) mother cpd.

matinal [mati'nal] a morning cpd.

matiz [ma'tiθ] nm shade; ~**ar** vt (dar tonos de) to tinge, tint; (variar) to vary; (ARTE) to blend.

matón [ma'ton] nm bully.

matorral [mato'rral] nm thicket.

matraca [ma'traka] nf rattle.

matrícula [ma'trikula] nf (registro) register; (AUTO) registration number; (: placa) licence plate; **matricular** vt to register, enrol.

matrimonial [matrimo'njal] a matrimonial.

matrimonio [matri'monjo] nm (boda) wedding; (pareja) (married) couple; (unión) marriage.

matriz [ma'triθ] nf womb; (TEC) mould; **casa ~** (COM) head office.

matrona [ma'trona] nf (persona de edad) matron; (partera) midwife.

matute [ma'tute] nm contraband.

maullar [mau'ʎar] vi to mew, miaow.

mausoleo [mauso'leo] nm mausoleum.

maxilar [maksi'lar] nm jaw(bone).

máxima ['maksima] ver **máximo**.

máxime ['maksime] ad especially.

máximo, a ['maksimo, a] a maximum; (más alto) highest; (más grande) greatest // nm maximum // af máxima.

mayo ['majo] nm May.

mayonesa [majo'nesa] nf mayonnaise.

mayor [ma'jor] a (gen) main, chief; (adulto) adult; (de edad avanzada) elderly; (MUS) major; (comparativo: de tamaño) bigger; (: de edad) older; (superlativo: de tamaño) biggest; (: de edad) oldest // nm chief, boss; **al por ~** wholesale; ~ **de edad** adult; ~**es** ampl ancestors.

mayoral [majo'ral] nm foreman.

mayordomo [major'ðomo] nm (criado) butler; (de hotel) steward.

mayoría [majo'ria] nf majority, greater part.

mayorista [majo'rista] nm/f wholesaler.

mayúsculo, a [ma'juskulo, a] a (fig) big, tremendous // nf capital (letter).

mazapán [maθa'pan] nm marzipan.

mazo ['maθo] nm (martillo) mallet; (de flores) bunch; (fig) bore; (DEPORTE) bat; (palo) club.

me [me] pron (directo) me; (indirecto) (to) me; (reflexivo) (to) myself; ¡**démelo**! give it to me!

mecánico, a [me'kaniko, a] a mechanical // nm/f mechanic // nf (estudio) mechanics sg; (mecaaísmo) mechanism.

mecanismo [meka'nismo] nm mechanism; (marcha) gear.

mecanografía [mekanoʂra'fia] *nf* typewriting; **mecanógrafo, a** *nm/f* typist.

mecedor, a [meθe'ðor, a] *a* rocking // *nm* (*columpio*) swing // *nf* rocking chair.

mecer [me'θer] *vt* (*cuna*) to rock; (*líquido*) to stir; ~**se** *vr* to rock; (*ramo*) to sway.

mechero [me'tʃero] *nm* (cigarette) lighter.

mechón [me'tʃon] *nm* (*gen*) tuft; (*manojo*) bundle; (*de pelo*) lock.

medalla [me'ðaʎa] *nf* medal.

media ['meðja] *nf ver* **medio.**

mediado, a [me'ðjaðo, a] *a* half-full; (*trabajo*) half-complete; **a** ~**s de** in the middle of, halfway through.

mediano, a [me'ðjano, a] *a* (*regular*) medium, average; (*mediocre*) mediocre; (*indiferente*) indifferent.

medianoche [meðja'notʃe] *nf* midnight.

mediante [me'ðjante] *ad* by (means of), through.

mediar [me'ðjar] *vi* (*llegar a la mitad*) to get to the middle, get halfway; (*estar en medio*) to be in the middle; (*interceder*) to mediate, intervene.

medicación [meðika'θjon] *nf* medication, treatment.

medicamento [meðika'mento] *nm* medicine, drug.

medicina [meði'θina] *nf* medicine.

medición [meði'θjon] *nf* measurement.

médico, a ['meðiko, a] *a* medical // *nm/f* doctor.

medida [me'ðiða] *nf* (*gen*) measure; (*medición*) measurement; (*prudencia*) moderation, prudence; **en cierta/gran** ~ up to a point/to a great extent; **un traje a la** ~ made-to-measure suit; ~ **de cuello** collar size; **a** ~ **de** in proportion to; (*de acuerdo con*) in keeping with.

medio, a [a 'meðjo, a] *a* half (a); (*punto*) mid, middle; (*promedio*) average // *ad* half // *nm* (*centro*) middle, centre; (*promedio*) average; (*DEPORTE*) half-back; (*método*) means, way; (*ambiente*) environment // *nf* (*prenda de vestir*) stocking; (*promedio*) average; ~**s** *nmpl* means, resources; ~ **litro** half a litre; **las tres y** ~**a** half past three; **M**~ **Oriente** Middle East; **a** ~ **terminar** half finished; **pagar a** ~**as** to share the cost; **hacer** ~**a** to knit.

mediocre [me'ðjokre] *a* middling, average; (*pey*) mediocre.

mediodía [meðjo'ðia] *nm* midday, noon.

medir [me'ðir] *vt* (*gen*) to measure; (*pesar*) to weigh up // *vi* to measure.

meditar [meði'tar] *vt* to ponder, think over, meditate (on); (*planear*) to think out.

mediterráneo, a [meðite'rraneo, a] *a* Mediterranean // *nm*: **el M**~ **the** Mediterranean.

medroso, a [me'ðroso, a] *a* fearful, timid.

medusa [me'ðusa] *nf* jellyfish.

megáfono [me'ɣafono] *nm* megaphone.

megalómano, a [meɣa'lomano, a] *nm/f* megalomaniac.

mejicano, a [mexi'kano, a] *a*, *nm/f* Mexican.

Méjico ['mexiko] *nm* Mexico.

mejilla [me'xiʎa] *nf* cheek.

mejor [me'xor] *a*, *ad* (*comparativo*) better; (*superlativo*) best; **a lo** ~ probably; (*quizá*) maybe; ~ **dicho** rather; **tanto** ~ so much the better.

mejora [me'xora] *nf* improvement; **mejorar** *vt* to improve, make better // *vi*, **mejorarse** *vr* to improve, get better.

melancólico, a [melan'koliko, a] *a* (*triste*) sad, melancholy; (*soñador*) dreamy.

melena [me'lena] *nf* (*de persona*) long hair; (*del león*) mane.

melocotón [meloko'ton] *nm* peach.

melodía [melo'ðia] *nf* melody; (*aire*) tune.

melodrama [melo'ðrama] *nm* melodrama; **melodramático, a** *a* melodramatic.

melón [me'lon] *nm* melon.

meloso, a [me'loso, a] *a* honeyed, sweet.

mellizo, a [me'ʎiðo, a] *a*, *nm/f* twin.

membrete [mem'brete] *nm* letterhead.

memorable [memo'raβle] *a* memorable.

memorándum [memo'randum] *nm* (*libro*) notebook; (*comunicación*) memorandum.

memoria [me'morja] *nf* (*gen*) memory; (*informe*) report; ~**s** *nfpl* (*de autor*) memoirs.

mencionar [menθjo'nar] *vt* to mention.

mendigar [mendi'xar] *vt* to beg (for).

mendigo, a [men'diɣo, a] *nm/f* beggar.

mendrugo [men'druɣo] *nm* crust.

menear [mene'ar] *vt* to move; (*fig*) to handle; ~**se** *vr* to shake; (*balancearse*) to sway; (*moverse*) to move; (*fig*) to get a move on.

menester [menes'ter] *nm* (*necesidad*) necessity; (*ocupación*) job; ~**es** *nmpl* (*deberes*) duties; (*instrumentos*) tackle *sg*, tools; **es** ~ it is necessary.

mengua ['mengwa] *nf* (*disminución*) decrease; (*falta*) lack; (*pobreza*) poverty; (*fig*) discredit; ~**do, a** a cowardly, timid; (*cicatero*) mean.

menguante [men'gwante] *a* decreasing, diminishing; **menguar** *vt* to lessen, diminish; (*fig*) to discredit // *vi* to diminish, decrease; (*fig*) to decline.

menopausia [meno'pausja] *nf* menopause.

menor [me'nor] *a* (*más pequeño*: *comparativo*) smaller; (: *superlativo*) smallest; (*más joven*: *comparativo*) younger; (: *superlativo*) youngest; (*MUS*) minor // *nm/f* (*joven*) young person, juvenile; **no tengo la** ~ **idea** I haven't the slightest idea; **al por** ~ retail; ~ **de edad** person under age.

menos ['menos] *a* (*comparativo*: *sg*) less; (: *pl*) fewer; (*superlativo*: *sg*) least; (: *pl*) fewest // *ad* (*comparativo*) less; (*superlativo*) least // *conj* except // *nm* (*MAT*) minus; **es lo** ~ **que puedo hacer**

it's the least I can do; **lo ~ posible** as little as possible; **a ~ que** unless; **te echo de ~** I miss you; **al o por lo ~** at least.

menoscabar [menoska'βar] vt (estropear) to damage, harm; (acortar) to lessen, reduce; (fig) to discredit.

menospreciar [menospre'θjar] vt to underrate, undervalue; (despreciar) to scorn, despise; **menosprecio** nm underrating, undervaluation; scorn, contempt.

mensaje [men'saxe] nm message; **~ro, a** nm/f messenger.

menstruar [mens'trwar] vi to menstruate; **menstruo** nm menstruation, period.

mensual [men'swal] a monthly; **100 ptas ~es** 100 ptas. a month.

menta ['menta] nf mint.

mental [men'tal] a mental.

mentar [men'tar] vt to mention, name.

mente ['mente] nf mind.

mentecato, a [mente'kato, a] a silly, stupid // nm/f fool, idiot.

mentir [men'tir] vi to lie; **~a** nf (una ~ε) lie; (acto) lying; (invención) fiction; **parece ~a que...** it seems incredible that..., I can't believe that...; **~oso, a** a lying; (texto) full of errors // nm/f liar.

mentís [men'tis] nm: **dar el ~ a** to deny.

menú [me'nu] nm menu.

menudeo [menu'ðeo] nm: **vender al ~** to sell retail.

menudo, a [me'nuðo, a] a (pequeño) small, tiny; (sin importancia) petty, insignificant; (exacto) exact, meticulous; **¡ ~ negocio!** (fam) some deal!; **a ~** often, frequently; **por ~** in detail.

meñique [me'nike] nm little finger.

meollo [me'oʎo] nm (gen) marrow; (fig) core.

mercadería [merkaðe'ria] nf commodity; **~s** nfpl goods, merchandise sg.

mercado [mer'kaðo] nm market; **M~ Común** Common Market.

mercadotecnia [merkaðo'teknja] nf marketing.

mercancía [merkan'θia] nf commodity; **~s** nfpl goods, merchandise sg.

mercantil [merkan'til] a mercantile, commercial.

mercenario, a [merθe'narjo, a] a, nm mercenary.

mercurio [mer'kurjo] nm mercury.

merecer [mere'θer] vt to deserve, merit // vi to be deserving, be worthy; **merece la pena** it's worthwhile; **merecido, a** a (well) deserved; **llevar su merecido** to get one's deserts.

merendar [meren'dar] vt to have for tea // vi to have tea; (en el campo) to have a picnic.

merengue [me'renge] nm meringue.

merienda [me'rjenda] nf (light) tea, afternoon snack; (de campo) picnic.

mérito ['merito] nm merit; (valor) worth, value.

merluza [mer'luθa] nf hake.

merma ['merma] nf decrease; (pérdida) wastage; **mermar** vt to reduce, lessen // vi, **mermarse** vr to decrease, dwindle; (fig) to waste away.

mermelada [merme'laða] nf jam.

mero, a ['mero, a] a mere.

mes [mes] nm month; (salario) month's pay.

mesa ['mesa] nf table; (de trabajo) desk; (GEO) plateau; (ARQ) landing; **~ directiva** board; **poner/quitar la ~** to lay/clear the table.

meseta [me'seta] nf (GEO) meseta, tableland; (ARQ) landing.

mesón [me'son] nm olde-worlde bar.

mestizo, a [mes'tiθo, a] a half-caste, of mixed race; (ZOOL) crossbred // nm/f half-caste, half-breed.

mesura [me'sura] nf (moderación) moderation, restraint; (dignidad) dignity, calm; (cortesía) courtesy.

meta ['meta] nf goal; (de carrera) finish.

metáfora [me'tafora] nf metaphor.

metal [me'tal] nm (materia) metal; (MUS) brass; (fig) quality; **metálico, a** a metallic; (de metal) metal // nm cash.

metalurgia [meta'lurxja] nf metallurgy.

meteoro [mete'oro] nm meteor.

meter [me'ter] vt (colocar) to put, place; (introducir) to put in, insert; (añadir) to add; (involucrar) to involve; (causar) to make, cause; **~se** vr: **~se en** to go into, enter; (fig) to interfere in, meddle in; **~se a** to start; **~se a escritor** to become a writer; **~se con alguien** to provoke sb, pick a quarrel with sb.

meticuloso, a [metiku'loso, a] a meticulous, thorough.

metódico, a [me'toðiko, a] a methodical.

metodismo [meto'ðismo] nm Methodism.

método ['metoðo] nm method.

metralleta [metra'ʎeta] nf submachine gun.

métrico, a ['metriko, a] a metric.

metro ['metro] nm metre; (tren) underground, subway.

México ['meksiko] nm Mexico.

mezcla ['meθkla] nf mixture; (ARQ) mortar; **mezclar** vt to mix (up); (naipes) to shuffle; **mezclarse** vr to mix, mingle; **mezclarse en** to get mixed up in, get involved in.

mezquino, a [meθ'kino, a] a (cicatero) mean; (pobre) miserable.

mezquita [meθ'kita] nf mosque.

mi [mi] det my.

mí [mi] pron me; myself.

miaja ['mjaxa] nf crumb.

microbús [mikro'βus] nm minibus.

micrófono [mi'krofono] nm microphone.

microlentillas [mikrolen'tiʎas] nfpl contact lenses.

microscopio [mikro'skopjo] nm microscope.

miedo ['mjeðo] nm fear; (nerviosismo) apprehension, nervousness; **tener ~** to be afraid; **de** ~ wonderful, marvellous; **hace un frío de** ~ (*fam*) it's terribly cold; ~**so, a** *a* fearful, timid.

miel [mjel] *nf* honey.

miembro ['mjembro] *nm* limb; (*socio*) member; ~ **viril** penis.

mientes ['mjentes] *nfpl:* **no parar** ~ **en** to pay no attention to; **traer a las** ~ to recall.

mientras ['mjentras] *conj* while; (*duración*) as long as // *ad* meanwhile; ~ **tanto** meanwhile; ~ **más tiene, más quiere** the more he has, the more he wants.

miércoles ['mjerkoles] *nm inv* Wednesday.

mierda ['mjerða] *nf* (*fam*) shit.

miga ['miɣa] *nf* crumb; (*fig*) essence; **hacer buenas** ~**s** (*fam*) to get on well.

migración [miɣra'θjon] *nf* migration.

mil [mil] *num* thousand; **dos** ~ **libras** two thousand pounds.

milagro [mi'laɣro] *nm* miracle; ~**so, a** *a* miraculous.

mili ['mili] *nf:* **hacer la** ~ (*fam*) to do one's military service.

milicia [mi'liθja] *nf* (*MIL*) militia; (: *arte*) art of war; (*servicio militar*) military service.

milímetro [mi'limetro] *nm* millimetre.

militante [mili'tante] *a* militant.

militar [mili'tar] *a* (*del ejército*) military; (*guerrero*) warlike // *nm/f* soldier // *vi* to serve in the army; (*fig*) to be a member of a party.

milla ['miʎa] *nf* mile.

millar [mi'ʎar] *nm* thousand.

millón [mi'ʎon] *num* million; **millonario, a** *nm/f* millionaire.

mimar [mi'mar] *vt* (*gen*) to spoil, pamper; (*al poderoso*) to flatter.

mimbre ['mimbre] *nm* wicker.

mímica [mi'mika] *nf* (*para comunicarse*) sign language; (*imitación*) mimicry.

mimo ['mimo] *nm* (*caricia*) affectionate caress; (*de niño*) spoiling; (*TEATRO*) mime.

mina ['mina] *nf* mine; **minar** *vt* to mine; (*fig*) to undermine.

mineral [mine'ral] *a* mineral // *nm* (*GEO*) mineral; (*mena*) ore.

minero, a [mi'nero, a] *a* mining // *nm/f* miner.

miniatura [minja'tura] *a inv, nf* miniature.

minifalda [mini'falda] *nf* miniskirt.

mínimo, a ['minimo, a] *a, nm* minimum.

ministerio [minis'terjo] *nm* Ministry; **M**~ **de Hacienda/del Exterior** Treasury/Foreign Office.

ministro [mi'nistro] *nm* minister.

minorar [mino'rar] *vt* to reduce.

minoría [mino'ria] *nf* minority.

minucioso, a [minu'θjoso, a] *a* thorough, meticulous; (*prolijo*) very detailed.

minúsculo, a [mi'nuskulo, a] *a* tiny, minute // *nf* small letter.

minuta [mi'nuta] *nf* (*de comida*) menu;

(*borrador*) rough draft; (*apunte*) note.

minutero [minu'tero] *nm* minute hand.

minuto [mi'nuto] *nm* minute.

mío, a ['mio, a] *pron:* **el** ~ mine; **un amigo** ~ a friend of mine; **lo** ~ what is mine.

miope [mi'ope] *a* short-sighted.

mira ['mira] *nf* (*de arma*) sight(s) (*pl*); (*fig*) aim, intention; **estar a la** ~ to be on the look-out, keep watch; ~**da** *nf* look, glance; (*expresión*) look, expression; **echar una** ~**da a** to glance at; ~**do, a** *a* (*sensato*) sensible; (*considerado*) considerate; **bien/mal** ~**do** well/not well thought of.

mirador [mira'ðor] *nm* viewpoint, vantage point.

mirar [mi'rar] *vt* to look at; (*observar*) to watch; (*considerar*) to consider, think over; (*vigilar, cuidar*) to look after // *vi* to look; (*ARQ*) to face; ~**se** *vr* (*dos personas*) to look at each other; ~ **bien/mal** to think highly of/have a poor opinion of; ~**se al espejo** to look at o.s. in the mirror.

mirlo ['mirlo] *nm* blackbird.

misa ['misa] *nf* mass.

miserable [mise'raβle] *a* (*avaro*) mean, stingy; (*nimio*) miserable, paltry; (*lugar*) squalid; (*fam*) vile, despicable // *nm/f* (*indigente*) wretch, poor person; (*perverso*) rotter.

miseria [mi'serja] *nf* misery; (*pobreza*) poverty; (*tacañería*) meanness, stinginess; (*condiciones*) squalor; **una** ~ a pittance.

misericordia [miseri'korðja] *nf* (*compasión*) compassion, pity; (*piedad*) mercy.

misil [mi'sil] *nm* missile.

misión [mi'sjon] *nf* mission; **misionero, a** *nm/f* missionary.

mismo, a ['mismo, a] *a* (*semejante*) same; (*después de pronombre*) -self; (*para énfasis*) very; **el** ~ **traje** the same suit; **en ese** ~ **momento** at that very moment; **vino el** ~ **Ministro** the minister himself came; **yo** ~ **lo vi** I saw it myself; **lo** ~ the same (thing); **da lo** ~ it's all the same; **quedamos en las** ~**as** we're no further forward // *ad:* **aquí/hoy** ~ right here/this very day; **ahora** ~ right now // *conj:* **lo** ~ **que** just like, just as; **por lo** ~ for the same reason.

misterio [mis'terjo] *nm* (*gen*) mystery; (*lo secreto*) secrecy.

mitad [mi'tað] *nf* (*medio*) half; (*centro*) middle; **a** ~ **de precio** (at) half-price; **en o a** ~ **del camino** halfway along the road; **cortar por la** ~ to cut through the middle.

mitin ['mitin] *nm* meeting.

mito ['mito] *nm* myth.

mixto, a ['miksto, a] *a* mixed.

mobiliario [moβi'ljarjo] *nm* furniture.

mocedad [moθe'ðað] *nf* youth.

moción [mo'θjon] *nf* motion.

mochila [mo'tʃila] *nf* rucksack.

moda ['moða] *nf* (*gen*) fashion; (*estilo*) style; **de** *o* **a la** ~ in fashion, fashionable; **pasado** *o* **fuera de** ~ out of fashion.

modales [mo'ðales] *nmpl* manners.

modalidad [moðali'ðað] *nf* kind, variety.

modelar [moðe'lar] *vt* to model.

modelo [mo'ðelo] *a inv, nm/f* model.

moderado, a [moðe'raðo, a] *a* moderate.

moderar [moðe'rar] *vt* to moderate; (*violencia*) to restrain, control; (*velocidad*) to reduce; ~**se** *vr* to restrain o.s., control o.s.

modernizar [moðerni'θar] *vt* to modernize.

moderno, a [mo'ðerno, a] *a* modern; (*actual*) present-day.

modestia [mo'ðestja] *nf* modesty; **modesto, a** *a* modest.

módico, a ['moðiko, a] *a* moderate, reasonable.

modificar [moðifi'kar] *vt* to modify.

modista [mo'ðista] *nm/f* dressmaker.

modo ['moðo] *nm* (*manera, forma*) way, manner; (*MUS*) mode; ~**s** *nmpl* manners; **de ningún** ~ in no way; **de todos** ~**s** at any rate; ~ **de empleo** directions *pl* (for use).

modorra [mo'ðorra] *nf* drowsiness.

modular [moðu'lar] *vt* to modulate.

mofa ['mofa] *nf* mockery, ridicule; **hacer** ~ **de** to mock; **mofar** *vi* to mock, scoff; **mofarse** *vr*: **mofarse de** to mock, scoff at.

mohino, a [mo'ino, a] *a* (*triste*) gloomy, depressed; (*enojado*) sulky.

moho ['moo] *nm* (*BOT*) mould; (*oxidación*) rust; ~**so, a** *a* mouldy; rusty.

mojar [mo'xar] *vt* to wet; (*humedecer*) to damp(en), moisten; (*calar*) to soak // *vi*: ~ **en** to get involved in; ~**se** *vr* to get wet.

mojón [mo'xon] *nm* (*en un camino*) signpost; (*montón*) heap, pile.

molde ['molde] *nm* mould; (*de costura*) pattern; (*fig*) model; **el vestido le está de** ~ the dress is just right for her; ~**ar** *vt* to mould.

mole ['mole] *nf* mass, bulk.

moledora [mole'ðora] *nf* grinder, mill.

moler [mo'ler] *vt* to grind, crush; (*cansar*) to tire out, exhaust; (*irritar*) to annoy.

molestar [moles'tar] *vt* (*gen*) to bother; (*fastidiar*) to annoy; (*incomodar*) to inconvenience, put out // *vi* to be a nuisance; ~**se** *vr* to bother; (*incomodarse*) to go to trouble; (*ofenderse*) to take offence.

molestia [mo'lestja] *nf* (*gen*) bother, trouble; (*incomodidad*) inconvenience; (*MED*) discomfort; **es una** ~ it's a nuisance; **molesto, a** *a* (*que causa molestia*) annoying; (*incómodo*) inconvenient; (*inquieto*) uncomfortable, ill at ease; (*enfadado*) annoyed.

molinillo [moli'niʎo] *nm*: ~ **de café/carne** coffee grinder/mincer.

molino [mo'lino] *nm* (*edificio*) mill; (*máquina*) grinder.

momentáneo, a [momen'taneo, a] *a* momentary.

momento [mo'mento] *nm* (*gen*) moment; (*TEC*) momentum; **de** ~ at the moment, for the moment.

momia ['momja] *nf* mummy.

monarca [mo'narka] *nm/f* monarch, ruler; **monarquía** *nf* monarchy; **monarquista** *nm/f* royalist, monarchist.

monasterio [monas'terjo] *nm* monastery.

mondar [mon'dar] *vt* (*limpiar*) to clean; (*podar*) to prune, trim; (*pelar*) to peel; ~**se** *vr*: ~**se los dientes** to pick one's teeth.

moneda [mo'neða] *nf* (*tipo de dinero*) currency, money; (*pieza*) coin; **una** ~ **de 5p** *a* **5p** piece; **monedero** *nm* purse; **monetario, a** *a* monetary, financial.

monja ['monxa] *nf* nun.

monje ['monxe] *nm* monk.

mono, a ['mono, a] *a* (*bonito*) lovely, pretty; (*gracioso*) nice, charming // *nm/f* monkey, ape // *nm* (*overoles*) overalls *pl*.

monopolio [mono'poljo] *nm* monopoly; **monopolizar** *vt* to monopolize.

monoriel [mono'riel] *nm* monorail.

monotonía [monoto'nia] *nf* (*sonido*) monotone; (*fig*) monotony.

monótono, a [mo'notono, a] *a* monotonous.

monstruo ['monstrwo] *nm* monster // *a* fantastic; ~**so, a** *a* monstrous.

monta ['monta] *nf* total, sum; **de poca** ~ unimportant, of little account.

montaje [mon'taxe] *nm* assembly; (*ARQ*) erection; (*TEATRO*) décor; (*CINE*) montage.

montaña [mon'tapa] *nf* (*monte*) mountain; (*sierra*) mountains *pl*, mountainous area; (*AM*) forest; ~ **rusa** roller coaster; **montañés, esa** *a* mountain *cpd* // *nm/f* highlander; (*de Santander*) native of the Santander region.

montar [mon'tar] *vt* (*subir a*) to mount, get on; (*caballo etc*) to ride; (*TEC*) to assemble, put together; (*ARQ*) to erect; (*negocio*) to set up; (*arma*) to cock; (*colocar*) to lift on to // *vi* to mount, get on; (*sobresalir*) to overlap; ~ **a** to amount to, come to; ~ **en cólera** to get angry.

montaraz [monta'raθ] *a* mountain *cpd*, highland *cpd* (*salvaje*) wild, untamed; (*pey*) uncivilized.

monte ['monte] *nm* (*montaña*) mountain; (*bosque*) woodland; (*área sin cultivar*) wild area, wild country; ~ **de Piedad** pawnshop; ~ **alto** forest; ~ **bajo** scrub(land).

monto ['monto] *nm* total, amount.

montón [mon'ton] *nm* heap, pile; (*fig*): **un** ~ **de** heaps of, lots of.

monumento [monu'mento] *nm* monument.

monzón [mon'θon] *nm* monsoon.

moña ['mopa] *nf* hair ribbon.

moño ['mopo] *nm* bun.

morado, a [mo'raðo, a] a purple; (violado)
violet // nm bruise // nf (casa) dwelling,
abode; (período) stay.
moral [mo'ral] a moral // nf (ética) ethics;
(moralidad) morals pl, morality; (ánimo)
morale.
moraleja [mora'lexa] nf moral.
moralizar [morali'θar] vt to moralize.
morboso, a [mor'βoso, a] a morbid.
morcilla [mor'θiʎa] nf blood sausage,
black pudding.
mordaz [mor'ðaθ] a biting, scathing.
mordaza [mor'ðaθa] nf (para la boca) gag;
(TEC) clamp.
morder [mor'ðer] vt to bite; (mordisquear)
to nibble; (consumir) to eat away, eat into;
mordisco nm bite.
moreno, a [mo'reno, a] a (color) (dark)
brown; (de tez) dark; (de pelo ~) dark-
haired; (negro) Negro.
moretón [more'ton] nm (fam) bruise.
morfina [mor'fina] nf morphine.
moribundo, a [mori'βundo, a] a dying.
morir [mo'rir] vi (gen) to die; (fuego) to
die down; (luz) to go out; ~se vr (gen) to
die; (pierna etc) to go to sleep, go numb;
(fig) to be dying; **fue muerto en un
accidente** he was killed in an accident;
~se por algo to be dying for sth.
morisco, a [mo'risko, a], **moro, a** ['moro,
a] a Moorish // nm/f Moor.
morral [mo'rral] nm haversack.
morsa ['morsa] nf walrus.
mortaja [mor'taxa] nf shroud; (TEC)
mortise; (AM) cigarette paper.
mortal [mor'tal] a mortal; (golpe) deadly;
~ **idad, mortandad** nf mortality.
mortero [mor'tero] nm mortar.
mortífero, a [mor'tifero, a] a deadly,
lethal.
mortificar [mortifi'kar] vt (MED) to
damage, affect seriously; (fig) to mortify;
~se vr to be (very) embarrassed.
mosca ['moska] nf fly.
Moscú [mos'ku] n Moscow.
mosquitero [moski'tero] nm mosquito
net.
mosquito [mos'kito] nm mosquito.
mostaza [mos'taθa] nf mustard.
mostrador [mostra'ðor] nm (de tienda)
counter; (de café) bar; (de reloj) face, dial.
mostrar [mos'trar] vt (gen) to show;
(exhibir) to display, exhibit; (explicar) to
explain; ~se vr: ~se amable to be kind,
to prove to be kind; **no se muestra muy
inteligente** he doesn't seem (to be) very
intelligent.
mostrenco, a [mos'trenko, a] a
ownerless, unclaimed; (perro) stray;
(persona) homeless; (fam) dense, slow.
mota ['mota] nf speck, tiny piece; (en
diseño) dot.
mote ['mote] nm (apodo) nickname;
(sentencia) motto.
motín [mo'tin] nm (del pueblo) revolt,
rising; (del ejército) mutiny.

motivar [moti'βar] vt (causar) to cause,
motivate; (explicar) to explain, justify;
motivo, a a motive // nm motive, reason.
moto ['moto] nf, **motocicleta** [motoθi-
'kleta] nf motorbike.
motoniveladora [motoniβela'ðora] nf
bulldozer.
motor [mo'tor] nm motor, engine; ~ **a
chorro de reacción/de explosión** jet
engine/internal combustion engine.
motora [mo'tora] nf, **motorbote** [motor-
'βote] nm motorboat.
motosierra [moto'sjerra] nf mechanical
saw.
movedizo, a [moβe'ðiθo, a] a easily
moved, movable; (inseguro) unsteady; (fig)
unsettled, changeable; (persona) fickle.
mover [mo'βer] vt (gen) to move; (cabeza)
to shake; (accionar) to drive; (fig) to cause,
provoke; ~se vr to move; (fig) to get a
move on.
móvil ['moβil] a mobile; (pieza de máquina)
moving; (mueble) movable // nm motive;
movilidad nf mobility; **movilizar** vt to
mobilize.
movimiento [moβi'mjento] nm (gen)
movement; (TEC) motion; (actividad)
activity; **el M~** the Falangist Movement.
mozo, a ['moθo, a] a (joven) young;
(soltero) single, unmarried // nm/f (joven)
youth, lad/girl; (criado) servant // nm
(camarero) waiter.
muchacho, a [mu'tʃatʃo, a] nm/f (niño)
boy/girl; (criado) servant/servant or maid.
muchedumbre [mutʃe'ðumbre] nf crowd.
mucho, a ['mutʃo, a] a (sg) a lot of; (gen en
frase negativa o interrogativa) much; (pl)
many, a lot of, lots of // ad (en cantidad) a
lot, a great deal, much; (del tiempo) long;
(muy) very // pron: **tengo ~ que hacer** I
have a lot to do; ~s **dicen que** a lot of
people say that; **ni ~ menos** far from it.
mudanza [mu'ðanθa] nf (cambio) change;
(de casa) move; ~s nfpl (fig) moodiness
sg.
mudar [mu'ðar] vt to change; (ZOOL) to
shed // vi to change; ~se vr (la ropa) to
change; (de casa) to move (house).
mudo, a ['muðo, a] a dumb; (callado, CINE)
silent.
mueble ['mweβle] nm piece of furniture;
~s nmpl furniture sg; ~ría nf furniture
shop.
mueca ['mweka] nf face, grimace; **hacer
~s a** to make faces at.
muela ['mwela] nf (diente) tooth; (: de
atrás) molar.
muelle ['mweʎe] a (blando) soft; (elástico)
springy; (fig) soft, easy // nm spring;
(NAUT) wharf; (malecón) jetty.
muero etc vb ver **morir**.
muerte ['mwerte] nf death; (homicidio)
murder; **dar ~ a** to kill.
muerto, a ['mwerto, a] pp de **morir** // a
dead; (color) dull // nm/f dead
man/woman; (difunto) deceased;

(*cadáver*) corpse; **estar ~ de cansancio** to be dead tired.

muestra ['mwestra] *nf* (*señal*) indication, sign; (*demostración*) demonstration; (*prueba*) proof; (*estadística*) sample; (*modelo*) model, pattern; (*testimonio*) token; **muestreo** *nm* sample, sampling.

muestro *etc vb ver* **mostrar**.

muevo *etc vb ver* **mover**.

mugir [mu'xir] *vi* (*vaca*) to moo; (*persona*) to roar, howl.

mugre ['muxre] *nf* dirt, filth; **mugriento**, a *a* dirty, filthy.

mujer [mu'xer] *nf* (*de sexo femenino*) woman; (*esposa*) wife; **~iego** *nm* womaniser.

mula ['mula] *nf* mule.

muladar [mula'ðar] *nm* dungheap, dunghill.

muleta [mu'leta] *nf* (*para andar*) crutch; (*TAUR*) stick with red cape attached; (*fig*) prop, support.

multa ['multa] *nf* fine; **multar** *vt* to fine.

multicopista [multiko'pista] *nm* duplicator.

múltiple ['multiple] *a* multiple; (*pl*) many, numerous.

multiplicar [multipli'kar] *vt* (*MAT*) to multiply; (*fig*) to increase; **~se** *vr* (*BIO*) to multiply; (*fig*) to attend to a lot of things at one time.

multitud [multi'tuð] *nf* (*gentío, muchedumbre*) crowd; **~ de** lots of.

mullido, a [mu'ʎiðo, a] *a* (*cama*) soft; (*hierba*) soft, springy // *nm* stuffing, filling.

mundano, a [mun'dano, a] *a* worldly; (*de moda*) fashionable.

mundial [mun'djal] *a* world-wide, universal; (*guerra, récord*) world *cpd*.

mundo ['mundo] *nm* world; **todo el ~** everybody; **tener ~** to be experienced, know one's way around.

munición [muni'θjon] *nf* (*MIL*) stores *pl*, supplies *pl*; (*de arma*) ammunition.

municipio [muni'θipjo] *nm* (*municipalidad*) town council, corporation; (*comuna*) town, municipality.

muñeca [mu'ɲeka] *nf* (*ANAT*) wrist; (*juguete*) doll; (*maniquí*) dummy.

muñeco [mu'ɲeko] *nm* (*figura*) figure; (*marioneta*) puppet; (*maniquí*) dummy; (*fig*) puppet, pawn.

muralla [mu'raʎa] *nf* (*city*) wall(s) (*pl*).

murciélago [mur'θjelaxo] *nm* bat.

murmullo [mur'muʎo] *nm* murmur(ing); (*cuchicheo*) whispering; (*de arroyo*) murmur, rippling.

murmuración [murmura'θjon] *nf* gossip; **murmurar** *vi* to murmur, whisper; (*criticar*) to criticize; (*cotillear*) to gossip.

muro ['muro] *nm* wall.

muscular [musku'lar] *a* muscular.

músculo ['muskulo] *nm* muscle.

museo [mu'seo] *nm* museum.

musgo ['musxo] *nm* moss.

músico, a ['musiko, a] *a* musical // *nm/f* musician // *nf* music.

musitar [musi'tar] *vt, vi* to mutter, mumble.

muslo ['muslo] *nm* thigh.

mustio, a ['mustjo, a] *a* (*persona*) depressed, gloomy; (*planta*) faded, withered.

musulmán, ana [musul'man, ana] *nm/f* Moslem.

mutación [muta'θjon] *nf* (*BIO*) mutation; (*cambio*) (sudden) change.

mutilar [muti'lar] *vt* to mutilate; (*a una persona*) to maim.

mutuamente [mutwa'mente] *ad* mutually; **mutuo, a** *a* mutual.

muy [mwi] *ad* very; (*demasiado*) too; **M~ Señor mío** Dear Sir; **~ de noche** very late at night; **eso es ~ de él** that's just like him.

N

N *abr de* **norte**.

n/ *abr de* **nuestro, a**.

nabo ['naβo] *nm* turnip; (*raíz*) root.

nácar ['nakar] *nm* mother-of-pearl.

nacer [na'θer] *vi* to be born; (*de huevo*) to hatch; (*vegetal*) to sprout; (*río*) to rise; **~ al amor** to awaken to love; **nació una sospecha en su mente** a suspicion formed in her mind; **nacido, a** *a* born; **recién nacido** newborn; **naciente** *a* new, emerging; (*sol*) rising; **nacimiento** *nm* birth; (*fig*) birth, origin; (*de Navidad*) Nativity; (*linaje*) descent, family; (*de río*) source.

nación [na'θjon] *nf* nation; **nacional** *a* national; **nacionalismo** *nm* nationalism; **nacionalista** *nm/f* nationalist; **nacionalizar** *vt* to nationalize; **nacionalizarse** *vr* to become naturalized.

nada ['naða] *pron* nothing // *ad* not at all, in no way; **no decir ~** to say nothing, not to say anything; **de ~** don't mention it.

nadaderas [naða'ðeras] *nfpl* waterwings

nadador, a [naða'ðor, a] *nm/f* swimmer.

nadar [na'ðar] *vi* to swim.

nadie ['naðje] *pron* nobody, no-one; **~ habló** nobody spoke; **no había ~** there was nobody there, there wasn't anybody there.

nado ['naðo]: **a ~** *ad*: **pasar a ~** to swim across.

naipe ['naipe] *nm* playing card; **~s** *nmpl* cards.

nalgas ['nalxas] *nfpl* buttocks.

nana ['nana] *nf* (*fam: abuela*) grandma (*fam*), granny (*fam*); (: *canción*) lullaby.

naranja [na'ranxa] *a, nf* orange; **media ~** (*fam*) better half (*fam*); **~do, a** *a* orange // *nf* orangeade; **naranjo** *nm* orange tree.

narciso [nar'θiso] *nm* narcissus.

narcótico, a [nar'kotiko, a] *a, nm* narcotic; **narcotizar** *vt* to drug.

nardo ['narðo] *nm* lily.

narigón, ona [nari'ɣon, ona], **narigudo, a** [nari'ɣuðo, a] a big-nosed.

nariz [na'riθ] *nf* nose; **narices** *nfpl* nostrils; **en las narices de uno** under one's (very) nose.

narración [narra'θjon] *nf* narration; **narrador, a** *nm/f* narrator.

narrar [na'rrar] *vt* to narrate, recount; **narrativa** *nf* narrative, story.

nata ['nata] *nf* cream.

natación [nata'θjon] *nf* swimming.

natal [na'tal] a: **ciudad ~** home town; **~icio** *nm* birthday; **~idad** *nf* birth rate.

natillas [na'tiʎas] *nfpl* custard *sg*.

natividad [natiβi'ðað] *nf* nativity.

nativo, a [na'tiβo, a] a native; (*innato*) innate, natural // *nm/f* native.

nato, a ['nato, a] a born; **un músico ~** a born musician.

natural [natu'ral] a natural; (*fruta etc*) fresh // *nm/f* native // *nm* nature; **~eza** *nf* nature; (*género*) nature, kind; **~eza muerta** still life; **~idad** *nf* naturalness; **~ización** *nf* naturalization; **~izarse** *vr* to become naturalized; (*aclimatarse*) to become acclimatized; **~mente** *ad* naturally.

naufragar [naufra'ɣar] *vi* to sink; **naufragio** *nm* shipwreck; **náufrago, a** *nm/f* castaway, shipwrecked person.

náusea ['nausea] *nf* nausea; **me da ~** it makes me feel sick; **nauseabundo, a** a nauseating, sickening.

náutico, a ['nautiko, a] a nautical.

nava ['naβa] *nf* (GEO) level plain.

navaja [na'βaxa] *nf* (*cortaplumas*) clasp knife, penknife; (*de barbero, peluquero*) razor.

navarro, a [na'βarro, a] a Navarrese.

nave ['naβe] *nf* (*barco*) ship, vessel; (ARQ) nave; **~ espacial** spaceship.

navegación [naβeɣa'θjon] *nf* navigation; (*viaje*) sea journey; **~ aérea** air traffic; **~ costera** coastal shipping; **navegante** *nm/f* navigator; **navegar** *vi* (*barco*) to sail; (*avión*) to fly // *vt* to sail; to fly; (*dirigir el rumbo*) to navigate.

navidad [naβi'ðað] *nf* Christmas; **navideño, a** a Christmas *cpd*.

navío [na'βio] *nm* ship.

nazi ['naθi] a, *nm/f* Nazi.

neblina [ne'βlina] *nf* mist.

nebuloso, a [neβu'loso, a] a foggy; (*calinoso*) misty; (*cielo*) cloudy; (*indefinido*) nebulous, vague // *nf* nebula.

necedad [neθe'ðað] *nf* foolishness; (*una ~*) foolish act.

necesario, a [neθe'sarjo, a] a necessary.

neceser [neθe'ser] *nm* vanity case; (*bolsa*) holdall; **~ de viaje** travelling case.

necesidad [neθesi'ðað] *nf* need; (*lo inevitable*) necessity; (*miseria*) poverty, need; **en caso de ~** in case of need *or* emergency; **hacer sus ~es** to relieve o.s.

necesitado, a [neθesi'taðo, a] a needy, poor; **~ de** in need of.

necesitar [neθesi'tar] *vt* to need, require // *vi*: **~ de** to have need of.

necio, a ['neθjo, a] a foolish.

necrología [nekrolo'xia] *nf* obituary.

necrópolis [ne'kropolis] *nf* cemetery.

nectarina [nekta'rina] *nf* nectarine.

nefando, a [ne'fando, a] a unspeakable.

nefasto, a [ne'fasto, a] a ill-fated, unlucky.

negación [neɣa'θjon] *nf* negation; (*rechazo*) refusal, denial.

negar [ne'ɣar] *vt* (*renegar, rechazar*) to refuse; (*prohibir*) to refuse, deny; (*desmentir*) to deny; **~se** *vr*: **~se a** to refuse to.

negativo, a [neɣa'tiβo, a] a, *nm* negative // *nf* (*gen*) negative; (*rechazo*) refusal, denial.

negligencia [neɣli'xenθja] *nf* negligence; **negligente** a negligent.

negociable [neɣo'θjaβle] a (COM) negotiable.

negociado [neɣo'θjaðo] *nm* department, section.

negociante [neɣo'θjante] *nm/f* businessman/woman; (*comerciante*) merchant.

negociar [neɣo'θjar] *vt, vi* to negotiate; **~ en** to deal in, trade in.

negocio [ne'ɣoθjo] *nm* (COM) business; (*asunto*) affair, business; (*operación comercial*) deal, transaction; (AM) firm; (*lugar*) place of business; **los ~s** business *sg*; **hacer ~** to do business.

negro, a ['neɣro, a] a black; (*suerte*) awful // *nm* black // *nm/f* Negro/Negress, black // *nf* (MUS) crotchet; **negrura** *nf* blackness.

nene, a ['nene, a] *nm/f* baby, small child; (*fam*) dear.

nenúfar [ne'nufar] *nm* water lily.

neologismo [neolo'xismo] *nm* neologism.

neoyorquino, a [neojor'kino, a] a (of) New York.

nepotismo [nepo'tismo] *nm* nepotism.

nervio ['nerβjo] *nm* (ANAT) nerve; (: *tendón*) tendon; (*fig*) vigour; **~sidad** *nf* nervousness, nerves *pl*; **~so, a, nervudo, a** a nervous.

neto, a ['neto, a] a clear; (*verdad etc*) pure; (*limpio*) clean; (COM) net.

neumático, a [neu'matiko, a] a pneumatic // *nm* tyre; **~ de recambio** spare tyre.

neuralgia [neu'ralxja] *nf* neuralgia.

neurastenia [neuras'tenja] *nf* nervous exhaustion.

neuritis [neu'ritis] *nf* neuritis.

neurólogo, a [neu'roloɣo, a] *nm/f* neurologist.

neurosis [neu'rosis] *nf inv* neurosis.

neutral [neu'tral] a neutral; **~izar** *vt* to neutralize; (*contrarrestar*) to counteract.

neutro, a ['neutro, a] a (BIO) neuter, sexless; (LING) neuter.

neutrón [neu'tron] *nm* neutron; **bomba de neutrones** neutron bomb.

nevada [ne'βaða] *nf* snowstorm; (*caída de nieve*) snowfall.

nevar [ne'βar] *vi* to snow; **nevasca** *nf* snowstorm.

nevera [ne'βera] *nf* refrigerator, icebox.

nevisca [ne'βiska] *nf* flurry of snow; (*aguaniere*) sleet; **neviscar** *vi* to snow lightly; to sleet.

ni [ni] *conj* nor, neither; (~ *siquiera*) not ... even; ~ **que** not even if; ~ **blanco** ~ **negro** neither white nor black.

Nicaragua [nika'raʀwa] *nf* Nicaragua; **nicaragüense** *a*, *nm/f* Nicaraguan.

nicotina [niko'tina] *nf* nicotine.

nicho [ˈnitʃo] *nm* niche.

nido [ˈniðo] *nm* nest; (*fig*) hiding place; (*lugar predilecto*) haunt.

niebla [ˈnjeβla] *nf* fog; (*neblina*) mist.

niego *etc vb ver* **negar**.

nieto, a [ˈnjeto, a] *nm/f* grandson/daughter; ~**s** *nmpl* grandchildren.

nieva *etc vb ver* **nevar**.

nieve [ˈnjeβe] *nf* snow.

nigromancia [niʀro'manθja] *nf* necromancy, black magic.

nihilismo [nii'lismo] *nm* nihilism.

Nilo [ˈnilo] *nm*: **el** ~ **the** Nile.

nimbo [ˈnimbo] *nm* (*aureola*) halo; (*nube*) nimbus.

nimiedad [nimje'ðað] *nf* small-mindedness; (*prolijidad*) long-windedness; (*trivialidad*) triviality.

nimio, a [ˈnimjo, a] *a* (*insignificante*) trivial, insignificant; (*escrupuloso*) fussy, overparticular.

ninfa [ˈninfa] *nf* nymph.

ninfómana [nin'fomana] *nf* nymphomaniac.

ninguno, a [nin'guno, a]. **ningún** [nin-'gun] *a* no // *pron* (*nadie*) nobody; (*ni uno*) none, not one; (*ni uno ni otro*) neither; **de** ~**a manera** by no means, not at all.

niña [ˈniɲa] *nf ver* **niño**.

niñera [ni'ɲera] *nf* nursemaid, nanny; **niñería** *nf* childish act.

niñez [ni'ɲeθ] *nf* childhood; (*infancia*) infancy.

niño, a [ˈniɲo, a] *a* (*joven*) young; (*inmaduro*) immature // *nm* (*chico*) boy, child // *nf* (*chica*) girl, child; (*ANAT*) pupil.

nipón, ona [ni'pon, ona] *a, nm/f* Japanese.

níquel [ˈnikel] *nm* nickel; **niquelar** *vt* (*TEC*) to nickel-plate.

nitidez [niti'ðeθ] *nf* (*claridad*) clarity; (: *de atmósfera*) brightness; (: *de imagen*) sharpness; **nítido, a** *a* clear; sharp.

nitrato [ni'trato] *nm* nitrate.

nitrógeno [ni'troxeno] *nm* nitrogen.

nitroglicerina [nitroxliθe'rina] *nf* nitroglycerine.

nivel [ni'βel] *nm* (*GEO*) level; (*norma*) level, standard; (*altura*) height; ~ **de aceite** oil level; ~ **de aire** spirit level; ~ **de vida** standard of living; ~**ar** *vt*

(*terreno*) to level out; (*equilibrar: mueble*) to even up; (*COM*) to balance.

NN. UU. *abr de* **Naciones Unidas** U.N. *sg* (United Nations).

no [no] *ad* no; not; (*con verbo*) not // *excl* no!; ~ **tengo nada** I don't have anything, I have nothing; ~ **es el mío** it's not mine; **ahora** ~ not now; ¿~ **lo sabes?** don't you know?; ~ **mucho** not much; ~ **bien termine, lo entregaré** as soon as I finish I'll hand it over; **¡a que** ~ **lo sabes!** I bet you don't know!; **¡cuándo** o **cómo** ~! of course!; **los países** ~ **alineados** the non-aligned countries; **el** ~ **conformismo** non-conformism; **la** ~ **intervención** non-intervention.

NO *abr de* **noroeste**.

no. *abr de* **número**.

noble [ˈnoβle] *a, nm/f* noble; ~**za** *nf* nobility.

noción [no'θjon] *nf* notion.

nocivo, a [no'θiβo, a] *a* harmful.

noctambulismo [noktam'βu'lismo] *nm* sleepwalking; **noctámbulo, a** *nm/f* sleepwalker.

nocturno, a [nok'turno, a] *a* (*de la noche*) nocturnal, night *cpd*; (*de la tarde*) evening *cpd* // *nm* nocturne.

noche [ˈnotʃe] *nf* night, night-time; (*la tarde*) evening; (*fig*) darkness; **de** ~, **por la** ~ at night.

nochebuena [notʃe'βwena] *nf* Christmas Eve.

nochevieja [notʃe'βjexa] *nf* New Year's Eve.

nodriza [no'ðriθa] *nf* wet nurse.

nogal [no'sal] *nm* walnut tree.

nómada [ˈnomaða] *a* nomadic // *nm/f* nomad.

nombradía [nombra'ðia] *nf* fame.

nombramiento [nombra'mjento] *nm* naming; (*a un empleo*) appointment.

nombrar [nom'brar] *vt* (*designar*) to name; (*mencionar*) to mention; (*dar puesto a*) to appoint.

nombre [ˈnombre] *nm* name; (*sustantivo*) noun; (*fama*) renown; ~ **y apellidos** name in full; ~ **común/propio** common/proper noun; ~ **de pila/de soltera** Christian/maiden name.

nomenclatura [nomenkla'tura] *nf* nomenclature.

nomeolvides [nomeol'βiðes] *nm inv* forget-me-not.

nómina [ˈnomina] *nf* (*lista*) list; (*COM*) payroll.

nominal [nomi'nal] *a* nominal.

nominativo, a [nomina'tiβo, a] *a* (*COM*): **cheque** ~ **a X** cheque made out to X.

non [non] *a* odd, uneven // *nm* odd number.

nonada [ao'naða] *nf* trifle.

nono, a [ˈnono, a] *a* ninth.

nordeste [nor'ðeste] *a* north-east, north-eastern, north-easterly // *am* north-east.

nórdico, a [ˈnorðiko, a] *a* (*del norte*) northern, northerly; (*escandinavo*) Nordic.

noria ['norja] nf (AGR) waterwheel; (de carnaval) big wheel.

normal [nor'mal] a (corriente) normal; (habitual) usual, natural; (gasolina) ~ two-star petrol; ~**idad** nf normality; **restablecer la** ~**idad** to restore order; ~**izar** vt (reglamentar) to normalize; (TEC) to standardize; ~**izarse** vr to return to normal.

normando, a [nor'mando, a] a, nm/f Norman.

noroeste [noro'este] a north-west, north-western, north-westerly // nm north-west.

norte ['norte] a north, northern, northerly // nm north; (fig) guide.

norteamericano, a [norteameri'kano, a] a, nm/f (North) American.

noruego, a [no'rweɣo, a] a, nm/f Norwegian; N~**a** nf Norway.

nos [nos] pron (directo) us; (indirecto) us; to us; for us; from us; (reflexivo) (to) ourselves; (recíproco) (to) each other; ~ **levantamos a las 7** we get up at 7.

nosotros [no'sotros] pron (sujeto) we; (después de prep) us.

nostalgia [nos'talxja] nf nostalgia.

nota ['nota] nf note; (ESCOL) mark.

notabilidad [notaβili'ðað] nf (persona) notable.

notable [no'taβle] a, nm/f notable.

notación [nota'θjon] nf (nota) note; (MAT, MUS) notation.

notar [no'tar] vt (advertir) to notice, note; (anotar, asentar) to note (down); (censurar) to criticize; ~ **se** vr to be obvious.

notarial [nota'rjal] a: **acta** ~ affidavit.

notario [no'tarjo] nm notary.

noticia [no'tiθja] nf (información) piece of news; **las** ~**s** the news sg; **tener** ~**s de alguien** to hear from sb.

noticiar [noti'θjar] vt to notify; ~**io** nm (CINE) newsreel; (TV) news bulletin; **noticioso, a** a well-informed.

notificación [notifika'θjon] nf notification; **notificar** vt to notify, inform.

notoriedad [notorje'ðað] nf fame, renown; **notorio, a** a (público) well-known; (evidente) obvious.

novato, a [no'βato, a] a inexperienced // nm/f beginner.

novecientos [noβe'θjentos] num nine hundred.

novedad [noβe'ðað] nf (calidad de nuevo) newness; (noticia) piece of news; (cambio) change, (new) development.

novedoso, a [noβe'ðoso, a] a novel.

novel [no'βel] a new; (inexperto) inexperienced // nm/f beginner.

novela [no'βela] nf novel.

novelero, a [noβe'lero, a] a highly imaginative; (voluble) fickle; (chismoso) gossipy.

novelesco, a [noβe'lesko, a] a fictional; (romántico) romantic; (fantástico) fantastic.

noveno, a [no'βeno, a] a ninth.

noventa [no'βenta] num ninety.

novia ['noβja] nf ver **novio**.

noviazgo [no'βjaθo] nm engagement.

novicio, a [no'βiθjo, a] nm/f novice.

noviembre [no'βjembre] nm November.

novilla [no'βiʎa] nf heifer; ~**da** nf (TAUR) bullfight with young bulls; **novillero** nm novice bullfighter; **novillo** nm young bull; **hacer novillos** (fam) to play truant.

novio, a ['noβjo, a] nm/f boyfriend/girlfriend; (prometido) fiancé/fiancée; (recién casado) bridegroom/bride **los** ~**s** the newly-weds.

N. S. abr de **Nuestro Señor**.

nubarrón [nuβa'rron] nm storm cloud.

nube ['nuβe] nf cloud.

nublado, a [nu'βlaðo, a] a cloudy // nm storm cloud; **nublar** vt (oscurecer) to darken; (confundir) to cloud; **nublarse** vr to grow dark.

nuca ['nuka] nf nape of the neck.

nuclear [nukle'ar] a nuclear.

núcleo ['nukleo] nm (centro) core; (FÍSICA) nucleus.

nudillo [nu'ðiʎo] nm knuckle.

nudo ['nuðo] nm (gen) knot; (unión) bond; (de problema) crux; (de comunicaciones) centre; ~ **so, a** a knotty.

nuera ['nwera] nf daughter-in-law.

nuestro, a ['nwestro, a] det our // pron ours; ~ **padre** our father; **un amigo** ~ a friend of ours; **es el** ~ it's ours.

nueva ['nweβa] nf ver **nuevo**.

nuevamente [nweβa'mente] ad (otra vez) again; (de nuevo) anew.

nueve ['nweβe] num nine.

nuevo, a ['nweβo, a] a (gen) new // nf piece of news; **de** ~ again; N~**a York** n New York; N~**a Zelandia** nf New Zealand.

nuez [nweθ] (pl **nueces**) nf (fruto) nut; (del nogal) walnut; ~ **de Adán** Adam's apple; ~ **moscada** nutmeg.

nulidad [nuli'ðað] nf (incapacidad) incompetence; (abolición) nullity.

nulo, a ['nulo a] a (inepto, torpe) useless; (inválido) (null and) void; (DEPORTE) drawn, tied.

núm. abr de **número**.

numen ['numen] nm inspiration.

numeración [numera'θjon] nf (cifras) numbers pl; (arábiga, romana etc) numerals pl.

numeral [nume'ral] nm numeral.

numerar [nume'rar] vt to number.

numerario [nume'rarjo] nm hard cash.

numérico, a [nu'meriko, a] a numerical.

número ['numero] nm (gen) number; (tamaño: de zapato) size; (ejemplar: de diario) number, issue; **sin** ~ numberless, unnumbered; ~ **de matrícula/telefónico** registration/telephone number; ~ **atrasado** back number.

numeroso, a [nume'roso, a] a numerous.

nunca ['nunka] ad (jamás) never; ~ **lo pensé** I never thought it; **no vino** ~ he never came; ~ **más** never again.

nuncio ['nunθjo] *nm* (*REL*) nuncio.

nupcias ['nupθjas] *nfpl* wedding *sg*,
nuptials.

nutria ['nutrja] *nf* otter.

nutrición [nutri'θjon] *nf* nutrition.

nutrido, a [nu'triðo, a] *a* (*alimentado*)
nourished; (*fig: grande*) large: (*abundante*)
abundant.

nutrir [nu'trir] *vt* (*alimentar*) to nourish;
(*dar de comer*) to feed; (*alentar*) to
encourage; (*esperanzas*) to cherish;
nutritivo, a *a* nourishing, nutritious.

nylon [ni'lon] *nm* nylon.

Ñ

ñame ['ɲame] *nm* yam.

ñaque ['ɲake] *nm* junk.

ñato, a ['ɲato, a] *a* (*AM*) snub-nosed.

ñoñería [ɲoɲe'ria], **ñoñez** [ɲo'ɲeθ] *nf*
insipidness.

ñoño, a ['ɲoɲo, a] *a* (*AM. tonto*) silly, stupid;
(*soso*) insipid; (*persona*) spineless.

O

o [o] *conj* or.

O *abr de* **oeste.**

o/ *abr de* **orden.**

oasis [o'asis] *nm* oasis.

obcecar [obθe'kar] *vt* to blind.

obedecer [oβeðe'θer] *vt* to obey;
obediencia *nf* obedience; **obediente** *a*
obedient.

obertura [oβer'tura] *nf* overture.

obesidad [oβesi'ðað] *nf* obesity; **obeso, a** *a*
obese.

obispo [o'βispo] *nm* bishop.

objeción [oβxe'θjon] *nf* objection; **objetar**
vt, vi to object.

objetivo, a [oβxe'tiβo, a] *a, nm* objective.

objeto [oβ'xeto] *nm* (*cosa*) object; (*fin*)
aim.

oblicuo, a [o'βlikwo, a] *a* oblique; (*mirada*)
sidelong.

obligación [oβlixa'θjon] *nf* obligation;
(*COM*) bond.

obligar [oβli'xar] *vt* to force; **~se** *vr* to
bind o.s.; **obligatorio, a** *a* compulsory,
obligatory.

oboe [o'βoe] *nm* oboe.

obra ['oβra] *nf* (*gen*) work; (*hechura*) piece
of work; (*ARQ*) construction, building;
(*TEATRO*) play; **~ maestra** masterpiece;
(Ministerio de) O~s Públicas Ministry
of Public Works; **en ~ de** in about; **por
~ de** thanks to (the efforts of); **obrar** *vt*
to work; (*tener efecto*) to have an effect on
// *vi* to act, behave; (*tener efecto*) to have
an effect; **la carta obra en su poder** the
letter is in his/her possession; **obrero, a** *a*
working, labour *cpd*; **clase obrera**
working class // *nm/f* (*gen*) worker; (*sin
oficio*) labourer.

obscenidad [obsθeni'ðað] *nf* obscenity;
obsceno, a *a* obscene.

obscu... = oscu... .

obsequiar [oβse'kjar] *vt* (*ofrecer*) to
present with; (*agasajar*) to make a fuss of,
lavish attention on; **obsequio** *nm* (*regalo*)
gift; (*cortesía*) courtesy, attention;
obsequioso, a *a* attentive.

observación [oβserβa'θjon] *nf*
observation; (*reflexión*) remark.

observancia [oβser'βanθja] *nf*
observance.

observar [oβser'βar] *vt* to observe;
(*anotar*) to notice; **~se** *vr* to keep to,
observe.

obsesión [oβse'sjon] *nf* obsession;
obsesionar *vt* to obsess.

obstaculizar [obstakuli'θar] *vt* (*dificultar*)
to hinder; (*impedir*) to stand in the way of.

obstáculo [oβ'stakulo] *nm* (*gen*) obstacle;
(*impedimento*) hindrance, drawback.

obstante [oβ'stante]: **no ~** *ad*
nevertheless // *prep* in spite of.

obstar [oβ'star] *vi* **~ a** to hinder.

obstetricia [oβste'triθja] *nf* obstetrics *sg*,
obstétrico, a *a* obstetric // *nm/f*
obstetrician.

obstinado, a [oβsti'naðo, a] *a* (*gen*)
obstirate; (*terco*) stubborn.

obstinarse [oβsti'narse] *vr* to be
obstinate; **~ en** to persist in.

obstrucción [oβstruk'θjon] *nf* obstruction;
obstruir *vt* to obstruct.

obtener [oβte'ner] *vt* (*conseguir*) to
obtain; (*ganar*) to gain.

obtuso, a [oβ'tuso, a] *a* (*filo*) blunt; (*MAT,
fig*) obtuse.

obviar [oβ'βjar] *vt* to clear away // *vi* to
stand in the way.

obvio, a ['oββjo, a] *a* obvious.

ocasión [oka'sjon] *nf* (*oportunidad*)
opportunity, chance; (*momento*) occasion,
time; (*causa*) cause; **de ~** secondhand;
ocasionar *vt* to cause.

ocaso [o'kaso] *nm* (*oeste*) west; (*fig*)
decline.

occidente [okθi'ðente] *nm* west.

océano [o'θeano] *nm* ocean; **el ~ Índico**
the Indian Ocean.

O.C.E.D. *nf abr de* **Organización de
Cooperación Económica y Desarrollo**
OECD (Organization for Economic
Cooperation and Development).

ocio ['oθjo] *nm* (*tiempo*) leisure; (*pey*)
idleness; **~s** *nmpl* pastime *sg*; **~sidad** *nf*
idleness; **~so, a** *a* (*inactivo*) idle (*inútil*)
useless.

octanaje [okta'naxe] *nm*: **de alto ~** high
octane; **octano** *nm* octane.

octavilla [okta'βiʎa] *nm* piccolo.

octavo, a [ok'taβo, a] *a* eighth.

octogenario, a [oktoxe'narjo, a] *a*
octogenarian.

octubre [ok'tuβre] *nm* October.

ocular [oku'lar] *a* ocular, eye *cpd*; **testigo
~** eyewitness.

oculista [oku'lista] nm/f oculist.

ocultar [okul'tar] vt (esconder) to hide; (callar) to withhold; **oculto, a** a hidden; (fig) secret.

ocupación [okupa'θjon] nf occupation.

ocupado, a [oku'paðo, a] a (persona) busy; (sitio) occupied; (teléfono) engaged; **ocupar** vt (gen) to occupy; **ocuparse** vr: **ocuparse con** o **de** o **en** (gen) to concern o.s. with; (cuidar) to look after.

ocurrencia [oku'rrenθja] nf (ocasión) occurrence; (agudeza) witticism.

ocurrir [oku'rrir] vi to happen; **~se** vr: **se me ocurre que...** it occurs to me that... .

ochenta [o'tʃenta] num eighty.

ocho ['otʃo] num eight.

odiar [o'ðjar] vt to hate; **odio** nm (gen) hate, hatred; (disgusto) dislike; **odioso, a** a (gen) hateful; (malo) nasty.

O.E.A. nf abr de **Organización de Estados Americanos** O.A.S. (Organization of American States).

oeste [o'este] nm west; **una película del ~** a western.

ofender [ofen'der] vt (agraviar) to offend; (ser ofensivo a) to be offensive to; **~se** vr to take offence; **ofensa** nf offence; **ofensivo, a** a (insultante) insulting; (MIL) offensive // nf offensive.

oferta [o'ferta] nf offer; (propuesta) proposal; **la ~ y la demanda** supply and demand; **artículos en ~** goods on offer.

oficial [ofi'θjal] a official // nm official; (MIL) officer.

oficina [ofi'θina] nf office; **oficinista** nm/f clerk.

oficio [o'fiθjo] nm (profesión) profession; (puesto) post; (REL) service; **ser del ~** to be an old hand; **tener mucho ~** to have a lot of experience; **~ de difuntos** funeral service; **de ~** officially.

oficiosidad [ofiθjosi'ðað] nf helpfulness; (pey) officiousness.

oficioso, a [ofi'θjoso, a] a (diligente) attentive; (pey) officious; (no oficial) unofficial, informal.

ofrecer [ofre'θer] vt (dar) to offer; (proponer) to propose; **~se** vr (persona) to offer o.s., volunteer; (situación) to present itself; **¿qué se le ofrece?, ¿se le ofrece algo?** what can I do for you?, can I get you anything?

ofrecimiento [ofreθi'mjento] nm offer, offering.

ofrendar [ofren'dar] vt to offer, contribute.

oftálmico, a [of'talmiko, a] a ophthalmic.

ofuscación [ofuska'θjon] nf, **ofuscamiento** [ofuska'mjento] nm (fig) bewilderment; **ofuscar** vt (confundir) to bewilder; (enceguecer) to dazzle, blind.

oída [o'iða] nf hearing; **de ~s** by hearsay.

oído [o'iðo] nm ear; (sentido) hearing.

oigo etc vb ver **oír**.

oír [o'ir] vt (gen) to hear; (atender a) to

listen to; **¡oiga!** listen!; **~ misa** to attend mass.

O.I.T. nf abr de **Organización Internacional del Trabajo** I.L.O. (International Labour Organization).

ojal [o'xal] nm buttonhole.

ojalá [oxa'la] excl if only it were so!, some hope(s)! // conj if only...!, would that...!; **~ que venga hoy** I hope he comes today.

ojeada [oxe'aða] nf glance; **ojear** vt (mirar fijo) to stare at; (examinar) to eye; (mirar de reojo) to glance at.

ojera [o'xera] nf: **tener ~s** to have rings or circles under the eyes.

ojeriza [oxe'riθa] nf ill-will.

ojeroso, a [oxe'roso, a] a haggard.

ojete [o'xete] nm eye(let).

ojo ['oxo] nm eye; (de puente) span; (de cerradura) keyhole // excl careful!; **tener ~ para** to have an eye for; **~ de buey** porthole.

ola ['ola] nf wave.

olé [o'le] excl bravo!, olé!

oleada [ole'aða] nf big wave, swell; (fig) surge.

oleaje [ole'axe] nm swell.

óleo ['oleo] nm oil; **oleoducto** nm (oil) pipeline.

oler [o'ler] vt (gen) to smell; (husmear) to pry into; (fig) to sniff out // vi: **~ a** to smell of.

olfatear [olfate'ar] vt to smell; (fig) to sniff out; (husmear) to pry into; **olfato** nm sense of smell.

oliente [o'ljente] a smelling; **bien/mal ~** sweet-/foul-smelling.

oligarquía [oliɣar'kia] nf oligarchy.

olimpíada [olim'piaða] nf: **las O~s** the Olympics.

oliva [o'liβa] nf (aceituna) olive; (árbol) olive tree; **aceite de ~** olive oil; **olivo** nm olive tree.

olmo ['olmo] nm elm (tree).

olor [o'lor] nm smell; **~oso, a** a scented.

olvidadizo, a [olβiða'ðiθo, a] a (desmemoriado) forgetful; (distraído) absent-minded

olvidar [olβi'ðar] vt to forget; (omitir) to omit; **~se** vr to forget o.s.; **se me olvidó** I forgot.

olvido [ol'βiðo] nm oblivion.

olla ['oʎa] nf pan; (comida) stew; **~ a presión** o **autopresión** pressure cooker; **~ podrida** Spanish stew.

ombligo [om'bliɣo] nm navel.

ominoso, a [omi'noso, a] a ominous.

omisión [omi'sjon] nf (abstención) omission; (descuido) neglect.

omiso, a [o'miso, a] a: **hacer caso ~ de** to ignore, pass over.

omitir [omi'tir] vt to omit.

omnipotente [omnipo'tente] a omnipotent.

omnívoro, a [om'niβoro, a] a omnivorous.

omóplato [o'moplato] nm shoulder blade.

O.M.S. nf abr de **Organización Mundial**

de la Salud W.H.O. (World Health Organization).

once ['onθe] *num* eleven; **las ~** *(fam)* elevenses.

onda ['onda] *nf* wave; **~ corta/larga/media** short/long/medium wave; **~s acústicas/ hertzianas** acoustic/Hertzian waves; **ondear** *vt* to wave // *vi* to wave; *(tener ondas)* to be wavy; *(pelo)* to flow; *(agua)* to ripple; **ondearse** *vr* to swing, sway.

ondulación [ondula'θjon] *nf* undulation; **ondulado, a** *a* wavy // *nm* wave; **ondulante** *a* undulating; *(cartón, chapa)* corrugated.

ondular [ondu'lar] *vt* (el pelo) to wave // *vi*, **~ se** *vr* to undulate.

oneroso, a [one'roso, a] *a* onerous.

ONU *nf abr de* **Organización de las Naciones Unidas** UNO (United Nations Organization).

O.P. *nfpl abr de* **Obras Públicas** Public Works.

opaco, a [o'pako, a] *a* opaque; *(fig)* dull.

opalescente [opales'θente] *a* opalescent.

ópalo ['opalo] *nm* opal.

opción [op'θjon] *nf* (gen) option; *(derecho* right, option.

ópera ['opera] *nf* opera; **~ bufa o cómica** comic opera.

operación [opera'θjon] *nf* (gen) operation; *(COM)* transaction, deal.

operador, a [opera'ðor, a] *nm/f* operator; *(en cine)* projectionist; *(de cine)* camera operator.

operante [ope'rante] *a* operating.

operar [ope'rar] *vt (producir)* to produce, bring about; *(MED)* to operate on // *vi (COM)* to operate, deal; **~se** *vr* to occur; *(MED)* to have an operation.

opereta [ope'reta] *nf* operetta.

opinar [opi'nar] *vt (estimar)* to think // *vi (enjuiciar)* to give one's opinion; **opinión** *nf (creencia)* belief; *(criterio)* opinion.

opio ['opjo] *nm* opium.

oponente [opo'nente] *nm/f* opponent.

oponer [opo'ner] *vt (resistencia)* to put up, offer; *(negativa)* to raise; **~se** *vr (objetar)* to object; *(estar frente a frente)* to be opposed; *(dos personas)* to oppose each other; **~ A a B** to set A against B; **me opongo a pensar que...** I refuse to believe or think that... .

oportunidad [oportuni'ðað] *nf (ocasión)* opportunity; *(posibilidad)* chance.

oportunismo [oportu'nismo] *nm* opportunism; **oportunista** *nm/f* opportunist.

oportuno, a [opor'tuno, a] *a (apto)* appropriate, suitable; *(en su tiempo)* opportune; *(conveniente)* convenient; **en el momento ~** at the right moment.

oposición [oposi'θjon] *nf* opposition; **oposiciones** *nfpl* public examinations.

opositor, a [oposi'tor, a] *nm/f (adversario)* opponent; *(concurrente)* competitor.

opresión [opre'sjon] *nf* oppression;

opresivo, a *a* oppressive; **opresor, a** *nm/f* oppressor.

oprimir [opri'mir] *vt* to squeeze; *(fig)* to oppress.

oprobio [o'proßjo] *nm (infamia)* ignominy; *(descrédito)* shame.

optar [op'tar] *vi (elegir)* to choose; **~ a** *o* **por** to opt for.

óptico, a ['optika, a] *a* optic(al) // *nm/f* optician.

optimismo [opti'mismo] *nm* optimism; **optimista** *nm/f* optimist.

óptimo, a ['optimo, a] *a (bueno)* very good; *(el mejor)* very best.

opuesto, a [o'pwesto, a] *a (contrario)* opposite; *(antagónico)* opposing.

opugnar [opuŋ'nar] *vt* to attack.

opulencia [opu'lenθja] *nf* opulence; **opulento, a** *a* opulent.

oquedad [oke'ðað] *nf (fig)* void.

ora ['ora] *ad*: **~ tú ~ yo** now you, now me.

oración [ora'θjon] *nf (discurso)* speech; *(REL)* prayer; *(LING)* sentence.

oráculo [o'rakulo] *nm* oracle.

orador, a [ora'ðor, a] *nm/f (predicador)* preacher; *(conferenciante)* speaker.

oral [o'ral] *a* oral.

orangután [oraŋgu'tan] *nm* orang-utan.

orar [o'rar] *vi (REL)* to pray; *(hablar)* to make a speech.

oratoria [ora'torja] *nf* oratory.

órbita ['orßita] *nf* orbit.

orden ['orðen] *nm (gen)* order // *nf (gen)* order; **~ del día** agenda; **de primer ~** first-rate; **en ~ de prioridad** in order of priority.

ordenado, a [orðe'naðo, a] *a (metódico)* methodical; *(arreglado)* orderly.

ordenador [orðena'ðor] *nm* computer.

ordenanza [orðe'nanθa] *nf* ordinance.

ordenar [orðe'nar] *vt (mandar)* to order; *(poner orden)* to put in order, arrange; **~se** *vr (REL)* to be ordained.

ordeñadora [orðeɲa'ðora] *nf* milking machine.

ordeñar [orðe'ɲar] *vt* to milk.

ordinario, a [orði'narjo, a] *a (común)* ordinary, usual; *(bajo)* vulgar, common.

orégano [o're ̇xano] *nm* oregano.

oreja [o'rexa] *nf* ear; *(de zapatos)* tongue; *(MECÁNICA)* lug, flange.

orfandad [orfan'dað] *nf* orphanhood.

orfebrería [orfeßre'ria] *nf* gold/silver work.

organillo [orɣa'niʎo] *nm* barrel organ.

organismo [orɣa'nismo] *nm (BIO)* organism; *(POL)* organization.

organista [orɣa'nista] *nm/f* organist.

organización [orɣaniθa'θjon] *nf* organization; **organizar** *vt* to organize.

órgano ['orɣano] *nm* organ.

orgasmo [or'ɣasmo] *nm* orgasm.

orgía [or'xia] *nf* orgy.

orgullo [or'ɣuʎo] *nm (altanería)* pride; *(autorespeto)* self-respect; **orgulloso, a** *a*

(gen) proud; (altanero) haughty.
orientación [orjenta'θjon] nf (posición)
position; (dirección) direction; (entrenamiento) training.
orientar [orjen'tar] vt (situar) to
orientate; (señalar) to point; (dirigir) to
direct; (informar) to guide; ~se vr to get
one's bearings; (decidirse) to decide on a
course of action.
oriente [o'rjente] nm east; Cer-
cano/Medio/Lejano O~ Near/
Middle/Far East.
origen [o'rixen] nm (germen) origin;
(nacimiento) lineage, birth.
original [orixi'nal] a (nuevo) original;
(extraño) odd, strange; ~idad nf
originality.
originar [orixi'nar] vt to originate; ~se
vr to originate; ~io, a a (nativo) native;
(primordial) original.
orilla [o'riʎa] nf (borde) border; (de río)
bank; (de bosque, tela) edge; (de taza etc)
rim, lip; (de calle) pavement; **orillar** vt
(bordear) to skirt, go round; (resolver) to
wind up; (tocar: asunto) to touch briefly on.
orín [o'rin] nm rust.
orina [o'rina] nf urine; **orinal** nm
(chamber) pot; **orinar** vi to urinate;
orinarse vr to wet o.s.; **orines** nmpl urine
sg.
oriundo, a [o'rjundo, a] a: ~ de native of.
orlar [or'lar] vt (adornar) to adorn,
decorate; (encuadrar) to frame.
ornamentar [ornamen'tar] vt (adornar,
ataviar) to adorn; (revestir) to bedeck.
ornamento [orna'mento] nm ornament.
ornar [or'nar] vt to adorn.
oro ['oro] nm gold; ~s nmpl (NAIPES)
hearts.
oropel [oro'pel] nm tinsel.
orozuz [oro'θuθ] nm liquorice.
orquesta [or'kesta] nf orchestra; ~ de
cámara/sinfónica chamber/symphony
orchestra.
orquídea [or'kiðea] nf orchid.
ortiga [or'tiɣa] nf nettle.
ortodoxo, a [orto'ðokso, a] a orthodox.
ortografía [ortoɣra'fia] nf spelling.
ortopedia [orto'peðja] nf orthopaedics sg.
oruga [o'ruɣa] nf caterpillar; (BOT) rocket.
orzuelo [or'θwelo] nm (MED) stye.
os [os] pron (gen) you; (a vosotros) to you.
osa ['osa] nf (she-)bear; O~
Mayor/Menor Great/Little Bear.
osadía [osa'ðia] nf daring.
osar [o'sar] vi to dare.
oscilación [osθila'θjon] nf (movimiento)
oscillation; (fluctuación) fluctuation;
(vacilación) hesitation; (columpio)
swinging, movement to and fro; **oscilar** vi
to oscillate; to fluctuate; to hesitate.
ósculo ['oskulo] nm kiss.
oscurecer [oskure'θer] vt to darken // vi
to grow dark; ~se vr to grow or get dark.
oscuridad [oskuri'ðað] nf obscurity;
(tinieblas) darkness.

oscuro, a [os'kuro, a] a dark; (fig)
obscure; a ~as in the dark.
óseo, a ['oseo, a] a bony.
oso ['oso] nm bear; ~ de peluche teddy
bear; ~ hormiguero anteater.
ostensible [osten'siβle] a obvious.
ostentación [ostenta'θjon] nf (gen)
ostentation; (acto) display; **ostentar** vt
(gen) to show; (pey) to flaunt, show off;
(poseer) to have, possess; **ostentoso, a** a
ostentatious, showy.
osteópata [oste'opata] nm/f osteopath.
ostra ['ostra] nf oyster.
ostracismo [ostra'θismo] nm ostracism.
osuno, a [o'suno, a] a bear-like.
OTAN ['otan] nf abr de **Organización del
Tratado del Atlántico Norte** NATO
(North Atlantic Treaty Organization).
otear [ote'ar] vt to observe; (fig) to look
into.
otitis [o'titis] nf earache.
otoñal [oto'ɲal] a autumnal.
otoño [o'toɲo] nm autumn.
otorgamiento [otorɣa'mjento] nm
conferring, granting; (JUR) execution.
otorgar [otor'ɣar] vt (conceder) to
concede; (dar) to grant.
otro, a ['otro, a] a (sg) another; (pl) other
// pron another one; ~s others; ~a cosa
something else; ~a manera
otherwise; en ~ tiempo formerly, once;
ni uno ni ~ neither one nor the other; ~
tanto the same again.
ovación [oβa'θjon] nf ovation.
oval [o'βal], **ovalado, a** [oβa'laðo, a] a
oval; **óvalo** nm oval.
oveja [o'βexa] nf sheep; **ovejuno, a** a
sheep cpd.
overol [oβe'rol] nm overalls pl.
ovillar [oβi'ʎar] vt to wind (into a ball);
~se vr to curl up into a ball.
OVNI ['oβni] nm abr de **objeto volante no
identificado** UFO (unidentified flying
object).
ovulación [oβula'θjon] nf ovulation; **óvulo**
nm ovum.
oxidación [oksiða'θjon] nf rusting; **oxidar**
vt to rust; **oxidarse** vr to become rusty.
óxido ['oksiðo] nm oxide.
oxigenado, a [oksixe'naðo, a] a (QUÍMICA)
oxygenated; (pelo) bleached // nm
peroxide.
oxígeno [ok'sixeno] nm oxygen.
oyente [o'jente] nm/f listener, hearer.
oyes, oyó etc vb ver **oír**.

P

P abr de **padre**.
pabellón [paβe'ʎon] nm bell tent; (ARQ)
pavilion; (de hospital etc) block, section;
(bandera) flag.
pábilo ['paβilo] nm wick.
pacer [pa'θer] vi to graze // vt to graze on.
paciencia [pa'θjenθja] nf patience.
paciente [pa'θjente] a, nm/f patient.

pacificación [paθifika'θjon] nf pacification; **pacificar** vt to pacify; (tranquilizar) to calm.

pacífico, a [pa'θifiko, a] a (persona) peace-loving; (existencia) pacific; **el (océano) P~** the Pacific (Ocean).

pacifismo [paθi'fismo] nm pacifism; **pacifista** nm/f pacifist.

pactar [pak'tar] vt to agree to, agree on // vi to come to an agreement.

pacto ['pakto] nm (tratado) pact; (acuerdo) agreement.

padecer [paðe'θer] vt (sufrir) to suffer; (soportar) to endure, put up with; (ser víctima de) to be a victim of; **padecimiento** nm suffering.

padrastro [pa'ðrastro] nm stepfather.

padre ['paðre] nm father // a (fam): un **éxito ~** a tremendous success; **~s** ampl parents.

padrino [pa'ðrino] nm (REL) godfather; (fig) sponsor, patron; **~s** nmpl godparents; **~ de boda** best man.

padrón [pa'ðron] nm (censo) census, roll; (de socios) register; (TEC) pattern.

paella [pa'eʎa] nf paella, dish of rice with meat, shellfish etc.

paga ['paxa] nf (dinero pagado) payment; (sueldo) pay, wages pl.

pagadero, a [paxa'ðero, a] a payable; **~ a la entrega/a plazos** payable on delivery/in instalments.

pagador, a [paxa'ðor, a] nm/f (quien paga) payer; (cajero) cashier.

pagano, a [pa'xano, a] a, nm/f pagan, heathen.

pagar [pa'xar] vt (gen) to pay; (las compras, crimen) to pay for; (fig: favor) to repay // vi to pay; **~ al contado/a plazos** to pay (in) cash/in instalments; **~se** vr: **~se con algo** to be content with sth; **~se de sí mismo** to be conceited.

pagaré [paxa're] nm I.O.U.

página ['paxina] nf page.

pago ['paxo] nm (dinero) payment; (fig) return; (barrio) district; (AM) home region, home area; **estar ~** to be even or quits; **~ anticipado/a cuenta/a la entrega/en especie** advance payment/payment on account/cash on delivery/payment in kind.

país [pa'is] nm (gen) country; (región) land; (paisaje) landscape; **los P~es Bajos** the Low Countries; **el P~ Vasco** the Basque Country; **paisaje** nm countryside, scenery.

paisano, a [pai'sano, a] a of the same country // nm/f (compatriota) fellow countryman/woman; (campesino) peasant; **vestir de ~** (soldado) to be in civvies (fam); (guardia) to be in plain clothes.

paja ['paxa] nf straw; (fig) trash, rubbish.

pájara ['paxara] nf hen bird; (cometa) kite; (mujer) thief.

pájaro ['paxaro] nm bird.

pajita [pa'xita] nf (drinking) straw.

pala ['pala] nf (de mango largo) spade; (de mango corto) shovel; (raqueta etc) bat; (: de tenis) racquet; (CULIN) slice; **~ matamoscas** fly swat.

palabra [pa'laβra] nf (gen) word; (facultad) (power of) speech; (derecho de hablar) right to speak; **palabrota** nf swearword.

palacio [pa'laθjo] nm palace; (mansión) mansion, large house; **~ de justicia** courthouse; **~ municipal** town/city hall.

paladar [pala'ðar] nm (gen) palate; **paladear** vt to taste.

palanca [pa'lanka] nf lever; (fig) pull, influence.

palangana [palan'gana] nf washbasin.

palco ['palko] nm box.

palenque [pa'lenke] nm (cerca) stockade, fence; (área) arena, enclosure; (de gallos) pit.

Palestina [pales'tina] nf Palestine.

paliar [pa'ljar] vt (mitigar) to mitigate; (disfrazar) to conceal; **paliativo** nm palliative.

palidecer [paliðe'θer] vi to turn pale; **palidez** nf paleness; **pálido, a** a pale.

palillo [pa'liʎo] nm small stick; (para dientes) toothpick.

paliza [pa'liθa] nf beating, thrashing.

palizada [pali'θaða] nf fence; (lugar cercado) enclosure.

palma ['palma] nf (ANAT) palm; (árbol) palm tree; **batir o dar ~s** to clap, applaud; **~da** nf slap; **~s** nfpl clapping sg, applause sg.

palmear [palme'ar] vt to clap.

palmo ['palmo] nm (medida) span; (fig) small amount; **~ a ~** inch by inch.

palmotear [palmote'ar] vi to clap, applaud; **palmoteo** nm clapping, applause; (palmada) slap.

palo ['palo] nm stick; (poste) post, pole; (mango) handle, shaft (golpe) blow, hit; (de golf) club; (de béisbol) bat; (NAUT) mast; (NAIPES) suit; **~ de tienda** tent pole.

paloma [pa'loma] nf dove, pigeon.

palomilla [palo'miʎa] nf moth; (TEC: tuerca) wing nut; (: hierro) angle iron.

palomitas [palo'mitas] nfpl popcorn sg.

palpar [pal'par] vt to touch, feel; (acariciar) to caress, fondle; (caminar a tientas) to grope one's way along; (fig) to appreciate, understand; **~ a uno** to frisk sb.

palpitación [palpita'θjon] nf palpitation; **palpitante** a palpitating; (fig) burning; **palpitar** vi to palpitate; (latir) to beat.

palúdico, a [pa'luðiko, a] a marshy.

paludismo [palu'ðismo] nm malaria.

pampa ['pampa] nf (AM) pampa(s), prairie.

pan [pan] nm (en general) bread; (una barra) loaf; (trigo) wheat; **de ~ llevar** arable; **~ integral** wholemeal bread; **~ molido** breadcrumbs pl.

pana ['pana] nf corduroy.

panadería [panaðe'ria] nf baker's (shop); **panadero, a** nm/f baker.

Panamá [pana'ma] *nm* Panama; **panameño, a** *a* Panamanian.
pancarta [pan'karta] *nf* placard, banner.
panda ['panda] *nf* panda.
pandereta [pande'reta] *nf* tambourine.
pandilla [pan'diʎa] *nf* set, group; *(de criminales)* gang; *(pey)* clique.
pando, a ['pando, a] *a* sagging.
panel [pa'nel] *nm* panel.
pánico ['paniko] *nm* panic.
panorama [pano'rama] *nm* panorama; *(vista)* view.
pantalones [panta'lones] *nmpl* trousers.
pantalla [pan'taʎa] *nf* *(de cine)* screen; *(cubre-luz)* lampshade.
pantano [pan'tano] *nm* *(ciénaga)* marsh, swamp; *(depósito: de agua)* reservoir; *(fig)* jam, fix, difficulty.
pantera [pan'tera] *nf* panther.
pantimedias [panti'meðjas] *nfpl* tights.
pantomima [panto'mima] *nf* pantomime.
pantorrilla [panto'rriʎa] *nf* calf (of the leg).
pantufla [pan'tufla] *nf* slipper.
panza ['panθa] *nf* belly, paunch; **panzudo, a, panzón, ona** *a* fat, potbellied.
pañal [pa'nal] *nm* nappy; **~es** *nmpl* *(fig)* early stages, infancy *sg*.
pañería [paɲe'ria] *nf* drapery; **pañero, a** *nm/f* draper.
paño ['paɲo] *nm* *(tela)* cloth; *(pedazo de tela)* (piece of) cloth; *(trapo)* duster, rag; **~ higiénico** sanitary towel; **~s menores** underclothes.
pañuelo [pa'ɲwelo] *nm* handkerchief, hanky *(fam)*; *(para la cabeza)* (head)scarf.
papa ['papa] *nf* *(AM)* potato // *nm*: **el P~** the Pope.
papá [pa'pa] *(pl* **~s)** *nm* *(fam)* dad, daddy.
papagayo [papa'xajo] *nm* parrot.
papamoscas [papa'moskas] *nm inv* fly-catcher.
papanatas [papa'natas] *nm inv* *(fam)* sucker, simpleton.
papar [pa'par] *vt* to swallow, gulp (down).
paparrucha [papa'rrutʃa] *nf* *(tontería)* piece of nonsense; *(engaño)* hoax.
papaya [pa'paja] *nf* papaya.
papel [pa'pel] *nm* *(en general)* paper; *(hoja de papel)* sheet of paper; *(TEATRO)* part, role; **~ de calcar/carbón/de cartas** tracing paper/carbon paper/stationery; **~ de envolver/de empapelar** brown paper, wrapping paper/wallpaper; **~ de estaño/higiénico** tinfoil/toilet paper; **~ de lija** sandpaper; **~ moneda** paper money; **~ secante** blotting paper.
papeleo [pape'leo] *nm* red tape.
papelera [pape'lera] *nf* *(cesto)* wastepaper basket; *(escritorio)* desk.
papelería [papele'ria] *nf* *(papeles)* mass of papers; *(tienda)* stationer's (shop).
papeleta [pape'leta] *nf* *(pedazo de papel)* slip *or* bit of paper; *(tarjeta de archivo)* index card; *(POL)* ballot paper; *(ESCOL)* report.

paperas [pa'peras] *nfpl* mumps.
paquete [pa'kete] *nm* *(caja)* packet; *(bulto)* parcel; *(AM, fam)* nuisance, bore.
par [par] *a* *(igual)* like, equal; *(MAT)* even // *nm* equal; *(de guantes)* pair; *(de veces)* couple; *(dignidad)* peer; *(GOLF, COM)* par; **abrir de ~ en ~** to open wide.
para ['para] *prep* *(gen)* for; **no es ~ comer** it's not for eating; **decir ~ sí** to say to o.s.; **¿~ qué lo quieres?** what do you want it for?; **se casaron ~ separarse otra vez** they married only to separate again; **lo tendré ~ mañana** I'll have it for tomorrow; **ir ~ casa** to go home, head for home; **~ profesor es muy estúpido** he's very stupid for a teacher; **¿quién es usted ~ gritar así?** who are you to shout like that?; **tengo bastante ~ vivir** I have enough to live on; **estoy ~ cantar** I'm about to sing.
parabién [para'βjen] *nm* congratulations *pl*.
parábola [pa'raβola] *nf* parable; *(MAT)* parabola.
parabrisas [para'βrisas] *nm inv* windscreen.
paracaídas [paraka'iðas] *nm inv* parachute; **paracaidista** *nm/f* parachutist; *(MIL)* paratrooper.
parachoques [para'tʃokes] *nm inv* bumper; *(en auto)* shock absorber.
parada [pa'raða] *nf* ver **parado**.
paradero [para'ðero] *nm* stopping-place; *(situación)* whereabouts; *(fin)* end.
parado, a [pa'raðo, a] *a* *(persona)* motionless, standing still; *(fábrica)* closed, at a standstill; *(coche)* stopped; *(AM)* standing (up); *(sin empleo)* unemployed, idle; *(confuso)* confused // *nf* *(gen)* stop; *(acto)* stopping; *(de industria)* shutdown, stoppage; *(de pagos)* suspension; *(lugar)* stopping-place; *(apuesta)* bet; **~a de autobús** bus stop.
paradoja [para'ðoxa] *nf* paradox.
parador [para'ðor] *nm* (luxury) hotel.
paráfrasis [pa'rafrasis] *nm inv* paraphrase.
paragolpes [para'xolpes] *nm inv* bumper.
paraguas [pa'raɣwas] *nm inv* umbrella.
Paraguay [para'xwai] *nm*: **el ~** Paraguay.
paraíso [para'iso] *nm* paradise, heaven.
paraje [pa'raxe] *nm* place, spot.
paralelo, a [para'lelo, a] *a* parallel.
parálisis [pa'ralisis] *nf* paralysis; **paralítico, a** *a, nm/f* paralytic; **paralizar** *vt* to paralyse; **paralizarse** *vr* to become paralysed; *(fig)* to come to a standstill.
paramilitar [paramili'tar] *a* para-military.
páramo ['paramo] *nm* bleak plateau.
parangón [paran'gon] *nm*: **sin ~** incomparable.
paranoico, a [para'noiko, a] *nm/f* paranoiac.
parapléjico, a [para'plexiko, a] *a, nm/f* paraplegic.

parar [pa'rar] vt to stop; (golpe) to ward off // vi to stop; ~se vr to stop (AM) to stand up; **ha parado de llover** it has stopped raining; **van a ~ en la comisaría** they're going to end up in the police station; ~**se en** to pay attention to.

parásito, a [pa'rasito, a] nm/f parasite.

parasol [para'sol] nm parasol, sunshade.

parcela [par'θela] nf plot, piece of ground.

parcial [par'θjal] a (pago) part-; (eclipse) partial; (juez) prejudiced, biased; ~**idad** nf (prejuicio) prejudice, bias; (partido, facción) party, faction.

parco, a ['parko, a] a (frugal) frugal; (mezquino) mean; (moderado) moderate.

parche ['partʃe] nm (MED) sticking plaster; (gen) patch.

parear [pare'ar] vt (juntar, hacer par) to match, put together; (calcetines) to put into pairs; (BIO) to mate, pair.

parecer [pare'θer] nm (opinión) opinion, view; (aspecto) looks pl // vi (tener apariencia) to seem, look; (asemejarse) to look like, seem like; (aparecer, llegar) to appear; ~**se** vr to look alike, resemble each other; ~**se a** to look like, resemble; **según** o **a lo que parece** evidently, apparently; **me parece que** I think (that), it seems to me that; **parecido, a** a similar // nm similarity, likeness, resemblance; **bien parecido** good-looking, nice-looking.

pared [pa'reð] nf wall.

parejo, a [pa'rexo, a] a (igual) equal; (liso) smooth, even // nf (dos) pair; (: de personas) couple; (el otro: de un par) other one (of a pair); (: persona) partner.

parentela [paren'tela] nf relations pl.

parentesco [paren'tesko] nm relationship.

paréntesis [pa'rentesis] nm inv parenthesis; (digresión) digression; (en escrito) bracket.

parezco etc vb ver **parecer.**

pariente, a [pa'rjente, a] nm/f relative, relation.

parihuela [pari'wela] nf stretcher.

parir [pa'rir] vt to give birth to // vi (mujer) to give birth, have a baby.

París [pa'ris] n Paris.

parlamentar [parlamen'tar] vi (hablar) to talk, converse; (negociar) to parley.

parlamentario, a [parlamen'tarjo, a] a parliamentary // nm/f member of parliament.

parlamento [parla'mento] nm (POL) parliament; (conversación) parley.

parlanchín, ina [parlan'tʃin, ina] a loose-tongued, indiscreet // nm/f chatterbox.

parlar [par'lar] vi to chatter (away), talk (a lot); (chismear) to gossip; **parlero, a** a talkative; gossipy; (pájaro) singing.

paro ['paro] nm (huelga) stoppage (of work), strike; (desempleo) unemployment; **subsidio de** ~ unemployment benefit; **hay** ~ **en la industria** work in the industry is at a standstill.

parodia [pa'roðja] nf parody; **parodiar** vt to parody.

parpadear [parpaðe'ar] vi (los ojos) to blink; (luz) to flicker.

párpado ['parpaðo] nm eyelid.

parque ['parke] nm (lugar verde) park; (depósito) depot; ~ **de atracciones/de estacionamiento/zoológico** fairground/car park/zoo.

parquímetro [par'kimetro] nm parking meter.

párrafo ['parrafo] nm paragraph; **echar un** ~ (fam) to have a chat.

parranda [pa'rranda] nf (fam) spree, binge.

parrilla [pa'rriʎa] nf (CULIN) grill; (de coche) grille; (carne de) ~ barbecue; ~**da** nf barbecue.

párroco ['parroko] nm parish priest.

parroquia [pa'rrokja] nf parish; (iglesia) parish church; (COM) clientele, customers pl; ~**no, a** nm/f parishioner; client, customer.

parte ['parte] nm message; (informe) report // nf (gen) part; (lado, cara) side; (de reparto) share; (POL) party; **en alguna** ~ **de Europa** somewhere in Europe; **en cualquier** ~ anywhere; **en gran** ~ to a large extent; **la mayor** ~ **de los españoles** most Spaniards; **de algún tiempo a esta** ~ for some time past; **de** ~ **de alguien** on sb's behalf; **por** ~ **de** on the part of; **yo por mi** ~ I for my part; **por otra** ~ on the other hand; **dar** ~ to inform; **tomar** ~ to take part.

partera [par'tera] nf midwife.

partición [parti'θjon] nf division, sharing-out; (POL) partition.

participación [partiθipa'θjon] nf (acto) participation, taking part (parte, COM) share; (de lotería) small prize; (aviso) notice, notification.

participante [partiθi'pante] nm/f participant; **participar** vt to notify, inform // vi to take part, participate; (compartir) to share.

partícipe [par'tiθipe] nm/f participant.

particular [partiku'lar] a (especial) particular, special; (individual, personal) private, personal // nm (punto, asunto) particular point; (individuo) individual; **tiene coche** ~ he has a car of his own; ~**izar** vt to distinguish; (especificar) to specify; (detallar) to give details about.

partida [par'tiða] nf (salida) departure; (COM) entry item; (juego) game; (apuesta) bet; (grupo, bando) band, group; **mala** ~ dirty trick; ~ **de nacimiento/matrimonio/defunción** birth/marriage/death certificate.

partidario, a [parti'ðarjo, a] a partisan // nm/f (DEPORTE) supporter; (POL) partisan.

partido [par'tiðo] nm (POL) party; (encuentro) game, match; (apoyo) support; (equipo) team; **sacar** ~ **de** to profit from, benefit from; **tomar** ~ to take sides.

partir [par'tir] vt (dividir) to split, divide;

(*compartir, distribuir*) to share (out), distribute; (*romper*) to break open, split open; (*rebanada*) to cut (off) // vi (*tomar camino*) to set off, set out; (*comenzar*) to start (off or out); ~**se** vr to crack or split or break (in two *etc*); **a** ~ **de** (starting) from.

parto ['parto] nm birth; (*fig*) product, creation; **estar de** ~ to be in labour.

parvulario [parβu'larjo] nm nursery school, kindergarten.

pasa ['pasa] nf raisin; ~ **de Corinto/de Esmirna** currant/sultana.

pasada [pa'saða] nf ver **pasado**.

pasadizo [pasa'ðiθo] nm (*pasillo*) passage, corridor; (*callejuela*) alley.

pasado, a [pa'saðo, a] a past; (*malo: comida, fruta*) bad; (*muy cocido*) overdone; (*anticuado*) out of date // nm past // nf passing, passage; (*acción de pulir*) rub, polish; ~**s** nmpl ancestors; ~ **mañana** the day after tomorrow; **el mes** ~ last month; **de** ~**a** in passing, incidentally; **una mala** ~**a** a dirty trick.

pasador [pasa'ðor] nm (*gen*) bolt; (*de pelo*) pin, grip; ~**es** nmpl cufflinks.

pasaje [pa'saxe] nm (*gen*) passage; (*pago de viaje*) fare; (*los pasajeros*) passengers pl; (*pasillo*) passageway.

pasajero, a [pasa'xero, a] a passing; (*calle*) busy // nm/f passenger; (*viajero*) traveller.

pasamanos [pasa'manos] nm rail, handrail; (*de escalera*) banister.

pasaporte [pasa'porte] nm passport.

pasar [pa'sar] vt (*gen*) to pass; (*tiempo*) to spend; (*durezas*) to suffer, endure; (*noticia*) to give, pass on; (*río*) to cross; (*barrera*) to pass through; (*falta*) to overlook, tolerate; (*contrincante*) to surpass, do better than; (*coche*) to overtake; (*enfermedad*) to give, infect with // vi (*gen*) to pass; (*terminarse*) to be over; (*ocurrir*) to happen; ~**se** vr (*flores*) to fade; (*comida*) to go bad, go off; (*fig*) to overdo it, go too far; ~ **de** to go beyond, exceed; ¡**pase!** come in!; ~**se al enemigo** to go over to the enemy; **se me pasó** I forgot; **no se le pasa nada** nothing escapes him, he misses nothing; **pase lo que pase** come what may.

pasarela [pasa'rela] nf footbridge; (*en barco*) gangway.

pasatiempo [pasa'tjempo] nm pastime; (*distracción*) amusement.

Pascua ['paskwa] nf: ~ (**de Resurrección**) Easter; ~ **de Navidad** Christmas; ~**s** nfpl Christmas time; ¡**felices** ~**s!** Merry Christmas.

pase ['pase] nm pass.

pasear [pase'ar] vt to take for a walk; (*exhibir*) to parade, show off // vi, ~**se** vr to walk, go for a walk; (*holgazanear*) to idle, loaf about; ~ **en coche** to go for a drive; **paseo** nm (*avenida*) avenue; (*distancia corta*) short walk; **dar un paseo** to go for a walk.

pasillo [pa'siʎo] nm passage, corridor.

pasión [pa'sjon] nf passion.

pasivo, a [pa'siβo, a] a passive; (*inactivo*) inactive // nm (*COM*) liabilities pl, debts pl.

pasmar [pas'mar] vt (*asombrar*) to amaze, astonish; (*enfriar*) to chill (*to* the bone); **pasmo** nm amazement, astonishment; chill; (*fig*) wonder, marvel; **pasmoso, a** a amazing, astonishing.

paso, a ['paso, a] a dried // nm (*gen*) step; (*modo de andar*) walk; (*huella*) footprint; (*rapidez*) speed, pace, rate; (*camino accesible*) way through, passage; (*cruce*) crossing; (*pasaje*) passing, passage; (*GEO*) pass; (*estrecho*) strait; **a ese** ~ (*fig*) at that rate; **salir al** ~ **de** o a to waylay; **estar de** ~ to be passing through; ~ **elevado** flyover; **prohibido el** ~ no entry; **ceda el** ~ give way.

pasta ['pasta] nf (*gen*) paste; (*CULIN: masa*) dough; (: *de bizcochos etc*) pastry; (*cartón*) cardboard; (*fam*) money, dough (*fam*); ~**s** nfpl (*bizcochos*) pastries, small cakes; (*fideos, espaguetis etc*) noodles, spaghetti sg etc; ~ **de dientes** o **dentífrica** toothpaste; ~ **de madera** wood pulp.

pastar [pas'tar], **pastear** [paste'ar] vt, vi to graze.

pastel [pas'tel] nm (*dulce*) cake; (*de carne*) pie; (*pintura*) pastel; ~**ería** nf cake shop, pastry shop.

pasteurizado, a [pasteuri'θaðo, a] a pasteurized.

pastilla [pas'tiʎa] nf (*de jabón, chocolate*) cake, bar; (*píldora*) tablet, pill.

pasto ['pasto] nm (*hierba*) grass; (*lugar*) pasture, field.

pastor, a [pas'tor, a] nm/f shepherd/ess // nm clergyman, pastor.

pata ['pata] nf (*pierna*) leg; (*pie*) foot; (*de muebles*) leg; ~**s arriba** upside down; **meter la** ~ to put one's foot in it; (*TEC*): ~ **de cabra** crowbar; **tener buena/mala** ~ to be lucky/unlucky; ~**da** nf stamp; (*puntapié*) kick.

patalear [patale'ar] vi to stamp one's feet.

patata [pa'tata] nf potato; ~**s fritas** o a **la española** chips, French fries; ~**s inglesas** crisps.

patear [pate'ar] vt (*pisar*) to stamp on, trample (on); (*pegar con el pie*) to kick // vi to stamp (with rage), stamp one's foot.

patente [pa'tente] a obvious, evident; (*COM*) patent // nf patent; **patentizar** vt to show, reveal, make evident.

paternal [pater'nal] a fatherly, paternal; **paterno, a** a paternal.

patético, a [pa'tetiko, a] a pathetic, moving.

patillas [pa'tiʎas] nfpl sideburns.

patín [pa'tin] nm skate; (*de tobogán*) runner; **patinaje** nm skating; **patinar** vi to skate; (*resbalarse*) to skid, slip; (*fam*) to slip up, blunder.

patio ['patjo] nm (*de casa*) patio, courtyard; ~ **de recreo** playground.

pato ['pato] nm duck; **pagar el** ~ (*fam*) to take the blame, carry the can.

patológico, a [pato'loxiko, a] *a* pathological.

patraña [pa'traɲa] *nf* story, fib.

patria ['patrja] *nf* native land, mother country.

patrimonio [patri'monjo] *nm* inheritance; *(fig)* heritage.

patriota [pa'trjota] *nm/f* patriot; **patriotismo** *nm* patriotism.

patrocinar [patroθi'nar] *vt* to sponsor; *(apoyar)* to back, support; **patrocinio** *nm* sponsorship; backing, support.

patrón, ona [pa'tron, ona] *nm/f* *(jefe)* boss, chief, master/mistress; *(propietario)* landlord/lady; *(REL)* patron saint // *nm (TEC, costura)* pattern; **patronal** *a:* **la clase patronal** management; **patronato** *nm* sponsorship; *(acto)* patronage; *(COM)* employers' association.

patrulla [pa'truʎa] *nf* patrol.

pausa ['pausa] *nf* pause; *(intervalo)* break; *(interrupción)* interruption.

pausado, a [pau'saðo, a] *a* slow, deliberate.

pauta ['pauta] *nf* line, guide line.

pavo ['paβo] *nm* turkey; ~ **real** peacock.

pavor [pa'βor] *nm* dread, terror.

payaso, a [pa'jaso, a] *nm/f* clown.

paz [paθ] *nf* peace; *(tranquilidad)* peacefulness, tranquillity; **hacer las paces** to make peace; *(fig)* to make up.

P.C.E. *abr de* **Partido Comunista Español.**

peaje [pe'axe] *nm* toll.

peatón [pea'ton] *nm* pedestrian.

peca ['peka] *nf* freckle.

pecado [pe'kaðo] *nm* sin; **pecador, a** *a* sinful // *nm/f* sinner.

pecaminoso, a [pekami'noso, a] *a* sinful.

pecar [pe'kar] *vi (REL)* to sin; *(fig)*: **peca de generoso** is too generous.

peculiar [peku'ljar] *a* special, peculiar; *(característico)* typical, characteristic; ~**idad** *nf* peculiarity; special feature, characteristic.

pecho ['petʃo] *nm (ANAT)* chest; *(de mujer)* breast(s) *(pl)*, bosom; *(corazón)* heart, breast; *(valor)* courage, spirit; **dar el** ~ **a** to breast-feed; **tomar algo a** ~ to take sth to heart.

pechuga [pe'tʃuɣa] *nf* breast (of chicken *etc*).

pedal [pe'ðal] *nm* pedal; ~**ear** *vi* to pedal.

pedante [pe'ðante] *a* pedantic // *nm/f* pedant; ~**ría** *nf* pedantry.

pedazo [pe'ðaθo] *nm* piece, bit; **hacerse** ~**s** to fall to pieces; *(romperse)* to smash, shatter.

pedernal [peðer'nal] *nm* flint.

pediatra [pe'ðjatra] *nm/f* pediatrician.

pedicuro, a [peði'kuro, a] *nm/f* chiropodist.

pedido [pe'ðiðo] *nm (COM. mandado)* order; *(petición)* request.

pedir [pe'ðir] *vt* to ask for, request; *(comida, COM. mandar)* to order; *(exigir:*

precio) to ask; *(necesitar)* to need, demand, require // *vi* to ask; **me pidió que cerrara la puerta** he asked me to shut the door; **¿cuánto piden por el coche?** how much are they asking for the car?

pegadizo, a [peɣa'ðiθo, a] *a* sticky; *(MED)* infectious // *nm/f* sponger, hanger-on *(fam)*.

pegajoso, a [peɣa'xoso, a] *a* sticky, adhesive; *(MED)* infectious.

pegamento [peɣa'mento] *nm* gum, sticky stuff.

pegar [pe'ɣar] *vt (papel, sellos)* to stick (on); *(cartel)* to post, stick up; *(coser)* to sew (on); *(unir: partes)* to join, fix together; *(MED)* to give, infect with; *(dar: golpe)* to give, deal // *vi (adherirse)* to stick, adhere; *(prender: fuego)* to catch; *(ir juntos: colores)* to match, go together; *(golpear)* to hit; *(quemar: el sol)* to strike hot, burn *(fig)*; ~**se** *vr (gen)* to stick; *(dos personas)* to hit each other, fight; *(fam)*: ~ **un grito** to let out a yell; ~ **un salto** to jump (with fright); ~ **en** to touch; ~**se un tiro** to shoot o.s.

peinado [pei'naðo] *nm (en peluquería)* hairdo; *(estilo)* hair style.

peinador, a [peina'ðor, a] *nm/f* hairdresser.

peinar [pei'nar] *vt* to comb; *(hacer estilo)* to style; ~**se** *vr* to comb one's hair.

peine ['peine] *nm* comb; ~**ta** *nf* ornamental comb.

Pekín [pe'kin] *n* Pekin(g).

pelado, a [pe'laðo, a] *a (cabeza)* shorn; *(fruta)* peeled; *(campo, fig)* bare // *nm* bare patch; *(fig)* wretch, poor devil.

pelaje [pe'laxe] *nm (ZOOL)* fur, coat; *(fig)* appearance.

pelambre [pe'lambre] *nm (pelo largo)* long hair, mop; *(piel de animal cortado)* fur; *(: de oveja)* fleece; *(parte sin piel)* bare patch.

pelar [pe'lar] *vt (cortar el pelo a)* to cut the hair of; *(quitar la piel: animal)* to skin; ~**se** *vr (la piel)* to peel off; *(persona)* to lose one's hair; **voy a** ~**me** I'm going to get my hair cut.

peldaño [pel'daɲo] *nm* step.

pelea [pe'lea] *nf (lucha)* fight; *(discusión)* quarrel, row; **pelear** *vi* to fight; **pelearse** *vr* to fight; *(reñirse)* to fall out, quarrel.

peletería [pelete'ria] *nf* furrier's, fur shop.

pelícano [peli'kano], **pelícano** [pe'likano] *nm* pelican.

pelicorto, a [peli'korto, a] *a* short-haired.

película [pe'likula] *nf (film)* film; *(cobertura ligera)* thin covering; *(FOTO. rollo)* roll *or* reel of film.

peligro [pe'liɣro] *nm* danger; *(riesgo)* risk; **correr** ~ **de** to be in danger of; ~**so, a** *a* dangerous; risky.

pelirrojo, a [peli'rroxo, a] *a* red-haired, red-headed.

pelo ['pelo] *nm (cabellos)* hair; *(de barba, bigote)* whisker; *(de animal: pellejo)* fur;

coat; (de perro etc) hair, coat; **al** ~ just right; **venir al** ~ to be exactly what one needs; **un hombre de** ~ **en pecho a** brave man; **por los** ~s by the skin of one's teeth; **no tener** ~s **en la lengua** to be outspoken, not mince words; **tomar el** ~ **a uno** to pull sb's leg.

pelón, ona [pe'lon, ona] a hairless, bald; (fig) broke, skint (fam).

pelota [pe'lota] nf ball; (fam: cabeza) nut (fam); **en** ~ stark naked; ~ **vasca** pelota.

pelotón [pelo'ton] nm (pelota) big ball; (muchedumbre) crowd; (MIL) squad, detachment.

peluca [pe'luka] nf wig.

peluche [pe'lutʃe] nm felt.

peludo, a [pe'luðo, a] a hairy, shaggy.

peluquería [peluke'ria] nf hairdresser's; (para hombres) barber's (shop); **peluquero, a** nm/f hairdresser; barber.

pelleja [pe'ʎexa] nf skin, hide; (fam) whore.

pellejo [pe'ʎexo] nm (de animal) skin, hide; (de fruta) skin, peel.

pellizcar [peʎiθ'kar] vt to pinch, nip.

pena ['pena] nf (congoja) grief, sadness; (ansia) anxiety; (remordimiento) regret; (dificultad) trouble; (dolor) pain; **merecer** o **valer la** ~ to be worthwhile; **a duras** ~s with great difficulty; ~ **de muerte** death penalty; ~ **pecuniaria** fine; ¡**qué** ~! what a shame!

penal [pe'nal] a penal // nm (cárcel) prison; (FÚTBOL) penalty.

penalidad [penali'ðað] nf (problema, dificultad) trouble, hardship; (JUR) penalty, punishment.

penar [pe'nar] vt to penalize; (castigar) to punish // vi to suffer; ~**se** vr to grieve, mourn.

pender [pen'der] vi (colgar) to hang; (JUR) to be pending.

pendiente [pen'djente] a (colgante) hanging; (por resolver) pending, unsettled // nm earring // nf hill, slope.

pene ['pene] nm penis.

penetración [penetra'θjon] nf (acto) penetration; (agudeza) sharpness, insight.

penetrante [pene'trante] a (herida) deep; (persona, arma) sharp; (sonido) penetrating, piercing; (mirada) searching; (viento, ironía) biting.

penetrar [pene'trar] vt to penetrate, pierce; (entender) to grasp // vi to penetrate, go in; (líquido) to soak in; (emoción) to pierce.

penicilina [peniθi'lina] nf penicillin.

península [pe'ninsula] nf peninsula; **peninsular** a peninsular.

penitencia [peni'tenθja] nf (remordimiento) penitence; (castigo) penance; **penitencial** a penitential; ~**ría** nf prison, penitentiary.

penoso, a [pe'noso, a] a (afligido) painful, distressing; (trabajoso) laborious, difficult.

pensador, a [pensa'ðor, a] nm/f thinker.

pensamiento [pensa'mjento] nm (gen) thought; (mente) mind; (idea) idea; (intento) intention.

pensar [pen'sar] vt to think; (considerar) to think over, think out; (proponerse) to intend, plan, propose; (imaginarse) to think up, invent // vi to think; ~ **en** to aim at, aspire to; **pensativo, a** a thoughtful, pensive.

pensión [pen'sjon] nf (casa) boarding house, guest house; (dinero) pension; (cama y comida) board and lodging; (beca) scholarship; **pensionista** nm/f (jubilado) (old-age) pensioner; (quien vive en pensión) lodger.

penúltimo, a [pe'nultimo, a] a penultimate, second last.

penumbra [pe'numbra] nf half-light, semi-darkness.

penuria [pe'nurja] nf shortage, want.

peña ['peɲa] nf (roca) rock; (cuesta) cliff, crag; (grupo) group, circle.

peñascal [peɲas'kal] nm rocky place; **peñasco** nm large rock, boulder.

peñón [pe'ɲon] nm mass of rock; **el P**~ the Rock of Gibraltar.

peón [pe'on] nm labourer; (AM) farm labourer, farmhand; (eje) spindle, shaft, axle; (AJEDREZ) pawn.

peor [pe'or] a (comparativo) worse; (superlativo) worst // ad worse; worst; **de mal en** ~ from bad to worse.

pepino [pe'pino] nm cucumber; (**no**) **me importa un** ~ I don't care two hoots.

pepita [pe'pita] nf (BOT) pip; (MINERÍA) nugget.

pequeñez [peke'ɲeθ] nf smallness, littleness; (infancia) infancy; (trivialidad) trifle, triviality.

pequeño, a [pe'keɲo, a] a small, little.

pera ['pera] nf pear; **peral** nm pear tree.

percance [per'kanθe] nm setback, misfortune.

percatarse [perka'tarse] vr: ~ **de** to notice, take note of.

percepción [perθep'θjon] nf (vista) perception; (idea) notion, idea; (colecta de fondos) collection.

perceptible [perθep'tiβle] a perceptible, noticeable; (COM) payable, receivable.

percibir [perθi'βir] vt to perceive, notice; (COM) to earn, receive, get.

percusión [perku'sjon] nf percussion.

percha ['pertʃa] nf (poste) pole, support; (ganchos) coat stand; (colgador) coat hanger; (de ave) perch.

perdedor, a [perðe'ðor, a] a (que pierde) losing; (olvidadizo) forgetful // nm/f loser.

perder [per'ðer] vt (gen) to lose; (tiempo, palabras) to waste; (oportunidad) to lose, miss; (tren) to miss // vi to lose; ~**se** vr (extraviarse) to get lost; (desaparecer) to disappear, be lost to view; (arruinarse) to be ruined; (hundirse) to sink; **echar a** ~ (comida) to spoil, ruin; (oportunidad) to waste.

perdición [perði'θjon] nf perdition, ruin.

pérdida ['perðiða] nf (gen) loss; (de tiempo) waste; ~s nfpl (COM) losses.

perdido, a [per'ðiðo, a] a lost; (incorregible) incorrigible; ~so, a a (que pierde) losing; (fácilmente ~) easily lost.

perdiz [per'ðiθ] nf partridge.

perdón [per'ðon] nm (disculpa) pardon, forgiveness; (clemencia) mercy; ¡~! sorry!, I beg your pardon!; **perdonar** vt to pardon, forgive; (la vida) to spare; (excusar) to exempt, excuse.

perdurable [perðu'raßle] a lasting; (eterno) everlasting; **perdurar** vi (resistir) to last, endure; (seguir existiendo) to stand, still exist.

perecer [pere'θer] vi (morir) to perish, die; (objeto) to shatter.

peregrinación [pereɣrina'θjon] nf long tour, travels pl; (REL) pilgrimage; **peregrino, a** a travelling; (nuevo) newly-introduced // nm/f pilgrim.

perejil [pere'xil] nm parsley.

perenne [pe'renne] a everlasting, perennial.

perentorio, a [peren'torjo, a] a (urgente) urgent, peremptory; (fijo) set, fixed.

pereza [pe'reθa] nf (flojera) laziness (lentitud) sloth, slowness; **perezoso, a** a lazy; slow, sluggish.

perfección [perfek'θjon] nf perfection; (acto) completion; **perfeccionar** vt to perfect; (acabar) to complete, finish.

perfecto, a [per'fekto, a] a perfect; (terminado) complete, finished.

perfidia [per'fiðja] nf perfidy, treachery.

perfil [per'fil] nm (parte lateral) profile; (silueta) silhouette, outline; (ARQ) (cross) section; ~es nmpl features; (fig) social graces; ~ado, a a (bien formado) well-shaped; (largo: cara) long; ~ar vt (trazar) to outline; (dar carácter a) to shape, give character to.

perforación [perfora'θjon] nf perforation; (con taladro) drilling; **perforadora** nf drill.

perforar [perfo'rar] vt to perforate; (agujero) to drill, bore; (papel) to punch a hole in // vi to drill, bore.

perfumado, a [perfu'maðo, a] a scented, perfumed.

perfume [per'fume] nm perfume, scent.

pericia [pe'riθja] nf skill, expertise.

periferia [peri'ferja] nf periphery; (de ciudad) outskirts pl.

perímetro [pe'rimetro] nm perimeter.

periódico, a [pe'rjoðiko, a] a periodic(al) // nm newspaper; **periodismo** nm journalism; **periodista** nm/f journalist.

periodo [pe'rjoðo], **período** [pe'rioðo] nm period.

perito, a [pe'rito, a] a (experto) expert; (diestro) skilled, skilful // nm/f expert; skilled worker; (técnico) technician.

perjudicar [perxuði'kar] vt (gen) to damage, harm; es vestido le perjudica that dress doesn't suit her; **perjudicial** a damaging, harmful; (en detrimento) detri-

mental; **perjuicio** nm damage, harm; (pérdidas) financial loss.

perjurar [perxu'rar] vi to commit perjury.

perla ['perla] nf pearl; me viene de ~ it suits me fine.

permanecer [permane'θer] vi (quedarse) to stay, remain; (seguir) to continue to be.

permanencia [perma'nenθja] nf (duración) permanence; (estancia) stay.

permanente [perma'nente] a (que queda) permanent; (constante) constant // nf perm.

permisible [permi'sißle] a permissible, allowable.

permiso [per'miso] nm permission; (licencia) permit, licence; con ~ excuse me; estar de ~ (MIL) to be on leave; ~ de conducir o conductor driving licence.

permitir [permi'tir] vt to permit, allow.

pernicioso, a [perni'θjoso, a] a (maligno, MED) pernicious; (persona) wicked.

pernio ['pernjo] nm hinge.

perno ['perno] nm bolt.

pero ['pero] conj but; (aún) yet // nm (defecto) flaw, defect; (reparo) objection.

perorar [pero'rar] vi to make a speech.

perpendicular [perpendiku'lar] a perpendicular; el camino es ~ al río the road is at right angles to the river.

perpetrar [perpe'trar] vt to perpetrate.

perpetuamente [perpetwa'mente] ad perpetually; **perpetuar** vt to perpetuate; **perpetuo, a** a perpetual.

perplejo, a [per'plexo, a] a perplexed, bewildered.

perra ['perra] nf bitch; (fam) mania, crazy idea.

perrera [pe'rrera] nf kennel.

perrillo [pe'rriʎo] nm puppy.

perro ['perro] nm dog; ~ caliente hot dog.

persa ['persa] a, nm/f Persian.

persecución [perseku'θjon] nf pursuit, hunt, chase; (REL, POL) persecution.

perseguir [perse'xir] vt to pursue, hunt; (cortejar) to chase after; (molestar) to pester, annoy; (REL, POL) to persecute.

perseverante [perseße'rante] a persevering, persistent; **perseverar** vi to persevere, persist; **perseverar en** to persevere in, persist with.

persiana [per'sjana] nf (Venecian) blind.

persignarse [persix'narse] vr to cross o.s.

persistente [persis'tente] a persistant; **persistir** vi to persist.

persona [per'sona] nf person; 10 ~s 10 people.

personaje [perso'naxe] nm important person, celebrity; (TEATRO) character.

personal [perso'nal] a (particular) personal; (para una persona) single, for one person // nm personnel, staff; ~idad nf personality.

personarse [perso'narse] vr to appear in person

personificar [personifi'kar] vt to personify.

perspectiva [perspek'tißa] nf perspective; (vista, panorama) view, panorama; (posibilidad futura) outlook, prospect.

perspicacia [perspi'kaθja] nf keen-sightedness; (fig) discernment, perspicacity.

perspicaz [perspi'kaθ] a (agudo: de la vista) keen; (fig) shrewd.

persuadir [perswa'ðir] vt (gen) to persuade; (convencer) to convince; ~se vr to become convinced; **persuasión** nf (acto) persuasion; (estado de mente) conviction; **persuasivo, a** a persuasive; convincing.

pertenecer [pertene'θer] vi to belong; (fig) to concern; **pertenencia** nf ownership; **pertenencias** nfpl possessions, property sg; **perteneciente** a: **pertenecer a** belonging to.

pertinaz [perti'naθ] a (persistente) persistent; (terco) obstinate.

pertinente [perti'nente] a relevant, pertinent; (apropiado) appropriate; ~ a concerning, relevant to.

perturbación [perturßa'θjon] nf (POL) disturbance; (MED) upset, disturbance.

perturbado, a [pertur'ßaðo, a] a mentally unbalanced.

perturbador, a [perturßa'ðor, a] a (que perturba) perturbing, disturbing; (subversivo) subversive.

perturbar [pertur'ßar] vt (el orden) to disturb; (MED) to upset, disturb; (mentalmente) to perturb.

Perú [pe'ru] nm: el ~ Peru; **peruano, a** a, nm/f Peruvian.

perversión [perßer'sjon] nf perversion; **perverso, a** a perverse; (depravado) depraved; **pervertido, a** a perverted // nm/f pervert; **pervertir** vt to pervert, corrupt; (distorsionar) to distort.

pesa ['pesa] nf weight; (DEPORTE) shot.

pesadez [pesa'ðeθ] nf (calidad de pesado) heaviness; (lentitud) slowness; (aburrimiento) tediousness.

pesadilla [pesa'ðiʎa] nf nightmare, bad dream.

pesado, a [pe'saðo, a] a (gen) heavy; (lento) slow; (difícil, duro) tough, hard; (aburrido) tedious, boring; (bochornoso) sultry.

pesadumbre [pesa'ðumbre] nf grief, sorrow.

pésame ['pesame] nm expression of condolence, message of sympathy.

pesar [pe'sar] vt to weigh // vi to weigh; (ser pesado) to weigh a lot, be heavy; (fig: opinión) to carry weight // nm (sentimiento) regret; (pena) grief, sorrow; **a ~ de** o **pese a (que)** in spite of, despite.

pesario [pe'sarjo] nm pessary.

pesca ['peska] nf (acto) fishing; (cantidad de pescado) catch; **ir de ~** to go fishing.

pescadería [peskaðe'ria] nf fish shop.

pescado [pes'kaðo] nm fish.

pescador, a [peska'ðor, a] nm/f fisherman/woman.

pescar [pes'kar] vt (coger) to catch; (tratar de coger) to fish for; (conseguir: trabajo) to manage to get // vi to fish, go fishing; **viene a ~ un marido** she's come to get a husband.

pescuezo [pes'kweθo] nm neck.

pesebre [pe'seßre] nm manger.

peseta [pe'seta] nf peseta.

pesimista [pesi'mista] a pessimistic // nm/f pessimist.

pésimo, a ['pesimo, a] a abominable, vile.

peso ['peso] nm weight; (balanza) scales pl; (moneda) peso; ~ **bruto/neto** gross/net weight; **vender a ~** to sell by weight.

pesquero, a [pes'kero, a] a fishing cpd.

pesquisa [pes'kisa] nf inquiry, investigation.

pestaña [pes'taɲa] nf (ANAT) eyelash; (borde) rim; **pestañear, pestañar** vi to blink.

peste ['peste] nf (gen) plague; (mal olor) stink, stench.

pesticida [pesti'θiða] nm pesticide.

pestilencia [pesti'lenθja] nf (plaga) pestilence, plague; (mal olor) stink, stench.

pétalo ['petalo] nm petal.

petardista [petar'ðista] nm/f (tramposo) cheat; (rompehuelgas) blackleg.

petición [peti'θjon] nf (pedido) request, plea; (memorial) petition; (JUR) plea.

petrificar [petrifi'kar] vt to petrify.

petróleo [pe'troleo] nm oil, petroleum; **petrolero, a** a petroleum cpd // nm (COM) oil man; (extremista) extremist, revolutionary; (buque) (oil) tanker.

peyorativo, a [pejora'tißo, a] a pejorative.

pez [peθ] nm fish.

pezón [pe'θon] nm teat, nipple; (MECÁNICA) nipple, lubrication point.

piadoso, a [pja'ðoso, a] a (devoto) pious, devout; (misericordioso) kind, merciful.

pianista [pja'nista] nm/f pianist.

piano ['pjano] nm piano.

piar [pi'ar] vi to cheep.

picadillo [pika'ðiʎo] nm mince, minced meat.

picado, a [pi'kaðo, a] a pricked, punctured; (mar) choppy; (diente) bad; (tabaco) cut; (enfadado) cross // nf prick; (de abeja) sting; (de mosquito) bite.

picador [pika'ðor] nm (TAUR) picador; (entrenador de caballos) horse trainer; (minero) faceworker.

picadura [pika'ðura] nf (diente) bad tooth; (pinchazo) puncture; (de abeja) sting; (de mosquito) bite; (tabaco picado) cut tobacco.

picante [pi'kante] a hot; (comentario) racy, spicy.

picar [pi'kar] vt (agujerear, perforar) to prick, puncture; (abeja) to sting; (mosquito, serpiente) to bite; (incitar) to incite, goad; (dañar, irritar) to annoy, bother; (quemar:

lengua) to burn, sting // *vi* (*pez*) to bite, take the bait; (*el sol*) to burn, scorch; (*abeja*, MED) to sting; (*mosquito*) to bite; ~**se** *vr* (*decaer*) to decay; (*agriarse*) to turn sour, go off; (*ofenderse*) to take offence; ~ **en** (*fig*) to dabble in.

picardía [pikar'ðia] *nf* villainy; (*astucia*) slyness, craftiness; (*una* ~) dirty trick; (*palabra*) rude/bad word or expression.

pícaro, a ['pikaro, a] *a* (*malicioso*) villainous; (*travieso*) mischievous // *nm* (*ladrón*) crook; (*astuto*) sly sort; (*sinvergüenza*) rascal, scoundrel.

pico ['piko] *nm* (*de ave*) beak; (*punto agudo*) peak, sharp point; (*TEC*) pick, pickaxe; (*GEO*) peak, summit; y ~ and a bit.

picotear [pikote'ar] *vt* to peck // *vi* to nibble, pick; (*fam*) to chatter; ~**se** *vr* to squabble.

picudo, a [pi'kuðo, a] *a* pointed, with a point.

pichón [pi'tʃon] *nm* young pigeon.

pido, pidió *etc vb ver* **pedir.**

pie [pje] (*pl* ~**s**) *nm* (*gen*) foot; (*fig: motivo*) motive, basis; (: *fundamento*) foothold; **ir a** ~ to go on foot, walk; **estar de** ~ to be standing (up); **ponerse de** ~ to stand up; **al** ~ **de la letra** (*citar*) literally, verbatim; (*copiar*) exactly, word for word; **en** ~ **de guerra** on a war footing; **dar** ~ **a** to give cause for.

piedad [pje'ðað] *nf* (*lástima*) pity, compassion; (*clemencia*) mercy; (*devoción*) piety, devotion.

piedra ['pjeðra] *nf* stone; (*roca*) rock; (*de mechero*) flint; (*METEOROLOGÍA*) hailstone.

piel [pjel] *nf* (*ANAT*) skin; (*ZOOL*) skin, hide; (*de oso*) fur; (*cuero*) leather; (*BOT*) skin, peel; ~ **de ante** o **de Suecia** suede.

pienso *etc vb ver* **pensar.**

pierdo *etc vb ver* **perder.**

pierna ['pjerna] *nf* leg.

pieza ['pjeθa] *nf* piece; (*habitación*) room; ~ **de recambio** o **repuesto** spare (part).

pigmeo, a [piɣ'meo, a] *a, nm/f* pigmy.

pijama [pi'xama] *nm* pyjamas *pl*.

pila ['pila] *nf* (*ELEC*) battery; (*montón*) heap, pile; (*fuente*) sink.

píldora ['pilðora] *nf* pill; **la** ~ (*anticonceptiva*) the pill.

pileta [pi'leta] *nf* basin, bowl; (*AM*) swimming pool.

pilón [pi'lon] *nm* pillar, post; (*ELEC*) pylon.

piloto [pi'loto] *nm* pilot; (*de aparato*) rear light, tail light; (*AUTO*) driver.

pillaje [pi'ʎaxe] *nm* pillage, plunder.

pillar [pi'ʎar] *vt* (*saquear*) to pillage, plunder; (*fam: coger*) to catch; (: *agarrar*) to grasp, seize; (: *entender*) to grasp, catch on to.

pillo, a ['piʎo, a] *a* villainous; (*astuto*) sly, crafty // *nm/f* rascal, rogue, scoundrel.

pimentón [pimen'ton] *nm* (*polvo*) paprika; (*pimiento*) red pepper.

pimienta [pi'mjenta] *nf* pepper.

pimiento [pi'mjento] *nm* pepper, pimiento.

pinacoteca [pinako'teka] *nf* art gallery.

pinar [pi'nar] *nm* pinewood.

pincel [pin'θel] *nm* paintbrush.

pinchar [pin'tʃar] *vt* (*perforar*) to prick, pierce; (*neumático*) to puncture; (*incitar*) to prod; (*herir*) to wound.

pinchazo [pin'tʃaθo] *nm* (*perforación*) prick; (*de llanta*) puncture; (*fig*) prod.

pinchitos [pin'tʃitos] *nmpl* bar snacks.

pingüino [pin'gwino] *nm* penguin.

pino ['pino] *nm* pine (tree); **en** ~ upright, vertical.

pinta ['pinta] *nf* spot; (*medida*) spot, drop; (*aspecto*) appearance, look(s) (*pl*); ~**do, a** a spotted; (*de muchos colores*) colourful.

pintar [pin'tar] *vt* to paint // *vi* to paint; (*fam*) to count, be important; ~**se** *vr* to put on make-up.

pintor, a [pin'tor, a] *nm/f* painter.

pintoresco, a [pinto'resko, a] *a* picturesque.

pintura [pin'tura] *nf* painting; ~ **a la acuarela** watercolour; ~ **al óleo** oil painting; ~ **rupestre** cave painting.

pinza ['pinθa] *nf* (*ZOOL*) claw; (*para colgar ropa*) clothes peg; (*TEC*) pincers *pl*; ~**s** *nfpl* (*para depilar*) tweezers *pl*.

piña ['pina] *nf* (*fruto del pino*) pine cone; (*fruta*) pineapple; (*fig*) group.

pío, a ['pio, a] *a* (*devoto*) pious, devout; (*misericordioso*) merciful // *nm* cheep, chirp.

piojo [pi'oxo] *nm* louse.

pionero, a [pjo'nero, a] *a* pioneering // *nm/f* pioneer.

pipa ['pipa] *nf* pipe; (*BOT*) edible sunflower seed.

pipí [pi'pi] *nm* (*fam*): **hacer** ~ to have a wee(wee).

pique ['pike] *nm* (*resentimiento*) pique, resentment; (*rivalidad*) rivalry, competition; **irse a** ~ to sink; (*familia*) to be ruined.

piquera [pi'kera] *nf* hole, vent.

piqueta [pi'keta] *nf* pick(axe).

piquete [pi'kete] *nm* (*herida*) prick, jab; (*agujerito*) small hole; (*MIL*) squad, party; (*de obreros*) picket.

piragua [pi'raɣwa] *nf* canoe; **piragüismo** *nm* (*DEPORTE*) canoeing.

pirámide [pi'ramiðe] *nf* pyramid.

pirata [pi'rata] *a, nm* pirate.

Pirineo(s) [piri'neo(s)] *nm(pl)* Pyrenees *pl*.

piropo [pi'ropo] *nm* compliment, (piece of) flattery.

pisada [pi'saða] *nf* (*paso*) footstep; (*huella*) footprint.

pisar [pi'sar] *vt* (*caminar sobre*) to walk on, tread on; (*apretar con el pie*) to press; (*fig*) to trample on, walk all over // *vi* to tread, step, walk.

piscina [pis'θina] *nf* swimming pool; (*para peces*) fishpond.

Piscis ['pisθis] *nm* Pisces.

piso ['piso] *nm* (*suelo, de edificio*) floor; (*apartamento*) flat, apartment.

pisotear [pisote'ar] *vt* to trample (on *or* underfoot).

pista ['pista] *nf* track, trail; (*indicio*) clue; ~ **de aterrizaje** runway; ~ **de baile** dance floor; ~ **de tenis** tennis court; ~ **de hielo** ice rink.

pistola [pis'tola] *nf* pistol; (*TEC*) spray-gun; **pistolero, a** *nm/f* gunman, gangster // *nf* holster.

pistón [pis'ton] *nm* (*TEC*) piston; (*MUS*) key.

pitar [pi'tar] *vt* (*hacer sonar*) to blow; (*rechiflar*) to whistle at, boo // *vi* to whistle; (*AUTO*) to sound *or* toot one's horn; (*AM*) to smoke.

pitillo [pi'tiʎo] *nm* cigarette.

pito ['pito] *nm* whistle; (*de coche*) horn.

pitón [pi'ton] *nm* (*ZOOL*) python; (*protuberancia*) bump, lump; (*de jarro*) spout.

pitonisa [pito'nisa] *nf* fortune-teller.

pizarra [pi'θarra] *nf* (*piedra*) slate; (*encerado*) blackboard.

pizca ['piθka] *nf* pinch, spot; (*fig*) spot, speck, trace; **ni** ~ not a bit.

placa ['plaka] *nf* plate; ~ **de matrícula** number plate.

placentero, a [plaθen'tero, a] *a* pleasant, agreeable.

placer [pla'θer] *nm* pleasure // *vt* to please.

plácido, a ['plaθiðo, a] *a* placid.

plaga ['playa] *nf* pest; (*MED*) plague; (*abundancia*) abundance; **plagar** *vt* to infest, plague; (*llenar*) to fill.

plagio ['plaxjo] *nm* plagiarism.

plan [plan] *nm* (*esquema, proyecto*) plan; (*idea, intento*) idea, intention; **tener** ~ (*fam*) to have a date; **tener un** ~ (*fam*) to have an affair; **en** ~ **económico** (*fam*) on the cheap; **vamos en** ~ **de turismo** we're going as tourists; **si te pones en ese** ~... if that's your attitude... .

plana ['plana] *nf ver* **plano**.

plancha ['plantʃa] *nf* (*para planchar*) iron; (*rótulo*) plate, sheet; (*NAUT*) gangway; ~**do** *nm* ironing; **planchar** *vt* to iron // *vi* to do the ironing.

planeador [planea'ðor] *nm* glider; ~**a** *nf* bulldozer.

planear [plane'ar] *vt* to plan // *vi* to glide.

planeta [pla'neta] *nm* planet.

planicie [pla'niθje] *nf* plain.

planificación [planifika'θjon] *nf* planning; ~ **familiar** family planning.

plano, a ['plano, a] *a* flat, level, even // *nm* (*MAT, TEC, AVIAT*) plane; (*FOTO*) shot; (*ARQ*) plan; (*GEO*) map; (*de ciudad*) map, street plan // *nf* sheet (of paper), page; (*TEC*) trowel; **primer** ~ close-up; **caer de** ~ to fall flat; **en primera** ~**a** on the front page; ~**a mayor** staff.

planta ['planta] *nf* (*BOT, TEC*) plant; (*ANAT*) sole of the foot, foot; ~ **baja** ground floor.

plantación [planta'θjon] *nf* (*AGR*) plantation; (*acto*) planting.

plantar [plan'tar] *vt* (*BOT*) to plant; (*levantar*) to erect, set up; ~ **se** *vr* to stand firm; ~ **a uno en la calle** to chuck sb out; **dejar plantado a uno** (*fam*) to stand sb up.

plantear [plante'ar] *vt* (*problema*) to pose; (*dificultad*) to raise; (*planificar*) to plan; (*institución*) to set up, establish; (*reforma*) to implant.

plantilla [plan'tiʎa] *nf* (*de zapato*) insole; (*de media*) sole; (*personal*) personnel; **ser de** ~ to be on the staff.

plantío [plan'tio] *nm* (*acto*) planting; (*lugar*) plot, bed, patch.

plantón [plan'ton] *nm* (*MIL*) guard, sentry; (*fam*) long wait; **dar (un)** ~ **a uno** to stand sb up.

plañidero, a [plaɲi'ðero, a] *a* mournful, plaintive.

plañir [pla'ɲir] *vi* to mourn.

plasmar [plas'mar] *vt* (*dar forma*) to mould, shape; (*representar*) to represent // *vi*: ~ **en** to take the form of.

plasticina [plasti'θina] *nf* plasticine.

plástico, a ['plastiko, a] *a* plastic // *nf* (*art of*) sculpture, modelling // *nm* plastic.

plata ['plata] *nf* (*metal*) silver; (*cosas hechas de plata*) silverware; (*AM*) money; **hablar en** ~ to speak bluntly *or* frankly.

plataforma [plata'forma] *nf* platform; ~ **de lanzamiento/perforación** launch(ing) pad/drilling rig.

plátano ['platano] *nm* (*fruta*) banana; (*árbol*) banana tree.

platea [pla'tea] *nf* (*TEATRO*) pit.

plateado, a [plate'aðo, a] *a* silver; (*TEC*) silver-plated.

platería [plate'ria] *nf* silversmith's.

plática ['platika] *nf* talk, chat; **platicar** *vi* to talk, chat.

platillo [pla'tiʎo] *nm* saucer; ~**s** *nmpl* cymbals; ~ **volador** *o* **volante** flying saucer.

platino [pla'tino] *nm* platinum; ~**s** *nmpl* (*AUTO*) contact points.

plato ['plato] *nm* plate, dish; (*parte de comida*) course; (*guiso*) dish.

playa ['plaja] *nf* beach; (*lugar veraniego*) seaside resort; (*costa*) seaside; ~ **de estacionamiento** (*AM*) car park.

playera [pla'jera] *nf* T-shirt.

plaza ['plaθa] *nf* square; (*mercado*) market(place); (*sitio*) room, space; (*en vehículo*) seat, place; (*colocación*) post, job.

plazco *etc vb ver* **placer**.

plazo ['plaθo] *nm* (*lapso de tiempo*) time, period, term; (*fecha de vencimiento*) expiry date; (*pago parcial*) instalment; **a corto/largo** ~ short-/long-term; **comprar a** ~**s** to buy on hire purchase, pay for in instalments.

plazoleta [plaθo'leta], **plazuela** [pla-'θwela] *nf* small square.

pleamar [plea'mar] *nf* high tide.

plebe ['pleβe] *nf*: **la** ~ the common

people *pl*, the masses *pl*; *(pey)* the plebs *pl*; ~yo, a *a* plebeian; *(pey)* coarse, common.

plebiscito [pleßis'θito] *nm* plebiscite.

plegable [ple'saßle] **plegadizo,** a [plexa'ðiθo, a] *a* pliable; *(silla)* folding.

plegar [ple'xar] *vt (doblar)* to fold, bend; *(COSTURA)* to pleat; ~se *vr* to yield, submit.

pleito ['pleito] *nm (JUR)* lawsuit, case; *(fig)* dispute, feud.

plenilunio [pleni'lunjo] *nm* full moon.

plenitud [pleni'tuð] *nf* plenitude, fullness; *(abundancia)* abundance.

pleno, a ['pleno, a] *a (gen)* full; *(completo)* complete // *nm* plenum; **en ~ día** in broad daylight; **en ~ verano** at the height of summer; **en ~ a cara** full in the face.

pleuresía [pleure'sia] *nf* pleurisy.

plexiglás [pleksi'ɣlas] *nm* perspex.

pliego ['pljeɣo] *nm (hoja)* sheet (of paper); *(carta)* sealed letter/document; **~ de condiciones** details *pl*, specifications *pl*.

pliegue ['pljeɣe] *nm* fold, crease; *(de vestido)* pleat.

plisado [pli'saðo] *nm* pleating; **~ de acordeón** accordion pleats *pl*.

plomero [plo'mero] *nm* plumber.

plomo ['plomo] *nm (metal)* lead; *(ELEC)* fuse.

pluma ['pluma] *nf (gen)* feather; *(para escribir)* pen.

plural [plu'ral] *a* plural; **~idad** *nf* plurality; **una ~idad de votos** a majority of votes.

plus [plus] *nm* bonus.

plutocracia [pluto'kraθja] *nf* plutocracy.

población [poßla'θjon] *nf* population; *(pueblo, ciudad)* town, city; **poblado,** a *a* inhabited // *nm (aldea)* village; *(pueblo)* (small) town; **densamente poblado** densely populated.

poblador, a [poßla'ðor, a] *nm/f* settler, colonist; *(fundador)* founder.

poblar [po'ßlar] *vt (colonizar)* to colonize; *(fundar)* to found; *(habitar)* to inhabit.

pobre [po'ßre] *a* poor // *nm/f* poor person; **¡~!** poor thing!; **~za** *nf* poverty.

pocilga [po'θilxa] *nf* pigsty.

poción [po'θjon] **pócima** ['poθima] *nf* potion.

poco, a ['poko, a] *a* little; **~s** few // *ad (no mucho)* little, not much // *nm*: **un ~ a** little, a bit; **tener a uno en ~** to think little *or* not think much of sb; **por ~** almost, nearly; **~ a ~** little by little, gradually; **dentro de ~** (+ *presente o futuro*) shortly; (+ *pasado*) soon after; **hace ~** a short time ago, not long ago.

podar [po'ðar] *vt* to prune.

podenco [po'ðenko] *nm* hound.

poder [po'ðer] *vi* can; *(sujeto: persona)* to be able to, can; *(permiso)* can, may; *(posibilidad, hipótesis)* may // *nm* power; *(autoridad)* authority; **puede que sea así** it may be, maybe; **¿se puede?** may I come in?; **¿puedes con eso?** can

you manage that?; **a más no ~** to the utmost; **no ~ menos de hacer algo** not to be able to help doing sth; **no ~ más** to have had enough; **~fo** *nm* power; *(autoridad)* authority; **~oso,** a *a* powerful.

podrido, a [po'ðriðo, a] *a* rotten, bad; *(fig)* rotten, corrupt.

podrir [po'ðrir] = **pudrir.**

poema [po'ema] *nm* poem.

poesía [poe'sia] *nf* poetry.

poeta [po'eta] *nm* poet; **poético,** a *a* poetical.

póker ['poker] *nm* poker.

polaco, a [po'lako, a] *a* Polish // *nm/f* Pole.

polar [po'lar] *a* polar; **~idad** *nf* polarity; **~izarse** *vr* to polarize.

polea [po'lea] *nf* pulley.

polémica [po'lemika] *nf (gen)* polemics *sg*; *(una ~)* controversy.

policía [poli'θia] *nm, f* policeman/woman // *nf* police; **~co,** a *a* police *cpd*; **novela ~ca** detective story.

poligamia [poli'xamja] *nf* polygamy.

polilla [po'liʎa] *nf* moth.

polio ['poljo] *nm* polio.

politécnico [poli'tekniko] *nm* polytechnic.

politene [poli'tene], **politeno** [poli'teno] *nm* polythene.

político, a [po'litiko, a] *a* political; *(discreto)* tactful; *(de familia)* in-law // *nm/f* politician // *nf* politics *sg*; *(económica, agraria)* policy; **padre ~** father-in-law; **políticastro** *nm (pey)* politician, politico.

póliza ['poliθa] *nf* insurance policy.

polo [polo] *nm (GEO, ELEC)* pole; *(helado)* iced lolly; *(DEPORTE)* polo; *(suéter)* polo-neck; **~ Norte/Sur** North/South Pole.

Polonia [po'lonja] *nf* Poland.

poltrona [pol'trona] *nf* reclining chair, easy chair.

polución [polu'θjon] *nf* pollution.

polvera [pol'ßera] *nf* powder compact, vanity case.

polvo ['polßo] *nm* dust; *(QUÍMICA, CULIN, MED)* powder; **~s** *nmpl* powder *sg*; **~ de talco** talcum powder; **estar hecho ~** to be worn out *or* exhausted.

pólvora ['polßora] *nf* gunpowder; *(fuegos artificiales)* fireworks *pl*.

polvoriento, a [polßo'rjento, a] *a (superficie)* dusty; *(sustancia)* powdery.

pollería [poʎe'ria] *nf* poulterer's (shop).

pollo ['poʎo] *nm* chicken.

pomada [po'maða] *nf* pomade.

pomelo [po'melo] *nm* grapefruit.

pómez ['pomeθ] *nf*: **piedra ~** pumice stone.

pompa ['pompa] *nf (burbuja)* bubble; *(bomba)* pump; *(esplendor)* pomp, splendour; **pomposo,** a *a* splendid, magnificent; *(pey)* pompous.

pómulo ['pomulo] *nm* cheekbone.

pon [pon] *vb ver* **poner.**

ponche ['ponʧe] *nm* punch.

poncho ['pontʃo] nm (AM) poncho, cape.

ponderado, a [ponde'raðo, a] a calm, steady, balanced.

ponderar [ponde'rar] vt (considerar) to weigh up, consider; (elogiar) to praise highly, speak in praise of.

pondré etc vb ver **poner**.

poner [po'ner] vt (gen) to put; (colocar) to place, set; (ropa) to put on; (problema, la mesa) to set; (telegrama) to send; (TELEC) to connect; (radio, TV) to switch on, turn on; (tienda) to open, set up; (nombre) to give; (añadir) to add; (TEATRO, CINE) to put on; (+ adjetivo) to make, turn; (suponer) to suppose // vi (ave) to lay (eggs); ~se vr to put or place o.s.; (ropa) to put on; (+ adjetivo) to turn, get, become; (el sol) to set; **póngame con el Señor X** get me Mr X, put me through to Mr X; ~se de **zapatero** to take a job as a shoemaker; ~se a bien con uno to get on good terms with sb; ~se con uno to quarrel with sb; ~se rojo to blush; ~se a to begin to.

pongo etc vb ver **poner**.

pontificado [pontifi'kaðo] nm papacy, pontificate; **pontífice** nm pope, pontiff.

pontón [pon'ton] nm pontoon.

ponzoña [pon'θoɲa] nf poison, venom; **ponzoñoso, a** a poisonous, venomous.

popa ['popa] nf stern.

popular [popu'lar] a popular; (del pueblo) of the people; ~idad nf popularity; ~izarse vr to become popular.

poquedad [poke'ðað] nf (escasez) scantiness; (una ~) small thing, trifle; (fig) timidity.

por [por] prep (con el fin de) in order to; (a favor de, hacia) for; (a causa de) out of, because of, from; (según) according to; (por agencia de) by; (a cambio de) for, in exchange for; (en lugar de) instead of, in place of; (durante) for; **10 ~ 10 son 100** 10 times 10 are 100; **será ~ poco tiempo** it won't be for long; ~ **correo/avión** by post/plane; ~ **centenares** by the hundred; **(el) 10 ~ ciento** 10 per cent; ~ **orden** in order; **ir a Bilbao ~ Santander** to go to Bilbao via Santander; **pasar ~ Madrid** to pass through Madrid; **camina ~ la izquierda** walk on the left; ~ **todo el país** throughout the country; **entra ~ delante/detrás** come/go in by the front/back (door); ~ **la calle** along the street; ~ **la mañana** in the morning; ~ **la noche** at night; **£2 ~ hora** £2 an hour; ~ **allí** over there; **está ~ el norte** it's somewhere in the north; ~ **mucho que quisiera, no puedo** much as I would like to, I can't; ~**que demasiado**; ¿**~ qué?** why?; ~ **(lo) tanto** so, therefore; ~ **cierto** (seguro) certainly; (a propósito) by the way; ~ **ejemplo** for example; ~ **favor** please; ~ **fuera/dentro** outside/inside; ~ **si (acaso)** just in case; ~ **sí mismo** o **sólo** by o.s.

porcelana [porθe'lana] nf porcelain; (china) china.

porcentaje [porθen'taxe] nm percentage.

porción [por'θjon] nf (parte) portion, share; (cantidad) quantity, amount.

pordiosear [porðjose'ar] vi to beg; **pordiosero, a** nm/f beggar.

porfía [por'fia] nf persistence; (terquedad) obstinacy; **porfiado, a** a persistent, obstinate; **porfiar** vi to persist, insist; (disputar) to argue stubbornly.

pormenor [porme'nor] nm detail, particular.

pornografía [pornoɣra'fia] nf pornography.

poro ['poro] nm pore; ~**so, a** a porous.

porque ['porke] conj (a causa de) because; (ya que) since; (con el fin de) so that, in order that.

porqué [por'ke] nm reason, cause.

porquería [porke'ria] nf (suciedad) filth, muck, dirt; (acción) dirty trick; (objeto) small thing, trifle; (fig) rubbish.

porro, a ['porro, a] a (fam) stupid // nf (arma) stick, club; (TEC) large hammer; (fam) bore.

porrón, ona [po'rron, ona] a slow, stupid // nm glass wine jar with a long spout.

portada [por'taða] nf (entrada) porch, doorway; (de revista) cover.

portador, a [porta'ðor, a] nm/f carrier, bearer.

portaequipajes [portaeki'paxes] nm inv boot; (arriba del coche) luggage rack.

portal [por'tal] nm (entrada) vestibule, hall; (portada) porch, doorway; (puerta de entrada) main door; (de ciudad) gate; (DEPORTE) goal.

portaligas [porta'liɣas] nm inv suspender belt.

portamaletas [portama'letas] nm inv boot.

portamonedas [portamo'neðas] nm inv purse.

portarse [por'tarse] vr to behave, conduct o.s.

portátil [por'tatil] a portable.

portaviones [porta'βjones] nm inv aircraft carrier.

portavoz [porta'βoθ] nm (megáfono) megaphone, loudhailer; (vocero) spokesman/woman.

portazo [por'taθo] nm: **dar un ~** to slam the door.

porte ['porte] nm (COM) transport; (precio) transport charges pl; (comportamiento) conduct, behaviour.

portento [por'tento] nm marvel, wonder; ~**so, a** a marvellous, extraordinary.

porteño, a [por'teɲo, a] a of or from Buenos Aires.

portería [porte'ria] nf (oficina) porter's office; (gol) goal.

portero, a [por'tero, a] nm/f porter; (conserje) caretaker; (ujier) doorman // nm goalkeeper.

pórtico ['portiko] *nm* (*patio*) portico, porch; (*fig*) gateway; (*arcada*) arcade.

portilla [por'tiʎa] *nf* porthole.

portillo [por'tiʎo] *nm* (*abertura*) gap, opening; (GEO) narrow pass.

portorriqueño, a [portorri'keɲo, a] *a* Puerto Rican.

Portugal [portu'xal] *nm* Portugal; **portugués, esa** *a, nm/f* Portuguese.

porvenir [porβe'nir] *nm* future.

pos [pos] *prep*: **en ~ de** after, in pursuit of.

posada [po'saða] *nf* (*refugio*) shelter, lodging; (*mesón*) guest house; **dar ~ a** to give shelter to, take in.

posaderas [posa'ðeras] *nfpl* backside *sg*, buttocks.

posar [po'sar] *vt* (*en el suelo*) to lay down, put down; (*la mano*) to place, put gently // *vi* to sit, pose; **~se** *vr* to settle; (*pájaro*) to perch; (*avión*) to land, come down.

posdata [pos'ðata] *nf* postscript.

pose ['pose] *nf* pose.

poseedor, a [posee'ðor, a] *nm/f* owner, possessor; (*de récord, puesto*) holder.

poseer [pose'er] *vt* to have, possess, own; (*ventaja*) to enjoy; (*récord, puesto*) to hold; **poseído, a** *a* possessed; **posesión** *nf* possession; **posesionarse** *vr*: **posesionarse de** to take possession of, take over; **posesivo, a** *a* possessive.

posibilidad [posiβili'ðað] *nf* possibility; (*oportunidad*) chance; **posibilitar** *vt* to make possible, permit; (*hacer factible*) to make feasible.

posible [po'siβle] *a* possible; (*factible*) feasible; **de ser ~** if possible; **en lo ~ as** far as possible.

posición [posi'θjon] *nf* (*gen*) position; (*rango social*) status.

positivo, a [posi'tiβo, a] *a* positive // *nf* (FOTO) print.

poso ['poso] *nm* sediment.

posponer [pospo'ner] *vt* to put behind/below; (AM) to postpone.

posta ['posta] *nf* (*de caballos*) relay, team; (*pedazo*) slice // *nm* courier.

postal [pos'tal] *a* postal // *nf* postcard.

poste ['poste] *nm* (*de telégrafos*) post, pole; (*columna*) pillar; **dar ~ a uno** (*fam*) to keep sb hanging about.

postergar [poster'xar] *vt* (AM: *posponer*) to postpone, delay.

posteridad [posteri'ðað] *nf* posterity.

posterior [poste'rjor] *a* back, rear; (*siguiente*) following, subsequent; (*más tarde*) later; **~idad** *nf*: **con ~idad** later, subsequently.

postizo, a [pos'tiθo, a] *a* false, artificial // *nm* hairpiece.

postor, a [pos'tor, a] *nm/f* bidder.

postrado, a [pos'traðo, a] *a* prostrate; **postrar** *vt* (*derribar*) to cast down, overthrow; (*humillar*) to humble; (MED) to weaken, exhaust.

postre ['postre] *nm* sweet, dessert.

postremo, a [pos'tremo, a], **postrer,**

ero, a [pos'trer, ero, a] *a* (*último*) last; (*que viene detrás*) rear.

postulado [postu'laðo] *nm* postulate; **postular** *vt* (*empleo*) to apply for; (*pedir*) to seek, demand; (*proponer*) to postulate.

póstumo, a ['postumo, a] *a* posthumous.

postura [pos'tura] *nf* (*del cuerpo*) posture, position; (*fig*) attitude, position.

potable [po'taβle] *a* drinkable.

potaje [po'taxe] *nm* stew; **~s** *nmpl* mixed vegetables.

pote ['pote] *nm* pot jar.

potencia [po'tenθja] *nf* power.

potencial [poten'θjal] *a, nm* potential.

potente [po'tente] *a* powerful.

pozo ['poθo] *nm* well; (*de río*) deep pool; (*de mina*) shaft.

práctica ['praktika] *nf ver* **práctico.**

practicable [prakti'kaβle] *a* practicable; (*camino*) passable, usable.

practicante [prakti'kante] *nm/f* (MED: *ayudante de doctor*) medical assistant; (: *enfermero*) male nurse; (*quien practica algo*) practitioner // *a* practising.

practicar [prakti'kar] *vt* to practise; (*deporte*) to go in for, play; (*realizar*) to carry out, perform.

práctico, a ['praktiko, a] *a* (*gen*) practical; (*conveniente*) handy; (*instruido: persona*) skilled, expert // *nf* practice; (*método*) method; (*arte, capacidad*) skill; **en la ~a** in practice.

pradera [pra'ðera] *nf* meadow; (*de Canadá*) prairie.

prado ['praðo] *nm* (*campo*) meadow, field; (*pastizal*) pasture.

Praga ['praxa] *n* Prague.

pragmático, a [prax'matiko, a] *a* pragmatic.

preámbulo [pre'ambulo] *nm* preamble, introduction.

precario, a [pre'karjo, a] *a* precarious.

precaución [prekau'θjon] *nf* (*medida preventiva*) preventive measure, precaution; (*prudencia*) caution, wariness.

precaver [preka'βer] *vt* to guard against; (*impedir*) to forestall; **~se** *vr*: **~se de o contra algo** to (be on one's) guard against sth; **precavido, a** *a* cautious, wary.

precedencia [preθe'ðenθja] *nf* precedence; (*prioridad*) priority; (*superioridad*) greater importance, superiority; **precedente** *a* preceding; (*anterior*) former // *nm* precedent; **preceder** *vt, vi* to precede, go/come before.

precepto [pre'θepto] *nm* precept.

preciado, a [pre'θjaðo, a] *a* (*estimado*) esteemed, valuable; (*vanidoso*) presumptuous; **preciar** *vt* to esteem, value; **preciarse** *vr* to boast **preciarse de** to pride o.s. on, boast of being.

precio ['preθjo] *nm* (*de mercado*) price; (*costo*) cost; (*valor*) value, worth; (*de viaje*) fare; **~ al contado/de coste/de**

oportunidad cash/cost/bargain price; ~ **tope** top price.

preciosidad [preθjosi'ðað] *nf* (*valor*) (high) value, (great) worth; (*encanto*) charm; (*cosa bonita*) beautiful thing; **es una** ~ it's lovely, it's really beautiful; **precioso, a** *a* precious; (*de mucho valor*) valuable; (*fam*) lovely, beautiful.

precipicio [preθi'piθjo] *nm* cliff, precipice; (*fig*) abyss.

precipitación [preθipita'θjon] *nf* haste; (*lluvia*) rainfall.

precipitado, a [preθipi'taðo, a] *a* hasty, rash; (*salida*) hasty, sudden.

precipitar [preθipi'tar] *vt* (*arrojar*) to hurl down, throw; (*apresurar*) to hasten; (*acelerar*) to speed up, accelerate; ~**se** *vr* to throw o.s.; (*apresurarse*) to rush; (*actuar sin pensar*) to act rashly.

precipitoso, a [preθipi'toso, a] *a* (*escarpado*) steep, sheer; (*a la carrera, imprudente*) hasty, rash.

precisamente [preθisa'mente] *ad* precisely; (*justo*) precisely, exactly, just.

precisar [preθi'sar] *vt* (*necesitar*) to need, require; (*fijar*) to determine exactly, fix; (*especificar*) to specify // *vi* to be necessary.

precisión [preθi'sjon] *nf* (*exactitud*) precision; (*necesidad*) need, necessity.

preciso, a [preθiso, a] *a* (*exacto*) precise; (*necesario*) necessary, essential.

preconcebido, a [prekonθe'βiðo, a] *a* preconceived.

preconizar [prekoni'θar] *vt* (*aconsejar*) to advise; (*prever*) to foresee.

precoz [pre'koθ] *a* (*persona*) precocious; (*calvicie*) premature.

precursor, a [prekur'sor, a] *nm/f* precursor.

predecir [preðe'θir] *vt* to predict, foretell, forecast.

predestinado, a [preðesti'naðo, a] *a* predestined.

predeterminar [preðetermi'nar] *vt* to predetermine.

prédica ['preðika] *nf* sermon; **predicador, a** *nm/f* preacher; **predicar** *vt, vi* to preach.

predicción [preðik'θjon] *nf* prediction.

predilecto, a [preði'lekto, a] *a* favourite.

predio ['preðjo] *nm* property, estate.

predisponer [preðispo'ner] *vt* to predispose; (*pey*) to prejudice; **predisposición** *nf* predisposition, inclination; prejudice, bias.

predominante [preðomi'nante] *a* predominant.

predominar [preðomi'nar] *vt* to dominate // *vi* to predominate; (*prevalecer*) to prevail; **predominio** *nm* predominance, prevalence.

prefabricado, a [prefaβri'kaðo, a] *a* prefabricated.

prefacio [pre'faθjo] *nm* preface.

preferencia [prefe'renθja] *nf* preference; **de** ~ preferably, for preference;

preferible *a* preferable; **preferir** *vt* to prefer.

prefigurar [prefixu'rar] *vt* to foreshadow, prefigure.

pregonar [prexo'nar] *vt* to proclaim, announce.

pregunta [pre'xunta] *nf* question; **hacer una** ~ to ask *or* put a question.

preguntar [prexun'tar] *vt* to ask; (*cuestionar*) to question // *vi* to ask; ~**se** *vr* to wonder; ~ **por alguien** to ask for sb; **preguntón, ona** *a* inquisitive.

prehistórico, a [preis'toriko, a] *a* prehistoric.

prejuicio [pre'xwiθjo] *nm* prejudgement; (*preconcepción*) preconception; (*pey*) prejudice, bias.

prelación [prela'θjon] *nf* priority.

preliminar [prelimi'nar] *a* preliminary.

preludio [pre'luðjo] *nm* prelude.

prematuro, a [prema'turo, a] *a* premature.

premeditación [premeðita'θjon] *nf* premeditation; **premeditar** *vt* to premeditate.

premiar [pre'mjar] *vt* to reward; (*en un concurso*) to give a prize to; **premio** *nm* reward; prize; (*COM*) premium.

premonición [premoni'θjon] *nf* premonition.

premura [pre'mura] *nf* (*aprieto*) pressure; (*prisa*) haste, urgency.

prenatal [prena'tal] *a* antenatal, prenatal.

prenda ['prenda] *nf* (*ropa*) garment, article of clothing; (*garantía*) pledge; ~**s** *nfpl* talents, gifts.

prendar [pren'dar] *vt* to captivate, enchant; ~**se de uno** to fall in love with sb.

prendedor [prende'ðor] *nm* brooch.

prender [pren'der] *vt* (*captar*) to catch, capture; (*detener*) to arrest; (*coser*) to pin, attach; (*sujetar*) to fasten // *vi* to catch; (*arraigar*) to take root; ~**se** *vr* (*encenderse*) to catch fire; (*engalanarse*) to dress up.

prensa ['prensa] *nf* press; **la P**~ the press; **prensar** *vt* to press.

preñado, a [pre'naðo, a] *a* (*mujer*) pregnant; ~ **de** pregnant with, full of; **preñez** *nf* pregnancy.

preocupación [preokupa'θjon] *nf* worry, concern; (*ansiedad*) anxiety; **preocupado, a** *a* worried, concerned; anxious.

preocupar [preoku'par] *vt* to worry; ~**se** *vr* to worry; ~**se de algo** (*hacerse cargo*) to worry about sth, take care of sth.

preparación [prepara'θjon] *nf* (*acto*) preparation; (*estado*) preparedness, readiness; (*entrenamiento*) training; **preparado, a** *a* (*dispuesto*) prepared; (*CULIN*) ready (to serve) // *nm* preparation.

preparador, a [prepara'ðor, a] *nm/f* trainer.

preparar [prepa'rar] *vt* (*disponer*) to prepare, get ready; (*TEC*: *tratar*) to prepare, process, treat; (*entrenar*) to teach, train; ~**se** *vr*: ~**se a** *o* **para** to prepare to *or* for, get ready to *or* for; **preparativo, a** *a* preparatory, preliminary; **preparativos** *nmpl* preparations; **preparatorio, a** *a* preparatory.

prerrogativa [prerroxa'tiβa] *nf* prerogative, privilege.

presa ['presa] *nf* (*captura*) capture, seizure; (*cosa apresada*) catch; (*víctima*) victim; (*de animal*) prey; (*de agua*) dam.

presbítero [pres'βitero] *nm* priest.

prescindible [presθin'diβle] *a* dispensable.

prescindir [presθin'dir] *vi*: ~ **de** (*privarse de*) to do without, go without; (*descartar*) to dispense with.

prescribir [preskri'βir] *vt* to prescribe; **prescripción** *nf* prescription.

presencia [pre'senθja] *nf* presence; **presencial** *a*: **testigo presencial** eyewitness; **presenciar** *vt* to be present at; (*asistir a*) to attend; (*ver*) to see, witness.

presentación [presenta'θjon] *nf* presentation; (*introducción*) introduction.

presentador, a [presenta'ðor, a] *nm/f* compère.

presentar [presen'tar] *vt* to present; (*ofrecer*) to offer; (*mostrar*) to show, display; (*a una persona*) to introduce; ~**se** *vr* (*llegar inesperadamente*) to appear, turn up; (*ofrecerse: como candidato*) to run, stand; (*aparecer*) to show, appear; (*solicitar empleo*) to apply.

presente [pre'sente] *a* present // *nm* present; **hacer** ~ to state, declare; **tener** ~ to remember, bear in mind.

presentimiento [presenti'mjento] *nm* premonition, presentiment; **presentir** *vt* to have a premonition of.

preservación [preserβa'θjon] *nf* protection, preservation; **preservar** *vt* to protect, preserve; **preservativo** *nm* sheath, condom.

presidencia [presi'ðenθja] *nf* presidency; (*de comité*) chairmanship; **presidente** *nm/f* president; chairman/woman.

presidiario [presi'ðjarjo] *nm* convict; **presidio** *nm* (*penitenciaría*) prison, penitentiary; (*trabajo forzoso*) hard labour; (*MIL*) garrison.

presidir [presi'ðir] *vt* (*dirigir*) to preside at, preside over; (: *comité*) to take the chair at; (*dominar*) to dominate, rule // *vi* to preside; to take the chair.

presión [pre'sjon] *nf* pressure; **presionar** *vt* to press; (*fig*) to press, put pressure on // *vi*: **presionar para o por** to press for.

preso, a ['preso, a] *nm/f* prisoner; **tomar** *o* **llevar** ~ **a uno** to arrest sb, take sb prisoner.

prestado, a [pres'taðo, a] *a* on loan; **pedir** ~ to borrow.

prestamista [presta'mista] *nm/f* moneylender.

préstamo ['prestamo] *nm* loan.

prestar [pres'tar] *vt* to lend, loan; (*atención*) to pay; (*ayuda*) to give // *vi* to give, stretch.

prestatario, a [presta'tarjo, a] *nm/f* borrower.

presteza [pres'teθa] *nf* speed, promptness.

prestigio [pres'tixjo] *nm* prestige; ~**so, a** *a* (*honorable*) prestigious; (*famoso, renombrado*) renowned, famous.

presto, a ['presto, a] *a* (*rápido*) quick, prompt; (*dispuesto*) ready // *ad* at once, right away.

presumir [presu'mir] *vt* to presume // *vi* (*tener aires*) to be conceited; **según cabe** ~ as may be presumed, presumably; **presunción** *nf* presumption; **presunto, a** (*supuesto*) supposed, presumed; (*así llamado*) so-called; **presuntuoso, a** *a* conceited, presumptuous.

presuponer [presupo'ner] *vt* to presuppose.

presupuesto [presu'pwesto] *nm* (*FINANZAS*) budget; (*estimación: de costo*) estimate.

presuroso, a [presu'roso, a] *a* (*rápido*) quick, speedy; (*que tiene prisa*) hasty.

pretencioso, a [preten'θjoso, a] *a* pretentious.

pretender [preten'der] *vt* (*intentar*) to try to, seek to; (*reivindicar*) to claim; (*buscar*) to seek, try for; (*cortejar*) to woo, court; ~ **que** to expect that; **pretendiente** *nm/f* (*candidato*) candidate, applicant; (*amante*) suitor; **pretensión** *nf* (*aspiración*) aspiration; (*reivindicación*) claim; (*orgullo*) pretension.

pretexto [pre'teksto] *nm* pretext; (*excusa*) excuse.

prevalecer [preβale'θer] *vi* to prevail; **prevaleciente** *a* prevailing, prevalent.

prevalerse [preβa'lerse] *vr*: ~ **de** to avail o.s. of.

prevención [preβen'θjon] *nf* (*preparación*) preparation; (*estado*) preparedness readiness; (*el evitar*) prevention; (*previsión*) foresight, forethought; (*prejuicio*) bias, prejudice; (*precaución*) precaution.

prevenido, a [preβe'niðo, a] *a* prepared, ready; (*cauteloso*) cautious.

prevenir [preβe'nir] *vt* (*impedir*) to prevent; (*prever*) to foresee, anticipate; (*predisponer*) to prejudice, bias; (*avisar*) to warn; (*preparar*) to prepare, get ready; ~**se** *vr* to get ready, prepare; ~**se contra** to take precautions against; **preventivo, a** *a* preventive, precautionary.

prever [pre'βer] *vt* to foresee.

previo, a ['preβjo, a] *a* (*anterior*) previous; (*preliminar*) preliminary // *prep*: ~ **acuerdo de los otros** subject to the agreement of the others.

previsión [preβi'sjon] *nf* (*perspicacia*) foresight; (*predicción*) forecast; ~ **social** social security.

prieto, a ['prjeto, a] *a* (*oscuro*) dark; (*fig*) mean; (*comprimido*) tight, compressed.

prima ['prima] *nf ver* **primo.**
primacía [prima'θia] *nf* primacy.
primario, a [pri'marjo, a] *a* primary.
primavera [prima'βera] *nf* (*temporada*) spring; (*período*) springtime.
primer, primero, a [pri'mer, pri'mero, a] *a* first; (*fig*) prime // *ad* first; (*más bien*) sooner, rather // *nf* (*AUTO*) first gear; (*FERRO*) first class; **de ~a** (*fam*) first-class, first-rate; **~a plana** front page.
primitivo, a [primi'tiβo, a] *a* primitive; (*original*) original.
primo, a ['primo, a] *nm/f* cousin; (*fam*) fool, dupe // *nf* (*COM*) bonus; **~ hermano** first cousin; **materias ~as** raw materials.
primogénito, a [primo'xenito, a] *a* first-born.
primordial [primor'δjal] *a* basic, fundamental.
primoroso, a [primo'roso, a] *a* exquisite, delicate.
princesa [prin'θesa] *nf* princess.
principal [prinθi'pal] *a* principal, main // *nm* (*jefe*) chief, principal.
príncipe ['prinθipe] *nm* prince.
principiante [prinθi'pjante] *nm/f* beginner; **principiar** *vt* to begin.
principio [prin'θipjo] *nm* (*comienzo*) beginning, start; (*origen*) origin; (*primera etapa*) rudiment, basic idea; (*moral*) principle; **a ~s de** at the beginning of; **tener o tomar en ~** to start from, be based on.
pringue ['pringe] *nm* (*grasa*) grease, fat, dripping; (*mancha*) grease stain.
prioridad [priori'δaδ] *nf* priority.
prisa ['prisa] *nf* (*apresuramiento*) hurry, haste; (*rapidez*) speed; (*urgencia*) (sense of) urgency; **a o de ~** quickly; **correr ~** to be urgent; **darse ~** to hurry up; **estar de o tener ~** to be in a hurry.
prisión [pri'sjon] *nf* (*cárcel*) prison; (*período de cárcel*) imprisonment; **prisionero, a** *nm/f* prisoner.
prismáticos [pris'matikos] *nmpl* binoculars.
privación [priβa'θjon] *nf* deprivation; (*falta*) want, privation.
privado, a [pri'βaδo, a] *a* private.
privar [pri'βar] *vt* to deprive; (*prohibir*) to forbid // *vi* (*gozar de favor*) to be in favour; (*prevalecer*) to prevail; **privativo, a** *a* exclusive.
privilegiado, a [priβile'xjaδo, a] *a* privileged; (*memoria*) very good; **privilegiar** *vt* to grant a privilege to; (*favorecer*) to favour.
privilegio [priβi'lexjo] *nm* privilege; (*concesión*) concession; **~ de invención** patent.
pro [pro] *nm o f* profit, advantage // *prep*: **asociación ~ ciegos** association for the blind // *pref*: **~ soviético/americano** pro-Soviet/American; **en ~ de** on behalf of, for; **los ~s y los contras** the pros and cons.

probabilidad [proβaβili'δaδ] *nf* probability, likelihood; (*oportunidad, posibilidad*) chance, prospect; **probable** *a* probable, likely.
probanza [pro'βanθa] *nf* proof, evidence.
probar [pro'βar] *vt* (*demostrar*) to prove; (*someter a prueba*) to test, try out; (*ropa*) to try on; (*comida*) to taste // *vi* to try; **~se un traje** to try on a suit.
probeta [pro'βeta] *nf* test tube.
problema [pro'βlema] *nm* problem.
procaz [pro'kaθ] *a* insolent, impudent.
procedente [proθe'δente] *a* (*razonable*) reasonable; (*conforme a derecho*) proper, fitting; **~ de** coming from, originating in.
proceder [proθe'δer] *vi* (*avanzar*) to proceed; (*actuar*) to act; (*ser correcto*) to be right (and proper), be fitting // *nm* (*acción*) course of action; (*comportamiento*) behaviour, conduct; **procedimiento** *nm* procedure; (*proceso*) process; (*método*) means, method.
procesado, a [proθe'saδo, a] *nm/f* accused (person); **procesar** *vt* to try, put on trial.
procesión [proθe'sjon] *nf* procession.
proceso [pro'θeso] *nm* process; (*JUR*) trial; (*lapso*) course (of time).
proclama [pro'klama] *nf* (*acto*) proclamation; (*cartel*) poster; **proclamar** *vt* to proclaim.
procreación [prokrea'θjon] *nf* procreation; **procrear** *vt*, *vi* to procreate.
procurador, a [prokura'δor, a] *nm/f* attorney.
procurar [proku'rar] *vt* (*intentar*) to try, endeavour; (*conseguir*) to get, obtain; (*asegurar*) to secure; (*producir*) to produce.
prodigio [pro'δixjo] *nm* prodigy; (*milagro*) wonder, marvel; **~so, a** *a* prodigious, marvellous.
pródigo, a ['proδixo, a] *a*: **hijo ~** prodigal son.
producción [proδuk'θjon] *nf* production; (*suma de productos*) output; (*producto*) product; **~ en serie** mass production.
producir [proδu'θir] *vt* to produce; (*generar*) to cause, bring about; **~se** *vr* (*gen*) to come about, happen; (*hacerse*) to be produced, be made; (*estallar*) to break out.
productividad [proδuktiβi'δaδ] *nf* productivity; **productivo, a** *a* productive; (*provechoso*) profitable.
producto [pro'δukto] *nm* product; (*producción*) production.
productor, a [proδuk'tor, a] *a* productive, producing // *nm/f* producer.
proeza [pro'eθa] *nf* exploit, feat.
profanar [profa'nar] *vt* to desecrate, profane; **profano, a** *a* profane // *nm/f* layman/woman.
profecía [profe'θia] *nf* prophecy.
proferir [profe'rir] *vt* (*palabra, sonido*) to utter; (*injuria*) to hurl, let fly.
profesar [profe'sar] *vt* (*declarar*) to profess; (*practicar*) to practise.

profesión [profe'sjon] nf profession;
profesional a professional.

profesor, a [profe'sor, a] nm/f teacher;
~**ado** nm teaching profession.

profeta [pro'feta] nm/f prophet;
profetizar vt, vi to prophesy.

prófugo, a [profuxo, a] nm/f fugitive;
(desertor) deserter.

profundidad [profundi'ðað] nf depth;
profundizar vt (fig) to go deeply into;
profundo, a a deep; (misterio, pensador)
profound.

progenie [pro'xenje] nf offspring.

progenitor [proxeni'tor] nm ancestor;
~**es** nmpl (fam) parents.

programa [pro'xrama] nm programme;
~**ción** nf programming; ~**dor, a** nm/f
programmer; **programar** vt to
programme.

progresar [proxre'sar] vi to progress
make progress; **progresista** a, nm/f
progressive; **progresivo, a** a progressive;
(gradual) gradual; (continuo) continuous;
progreso nm progress.

prohibición [proiβi'θjon] nf prohibition,
ban; **prohibir** vt to prohibit, ban, forbid;
se prohibe fumar no smoking.

prohijar [proi'xar] vt to adopt.

prójimo, a ['proximo, a] nm/f fellow man,
neighbour.

proletariado [proleta'rjaðo] nm
proletariat; **proletario, a** a, nm/f
proletarian.

proliferación [prolifera'θjon] nf
proliferation; **proliferar** vi to proliferate;
prolífico, a a prolific.

prolijo, a [pro'lixo, a] a long-winded,
tedious.

prólogo ['proloxo] nm prologue.

prolongación [prolonga'θjon] nf
extension; **prolongado, a** a (largo) long;
(alargado) lengthy; **prolongar** vt (gen) to
extend; (en el tiempo) to prolong; (calle,
tubo) to make longer, extend.

promedio [pro'meðjo] nm average; (de
distancia) middle, mid-point.

promesa [pro'mesa] nf promise.

prometer [prome'ter] vt to promise // vi
to show promise; ~**se** vr (dos personas) to
get engaged; **prometido, a** a promised;
engaged // nm/f fiancé/fiancée.

prominente [promi'nente] a prominent.

promiscuo, a [pro'miskwo, a] a
(mezclado) mixed(-up), in disorder;
(ambiguo) ambiguous.

promoción [promo'θjon] nf promotion.

promotor [promo'tor] nm promoter;
(instigador) instigator.

promover [promo'βer] vt to promote;
(causar) to cause; (instigar) to instigate,
stir up.

promulgar [promul'xar] vt to promulgate;
(fig) to proclaim.

pronosticar [pronosti'kar] vt to predict,
foretell, forecast; **pronóstico** nm
prediction, forecast.

prontitud [pronti'tuð] nf speed, quickness;

(de ingenio) quickness, sharpness.

pronto, a ['pronto, a] a (rápido) prompt,
quick; (preparado) ready; (astuto) quick,
sharp // ad quickly, promptly; (en seguida)
at once, right away; (dentro de poco) soon;
(temprano) early // nm: **tener** ~**s de
enojo** to be quick-tempered; **al** ~ at first;
de ~ suddenly; **por lo** ~ meanwhile, for
the present.

pronunciación [pronunθja'θjon] nf
pronunciation; **pronunciar** vt to
pronounce; (discurso) to make, deliver;
pronunciarse vr to revolt, rise, rebel;
(declararse) to declare o.s.

propagación [propaxa'θjon] nf
propagation.

propaganda [propa'xanda] nf (política)
propaganda (comercial) advertising.

propagar [propa'xar] vt to propagate.

propensión [propen'sjon] nf inclination,
propensity; **propenso, a** a inclined to; **ser
propenso a** to be inclined to, have a
tendency to.

propiamente [propja'mente] ad properly;
(realmente) really exactly.

propicio, a [pro'piθjo, a] a favourable,
propitious.

propiedad [propje'ðað] nf (gen) property;
(posesión) possession, ownership; ~
industrial patent rights pl; ~ **literaria**
copyright; ~ **particular** private
property.

propietario, a [propje'tarjo, a] nm/f
owner, proprietor.

propina [pro'pina] nf tip.

propio, a ['propjo, a] a own, of one's own;
(característico) characteristic, typical;
(conveniente) proper; (mismo) selfsame,
very; **el** ~ **ministro** the minister himself;
¿**tienes casa** ~**a**? have you a house of
your own?

proponer [propo'ner] vt to propose, put
forward; (problema) to pose; ~**se** vr to
propose, plan, intend

proporción [propor'θjon] nf proportion;
(MAT) ratio; (oportunidad) chance,
opportunity; **proporciones** nfpl
dimensions; (fig) size ; **proporcionado,
a** a proportionate; (regular) medium,
middling; (justo) just right; **proporcionar**
vt (dar) to give, supply, provide; (adaptar)
to adjust, adapt.

proposición [proposi'θjon] nf proposition;
(propuesta) proposal.

propósito [pro'posito] nm purpose;
(intento) aim, intention // a: a ~
appropriate, suitable; ad: a ~ by the
way, incidentally; a ~ **de** about, with
regard to; **de** ~ on purpose, deliberately.

propuesta [pro'pwesta] nf proposal.

propulsar [propul'sar] vt to drive, propel;
(fig) to promote, encourage; **propulsión**
nf propulsion; **propulsión a chorro** o **por
reacción** jet propulsion

prórroga ['prorroxa] nf (gen) extension;
(JUR) stay; (COM) deferment; **prorrogar** vt

(período) to extend; *(decisión)* to defer, postpone.

prorrumpir [prorrum'pir] *vi* to burst forth, break out.

prosa ['prosa] *nf* prose.

proscribir [proskri'ⲃir] *vt* to prohibit, ban; *(desterrar)* to exile, banish; *(partido)* to proscribe; **proscripción** *nf* prohibition, ban; banishment; proscription.

prosecución [proseku'θjon] *nf* continuation; *(persecución)* pursuit.

proseguir [prose'ⲅir] *vt* to continue, carry on, proceed with // *vi* to continue, go on.

prospección [prospek'θjon] *nf* exploration; *(del petróleo, del oro)* prospecting.

prospecto [pros'pekto] *nm* prospectus.

prosperar [prospe'rar] *vi* to prosper, thrive, flourish; **prosperidad** *nf* prosperity; *(éxito)* success; **próspero, a** *a* prosperous, thriving, flourishing; *(que tiene éxito)* successful.

prostíbulo [pros'tiⲃulo] *nm* brothel.

prostitución [prostitu'θjon] *nf* prostitution; **prostituir** *vt* to prostitute; **prostituirse** *vr* to prostitute o.s., become a prostitute; **prostituta** *nf* prostitute.

protagonista [protaɣo'nista] *nm/f* protagonist.

protección [protek'θjon] *nf* protection.

protector, a [protek'tor, a] *a* protective, protecting // *nm/f* protector.

proteger [prote'xer] *vt* to protect; **protegido, a** *nm/f* protégé/ protégée.

proteína [prote'ina] *nf* protein.

protesta [pro'testa] *nf* protest; *(declaración)* protestation.

protestante [protes'tante] *a* Protestant.

protestar [protes'tar] *vt* to protest, declare; *(fé)* to protest // *vi* to protest.

protocolo [proto'kolo] *nm* protocol.

prototipo [proto'tipo] *nm* prototype.

provecho [pro'ⲃetʃo] *nm* advantage, benefit; *(FINANZAS)* profit; ¡**buen ~!** bon appétit!; **en ~ de** to the benefit of; **sacar ~ de** to benefit from, profit by.

proveer [proⲃe'er] *vt* to provide, supply; *(preparar)* to provide, get ready; *(vacante)* to fill; *(negocio)* to transact, dispatch // *vi*: **~ a** to provide for.

provenir [proⲃe'nir] *vi*: **~ de** to come from, stem from.

proverbio [pro'ⲃerⲃjo] *nm* proverb.

providencia [proⲃi'ðenθja] *nf* providence; *(previsión)* foresight; **~s** *nfpl* measures, steps.

provincia [pro'ⲃinθja] *nf* province; **~no, a** a provincial; *(del campo)* country *cpd*.

provisión [proⲃi'sjon] *nf* provision; *(abastecimiento)* provision, supply; *(medida)* measure, step.

provisional [proⲃisjo'nal] *a* provisional.

provocación [proⲃoka'θjon] *nf* provocation; **provocar** *vt* to provoke; *(alentar)* to tempt, invite; *(causar)* to bring about, lead to; *(promover)* to promote;

(estimular) to rouse, stir, stimulate; **provocativo, a** a provocative.

próximamente [proksima'mente] *ad* shortly, soon.

proximidad [proksimi'ðað] *nf* closeness, proximity; **próximo, a** a near, close; *(vecino)* neighbouring; *(el que viene)* next.

proyectar [projek'tar] *vt* *(objeto)* to hurl, throw; *(luz)* to cast, shed; *(CINE)* to screen, show; *(planear)* to plan.

proyectil [projek'til] *nm* projectile, missile; *(MIL)* missile.

proyecto [pro'jekto] *nm* plan; *(estimación de costo)* detailed estimate.

proyector [projek'tor] *nm* *(CINE)* projector; *(MIL)* searchlight; *(de teatro)* spotlight.

prudencia [pru'ðenθja] *nf* *(sabiduría)* wisdom, prudence; *(cautela)* care; **prudente** a sensible, wise, prudent; *(conductor)* careful.

prueba ['prweⲃa] *nf* proof; *(ensayo)* test, trial; *(saboreo)* testing, sampling; *(de ropa)* fitting; **~s** *nfpl* trials; **a ~** on trial; **a ~ de** proof against; **a ~ de agua/fuego** waterproof/fireproof; **sala de ~s** fitting room; **someter a ~** to put to the test.

prurito [pru'rito] *nm* itch; *(de bebé)* nappy rash.

psico... [siko] *pref* psycho...; **~análisis** *nm* psychoanalysis; **~logía** *nf* psychology; **~lógico, a** a psychological; **psicólogo, a** *nm/f* psychologist; **psicópata** *nm/f* psychopath; **~sis** *nf inv* psychosis.

psiquiatra [si'kjatra] *nm/f* psychiatrist; **psiquiátrico, a** a psychiatric.

psíquico, a ['sikiko, a] a psychic(al).

PSOE *abr de* **Partido Socialista Obrero Español.**

púa ['pua] *nf* sharp point; *(para guitarra)* plectrum; **alambre de ~** barbed wire.

pubertad [puⲃer'tað] *nf* puberty.

publicación [puⲃlika'θjon] *nf* publication; **publicar** *vt* *(editar)* to publish; *(hacer público)* to publicize; *(vulgarizar)* to make public, divulge.

publicidad [puⲃliði'ðað] *nf* publicity; *(COM)* advertising; **publicitario, a** a publicity *cpd*; advertising *cpd*.

público, a ['puⲃliko, a] a public // *nm* public; *(TEATRO etc)* audience.

puchero [pu'tʃero] *nm* stew; **hacer ~s** to pout.

pude *etc vb ver* **poder.**

púdico, a ['puðiko, a] a modest.

pudiera *etc vb ver* **poder.**

pudor [pu'ðor] *nm* modesty.

pudrir [pu'ðrir] *vt* to rot; *(fam)* to upset, annoy; **~se** *vr* to rot, decay.

pueblo ['pweⲃlo] *nm* people; *(nación)* nation; *(aldea)* village.

puedo *etc vb ver* **poder.**

puente ['pwente] *nm* *(gen)* bridge; **~ aéreo** airlift; **~ colgante** suspension bridge; **hacer el ~** *(fam)* to take an extra day off work between 2 public holidays.

puerco, a ['pwerko, a] *nm/f* pig/sow // a

(*sucio*) dirty, filthy; (*obsceno*) disgusting; ~ **de mar** porpoise; ~ **marino** dolphin.

pueril [pwe'ril] *a* childish.

puerro ['pwerro] *nm* leek.

puerta ['pwerta] *nf* door; (*de jardín* gate; (*portal*) doorway; (*fig*) gateway; (*gol*) goal; **a** ~ **cerrada** behind closed doors; ~ **giratoria** swing door, revolving door.

puertaventana [pwerta'ßen'tana] *nf* shutter.

puerto ['pwerto] *nm* port; (*paso*) pass; (*fig*) haven, refuge.

Puerto Rico [pwerto'riko] *nm* Puerto Rico; **puertorriqueño, a** *a* Puerto Rican.

pues [pwes] *ad* (*entonces*) then; (*¡entonces!*) well, well then; (*así que*) so // *conj* (*ya que*) since; ¡~! (*sí*) yes!, certainly!

puesto, a ['pwesto, a] *pp de* **poner** // *a* dressed // *nm* (*lugar, posición*) place; (*trabajo*) post, job; (*COM*) stall // *conj* ~ **que** since, as // *nf* (*apuesta*) bet, stake; ~**a en marcha** starting; ~**a del sol** sunset.

púgil ['puxil] *nm* boxer.

pugna ['puxna] *nf* battle, conflict; ~**cidad** *nf* pugnacity, aggressiveness; **pugnar** *vi* (*luchar*) to struggle, fight; (*pelear*) to fight.

pulcro, a ['pulkro, a] *a* neat, tidy; (*bello*) exquisite.

pulga ['pulxa] *nf* flea.

pulgada [pul'xaða] *nf* inch.

pulgar [pul'xar] *nm* thumb.

pulir [pu'lir], **pulimentar** [pulimen'tar] *vt* to polish; (*alisar*) to smooth; (*fig*) to polish up, touch up.

pulmón [pul'mon] *nm* lung; **pulmonía** *nf* pneumonia.

pulpa ['pulpa] *nf* pulp; (*de fruta*) flesh, soft part.

púlpito ['pulpito] *nm* pulpit.

pulpo ['pulpo] *nm* octopus.

pulsación [pulsa'θjon] *nf* beat, pulsation; (*ANAT*) throb(bing).

pulsador [pulsa'ðor] *nm* button, push button.

pulsar [pul'sar] *vt* (*tecla*) to touch, tap (*MUS*) to play; (*botón*) to press, push // *vi* to pulsate; (*latir*) to beat, throb; (*MED*): ~ **a uno** to take sb's pulse.

pulsera [pul'sera] *nf* bracelet.

pulso ['pulso] *nm* (*ANAT*) pulse; (: *muñeca*) wrist; (*fuerza*) strength; (*firmeza*) steadiness, steady hand; (*tacto*) tact, good sense.

pulverizador [pulßeriθa'ðor] *nm* spray, spray gun; **pulverizar** *vt* to pulverize; (*líquido*) to spray.

pulla ['puʎa] *nf* cutting remark; (*expresión grosera*) obscene remark.

pungir [pun'xir] *vt* to puncture, prick, pierce; (*fig*) to cause suffering to.

punición [puni'θjon] *nf* punishment; **punitivo, a** *a* punitive.

punta ['punta] *nf* point, tip; (*extremidad*) end; (*fig*) touch, trace; **horas** ~**s** peak hours, rush hours; **sacar** ~ **a** to sharpen; **estar de** ~ to be edgy.

puntada [pun'taða] *nf* (*COSTURA*) stitch; (*fam*) hint; **no ha dado** ~ he hasn't done a stroke.

puntal [pun'tal] *nm* prop, support.

puntapié [punta'pje] *nm* kick.

puntear [punte'ar] *vt* (*marcar*) to tick, mark; (*coser*) to stitch (up).

puntería [punte'ria] *nf* (*de arma*) aim, aiming; (*destreza*) marksmanship.

puntiagudo, a [puntja'xuðo, a] *a* sharp, pointed.

puntilla [pun'tiʎa] *nf* (*de pluma*) point, nib; (**andar**) **de** ~**s** (to walk) on tiptoe.

punto ['punto] *nm* (*gen*) point; (*señal diminuta*) spot, dot; (*lugar*) spot, place; (*momento*) point, moment; **a** ~ ready; **estar a** ~ **de** to be on the point of *or* about to; **en** ~ on the dot; ~ **de arranque** starting point; ~ **muerto** dead centre; (*AUTO*) neutral (gear); ~ **y coma** semicolon; ~ **de interrogación** question mark.

puntuación [puntwa'θjon] *nf* punctuation; (*puntos: en examen*) mark(s) (*pl*); (: *DEPORTE*) score.

puntual [pun'twal] *a* (*a tiempo*) punctual; (*exacto*) exact, accurate; (*seguro*) reliable; ~**idad** *nf* punctuality; exactness, accuracy; reliability; ~**izar** *vt* to fix, specify; (*en la memoria*) to fix in one's mind/memory.

punzante [pun'θante] *a* (*dolor*) shooting, sharp; (*herramienta*) sharp; **punzar** *vt* to prick, pierce // *vi* to shoot, stab.

puñado [pu'ɲaðo] *nm* handful.

puñal [pu'ɲal] *nm* dagger; ~**ada** *nf* stab; ~**ada de misericordia** coup de grâce.

puñetazo [puɲe'taðo] *nm* punch.

puño ['puɲo] *nm* (*ANAT*) fist; (*cantidad*) fistful, handful; (*COSTURA*) cuff; (*de herramienta*) handle.

pupila [pu'pila] *nf* pupil.

pupitre [pu'pitre] *nm* desk.

puré [pu're] *nm* puree; (*sopa*) (thick) soup; ~ **de patatas** mashed potatoes.

pureza [pu'reθa] *nf* purity.

purga ['purxa] *nf* purge; **purgante** *a*, *nm* purgative, **purgar** *vt* to purge.

purgatorio [purxa'torjo] *nm* purgatory.

purificar [purifi'kar] *vt* to purify; (*refinar*) to refine.

puritano, a [puri'tano, a] *a* (*actitud*) puritanical; (*iglesia, tradición*) puritan // *nm,f* puritan.

puro, a ['puro, a] *a* pure; (*cielo*) clear; (*verdad*) simple, plain // *ad*: **de** ~ **cansado** out of sheer tiredness // *nm* cigar.

púrpura ['purpura] *nf* purple; **purpúreo, a** *a* purple.

puse, pusiera *etc vb ver* **poner.**

pústula ['pustula] *nf* pimple, sore.

puta ['puta] *nf* whore, prostitute.

putrefacción [putrefak'θjon] *nf* rotting, putrefaction

pútrido, a ['putriðo, a] *a* rotten.

Q

q.e.p.d. *abr de* que en paz descanse.

q.e.s.m. *abr de* que estrecha su mano.

que [ke] *pron (sujeto)* who, that; (: *cosa*) which, that; (*complemento*) whom, that; (: *cosa*) which, that // *conj* that; **el momento en ~ llegó** the moment he arrived; **lo ~ digo** what I say; **dar ~ hablar** to give cause to talk, cause talk; **le ruego ~ se calle** I'm asking you to keep quiet; **te digo ~ sí** I'm telling you, I assure you; **yo ~ tú** if I were you.

qué [ke] *a* what?, which? // *pron* what?; ¡ **divertido!** how funny!; ¿ **~ edad tiene Ud?** how old are you?; ¿**de ~ me hablas?** what are you saying to me?; ¿ **~ tal?** how are you?, how are things?; ¿ **~ hay (de nuevo)?** what's new?

quebrada [ke'βraða] *nf ver* **quebrado.**

quebradizo, a [keβra'ðiθo, a] *a* fragile; (*persona*) frail.

quebrado, a [ke'βraðo, a] *a (roto)* broken; (*pálido*) pale; (*COM*) bankrupt // *nm/f* bankrupt // *nf* ravine.

quebradura [keβra'ðura] *nf (fisura)* fissure; (*GEO*) gorge; (*MED*) rupture.

quebrantadura [keβranta'ðura] *nf*, **quebrantamiento** [keβranta'mjento] *nm* (*acto*) breaking; (*estado*) exhaustion.

quebrantar [keβran'tar] *vt (romper)* to break; (*infringir*) to violate, transgress; **~se** *vr (persona)* to fail in health; (*deshacerse*) to break.

quebranto [ke'βranto] *nm* damage, harm; (*decaimiento*) exhaustion; (*debilidad*) weakness; (*dolor*) grief, pain.

quebrar [ke'βrar] *vt* to break, smash; (*interrumpir*) to interrupt // *vi* to go bankrupt; **~se** *vr* to break, get broken; (*MED*) to be ruptured.

quedar [ke'ðar] *vi (permanecer)* to stay; (*seguir siendo*) to remain; (*encontrarse*) to be; (*restar*) to remain, be left; **~se** *vr* to remain, stay (behind); **~se con** to keep; **~ en** (*acordar*) to agree on/to; (*acabar siendo*) to end up as; **~ por hacer** to be still to be done; **~ ciego/mudo** to be left blind/dumb; **no te queda bien ese vestido** that dress doesn't suit you; **quedamos a las seis** we agreed to meet at six.

quedo, a ['keðo, a] *a* still // *ad* softly, gently.

quehacer [kea'θer] *nm* task, job; (*doméstico*) chore.

queja ['kexa] *nf* complaint; **quejarse** *vr* (*enfermo*) to moan, groan; (*protestar*) to complain; **quejido** [ke'xiðo] *nm* moan; **quejoso, a** *a* complaining.

quemado, a [ke'maðo, a] *a* burnt.

quemadura [kema'ðura] *nf* burn, scald.

quemar [ke'mar] *vt* to burn; (*fig*) to burn up, squander // *vi* to be burning hot; **~se** *vr* to burn (up); (*del sol*) to get sunburnt.

quemarropa [kema'rropa]: **a ~** *ad* point-blank.

quemazón [kema'θon] *nf* burn; (*calor*) intense heat; (*sensación*) itch.

quepo *etc vb ver* **caber.**

querella [ke'reʎa] *nf (JUR)* charge; (*disputa*) dispute.

querer [ke'rer] *vt (desear)* to want, wish; (*amar a*) to love; **~ hacer algo** to want to do sth; **querido, a** *a* dear // *nm/f* darling // *nf* mistress.

quesería [kese'ria] *nf* dairy, cheese factory.

queso ['keso] *nm* cheese; **~ crema** cream cheese; **~ helado** ice-cream brick.

quicio ['kiθjo] *nm* hinge; **sacar a uno de ~** to get on sb's nerves.

quiebra ['kjeβra] *nf* break, split; (*COM*) bankruptcy; (*ECON*) slump.

quiebro ['kjeβro] *nm (del cuerpo)* swerve.

quien [kjen] *pron* who; **hay ~ piensa que** there are those who think that; **no hay ~ lo haga** no-one will do it.

quién [kjen] *pron* who, whom; ¿**~ es?** who's there?

quienquiera [kjen'kjera] (*pl* **quienesquiera**) *pron* whoever.

quiero *etc vb ver* **querer.**

quieto, a ['kjeto, a] *a* still; (*carácter*) placid; **quietud** *nf* stillness.

quijada [ki'xaða] *nf* jaw, jawbone.

quilate [ki'late] *nm* carat.

quimera [ki'mera] *nf* chimera; **quimérico, a** *a* fantastic.

químico, a ['kimiko, a] *a* chemical // *nm/f* chemist // *nf* chemistry.

quincalla [kin'kaʎa] *nf* hardware, ironmongery.

quince ['kinθe] *num* fifteen; **~na** *nf* fortnight; (*pago*) fortnightly pay; **~nal** *a* fortnightly.

quiniela [ki'njela] *nf* pools coupon; **~s** *nfpl* football pools.

quinientos [ki'njentos] *num* five hundred.

quinina [ki'nina] *nf* quinine.

quinqui ['kinki] *nm* gangster.

quinto, a ['kinto, a] *a* fifth // *nf* country house; (*MIL*) call-up, draft.

quiosco ['kjosko] *nm (de música)* bandstand; (*de periódicos*) news stand.

quirúrgico, a [ki'ruxiko, a] *a* surgical.

quise, quisiera *etc vb ver* **querer.**

quisquilloso, a [kiski'ʎoso, a] *a* touchy; (*fam*) pernickety.

quiste ['kiste] *nm* cyst.

quita ['kita] *nf* remission of debt; **de ~ y pon** detachable.

quitaesmalte [kitaes'malte] *nm* nail-polish remover.

quitamanchas [kita'mantʃas] *nm inv* stain remover.

quitar [ki'tar] *vt* to remove, take away; (*ropa*) to take off; (*dolor*) to kill, stop; **¡quita de ahí!** get away!; **~se** *vr* to

withdraw; **se quitó el sombrero** he took off his hat.
quitasol [kita'sol] *nm* sunshade.
quite ['kite] *nm* (*esgrima*) parry; (*evasión*) dodge.
quizá(s) [ki'θa(s)] *ad* perhaps, maybe.

R

rábano ['raβano] *nm* radish; **me importa un** ~ I don't give a damn.
rabia ['raβja] *nf* (*MED*) rabies; (*fig*) fury, rage; **rabiar** *vi* to have rabies; to rage, be furious; **rabiar por algo** to be dying for or long for sth.
rabieta [ra'βjeta] *nf* tantrum, fit of temper.
rabino [ra'βino] *nm* rabbi.
rabioso, a [ra'βjoso, a] *a* rabid; (*fig*) furious.
rabo ['raβo] *nm* tail.
racial [ra'θjal] *a* racial, race *cpd*.
racimo [ra'θimo] *nm* bunch.
raciocinio [raθjo'θinjo] *nm* reason.
ración [ra'θjon] *nf* portion; **raciones** *afpl* rations.
racional [raθjo'nal] *a* (*razonable*) reasonable; (*lógico*) rational; ~**izar** *vt* to rationalize.
racionar [raθjo'nar] *vt* to ration (out).
racismo [ra'θismo] *nm* racialism, racism; **racista** *a, nm/f* racist.
racha ['ratʃa] *nf* gust of wind.
radar [ra'ðar] *nm* radar.
radiador [raðja'ðor] *nm* radiator.
radiante [ra'ðjante] *a* radiant.
radical [raði'kal] *a, nm/f* radical.
radicar [raði'kar] *vi* to take root; ~ **en** to lie or consist in; ~**se** *vr* to establish o.s., put down (one's) roots.
radio ['raðjo] *nf* radio; (*aparato*) radio (set) // *nm* (*MAT*) radius; (*QUÍMICA*) radium; ~**activo, a** *a* radioactive; ~**difusión** *nf* broadcasting; ~**emisora** *nf* transmitter, radio station; ~**escucha** *nm/f* listener; ~**grafía** *nf* X-ray; ~**grafiar** *vt* to X-ray; ~**terapia** *nf* radiotherapy; **radioyente** *nm/f* listener.
raer [ra'er] *vt* to scrape (off).
ráfaga ['rafaxa] *nf* gust; (*de luz*) flash; (*de tiros*) burst.
raído, a [ra'iðo, a] *a* (*ropa*) threadbare; (*persona*) shameless.
raigambre [rai'xambre] *nf* (*BOT*) roots *pl*; (*fig*) tradition.
raíz [ra'iθ] (*pl* **raíces**) *nf* root; ~ **cuadrada** square root; **a** ~ **de** as a result of.
raja ['raxa] *nf* (*de melón etc*) slice; (*grieta*) crack; **rajar** *vt* to split; (*fam*) to slash; (*fruta etc*) to slice; **rajarse** *vr* to split, crack; (*AM*) to quit.
rajatabla [raxa'taβla]: **a** ~ *ad* (*estrictamente*) strictly, to the letter; (*cueste lo que cueste*) at all costs.
ralo, a ['ralo, a] *a* thin, sparse.

rallado, a [ra'ʎaðo, a] *a* grated; **rallador** *nm* grater; **rallar** *vt* to grate.
rama ['rama] *nf* branch; ~**da** *nf*, ~**je** *nm* branches *pl*, foliage; **ramal** *nm* (*de cuerda*) strand, (*FERRO*) branch line; (*AUTO*) branch (road).
rambla ['rambla] *nf* (*de agua*) stream; (*avenida*) avenue.
ramera [ra'mera] *nf* whore.
ramificación [ramifika'θjon] *nf* ramification; **ramificarse** *vr* to branch out.
ramillete [rami'ʎete] *nm* bouquet; (*fig*) select group.
ramo ['ramo] *nm* branch; (*COM*) department, section.
rampa ['rampa] *nf* (*MED*) cramp; (*plano*) ramp.
ramplón, ona [ram'plon, ona] *a* uncouth, coarse.
rana ['rana] *nf* frog; ~ **toro** bullfrog; **salto de** ~ leapfrog.
rancio, a [ra'nθjo, a] *a* rancid; (*vino*) aged, mellow; (*fig*) ancient.
rancho ['rantʃo] *nm* grub (*fam*); (*AM*) farm.
rango ['rango] *nm* rank, standing.
ranura [ra'nura] *nf* groove; (*de teléfono*) slot.
rapacidad [rapaθi'ðað] *nf* rapacity.
rapar [ra'par] *vt* to shave; (*los cabellos*) to crop; (*fam*) to pinch, nick (*fam*).
rapaz [ra'paθ] *a* (*ladrón*) thieving; (*ZOOL*) predatory.
rapaz, a [ra'paθ, a] *nm/f* young boy/girl.
rape ['rape] *nm* quick shave; **al** ~ cropped.
rapé [ra'pe] *nm* snuff.
rapidez [rapi'ðeθ] *nf* speed, rapidity; **rápido, a** *a* rapid, fast, quick // *ad* quickly // *nm* (*tren*) express; **rápidos** *nmpl* rapids.
rapiña [ra'pina] *nm* robbery; **ave de** ~ bird of prey.
raptar [rap'tar] *vt* to kidnap; **rapto** *nm* kidnapping; (*impulso*) sudden impulse; (*éxtasis*) ecstasy, rapture.
raqueta [ra'keta] *nf* racquet.
raquítico, a [ra'kitiko, a] *a* stunted; (*fig*) poor, inadequate; **raquitismo** *nm* rickets *sg*.
rareza [ra'reθa] *nf* rarity; (*fig*) eccentricity.
raro, a ['raro, a] *a* (*poco común*) rare; (*extraño*) odd, strange; (*excepcional*) remarkable.
ras [ras] *nm*: **a** ~ **de** level with; **a** ~ **de tierra** at ground level.
rasar [ra'sar] *vt* (*igualar*) to level; (*frotar*) to graze.
rascacielos [raska'θjelos] *nm inv* skyscraper.
rascar [ras'kar] *vt* (*con las uñas*) to scratch; (*raspar*) to scrape; ~**se** *vr* to scratch (o.s.).
rasgadura [rasxa'ðura] *nf* tear, rip; **rasgar** *vt* to tear, rip (up).
rasgo ['rasxo] *nm* stroke; ~**s** *nmpl*

features, characteristics; **a grandes ~s** in outline, broadly.

rasguñar [rasɣu'ɲar] *vt* to scratch; **rasguño** *nm* scratch.

raso, a ['raso, a] *a* (*liso*) flat, level; (*a baja altura*) very low // *nm* satin; **cielo ~** clear sky; **soldado ~** private.

raspador [raspa'ðor] *nm* scraper.

raspadura [raspa'ðura] *nf* scrape; (*marca*) scratch; **~s** *nfpl* scrapings; **raspar** *vt* to scrape; (*arañar*) to scratch; (*limar*) to file.

rastra ['rastra] *nf* (*huella*) track; (AGR) rake; **a ~s** by dragging; (*fig*) unwillingly; **pescar a la ~** to trawl.

rastreador [rastrea'ðor] *nm* tracker; (NAUT) trawler; **~ de minas** minesweeper; **rastrear** *vt* to track; (*laguna, río*) to dredge, drag.

rastrero, a [ras'trero, a] *a* creeping; (*vestido*) trailing; (*fig*) despicable, mean.

rastrillar [rastri'ʎar] *vt* to rake; **rastrillo** *nm* rake.

rastro ['rastro] *nm* (AGR) rake; (*pista*) track, trail; (*curso*) course; (*vestigio*) trace; (*matadero*) slaughterhouse; **el R~** the Madrid fleamarket.

rastrojo [ras'troxo] *nm* stubble.

rasurador [rasura'ðor] *nm*, **rasuradora** [rasura'ðora] *nf* electric shaver; **rasurarse** *vr* to shave.

rata ['rata] *nf* rat.

ratear [rate'ar] *vt* (*robar*) to steal; (*distribuir*) to share out.

ratería [rate'ria] *nf* petty theft.

ratero, a [ra'tero, a] *a* light-fingered // *nm/f* pickpocket.

ratificar [ratifi'kar] *vt* to ratify.

rato ['rato] *nm* while, short time; **a ~s** at times; **hay para ~** there's still a long way to go; **pasar el ~** to kill time; **pasar un buen/mal ~** to have a good/rough time.

ratón [ra'ton] *nm* mouse; **ratonera** *nf* mousetrap.

raudal [rau'ðal] *nm* torrent; **a ~es** in abundance.

raya ['raja] *nf* line; (*marca*) scratch; (*en tela*) stripe; (*de pelo*) parting; (*límite*) boundary; **tener a ~** to keep in check; **rayar** *vt* to line; to scratch; (*talón*) to cross; (*subrayar*) to underline // *vi*: **rayar en** *o* **con** to border on.

rayo ['rajo] *nm* (*del sol*) ray, beam; (*de luz*) shaft; (*en una tormenta*) lightning, flash of lightning; **~s X** X-rays.

rayón [ra'jon] *nm* rayon.

raza ['raθa] *nf* race; **~ humana** human race.

razón [ra'θon] *nf* (*gen*) reason; (*justicia*) right, justice; (*razonamiento*) reasoning; (*motivo*) course; (MAT) ratio; **a ~ de 10 cada día** at the rate of 10 a day; **'~: ...'** "inquiries to ..."; **en ~ de** with regard to; **dar ~ a uno** to agree that sb is right; **tener ~** to be right; **~ directa/inversa** direct/inverse proportion; **~ de ser**

raison d'être; **razonable** *a* reasonable; (*justo, moderado*) fair; **razonamiento** *nm* (*juicio*) judgement; (*argumento*) reasoning; **razonar** *vt* to reason, argue; (*cuenta*) to itemize // *vi* to reason, argue.

reabastecer [reaβaste'θer] *vt* to refuel.

reabrir [rea'βrir] *vt* to reopen.

reacción [reak'θjon] *nf* reaction; **avión a ~ jet plane**; **~ en cadena** chain reaction; **reaccionar** *vi* to react; **reaccionario, a** *a* reactionary.

reacio, a [re'aθjo, a] *a* stubborn.

reactor [reak'tor] *nm* reactor.

readaptación [reaðapta'θjon] *nf*: **~ profesional** industrial retraining.

reafirmar [reafir'mar] *vt* to reaffirm.

reagrupar [reaɣru'par] *vt* to regroup.

reajuste [rea'xuste] *nm* readjustment.

real [re'al] *a* real; (*del rey, fig*) royal.

realce [re'alθe] *nm* (TEC) embossing; (*lustre, fig*) splendour; (ARTE) highlight; **poner de ~** to emphasize.

realidad [reali'ðað] *nf* reality, fact; (*verdad*) truth.

realista [rea'lista] *nm/f* realist.

realización [realiθa'θjon] *nf* fulfilment; (COM) sale, selling-up.

realizador, a [realiθa'ðor, a] *nm/f* (TV etc) producer.

realizar [reali'θar] *vt* (*objetivo*) to achieve; (*plan*) to carry out; (*viaje*) to make, undertake; (COM) to sell up; **~se** *vr* to come about, come true.

realmente [real'mente] *ad* really, actually.

realzar [real'θar] *vt* (TEC) to raise; (*embellecer*) to enhance; (*acentuar*) to highlight.

reanimar [reani'mar] *vt* to revive; (*alentar*) to encourage; **~se** *vr* to revive.

reanudar [reanu'ðar] *vt* (*renovar*) to renew; (*retomar*) to resume.

reaparición [reapari'θjon] *nf* reappearance.

rearme [re'arme] *nm* rearmament.

reata [re'ata] *nf* rope, rein; **de ~** in single file.

rebaja [re'βaxa] *nf* (COM) reduction; (*menoscabo*) lessening; **rebajar** *vt* (*bajar*) to lower; (*reducir*) to reduce; (*disminuir*) to lessen; (*humillar*) to humble.

rebanada [reβa'naða] *nf* slice.

rebaño [re'βaɲo] *nm* herd; (*de ovejas*) flock.

rebasar [reβa'sar] *vt* (*también ~ de*) to exceed; (AUTO) to overtake.

rebatir [reβa'tir] *vt* to refute; (*descontar*) to deduct.

rebato [re'βato] *nm* alarm; (*ataque*) surprise attack.

rebelarse [reβe'larse] *vr* to rebel, revolt.

rebelde [re'βelde] *a* rebellious; (*indócil*) unruly // *nm/f* rebel; **rebeldía** *nf* rebelliousness; (*desobediencia*) disobedience; **rebelión** *nf* rebellion.

reblandecer [reβlande'θer] *vt* to soften.

rebosante [reβo'sante] a overflowing.
rebosar vi to overflow; (abundar) to abound, be plentiful.
rebotar [reβo'tar] vt to bounce; (rechazar) to repel; ~**se** vr (pelota) to rebound; (bala) to ricochet; **rebote** nm rebound; **de rebote** on the rebound.
rebozar [reβo'θar] vt to wrap up; (CULIN) to fry in batter; **rebozo** nm muffler; (AM) shawl; **decir algo sin rebozo** o call a spade a spade.
rebuscado, a [reβus'kaδo, a] a affected.
rebuscar [reβus'kar] vt to search carefully; (objeto) to search for carefully.
rebuznar [reβuθ'nar] vi to bray.
recabar [reka'βar] vt to manage to get.
recado [re'kaδo] nm errand; (mensaje) message; **tomar un** ~ (TELEC) to take a message.
recaer [reka'er] vi to relapse; ~ **en** to fall to or on; **recaída** nf relapse.
recalcar [rekal'kar] vt (fig) to stress, emphasize.
recalcitrante [rekalθi'trante] a recalcitrant.
recalcitrar [rekalθi'trar] vi (echarse atrás) to step back; (resistir) to resist, be stubborn.
recalentar [rekalen'tar] vt (volver a calentar) to reheat; (demasiado) to overheat.
recambio [re'kambjo] nm spare; (de pluma) refill.
recapacitar [rekapaθi'tar] vt to think over // vi to reflect.
recargado, a [rekar'xaδo, a] a overloaded; **recargar** vt to overload; (batería) to recharge; **recargar los precios** to increase prices; **recargo** nm surcharge; (aumento) increase.
recatado, a [reka'taδo, a] a modest, demure; (prudente) cautious.
recatar [reka'tar] vt to hide; ~**se** vr to hide o.s.
recato [re'kato] nm modesty, demureness; (cautela) caution.
recaudación [rekauδa'θjon] nf collection; (suma) takings pl; (en deporte) gate; **recaudador** nm tax collector.
recelar [reθe'lar] vt: ~ **que** (sospechar) to suspect that; (temer) to fear that // vi, ~**se** vr: ~**(se) de** to distrust; **recelo** nm distrust, suspicion; **receloso, a** a distrustful, suspicious.
recepción [reθep'θjon] nf reception; **recepcionista** nm/f receptionist.
receptáculo [reθep'takulo] nm receptacle.
receptivo, a [reθep'tiβo, a] a receptive.
receptor, a [reθep'tor, a] nm/f recipient // nm receiver.
recesión [reθe'sjon] nf recession.
receta [re'θeta] nf (CULIN) recipe; (MED) prescription.
recibidor, a [reθiβi'δor, a] nm/f receiver, recipient.
recibimiento [reθiβi'mjento] nm

(recepción) reception; (acogida) welcome.
recibir [reθi'βir] vt (gen) to receive; (dar la bienvenida) to welcome // vi to entertain; ~**se** vr: ~**se de** to qualify as; **recibo** nm receipt.
reciedumbre [reθje'δumbre] nf strength; (vigor) vigour.
recién [re'θjen] ad recently, newly; **el** ~ **llegado** the newcomer; **el** ~ **nacido** the newborn child.
reciente [re'θjente] a recent; (fresco) fresh.
recinto [re'θinto] nm (gen) enclosure; (área) area, place.
recio, a ['reθjo, a] a strong, tough; (voz) loud; (tiempo) harsh // ad hard; loud(ly).
recipiente [reθi'pjente] nm receptacle.
reciprocidad [reθiproθi'δaδ] nf reciprocity; **recíproco, a** a reciprocal.
recital [reθi'tal] nm (MUS) recital; (LITERATURA) reading; **recitar** vt to recite.
reclamación [reklama'θjon] nf claim, demand; (queja) complaint.
reclamar [rekla'mar] vt to claim, demand // vi: ~ **contra** to complain about; ~ **en justicia** to take to court; **reclamo** nm (anuncio) advertisement; (tentación) attraction.
reclinar [rekli'nar] vt to recline, lean; ~**se** vr to lean back.
recluir [reklu'ir] vt to intern, confine.
reclusión [reklu'sjon] nf (prisión) prison; (refugio) seclusion; ~ **perpetua** life imprisonment.
recluta [re'kluta] nm/f recruit // nf recruitment.
reclutamiento [rekluta'mjento] nm recruitment.
recobrar [reko'βrar] vt (recuperar) to recover; (rescatar) to get back; ~**se** vr to recover.
recodo [re'koδo] nm (de río, camino) bend.
recogedor, a [rekoxe'δor, a] nm/f picker, harvester.
recoger [reko'xer] vt (gen) to collect; (AGR) to harvest; (levantar) to pick up; (juntar) to gather; (pasar a buscar) to come for, fetch; (dar asilo) to give shelter to; (faldas) to gather up; (pelo) to put up; ~**se** vr (retirarse) to retire; **recogido, a** a (lugar) quiet, secluded; (persona) modest, retiring; (pequeño) small // nf (del correo) collection; (AGR) harvest.
recolección [rekolek'θjon] nf (de las mieses) harvesting; (colecta) collection.
recomendación [rekomenda'θjon] nf (sugerencia) suggestion, recommendation; (elogio) praise; **recomendar** vt to suggest, recommend; to praise; (confiar) to entrust.
recompensa [rekom'pensa] nf reward, recompense; **recompensar** vt to reward, recompense; (por pérdidas) to compensate.
recomponer [rekompo'ner] vt to mend; ~**se** vr (fam) to doll up.
reconciliación [rekonθilja'θjon] nf reconciliation; **reconciliar** vt to

reconcile; reconciliarse vr to become reconciled.

reconfortar [rekonfor'tar] vt to comfort; ~**se** vr: ~**se con** to fortify o.s. with.

reconocer [rekono'θer] vt to recognize; (registrar) to search; (MED) to examine; **reconocido, a** recognized; (agradecido) grateful; **reconocimiento** nm recognition; search; examination; gratitude; (confesión) admission.

reconquista [rekon'kista] nf reconquest.

reconstituyente [rekonstitu'jente] nm tonic.

reconstruir [rekonstru'ir] vt to reconstruct.

recopilación [rekopila'θjon] nf (sumario) summary; (compendio) compilation; **recopilar** vt to compile.

récord ['rekorð] a inv, nm record.

recordar [rekor'ðar] vt (acordarse de) to remember; (acordar a otro) to remind // vi to remember.

recorrer [reko'rrer] vt (país) to cross, travel through; (distancia) to cover; (repasar) to go over, look over; **recorrido** nm run, journey; **tren de largo recorrido** main-line train.

recortado, a [rekor'taðo, a] a uneven, irregular.

recortar [rekor'tar] vt to cut out; **recorte** nm (acción) cutting; (de prensa) cutting, clipping; (de telas, chapas) trimming.

recostado, a [rekos'taðo, a] a leaning; **estar** ~ to be lying down.

recostar [rekos'tar] vt to lean; ~**se** vr to lie down.

recoveco [reko'ßeko] nm bend; (en casa) cubby hole.

recreación [rekrea'θjon] nf recreation; (TEATRO, CINE) interval, intermission.

recrear [rekre'ar] vt (entretener) to entertain; (volver a crear) to recreate; **recreativo, a** a recreational; **recreo** nm recreation; (ESCOL) break, playtime.

recriminar [rekrimi'nar] vt to reproach // vi to recriminate; ~**se** vr to reproach each other.

recrudecer [rekruðe'θer] vt, vi, ~**se** vr to worsen.

recrudecimiento [rekruðeθi'mjento] nm, **recrudescencia** [rekruðes'θenθja] nf upsurge.

recta ['rekta] nf ver **recto**.

rectángulo, a [rek'tangulo, a] a rectangular // nm rectangle.

rectificar [rektifi'kar] vt to rectify; (volverse recto) to straighten // vi to correct o.s.

rectitud [rekti'tuð] nf (exactitud) correctness; (fig) rectitude.

recto, a ['rekto, a] a straight; (persona) honest, upright // nm rectum // nf straight line.

rector, a [rek'tor, a] a governing.

recua ['rekwa] nf mule train.

recuento [re'kwento] nm inventory; **hacer el** ~ **de** to count or reckon up.

recuerdo [re'kwerðo] nm souvenir; ~**s** nmpl memories; ¡~**s a tu madre!** give my regards to your mother.

recular [reku'lar] vi to fall back; (fig) to back down.

recuperable [rekupe'raßle] a recoverable; **recuperación** nf recovery.

recuperar [rekupe'rar] vt to recover; (tiempo) to make up; ~**se** vr to recuperate.

recurrir [reku'rrir] vi (JUR) to appeal; ~ **a** to resort to; (persona) to turn to; **recurso** nm resort; (medios) means pl, resources pl; (JUR) appeal.

recusar [reku'sar] vt to reject, refuse.

rechazar [retʃa'θar] vt to repel, drive back; (idea) to reject; (oferta) to turn down.

rechazo [re'tʃaßo] nm (retroceso) recoil; (rebote) rebound; (negación) rebuff.

rechifla [re'tʃifla] nf hissing, booing; (fig) derision; **rechiflar** vt to hiss, boo; **rechiflarse** vr to take things as a joke.

rechinar [retʃi'nar] vi to creak; (gruñir) to grumble; (dientes) to grind.

rechoncho, a [re'tʃontʃo, a] a (fam) chubby, thickset.

red [reð] nf net, mesh; (de ferrocarriles etc) network; (trampa) trap.

redacción [reðak'θjon] nf editing; (oficina) newspaper office; (personal) editorial staff.

redactar [reðak'tar] vt to draw up, draft; (periódico) to edit.

redada [re'ðaða] nf: **~ policíaca** police raid, round-up.

rededor [reðe'ðor] nm: **al o en** ~ around, round about.

redención [reðen'θjon] nf redemption; **redentor, a** a redeeming.

redescubrir [reðesku'ßrir] vt to rediscover.

redicho, a [re'ðitʃo, a] a affected, stilted.

redil [re'ðil] nm sheepfold.

redimir [reði'mir] vt to redeem.

rédito ['reðito] nm interest, yield.

redoblar [reðo'ßlar] vt to redouble; (plegar) to fold back // vi (tambor) to play a roll on the drums.

redomado, a [reðo'maðo, a] a sly, crafty.

redonda [re'ðonda] nf ver **redondo**.

redondear [reðonde'ar] vt to round, round off; ~**se** vr to become wealthy.

redondel [reðon'del] nm (círculo) circle; (TAUR) bullring, arena.

redondo, a [re'ðondo a] a (circular) round; (directo) straight; (completo) complete // nf: **a la** ~**a** around, round about.

reducción [reðuk'θjon] nf reduction; (MED) setting.

reducido, a [reðu'θiðo, a] a reduced; (limitado) limited; (pequeño) small; **reducir** vt to reduce; to limit; (MED) to set a bone; **reducirse** vr to diminish.

redundancia [reðun'danθja] *nf* redundancy.

reembolsar [reembol'sar] *vt* to reimburse; (*depósito*) to refund; **reembolso** *nm* reimbursement; refund.

reemplazar [reempla'θar] *vt* to replace; **reemplazo** *nm* replacement; **de reemplazo** (*MIL*) reserve.

refacción [refak'θjon] *nf* (*AM*) repair(s) (*pl*).

refajo [re'faxo] *nm* (*enagua*) flannel underskirt; (*falda*) short skirt.

referencia [refe'renθja] *nf* reference; (*informe*) report; **con ~ a** with reference to.

referente [refe'rente] *a*: **~ a** concerning, relating to.

referir [refe'rir] *vt* (*contar*) to tell, recount; (*relacionar*) to refer, relate; **~se** *vr*: **~se a** to refer to.

refilón [refi'lon]: **de ~** *ad* obliquely, aslant.

refinado, a [refi'naðo, a] *a* refined; **refinamiento** *nm* refinement; **refinar** *vt* to refine; (*fig*) to perfect, polish.

reflejar [refle'xar] *vt* (*gen*) to reflect; **reflejo, a** reflected; (*movimiento*) reflex // *nm* reflection; (*ANAT*) reflex.

reflexión [reflek'sjon] *nf* reflection; **reflexionar** *vt* to reflect on // *vi* to reflect; (*detenerse*) to pause (to think).

reflexivo, a [reflek'siβo, a] *a* thoughtful; (*LING, fig*) reflexive.

reflujo [re'fluxo] *nm* ebb.

refocilar [refoθi'lar] *vt* to cheer up.

reforma [re'forma] *nf* reform; (*ARQ etc*) repair; **~ agraria** agrarian reform.

reformar [refor'mar] *vt* (*modificar*) to change, alter; (*formar de nuevo*) to reform; (*ARQ*) to repair; **~se** *vr* to mend one's ways.

reformatorio [reforma'torjo] *nm* reformatory.

reforzar [refor'θar] *vt* (*gen*) to strengthen; (*ARQ*) to reinforce; (*fig*) to encourage.

refractario, a [refrak'tarjo, a] *a* stubborn; (*TEC*) heat-resistant.

refrán [re'fran] *nm* proverb, saying.

refregar [refre'xar] *vt* to scrub.

refrenar [refre'nar] *vt* to check, restrain.

refrendar [refren'dar] *vt* (*firma*) to endorse, countersign; (*pasaporte*) to stamp; (*ley*) to approve.

refrescar [refres'kar] *vt* (*gen*) to refresh // *vi* to cool down; **~se** *vr* to get cooler; (*tomar aire fresco*) to go out for a breath of fresh air.

refresco [re'fresko] *nm* soft drink, cool drink; "**~s**" "refreshments".

refriega [re'frjexa] *nf* scuffle, brawl.

refrigeración [refrixera'θjon] *nf* refrigeration; (*de casa*) air-conditioning; **refrigerador** *nm* refrigerator; **refrigerar** *vt* to refrigerate; to air-condition.

refuerzo [re'fwerθo] *nm* reinforcement; (*TEC*) support.

refugiado, a [refu'xjaðo, a] *nm/f* refugee; **refugiarse** *vr* to take refuge, shelter; **refugio** *nm* refuge; (*protección*) shelter.

refulgencia [reful'xenθja] *nf* brilliance; **refulgir** *vi* to shine, be dazzling.

refundición [refundi'θjon] *nf* recasting, revision; **refundir** *vt* to recast.

refunfuñar [refunfu'nar] *vi* to grunt, growl; (*quejarse*) to grumble.

refutación [refuta'θjon] *nf* refutation; **refutar** *vt* to refute.

regadera [rexa'ðera] *nf* watering can.

regadío [rexa'ðio] *nm* irrigated land.

regalado, a [rexa'laðo, a] *a* comfortable, luxurious; (*gratis*) free, for nothing; (*pey*) soft.

regalar [rexa'lar] *vt* (*dar*) to give, present; (*entregar*) to give away; (*mimar*) to pamper, make a fuss of.

regalía [rexa'lia] *nf* privilege, prerogative; (*COM*) bonus; (*de autor*) royalty.

regaliz [rexa'liθ] *nm*, **regaliza** [rexa'liθa] *nf* liquorice.

regalo [re'xalo] *nm* (*obsequio*) gift, present; (*gusto*) pleasure; (*comodidad*) comfort.

regalón, ona [rexa'lon, ona] *a* spoiled, pampered.

regañadientes [rexana'ðjentes]: **a ~** *ad* reluctantly.

regañar [rexa'nar] *vt* to scold // *vi* to grumble; **regaño** *nm* scolding, telling-off; (*queja*) grumble; **regañón, ona** *a* grumbling; (*mujer*) nagging.

regar [re'xar] *vt* to water, irrigate; (*fig*) to scatter, sprinkle.

regatear [rexate'ar] *vt* to bargain over; (*guardar*) to be mean with // *vi* to bargain, haggle; (*DEPORTE*) to dribble; **regateo** *nm* bargaining; dribbling; (*del cuerpo*) swerve, dodge.

regazo [re'xaθo] *nm* lap.

regeneración [rexenera'θjon] *nf* regeneration; **regenerar** *vt* to regenerate.

regentar [rexen'tar] *vt* to direct, manage; **regente** *nm* manager; (*POL*) regent.

régimen ['reximen] (*pl* **regímenes**) *nm* regime; (*MED*) diet.

regimiento [rexi'mjento] *nm* regiment; (*organización*) administration.

regio, a ['rexjo, a] *a* royal, regal; (*fig: suntuoso*) splendid.

región [re'xjon] *nf* region; **regionalista** *nm/f* regionalist.

regir [re'xir] *vt* to govern, rule; (*dirigir*) to manage, run // *vi* to apply, be in force.

registrador [rexistra'ðor] *nm* registrar, recorder.

registrar [rexis'trar] *vt* (*buscar en cajón*) to look through, search; (*inspeccionar*) to inspect; (*anotar*) to register, record; **~se** *vr* to register; (*ocurrir*) to happen.

registro [re'xistro] *nm* registration; (*MUS, libro*) register; (*inspección*) inspection,

search; ~ **civil** registry office.
regla ['rexla] nf (ley) rule, regulation; (de medir) ruler, rule; **la** ~ (MED) periods pl; **salir de** ~ to step out of line.
reglamentación [reʌlamenta'θjon] nf (acto) regulation; (lista) rules pl; **reglamentar** vt to regulate; **reglamentario, a** a statutory; **reglamento** nm rules pl, regulations pl.
reglar [re'ʌlar] vt (papel) to rule; (actos) to regulate.
regocijado, a [rexoθi'xaðo, a] a merry; **regocijar** vt to cheer up, gladden; **regocijarse** vr to have a good time, make merry; (alegrarse) to rejoice; **regocijo** nm joy, happiness.
regodearse [rexoðe'arse] vr to be glad, be delighted; **regodeo** nm delight.
regresar [rexre'sar] vi to come/go back, return; **regresivo, a** a backward; (fig) regressive; **regreso** nm return.
reguero [re'xero] nm irrigation ditch.
regulador [rexula'ðor] nm (gen) regulator; (de radio etc) knob, control.
regular [rexu'lar] a (gen) regular; (normal) normal, usual; (común) ordinary; (organizado) regular, orderly; (mediano) average; (fam) not bad, so-so // ad so-so, alright // vt (controlar) to control, regulate; (TEC) to adjust; **por lo** ~ as a rule; ~**idad** nf regularity; ~**izar** vt to regularize.
regusto [re'xusto] nm aftertaste.
rehabilitación [reaβilita'θjon] nf rehabilitation; (ARQ) restoration; **rehabilitar** vt to rehabilitate; to restore; (reintegrar) to reinstate.
rehacer [rea'θer] vt (reparar) to mend, repair; (volver a hacer) to redo, repeat; ~**se** vr (MED) to recover; (dominarse) to pull o.s. together.
rehén [re'en] nm hostage.
rehilete [rei'lete] nm (dardo) dart; (DEPORTE) badminton, shuttlecock.
rehuir [reu'ir] vt to avoid, shun.
rehusar [reu'sar] vt, vi to refuse.
reina ['reina] nf queen; ~**do** nm reign; **reinante** a (fig) prevailing; **reinar** vi to reign.
reincidir [reinθi'ðir] vi to relapse.
reincorporarse [reinkorpo'rarse] vr: ~ **a** to rejoin.
reino ['reino] nm kingdom; **el R**~ **Unido** the United Kingdom.
reintegrar [reinte'xrar] vt (reconstituir) to reconstruct; (persona) to reinstate; (dinero) to return, pay back; ~**se** vr: ~**se a** to return to.
reír [re'ir] vi, ~**se** vr to laugh; ~**se de** to laugh at.
reiterar [reite'rar] vt to reiterate.
reivindicación [reiβindika'θjon] nf (demanda) claim, demand; (justificación) vindication; **reivindicar** vt to claim; (restaurar) to restore.
reja ['rexa] nf (de ventana) grille, bars pl;

(en la calle) grating; (del arado) ploughshare.
rejilla [re'xiʎa] nf (de ventana) grille; (de silla) wickerwork; (de ventilación) vent; (de coche) luggage rack.
rejoneador [rexonea'ðor] nm mounted bullfighter.
rejuvenecer [rexuβene'θer] vt, vi to rejuvenate; ~**se** vr to be rejuvenated.
relación [rela'θjon] nf relation, relationship; (MAT) ratio; (informe) report; **relaciones públicas** public relations; **con** ~ **a** o **en** ~ **con** in relation to; **relacionar** vt to relate, connect; **relacionarse** vr to be connected, be linked.
relajación [relaxa'θjon] nf relaxation; **relajado, a** a (disoluto) loose; (cómodo) relaxed; (MED) ruptured; **relajar** vt, **relajarse** vr to relax.
relamer [rela'mer] vt to lick (repeatedly); ~**se** vr to lick one's lips.
relamido, a [rela'miðo, a] a (pulcro) overdressed; (afectado) affected.
relámpago [re'lampaxo] nm flash of lightning; **visita/huelga** ~ lightning visit/strike; **relampaguear** vi to flash.
relatar [rela'tar] vt to tell, relate.
relativo, a [rela'tiβo, a] a relative; **en lo** ~ **a** concerning.
relato [re'lato] nm (narración) story, tale; (informe) report.
relegar [rele'xar] vt to relegate.
relevante [rele'βante] a eminent, outstanding.
relevar [rele'βar] vt (sustituir) to relieve; ~**se** vr to relay; ~ **a uno de un cargo** to relieve sb of his post.
relevo [re'leβo] nm relief; **carrera de** ~**s** relay race.
relieve [re'ljeβe] nm (ARTE, TEC) relief; (fig) prominence, importance; ~**s** nmpl left-overs; **bajo** ~ bas-relief.
religión [reli'xjon] nf religion; **religiosidad** nf religiosity; **religioso, a** a religious // nm/f monk/nun // nm cleric.
relinchar [relin'tʃar] vi to neigh; **relincho** nm neigh; (acto) neighing.
reliquia [re'likja] nf relic; ~ **de familia** family heirloom.
reloj [re'lo(x)] nm watch; (de iglesia etc) clock; ~ **de pulsera** wristwatch; ~ **despertador** alarm clock; ~**ero, a** nm/f watchmaker; clockmaker.
reluciente [relu'θjente] a brilliant, shining; **relucir** vi to shine; (fig) to excel.
relumbrante [relum'brante] a dazzling; **relumbrar** vi to dazzle, shine brilliantly.
rellano [re'ʎano] nm (ARQ) landing.
rellenar [reʎe'rar] vt (llenar) to fill up; (CULIN) to stuff; (COSTURA) to pad; **relleno, a** a full up; **stuffed** // nm stuffing; (de tapicería) padding.
remachar [rema'tʃar] vt to rivet; (fig) to hammer home, drive home; **remache** nm rivet.
remanente [rema'nente] nm remainder;

(COM) balance; (de producto) surplus.

remanso [re'manso] nm pool; (fig) quiet place.

remar [re'mar] vi to row.

rematado, a [rema'taðo, a] a complete, utter.

rematar [rema'tar] vt to finish off; (COM) to sell off cheap // vi to end, finish off.

remate [re'mate] nm end, finish; (punta) tip; (DEPORTE) shot; (ARQ) top; (COM) auction sale; **de** o **para** ~ to crown it all.

remedar [reme'ðar] vt to imitate.

remediar [reme'ðjar] vt (gen) to remedy; (subsanar) to make good, repair; (ayudar) to help; (evitar) to avoid.

remedio [re'meðjo] nm remedy; (alivio) relief, help; (JUR) recourse, remedy; **poner** ~ **a** to correct, stop; **no tener más** ~ to have no alternative; **¡qué** ~! there's no choice; **sin** ~ hopeless, incurable.

remedo [re'meðo] nm imitation; (pey) parody.

remendar [remen'dar] vt to repair; (con parche) to patch.

remesa [re'mesa] nf remittance; (COM) shipment; **remesar** vt to remit, send.

remiendo [re'mjendo] nm (gen) mend; (con parche) patch; (cosido) darn.

remilgado, a [remil'xaðo, a] a prim; (afectado) affected; **remilgo** nm primness; affectation.

reminiscencia [reminis'θenθja] nf reminiscence.

remisión [remi'sjon] nf (acto) sending, shipment.

remiso, a [re'miso, a] a remiss.

remitir [remi'tir] vt to remit, send; (perdonar) to pardon; (posponer) to postpone // vi to slacken; (en carta): **remite: X** sender: X; **remitente** nm/f sender.

remo ['remo] nm (de barco) oar; (deporte) rowing.

remoción [remo'θjon] nf removal.

remojar [remo'xar] vt to steep, soak; (galleta etc) to dip.

remojo [re'moxo] nm: **dejar la ropa a** ~ to leave clothes to soak.

remolacha [remo'latʃa] nf beet, beetroot.

remolcador [remolka'ðor] nm (NAUT) tug; (AUTO) breakdown lorry.

remolinar [remoli'nar] vi to whirl, eddy; **remolino** nm (gen) eddy; (de agua) whirlpool; (de viento) whirlwind; (de gente) throng.

remolque [re'molke] nm tow, towing; (cuerda) towrope; **llevar a** ~ to tow.

remontar [remon'tar] vt to mend; ~**se** vr to soar; ~**se a** (COM) to amount to; ~ **el vuelo** to soar.

rémora ['remora] nf hindrance.

remorder [remor'ðer] vt to distress, disturb; ~**se** vr to suffer remorse; ~**se la conciencia** to have a troubled conscience; **remordimiento** nm remorse.

remoto, a [re'moto, a] a remote.

remover [remo'ßer] vt to stir; (tierra) to turn over, (objetos) to move around; (quitar) to remove.

remozar [remo'θar] vt to rejuvenate; ~**se** vr to be rejuvenated, look younger.

remuneración [remunera'θjon] nf remuneration; **remunerar** vt to remunerate, (premiar) to reward.

renacer [rena'θer] vi to be reborn; (fig) to revive; **renacimiento** nm rebirth; **el Renacimiento** the Renaissance.

renal [re'nal] a renal, kidney cpd.

rencilla [ren'ðiʎa] nf quarrel.

rencor [ren'kor] nm rancour, bitterness; ~**oso, a** a spiteful.

rendición [rendi'θjon] nf surrender.

rendido, a [ren'diðo, a] a (sumiso) submissive; (cansado) worn-out.

rendimiento [rendi'mjento] nm (MIL) surrender; (producción) output; (agotamiento) exhaustion; (TEC, COM) efficiency.

rendir [ren'dir] vt (vencer) to defeat; (producir) to produce; (dar beneficio) to yield; (agotar) to exhaust; (dominar) to dominate // vi to pay; ~**se** vr (someterse) to surrender; (cansarse) to wear o.s. out; ~ **homenaje** o **culto a** to pay homage to.

renegado, a [rene'xaðo, a] a, nm/f renegade.

renegar [rene'xar] vi (renunciar) to renounce; (blasfemar) to blaspheme; (fam) to curse; (quejarse) to complain.

RENFE nf abr de **Red Nacional de los Ferrocarriles Españoles**.

renglón [ren'glon] nm (línea) line; (COM) item, article; **a** ~ **seguido** immediately after.

reniego [re'njexo] nm curse, oath; (queja) grumble, complaint.

renombrado, a [renom'braðo, a] a renowned; **renombre** nm renown.

renovación [renoßa'θjon] nf (de contrato) renewal; (ARQ) renovation; **renovar** vt to renew; to renovate.

renta ['renta] nf (ingresos) income; (beneficio) profit; (alquiler) rent; ~ **vitalicia** annuity; **rentable** a profitable; **rentar** vt to produce, yield.

rentero, a [ren'tero, a] a nm/f tenant farmer.

rentista [ren'tista] nm/f stockholder.

renuencia [re'nwenθja] nf reluctance; **renuente** a inv reluctant.

renuncia [re'nunθja] nf (gen) resignation.

renunciar [renun'θjar] vt to renounce // vi to resign; ~ **a hacer algo** to give up doing sth.

reñido, a [re'niðo, a] a (batalla) bitter, hard-fought; **estar** ~ **con uno** to be on bad terms with sb.

reñir [re'nir] vt (regañar) to scold // vi (estar peleado) to quarrel, fall out; (combatir) to fight.

reo ['reo] nm/f culprit, offender; ~ **de muerte** prisoner condemned to death.

reojo [re'oxo]: **de** ~ out of the corner of one's eye; (fig) askance.

reorganizar [reorɣani'θar] *vt* to reorganize.

reorientar [reorjen'tar] *vt* to reorientate; *(reajustar)* to readjust.

reparación [repara'θjon] *nf* (*acto*) mending, repairing; (*TEC*) repair; (*fig*) amends, reparation; **reparar** *vt* to repair; to make amends for; (*suerte*) to retrieve; (*observar*) to observe // *vi*: **reparar en** (*darse cuenta de*) to notice; (*poner atención en*) to pay attention to.

reparo [re'paro] *nm* (*reparación*) repair; (*advertencia*) observation; (*duda*) doubt; (*dificultad*) difficulty; (*resguardo*) defence.

reparón, ona [repa'ron, ona] *a* carping.

repartición [reparti'θjon] *nf* distribution; (*división*) division; **repartidor, a** *nm/f* distributor.

repartir [repar'tir] *vt* to distribute, share out; (*correo*) to deliver; **reparto** *nm* distribution; delivery; (*TEATRO, CINE*) cast.

repasar [repa'sar] *vt* (*sitio*) to pass by again; (*lección*) to revise; (*MECÁNICA*) to check; **repaso** *nm* revision; overhaul, checkup; (*de ropa*) mending.

repatriar [repa'trjar] *vt* to repatriate.

repecho [re'petʃo] *nm* steep incline; **a ~** uphill.

repelente [repe'lente] *a* repellent, repulsive; **repeler** *vt* to repel.

repensar [repen'sar] *vt* to reconsider.

repente [re'pente] *nm*: **de ~** suddenly; **un ~ de ira** a fit of anger.

repentino, a [repen'tino, a] *a* sudden.

repercusión [reperku'sjon] *nf* repercussion.

repercutir [reperku'tir] *vi* to rebound; (*sonido*) to echo; **~se** *vr* to reverberate; **~ en** to have repercussions on.

repertorio [reper'torjo] *nm* list; (*TEATRO*) repertoire.

repetición [repeti'θjon] *nf* repetition; **repetir** *vt* to repeat; (*plato*) to have a second helping // *vi* to repeat; **repetirse** *vr* (*volver sobre tema*) to repeat o.s.; (*sabor*) to come back.

repicar [repi'kar] *vt* (*desmenuzar*) to chop up finely; (*campanas*) to ring; **~se** *vr* to boast.

repique [re'pike] *nm* pealing, ringing; **~teo** *nm* pealing; (*de tambor*) drumming.

repisa [re'pisa] *nf* ledge, shelf; **~ de chimenea** mantelpiece.

repito *etc vb ver* **repetir**.

replegar [reple'ɣar] *vt* to fold over; **~se** *vr* to fall back, retreat.

repleto, a [re'pleto, a] *a* replete, full up.

réplica ['replika] *nf* answer; (*ARTE*) replica.

replicar [repli'kar] *vi* to answer; (*objetar*) to argue, answer back.

repliegue [re'pljeɣe] *nm* (*MIL*) withdrawal.

repoblación [repoβla'θjon] *nf* repopulation; (*de río*) restocking; **~ forestal** reafforestation; **repoblar** *vt* to repopulate; to reafforest.

repollo [re'poʎo] *nm* cabbage.

reponer [repo'ner] *vt* to replace, put back; (*TEATRO*) to revive; **~se** *vr* to recover; **~ que** to reply that.

reportaje [repor'taxe] *nm* report, article.

reposacabezas [reposaka'βeθas] *nm inv* headrest.

reposado, a [repo'saðo, a] *a* (*descansado*) restful; (*tranquilo*) calm; **reposar** *vi* to rest, repose.

reposición [reposi'θjon] *nf* replacement; (*CINE*) remake.

repositorio [reposi'torjo] *nf* repository.

reposo [re'poso] *nm* rest.

repostar [repos'tar] *vt* to replenish; (*AUTO*) to fill up (with petrol).

repostería [reposte'ria] *nf* confectioner's (shop); (*depósito*) pantry, larder; **repostero, a** *nm/f* confectioner.

reprender [repren'der] *vt* to reprimand; **reprensión** *nf* rebuke, reprimand.

represa [re'presa] *nf* dam; (*lago artificial*) lake, pool.

represalia [repre'salja] *nf* reprisal.

representación [representa'θjon] *nf* representation; (*TEATRO*) performance; **representante** *nm/f* representative; performer.

representar [represen'tar] *vt* to represent; (*TEATRO*) to play; (*edad*) to look; **~se** *vr* to imagine; **representativo, a** *a* representative.

represión [repre'sjon] *nf* repression.

reprimir [repri'mir] *vt* to repress.

reprobar [repro'βar] *vt* to censure, reprove.

réprobo, a ['reproβo, a] *nm/f* reprobate.

reprochar [repro'tʃar] *vt* to reproach; **reproche** *nm* reproach.

reproducción [reproðuk'θjon] *nf* reproduction.

reproducir [reproðu'θir] *vt* to reproduce; **~se** *vr* to breed; (*situación*) to recur.

reptil [rep'til] *nm* reptile.

república [re'puβlika] *nf* republic; **republicano, a** *a, nm/f* republican.

repudiar [repu'ðjar] *vt* to repudiate; (*fe*) to renounce; **repudio** *nm* repudiation.

repuesto [re'pwesto] *nm* (*pieza de recambio*) spare (part); (*abastecimiento*) supply; **rueda de ~** spare wheel.

repugnancia [repuɣ'nanθja] *nf* repugnance; **repugnante** *a* repugnant, repulsive.

repugnar [repuɣ'nar] *vt* to disgust // *vi*, **~se** *vr* (*contradecirse*) to conflict; (*dar asco*) to be disgusting.

repujar [repu'xar] *vt* to emboss.

repulgar [repul'xar] *vt* to hem.

repulido, a [repu'liðo, a] *a* (*gen*) polished; (*persona*) dressed up, dolled up.

repulsa [re'pulsa] *nf* rebuff; (*fig*) reprimand.

repulsión [repul'sjon] *nf* repulsion, aversion; **repulsivo, a** *a* repulsive.

reputación [reputa'θjon] *nf* reputation.

reputar [repu'tar] *vt* to consider deem.

requemado, a [reke'maðo a] *a* (*quemado*) scorched; (*bronceado*) tanned.

requerimiento [rekeri'mjento] *nm* request; (*JUR*) summons.

requerir [reke'rir] *vt* (*rogar*) to ask, request; (*exigir*) to require; (*llamar*) to send for, summon.

requesón [reke'son] *nm* cottage cheese.

requete... [re'kete] *pref* extremely.

réquiem ['rekjem] *nm* requiem.

requisa [re'kisa] *nf* (*inspección*) survey, inspection; (*MIL*) requisition.

requisito [reki'sito] *nm* requirement, requisite.

res [res] *nf* beast, head of cattle.

resabio [re'saßjo] *nm* (*maña*) vice, bad habit; (*dejo*) aftertaste.

resaca [re'saka] *nf* (*en el mar*) undertow, undercurrent; (*fig*) backlash; (*fam*) hangover.

resalado, a [resa'laðo, a] *a* (*fam*) lively.

resaltar [resal'tar] *vi* to project, stick out; (*persona*) to stand out, be conspicuous.

resarcimiento [resarθi'mjento] *nm* compensation; **resarcir** *vt* to compensate; **resarcirse** *vr* to make up for.

resbaladero [resßala'ðero] *nm* (*gen*) slippery place; (*en parque infantil*) slide.

resbaladizo, a [resßala'ðiθo, a] *a* slippery.

resbalar [resßa'lar] *vi*, **~se** *vr* to slip, slide; (*fig*) to slip (up).

rescatar [reska'tar] *vt* (*heridos*) to save, rescue; (*objeto*) to get back, recover; (*cautivos*) to ransom.

rescate [res'kate] *nm* rescue, recovery; **pagar un ~** to pay a ransom.

rescindir [resθin'dir] *vt* to rescind.

rescisión [resθi'sjon] *nf* cancellation.

rescoldo [res'koldo] *nm* embers *pl*; (*fig*) scruple.

resecar [rese'kar] *vt* to dry thoroughly; (*MED*) to remove; **~se** *vr* to dry up.

reseco, a [re'seko, a] *a* very dry; (*fig*) skinny.

resentido, a [resen'tiðo, a] *a* resentful; **resentimiento** *nm* resentment, bitterness.

resentirse [resen'tirse] *vr* (*debilitarse: persona*) to suffer; **~ con** to resent; **~ de** (*consecuencias*) to feel the effects of.

reseña [re'seɲa] *nf* (*cuenta*) account; (*informe*) report; (*LITERATURA*) review; **reseñar** *vt* to describe; to review.

reserva [re'serßa] *nf* (*gen*) reserve; (*reservación*) reservation; **a ~ de** except for; **con toda ~** in strictest confidence.

reservado, a [reser'ßaðo, a] *a* reserved; (*retraído*) cold, distant // *nm* private room.

reservar [reser'ßar] *vt* (*guardar*) to keep; (*habitación, entrada*) to reserve; (*callar*) to keep to o.s.; **~se** *vr* to save o.s.

resfriado [resfri'aðo] *nm* cold; **resfriarse** *vr* to cool; (*MED*) to catch (a) cold.

resguardar [reswar'ðar] *vt* to protect,

shield; **~se** *vr*: **~se de** to guard against; **resguardo** *nm* defence; (*custodia*) protection; (*garantía*) guarantee; (*vale*) voucher.

residencia [resi'ðenθja] *nf* residence.

residente [resi'ðente] *a, nm/f* resident.

residir [resi'ðir] *vi* to reside, live; **~ en** to reside in, lie in.

residuo [re'siðwo] *nm* residue.

resignación [resiɣna'θjon] *nf* resignation; **resignar** *vt* to resign; **resignarse** *vr*: **resignarse a ó con** to resign o.s. to, be resigned to.

resistencia [resis'tenθja] *nf* (*dureza*) endurance, strength; (*oposición, eléctrica*) resistance; **resistente** *a* strong hardy; resistant.

resistir [resis'tir] *vt* (*soportar*) to bear; (*oponerse a*) to resist, oppose; (*aguantar*) to put up with // *vi* to resist; (*aguantar*) to last, endure; **~se** *vr*: **~se a** to refuse to, resist.

resma ['resma] *nf* ream.

resol [re'sol] *nm* glare of the sun.

resolución [resolu'θjon] *nf* (*gen*) resolution; (*decisión*) decision; **resoluto, a** *a* resolute.

resolver [resol'ßer] *vt* to resolve; (*solucionar*) to solve, resolve; (*decidir*) to decide, settle; **~se** *vr* to make up one's mind.

resollar [reso'ʎar] *vi* to breathe noisily, wheeze.

resonancia [reso'nanθja] *nf* (*del sonido*) resonance; (*repercusión*) repercussion; **resonante** *a* resonant, resounding; (*fig*) tremendous; **resonar** *vi* to ring, echo.

resoplar [reso'plar] *vi* to snort; **resoplido** *nm* heavy breathing.

resorte [re'sorte] *nm* (*pieza*) spring; (*elasticidad*) elasticity, (*fig*) lever.

respaldar [respal'dar] *vt* to endorse; (*fig*) to back (up), support; **~se** *vr* to lean back; **~se con o en** to take one's stand on; **respaldo** *nm* (*de cama*) headboard; (*de sillón*) back; (*fig*) support, backing.

respectivo, a [respek'tißo, a] *a* respective; **en lo ~ a** with regard to.

respecto [res'pekto] *nm*: **al ~** on this matter; **con ~ a, ~ de** with regard to, in relation to.

respetable [respe'taßle] *a* respectable; **respetar** *vt* to respect; **respeto** *nm* respect; (*acatamiento*) deference; **respetos** *nmpl* respects; **respetuoso, a** *a* respectful.

respingar [respin'gar] *vi* to shy; **respingo** *nm* start, jump; (*fig*) gesture of disgust.

respiración [respira'θjon] *nf* breathing; (*MED*) respiration; (*ventilación*) ventilation; **respirar** *vi* to breathe; (*inhalar*) to inhale; **respiratorio, a** *a* respiratory; **respiro** *nm* breathing; (*fig*) respite.

resplandecer [resplande'θer] *vi* to shine; **resplandeciente** *a* resplendent, shining;

resplandor nm brilliance, brightness; (del fuego) blaze.

responder [respon'der] vt to answer // vi to answer; (fig) to respond; (pey) to answer back; ~ **de** o **por** to answer for.

responsabilidad [responsaβili'ðað] nf responsibility; **responsable** a responsible.

respuesta [res'pwesta] nf answer, reply.

resquebrajar [reskeβra'xar] vt, ~**se** vr to crack, split.

resquemor [reske'mor] nm resentment.

resquicio [res'kiθjo] nm chink; (hendedura) crack.

restablecer [restaβle'θer] vt to re-establish, restore; ~**se** vr to recover.

restallar [resta'ʎar] vi to crack.

restante [res'tante] a remaining; **lo** ~ the remainder.

restar [res'tar] vt (MAT) to subtract; (fig) to take away // vi to remain, be left.

restauración [restaura'θjon] nf restoration.

restaurán [restau'ran], **restaurante** [restau'rante] nm restaurant.

restaurar [restau'rar] vt to restore.

restitución [restitu'θjon] nf return, restitution.

restituir [restitu'ir] vt (devolver) to return, give back; (rehabilitar) to restore; ~**se** vr: ~**se a** to rejoin.

resto ['resto] nm (residuo) rest, remainder; (apuesta) stake; ~**s** nmpl remains.

restregar [restre'xar] vt to scrub, rub.

restricción [restrik'θjon] nf restriction.

restrictivo, a [restrik'tiβo, a] a restrictive.

restringir [restrin'xir] vt to restrict, limit.

resucitar [resuθi'tar] vt, vi to resuscitate, revive.

resuelto, a [re'swelto, a] pp de **resolver** // a resolute, determined.

resuello [re'sweʎo] nm breath.

resultado [resul'taðo] nm (conclusión) outcome; (consecuencia) result, consequence; **resultante** a resulting, resultant.

resultar [resul'tar] vi (llegar a ser) to turn out to be; (salir bien) to turn out well; (COM) to amount to; ~ **de** to stem from; **me resulta difícil hacerlo** it's difficult for me to do it.

resumen [re'sumen] nm summary, résumé; **en** ~ in short.

resumir [resu'mir] vt to sum up; (cortar) to abridge, cut down.

retablo [re'taβlo] nm altarpiece.

retaguardia [reta'ywarðja] nf rearguard.

retahíla [reta'ila] nf series, string.

retal [re'tal] nm remnant.

retama [re'tama] nf (AM) broom.

retar [re'tar] vt (gen) to challenge; (desafiar) to defy, dare.

retardar [retar'ðar] vt (demorar) to delay; (hacer más lento) to slow down; (retener) to hold back; **retardo** nm delay.

retazo [re'taθo] nm snippet.

rete... ['rete] pref very, extremely.

retén [re'ten] nm (TEC) catch; (reserva) store, reserve.

retener [rete'ner] vt (guardar) to retain, keep; (intereses) to withhold.

retina [re'tina] nf retina.

retintín [retin'tin] nm jangle.

retirada [reti'raða] nf (MIL, refugio) retreat; (de dinero) withdrawal; (de embajador) recall; **retirado, a** a (distante) remote; (tranquilo) quiet; (jubilado) retired.

retirar [reti'rar] vt to withdraw; (quitar) to remove; (jubilar) to retire, pension off; ~**se** vr to retreat, withdraw; to retire; (acostarse) to retire, go to bed; **retiro** nm retreat; retirement; (pago) pension.

reto ['reto] nm dare, challenge.

retocar [reto'kar] vt (fotografía) to touch up, retouch.

retoño [re'toɲo] nm sprout, shoot; (fig) offspring, child.

retoque [re'toke] nm retouching; (MED) symptom.

retorcer [retor'θer] vt (gen) to twist; (manos, lavado) to wring; ~**se** vr to become twisted; (mover el cuerpo) to writhe.

retorcimiento [retorθi'mjento] nm twist, twisting; (fig) deviousness.

retórica [re'torika] nf rhetoric; (fig) affectedness.

retornar [retor'nar] vt to return, give back // vi to return, go/come back; **retorno** nm return.

retortijón [retorti'xon] nm twist, twisting.

retozar [reto'θar] vi (juguetear) to frolic, romp; (saltar) to gambol; **retozón, ona** a playful.

retracción [retrak'θjon] nf, **retractación** [retrakta'θjon] nf retraction.

retractar [retrak'tar] vt to retract; ~**se** vr to retract; **me retracto** I take that back.

retraer [retra'er] vt to dissuade; ~**se** vr to retreat, withdraw; **retraído, a** a shy, retiring; **retraimiento** nm (gen) retirement; (timidez) shyness; (lugar) retreat.

retransmisión [retransmi'sjon] nf repeat (broadcast); **retransmitir** vt (mensaje) to relay; (TV etc) to retransmit; (: en vivo) to broadcast live.

retrasado, a [retra'saðo, a] a late; (MED) mentally retarded; (país etc) backward, underdeveloped; **retrasar** vt (demorar) to postpone, put off; (retardar) to slow down // vi, **retrasarse** vr (atrasarse) to be late; (reloj) to be slow; (producción) to fall (away); (quedarse atrás) to lag behind.

retraso [re'traso] nm (demora) delay; (lentitud) slowness; (tardanza) lateness; (atraso) backwardness; **llegar con** ~ to arrive late; ~ **mental** mental deficiency.

retratar [retra'tar] vt (ARTE) to paint the portrait of; (fotografiar) to photograph; (fig) to depict; ~**se** vr to have one's portrait painted; to have one's photograph taken; **retrato** *nm* portrait; *(fig)* likeness; **retrato-robot** *nm* identikit picture.

retreta [re'treta] *nf* retreat.

retrete [re'trete] *nm* toilet, lavatory.

retribución [retriβu'θjon] *nf* (*recompensa*) reward; (*pago*) pay, payment; **retribuir** *vt* to reward; to pay.

retro... [retro] *pref* retro... .

retroactivo, a [retroak'tiβo, a] *a* retroactive, retrospective.

retroceder [retroθe'ðer] *vi* (*echarse atrás*) to move back(wards); (*tropas*) to fall back, retreat; (*arma de fuego*) to recoil; *(fig)* to back down.

retroceso [retro'θeso] *nm* backward movement; (*MIL*) withdrawal, retreat; (*MED*) relapse; *(fig)* backing down.

retrógrado, a [re'troxraðo, a] *a* (*atrasado*) retrograde; (*POL*) reactionary.

retropropulsión [retropropul'sjon] *nf* jet propulsion.

retrospectivo, a [retrospek'tiβo, a] *a* retrospective.

retrovisor [retroβi'sor] *nm* driving *or* rear-view mirror.

retumbante [retum'bante] *a* resounding; **retumbar** *vi* to echo, resound.

reuma ['reuma] *nm* rheumatism; **reumático, a** *a* rheumatic; **reumatismo** *nm* rheumatism.

reunificar [reunifi'kar] *vt* to reunify.

reunión [reu'njon] *nf* (*asamblea*) meeting; (*fiesta*) party; (*reencuentro*) reunion.

reunir [reu'nir] *vt* (*juntar*) to reunite, join; (*recoger*) to gather; (*personas*) to assemble; (*cualidades*) to combine; **~se** *vr* to meet, gather.

revalidar [reβali'ðar] *vt* to confirm, ratify.

revalorar [reβalo'rar] *vt* to revalue, reassess.

revancha [re'βantʃa] *nf* revenge.

revelación [reβela'θjon] *nf* revelation.

revelado [reβe'laðo] *nm* developing.

revelar [reβe'lar] *vt* to reveal; (*FOTO*) to develop.

revendedor, a [reβende'ðor, a] *nm/f* retailer; (*pey*) ticket tout.

reventar [reβen'tar] *vt* to burst, explode; (*fam: plan*) to ruin // *vi*, **~se** *vr* (*estallar*) to burst, explode; (*fam: morirse*) to kick the bucket (*fam*); **~ por** to be bursting to.

reventón [reβen'ton] *nm* burst, explosion; (*AUTO*) blow-out, puncture.

reverberación [reβerβera'θjon] *nf* reverberation; **reverberar** *vi* to reverberate; **reverbero** *nm* reverberation.

reverdecer [reβerðe'θer] *vi* (*tig*) to revive, come to life again.

reverencia [reβe'renθja] *nf* reverence; **reverenciar** *vt* to revere.

reverendo, a [reβe'renðo, a] *a* reverend; **reverente** *a* reverent.

reversión [reβer'sjon] *nf* reversion.

reverso [re'βerso] *nm* back, wrong side; (*de moneda*) reverse.

revertir [reβer'tir] *vi* to revert.

revés [re'βes] *nm* back, wrong side; *(fig)* reverse, setback; (*DEPORTE*) backhand; **hacer al ~** to do sth the wrong way round; **volver algo al ~** to turn sth round; (*ropa*) to turn sth inside out.

revestir [reβes'tir] *vt* to put on; (*cubrir*) to cover, coat; **~ con** *o* **de** to invest with.

revisar [reβi'sar] *vt* (*examinar*) to check; (*rever*) to revise; **revisión** *nf* revision.

revisor [reβi'sor, a] *nm/f* inspector; (*FERRO*) ticket collector.

revista [re'βista] *nf* magazine, review; (*TEATRO*) revue; (*inspección*) inspection; **pasar ~ a** to review, inspect.

revivir [reβi'βir] *vi* to revive.

revocación [reβoka'θjon] *nf* repeal; **revocar** *vt* to revoke.

revolcar [reβol'kar] *vt* to knock down, send flying; **~se** *vr* to roll about.

revolotear [reβoloɪe'ar] *vi* to flutter; **revoloteo** *nm* fluttering.

revoltijo [reβol'tixo] *nm* mess, jumble.

revoltoso, a [reβol'toso, a] *a* (*travieso*) naughty, unruly; (*rebelde*) rebellious.

revolución [reβolu'θjon] *nf* revolution; **revolucionar** *vt* to revolutionize; **revolucionario, a** *a, nm/f* revolutionary.

revólver [re'βolβer] *nm* revolver.

revolver [reβol'βer] *vt* (*desordenar*) to disturb, mess up; (*mover*) to move about; (*poner al revés*) to turn over; (*investigar*) to look through; (*adentrarse en*) to go into; (*POL*) to stir up; (*hacer paquete*) to wrap up // *vi*: **~ en** to go through, rummage (about) in; **~se** *vr* to turn round; (*por dolor*) to writhe; (*volver contra*) to turn on *or* against.

revuelco [re'βwelko] *nm* fall, tumble.

revuelo [re'βwelo] *nm* fluttering; *(fig)* commotion.

revuelto, a [re'βwelto, a] *pp de* **revolver** // *a* (*mezclado*) mixed-up; (*huevos*) scrambled; (*descontento*) discontented; (*travieso*) mischievous // *nf* (*motín*) revolt; (*conmoción*) commotion.

revulsivo [reβul'siβo] *nm* enema.

rey [rei] *nm* king.

reyerta [re'jerta] *nf* quarrel, brawl.

rezagado, a [reθa'xaðo, a] *nm/f* straggler.

rezagar [reθa'xar] *vt* (*dejar atrás*) to leave behind; (*retrasar*) to delay, postpone.

rezar [re'θar] *vi* to pray; **~ con** (*fam*) to concern, have to do with; **rezo** *nm* prayer.

rezongar [reθoŋ'gar] *vi* to grumble.

rezumar [reθu'mar] *vt* to ooze // *vi* to leak; **~se** *vr* to leak out.

ría ['ria] *nf* estuary.

riada [ri'aða] *nf* flood.

ribera [ri'βera] *nf* (*de río*) bank; (*: área*) riverside; (*del mar*) shore.

ribete [ri'βete] *nm* (*de vestido*) border; *(fig)* addition; **~ar** *vt* to edge, border.

rico, a ['riko, a] *a* (*gen*) rich; (*adinerado*)

wealthy; (*lujoso*) luxurious; (*comida*) tasty, delicious // *nm/f* rich person.

rictus ['riktus] *nm* (*mueca*) sneer, grin.

ridiculez [riðiku'leθ] *nf* absurdity; **ridiculizar** *vt* to ridicule.

ridículo, a [ri'ðikulo, a] *a* ridiculous; **hacer el ~** to make o.s. ridiculous; **poner a uno en ~** to ridicule sb.

riego ['rjexo] *nm* (*aspersión*) watering; (*irrigación*) irrigation.

riel [rjel] *nm* rail.

rienda ['rjenda] *nf* rein; **dar ~ suelta a** to give free rein to.

riente ['rjente] *a* laughing.

riesgo ['rjesxo] *nm* risk; **correr el ~ de** to run the risk of.

rifa ['rifa] *nf* (*lotería*) raffle; (*disputa*) quarrel; **rifar** *vt* to raffle // *vi* to quarrel; **rifarse** *vr*: **rifarse algo** to fight over sth.

rifle ['rifle] *nm* rifle.

rigidez [rixi'ðeθ] *nf* rigidity, stiffness; (*fig*) strictness; **rígido, a** *a* rigid, stiff; strict, inflexible.

rigor [ri'xor] *nm* strictness, rigour; (*inclemencia*) harshness; **de ~ de rigueur**, essential; **riguroso, a** *a* rigorous; harsh; (*severo*) severe.

rimar [ri'mar] *vi* to rhyme.

rimbombante [rimbom'bante] *a* resounding; (*fig*) pompous.

rincón [rin'kon] *nm* (inside) corner.

rinoceronte [rinoθe'ronte] *nm* rhinoceros.

riña ['riɲa] *nf* (*disputa*) argument; (*pelea*) brawl.

riñón [ri'ɲon] *nm* (*gen*) kidney; **tener riñones** to have guts.

río *etc vb ver* **reír** // ['rio] *nm* river; (*fig*) torrent, stream; **~ abajo/arriba** downstream/upstream.

rioplatense [riopla'tense] *a* of the River Plate region.

ripio ['ripjo] *nm* (*residuo*) refuse, waste; (*cascotes*) rubble, debris.

riqueza [ri'keθa] *nf* wealth, riches *pl*; (*cualidad*) richness.

risa ['risa] *nf* (*una ~*) laugh; (*gen*) laughter.

risco ['risko] *nm* crag, cliff; **~so, a** *a* steep.

risible [ri'siβle] *a* (*ridículo*) ludicrous; (*jocoso*) laughable.

risotada [riso'taða] *nf* guffaw.

ristra ['ristra] *nf* string.

risueño, a [ri'sweɲo, a] *a* (*sonriente*) smiling; (*contento*) cheerful.

ritmo ['ritmo] *nm* rhythm; **a ~ lento** slowly; **trabajar a ~ lento** to go slow.

rito ['rito] *nm* rite.

ritual [ri'twal] *a, nm* ritual.

rival [ri'βal] *a, nm/f* rival; **~idad** *nf* rivalry; **~izar** *vi*: **~izar con** to rival, vie with.

rizado, a [ri'θaðo, a] *a* curly // *nm* curls *pl*; **rizar** *vt* to curl; **rizarse** *vr* (*el pelo*) to

curl; (*el mar*) to ripple; **rizo** *nm* curl; ripple.

RNE *nf abr de* **Radio Nacional de España.**

robar [ro'βar] *vt* to rob; (*objeto*) to steal; (*casa etc*) to break into; (*NAIPES*) to draw.

roble ['roβle] *nm* oak; **~do, ~dal** *nm* oakwood.

roblón [ro'βlon] *nm* rivet.

robo ['roβo] *nm* robbery, theft; **~ relámpago** smash-and-grab raid.

robot [ro'βo(t)] *nm* robot.

robustecer [roβuste'θer] *vt* to strengthen.

robusto, a [ro'βusto, a] *a* robust, strong.

roca ['roka] *nf* rock.

rocalla [ro'kaʎa] *nf* pebbles *pl*.

roce ['roθe] *nm* (*caricia*) brush; (*TEC*) friction; (*en la piel*) graze; **tener ~ con** to be in close contact with.

rociada [ro'θjaða] *nf* (*aspersión*) sprinkling; (*fig*) hail, shower; **rociar** *vt* to spray.

rocín [ro'θin] *nm* nag, hack.

rocío [ro'θio] *nm* dew.

rocoso, a [ro'koso, a] *a* rocky.

rodado, a [ro'ðaðo, a] *a* (*con ruedas*) wheeled; (*redondo*) round // *nf* rut.

rodaja [ro'ðaxa] *nf* (*raja*) slice; (*rueda*) small wheel.

rodaje [ro'ðaxe] *nm* (*TEC*) wheels *pl*, set of wheels; (*CINE*) shooting, filming, (*AUTO*): **en ~** running in.

rodar [ro'ðar] *vt* (*vehículo*) to wheel; (*escalera*) to roll down; (*viajar por*) to travel (over) // *vi* to roll; (*coche*) to go, run; (*CINE*) to shoot, film.

rodear [roðe'ar] *vt* to surround // *vi* to go round; **~se** *vr*: **~se de amigos** to surround o.s. with friends.

rodeo [ro'ðeo] *nm* (*ruta indirecta*) detour; (*evasión*) evasion; (*AM*) rodeo; **hablar sin ~s** to come to the point, speak plainly.

rodilla [ro'ðiʎa] *nf* knee; **de ~s** kneeling.

rodillo [ro'ðiʎo] *nm* roller; (*CULIN*) rolling-pin; **~ apisonador** *o* **de vapor** steamroller.

rododendro [roðo'ðendro] *nm* rhododendron.

roedor, a [roe'ðor, a] *a* gnawing // *nm* rodent.

roer [ro'er] *vt* (*masticar*) to gnaw; (*corroer, fig*) to corrode.

rogar [ro'xar] *vt, vi* (*pedir*) to ask for; (*suplicar*) to beg, plead; **se ruega no fumar** please do not smoke.

rojete [ro'xete] *nm* rouge.

rojizo, a [ro'xiθo, a] *a* reddish.

rojo, a ['roxo, a] *a, nm* red; **al ~ vivo** red-hot; **~ de labios** lipstick.

rol [rol] *nm* list, roll; (*AM: papel*) role.

rollizo, a [ro'ʎiθo, a] *a* (*objeto*) cylindrical; (*persona*) plump.

rollo ['roʎo] *nm* (*gen*) roll; (*de cuerda*) coil; (*madera*) log; (*fam*) bore; **¡qué ~!** what a carry-on!

Roma ['roma] *n* Rome.

romance [ro'manθe] *nm* Romance language; (*LITERATURA*) ballad; **hablar en** ~ to speak plainly.

romántico, a [ro'mantiko, a] *a* romantic.

romería [rome'ria] *nf* (*REL*) pilg image; (*excursión*) trip, outing.

romero, a [ro'mero, a] *nm/f* pilgrim // *nm* rosemary.

romo, a ['romo, a] *a* blunt; (*fig*) dull.

rompecabezas [rompeka'βeθas] *nm inv* riddle, puzzle; (*juego*) jigsaw.

rompehuelgas [rompe'welɣas] *nm inv* strikebreaker, blackleg.

rompeolas [rompe'olas] *nm inv* breakwater.

romper [rom'per] *vt* (*gen*) to break; (*hacer pedazos*) to smash; (*papel etc*) to tear, rip // *vi* (*olas*) to break; (*sol, diente*) to break through; ~ **un contrato** to break a contract; ~ **a** to start (suddenly) to; ~ **en llanto** to burst into tears; ~ **con uno** to fall out with sb.

rompimiento [rompi'mjento] *nm* breaking; (*fig*) break; (*quiebra*) crack; ~ **de hostilidades** outbreak of hostilities.

ron [ron] *nm* rum.

roncar [ron'kar] *vi* to snore.

ronco, a ['ronko, a] *a* (*sin voz*) hoarse; (*áspero*) raucous.

roncha ['rontʃa] *nf* weal; (*contusión*) bruise.

ronda ['ronda] *nf* (*gen*) round; (*partrulla*) patrol; **rondar** *vt* to patrol // *vi* to patrol; (*fig*) to prowl round.

rondón [ron'don]: **de** ~ *ad* unexpectedly.

ronquear [ronke'ar] *vi* to be hoarse; **ronquedad** *nf* hoarseness.

ronquido [ron'kiðo] *nm* snore, snoring.

ronronear [ronrone'ar] *vi* to purr; **ronroneo** *nm* purr.

ronzal [ron'θal] *nm* halter.

roña ['roɲa] *nf* scab; (*mugre*) crust (of dirt).

roñoso, a [ro'ɲoso, a] *a* (*mugriento*) filthy; (*inútil*) useless; (*tacaño*) mean.

ropa ['ropa] *nf* clothes *pl*, clothing; ~ **blanca** linen; ~ **de cama** bed linen; ~ **interior** underwear; ~**je** *nm* gown, robes *pl*; ~**vejero, a** *nm/f* second-hand clothes dealer.

ropero [ro'pero] *nm* linen cupboard; (*guardarropa*) wardrobe.

roque ['roke] *nm* rook, castle.

roquedal [roke'ðal] *nm* rocky place.

rosa ['rosa] *a inv* pink // *nf* rose; (*ANAT*) red birthmark; ~ **de los vientos** the compass; ~**s** *nfpl* popcorn *sg*.

rosado, a [ro'saðo, a], **rosáceo, a** [ro'saθeo, a] *a* pink // *nm* rosé.

rosal [ro'sal] *nm* rosebush.

rosario [ro'sarjo] *nm* (*REL*) rosary; **rezar el** ~ to say the rosary.

rosca ['roska] *nf* (*de tornillo*) thread; (*de humo*) coil, spiral; (*pan, postre*) ring-shaped roll/pastry.

rosetón [rose'ton] *nm* rosette; (*ARQ*) rose

window; (*AUTO*) cloverleaf (junction).

rostro ['rostro] *nm* (*cara*) face.

rotación [rota'θjon] *nf* rotation; ~ **de cultivos** crop rotation.

rotativo, a [rota'tiβo, a] *a* rotary.

roto, a ['roto, a] *pp de* **romper** // *a* broken; (*disipado*) debauched.

rótula ['rotula] *nf* kneecap; (*TEC*) ball-and-socket joint.

rotular [rotu'lar] *vt* (*titular, encabezar*) to head, entitle; (*etiquetar*) to label; **rótulo** *nm* heading, title; label.

rotundo, a [ro'tundo, a] *a* round; (*enfático*) emphatic.

rotura [ro'tura] *nf* (*rompimiento*) breaking; (*quiebra*) crack; (*MED*) fracture.

roturar [rotu'rar] *vt* to plough.

rozado, a [ro'θaðo, a] *a* worn.

rozadura [roθa'ðura] *nf* abrasion, graze.

rozar [ro'θar] *vt* (*frotar*) to rub; (*arañar*) to scratch; (*arrugar*) to crumple; (*AGR*) to graze; (*tocar ligeramente*) to shave, touch lightly, ~**se** *vr* to rub (together); (*trabarse*) to trip over one's own feet; ~ **con** (*fam*) to rub shoulders with.

roznar [roθ'nar] *vi* to bray.

rte *abr de* **remite, remitente** sender.

rubí [ru'βi] *nm* ruby.

rubicundo, a [ruβi'kundo, a] *a* ruddy; (*de salud*) rosy with health.

rubio, a ['ruβjo, a] *a* fair-haired // *nm/f* blond/blonde; **tabaco** ~ Virginia tobacco.

rubor [ru'βor] *nm* (*timidez*) bashfulness; (*sonrojo*) blush; ~**izarse** *vr* to blush; ~**oso, a** *a* blushing.

rúbrica ['ruβrika] *nf* title, heading; (*de la firma*) flourish; **rubricar** *vt* (*firmar*) to sign with a flourish; (*concluir*) to sign and seal.

rucio, a ['ruθjo, a] *a* grey.

rudeza [ru'ðeθa] *nf* (*tosquedad*) coarseness; (*sencillez*) simplicity.

rudimento [ruði'mento] *nm* rudiment.

rudo, a ['ruðo, a] *a* (*sin pulir*) unpolished; (*tosco*) coarse; (*violento*) violent; (*vulgar*) common; (*estúpido*) stupid.

rueda ['rweða] *nf* (*gen*) wheel; (*círculo*) ring, circle; (*rodaja*) slice, round; ~ **delantera/trasera/de repuesto** front/back/spare wheel; ~ **de prensa** press conference.

ruedo ['rweðo] *nm* (*contorno*) edge, border; (*de vestido*) hem; (*círculo*) circle; (*TAUR*) arena, bullring.

~**uego** *etc vb ver* **rogar** // ['rweɣo] *nm* request.

rufián [ru'fjan] *nm* scoundrel

rugby ['ruxβi] *nm* rugby.

rugido [ru'xiðo] *nm* roar; **rugir** *vi* to roar.

rugoso, a [ru'ɣoso, a] *a* (*arrugado*) wrinkled; (*áspero*) rough; (*desigual*) ridged.

ruibarbo [rui'βarβo] *nm* rhubarb.

ruido ['rwiðo] *nm* (*gen*) noise; (*sonido*) sound; (*alboroto*) racket, row; (*escándalo*) commotion, rumpus; ~**so, a** a noisy, loud; (fig) sensational.

ruin [ru'in] a contemptible, mean.

ruina ['rwina] nf (gen) ruin; (colapso) collapse; (de persona) ruin, downfall; (de imperio) decline.

ruindad [rwin'ðað] nf lowness, meanness; (acto) low or mean act.

ruinoso, a [rui'noso, a] a ruinous; (destartalado) dilapidated, tumbledown; (COM) disastrous.

ruiseñor [rwise'ɲor] nm nightingale.

rula ['rula], **ruleta** [ru'leta] nf roulette.

Rumania [ru'manja] nf Rumania.

rumba ['rumba] nf rumba.

rumbo ['rumbo] nm (ruta) route, direction; (ángulo de dirección) course, bearing; (fig) course of events.

rumboso, a [rum'boso, a] a generous.

rumiante [ru'mjante] nm ruminant.

rumiar [rumi'nar] vt to chew; (fig) to chew over // vi to chew the cud.

rumor [ru'mor] nm (ruido sordo) low sound; (murmuración) murmur, buzz; ~**earse** vr: **se ~ea que** it is rumoured that; ~**eo** nm murmur.

rupestre [ru'pestre] a rock cpd.

ruptura [rup'tura] nf (MED) fracture; (fig) rupture.

rural [ru'ral] a rural.

Rusia ['rusja] nf Russia; **ruso, a** a, nm/f Russian.

rústico, a ['rustiko, a] a rustic; (ordinario) coarse, uncouth // nm/f yokel // nf: **libro en ~a** paperback.

ruta ['ruta] nf route.

rutina [ru'tina] nf routine; ~**rio, a** a routine.

S

S abr de **santo, a; sur**.

s. abr de **siglo; siguiente**.

sábado ['saβaðo] nm Saturday.

sábana ['saβana] nf sheet.

sabandija [saβan'dixa] nf bug, insect.

sabañón [saβa'ɲon] nm chilblain.

sabelotodo [saβelo'toðo] nm/f inv know-all.

saber [sa'βer] vt to know; (llegar a conocer) to find out, learn; (tener capacidad de) to know how to // vi: ~ **a** to taste of, taste like // nm knowledge, learning; a ~ namely; **¿sabes nadar?** can you swim?; **¿sabes ir?** do you know the way?

sabiduría [saβiðu'ria] nf (conocimientos) wisdom; (instrucción) knowledge, learning.

sabiendas [sa'βjendas]: **a ~** ad knowingly.

sabio, a ['saβjo,a] a (docto) learned; (prudente) wise, sensible.

sabor [sa'βor] nm taste, flavour; ~**ear** vt to savour, relish; (dar ~ a) to flavour.

sabotaje [saβo'taxe] nm sabotage; **sabotear** vt to sabotage.

sabré etc vb ver **saber**.

sabroso, a [sa'βroso, a] a tasty; (fig: fam) racy, salty.

sacacorchos [saka'kortʃos] nm inv corkscrew.

sacapuntas [saka'puntas] nm inv pencil sharpener.

sacar [sa'kar] vt (gen) to take out; (fig) to get (out); (quitar) to remove, get out; (hacer salir) to bring out; (conclusión) to draw; (novela etc) to publish, bring out; (ropa) to take off; (obra) to make; (FOTO) to take; (premio) to receive; (entradas) to get; ~ **adelante** to bring up; ~ **a alguien a bailar** to get sb up to dance; ~ **apuntes** to take notes; ~ **la cara por alguien** to stick up for sb; ~ **la lengua** to stick out one's tongue.

sacarina [saka'rina] nf saccharin(e).

sacerdote [saθer'ðote] nm priest.

saco ['sako] nm (gen) bag; (grande) sack; (su contenido) bagful; (AM) jacket; ~ **de dormir** sleeping bag.

sacramento [sakra'mento] nm sacrament.

sacrificar [sakrifi'kar] vt to sacrifice; **sacrificio** nm sacrifice.

sacrilegio [sakri'lexjo] nm sacrilege; **sacrílego, a** a sacrilegious.

sacristía [sakris'tia] nf sacristy.

sacro, a ['sakro, a] a sacred.

sacudida [saku'ðiða] nf (zarandeada) shake, shaking; (sacudimiento) jolt, bump; ~ **eléctrica** electric shock; **sacudir** vt to shake; (golpear) to hit.

sádico, a ['saðiko, a] a sadistic; **sadismo** nm sadism.

saeta [sa'eta] nf (flecha) arrow; (de reloj) hand; (brújula) magnetic needle.

sagacidad [saxaθi'ðað] nf shrewdness, cleverness; **sagaz** a shrewd, clever; (astuto) astute.

sagrado, a [sa'xraðo, a] a sacred, holy // nm sanctuary, asylum.

Sáhara ['saara] nm: **el ~** the Sahara (desert).

sahumar [sau'mar] vt to fumigate.

sal [sal] vb ver **salir** // nf salt; ~ **de la Higuera** Epsom salts.

sala ['sala] nf (cuarto grande) large room; (~ de estar) living room; (TEATRO) house, auditorium; (de hospital) ward; ~ **de apelación** court; ~ **de espera** waiting room.

salado, a [sa'laðo, a] a salty; (fig) witty, amusing; **agua ~a** salt water; **salar** vt to salt, add salt to.

salario [sa'larjo] nm wage, pay.

salchicha [sal'tʃitʃa] nf pork sausage; **salchichón** nm (salami-type) sausage.

saldar [sal'dar] vt to pay; (vender) to sell off; (fig) to settle, resolve; **saldo** nm (pago) settlement; (de una cuenta) balance; (lo restante) remnant(s) (pl), remainder.

saldré etc vb ver **salir**.

salero [sa'lero] nm salt cellar.

salgo etc vb ver **salir**.

salida [sa'liða] *nf* exit, way out; (*acto*) leaving, going out; (*de tren, AVIAT*) departure; (*TEC*) output, production; (*fig*) way out; (*COM*) opening; (*GEO, válvula*) outlet; (*de gas, aire*) escape, leak; **calle sin ~** cul-de-sac; **~ de emergencia** emergency exit.

saliente [sa'ljente] *a* (*ARQ*) projecting; (*que se retira*) outgoing, retiring; (*el sol*) rising; (*fig*) outstanding.

salir [sa'lir] *vi* (*gen*) to come/go out; (*resultar*) to turn out; (*partir*) to leave, depart; (*aparecer*) to appear; (*sobresalir*) to project, jut out; **~se** *vr* (*vasija*) to leak; (*animal*) to escape, get out; **~ con** to go out with; **~ a la superficie** to come to the surface; **~ caro/barato** to work out expensive/cheap.

saliva [sa'liβa] *nf* saliva.

salmantino, a [salman'tino, a] *a* of Salamanca.

salmo ['salmo] *nm* psalm.

salmón [sal'mon] *nm* salmon.

salmuera [sal'mwera] *nf* pickle, brine.

salón [sa'lon] *nm* (*de casa*) living-room, lounge; (*muebles*) lounge suite; **~ de belleza** beauty parlour; **~ de pintura** art gallery; **~ de baile** dance hall.

salpicadero [salpika'ðero] *nm* dashboard.

salpicar [salpi'kar] *vt* (*rociar*) to sprinkle, spatter; (*esparcir*) to scatter.

salsa ['salsa] *nf* sauce; (*con carne asada*) gravy; (*fig*) spice.

saltamontes [salta'montes] *nm inv* grasshopper.

saltar [sal'tar] *vt* to jump (over), leap (over); (*dejar de lado*) to skip, miss out // *vi* to jump, leap; (*pelota*) to bounce; (*al aire*) to fly up; (*quebrarse*) to break; (*al agua*) to dive; (*fig*) to explode, blow up.

saltear [salte'ar] *vt* (*robar*) to rob (in a holdup); (*asaltar*) to assault, attack; (*CULIN*) to sauté.

saltimbanqui [saltim'banki] *nm/f* acrobat.

salto ['salto] *nm* jump, leap; (*al agua*) dive; (*DEPORTE*) jump; **~ de agua** waterfall.

saltón, ona [sal'ton, ona] *a* (*ojos*) bulging, popping; (*dientes*) protruding.

salubre [sa'luβre] *a* healthy, salubrious.

salud [sa'luð] *nf* health; ¡(**a su**) ~**!** good health!; **~able** *a* (*de buena* ~) healthy; (*provechoso*) good, beneficial.

saludar [salu'ðar] *vt* to greet; (*MIL*) to salute; **saludo** *nm* greeting; **saludos** (*en carta*) best wishes, regards, greetings.

salvación [salβa'θjon] *nf* (*gen*) salvation; (*rescate*) rescue.

salvaguardar [salβaxwar'ðar] *vt* to safeguard.

salvaje [sal'βaxe] *a* wild; (*tribú*) savage; **salvajismo** *nm*, **salvajez** *nf* savagery.

salvar [sal'βar] *vt* (*rescatar*) to save, rescue; (*resolver*) to overcome, resolve; (*cubrir distancias*) to cover, travel; (*hacer excepción*) to except, exclude; (*un barco*) to salvage.

salvavidas [salβa'βiðas] *nm inv* lifebelt // *a*: **bote/chaleco/cinturón ~** lifeboat/jacket/belt.

salvia ['salβja] *nf* sage.

salvo, a ['salβo, a] *a* safe // *ad* except (for), save; **a ~** out of danger; **~ que** unless; **~ conducto** *nm* safe-conduct.

san [san] *a* saint; **~ Juan** St. John.

sanar [sa'nar] *vt* (*herida*) to heal; (*persona*) to cure // *vi* (*persona*) to get well, recover; (*herida*) to heal.

sanatorio [sana'ɔrjo] *nm* sanatorium.

sanción [san'θjon] *nf* sanction; **sancionar** *vt* to sanction.

sandalia [san'dalja] *nf* sandal.

sandía [san'dia] *nf* watermelon.

sandwich ['sandwitʃ] *nm* sandwich.

saneamiento [sanea'mjento] *nm* sanitation; (*de la tierra*) drainage; (*indemnización*) compensation; (*fig*) remedy; **sanear** *vt* to drain; to compensate; to remedy, repair; (*garantizar*) to guarantee; (*asegurar*) to insure.

sangrar [san'grar] *a, vi* to bleed; **sangre** *nf* blood.

sangría [san'gria] *nf* sangria, sweetened drink of red wine with fruit.

sangriento, a [san'grjento, a] *a* (*herido*) bleeding; (*batalla*) bloody.

sanguinario, a [sangi'narjo, a] *a* bloodthirsty.

sanguíneo, a [san'gineo, a] *a* blood *cpd*.

sanidad [sani'ðað] *nf* sanitation; (*calidad de sano*) health, healthiness; **~ pública** public health.

sanitario, a [sani'tarjo, a] *a* sanitary; (*de la salud*) health *cpd*.

sano, a ['sano, a] *a* healthy; (*sin daños*) sound; (*comida*) good; (*entero*) whole, intact; **~ y salvo** safe and sound.

santidad [santi'ðað] *nf* holiness, sanctity; **santificar** *vt* to sanctify, make holy.

santiguar [santi'ɣwar] *vt* (*fig*) to slap, hit; **~se** *vr* to make the sign of the cross.

santo, a ['santo, a] *a* holy; (*fig*) wonderful, miraculous // *nm/f* saint *f*; *nm* saint's day; **~ y seña** password.

santuario [san'twarjo] *nm* sanctuary, shrine.

saña ['sana] *nf* rage, fury.

sapo ['sapo] *nm* toad.

saque ['sake] *nm* (*TENIS*) service, serve; (*FÚTBOL*) throw-in; **~ de esquina** corner (kick).

saquear [sake'ar] *vt* (*MIL*) to sack; (*robar*) to loot, plunder; (*fig*) to ransack; **saqueo** *nm* sacking; looting, plundering, ransacking.

sarampión [saram'pjon] *nm* measles *sg*.

sarcasmo [sar'kasmo] *nm* sarcasm; **sarcástico, a** *a* sarcastic.

sardina [sar'ðina] *nf* sardine.

sardónico, a [sar'ðoniko, a] *a* sardonic; (*irónico*) ironical, sarcastic.

sargento [sar'xento] *nm* sergeant.

sarna ['sarna] *nf* itch; (*MED*) scabies.
sartén [sar'ten] *nf* frying pan.
sastre ['sastre] *nm* tailor; ~**ría** *nf* (*arte*) tailoring; (*tienda*) tailor's (shop).
satélite [sa'telite] *nm* satellite.
sátira ['satira] *nf* satire.
satisfacción [satisfak'θjon] *nf* satisfaction; **satisfacer** *vt* to satisfy; (*gastos*) to meet; (*pérdida*) to make good; **satisfacerse** *vr* to satisfy o.s., be satisfied; (*vengarse*) to take revenge; **satisfecho, a** *a* satisfied; (*contento*) content(ed), happy; (*vanidoso*) self-satisfied, smug.
saturar [satu'rar] *vt* to saturate.
sauce ['sauθe] *nm* willow; ~ **llorón** weeping willow.
sauna ['sauna] *nf* sauna.
savia ['saβja] *nf* sap.
saxofón [sakso'fon], **saxófono** [sak-'sofono] *nm* saxophone.
sayo ['sajo] *nm* smock.
sazonado, a [saθo'naðo, a] *a* (*fruta*) ripe; (*CULIN*) flavoured, seasoned; **sazonar** *vt* to ripen; to flavour, season.
se [se] *pron reflexivo* oneself; (*sg: m*) himself; (: *f*) herself; (: *de una cosa*) itself; (: *de Ud*) yourself; (*pl*) themselves; (: *de Uds*) yourselves; (*de uno*) oneself; ~ **mira en el espejo** he looks at himself in the mirror; (*recíproco*) each other, one another; ~ **ayudan** they help each other; ~ **miraron (el uno al otro)** they looked at one another; (*uso impersonal*): ~ **compró hace 3 años it** was bought 3 years ago; **en esa parte** ~ **habla francés** in that area French is spoken *or* people speak French; (*dativo*): ~ **lo daré** I'll give it to him/her/you; **él** ~ **ha comprado un sombrero** he has bought himself a hat.
SE *abr de* **sudeste.**
sé *vb ver* **saber, ser.**
sea *etc vb ver* **ser.**
sebo ['seβo] *nm* fat, grease.
seca ['seka] *nf ver* **seco.**
secador [seka'ðor] *nm*: ~ **de cabello** *o* **para el pelo** hair-dryer.
secadora [seka'ðora] *nf* wringer; ~ **centrífuga** spin-dryer.
secar [se'kar] *vt* to dry; ~**se** *vr* to dry (off); (*río, planta*) to dry up.
sección [sek'θjon] *nf* section.
seco, a ['seko, a] *a* dry; (*carácter*) cold; (*respuesta*) sharp, curt; (*coñac*) straight // *nf* drought; **vivir a pan** ~ to live by bread alone; **habrá pan a** ~**as** there will be just bread; **decir algo a** ~**as** to say sth curtly; **parar en** ~ to stop dead.
secretaría [sekreta'ria] *nf* secretariat; **secretario, a** *nm/f* secretary.
secreto, a [se'kreto, a] *a* secret; (*persona*) secretive // *nm* secret; (*calidad*) secrecy.
secta ['sekta] *nf* sect; ~**rio, a** *a* sectarian.
sector [sek'tor] *nm* sector.
secuela [se'kwela] *nf* consequence.
secuestrar [sekwes'trar] *vt* to kidnap; (*bienes*) to seize, confiscate; **secuestro** *nm* kidnapping; seizure, confiscation.
secular [seku'lar] *a* secular.
secundar [sekun'dar] *vt* to second, support.
secundario, a [sekun'darjo, a] *a* secondary.
sed [seð] *nf* thirst; **tener** ~ to be thirsty.
seda ['seða] *nf* silk.
sedal [se'ðal] *nm* fishing line.
sedante [se'ðante], **sedativo** [seða'tiβo] *nm* sedative.
sede ['seðe] *nf* (*de gobierno*) seat; (*de compañía*) headquarters *pl*; **Santa S**~ Holy See.
sediento, a [se'ðjento, a] *a* thirsty.
sedimentar [seðimen'tar] *vt* to deposit; ~**se** *vr* to settle; **sedimento** *nm* sediment.
seducción [seðuk'θjon] *nf* seduction; **seducir** *vt* to seduce; (*sobornar*) to bribe; (*cautivar*) to charm, fascinate; **seductor, a** *a* seductive; charming, fascinating; (*engañoso*) deceptive, misleading // *nm/f* seducer.
segadora-trilladora [seɣa'ðora triʎa-'ðora] *nf* combine harvester.
seglar [se'ɣlar] *a* secular, lay.
segregación [seɣreɣa'θjon] *nf* segregation; ~ **racial** racial segregation; **segregar** *vt* to segregate, separate.
seguido, a [se'ɣiðo, a] *a* (*continuo*) continuous, unbroken; (*recto*) straight; ~**s** consecutive, successive // *ad* (*directo*) straight (on); (*después*) after // *nf*: **en** ~**a** at once, right away; **5 días** ~**s** 5 days running, 5 days in a row.
seguimiento [seɣi'mjento] *nm* chase, pursuit; (*continuación*) continuation.
seguir [se'ɣir] *vt* (*gen*) to follow; (*venir después*) to follow on, come after; (*proseguir*) to continue; (*perseguir*) to chase, pursue // *vi* (*gen*) to follow; (*continuar*) to continue, carry *or* go on; ~**se** *vr* to follow; **sigo sin comprender** I still don't understand; **sigue lloviendo** it's still raining.
según [se'ɣun] *prep* according to // *ad* according to circumstances; ~ **y conforme** it all depends; ~ **esté el tiempo** depending on the weather.
segundo, a [se'ɣundo, a] *a* second // *nm* second // *nf* second meaning; **de** ~**a mano** second hand.
segur [se'ɣur] *nf* (*hacha*) axe; (*hoz*) sickle.
seguramente [seɣura'mente] *ad* surely; (*con certeza*) for sure, with certainty.
seguridad [seɣuri'ðað] *nf* (*gen*) safety; (*del estado, de casa etc*) security; (*certidumbre*) certainty; (*confianza*) confidence; (*estabilidad*) stability; ~ **social** social security.
seguro, a [se'ɣuro, a] *a* (*cierto*) sure, certain; (*fiel*) trustworthy; (*libre del peligro*) safe; (*bien defendido, firme*) secure // *ad* for sure, certainly // *nm* (*COM*) insurance; ~ **contra terceros/a todo riesgo** third party/comprehensive insurance; ~**s sociales** social security *sg*.

seis [seis] *num* six.
seismo ['seismo] *nm* tremor, earthquake.
selección [selek'θjon] *nf* selection;
seleccionar *vt* to pick, choose, select;
selecto, a *a* select, choice; *(escogido)*
selected.
selva ['selβa] *nf (bosque)* forest, woods *pl*.
(jungla) jungle.
sello ['seʎo] *nm* stamp; *(medicinal)*
capsule, pill.
semáforo [se'maforo] *nm (AUTO)* traffic
lights *pl*; *(FERRO)* signal.
semana [se'mana] *nf* week; **entre ~**
during the week; **semanal, semanario, a**
a weekly.
semblante [sem'blante] *nm* face; *(fig)*
face, appearance.
sembrar [sem'brar] *vt* to sow; *(objetos)* to
sprinkle, scatter about; *(noticias)* to
spread.
semejante [seme'xante] *a (parecido)*
similar; **~s alike**, similar // *nm* fellow
man, fellow creature; **no he dicho cosa
~** I have not said any such thing;
semejanza *nf* similarity, resemblance.
semejar [seme'xar] *vi* to seem like,
resemble; **~se** *vr* to look alike, be similar.
semen ['semen] *nm* semen; **~tal** *nm* stud.
semestral [semes'tral] *a* half-yearly, bi-
annual.
semicírculo [semi'θirkulo] *nm* semicircle.
semiconsciente [semikons'θjente] *a*
semiconscious.
semilla [se'miʎa] *nf* seed.
seminario [semi'narjo] *nm (REL)*
seminary; *(en universidad)* seminar.
sémola ['semola] *nf* semolina.
sempiterno, a [sempi'terno, a] *a*
everlasting // *nf* evergreen.
Sena ['sena] *nm*: **el ~** the (river) Seine.
senado [se'naðo] *nm* senate; **senador, a**
nm/f senator.
sencillez [senθi'ʎeθ] *nf (gen)* simplicity;
(naturalidad) naturalness; **sencillo, a** *a*
simple; natural, unaffected.
senda ['senda] *nf*, **sendero** [sen'dero] *nm*
path, track.
sendos, as ['sendos, as] *apl*: **les dio ~**
golpes he hit both of them.
senil [se'nil] *a* senile.
seno ['seno] *nm (ANAT)* bosom, bust; *(fig)*
bosom; *(vacío)* hollow; **~s** breasts.
sensación [sensa'θjon] *nf (gen)* sensation;
(sentido) sense; *(sentimiento)* feeling.
sensato, a [sen'sato, a] *a* sensible.
sensible [sen'sible] *a* sensitive;
(apreciable) perceptible, appreciable;
(pérdida) considerable.
sensitivo, a [sensi'tiβo, a], **sensorio, a**
[sen'sorjo, a], **sensorial** [senso'rjal] *a*
sensory.
sensual [sen'swal] *a* sensual.
sentado, a [sen'taðo, a] *a (establecido)*
settled; *(carácter)* sensible; **estar ~** to sit,
be sitting (down) // *nf* sitting; **dar por ~**
to take for granted, assume.

sentar [sen'tar] *vt* to sit, seat; *(fig)* to
establish // *vi (vestido)* to suit; *(alimento)*:
~ bien/mal a to agree/disagree with;
~se *vr (persona)* to sit, sit down; *(el
tiempo)* to settle (down); *(los depósitos)* to
settle.
sentencia [sen'tenθja] *nf (máxima)*
maxim, saying; *(JUR)* sentence;
sentenciar *vt* to sentence // *vi* to give
one's opinion.
sentido, a [sen'tiðo, a] *a (pérdida)*
regrettable; *(carácter)* sensitive // *nm*
(gen) sense; *(sentimiento)* feeling;
(significado) sense, meaning; *(dirección)*
direction; **mi más ~ pésame** my
deepest sympathy; **~ del humor** sense of
humour; **~ único** one-way (street).
sentimental [sentimen'tal] *a* sentimental;
vida ~ love life.
sentimiento [senti'mjento] *nm (emoción)*
feeling, emotion; *(sentido)* sense; *(pesar)*
regret, sorrow.
sentir [sen'tir] *vt (gen)* to feel; *(percibir)*
to perceive, sense; *(lamentar)* to regret, be
sorry for // *vi (tener la sensación)* to feel;
(lamentarse) to feel sorry // *nm* opinion,
judgement; **~se bien/mal** to feel
well/ill; **lo siento** I'm sorry.
seña ['sena] *nf* sign; *(MIL)* password; **~s**
nfpl address *sg*; **~s personales** personal
details.
señal [se'nal] *nf (gen)* sign; *(síntoma)*
symptom; *(FERRO, TELEC)* signal; *(marca)*
mark; *(COM)* deposit; **en ~ de** as a sign
of, as a sign of; **~ar** *vt* to mark; *(indicar)*
to point out, indicate; *(fijar)* to fix, settle;
~arse *vr* to make one's mark.
señor [se'nor] *nm (hombre)* man;
(caballero) gentleman; *(dueño)* owner,
master; *(trato: antes de nombre propio)* Mr;
(: directo) sir; **muy ~ mío** Dear Sir; **el ~
alcalde/presidente** the mayor/presi-
dent.
señora [se'nora] *nf (dama)* lady; *(trato)*
Mrs; *(tratamiento de cortesía)* madam;
(fam) wife; **Nuestra S~** Our Lady.
señorita [seno'rita] *nf (gen.* Miss; *(mujer
joven)* young lady.
señuelo [se'nwelo] *nm* decoy.
sepa *etc vb ver* **saber**.
separación [separa'θjon] *nf* separation;
(división) division; *(distancia)* gap,
distance.
separar [sepa'rar] *vt* to separate; *(dividir)*
to divide; **~se** *vr (parte)* to come away;
(partes) to come apart; *(persona)* to leave,
go away; *(matrimonio)* to separate; **sepa-
ratismo** *nm* separatism.
sepia ['sepja] *nf* cuttlefish.
séptico, a [a ['septiko, a] *a* septic.
septiembre [sep'tjembre] *nm* September.
séptimo, a [a ['septimo, a] *a, nm* seventh.
sepultar [sepul'tar] *vt* to bury; **sepultura**
nf (acto) burial; *(tumba)* grave, tomb;
sepulturero, a *nm/f* gravedigger.
sequedad [seke'ðað] *nf* dryness; *(fig)*
brusqueness, curtness.

sequía [se'kia] nf drought.

séquito ['sekito] nm followers pl, retinue.

ser [ser] vi (gen) to be; (devenir) to become // nm being; ~ **de** (origen) to be from, come from; (hecho de) to be (made) of; (pertenecer a) to belong to; **es la una** it is one o'clock; **es de esperar que** it is to be hoped that; **era de ver** it was worth seeing, you should have seen it; **a no ~ que** unless; **de no ~ así** if it were not so, were it not so; **o sea** that is to say; **sea como sea** be that as it may.

serenarse [sere'narse] vr to calm down.

sereno, a [se'reno, a] a (persona) calm, unruffled; (el tiempo) fine, settled; (ambiente) calm, peaceful // nm night watchman.

serie ['serje] nf series; (cadena) sequence, succession; **fuera de ~** out of order; **fabricación en ~** mass production.

seriedad [serje'ðað] nf seriousness; (formalidad) reliability; (de crisis) gravity, seriousness; **serio, a** a serious; reliable, dependable; grave, serious; **en serio** ad seriously.

sermón [ser'mon] nm (REL) sermon.

serpentear [serpente'ar] vi to wriggle; (fig) to wind, snake.

serpentina [serpen'tina] nf streamer.

serpiente [ser'pjente] nf snake; ~ **boa** boa constrictor; ~ **pitón** python; ~ **de cascabel** rattlesnake.

serranía [serra'nia] nf mountainous area; **serrano, a** a highland cpd, hill cpd // nm/f highlander.

serrar [se'rrar] vt = **aserrar**.

serrín [se'rrin] nm = **aserrín**.

serrucho [se'rrutʃo] nm saw.

servicio [ser'βiθjo] nm service; ~**s** toilet(s).

servidor, a [serβi'ðor, a] nm/f servant; **su seguro ~** (s.s.s.) yours faithfully; **servidumbre** nf (sujeción) servitude; (criados) servants pl, staff.

servil [ser'βil] a servile.

servilleta [serβi'ʎeta] nf serviette, napkin.

servir [ser'βir] vt to serve // vi to serve; (tener utilidad) to be of use, be useful; ~**se** vr to serve or help o.s.; ~**se de algo** to make use of sth, use sth; **sírvase pasar** please come in.

sesenta [se'senta] num sixty.

sesgado, a [ses'xaðo, a] a slanted, slanting; **sesgo** nm slant; (fig) slant, twist.

sesión [se'sjon] nf (POL) session, sitting; (CINE) showing.

seso ['seso] nm brain; **sesudo, a** a sensible, wise.

seta ['seta] nf mushroom.

setenta [se'tenta] num seventy.

seudo... ['seuðo] pref pseudo... .

seudónimo [seu'ðonimo] nm pseudonym.

severidad [seβeri'ðað] nf severity; **severo, a** a severe.

Sevilla [se'βiʎa] n Seville.

sexo ['sekso] nm sex.

sexto, a ['seksto, a] a, nm sixth.

sexual [sek'swal] a sexual; **vida ~ sex** life.

si [si] conj if; **me pregunto ~...** I wonder if or whether... .

sí [si] ad yes // nm consent // pron (gen) oneself; (sg: m) himself; (: f) herself; (: de cosa) itself; (de usted) yourself; (pl) themselves; (de ustedes) yourselves; (recíproco) each other; **él no quiere pero yo ~** he doesn't want to but I do; **ella ~ vendrá** she will certainly come, she is sure to come; **claro que ~** of course; **creo que ~** I think so.

siderúrgico, a [siðe'rurxico, a] a iron and steel cpd // nf: **la ~a** the iron and steel industry.

sidra ['siðra] nf cider.

siembra ['sjembra] nf sowing.

siempre ['sjempre] ad (gen) always; (todo el tiempo) all the time; ~ **que** conj (cada vez) whenever; (dado que) provided that; **para ~** for ever.

sien [sjen] nf temple.

siento etc vb ver **sentar, sentir**.

sierra ['sjerra] nf (TEC) saw; (cadena de montañas) mountain range.

siervo, a ['sjerβo, a] nm/f slave.

siesta ['sjesta] nf siesta, nap.

siete ['sjete] num seven.

sífilis ['sifilis] nf syphilis.

sifón [si'fon] nm syphon; **whisky con ~** whisky and soda.

sigla ['sixla] nf symbol.

siglo ['sixlo] nm century; (fig) age.

significación [sixnifika'θjon] nf significance.

significado [sixnifi'kaðo] nm significance; (de palabra) meaning.

significar [sixnifi'kar] vt to mean, signify; (notificar) to make known, express; ~**se** vr to become known, make a name for o.s.; **significativo, a** a significant.

signo ['sixno] nm sign; ~ **de admiración** o **exclamación** exclamation mark; ~ **de interrogación** question mark.

sigo etc vb ver **seguir**.

siguiente [si'xjente] a next, following.

siguió etc vb ver **seguir**.

sílaba ['silaβa] nf syllable.

silbar [sil'βar] vt, vi to whistle; **silbato** nm whistle; **silbido** nm whistle, whistling.

silenciador [silenθja'ðor] nm silencer.

silenciar [silen'θjar] vt (persona) to silence; (escándalo) to hush up; **silencio** nm silence, quiet; **silencioso, a** a silent, quiet.

silicio [si'liθjo] nm silicon.

silueta [si'lweta] nf silhouette; (de edificio) outline; (figura) figure.

silvestre [sil'βestre] a rustic, rural; (salvaje) wild.

silla ['siʎa] nf (asiento) chair; (de jinete) saddle.

sillón [si'ʎon] *nm* armchair, easy chair; ~ **de ruedas** wheelchair.
simbólico, a [sim'boliko, a] *a* symbolic(al); **símbolo** *nm* symbol.
simetría [sime'tria] *nf* symmetry.
simiente [si'mjente] *nf* seed.
similar [simi'lar] *a* similar.
simio ['simjo] *nm* ape.
simpatía [simpa'tia] *nf* liking; (*afecto*) affection; (*amabilidad*) kindness; (*solidaridad*) mutual support, solidarity; **simpático, a** *a* nice, pleasant; (*kind*) **simpatizante** *nm/f* sympathiser; **simpatizar** *vi*: **simpatizar con** to get on well with.
simple ['simple] *a* (*gen*) simple; (*elemental*) simple, easy; (*mero*) mere; (*puro*) pure, sheer // *nm/f* simpleton; ~**za** *nf* simpleness; (*necedad*) silly thing; **simplicidad** *nf* simplicity; **simplificar** *vt* to simplify.
simular [simu'lar] *vt* to simulate.
simultáneo, a [simul'taneo, a] *a* simultaneous.
sin [sin] *prep* without; **la ropa está** ~ **lavar** the clothes are unwashed; ~ **que** *conj* without; ~ **embargo** however, still.
sinagoga [sina'ɣoɣa] *nf* synagogue.
sinceridad [sinθeri'ðað] *nf* sincerity; **sincero, a** *a* sincere.
sincronizar [sinkroni'θar] *vt* to synchronize.
sindical [sindi'kal] *a* union *cpd*, trade-union *cpd*; ~**ista** *nm/f* trade-unionist; **sindicato** *nm* (*de trabajadores*) trade(s) union; (*de negociantes*) syndicate.
sinfín [sin'fin] *nm*: **un** ~ **de** a great many, no end of.
sinfonía [sinfo'nia] *nf* symphony.
singular [singu'lar] *a* singular; (*fig*) outstanding, exceptional; (*pey*) peculiar, odd; ~**idad** *nf* singularity, peculiarity; ~**izar** *vt* to single out; ~**izarse** *vr* to distinguish o.s., stand out.
siniestro, a [si'njestro, a] *a* left; (*fig*) sinister.
sinnúmero [sin'numero] *nm* = **sinfín**.
sino ['sino] *nm* fate, destiny // *conj* (*pero*) but; (*salvo*) except, save.
sinónimo [si'nonimo] *nm* synonym.
sinrazón [sinra'θon] *nf* wrong, injustice.
síntesis ['sintesis] *nf* synthesis; **sintético, a** *a* synthetic; **sintetizar** *vt* to synthesize.
sintió *vb ver* **sentir**.
síntoma ['sintoma] *nm* symptom.
sinvergüenza [sinβer'ɣwenθa] *nm/f* shameless person.
sionismo [sjo'nismo] *nm* Zionism.
siquiera [si'kjera] *conj* even if, even though // *ad* at least; **ni** ~ not even.
sirena [si'rena] *nf* siren.
sirviente, a [sir'βjente, a] *nm/f* servant.
sirvo *etc vb ver* **servir**.
sisear [sise'ar] *vt, vi* to hiss.
sismógrafo [sis'moɣrafo] *nm* seismograph.

sistema [sis'tema] *nm* system; (*método*) method; **sistemático, a** *a* systematic.
sitiar [si'tjar] *vt* to beseige, lay seige to.
sitio ['sitjo] *nm* (*lugar*) place; (*espacio*) room, space; (*MIL*) siege.
situación [sitwa'θjon] *nf* situation, position; (*estatus*) position, standing.
situar [si'twar] *vt* to place, put; (*edificio*) to locate, situate.
slip [slip] *nm* pants *pl*, briefs *pl*.
smoking ['smokin] (*pl* ~**s**) *nm* dinner jacket.
so [so] *prep* under.
SO *abr de* **sudoeste**.
sobaco [so'βako] *nm* armpit.
soberanía [soβera'nia] *nf* sovereignty; **soberano, a** *a* sovereign; (*fig*) supreme // *nm/f* sovereign.
soberbio, a [so'βerβjo, a] *a* (*orgulloso*) proud; (*altivo*) haughty, arrogant; (*fig*) magnificent, superb // *nf* pride; haughtiness, arrogance; magnificence; (*cólera*) anger.
sobornar [soβor'nar] *vt* to bribe; **soborno** *nm* bribe.
sobra ['soβra] *nf* excess, surplus; ~**s** *nfpl* left-overs, scraps; **de** ~ surplus, extra; **tengo de** ~ I've more than enough; ~**do**, **a** *a* (*de** ~) more than enough; (*excesivo*) excessive // *ad* too, exceedingly; **sobrante** *a* remaining, extra // *nm* surplus, remainder; **sobrar** *vt* to exceed, surpass // *vi* (*tener de más*) to be more than enough; (*quedar*) to remain, be left (over).
sobre ['soβre] *prep* (*gen*) on; (*encima*) on (top of); (*por encima de, arriba de*) over, above; (*más que*) more than; (*además*) in addition to, besides; (*alrededor de, tratando de*) about // *nm* envelope.
sobrecama [soβre'kama] *nf* bedspread.
sobrecargar [soβrekar'ɣar] *vt* (*camión*) to overload; (*COM*) to surcharge.
sobrehumano, a [soβreu'mano, a] *a* superhuman.
sobrellevar [soβreʎe'βar] *vt* (*fig*) to bear, endure.
sobremarcha [soβre'martʃa] *nf* (*AUTO*) overdrive.
sobrenatural [soβrenatu'ral] *a* supernatural.
sobrepasar [soβrepa'sar] *vt* to exceed, surpass.
sobreponer [soβrepo'ner] *vt* (*poner encima*) to put on top; (*añadir*) to add; ~**se** *vr*: ~**se a** to win through, pull through.
sobreprecio [soβre'preθjo] *nm* surcharge.
sobresaliente [soβresa'ljente] *a* projecting; (*fig*) outstanding, excellent; **sobresalir** *vi* to project, jut out; to stand out, excel.
sobresaltar [soβresal'tar] *vt* (*asustar*) to scare, frighten; (*sobrecoger*) to startle; **sobresalto** *nm* (*movimiento*) start; (*susto*) scare; (*turbación*) sudden shock; **de sobresalto** suddenly.

sobrescrito [soßres'krito] *nm* address.
sobretodo [soßre'toðo] *nm* overcoat.
sobreviviente [soßreßi'ßjente] *a* surviving // *nm/f* survivor; **sobrevivir** *vi* to survive.
sobriedad [soßrje'ðað] *nf* sobriety, soberness; (*moderación*) moderation, restraint.
sobrino, a [so'ßrino, a] *nm/f* nephew/niece.
sobrio, a ['soßrjo, a] *a* sober; (*moderado*) moderate, restrained.
socarrón, ona [soka'rron, ona] *a* (*sarcástico*) sarcastic, ironic(al); (*astuto*) crafty, cunning.
sociable [so'θjaßle] *a* (*persona*) sociable, friendly; (*animal*) social.
social [so'θjal] *a* social; (*COM*) company *cpd.*
socialdemócrata [soθjalde'mokrata] *nm/f* social democrat.
socialista [soθja'lista] *a, nm/f* socialist.
socializar [soθjali'θar] *vt* to socialize.
sociedad [soθje'ðað] *nf* (*gen*) society; (*COM*) company; ~ **anónima** (**SA**) limited company.
socio, a ['soθjo, a] *nm/f* (*miembro*) member; (*COM*) partner; ~ **comandatario** sleeping partner.
sociología [soθjolo'xia] *nf* sociology.
socorrer [soko'rrer] *vt* to help; **socorro** *nm* (*ayuda*) help, aid; (*MIL*) relief; ¡**socorro!** help!
soda ['soða] *nf* (*sosa*) soda; (*bebida*) soda water.
sofá [so'fa] (*pl* ~**s**) *nm* sofa, settee; ~**-cama** *nm* studio couch.
sofisticación [sofistika'θjon] *nf* sophistication.
sofocar [sofo'kar] *vt* to suffocate; (*apagar*) to smother, put out; ~**se** *vr* to suffocate; (*fig*) to blush, feel embarrassed; **sofoco** *nm* suffocation; embarrassment.
soga ['soxa] *nf* rope.
sois *vb ver* **ser.**
sojuzgar [soxuθ'xar] *vt* to subdue, rule despotically.
sol [sol] *nm* sun; (*luz*) sunshine, sunlight; **hace** ~ it is sunny.
solamente [sola'mente] *ad* only, just.
solapa [so'lapa] *nf* (*de ropa*) lapel; (*de libro*) jacket.
solar [so'lar] *a* solar, sun *cpd.*
solaz [so'laθ] *nm* recreation, relaxation; (*alivio*) solace; ~**ar** *vt* (*divertir*) to amuse; (*aliviar*) to console.
soldada [sol'daða] *nf* pay.
soldado [sol'daðo] *nm* soldier.
soldador [solda'ðor] *nm* soldering iron; (*persona*) welder; **soldar** *vt* to solder, weld; (*unir*) to join, unite.
soledad [sole'ðað] *nf* solitude; (*estado infeliz*) loneliness; (*nostalgia*) grieving, mourning.
solemne [so'lemne] *a* solemn; **solemnidad** *nf* solemnity.

soler [so'ler] *vi* to be in the habit of, be accustomed to.
solfa ['solfa] *nf*, **solfeo** [sol'feo] *nm* solfa; (*conjunto de signos*) musical notation.
solicitación [soliθita'θjon] *nf* request; (*de votos*) canvassing; **solicitar** *vt* (*permiso*) to ask for, seek; (*puesto*) to apply for; (*votos*) to canvass; (*atención*) to attract; (*persona*) to pursue, chase after.
solícito, a [so'liθito, a] *a* (*diligente*) diligent; (*cuidadoso*) careful; **solicitud** *nf* (*calidad*) great care; (*petición*) request; (*memorial*) petition; (*a un puesto*) application.
solidaridad [soliðari'ðað] *nf* solidarity; **solidario, a** *a* (*participación*) joint, common; (*compromiso*) mutually binding.
solidez [soli'ðeθ] *nf* solidity; **sólido, a** *a* solid.
soliloquio [soli'lokjo] *nm* soliloquy, monologue.
solista [so'lista] *nm/f* soloist.
solitario, a [soli'tarjo, a] *a* lonely, solitary // *nm/f* recluse; (*en la sociedad*) loner // *nm* solitaire.
soliviar [soli'ßjar] *vt* to lift.
solo, a ['solo, a] *a* (*único*) single, sole; (*sin compañía*) alone; (*solitario*) lonely; **hay una** ~**a dificultad** there is just one difficulty; **a** ~**as** alone, by o.s.
sólo ['solo] *ad* only, just.
solomillo [solo'miʎo] *nm* sirloin.
soltar [sol'tar] *vt* (*dejar ir*) to let go of; (*desprender*) to unfasten, loosen; (*librar*) to release, set free; (*estornudo, risa*) to let out.
soltero, a [sol'tero, a] *a* single, unmarried // *nm* bachelor // *nf* single woman, spinster.
soltura [sol'tura] *nf* looseness, slackness; (*de los miembros*) agility, ease of movement; (*en el hablar*) fluency, ease; (*MED*) diarrhoea.
soluble [so'lußle] *a* (*QUÍMICA*) soluble; (*problema*) solvable.
solución [solu'θjon] *nf* solution; **solucionar** *vt* (*problema*) to solve; (*asunto*) to settle.
solventar [solßen'tar] *vt* (*pagar*) to settle, pay; (*resolver*) to resolve.
sollozar [soʎo'θar] *vi* to sob; **sollozo** *nm* sob.
sombra ['sombra] *nf* shadow; (*como protección*) shade; ~**s** *nfpl* darkness *sg*; **tener buena/mala** ~ to be lucky/unlucky.
sombreador [sombrea'ðor] *nm*: ~ **de ojos** eyeshadow.
sombrero [som'brero] *nm* hat.
sombrilla [som'briʎa] *nf* parasol, sunshade.
sombrío, a [som'brio, a] *a* (*oscuro*) dark; (*sombreado*) shaded; (*fig*) sombre, sad; (*persona*) gloomy.
somero, a [so'mero, a] *a* superficial.
someter [some'ter] *vt* (*país*) to conquer; (*persona*) to subject to one's will; (*informe*) to present, submit; ~**se** *vr* to give in,

yield, submit; ~ **a** to subject to.

somnambulismo [somnambu'lismo] *nm* sleepwalking; **somnámbulo**, **a** *nm/f* sleepwalker.

somnífero [som'nifero] *nm* sleeping pill.

somos *vb ver* **ser.**

son [son] *vb ver* **ser** // *nm* sound; **en ~ de broma** as a joke.

sonar [so'nar] *vt* to ring // *vi* to sound; (*hacer ruido*) to make a noise; (*pronunciarse*) to be sounded, be pronounced; (*ser conocido*) to sound familiar; (*campana*) to ring; (*reloj*) to strike, chime; **~se** *vr*: **~se (las narices)** to blow one's nose; **me suena ese nombre** that name rings a bell.

sonda ['sonda] *nf* (*NAUT*) sounding; (*TEC*) bore, drill; (*MED*) probe; **sondear** *vt* to sound; to bore (into), drill; to probe, sound (*fig*) to sound out; **sondeo** *nm* sounding, boring, drilling; (*fig*) poll, enquiry.

sónico, a ['soniko, a] *a* sonic, sound *cpd*.

sonido [so'niðo] *nm* sound.

sonoro, a [so'noro, a] *a* sonorous; (*resonante*) loud, resonant.

sonreír [sonre'ir] *vi*, **~se** *vr* to smile; **sonriente** *a* smiling; **sonrisa** *nf* smile.

sonrojo [son'roxo] *nm* blush.

soñador, a [soɲa'ðor, a] *nm/f* dreamer; **soñar** *vt*, *vi* to dream; **soñar con** to dream about, dream of.

soñoliento, a [soɲo'ljento, a] *a* sleepy, drowsy.

sopa ['sopa] *nf* soup.

soplador [sopla'ðor] *nm* fan, ventilator.

soplar [so'plar] *vt* (*polvo*) to blow away, blow off; (*inflar*) to blow up; (*vela*) to blow out // *vi* to blow; **~se** *vr* (*fam: ufanarse*) to get conceited; **soplo** *nm* blow, puff; (*de viento*) puff, gust.

soporífero [sopo'rifero] *nm* sleeping pill.

soportable [sopor'taßle] *a* bearable; **soportar** *vt* to bear, carry; (*fig*) to bear, put up with; **soporte** *nm* support; (*fig*) pillar, support.

soprano [so'prano] *nf* soprano.

sorber [sor'ßer] *vt* (*chupar*) to sip; (*inhalar*) to inhale; (*tragar*) to swallow (up); (*absorber*) to soak up, absorb.

sorbete [sor'ßete] *nm* iced fruit drink.

sorbo ['sorßo] *nm* (*trago*) gulp, swallow; (*chupada*) sip.

sordera [sor'ðera] *nf* deafness.

sórdido, a ['sorðiðo, a] *a* dirty, squalid; (*palabra*) nasty, dirty; (*fig*) mean.

sordo, a ['sorðo, a] *a* (*persona*) deaf; (*máquina*) quiet // *nm/f* deaf person; **a ~as** on the quiet; **~mudo, a** *a* deaf and dumb.

sorprendente [sorpren'dente] *a* surprising; **sorprender** *vt* to surprise; **sorpresa** *nf* surprise.

sortear [sorte'ar] *vt* to draw lots for; (*objeto*) to raffle; (*dificultad*) to avoid; **sorteo** *nm* drawing lots; raffle.

sosegado, a [sose'ɣaðo, a] *a* quiet, calm; (*el ánimo*) to **sosegar** *vt* to quieten, calm; (*el ánimo*) to

reassure // *vi* to rest; **sosiego** *nm* quiet(ness), calm(ness).

soslayo [sos'lajo]: **al o de ~** *ad* obliquely, sideways.

soso, a ['soso, ε] *a* (*CULIN*) tasteless; (*fig*) dull, uninteresting.

sospecha [sos'petʃa] *nf* suspicion; **sospechar** *vt* to suspect; **sospechoso, a** *a* suspicious; (*testimonio, opinión*) suspect // *nm/f* suspect.

sostén [sos'ten] *nm* (*apoyo*) support; (*prenda femenina*) bra, brassière; (*alimentación*) sustenance, food.

sostener [soste'ner] *vt* to support; (*mantener*) to keep up, maintain; (*alimentar*) to sustain, keep going; **~se** *vr* to support o.s.; (*seguir*) to continue, remain; **sostenido, a** *a* continuous, sustained; (*prolongado*) prolonged.

sótano ['sotano] *nm* basement.

soterrar [sote'rrar] *vt* to bury.

soviético, a [so'ßjetika, a] *a* Soviet.

soy *vb ver* **ser.**

sport [sport] *nm* sport.

Sr *abr de* **Señor.**

Sra *abr de* **Señora.**

S.R.C. *abr de* **se ruega contestación** R.S.V.P.

Sta *abr de* **Santa; Señorita.**

status ['status] *nm inv* status.

Sto *abr de* **Santo.**

su [su] *pron* (*de él*) his; (*de ella*) her; (*de una cosa*) its; (*de ellos, ellas*) their; (*de usted, ustedes*) your.

suave ['swaße] *a* gentle; (*superficie*) smooth; (*trabajo*) easy; (*música, voz*) soft, sweet; **suavidad** *nf* gentleness; smoothness; softness, sweetness; **suavizar** *vt* to soften; (*quitar la aspereza*) to smooth (out).

subalimentado, a [sußalimen'taðo, a] *a* undernourished.

subasta [su'ßasta] *nf* auction; **subastar** *vt* to auction (off).

subconsciencia [sußkons'θjenθja] *nf* subconscious; **subconsciente** *a* subconscious.

subdesarrollado, a [sußðesarro'λaðo, a] *a* underdeveloped; **subdesarrollo** *nm* underdevelopment.

súbdito, a ['sußðito, a] *nm/f* subject.

subdividir [sußðißi'ðir] *vt* to subdivide.

subestimar [sußesti'mar] *vt* to underestimate, underrate; (*propiedad*) to undervalue.

subexpuesto, a [sußeks'pwesto, a] *a* underexposed.

subido, a [su'ßiðo, a] *a* (*color*) bright, strong; (*precio*) high // *nf* (*gen*) ascent, climb; (*de precio*) rise, increase; (*camino*) way up; (*pendiente*) slope, hill.

subir [su'ßir] *vt* (*objeto*) to raise, lift up; (*cuesta, calle*) to go up; (*montaña*) to climb; (*precio*) to raise, put up // *vi* to go/come up; (*a un coche*) to get in; (*a un autobús*) to get on; (*precio*) to rise, go up; (*río*) to rise; **~se** *vr* to get up, climb.

súbito, a ['suβito, a] a (repentino) sudden; (imprevisto) unexpected; (precipitado) hasty, rash // ad: **(de)** ~ suddenly.
sublevación [suβleβa'θjon] nf revolt, rising.
sublime [su'βlime] a sublime.
submarino, a [suβma'rino, a] a underwater // nm submarine.
subordinado, a [suβorði'naðo, a] a, nm/f subordinate.
subrayar [suβra'jar] vt to underline.
subrepticio, a [suβrep'tiθjo, a] a surreptitious.
subsanar [suβsa'nar] vt (reparar) to make good; (perdonar) to excuse; (sobreponerse a) to overcome.
subscribir [suβskri'βir] vt = **suscribir.**
subsidiario, a [suβsi'ðjarjo, a] a subsidiary.
subsidio [suβ'siðjo] nm (ayuda) aid, financial help; (subvención) subsidy, grant; (de enfermedad, paro etc) benefit.
subsistencia [suβsis'tenθja] nf subsistence; **subsistir** vi (gen) to subsist; (vivir) to live; (sobrevivir) to survive, endure.
subterráneo, a [suβte'rraneo, a] a underground, subterranean // nm underpass, underground passage.
suburbano, a [suβur'βano, a] a suburban.
suburbio [su'βurβjo] nm (barrio) slum quarter; (afueras) suburbs pl.
subvencionar [suββenθjo'nar] vt to subsidize.
subversión [suββer'sjon] nf subversion; **subversivo, a** a subversive.
subyugar [suβju'xar] vt (país) to subjugate, subdue; (enemigo) to overpower; (voluntad) to dominate.
suceder [suθe'ðer] vt, vi to happen; (seguir) to succeed, follow; **lo que sucede es que...** the fact is that...; **sucesión** nf succession; (serie) sequence, series.
sucesivamente [suθesiβa'mente] ad: **y así** ~ and so on.
sucesivo, a [suθe'siβo, a] a successive, following; **en lo** ~ in future, from now on.
suceso [su'θeso] nm (hecho) event, happening; (incidente) incident; (resultado) outcome.
suciedad [suθje'ðað] nf (estado) dirtiness; (mugre) dirt, filth.
sucinto, a [su'θinto, a] a succinct, concise.
sucio, a ['suθjo, a] a dirty.
suculento, a [suku'lento, a] a succulent.
sucumbir [sukum'bir] vi to succumb.
sucursal [sukur'sal] nf branch (office).
sudamericano, a [suðameri'kano, a] a South American.
sudar [su'ðar] vt, vi to sweat.
sudeste [su'ðeste] nm south-east; **sudoeste** nm south-west.
sudor [su'ðor] nm sweat; ~**oso, a, sudoso, a,** ~**iento, a** a sweaty, sweating.
Suecia ['sweθja] nf Sweden; **sueco, a** a Swedish // nm/f Swede.

suegro, a ['sweɤro, a] nm/f father-/mother-in-law.
suela ['swela] nf sole.
sueldo ['sweldo] nm pay, wage(s) (pl); **el** ~ **mínimo** the minimum wage.
suele etc vb ver **soler.**
suelo ['swelo] nm (tierra) ground; (de casa) floor.
suelto, a ['swelto, a] a loose; (libre) free; (separado) detached, individual; (ágil) quick, agile; (corriente) fluent, flowing // nm (loose) change, small change.
sueño etc vb ver **soñar** // ['sweɲo] nm sleep; (somnolencia) sleepiness, drowsiness; (lo soñado, fig) dream; **tener** ~ to be sleepy.
suero ['swero] nm serum.
suerte ['swerte] nf (fortuna) luck; (azar) chance; (destino) fate, destiny; (condición) lot; (género) sort, kind; **tener** ~ to be lucky; **de otra** ~ otherwise, if not; **de** ~ **que** so that, in such a way that.
suéter ['sweter] nm sweater.
suficiente [sufi'θjente] a enough, sufficient; (capaz) capable.
sufragio [su'fraxjo] nm (voto) vote; (derecho de voto) suffrage; (ayuda) help, aid.
sufrimiento [sufri'mjento] nm (dolor) suffering; (paciencia) patience; (tolerancia) tolerance.
sufrir [su'frir] vt (padecer) to suffer; (soportar) to bear, stand, put up with; (apoyar) to hold up, support // vi to suffer.
sugerencia [suxe'renθja] nf suggestion; **sugerir** vt to suggest; (sutilmente) to hint.
sugestión [suxes'tjon] nf suggestion; (sutil) hint; **sugestionar** vt to influence.
sugestivo, a [suxes'tiβo, a] a stimulating; (fascinante) fascinating.
suicida [sui'θiða] a suicidal // nm/f suicidal person; (muerto) suicide, person who has committed suicide; **suicidio** nm suicide.
Suiza ['swiθa] nf Switzerland; **suizo, a** a, nm/f Swiss.
sujeción [suxe'θjon] nf subjection.
sujetador [suxeta'ðor] nm fastener, clip; (de papeles) paper clip.
sujetar [suxe'tar] vt (fijar) to fasten; (detener) to hold down; (fig) to subject, subjugate; ~**se** vr to subject o.s.; **sujeto, a** a fastened, secure // nm subject; (individuo) individual; **sujeto a** subject to.
suma ['suma] nf (cantidad) total, sum; (de dinero) sum; (acto) adding (up), addition; (resumen) summary; (esencia) essence; **en** ~ in short; ~**dora** nf adding machine.
sumamente [suma'mente] ad extremely, exceedingly.
sumar [su'mar] vt to add (up); (reunir) to collect, gather; (abreviar) to summarize, sum up // vi to add up.
sumario, a [su'marjo, a] a brief, concise // nm summary.
sumergir [sumer'xir] vt to submerge; (hundir) to sink; (bañar) to immerse, dip;

sumersión *nf* submersion; *(fig)* absorption.

sumidero [sumi'ðero] *nm* drain; *(TEC)* sump.

suministrador, a [suministra'ðor, a] *nm/f* supplier; **suministrar** *vt* to supply, provide; **suministro** *nm* supply; *(acto)* supplying, providing.

sumir [su'mir] *vt* to sink, submerge; *(fig)* to plunge.

sumisión [sumi'sjon] *nf (acto)* submission; *(calidad)* submissiveness, docility; **sumiso, a** *a* submissive, docile.

sumo, a ['sumo, a] *a* great, extreme; *(mayor)* highest, supreme.

supe *etc vb ver* **saber**.

super... [super] *pref* super..., over... // *nm* high-grade fuel.

superar [supe'rar] *vt (sobreponerse a)* to overcome; *(rebasar)* to surpass, do better than; *(pasar)* to go beyond; **~se** *vr* to excel o.s.

superávit [supe'raßit] *nm* surplus.

supercarburante [superkarßu'rante] *nm* high-grade fuel.

superestructura [superestruk'tura] *nf* superstructure.

superficial [superfi'θjal] *a* superficial; *(medida)* surface *cpd*, of the surface.

superficie [super'fiθje] *nf* surface; *(área)* area.

superfluo, a [su'perflwo, a] *a* superfluous.

superintendente [superinten'dente] *nm/f* supervisor, superintendent.

superior [supe'rjor] *a (piso, clase)* upper; *(temperatura, número, nivel)* higher; *(mejor: calidad, producto)* superior, better // *nm/f* superior; **~idad** *nf* superiority.

supermercado [supermer'kaðo] *nm* supermarket.

supersónico, a [super'soniko, a] *a* supersonic.

superstición [supersti'θjon] *nf* superstition; **supersticioso, a** *a* superstitious.

supervisor, a [superßi'sor, a] *nm/f* supervisor.

supervivencia [superßi'ßenθja] *nf* survival.

supiera *etc vb ver* **saber**.

suplementario, a [suplemen'tarjo, a] *a* supplementary; **suplemento** *nm* supplement.

suplente [su'plente] *a, nm/f* substitute.

súplica ['suplika] *nf* request; *(REL)* supplication.

suplicante [supli'kante] *nm/f* applicant.

suplicar [supli'kar] *vt (cosa)* to beg (for), plead for; *(persona)* to beg, plead with.

suplicio [su'pliθjo] *nm* torture.

suplir [su'plir] *vt (compensar)* to make good, make up for; *(reemplazar)* to replace, substitute // *vi:* **~ a o por** to take the place of, substitute for.

suponer [supo'ner] *vt* to suppose // *vi* to have authority; **suposición** *nf* supposition; *(autoridad)* authority.

supremacía [suprema'θia] *nf* supremacy.

supremo, a [su'premo, a] *a* supreme.

supresión [supre'sjon] *nf* suppression; *(de derecho)* abolition; *(de dificultad)* removal; *(de palabra)* deletion; *(de restricción)* cancellation, lifting.

suprimir [supri'mir] *vt* to suppress; *(derecho, costumbre)* to abolish; *(dificultad)* to remove; *(palabra)* to delete; *(restricción)* to cancel, lift.

supuesto, a [su'pwesto, a] *a (hipotético)* supposed; *(falso)* false // *nm* assumption, hypothesis; **~ que** *conj* since; **por ~** of course.

sur [sur] *nm* south.

surcar [sur'kar] *vt* to plough, furrow; *(superficie)* to cut, score; **surco** *nm* groove; *(AGR)* furrow.

surgir [sur'xir] *vi* to arise, emerge; *(dificultad)* to come up, crop up.

surtido, a [sur'tiðo, a] *a* mixed, assorted // *nm (gen)* selection, assortment; *(abastecimiento)* supply, stock.

surtir [sur'tir] *vt* to supply, provide // *vi* to spout, spurt.

susceptible [susθep'tiβle] *a* susceptible; *(sensible)* sensitive; **~ de** capable of.

suscitar [susθi'tar] *vt* to cause, provoke; *(interés)* to arouse.

suscribir [suskri'ßir] *vt (firmar)* to sign; *(respaldar)* to subscribe to; endorse; **~se** *vr* to subscribe; **suscripción** *nf* subscription.

suspender [suspen'der] *vt (objeto)* to hang (up), suspend, *(trabajo)* to stop, suspend; *(a estudiante)* to fail; **suspensión** *nf* suspension; *(fig)* stoppage, suspension.

suspenso, a [sus'penso, a] *a* hanging, suspended; *(estudiante)* failed; *(admirado)* astonished, amazed // *nm* **quedar o estar en ~** to be pending.

suspicacia [suspi'kaθja] *nf* suspicion, mistrust; **suspicaz** *a* suspicious, distrustful.

suspirar [suspi'rar] *vi* to sigh; **suspiro** *nm* sigh.

sustancia [sus'tanθja] *nf* substance.

sustentar [susten'tar] *vt (alimentar)* to sustain, nourish; *(objeto)* to hold up, support; *(idea, teoría)* to maintain, uphold; *(fig)* to sustain, keep going; **sustento** *nm* support; *(alimento)* sustenance, food.

sustituir [sustitu'ir] *vt* to substitute, replace; **sustituto, a** *nm/f* substitute, replacement.

susto ['susto] *nm* fright, scare.

sustraer [sustra'er] *vt* to remove, take away; *(MAT)* to subtract; **~se** *vr (evitar)* to avoid; *(retirarse)* to withdraw.

susurrar [susu'rrar] *vi* to whisper; **susurro** *nm* whisper.

sutil [su'til] *a* subtle; *(teue)* thin; **~eza** *nf* subtlety, thinness.

suyo, a ['sujo, a] *a (con artículo o después del verbo-ser: de él)* his; *(: de ella)* hers; *(: de ellos, ellas)* theirs; *(: de Ud, Uds)* yours; *(después de un nombre: de él)* of his; *(: de* *ella*) of hers; (: *de ellos, ellas*) of theirs; (: *de Ud, Uds*) of yours.

T

t *abr de* **tonelada.**

taba ['taβa] *nf* (ANAT) ankle bone; (*juego*) jacks *sg*.

tabaco [ta'βako] *nm* tobacco; (*fam*) cigarettes *pl*.

taberna [ta'βerna] *nf* bar; **tabernero, a** *nm/f* (*encargado*) publican; (*camarero*) barman.

tabique [ta'βike] *nm* (*pared*) thin wall; (*para dividir*) partition.

tabla ['taβla] *nf* (*de madera*) plank; (*estante*) shelf; (*de anuncios*) board; (*lista, catálogo*) list; (*mostrador*) counter; (*de vestido*) pleat; (ARTE) panel; ~**s** (TAUR, TEATRO) boards; **hacer** ~**s** to draw; ~**do** *nm* (*plataforma*) platform; (*suelo*) plank floor; (TEATRO) stage.

tablero [ta'βlero] *nm* (*de madera*) plank, board; (*pizarra*) blackboard; (*de ajedrez, damas*) board; (AUTO) dashboard.

tablilla [ta'βliʎa] *nf* small board; (MED) splint.

tablón [ta'βlon] *nm* (*de suelo*) plank; (*de techo*) beam; (*de anuncios*) notice board.

tabú [ta'βu] *nm* taboo.

tabular [taβu'lar] *vt* to tabulate.

taburete [taβu'rete] *nm* stool.

tacaño, a [ta'kaɲo, a] *a* (*avaro*) mean; (*astuto*) crafty.

tácito, a ['taθito, a] *a* tacit.

taciturno, a [taθi'turno, a] *a* (*callado*) silent; (*malhumorado*) sullen.

taco ['tako] *nm* (BILLAR) cue; (*libro de billetes*) book; (*manojo de billetes*) wad; (AM) heel; (*tarugo*) peg; (*fam: bocado*) snack; (: *palabrota*) swear word; (: *trago de vino*) swig.

tacón [ta'kon] *nm* heel; **de** ~ **alto** high heeled; **taconeo** *nm* (heel) stamping.

táctico, a ['taktiko, a] *a* tactical // *nf* tactics *pl*.

tacto ['takto] *nm* touch; (*acción*) touching.

tacha ['tatʃa] *nf* flaw; (TEC) stud; **poner** ~ **a** to find fault with; **tachar** *vt* (*borrar*) to cross out; (*corregir*) to correct; (*criticar*) to criticize; **tachar de** to accuse of.

tafetán [tafe'tan] *nm* taffeta; **tafetanes** *nmpl* (*fam*) frills; ~ **adhesivo** *o* **inglés** sticking plaster.

tafilete [tafi'lete] *nm* morocco leather.

tahona [ta'ona] *nf* (*panadería*) bakery; (*molino*) flourmill.

tahur [ta'ur] *nm* gambler; (*pey*) cheat.

taimado, a [tai'maðo, a] *a* (*astuto*) sly; (*resentido*) sullen.

taja ['taxa] *nf* (*corte*) cut; (*repartición*) division; ~**da** *nf* slice; ~**dera** *nf* (*instrumento*) chopper; (*madera*) chopping block; **tajante** *a* sharp.

tajar [ta'xar] *vt* to cut; **tajo** *nm* (*corte*) cut; (*filo*) cutting edge; (GEO) cleft.

tal [tal] *a* such; ~ **vez** perhaps // *pron* (*persona*) someone, such a one; (*cosa*) something, such a thing; ~ **como** such as; ~ **para cual** tit for tat; (*dos iguales*) two of a kind // *ad*: ~ **como** (*igual*) just as; ~ **cual** (*como es*) just as it is; ~ **el padre, cual el hijo** like father, like son; ¿**qué** ~? how are things?; ¿**qué** ~ **te gusta?** how do you like it? // *conj*: **con** ~ **de que** provided that.

talabartero [talaβar'tero] *nm* saddler.

taladrar [tala'ðrar] *vt* to drill; **taladro** *nm* (*gen*) drill; (*hoyo*) drill hole; **taladro neumático** pneumatic drill.

talante [ta'lante] *nm* (*humor*) mood; (*voluntad*) will, willingness.

talar [ta'lar] *vt* to fell, cut down; (*fig*) to devastate.

talco ['talko] *nm* (*polvos*) talcum powder; (MINEROLOGÍA) talc.

talego [ta'leɣo] *nm*, **talega** [ta'leɣa] *nf* sack.

talento [ta'lento] *nm* talent; (*capacidad*) ability; (*don*) gift.

talidomida [taliðo'miða] *nm* thalidomide.

talismán [talis'man] *nm* talisman.

talmente [tal'mente] *a* (*de esta forma*) in such a way; (*hasta tal punto*) to such an extent; (*exactamente*) exactly.

talón [ta'lon] *nm* (*gen*) heel; (COM) counterfoil.

talonario [talo'narjo] *nm* (*de cheques*) chequebook; (*de billetes*) book of tickets; (*de recibos*) receipt book.

talud [ta'luð] *nm* slope.

talla ['taʎa] *nf* (*estatura, fig, MED*) height, stature; (*palo*) measuring rod; (ARTE) carving.

tallado, a [ta'ʎaðo, a] *a* carved // *nm* carving; **tallar** *vt* (*trabajar*) to work, carve; (*grabar*) to engrave; (*medir*) to measure; (*repartir*) to deal // *vi* to deal.

tallarín [taʎa'rin] *nm* noodle.

talle ['taʎe] *nm* (ANAT) waist; (*medida*) size; (*física*) build; (: *de mujer*) figure; (*fig*) appearance.

taller [ta'ʎer] *nm* (TEC) workshop; (*de artista*) studio.

tallo ['taʎo] *nm* (*de planta*) stem; (*de hierba*) blade; (*brote*) shoot; (*col*) cabbage; (CULIN) candied peel.

tamaño [ta'maɲo] *a* such a (big/small) // *nm* size; **de** ~ **natural** full-size.

tamarindo [tama'rindo] *nm* tamarind.

tambalearse [tambale'arse] *vr* (*persona*) to stagger; (*vehículo*) to sway.

también [tam'bjen] *ad* (*igualmente*) also, too, as well; (*además*) besides.

tambor [tam'bor] *nm* drum; (ANAT) eardrum; ~ **del freno** brake drum.

tamiz [ta'miθ] *nm* sieve; ~ **ar** *vt* to sieve.

tamo ['tamo] *nm* fluff.

tampoco [tam'poko] *ad* nor, neither; **yo** ~ **lo compré** I didn't buy it either.

tampón [tam'pon] *nm* plug; (MED) tampon.

tan [tan] *ad* so; ~ **es así que** so much so that.

tanda ['tanda] *nf* (*gen*) series; (*juego*) set; (*turno*) shift; (*grupo*) gang.

tangente [tan'xente] *nf* tangent.

Tánger ['tanxer] *n* Tangier(s).

tangible [tan'xiβle] *a* tangible.

tanque ['tanke] *nm* (*gen*) tank; (*AUTO, NAUT*) tanker.

tantear [tante'ar] *vt* (*calcular*) to reckon (up); (*medir*) to take the measure of; (*probar*) to test, try out; (*tomar la medida: persona*) to take the measurements of; (*considerar*) to weigh up // *vi* (*DEPORTE*) to score; **tanteo** *nm* (*cálculo*) (rough) calculation; (*prueba*) test, trial; (*DEPORTE*) scoring; (*adivinanzas*) guesswork; **al tanteo** by trial and error.

tanto, a ['tanto, a] *a* (*cantidad*) so much, as much; ~s so many, as many; **20 y ~s** 20-odd // *ad* (*cantidad*) so much, as much; (*tiempo*) so long, as long; ~ **tú como yo** both you and I; ~ **como eso** it's not as bad as that; ~ **más ... cuanto que** it's all the more ... because; ~ **mejor/peor** so much the better/the worse; ~ **si viene como si va** whether he comes or whether he goes; ~ **es así que** so much so that; **por o por lo** ~ therefore; **me he vuelto ronco de o con** ~ **hablar** I have become hoarse with so much talking // *conj*: **con** ~ **que** provided (that); **en** ~ **que while**; **hasta** ~ **(que)** until such time as // *nm* (*suma*) certain amount; (*proporción*) so much; (*punto*) point; (*gol*) goal; **al** ~ up to date; **un** ~ **perezoso** somewhat lazy; **al** ~ **de que** because of the fact that // *pron*: **cada uno paga** ~ each one pays so much; **a** ~**s de agosto** on such and such a day in August.

tapar [ta'par] *vt* (*cubrir*) to cover; (*envolver*) to wrap or cover up; (*la vista*) to obstruct; (*persona, falta*) to conceal; (*AM*) to fill; ~**se** *vr* to wrap o.s. up.

taparrabo [tapa'rraβo] *nm* (*bañador*) (bathing or swimming) trunks *pl*.

tapete [ta'pete] *nm* table cover.

tapia ['tapja] *nf* (garden) wall; **tapiar** *vt* to wall in.

tapicería [tapiθe'ria] *nf* tapestry; (*para muebles*) upholstery; (*tienda*) upholsterer's (shop); **tapiz** *nm* (*alfombra*) carpet; (*tela tejida*) tapestry; **tapizar** *vt* (*pared*) to wallpaper; (*suelo*) to carpet; (*muebles*) to upholster.

tapón [ta'pon] *nm* (*corcho*) stopper; (*TEC*) plug; (*MED*) tampon; ~ **de rosca o de tuerca** screw-top.

taquigrafía [takixra'fia] *nf* shorthand; **taquígrafo, a** *nm/f* shorthand writer.

taquilla [ta'kiʎa] *nf* (*donde se compra*) booking office; (*suma recogida*) takings *pl*; **taquillero, a** *a*: **función taquillera** box office success // *nm/f* ticket clerk.

taquímetro [ta'kimetro] *nm* speed-ometer; (*de control*) tachymeter.

tara ['tara] *nf* (*defecto*) defect; (*COM*) tare.

tarántula [ta'rantula] *nf* tarantula.

tararear [tarare'ar] *vi* to hum.

tardanza [tar'ðanθa] *nf* (*demora*) delay; (*lentitud*) slowness.

tardar [tar'ðar] *vi* (*tomar tiempo*) to take a long time; (*llegar tarde*) to be late; (*demorar*) to delay; **¿tarda mucho el tren?** does the train take long?; **a más** ~ at the latest; **no tardes en venir** come soon, come before long.

tarde ['tarðe] *ad* (*hora*) late; (*después de tiempo*) too late // *nf* (*de día*) afternoon; (*al anochecer*) evening; **de** ~ **en** ~ from time to time; **¡buenas** ~**s!** (*de día*) good afternoon!; (*de noche*) good evening!; **a o por la** ~ in the afternoon; in the evening.

tardío, a [tar'ðio] *a* (*retrasado*) late; (*lento*) slow (to arrive).

tardo, a ['tarðo, a] *a* (*lento*) slow; (*torpe*) dull.

tarea [ta'rea] *nf* task; (*ESCOL*) homework; ~ **de ocasión** chore.

tarifa [ta'rifa] *nf* (*lista de precios*) price list; (*COM*) tariff; ~ **completa** all-in cost.

tarima [ta'rima] *nf* (*plataforma*) platform; (*taburete*) stool; (*litera*) bunk.

tarjeta [tar'xeta] *nf* card; ~ **postal/de crédito/de Navidad** postcard/credit card/Christmas card.

tarro ['tarro] *nm* jar, pot.

tarta ['tarta] *nf* (*pastel*) cake; (*torta*) tart.

tartamudear [tartamuðe'ar] *vi* to stammer; **tartamudo, a** a stammering // *nm/f* stammerer.

tartana [tar'tana] *nf* (*barco*) dinghy.

tartárico, a [tar'tariko, a] *a*: **ácido** ~ tartaric acid.

tártaro ['tartaro] *a, nm* Tartar.

tasa ['tasa] *nf* (*precio*) (fixed) price, rate; (*valoración*) valuation; (*medida, norma*) measure, standard; ~ **de interés** rate of interest; ~**ción** *nf* (*gen*) valuation; (*de oro etc*) appraisal; ~**dor** *nm* valuer.

tasajo [ta'saxo] *nm* dried beef.

tasar [ta'sar] *vt* (*arreglar a precio*) to fix a price for; (*valorar*) to value, assess; (*limitar*) to limit.

tasca [taska] *nf* (*fam*) pub.

tatarabuelo [tatara'βwelo] *nm* great-great-grandfather.

tatuaje [ta'twaxe] *nm* (*dibujo*) tattoo; (*acto*) tattooing; **tatuar** *vt* to tattoo.

taumaturgo [tauma'turxo] *nm* miracle-worker.

taurino, a [tau'rino, a] *a* bullfighting *cpd*.

Tauro ['tauro] *nm* Taurus.

tauromaquia [tauro'makja] *nf* tauromachy.

tautología [tautolo'xia] *nf* tautology.

taxi ['taksi] *nm* taxi.

taxidermia [taksi ðermja] *nf* taxidermy.

taxista [tak'sista] *nm/f* taxi driver.

taza ['taθa] *nf* cup; (*de retrete*) bowl; ~ **para café** coffee cup; **tazón** *nm* (~ *grande*) large cup; (*escudilla*) basin.

te [te] *pron* (*complemento de objeto*) you; (*complemento indirecto*) (to) you; (*reflexivo*) (to) yourself; **¿~ duele**

mucho el brazo? does your arm hurt a lot?; ~ **equivocas** you're wrong; ¡**cálma**~! calm yourself!

té [te] *nm* tea.

tea ['tea] *nf* torch.

teatral [tea'tral] *a* theatre *cpd*; (*fig*) theatrical; **teatro** *nm* (*gen*) theatre; (*LITERATURA*) plays *pl*, drama.

tebeo [te'βeo] *nm* children's comic.

tecla ['tekla] *nf* key; ~**do** *nm* keyboard; **teclear** *vi* to strum; (*fam*) to drum; **tecleo** *nm* (*MUS*; *sonido*) strumming; (*forma de tocar*) fingering; (*fam*) drumming.

técnico, a ['tekniko, a] *a* technical // *nm* technician; (*experto*) expert // *nf* (*procedimientos*) technique; (*arte, oficio*) craft.

tecnócrata [tek'nokrata] *nm/f* technocrat.

tecnología [teknolo'xia] *nf* technology; **tecnológico, a** *a* technological; **tecnólogo** *nm* technologist.

techo ['tetʃo] *nm* (*externo*) roof; (*interno*) ceiling; **techumbre** *nf* roof.

tedio ['teðjo] *nm* (*aburrimiento*) boredom; (*apatía*) apathy; (*fastidio*) depression; ~**so, a** *a* boring; (*cansado*) wearisome, tedious.

teja ['texa] *nf* (*azulejo*) tile; (*BOT*) lime (tree); ~**do** *nm* (tiled) roof.

tejanos [te'xanos] *nmpl* jeans.

tejemaneje [texema'nexe] *nm* (*bullicio*) bustle; (*lío*) fuss; (*aspaviento*) to-do; (*intriga*) intrigue.

tejer [te'xer] *vt* to weave; (*AM*) to knit; (*fig*) to fabricate; **tejido** *nm* fabric; (*telaraña*) web; (*estofa, tela*) (knitted) material; (*ANAT*) tissue; (*textura*) texture.

tel, teléf *abr de* **teléfono.**

tela ['tela] *nf* (*material*) material; (*telaraña*) web; (*de fruta, en líquido*) skin; (*del ojo*) film; **telar** *nm* (*máquina*) loom; (*de teatro*) gridiron; **telares** *nmpl* textile mill *sg*.

telaraña [tela'raŋa] *nf* cobweb.

tele ['tele] *nf* (*fam*) TV.

tele... [tele] *pref* tele...; ~**comunicación** *nf* telecommunication; ~**control** *nm* remote control; ~**diario** *nm* television news; ~**difusión** *nf* (television) broadcast; ~**dirigido, a** *a* remote-controlled; ~**férico** *nm* (*tren*) cable-railway; (*de esquí*) ski-lift; ~**fonear** *vi* to telephone; ~**fónico, a** *a* telephone *cpd*; ~**fonista** *nm/f* telephonist; **teléfono** *nm* telephone; ~**foto** *nf* telephoto; ~**grafía** *nf* telegraphy; **telégrafo** *nm* telegraph; (*fam: persona*) telegraph boy; ~**grama** *nm* telegram; ~**impresor** *nm* teleprinter; **telémetro** *nm* rangefinder; ~**objetivo** *nm* telephoto lens; ~**pático, a** *a* tele-pathic; ~**scópico, a** *a* telescopic; ~**scopio** *nm* telescope; ~**silla** *nf* chairlift; ~**spectador, a** *nm/f* viewer; ~**squí** *nm* ski-lift; ~**tipista** *nm/f* teletypist; ~**tipo** *nm* teletype; ~**vidente** *nm/f* viewer; ~**visar** *vt* to televise;

~**visión** *nf* television; ~**visión en colores** colour television; ~**visor** *nm* television set.

telex [te'leks] *nm* telex.

telón [te'lon] *nm* curtain; ~ **de boca/seguridad** front/safety curtain; ~ **de acero** (*POL*) iron curtain; ~ **de fondo** backcloth, background.

tema ['tema] *nm* (*asunto*) subject, topic; (*MUS*) theme // *nf* (*obsesión*) obsession; (*manía*) ill-will; **tener** ~ **a uno** to have a grudge against sb; **temático, a** *a* thematic.

tembladera [tembla'ðera] *nf* shaking; (*AM*) quagmire.

temblar [tem'blar] *vi* to shake, tremble; (*de frío*) to shiver; **tembleque** *a* shaking // *nm* = **tembladera; temblón, ona** *a* shaking; **temblor** *nm* trembling; (*AM: de tierra*) earthquake; **tembloroso, a** *a* trembling.

temer [te'mer] *vt* to fear // *vi* to be afraid; **temo que llegue tarde** I am afraid he may be late.

temerario, a [teme'rarjo, a] *a* (*descuidado*) reckless; (*arbitrario*) hasty; **temeridad** *nf* (*imprudencia*) rashness; (*audacia*) boldness.

temeroso, a [teme'roso, a] *a* (*miedoso*) fearful; (*que inspira temor*) frightful.

temible [te'miβle] *a* fearsome.

temor [te'mor] *nm* (*miedo*) fear; (*duda*) suspicion.

témpano ['tempano] *nm* (*MUS*) kettledrum; ~ **de hielo** ice-floe; ~ **de tocino** flitch of bacon.

temperamento [tempera'mento] *nm* temperament.

temperatura [tempera'tura] *nf* temperature.

temperie [tem'perje] *nf* state of the weather.

tempestad [tempes'tað] *nf* storm; **tempestuoso, a** *a* stormy.

templado, a [tem'plaðo, a] *a* (*moderado*) moderate; (: *en el comer*) frugal; (: *en el beber*) abstemious; (*agua*) lukewarm; (*clima*) mild; (*MUS*) well-tuned; **templanza** *nf* moderation; abstemiousness; mildness.

templar [tem'plar] *vt* (*moderar*) to moderate; (*furia*) to restrain; (*calor*) to reduce; (*solución*) to dilute; (*afinar*) to tune (up); (*acero*) to temper; (*tuerca*) to tighten up // *vi* to moderate; ~**se** *vr* to be restrained; **temple** *nm* (*humor*) mood; (*ajuste*) tempering; (*afinación*) tuning; (*clima*) temperature; (*pintura*) tempera.

templete [tem'plete] *nm* bandstand.

templo ['templo] *nm* (*iglesia*) church; (*pagano etc*) temple.

temporada [tempo'raða] *nf* time, period; (*estación*) season.

temporal [tempo'ral] *a* (*no permanente*) temporary; (*REL*) temporal // *nm* storm.

tempranero, a [tempra'nero, a] *a* (*BOT*) early; (*persona*) early-rising.

temprano, a [tem'prano, a] *a* early;

(*demasiado pronto*) too soon, too early.

ten *vb ver* **tener.**

tenacidad [tena θi'ðað] *nf* (*gen*) tenacity; (*dureza*) toughness; (*terquedad*) stubbornness.

tenacillas [tena'θiʎas] *nfpl* (*gen*) tongs; (*para el pelo*) curling tongs; (*MED*) forceps.

tenaz [te'naθ] *a* (*material*) tough; (*persona*) tenacious; (*pegajoso*) sticky; (*terco*) stubborn.

tenaza(s) [te'naθa(s)] *nf(pl)* (*MED*) forceps; (*TEC*) pliers; (*ZOOL*) pincers.

tendal [ten'dal] *nm* awning.

tendedero [tende'ðero] *nm* (*para ropa*) drying-place; (*cuerda*) clothes line.

tendencia [ten'denθja] *nf* tendency; (*proceso*) trend; **tener ~** to tend or have a tendency to; **tendencioso, a** *a* tendentious.

tender [ten'der] *vt* (*extender*) to spread out; (*colgar*) to hang out; (*vía férrea, cable*) to lay; (*cuerda*) to stretch // *vi* to tend; **~se** *vr* to lie down; (*fig: dejarse llevar*) to let o.s. go; (: *dejar ir*) to let things go; **~ la cama/la mesa** (*AM*) to make the bed/lay the table.

ténder ['tender] *nm* tender.

tenderete [tende'rete] *nm* (*puesto*) stall; (*carretilla*) barrow; (*exposición*) display of goods; (*jaleo*) mess.

tendero, a [ten'dero, a] *nm/f* shopkeeper.

tendido, a [ten'diðo, a] *a* (*acostado*) lying down, flat; (*colgado*) hanging // *nm* (*ropa*) washing; (*TAUR*) front rows of seats; (*colocación*) laying; (*ARQ: enyesado*) coat of plaster; **a galope ~** flat out.

tendón [ten'don] *nm* tendon.

tendré *etc vb ver* **tener.**

tenducho [ten'dutʃo] *nm* small dirty shop.

tenebroso, a [tene'βroso, a] *a* (*oscuro*) dark; (*fig*) gloomy; (*siniestro*) sinister.

tenedor [tene'ðor] *nm* (*CULIN*) fork; (*poseedor*) holder; **~ de libros** bookkeeper.

teneduría [teneðu'ria] *nf* keeping; **~ de libros** book-keeping.

tenencia [te'nenθja] *nf* (*de casa*) tenancy; (*de oficio*) tenure; (*de propiedad*) possession.

tener [te'ner] *vt* (*poseer*) to have; (*en la mano*) to hold; (*caja*) to hold, contain; (*considerar*) to consider; **~ suerte** to be lucky; **~ permiso** to have permission; **tiene 10 años** he is 10 years old; **¿cuántos años tienes?** how old are you?; **~ sed/hambre/frío/calor** to be thirsty/hungry/cold/hot; **~ ganas (de)** to want (to); **~ celos** to be jealous; **~ cuidado** to be careful; **~ razón** to be right; **~ un metro de ancho/de largo** to be one metre wide/long; **~ a bien** to see fit to; **~ en cuenta** to bear in mind, take into account; **~ a menos** to consider it beneath o.s.; **~ a uno en más (estima)** to think all the more of sb; **~ a uno por...** to think sb...; **~ por seguro** to be sure; **~ presente** to remember, bear in mind; **~**

que (*obligación*) to have to; **tiene que ser así** it has to be this way; **nos tiene preparada una sorpresa** he has prepared a surprise for us; **¿qué tiene?** what's the matter with him?; **¿ésas tenemos?** what's all this?; **tiene un mes de muerto** he has been dead for a month; **~se** *vr* (*erguirse*) to stand; (*apoyarse*) to lean (*on*); (*fig*) to control o.s.; (*considerarse*) to consider o.s.

tenería [tene'ria] *nf* tannery.

tengo *etc vb ver* **tener.**

tenia ['tenja] *nf* tapeworm.

teniente [te'njente] *nm* (*rango*) lieutenant; (*ayudante*) deputy.

tenis ['tenis] *nm* tennis; **~ta** *nm/f* tennis player.

tenor [te'nor] *nm* (*tono*) tone; (*sentido*) meaning; (*MUS*) tenor; **a ~ de** on the lines of.

tensar [ten'sar] *vt* to tauten; (*arco*) to draw.

tensión [ten'sjon] *nf* (*gen*) tension; (*TEC*) stress, (*MED*): **~ arterial** blood pressure; **tener la ~ alta** to have high blood pressure; **tenso, a** *a* tense.

tentación [tenta'θjon] *nf* temptation.

tentáculo [ten'takulo] *nm* tentacle.

tentador, a [tenta'ðor, a] *a* tempting // *nm/f* tempter/tempress.

tentar [ten'tar] *vt* (*tocar*) to touch, feel; (*seducir*) to tempt; (*atraer*) to attract; (*probar*) to try (out); (*lanzarse a*) to venture; (*MED*) to probe; **tentativa** *nf* attempt; **tentativa de asesinato** attempted murder.

tentempié [tentem'pje] *nm* (*fam*) snack.

tenue ['tenwe] *a* (*delgado*) thin, slender; (*alambre*) fine; (*insustancial*) tenuous; (*sonido*) faint; (*neblina*) light; (*lazo, vínculo*) slight; **tenuidad** *nf* thinness; fineness; (*ligereza*) lightness; (*sencillez*) simplicity.

teñir [te'nir] *vt* to dye; (*fig*) to tinge; **~se** *vr* to dye; **~se el pelo** to dye one's hair.

teología [teolo'xia] *nf* theology.

teorema [teo'rema] *nm* theorem.

teoría [teo'ria] *nf* theory; **en ~** in theory; **teóricamente** *ad* theoretically; **teórico, a** *a* theoretic(al) // *nf* theoretician, theorist; **teorizar** *vi* to theorize.

terapéutico, a [tera'peutiko, a] *a* therapeutic.

terapia [te'rapja] *nf* therapy; **~ laboral** occupational therapy.

tercer [ter'θer] *a ver* **tercero.**

tercería [terθe'ria] *nf* (*mediación*) mediation; (*arbitraje*) arbitration.

tercero, a [ter'θero, a] *a* third // *nm* (*árbitro*) mediator; (*JUR*) third party.

terceto [ter'θeto] *nm* trio.

terciado, a [ter'θjaðo, a] *a* slanting; **azúcar ~** brown sugar.

terciar [ter'θjar] *vt* (*MAT*) to divide into three; (*inclinarse*) to slope; (*llevar*) to wear (*across the shoulder*) // *vi* (*participar*) to take part; (*hacer de árbitro*) to mediate;

~se vr to come up; **~io, a** a tertiary.
tercio ['terθjo] nm third.
terciopelo [terθjo'pelo] nm velvet.
terco, a ['terko, a] a obstinate; (material) tough.
tergiversación [terxiβersa'θjon] nf (deformación) distortion; (evasivas) prevarication; **tergiversar** vt to distort // vi to prevaricate.
termas ['termas] nfpl hot springs.
terminación [termina'θjon] nf (final) end; (conclusión) conclusion, ending; **terminal** a, nm, nf terminal; **terminante** a (final) final, definitive; (tajante) categorical; **terminar** vt (completar) to complete, finish; (concluir) to end // vi (llegar a su fin) to end; (parar) to stop; (acabar) to finish; **terminarse** vr to come to an end; **terminar por hacer algo** to end up (by) doing sth; **término** nm end, conclusion; (parada) terminus; (límite) boundary; **término medio** average; (fig) middle way; **en último término** (a fin de cuentas) in the last analysis; (como último recurso) as a last resort; **en términos de** in terms of.
terminología [terminolo'xia] nf terminology.
termodinámico, a [termoði'namiko, a] a thermodynamic.
termómetro [ter'mometro] nm thermometer.
termonuclear [termonukle'ar] a thermonuclear.
termo(s) ['termo(s)] nm thermos.
termostato [termo'stato] nm thermostat.
ternero, a [ter'nero, a] nm/f (animal) calf // nf (carne) veal.
terneza [ter'neθa] nf tenderness.
terno ['terno] nm (traje) three-piece suit; (conjunto) set of three.
ternura [ter'nura] nf (trato) tenderness; (palabra) endearment; (cariño) fondness.
terquedad [terke'ðað] nf obstinacy; (dureza) harshness.
terrado [te'rraðo] nm terrace.
terraplén [terra'plen] nm (AGR) terrace; (FERRO) embankment; (MIL) rampart; (cuesta) slope.
terrateniente [terrate'njente] nm landowner.
terraza [te'rraθa] nf (balcón) balcony; (techo) flat roof; (AGR) terrace.
terremoto [terre'moto] nm earthquake.
terrenal [terre'nal] a earthly.
terreno [te'rreno] nm (tierra) land; (parcela) plot; (suelo) soil; (fig) field; **un ~** a piece of land.
terrero, a [te'rrero, a] a (de la tierra) earthly; (vuelo) low; (fig) humble.
terrestre [te'rrestre] a terrestrial; (ruta) land cpd.
terrible [te'rriβle] a (espantoso) terrible; (aterrador) dreadful; (tremendo) awful.
territorio [terri'torjo] nm territory.
terrón [te'rron] nm (de azúcar) lump; (de tierra) clod, lump; **terrones** nmpl land sg.

terror [te'rror] nm terror; **~ífico, a** a terrifying; **~ista** a, nm/f terrorist.
terroso, a [te'rroso, a] a earthy.
terruño [te'rruno] nm (pedazo) clod; (parcela) plot; (fig) native soil.
terso, a ['terso, a] a (liso) smooth; (pulido) polished; (fig: estilo) flowing; **tersura** nf smoothness; (brillo) shine.
tertulia [ter'tulja] nf (reunión informal) social gathering; (grupo) group, circle; (sala) clubroom.
tesar [te'sar] vt to tighten up.
tesis ['tesis] nf inv thesis.
tesón [te'son] nm (firmeza) firmness; (tenacidad) tenacity.
tesorero, a [teso'rero, a] nm/f treasurer; **tesoro** nm (gen) treasure; (FIN, POL) treasury.
testaferro [testa'ferro] nm figurehead.
testamentaría [testamenta'ria] nf execution of a will.
testamentario, a [testamen'tarjo, a] a testamentary // nm/f executor/executrix; **testamento** nm will; **testar** vi to make a will.
testarudo, a [testa'ruðo, a] a stubborn.
testero, a [tes'tero, a] nm/f (gen) front // nm (ARQ) front wall.
testes ['testes] nmpl testes.
testículo [tes'tikulo] nm testicle.
testificar [testifi'kar] vt to testify; (fig) to attest // vi to give evidence.
testigo [tes'tixo] nm/f witness; **~ de cargo/descargo** witness for the prosecution/defence; **~ ocular** eye witness.
testimoniar [testimo'njar] vt to testify to; (fig) to show; **testimonio** nm testimony.
teta ['teta] nf (de biberón) teat; (ANAT) nipple; (fam) breast.
tétanos ['tetanos] nm tetanus.
tetera [te'tera] nf teapot.
tetilla [te'tiΛa] nf (ANAT) nipple; (de biberón) teat.
tétrico, a ['tetriko, a] a gloomy, dismal.
textil [teks'til] a textile; **~es** nmpl textiles.
texto ['teksto] nm text; **textual** a textual.
textura [teks'tura] nf (de tejido) texture; (de mineral) structure.
tez [teθ] nf (cutis) complexion; (color) colouring.
ti [ti] pron you; (reflexivo) yourself.
tía ['tia] nf (pariente) aunt; (mujer cualquiera) girl, bird (col); (fam: pej: vieja) old bag; (: prostituta) whore.
tibia ['tiβja] nf tibia.
tibieza [ti'βjeθa] nf (temperatura) tepidness; (fig) coolness; **tibio, a** a lukewarm.
tiburón [tiβu'ron] nm shark.
tic [tik] nm (ruido) click; (de reloj) tick; (MED): **~ nervioso** nervous tic.
tictac [tik'tak] nm (de reloj) tick tock.
tiempo ['tjempo] nm (gen) time; (época, período) age period; (METEOROLOGÍA) weather; (LING) tense; (edad) age; (de

juego) half; **a** ~ in time; **a un o al mismo** ~ at the same time; **al poco** ~ very soon (after); **de** ~ **en** ~ from time to time; **hace buen/mal** ~ the weather is fine/bad; **estar a** ~ to be in time; **hace** ~ some time ago; **hacer** ~ to while away the time; **motor de 2** ~**s** two-stroke engine.

tienda ['tjenda] *nf* (*gen*) shop; (*más grande*) store; (*NAUT*) awning; ~ **de campaña** tent.

tienes *etc vb ver* **tener.**

tienta ['tjenta] *nf* (*MED*) probe; (*fig*) tact; **andar a** ~**s** to grope one's way along.

tiento ['tjento] *nm* (*tacto*) touch; (*precaución*) wariness; (*pulso*) steady hand; (*ZOOL*) feeler; (*de ciego*) blind man's stick.

tierno, a ['tjerno, a] *a* (*blando, dulce*) tender; (*fresco*) fresh.

tierra ['tjerra] *nf* earth; (*suelo*) soil; (*mundo*) world; (*país*) country, land; ~ **adentro** inland.

tieso, a ['tjeso, a] *a* (*rígido*) rigid; (*duro*) stiff; (*fig: testarudo*) stubborn; (*fam: orgulloso*) conceited // *ad* strongly.

tiesto ['tjesto] *nm* flowerpot; (*pedazo*) piece of pottery.

tiesura [tje'sura] *nf* rigidity; (*fig*) stubbornness; (*fam*) conceit.

tifo ['tifo] *nm* typhus.

tifoidea [tifoi'ðea] *nf* typhoid.

tifón [ti'fon] *nm* (*huracán*) typhoon; (*de mar*) tidal wave.

tifus ['tifus] *nm* typhus.

tigre ['tixre] *nm* tiger.

tijera [ti'xera] *nf* (*AM*) scissors *pl*; (*ZOOL*) claw; (*persona*) gossip; **de** ~ folding; ~**s** *nfpl* scissors; (*para plantas*) shears; **tijeretear** *vt* to snip // *vi* (*fig*) to meddle.

tildar [til'dar] *vt*: ~ **de** to brand as.

tilde ['tilde] *nf* (*defecto*) defect; (*trivialidad*) triviality; (*TIPOGRAFÍA*) tilde.

tilín [ti'lin] *nm* tinkle.

tilo ['tilo] *nm* lime tree.

timar [ti'mar] *vt* (*robar*) to steal; (*estafar*) to swindle; ~**se** *vr* (*fam*) to make eyes (*con uno* at sb).

timbal [tim'bal] *nm* small drum.

timbrar [tim'brar] *vt* to stamp.

timbre ['timbre] *nm* (*sello*) stamp; (*campanilla*) bell; (*tono*) timbre; (*COM*) stamp duty.

timidez [timi'ðeθ] *nf* shyness; **tímido, a** *a* shy.

timo ['timo] *nm* swindle.

timón [ti'mon] *nm* helm, rudder; **timonel** *nm* helmsman.

tímpano ['timpano] *nm* (*ANAT*) eardrum; (*MUS*) small drum.

tina ['tina] *nf* tub; (*baño*) bathtub; **tinaja** *nf* large jar.

tinglado [tin'glaðo] *nm* (*cobertizo*) shed; (*fig: truco*) trick; (*intriga*) intrigue.

tinieblas [ti'njeßlas] *nfpl* (*gen*) darkness *sg*; (*sombras*) shadows.

tino ['tino] *nm* (*habilidad*) skill; (*MIL*) marksmanship; (*juicio*) insight; (*moderación*) moderation.

tinta ['tinta] *nf* ink; (*TEC*) dye; (*ARTE*) colour.

tinte ['tinte] *nm* (*acto*) dyeing; (*carácter*) tinge; (*barniz*) veneer.

tinterillo [tinte'riʎo] *nm* penpusher.

tintero [tin'tero] *nm* inkwell.

tintinear [tintine'ar] *vt* to tinkle.

tinto, a ['tinto, a] *a* (*teñido*) dyed; (*manchado*) stained // *nm* red wine.

tintorera [tinto'rera] *nf* shark.

tintorería [tintore'ria] *nf* dry cleaner's.

tintura [tin'tura] *nf* (*acto*) dyeing; (*QUÍMICA*) dye; (*farmacéutico*) tincture.

tío ['tio] *nm* (*pariente*) uncle; (*fam: viejo*) old fellow; (: *individuo*) bloke, chap.

tiovivo [tio'ßißo] *nm* roundabout.

típico, a ['tipiko, a] *a* typical.

tiple ['tiple] *nm* soprano (voice) // *nf* soprano.

tipo ['tipo] *nm* (*clase*) type, kind; (*norma*) norm; (*patrón*) pattern; (*hombre*) fellow; (*ANAT*) build; (: **de mujer**) figure; (*IMPRENTA*) type; ~ **bancario/de descuento/de interés/de cambio** bank/discount/interest/exchange rate.

tipografía [tipoɣra'fia] *nf* (*tipo*) printing; (*lugar*) printing press; **tipográfico, a** *a* printing; **tipógrafo, a** *nm/f* printer.

tiquismiquis [tikis'mikis] *nm* fussy person // *nmpl* (*querellas*) squabbling *sg*; (*escrúpulos*) silly scruples.

tira ['tira] *nf* strip; (*fig*) abundance; ~ **y afloja** give and take.

tirabuzón [tiraßu'θon] *nm* corkscrew.

tirado, a [ti'raðo, a] *a* (*barato*) dirt-cheap; (*fam: fácil*) very easy // *nf* (*acto*) cast, throw; (*distancia*) distance; (*serie*) series; (*TIPOGRAFÍA*) printing, edition; **de una** ~**a** at one go.

tirador [tira'ðor] *nm* (*mango*) handle; (*ELEC*) flex.

tiranía [tira'nia] *nf* tyranny, **tirano, a** *a* tyrannical // *nm/f* tyrant.

tirante [ti'rante] *a* (*cuerda*) tight, taut; (*relaciones*) strained // *nm* (*ARQ*) brace; (*TEC*) stay; (*correa*) shoulder strap; ~**s** *nmpl* braces; **tirantez** *nf* tightness; (*fig*) tension.

tirar [ti'rar] *vt* (*aventar*) to throw; (*dejar caer*) to drop; (*volcar*) to upset; (*derribar*) to knock down *or* over; (*jalar*) to pull; (*desechar*) to throw out *or* away; (*disipar*) to squander; (*imprimir*) to print; (*dar: golpe*) to deal // *vi* (*disparar*) to shoot; (*jalar*) to pull; (*fig*) to draw; (*fam: andar*) to go; (*tender a, buscar realizar*) to tend to; (*DEPORTE*) to shoot; ~**se** *vr* to throw o.s.; (*fig*) to cheapen o.s.; ~ **abajo** to bring down, destroy; **tira más a su padre** he takes more after his father; **ir tirando** to manage; **a todo** ~ at the most.

irita [ti'rita] *nf* (*sticking*) plaster.

iritar [tiri'tar] *vi* to shiver.

tiro ['tiro] *nm* (*lanzamiento*) throw;

(*disparo*) shot; (*disparar*) shooting; (*DEPORTE*) drive; (*alcance*) range; (*de escalera*) flight (of stairs); (*golpe*) blow; (*engaño*) hoax; ~ **al blanco** target practice; **caballo de** ~ cart-horse; **andar de** ~**s largos** to be all dressed up; **al** ~ (*AM*) at once.

tirón [ti'ron] *nm* (*sacudida*) pull, tug; **de un** ~ in one go.

tirotear [tirote'ar] *vt* to shoot at; ~**se** *vr* to exchange shots; **tiroteo** *nm* exchange of shots, shooting.

tísico, a ['tisiko, a] *a* consumptive.

títere ['titere] *nm* puppet.

titilar [titi'lar] *vi* (*luz, estrella*) to twinkle; (*parpado*) to flutter.

titiritero, a [titiri'tero, a] *nm/f* puppeteer.

titubeante [tituße'ante] *a* (*inestable*) shaky, tottering; (*farfullante*) stammering; (*dudoso*) hesitant; **titubear** *vi* to stagger; (*fig*) to hesitate; **titubeo** *nm* staggering; stammering; hesitation.

titulado, a [titu'lado, a] *a* (*libro*) entitled; (*persona*) titled; **titular** *a* titular // *nm/f* occupant // *nm* headline // *vt* to title; **titularse** *vr* to be entitled; **título** *nm* (*gen*) title; (*de diario*) headline; (*certificado*) professional qualification; (*universitario*) university degree; (*fig*) right; **a título de** in the capacity of.

tiza ['tiθa] *nf* chalk.

tizna ['tiθna] *nf* grime; **tiznar** *vt* to blacken; (*fig*) to tarnish.

tizón [ti'θon], **tizo** ['tiθo] *nm* brand; (*fig*) stain.

toalla [to'aʎa] *nf* towel.

tobillo [to'ßiʎo] *nm* ankle.

tobogán [toßo'van] *nm* toboggan; (*montaña rusa*) switchback; (*resbaladilla*) chute, slide.

toca ['toka] *nf* headdress.

tocadiscos [toka'ðiskos] *nm inv* record player.

tocado, a [to'kaðo, a] *a* rotten; (*fam*) touched // *nm* headdress.

tocador [toka'ðor] *nm* (*mueble*) dressing table; (*cuarto*) boudoir; (*neceser*) toilet case; (*fam*) ladies' toilet.

tocante [to'kante]: ~ **a** *prep* with regard to.

tocar [to'kar] *vt* to touch; (*MUS*) to play; (*topar con*) to run into, strike; (*referirse a*) to allude to; (*padecer*) to suffer; (*el pelo*) to do // *vi* (*a la puerta*) to knock (on or at the door); (*ser de turno*) to fall to, be the turn of; (*ser hora*) to be due; (*barco, avión*) to call at; (*atañer*) to concern; ~**se** *vr* (*cubrirse la cabeza*) to cover one's head; (*tener contacto*) to touch (each other); **por lo que a mí me toca** as far as I am concerned; **esto toca en la locura** this verges on madness.

tocayo, a [to'kajo, a] *nm/f* namesake.

tocino [to'θino] *nm* bacon.

todavía [toða'ßia] *ad* (*aun*) still; (*aún*) yet; ~ **más** yet more; ~ **no** not yet.

todo, a ['toðo, a] *a* all; (*cada*) every;

(*entero*) whole; (*sentido negativo*): **en** ~ **el día lo he visto** I haven't seen him all day; ~**as las semanas/**~**s los martes** every week/Tuesday // *ad* all, completely // *nm* everything // *pron*: ~**s/**~**as** everyone; **a** ~**a velocidad** at full speed; **estaba** ~ **ojos** he was all eyes; **puede ser** ~ **lo honesto que quiera** he can be as honest as he likes; **ante** ~ above all; **en un** ~ as a whole; **corriendo y** ~, **no llegaron a tiempo** even though they ran, they still didn't arrive in time; **con** ~ still, even so; **del** ~ completely.

todopoderoso, a [todopoðe'roso, a] *a* all powerful; (*REL*) almighty.

toga ['toxa] *nf* toga; (*ESCOL*) gown.

Tokio ['tokjo] *n* Tokyo.

toldo ['toldo] *nm* (*para el sol*) sunshade; (*tienda*) marquee; (*fig*) pride.

tole ['tole] *nm* (*fam*) commotion.

tolerable [tole'raßle] *a* tolerable; **tolerancia** *nf* tolerance; **tolerar** *vt* to tolerate; (*resistir*) to endure.

toma ['toma] *nf* (*gen*) taking; (*MED*) dose.

tomar [to'mar] *vt* (*gen*) to take; (*aspecto*) to take on; (*beber*) to drink // *vi* to take; (*AM*) to drink; ~**se** *vr* to take; ~**se por** to consider o.s. to be; ~ **a bien/a mal** to take well/badly; ~ **en serio** to take seriously; ~ **el pelo a alguien** to pull sb's leg; ~**la con uno** to pick a quarrel with sb.

tomate [to'mate] *nm* tomato; ~**ra** *nf* tomato plant.

tomillo [to'miʎo] *nm* thyme.

tomo ['tomo] *nm* (*libro*) volume; (*tamaño*) size; (*fig*) importance.

ton [ton] *abr de* **tonelada** // *nm*: **sin** ~ **ni son** without rhyme or reason.

tonada [to'naða] *nf* tune.

tonalidad [tonali'ðað] *nf* tone.

tonel [to'nel] *nm* barrel.

tonelada [tone'laða] *nf* ton; **tonelaje** *nm* tonnage.

tonelero [tone'lero] *nm* cooper.

tónico, a ['toniko, a] *a* tonic // *nm* (*MED*) tonic // *nf* (*MUS*) tonic; (*fig*) keynote.

tonificar [tonifi'kar] *vt* to tone up.

tonillo [to'niʎo] *nm* monotonous voice.

tono ['tono] *nm* tone; **fuera de** ~ inappropriate; **darse** ~ to put on airs.

tontería [tonte'ria] *nf* (*estupidez*) foolishness; (*una* ~) stupid remark; ~**s** *nfpl* rubbish *sg*, nonsense *sg*.

tonto, a ['tonto, a] *a* stupid; (*sentimental*) silly // *nm/f* fool; (*payaso*) clown.

topacio [to'paθjo] *nm* topaz.

topar [to'par] *vt* (*tropezar*) to bump into; (*encontrar*) to find, come across; (*ZOOL*) to butt // *vi*: ~ **contra** *o* **en** to run into; ~ **con** to run up against; **el problema topa en eso** that's where the problem lies.

tope ['tope] *a* maximum // *nm* (*fin*) end; (*límite*) limit; (*riña*) quarrel; (*FERRO*) buffer; (*AUTO*) bumper; **al** ~ **end to end.

tópico, a ['topiko, a] *a* topical // *nm* platitude.

topo ['topo] nm (ZOOL) mole; (fig) blunderer.

topografía [topoxra'fia] nf topography; **topógrafo, a** nm/f topographer.

toque ['toke] nm touch; (MUS) beat; (de campana) peal; (fig) crux; **dar un** ~ **a** to test; ~ **de queda** curfew; ~**tea** vt to handle.

toquilla [to'kiʎa] nf (bufanda) headscarf; (chal) shawl.

torbellino [torbe'ʎino] nm whirlwind; (fig) whirl.

torcedura [torθe'ðura] nf twist; (MED) sprain.

torcer [tor'θer] vt to twist; (la esquina) to turn; (MED) to sprain; (cuerda) to plait; (ropa, manos) to wring; (persona) to corrupt // vi (desviar) to turn off; (pelota) to spin; ~**se** vr (ladearse) to bend; (desviarse) to go astray; (fracasar) to go wrong; **torcido, a** a twisted; (fig) crooked // nm curl.

tordo, a ['torðo, a] a dappled // nm thrush.

torear [tore'ar] vt (fig: evadir) to avoid; (jugar con) to tease // vi to fight bulls; **toreo** nm bullfighting; **torero, a** nm/f bullfighter.

tormenta [tor'menta] nf storm; (fig: confusión) turmoil; (desgracia) misfortune.

tormento [tor'mento] nm torture; (fig) anguish.

tornar [tor'nar] vt (devolver) to return, give back; (transformar) to transform // vi to go back; ~**se** vr (ponerse) to become; (volver) to return.

tornasol [torna'sol] nm (BOT) sunflower; **papel de** ~ litmus paper; ~**ado, a** a (brillante) iridescent; (reluciente) shimmering.

torneo [tor'neo] nm tournament.

tornero, a [tor'nero, a] nm/f machinist.

tornillo [tor'niʎo] nm screw.

torniquete [torni'kete] nm (puerta) turnstile; (MED) tourniquet.

torno ['torno] nm (TEC) winch; (tambor) drum; **en** ~ **(a)** round, about.

toro ['toro] nm bull; (fam) he-man; **los** ~**s** bullfighting.

toronja [to'ronxa] nf grapefruit.

torpe ['torpe] a (poco hábil) clumsy, awkward; (necio) dim; (lento) slow; (indecente) crude; (no honrado) dishonest.

torpedo [tor'peðo] nm torpedo.

torpeza [tor'peθa] nf (falta de agilidad) clumsiness; (lentitud) slowness; (rigidez) stiffness; (error) mistake; (crudeza) obscenity.

torre ['torre] nf tower; (de petróleo) derrick.

torrente [to'rrente] nm torrent.

tórrido, a ['torriðo, a] a torrid.

torrija [to'rrixa] nf fried bread; ~**s** French toast sg.

torsión [tor'sjon] nf twisting.

torso ['torso] nm torso.

torta ['torta] nf cake; (fam) slap.

tortícolis [tor'tikolis] nm stiff neck.

tortilla [tor'tiʎa] nf omelette; (AM) maize pancake; ~ **francesa/española** plain/potato omelette.

tórtola ['tortola] nf turtledove.

tortuga [tor'tuɣa] nf tortoise.

tortuoso, a [tor'twoso, a] a winding.

tortura [tor'tura] nf torture; **torturar** vt to torture.

tos [tos] nf cough; ~ **ferina** whooping cough.

tosco, a ['tosko, a] a coarse.

toser [to'ser] vi to cough.

tostado, a [tos'taðo, a] a toasted; (por el sol) dark brown; (piel) tanned // nf tan; **tostador** nm toaster; **tostar** vt to toast; (café) to roast; (el sol) to tan; **tostarse** vr to get brown.

total [to'tal] a total // ad in short; (al fin y al cabo) when all is said and done // nm total; ~ **que** to cut a long story short.

totalidad [totali'ðað] nf whole.

totalitario, a [totali'tarjo, a] a totalitarian.

tóxico, a ['toksiko, a] a toxic // nm poison.

tozudo, a [to'θuðo, a] a obstinate.

traba ['traβa] nf bond, tie; (cadena) fetter.

trabajador, a [traβaxa'ðor, a] nm/f worker // a hard-working.

trabajar [traβa'xar] vt (arar) to till; (empeñarse en) to work at; (empujar: persona) to push; (convencer) to persuade // vi to work; (esforzarse) to strive; **trabajo** nm work; (tarea) task; (POL) labour; (fig) effort; **tomarse el trabajo de** to take the trouble to; **trabajo por turno/a destajo** shift work/ piecework; **trabajoso, a** a hard; (MED) pale.

trabalenguas [traβa'lengwas] nm inv tongue twister.

trabar [tra'βar] vt (juntar) to join, unite; (atar) to tie down, fetter; (agarrar) to seize; (amistad) to strike up; ~**se** vr to become entangled; (reñir) to squabble; **trabazón** nf (TEC) joining, assembly; (fig) bond, link.

trabucar [traβu'kar] vt (confundir) to confuse, mix up; (palabras) to misplace.

tracción [trak'θjon] nf traction; ~ **delantera/trasera** front-wheel/rear-wheel drive.

tractor [trak'tor] nm tractor.

tradición [traði'θjon] nf tradition; **tradicional** a traditional.

traducción [traðuk'θjon] nf translation; **traducir** vt to translate; **traductor, a** nm/f translator.

traer [tra'er] vt (gen) to bring; (llevar) to carry; (ropa) to wear; (incluir) to carry; (fig) to cause; ~**se** vr: ~**se algo** to be up to sth; ~**se bien/mal** to dress well/badly.

traficar [trafi'kar] vi to trade.

tráfico ['trafiko] nm (COM) trade; (AUTO) traffic.

tragaluz [traɣa'luθ] nm skylight.

tragamonedas [traɣamo'neðas] nm inv,

tragaperras [traɣa'perras] nm inv slot machine.

tragar [tra'ɣar] vt to swallow; (devorar) to devour, bolt down; ~**se** vr to swallow.

tragedia [tra'xeðja] nf tragedy; **trágico, a** a tragic.

trago ['traɣo] nm (líquido) drink; (comido de golpe) gulp; (fam: de bebida) swig; (desgracia) blow.

traición [trai'θjon] nf treachery; (JUR) treason; (una ~) act of treachery; **traicionar** vt to betray; **traidor, a, traicionero, a** a treacherous // nm/f traitor.

traigo etc vb ver **traer.**

traje ['traxe] vb ver **traer** // nm (gen) dress; (de hombre) suit; (vestimenta típica) costume; (fig) garb; ~ **de baño** swimsuit; ~ **de luces** bullfighter's costume.

trajera etc vb ver **traer.**

trajín [tra'xin] nm haulage; (fam: movimiento) bustle; **trajines** nmpl goings-on; **trajinar** vt (llevar) to carry, transport // vi (moverse) to bustle about; (viajar) to travel around.

trama ['trama] nf (fig) link; (: intriga) plot; (de tejido) weft; **tramar** vt to plot; (TEC) to weave.

tramitar [trami'tar] vt (asunto) to transact; (negociar) to negotiate; (manejar) to handle; **trámite** nm (paso) step; (JUR) transaction; **trámites** nmpl (burocracia) paperwork sg, procedures; (JUR) proceedings.

tramo ['tramo] nm (de tierra) plot; (de escalera) flight; (de vía) section.

tramoya [tra'moja] nf (TEATRO) piece of stage machinery; (fig) trick; **tramoyista** nm/f scene shifter; (fig) trickster.

trampa ['trampa] nf (gen) trap; (en el suelo) trapdoor; (prestidigitación) conjuring trick; (engaño) trick; (fam) fiddle; (de pantalón) fly; **trampear** vt, vi to cheat; **trampista** nm/f = **tramposo.**

trampolín [trampo'lin] nm trampoline; (de piscina etc) diving board.

tramposo, a [tram'poso, a] a crooked, cheating // nm/f crook, cheat.

tranca ['tranka] nf (palo) stick; (viga) beam; (de puerta, ventana) bar; **trancar** vt to bar // vi to stride along.

trance ['tranθe] nm (momento difícil) difficult moment; (situación crítica) critical situation; (estado hipnotizado) trance.

tranco ['tranko] nm stride.

tranquilidad [trankili'ðað] nf (calma) calmness, stillness; (paz) peacefulness; **tranquilizar** vt (calmar) to calm (down); (asegurar) to reassure; **tranquilo, a** a (calmado) calm; (apacible) peaceful; (mar) calm; (mente) untroubled.

transacción [transak'θjon] nf transaction.

transar [tran'sar] vt = **transigir.**

transbordador [transβorða'ðor] nm ferry.

transbordar [transβor'ðar] vt to transfer; ~**se** vr to change; **transbordo** nm

transfer; **hacer transbordo** to change (trains).

transcurrir [transku'rrir] vi (tiempo) to pass; (hecho) to turn out.

transcurso [trans'kurso] nm: ~ **del tiempo** lapse (of time).

transeúnte [transe'unte] a transient // nm/f passer-by.

transferencia [transfe renθja] nf transference; (COM) transfer; **transferir** vt to transfer; (de tiempo) to postpone.

transfigurar [transfiɣu'rar] vt to transfigure.

transformador [transforma'ðor] nm transformer.

transformar [transfor'mar] vt to transform; (convertirse) to convert.

tránsfuga ['transfuɣa] nm/f (MIL) deserter; (POL) turncoat.

transgresión [transɣre'sjon] nf transgression.

transición [transi'θjon] nf transition.

transido, a [tran'siðo, a] a overcome.

transigir [transi'xir] vi to compromise, make concessions.

transistor [transis'tor] nm transistor.

transitar [transi'tar] vi to go (from place to place); **tránsito** nm transit; (AUTO) traffic; (parada) stop; **transitorio, a** a transitory.

transmisión [transmi'sjon] nf (TEC) transmission; (transferencia) transfer; ~ **en directo/exterior** live/outside broadcast; **transmitir** vt (gen) to transmit; (RADIO, TV) to broadcast.

transparencia [transpa'renθja] nf transparency; (claridad) clearness, clarity; (foto) slide; **transparentar** vt to reveal // vi to be transparent; **transparente** a transparent; clear; (ligero) diaphanous // nm curtain.

transpirar [transpi rar] vi to perspire; (fig) to transpire.

transponer [transpo'ner] vt to transpose; (cambiar de sitio) to change the place of // vi (desaparecer) to disappear; (ir más allá) to go beyond; ~**se** vr to change places; (ocultarse) to hide; (sol) to go down.

transportación [transporta'θjon] nf transportation; **transportar** vt to transport; (llevar) to carry; **transporte** nm transport; (COM) haulage.

tranvía [tran'βia] nm tram.

trapecio [tra'peθjo] nm trapeze; **trapecista** nm/f trapeze artist.

trapero, a [tra'pero, a] nm/f ragman.

trapicheos [trapi'tʃeos] nmpl (fam) schemes, fiddles.

trapisonda [trapi'sonda] nf (jaleo) row; (estafa) swindle.

trapo ['trapo] nm (tela) rag; (de cocina) cloth.

traqueteo [trake'teo] nm (crujido) crack; (golpeteo) rattling.

tras [tras] prep (detrás) behind; (después) after; ~ **de besides.**

trascendencia [trasθen'denθja] nf

(*importancia*) importance; (*filosofía*) transcendence; **trascendental** *a* important; transcendental; **trascender** *vi* (*oler*) to smell; (*evocar*) to evoke, suggest; (*noticias*) to come out; (*suceso*) to have a wide effect; **trascender a** to smack of.

trasegar [trase'var] *vt* (*moverse*) to move about; (*vino*) to decant.

trasero, a [tra'sero, a] *a* back // *nm* (*ANAT*) bottom; ~s *nmpl* ancestors.

trasfondo [tras'fondo] *nm* background.

trasgredir [trasvre'ðir] *vt* to contravene.

trashumante [trasu'mante] *a* migrating.

trasladar [trasla'ðar] *vt* (*gen*) to move; (*persona*) to transfer; (*postergar*) to postpone; (*copiar*) to copy; (*interpretar*) to interpret; **traslado** *nm* (*gen*) move; (*mudanza*) move, removal; (*copia*) copy.

traslucir [traslu'θir] *vt* to show; ~se *vr* to be translucent; (*fig*) to be revealed.

trasluz [tras'luθ] *nm* reflected light; **al** ~ against *or* up to the light.

trasnochar [trasno'tʃar] *vi* (*acostarse tarde*) to stay up late; (*no dormir*) to have a sleepless night; (*pasar la noche*) to stay the night.

traspasar [traspa'sar] *vt* (*bala*) to pierce, go through; (*propiedad*) to sell, transfer; (*calle*) to cross over; (*límites*) to go beyond; (*ley*) to break; **traspaso** *nm* transfer; (*fig*) anguish.

traspié [tras'pje] *nm* (*caída*) stumble; (*tropezón*) trip; (*fig*) blunder.

trasplantar [trasplan'tar] *vt* to transplant.

traste ['traste] *nm* (*MUS*) fret; **dar al** ~ **con algo** to ruin sth.

trastienda [tras'tjenda] *nf* backshop; **obtener algo por la** ~ to get sth by underhand means.

trasto ['trasto] *nm* (*mueble*) piece of furniture; (*tarro viejo*) old pot; (*pey: cosa*) piece of junk; (: *persona*) dead loss; ~s *nmpl* (*TEATRO*) scenery sg.

trastornado, a [trastor'naðo, a] *a* (*loco*) mad; (*agitado*) crazy; **trastornar** *vt* to overturn, upset; (*fig: ideas*) to confuse; (: *nervios*) to shatter; (: *persona*) to drive crazy; **trastornarse** *vr* (*plan*) to fall through; **trastorno** *nm* (*acto*) overturning; (*confusión*) confusion.

trasunto [tra'sunto] *nm* copy.

tratable [tra'taβle] *a* friendly.

tratado [tra'taðo] *nm* (*POL*) treaty; (*COM*) agreement.

tratamiento [trata'mjento] *nm* treatment.

tratar [tra'tar] *vt* (*ocuparse de*) to treat; (*manejar, TEC*) to handle; (*MED*) to treat; (*dirigirse a: persona*) to address // *vi*: ~ **de** (*hablar sobre*) to be about, be about; (*intentar*) to try to; ~ **con** (*COM*) to trade in; (*negociar*) to negotiate with; (*tener contactos*) to have dealings with; ~se *vr* to treat each other; **trato** *nm* dealings *pl*; (*relaciones*) relationship; (*comportamiento*)

manner; (*COM*) agreement; (*título*) (form of) address.

trauma ['trauma] *nm* trauma.

través [tra'βes] *nm* (*fig*) reverse; **al** ~ *ad* across, crossways; **a** ~ **de** *prep* across; (*sobre*) over; (*por*) through.

travesaño [traβe'saɲo] *nm* (*ARQ*) crossbeam; (*DEPORTE*) crossbar.

travesía [traβe'sia] *nf* (*calle*) cross-street; (*NAUT*) crossing.

travesura [traβe'sura] *nf* (*broma*) prank; (*ingenio*) wit, **travieso, a** (*niño*) naughty; (*adulto*) restless; (*ingenioso*) witty // *nf* crossing; (*ARQ*) crossbeam.

trayecto [tra'jekto] *nm* (*ruta*) road, way; (*viaje*) journey; (*tramo*) stretch; (*curso*) course; ~**ria** *nf* trajectory; (*fig*) path.

traza ['traθa] *nf* (*ARQ*) plan, design; (*aspecto*) looks *pl*; (*señal*) sign; (*engaño*) trick; (*habilidad*) skill; ~**do, a** *a*: **bien** ~**do** shapely, well-formed // *nm* (*ARQ*) plan, design; (*fig*) outline; **trazar** *vt* (*ARQ*) to plan; (*ARTE*) to sketch; (*fig*) to trace; (*plan*) to follow; **trazo** *nm* (*línea*) line; (*bosquejo*) sketch.

trébol ['treβol] *nm* (*BOT*) clover.

trece ['treθe] *num* thirteen.

trecho ['tretʃo] *nm* (*distancia*) distance; (*de tiempo*) while; (*fam*) piece; **de** ~ **en** ~ at intervals.

tregua ['treɣwa] *nf* (*MIL*) truce; (*fig*) lull.

treinta ['treinta] *num* thirty.

tremendo, a [tre'mendo, a] *a* (*terrible*) terrible; (*imponente: cosa*) imposing; (*fam: fabuloso*) tremendous; (*divertido*) entertaining.

trémulo, a ['tremulo, a] *a* quivering.

tren [tren] *nm* train; ~ **de aterrizaje** undercarriage

trenza ['trenθa] *nf* (*de pelo*) plait; **trenzar** *vt* (*el pelo*) to plait /; *vi* (*en baile*) to weave in and out; **trenzarse** *vr* (*AM*) to become involved with.

trepadora [trepa'ðora] *nf* (*BOT*) climber; **trepar** *vt, vi* to climb (*TEC*) to drill.

trepidación [trepiða'θjon] *nf* shaking, vibration; **trepidar** *vi* to shake, vibrate.

tres [tres] *num* three.

tresillo [tre'siʎo] *nm* three-piece suite; (*MUS*) triplet.

treta ['treta] *nf* (*COM etc*) gimmick; (*fig*) trick.

triángulo ['trjangulo] *nm* triangle.

tribu ['triβu] *nf* tribe.

tribuna [tri'βuna] *nf* (*plataforma*) platform; (*DEPORTE*) stand; (*fig*) public speaking.

tribunal [triβu'nal] *nm* (*juicio*) court; (*comisión, fig*) tribunal.

tributar [triβu'tar] *vt* to pay; (*las gracias*) to give; (*cariño*) to show; **tributo** *nm* (*COM*) tax.

trigal [tri'val] *nm* wheat field; **trigo** *nm* wheat; **trigos** *nmpl* wheat field(s) (*pl*).

trigueño, a [tri'veɲo, a] *a* (*pelo*) corn-coloured; (*piel*) olive-skinned.

trillado, a [tri'ʎaðo, a] *a* threshed; (*fig*)

trite, hackneyed; **trilladora** *nf* threshing machine; **trillar** *vt* (*fig*) to frequent; (*AGR*) to thresh.

trimestral [trimes'tral] *a* quarterly; (*ESCOL*) termly; **trimestre** *nm* (*ESCOL*) term.

trincar [trin'kar] *vt* (*atar*) to tie up; (*NAUT*) to lash; (*agarrar*) to pinion.

trinchar [trin'tʃar] *vt* to carve.

trinchera [trin'tʃera] *nf* (*fosa*) trench; (*para vía*) cutting; (*impermeable*) trench-coat.

trineo [tri'neo] *nm* sledge.

trinidad [trini'ðað] *nf* trio; (*REL*): **la T~** the Trinity.

trino ['trino] *nm* trill.

trinquete [trin'kete] *nm* (*TEC*) pawl; (*NAUT*) foremast.

tripa ['tripa] *nf* (*ANAT*) intestine; (*fam*) insides *pl*.

triple ['triple] *a* triple.

triplicado [tripli'kaðo] *a*: **por ~** in triplicate.

tripulación [tripula'θjon] *nf* crew; **tripulante** *nm/f* crewman/woman; **tripular** *vt* (*barco*) to man; (*AUTO*) to drive.

triquiñuela [triki'ɲwela] *nf* trick.

tris [tris] *nm* crack; **en un ~** in an instant.

triste ['triste] *a* (*afligido*) sad; (*sombrío*) melancholy, gloomy; (*desolado*) desolate; (*lamentable*) sorry, miserable; (*viejo*) old; **~za** *nf* (*aflicción*) sadness; (*melancolía*) melancholy.

triturar [tritu'rar] *vt* (*moler*) to grind; (*mascar*) to chew.

triunfar [trjun'far] *vi* (*tener éxito*) to triumph; (*ganar*) to win; **triunfo** *nm* triumph.

trivial [tri'βjal] *a* trivial; **~izar** *vt* to minimize, play down.

triza ['triθa] *nf* bit, piece; **hacer ~s** to smash to bits; **trizar** *vt* to smash to bits.

trocar [tro'kar] *vt* (*COM*) to exchange; (*dinero, de lugar*) to change; (*palabras*) to exchange; (*confundir*) to confuse; (*vomitar*) to vomit.

trocha ['trotʃa] *nf* (*sendero*) by-path; (*atajo*) short cut.

troche ['trotʃe]: **a ~ y moche** *ad* helter-skelter, pell-mell.

trofeo [tro'feo] *nm* (*premio*) trophy; (*éxito*) success.

troj(e) ['trox(e)] *nf* granary.

tromba ['tromba] *nf* whirlwind.

trombón [trom'bon] *nm* trombone.

trombosis [trom'bosis] *nf* thrombosis.

trompa ['trompa] *nf* horn; (*trompo*) humming top; (*hocico*) snout; (*fam*): **cogerse una ~** to get tight.

trompeta [trom'peta] *nf* trumpet; (*clarín*) bugle.

trompo ['trompo] *nm* spinning top.

trompón [trom'pon] *nm* bump.

tronado, a [tro'naðo, a] *a* broken-down.

tronar [tro'nar] *vt* (*AM*) to shoot // *vi* to

thunder; (*fig*) to rage; (*fam*) to go broke.

tronco ['tronko] *nm* (*de árbol*, *ANAT*) trunk; (*de planta*) stem.

tronchar [tron'tʃar] *vt* (*árbol*) to chop down; (*fig*: *vida*) to cut short; (*esperanza*) to shatter; (*persona*) to tire out; **~se** *vr* to fall down.

tronera [tro'nera] *nf* (*MIL*) loophole; (*ARQ*) small window.

trono ['trono] *nm* throne.

tropa ['tropa] *nf* (*MIL*) troop; (*soldados*) soldiers *pl*; (*gentío*) mob.

tropel [tro'pel] *nm* (*muchedumbre*) crowd; (*prisa*) rush; (*montón*) throng.

tropelía [trope'lia] *nm* outrage.

tropezar [trope'θar] *vi* to trip, stumble; (*fig*) to slip up; **~ con** (*encontrar*) to run into; (*topar con*) to bump into; (*reñir*) to fall out with; **tropezón** *nm* tripe; (*fig*) blunder.

tropical [tropi'kal] *a* tropical; **trópico** *nm* tropic.

tropiezo [tro'pjeθo] *nm* (*error*) slip, blunder; (*desgracia*) misfortune; (*obstáculo*) snag; (*discusión*) quarrel.

trotamundos [trota'mundos] *nm inv* globetrotter.

trotar [tro'tar] *vi* to trot; **trote** *nm* trot; (*fam*) travelling; **de mucho trote** hard-wearing.

trozo ['troθo] *nm* bit, piece.

truco ['truko] *nm* (*habilidad*) knack; (*engaño*) trick; **~s** *nmpl* billiards *sg*.

trucha ['trutʃa] *nf* (*pez*) trout; (*TEC*) crane.

trueno ['trweno] *nm* (*gen*) thunder; (*estampido*) boom; (*de arma*) bang.

trueque ['trweke] *nm* exchange; (*COM*) barter.

trufa ['trufa] *nf* (*BOT*) truffle; (*fig*: *fam*) fib.

truhán, ana [tru'an, ana] *nm/f* rogue.

truncado, a [trun'kaðo, a] *a* truncated; **truncar** *vt* (*cortar*) to truncate; (*la vida etc*) to cut short; (*el desarrollo*) to stunt.

tu [tu] *a* your.

tú [tu] *pron* you.

tubérculo [tu'βerkulo] *nm* (*BOT*) tuber.

tuberculosis [tuβerku'losis] *nf* tuberculosis.

tubería [tuβe'ria] *nf* pipes *pl*; (*conducto*) pipeline; **tubo** *nm* tube, pipe; **tubo de ensayo** test-tube; **tubo de escape** exhaust (pipe).

tuerca ['twerka] *nf* nut.

tuerto, a ['twerto, a] *a* (*torcido*) twisted; (*ciego*) blind in one eye // *nm* one-eyed person; (*ofensa*) wrong; **a ~as** upside-down.

tuétano ['twetano] *nm* (*gen*) marrow; (*BOT*) pith.

tufo ['tufo] *nm* vapour; (*fig*: *pey*) stench.

tul [tul] *nm* tulle.

tulipán [tuli'pan] *nm* tulip.

tullido, a [tu'ʎiðo, a] *a* crippled; (*cansado*) exhausted.

tumba ['tumba] *nf* (*sepultura*) tomb; (*sacudida*) shake; (*voltereta*) somersault.

tumbar [tum'bar] *vt* to knock down; (*doblar*) to knock over; (*fam: suj: olor*) to overpower // *vi* to fall down; ~**se** *vr* (*echarse*) to lie down; (*extenderse*) to stretch out.

tumbo ['tumbo] *nm* (*caída*) fall; (*de vehículo*) jolt; (*momento crítico*) critical moment.

tumido, a [tu'miðo, a] *a* swollen.

tumor [tu'mor] *nm* tumour.

tumulto [tu'multo] *nm* turmoil.

tuna ['tuna] *nf ver* **tuno.**

tunante [tu'nante] *a* rascally.

tunda ['tunda] *nf* (*de tela*) shearing; (*golpeo*) beating; **tundir** *vt* (*tela*) to shear; (*hierba*) to mow; (*fig*) to exhaust; (*fam: golpear*) to beat.

túnel ['tunel] *nm* tunnel.

Túnez ['tuneθ] *nm* Tunisia; (*ciudad*) Tunis.

tuno, a ['tuno, a] *nm/f* (*fam*) rogue // *nf* (*BOT*) prickly pear; (*MUS*) student music group.

tuntún [tun'tun]: **al** ~ *ad* thoughtlessly.

tupido, a [tu'piðo, a] *a* (*denso*) dense; (*fig*) dim; (*tela*) close-woven.

turba ['turßa] *nf* crowd.

turbación [turßa'θjon] *nf* (*molestia*) disturbance; (*preocupación*) worry; **turbado, a** *a* (*molesto*) disturbed; (*preocupado*) worried; **turbar** *vt* (*molestar*) to disturb; (*incomodar*) to upset; **turbarse** *vr* to be disturbed.

turbina [tur'ßina] *nf* turbine.

turbio, a ['turßjo, a] *a* cloudy; (*lenguaje*) confused // *ad* indistinctly.

turbión [tur'ßjon] *nf* (*fig*) shower.

turbohélice [turßo'eliθe] *nm* turboprop.

turbulencia [turßu'lenθja] *nf* turbulence; (*fig*) restlessness; **turbulento, a** *a* turbulent; (*fig: intranquilo*) restless; (*: ruidoso*) noisy.

turco, a ['turko, a] *a* Turkish.

turismo [tu'rismo] *nm* tourism; (*coche*) saloon car; **turista** *nm/f* tourist; **turístico, a** *a* tourist *cpd*.

turnar [tur'nar] *vi*, ~**se** *vr* to take (it in) turns; **turno** *nm* (*INDUSTRIA*) shift; (*oportunidad*, *orden de prioridad*) opportunity; (*DEPORTE etc*) turn.

turquesa [tur'kesa] *nf* turquoise.

Turquía [tur'kia] *nf* Turkey.

turrón [tu'rron] *nm* (*dulce*) nougat; (*fam*) sinecure.

tutear [tute'ar] *vt* to address as familiar 'tú'; ~**se** *vr* to be on familiar terms.

tutela [tu'tela] *nf* (*legal*) guardianship; (*instrucción*) guidance; **tutelar** *a* tutelary // *vt* to protect.

tutor, a [tu'tor, a] *nm/f* (*legal*) guardian; (*ESCOL*) tutor.

tuve, tuviera *etc vb ver* **tener.**

tuyo, a ['tujo, a] *a* yours, of yours // *pron* yours; **los** ~**s** (*fam*) your relations, your family.

TVE *nf abr de* **Televisión Española.**

U

u [u] *conj* or.

ubérrimo, a [u'ßerrimo, a] *a* very rich, fertile.

ubicar [ußi'kar] *vt* (*AM*) to place, situate; (*: fig*) to install in a post; ~**se** *vr* to lie, be located.

ubicuo, a [u'ßikwo, a] *a* ubiquitous.

ubre ['ußre] *nf* udder.

U.C.D. *abr de* **Unión del Centro Democrático.**

Ud(s) *abr de* **usted(es).**

ufanarse [ufa'narse] *vr* to boast; ~ **de** to pride o.s. on; **ufano, a** *a* (*arrogante*) arrogant; (*presumido*) conceited.

U.G.T. *abr de* **Unión General de Trabajadores.**

ujier [u'xjer] *nm* usher; (*portero*) doorkeeper.

úlcera ['ulθera] *nf* ulcer; **ulcerar** *vt* to make sore; **ulcerarse** *vr* to ulcerate.

ulterior [ulte'rjor] *a* (*más allá*) farther, further; (*subsecuente*, *siguiente*) subsequent; ~**mente** *ad* later, subsequently.

últimamente [ultima'mente] *ad* (*recientemente*) lately, recently; (*finalmente*) finally; (*como último recurso*) as a last resort.

ultimar [ulti'mar] *vt* to finish; (*finalizar*) to finalize; (*AM: rematar*) to finish off.

último, a ['ultimo, a] *a* last; (*más reciente*) latest, most recent; (*más bajo*) bottom; (*más alto*) top; (*fig*) final, extreme; **en las** ~**as** on one's last legs; **por** ~ finally.

ultra ['ultra] *a* ultra // *nm/f* extreme right-winger.

ultrajar [ultra'xar] *vt* (*escandalizar*) to outrage; (*insultar*) to insult, abuse; **ultraje** *nm* outrage, insult.

ultramar [ultra'mar] *nm*: **de** *o* **en** ~ abroad, overseas; ~**ino, a** *a* overseas, foreign; ~**inos** *nmpl* groceries; **tienda de** ~**inos** grocer's (shop).

ultranza [ul'tranθa]: **a** ~ *ad* to the death; (*a todo trance*) at all costs; (*completo*) outright.

ultrasónico, a [ultra'soniko, a] *a* ultrasonic.

ulular [ulu'lar] *vi* to howl; (*búho*) to hoot.

umbral [um'bral] *nm* (*gen*) threshold.

umbroso, a [um'broso, a], **umbrío, a** [um'brio, a] *a* shady.

un, una [un, 'una] *det a* // *num* one; *ver* **uno.**

unánime [u'nanime] *a* unanimous; **unanimidad** *nf* unanimity.

unción [un'θjon] *nf* anointing; **extrema** ~ Extreme Unction.

undécimo, a [un'deθimo, a] *a* eleventh.

undular [undu'lar] *vi ver* **ondular.**

ungir [un'xir] *vt* to rub with ointment; (*REL*) to anoint.

ungüento [un'gwento] *nm* ointment; *(fig)* salve, balm.

únicamente ['unikamente] *ad* solely; *(solamente)* only; **único, a** *a* only; *(solo)* sole, single; *(sin par)* unique.

unidad [uni'ðað] *nf* unity; *(TEC)* unit.

unido, a [u'niðo, a] *a* joined, linked; *(fig)* united.

unificar [unifi'kar] *vt* to unite, unify.

uniformar [unifor'mar] *vt* to make uniform, level up; *(persona)* to put into uniform; **uniforme** *a* uniform, equal; *(superficie)* even // *nm* uniform; **uniformidad** *nf* uniformity; *(llaneza)* levelness, evenness.

unilateral [unilate'ral] *a* unilateral.

unión [u'njon] *nf* (*gen*) union; *(acto)* uniting, joining; *(calidad)* unity; *(TEC)* joint; *(fig)* closeness, togetherness; **la U~ Soviética** the Soviet Union.

unir [u'nir] *vt* (*juntar*) to join, unite; *(atar)* to tie, fasten; *(combinar)* to combine // *vi* to mix well; **~se** *vr* to join together, unite; *(empresas)* to merge.

unísono [u'nisono] *nm*: **al ~** in unison.

universal [uniβer'sal] *a* universal; *(mundial)* world *cpd*.

universidad [uniβersi'ðað] *nf* university.

universo [uni'βerso] *nm* universe.

uno ['uno] *num, det* one // *pron* one; *(alguien)* someone, somebody; **~s some, a few; ~ a ~, ~ por ~** one by one; **cada ~** each *or* every one; **estar en ~** to be at one; **~ que otro** some, a few; **~s y otros** all of them; **~ y otro** both.

untar [un'tar] *vt* (*gen*) to rub; *(engrasar)* to grease, oil; *(MED)* to rub with ointment; *(fig)* to bribe; **~se** *vr* to be crooked; **unto** *nm* animal fat; *(MED)* ointment; *(fam)* slush fund.

uña ['uɲa] *nf* (*ANAT*) nail; *(garra)* claw; *(casco)* hoof; *(arrancaclavos)* claw.

uranio [u'ranjo] *nm* uranium.

urbanidad [urβani'ðað] *nf* courtesy, politeness.

urbanismo [urβa'nismo] *nm* town planning.

urbanización [urβaniθa'θjon] *nf* housing scheme.

urbano, a [ur'βano, a] *a* (*de ciudad*) urban; *(cortés)* courteous, polite.

urbe ['urβe] *nf* large city.

urdimbre [ur'ðimbre] *nf* (*de tejido*) warp; *(intriga)* intrigue; **urdir** *vt* to warp; *(fig)* to plot, contrive.

urgencia [ur'xenθja] *nf* urgency; *(prisa)* haste, rush; **servicios de ~** emergency services; **urgente** *a* urgent; *(insistente)* insistent; **urgir** *vi* to be urgent.

urinario, a [uri'narjo, a] *a* urinary // *nm* urinal.

urna ['urna] *nf* urn; *(POL)* ballot box.

urraca [u'rraka] *nf* magpie.

URSS *nf*: **la ~** the USSR.

Uruguay [uru'xwai] *nm*: **el ~** Uruguay; **uruguayo, a** *a, nm/f* Uruguayan.

usado, a [u'saðo, a] *a* (*gen*) used; *(ropa etc)* worn.

usanza [u'sanθa] *nf* custom, usage.

usar [u'sar] *vt* to use; *(ropa)* to wear; *(tener costumbre)* to be in the habit of; **~se** *vr* to be used; **uso** *nm* use; wear; *(costumbre)* usage, custom; *(moda)* fashion; **al uso** in keeping with custom; **al uso de** in the style of.

usted [us'teð] *pron* you.

usual [u'swal] *a* usual.

usuario, a [u'swarjo, a] *nm/f* user.

usura [u'sura] *nf* usury; **usurero, a** *nm/f* usurer.

usurpar [usur'par] *vt* to usurp.

utensilio [uten'siljo] *nm* tool; *(CULIN)* utensil.

útero ['utero] *nm* uterus, womb.

útil ['util] *a* useful // *nm* tool; **utilidad** *nf* usefulness; *(COM)* profit; **utilizar** *vt* to use, utilize.

utopía [uto'pia] *nf* Utopia; **utópico, a** *a* Utopian.

uva ['uβa] *nf* grape.

V

v *abr de* **voltio.**

va *vb ver* **ir.**

vaca ['baka] *nf* (*animal*) cow; *(carne)* beef; *(cuero)* cowhide.

vacaciones [baka'θjones] *nfpl* holidays.

vacante [ba'kante] *a* vacant, empty // *nf* vacancy.

vacar [ba'kar] *vi* to fall vacant; **~ a o en** to devote o.s. to.

vaciado, a [ba'θjaðo, a] *a* (*hecho en molde*) cast in a mould; *(hueco)* hollow // *nm* cast.

vaciar [ba'θjar] *vt* to empty out; *(ahuecar)* to hollow out; *(moldear)* to cast // *vi* (*río*) to flow (*en* into); **~se** *vr* to empty; *(fig)* to blab, spill the beans.

vaciedad [baθje'ðað] *nf* emptiness.

vacilación [baθila'θjon] *nf* hesitation; **vacilante** *a* unsteady; *(habla)* faltering; *(fig)* hesitant; **vacilar** *vi* to be unsteady; to falter; to hesitate, waver; *(persona)* to stagger, stumble; *(memoria)* to fail.

vacío, a [ba'θio, a] *a* empty; *(puesto)* vacant; *(desocupado)* idle; *(vano)* vain // *nm* emptiness; *(FISICA)* vacuum; *(un ~)* (empty) space.

vacuna [ba'kuna] *nf* vaccine; **vacunar** *vt* to vaccinate.

vacuno, a [ba'kuno, a] *a* bovine.

vacuo, a ['bakwo, a] *a* empty.

vadear [baðe'ar] *vt* (*río*) to ford; *(problema)* to overcome; *(persona)* to sound out; **vado** *nm* ford; *(solución)* solution; *(descanso)* respite.

vagabundo, a [baxa'βundo, a] *a* wandering; *(pey)* vagrant // *nm* tramp.

vagamente [baxa'mente] *ad* vaguely.

vagancia [ba'xanθja] *nf* vagrancy; **vagar** *vi* (*gen*) to wander; *(no hacer nada)* to idle // *nm* leisure.

vagido [ba'xiðo] *nm* wail.

vagina [ba'xina] *nf* vagina.

vago, a ['baxo, a] *a* vague; (*perezoso*) lazy; (*ambulante*) wandering // *nm/f* (*vagabundo*) tramp; (*flojo*) lazybones *sg*, idler.

vagón [ba'xon] *nm* (*de pasajeros*) carriage; (*de mercancías*) wagon.

vaguedad [baxe'ðað] *nf* vagueness.

vaho ['bao] *nm* (*vapor*) vapour, steam; (*olor*) smell; (*respiración*) breath.

vaina ['baina] *nf* sheath.

vainilla [bai'niʎa] *nf* vanilla.

vais *vb ver* **ir.**

vaivén [bai'ßen] *nm* to-and-fro movement; (*de tránsito*) coming and going; **vaivenes** *nmpl* (*fig*) ups and downs.

vajilla [ba'xiʎa] *nf* crockery, dishes *pl.*

val, valdré *etc vb ver* **valer.**

vale ['bale] *nm* voucher; (*recibo*) receipt; (*pagaré*) I.O.U.

valedero, a [bale'ðero, a] *a* valid.

valenciano, a [balen θjano, a] *a* Valencian.

valentía [balen'tia] *nf* courage, bravery; (*pey*) boastfulness; (*acción*) heroic deed; **valentón, ona** *a* blustering.

valer [ba'ler] *vt* to aid, protect; (*MAT*) to equal // *vi* to be worth; (*costar*) to cost; (*ser útil*) to be useful; (*ser válido*) to be valid; **~se** *vr* to defend o.s.; **~se de** to make use of, take advantage of // *nm* worth, value; **~ la pena** to be worthwhile; ¿**vale?** O. K.?

valgo *etc vb ver* **valer.**

validar [bali'ðar] *vt* to validate; **validez** *nf* validity; **válido, a** *a* valid.

valiente [ba'ljente] *a* brave, valiant; (*pey*) boastful // *nm* hero.

valija [ba'lixa] *nf* case; (*mochila*) satchel.

valioso, a [ba'ljoso, a] *a* valuable; (*rico*) wealthy.

valor [ba'lor] *nm* value, worth; (*precio*) price; (*valentía*) valour, courage; (*importancia*) importance; **~es** *nmpl* (*COM*) securities; **~ación** *nf* valuation; **~ar** *vt* to value.

vals [bals] *nm* waltz.

válvula ['baißula] *nf* valve.

valla ['baʎa] *nf* fence; (*DEPORTE*) hurdle; (*fig*) barrier; **vallar** *vt* to fence in.

valle ['baʎe] *nm* valley, vale.

vamos *vb ver* **ir.**

vampiro, resa [bam'piro, i'resa] *nm/f* vampire.

van *vb ver* **ir.**

vanagloriarse [banaxlo'rjarse] *vr* to boast.

vándalo, a ['bandalo, a] *nm/f* vandal; **vandalismo** *nm* vandalism.

vanguardia [ban'gwardja] *nf* vanguard; (*ARTE*) avant-garde.

vanidad [bani'ðað] *nf* vanity; (*irrealidad*) unreality; **vanidoso, a** *a* vain, conceited.

vano, a ['bano, a] *a* (*irreal*) unreal; (*irracional*) unreasonable; (*inútil*) useless;

(*persona*) vain, conceited; (*frívolo*) frivolous.

vapor [ba'por] *nm* vapour; (*vaho*) steam; (*neblina*) mist; **~es** *nmpl* (*MED*) hysterics; **al ~** (*CULIN*) steamed; **~izar** *vt* to vaporize; **~oso, a** *a* vaporous; (*vahoso*) steamy.

vaquero, a [ba'kero, a] *a* cattle *cpd* // *nm* cowboy; **~s** *mpl* jeans.

vara ['bara] *nf* stick, wand; (*TEC*) rod.

varear [bare'ar] *vt* to hit, beat.

variable [ba'rjaßle] *a, nf* variable; **variación** *nf* variation; **variar** *vt* to vary; (*modificar*) to modify; (*cambiar de posición*) to switch around // *vi* to vary; **variedad** *nf* variety.

varilla [ba'riʎe] *nf* stick; (*BOT*) twig; (*TEC*) rod; (*de rueda*) spoke.

vario, a ['bario, a] *a* (*variado*) varied; (*multicolor*) motley; (*cambiable*) changeable; **~s** various, several.

varón [ba'ron] *nm* male, man; **varonil** *a* manly.

Varsovia [bar'soßja] *n* Warsaw.

vas *vb ver* **ir.**

vascongado, a [baskon'xaðo, a], **vascuence** [bas'kwenθe], **vasco, a** ['basko, a] *a* Basque; **las Vascongadas** the Basque Country.

vaselina [base'lina] *nf* vaseline.

vasija [ba'sixa] *nf* container, vessel.

vaso ['baso] *nm* glass, tumbler; (*ANAT*) vessel.

vástago ['bastaxo] *nm* (*BOT*) shoot; (*TEC*) rod; (*fig*) offspring.

vasto, a ['basto, a] *a* vast, huge.

Vaticano [bati'kano] *nm*: **el ~** the Vatican.

vaticinio [bati'θinjo] *nm* prophecy.

vatio ['batjo] *nm* (*ELEC*) watt.

vaya *etc vb ver* **ir.**

Vd(s) *abr de* **usted(es).**

ve *vb ver* **ir, ver.**

vecindad [beθin'dað] *nf*, **vecindario** [beθin'darjo] *nm* neighbourhood; (*habitantes*) residents *pl*; **vecino, a** *a* neighbouring // *nm/f* neighbour; (*residente*) resident.

veda ['beða] *nf* prohibition.

vedado [be'ðaðo] *nm* preserve.

vedar [be'ðar] *vt* (*prohibir*) to ban, prohibit; (*impedir*) to stop, prevent.

vegetación [bexeta'θjon] *nf* vegetation.

vegetal [bexe'tal] *a nm* vegetable.

vehemencia [bee'menθja] *nf* (*insistencia*) vehemence; (*pasión*) passion; (*fervor*) fervour; (*violencia*) violence; **vehemente** *a* vehement; passionate; fervent.

vehículo [be'ikulo] *nm* vehicle; (*MED*) carrier.

veía *etc vb ver* **ver.**

veinte ['beinte] *num* twenty.

vejación [bexa'θjon] *nf* vexation; (*humillación*) humiliation.

vejamen [be'xamen] *nm* satire.

vejar [be'xar] vt (irritar) to annoy, vex; (humillar) to humiliate.
vejez [be'xeθ] nf old age.
vejiga [be'xiɣa] nf (ANAT) bladder.
vela ['bela] nf (de cera) candle; (NAUT) sail; (insomnio) sleeplessness; (vigilia) vigil; (MIL) sentry duty; (fam) snot; **estar a dos ~s** (fam) to be skint (fam).
velado, a [be'laðo, a] a veiled; (sonido) muffled; (FOTO) blurred // nf soirée.
velador [bela'ðor] nm watchman; (candelero) candlestick.
velar [be'lar] vt (hacer guardia) to keep watch over; (cubrir) to veil // vi to stay awake; **~ por** to watch over, look after.
veleidad [belei'ðað] nf (ligereza) fickleness; (capricho) whim.
velero [be'lero] nm (NAUT) sailing ship; (AVIAT) glider.
veleta [be'leta] nf weather vane.
velo ['belo] nm veil.
velocidad [beloθi'ðað] nf speed; (TEC, AUTO) gear.
velocímetro [belo'θimetro] nm speedometer.
velódromo [be'loðromo] nm cycle track.
veloz [be'loθ] a fast.
vello ['beʎo] nm down, fuzz; **vellón** nm fleece; **~so, a** a fuzzy; **velludo, a** a shaggy // nm plush, velvet.
ven vb ver **venir**.
vena ['bena] nf vein.
venablo [be'naβlo] nm javelin.
venado [be'naðo] nm deer.
venal [be'nal] a (ANAT) venous; (pey) venal; **~idad** nf venality.
vencedor, a [benθe'ðor, a] a victorious // nm/f victor, winner.
vencer [ben'θer] vt (dominar) to defeat, beat; (derrotar) to vanquish; (superar, controlar) to overcome, master // vi (triunfar) to win (through), triumph; (plazo) to expire; **vencido, a** a (derrotado) defeated, beaten; (COM) due // ad: **pagar vencido** to pay in arrears; **vencimiento** nm collapse; (COM) maturity.
venda ['benda] nf bandage; **~je** nm bandage, dressing; **vendar** vt to bandage; **vendar los ojos** to blindfold.
vendaval [benda'βal] nm (viento) gale; (huracán) hurricane.
vendedor, a [bende'ðor, a] nm/f seller.
vender [ben'der] vt to sell; **~ al contado/al por mayor/al por menor** to sell for cash/wholesale/retail.
vendimia [ben'dimja] nf grape harvest.
vendré etc vb ver **venir**.
veneno [be'neno] nm poison, venom; **~so, a** a poisonous.
venerable [bene'raβle] a venerable; **veneración** nf veneration; **venerar** vt (reconocer) to venerate; (adorar) to worship.
venéreo, a [be'nereo, a] a venereal.
venero [be'nero] nm (veta) seam, lode; (fuente) spring.

venezolano, a [beneθo'lano, a] a Venezuelan.
Venezuela [bene'θwela] nf Venezuela.
venganza [ben'ganθa] nf vengeance, revenge; **vengar** vt to avenge; **vengarse** vr to take revenge; **vengativo, a** a (persona) vindictive.
vengo etc vb ver **venir**.
venia ['benja] nf (perdón) pardon; (permiso) consent.
venial [be'njal] a venial.
venida [be'niða] nf (llegada) arrival; (regreso) return; (fig) rashness.
venidero, a [beni'ðero, a] a coming, future.
venir [be'nir] vi to come; (llegar) to arrive; (fig) to stem from; (ocurrir) to happen; **~ bien/mal** to be suitable/unsuitable; **el año que viene** next year; **~se abajo** to collapse.
venta ['benta] nf (COM) sale; **~ a plazos** hire purchase; **~ al contado/al por mayor/al por menor o al detalle** cash sale/ wholesale/retail; **~ de liquidación** clearance sale.
ventaja [ben'taxa] nf advantage; **ventajoso, a** a advantageous.
ventana [ben'tana] nf window; **~ de guillotina/saltediza** sash/bay window; **ventanilla** nf (de taquilla) window (of booking office etc).
ventear [bente'ar] vt (ropa) to hang out to dry; (oler) to sniff // vi (investigar) to investigate; (soplar) to blow; **~se** vr (romperse) to crack; (ANAT) to break wind.
ventilación [bentila'θjon] nf ventilation; (corriente) draught; **ventilar** vt to ventilate; (a secar) to put out to dry; (fig) to air, discuss.
ventisca [ben'tiska] nf, **ventisquero** [bentis'kero] nm blizzard; (nieve amontonada) snowdrift.
ventosear [bentose'ar] vi to break wind.
ventoso, a [ben'toso, a] a windy.
ventrílocuo, a [ben'trilokwo, a] nm/f ventriloquist; **ventriloquia** nf ventriloquism.
ventura [ben'tura] nf (felicidad) happiness; (buena suerte) luck; (destino) fortune; **a la (buena) ~** at random; **venturoso, a** a happy; (afortunado) lucky, fortunate.
veo etc vb ver **ver**.
ver [ber] vt, vi to see; (mirar) to look at, watch; (investigar) to look into; **~se** vr (encontrarse) to meet; (dejarse) to be seen; (hallarse: en un apuro) to find o.s., be // nm looks pl, appearance; **a ~** let's see; **dejarse ~** to become apparent; **no tener nada que ~ con** to have nothing to do with; **a mi modo de ~** as I see it.
vera ['bera] nf edge, verge; (de río) bank.
veracidad [beraθi'ðað] nf truthfulness.
veranear [berane'ar] vi to spend the summer; **veraneo** nm summer holiday; **veraniego, a** a summer cpd; **verano** nm summer.

veras ['beras] *nfpl* truth *sg*; **de ~** really, truly.

veraz [be'raθ] *a* truthful.

verbal [ber'ßal] *a* verbal.

verbena [ber'ßena] *nf* street party.

verbigracia [berßi'xraθja] *ad* for example.

verbo [ber'ßo] *nm* verb; **~so, a** *a* verbose.

verdad [ber'ðað] *nf* (*lo verídico*) truth; (*fiabilidad*) reliability // *ad* really; **de ~** *a* real, proper; **a decir ~** to tell the truth; **~ero, a** *a* (*veraz*) true, truthful; (*fiable*) reliable; (*fig*) real.

verde ['berðe] *a* green; (*sucio*) blue, dirty // *nm* green; **viejo ~** dirty old man; **~ar, ~cer** *vi* to turn green; **verdor** *nm* (*lo ~*) greenness; (*BOT*) verdure; (*fig*) youthful vigour.

verdugo [ber'ðuxo] *nm* executioner; (*BOT*) shoot; (*cardenal*) weal.

verdulero, a [berðu'lero, a] *nm/f* greengrocer.

verdura [ber'ðura] *nf* greenness; **~s** *nfp.* (*CULIN*) greens.

vereda [be'reða] *nf* path.

veredicto [bere'ðikto] *nm* verdict.

vergonzoso, a [berxon'θoso, a] *a* shameful; (*tímido*) timid, bashful.

vergüenza [ber'xwenθa] *nf* shame, sense of shame; (*timidez*) bashfulness; (*pudor*) modesty.

verídico, a [be'riðiko, a] *a* true, truthful.

verificar [berifi'kar] *vt* to check; (*corroborar*) to verify; (*llevar a cabo*) to carry out; **~se** *vr* to occur, happen.

verja ['berxa] *nf* grating.

vermut [ber'mut] *nm* vermouth.

verosímil [bero'simil] *a* likely, probable; (*relato*) credible.

verruga [be'rruxa] *nf* wart.

versado, a [ber'saðo, a] *a*: **~ en** versed in.

versar [ber'sar] *vi* to go round, turn.

versátil [ber'satil] *a* versatile.

versión [ber'sjon] *nf* version; (*traducción*) translation.

verso ['berso] *nm* (*gen*) verse; **un ~** a line of poetry.

vértebra ['berteßra] *nf* vertebra.

verter [ber'ter] *vt* (*vaciar*) to empty, pour (out); (*tirar*) to dump // *vi* to flow.

vertical [berti'kal] *a* vertical.

vértice ['bertiθe] *nm* vertex, apex.

vertiente [ber'tjente] *nf* slope.

vertiginoso, a [bertixi'noso, a] *a* giddy, dizzy; **vértigo** *nm* vertigo; (*mareo*) dizziness.

vesícula [be'sikula] *nf* blister.

vespertino, a [besper'tino, a] *a* evening *cpd*.

vestíbulo [bes'tißulo] *nm* hall; (*de teatro*) foyer.

vestido [bes'tiðo] *nm* (*ropa*) clothes *pl*, clothing; (*de mujer*) dress, frock.

vestigio [bes'tixjo] *nm* (*trazo*) trace; (*señal*) sign; **~s** *nmpl* remains.

vestimenta [besti'menta] *nf* clothing.

vestir [bes'tir] *vt* (*poner: ropa*) to put on; (*llevar: ropa*) to wear; (*cubrir*) to clothe, cover; (*pagar: la ropa*) to pay for the clothing of; (*sastre*) to make clothes for // *vi* (*ponerse: ropa*) to dress; (*verse bien*) to look good; **~se** *vr* to get dressed, dress o.s.

vestuario [bes'twarjo] *nm* clothes *pl*, wardrobe; (*TEATRO*) dressing room; (*DEPORTE*) changing room.

veta ['beta] *nf* (*vena*) vein, seam; (*raya*) streak; (*de madera*) grain.

vetar [be'tar] *vt* to veto.

veterano, a [bete'rano, a] *a, nm* veteran.

veterinario, a [beteri'narjo, a] *nm/f* vet(erinary surgeon) // *nf* veterinary science.

veto ['beto] *nm* veto.

vetusto, a [be'tusto, a] *a* ancient.

vez [beθ] *nf* time; (*turno*) turn; **a la ~ que** at the same time as; **a su ~** in its turn; **cada ~ más/menos** more and more/less and less; **una ~** once; **de una ~** in one go; **de una ~ para siempre** once and for all; **en ~ de** instead of; **a veces** sometimes; **una y otra ~** repeatedly; **de ~ en cuando** from time to time; **7 veces 9** 7 times 9; **hacer las veces de** to stand in for; **tal ~** perhaps.

v. g., v. gr. *abr de* **verbigracia**.

vía ['bia] *nf* track, route; (*FERRO*) line; (*fig*) way; (*ANAT*) passage, tube // *prep* via, by way of; **por ~ judicial** by legal means; **por ~ oficial** through official channels; **por ~** by way of; **en ~s de** in the process of; **~ aérea** airway.

viaducto [bja'ðukto] *nm* viaduct.

viajante [bja'xante] *nm* commercial traveller.

viajar [bja'xar] *vi* to travel; **viaje** *nm* journey; (*gira*) tour; (*NAUT*) voyage; **estar de viaje** to be on a journey; **viaje de ida y vuelta** round trip; **viaje de novios** honeymoon; **viajero, a** *a* travelling; (*ZOOL*) migratory // *nm/f* (*quien viaja*) traveller; (*pasajero*) passenger.

vial [bjal] *a* road *cpd*, traffic *cpd*.

víbora ['bißora] *nf* viper.

vibración [bißra'θjon] *nf* vibration; **vibrador** *nm* vibrator; **vibrante** *a* vibrant; **vibrar** *vt, vi* to vibrate.

vicario [bi'karjo] *nm* curate.

vicepresidente [biθepresi'ðente] *nm/f* vice president.

viciado, a [bi'θjaðo, a] *a* (*corrompido*) corrupt; (*contaminado*) foul, contaminated; **viciar** *vt* (*pervertir*) to pervert; (*adulterar*) to adulterate; (*falsificar*) to falsify; (*JUR*) to nullify; (*estropear*) to spoil; (*sentido*) to twist; **viciarse** *vr* to become corrupted.

vicio ['biθjo] *nm* (*libertinaje*) vice; (*mala costumbre*) bad habit; (*mimo*) spoiling; (*alabeo*) warp, warping; **~so, a** *a* (*muy malo*) vicious; (*corrompido*) depraved; (*mimado*) spoiled // *nm/f* depraved person.

vicisitud [biθisi'tuð] *nf* vicissitude.

víctima ['biktima] *nf* victim.
victoria [bik'torja] *nf* victory; **victorioso, a** *a* victorious.
vicuña [bi'kuɲa] *nf* vicuna.
vid [bið] *nf* vine.
vida ['biða] *nf* (*gen*) life; (*duración*) lifetime; **de por** ~ for life; **en la/mi** ~ never; **estar con** ~ to be still alive; **ganarse la** ~ to earn one's living.
vidriero, a [bi'ðrjero, a] *nm/f* glazier // *nf* (*ventana*) stained-glass window; (*puerta*) glass door.
vidrio ['biðrjo] *nm* glass; ~**so, a** *a* glassy; (*frágil*) fragile, brittle; (*resbaladizo*) slippery.
viejo, a ['bjexo, a] *a* old // *nm/f* old man/woman.
vienes *etc vb ver* **venir**.
vienés, esa [bje'nes, esa] *a* Viennese.
viento ['bjento] *nm* wind; (*olfato*) scent.
vientre ['bjentre] *nm* belly; (*matriz*) womb; ~**s** *nmpl* bowels.
viernes ['bjernes] *nm inv* Friday.
Vietnam [bjet'nam] *nm*: **el** ~ Vietnam; **vietnamita** *a* Vietnamese.
viga ['bixa] *nf* beam, rafter.
vigencia [bi'xenθja] *nf* validity; **estar en** ~ to be in force; **vigente** *a* valid, in force; (*imperante*) prevailing.
vigésimo, a [bi'xesimo, a] *a* twentieth.
vigía [bi'xia] *nm* look-out // *nf* (*atalaya*) watchtower; (*acción*) watching.
vigilancia [bixi'lanθja] *nf* vigilance; **vigilar** *vt* to watch over // *vi* (*gen*) to be vigilant; (*hacer guardia*) to keep watch.
vigilia [vi'xilja] *nf* wakefulness, being awake; (*REL*) fast; **comer de** ~ to fast.
vigor [bi'xor] *nm* vigour, vitality; **en** ~ in force; **entrar/poner en** ~ to take/put into effect; ~**oso, a** *a* vigorous.
vil [bil] *a* vile, low; ~**eza** *nf* vileness; (*acto*) base deed.
vilipendiar [bilipen'djar] *vt* to vilify, revile.
vilo ['bilo]: **en** ~ *ad* in the air, suspended.
villa ['biʎa] *nf* (*pueblo*) small town; (*municipalidad*) municipality.
villorrio [bi'ʎorrjo] *nm* one-horse town, dump (*fam*).
vinagre [bi'naxre] *nm* vinegar.
vinculación [binkula'θjon] *nf* (*lazo*) link, bond; (*acción*) linking; **vincular** *vt* to link, bind; **vínculo** *nm* link, bond.
vindicar [bindi'kar] *vt* to vindicate; (*vengar*) to avenge; (*JUR*) to claim.
vine *etc vb ver* **venir**.
vinicultura [binikul'tura] *nf* wine growing.
viniera *etc vb ver* **venir**.
vino ['bino] *nm* wine.
viña ['biɲa] *nf*, **viñedo** [bi'ɲeðo] *nm* vineyard.
violación [bjola'θjon] *nf* violation; ~ **(sexual)** rape; **violar** *vt* to violate; to rape.
violencia [bjo'lenθja] *nf* (*fuerza*) violence,

force; (*embarazo*) embarrassment; (*acto injusto*) unjust act; **violentar** *vt* to force; (*casa*) to break into; (*agredir*) to assault; (*violar*) to violate; **violento, a** *a* violent; (*furioso*) furious; (*situación*) embarrassing; (*acto*) forced, unnatural; (*difícil*) awkward.
violeta [bjo'leta] *nf* violet.
violín [bjo'lin] *r.m* violin.
violón [bjo'lon] *nm* double bass.
viraje [bi'raxe] *nm* turn; (*de vehículo*) swerve; (*de carretera*) bend; (*fig*) change of direction; **virar** *vt, vi* to change direction.
virgen ['birxen] *a, nf* virgin.
Virgo ['birxo] *nm* Virgo.
viril [bi'ril] *a* virile; ~**idad** *nf* virility.
virtualmente [birtwal'mente] *ad* virtually.
virtud [bir'tuð] *nf* virtue; **virtuoso, a** *a* virtuous // *nm/f* virtuoso.
viruela [bi'rwela] *nf* smallpox; ~**s** *nfpl* pockmarks; ~**s locas** chickenpox.
virulento, a [biru'lento, a] *a* virulent.
virus ['birus] *nm* virus.
visado [bi'saðo] *nm* visa.
viscoso, a [bis'koso, a] *a* viscous.
visera [bi'sera] *nf* visor.
visibilidad [bisiβili'ðað] *nf* visibility; **visible** *a* visible; (*fig*) obvious.
visión [bi'sjon] *nf* (*ANAT*) vision, (eye)sight; (*fantasía*) vision, fantasy; (*panorama*) view; **visionario, a** *a* (*que prevee*) visionary; (*alucinado*) deluded // *nm/f* visionary; (*chalado*) lunatic.
visita [bi'sita] *nf* call, visit; (*persona*) visitor; **visitar** *vt* to visit, call on; (*inspeccionar*) to inspect.
vislumbrar [bislum'brar] *vt* to glimpse, catch a glimpse of; **vislumbre** *nf* glimpse; (*centelleo*) gleam; (*idea vaga*) glimmer.
viso ['biso] *nm* (*del metal*) glint, gleam; (*de tela*) sheen; (*aspecto*) appearance.
visón [bi'son] *nm* mink.
visor [bi'sor] *nm* (*FOTO*) viewfinder.
víspera ['bispera] *nf* eve, day before.
vista ['bista] *nf* sight, vision; (*capacidad de ver*) (eye)sight; (*mirada*) look(s) (*pl*) // *nm* customs officer; **a primera** ~ at first glance; **hacer la** ~ **gorda** to turn a blind eye; **volver la** ~ to look back; **está a la** ~ **que** it's obvious that; **en** ~ **de** in view of; **en** ~ **de que** in view of the fact that; **¡hasta la** ~! so long!, see you!; **con** ~**s a** with a view to; ~**zo** *nm* glance; **dar** *o* **echar un** ~**zo a** to glance at.
visto *etc vb ver* **vestir**.
visto, a ['bisto, a] *pp de* **ver** // *a* seen; (*considerado*) considered // *nm*: ~ **bueno** approval; **'**~ **bueno'** approved; **por lo** ~ evidently; **está** ~ **que** it's clear that; **está bien/mal** ~ it's acceptable/unacceptable; ~ **que** *conj* since, considering that.
vistoso, a [bis'toso, a] *a* colourful; (*alegre*) gay; (*pey*) gaudy.
vital [bi'tal] *a* life *cpd*, living *cpd*; (*fig*) vital; (*persona*) lively, vivacious; ~**icio, a** *a* for life.

vitamina [bita'mina] *nf* vitamin.

viticultor, a [bitikul'tor, a] *nm/f* vine grower; **viticultura** *nf* vine growing.

vitorear [bitore'ar] *vt* to cheer, acclaim.

vítreo, a [ˈbitreo, a] *a* vitreous.

vitrina [bi'trina] *nf* glass case.

vituperar [bitupe'rar] *vt* to condemn; **vituperio** *nm* (*condena*) condemnation; (*censura*) censure; (*insulto*) insult.

viudo, a [ˈbjuðo, a] *nm/f* widower/widow; **viudez** *nf* widowhood.

vivacidad [biβaθi'ðað] *nf* (*vigor*) vigour; (*vida*) vivacity.

vivaracho, a [biβa'ratʃo, a] *a* jaunty, lively; (*ojos*) bright, twinkling.

vivaz [bi'βaθ] *a* (*que dura*) enduring; (*vigoroso*) vigorous; (*vivo*) lively.

víveres [ˈbiβeres] *nmpl* provisions.

viveza [bi'βeθa] *nf* liveliness; (*agudeza*) sharpness.

vivienda [bi'βjenda] *nf* (*alojamiento*) housing; (*morada*) dwelling.
0**Aviviente** [bi'βjente] *a* living.

vivificar [biβifi'kar] *vt* to give life to.

vivir [bi'βir] *vt, vi* to live // *nm* life, living.

vivo, a [ˈbiβo, a] *a* living, live, alive; (*fig*) vivid; (*astuto*) smart, clever; **llegar a lo** ~ to cut to the quick.

vocablo [bo'kaβlo] *nm* (*palabra*) word; (*término*) term.

vocabulario [bokaβu'larjo] *nm* vocabulary.

vocación [boka'θjon] *nf* vocation.

vocal [bo'kal] *a* vocal // *nf* vowel; ~**izar** *vt* to vocalize.

vocear [boθe'ar] *vt* (*para vender*) to cry; (*aclamar*) to acclaim; (*fig*) to proclaim // *vi* to yell; **vocerío** *nm*, **vocería** *nf* shouting.

vocero [bo'θero] *nm/f* spokesman/woman.

vociferar [boθife'rar] *vt* to shout; (*jactarse*) to proclaim boastfully // *vi* to yell.

vocinglero, a [boθin'glero, a] *a* vociferous; (*gárrulo*) garrulous; (*fig*) blatant.

vodka [ˈboðka] *nf* vodka.

vol *abr de* **volumen**.

volador, a [bola'ðor, a] *a* flying.

volante [bo'lante] *a* flying // *nm* (*de máquina, coche*) steering wheel; (*de reloj*) balance.

volar [bo'lar] *vt* (*demoler*) to blow up, demolish // *vi* to fly.

volátil [bo'latil] *a* volatile; (*fig*) changeable.

volcán [bol'kan] *nm* volcano; ~**ico, a** *a* volcanic.

volcar [bol'kar] *vt* to upset, overturn (*tumbar, derribar*) to knock over; (*vaciar*) to empty out // *vi* to overturn; ~**se** *vr* to tip over.

volibol [boli'βol] *nm* volleyball.

volición [boli'θjon] *nf* volition.

voltaje [bol'taxe] *nm* voltage.

volteador, a [boltea'ðor, a] *nm/f* acrobat.

voltear [bolte'ar] *vt* to turn over; (*volcar*) to turn upside down; (*doblar*) to peal // *vi* to roll over.

voltio [ˈboltjo] *nm* volt.

voluble [bo'luβle] *a* fickle.

volumen [bo'lumen] *nm* volume; **voluminoso, a** *a* voluminous; (*enorme*) massive.

voluntad [bolun'tað] *nf* will, willpower; (*deseo*) desire, wish; (*afecto*) fondness.

voluntario, a [bolun'tarjo, a] *a* voluntary // *nm/f* volunteer.

voluntarioso, a [bolunta'rjoso, a] *a* headstrong.

voluptuoso, a [bolup'twoso, a] *a* voluptuous.

volver [bol'βer] *vt* (*gen*) to turn; (*dar vuelta*) to turn (over); (*voltear*) to turn round, turn upside down; (*poner al revés*) to turn inside out; (*devolver*) to return; (*transformar*) to change, transform // *vi* to return, go/come back; ~**se** *vr* to turn round; (*llegar a ser*) to become; ~ **la espalda** to turn one's back; ~ **bien por mal** to return good for evil; ~ **a hacer** to do again; ~ **en sí** to come to; ~**se loco** to go mad.

vomitar [bomi'tar] *vt, vi* to vomit; **vómito** *nm* (*acto*) vomiting; (*resultado*) vomit.

voraz [bo'raθ] *a* voracious; (*fig*) fierce.

vórtice [ˈbortiθe] *nm* whirlpool; (*de aire*) whirlwind.

vosotros [bo'sotros] *pron* you.

votación [bota'θjon] *nf* (*acto*) voting; (*voto*) vote; **votar** *vi* to vote; **voto** *nm* vote; (*promesa*) vow; (*maldición*) oath, curse; **votos** (*good*) wishes.

voy *vb ver* **ir**.

voz [boθ] *nf* voice; (*grito*) shout; (*chisme*) rumour; (*LING*) word; **dar voces** to shout, yell; **a media** ~ in a low voice; **a** ~ **en cuello** *o* **en grito** at the top of one's voice; **de viva** ~ verbally; **en** ~ **alta** aloud; ~ **de mando** command.

vuelco [ˈbwelko] *nm* spill, overturning; (*fig*) collapse.

vuelo [ˈbwelo] *vb ver* **volar** // *nm* flight; (*encaje*) lace, frill; (*fig*) importance; **coger al** ~ to catch in flight.

vuelta [ˈbwelta] *nf* (*gen*) turn; (*curva*) bend, curve; (*regreso*) return; (*revolución*) revolution (*paseo*) stroll; (*circuito*) lap; (*de papel, tela*) reverse; (*cambio*) change; **V** ~ **de Francia** Tour de France; ~ **cerrada** hairpin bend; **a la** ~ on one's return; **a** ~ **de correo** by return of post; **dar** ~**s** to turn, revolve; **dar** ~**s a una idea** to turn over an idea (in one's head); **estar de** ~ (*fam*) to be back; **dar una** ~ to go for a walk.

vuelto *pp de* **volver**.

vuelvo *etc vb ver* **volver**.

vuestro, a [ˈbwestro, a] *a* your; **un amigo** ~ a friend of yours // *pron*: **el** ~/**la** ~ a/**los** ~**s**/**las** ~**s** as yours.

vulgar [bul'xar] *a* (*ordinario*) vulgar; (*común*) common; ~**idad** *nf* commonness; (*acto*) vulgarity; (*expresión*) coarse

expression; ~**idades** nfpl banalities;
~**izar** vt to popularize.
vulgo ['bulɣo] nm common people.
vulnerable [bulne'raβle] a vulnerable.
vulnerar [bulne'rar] vt to harm, damage.
vulpino, a [bul'pino, a] a vulpine; (fig)
foxy.

W

wáter ['bater] nm lavatory.
wátman ['watman] a inv (fam) cool.
whisky ['wiski] nm whisky.

X

xenofobia [kseno'foβja] nf xenophobia.
xilófono [ksi'lofono] nm xylophone.

Y

y [i] conj and.
ya [ja] ad (gen) already; (ahora) now; (en
seguida) at once; (pronto) soon // excl all
right! // conj (ahora que) now that; ~ **lo**
sé I know; ~ **dice que sí,** ~ **dice que**
no first he says yes, then he says no; ~
que since.
yacer [ja'θer] vi to lie.
yacimiento [jaθi'mjento] nm bed, deposit.
yanqui ['janki] a Yankee.
yate ['jate] nm yacht.
yazco etc vb ver **yacer.**
yedra ['jeðra] nf ivy.
yegua ['jeɣwa] nf mare.
yema ['jema] nf (del huevo) yoke; (BOT)
leaf bud; (fig) best part; ~ **del dedo**
fingertip.
yergo etc vb ver **erguir.**
yermo, a ['jermo, a] a uninhabited // nm
waste land.
yerno ['jerno] nm son-in-law.
yerro etc vb ver **errar.**
yerto, a ['jerto, a] a stiff.
yesca ['jeska] nf tinder.
yeso ['jeso] nm (GEO) gypsum; (ARQ)
plaster.
yodo ['joðo] nm iodine.
yugo ['juɣo] nm yoke.
Yugoslavia [juɣos'laβja] nf Yugoslavia.
yugular [juɣu'lar] a jugular.
yunque ['junke] nm anvil.
yunta ['junta] nf yoke; **yuntero** nm
ploughman.
yute ['jute] nm jute.
yuxtaponer [jukstapo'ner] vt to
juxtapose; **yuxtaposición** nf juxta-
position.

Z

zafar [θa'far] vt (soltar) to untie;
(superficie) to clear; ~**se** vr (escaparse) to
escape; (ocultarse) to hide o.s. away; (TEC)
to slip off.
zafio, a ['θafjo, a] a coarse.

zafiro [θa'firo] nm sapphire.
zaga ['θaɣa] nf rear; **a la** ~ behind, in the
rear.
zagal, a [θa'ɣal, a] nm/f boy/girl, lad/lass.
zaguán [θa'ɣwan] nm hallway.
zahareño, a [θaa'reɲo, a] a (salvaje) wild;
(arisco) unsociable.
zaherir [θae'rir] vt (criticar) to criticize;
(fig: herir) to wound.
zahorí [θao'ri] nm clairvoyant.
zaino, a ['θaino, a] a (color de caballo)
chestnut; (pérfido) treacherous; (animal)
vicious.
zalamería [θala'merja] nf flattery;
zalamero, a a flattering; (relamido)
suave.
zamarra [θa'marra] nf (piel) sheepskin;
(saco) sheepskin jacket.
zambra ['θambra] nf gypsy dance.
zambullirse [θambu'ʎirse] vr to dive;
(ocultarse) to hide o.s.
zampar [θam'par] vt (esconder) to hide or
put away (hurriedly); (comer) to gobble;
(arrojar) to hurl // vi to eat voraciously;
~**se** vr (chocar) to bump; (fig) to
gatecrash.
zanahoria [θana'orja] nf carrot.
zancada [θan'kaða] nf stride.
zancadilla [θanka'ðiʎa] nf trip; (fig)
stratagem.
zancajo [θan'kaxo] nm (ANAT) heel; (fig)
dwarf.
zanco ['θanko] nm stilt.
zancudo, a [θan'kuðo, a] a long-legged //
nm (AM) mosquito.
zángano ['θangano] nm drone.
zanja ['θanxa] nf (fosa) ditch; (tumba)
grave; (zanjar vt (fosa) to ditch, trench;
(problema) to surmount; (conflicto) to
resolve.
zapapico [θapa'piko] nm pick pickaxe.
zapata [θa'pata] nf half-boot; (MECÁNICA)
shoe.
zapatear [θapate'ar] vt (tocar) to tap with
one's foot; (patear) to kick; (fam) to ill-
treat // vi to tap with one's feet.
zapatería [θapate'ria] nf (oficio)
shoemaking; (tienda) shoe-shop; (fábrica)
shoe factory; **zapatero, a** nm/f
shoemaker.
zapatilla [θapa'tiʎa] nf slipper.
zapato [θa'pato] nm shoe.
zarabanda [θara'βanda] nf saraband; (fig)
whirl.
zaranda [θa'randa] nf sieve; **zarandear** vt
to sieve; (fam) to shake vigorously.
zarcillo [θar'θiʎo] nm earring.
zarpa ['θarpa] nf (garra) claw.
zarpar [θar'par] vi to weigh anchor.
zarza ['θarθa] nf (BOT) bramble; **zarzal** nm
(matorral) bramble patch.
zarzamora [θarθa'mora] nf blackberry.
zarzuela [θar'θwela] nf Spanish light
opera.
zigzag [θiɣ'θaɣ] a zigzag; **zigzaguear** vi to
zigzag.

zinc [θink] nm zinc.
zócalo ['θokalo] nm (ARQ) plinth, base.
zona ['θona] nf zone; ~ fronteriza border
area.
zoología [θoolo'xia] nf zoology; zoológico,
a a zoological // nm zoo; zoólogo, a nm/f
zoologist.
zopilote [θopi'lote] nm (AM) buzzard.
zoquete [θo'kete] nm (madera) block;
(pan) crust; (fam) blockhead.
zorro, a ['θorro, a] a crafty // nm/f
fox/vixen.
zozobra [θo'θoßra] nf (fig) anxiety;
zozobrar vi (hundirse) to capsize; (fig) to
fail.
zueco ['θweko] nm clog.

zumbar [θum'bar] vt (burlar) to tease;
(golpear) to hit // vi to buzz; (fam) to be
very close; ~se vr: ~se de to tease;
zumbido nm buzzing; (fam) punch.
zumo ['θumo] nm juice; (ganancia) profit.
zurcir [θur'θir] vt (coser) to darn; (fig) to
put together.
zurdo, a ['θurðo, a] a (mano) left; (persona)
left-handed.
zurrar [θu'rrar] vt (TEC) to dress; (fam:
pegar duro) to wallop; (: aplastar) to
flatten; (: criticar) to criticize harshly.
zurriago [θu'rrjaɣo] nm whip, lash.
zurrón [θu'rron] nm pouch.
zutano, a [θu'tano, a] nm/f so-and-so.

ENGLISH - SPANISH
INGLÉS - ESPAÑOL

A

a, an [eɪ, ə, æn, ɔn, n] *det* un(ε); **3 a day/week** 3 por día/semana; **10 km an hour** 10 km por hora.

A.A. *n abbr of* **Automobile Association; Alcoholics Anonymous.**

aback [ə'bæk] *ad*: **to be taken ~** quedar desconcertado.

abandon [ə'bændən] *vt* abandonar; (*renounce*) renunciar a // *n* abandono; (*wild behaviour*) desenfreno.

abashed [ə'bæʃt] *a* avergonzado, confuso.

abate [ə'beɪt] *vi* moderarse; (*lessen*) disminuir; (*calm down*) calmarse.

abattoir ['æbətwɑ:*] *n* matadero.

abbey ['æbɪ] *n* monasterio.

abbot ['æbət] *n* abad *m*.

abbreviate [ə'bri:vɪeɪt] *vt* abreviar; **abbreviation** [-'eɪʃən] *n* (*short form*) abreviatura; (*act*) abreviación *f*.

abdicate ['æbdɪkeɪt] *vt, vi* abdicar; **abdication** [-'keɪʃən] *n* abdicación *f*.

abdomen ['æbdəmən] *n* abdomen *m*.

abduct [æb'dʌkt] *vt* raptar, secuestrar; **~ion** [-'dʌkʃən] *n* rapto, secuestro.

aberration [æbə'reɪʃən] *n* aberración *f*.

abet [ə'bet] *vt* (*incite*) incitar; (*aid*) ser cómplice de.

abeyance [ə'beɪəns] *n*: **in ~** (*law*) en desuso; (*matter*) en suspenso.

abhor [əb'hɔ:*] *vt* aborrecer, abominar (de); **~rent** *a* aborrecible, detestable.

abide [ə'baɪd] *pt, pp* **abode** *or* **abided** *vt* aguantar, soportar, **to ~ by** *vt fus* atenerse a.

ability [ə'bɪlɪtɪ] *n* habilidad *f*, capacidad *f*; (*talent*) talento.

ablaze [ə'bleɪz] *a* en llamas, ardiendo.

able ['eɪbl] *a* capaz; (*skilled*) hábil; **to be ~ to do sth** poder hacer algo; **~-bodied** *a* sano; **ably** *ad* hábilmente.

abnormal [æb'nɔ:məl] *a* anormal; **~ity** [-'mælɪtɪ] *n* anormalidad *f*.

aboard [ə'bɔ:d] *ad* a bordo // *prep* a bordo de.

abode [ə'bəud] *pt, pp of* **abide** // *n* domicilio.

abolish [ə'bɔlɪʃ] *vt* suprimir, abolir; **abolition** [æbəu'lɪʃən] *n* supresión *f*, abolición *f*.

abominable [ə'bɔmɪnəbl] *a* abominable.

aborigine [æbə'rɪdʒɪnɪ] *n* aborigen *m*.

abort [ə'bɔ:t] *vt* abortar; **~ion** [ə'bɔ:ʃən] *n* aborto (provocado); **to have an ~ion** abortarse, hacerse abortar; **~ive** *a* fracasado.

abound [ə'baund] *vi* abundar.

about [ə'baut] *prep* (*subject*) acerca de, sobre; (*place*) alrededor de, por // *ad* casi, más o menos, a eso de; **to walk ~ the town** andar por la ciudad; **it takes ~ 10 hours** es cosa de 10 horas más o menos; **at ~ 2 o'clock** a eso de las 2; **to be ~ to** estar a punto de; **what** *or* **how ~ doing this?** ¿qué tal si hacemos esto?; **~ turn** *n* media vuelta.

above [ə'bʌv] *ad* encima, por encima, arriba // *prep* encima de; **mentioned ~** susodicho; **~ all** sobre todo; **~ board** *a* legítimo.

abrasion [ə'breɪʒən] *n* (*on skin*) abrasión *f*; **abrasive** [ə'breɪzɪv] *a* abrasivo.

abreast [ə'brest] *ad* de frente; **to keep ~ of** mantenerse a corriente de.

abridge [ə'brɪdʒ] *vt* abreviar.

abroad [ə'brɔ:d] *ad* (*to be*) en el extranjero; (*to go*) al extranjero.

abrupt [ə'brʌpt] *a* (*sudden*) brusco; (*gruff*) áspero.

abscess ['æbsɪs] *n* absceso.

abscond [əb'skɔnd] *vi* fugarse.

absence ['æbsəns] *n* ausencia.

absent ['æbsənt] *a* ausente; **~ee** [-'ti:] *n* ausente *m/f*; **~eeism** [-'ti:ɪzm] *n* absentismo; **~-minded** *a* distraído.

absolute ['æbsəlu:t] *a* absoluto; **~ly** [-'lu:tlɪ] *ad* absolutamente.

absolve [əb'zɔlv] *vt* **to ~ sb (from)** absolver a alguien (de).

absorb [əb'zɔːb] *vt* absorber; **to be ~ed in a book** estar absorto en un libro; **~ent** *a* absorbente; **~ing** *a* absorbente.

abstain [əb'steɪn] *vi*: **to ~ (from)** abstenerse (de).

abstention [əb'stenʃən] *n* abstención *f*.

abstinence ['æbstɪnəns] *n* abstinencia.

abstract ['æbstrækt] *a* abstracto.

absurd [əb'sɔːd] *a* absurdo; **~ity** *n* absurdo.

abundance [ə'bʌndəns] *n* abundancia; **abundant** [-dənt] *a* abundante.

abuse [ə'bju:s] *n* (*insults*) improperios *mpl*, injurias *fpl*; (*misuse*) abuso // *vt* [ə'bju:z] (*ill-treat*) maltratar; (*take advantage of*) abusar de; **abusive** *a* ofensivo.

abysmal [ə'bɪzməl] *a* abismal; (*ignorance etc*) profundo.

abyss [ə'bɪs] *n* abismo.

academic [ækə'demɪk] *a* académico, universitario; (*pej: issue*) puramente teórico.

academy [ə'kædəmɪ] *n* (*learned body*) academia; (*school*) instituto, colegio.

accede [æk'si:d] *vi*: **to ~ to** (*request*) consentir en; (*throne*) subir a.

accelerate [æk'sɛləreɪt] vt acelerar // vi acelerarse; **acceleration** [-'reɪʃən] n aceleración f; **accelerator** n acelerador m.

accent ['æksɛnt] n acento.

accept [ək'sɛpt] vt aceptar; (approve) aprobar; (permit) admitir; **~able** a aceptable; admisible; **~ance** n aceptación f; aprobación f.

access ['æksɛs] n acceso; **to have ~ to** tener libre acceso a; **~ible** [-'sɛsəbl] a accesible.

accessory [æk'sɛsərɪ] n accesorio; **toilet accessories** npl artículos mpl de tocador.

accident ['æksɪdənt] n accidente m; (chance) casualidad f; **by ~** (unintentionally) sin querer; (by coincidence) por casualidad; **~al** [-'dɛntl] a accidental, fortuito; **~ally** [-'dɛntəlɪ] ad sin querer; por casualidad; **~-prone** a con tendencia a sufrir/causar accidentes.

acclaim [ə'kleɪm] vt aclamar, aplaudir // n aclamación f, aplausos mpl.

acclimatize [ə'klaɪmətaɪz] vt: **to become ~d** aclimatarse.

accommodate [ə'kɔmədeɪt] vt alojar, hospedar; (reconcile) componer; (oblige, help) complacer; (adapt): **to ~ one's plans** acomodar sus proyectos a; **accommodating** a servicial, complaciente.

accommodation [əkɔmə'deɪʃən] n alojamiento; (space) sitio.

accompaniment [ə'kʌmpənɪmənt] n acompañamiento; **accompany** [-nɪ] vt acompañar.

accomplice [ə'kʌmplɪs] n cómplice m/f.

accomplish [ə'kʌmplɪʃ] vt (finish) acabar, alcanzar; (achieve) realizar, llevar a cabo; **~ed** a experto, hábil; **~ment** n (ending) conclusión f; (bringing about) realización f; (skill) talento.

accord [ə'kɔːd] n acuerdo // vt concordar; **of his own ~** espontáneamente; **~ance** n: **in ~ance with** de acuerdo con; **~ing to** prep según; (in accordance with) conforme a; **~ingly** ad (thus) por consiguiente.

accordion [ə'kɔːdɪən] n acordeón m.

accost [ə'kɔst] vt abordar, dirigirse a.

account [ə'kaunt] n (COMM) cuenta, factura; (report) informe m; **of little ~** de poca importancia; **on ~** a cuenta; **on no ~** de ninguna manera, bajo ningún concepto; **on ~ of** a causa de, por motivo de; **to take into ~, take ~ of** tomar o tener en cuenta; **to ~ for** (answer for) responder de; (explain) dar cuenta o razón de; **~able** a responsable.

accountancy [ə'kauntənsɪ] n contabilidad f; **accountant** [-tənt] n contador/a m/f.

accumulate [ə'kjuːmjuleɪt] vt acumular // vi acumularse; **accumulation** [-'leɪʃən] n acumulación f.

accuracy ['ækjurəsɪ] n exactitud f, precisión f; **accurate** [-rɪt] a (number) exacto; (answer) acertado; (shot) certero.

accusation [ækju'zeɪʃən] n acusación f; **accuse** [ə'kjuːz] vt acusar; (blame) echar la culpa a; **accused** [ə'kjuːzd] n acusado/a.

accustom [ə'kʌstəm] vt acostumbrar; **~ed a: ~ed to** acostumbrado a.

ace [eɪs] n as m.

ache [eɪk] n dolor m // vi doler; **my head ~s** me duele la cabeza.

achieve [ə'tʃiːv] vt (reach) alcanzar; (realize) llevar a cabo; (victory, success) lograr, conseguir; **~ment** n (completion) realización f; (success) éxito.

acid ['æsɪd] a ácido; (bitter) agrio // n ácido; **~ity** [ə'sɪdɪtɪ] n acidez f; (MED) acedía.

acknowledge [ək'nɔlɪdʒ] vt (letter) acusar recibo de; (fact) reconocer; **~ment** n acuse m de recibo; reconocimiento.

acne ['æknɪ] n acné m.

acorn ['eɪkɔːn] n bellota.

acoustic [ə'kuːstɪk] a acústico; **~s** n, npl acústica sg.

acquaint [ə'kweɪnt] vt: **to ~ sb with sth** (warn) avisar a uno de algo; (inform) poner a uno al corriente de algo; **to be ~ed with** (person) conocer; (fact) estar al corriente de; **~ance** n conocimiento; (person) conocido/a.

acquiesce [ækwɪ'ɛs] vt: **to ~ in** consentir en, conformarse con.

acquire [ə'kwaɪə*] vt adquirir; (achieve) conseguir; **acquisition** [ækwɪ'zɪʃən] n adquisición f; **acquisitive** [ə'kwɪzɪtɪv] a codicioso.

acquit [ə'kwɪt] vt absolver, exculpar; **to ~ o.s. well** defenderse, salir con éxito; **~tal** n absolución f, exculpación f.

acre ['eɪkə*] n acre m.

acrimonious [ækrɪ'məunɪəs] a (remark) mordaz; (argument) reñido.

acrobat ['ækrəbæt] n acróbata m/f; **~ics** [ækrəu'bætɪks] n, npl acrobacia sg.

across [ə'krɔs] prep (on the other side of) al otro lado de, del otro lado de; (crosswise) a través de // ad de un lado a otro, de una parte a otra; a través, al través; **to run/swim ~** atravesar corriendo/nadando; **~ from** enfrente de.

act [ækt] n acto, acción f; (THEATRE) acto; (in music-hall etc) número; (LAW) decreto, ley f // vi (machine) funcionar, marchar; (person) actuar, comportarse; (THEATRE) actuar, trabajar; (pretend) fingir; (take action) obrar // vt (part) hacer el papel de, representar; **to ~** as actuar o hacer de; **~ing** a suplente // n: **to do some ~ing** ser actor/actriz.

action ['ækʃən] n acción f, acto; (MIL) acción f, batalla; (LAW) proceso, demanda; **to take ~** tomar medidas.

activate ['æktɪveɪt] vt (mechanism) activar.

active ['æktɪv] a activo, enérgico; (volcano) en actividad; **activity** [-'tɪvɪtɪ] n actividad f.

actor ['æktə*] n actor m; **actress** [-trıs] n actriz f.

actual ['æktjuəl] a verdadero, real; **~ly** ad realmente, en realidad.

acupuncture ['ækjupʌŋktjə*] n acupuntura.

acute [ə'kju:t] a (gen) agudo.

ad [æd] n abbr of **advertisement**

A.D. ad abbr of **Anno Domini** A.C (año de Cristo).

Adam ['ædəm] n Adán; **~'s apple** n nuez f de la garganta.

adamant ['ædəmənt] a firme, inflexible.

adapt [ə'dæpt] vt adaptar; (re-oncile) acomodar // vi: **to ~ (to)** adapta se (a), ajustarse (a); **~able** a (device) adaptable; (person) que se adapta; **~ation** ædæp-'teɪʃən] n adaptación f, **~er** n (ELEC) adaptador m.

add [æd] vt añadir, agregar; (figures also: **~ up**) sumar // vi: **to ~ to** (increase) aumentar, acrecentar; **it doesn't ~ up** no tiene sentido.

adder ['ædə*] n víbora.

addict ['ædıkt] n (enthusiast) entusiasta m/f; (to drugs etc) adicto/a; **~ed** [ə'dıktıd] a: **to be ~ed to** ser aficionado de; ser adicto a; **addiction** [ə'dıkʃən] n (enthusiasm) afición f; (dependence) hábito morboso.

adding machine ['ædıŋməʃiːn] n calculadora.

addition [ə'dıʃən] n (adding up) adición f; (thing added) añadidura, añadido; **in ~** además, por añadidura; **in ~ to** además de; **~al** a adicional.

additive ['ædıtıv] n aditivo.

address [ə'drɛs] n dirección f, señas fp ; (speech) discurso // vt (letter) dirigir (speak to) dirigirse a, dirigir la palabra a **~ee** [ædrɛ'si:] n destinatario/a.

adenoids ['ædınɔıdz] npl vegetaciones fp; adenoideas.

adept ['ædɛpt] a: **~ at** experto o hábil en.

adequate ['ædıkwıt] a (apt) adecuado; (enough) suficiente.

adhere [əd'hıə*] vi: **to ~ to** pegarse a; (fig: abide by) observar; (: hold to) adherirse a; **adherent** n partidario/a.

adhesive [əd'hi:zıv] a, n adhesivo.

adjacent [ə'dʒeısənt] a: **~ to** contiguo a, inmediato a.

adjective ['ædʒɛktıv] n adjetivo.

adjoining [ə'dʒɔınıŋ] a contiguo, vecino.

adjourn [ə'dʒəːn] vt aplazar; (session) suspender, levantar // vi suspenderse.

adjudicate [ə'dʒu:dıkeıt] vi sentenciar; **adjudicator** n juez m, árbitro.

adjust [ə'dʒʌst] vt (change) modificar; (arrange) arreglar; (machine) ajustar // vi: **to ~ (to)** adaptarse (a); **~able** a ajustable; **~ment** n modificación f; arreglo; (of prices, wages) ajuste m.

adjutant ['ædʒətənt] n ayudante m.

ad-lib [æd'lıb] vt, vi improvisar; **ad lib** ad a voluntad, a discreción.

administer [əd'mınıstə*] vt proporcionar;

(justice) administrar; **administration** [-'treıʃən] n administración f; (government) gobierno; **administrative** [-trətıv] a administrativo; **administrator** [-treıtə*] n administrador/a m/f.

admirable ['ædmərəbl] a admirable.

admiral ['ædmərəl] n almirante m; **A~ty** n Ministerio de Marina, Almirantazgo.

admiration [ædmə'reıʃən] n admiración f.

admire [əd'maıə*] vt admirar; **admirer** n admirador/a m/f; (suitor) pretendiente m.

admission [əd'mıʃən] n (entry) entrada; (enrolment) ingreso; (confession) confesión f.

admit [əd'mıt] vt dejar entrar, dar entrada a; (permit) admitir; (acknowledge) reconocer; (accept) aceptar; **to ~** confesarse culpable de; **~tance** n entrada; **~tedly** ad de acuerdo que.

admonish [əd'mɔnıʃ] vt amonestar; (advise) aconsejar.

ado [ə'du:] n: **without (any) more ~** sin más (ni más).

adolescence [ædəu'lɛsns] n adolescencia; **adolescent** [-'lɛsnt] a, n adolescente m/f.

adopt [ə'dɔpt] vt adoptar; **~ion** [ə'dɔpʃən] n adopción f; **~ed** a adoptivo.

adore [ə'dɔ:*] vt adorar.

adorn [ə'dɔ:n] vt adornar.

adrenalin [ə'drɛnəlın] n adrenalina.

Adriatic [eıdrı'ætık] n: **the ~ (Sea)** el (Mar) Adriático.

adrift [ə'drıft] ad a la deriva; **to come ~** desprenderse.

adult ['ædʌlt] n (gen) adulto.

adulterate [ə'dʌltəreıt] vt adulterar.

adultery [ə'dʌltərı] n adulterio.

advance [əd'vɑːns] n (gen) adelanto, progreso; (money) anticipo, préstamo; (MIL) avance m // vt avanzar, adelantar; anticipar, prestar // vi avanzar, adelantarse; **in ~** por adelantado; **~d** a avanzado; (SCOL: studies) adelantado; **~ment** n progreso; (in rank) ascenso.

advantage [əd'vɑːntıdʒ] n (also TENNIS) ventaja; **to take ~ of** (use) aprovecharse de; (gain by) sacar partido de; **~ous** [ædvən'teıdʒəs] a ventajoso, provechoso.

advent ['ædvənt] n advenimiento; **A~** Adviento.

adventure [əd'vɛntʃə*] n aventura; **adventurous** [-tʃərəs] a aventurero.

adverb ['ædvə:b] n adverbio.

adversary ['ædvəsərı] n adversario, contrario.

adverse ['ædvə:s] a adverso, contrario; **~ to** adverso a.

adversity [əd'və:sıtı] n infortunio.

advert ['ædvə:t] n abbr of **advertisement**.

advertise ['ædvətaız] vi hacer propaganda; (in newspaper etc) poner un anuncio // vt anunciar; **~ment** [əd-'və:tısmənt] n (COMM) anuncio; **advertising** n publicidad f, propaganda; anuncios mpl.

advice [əd'vaɪs] *n* consejo, consejos *mpl*; (*notification*) aviso; **to take legal ~** consultar a un abogado.
advisable [əd'vaɪzəbl] *a* aconsejable, conveniente.
advise [əd'vaɪz] *vt* aconsejar; (*inform*) avisar; **adviser** *n* consejero; (*business adviser*) asesor *m*; **advisory** *a* consultivo.
advocate ['ædvəkeɪt] *vt* (*argue for*) abogar por; (*give support to*) ser partidario de // *n* [-kɪt] abogado.
aerial ['ɛərɪəl] *n* antena // *a* aéreo.
aeroplane ['ɛərəpleɪn] *n* avión *m*.
aerosol ['ɛərəsɔl] *n* aerosol *m*.
aesthetic [iːs'θɛtɪk] *a* estético.
afar [ə'fɑː*] *ad*: **from ~** desde lejos.
affable ['æfəbl] *a* afable.
affair [ə'fɛə*] *n* asunto; (*also*: **love ~**) aventura *o* relación *f* (amorosa).
affect [ə'fɛkt] *vt* afectar, influir en; (*move*) conmover; **~ation** [æfɛk'teɪʃən] *n* afectación *f*; **~ed** *a* afectado.
affection [ə'fɛkʃən] *n* afecto, cariño; **~ate** *a* afectuoso, cariñoso.
affiliated [ə'fɪlɪeɪtɪd] *a* afiliado.
affinity [ə'fɪnɪtɪ] *n* afinidad *f*.
affirmation [æfə'meɪʃən] *n* afirmación *f*.
affirmative [ə'fəːmətɪv] *a* afirmativo.
affix [ə'fɪks] *vt* (*signature*) poner, añadir; (*stamp*) pegar.
afflict [ə'flɪkt] *vt* afligir; **~ion** [ə'flɪkʃən] *n* enfermedad *f*, aflicción *f*.
affluence ['æfluəns] *n* opulencia, riqueza; **affluent** [-ənt] *a* opulento, acaudalado.
afford [ə'fɔːd] *vt* (*provide*) dar, proporcionar; **can we ~ it?** ¿tenemos bastante dinero para comprarlo?
affront [ə'frʌnt] *n* afrenta, ofensa.
afield [ə'fiːld] *ad*: **far ~** muy lejos.
afloat [ə'fləʊt] *ad* (*floating*) a flote; (*at sea*) en el mar.
afoot [ə'fʊt] *ad*: **there is something ~** algo se está tramando.
aforesaid [ə'fɔːsɛd] *a* susodicho.
afraid [ə'freɪd] *a*: **to be ~ of** (*person*) tener miedo a; (*thing*) tener miedo de; **to be ~ to** tener miedo de, temer; **I am ~ that** me temo que.
afresh [ə'frɛʃ] *ad* de nuevo, otra vez.
Africa ['æfrɪkə] *n* África; **~n** *a*, *n* africano/a.
aft [ɑːft] *ad* (*to be*) en popa; (*to go*) a popa.
after ['ɑːftə*] *prep* (*time*) después de; (*place*, *order*) detrás de, tras // *ad* después // *conj* después (de) que; **what/who are you ~?** ¿qué/a quién busca Usted?; **to ask ~ sb** preguntar por alguien; **~ all** después de todo, al fin y al cabo; **~ you!** ¡pase Usted!; **~birth** *n* secundinas *fpl*; **~effects** *npl* consecuencias *fpl*, efectos *mpl*; **~life** *n* vida futura; **~math** *n* consecuencias *fpl*, resultados *mpl*; **~noon** *n* tarde *f*; **~shave** (*lotion*) *n* loción *f* para después del afeitado; **~thought** *n* ocurrencia (tardía); **~wards** *ad* después, más tarde.

again [ə'gɛn] *ad* otra vez, de nuevo; **to do sth ~** volver a hacer algo; **~ and ~** una y otra vez; **now and ~** de vez en cuando.
against [ə'gɛnst] *prep* (*opposed*) contra, en contra de; (*close to*) contra, junto a.
age [eɪdʒ] *n* (*gen*) edad *f*; (*old ~*) vejez *f*; (*period*) época // *vi* envejecer(se) // *vt* envejecer; **to come of ~** llegar a la mayoría de edad; **it's been ~s since** hace muchísimo tiempo que; **~d** *a* ['eɪdʒɪd] viejo, anciano // *a* [eɪdʒd]: **~d 10** de 10 años de edad; **~ group** *n*: **to be in the same ~ group** tener la misma edad; **~less** *a* (*eternal*) eterno; (*ever young*) siempre joven; **~ limit** *n* edad mínima/máxima.
agency ['eɪdʒənsɪ] *n* agencia; **through** *or* **by the ~ of** por medio de.
agenda [ə'dʒɛndə] *n* orden *m* del día.
agent ['eɪdʒənt] *n* (*gen*) agente *m/f*; (*representative*) representante *m/f*, delegado/a.
aggravate ['ægrəveɪt] *vt* agravar; (*annoy*) irritar, exasperar; **aggravation** [-'veɪʃən] *n* agravación *f*.
aggregate ['ægrɪgeɪt] *n* (*whole*) conjunto; (*collection*) agregado.
aggression [ə'grɛʃən] *n* agresión *f*; **aggressive** [ə'grɛsɪv] *a* agresivo; (*zealous*) enérgico.
aggrieved [ə'griːvd] *a* ofendido, agraviado.
aghast [ə'gɑːst] *a* horrorizado; **to be ~** pasmarse.
agile ['ædʒaɪl] *a* ágil.
agitate ['ædʒɪteɪt] *vt* (*shake*) agitar; (*trouble*) inquietar; **to ~ for** hacer campaña pro *o* en favor de; **agitator** *n* agitador/a *m/f*.
ago [ə'gəʊ] *ad*: **2 days ~** hace 2 días; **not long ~** hace poco; **how long ~?** ¿hace cuánto tiempo?
agog [ə'gɔg] *a* (*anxious*) ansiado; (*excited*) emocionado.
agonizing ['ægənaɪzɪŋ] *a* (*pain*) atroz, agudo; (*suspense*) angustioso.
agony ['ægənɪ] *n* (*pain*) dolor *m* agudo; (*distress*) angustia; **to be in ~** sufrir atrozmente.
agree [ə'griː] *vt* (*price*) acordar, quedar en // *vi* (*statements etc*) coincidir, concordar; **to ~ (with)** (*person*) estar de acuerdo (con), ponerse de acuerdo (con); **to ~ to do** aceptar hacer; **to ~ to sth** consentir en algo; **to ~ that** (*admit*) estar de acuerdo en que; **garlic doesn't ~ with me** el ajo no me sienta bien; **~able** *a* agradable; (*person*) simpático; (*willing*) de acuerdo, conforme; **~d** *a* (*time*, *place*) convenido; **~ment** *n* acuerdo; (*COMM*) contrato; **in ~ment** de acuerdo, conforme.
agricultural [ægrɪ'kʌltʃərəl] *a* agrícola; **agriculture** ['ægrɪkʌltʃə*] *n* agricultura.
aground [ə'graʊnd] *ad*: **to run ~** encallar, embarrancar.
ahead [ə'hɛd] *ac* delante; **~ of** delante de;

(*fig: schedule etc*) antes de; ~ **of time** antes de la hora; **to be** ~ **of sb** (*fig*) llevar la ventaja a alguien; **go right** *er* **straight** ~ ¡siga adelante!

aid [eɪd] *n* ayuda, auxilio // *vt* ayudar, auxiliar; **in** ~ **of** a beneficio de; **to** ~ **and abet** (*LAW*) ser cómplice de.

aide [eɪd] *n* (*person*) edecán *m*.

ailment ['eɪlmənt] *n* enfermedad *f*, achaque *m*.

aim [eɪm] *vt* (*gun, camera*) apuntar; (*missile, remark*) dirigir; (*blow*) asestar // *vi* (*also*: **take** ~) apuntar // *n* puntería; (*objective*) propósito, meta; **to** ~ **at** (*objective*) aspirar a, pretender; **to** ~ **to do** tener la intención de hacer; ~**less** *a* sin propósito, sin objeto; ~**lessly** *ad* a la ventura, a la deriva.

air [ɛə*] *n* aire *m*; (*appearance*) aspecto // *vt* ventilar; (*grievances, ideas*) airear // *cpd* (*currents, attack etc*) aéreo; ~**borne** *a* (*in the air*) en el aire; (*MIL*) aerotransportado; ~**-conditioned** *a* con aire acondicionado; ~ **conditioning** *n* aire acondicionado; ~**craft**(*n, pl inv*) avión *m*; ~**craft carrier** *n* porta(a)viones *m inv*; **A**~ **Force** *n* Fuerzas Aéreas *fpl*, aviación *f*; ~**gun** *n* escopeta de aire comprimido; ~ **hostess** *n* azafata; ~ **letter** *n* carta aérea; ~**lift** *n* puente *m* aéreo; ~**line** *n* línea aérea; ~**liner** *n* avión *m* de pasajeros; ~**lock** *n* esclusa de aire; ~ **mail** *n*: **by** ~ **mail** por avión; ~**port** *n* aeropuerto; ~ **raid** *n* ataque *m* aéreo; ~**sick** *a*: **to be** ~**sick** marearse (en un avión); ~**strip** *n* pista de aterrizaje; ~**tight** *a* hermético; ~**y** *a* (*room*) bien ventilado; (*manners*) ligero.

aisle [aɪl] *n* (*of church*) nave *f*; (*of theatre*) pasillo.

ajar [ə'dʒɑ:*] *a* entreabierto.

akin [ə'kɪn] *a*: ~ **to** relacionado con.

alarm [ə'lɑ:m] *n* alarma; (*anxiety*) inquietud *f* // *vt* asustar, inquietar; ~ **clock** *n* despertador *m*.

Albania [æl'beɪnɪə] *n* Albania.

album ['ælbəm] *n* álbum *m*; (*L.P.*) elepé *m*.

alcohol ['ælkəhɔl] *n* alcohol *m*; ~**ic** [-'hɔlɪk] *a, n* alcohólico/a; ~**ism** *n* alcoholismo.

alcove ['ælkəuv] *n* nicho, hueco.

alderman ['ɔ:ldəmən] *n, pl* **-men** concejal *m*.

ale [eɪl] *n* cerveza.

alert [ə'lə:t] *a* alerta; (*sharp*) despierto, despabilado // *n* alerta *m*, alarma // *vt* poner sobre aviso; **to be on the** ~ estar alerta *o* sobre aviso.

algebra ['ældʒɪbrə] *n* álgebra.

Algeria [æl'dʒɪərɪə] *n* Argelia; ~**n** *a, n* argelino/a.

alias ['eɪlɪəs] *ad* alias, por otro nombre // *n* alias *m*.

alibi ['ælɪbaɪ] *n* coartada.

alien ['eɪlɪən] *n* extranjero/a // *a*: ~ **to** distinto de, ajeno a; ~**ate** *vt* enajenar, alejar; ~**ation** [-'neɪʃən] *n* enajenación *f*.

alight [ə'laɪt] *a* ardiendo, quemando // *vi* apearse, bajar.

align [ə'laɪn] *vt* alinear; ~**ment** *n* alineación *f*.

alike [ə'laɪk] *a* semejantes, iguales // *ad* igualmente, del mismo modo; **to look** ~ parecerse.

alimony ['ælɪmənɪ] *n* (*payment*) alimentos *mpl*.

alive [ə'laɪv] *a* (*gen*) vivo; (*lively*) activo, enérgico.

alkali ['ælkəlaɪ] *n* álcali *m*.

all [ɔ:l] *a* todo; (*pl*) todos(as) // *pron* todo; (*pl*) todos(as) // *ad* completamente, del todo; ~ **alone** completamente solo; **at** ~ en absoluto, del todo; ~ **the time**/**his life** todo el tiempo/toda su vida; ~ **five** todos los cinco; ~ **of them** todos (ellos); ~ **of us went** fuimos todos; **not as hard as** ~ **that** no tan difícil; ~ **in** ~ con todo, así y todo.

allay [ə'leɪ] *vt* (*fears*) aquietar; (*pain*) aliviar.

allegation [ælɪ'geɪʃən] *n* aseveración *f*, alegación *f*.

allege [ə'ledʒ] *vt* afirmar, pretender.

allegiance [ə'li:dʒəns] *n* lealtad *f*.

allegory ['ælɪgərɪ] *n* alegoría.

allergic [ə'lə:dʒɪk] *a*: ~ **to** alérgico a; **allergy** ['ælədʒɪ] *n* alergia.

alleviate [ə'li:vɪeɪt] *vt* aliviar, mitigar.

alley ['ælɪ] *n* (*street*) callejuela; (*in garden*) paseo.

alliance [ə'laɪəns] *n* alianza *f*; **allied** ['ælaɪd] *a* aliado; (*related*) relacionado.

alligator ['ælɪgeɪtə*] *n* caimán *m*.

all-in [ɔ:lɪn] *a* (*also ad: charge*) todo incluido; ~ **wrestling** *n* lucha libre.

alliteration [əlɪtə'reɪʃən] *n* aliteración *f*.

all-night ['ɔ:l'naɪt] *a* (*café*) abierto toda la noche; (*party*) que dura toda la noche.

allocate ['æləkeɪt] *vt* (*share out*) repartir, distribuir; (*devote*) asignar; **allocation** [-'keɪʃən] *n* (*of money*) ración *f*, cuota; (*distribution*) reparto.

allot [ə'lɔt] *vt* asignar; ~**ment** *n* ración *f*, porción *f*; (*garden*) parcela.

all-out ['ɔ:laut] *a* (*effort etc*) máximo; **all out** *ad* con todas sus fuerzas; (*speed*) a máxima velocidad.

allow [ə'lau] *vt* (*practice, behaviour*) permitir, dejar; (*sum to spend etc*) pagar, dar; (*a claim*) admitir; (*sum, time estimated*) dar, conceder; (*concede*): **to** ~ **that** reconocer que; **to** ~ **sb to do** permitir a alguien hacer; **to** ~ **for** *vt fus* tener en cuenta, tomar en consideración; ~**ance** *n* (*gen*) concesión *f*; (*payment*) subvención *f*, pensión *f*; (*discount*) descuento, rebaja; **family** ~**ance** subsidio familiar; **to make** ~**ances for** ser indulgente con; tener en cuenta.

alloy ['ælɔɪ] *n* (*mix*) mezcla.

all: ~ **right** *ad* (*well*) bien; (*correct*) correcto; (*as answer*) ¡conforme!, ¡está bien!; ~**-round** *a* (*gen*) completo; (*view*) amplio; (*person*) que hace de todo;

~-time a (record) de todos los tiempos.

allude [ə'luːd] vi: **to ~ to** aludir a.

alluring [ə'ljuərɪŋ] a seductor(a), atractivo.

allusion [ə'luːʒən] n referencia, alusión f.

ally ['ælaɪ] n aliado/a // vr [ə'laɪ]: **to ~ o.s. with** aliarse con.

almighty [ɔːl'maɪtɪ] a todopoderoso, omnipotente.

almond ['ɑːmənd] n (fruit) almendra; (tree) almendro.

almost ['ɔːlməust] ad casi, por poco.

alms [ɑːmz] npl limosna sg.

aloft [ə'lɒft] ad arriba, en alto.

alone [ə'ləun] a solo // ad sólo, solamente; **to leave sb ~** dejar a uno solo o en paz; **to leave sth ~** no tocar algo, dejar algo sin tocar; **let ~** sin hablar de.

along [ə'lɒŋ] prep a lo largo de, por // ad: **is he coming ~ with us?** ¿nos acompaña?; **he was limping ~** iba cojeando; **~ with** junto con, además de; **~side** prep junto a, al lado de // ad (NAUT) al costado.

aloof [ə'luːf] a reservado // ad: **to stand ~** mantenerse a distancia.

aloud [ə'laud] ad en voz alta.

alphabet ['ælfəbet] n alfabeto; **~ical** [-'betɪkəl] a alfabético.

alpine ['ælpaɪn] a alpino, alpestre.

Alps [ælps] npl: **the ~** los Alpes.

already [ɔːl'redɪ] ad ya.

alright ['ɔːl'raɪt] ad = **all right.**

also ['ɔːlsəu] ad también, además.

altar ['ɔːltə*] n altar m.

alter ['ɔːltə*] vt cambiar, modificar // vi cambiarse, mudarse; (worsen) alterarse; **~ation** [ɔːltə'reɪʃən] n cambio, modificación f; alteración f.

alternate [ɔl'təːnɪt] a alterno, alternativo // vi ['ɔltəneɪt] alternarse; **on ~ days** un día sí y otro no; **~ly** ad alternativamente, por turno; **alternating** [-'neɪtɪŋ] a (current) alterno.

alternative [ɔl'təːnətɪv] a alternativo // n alternativa; **~ly** ad: **~ly one could...** por otra parte se podría... .

alternator ['ɔltəneɪtə*] n (AUT) alternador m.

although [ɔːl'ðəu] conj aunque; (given that) si bien.

altitude ['æltɪtjuːd] n altitud f, altura.

alto ['æltəu] n (female) contralto f; (male) alto.

altogether [ɔːltə'geðə*] ad enteramente, del todo; (on the whole, in all) en total, en conjunto.

aluminium [ælju'mɪnɪəm], **aluminum** [ə'luːmɪnəm] (US) n aluminio.

always ['ɔːlweɪz] ad siempre.

am [æm] vb see **be.**

a.m. ad abbr of **ante meridiem** de la mañana, antes de mediodía.

amalgamate [ə'mælgəmeɪt] vi amalgamarse, unirse // vt amalgamar,

unir; **amalgamation** [-'meɪʃən] n (COMM) amalgamación f, unión f.

amass [ə'mæs] vt amontonar, acumular.

amateur ['æmətə*] n aficionado/a, amateur m/f.

amaze [ə'meɪz] vt asombrar, pasmar; **~ment** n asombro, sorpresa.

Amazon ['æməzən] n (GEO) Amazonas m.

ambassador [æm'bæsədə*] n embajador m.

amber ['æmbə*] n ámbar m; **at ~** (AUT) en el amarillo.

ambidextrous [æmbɪ'dekstrəs] a ambidextro.

ambiguity [æmbɪ'gjuɪtɪ] n ambigüedad f; (of meaning) doble sentido; **ambiguous** [-'bɪgjuəs] a ambiguo.

ambition [æm'bɪʃən] n ambición f; **ambitious** [-ʃəs] a ambicioso; (plan) grandioso.

ambivalent [æm'bɪvələnt] a ambivalente; (pej) equívoco.

amble ['æmbl] vi (gen: **~ along**) deambular, andar sin prisa.

ambulance ['æmbjuləns] n ambulancia.

ambush ['æmbuʃ] n emboscada // vt tender una emboscada a; (fig) coger por sorpresa.

amenable [ə'miːnəbl] a: **~ to** (advice etc) sensible a.

amend [ə'mend] vt (law, text) enmendar; (habits) corregir, mejorar; **to make ~s** compensar, dar satisfacción por; **~ment** n enmienda.

amenities [ə'miːnɪtɪz] npl conveniencias fpl, comodidades fpl.

America [ə'merɪkə] n Estados Unidos mpl; **~n** a, n norteamericano/a.

amiable ['eɪmɪəbl] a (kind) amable, simpático; (hearty) bonachón(ona).

amicable ['æmɪkəbl] a amistoso, amigable.

amid(st) [ə'mɪd(st)] prep entre, en medio de.

amiss [ə'mɪs] ad: **to take sth ~** tomar algo a mal.

ammonia [ə'məunɪə] n amoníaco.

ammunition [æmju'nɪʃən] n municiones fpl.

amnesia [æm'niːzɪə] n amnesia.

amnesty ['æmnɪstɪ] n amnistía.

amok [ə'mɔk] ad: **to run ~** enloquecerse, desbocarse.

among(st) [ə'mʌŋ(st)] prep entre, en medio de

amoral [æ'mɒrəl] a amoral.

amorous ['æmərəs] a amoroso; (in love) enamorado.

amount [ə'maunt] n (gen) cantidad f; (of bill etc* suma, importe m // vi: **to ~ to** (reach) alcanzar; (total) sumar; (be same as) equivaler a, significar.

amp(ère) ['æmp(ɛə*)] n amperio.

amphibian [æm'fɪbɪən] n anfibio; **amphibious** [-bɪəs] a anfibio.

amphitheatre ['æmfɪθɪətə*] n anfiteatro.

ample ['æmpl] a (*spacious*) amplio, ancho; (*abundant*) abundante; (*enough*) bastante, suficiente.

amplifier ['æmplɪfaɪə*] n amplificador m.

amplify ['æmplɪfaɪ] vt amplificar, aumentar; (*explain*) explicar.

amputate ['æmpjuteɪt] vt amputar.

amuck [ə'mʌk] ad = **amok**.

amuse [ə'mjuːz] vt divertir; (*distract*) distraer, entretener; ~**ment** n diversión f; (*pastime*) pasatiempo; (*laughter*) risa.

an [æn, ən, n] det see **a**.

anaemia [ə'niːmɪə] n anemia; **anaemic** [-mɪk] a anémico; (*fig*) soso, insípido.

anaesthetic [ænɪs'θetɪk] n anestesia; **anaesthetist** [æ'niːsθɪtɪst] n anestesista m/f.

analgesic [ænæl'dʒiːsɪk] a, n analgésico.

analogy [ə'nælədʒɪ] n análogo.

analyse ['ænəlaɪz] vt analizar; **analysis** [ə'næləsɪs], pl **-ses** [-siːz] n análisis m inv; **analyst** [-lɪst] n (US) analista m/f; **analytic(al)** [-'lɪtɪk(əl)] a analítico.

anarchist ['ænəkɪst] a, n anarquista m/f; **anarchy** [-kɪ] n anarquía, desorden m.

anatomy [ə'nætəmɪ] n anatomía.

ancestor ['ænsɪstə*] n antepasado; **ancestry** [-trɪ] n ascendencia, abolengo.

anchor ['æŋkə*] n ancla, áncora // vi anclar // vt (*fig*) sujetar, asegurar; **to weigh** ~ levar anclas; ~**age** n ancladero.

anchovy ['æntʃəvɪ] n anchoa.

ancient ['eɪnʃənt] a antiguo.

and [ænd] conj y; (*before i, hi*) e; ~ **so on** etcétera, y así sucesivamente; **try** ~ **come** procure o intente venir; **better** ~ **better** cada vez mejor.

Andes ['ændiːz] npl: the ~ los Andes.

anecdote ['ænɪkdəut] n anécdota.

anew [ə'njuː] ad de nuevo, otra vez.

angel ['eɪndʒəl] n ángel m.

anger ['æŋgə*] n cólera, ira // vt enojar, provocar.

angina [æn'dʒaɪnə] n angina (de pecho).

angle ['æŋgl] n ángulo; **from their** ~ desde su punto de vista.

angler ['æŋglə*] n pescador/a m/f (de caña).

Anglican ['æŋglɪkən] a, n anglicano/a.

angling ['æŋglɪŋ] n pesca con caña.

Anglo- ['æŋgləu] pref anglo... .

angrily ['æŋgrɪlɪ] ad con enojo, airadamente.

angry ['æŋgrɪ] a enfadado, enojado; **to be** ~ **with sb/at sth** estar enfadado con alguien/por algo; **to get** ~ enfadarse, enojarse.

anguish ['æŋgwɪʃ] n (*physical*) dolor m agudo; (*mental*) angustia.

angular ['æŋgjulə*] a (*shape*) angular; (*features*) anguloso.

animal ['ænɪməl] n animal m, bestia; (*insect*) bicho // a animal.

animate ['ænɪmeɪt] vt (*enliven*) animar;

(*encourage*) estimular, alentar; ~**d** a vivo, animado.

animosity [ænɪ'mɔsɪtɪ] n animosidad f, rencor m.

aniseed ['ænɪsiːd] n anís m.

ankle ['æŋkl] n tobillo m.

annex ['ænɛks] n (*also*: **annexe**) (*edificio*) anexo, dependencia // vt (*æ'neks*) (*territory*) anexar; (*document*) adjuntar.

annihilate [ə'naɪəleɪt] vt aniquilar.

anniversary [ænɪ'vɜːsərɪ] n aniversario.

annotate ['ænəuteɪt] vt anotar, comentar.

announce [ə'nauns] vt comunicar, anunciar; ~**ment** n anuncio, aviso, declaración f; **announcer** n (*RADIO, TV*) locutor/a m/f.

annoy [ə'nɔɪ] vt molestar, fastidiar; irritar; **don't get** ~**ed!** ¡no se enfade!; ~**ance** n enojo; (*thing*) molestia; ~**ing** a molesto, fastidioso; (*person*) pesado.

annual ['ænjuəl] a anual // n (*BOT*) anual m; (*book*) anuario; ~**ly** ad anualmente, cada año.

annuity [ə'njuːɪtɪ] n renta o pensión f vitalicia.

annul [ə'nʌl] vt anular, cancelar; (*law*) revocar; ~**ment** n anulación f, cancelación f.

annum ['ænəm] n see **per**.

anoint [ə'nɔɪnt] vt untar.

anomaly [ə'nɔməlɪ] n anomalía.

anonymity [ænə'nɪmɪtɪ] n anonimato; **anonymous** [ə'nɔnɪməs] a anónimo.

anorak ['ænəræk] n anorak m.

anorexia [ænə'reksɪə] n (*MED*) anorexia.

another [ə'nʌðə*] a: ~ **book** (*one more*) otro libro; (*a different one*) un libro distinto // pron otro; see also **one**.

answer ['ɑːnsə*] n contestación f, respuesta; (*to problem*) solución f // vi contestar, responder // vt (*reply to*) contestar a, responder a; (*problem*) resolver; **to** ~ **the phone** contestar el teléfono; **in** ~ **to your letter** contestando o en contestación a su carta; **to** ~ **the bell** or **the door** acudir a la puerta; **to** ~ **back** vi replicar, ser respondón(ona); **to** ~ **for** vt fus responder de o por; **to** ~ **to** vt fus (*description*) corresponder a; (*needs*) satisfacer; ~**able** a: ~**able to sb for sth** responsable ante uno de algo.

ant [ænt] n hormiga.

antacid [ænt'æsɪd] a antiácido.

antagonist [æn'tægənɪst] n antagonista m/f, adversario/a; ~**ic** [-'nɪstɪk] a antagónico; (*opposed*) contrario, opuesto; **antagonize** [-naɪz] vt enemistarse con.

Antarctic [ænt'ɑːktɪk] n: the ~ el Antártico; ~**a** n Antártida.

antelope ['æntɪləup] n antílope m.

antenatal ['æntɪ'neɪtl] a antenatal, prenatal; ~ **clinic** a clínica prenatal.

antenna [æn'tenə] pl ~**e** [-niː] n antena.

anthem ['ænθəm] n: **national** ~ himno nacional.

anthology [æn'θɔlədʒɪ] n antología.

anthropologist [ænθrə'pɔlədʒɪst] n antropólogo; **anthropology** [-dʒɪ] n antropología.
anti... [æntɪ] pref anti...; **~-aircraft** a antiaéreo.
antibiotic [æntɪbaɪ'ɔtɪk] a, n antibiótico.
anticipate [æn'tɪsɪpeɪt] vt (foresee) prever; (expect) esperar, contar con; (forestall) anticiparse a, adelantarse a; (look forward to) prometerse; **anticipation** [-'peɪʃən] n previsión f; esperanza; anticipación f, prevención f.
anticlimax [æntɪ'klaɪmæks] n decepción f.
anticlockwise [æntɪ'klɔkwaɪz] ad en dirección contraria a la de las agujas del reloj.
antics ['æntɪks] npl payasadas fpl; (of child) travesuras fpl.
anticyclone [æntɪ'saɪkloun] n anticiclón m.
antidote ['æntɪdout] n antídoto.
antifreeze ['æntɪfriːz] n anticongelante m, solución f anticongelante.
antihistamine [æntɪ'hɪstəmiːn] n antihistamínico.
antiquated ['æntɪkweɪtɪd] a anticuado.
antique [æn'tiːk] n antigüedad f, antigualla // a antiguo, anticuado; **~ dealer** n anticuario; **~ shop** n tienda de antigüedades.
antiquity [æn'tɪkwɪtɪ] n antigüedad f.
antiseptic [æntɪ'septɪk] a, n antiséptico.
antisocial [æntɪ'souʃəl] a antisocial.
antlers ['æntləz] npl cuernas fpl.
anus ['eɪnəs] n ano.
anvil ['ænvɪl] n yunque m.
anxiety [æŋ'zaɪətɪ] n (worry) inquietud f; (eagerness) ansia, anhelo; (MED) ansiedad f.
anxious ['æŋkʃəs] a (worried) inquieto; (keen) deseoso; **~ly** ad con inquietud, de manera angustiada.
any ['enɪ] a (in negative and interrogative sentences = some) algún, alguno, alguna; (negative sense) ningún, ninguno, ninguna; (no matter which) cualquier(a); (each and every) todo; **I haven't ~ money/books** no tengo dinero/libros; **have you ~ butter/children?** ¿tiene mantequilla/hijos?; **at ~ moment** en cualquier momento; **in ~ case** de todas formas, de todas maneras; **at ~ rate** de todas formas, sea como sea // pron alguno; ninguno; (anybody) cualquiera; (in negative and interrogative sentences): **I haven't ~** no tengo ninguno; **have you got ~?** ¿tiene algunos?; **can ~ of you sing?** ¿alguno de Ustedes sabe cantar? // ad (in negative sentences) nada; (in interrogative and conditional constructions) algo; **I can't hear him ~ more** no le oigo más; **do you want ~ more soup?** ¿quiere más sopa?; **~body** pron cualquiera, cualquier persona; (in interrogative sentences) alguien; (in negative sentences): **I don't see ~body** no veo a nadie; **~how** ad de todos modos, de todas maneras;

(carelessly) de cualquier manera; **~one** = **~body**; **~thing** pron (see **~body**) algo, cualquier cosa; algo; (in negative sentences) nada; (everything) todo; **~time** ad (at any moment) en cualquier momento, de un momento a otro; (whenever) no importa cuándo, cuando quiera; **~way** ad de todas maneras; de cualquier modo; **~where** ad (see **~body**) dondequiera; en algún sitio; (negative sense) en ningún sitio; (everywhere) en or por todas partes; **I don't see him ~where** no le veo en ningún sitio.
apart [ə'pɑːt] ad aparte, separadamente; **10 miles ~** separados por 10 millas; **~ from** prep aparte de.
apartheid [ə'pɑːteɪt] n apartheid m.
apartment [ə'pɑːtmənt] n (US) piso, apartamento; (room) cuarto.
apathetic [æpə'θetɪk] a apático, indiferente; **apathy** ['æpəθɪ] n apatía, indiferencia.
ape [eɪp] n mono // vt imitar, remedar.
aperitif [ə'perɪtɪv] n aperitivo.
aperture ['æpətjuə*] n rendija, resquicio; (PHOT) abertura.
apex ['eɪpeks] n ápice m; (fig) cumbre f.
aphrodisiac [æfrəu'dɪzɪæk] a, n afrodisíaco.
apiece [ə'piːs] ad cada uno.
apologetic [əpɔlə'dʒetɪk] a (tone, letter) lleno de disculpas.
apologize [ə'pɔlədʒaɪz] vi: **to ~ (for sth to sb)** disculparse (con alguien de algo); **apology** [-dʒɪ] n disculpa, excusa.
apostle [ə'pɔsl] n apóstol m/f.
apostrophe [ə'pɔstrəfɪ] n apóstrofe m.
appal [ə'pɔːl] vt horrorizar, espantar; **~ling** a espantoso; (awful) pésimo.
apparatus [æpə'reɪtəs] n aparato.
apparent [ə'pærənt] a aparente; (obvious) manifiesto, claro; **~ly** ad por lo visto, al parecer.
apparition [æpə'rɪʃən] n aparición f; (ghost) fantasma m.
appeal [ə'piːl] vi (LAW) apelar // n (LAW) apelación f; (request) llamamiento; (plea) súplica, ruego; (charm) atractivo, encanto; **to ~ for** suplicar, reclamar; **to ~ to** (subj: person) rogar a, suplicar a; (subj: thing) atraer, interesar; **to ~ to sb for mercy** rogarle misericordia a alguien; **it doesn't ~ to me** no me atrae, no me llama la atención; **~ing** a (nice) atrayente, atractivo; (touching) conmovedor(a), emocionante.
appear [ə'pɪə*] vi aparecer, presentarse; (LAW) comparecer; (publication) salir (a luz), publicarse; (seem) parecer; **it would ~ that** parecería que; **~ance** n aparición f; (look, aspect) apariencia, aspecto.
appease [ə'piːz] vt (pacify) apaciguar; (satisfy) satisfacer, saciar.
appendicitis [əpendɪ'saɪtɪs] n apendicitis f.
appendix [ə'pendɪks] pl **-dices** [-dɪsiːz] n apéndice m.

appetite ['æpɪtaɪt] n apetito; (fig) deseo, anhelo.

appetizing ['æpɪtaɪzɪŋ] a apetitoso.

applaud [ə'plɔːd] vt, vi aplaudir; **applause** [-ɔːz] n aplausos mpl.

apple ['æpl] n manzana; ~ **tree** n manzano.

appliance [ə'plaɪəns] n aparato.

applicable [ə'plɪkəbl] a aplicable, pertinente.

applicant ['æplɪkənt] n candidato/a, solicitante m/f.

application [æplɪ'keɪʃən] n aplicación f; (for a job, a grant etc) solicitud f, petición f; ~ **form** n formulario.

apply [ə'plaɪ] vt: **to** ~ **(to)** aplicar (a); (fig) emplear (para) // vi: **to** ~ **to** (ask) presentarse a, ser candidato a; (be suitable for) ser aplicable a; (be relevant to) tener que ver con; **to** ~ **for** (permit, grant, job) solicitar; **to** ~ **the brakes** aplicar los frenos; **to** ~ **o.s. to** aplicarse a, dedicarse a.

appoint [ə'pɔɪnt] vt (to post) nombrar; (date, place) fijar, señalar; ~**ment** n (engagement) cita; (date) compromiso; (act) nombramiento; (post) puesto.

apportion [ə'pɔːʃən] vt repartir, distribuir; (blame) dar.

appraisal [ə'preɪzl] n tasación f, valoración f.

appreciable [ə'priːʃəbl] a sensible.

appreciate [ə'priːʃieɪt] vt (like) apreciar, tener en mucho; (be grateful for) agradecer; (assess) valorar, apreciar; (be aware of) comprender, percibir // vi (COMM) aumentar(se) en valor, subir; **appreciation** [-'eɪʃən] n aprecio; reconocimiento, agradecimiento; aumento en valor.

appreciative [ə'priːʃiətɪv] a (person) agradecido; (comment) elogioso.

apprehend [æprɪ'hɛnd] vt percibir, comprender; (arrest) detener.

apprehension [æprɪ'hɛnʃən] n (fear) recelo, aprensión f; **apprehensive** [-'hɛnsɪv] a aprensivo.

apprentice [ə'prɛntɪs] n aprendiz/a m/f, ~**ship** n aprendizaje m.

approach [ə'prəʊtʃ] vi acercarse // vt acercarse a; (be approximate) aproximarse a; (ask, apply to) dirigirse a // n acercamiento; aproximación f; (access) acceso; (proposal) proposición f; ~**able** a (person) abordable; (place) accesible.

appropriate [ə'prəʊprieɪt] vt (take) apropiarse; (allot): **to** ~ **sth for** destinar algo a // a [-rɪɪt] (apt) apropiado, conveniente; (relevant) competente.

approval [ə'pruːvəl] n aprobación f, visto bueno; **on** ~ (COMM) a prueba.

approve [ə'pruːv] vt aprobar; ~**d school** n correccional m.

approximate [ə'prɒksɪmɪt] a aproximado // vt [-meɪt] aproximarse a, acercarse a;

approximation [-'meɪʃən] n aproximación f.

apricot ['eɪprɪkɒt] n albaricoque m.

April ['eɪprəl] n abril m; ~ **Fool's Day** n Día m de los inocentes.

apron ['eɪprən] n delantal m.

apt [æpt] a (suitable) acertado, oportuno; (appropriate) conveniente; (likely): ~ **to** do con tendencia a hacer.

aptitude ['æptɪtjuːd] n aptitud f, capacidad f.

aqualung ['ækwəlʌŋ] n aparato de buceo autónomo.

aquarium [ə'kwɛərɪəm] n acuario.

Aquarius [ə'kwɛərɪəs] n Acuario.

aquatic [ə'kwætɪk] a acuático.

aqueduct ['ækwɪdʌkt] n acueducto.

Arab ['ærəb] a árabe m/f.

Arabia [ə'reɪbiə] n Arabia; ~**n** a árabe.

Arabic ['ærəbɪk] n árabe m.

arable ['ærəbl] a cultivable.

arbitrary ['ɑːbɪtrərɪ] a arbitrario.

arbitrate ['ɑːbɪtreɪt] vi arbitrar; **arbitration** [-'treɪʃən] n arbitraje m; **arbitrator** n juez m árbitro.

arc [ɑːk] n arco.

arcade [ɑː'keɪd] n arcada; (round a square) soportales mpl; (passage with shops) galería, pasaje m.

arch [ɑːtʃ] n arco; (vault) bóveda; (of foot) empeine m // vt arquear.

archaeologist [ɑːkɪ'ɒlədʒɪst] n arqueólogo; **archaeology** [-dʒɪ] n arqueología.

archaic [ɑː'keɪɪk] a arcaico.

archbishop [ɑːtʃ'bɪʃəp] n arzobispo.

arch-enemy ['ɑːtʃ'ɛnɪmɪ] n enemigo jurado.

archer ['ɑːtʃə*] n arquero; ~**y** n tiro con arco.

archetype ['ɑːkɪtaɪp] n arquetipo.

archipelago [ɑːkɪ'pɛlɪgəʊ] n archipiélago.

architect ['ɑːkɪtɛkt] n arquitecto; ~**ural** [-'tɛktʃərəl] a arquitectónico; ~**ure** n arquitectura.

archives ['ɑːkaɪvz] npl archivo sg.

archway ['ɑːtʃweɪ] n arco, arcada.

Arctic ['ɑːktɪk] a ártico // n: **the** ~ el Ártico.

ardent ['ɑːdənt] a (passionate) ardiente, apasionado; (fervent) fervoroso; **ardour** ['ɑːdə*] n ardor m; fervor m.

arduous ['ɑːdjʊəs] a (gen) arduo; (journey) penoso.

are [ɑː*] vb see be.

area ['ɛərɪə] n (gen) área; (MATH etc) superficie f, extensión f; (zone) región f, zona.

arena [ə'riːnə] n arena; (of circus, pista, (for bullfight) plaza, ruedo.

aren't [ɑːnt] = are not.

Argentina [ɑːdʒən'tiːnə] n Argentina; **Argentinian** [-'tɪnɪən] a, n argentino/a.

argue ['ɑːgjuː] vi (quarrel) discutir; (reason) argüir, discurrir; **to** ~ **that** sostener que; **argument** n (reasons) argumento; (*quarrel*) discusión f; (*debate*) debate m, disputa; **argumentative** [-mɛntətɪv] a discutidor(a).

aria ['ɑːrɪə] n (MUS) aria.

arid ['ærɪd] a árido.

Aries ['ɛərɪz] n Aries m.

arise [ə'raɪz], pt **arose**, pp **arisen** [ə'rɪzn] vi (*rise up*) levantarse, alzarse; (*emerge*) surgir, presentarse; **to ~ from** resultar de.

aristocracy [ærɪs'tɔkrəsɪ] n aristocracia; **aristocrat** ['ærɪstəkræt] n aristócrata m/f.

arithmetic [ə'rɪθmətɪk] n aritmética.

ark [ɑːk] n: **Noah's A ~** Arca de Noé.

arm [ɑːm] n (ANAT) brazo; (*weapon*, MIL: *branch*) arma // vt armar; **~s** npl (*weapons*) armas fpl; (HERALDRY) escudo sg; **~s race** carrera de armamentos; **~ in ~** cogidos del brazo; **~band** n brazalete m; **~chair** n sillón m; **~ed** a armado; **~ed robbery** n robo a mano armada; **~ful** n brazado, brazada.

armistice ['ɑːmɪstɪs] n armisticio.

armour ['ɑːmə*] n armadura; **~ed car** n coche m blindado; **~y** n armería, arsenal m.

armpit ['ɑːmpɪt] n sobaco, axila.

army ['ɑːmɪ] n ejército.

aroma [ə'rəumə] n aroma m, fragancia; **~tic** [ærə'mætɪk] a aromático, fragante.

arose [ə'rəuz] pt of **arise**.

around [ə'raund] ad alrededor; (*in the area*) a la redonda // prep alrededor de, en torno de; (*fig: about*) alrededor de.

arouse [ə'rauz] vt despertar.

arrange [ə'reɪndʒ] vt arreglar, ordenar; (*programme*) organizar; **~ment** n arreglo; (*agreement*) acuerdo; **~ments** npl (*plans*) planes mpl, medidas fpl; (*preparations*) preparativos mpl.

arrears [ə'rɪəz] npl atrasos mpl; **to be in ~ with one's rent** atrasarse en el arriendo.

arrest [ə'rɛst] vt detener; (*sb's attention*) llamar // n detención f; **under ~** detenido.

arrival [ə'raɪvəl] n llegada; **new ~** recién llegado.

arrive [ə'raɪv] vi llegar.

arrogance ['ærəgəns] n arrogancia; **arrogant** [-gənt] a arrogante.

arrow ['ærəu] n flecha.

arsenal ['ɑːsɪnl] n arsenal m.

arsenic ['ɑːsnɪk] n arsénico.

arson ['ɑːsn] n delito de incendiar.

art [ɑːt] n arte m; (*craft*) artes fpl y oficios mpl; (*skill*) destreza; (*technique*) técnica; **A ~s** npl (SCOL) Letras fpl; **~ gallery** n museo de bellas artes; (*small and private*) galería de arte.

artery ['ɑːtərɪ] n (MED) arteria; (*fig*) vía principal.

arthritis [ɑː'θraɪtɪs] n artritis f.

artichoke ['ɑːtɪtʃəuk] n alcachofa; **Jerusalem ~** aguaturma.

article ['ɑːtɪkl] n artículo, objeto, cosa; (*in*

newspaper) artículo; (LAW: *training*): **~s** npl contrato sg de aprendizaje.

articulate [ɑː'tɪkjulɪt] a claro o distinto en el hablar // vt [-leɪt] articular; **~d lorry** n camión m articulado.

artificial [ɑːtɪ'fɪʃəl] a artificial; (*teeth etc*) postizo; **~ respiration** n respiración f artificial.

artillery [ɑː'tɪlərɪ] n artillería.

artisan ['ɑːtɪzæn] n artesano.

artist ['ɑːtɪst] n artista m/f; (MUS) intérprete m/f; (~**ic** [ɑː'tɪstɪk] a artístico; **~ry** n arte m, habilidad f artística.

artless ['ɑːtlɪs] a (*innocent*) natural, sencillo; (*clumsy*) desmañado.

as [æz, əz] conj (*cause*) como, ya que; (*time: moment*) como, cuando: (: *duration*) mientras; (*manner*) como, lo mismo que, tal como; (*in the capacity of*) como; **~ big ~ tan** grande como; **twice ~ big ~** dos veces más grande que; **~ she said** como ella dijo; **~ if** o **though** como si; **~ for** or **to that** en cuanto a eso, en lo que a eso se refiere; **~ or so long ~** conj mientras (que); **~ much/many ~** tanto(s)... como; **~ soon ~** con: tan pronto como; **~ such** ad como tal; **~ well** ad también, además; **~ well ~** conj así como; see also **such.**

asbestos [æz'bɛstɔs] n asbesto, amianto.

ascend [ə'sɛnd] vt subir; **~ancy** n ascendiente n, dominio.

ascent [ə'sɛnt] n subida; (*slope*) cuesta, pendiente m; (*promotion*) ascenso.

ascertain [æsə'teɪn] vt averiguar, determinar.

ascetic [ə'sɛtɪk] a ascético.

ascribe [ə'skraɪb] vt: **to ~ sth to** atribuir algo a.

ash [æʃ] n ceniza; (*tree*) fresno.

ashamed [ə'ʃeɪmd] a avergonzado; **to be ~ of** avergonzarse de.

ashen ['æʃn] a ceniciento, pálido.

ashore [ə'ʃɔː*] ad en tierra.

ashtray ['æʃtreɪ] n cenicero.

Asia ['eɪʃə] n Asia; **~n, ~tic** [eɪsɪ'ætɪk] a, n asiático/a.

aside [ə'saɪd] ad aparte, a un lado.

ask [ɑːsk] vt (*question*) preguntar; (*demand*) pedir; (*invite*) invitar; **to ~ sb sth/to do sth** preguntar algo a alguien/pedir a alguien que haga algo; **to ~ sb about sth** preguntar algo a alguien; **to ~ (sb) a question** hacer una pregunta (a alguien); **to ~ sb out to** dinner invitar a comer a uno; **to ~ for** vt fus pedir.

askance [ə'skɑːns] ad: **to look ~ at sb** mirar con recelo a uno.

askew [ə'skjuː] ad sesgado, ladeado, oblicuamente.

asleep [ə'sliːp] a dormido; **to fall ~** dormirse, quedarse dormido.

asparagus [əs'pærəgəs] n espárragos mpl.

aspect ['æspɛkt] n aspecto, apariencia; (*direction in which a building etc faces*) orientación f.

aspersions [əs'pəːʃənz] npl: **to cast ~ on** difamar a, calumniar a.

asphalt ['æsfælt] n asfalto; (place) pista asfaltada.

asphyxiate [æs'fɪksɪeɪt] vt asfixiar // vi asfixiarse; **asphyxiation** [-'eɪʃən] n asfixia.

aspiration [æspə'reɪʃən] n (fig) anhelo, deseo, ambición f.

aspire [əs'paɪə*] vi: **to ~ to** aspirar a, ambicionar.

aspirin ['æsprɪn] n aspirina.

ass [æs] n asno, burro; (col) imbécil m.

assailant [ə'seɪlənt] n asaltador/a m/f, agresor/a m/f.

assassin [ə'sæsɪn] n asesino; **~ate** vt asesinar; **~ation** [-'neɪʃən] n asesinato.

assault [ə'sɔːlt] n (gen: attack) asalto, ataque m // vt asaltar, atacar; (sexually) violar.

assemble [ə'sɛmbl] vt reunir, juntar; (TECH) montar // vi reunirse, juntarse.

assembly [ə'sɛmblɪ] n (meeting) reunión f asamblea; (people) concurrencia; (construction) montaje m; **~ line** n línea de producción.

assent [ə'sɛnt] n asentimiento, aprobación f // vi consentir, asentir.

assert [ə'səːt] vt afirmar; (claim etc) hacer valer; **~ion** [ə'səːʃən] n afirmación f.

assess [ə'sɛs] vt valorar, calcular; (tax, damages) fijar; (property etc: for tax) gravar; **~ment** n valoración f; gravamen m; **~or** n asesor/a m/f; (of tax) tasador/a m/f.

asset ['æsɛt] n posesión f; (quality) ventaja sg; **~s** npl (funds) activo sg, fondos mpl.

assiduous [ə'sɪdjuəs] a asiduo.

assign [ə'saɪn] vt (date) fijar; (task) asignar; (resources) destinar; (property) traspasar; **~ment** n asignación f; (task) tarea.

assimilate [ə'sɪmɪleɪt] vt asimilar.

assist [ə'sɪst] vt ayudar; (progress etc) fomentar; **~ance** n ayuda, auxilio; (welfare) subsidio; **~ant** n ayudante m/f, auxiliar m/f; (also: **shop ~ant**) dependiente/a m/f.

assizes [ə'saɪzɪz] npl sesión f de un tribunal.

associate [ə'səuʃɪt] a asociado // n asociado, colega m; (in crime) cómplice m/f; (member) miembro f // (vb: [-ʃieɪt]) vt asociar, relacionar // vi: **to ~ with sb** tratar con alguien.

association [əsəusɪ'eɪʃən] n asociación f; (COMM) sociedad f.

assorted [ə'sɔːtɪd] a surtido, variado.

assortment [ə'sɔːtmənt] n surtido.

assume [ə'sjuːm] vt (suppose) suponer, dar por sentado; (responsibilities etc) asumir; (attitude, name) adoptar, tomar.

assumption [ə'sʌmpʃən] n (supposition) suposición f, presunción f; (act) asunción f.

assurance [ə'ʃuərəns] n garantía, promesa; (confidence) confianza, aplomo; (certainty) certeza; (insurance) seguro f.

assure [ə'ʃuə*] vt asegurar.

asterisk ['æstərɪsk] n asterisco.

astern [ə'stəːn] ad a popa, por la popa.

asteroid ['æstərɔɪd] n asteroide m.

asthma ['æsmə] n asma; **~tic** [æs'mætɪk] a, n asmático/a.

astonish [ə'stɔnɪʃ] vt asombrar, pasmar; **~ment** n asombro, sorpresa.

astound [ə'staund] vt asombrar, pasmar.

astray [ə'streɪ] ad: **to go ~** extraviarse; **to lead ~** llevar por mal camino.

astride [ə'straɪd] ad a horcajadas // prep a caballo o horcajadas sobre.

astrologer [əs'trɔlədʒə*] n astrólogo; **astrology** [-dʒɪ] n astrología.

astronaut ['æstrənɔːt] n astronauta m/f.

astronomer [əs'trɔnəmə*] n astrónomo; **astronomical** [æstrə'nɔmɪkəl] a astronómico; (fig) tremendo, enorme; **astronomy** [-mɪ] n astronomía.

astute [əs'tjuːt] a astuto.

asunder [ə'sʌndə*] ad: **to tear ~** romper en dos, hacer pedazos.

asylum [ə'saɪləm] n (refuge) asilo; (hospital) manicomio.

at [æt] prep en, a; **~ the top** en la cumbre; **~ 4 o'clock** a las cuatro; **~ £1 a kilo** a libra el kilo; **~ night** de noche, por la noche; **~ a stroke** de un golpe; **two ~ a time** de dos en dos; **~ times** a veces.

ate [eɪt] pt of eat.

atheist ['eɪθɪɪst] n ateo/a.

Athens ['æθɪnz] n Atenas f.

athlete ['æθliːt] n atleta m/f.

athletic [æθ'lɛtɪk] a atlético; **~s** n atletismo.

Atlantic [ət'læntɪk] n: **the ~ (Ocean)** el (Océano) Atlántico.

atlas ['ætləs] n atlas m.

atmosphere ['ætməsfɪə*] n atmósfera; (fig) ambiente m.

atom ['ætəm] n átomo; **~ic** [ə'tɔmɪk] a atómico; **~(ic) bomb** n bomba atómica; **~izer** ['ætəmaɪzə*] n atomizador m.

atone [ə'təun] vi: **to ~ for** expiar.

atrocious [ə'trəuʃəs] a (very bad) atroz; (fig) horrible, infame.

atrocity [ə'trɔsɪtɪ] n atrocidad f.

attach [ə'tætʃ] vt (gen) sujetar, pegar; (document, letter) adjuntar; **to be ~ed to sb/sth** (to like) tener cariño a alguien/algo.

attaché [ə'tæʃeɪ] n agregado; **~ case** n maletín m.

attachment [ə'tætʃmənt] n (tool) accesorio; (love): **~ (to)** cariño (a).

attack [ə'tæk] vt (MIL) atacar; (criminal) agredir, asaltar; (task etc) emprender // n ataque m, asalto; (on sb's life) atentado; **heart ~** ataque al corazón o cardíaco; **~er** n agresor/a m/f, asaltante m/f.

attain [ə'teɪn] vt (also: **~ to**) alcanzar; (achieve) lograr, conseguir; **~ments** npl dotes fpl, talento sg.

attempt [ə'tɛmpt] n tentativa, intento; (attack) atentado // vt intentar, tratar de.

attend [ə'tɛnd] vt asistir a; (patient) atender; **to ~ to** vt fus (needs, affairs etc) ocuparse de; (speech etc) prestar atención a; (customer) atender a; **~ance** n asistencia, presencia; (people present) concurrencia; **~ant** n sirviente/a m/f, mozo/a; (THEATRE) acomodador/a m/f // a concomitante.

attention [ə'tɛnʃən] n atención f // excl (MIL) ¡firme(s)!; **for the ~ of...** (ADMIN) atención... .

attentive [ə'tɛntɪv] a atento; (polite) cortés.

attest [ə'tɛst] vi: **to ~ to** dar fe de.

attic ['ætɪk] n desván m, ático.

attitude ['ætɪtjuːd] n (gen) actitud f; (disposition) disposición f.

attorney [ə'tɜːnɪ] n (lawyer) abogado; (having proxy) apoderado; **A~ General** n (Brit) fiscal m de la corona; (US) procurador m general.

attract [ə'trækt] vt atraer; (attention) llamar; **attraction** [ə'trækʃən] n (gen pl) encantos mpl; (amusements) diversiones fpl; (PHYSICS) atracción f; (fig: towards sth) atractivo; **~ive** a atractivo; (interesting) atrayente; (pretty) guapo, mono.

attribute ['ætrɪbjuːt] n atributo // vt [ə'trɪbjuːt]: **to ~ sth to** atribuir o achacar algo a.

aubergine ['əʊbəʒiːn] n berenjena.

auburn ['ɔːbən] a castaño rojizo.

auction ['ɔːkʃən] n (also: **sale by ~**) subasta // vt subastar; **~eer** [-'nɪə*] n subastador/a m/f.

audacious [ɔː'deɪʃəs] a audaz, atrevido; (pej) descarado; **audacity** [ɔː'dæsɪtɪ] n audacia, atrevimiento; (pej) descaro.

audible ['ɔːdɪbl] a audible, que se puede oír.

audience ['ɔːdɪəns] n auditorio, público; (interview) audiencia.

audio-visual [ɔːdɪəʊ'vɪzjuəl] a audiovisual.

audit ['ɔːdɪt] vt revisar, intervenir.

audition [ɔː'dɪʃən] n audición f.

auditor ['ɔːdɪtə*] n interventor/a m/f, censor/a m/f de cuentas.

auditorium [ɔːdɪ'tɔːrɪəm] n auditorio.

augment [ɔːg'mɛnt] vt aumentar // vi aumentarse.

augur ['ɔːgə*] vi: **it ~s well** es de buen agüero.

August ['ɔːgəst] n agosto.

aunt [ɑːnt] n tía; **~ie, ~y** n diminutive of **aunt**.

au pair ['əʊ'pɛə*] n (also: **~ girl**) au pair f.

aura ['ɔːrə] n emanación f; (atmosphere) ambiente m.

auspices ['ɔːspɪsɪz] npl: **under the ~ of** bajo los auspicios de.

auspicious [ɔːs'pɪʃəs] a propicio, de buen augurio.

austere [ɒs'tɪə*] a austero; (manner) adusto; **austerity** [ɔ'stɛrɪtɪ] n austeridad f.

Australia [ɒs'treɪlɪə] n Australia; **~n** a, n australiano/a.

Austria ['ɒstrɪə] n Austria; **~n** a, n austríaco/a.

authentic [ɔː'θɛntɪk] a auténtico.

author ['ɔːθə] n autor/a m/f.

authoritarian [ɔːθɔrɪ'tɛərɪən] a autoritario.

authoritative [ɔː'θɔrɪtətɪv] a autorizado; (manner) autoritario.

authority [ɔː'θɔrɪtɪ] n autoridad f; **the authorities** npl las autoridades.

authorize ['ɔːθəraɪz] vt autorizar.

auto ['ɔːtəʊ] n (US) coche m, automóvil m.

autobiography [ɔːtəbaɪ'ɔgrəfɪ] n autobiografía.

autocratic [ɔːtə'krætɪk] a autocrático.

autograph ['ɔːtəgrɑːf] n autógrafo // vt firmar; (photo etc) dedicar.

automatic [ɔːtə'mætɪk] a automático // n (gun) pistola automática.

automation [ɔːtə'meɪʃən] n automatización f.

automaton [ɔː'tɔmətən], pl **-mata** [-tə] n autómata m/f.

automobile ['ɔːtəməbiːl] n (US) coche m, automóvil m.

autonomous [ɔː'tɔnəməs] a autónomo.

autopsy ['ɔːtɔpsɪ] n autopsia.

autumn ['ɔːtəm] n otoño.

auxiliary [ɔːg'zɪlɪərɪ] a auxiliar.

Av. abbr of **avenue**.

avail [ə'veɪl] vt: **to ~ o.s. of** aprovechar(se) de, valerse de // n: **to no ~** en vano, sin resultado.

availability [əveɪlə'bɪlɪtɪ] n disponibilidad f.

available [ə'veɪləbl] a disponible; (usable) asequible.

avalanche ['ævəlɑːnʃ] n alud m, avalancha.

avant-garde ['ævãŋ'gɑːd] a de vanguardia.

avaricious [ævə'rɪʃəs] a avaro, avariento.

Ave. abbr of **avenue**.

avenge [ə'vɛndʒ] vt vengar.

avenue ['ævənjuː] n avenida; (path) camino.

average ['ævərɪdʒ] n promedio, término medio // a (mean) medio, de término medio; (ordinary) regular, corriente // vt calcular el promedio de, prorratear; **on ~** por regla general; **to ~ out** vi: **to ~ out at** resultar por promedio, ser por regla general.

averse [ə'vɜːs] a: **to be ~ to sth/doing** sentir aversión o antipatía por algo/por hacer; **aversion** [ə'vɜːʃən] n aversión f, repugnancia.

avert [ə'vɜːt] vt prevenir; (blow) desviar; (one's eyes) apartar.

aviary ['eɪvɪərɪ] n pajarera, avería.

aviation [eɪvɪ'eɪʃən] n aviación f.

avid ['ævɪd] a ávido, ansioso.

avocado [ævə'kɑːdəʊ] n (also: **~ pear**) aguacate m.

avoid [ə'vɔɪd] vt evitar, eludir; **~able** a

evitable, eludible; ~**ance** n el evitar, evitación f.

await [ə'weɪt] vt esperar, aguardar.

awake [ə'weɪk] a despierto // vb: pt **awoke**, pp **awoken** or **awaked**) vt despertar // vi despertarse; ~**ning** n el despertar.

award [ə'wɔːd] n (prize) premio, condecoración f; (LAW) fallo, sentencia; (act) concesión f // vt (prize) otorgar, conceder; (LAW: damages) adjudicar, decretar.

aware [ə'wɛə*] a consciente; (awake) despierto; (informed) enterado; to **become** ~ of darse cuenta de, enterarse de; ~**ness** n conciencia, conocimiento.

awash [ə'wɒʃ] a inundado.

away [ə'weɪ] ad (gen) fuera; (far ~) lejos; **two kilometres** ~ a dos kilómetros de distancia; **two hours** ~ **by car** a dos horas en coche; **the holiday was two weeks** ~ faltaba dos semanas para las vacaciones; ~ **from** lejos de, fuera de; **he's** ~ **for a week** estará ausente una semana; to **take** ~ vt llevar(se); to **work/pedal** ~ seguir trabajando/pedaleando; to **fade** ~ desvanecerse; (sound) apagarse; ~ **match** n (SPORT) partido de fuera.

awe [ɔː] n pavor m, respeto, temor m reverencial; ~**inspiring**, ~**some** a imponente, pasmoso; ~**struck** a pasmado.

awful ['ɔːfəl] a tremendo, terrible, pasmoso; ~**ly** ad (very) terriblemente.

awhile [ə'waɪl] ad durante un rato, un rato, algún tiempo.

awkward ['ɔːkwəd] a (clumsy) desmañado, torpe; (shape) incómodo; (problem) difícil; (embarrassing) delicado, desagradable.

awning ['ɔːnɪŋ] n (of shop) toldo; (of window etc) marquesina.

awoke [ə'wəuk], **awoken** [-kən] pt, pp of **awake**.

awry [ə'raɪ] ad: to **be** ~ estar de través o al sesgo; to **go** ~ salir mal, fracasar.

axe, ax (US) [æks] n hacha // vt (employee) despedir; (project etc) parar, cortar; (jobs) reducir.

axiom ['æksɪəm] n axioma m.

axis ['æksɪs], pl **axes** [-siːz] n eje m.

axle ['æksl] n eje m, árbol m.

ay(e) [aɪ] excl (yes) sí; **the ayes** npl los que votan a favor.

Aztec ['æztɛk] n azteca m/f.

B

B.A. abbr of **Bachelor of Arts** licenciado en letras.

babble ['bæbl] vi barbullar.

baboon [bə'buːn] n mandril m.

baby ['beɪbɪ] n nene/a m/f; ~ **carriage** (US) cochecito; ~**ish** a infantil; ~**sit** vi hacer de canguro; ~**sitter** n canguro m/f.

bachelor ['bætʃələ*] n soltero.

back [bæk] n (of person) espalda; (of animal) lomo; (of hand) dorso; (of house, car, train) parte f de atrás; (of chair) respaldo; (of page) reverso; (FOOTBALL) defensa m // ~ (candidate: also: ~ **up**) respaldar, apoyar; (horse: at races) apostar a; (car) dar marcha atrás a o con // vi (car etc) dar marcha atrás // a (in compounds) tras; ~ **seats/wheels** (AUT) asientos mpl/ruedas fpl de atrás; ~ **payments** pagos mpl con efecto retroactivo; ~ **rent** renta atrasada // ad (not forward) (hacia) atrás; (returned): **he's** ~ está de vuelta, ha vuelto; **he ran** ~ retrocedió corriendo; (restitution): **throw the ball** ~ devuelva la pelota; **can I have it** ~? ¿me lo devuelve?; (again): **he called** ~ llamó de nuevo; to ~ **down** vi echarse atrás; to ~ **out** vi (of promise) volverse atrás.

back: ~**ache** n dolor m de espalda; ~**bencher** n miembro del parlamento sin portafolio; ~**biting** a murmuración f; ~**bone** n columna vertebral; ~**cloth** n telón m de foro; ~**date** vt (letter) poner fecha atrasada a; ~**dated pay rise** alza de sueldo con efecto retroactivo; ~ **fire** vi (AUT) petardear; (plans) fallar, salir al revés; ~**gammon** n backgammon m; ~**ground** n fondo; (of events) antecedentes mpl; (basic knowledge) bases fpl; (experience) conocimientos mpl, educación f; **family** ~ **ground** origen m, antecedentes mpl; ~**hand** n (TENNIS: also: ~**hand stroke**) revés m; ~**handed** a (fig) ambiguo, equívoco; ~**hander** n (bribe) soborno; ~**ing** n (fig) apoyo, respaldo; ~**lash** n reacción f, resaca; ~**log** n: ~**log of work** atrasos mpl; ~ **number** n (of magazine etc) número atrasado; ~ **pay** n pago atrasado; ~**side** n (col) trasero, culo; ~**stage** ad entre bastidores; ~**stroke** n braza de espaldas; ~**ward** a (movement) hacia atrás; (person, country) atrasado; (shy) tímido; ~**wards** ad (move, go) hacia atrás; (read a list) al revés; (fall) de espaldas; ~**water** n (fig) lugar m atrasado o apartado; ~**yard** n traspatio.

bacon ['beɪkən] n tocino.

bacteria [bæk'tɪərɪə] npl bacteria sg.

bad [bæd] a malo; (serious) grave (meat food) podrido, pasado; to **go** ~ echarse a perder.

badge [bædʒ] n insignia; (of policeman) chapa, placa.

badger ['bædʒə*] n tejón m.

badly ['bædlɪ] ad (work, dress etc) mal; ~ **wounded** gravemente herido; **he needs it** ~ le hace gran falta; to **be** ~ **off (for money)** andar mal de dinero.

badminton ['bædmɪntən] n badminton m.

bad-tempered ['bæd'tempəd] a de mal genio o carácter; (temporary) de mal humor.

baffle ['bæfl] vt (puzzle) desconcertar, confundir.

bag [bæg] n bolsa, saco; (handbag) bolso; (satchel) mochila; (case) maleta; (of hunter) caza // vt (col: take) coger, pescar; ~**ful** n saco (lleno); ~**gage** n equipaje m; ~**gy** a que hace bolsas; ~**pipes** npl gaita sg.

bail [beɪl] n fianza, caución f // vt (prisoner: gen: give ~ to) poner en libertad bajo fianza; (boat: also: ~ out) achicar; **to ~ sb out** obtener la libertad de uno bajo fianza; see also **bale**.

bailiff ['beɪlɪf] n alguacil m.

bait [beɪt] n cebo // vt cebar, poner el cebo en.

bake [beɪk] vt cocer (al horno) // vi (cook) cocerse; (be hot) hacer un calor terrible; ~**d beans** npl judías fpl en salsa de tomate; **baker** n panadero; ~**ry** n (for bread) panadería; (for cakes) pastelería; **baking** n (act) cocción f; (batch) hornada; **baking powder** n polvos mpl de levadura.

balaclava [bælə'klɑːvə] n (also: ~ **helmet**) pasamontañas m inv.

balance ['bæləns] n equilibrio; (COMM. sum) balance m; (remainder) resto; (scales) balanza // vt equilibrar; (budget) nivelar; (account) saldar; (compensate) contrapesar; ~ **of trade/payments** balanza de comercio/pagos; ~**d** a (personality, diet) equilibrado; ~ **sheet** n balance m.

balcony ['bælkənɪ] n (open) balcón m; (closed) galería.

bald [bɔːld] a calvo; ~**ness** n calvicie f.

bale [beɪl] n (AGR) paca, fardo; **to ~ out** (of a plane) lanzarse en paracaídas; **to ~ sb out of a difficulty** sacar a uno de un problema.

baleful ['beɪlful] a (look) triste; (sinister) funesto, siniestro.

ball [bɔːl] n bola; (football) balón m; (for tennis, golf) pelota; (dance) baile m.

ballad ['bæləd] n balada, romance m.

ballast ['bæləst] n lastre m.

ballerina [bælə'riːnə] n bailarina.

ballet ['bæleɪ] n ballet m, baile m; ~ **dancer** n bailarín/ina m/f.

balloon [bə'luːn] n globo; ~**ist** n ascensionista m/f.

ballot ['bælət] n votación f; ~ **box** n urna (electoral); ~ **paper** n papeleta.

ball-point pen ['bɔːlpɔɪnt'-] n bolígrafo.

ballroom ['bɔːlrum] n salón m de baile.

balmy ['bɑːmɪ] a (breeze, air) suave, fragante; (col) = **barmy**.

Baltic ['bɔːltɪk] n: **the ~ (Sea)** el (Mar) Báltico.

balustrade ['bæləstreɪd] n barandilla.

bamboo [bæm'buː] n bambú m.

ban [bæn] n prohibición f, proscripción f // vt prohibir, proscribir; (exclude) excluir.

banal [bə'nɑːl] a banal, vulgar.

banana [bə'nɑːnə] n plátano.

band [bænd] n (group) banda; (gang) pandilla; (strip) faja, tira; (at a dance)

orquesta; (MIL) banda; **to ~ together** vi juntarse, asociarse.

bandage ['bændɪdʒ] n venda, vendaje m // vt vendar.

bandit ['bændɪt] n bandido; **one-armed ~** máquina tragaperras.

bandstand ['bændstænd] n quiosco.

bandwagon ['bændwægən] n: **to jump on the ~** (fig) seguir la corriente o la moda.

bandy ['bændɪ] vt (jokes, insults) cambiar.

bandy-legged ['bændɪ'lɛgd] a estevado.

bang [bæŋ] n estallido; (cf door) portazo; (blow) golpe m // vt hacer estallar; (door) cerrar de golpe // vi estallar.

banger ['bæŋə*] n (car: gen: old ~) chatarra.

bangle ['bæŋgl] n ajorca.

banish ['bænɪʃ] vt desterrar.

banister(s) ['bænɪstə(z)] n(pl) pasamanos m inv.

banjo ['bændʒəu], pl ~**es** or ~**s** n banjo.

bank [bæŋk] n (COMM) banco; (of river, lake) ribera, orilla; (of earth) terraplén m // vi (AVIAT) ladearse; **to ~ on** vt fus contar con; **to ~ with** tener la cuenta con; ~ **account** n cuenta de banco; ~ **B~ holiday** n día m festivo; ~**ing** n banca; ~**note** n billete m de banco; ~ **rate** n tipo de interés bancario.

bankrupt ['bæŋkrəpt] n quebrado/a // a quebrado, insolvente; **to go ~** quebrar; **to be ~** estar en quiebra; ~**cy** n quiebra; (fraudulent) bancarrota.

banner ['bænə*] n bandera; (in demonstration) pancarta.

banns [bænz] npl amonestaciones fpl.

banquet ['bæŋkwɪt] n banquete m.

baptism ['bæptɪzəm] n bautismo.

baptize [bæp'taɪz] vt bautizar.

bar [bɑː*] n barra; (of window etc) tranca; (of soap) pastilla; (fig: hindrance) obstáculo; (prohibition) proscripción f; (pub) bar m; (counter: in pub) mostrador m; (MUS) barra // vt (road) obstruir; (window) atrancar; (person) excluir; (activity) prohibir; **behind ~s** en la cárcel; **the B~** (LAW: profession) la abogacía; (people) el cuerpo de abogados; ~ **none** sin excepción.

barbaric [bɑː'bærɪk] a bárbaro.

barbarous ['bɑːbərəs] a bárbaro.

barbecue ['bɑːbɪkjuː] n barbacoa.

barbed wire ['bɑːbd-] n alambre m de púas.

barber ['bɑːbə*] n peluquero, barbero.

barbiturate [bɑː'bɪtjurɪt] n barbitúrico.

bare [bɛə*] a desnudo; (head) descubierto // vt desnudar; **to ~ one's teeth** enseñar los dientes; ~**back** ad sin montura; ~**faced** a descarado; ~**foot** a, ad descalzo; ~**ly** ad apenas.

bargain ['bɑːgɪn] n pacto, negocio; (good buy) ganga // vi negociar; (haggle) regatear; **into the ~** además, por añadidura.

barge [bɑːdʒ] n barcaza; **to ~ in** vi

irrumpir, entrar sin permiso; **to ~ into** vt fus dar contra.

baritone [ˈbærɪtəun] n barítono.

bark [bɑːk] n (of tree) corteza; (of dog) ladrido // vi ladrar.

barley [ˈbɑːlɪ] n cebada.

barmaid [ˈbɑːmeɪd] n camarera.

barman [ˈbɑːmən] n camarero, barman m.

barmy [ˈbɑːmɪ] a (col) chiflado, ledo.

barn [bɑːn] n granero.

barnacle [ˈbɑːnəkl] n percebe m.

barometer [bəˈrɔmɪtə*] n barómetro.

baron [ˈbærən] n barón m; **~ess** n baronesa.

barracks [ˈbærəks] npl cuartel m.

barrage [ˈbærɑːʒ] n (MIL) descarga, bombardeo; (dam) presa.

barrel [ˈbærəl] n tonel m, barril m; (of gun) cañón m.

barren [ˈbærən] a estéril, árido.

barricade [bærɪˈkeɪd] n barricada // vt levantar barricadas.

barrier [ˈbærɪə*] n barrera.

barring [ˈbɑːrɪŋ] prep excepto, salvo.

barrister [ˈbærɪstə*] n abogado m/f.

barrow [ˈbærəu] n (cart) carretilla (de mano).

bartender [ˈbɑːtendə*] n (US) camarero, barman m.

barter [ˈbɑːtə*] vt: **to ~ sth for sth** trocar algo por algo.

base [beɪs] n base f // vt: **to ~ sth on** basar o fundar algo en // a bajo, infame; **~ball** n béisbol m; **~ment** n sótano.

bash [bæʃ] vt (col) golpear.

bashful [ˈbæʃful] a tímido, vergonzoso.

bashing [ˈbæʃɪŋ] n (col) tunda.

basic [ˈbeɪsɪk] a básico; **~ally** ad fundamentalmente, en el fondo.

basil [ˈbæzɪl] n albahaca.

basin [ˈbeɪsn] n (vessel) cuenco, tazón m; (GEO) cuenca; (also: **wash~**) palangana, jofaina.

basis [ˈbeɪsɪs], pl **-ses** [-siːz] n base f.

bask [bɑːsk] vi: **to ~ in the sun** tomar el sol.

basket [ˈbɑːskɪt] n cesta, cesto; (with handle) canasta; **~ball** n baloncesto; **~work** n cestería.

Basque [bæsk] a, n vasco/a; **~ Country** Euskadi m, País m Vasco.

bass [beɪs] n (MUS) contrabajo.

bassoon [bəˈsuːn] n bajón m.

bastard [ˈbɑːstəd] n bastardo.

baste [beɪst] vt (CULIN) pringar.

bastion [ˈbæstɪən] n baluarte m.

bat [bæt] n (ZOOL) murciélago; (for ball games) palo; (for cricket, baseball) bate m; (for table tennis) raqueta; **he didn't ~ an eyelid** ni pestañeó.

batch [bætʃ] n (of bread) hornada; (of papers) colección f, lote m.

bated [ˈbeɪtɪd] a: **with ~ breath** sin respiración.

bath [bɑːθ, pl bɑːðz] n (~ tub) baño, bañera; (also: **~s** pl) baño, piscina // vt bañar;

have a ~ bañarse, tomar un baño; **~chair** n silla de ruedas.

bathe [beɪð] vi bañarse // vt bañar; **bather** n bañista m/f.

bathing [ˈbeɪðɪŋ] n el bañarse; **~ cap** n gorro de baño; **~ costume** n traje m de baño; **~ trunks** npl bañador m.

bath: ~mat n estera de baño; **~room** n (cuarto de) baño; **~s** npl piscina sg; **~ towel** n toalla de baño.

baton [ˈbætən] n (MUS) batuta.

battalion [bəˈtælɪən] n batallón m.

batter [ˈbætə*] vt apalear, azotar // n batido; **~ed** a (hat, pan) estropeado.

battery [ˈbætərɪ] n batería; (of torch) pila.

battle [ˈbætl] n batalla; (fig) lucha // vi luchar; **~field** n campo m de batalla; **~ments** npl almenas fpl; **~ship** n acorazado.

bawdy [ˈbɔːdɪ] a indecente; (joke) verde.

bawl [bɔːl] vi chillar, gritar.

bay [beɪ] n (GEO) bahía; (BOT) laurel m // vi aullar; **to hold sb at ~** mantener a alguien a raya.

bayonet [ˈbeɪənɪt] n bayoneta.

bay window [beɪ-] n ventana satrrza.

bazaar [bəˈzɑː*] n bazar m.

bazooka [bəˈzuːkə] n bazuca.

b. & b., B. & B. abbr of bed and breakfast cama y desayuno.

BBC n abbr of British Broadcasting Corporation.

B.C. ad abbr of before Christ a. de J.C. (antes de Jesucristo).

be [biː] pt was, were, pp been vi (of state) ser; (of place, temporary condition) estar; **I am English** soy inglés; **I am tired** estoy cansado; **how are you?** ¿cómo está Usted?; **who is it?** ¿quién es?; **it is raining** está lloviendo; **I am warm** tengo calor, **it is cold** hace frío; **how much is it?** ¿cuánto es o cuesta?; **he is four (years old)** tiene cuatro años; **2 and 2 are 4** dos más dos son cuatro; **where have you been?** ¿dónde has estado?, ¿de dónde vienes?

beach [biːtʃ] n playa // vt varar.

beacon [ˈbiːkən] n (lighthouse) faro; (marker) guía.

bead [biːd] n cuenta, abalorio; (of sweat) gota.

beak [biːk] n pico.

beaker [ˈbiːkə*] n jarra.

beam [biːm] n (ARCH) viga, travesaño; (of light) rayo, haz m de luz // vi brillar; (smile) sonreír; **~ing** a (sun, smile) radiante.

bean [biːn] n judía; **runner/broad ~** habichuela/haba; **coffee ~** grano de café.

bear [beə*] n oso // vb (pt bore, pp borne) vt (weight etc) llevar; (cost) pagar; (responsibility) tener; (endure) soportar, aguantar; (stand up to) resistir a; (children) parir // vi: **to ~ right/left** torcer a la derecha/izquierda; **~able** a soportable.

beard [bɪəd] n barba; **~ed** a barbado.

bearing ['bɛərɪŋ] *n* porte *m*, comportamiento; (*connection*) relación *f*; (**ball**) ~**s** *npl* cojinetes *mpl* a bolas; **to take a** ~ marcarse; **to find one's** ~**s** orientarse.

beast [biːst] *n* bestia; (*col*) bruto, salvaje *m*; ~**ly** *a* bestial; (*awful*) horrible.

beat [biːt] *n* (*of heart*) latido; (*MUS*) ritmo, compás *m*; (*of policeman*) ronda // (*vb: pt* **beat**, *pp* **beaten**) *vt* (*hit*) golpear; (*eggs*) batir; (*defeat*) vencer, derrotar; (*better*) sobrepasar; (*drum*) tocar; (*rhythm*) marcar // *vi* (*heart*) latir; **to** ~ **about the bush** ir por rodeos; **to** ~ **it** largarse; **to** ~ **off** *vt* rechazar; **to** ~ **up** *vt* (*col: person*) dar una paliza a; ~**er** *n* (*for eggs, cream*) batidora; ~**ing** *n* golpeo.

beautiful ['bjuːtɪful] *a* hermoso, bello; ~**ly** *ad* maravillosamente; **beautify** [-faɪ] *vt* embellecer.

beauty ['bjuːtɪ] *n* belleza, hermosura; (*person*) belleza; ~ **salon** *n* salón *m* de belleza; ~ **spot** *n* lunar *m* postizo; (*TOURISM*) lugar *m* de excepcional belleza.

beaver ['biːvə*] *n* castor *m*.

becalmed [bɪ'kɑːmd] *a* encalmado.

became [bɪ'keɪm] *pt of* **become.**

because [bɪ'kɔz] *conj* porque; ~ **of** *prep* debido a, a causa de.

beck [bɛk] *n*: **to be at the** ~ **and call of** estar a disposición de.

beckon ['bɛkən] *vt* (*also*: ~ **to**) llamar con señas.

become [bɪ'kʌm] (*irg: like* **come**) *vt* (*suit*) favorecer, sentar a // *vi* (+ *noun*) hacerse, llegar a ser; (+ *adj*) ponerse, volverse; **to** ~ **fat** engordarse.

becoming [bɪ'kʌmɪŋ] *a* (*behaviour*) decoroso; (*clothes*) favorecedor(a).

bed [bɛd] *n* cama; (*of flowers*) macizo; (*of coal, clay*) capa; **to go to** ~ acostarse; **single/double** ~ cama individual/matrimonial; ~**clothes** *npl* ropa *sg* de cama; ~**ding** *n* ropa de cama.

bedlam ['bɛdləm] *n* confusión *f*.

bedraggled [bɪ'drægld] *a* mojado, ensuciado.

bed: ~**ridden** *a* postrado (en cama); ~**room** *n* dormitorio, alcoba; ~**side** *n*: **at sb's** ~**side** a la cabecera de alguien; ~**sit(ter)** *n* apartamento; ~**spread** *n* sobrecama *m*, colcha.

bee [biː] *n* abeja.

beech [biːtʃ] *n* haya.

beef [biːf] *n* carne *f* de vaca; **roast** ~ rosbif *m*.

bee: ~**hive** *n* colmena; ~**line** *n*: **to make a** ~**line for** ir derecho a.

been [biːn] *pp of* **be.**

beer [bɪə*] *n* cerveza.

beetle ['biːtl] *n* escarabajo.

beetroot ['biːtruːt] *n* remolacha.

before [bɪ'fɔː*] *prep* (*of time*) antes de; (*of space*) delante de // *conj* antes (de) que // *ad* (*time*) antes, anteriormente; (*space*) delante, adelante; **the week** ~ la semana

anterior; **I've never seen it** ~ no lo he visto nunca.

befriend [bɪ'frɛnd] *vt* ofrecer amistad a, ayudar.

beg [bɛg] *vi* pedir, rogar; (*as beggar*) pedir limosna // *vt* pedir, rogar; (*entreat*) suplicar.

began [bɪ'gæn] *pt of* **begin.**

beggar ['bɛgə*] *n* mendigo.

begin [bɪ'gɪn], *pt* **began**, *pp* **begun** *vt, vi* empezar, comenzar; ~**ner** *n* principiante *m/f*; ~**ning** *n* principio, comienzo.

begrudge [bɪ'grʌdʒ] *vt*: **to** ~ **sb sth** tenerle envidia a alguien por algo.

begun [bɪ'gʌn] *pp of* **begin.**

behalf [bɪ'hɑːf] *n*: **on** ~ **of** en nombre de, por.

behave [bɪ'heɪv] *vi* (*person*) portarse, comportarse; (*thing*) funcionar; (*well: also*: ~ **o.s.**) portarse bien; **behaviour, behavior** (*US*) *n* comportamiento, conducta.

behind [bɪ'haɪnd] *prep* detrás de // *ad* detrás, por detrás, atrás // *n* trasero; ~ **time** atrasado.

behold [bɪ'həuld] (*irg: like* **hold**) *vt* contemplar.

beige [beɪʒ] *a* beige.

being ['biːɪŋ] *n* ser *m*; **to come into** ~ nacer, aparecer.

belated [bɪ'leɪtɪd] *a* atrasado, tardío.

belch [bɛltʃ] *vi* eructar // *vt* (*gen*: ~ **out**: *smoke etc*) arrojar.

belfry ['bɛlfrɪ] *n* campanario.

Belgian ['bɛldʒən] *a, n* belga *m/f*.

Belgium ['bɛldʒəm] *n* Bélgica.

belie [bɪ'laɪ] *vt* desmentir, contradecir.

belief [bɪ'liːf] *n* (*opinion*) opinión *f*; (*trust, faith*) fe *f*; (*acceptance as true*) creencia.

believable [bɪ'liːvəbl] *a* creíble.

believe [bɪ'liːv] *vt, vi* creer; **believer** *n* creyente *m/f*, fiel *m/f*; (*POL*) partidario/a.

belittle [bɪ'lɪtl] *vt* minimizar, despreciar.

bell [bɛl] *n* campana; (*small*) campanilla; (*on door*) timbre *m*; (*animal's*) cencerro; (*on toy etc*) cascabel *m*.

belligerent [bɪ'lɪdʒərənt] *a* (*at war*) beligerante; (*fig*) agresivo.

bellow ['bɛləu] *vi* bramar; (*person*) rugir // *vt* (*orders*) gritar, vociferar.

bellows ['bɛləuz] *npl* fuelle *m*.

belly ['bɛlɪ] *n* barriga, panza.

belong [bɪ'lɔŋ] *vi*: **to** ~ **to** pertenecer a; (*club etc*) ser socio de; ~**ings** *npl* pertenencias *fpl*.

beloved [bɪ'lʌvɪd] *a, n* querido/a, amado/a.

below [bɪ'ləu] *prep* bajo, debajo de // *ad* abajo, (por) debajo; **see** ~ véase más abajo.

belt [bɛlt] *n* cinturón *m*; (*MED*) faja; (*TECH*) correa, cinta // *vt* (*thrash*) golpear con correa.

bench [bɛntʃ] *n* banco; **the B**~ (*LAW*) tribunal *m*; (*people*) judicatura.

bend [bɛnd], *pt, pp* **bent** *vt* doblar, inclinar;

(leg, arm) torcer // vi doblarse, inclinarse // n (in road) recodo, vuelta (in pipe, river) ángulo, curva; **to ~ down** vi inclinar, doblar; **to ~ over** vi inclinarse.

beneath [bɪ'ni:θ] prep bajo, debajo de; (unworthy of) indigno de // ad abajo, (por) debajo.

benefactor ['benɪfæktə*] n bienhechor m.

beneficial [benɪ'fɪʃəl] a provechoso, beneficioso.

benefit ['benɪfɪt] n beneficio, provecho; (profit) utilidad f; (money) subsidio // vt beneficiar, aprovechar // vi: **he'll ~ from it** le sacará provecho.

Benelux ['benɪlʌks] n Benelux m.

benevolent [bɪ'nevələnt] a benévolo.

bent [bent] pt, pp of **bend** // n inclinación f // a: **to be ~ on** estar empeñado en.

bequeath [bɪ'kwi:ð] vt legar.

bequest [bɪ'kwest] n legado.

bereaved [bɪ'ri:vd] n: **the ~** los afligidos mpl; **bereavement** [-'ri:vmənt] n aflicción f.

beret ['bereɪ] n boina.

berry ['berɪ] n baya.

berserk [bə'sə:k] a: **to go ~** perder los estribos.

berth [bə:θ] n (bed) litera; (cabin) camarote m; (for ship) amarradero // vi atracar, amarrar.

beseech [bɪ'si:tʃ], pt, pp **besought** [-'sɔ:t] vt suplicar.

beset [bɪ'set], pt, pp **beset** vt rodear; (person) acosar.

beside [bɪ'saɪd] prep junto a, al lado de; **to be ~ o.s. (with anger)** estar fuera de sí.

besides [bɪ'saɪdz] ad además // prep (as well as) además de; (except) fuera de, excepto.

besiege [bɪ'si:dʒ] vt (town) sitiar; (fig) asediar.

best [best] a (el/la) mejor // ad (lo) mejor; **the ~ part of** (quantity) la mayor parte de; **at ~** en el mejor de los casos; **to make the ~ of sth** sacar el mejor partido de algo; **to the ~ of my knowledge** que yo sepa; **to the ~ of my ability** como mejor puedo; **~ man** n padrino de boda.

bestow [bɪ'stəu] vt otorgar; (affection) ofrecer.

bestseller ['best'selə*] n éxito de librería, bestseller m.

bet [bet] n apuesta // vt, vi, pt, pp **bet** or **betted** apostar, jugar.

betray [bɪ'treɪ] vt traicionar; (denounce) delatar; **~al** n traición f.

better ['betə*] a mejor // ad mejor // vt mejorar; (go above) superar // n: **to get the ~ of** quedar por encima de alguien; **you had ~ do it** más vale que lo haga; **he thought ~ of it** cambió de parecer; **to get ~** mejorar(se); (MED) reponerse; **~ off** a más acomodado.

betting ['betɪŋ] n juego, el apostar; **~ shop** n agencia de apuestas.

between [bɪ'twi:n] prep entre // ad en medio.

beverage ['bevərɪdʒ] n bebida.

bevy ['bevɪ] n: **a ~ of** una bandada de.

beware [bɪ'wɛə*] vi: **to ~ (of)** precaverse de, tener cuidado con // excl ¡cuidado!

bewildered [bɪ'wɪldəd] a aturdido, perplejo.

bewitching [bɪ'wɪtʃɪŋ] a hechicero, encantador(a).

beyond [bɪ'jɔnd] prep (in space) más allá de; (exceeding) además de, fuera de; (above) superior a // ad más allá, más lejos; **~ doubt** fuera de toda duda; **~ repair** irreparable.

bias ['baɪəs] n (prejudice) prejuicio, pasión f; (preference) predisposición f; **~(s)ed** a (against) con prejuicios; (towards) partidario.

bib [bɪb] n babero.

Bible ['baɪbl] n Biblia.

bibliography [bɪb'lɪəgrəfɪ] n bibliografía.

bicker ['bɪkə*] vi reñir.

bicycle ['baɪsɪkl] n bicicleta.

bid [bɪd] n (at auction) oferta, postura; (attempt) tentativa, conato // (vb: pt **bade** [bæd] or **bid**, pp **bidden** ['bɪdn] or **bid**) vi hacer una oferta // vt mandar, ordenar; **to ~ sb good day** dar a uno los buenos días; **~der** n: **the highest ~der** el mejor postor; **~ding** n (at auction) ofertas fpl; (order) orden f, mandato.

bide [baɪd] vt: **to ~ one's time** esperar el momento adecuado.

bidet ['bi:deɪ] n bidet m.

bier [bɪə*] n féretro.

big [bɪg] a grande.

bigamy ['bɪgəmɪ] n bigamía.

bigheaded ['bɪg'hedɪd] a engreído.

bigot ['bɪgət] n fanático, intolerante m/f; **~ed** a fanático, intolerante; **~ry** n fanatismo, intolerancia.

bike [baɪk] n bici f.

bikini [bɪ'ki:nɪ] n bikini m.

bile [baɪl] n bilis f.

bilingual [baɪ'lɪŋgwəl] a bilingüe.

bill [bɪl] n (account) cuenta; (invoice) factura; (POL) proyecto de ley; (US: banknote) billete m; (of bird) pico; **stick no ~s** prohibido fijar carteles.

billet ['bɪlɪt] n alojamiento.

billfold ['bɪlfəuld] n (US) cartera.

billiards ['bɪljədz] n billar m.

billion ['bɪljən] n (Brit) billón m; (US) mil millones.

billy goat ['bɪlɪ-] n macho cabrío.

bin [bɪn] n (gen) cubo; **bread/litter ~** nasa/papelera.

bind [baɪnd], pt, pp **bound** vt atar, liar; (wound) vendar; (book) encuadernar; (oblige) obligar; **~ing** a (contract) obligatorio.

binge [bɪndʒ] n borrachera, juerga.

bingo ['bɪŋgəu] n bingo m.

binoculars [bɪ'nɔkjuləz] npl gemelos mpl, prismáticos mpl.

bio... [baɪə] *pref*: **~chemistry** *n* bioquímica; **~graphy** [baɪˈɒɡrəfi] *n* biografía; **~logical** *a* biológico; **~logy** [baɪˈɒlədʒɪ] *n* biología.

birch [bəːtʃ] *n* abedul *m*; (*cά.:ψ*) vara.

bird [bəːd] *n* ave *f*, pájaro; (*col: girl*) chica; **~cage** *n* jaula; **~'s eye view** *n* vista de pájaro; **~ watcher** *n* ornitólogo.

birth [bəːθ] *n* nacimiento; (*MED*) parto; **to give ~ to** parir, dar a luz; **~ certificate** *n* partida de nacimiento; **~ control** *n* control *m* de natalidad; (*methods*) métodos *mpl* anticonceptivos; **~day** *n* cumpleaños *m*; **~place** *n* lugar *m* de nacimiento; **~ rate** *n* (tasa de) natalidad *f*.

biscuit ['bɪskɪt] *n* galleta.

bisect [baɪˈsɛkt] *vt* bisecar.

bishop ['bɪʃəp] *n* obispo.

bit [bɪt] *pt of* **bite** // *n* trozo, pedazo, pedacito; (*of horse*) freno, bocado; **a ~ of** un poco de; **a ~ mad** algo loco; **~ by ~** poco a poco.

bitch [bɪtʃ] *n* (*dog*) perra.

bite [baɪt], *pt* **bit**, *pp* **bitten** *vt*, *vi* morder; (*insect etc*) picar // *n* mordedura; (*insect ~*) picadura; (*mouthful*) bocado; **let's have a ~ (to eat)** comamos algo.

biting ['baɪtɪŋ] *a* penetrante, cortante; (*sharp*) mordaz.

bitten ['bɪtn] *pp of* **bite**.

bitter ['bɪtə*] *a* amargo; (*wind, criticism*) cortante, penetrante; (*battle*) encarnizado // *n* (*beer*) cerveza clara; **~ness** *n* amargura; (*anger*) rencor *m*.

bizarre [bɪˈzɑː*] *a* raro, estrafalario.

blab [blæb] *vi* chismear, soplar // *vt* (*also: ~ out*) revelar, contar.

black [blæk] *a* (*colour*) negro; (*dark*) oscuro // *n* negro; (*colour*) color *m* negro // *vt* (*shoes*) lustrar; (*INDUSTRY*) boicotear; **to give sb a ~ eye** darle a uno una bofetada (en el ojo); **~ and blue** *a* amoratado; **~berry** *n* zarzamora; **~bird** *n* mirlo; **~board** *n* pizarra; **~currant** *n* grosella negra; **~en** *vt* ennegrecer; (*fig*) denigrar; **~leg** *n* esquirol *m*, rompehuelgas *m inv*; **~list** *n* lista negra; **~mail** *n* chantaje *m* // *vt* chantajear; **~mailer** *n* chantajista *m/f*; **~ market** *n* mercado negro; **~out** *n* apagón *m*; (*fainting*) desmayo, pérdida de conocimiento; **~smith** *n* herrero.

bladder ['blædə*] *n* vejiga.

blade [bleɪd] *n* hoja; (*cutting edge*) filo; **a ~ of grass** una brizna de hierba.

blame [bleɪm] *n* culpa // *vt*: **to ~ sb for sth** echar a uno la culpa de algo; **to be to ~** tener la culpa de; **~less** *a* (*person*) inocente.

bland [blænd] *a* suave; (*taste*) soso.

blank [blæŋk] *a* en blanco; (*shot*) sin bala; (*look*) sin expresión // *n* blanco, espacio en blanco; cartucho sin bala o de fogueo.

blanket ['blæŋkɪt] *n* manta // *vt* envolver.

blare [blɛə*] *vi* (*brass band, horns, radio*) resonar.

blasé ['blɑːzeɪ] *a* hastiado.

blasphemy ['blæsfɪmɪ] *n* blasfemia.

blast [blɑːst] *n* (*of wind*) ráfaga, soplo; (*of whistle*) toque *m*; (*of explosive*) carga explosiva; (*force*) choque *m* // *vt* (*blow up*) volar; (*blow open*) abrir con carga explosiva; **~-off** *n* (*SPACE*) lanzamiento.

blatant ['bleɪtənt] *a* descarado.

blaze [bleɪz] *n* (*fire*) fuego; (*flames*) llamarada; (*fig*) arranque *m* // *vi* (*fire*) arder en llamas; (*fig*) brillar // *vt*: **to ~ a trail** (*fig*) abrir (un) camino.

blazer ['bleɪzə*] *n* chaqueta ligera.

bleach [bliːtʃ] *n* (*also: household ~*) lejía // *vt* (*linen*) blanquear; **~ed** *a* (*hair*) decolorado.

bleak [bliːk] *a* (*countryside*) desierto; (*prospect*) poco prometedor(a).

bleary-eyed ['blɪərɪ'aɪd] *a* de ojos legañosos.

bleat [bliːt] *vi* balar.

bleed [bliːd], *pt*, *pp* **bled** [blɛd] *vt*, *vi* sangrar.

blemish ['blɛmɪʃ] *n* mancha, tacha.

blend [blɛnd] *n* mezcla // *vt* mezclar // *vi* (*colours etc*) combinarse, mezclarse.

bless [blɛs], *pt*, *pp* **blessed** *o* **blest** [blɛst] *vt* bendecir; **~ing** *n* bendición *f*; (*advantage*) beneficio, ventaja.

blew [bluː] *pt of* **blow**.

blight [blaɪt] *vt* (*hopes etc*) frustrar, arruinar.

blimey ['blaɪmɪ] *excl* (*col*) ¡caray!

blind [blaɪnd] *a* ciego // *n* (*for window*) persiana // *vt* cegar; (*dazzle*) deslumbrar; **~ alley** *n* callejón *m* sin salida; **~ corner** *n* esquina escondida; **~fold** *n* venda // *a*, *ad* con los ojos vendados // *vt* vendar los ojos a; **~ly** *ad* a ciegas, ciegamente; **~ness** *n* ceguera; **~ spot** *n* mácula.

blink [blɪŋk] *vi* parpadear; pestañear; (*light*) oscilar; **~ers** *npl* anteojeras *fpl*.

blinking ['blɪŋkɪŋ] *a* (*col*): **this ~...** este condenado... .

bliss [blɪs] *n* felicidad *f*; (*fig*) éxtasis *m*.

blister ['blɪstə*] *n* (*on skin*) ampolla // *vi* (*paint*) ampollarse; **~ing** *a* (*heat*) abrasador(a).

blithe [blaɪð] *a* alegre.

blithering ['blɪðərɪŋ] *a* (*col*): **this ~ idiot** este tonto perdido.

blitz [blɪts] *n* bombardeo aéreo.

blizzard ['blɪzəd] *n* ventisca.

bloated ['bləʊtɪd] *a* hinchado.

blob [blɒb] *n* (*drop*) gota; (*stain, spot*) mancha.

block [blɒk] *n* bloque *m*; (*in pipes*) obstáculo; (*of buildings*) manzana // *vt* (*gen*) obstruir, cerrar; (*progress*) estorbar; **~ade** [-'keɪd] *n* bloqueo // *vt* bloquear; **~age** *n* estorbo, obstrucción *f*; **~ of flats** *n* bloque *m* de pisos; **~ letters** *npl* letras *fpl* de molde.

bloke [bləʊk] *n* (*col*) tipo, tío.

blond(e) [blɒnd] *a*, *n* rubio/a.

blood [blʌd] *n* sangre *f*; **~ donor** *n*

donador/a m/f de sangre; ~ **group** n
grupo sanguíneo; ~ **hound** n sabueso;
pressure n presión f sanguínea, ~**shed** a
matanza; ~**shot** a inyectado er sangre;
~**stained** a manchado de sangre;
~**stream** n corriente f sanguínea;
~**thirsty** a sanguinario; ~ **transfusion**
n transfusión f de sangre; ~**y** a
sangriento; (col!): **this** ~**y...** este
condenado/puñetero...; ~**y strong/ good**
(col!) terriblemente fuerte/ buena; ~**y-**
minded a (col) malintencionado.

bloom [blu:m] n floración f; (fig)
perfección f, plenitud f // vi florecer;
~**ing** a (col): **this** ~**ing...** este
condenado.

blossom ['blɔsəm] n flor f // vi florecer;
(fig) desarrollarse.

blot [blɔt] n borrón m // vt secar; (ink)
manchar; **to** ~ **out** vt (view) oscurecer,
hacer desaparecer.

blotchy ['blɔtʃi] a (complexion) enrojecido,
lleno de manchas.

blotting paper ['blɔtɪŋ-] n papel m
secante.

blouse [blauz] n blusa.

blow [bləu] n golpe m // (vb: pt blew, pp
blown [bləun]) vi soplar // vt (glass)
soplar; (fuse) quemar; (instrument) tocar;
to ~ **one's nose** sonarse; **to** ~ **away** vt
llevarse, arrancar; **to** ~ **down** vt
derribar; **to** ~ **off** vt arrebatar; **to** ~ **out**
vi apagarse; **to** ~ **over** vi pasar, quedar
olvidado; **to** ~ **up** vi estallar // vt volar
(tyre) inflar; (PHOT) ampliar; ~**lamp** n
soplete m, lámpara de soldar; ~**-out** n (of
tyre) pinchazo.

blubber ['blʌbə*] n grasa de ballena // vi
(pej) lloriquear.

blue [blu:] a azul; ~ **film/joke** film/chiste
verde; **to have the** ~**s** estar melancólico;
~**bell** n campanilla, campánula azul;
~**bottle** n moscarda, mosca azul; ~
jeans npl bluejean m inv, vaqueros mpl;
~**print** n (fig) anteproyecto.

bluff [blʌf] vi hacer un bluff, farolear // n
bluff m, farol m.

blunder ['blʌndə*] n error m garrafal,
metedura de pata // vi cometer un error,
meter la pata.

blunt [blʌnt] a embotado, desafilado;
(person) franco, directo // vt embotar,
desafilar; ~**ness** n (of person) franqueza,
brusquedad f.

blur [blə:*] n aspecto borroso // vt hacer
borroso, desdibujar.

blurt [blə:t] **to** ~ **out** vt (say) descolgarse
con, dejar escapar.

blush [blʌʃ] vi ruborizarse, ponerse
colorado // n rubor m.

blustering ['blʌstərɪŋ] a (person)
fanfarrón(ona).

blustery ['blʌstəri] a (weather)
tempestuoso, tormentoso.

board [bɔ:d] n tabla, tablero; (on wall)
tablón m; (for chess etc) tablero; (committee) junta, consejo; (in firm) mesa o junta

directiva // vt (ship) embarcarse en;
(train) subir a; **ful**. ~ pensión f completa;
to go by the ~ (fig) ser
abandonado/olvidado; **to** ~ **up** vt (door)
entablar, enmaderar; ~ **and lodging** n
pensión f; ~**er** n huésped/a m/f; (SCOL)
interno; ~**ing house** n casa de
huéspedes; ~**ing school** n internado; ~
room n sala de juntas.

boast [bəust] vi jactarse, presumir // vt
ostentar // n alarde m, baladronada; ~**ful**
a presumido, jactancioso.

boat [bəut] n barco, buque m; (small)
barca, bote m; ~**er** a (hat) sombrero de
paja; ~**ing** n canotaje m; ~**man** n
barquero; ~**swain** ['bəusn] n
contramaestre m.

bob [bɔb] vi (boat, cork on water: also: ~ **up**
and down) menearse, balancearse; **to** ~
up vi aparecer, levantarse // n (col) =
shilling.

bobbin ['bɔbɪn] n (of sewing machine)
carrete m, bobina.

bobby ['bɔbɪ] n (col) poli m/f.

bobsleigh ['bɔbsleɪ] n bob m.

bodice ['bɔdɪs] n corpiño.

bodily ['bɔdɪli] a corpóreo, corporal // ad
(in person) en persona; (lif) en peso.

body ['bɔdɪ] n cuerpo; (corpse) cadáver m;
(of car) caja, carrocería; (fig: society) conjunto; (fig: quantity) parte f principal; **in a**
~ en bloque, en conjunto; ~**guard** n
guardaespaldas m inv; ~**work** n
carrocería.

bog [bɔg] a pantano, ciénaga // vt: **to get**
~**ged down** (fig) empantanarse,
atascarse.

boggle ['bɔgl] vi: **the mind** ~**s** le deja
boquiabierto a uno.

bogus ['bəugəs] a falso, fraudulento;
(person) fingido.

boil [bɔɪl] vt cocer; (eggs) pasar por agua
// vi hervir // n (MED) furúnculo, divieso;
to come to the ~ comenzar a hervir; **to**
~ **down to** (fig) reducirse a; ~**er** n
caldera; ~**er suit** n mono; ~**ing point** n
punto de ebullición f.

boisterous ['bɔɪstərəs] a (noisy) bullicioso;
(excitable) exuberante; (crowd)
tumultuoso.

bold [bəuld] a (brave) valiente, audaz;
(excessively) atrevido; (pej) descarado;
(outline, colour) fuerte; ~**ness** n valor m,
audacia; (cheek) descaro.

Bolivia [bə'lɪvɪə] n Bolivia.

bollard ['bɔləd] a (AUT) poste m.

bolster ['bəulstə*] n travesero, cabezal m;
to ~ **up** vt reforzar; (fig) alentar.

bolt [bəult] n (lock) cerrojo; (with nut)
perno, tornillo // vt (door) echar el
cerrojo a; (food) engullir // vi fugarse;
(horse) desbocarse.

bomb [bɔm] n bomba // vt bombardear;
~**ard** [-'bɑ:d] vt bombardear; (fig)
asediar; ~**ardment** [-'bɑ:dmənt] n
bombardeo.

bombastic [bɔm'bæstɪk] a rimbombante; (*person*) farolero.

bomb: ~ **disposal** n desmontaje m de explosivos; ~**er** n (AVIAT) bombardero; ~**shell** n obús m, granada; (*fig*) bomba.

bona fide ['bəunə'faɪdɪ] a genuino, auténtico.

bond [bɔnd] n (*binding promise*) fianza; (FINANCE) bono; (*link*) vínculo, lazo.

bondage [bɔndɪdʒ] n esclavitud f.

bone [bəun] n hueso; (*of fish*) espina // vi deshuesar; quitar las espinas a; ~-**dry** a completamente seco; ~ **idle** a gandul.

bonfire ['bɔnfaɪə*] n hoguera, fogata.

bonnet ['bɔnɪt] n gorra; (*Brit: of car*) capó m.

bonus ['bəunəs] n sobrepaga, prima.

bony ['bəunɪ] a (arm, face, MED. *tissue*) huesudo; (*meat*) lleno de huesos; (*fish*) lleno de espinas.

boo [bu:] vt abuchear, rechiflar.

booby trap ['bu:bɪ-] n trampa explosiva.

book [buk] n libro; (*notebook*) libreta; (*of stamps etc*) librito; (COMM) ~**s** las cuentas, el balance // vt (*ticket*) sacar; (*seat, room*) reservar; (*driver*) fichar; ~**case** n librería, estante m para libros; ~**ing office** n (RAIL) despacho de billetes; (THEATRE) taquilla; ~**-keeping** n teneduría de libros; ~**let** n folleto; ~**maker** n corredor m de apuestas; ~**seller** n librero; ~**shop** n librería; ~**stall** n quiosco de libros.

boom [bu:m] n (*noise*) trueno, estampido; (*in prices etc*) alza rápida; (ECON) boom m, prosperidad f repentina.

boomerang ['bu:məræŋ] n bumerang m.

boon [bu:n] n favor m, beneficio.

boost [bu:st] n estímulo, empuje m // vt estimular, empujar; ~**er** n (MED) reinyección f.

boot [bu:t] n bota; (*Brit: of car*) maleta, maletero // vt dar un puntapié a; **to** ~ (*in addition*) además, por añadidura.

booth [bu:ð] n (*at fair*) barraca; (*telephone* ~, *voting* ~) cabina.

booty ['bu:tɪ] n botín m.

booze [bu:z] (*col*) n bebida, trago // vi emborracharse.

border ['bɔ:də*] n borde m, margen m, orilla; (*of a country*) frontera // a fronterizo; **the B**~**s** región fronteriza entre Escocia e Inglaterra; **to** ~ **on** vt fus lindar con; (*fig*) frontera.

bore [bɔ:*] pt of **bear** // vt (*hole*) taladrar, agujerear; (*person*) aburrir // n (*person*) pelmazo, pesado; (*of gun*) calibre m; ~**dom** n aburrimiento.

boring ['bɔ:rɪŋ] a aburrido.

born [bɔ:n] a: **to be** ~ nacer; **I was** ~ **in 1960** nací en 1960.

borne [bɔ:n] pp of **bear**.

borough ['bʌrə] n municipio.

borrow ['bɔrəu] vt: **to** ~ **sth (from sb)** pedir algo prestado a alguien.

borstal ['bɔ:stl] n reformatorio (de menores).

bosom ['buzəm] n pecho; (*fig*) seno; ~ **friend** n amigo del alma o íntimo.

boss [bɔs] n jefe m; (*employer*) patrón/ona m/f; (*political etc*) cacique m // vt regentar, dar órdenes a; ~**y** a mandón(ona).

bosun ['bəusn] n contramaestre m.

botanist ['bɔtənɪst] n botanista m/f; **botany** [-nɪ] n botánica.

botch [bɔtʃ] vt (*also*: ~ **up**) arruinar, estropear.

both [bəuθ] a, pron ambos(as), los dos; ~ **of us went, we** ~ **went** fuimos los dos, ambos fuimos // ad: ~ **A and B** tanto A como B.

bother ['bɔðə*] vt (*worry*) preocupar; (*disturb*) molestar, fastidiar // vi (*gen*: ~ **o.s.**) molestarse; **to** ~ **doing** tomarse la molestia de hacer // n: **what a** ~! ¡qué lata!

bottle ['bɔtl] n botella; (*small*) frasco; (*baby's*) biberón m // vt embotellar; **to** ~ **up** vt embotellar, contener; ~**neck** n embotellamiento; ~-**opener** n destapador m, abrebotellas m inv.

bottom ['bɔtəm] n (*of box, sea*) fondo; (*buttocks*) trasero, culo; (*of page, list*) pie m // a (*low*) inferior, más bajo; (*last*) último; ~**less** a sin fondo, insondable.

bough [bau] n rama.

bought [bɔ:t] pt, pp of **buy.**

boulder ['bəuldə*] n canto rodado.

bounce [bauns] vi (*ball*) (re)botar; (*cheque*) ser rechazado o incobrable // vt hacer (re)botar // n (*rebound*) (re)bote m.

bound [baund] pt, pp of **bind** // n (*leap*) salto; (*gen pl: limit*) límite m // vi (*leap*) saltar // a: ~ **by** (*limited by*) rodeado de, confinado con; **to be** ~ **to do sth** (*obliged*) tener el deber de hacer algo; (*likely*) estar seguro de hacer algo; **out of** ~**s** prohibido el paso; ~ **for** con destino a.

boundary ['baundrɪ] n límite m, lindero.

boundless ['baundlɪs] a ilimitado.

bouquet ['bukeɪ] n (*of flowers*) ramo; (*of wine*) aroma m.

bout [baut] n (*of malaria etc*) ataque m; (BOXING etc) combate m, encuentro.

bow [bəu] n (*knot*) lazo; (*weapon, MUS*) arco // n [bau] (*of the head*) reverencia; (NAUT) proa // vi [bau] inclinarse, hacer una reverencia; (*yield*): **to** ~ **to** o **before** ceder ante, someterse a.

bowels [bauəlz] npl intestinos mpl, vientre m.

bowl [bəul] n tazón m, cuenco; (*for washing*) palangana, jofaina; (*ball*) bola // vi (CRICKET) arrojar la pelota; ~**s** n juego de las bochas, bolos mpl.

bow-legged ['bəu'legɪd] a estevado.

bowler ['bəulə*] n (CRICKET) lanzador m (de la pelota); (*also*: ~ **hat**) hongo, bombín m.

bowling ['bəulɪŋ] n (*game*) bochas fpl, bolos mpl; ~ **alley** n bolera; ~ **green** n pista para bochas.

bow tie ['bəʊ-] *n* corbata de lazo.

box [bɒks] *n* (*also:* **cardboard** ~) caja, cajón *m*; (*for jewels*) estuche *m*; (*for money*) cofre *m*; (*THEATRE*) palco *m* // *vt* encajonar // *vi* (*SPORT*) boxear; **~er** *n* (*person*) boxeador *m*; (*dog*) bóxer *m*; **~ing** *n* (*SPORT*) boxeo; **B~ing Day** *n* Día de San Esteban, 26 de diciembre; **~ing gloves** *npl* guantes *mpl* de boxeo; **~ing ring** *n* ring *m*, cuadrilátero; ~ **office** *n* taquilla; **~room** *n* trastero.

boy [bɔɪ] *n* (*young*) niño *m*; (*older*) muchacho; (*servant*) criado.

boycott ['bɔɪkɒt] *n* boicot *m* // *vt* boicotear.

boyfriend ['bɔɪfrɛnd] *n* novio.

boyish ['bɔɪɪʃ] *a* muchachil.

B.R. *abbr of* **British Rail.**

bra [brɑ:] *n* sostén *m*.

brace [breɪs] *n* refuerzo, abrazadera; (*on teeth*) aparato; (*tool*) berbiquí *m* // *vt* asegurar, reforzar; **~s** *npl* tirantes *mpl*; **to ~ o.s.** (*fig*) fortalecer el ánimo.

bracelet ['breɪslɪt] *n* pulsera, brazalete *m*.

bracing ['breɪsɪŋ] *a* vigorizante, tónico.

bracken ['brækən] *n* helecho.

bracket ['brækɪt] *n* (*TECH*) soporte *m*, puntal *m*; (*group*) clase *f*, categoría; (*also:* **brace** ~) soporte *m*, abrazadera; (*also:* **round** ~) paréntesis *m inv*; (*gen:* **square** ~) corchete *m* // *vt* (*group*) agrupar.

brag [bræg] *vi* jactarse.

braid [breɪd] *n* (*trimming*) galón *m*; (*of hair*) trenza.

Braille [breɪl] *n* Braille *m*.

brain [breɪn] *n* cerebro; **~s** *npl* sesos *mpl*; **~child** *n* parto del ingenio; **~wash** *vt* lavar el cerebro a; **~wave** *n* idea luminosa; **~y** *a* muy listo o inteligente.

braise [breɪz] *vt* cocer a fuego lento.

brake [breɪk] *n* (*on vehicle*) freno // *vt*, *vi* frenar; ~ **drum** *n* tambor *m* de freno; ~ **fluid** *n* líquido para freno.

bramble ['bræmbl] *n* zarza.

branch [brɑ:ntʃ] *n* rama; (*fig*) ramo; (*road*) ramal *m*; (*COMM*) sucursal *f* // *vi* (*also:* ~ **out**) ramificarse; (: *fig*) extenderse.

brand [brænd] *n* marca; (*iron*) hierro de marcar // *vt* (*cattle*) marcar con hierro candente.

brandish ['brændɪʃ] *vt* blandir.

brand-new ['brænd'nju:] *a* flamante, completamente nuevo.

brandy ['brændɪ] *n* coñac *m*, brandy *m*.

brash [bræʃ] *a* (*rough*) tosco; (*cheeky*) descarado.

brass [brɑ:s] *n* latón *m*; ~ **band** *n* banda de metal.

brassière ['bræsɪə*] *n* sostén *m*.

brat [bræt] *n* (*pej*) mocoso.

bravado [brə'vɑ:dəʊ] *n* baladronada.

brave [breɪv] *a* valiente, valeroso // *n* valiente *m* // *vt* (*challenge*) desafiar; (*resist*) aguantar; **~ry** *n* valor *m*, valentía.

brawl [brɔ:l] *n* pendencia, reyerta // *vi* pelearse.

brawn [brɔ:n] *n* fuerza; (*meat*) carne *f* en gelatina; **~y** *a* fornido, musculoso.

bray [breɪ] *n* rebuzno // *vi* rebuznar.

brazen ['breɪzn] *a* descarado, cínico // *vt*: **to ~ it out** defenderse con descaro.

brazier ['breɪzɪə*] *n* brasero.

Brazil [brə'zɪl] *n* (el) Brasil; **~ian** *a*, *n* brasileño/a.

breach [bri:tʃ] *vt* abrir brecha en // *n* (*gap*) brecha; (*breaking*): ~ **of contract** infracción *f* de contrato; ~ **of the peace** perturbación *f* del orden público.

bread [brɛd] *n* pan *m*; ~ **and butter** *n* pan con mantequilla; (*fig*) pan (de cada día) // *a* común y corriente; **~crumbs** *apl* migajas *fpl*; (*CULIN*) pan molido.

breadth [brɛtθ] *n* anchura; (*fig*) amplitud *f*.

breadwinner ['brɛdwɪnə*] *n* sostén *m* de la familia.

break [breɪk], *pt* **broke**, *pp* **broken** *vt* (*gen*) romper; (*promise*) faltar a; (*fall*) amortiguar; (*journey*) interrumpir; (*law*) violar, infringir; (*record*) batir; (*news*) comunicar // *vi* romperse, quebrarse; (*storm*) estallar // *n* (*gap*) abertura; (*crack*) grieta; (*fracture*) fractura; (*breakdown*) ruptura, rompimiento; (*rest*) descanso; (*time*) intervalo; (: *at school*) (período de) recreo; (*chance*) oportunidad *f*; (*escape*) evasión *f*, fuga; **to ~ down** *vt* (*figures, data*) analizar, descomponer; (*undermine*) acabar con // *vi* estropearse; (*MED*) sufrir un colapso; (*AUT*) averiarse; (*person*) romper a llorar; **to ~ even** *vi* salir sin ganar ni perder; **to ~ free** *or* **loose** *vi* abrirse paso; **to ~ in** *vt* (*horse etc*) domar // *vi* (*burglar*) forzar una entrada; **to ~ into** *vt fus* (*house*) forzar; **to ~ off** *vi* (*speaker*) pararse, detenerse; (*branch*) partir; **to ~ open** *vt* (*door etc*) abrir por la fuerza, forzar; **to ~ out** *vi* estallar; **to ~ out in spots** salir a uno granos; **to ~ up** *vi* romperse // *vt* romper, intervenir en; **~able** *a* quebradizo; **~age** *n* rotura; **~down** *n* (*AUT*) avería; (*in communications*) interrupción *f*; (*MED: also:* **nervous ~down**) colapso, crisis *f* nerviosa; **~down lorry** *n* grúa, camión *m* grúa; **~er** *n* rompiente *m*, ola grande.

breakfast ['brɛkfəst] *n* desayuno.

break: **~through** *n* ruptura; (*fig*) avance *m*, adelanto; **~water** *n* rompeolas *m inv*.

breast [brɛst] *n* (*of woman*) pecho, seno; (*chest*) pecho; (*of bird*) pechuga; **~stroke** *n* braza de pecho.

breath [brɛθ] *n* aliento, respiración; **out of ~** sin aliento, sofocado; **~alyser** *n* prueba de alcohol por el aliento.

breathe [bri:ð] *vt*, *vi* respirar; (*noisily*) resollar; **breather** *n* respiro.

breath: **~less** *a* sin aliento, jadeante; **~taking** *a* imponente, pasmoso.

breed [bri:d], *pt*, *pp* **bred** [brɛd] *vt* criar, engendrar // *vi* reproducirse, procrear // *n* raza, casta; **~er** *a* (*person*) criador/a *m/f*; **~ing** *n* (*of person*) educación *f*.

breeze [bri:z] n brisa.

breezy ['bri:zı] a de mucho viento, ventoso; (person) despreocupado.

brevity ['brevıtı] n brevedad f.

brew [bru:] vt (tea) hacer; (beer) elaborar // vi hacerse, prepararse; (fig) amenazar; ~er n cervecero; ~ery n fábrica de cerveza.

bribe [braıb] n soborno // vt sobornar, cohechar; ~ry n soborno, cohecho.

brick [brık] n ladrillo; ~layer n albañil m; ~works n ladrillar m.

bridal ['braıdl] a nupcial.

bride [braıd] n novia; ~groom n novio; **bridesmaid** n dama de honor.

bridge [brıdʒ] n puente m; (NAUT) puente m de mando; (of nose) caballete m; (CARDS) bridge m // vt (river) tender un puente sobre; ~head n cabeza de puente.

bridle ['braıdl] n brida, freno // vt poner la brida a; (fig) reprimir, refrenar; ~ path n camino de herradura.

brief [bri:f] a breve, corto // n (LAW) escrito // vt (inform) informar; (instruct) dar órdenes a; ~s npl (for men) calzoncillos mpl; (for women) bragas fpl; ~case n cartera; ~ing n (PRESS) informe m.

brigade [brı'geıd] n (MIL) brigada.

brigadier [brıgə'dıə*] n general m de brigada.

bright [braıt] a claro, luminoso; (weather) de sol; (person: clever) listo, inteligente; (: lively) alegre, animado; (colour) vivo; ~en vt (room) hacer más alegre // vi (weather) despejarse; (person: gen: ~en up) animarse, alegrarse.

brilliance ['brıljəns] n brillo, brillantez f; **brilliant** [-ənt] a brillante; (clever) genial.

brim [brım] n borde m; (of hat) ala; ~ful a lleno hasta el borde; (fig) rebosante (de).

brine [braın] n (CULIN) salmuera.

bring [brıŋ], pt, pp **brought** vt (thing) traer; (person) conducir; **to ~ about** vt ocasionar, producir; **to ~ back** vt volver a traer; (return) devolver; **to ~ down** vt bajar; (price) rebajar; **to ~ forward** vt adelantar; **to ~ in** vt (harvest) recoger; **to ~ off** vt (task, plan) lograr, conseguir; **to ~ out** vt (object) sacar; **to ~ round** vt (unconscious person) hacer volver en sí; (convince) convencer, ganar; **to ~ up** vt (person) educar, criar; (carry up) subir; (question) sacar a colación.

brink [brıŋk] n borde m.

brisk [brısk] a enérgico, vigoroso; (speedy) rápido; (trade) activo.

brisket ['brıskıt] n carne f de vaca para asar.

bristle ['brısl] n cerda // vi erizarse.

Britain ['brıtən] n Gran Bretaña.

British ['brıtıʃ] a británico; **the ~** npl los británicos; **the ~ Isles** npl las Islas Británicas.

Briton ['brıtən] n británico/a.

brittle ['brıtl] a quebradizo, frágil.

broach [brəutʃ] vt (subject) abordar.

broad [brɔ:d] a ancho, amplio; (accent) cerrado; **in ~ daylight** en pleno día; ~cast n emisión f // (vb: pt, pp ~cast) vt (RADIO) emitir; (TV) transmitir // vi hablar o tocar por la radio; ~casting n radiodifusión f, difusión f, ~en vt ensanchar // vi ensancharse; ~ly ad en general; ~minded a tolerante, liberal.

brochure ['brəuʃuə*] n folleto.

broke [brəuk] pt of **break** // a (col) pelado, sin blanca.

broken ['brəukən] pp of **break** // a: ~ **leg** pierna rota; **in ~ English** en un inglés imperfecto; ~hearted con el corazón partido.

broker ['brəukə*] n agente m/f, bolsista m/f.

bronchitis [brɔŋ'kaıtıs] n bronquitis f.

bronze [brɔnz] n bronce m.

brooch [brəutʃ] n prendedor m.

brood [bru:d] n camada, cría; (children) progenie f; (: pej) prole f // vi (hen) empollar; (obsessively) darle vueltas (a).

brook [bruk] n arroyo.

broom [brum] n escoba; (BOT) retama; ~stick n palo de escoba.

Bros. abbr of **Brothers.**

broth [brɔθ] n caldo.

brothel ['brɔθl] n burdel m.

brother ['brʌðə*] n hermano; ~-in-law n cuñado.

brought [brɔ:t] pt, pp of **bring.**

brow [brau] n ceja; (forehead) frente m; (of hill) cumbre f.

brown [braun] a moreno; (hair) castaño; (tanned) bronceado // n (colour) color m moreno o pardo // vt (skin) poner moreno; (tan) broncear; (CULIN) dorar; ~ie n niña Girl Guide.

browse [brauz] vi (among books) hojear libros.

bruise [bru:z] n cardenal m, contusión f // vt magular.

brunette [bru:'net] n morena.

brunt [brʌnt] n: **the ~ of** lo más fuerte de, lo peor de.

brush [brʌʃ] n cepillo; (large) escoba; (for painting, shaving etc) brocha; (artist's) pincel m; (BOT) maleza; (quarrel) escaramuza, encuentro // vt cepillar; (gen: ~ past, ~ against) rozar al pasar; **to ~ aside** vt rechazar, no hacer caso a; **to ~ up** vt (knowledge) repasar, refrescar; ~wood n (bushes) maleza; (sticks) leña.

brusque [bru:sk] a brusco, áspero.

Brussels ['brʌslz] n Bruselas; ~ **sprout** n colecilla de Bruselas.

brutal ['bru:tl] a brutal; ~ity [-'tælıtı] n brutalidad f.

brute [bru:t] n bruto; (person) bestia.

B.Sc. abbr of **Bachelor of Science** licenciado en ciencias.

bubble ['bʌbl] n burbuja, ampolla // vi burbujear, borbotar; ~ **gum** n chicle m de globo.

buck [bʌk] n macho; (us: col) dólar m // vi

corcovear; **to pass the** ~ **(to sb)** echar (a uno) el muerto; **to** ~ **up** vi (cheer up) animarse, cobrar ánimo.

bucket ['bʌkɪt] n cubo, balde m.

buckle ['bʌkl] n hebilla // vt abrochar con hebilla // vi torcerse, combarse.

bud [bʌd] n brote m, yema; (of flower) capullo // vi brotar, echar brotes; (fig) florecer.

Buddhism ['budɪzm] n Budismo.

budding ['bʌdɪŋ] a en ciernes, en embrión.

buddy ['bʌdɪ] n (US) compañero, compinche m.

budge [bʌdʒ] vt mover; (fig) hacer ceder // vi moverse.

budgerigar ['bʌdʒərɪgɑː*] n periquito.

budget ['bʌdʒɪt] n presupuesto.

budgie ['bʌdʒɪ] n = **budgerigar.**

buff [bʌf] a (colour) color m de ante // n (enthusiast) entusiasta m/f.

buffalo ['bʌfələu], pl ~ or ~es n búfalo.

buffer ['bʌfə*] n amortiguador m.

buffet ['bufeɪ] n (bar) bar m, cafetería; (food) buffet m // vt ['bʌfɪt] (strike) abofetear; (wind etc) golpear; ~ **car** n coche-comedor m.

buffoon [bə'fuːn] n bufón m.

bug [bʌg] n (insect) chinche m; (: gen) bicho, sabandija; (: fig: germ) microbio, bacilo; (spy device) micrófono oculto; (tap) intervención f; (machine for tapping) aparato de intervención // vt (zam) fastidiar; (spy on) poner micrófono oculto en.

bugle ['bjuːgl] n corneta, clarín m.

build [bɪld] n (of person) talle m, tipo // vt, pt, pp built construir, edificar; ~**er** n constructor m; (contractor) contratista m/f; ~**ing** n (act of) construcción f; (habitation, offices) edificio; ~**ing society** n sociedad f inmobiliaria, cooperativa de construcciones; **to** ~ **up** vt (MED) fortalecer; (stocks) acumular.

built [bɪlt] pt, pp of **build** // a: ~-**in** (cupboard) empotrado; (device) interior, incorporado; ~-**up** (area) urbanizado.

bulb [bʌlb] n (BOT) bulbo; (ELEC) bombilla.

Bulgaria [bʌl'gɛərɪə] n Bulgaria; ~**n** a, n búlgaro/a.

bulge [bʌldʒ] n bombeo, pandeo // vi bombearse, pandearse; (pocket etc) hacer bulto.

bulk [bʌlk] n (mass) bulto, volumen m; (major part) grueso; **in** ~ (COMM) a granel; **the** ~ **of** la mayor parte de; ~**head** n mamparo; ~**y** a voluminoso, abultado.

bull [bul] n toro; ~**dog** n dogo.

bulldozer ['buldəuzə*] n aplanadora, motoniveladora.

bullet ['bulɪt] n bala; ~**proof** a a prueba de balas; ~ **wound** n balazo.

bulletin ['bulɪtɪn] n anuncio, parte m.

bullfight ['bulfaɪt] n corrida de toros; ~**er** n torero; ~**ing** n los toros mpl, el toreo; (art of ~ing) tauromaquia.

bullion ['buljən] n oro o plata en barras.

bullock ['bulək] n novillo.

bull's-eye ['bulzaɪ] n centro del blanco.

bully ['bulɪ] n valentón m, matón m // vt intimidar, tiranizar.

bum [bʌm] n (col: backside) culo, trasero; (tramp) vagabundo.

bumblebee ['bʌmblbiː] n (ZOOL) abejorro.

bump [bʌmp] n (blow) tope m, choque m; (jolt) sacudida; (on road etc, on head) boilo, abolladura // vt (strike) chocar contra, topetar // vi dar sacudidas; **to** ~ **into** vt fus chocar contra, tropezar con; (person) topar; ~**er** n (Brit) parachoques m inv // a: ~**er crop/harvest** cosecha abundante.

bumpy ['bʌmpɪ] a (road) lleno de baches; (journey) zarandeado.

bun [bʌn] n bollo; (of hair) moño.

bunch [bʌntʃ] n (of flowers) ramo; (of keys) manojo; (of bananas) piña; (of people) grupo; (pej) pandilla.

bundle ['bʌndl] n (gen) bulto, fardo; (of sticks) haz f; (of papers) legajo // vt (also: ~ **up**) atar, envolver; (put): **to** ~ **sth/sb into** meter algo/a alguien precipitadamente en.

bung [bʌŋ] n tapón m, bitoque m // vt (throw: gen: ~ **into**) arrojar.

bungalow ['bʌŋgələu] n bungalow m, chalé m.

bungle ['bʌŋgl] vt chapucear.

bunion ['bʌnjən] n juanete m.

bunk [bʌŋk] n tonterías fpl; ~ **beds** npl literas fpl.

bunker ['bʌŋkə*] n (coal store) carbonera; (MIL) refugio; (GOLF) bunker m.

bunny ['bʌnɪ] n (also: ~ **rabbit**) conejito.

bunting ['bʌntɪŋ] n empavesada, banderas fpl.

buoy [bɔɪ] n boya; **to** ~ **up** vt mantener a flote; (fig) animar; ~**ant** a boyante.

burden ['bəːdn] n carga // vt cargar.

bureau [bjuə'rəu], pl ~**x** [-z] n (furniture) escritorio, buró m; (office) oficina, agencia.

bureaucracy [bjuə'rɔkrəsɪ] n burocracia; **bureaucrat** ['bjuərəkræt] n burócrata m/f.

burglar ['bəːglə*] n ladrón/ona m/f; ~ **alarm** n alarma f de ladrones; ~**y** n robo con allanamiento, robo de una casa; **burgle** ['bəːgl] vt robar (con allanamiento).

burial ['berɪəl] n entierro; ~ **ground** n cementerio.

burlesque [bəː'lɛsk] n parodia.

burly ['bəːlɪ] a fornido, membrudo.

Burma ['bəːmə] n Birmania.

burn [bəːn], pt, pp burned or burnt vt quemar; (house) incendiar // vi quemarse, arder; incendiarse; (sting) escocer // n quemadura; **to** ~ **down** vt incendiar; ~**er** n (gas) quemador m, fuego; ~**ing** a ardiente.

burp [bəːp] (col) n eructo // vi eructar.

burrow ['bʌrəu] n madriguera // vt hacer una madriguera.

bursar ['bɔːsə*] *n* tesorero; (*student*) becario; ~**y** *n* beca.

burst [bɔːst], *pt, pp* **burst** *vt* (*balloon, pipe*) reventar; (*banks etc*) romper // *vi* reventarse; romperse; (*tyre*) pincharse; (*bomb*) estallar // *n* (*gen*) reventón *m*; (*explosion*) estallido; (*shots*) ráfaga de tiros; a ~ of energy una explosión f de energía; to ~ into flames estallar en llamas; to ~ into laughter soltar la carcajada; to ~ into tears deshacerse en lágrimas; to be ~ing with reventar por *o* de; to ~ into *vt fus* (*room etc*) irrumpir en; to ~ open *vi* abrirse de golpe.

bury ['bɛrɪ] *vt* enterrar; (*body*) enterrar, sepultar.

bus [bʌs] *n* autobús *m*.

bush [buʃ] *n* arbusto; (*scrub land*) monte *m*; to beat about the ~ ir por rodeos; ~**y** *a* (*thick*) espeso, poblado.

busily ['bɪzɪlɪ] *ad* atareadamente, afanosamente.

business ['bɪznɪs] *n* (*matter*) negocio; (*trading*) comercio, negocios *mpl*; (*firm*) empresa, casa; (*occupation*) oficio; (*affair*) asunto; **it's my ~ to...** me toca *o* corresponde...; **it's none of my ~** yo no tengo nada que ver; **he means ~** habla en serio; ~**like** *a* formal, metódico; ~**man** *n* hombre *m* de negocios.

bus-stop ['bʌsstɔp] *n* parada de autobús.

bust [bʌst] *n* (ANAT) pecho // *a* (*broken*) roto, estropeado; to go ~ quebrarse.

bustle ['bʌsl] *n* bullicio, movimiento // *vi* menearse, apresurarse; **bustling** *a* (*town*) animado, bullicioso.

busy ['bɪzɪ] *a* ocupado, atareado; (*shop, street*) concurrido, animado // *vr*: to ~ **o.s. with** ocuparse en; ~**body** *n* entrometido.

but [bʌt] *conj* pero // *prep* excepto, menos; **nothing** ~ nada más que; ~ **for** a no ser por, si no fuera por; ~ **finished** casi terminado.

butane ['bjuːteɪn] *n* butano.

butcher ['butʃə*] *n* carnicero // *vt* hacer una carnicería con; (*cattle etc for meat*) matar; ~**'s (shop)** *n* carnicería.

butler ['bʌtlə*] *n* mayordomo.

butt [bʌt] *n* (*cask*) tonel *m*; (*for rain*) tina; (*thick end*) cabo, extremo; (*of gun*) culata; (*of cigarette*) colilla; (*fig: target*) blanco // *vt* dar cabezadas contra, topetar.

butter ['bʌtə*] *n* mantequilla // *vt* untar con mantequilla; ~ **bean** *n* judía blanca; ~**cup** *n* ranúnculo.

butterfly ['bʌtəflaɪ] *n* mariposa.

buttocks ['bʌtəks] *npl* nalgas *fpl*.

button ['bʌtn] *n* botón *m* // *vt* abotonar, abrochar // *vi* abrocharse; ~**hole** *n* ojal *m*; (*flower*) flor f que se lleva en el ojal // *vt* obligar a escuchar.

buttress ['bʌtrɪs] *n* contrafuerte *m*; (*fig*) apoyo, sostén *m*.

buxom ['bʌksəm] *a* (*baby*) rollizo; (*woman*) frescachona.

buy [baɪ], *pt, pp* **bought** *vt* comprar // *n* compra; to ~ **sb sth/sth from sb** comprar algo para alguien/comprarle algo a alguien; ~**er** *n* comprador/a *m/f*.

buzz [bʌz] *n* zumbido; (*col: phone call*) llamada (por teléfono) // *vi* zumbar.

buzzard ['bʌzəd] *n* águila ratonera.

buzzer ['bʌzə*] *n* zumbador *m*, vibrador *m*.

by [baɪ] *prep* por; (*beside*) junto a, cerca de; (*according to*) según, de acuerdo con; (*before*): ~ **4 o'clock** para las cuatro // **ad see pass, go etc**; ~ **bus/car** en autobús/coche; **paid** ~ **the hour** pagado por horas; ~ **night/day** de noche/día; (**all**) ~ **oneself** (completamente) solo; ~ **the way** a propósito, por cierto; ~ **and large** en general; ~ **and** ~ luego, más tarde.

bye(-bye) ['baɪ('baɪ)] *excl* adiós, hasta luego.

by(e)-law ['baɪlɔː] *n* ordenanza municipal.

by-election ['baɪɪlɛkʃən] *n* elección f parcial.

bygone ['baɪɡɔn] *a* pasado del pasado // *n*: **let** ~**s be** ~**s** lo pasado, pasado está.

bypass ['baɪpɑːs] *n* carretera de circunvalación // *vt* evitar.

by-product ['baɪprɔdʌkt] *n* subproducto, derivado.

bystander ['baɪstændə*] *n* espectador/a *m/f*.

byword ['baɪwɔːd] *n*: to be a ~ for ser conocidísimo por.

C

C. *abbr of* centigrade.

C.A. *abbr of* chartered accountant.

cab [kæb] *n* taxi *m*; (*of truck*) cabina.

cabaret ['kæbəreɪ] *n* cabaret *m*.

cabbage ['kæbɪdʒ] *n* col *m*, berza.

cabin ['kæbɪn] *n* cabaña; (*on ship*) camarote *m*; ~ **cruiser** *n* yate *m* de motor.

cabinet ['kæbɪnɪt] *n* (POL) consejo de ministros; (*furniture*) armario; (*also*: **display** ~) vitrina; ~**-maker** *n* ebanista *m*.

cable ['keɪbl] *n* cable *m* // *vt* cablegrafiar; ~**-car** *n* coche *m* de teleférico, tren *m* aéreo.

cackle ['kækl] *vi* cacarear.

cactus ['kæktəs], *pl* -**ti** [-taɪ] *n* cacto.

caddie ['kædɪ] *n* cadi *m*.

cadet [kə'dɛt] *n* (MIL) cadete *m*.

cadge [kædʒ] *vt* gorronear; **cadger** *n* gorrón/ona *m/f*.

Caesarean (section) [siːˈzɛərɪən] *n* cesárea.

café ['kæfeɪ] *n*, **cafeteria** [kæfɪˈtɪərɪə] *n* café *m*.

caffein(e) ['kæfiːn] *n* cafeína.

cage [keɪdʒ] *n* jaula // *vt* enjaular.

cagey ['keɪdʒɪ] *a* (*col*) cauteloso, reservado.

Cairo ['kaɪərəu] *n* el Cairo.

cajole [kə'dʒəul] vt engatusar.

cake [keɪk] n (large) pastel m; (small) pasta, bizcocho; (of soap) pastilla; ~d with cubierto de.

calamitous [kə'læmɪtəs] a calamitoso; **calamity** [-ɪtɪ] n calamidad f.

calcium ['kælsɪəm] n calcio.

calculate ['kælkjulert] vt calcular; **calculating** a (clever) astuto (devious) calculador(a); **calculation** ['leɪʃən] n cálculo, cómputo; **calculator** n calculadora.

calculus ['kælkjuləs] n cálculo.

calendar ['kæləndə*] n calendario; ~ month/year mes m/año civil.

calf [kɑːf], pl **calves** n (of cow) ternero, becerro; (of other animals) cría; (also: ~skin) piel m de becerro; (ANAT) pantorrilla.

calibre, caliber (US) ['kælɪbə*] n calibre m.

call [kɔːl] vt (gen, also TEL) llamar // vi (shout) llamar; (telephone) llamar por teléfono; (visit: also: ~ in, ~ round) hacer una visita // n (shout, TEL) llamada; (of bird) canto; (appeal) llamamiento; to ~ for vt fus (demand) pedir, exigir; (fetch) venir por; to ~ off vt suspender; (cancel) cancelar; to ~ on vt fus (visit) visitar; (turn to) acudir a; to ~ out vi gritar, dar voces; to ~ up vt (MIL) llamar al servicio militar; ~box n cabina telefónica; ~er n visita m/f; (TEL) usuario; ~ girl n prostituta; ~ing n vocación f, profesión f.

callous ['kæləs] a insensible, cruel.

calm [kɑːm] n calma, tranquilidad f // vt calmar, tranquilizar // a (gen) tranquilo; (sea) liso, en calma; ~ly ad tranquilamente, con calma; ~ness n calma; to ~ down vi calmarse, tranquilizarse // vt calmar, tranquilizar.

calorie ['kælərɪ] n caloría.

calve [kɑːv] vi parir.

calves [kɑːvz] pl of **calf**.

camber ['kæmbə*] n (of road) combadura, comba.

Cambodia [kæm'bəudjə] n Camboya.

came [keɪm] pt of **come**.

camel ['kæməl] n camello.

cameo ['kæmɪəu] n camafeo.

camera ['kæmərə] n máquina fotográfica; (CINEMA, TV) cámara; **in ~** en secreto; ~man n cámaraman m, cámara m/f.

camouflage ['kæməflɑːʒ] n camuflaje m // vt camuflar.

camp [kæmp] n campo, campamento // vi acampar // a afectado, afeminado.

campaign [kæm'peɪn] n (MIL, POL etc) campaña // vi hacer campaña.

camp: ~bed n cama de campaña; ~er n campista m/f; (vehicle) caravana; ~ing n camping m; to go ~ing hacer camping; ~site n camping m.

campus ['kæmpəs] n ciudad f universitaria.

can [kæn] auxiliary vb (gen) poder; (know

how to) saber; I ~ swim sé nadar // n (of oil, water) lata, bote m // vt enlatar; (preserve) conservar en lata.

Canada ['kænədə] n el Canadá; **Canadian** [kə'neɪdɪən] a, n canadiense m/f.

canal [kə'næl] n canal m.

canary [kə'neərɪ] n canario; **C~ Islands** npl las (Islas) Canarias fpl.

cancel ['kænsəl] vt cancelar; (train) suprimir; (appointment) anular; (cross out) tachar, borrar; ~lation ['leɪʃən] n cancelación f; supresión f.

cancer ['kænsə*] n cáncer m; **C~** (ASTRO) Cáncer m.

candid ['kændɪd] a franco, abierto.

candidate ['kændɪdeɪt] n candidato.

candle ['kændl] n vela; (in church) cirio; ~stick n (also: ~ holder) (single) candelero; (low) palmatoria; (bigger, ornate) candelabro.

candour ['kændə*] n franqueza.

candy ['kændɪ] n azúcar m cande; (US) dulce m, caramelo.

cane [keɪn] n (BOT) caña; (stick) vara, palmeta // vt (SCOL) castigar (con palmeta).

canine ['kænaɪn] a canino.

canister ['kænɪstə*] n bote m, lata.

cannabis ['kænəbɪs] n cáñamo, marijuana.

canned [kænd] a en lata, de lata.

cannibal ['kænɪbəl] n caníbal m/f; ~ism n canibalismo.

cannon ['kænən], pl ~ or ~s n cañón m; ~ball n bala (de cañón).

cannot ['kænɒt] = **can not**.

canny ['kænɪ] a astuto.

canoe [kə'nuː] n canoa; (SPORT) piragua; ~ing n (SPORT) piragüismo; ~ist n piragüista m/f.

canon ['kænən] n (clergyman) canónigo; (standard) canon m.

canonize ['kænənaɪz] vt canonizar.

can opener ['kænəupnə*] n abrelatas m inv.

canopy ['kænəpɪ] n dosel m, toldo; (ARCH) baldaquín m.

can't [kænt] = **can not**.

cantankerous [kæn'tæŋkərəs] a arisco, malhumorado.

canteen [kæn'tiːn] n cantina; (bottle) cantimplora; (of cutlery) juego (de cubiertos).

canter ['kæntə*] n medio galope // vi ir a medio galope.

canvas ['kænvəs] n (gen) lona; (painting) lienzo; (NAUT) velas fpl; under ~ (camping) bajo lona.

canvass ['kænvəs] vt (POL) solicitar votos de.

canyon ['kænjən] n cañón m.

cap [kæp] n gorra; (of pen) capuchón m; (of bottle) tapa, cápsula; (MED) diafragma m // vt coronar, poner remate a; (outdo) superar; (FOOTBALL) seleccionar (para el equipo nacional).

capability [keɪpə'bɪlɪtɪ] n capacidad f; **capable** ['keɪpəbl] a capaz.

capacity [kə'pæsɪtɪ] n capacidad f; (position) calidad f.

cape [keɪp] n capa; (GEO) cabo.

caper ['keɪpə*] n (CULIN: gen: ~s) alcaparra; (prank) travesura.

capital ['kæpɪtl] n (also: ~ city) capital f; (money) capital m; (also: ~ letter) mayúscula; ~**ism** n capitalismo; ~**ist** a, n capitalista m/f; ~ **punishment** n pena de muerte.

capitulate [kə'pɪtjuleɪt] vi capitular, rendirse; **capitulation** [-'leɪʃən] n capitulación f, rendición f.

capricious [kə'prɪʃəs] a caprichoso.

Capricorn ['kæprɪkɔ:n] n Capricornio.

capsize [kæp'saɪz] vt volcar, hacer zozobrar // vi volcarse, zozobrar.

capstan ['kæpstən] n cabrestante m.

capsule ['kæpsju:l] n cápsula.

captain ['kæptɪn] n capitán m // vt capitanear, ser el capitán de.

caption ['kæpʃən] n (heading) título; (to picture) leyenda.

captivate ['kæptɪveɪt] vt cautivar, encantar.

captive ['kæptɪv] a, n cautivo/a; **captivity** [-'tɪvɪtɪ] n cautiverio.

capture ['kæptʃə*] vt prender, apresar; (place) tomar; (attention) captar, llamar // n apresamiento; toma; (thing taken) presa.

car [ka:*] n coche m, automóvil m; (RAIL) vagón m.

carafe [kə'ræf] n garrafa.

caramel ['kærəməl] n caramelo.

carat ['kærət] n quilate m.

caravan ['kærəvæn] n caravana, rulota; (of camels) caravana.

caraway ['kærəweɪ] n: ~ **seed** carvi m.

carbohydrate [ka:bəu'haɪdreɪt] n hidrato de carbono; (food) fécula.

carbon ['ka:bən] n carbono; ~ **copy** n copia al carbón; ~ **paper** n papel m carbón.

carburettor [ka:bju'retə*] n carburador m.

carcass ['ka:kəs] n cadáver m de animal.

card [ka:d] n carta, naipe m; (visiting ~, post~ etc) tarjeta; ~**board** n cartón m, cartulina; ~ **game** n juego de naipes.

cardiac ['ka:dɪæk] a cardíaco.

cardigan ['ka:dɪgən] n rebeca.

cardinal ['ka:dɪnl] a cardinal // n cardenal m.

card index n fichero.

care [kɛə*] n (gen) cuidado; (worry) inquietud f, solicitud f; (charge) cargo, custodia // vi: **to** ~ **about** preocuparse de, tener interés en; **in sb's** ~ a cargo de alguien; **to take** ~ **to** cuidarse o tener cuidado de; **to take** ~ **of** vt cuidar; **to** ~ **for** vt fus cuidar a; (like) querer; **I don't** ~ no me importa.

career [kə'rɪə*] n carrera // vi (also: ~

along) correr a toda velocidad.

carefree ['kɛəfri:] a despreocupado.

careful ['kɛəful] a cuidadoso; (cautious) cauteloso; **(be)** ~! ¡tenga cuidado!; ~**ly** ad con cuidado, cuidadosamente.

careless ['kɛəlɪs] a descuidado (heedless) poco atento; ~**ly** ad sin cuidado, a la ligera; ~**ness** n descuido, falta de atención.

caress [kə'rɛs] n caricia // vt acariciar.

caretaker ['kɛəteɪkə*] n portero, conserje m/f.

car-ferry ['ka:fɛrɪ] n transbordador m para coches.

cargo ['ka:gəu], pl ~**es** n cargamento, carga.

Caribbean [kærɪ'bi:ən] n: **the** ~ **(Sea)** el Caribe.

caricature ['kærɪkətjuə*] n caricatura.

carnal ['ka:nl] a carnal.

carnation [ka:'neɪʃən] n clavel m.

carnival ['ka:nɪvəl] n fiesta, feria, carnaval m.

carnivore ['ka:nɪvɔ:*] n carnívoro.

carol ['kærəl] n: **(Christmas)** ~ villancico.

carp [ka:p] n (fish) carpa; **to** ~ **at** vt fus quejarse de.

car park n aparcamiento, parking m.

carpenter ['ka:pɪntə*] n carpintero; **carpentry** [-trɪ] n carpintería.

carpet ['ka:pɪt] n alfombra // vt alfombrar; ~ **slippers** npl zapatillas fpl.

carriage ['kærɪdʒ] n coche m; (RAIL) vagón m; (for goods) transporte m; (bearing) porte m; ~**way** n (part of road) carretera; **dual** ~**way** carretera de doble calzada.

carrier ['kærɪə*] n trajinista m/f; (company) empresa de transportes; ~ **bag** n bolsa de papel.

carrot ['kærət] n zanahoria.

carry ['kærɪ] vt (gen) llevar; (transport) transportar; (a motion, bill) aprobar; (involve: responsibilities etc) entrañar, implicar // vi (sound) oírse; **to** ~ **on** vi (continue) seguir (adelante), continuar; (fam: complain) quejarse, protestar // vt proseguir, continuar; **to** ~ **out** vt (orders) cumplir; (investigation) llevar a cabo, realizar.

cart [ka:t] n carro, carreta // vt acarrear, llevar (en carro).

cartilage ['ka:tɪlɪdʒ] n cartílago.

cartographer [ka:'tɔgrəfə*] n cartógrafo.

carton ['ka:tən] n (box) caja (de cartón); (of yogurt) pote m.

cartoon [ka:'tu:n] n (PRESS) caricatura; (comic strip) tira cómica; (film) dibujos mpl animados; ~**ist** n caricaturista m/f, dibujante m/f.

cartridge ['ka:trɪdʒ] n cartucho.

carve [ka:v] vt (meat) trinchar; (wood, stone) cincelar, esculpir; (on tree) grabar; **to** ~ **up** dividir, repartir; **carving** n (in wood etc) escultura, (obra de) talla; **carving knife** n trinchante m.

car wash n lavado de coches.

cascade [kæs'keɪd] n salto de agua, cascada; (fig) chorro // vi caer a chorros o en forma de cascada.

case [keɪs] n (container) caja; (MED) caso; (for jewels etc) estuche m; (LAW) causa, proceso; (also: **suit**~) maleta, **in** ~ (of) en caso de (que), por si; **in any** ~ en todo caso; **just in** ~ por si acaso; **to make a good** ~ tener buenos argumentos.

cash [kæʃ] n (dinero en) efectivo, dinero contante // vt cobrar, hacer efectivo; to **pay (in)** ~ pagar al contado; ~ **on delivery** cóbrese al entregar; ~**book** n libro de caja; ~**desk** n caja.

cashew [kæ'ʃuː] n (also: ~ **nut**) anacardo.

cashier [kæ'ʃɪə*] n cajero.

cashmere [kæʃ'mɪə*] n casimir m, cachemira.

cash register n caja.

casing ['keɪsɪŋ] n envoltura; (of boiler etc) revestimiento.

casino [kə'siːnəʊ] n casino.

cask [kɑːsk] n tonel m, barril m.

casket ['kɑːskɪt] n cofre m, estuche m; (US: coffin) ataúd m.

casserole ['kæsərəʊl] n cacerola; (food) cazuela.

cassette [kæ'sɛt] n cassette m; ~ **player** n tocacassettes m inv.

cassock ['kæsək] n sotana.

cast [kɑːst], pt, pp **cast** vt (throw) echar, arrojar, lanzar; (skin) mudar, perder; (metal) fundir; (THEATRE) hacer el reparto de // vi (FISHING) lanzar // n (THEATRE) reparto; (mould) forma, molde m; (also: **plaster** ~) vaciado; **to** ~ **away** vt desechar; **to** ~ **down** vt derribar; **to** ~ **loose** soltar; **to** ~ **one's vote** dar el voto; **to** ~ **off** vi (NAUT) desamarrar.

castanets [kæstə'nɛts] npl castañuelas fpl.

castaway ['kɑːstəwəɪ] n náufrago.

caste [kɑːst] n casta.

casting vote ['kɑːstɪŋ-] n voto decisivo.

cast iron n hierro fundido.

castle ['kɑːsl] n castillo; (CHESS) torre f.

castor ['kɑːstə*] n (wheel) ruedecilla; ~ **oil** n aceite m de ricino; ~ **sugar** n azúcar m extrafino.

castrate [kæs'treɪt] vt castrar.

casual ['kæʒjul] a (by chance) fortuito; (irregular: work etc) eventual, temporero; (unconcerned) despreocupado; (informal: clothes) de sport; ~**ly** ad por casualidad; de manera despreocupada.

casualty ['kæʒjultɪ] n víctima m/f, herido; (dead) muerto; (MIL) baja; **casualties** npl pérdidas fpl.

cat [kæt] n gato.

Catalan ['kætəlæn] a, n Catalán/ana m/f.

catalogue, catalog (US) ['kætəlɔg] n catálogo // vt catalogar.

Catalonia [kætə'ləʊnɪə] n Cataluña.

catalyst ['kætəlɪst] n catalizador m.

catapult ['kætəpʌlt] n tirador m.

cataract ['kætərækt] n (also MED) catarata.

catarrh [kə'tɑː*] n catarro.

catastrophe [kə'tæstrəfi] n catástrofe m; **catastrophic** [kætə'strɔfɪk] a catastrófico.

catch [kætʃ], pt, pp **caught** vt (gen) coger; (arrest) detener; (grasp) asir; (breath) suspender; (person: by surprise) sorprender; (attract: attention) ganar; (MED) contagiarse de, coger; (also: ~ **up**) alcanzar // vi (fire) encenderse; (in branches etc) enredarse // n (fish etc) pesca; (act of catching) cogida; (trick) trampa; (of lock) pestillo, cerradura; **to** ~ **on** vi (understand) caer en la cuenta; (grow popular) hacerse popular; **to** ~ **sight of** divisar; **to** ~ **up** vi (fig) ponerse al día.

catch: ~**ing** a (MED) contagioso; ~**ment area** n zona de captación; ~ **phrase** n lema m, slogan m; ~**y** a (tune) pegadizo.

catechism ['kætɪkɪzəm] n (REL) catequismo.

categoric(al) [kætɪ'gɔrɪk(əl)] a categórico, terminante.

categorize ['kætɪgəraɪz] vt clasificar; **category** [-rɪ] n categoría, clase f.

cater ['keɪtə*] vi: **to** ~ **for** abastecer a; (needs) atender a; (consumers) proveer a; ~**er** n abastecedor m, proveedor m; ~**ing** n servicio de comidas; (trade) abastecimiento.

caterpillar ['kætəpɪlə*] n oruga, gusano; ~ **track** n rodado de oruga.

cathedral [kə'θiːdrəl] n catedral f.

catholic ['kæθəlɪk] a católico; **C**~ a, n (REL) católico/a.

cattle ['kætl] npl ganado sg.

catty ['kætɪ] a malicioso, rencoroso.

Caucasus ['kɔːkəsəs] n Cáucaso.

caught [kɔːt] pt, pp of **catch.**

cauliflower ['kɔlɪflaʊə*] n coliflor f.

cause [kɔːz] n causa, motivo, razón f // vt causar; (provoke) provocar.

causeway ['kɔːzweɪ] n (road) carretera elevada; (embankment) terraplén m.

caustic ['kɔːstɪk] a cáustico; (fig) mordaz.

caution ['kɔːʃən] n cautela, prudencia; (warning) advertencia, amonestación f // vt amonestar.

cautious ['kɔːʃəs] a cauteloso, prudente, precavido; ~**ly** ad con cautela; ~**ness** n cautela.

cavalier [kævə'lɪə*] a arrogante, desdeñoso.

cavalry ['kævəlrɪ] n caballería.

cave [keɪv] n cueva, caverna; **to** ~ **in** vi (roof etc) derrumbarse, hundirse; ~**man** n cavernícola m/f, troglodita m/f.

cavern ['kævən] n caverna.

caviar(e) ['kævɪɑː*] n caviar m.

cavity ['kævɪtɪ] n hueco, cavidad f.

cavort [kə'vɔːt] vi dar cabriolas.

caw [kɔː] vi graznar.

CBI n abbr of **Confederation of British Industries.**

cc *abbr of* **cubic centimetres; carbon copy.**

cease [si:s] *vt, vi* cesar; **~fire** *n* cese *m* de hostilidades *o* fuego; **~less** *a* incesante; **~lessly** *ad* sin cesar.

cedar ['si:də*] *n* cedro.

cede [si:d] *vt* ceder.

ceiling ['si:lɪŋ] *n* techo; (*fig*) límite *m*.

celebrate ['sɛlɪbreɪt] *vt* celebrar; (*marriage*) solemnizar // *vi* divertirse; **~d** *a* célebre; **celebration** [-'breɪʃən] *n* fiesta, celebración *f*.

celebrity [sɪ'lɛbrɪtɪ] *n* celebridad *f*.

celery ['sɛlərɪ] *n* apio.

celestial [sɪ'lɛstɪəl] *a* (*of sky*) celeste; (*divine*) celestial.

celibacy ['sɛlɪbəsɪ] *n* celibato.

cell [sɛl] *n* celda; (*BIOL*) célula; (*ELEC*) elemento.

cellar ['sɛlə*] *n* sótano; (*for wine*) bodega.

'cello ['tʃɛləu] *n* violoncelo.

cellophane ['sɛləfeɪn] *n* celofán *m*.

cellular ['sɛljulə*] *a* celular.

cellulose ['sɛljuləus] *n* celulosa.

Celt [kɛlt, sɛlt] *a, n* celta *m/f*; **~ic** *a* celta.

cement [sə'mɛnt] *n* cemento // *vt* cementar; (*fig*) cimentar, fortalecer.

cemetery ['sɛmɪtrɪ] *n* cementerio.

cenotaph ['sɛnətɑ:f] *n* cenotafio.

censor ['sɛnsə*] *n* censor // *vt* (*cut*) tachar, suprimir; **~ship** *n* censura.

censure ['sɛnʃə*] *vt* censurar.

census ['sɛnsəs] *n* censo.

cent [sɛnt] *n* (*US: coin*) centavo, céntimo; *see also* **per.**

centenary [sɛn'ti:nərɪ] *n* centenario.

centi... [sɛntɪ] *pref:* **~grade** a centígrado; **~litre** *n* centilitro; **~metre** *n* centímetro; **~pede** *n* ciempiés *m*.

central ['sɛntrəl] *a* central; (*of town*) céntrico; **C~ American** *a* centroamericano; **~ heating** *n* calefacción *f* central; **~ize** *vt* centralizar.

centre ['sɛntə*] *n* centro; **~- forward** *n* (*SPORT*) delantero centro; **~-half** *n* (*SPORT*) medio centro.

century ['sɛntjurɪ] *n* siglo; **20th ~** siglo veinte.

ceramic [sɪ'ræmɪk] *a* cerámico; **~s** *n* cerámica.

cereal ['si:rɪəl] *n* cereal *m*.

ceremony ['sɛrɪmənɪ] *n* ceremonia.

certain ['sə:tən] *a* (*gen*) seguro; (*correct*) cierto; (*person*) seguro; (*a particular*) cierto; **for ~** a ciencia cierta; **~ly** *ad* desde luego, por cierto; **~ty** *n* certeza, certidumbre *f*, seguridad *f*.

certificate [sə'tɪfɪkɪt] *n* certificado.

certify ['sə:tɪfaɪ] *vt* certificar.

cervix ['sə:vɪks] *n* cerviz *f*.

cessation [sə'seɪʃən] *n* cesación *f*, suspensión *f*.

cf. *abbr* **= compare** cfr.

chafe [tʃeɪf] *vt* (*rub*) rozar; (*wear*) desgastar; (*irritate*) irritar.

chaffinch ['tʃæfɪntʃ] *n* pinzón *m* vulgar.

chagrin ['ʃægrɪn] *n* disgusto, desazón *f*.

chain [tʃeɪn] *n* (*gen*) cadena // *vt* (*also:* **~ up**) encadenar; **~ reaction** *n* reacción *f* en cadena; **~ store** *n* tienda de una cadena.

chair [tʃɛə*] *n* silla; (*armchair*) sillón *m*; (*of university*) cátedra // *vt* (*meeting*) presidir; **~lift** *n* telesilla; **~man** *n* presidente *m*.

chalet ['ʃæleɪ] *n* chalet *m*.

chalice ['tʃælɪs] *n* cáliz *m*.

chalk [tʃɔ:k] *n* (*GEO*) creta; (*for writing*) tiza.

challenge ['tʃælɪndʒ] *n* desafío, reto // *vt* desafiar, retar; (*statement, right*) poner en duda, cuestionar; **to ~ sb to do sth** retar a uno a que haga algo; **challenger** *n* (*SPORT*) contrincante *m/f*; **challenging** *a* desafiante; (*tone*) de desafío.

chamber ['tʃeɪmbə*] *n* cámara, sala; **~ of commerce** cámara de comercio; **~maid** *n* camarera; **~ music** *n* música de cámara.

chamois ['ʃæmwɑ:] *n* gamuza.

champagne [ʃæm'peɪn] *n* champaña, champán *m*.

champion ['tʃæmpɪən] *n* campeón/ona *m/f*; **~ship** *n* campeonato.

chance [tʃɑ:ns] *n* (*luck*) casualidad *f*, suerte *f*; (*fate*) azar *m*; (*opportunity*) ocasión *f*, oportunidad *f*; (*likelihood*) posibilidad *f*; (*risk*) riesgo // *vt* arriesgar, probar // *a* fortuito, casual; **to ~ it** aventurarse, arriesgarse; **to take a ~** arriesgarse; **by ~** por casualidad.

chancel ['tʃɑ:nsəl] *n* coro y presbiterio.

chancellor ['tʃɑ:nsələ*] *n* canciller *m*; **C~ of the Exchequer** *n* Ministro de Hacienda.

chandelier [ʃændə'lɪə*] *n* araña (de luces).

change [tʃeɪndʒ] *vt* (*gen*) cambiar; (*replace*) reemplazar; (*gear, clothes, house*) cambiar de, mudar de; (*exchange*) trocar; (*transform*) transformar // *vi* (*gen*) cambiar(se), mudar; (*trains*) hacer transbordo; **to ~ into** transformarse en // *n* cambio, modificación *f*, transformación *f*; (*coins*) moneda suelta, suelto; (*money returned*) vuelta; **for a ~** para variar; **~able** *a* (*weather*) cambiable, mudable; **~less** *a* inmutable; **~over** *n* (*to new system*) cambio.

changing ['tʃeɪndʒɪŋ] *a* cambiante; **~ room** *n* vestuario.

channel ['tʃænl] *n* (*TV*) canal *m*; (*of river*) cauce *m*; (*of sea*) estrecho; (*groove, fig: medium*) conducto, medio // *vt* canalizar, encauzar; **the (English) C~** el Canal (de la Mancha); **the C~ Islands** las Islas Normandas *fpl*.

chant [tʃɑ:nt] *n* canto // *vt* cantar; (*fig*) recitar en tono monótono.

chaos ['keɪɔs] *n* caos *m*; **chaotic** [keɪ'ɔtɪk] *a* caótico, desordenado.

chap [tʃæp] *n* (*col: man*) tío, tipo // *vi* (*skin*) agrietarse.

chapel ['tʃæpəl] n capilla.
chaperon ['ʃæpərəun] n carabina.
chaplain ['tʃæplɪn] n capellán m.
chapter ['tʃæptə*] n capítulo.
char [tʃɑ:*] vt (burn) carbonizar, chamuscar // n = **charlady**.
character ['kærɪktə*] n carácter m, naturaleza, índole f, calidad f; (in novel, film) personaje m; (role) papel m; ~**istic** [-'rɪstɪk] a característico // n característica; ~**ize** vt caracterizar.
charade [ʃə'rɑ:d] n charada.
charcoal ['tʃɑ:kəul] n carbón m vegetal; (ART) carboncillo.
charge [tʃɑ:dʒ] n carga; (LAW) cargo, acusación f; (cost) precio, coste m; (responsibility) cargo; (task) encargo // vt (LAW) acusar (with de); (gun, battery, MIL enemy) cargar; (price) pedir; (customer) cobrar; (sb with task) encargar // vi cargar, precipitarse; (make pay) cobrar; ~**s** npl: bank ~s suplemento cobrado por el banco; free of ~ gratis; to reverse the ~s (TEL) poner una conferencia por cobrar; to take ~ of hacerse cargo de, encargarse de; to be in ~ of estar a cargo de o encargado de; how much do you ~? ¿cuánto cobra Usted?; to ~ an expense (up) to sb's account cargar algo a cuenta de alguien.
charitable ['tʃærɪtəbl] a caritativo.
charity ['tʃærɪtɪ] n (gen) caridad f; (sympathy) compasión f; (organization) sociedad f benéfica.
charlady ['tʃɑ:leɪdɪ] n mujer f de la limpieza.
charm [tʃɑ:m] n encanto, atractivo; (spell) hechizo; (object) amuleto // vt encantar, hechizar; ~**ing** a encantador(a), simpático.
chart [tʃɑ:t] n cuadro; (graph) gráfica; (map) carta de navegación // vt (course) trazar.
charter ['tʃɑ:tə*] vt (plane) alquilar; (ship) fletar // n (document) carta; ~**ed accountant** n perito contable; ~ **flight** n vuelo charter.
charwoman ['tʃɑ:wumən] n = **charlady**.
chase [tʃeɪs] vt (follow) perseguir; (hunt) cazar // n persecución f, caza; to ~ after correr tras.
chasm ['kæzəm] n abismo.
chassis ['ʃæsɪ] n chasis m.
chaste [tʃeɪst] a casto; **chastity** ['tʃæstɪtɪ] n castidad f.
chat [tʃæt] vi (also: **have a** ~) charlar // n charla.
chatter ['tʃætə*] vi (person) charlar; (teeth) castañetear // n (of birds) parloteo; (of people) charla, cháchara; ~**box** n parlanchín/ina m/f.
chatty ['tʃætɪ] a (style) familiar; (person) hablador(a), locuaz.
chauffeur ['ʃəufə*] n chófer m.
cheap [tʃi:p] a barato; (trick) malo; (poor quality) barato, de poca calidad // ad barato; ~**en** vt rebajar el precio, abaratar; to ~**en o.s.** rebajarse; ~**ly** ad barato, a bajo precio.

cheat [tʃi:t] vi hacer trampa // vt defraudar, timar // n trampa, fraude m; (person) tramposo; ~**ing** n trampa, fraude m.
check [tʃek] vt (examine) controlar; (facts) comprobar; (count) contar; (halt) parar, detener; (restrain) refrenar, restringir // n (inspection) control m, inspección f; (curb) freno; (bill) nota, cuenta; (obstacle) impedimento, estorbo; (token) ficha; (pattern: gen p*) cuadro; to ~ in vi (in hotel, airport) registrarse // vt (luggage) facturar; to ~ out vi (of hotel) pagar la cuenta y marcharse; to ~ up vi: to ~ up on sth comprobar algo; to ~ up on sb investigar a una persona; ~**mate** n jaque m mate; ~**out** n caja; ~**point** n (punto de) control m; ~**up** n (MED) reconocimiento general; (of machine) repaso.
cheek [tʃi:k] n mejilla; (impudence) descaro; ~**bone** n pómulo; ~**y** a fresco, descarado.
cheer [tʃɪə*] vi vitorear, aplaudir; (gladden) alegrar, animar // vi aplaudir, gritar con entusiasmo // n grito (de entusiasmo); ~**s** npl aplausos mpl; ~**s!** ¡salud!; to ~ **up** vi animarse, cobrar ánimos // vt alegrar, animar; ~**ful** a alegre; ~**fulness** n alegría; **cheerio** excl ¡hasta luego!; ~**less** a triste, sombrío.
cheese [tʃi:z] n queso.
chef [ʃef] n jefe/a m/f de cocina.
chemical ['kemɪkəl] a químico // n elemento químico.
chemist ['kemɪst] n farmacéutico; (scientist) químico; ~**ry** n química; ~**'s (shop)** n farmacia.
cheque [tʃek] n cheque m; ~**book** n libro de cheques, chequera.
chequered ['tʃekəd] a (fig) variado, accidentado.
cherish ['tʃerɪʃ] vt (love) querer, apreciar; (protect) cuidar; (hope etc) abrigar.
cherry ['tʃerɪ] n cereza.
chess [tʃes] n ajedrez m; ~**board** n tablero (de ajedrez); ~**man** n pieza, trebejo.
chest [tʃest] n (ANAT) pecho; (box) cofre m, cajón m; ~ **of drawers** n cómoda.
chestnut ['tʃesnʌt] n castaña; ~ **(tree)** n castaño.
chew [tʃu:] vt mascar, masticar; ~**ing gum** n chicle m.
chic [ʃi:k] a elegante.
chick [tʃɪk] n pollito, polluelo; (fam) chica.
chicken ['tʃɪkɪn] n gallina, pollo; (food) pollo; ~**pox** n varicela.
chickpea ['tʃɪkpi:] n garbanzo.
chicory ['tʃɪkərɪ] n (for coffee) achicoria; (salad) escarola.
chief [tʃi:f] n jefe/a m/f // a principal; ~**ly** ad principalmente.
chiffon ['ʃɪfɔn] n gasa.
chilblain ['tʃɪlbleɪn] n sabañón m.

child [tʃaɪld], pl **~ren** ['tʃɪldrən] n niño/a; (offspring) hijo/a; **~birth** n parto; **~hood** n niñez f, infancia; **~ish** a pueril, aniñado; **~like** a como (de) niño; **~ minder** n cuidadora de niños.

Chile ['tʃɪli] n Chile m; **~an** a, n chileno/a.

chill [tʃɪl] n frío; (MED) escalofrío, resfriado // vt enfriar; (CULIN) congelar; **~y** a frío.

chime [tʃaɪm] n (peal) repique m, campanada // vi repicar, sonar.

chimney ['tʃɪmnɪ] n chimenea; **~ sweep** n deshollinador m.

chimpanzee [tʃɪmpæn'zi:] n chimpancé m.

chin [tʃɪn] n barba, barbilla.

china ['tʃaɪnə] n porcelana; (gen) loza.

China ['tʃaɪnə] n China; **Chinese** [tʃaɪ'ni:z] a chino // n chino/a; (LING) el chino.

chink [tʃɪŋk] n (opening) grieta, hendedura; (noise) tintineo.

chip [tʃɪp] n (gen pl: CULIN) patata frita; (of wood) astilla; (of glass, stone) lasca; (at poker) ficha // vt (cup, plate) astillar; **to ~ in** vi interrumpir; (contribute) compartir los gastos.

chiropodist [kɪ'rɔpədɪst] n pedicuro.

chirp [tʃə:p] vi gorjear, piar; (cricket) chirriar.

chisel ['tʃɪzl] n (for wood) formón m; (for stone) cincel m.

chit [tʃɪt] n nota.

chitchat ['tʃɪttʃæt] n chismes mpl, habladurías fpl.

chivalrous ['ʃɪvəlrəs] a caballeroso; **chivalry** [-rɪ] n caballerosidad f.

chives [tʃaɪvz] npl cebollino sg.

chlorine ['klɔ:ri:n] n cloro.

chock [tʃɔk]: **~-a-block**, **~-full** a de bote en bote, atestado.

chocolate ['tʃɔklɪt] n chocolate m.

choice [tʃɔɪs] n elección f, selección f; (preference) preferencia // a selecto, elegido.

choir ['kwaɪə*] n coro; **~boy** n corista m.

choke [tʃəuk] vi sofocarse; (on food) atragantarse // vt ahogar, sofocar; (block) obstruir // n (AUT) estrangulador m; **choker** n (necklace) gargantilla.

cholera ['kɔlərə] n cólera m.

choose [tʃu:z], pt **chose**, pp **chosen** vt escoger, elegir; (team) seleccionar.

chop [tʃɔp] vt (wood) cortar, tajar; (CULIN: also: ~ **up**) desmenuzar; (meat) picar // n golpe m cortante; (CULIN) chuleta; **~s** npl (jaws) boca sg, labios mpl; **~py** a (sea) picado, agitado; **~sticks** npl palillos mpl.

choral ['kɔ:rəl] a coral.

chord [kɔ:d] n (MUS) acorde m.

chore [tʃɔ:*] n faena, tarea; (routine task) trabajo rutinario.

choreographer [kɔrɪ'ɔgrəfə*] n coreógrafo.

chorister ['kɔrɪstə*] n corista m/f.

chortle ['tʃɔ:tl] vi reír entre dientes.

chorus ['kɔ:rəs] n coro; (repeated part of song) estribillo.

chose [tʃəuz], **chosen** ['tʃəuzn] pt, pp of **choose**.

Christ [kraɪst] n Cristo.

christen ['krɪsn] vt bautizar; **~ing** n bautizo.

Christian ['krɪstɪən] a, n cristiano/a; **~ity** [-'ænɪtɪ] n cristianismo; **~ name** n nombre m de pila.

Christmas ['krɪsməs] n Navidad f; Merry **~!** ¡Felices Pascuas!; **~ Eve** n Nochebuena.

chrome [krəum], **chromium** ['krəumɪəm] n cromo.

chromosome ['krəuməsəum] n cromosoma m.

chronic ['krɔnɪk] a crónico.

chronicle ['krɔnɪkl] n crónica.

chronological [krɔnə'lɔdʒɪkəl] a cronológico.

chrysanthemum [krɪ'sænθəməm] n crisantemo.

chubby ['tʃʌbɪ] a rechoncho.

chuck [tʃʌk] vt lanzar, arrojar; **to ~ out** vt echar (fuera), tirar; **to ~ (up)** vt abandonar.

chuckle ['tʃʌkl] vi reírse entre dientes.

chug [tʃʌg] vi resoplar; **to ~ along** vi (fig) ir tirando.

chum [tʃʌm] n compinche m, compañero.

chunk [tʃʌŋk] n pedazo, trozo.

church [tʃə:tʃ] n iglesia; **~yard** n campo santo.

churlish ['tʃə:lɪʃ] a grosero, hosco.

churn [tʃə:n] n (for butter) mantequera; (for milk) lechera // vt revolver, agitar.

chute [ʃu:t] n (also: rubbish ~) vertedero; (children's slide) tobogán m.

chutney ['tʃʌtnɪ] n salsa picante.

CID n abbr of Criminal Investigation Department B.I.C. (Brigada de Investigación Criminal).

cider ['saɪdə*] n sidra.

cigar [sɪ'gɑ:*] n puro.

cigarette [sɪgə'rɛt] n cigarrillo; (fam) pitillo; **~ case** n pitillera; **~ end** n colilla; **~ holder** n boquilla.

Cinderella [sɪndə'rɛlə] n la Cenicienta.

cinders ['sɪndəz] npl cenizas fpl.

cine [sɪnɪ]: **~camera** n cámara cinematográfica; **~-film** n película cinematográfica.

cinema ['sɪnəmə] n cine m.

cinnamon ['sɪnəmən] n canela.

cipher ['saɪfə*] n cifra.

circle ['sə:kl] n círculo; (in cinema) anfiteatro // vi dar vueltas // vt (surround) rodear, cercar; (move round) dar la vuelta a.

circuit ['sə:kɪt] n circuito; (tour) gira; (track) pista; (lap) vuelta; **~ous** [sə:'kjuɪtəs] a tortuoso, indirecto.

circular ['sə:kjulə*] a circular // n circular f.

circulate ['sə:kjuleɪt] vi circular // vt poner en circulación, hacer circular;

circulation [-'leɪʃən] a circulación f; (of newspaper) tirada.

circumcise ['səːkəmsaɪz] vt circuncidar.

circumference [səˈkʌmfərəns] n circunferencia.

circumspect ['səːkəmspekt] a circunspecto, prudente.

circumstances ['səːkəmstənsɪz] npl circunstancias fpl; (financial condition) situación f económica.

circus ['səːkəs] n circo; (roundabout) glorieta.

cistern ['sɪstən] n tanque m, depósito; (in toilet) cisterna.

cite [saɪt] vt citar.

citizen ['sɪtɪzn] n (POL) ciudadano/a; (resident) vecino/a, habitante m/f; ~ship n ciudadanía.

citrus fruit ['sɪtrəs-] n agrios mpl.

city ['sɪtɪ] n ciudad f; the C~ centro financiero de Londres.

civic ['sɪvɪk] a cívico, municipal.

civil ['sɪvɪl] a civil; (polite) atento, cortés; (defence) pasivo; (well-bred) educado; ~ **engineer** n ingeniero civil; C~ **Service** administración f pública; ~**ian** [sɪ'vɪlɪən] a civil, de paisano // n civil m/f, paisano.

civilization [sɪvɪlaɪ'zeɪʃən] n civilización f.

civilized ['sɪvɪlaɪzd] a civilizado.

claim [kleɪm] vt exigir, reclamar; (rights etc) reivindicar; (assert) pretender // vt (for insurance) reclamar // n reclamación f; (LAW) demanda; (pretension) pretensión f; ~**ant** n (ADMIN, LAW) demandante m/f.

clairvoyant [kleə'vɔɪənt] n clarividente m/f.

clam [klæm] n almeja.

clamber ['klæmbə*] vi subir gateando, trepar.

clammy ['klæmɪ] a (cold) frío y húmedo; (sticky) pegajoso.

clamp [klæmp] n abrazadera, grapa // vt afianzar (con abrazadera); to ~ **down on** vt fus suprimir, restringir.

clan [klæn] n clan m.

clang [klæŋ] n sonido metálico // vi sonar, hacer estruendo.

clap [klæp] vi aplaudir // vt (hands) batir; (put) poner // n (of hands) palmada; (of thunder) estampido (de trueno); ~**ping** n aplausos mpl.

claret ['klærət] n clarete m.

clarification [klærɪfɪ'keɪʃən] n aclaración f; **clarify** ['klærɪfaɪ] vt aclarar.

clarinet [klærɪ'net] n clarinete m.

clarity ['klærɪtɪ] n claridad f.

clash [klæʃ] n estruendo; (fig) choque m // vi (meet) encontrarse; (battle) chocar; (disagree) estar en desacuerdo.

clasp [klɑːsp] n broche m; (on jewels) cierre m // vt abrochar; (hand) apretar, estrechar; (embrace) abrazar.

class [klɑːs] n (gen) clase f // a clasista, de clase // vt clasificar.

classic ['klæsɪk] a clásico // n (work) obra clásica; ~**al** a clásico.

classification [klæsɪfɪ'keɪʃən] n clasificación f; **classify** ['klæsɪfaɪ] vt clasificar.

class: ~**mate** n compañero de clase; ~**room** n aula.

clatter ['klætə*] n ruido, estruendo; (of hooves) trápala // vi hacer ruido o estruendo.

clause [klɔːz] n cláusula; (LING) oración f.

claustrophobia [klɔːstrə'fəubɪə] n claustrofobia.

claw [klɔː] n (of cat) uña; (of bird of prey) garra; (of lobster) pinza; (TECH) garfio // vt: to ~ **at** arañar; (tear) desgarrar.

clay [kleɪ] n arcilla.

clean [kliːn] a limpio; (clear) neto, bien definido // vt limpiar; to ~ **out** vt limpiar; to ~ **up** vt limpiar, asear; ~**-cut** a (person) de buen parecer; (clear) nítido; ~**er** n (person) asistenta; ~**ing** n (gen) limpieza; (clothes) limpieza en seco; ~**liness** ['klenlɪnɪs] a limpieza; ~**-shaven** a sin barba, lampiño.

cleanse [klenz] vt limpiar; **cleanser** n agente m de limpieza; (for face) desmaquillador m; **cleansing department** n departamento de limpieza.

clear [klɪə*] a claro; (road, way) limpio, libre; (complete) completo // vt (space) despejar, limpiar; (LAW: suspect) absolver; (obstacle) salvar, saltar por encima de; (debt) liquidar // vi (gen) aclararse; (fog etc) despejarse // ad: ~ **of** a distancia de; to ~ **up** vt limpiar; (mystery) aclarar, resolver; ~**ance** n (removal) despeje m; (permission) acreditación f; ~**-cut** a bien definido, nítido; ~**ing** n (in wood) claro; ~**ing bank** n cámara de compensación; ~**ly** ad claramente; ~**way** n (Brit) carretera donde no se puede aparcar.

cleaver ['kliːvə] n cuchilla (de carnicero).

clef [klef] n (MUS) clave f.

clemency ['klemənsɪ] n clemencia.

clench [klentʃ] vt apretar, cerrar.

clergy ['kləːdʒɪ] n clero; ~**man** n clérigo.

clerical ['klerɪkəl] a oficinista; (REL) clerical.

clerk [klɑːk, (US) klɔːrk] n empleado, oficinista m/f.

clever ['klevə*] a (mentally) inteligente, listo; (deft, crafty) hábil; (device, arrangement) ingenioso.

cliché ['kliːʃeɪ] n cliché m, frase f hecha.

click [klɪk] vt (tongue) chasquear; (heels) taconear.

client ['klaɪənt] n cliente m/f, ~**ele** [kliːɑːn'tel] n clientela.

cliff [klɪf] n acantilado.

climate ['klaɪmɪt] n clima m; (fig) ambiente m.

climax ['klaɪmæks] n clímax, punto culminante; (sexual) clímax m.

climb [klaɪm] vt (stairs) subir; (tree) trepar a; (hill) escalar // n subida; ~**er** n alpinista m/f, montañista m/f; ~**ing** n alpinismo.

clinch [klɪntʃ] vt (deal) cerrar; (argument) remachar.

cling [klɪŋ], pt, pp **clung** [klʌŋ] vi: **to ~ to** pegarse a, quedar pegado a; (of clothes) ajustarse a.

clinic ['klɪnɪk] n clínica; ~**al** a clínico.

clink [klɪŋk] vi tintinar.

clip [klɪp] n (for hair) prendido; (also: **paper ~**) sujetapapeles m inv; (clamp) grapa // vt (cut) cortar; (shorten) acortar; (clamp) sujetar; ~**pers** npl (for gardening) tijeras fpl; (for hair) maquinilla sg; (for nails) cortauñas m inv; ~**ping** n recorte m.

clique [kliːk] n camarilla, pandilla.

cloak [klɔuk] n capa, manto // vt (fig) encubrir, disimular; ~**room** n guardarropa; (in station) consigna; (WC) lavabo, aseos mpl.

clock [klɔk] n reloj m; (in taxi) taxímetro; (fam) cara; ~**wise** ad en el sentido de las agujas del reloj; ~**work** n aparato de relojería // a de cuerda.

clog [klɔg] n zueco, chanclo // vt atascar // vi atascarse.

cloister ['klɔɪstə*] n claustro.

close a, ad and derivatives [klɔus] a cercano, próximo; (print, weave) tupido, compacto; (friend) íntimo; (connection) estrecho; (examination) detallado, minucioso; (weather) bochornoso; (atmosphere) sofocante; (room) mal ventilado // ad cerca // vb and derivatives [klɔuz] vt (shut) cerrar; (end) concluir, terminar // vi (shop etc) cerrarse; (end) concluirse, terminarse // n (end) fin m, final m, conclusión f; **to ~ down** vi cerrarse definitivamente; **to ~ up** vi (crowd) arrimarse; ~**d** a (shop etc) cerrado; ~**d shop** n acuerdo de emplear sólo trabajadores sindicados; ~**ly** ad (exactly) fielmente; (carefully) atentamente.

closet ['klɔzɪt] n (cupboard) armario; (wc) lavabo.

close-up ['klɔusʌp] n primer plano.

closure ['klɔuʒə*] n (close-down) cierre m, clausura; (end) fin m.

clot [klɔt] n (gen: blood ~) embolia; (fam: idiot) imbécil m/f // vi (blood) cuajarse, coagularse.

cloth [klɔθ] n (material) tela, paño; (rag) trapo.

clothe [klɔuð] vt vestir; (fig) revestir; ~**s** npl ropa sg; ~**s brush** n cepillo (para la ropa); ~**s line** n cuerda (para tender la ropa); ~**s peg** n pinza; **clothing** n = **clothes.**

cloud [klaud] n nube f; (storm~) nubarrón m; ~**burst** n chaparrón m; ~**y** a nublado, nubloso; (liquid) turbio.

clout [klaut] vt dar un tortazo a.

clove [klɔuv] n clavo; ~ **of garlic** diente m de ajo.

clover ['klɔuvə*] n trébol m.

clown [klaun] n payaso // vi (also: ~ **about,** ~ **around**) hacer el payaso.

club [klʌb] n (society) club m; (weapon)

porra, cachiporra; (also: **golf ~**) palo // vt aporrear // vi: **to ~ together** hacer una colecta; ~**s** npl (CARDS) tréboles mpl; ~**house** n sala de reunión.

cluck [klʌk] vi cloquear.

clue [kluː] n pista; (in crosswords) indicación f; **I haven't a ~** no tengo idea.

clump [klʌmp] n (of trees) grupo.

clumsy ['klʌmzɪ] a (person) torpe, desmañado; (movement) pesado.

cluster ['klʌstə*] n grupo; (BOT) racimo // vi agruparse, apiñarse.

clutch [klʌtʃ] n (grip, grasp) apretón m, agarro; (AUT) embrague m; (pedal) pedal m de embrague // vt sujetar, empuñar.

clutter ['klʌtə*] vt atestar, llenar desordenadamente.

Co. abbr of **county; company.**

c/o abbr of **care of** c/a (en casa de), a/c (a cuidado de).

coach [kɔutʃ] n (bus) autocar m; (horse-drawn) coche m; (of train) vagón m, coche m; (SPORT) entrenador m, instructor m // vt (SPORT) entrenar; (student) preparar, enseñar.

coagulate [kɔu'ægjuleɪt] vi coagularse.

coal [kɔul] n carbón m; ~ **face** n frente m de carbón; ~**field** n yacimiento de carbón.

coalition [kɔuə'lɪʃən] n coalición f.

coal: ~**man,** ~ **merchant** n carbonero; ~**mine** n mina de carbón.

coarse [kɔːs] a basto, burdo; (vulgar) grosero, ordinario.

coast [kɔust] n costa, litoral m // vi (AUT) ir en punto muerto; ~**al** a costero, costanero; ~**er** n buque m costero, barco de cabotaje; ~**guard** n guardacostas m inv; ~**line** n litoral m.

coat [kɔut] n (jacket) chaqueta; (overcoat) abrigo; (of animal) pelo, lana; (of paint) mano f, capa // vt cubrir, revestir; ~ **of arms** n escudo de armas; ~ **hanger** n percha; ~**ing** n capa, baño.

coax [kɔuks] vt engatusar.

cob [kɔb] n see **corn.**

cobbler ['kɔblə] n zapatero remendón.

cobbles ['kɔblz], **cobblestones** ['kɔblstəunz] npl guijarros mpl.

cobra ['kɔubrə] n cobra.

cobweb ['kɔbwɛb] n telaraña.

cocaine [kɔ'keɪn] n cocaína.

cock [kɔk] n (rooster) gallo; (male bird) macho // vt (gun) amartillar; ~**atoo** n cacatúa; ~**erel** n gallito.

cockle ['kɔkl] n berberecho.

cockney ['kɔknɪ] n habitante m/f de ciertos barrios bajos de Londres.

cockpit ['kɔkpɪt] n (in aircraft) carlinga, cabina.

cockroach ['kɔkrəutʃ] n cucaracha.

cocktail ['kɔkteɪl] n combinado, coctel m; ~ **cabinet** n mueble-bar m; ~ **party** n coctel m, cóctel m.

cocoa ['kɔukɔu] n cacao; (drink) chocolate m.

coconut ['kəukənʌt] n coco.

cocoon [kə'ku:n] n capullo.

cod [kɔd] n bacalao.

code [kəud] n código; (cipher) clave f;
codify vt codificar.

coerce [kəu'ə:s] vt forzar, obligar;
coercion [-'ə:ʃən] n coacción f.

coexistence ['kəuɪg'zɪstəns] n
coexistencia.

coffee ['kɔfɪ] n café m; ~ **bean** n grano de
café; ~ **grounds** npl heces fpl de café;
~ **pot** n cafetera.

coffin ['kɔfɪn] n ataúd m.

cog [kɔg] n diente m; ~**wheel** n rueda
dentada.

cognac ['kɔnjæk] n coñac m.

coherent [kəu'hɪərənt] a coherente.

coil [kɔɪl] n rollo; (rope) adujada; (ELEC)
bobina, carrete m; (contraceptive) espiral f
// vi enrollarse, arrollarse.

coin [kɔɪn] n moneda // vt (word) inventar,
idear; ~**age** n moneda; ~**-box** n caja de
monedas.

coincide [kəuɪn'saɪd] vi coincidir; (agree)
estar de acuerdo; **coincidence** [kəu-
'ɪnsɪdəns] n casualidad f.

coke [kəuk] n (coal) coque m; (drink) Coca
Cola f.

colander ['kɔləndə*] n colador m,
escurridor m.

cold [kəuld] a frío // n frío; (MED) resfriado;
it's ~ hace frío; **to be** ~ tener frío; **to
catch** ~ resfriarse, acatarrarse; **to**
~**-shoulder** tratar con frialdad; ~**ly** a
fríamente; ~ **sore** n herpes m labial.

coleslaw ['kəulslɔ:] n ensalada de col.

colic ['kɔlɪk] n cólico.

collaborate [kə'læbəreɪt] vi colaborar;
collaboration [-'reɪʃən] n colaboración f.

collage [kɔ'lɑ:ʒ] n collage m.

collapse [kə'læps] vi (gen) hundirse,
derrumbarse; (MED) sufrir colapso // n
(gen) hundimiento; (MED) colapso;
collapsible a plegable.

collar ['kɔlə*] n (of coat, shirt) cuello;
~**bone** n clavícula.

collate [kɔ'leɪt] vt cotejar.

colleague ['kɔli:g] n colega m/f.

collect [kə'lɛkt] vt reunir; (as a hobby)
coleccionar; (call and pick up) recoger;
(wages) cobrar; (debts) recaudar;
(donations, subscriptions) colectar // vi
reunirse; coleccionar; ~**ion** [kə'lɛkʃən] n
colección f; cobro; (of people) grupo; (of
donations) recaudación f; (of post)
recogida.

collective [kə'lɛktɪv] a colectivo.

collector [kə'lɛktə*] n coleccionista m/f;
(of taxes etc) recaudador m.

college ['kɔlɪdʒ] n colegio.

collide [kə'laɪd] vi chocar.

collie ['kɔlɪ] n perro pastor.

collision [kə'lɪʒən] n choque m.

colloquial [kə'ləukwɪəl] a familiar,
coloquial.

colon ['kəulən] n (sign) dos puntos; (MED)
colón m.

colonel ['kə:nl] n coronel m.

colonial [kə'əunɪəl] a colonial.

colonize ['kɔlənaɪz] vt colonizar.

colony ['kɔlənɪ] n colonia.

colossal [kə'lɔsl] a colosal.

colour, color (US) ['kʌlə*] n color m // vt
color(e)ar; (with crayons) pintar; (dye)
teñir // vi (blush) sonrojarse; ~**s** npl (of
party, club) colores mpl; ~**-blind** a
daltoniano; ~**ed** a de color; (photo) a
colores; ~**ed** npl gente f de color; ~**
film** n película en colores; ~**ful** a lleno de
color; (personality) animado; ~**ing** n
colorido; ~**less** a incoloro, sin color; ~**
scheme** n combinación f de colores; ~**
television** n televisión f en color(es).

colt [kəult] n potro.

column ['kɔləm] n columna; ~**ist**
['kɔləmnɪst] n columnista m/f.

coma ['kəumə] n coma m.

comb [kəum] n peine m; (ornamental)
peineta // vt (hair) peinar; (area)
registrar.

combat ['kɔmbæt] n combate m // vt
combatir.

combination [kɔmbɪ'neɪʃən] n (gen)
combinación f.

combine [kəm'baɪn] vt combinar;
(qualities) reunir // vi combinarse //
['kɔmbaɪn] (ECON) asociación f; (pej)
monopolio; ~ (**harvester**) n
cosechadora.

combustion [kəm'bʌstʃən] n combustión f.

come [kʌm], pt **came**, pp **come** vi venir;
to ~ **about** vi suceder, ocurrir; **to** ~
across vt fus (person) topar; (thing) dar
con; **to** ~ **away** vi marcharse; **to** ~ **back**
vi volver; **to** ~ **by** vt fus (acquire)
conseguir; **to** ~ **down** vi bajar; (plane)
aterrizarse; (crash) estrellarse; (buildings)
desplomarse; **to** ~ **forward** vi
presentarse; **to** ~ **in** vi entrar; (train)
llegar; (fashion) ponerse de moda; **to** ~ **in
for** vt fus (criticism etc) merecer; **to** ~
into vt fus (money) heredar; **to** ~ **off** vi
(button) soltarse, desprenderse; (attempt)
tener lugar; **to** ~ **on** vi (pupil, undertaking)
crecer, desarrollarse // vt (find)
encontrar; ~ **on!** ¡vamos!; **to** ~ **out** vi
salir, aparecer; (be revealed) salir a luz; **to**
~ **out for/against** vi declararse
por/contra; **to** ~ **to** vi volver en sí; (total)
sumar; **to** ~ **up** vi subir; (sun) salir;
(problem) surgir; **to** ~ **up against** vt fus
(resistance, difficulties) tropezar con; **to** ~
up with vt fus (idea) sugerir, proponer; **to**
~ **upon** vt fus dar o topar con; ~**back** n
(THEATRE) reaparición f.

comedian [kə'mi:dɪən] n cómico;
comedienne [-'ɛn] n cómica.

comedown ['kʌmdaun] n (fam) revés m,
bajón m.

comedy ['kɔmɪdɪ] n comedia.

comet ['kɔmɪt] n cometa m.

comfort ['kʌmfət] n comodidad f, confort

m; (*well-being*) bienestar *m*; (*solace*) consuelo; (*relief*) alivio // *vt* consolar; aliviar; ~**able** *a* cómodo.

comic ['kɔmik] *a* (*also*: ~**al**) cómico // *n* (*magazine*) tebeo; ~ **strip** *n* tira cómica.

coming ['kʌmiŋ] *n* venida, llegada // *a* que viene; ~**(s) and going(s)** *n*(*pl*) ir y venir *m*, ajetreo.

comma ['kɔmə] *n* coma.

command [kə'mɑ:nd] *n* orden *f*, mandato; (*MIL*: *authority*) mando; (*mastery*) dominio // *vt* (*troops*) mandar; (*give orders to*) mandar, ordenar; (*dispose of*) disponer de; (*deserve*) merecer; ~**eer** [kɔmən'diə*] *vt* requisar; ~**er** *n* (*MIL*) comandante *m/f*, jefe/a *m/f*.

commando [kə'mɑ:ndəu] *n* comando.

commemorate [kə'meməreit] *vt* conmemorar; **commemoration** [-'reiʃən] *n* conmemoración *f*; **commemorative** [-rətiv] *a* conmemorativo.

commence [kə'mens] *vt*, *vi* comenzar, empezar.

commend [kə'mend] *vt* (*praise*) elogiar, alabar; (*recommend*) recomendar; (*entrust*) encomendar; ~**ation** [kɔmən-'deiʃən] *n* elogio, encomio; recomendación *f*.

commensurate [kə'menʃərit] *a* equivalente (*with a*).

comment ['kɔment] *n* comentario // *vi* hacer comentarios; ~**ary** ['kɔməntəri] *n* comentario; ~**ator** ['kɔmənteitə*] *n* comentador *m*.

commerce ['kɔmə:s] *n* comercio.

commercial [kə'mə:ʃəl] *a* comercial // *n* (*TV*) anuncio (comercial); ~ **break** *n* emisión *f* publicitaria; ~**ize** *vt* comercializar.

commiserate [kə'mizəreit] *vi*: to ~ **with** compadecerse de, condolerse de.

commission [kə'miʃən] *n* (*fee*) comisión *f*; (*act*) perpetración *f* // *vt* (*MIL*) nombrar; (*work of art*) encargar; **out of** ~ inutilizado; ~**aire** [kɔmiʃə'neə*] *n* portero; ~**er** *n* comisario; (*POLICE*) jefe/a *m/f* de policía.

commit [kə'mit] *vt* (*act*) cometer; (*to sb's care*) entregar; **to** ~ **o.s. (to do)** comprometerse (a hacer); **to** ~ **suicide** suicidarse; ~**ment** *n* compromiso.

committee [kə'miti] *n* comité *m*.

commodity [kə'mɔditi] *n* mercancía.

common ['kɔmən] *a* (*gen*) común; (*pej*) ordinario // *n* campo común; **the C~s** *npl* (la Cámara de) los Comunes; **in** ~ en común; ~**er** *n* plebeyo; ~ **law** *n* ley *f* consuetudinaria; ~**ly** *ad* comúnmente; **C~ Market** *n* Mercado Común; ~**place** *a* vulgar, trivial; ~**room** *n* salón *m* común; ~ **sense** *n* sentido común; **the C~wealth** *n* la Mancomunidad.

commotion [kə'məuʃən] *n* tumulto, confusión *f*.

communal ['kɔmju:nl] *a* comunal.

commune ['kɔmju:n] *n* (*group*) comuna // *vi* [kə'mju:n]: to ~ **with** comulgar o conversar con.

communicate [kə'mju:nikeit] *vt* comunicar // *vi*: to ~ **(with)** comunicarse (con).

communication [kəmju:ni'keiʃən] *n* comunicación *f*; ~ **cord** *n* timbre *m* de alarma.

communion [kə'mju:niən] *n* (*also*: **Holy C~**) comunión *f*.

communiqué [kə'mju:nikei] *n* comunicado, parte *m*.

communism ['kɔmjunizəm] *n* comunismo; **communist** *a*, *n* comunista *m/f*.

community [kə'mju:niti] *n* comunidad *f*; (*large group*) colectividad *f*; (*locals*) vecindario; ~ **centre** *n* centro social.

commute [kə'mju:t] *vi* viajar a diario // *vt* conmutar; **commuter** *n* persona que viaja a menudo.

compact [kəm'pækt] *a* compacto; (*style*) conciso; (*packed*) apretado // *n* ['kɔmpækt] (*pact*) pacto; (*for powder*) polvera.

companion [kəm'pæniən] *n* compañero; ~**ship** *n* compañerismo.

company ['kʌmpəni] *n* (*gen*) compañía; (*COMM*) sociedad *f*, compañía; **to keep sb** ~ acompañar a uno; **limited** ~ sociedad *f* anónima.

comparable ['kɔmpərəbl] *a* comparable.

comparative [kəm'pærətiv] *a* relativo.

compare [kəm'peə*] *vt* comparar; (*set side by side*) cotejar // *vi*: to ~ **(with)** compararse (con); **comparison** [-'pærisn] *n* comparación *f*; cotejo; **in comparison (with)** en comparación (con).

compartment [kəm'pɑ:tmənt] *n* (*also RAIL*) departamento.

compass ['kʌmpəs] *n* brújula; ~**es** *npl* compás *m*.

compassion [kəm'pæʃən] *n* compasión *f*; ~**ate** *a* compasivo.

compatible [kəm'pætibl] *a* compatible.

compel [kəm'pel] *vt* obligar; ~**ling** *a* (*fig*: *argument*) convincente.

compendium [kəm'pendiəm] *n* compendio.

compensate ['kɔmpənseit] *vt* compensar // *vi*: to ~ **for** compensar; **compensation** [-'seiʃən] *n* (*for loss*) indemnización *f*.

compère ['kɔmpeə*] *n* presentador *m*.

compete [kəm'pi:t] *vi* (*take part*) tomar parte, concurrir; (*vie with*) competir, hacer competencia.

competence ['kɔmpitəns] *n* capacidad *f*, aptitud *f*; **competent** [-ənt] *a* competente, capaz.

competition [kɔmpi'tiʃən] *n* (*contest*) concurso; (*ECON*) competencia; (*rivalry*) competencia.

competitive [kəm'petitiv] *a* (*ECON*) competitivo; (*spirit*) competidor(a), de competencia.

competitor [kəm'petitə*] *n* (*rival*)

competidor/a *m/f*; (*participant*)
concursante *m/f*.
compile [kəm'paɪl] *vt* recopilar, compilar.
complacency [kəm'pleɪsnsɪ] *n*
satisfacción *f* de sí mismo; **complacent**
[-sənt] *a* complacido.
complain [kəm'pleɪn] *vi* (*gen*) quejarse;
~**t** *n* (*gen*) queja; (*JUR*) demanda,
querella; (*MED*) enfermedad *f*.
complement ['kɒmplɪmənt] *n*
complemento; (*esp ship's crew*) dotación *f*;
~**ary** [kɒmplɪ'mentərɪ] *a* complementario.
complete [kəm'pliːt] *a* (*full*) completo;
(*finished*) acabado // *vt* (*fulfil*) completar;
(*finish*) acabar; (*a form*) llenar ~**ly** *ad*
completamente; **completion** *n* (*gen*)
conclusión *f*, terminación *f*; (*of contract
etc*) realización *f*.
complex ['kɒmpleks] *a* complejo // *n*
(*gen*) complejo.
complexion [kəm'plekʃən] *n* (*of face*) tez
f, cutis *m*; (*fig*) aspecto.
complexity [kəm'pleksɪtɪ] *n* complejidad
f.
compliance [kəm'plaɪəns] *n* (*submission*)
sumisión *f*; (*agreement*) conformidad *f*; **in**
~ **with** de acuerdo con; **compliant** [-ənt]
a sumiso; conforme.
complicate ['kɒmplɪkeɪt] *vt* complicar;
~**d** *a* complicado; **complication**
[-'keɪʃən] *n* complicación *f*.
compliment *n* ['kɒmplɪmənt] (*formal*)
cumplido; (*lovers'*) piropo; ~**s** *npl* saludos
mpl; **to pay sb a** ~ (*amorously*) piropear,
echar piropos a alguien; ~**ary** [-'mentərɪ]
a lisonjero; (*free*) de favor.
comply [kəm'plaɪ] *vi*: **to** ~ **with** cumplir
con.
component [kəm'pəunənt] *a* componente
// *n* (*TECH*) pieza.
compose [kəm'pəuz] *vt* componer; **to be**
~**d of** componerse de, constar de; **to** ~
o.s. tranquilizarse; ~**d** *a* sosegado;
composer *n* (*MUS*) compositor *m*.
composite ['kɒmpəzɪt] *a* compuesto.
composition [kɒmpə'zɪʃən] *n* composición
f.
compost ['kɒmpɒst] *n* abono compuesto.
composure [kəm'pəuʒə*] *n* serenidad *f*,
calma.
compound ['kɒmpaund] *n* (*CHEM, LING*)
compuesto; (*enclosure*) recinto // *a* (*gen*)
compuesto; (*fracture*) complicado.
comprehend [kɒmprɪ'hend] *vt*
comprender; **comprehension** [-'henʃən] *n*
comprensión *f*.
comprehensive [kɒmprɪ'hensɪv] *a*
(*broad*) extenso; (*general*) de conjunto;
(*INSURANCE*) contra todo riesgo; ~
(**school**) *n* integrado.
compress [kəm'pres] *vt* comprimir // *n*
['kɒmpres] (*MED*) compresa; ~**ion**
[-'preʃən] *n* compresión *f*.
comprise [kəm'praɪz] *vt* (*also:* **be** ~**d of**)
comprender, constar de.
compromise ['kɒmprəmaɪz] *n*

(*agreement*) componenda, arreglo;
(*midpoint*) término medio // *vt*
comprometer // *vi* transigir.
compulsion [kəm'pʌlʃən] *n* obligación *f*.
compulsive [kəm'pʌlsɪv] *a* compulsivo;
(*PSYCH*) empedernido.
compulsory [kəm'pʌlsərɪ] *a* obligatorio.
computer [kəm'pjuːtə*] *n* ordenador *m*,
computador *m*, computadora; ~**ize** *vt*
computerizar; ~ **programmer** *n*
programador/a *m/f*; ~ **programming** *n*
programación *f*; ~ **science** *n* ciencia de
computadoras.
comrade ['kɒmrɪd] *n* camarada *m/f*;
~**ship** *n* camaradería, compañerismo.
con [kɒn] *vt* estafar // *n* estafa.
concave ['kɒn'keɪv] *a* cóncavo.
conceal [kən'siːl] *vt* ocultar.
concede [kən'siːd] *vt* conceder // *vi* ceder,
darse por vencido.
conceit [kən'siːt] *n* presunción *f*; ~**ed** *a*
presumido.
conceivable [kən'siːvəbl] *a* concebible.
conceive [kən'siːv] *vt*, *vi* concebir.
concentrate ['kɒnsəntreɪt] *vi*
concentrarse // *vt* concentrar.
concentration [kɒnsən'treɪʃən] *n*
concentración *f*, ~ **camp** *n* campo de
concentración.
concept ['kɒnsept] *n* concepto.
conception [kən'sepʃən] *n* (*idea*)
concepto, idea; (*biol*) concepción *f*.
concern [kən'səːn] *n* (*matter*) asunto;
(*COMM*) empresa; (*anxiety*) preocupación *f*
// *vt* tener que ver con; **to be** ~**ed**
(**about**) interesarse (por), preocuparse
(por); ~**ing** *prep* sobre, acerca de.
concert ['kɒnsət] *n* concierto; ~ **hall** *n*
sala de conciertos.
concertina [kɒnsə'tiːnə] *n* concertina.
concerto [kən'tʃəːtəu] *n* concierto.
concession [kən'seʃən] *n* concesión *f*; **tax**
~ privilegio fiscal.
conciliation [kənsɪlɪ'eɪʃən] *n* conciliación
f; **conciliatory** [-'sɪlɪətrɪ] *a* conciliador(a).
concise [kən'saɪs] *a* conciso.
conclude [kən'kluːd] *vt* (*finish*) concluir;
(*treaty etc*) firmar; (*agreement*) llegar a;
(*decide*) llegar a la conclusión de;
conclusion [-'kluːʒən] *n* conclusión *f*;
conclusive [-'kluːsɪv] *a* decisivo,
concluyente.
concoct [kən'kɒkt] *vt* (*gen*) confeccionar;
(*plot*) tramar.
concrete ['kɒnkriːt] *n* hormigón *m* // *a*
concreto.
concur [kən'kəː*] *vi* estar de acuerdo,
asentir.
concurrently [kən'kʌrntlɪ] *ad* al mismo
tiempo.
concussion [kən'kʌʃən] *n* conmoción *f*
cerebral.
condemn [kən'dem] *vt* condenar; ~**ation**
[kɒndem'neɪʃən] *n* (*gen*) condenación *f*;
(*blame*) censura.

condensation [kɔndɛn'seiʃən] n condensación f.

condense [kən'dɛns] vi condensarse // vt condensar, abreviar; ~**d milk** n leche f condensada.

condescend [kɔndı'sɛnd] vi condescender, dignarse; ~**ing** a condescendiente.

condition [kən'dıʃən] n condición f // vt condicionar; **on** ~ **that** a condición (de) que.

condolences [kən'dəulənsız] npl pésame m.

condone [kən'dəun] vt condonar.

conducive [kən'djuːsıv] a: ~ **to** conducente a.

conduct ['kɔndʌkt] n conducta, comportamiento // vt [kən'dʌkt] (lead) conducir; (manage) llevar, dirigir; (MUS) dirigir // vi (MUS) llevar la batuta; **to** ~ **o.s.** comportarse; ~**or** n (of orchestra) director m; (on bus) cobrador m; (ELEC) conductor m; ~**ress** n (on bus) cobradora.

cone [kəun] n cono; (for ice-cream) barquillo.

confectioner [kən'fɛkʃənə*] n pastelero; ~**'s (shop)** n pastelería; (sweet shop) confitería; ~**y** n (cakes) pasteles mpl; (sweets) dulces mpl.

confederation [kənfɛdə'reiʃən] n confederación f.

confer [kən'fəː*] vt otorgar (on a) // vi conferenciar.

conference ['kɔnfərns] n (meeting) congreso.

confess [kən'fɛs] vt confesar // vi confesarse; ~**ion** [-'fɛʃən] n confesión f; ~**ional** [-'fɛʃənl] n confesionario; ~**or** n confesor m.

confetti [kən'fɛti] n confeti m.

confide [kən'faid] vi: **to** ~ **in** confiar en, fiarse de.

confidence ['kɔnfıdns] n (gen) confianza; (secret) confidencia; ~ **trick** n timo; **confident** a seguro de sí mismo; **confidential** [kɔnfı'dɛnʃəl] a confidencial; (secretary) de confianza.

confine [kən'fain] vt (limit) limitar; (shut up) encerrar; ~**d** a (space) reducido; ~**ment** n (prison) prisión f; (enclosure) encierro; (MED) parto, sobreparto; ~**s** ['kɔnfainz] npl confines mpl.

confirm [kən'fəːm] vt confirmar; ~**ation** [kɔnfə'meiʃən] n confirmación f; ~**ed** a empedernido.

confiscate ['kɔnfıskeıt] vt confiscar; **confiscation** [-'keiʃən] n incautación f.

conflict ['kɔnflıkt] n conflicto // vi [kən'flıkt] (opinions) chocar; ~**ing** a contrario.

conform [kən'fɔːm] vi conformarse; **to** ~ **to** ajustarse a, cuadrar con; ~**ist** n conformista m/f.

confound [kən'faund] vt confundir; ~**ed** a condenado.

confront [kən'frʌnt] vt (problems) encararse con; (enemy, danger) enfrentarse con; ~**ation** [kɔnfrən'teiʃən] n enfrentamiento.

confuse [kən'fjuːz] vt (perplex) aturdir, desconcertar; (mix up) confundir; ~**d** a confuso; (person) perplejo, despistado; **confusing** a confuso; **confusion** [-'fjuːʒən] n confusión f.

congeal [kən'dʒiːl] vi (freeze) congelarse; (coagulate) coagularse.

congenial [kən'dʒiːnıəl] a simpático, agradable.

congenital [kən'dʒɛnıtl] a congénito.

congested [kən'dʒɛstıd] a (gen) lleno; (area) superpoblado; **congestion** [-'dʒɛstʃən] n congestión f.

conglomeration [kənglɔmə'reiʃən] n conglomeración f.

congratulate [kən'grætjuleıt] vt felicitar; **congratulations** [-'leiʃənz] npl felicidades fpl.

congregate ['kɔngrıgeıt] vi congregarse; **congregation** [-'geıʃən] n (in church) fieles mpl; (assembly) reunión f.

congress ['kɔngrɛs] n congreso; ~**man** n (US) diputado.

conical ['kɔnıkl] a cónico.

conifer ['kɔnıfə*] n conífera; ~**ous** [kə'nıfərəs] a (forest) conífero.

conjecture [kən'dʒɛktʃə*] n conjetura.

conjugal ['kɔndʒugl] a conyugal.

conjugate ['kɔndʒugeıt] vt conjugar.

conjunction [kən'dʒʌŋkʃən] n conjunción f.

conjure ['kʌndʒə*] vi hacer juegos de manos; **to** ~ **up** vt (ghost, spirit) hacer aparecer; (memories) evocar; **conjurer** n ilusionista m/f; **conjuring trick** n ilusionismo, juego de manos.

conk [kɔŋk]: ~ **out** vi (col) estropearse.

con man ['kɔn-] n timador m.

connect [kə'nɛkt] vt juntar, unir; (ELEC) conectar; (fig) relacionar, asociar // vi: **to** ~ **with** (train) enlazar con; ~**ion** [-ʃən] n juntura, unión f; (ELEC) conexión f; (RAIL) correspondencia; (TEL) comunicación f; (fig) relación f.

connive [kə'naıv] vi: **to** ~ **at** hacer la vista gorda a.

connoisseur [kɔnı'sə*] n experto, entendido.

connotation [kɔnə'teıʃən] n connotación f.

conquer ['kɔŋkə*] vt (gen) conquistar; (enemy) vencer; (feelings) dominar; ~**or** n conquistador m.

conquest ['kɔŋkwɛst] n conquista.

cons [kɔnz] npl see **pro.**

conscience ['kɔnʃəns] n conciencia.

conscientious [kɔnʃı'ɛnʃəs] a concienzudo; (objection) de conciencia.

conscious ['kɔnʃəs] a consciente; ~**ness** n conciencia; (MED) conocimiento.

conscript ['kɔnskrıpt] n recluto m/f; ~**ion** [kən'skrıpʃən] n servicio militar (obligatorio).

consecrate ['kɔnsıkreıt] vt consagrar.

consecutive [kən'sɛkjutɪv] a sucesivo, seguido.

consensus [kən'sɛnsəs] n consenso.

consent [kən'sɛnt] n consentimiento // vi: **to ~ to** consentir en.

consequence ['kɔnsɪkwəns] n consecuencia.

consequently ['kɔnsɪkwəntlɪ] ad por consiguiente.

conservation [kɔnsə'veɪʃən] a conservación f.

conservative [kən'sɜːvətɪv] a conservador(a); (cautious) cauteloso; C~ a, n conservador/a m/f.

conservatory [kən'sɜːvətrɪ] n (greenhouse) invernadero.

conserve [kən'sɜːv] vt conservar // n conserva.

consider [kən'sɪdə*] vt (gen) considerar; (take into account) tomar en cuenta; (study) estudiar, examinar; **~able** a considerable; (sum) importante.

considerate [kən'sɪdərɪt] a considerado; **consideration** [-'reɪʃən] n consideración f; (reward) retribución f.

considering [kən'sɪdərɪŋ] prep en consideración a.

consign [kən'saɪn] vt consignar; **~ment** n envío.

consist [kən'sɪst] vi: **to ~ of** consistir en.

consistency [kən'sɪstənsɪ] n (of person etc) consecuencia; (thickness) consistencia.

consistent [kən'sɪstənt] a (person) consecuente; (even) constante.

consolation [kɔnsə'leɪʃən] n consuelo.

console [kən'səul] vt consolar // n ['kɔnsəul] consola.

consolidate [kən'sɔlɪdeɪt] vt consolidar.

consommé [kən'sɔmeɪ] n consomé m, caldo.

consonant ['kɔnsənənt] n consonante f.

consortium [kən'sɔːtɪəm] n consorcio.

conspicuous [kən'spɪkjuəs] a (visible) visible; (garish etc) llamativo; (outstanding) notable.

conspiracy [kən'spɪrəsɪ] n conjura, complot m.

conspire [kən'spaɪə*] vi conspirar.

constable ['kʌnstəbl] n policía m/f; **chief ~** jefe m de policía.

constabulary [kən'stæbjulərɪ] n policía.

constant ['kɔnstənt] a (gen) constante; (loyal) leal, fiel.

constellation [kɔnstə'leɪʃən] n constelación f.

consternation [kɔnstə'neɪʃən] n consternación f.

constipated ['kɔnstɪpeɪtɪd] a estreñido.

constituency [kən'stɪtjuənsɪ] n (POL) distrito electoral; **constituent** [-ənt] n (POL) elector/a m/f; (part) componente m.

constitute ['kɔnstɪtjuːt] vt constituir.

constitution [kɔnstɪ'tjuːʃən] n constitución f; **~al** a constitucional.

constrain [kən'streɪn] vt obligar; **~ed** a:

to feel ~ed to... sentirse en la necesidad de...; **~t** a (force) fuerza; (confinement) encierro; (shyness) reserva.

constrict [kən'strɪkt] vt apretar, estrechar.

construct [kən'strʌkt] vt construir; **~ion** [-ʃən] n construcción f; **~ive** a constructivo.

construe [kən'struː] vt interpretar.

consul ['kɔnsl] n cónsul m/f; **~ate** ['kɔnsjulɪt] n consulado.

consult [kən'sʌlt] vt, vi consultar; **~ant** n (MED) especialista m/f; (other specialist) asesor m; **~ation** [kɔnsəl'teɪʃən] n consulta; **~ing room** a consultorio.

consume [kən'sjuːm] vt (eat) comerse; (drink) beberse; (fire etc, COMM) consumir; **consumer** n consumidor/a m/f; **consumer goods** npl bienes mpl de consumo; **consumer society** n sociedad f de consumo.

consummate ['kɔnsʌmeɪt] vt consumar.

consumption [kən'sʌmpʃən] n consumo.

cont. abbr of **continued**.

contact ['kɔntækt] n contacto; (pej) enchufe m // vt ponerse en contacto con; **he has good ~s** tiene buenas relaciones; **~ lenses** npl lentes fpl de contacto, microlentillas fpl.

contagious [kən'teɪdʒəs] a contagioso.

contain [kən'teɪn] vt contener; **to ~ o.s.** contenerse; **~er** n recipiente m; (for shipping etc) contenedor m.

contaminate [kən'tæmɪneɪt] vt contaminar; **contamination** [-'neɪʃən] n contaminación f.

cont'd abbr of **continued**.

contemplate ['kɔntəmpleɪt] vt (gen) contemplar; (expect) contar con; (intend) pensar; **contemplation** [-'pleɪʃən] n contemplación f.

contemporary [kən'tempərərɪ] a, n contemporáneo/a.

contempt [kən'tempt] n desprecio; **~ible** a despreciable; **~uous** a despectivo, desdeñoso.

contend [kən'tend] vt (argue) afirmar // vi (struggle) luchar; **~er** n contendiente m/f.

content [kən'tent] a (happy) contento; (satisfied) satisfecho // vt contentar; satisfacer // n ['kɔntent] contento; satisfacción f; **~s** npl contenido sg; **~ed** a contento, satisfecho.

contention [kən'tenʃən] n contienda; (argument) argumento.

contentment [kən'tentmənt] a contento.

contest ['kɔntest] n concurso; (competition) concurso // vt [kən'test] (dispute) impugnar; (legal case) defender; (POL) ser candidato en; **~ant** [kən'testənt] n concursante m/f; (in fight) contendiente m/f.

context ['kɔntekst] n contexto.

continent ['kɔntɪnənt] n continente m; **the C~** el continente europeo; **~al** [-'nentl] a continental.

contingency [kən'tɪndʒənsɪ] n
contingencia; **contingent** [-ənt] n
contingente m.
continual [kən'tɪnjʊəl] a continuo; ～**ly** ad
constantemente.
continuation [kəntɪnju'eɪʃən] n
prolongación f; (after interruption)
continuación f.
continue [kən'tɪnju:] vi seguir, continuar
// vt seguir, continuar; (start again)
proseguir.
continuity [kɒntɪ'njuɪtɪ] n continuidad f.
continuous [kən'tɪnjuəs] a continuo.
contort [kən'tɔ:t] vt retorcer; ～**ion**
[-'tɔ:ʃən] n contorsión f; ～**ionist**
[-'tɔ:ʃənɪst] n contorsionista m/f.
contour ['kɒntʊə*] n contorno; (also: ～
line) curva de nivel.
contraband ['kɒntrəbænd] n contrabando.
contraception [kɒntrə'sepʃən] n
contracepción f; **contraceptive** [-'septɪv]
a, n anticonceptivo.
contract ['kɒntrækt] n contrato // (vb:
[kən'trækt]) vi (COMM): to ～ to do sth
comprometerse por contrato a hacer algo;
(become smaller) contraerse, encogerse //
vt contraer; ～**ion** [-ʃən] n contracción f;
～**or** n contratista m/f.
contradict [kɒntrə'dɪkt] vt (deny)
desmentir; (be contrary to) contradecir;
～**ion** [-ʃən] n contradicción f.
contralto [kən'træltəʊ] n contralto.
contraption [kən'træpʃən] n (pej)
armatoste m.
contrary ['kɒntrərɪ] a, n contrario.
contrast ['kɒntrɑ:st] n contraste m // vt
[kən'trɑ:st] comparar; ～**ing** a opuesto.
contravene [kɒntrə'vi:n] vt oponerse a;
(law) contravenir.
contribute [kən'trɪbju:t] vi contribuir //
vt: to ～ to (gen) contribuir a; (newspaper)
escribir para; **contribution**
[kɒntrɪ'bju:ʃən] n (money) aportación f; (to
debate) intervención f; (to journal)
colaboración f; **contributor** n (to
newspaper) colaborador m.
contrive [kən'traɪv] vt (invent) idear;
(carry out) efectuar; (plot) tramar // vi: to
～ to do lograr hacer.
control [kən'trəʊl] vt (gen) controlar;
(traffic etc) dirigir; (machinery) regular;
(temper) dominar // n (command) control
m; (of car) conducción f; (check) freno;
～**s** npl mando sg; ～ **panel** n tablero de
instrumentos; ～ **room** n sala de mando;
～ **tower** n (AVIAT) torre f de control.
controversial [kɒntrə'vɜ:ʃl] a discutible;
controversy ['kɒntrəvɜ:sɪ] n controversia.
convalesce [kɒnvə'les] vi convalecer;
convalescence n convalecencia;
convalescent a, n convaleciente m/f.
convector [kən'vektə*] n (heater)
calentador m de convección.
convene [kən'vi:n] vt convocar // vi
reunirse.
convenience [kən'vi:nɪəns] n (comfort)
comodidad f; (advantage) ventaja; **at your**

～ cuando le sea conveniente; **public** ～
aseos públicos mpl; **convenient** [-ənt] a
cómodo; (useful) útil; (place) accesible;
(time) oportuno, conveniente.
convent ['kɒnvənt] n convento; ～ **school**
n colegio de monjas.
convention [kən'venʃən] n convención f;
(meeting) asamblea; ～**al** a convencional.
converge [kən'vɜ:dʒ] vi converger.
conversant [kən'vɜ:snt] a: to be ～ with
ser enterado de.
conversation [kɒnvə'seɪʃən] n
conversación f; ～**al** a (familiar) familiar;
(talkative) locuaz.
converse ['kɒnvɜ:s] n inversa // vi [kən-
'vɜ:s] conversar; ～**ly** [-'vɜ:slɪ] ad a la
inversa.
conversion [kən'vɜ:ʃən] n conversión f; ～
table n tabla de conversión.
convert [kən'vɜ:t] vt (REL, COMM)
convertir; (alter) transformar // n
['kɒnvɜ:t] converso/a; ～**ible** a
convertible // n descapotable m.
convex ['kɒn'veks] a convexo.
convey [kən'veɪ] vt (gen) llevar; (thanks)
comunicar; (idea) expresar; ～**or belt** n
cinta transportadora.
convict [kən'vɪkt] vt (gen) condenar;
(sentence) declarar culpable // n
['kɒnvɪkt] presidiario; ～**ion** [-ʃən] n
condena; (belief) creencia, convicción f.
convince [kən'vɪns] vt convencer;
convincing a convincente.
convoy ['kɒnvɔɪ] n convoy m.
convulse [kən'vʌls] vt convulsionar;
(laughter) hacer morir de la risa;
convulsion [-'vʌlʃən] n convulsión f;
(laughter) paroxismo.
coo [ku:] vi arrullar.
cook [kuk] vt (gen) cocinar; (stew etc)
guisar; (meal) preparar // vi cocer;
(person) cocinar // n cocinero; ～**er** n
cocina; ～**ery** n (dishes) cocina; (art) arte
m de cocinar; ～**ery book** n libro de
cocina; ～**ie** n (US) bizcocho; ～**ing** n
cocina.
cool [ku:l] a fresco; (not hot) tibio; (not
afraid) tranquilo; (unfriendly) frío // vt
enfriar // vi enfriarse; ～**ness** n frescura,
tranquilidad f; (hostility) frialdad f; (indifference) falta de entusiasmo.
coop [ku:p] n gallinero // vt: to ～ **up** (fig)
encerrar.
co-op ['kəʊɒp] n abbr of **Cooperative
(Society)**.
cooperate [kəʊ'ɒpəreɪt] vi cooperar,
colaborar; **cooperation** [-'reɪʃən] n
cooperación f, colaboración f;
cooperative [-rətɪv] a cooperativo // n
cooperativa.
coordinate [kəʊ'ɔ:dɪneɪt] vt coordinar;
coordination [-'neɪʃən] n coordinación f.
cop [kɒp] n (col) poli m.
cope [kəʊp] vi: to ～ **with** poder con;
(problem) hacer frente a.
co-pilot ['kəʊ'paɪlət] n copiloto.
copious ['kəʊpɪəs] a copioso, abundante.

copper ['kɔpə*] n (metal) cobre m; (col: policeman) poli m; ~s npl monedas fpl de poco valor.

coppice ['kɔpɪs], **copse** [kɔps] n bosquecillo.

copulate ['kɔpjuleɪt] vi copularse; **copulation** [-'leɪʃən] n cópula.

copy ['kɔpɪ] n copia; (of book etc) ejemplar m; (of writing) original m // vt copiar; ~**right** n derechos mpl de autor.

coral ['kɔrəl] n coral m; ~ **reef** n arrecife m (de coral).

cord [kɔːd] n cuerda; (ELEC) cordón m; (fabric) pana.

cordial ['kɔːdɪəl] a afectuoso // n cordial m.

cordon ['kɔːdn] n cordón m; to ~ **off** vt acordonar.

corduroy ['kɔːdərɔɪ] n pana.

core [kɔː*] n (gen) centro, núcleo; (of fruit) corazón m // vt quitar el corazón de.

coriander [kɔrɪ'ændə*] n culantro.

cork [kɔːk] n corcho; (tree) alcornoque m; ~**screw** n sacacorchos pl inv.

cormorant ['kɔːmərnt] n cormorán m grande.

corn [kɔːn] n (wheat) trigo; (US: maize) maíz m; (cereals) granos mpl; (on foot) callo; ~ **on the cob** (CULIN) maíz en la mazorca.

corned beef ['kɔːnd-] n carne f de vaca acecinada.

corner ['kɔːnə*] n (gen) ángulo; (outside) esquina; (inside) rincón m; (in road) curva; (FOOTBALL) córner m // vt (trap) arrinconar; (COMM) acaparar // vi (in car) tomar una curva; ~**stone** n piedra angular.

cornet ['kɔːnɪt] n (MUS) corneta; (of ice-cream) barquillo.

cornflour ['kɔːnflauə*] n harina de maíz.

Cornwall ['kɔːnwəl] n Cornualles m.

corny ['kɔːnɪ] a (col) viejo, gastado.

corollary [kə'rɔlərɪ] n corolario.

coronary ['kɔrənərɪ] n: ~ **(thrombosis)** trombosis f coronaria.

coronation [kɔrə'neɪʃən] n coronación f.

coroner ['kɔrənə*] n juez m de primera instancia.

coronet ['kɔrənɪt] n corona.

corporal ['kɔːpərl] n cabo // a corporal.

corporate ['kɔːpərɪt] a corporativo.

corporation [kɔːpə'reɪʃən] n (of town) ayuntamiento; (COMM) corporación f.

corps [kɔː*], pl **corps** [kɔːz] n cuerpo.

corpse [kɔːps] n cadáver m.

corpuscle ['kɔːpʌsl] n corpúsculo.

corral [kə'rɑːl] n corral m.

correct [kə'rɛkt] a (accurate) justo, exacto; (proper) correcto // vt corregir; (exam) calificar; ~**ion** [-ʃən] n rectificación f; (erasure) tachadura.

correlate ['kɔrɪleɪt] vt correlacionar.

correspond [kɔrɪs'pɔnd] vi (write) escribirse; (be equal to) corresponder; ~**ence** n correspondencia; ~**ence**

course n curso por correspondencia; ~**ent** n corresponsal m/f; ~**ing** a correspondiente.

corridor ['kɔrɪdɔː*] n pasillo.

corroborate [kə'rɔbəreɪt] vt corroborar.

corrode [kə'rəud] vt corroer // vi corroerse; **corrosion** [-'rəuʒən] n corrosión f.

corrugated ['kɔrəgeɪtɪd] a ondulado; ~ **iron** n chapa ondulada.

corrupt [kə'rʌpt] a corrompido; (person) venal // vt corromper; (bribe) sobornar; ~**ion** [-ʃən] n corrupción f.

corset ['kɔːsɪt] n faja.

Corsica ['kɔːsɪkə] n Córcega.

cortège [kɔː'teːʒ] n cortejo, desfile m.

cortisone ['kɔːtɪzəun] n cortisona.

cosh [kɔʃ] n cachiporra.

cosiness ['kəuzɪnɪs] n comodidad f; (atmosphere) lo holgado.

cos lettuce [kɔs-] n lechuga cos.

cosmetic [kɔz'mɛtɪk] n cosmético.

cosmic ['kɔzmɪk] a cósmico.

cosmonaut ['kɔzmənɔːt] n cosmonauta m/f.

cosmopolitan [kɔzmə'pɔlɪtn] a cosmopolita.

cosmos ['kɔzmɔs] n cosmos m.

cost [kɔst] n (gen) coste m, costo; (price) precio; ~s npl costes mpl // vi, pt, pp **cost** costar, valer // vt preparar el presupuesto de; at the ~ of a costa de; how much does it ~? ¿cuánto cuesta?

co-star ['kəustɑː*] n colega m/f de reparto.

Costa Rican ['kɔstə'riːkən] a costarriqueño.

costly ['kɔstlɪ] a (expensive) costoso; (valuable) suntuoso.

cost price n precio de coste.

costume ['kɔstjuːm] n traje m; (also: swimming ~) traje de baño.

cosy ['kəuzɪ] a cómodo; (atmosphere) acogedor(a); (life) holgado.

cot [kɔt] n (child's) cuna.

cottage ['kɔtɪdʒ] n casita de campo; (rustic) barraca; ~ **cheese** n requesón m.

cotton ['kɔtn] n algodón m; (thread) hilo; to ~ **on** to vt (col) caer en la cuenta de; ~ **wool** a algodón m (hidrófilo).

couch [kautʃ] n sofá m.

cough [kɔf] vi toser // n tos f; to ~ **up** vt escupir; ~ **drop** n pastilla para la tos.

could [kud] pt of **can**; ~**n't** = could not.

council ['kaunsl] n consejo; city or town ~ consejo municipal; ~ **estate** n polígono de renta limitada; ~ **house** n vivienda de renta limitada; ~**lor** n concejal m/f.

counsel ['kaunsl] n (advice) consejo; (lawyer) abogado // vt aconsejar; ~**lor** n consejero.

count [kaunt] vt (gen) contar; (include) incluir // vi contar // n (gen) cuenta; (of votes) escrutinio; (nobleman) conde m; (sum) total m, suma; to ~ **on** vt fus contar con; **that doesn't** ~! ¡eso no vale!;

~**down** n cuenta hacia atrás.

counter ['kauntə*] n (in shop) mostrador m; (in games) ficha // vt contrarrestar; (blow) parar; (attack) contestar a // ad: ~ **to** contrario a; ~**act** vt contrarrestar; ~**attack** n contrataque m // vi contratacar; ~**balance** n contrapeso; ~**espionage** n contraespionaje m.

counterfeit ['kauntəfɪt] n moneda falsa // vt falsificar // a falso, falsificado.

counterfoil ['kauntəfɔɪl] n talón m.

counterpart ['kauntəpɑːt] n (of person) colega m/f.

counter-revolution [kauntərevə'luːʃən] n contrarrevolución f.

countersign ['kauntəsaɪn] vt refrendar.

countess ['kauntɪs] n condesa.

countless ['kauntlɪs] a incontable.

country ['kʌntrɪ] n país m; (native land) patria; (as opposed to town) campo; (region) región f, tierra; ~ **dancing** n baile m regional; ~ **house** n quinta, finca; ~**side** n campo.

county ['kauntɪ] n condado; ~ **town** n cabeza de partido.

coup [kuː], pl ~**s** [-z] n golpe m; ~ **d'état/de grâce** golpe de estado/de gracia.

coupé [kuː] n cupé m.

couple ['kʌpl] n (of things) par m; (of people) pareja; (married ~) matrimonio // vt (ideas, names) unir, juntar; (machinery) acoplar; **a** ~ **of** un par de.

coupling ['kʌplɪŋ] n (RAIL) enganche m.

coupon ['kuːpɔn] n cupón m; (pools ~) boleto.

courage ['kʌrɪdʒ] n valor m, valentía; ~**ous** [kə'reɪdʒəs] a valiente.

courier ['kurɪə*] n estafeta; (diplomatic) correo; (for tourists) agente m/f de turismo.

course [kɔːs] n (direction) dirección f; (of river, ESCOL) curso; (of ship) rumbo, derrota; (of bullet) trayectoria; (fig) proceder m; (GOLF) campo; (part of meal) plato; **of** ~ **ad** desde luego, naturalmente; **of** ~! ¡claro!; **in due** ~ en el momento oportuno.

court [kɔːt] n (royal) corte m; (LAW) tribunal m, juzgado; (TENNIS) pista, cancha // vt (woman) cortejar, hacer la corte a; (danger etc) buscar; **to take to** ~ demandar.

courteous ['kɔːtɪəs] a cortés.

courtesan [kɔːtɪ'zæn] n cortesana.

courtesy ['kɔːtəsɪ] n cortesía; **by** ~ **of** con permiso de.

court-house ['kɔːthaus] n (US) palacio de justicia.

courtier ['kɔːtɪə*] n cortesano.

court: ~**-martial**, pl ~**s-martial** n consejo de guerra // vt someter a consejo de guerra; ~**room** n sala de justicia; ~**yard** n patio.

cousin ['kʌzn] n primo/a; **first** ~ primo carnal.

cove [kəuv] n cala, ensenada.

covenant ['kʌvənənt] n convenio.

cover ['kʌvə*] vt (gen) cubrir; (with lid) tapar; (chairs etc) revestir; (distance) recorrer; (include) abarcar; (protect) abrigar; (journalist) investigar; (issues) tratar // n (gen) cubierta; (lid) tapa; (for chair etc) funda; (for bed) cobertor m; (envelope) sobre m; (for book) forro; (of magazine) portada; (shelter) abrigo; (insurance) cobertura; **under** ~ (indoors) bajo techo; **under** ~ **of** al abrigo de; (fig) so capa de; **to** ~ **up for sb** encubrir a uno; ~**age** n alcance m, ~ **charge** n precio del cubierto; ~**ing** n cubierta, envoltura; ~**ing letter** n carta explicatoria.

covet ['kʌvɪt] vt codiciar.

cow [kau] n vaca // vt intimidar.

coward ['kauəd] n cobarde m/f; ~**ice** [-ɪs] n cobardía; ~**ly** a cobarde.

cowboy ['kaubɔɪ] n vaquero.

cower ['kauə*] vi encogerse (de miedo).

cowshed ['kauʃed] n establo.

coxswain ['kɔksn] n (abbr: **cox**) timonel m/f.

coy [kɔɪ] a tímido.

coyote [kɔɪ'əutɪ] n coyote m.

crab [kræb] n cangrejo; ~ **apple** n manzana silvestre

crack [kræk] n grieta; (noise) crujido; (: of whip) chasquido; (fam) chiste m // vt agrietar, romper; (nut) cascar; (safe) forzar; (whip etc) chasquear; (knuckles) crujir; (joke) contar // a (expert) experto; **to** ~ **up** vi (MED) sufrir un colapso nervioso; ~**er** n (biscuit) cracker m; (Christmas cracker) sorpresa.

crackle ['krækl] vi crepitar; **crackling** n (of fire) crepitación f; (of leaves etc) crujido; (of pork) chicharrón m.

cradle ['kreɪdl] n cuna.

craft [krɑːft] n (skill) arte m; (trade) oficio; (cunning) astucia; (boat) barco.

craftsman ['krɑːftsmən] n artesano; ~**ship** n artesanía.

crafty ['krɑːftɪ] a astuto.

crag [kræg] n peñasco; ~**gy** a escarpado.

cram [kræm] vt (fill) llenar, henchir; ~**med** a atestado.

cramp [kræmp] n (MED) calambre m; (TECH) grapa // vt (limit) restringir; (annoy) estorbar; ~**ed** a apretado, estrecho.

crampon ['kræmpən] n crampón m.

cranberry ['krænbərɪ] n arándano agrio.

crane [kreɪn] n (TECH) grúa; (bird) grulla.

crank [kræŋk] n manivela; (person) chiflado; ~**shaft** n eje m del cigüeñal.

cranky ['kræŋkɪ] a (eccentric) maniático; (bad-tempered) irritable.

cranny ['krænɪ] n see **nook**.

crash [kræʃ] n (noise) estruendo; (of cars etc) choque m; (of plane) accidente m de avión; (COMM) quiebra // vt (plane) estrellar // vi (plane) estrellarse; (two cars) chocar; (fall noisily) caer con estrépito; ~ **course** n curso acelerado; ~

helmet n casco (protector); ~ **landing** n aterrizaje m forzoso.

crate [kreit] n cajón m de embalaje; (fam) armatoste m.

crater ['kreitə*] n cráter m.

cravat(e) [krə'væt] n pañuelo.

crave [kreiv] vt: to ~ **for** ansiar, anhelar; **craving** n (of pregnant woman) antojo.

crawl [krɔ:l] vi (gen) arrastrarse; (child) andar a gatas, gatear; (vehicle) avanzar a paso de tortuga // n (SWIMMING) crol m.

crayfish ['kreifiʃ] n, pl inv langostino.

crayon ['kreiən] n pastel m, lápiz m de color.

craze [kreiz] n manía; (fashion) moda.

crazy ['kreizi] a (person) loco; (idea) disparatado.

creak [kri:k] vi chirriar, rechinar; (door etc) crujir.

cream [kri:m] n (of milk) nata; (gen) crema; (fig) flor y nata // a (colour) color m (de) crema; ~ **cake** n pastel m de nata; ~ **cheese** n queso de nata; ~**y** a cremoso.

crease [kri:s] n (fold) pliegue m; (in trousers) raya; (wrinkle) arruga // vt (fold) doblar, plegar; (wrinkle) arrugar // vi (wrinkle up) arrugarse.

create [kri:'eit] vt crear; **creation** [-ʃən] n creación f; **creative** a creador(a); **creator** n creador m.

creature ['kri:tʃə*] n (animal) animal m, bicho; (living thing) criatura.

crèche, creche [kreʃ] n guardería infantil.

credentials [kri'dɛnʃlz] npl credenciales fpl.

credibility [krɛdɪ'bɪlɪti] n credibilidad f.

credible ['krɛdɪbl] a creíble.

credit ['krɛdɪt] n (gen) crédito; (merit) honor m, mérito // vt (COMM) abonar; (believe) creer, prestar fe a // a crediticio; ~**s** npl (CINEMA) fichas técnicas; ~**able** a estimable, digno de elogio; ~ **card** n tarjeta de crédito; ~**or** n acreedor m.

credulity [kri'dju:lɪti] n credulidad f.

creed [kri:d] n credo.

creek [kri:k] n cala, ensenada; (US) riachuelo.

creep [kri:p], pt, pp **crept** vi (animal) deslizarse; (gen) arrastrarse; (plant) trepar; ~**er** n enredadera; ~**y** a (frightening) horripilante.

cremate [kri'meit] vt incinerar; **cremation** [-ʃən] n incineración f.

crematorium [krɛmə'tɔ:rɪəm], pl **-ria** [-riə] n (horno) crematorio.

creosote ['kriəsəut] n creosota.

crêpe [kreip] n (fabric) crespón m; (rubber) crepé m; ~ **bandage** n venda de crepé.

crept [krept] pt, pp of **creep**.

crescent ['krɛsnt] n media luna; (street) calle f en semicírculo.

cress [krɛs] n mastuerzo.

crest [krɛst] n (of bird) cresta; (of hill)

cima, cumbre f; (of helmet) cimera; (of coat of arms) blasón m; ~**fallen** a alicaído.

Crete [kri:t] n Creta.

crevasse [kri'væs] n grieta.

crevice ['krɛvis] n grieta, hendedura.

crew [kru:] n (of ship etc) tripulación f; (gang) banda; (MIL) dotación f; ~**-cut** n corte m al rape; ~**-neck** n cuello plano.

crib [krib] n pesebre m // vt (col) plagiar.

crick [krik] n (in neck) tortícolis m.

cricket ['krikit] n (insect) grillo; (game) críquet m.

crime [kraim] n crimen m; (less serious) delito; **criminal** ['kriminl] n criminal m, delincuente m // a criminal, delictivo; (law) penal; **the Criminal Investigation Department** (CID) Brigada de Investigación Criminal (B.I.C.).

crimson ['krimzn] a carmesí.

cringe [krindʒ] vi agacharse, encogerse.

crinkle ['kriŋkl] vt arrugar.

cripple ['kripl] n lisiado, mutilado // vt lisiar, tulir.

crisis ['kraisis], pl **-ses** [-si:z] n crisis f.

crisp [krisp] a fresco; (cooked) tostado; (hair) crespo; (manner) seco; ~**s** npl papas fritas fpl.

criss-cross ['kriskrɔs] a entrecruzado.

criterion [krai'tiəriən], pl **-ria** [-riə] n criterio.

critic ['kritik] n (gen) criticón-ona m/f; (paper) crítico; ~**al** a (gen) crítico; (illness) grave; ~**ally** ad (ill) gravemente; ~**ism** ['kritisizm] n crítica; ~**ize** ['kritisaiz] vt criticar.

croak [krəuk] vi (frog) croar; (raven) graznar // n graznido.

crochet ['krəuʃei] n ganchillo.

crockery ['krɔkəri] n loza, vajilla.

crocodile ['krɔkədail] n cocodrilo.

crocus ['krəukəs] n azafrán m.

croft [krɔft] n granja pequeña; ~**er** n pequeño granjero.

croissant ['krwasã] n croissant m, medialuna.

crone [krəun] n bruja.

crony ['krəuni] n compinche m/f.

crook [kruk] n (fam) maleante m/f; (of shepherd) cayado; (of arm) pliegue m; ~**ed** ['krukid] a torcido; (path) tortuoso; (action) poco limpio.

crop [krɔp] n (species) cultivo; (quantity) cosecha // vt cortar, recortar; to ~ **up** vi surgir, presentarse.

croquet ['krəukei] n croquet m.

croquette [krə'kɛt] n croqueta.

cross [krɔs] n cruz f // vt (street etc) cruzar, atravesar // a de mal humor, malhumorado; to ~ **o.s.** santiguarse; to ~ **out** vt tachar; to ~ **over** vi cruzar; ~**bar** n travesaño; (SPORT) larguero; ~**country** (race) n carrera a campo traviesa, cross m; ~**-examination** n repregunta, interrogatorio; ~**-examine** vt repreguntar; ~**-eyed** a bizco; ~**ing** n (*road*) cruce *m*; (*rail*) paso a nivel; (*sea-passage*) travesía; (*also*: **pedestrian ~ing**) paso para peatones; **~ purposes** *npl*: **to be at ~ purposes** malentenderse uno a otro; **~-reference** *n* contra-rreferencia; **~roads** *n* cruce *m*, encrucijada; **~ section** *n* corte *m* transversal; (*of population*) sección *f* representativa; **~wind** *n* viento de costado; **~word** *n* crucigrama *m*.

crotch [krɔtʃ] *n* (*of garment*) entrepierna.

crotchet ['krɔtʃit] *n* (*MUS*) negra.

crotchety ['krɔtʃiti] *a* (*person*) arisco.

crouch [krautʃ] *vi* agacharse, acurrucarse.

croupier ['kru:piə] *n* crupier *m/f*.

crow [krəu] *n* (*bird*) cuervo; (*of cock*) canto, cacareo // *vi* (*cock*) cantar, cacarear.

crowbar ['krəuba:*] *n* palanca.

crowd [kraud] *n* muchedumbre *f*; (*SPORT*) público; (*unruly*) tropel *m*; (*common herd*) vulgo // *vt* (*gather*) amontonar; (*fill*) llenar // *vi* (*gather*) reunirse; (*pile up*) amontonarse; **~ed** *a* (*full*) atestado; (*well-attended*) concurrido.

crown [kraun] *n* corona; (*of head*) coronilla; (*of hat*) copa; (*of hill*) cumbre *f* // *vt* coronar; **~ jewels** *npl* joyas *fpl* reales; **~ prince** *n* príncipe *m* heredero.

crucial ['kru:ʃl] *a* decisivo.

crucifix ['kru:sifiks] *n* crucifijo; **~ion** [-'fikʃən] *n* crucifixión *f*; **crucify** [-fai] *vt* crucificar.

crude [kru:d] *a* (*materials*) bruto; (*fig: basic*) tosco; (*: vulgar*) ordinario; **~ (oil)** *n* aceite *m* crudo.

cruel ['kruəl] *a* cruel; **~ty** *n* crueldad *f*.

cruet ['kru:it] *n* angarillas *fpl*.

cruise [kru:z] *n* crucero, viaje *m* por mar // *vi* (*ship*) hacer un crucero; (*car*) circular lentamente; **cruiser** *n* crucero.

crumb [krʌm] *n* miga, migaja.

crumble ['krʌmbl] *vt* desmenuzar // *vi* (*gen*) desmenuzarse; (*building*) desmoro-narse; **crumbly** *a* desmenuzable.

crumpet ['krʌmpit] *n* bollo blando.

crumple ['krʌmpl] *vt* (*paper*) estrujar; (*material*) arrugar.

crunch [krʌntʃ] *vt* (*food etc*) mascar; (*underfoot*) hacer crujir // *n* (*fig*) crisis *f*; **~y** *a* crujiente.

crusade [kru:'seid] *n* cruzada.

crush [krʌʃ] *n* (*people*) agolpamiento; (*crowd*) aglomeración *f*; (*drink*): **lemon ~** limonada // *vt* (*gen*) aplastar; (*paper*) estrujar; (*cloth*) arrugar; (*fruit*) exprimir; **~ing** *a* aplastante; (*burden*) agobiador(a).

crust [krʌst] *n* corteza; (*MED*) costra.

crutch [krʌtʃ] *n* muleta.

crux [krʌks] *n* lo esencial.

cry [krai] *vi* llorar; (*shout*) gritar // *n* grito.

crypt [kript] *n* cripta.

cryptic ['kriptik] *a* enigmático, secreto.

crystal ['kristl] *n* cristal *m*; **~-clear** *a* transparente, claro como el agua; **crystallize** *vt* cristalizar // *vi* cristalizarse.

cub [kʌb] *n* cachorro.

Cuba ['kju:bə] *n* Cuba; **~n** *a*, *n* cubano/a.

cubbyhole ['kʌbihəul] *n* chiribitil *m*.

cube [kju:b] *n* cubo; (*of sugar*) terrón *m* // *vt* (*MATH*) cubicar; **~ root** *n* raíz *f* cúbica; **cubic** *a* cúbico.

cubicle ['kju:bikl] *n* (*at pool*) caseta; (*for bed*) camarilla.

cuckoo ['kuku:] *n* cuco; **~ clock** *n* reloj *m* de cuclillo.

cucumber ['kju:kʌmbə*] *n* pepino.

cuddle ['kʌdl] *vt* abrazar amorosamente // *vi* abrazarse; **cuddly** *a* mimoso.

cue [kju:] *n* (*snooker*) taco; (*THEATRE etc*) entrada, apunte *m*.

cuff [kʌf] *n* (*of shirt, coat etc*) puño; (*blow*) bofetada; **off the ~** *ad* de improviso; **~links** *npl* gemelos *mpl*.

cuisine [kwi'zi:n] *n* cocina.

cul-de-sac ['kʌldəsæk] *n* callejón *m* sin salida.

culinary ['kʌlinəri] *a* culinario.

cull [kʌl] *vt* (*flowers*) coger; (*select*) entresacar.

culminate ['kʌlmineit] *vi*: **to ~ in** terminar en; **culmination** [-'neiʃən] *n* culminación *f*, colmo.

culpable ['kʌlpəbl] *a* culpable.

culprit ['kʌlprit] *n* (*persona*) culpable, delincuente *m/f*.

cult [kʌlt] *n* culto.

cultivate ['kʌltiveit] *vt* (*also fig*) cultivar; **cultivation** [-'veiʃən] *n* cultivo; (*fig*) cultura.

cultural ['kʌltʃərəl] *a* cultural.

culture ['kʌltʃə*] *n* (*also fig*) cultura; **~d** *a* culto.

cumbersome ['kʌmbəsəm] *a* molesto, incómodo.

cumulative ['kju:mjulətiv] *a* cumulativo.

cunning ['kʌniŋ] *n* astucia // *a* astuto.

cup [kʌp] *n* taza; (*prize, event*) copa.

cupboard ['kʌbəd] *n* armario; (*on wall*) alacena.

Cupid ['kju:pid] *n* Cupido.

cupola ['kju:pələ] *n* cúpula.

cup-tie ['kʌptai] *n* partido de copa.

cur [kə*] *n* perro de mala raza; (*person*) canalla *m/f*.

curable ['kjuərəbl] *a* curable.

curate ['kjuərit] *n* cura *m*.

curator [kjuə'reitə*] *n* director *m*.

curb [kə:b] *vt* refrenar // *n* freno.

curdle ['kə:dl] *vi* cuajarse.

curds [kə:dz] *npl* requesón *m*.

cure [kjuə*] *vt* curar // *n* cura, curación *f*.

curfew ['kə:fju:] *n* toque *m* de queda.

curio ['kjuəriəu] *n* curiosidad *f*.

curiosity [kjuəri'ositi] *n* curiosidad *f*; **curious** ['kjuəriəs] *a* curioso.

curl [kə:l] *n* rizo, bucle *m* // *vt* (*hair*) rizar; (*paper*) arrollar; (*lip*) fruncir // *vi* rizarse; arrollarse; **~ up** *vi* arrollarse; (*person*) hacer un ovillo; (*fam*) morirse de risa; **~er** *n* bigudí *m*, chincho; **~y** *a* rizado.

currant ['kʌrnt] n pasa; (black, red) grosella.
currency ['kʌrnsɪ] n moneda.
current ['kʌrnt] n corriente f // a corriente, actual; ~ **account** n cuenta corriente; ~ **affairs** npl actualidades fpl; ~**ly** ad actualmente.
curriculum [kə'rɪkjuləm] pl ~s or ~la [-lə] n plan m de estudios; ~ **vitae** n currículum m.
curry ['kʌrɪ] n curry m // vt: to ~ **favour with** buscar favores con; ~ **powder** n polvos mpl de curry.
curse [kəs] vi echar pestes // vt maldecir, echar pestes de // n maldición f; (swearword) palabrota.
cursory ['kɔ:sərɪ] a rápido, superficial.
curt [kə:t] a corto, seco.
curtail [kə:'teɪl] vt (visit etc) acortar; (expenses etc) restringir.
curtain ['kə:tn] n cortina; (THEATRE) telón m; ~ **ring** n anilla.
curts(e)y ['kə:tsɪ] n reverencia // vi hacer una reverencia.
curve [kə:v] n curva // vt encorvar, torcer // vi encorvarse, torcerse; (road) hacer (una) curva.
cushion ['kuʃən] n cojín m; (SNOOKER) banda // vt (seat) acolchar; (shock) amortiguar.
custard ['kʌstəd] n (for pouring) natilla.
custodian [kʌs'təudɪən] n custodio.
custody ['kʌstədɪ] n custodia; **to take into** ~ detener.
custom ['kʌstəm] n costumbre f; (COMM) clientela; ~**ary** a acostumbrado.
customer ['kʌstəmə*] n cliente m/f.
custom-made ['kʌstəm'meɪd] a hecho a la medida.
customs ['kʌstəmz] npl aduana sg; ~ **duty** n derechos mpl de aduana; ~ **officer** n aduanero.
cut [kʌt], pt, pp **cut** vt cortar; (price) rebajar; (record) grabar; (reduce) reducir // vi cortar; (intersect) cruzarse // n (gen) corte m; (in skin) cortadura; (with sword) tajo; (of knife) cuchillada; (in salary etc) rebaja; (of meat) tajada; **power** ~ apagón m; to ~ **a tooth** salirle a uno un diente; **to** ~ **down** vt (tree) derribar; (reduce) reducir; **to** ~ **off** vt (gen) cortar; (retreat) impedir; (troops) cercar; **to** ~ **out** vt (shape) recortar; (delete) suprimir; **to** ~ **through** vi abrirse camino; ~**back** n reducción f.
cute [kju:t] a lindo; (shrewd) listo.
cuticle ['kju:tɪkl] n cutícula.
cutlery ['kʌtlərɪ] n cubiertos mpl.
cutlet ['kʌtlɪt] n chuleta.
cut: ~**out** n recortable m; ~**price** a a precio reducido; ~**throat** n asesino // a intenso.
cutting ['kʌtɪŋ] a (gen) cortante; (remark) mordaz // n (PRESS) recorte m; (RAIL) desmonte m.
cwt abbr of **hundredweight(s)**.
cyanide ['saɪənaɪd] n cianuro.

cyclamen ['sɪkləmən] n ciclamen m.
cycle ['saɪkl] n ciclo; (bicycle) bicicleta // vi ir en bicicleta; **cycling** n ciclismo; **cyclist** n ciclista m/f.
cyclone ['saɪkləun] n ciclón m.
cygnet ['sɪgnɪt] n pollo de cisne.
cylinder ['sɪlɪndə*] n cilindro; ~ **block** n bloque m de cilindros; ~ **capacity** n cilindrada; ~ **head** n culata de cilindro; ~**head gasket** n junta de culata.
cymbals ['sɪmblz] npl platillos mpl.
cynic ['sɪnɪk] n cínico; ~**al** a cínico; ~**ism** ['sɪnɪsɪzəm] n cinismo.
cypress ['saɪprɪs] n ciprés m.
Cypriot ['sɪprɪət] a, n chipriota m/f.
Cyprus ['saɪprəs] n Chipre f.
cyst [sɪst] n quiste m; ~**itis** n cistitis f.
czar [zɑ:*] n zar m.
Czech [tʃɛk] a, n checo/a.
Czechoslovakia [tʃɛkəslə'vækɪə] n Checoslovaquia.

D

dab [dæb] vt (eyes, wound) tocar (ligeramente); (paint, cream) mojar ligeramente // n (of paint) brochazo; (of liquid) gota; (amount) pequeña cantidad f.
dabble ['dæbl] vi: to ~ **in** interesarse por.
dad [dæd], **daddy** ['dædɪ] n papá m; **daddy-long-legs** n típula.
daffodil ['dæfədɪl] n narciso trompón.
daft [dɑ:ft] a estúpido, tonto.
dagger ['dægə*] n puñal m, daga; **to look** ~**s at sb** apuñalar a alguien con la mirada.
daily ['deɪlɪ] a diario, cotidiano // n (paper) diario; (domestic help) asistenta // ad a diario, cada día.
dainty ['deɪntɪ] a delicado; (tasteful) elegante, primoroso.
dairy ['dɛərɪ] n (shop) lechería; (on farm) vaquería // a lechero; ~ **farm** n granja; ~ **produce** n productos mpl lácteos.
daisy ['deɪzɪ] n margarita.
dale [deɪl] n valle m.
dam [dæm] n presa // vt represar.
damage ['dæmɪdʒ] n daño, perjuicio; (to machine) avería // vt dañar, perjudicar; averiar; ~**s** npl (LAW) daños y perjuicios.
damn [dæm] vt condenar; (curse) maldecir // n (col): **I don't give a** ~ me trae sin cuidado // a (col) maldito; ~ (it)! ¡mecachis!; ~**ing** a (evidence) irrecusable.
damp [dæmp] a húmedo, mojado // n humedad f // vt (also: ~**en**) (cloth, rag) mojar; (enthusiasm etc) desalentar; ~**ness** n humedad f.
damson ['dæmzən] n ciruela damascena.
dance [dɑ:ns] n baile m // vi bailar; ~ **hall** n salón m de baile; **dancer** n bailador/a m/f; (professional) bailarín/ina m/f; **dancing** n baile m.
dandelion ['dændɪlaɪən] n diente m de león.

dandruff ['dændrəf] n caspa.

Dane [deɪn] n danés/esa m/f.

danger ['deɪndʒə*] n peligro; (risk) riesgo; ~! (on sign) ¡peligro de muerte!; to be in ~ of correr riesgo de; ~ous a peligroso; ~ously ad peligrosamente.

dangle ['dæŋgl] vt colgar // vi pender, estar colgado.

Danish ['deɪnɪʃ] a, n danés/esa m/f.

dare [dɛə*] vt: to ~ sb to do desafiar a uno a hacer algo // vi: to ~ (to) do sth atreverse a hacer algo; ~devil n temerario, atrevido; **daring** a atrevido, osado // n atrevimiento, osadía.

dark [dɑːk] a (gen) oscuro; (hair, complexion) moreno; (cheerless) triste, sombrío; (fig) secreto, escondido // n (gen) oscuridad f; (night) tinieblas fpl; to be left in the ~ about (fig) quedar sin saber nada de; **after** ~ después del anochecer; ~en vt oscurecer; (colour) hacer más oscuro // vi oscurecerse; (sky) anublarse; ~ glasses npl gafas fpl oscuras; ~ness n oscuridad f, tinieblas fpl; ~ room n cuarto oscuro.

darling ['dɑːlɪŋ] a, n querido/a.

darn [dɑːn] vt zurcir.

dart [dɑːt] n dardo; (in game) rehilete m; (in sewing) sisa // vi precipitarse; to ~ away/along n blanco; ~s n juego de rehiletes.

dash [dæʃ] n (sign) guión m; (: long) raya; (rush) carrera // vt (break) romper, estrellar; (hopes) defraudar // vi precipitarse, ir de prisa; to ~ away or off vi marcharse apresuradamente; ~board n tablero de instrumentos; ~ing a gallardo.

data ['deɪtə] npl datos mpl; ~ processing n procesamiento de datos.

date [deɪt] n (day) fecha; (with friend) cita; (fruit) dátil m; (tree) palmera // vt fichar; citar; to ~ ad hasta la fecha; out of ~ fuera de moda; up to ~ moderno, al día; ~d a anticuado.

daub [dɔːb] vt manchar.

daughter ['dɔːtə*] n hija; ~-in-law n nuera, hija política.

daunting ['dɔːntɪŋ] a desalentador(a).

dawdle ['dɔːdl] vi (waste time) perder el tiempo; (go slow) andar muy despacio.

dawn [dɔːn] n alba, amanecer m // vi (day) amanecer; (fig): **it ~ed on him that...** cayó en la cuenta de que... .

day [deɪ] n día m; (working ~) jornada; **the ~ before** el día anterior; **the following ~** el día siguiente; **by** ~ de día; ~**break** n amanecer m; ~**dream** n ensueño // vi soñar despierto; ~**light** n luz f (del día); ~**time** n día m // a de día.

daze [deɪz] vt (stun) aturdir // n: in a ~ aturdido.

dazzle ['dæzl] vt deslumbrar; **dazzling** a deslumbrante.

dead [dɛd] a (gen) muerto; (deceased) difunto; (telephone) cortado; (ELEC) sin corriente // ad (gen) totalmente; (exactly) justo; ~ **tired** muerto de cansancio; **to stop** ~ parar en seco; **the** ~ los muertos; ~**en** vt (blow, sound) amortiguar; (make numb) calmar, aliviar; ~ **end** n callejón m sin salida; ~ **heat** n (SPORT) empate m; ~**line** n fecha o hora tope; ~**lock** n punto muerto; ~**ly** a mortal, fatal; ~**pan** a sin expresión.

deaf [dɛf] a sordo; ~-**aid** n audífono; ~**en** vt ensordecer; ~**ening** a ensordecedor(a); ~**ness** n sordera; ~-**mute** n sordomudo/a.

deal [diːl] n (agreement) pacto, convenio; (business) negocio, trato; (CARDS) reparto // vt, pt, pp **dealt** [dɛlt] (gen) dar; **a great** ~ (of) bastante, mucho; **to** ~ **in** tratar en, comerciar en; **to** ~ **with** vt fus (people) tratar con; (problem) ocuparse de; (subject) tratar de; (punish) castigar; ~**er** n comerciante m, tratante m; (CARDS) mano f; ~**ings** npl transacciones fpl; (relations) relaciones fpl.

dear [dɪə*] a querido; (expensive) caro // n: **my** ~ mi querido/a f, excl: ~ **me!** ¡Dios mío!; **D**~ **Sir/Madam** (in letter) Muy Señor Mío, estimado Señor/estimada Señora; ~**ly** ad (love) tiernamente; (pay) caro.

death [dɛθ] n muerte f; ~**bed** n lecho de muerte; ~ **certificate** n partida de defunción; ~ **duties** npl (Brit) derechos mpl de herencia; ~**ly** a mortal; (silence) profundo; ~ **penalty** n pena de muerte; ~ **rate** n mortalidad f.

debar [dɪ'bɑː*] vt (exclude) excluir.

debase [dɪ'beɪs] vt degradar.

debate [dɪ'beɪt] n debate m // vt discutir.

debauchery [dɪ'bɔːtʃərɪ] n libertinaje m.

debit ['dɛbɪt] n debe m // vt: to ~ **a sum to sb** or **sb's account** cargar una suma en cuenta a alguien.

debris ['dɛbriː] n escombros mpl.

debt [dɛt] n deuda; **to be in** ~ tener deudas; ~**or** n deudor/a m/f.

début ['deɪbjuː] n presentación f.

decade ['dɛkeɪd] n decenio.

decadence ['dɛkədəns] n decadencia.

decay [dɪ'keɪ] n decadencia; (of building) desmoronamiento; (fig) deterioro; (rotting) pudrición f; (of tooth) caries f // vi (rot) pudrirse; (fig) decaer.

deceased [dɪ'siːst] a difunto.

deceit [dɪ'siːt] n engaño; ~**ful** a engañoso.

deceive [dɪ'siːv] vt engañar.

decelerate [diː'sɛləreɪt] vt moderar la marcha de // vi decelerar.

December [dɪ'sɛmbə*] n diciembre m.

decency ['diːsənsɪ] n decencia.

decent ['diːsənt] a (proper) decente; (person) amable, bueno.

decentralize [diː'sɛntrəlaɪz] vt descentralizar.

deception [dɪ'sɛpʃən] n engaño; **deceptive** [-tɪv] a engañoso.

decibel ['dɛsɪbɛl] n decibel(io) m.

decide [dɪ'saɪd] vt (person) decidir;

(*question, argument*) resolver // *vi* decidir;
to ~ on sth decidir por algo; **~d** a
(*resolute*) decidido; (*clear, definite*)
indudable; **~dly** [-dɪdlɪ] *ad* decididamente.
deciduous [dɪˈsɪdjuəs] a de hoja caduca.
decimal [ˈdesɪməl] a decimal // *n* decimal
f; **~ point** *n* coma de decimales.
decimate [ˈdesɪmeɪt] *vt* diezmar.
decipher [dɪˈsaɪfə*] *vt* descifrar.
decision [dɪˈsɪʒən] *n* decisión f.
decisive [dɪˈsaɪsɪv] a decisivo; (*conclusive*)
terminante; (*manner*) tajante.
deck [dek] *n* (*NAUT*) cubierta; (*of bus*) piso;
(*of cards*) baraja; **~chair** *n* tumbona,
hamaca.
declaration [dekləˈreɪʃən] *n* declaración f;
declare [dɪˈkleə*] *vt* (*gen*) declarar.
decline [dɪˈklaɪn] *n* decaimiento
decadencia; (*lessening*) disminución f // *vt*
rehusar // *vi* decaer; disminuir; (*fall*)
bajar.
declutch [ˈdiːˈklʌtʃ] *vi* desembragar.
decode [diːˈkəud] *vt* descifrar.
decompose [diːkəmˈpəuz] *vi*
descomponerse; **decomposition**
[diːkɔmpəˈzɪʃən] *n* descomposición f.
decontaminate [diːkənˈtæmɪneɪt] *vt*
descontaminar.
décor [ˈdeɪkɔː*] *n* decoración f; (*THEATRE*)
decorado.
decorate [ˈdekəreɪt] *vt* adornar, decorar;
(*paint*) pintar; (*paper*) empapelar;
decoration [-ˈreɪʃən] *n* adorno; (*act*,
decoración f; (*medal*) condecoración f,
decorator *n* (*painter*) pintor *m*.
decoy [ˈdiːkɔɪ] *n* señuelo.
decrease [diːˈkriːs] *n* disminución f // (*vb*:
[diːˈkriːs]) *vt* disminuir, reducir // *vi*
reducirse.
decree [dɪˈkriː] *n* decreto; **~ nisi** *n* orden
f provisional de divorcio.
decrepit [dɪˈkrepɪt] a decrépito.
dedicate [ˈdedɪkeɪt] *vt* dedicar;
dedication [-ˈkeɪʃən] *n* (*devotion*)
dedicación f; (*in book*) dedicatoria.
deduce [dɪˈdjuːs] *vt* deducir.
deduct [dɪˈdʌkt] *vt* restar; (*from wage etc*)
descontar; **~ion** [dɪˈdʌkʃən] *n* descuento;
(*conclusion*) deducción f, conclusión f.
deed [diːd] *n* hecho, acto; (*feat*) hazaña;
(*LAW*) escritura.
deem [diːm] *vt* juzgar.
deep [diːp] a (*gen*) profundo; (*voice*) bajo;
(*breath*) profundo, a pleno pulmón;
(*person*) insondable // *ad*: **the spectators
stood 20 —** los espectadores se formaron
de 20 en fondo; **to be 4 metres —** tener 4
metros de profundo; **~en** *vt* ahondar,
profundizar // *vi* (*darkness*) intensificarse;
~freeze *n* congeladora; **~fry** *vt* freír
en aceite abundante; **~sea diving** *n*
buceo de altura; **~seated** a (*beliefs*)
(*profundamente*) arraigado; **~set** a
(*eyes*) hundido.
deer [dɪə*] *n*, *pl inv* ciervo; **~skin** *n*
gamuza, piel f de ciervo.
deface [dɪˈfeɪs] *vt* desfigurar, mutilar.

defamation [defəˈmeɪʃən] *n* difamación f.
default [dɪˈfɔːlt] *vi* no pagar; (*SPORT*) dejar
de presentarse // *n*: **by ~** (*LAW*) en
rebeldía; (*SPORT*) por no presentarse el
adversario; **~er** *n* (*in debt*) moroso/a.
defeat [dɪˈfiːt] *n* derrota // *vt* derrotar,
vencer; (*fig*: *efforts*) frustrar; **~ist** a, *n*
derrotista *m/f*.
defect [ˈdiːfekt] *n* defecto // *vi* [dɪˈfekt]
desertar; **~ive** [dɪˈfektɪv] a (*gen*)
defectuoso; (*person*) anormal.
defence [dɪˈfens] *n* defensa; **~less** a
indefenso.
defend [dɪˈfend] *vt* defender; **~ant** *n*
acusado/a; (*in civil case*) demandado/a;
~er *n* defensor *m*.
defensive [dɪˈfensɪv] a defensivo; **on the
~** a la defensiva.
defer [dɪˈfɜː*] *vt* (*postpone*) aplazar; **to ~
to** diferir a; **~ence** [ˈdefərəns] *n*
deferencia, respeto.
defiance [dɪˈfaɪəns] *n* desafío; **in ~ of** en
contra de; **defiant** [-ənt] a (*insolent*)
insolente; (*challenging*) retador(a).
deficiency [dɪˈfɪʃənsɪ] *n* (*lack*) falta;
(*defect*) defecto; **deficient** [-ənt] a
(*lacking*) insuficiente; (*incomplete*)
incompleto; (*defective*) defectuoso;
(*mentally*) anormal; **deficient in** falto de.
deficit [ˈdefɪsɪt] *n* déficit *m*.
defile [dɪˈfaɪl] *vt* marchar, deshonrar.
define [dɪˈfaɪn] *vt* definir.
definite [ˈdefɪnɪt] a (*fixed*) determinado;
(*clear, obvious*) claro, categórico; **he was
~ about it** no dejó lugar a dudas (sobre
ello); **~ly** *ad* claramente.
definition [defɪˈnɪʃən] a definición f.
definitive [dɪˈfɪnɪtɪv] a definitivo.
deflate [diːˈfleɪt] *vt* (*gen*) desinflar;
(*person*) quitar los humos a.
deflect [dɪˈflekt] *vt* desviar.
deform [dɪˈfɔːm] *vt* deformar; **~ed** a
deformado; **~ity** *n* deformación f.
defraud [dɪˈfrɔːd] *vt* estafar; **to ~ sb of
sth** estafar algo a uno.
defrost [diːˈfrɔst] *vt* (*fridge*) deshelar,
descongelar.
deft [deft] a diestro, hábil.
defunct [dɪˈfʌŋkt] a difunto.
defuse [diːˈfjuːz] *vt* quitar el fusible a.
defy [dɪˈfaɪ] *vt* (*resist*) oponerse
resueltamente a; (*challenge*) desafiar;
(*order*) contravenir.
degenerate [dɪˈdʒenəreɪt] *vi* degenerar //
a [dɪˈdʒenərɪt] degenerado.
degradation [degrəˈdeɪʃən] *n* degradación
f; **degrading** [dɪˈgreɪdɪŋ] a degradante.
degree [dɪˈgriː] *n* grado; (*scol*) título; **~ in
maths** licencia en matemáticas.
dehydrated [diːhaɪˈdreɪtɪd] a
deshidratado; (*milk*) en polvo.
de-ice [diːˈaɪs] *vt* (*windscreen*) deshelar.
deign [deɪn] *vi*: **to ~ to do** dignarse
hacer.
deity [ˈdiːɪtɪ] *n* deidad f, divinidad f.
dejected [dɪˈdʒektɪd] a abatido,

desanimado; (face) cariacontecido; **dejection** [-'ʃən] n abatimiento.

delay [dɪ'leɪ] vt demorar, aplazar; (person) entretener; (trains) retrasar // vi tardar // n (gen) dilación f; (a ~) demora, retraso; **without** ~ en seguida, sin tardar.

delegate ['dɛlɪgɪt] n delegado/a // vt ['dɛlɪgeɪt] delegar; **delegation** [-'geɪʃən] n delegación f.

delete [dɪ'liːt] vt suprimir, tachar.

deliberate [dɪ'lɪbərɪt] a (intentional) intencionado; (slow) pausado, lento // vi [dɪ'lɪbəreɪt] deliberar; ~ly ad (on purpose) a propósito; (slowly) pausadamente.

delicacy ['dɛlɪkəsɪ] n delicadeza; (choice food) golosina.

delicate ['dɛlɪkɪt] a (gen) delicado; (fragile) frágil; (skilled) fino.

delicatessen [dɛlɪkə'tɛsn] n tienda especializada en comida exótica.

delicious [dɪ'lɪʃəs] a delicioso, rico.

delight [dɪ'laɪt] n (feeling) placer m, deleite m; (object) encanto, delicia // vt encantar, deleitar; **to take** ~ **in** deleitarse con; ~**ful** a encantador(a), delicioso.

delinquency [dɪ'lɪŋkwənsɪ] n delincuencia; **delinquent** [-ənt] a, n delincuente m/f.

delirious [dɪ'lɪrɪəs] a delirante; **delirium** [-ɪəm] n delirio.

deliver [dɪ'lɪvə*] vt (distribute) repartir; (hand over) entregar; (message) comunicar; (speech) pronunciar; (blow) lanzar, dar; (MED): **to be** ~**ed** dar a luz; ~**y** n reparto; entrega; (distribution) distribución f; (of speaker) modo de expresarse; (MED) parto, alumbramiento; (saving) liberación f; **to take** ~**y of** recibir.

delta ['dɛltə] n delta m.

delude [dɪ'luːd] vt engañar.

deluge ['dɛljuːdʒ] n diluvio // vt inundar.

delusion [dɪ'luːʒən] n ilusión f, engaño.

de luxe [də'lʌks] a de lujo.

delve [dɛlv] vi: **to** ~ **into** ahondar en.

demand [dɪ'mɑːnd] vt (gen) exigir; (rights) reclamar // n (gen) exigencia; (claim) reclamación f; (ECON) demanda; **to be in** ~ ser muy solicitado; **on** ~ a solicitud; ~**ing** a (boss) exigente; (work) absorbente.

demarcation [diːmɑː'keɪʃən] n demarcación f.

demean [dɪ'miːn] vt: **to** ~ **o.s.** rebajarse.

demeanour [dɪ'miːnə*] n porte m, conducta.

demented [dɪ'mɛntɪd] a demente.

demister [diː'mɪstə*] n (AUT) de(s)fuminador m de vapores.

democracy [dɪ'mɒkrəsɪ] n democracia; **democrat** ['dɛmɔkræt] n demócrata m/f; **democratic** [dɛmɔ'krætɪk] a democrático.

demolish [dɪ'mɒlɪʃ] vt derribar, demoler; **demolition** [dɛmə'lɪʃən] n derribo, demolición f.

demonstrate ['dɛmənstreɪt] vt demostrar

// vi manifestarse; **demonstration** [-'streɪʃən] n (POL) manifestación f; (proof) prueba, demostración f; **demonstrator** n (POL) manifestante m/f.

demoralize [dɪ'mɒrəlaɪz] vt desmoralizar.

demote [dɪ'məut] vt degradar.

demure [dɪ'mjuə*] a recatado.

den [dɛn] n (of animal) guarida; (study) estudio.

denial [dɪ'naɪəl] n (refusal) negativa; (of report etc) desmentimiento; **self-~** abnegación f.

denim ['dɛnɪm] n dril m; ~**s** npl vaqueros mpl.

Denmark ['dɛnmɑːk] n Dinamarca.

denomination [dɪnɒmɪ'neɪʃən] n valor m; (REL) confesión f.

denominator [dɪ'nɒmɪneɪtə*] n denominador m.

denote [dɪ'nəut] vt indicar, significar.

denounce [dɪ'nauns] vt denunciar.

dense [dɛns] a (thick) espeso; (: foliage etc) tupido; (stupid) torpe, duro de mollera; ~**ly** ad: ~**ly populated** con gran densidad de población.

density ['dɛnsɪtɪ] n densidad f.

dent [dɛnt] n abolladura // vt (also: **make a** ~ **in**) abollar.

dental ['dɛntl] a dental; ~ **surgeon** n odontólogo.

dentist ['dɛntɪst] n dentista m/f; ~**ry** n odontología.

dentures ['dɛntʃəz] npl dentadura sg (postiza).

deny [dɪ'naɪ] vt (gen) negar; (charge) rechazar; (report) desmentir; **to** ~ **o.s.** privarse de.

deodorant [diː'əudərənt] n desodorante m.

depart [dɪ'pɑːt] vi irse, marcharse; (train) salir; **to** ~ **from** (fig: differ from) apartarse de.

department [dɪ'pɑːtmənt] n (COMM) sección f; (SCOL) ramo; (POL) ministerio; ~ **store** n gran almacén m.

departure [dɪ'pɑːtʃə*] n partida, ida; (of train) salida; **a new** ~ un nuevo rumbo.

depend [dɪ'pɛnd] vi: **to** ~ **on** depender de; (rely on) contar con; **it** ~**s** ¡depende!, ¡según!; ~**able** a (person) formal, serio; ~**ence** n dependencia; ~**ant**, ~**ent** n dependiente m/f.

depict [dɪ'pɪkt] vt (in picture) pintar; (describe) representar.

depleted [dɪ'pliːtɪd] a reducido.

deplorable [dɪ'plɔːrəbl] a lamentable, deplorable; **deplore** [dɪ'plɔː*] vt lamentar, deplorar.

deploy [dɪ'plɔɪ] vt desplegar.

depopulation ['diːpɒpju'leɪʃən] n despoblación f.

deport [dɪ'pɔːt] vt deportar; ~**ation** [-'teɪʃən] n deportación f; ~**ment** n comportamiento.

depose [dɪ'pəuz] vt deponer.

deposit [dɪ'pɒzɪt] n (gen) depósito; (CHEM) sedimento; (of ore, oil) yacimiento // vt (*gen*) depositar; ~ **account** *n* cuenta de ahorros; ~**or** *n* cuentacorrentista *m/f*.

depot ['dɛpəu] *n* (*storehouse*) depósito; (*for vehicles*) parque *m*.

depraved [dɪ'preɪvd] *a* depravado, vicioso; **depravity** [-'prævɪti] *n* depravación *f*, vicio.

depreciate [dɪ'priːʃɪeɪt] *vi* depreciarse, perder valor; **depreciation** [-'eɪʃən] *n* depreciación *f*.

depress [dɪ'prɛs] *vt* deprimir; (*press down*) presionar; ~**ed** *a* deprimido; ~**ing** *a* deprimente; ~**ion** [dɪ'prɛʃən] *n* depresión *f*.

deprivation [dɛprɪ'veɪʃən] *n* privación *f*; (*loss*) pérdida.

deprive [dɪ'praɪv] *vt*: **to** ~ **sb of** privar a alguien de; ~**d** *a* pobre.

depth [dɛpθ] *n* (*gen*) profundidad *f*; (*of room etc*) fondo; **in the** ~**s of** en lo más hondo de.

deputation [dɛpju'teɪʃən] *n* delegación *f*.

deputize ['dɛpjutaɪz] *vi*: **to** ~ **for sb** sustituir por uno.

deputy ['dɛpjuti] *a*: ~ **head** subdirector/a *m/f* // *n* sustituto/a, suplente *m*; (*POL*) diputado; (*agent*) representante *m*.

derail [dɪ'reɪl] *vt*: **to be** ~**ed** descarrilarse; ~**ment** *n* descarrilamiento.

deranged [dɪ'reɪndʒd] *a* (*person*) vuelto loco, trastornado (mentalmente).

derelict ['dɛrɪlɪkt] *a* abandonado.

deride [dɪ'raɪd] *vt* ridiculizar, mofarse de; **derision** [-'rɪʒən] *n* irrisión *f*, mofas *fpl*.

derivative [dɪ'rɪvətɪv] *n* derivado // *a* derivado; (*work*) poco original.

derive [dɪ'raɪv] *vt* derivar // *vi*: **to** ~ **from** derivarse de.

dermatitis [dəːmə'taɪtɪs] *n* dermatitis *f*; **dermatology** [-'tɒlədʒɪ] *n* dermatología.

derogatory [dɪ'rɒgətərɪ] *a* despectivo.

derrick ['dɛrɪk] *n* torre *f* de perforación.

descend [dɪ'sɛnd] *vt*, *vi* descender, bajar; **to** ~ **from** descender de; ~**ant** *n* descendiente *m/f*.

descent [dɪ'sɛnt] *n* descenso; (*GEO*) pendiente *m*, declive *m*; (*origin*) descendencia.

describe [dɪs'kraɪb] *vt* describir; **description** [-'krɪpʃən] *n* descripción *f*; (*sort*) clase *f*, género; **descriptive** [-'krɪptɪv] *a* descriptivo.

desecrate ['dɛsɪkreɪt] *vt* profanar.

desert ['dɛzət] *n* desierto // (*vb*: [dɪ'zəːt]) *vt* abandonar, desamparar // *vi* (*MIL*) desertar; ~**er** *n* desertor *m*; ~**ion** [dɪ'zəːʃən] *n* deserción *f*.

deserve [dɪ'zəːv] *vt* merecer, ser digno de; **deserving** *a* (*person*) digno; (*action, cause*) meritorio.

design [dɪ'zaɪn] *n* (*sketch*) bosquejo; (*layout, shape*) diseño; (*pattern*) dibujo; (*intention*) propósito, intención *f* // *vt* (*gen*) diseñar; (*plan*) proyectar.

designate ['dɛzɪgneɪt] *vt* (*point to*) señalar; (*appoint*) nombrar; (*destine*)

designar // *a* ['dɛzɪgnɪt] designado; **designation** [-'neɪʃən] *n* (*appointment*) nombramiento; (*name*) denominación *f*.

designer [dɪ'zaɪnə*] *n* (*ART*) dibujante *m*; (*TECH*) diseñador *m*; (*fashion* ~) modista *m/f*.

desirable [dɪ'zaɪərəbl] *a* (*proper*) deseable; (*attractive*) atractivo.

desire [dɪ'zaɪə*] *n* deseo // *vt* desear.

desk [dɛsk] *n* (*in office*) escritorio; (*for pupil*) pupitre *m*; (*in hotel, at airport*) recepción *f*.

desolate ['dɛsəlɪt] *a* (*place*) desierto; (*person*) afligido; **desolation** [-'leɪʃən] *n* (*of place*) desolación *f*; (*of person*) aflicción *f*.

despair [dɪs'pɛə*] *n* desesperación *f* // *vi*: **to** ~ **of** desesperarse de.

despatch [dɪs'pætʃ] *n*, *vt* = **dispatch**.

desperate ['dɛspərɪt] *a* desesperado; (*fugitive*) peligroso; ~**ly** *ad* desesperadamente; (*very*) terriblemente, gravemente.

desperation [dɛspə'reɪʃən] *n* desesperación *f*; **in** ~ desesperado.

despicable [dɪs'pɪkəbl] *a* vil, despreciable.

despise [dɪs'paɪz] *vt* despreciar.

despite [dɪs'paɪt] *prep* a pesar de, pese a.

despondent [dɪs'pɒndənt] *a* deprimido, abatido.

dessert [dɪ'zəːt] *n* postre *m*; ~**spoon** *n* cuchara (de postre).

destination [dɛstɪ'neɪʃən] *n* destino.

destiny ['dɛstɪnɪ] *a* destino.

destitute ['dɛstɪtjuːt] *a* desamparado, indigente.

destroy [dɪs'trɔɪ] *vt* (*gen*) destruir; (*finish*) acabar con; ~**er** *n* (*NAUT*) destructor *m*.

destruction [dɪs'trʌkʃən] *n* destrucción *f*; (*fig*) ruina; **destructive** [-tɪv] *a* destructivo, destructor(a).

detach [dɪ'tætʃ] *vt* separar; (*unstick*) despegar; ~**able** *a* separable; (*TECH*) desmontable; ~**ed** *a* (*attitude*) objetivo, imparcial; (*house*) independiente, solo; ~**ment** *n* (*gen*) separación *f*; (*MIL*) destacamento; (*fig*) objetividad *f*, imparcialidad *f*.

detail ['diːteɪl] *n* detalle *m* // *vt* (*gen*) detallar; (*MIL*) destacar; **in** ~ en detalle; ~**ed** *a* detallado.

detain [dɪ'teɪn] *vt* retener; (*in captivity*) detener.

detect [dɪ'tɛkt] *vt* (*gen*) descubrir; (*MED, POLICE*) identificar; (*MIL, RADAR, TECH*) detectar; ~**ion** [dɪ'tɛkʃən] *n* descubrimiento, identificación *f*; ~**ive** *n* detective *m*; ~**ive story** *n* novela policíaca; ~**or** *n* detector *m*.

detente [deɪ'tɑːnt] *n* détente *f*.

detention [dɪ'tɛnʃən] *n* detención *f*, arresto.

deter [dɪ'təː*] *vt* (*discourage*) desalentar; (*dissuade*) disuadir; (*prevent*) impedir.

detergent [dɪ'təːdʒənt] *n* detergente.

deteriorate [dɪ'tɪərɪəreɪt] *vi* deteriorarse; **deterioration** [-'reɪʃən] *n* deterioro.

determination [dɪtəːmɪ'neɪʃən] *n* (*gen*)

determinación f; (*resolve*) resolución f.
determine [dɪ'tɜːmɪn] vt (*gen*)
determinar; (*limits etc*) definir; (*dispute*)
resolver; ~**d** a (*person*) resuelto.
deterrent [dɪ'tɛrənt] n fuerza de
disuasión.
detest [dɪ'tɛst] vt aborrecer; ~**able** a
aborrecible.
detonate ['dɛtəneɪt] vi estallar // vt hacer
detonar; **detonator** n detonador m,
fulminante m.
detour ['diːtuə*] n rodeo.
detract [dɪ'trækt] vt: to ~ **from** quitar
mérito a, desvirtuar.
detriment ['dɛtrɪmənt] n: to the ~ **of** en
perjuicio de; ~**al** [dɛtrɪ'mɛntl] a
perjudicial (*to* a).
devaluation [diːvæljuˈeɪʃən] n devaluación
f; **devalue** [-'væljuː] vt devaluar.
devastate ['dɛvəsteɪt] vt devastar; **he was**
~**d by** the news las noticias le dejaron
desolado; **devastating** a devastador(a);
(*fig*) arrollador(a).
develop [dɪ'vɛləp] vt (*gen*) desarrollar;
(*PHOT*) revelar; (*disease*) coger; (*engine*
trouble) empezar a tener // vi
desarrollarse; (*advance*) progresar;
(*appear*) aparecer; ~**ing country** país m
en desarrollo; ~**ment** n desarrollo;
(*advance*) progreso; (*of affair, case*)
desenvolvimiento; (*of land*) urbanización f.
deviate ['diːvɪeɪt] vi desviarse; **deviation**
[-'eɪʃən] n desviación f.
device [dɪ'vaɪs] n (*scheme*) estratagema f,
recurso; (*apparatus*) aparato, mecanismo.
devil ['dɛvl] n diablo, demonio; ~**ish** a
diabólico.
devious ['diːvɪəs] a intricado, enrevesado;
(*person*) taimado.
devise [dɪ'vaɪz] vt idear, inventar.
devoid [dɪ'vɔɪd] a: ~ **of** desprovisto de.
devote [dɪ'vəʊt] vt: to ~ **sth to** dedicar
algo a; ~**d** a (*loyal*) leal, fiel; **the book is**
~**d to politics** el libro trata de la
política; **devotee** [dɛvəʊ'tiː] n devoto/a.
devotion [dɪ'vəʊʃən] n dedicación f; (*REL*)
devoción f.
devour [dɪ'vaʊə*] vt devorar.
devout [dɪ'vaʊt] a devoto.
dew [djuː] n rocío.
dexterity [dɛks'tɛrɪtɪ] n destreza.
diabetes [daɪə'biːtiːz] n diabetes f;
diabetic [-'bɛtɪk] a, n diabético/a.
diagnose [daɪəg'nəʊz] vt diagnosticar;
diagnosis [-'nəʊsɪs], pl -**ses** [-'nəʊsiːz] n
diagnóstico.
diagonal [daɪ'ægənl] a diagonal // n
diagonal f.
diagram ['daɪəgræm] n diagrama m,
esquema m.
dial ['daɪəl] n esfera, cuadrante m // vt
(*number*) marcar; ~**ling tone** n tono de
marcar.
dialect ['daɪəlɛkt] n dialecto.
dialogue ['daɪələg] n diálogo.
diameter [daɪ'æmɪtə*] n diámetro.

diamond ['daɪəmənd] n diamante m; ~**s**
npl (*CARDS*) oros mpl.
diaper ['daɪəpə*] n (*US*) pañal m.
diaphragm ['daɪəfræm] n diafragma m.
diarrhoea, diarrhea (*US*) [daɪə'riːə] n
diarrea.
diary ['daɪərɪ] n (*daily account*) diario;
(*book*) agenda m.
dice [daɪs] n, pl inv dados mpl // vt (*CULIN*)
cortar en cuadritos.
dictate [dɪk'teɪt] vt dictar; ~**s** ['dɪkteɪts]
npl dictados mpl; **dictation** [-'teɪʃən] n
dictado.
dictator [dɪk'teɪtə*] n dictador m; ~**ship**
n dictadura.
diction ['dɪkʃən] n dicción f.
dictionary ['dɪkʃənrɪ] n diccionario.
did [dɪd] pt of **do**.
die [daɪ] vi morir; to ~ **away** vi (*sound,*
light) extinguirse lentamente; to ~ **down**
vi (*gen*) apagarse; (*wind*) amainar; to ~
out vi desaparecer, extinguirse.
diesel ['diːzəl]: ~ **engine** n motor m
Diesel; ~ **(oil)** n gas-oil m.
diet ['daɪət] n dieta (*restricted food*)
régimen m // vi (*also:* be on a ~) estar a
dieta, hacer régimen.
differ ['dɪfə*] vi (*be different*) ser distinto
de, diferenciarse de; (*disagree*) discrepar;
~**ence** n diferencia; (*quarrel*)
desacuerdo; ~**ent** a diferente, distinto;
~**entiate** ['rɛnʃɪeɪt] vt distinguir // vi
diferenciarse; to ~**entiate between**
distinguir entre; ~**ently** ad de otro modo,
en forma distinta.
difficult ['dɪfɪkəlt] a difícil; ~**y** n
dificultad f.
diffidence ['dɪfɪdəns] n timidez f;
diffident [-ənt] a tímido.
diffuse [dɪ'fjuːs] a difuso // vt [dɪ'fjuːz]
difundir.
dig [dɪg], pt, pp **dug** vt (*hole*) cavar;
(*garden*) cultivar; (*coal*) extraer; (*nails etc*)
hincar // n (*prod*) empujón m;
(*archaeological*) excavación f; (*remark*)
indirecta; to ~ **in** vi atrincherarse; to ~
into vt (*savings*) consumir; to ~ **out** vt
(*hole*) excavar; (*fig*) sacar; to ~ **up** vt
desenterrar; (*plant*) desarraigar.
digest [daɪ'dʒɛst] vt (*food*) digerir; (*facts*)
asimilar // n ['daɪdʒɛst] resumen m;
~**ion** [dɪ'dʒɛstʃən] n digestión f.
digital ['dɪdʒɪtəl] a digital.
dignified ['dɪgnɪfaɪd] a grave, solemne;
(*action*) decoroso.
dignity ['dɪgnɪtɪ] n dignidad f.
digress [daɪ'grɛs] vi: to ~ **from**
apartarse de; ~**ion** [daɪ'grɛʃən] n
digresión f.
digs [dɪgz] npl (*Brit: col*) pensión f,
alojamiento.
dilapidated [dɪ'læpɪdeɪtɪd] a
desmoronado, ruinoso.
dilate [daɪ'leɪt] vt dilatar // vi dilatarse.
dilemma [daɪ'lɛmə] n dilema m.
diligent ['dɪlɪdʒənt] a diligente.
dilute [daɪ'luːt] vt diluir // a diluido.

dim [dɪm] a (*light*) débil; (*sight*) turbio; (*outline*) indistinto; (*stupid*) lerdo; (*room*) oscuro // vt (*light*) bajar; (AUT) poner a media luz.

dime [daɪm] n (US) *moneda de diez centavos.*

dimension [dɪ'menʃən] n dimensión f.

diminish [dɪ'mɪnɪʃ] vi disminuirse.

diminutive [dɪ'mɪnjutɪv] a diminuto // n (LING) diminutivo.

dimly ['dɪmlɪ] ad débilmente; (*not clearly*) indistintamente.

dimple ['dɪmpl] n hoyuelo.

din [dɪn] n estruendo, estrépito.

dine [daɪn] vi cenar; **diner** n (*person*) comensal m/f; (RAIL) = **dining car.**

dinghy ['dɪŋgɪ] n bote m; **rubber ~** lancha (neumática).

dingy ['dɪndʒɪ] a (*room*) sombrío; (*dirty*) sucio; (*dull*) deslucido.

dining ['daɪnɪŋ] **~ car** n coche-comedor m; **~ room** n comedor m.

dinner ['dɪnə*] n (*evening meal*) cena; (*lunch*) comida; (*public*) cena, banquete m; **~ jacket** n smoking m; **~ party** n cena; **~ time** n hora de cenar o comer.

diocese ['daɪəsɪs] n diócesis f.

dip [dɪp] n (*slope*) pendiente m; (*in sea*) baño // vt (*in water*) mojar; (*ladle etc*) meter; (AUT: *lights*) poner a media luz // vi inclinarse hacia abajo.

diphtheria [dɪf'θɪərɪə] n difteria.

diploma [dɪ'pləumə] n diploma m.

diplomacy [dɪ'pləuməsɪ] n diplomacia.

diplomat ['dɪpləmæt] n diplomático.

diplomatic [dɪplə'mætɪk] a diplomático.

dipstick ['dɪpstɪk] n (AUT) varilla graduada, indicador m de nivel (del aceite).

dire [daɪə*] a calamitoso.

direct [daɪ'rekt] a (*gen*) directo // vt dirigir; **can you ~ me to...?** ¿puede indicarme dónde está...?

direction [dɪ'rekʃən] n dirección f; **~s** npl (*advice*) órdenes fpl, instrucciones fpl; **~s for use** n modo de empleo.

directly [dɪ'rektlɪ] ad (*in straight line*) directamente; (*at once*) en seguida.

director [dɪ'rektə*] n director m; **managing ~** director gerente.

directory [dɪ'rektərɪ] n (TEL) guía (telefónica).

dirt [dɜːt] n suciedad f; **~-cheap** a tirado, muy barato; **~y** a sucio; (*joke*) verde // vt ensuciar; (*stain*) manchar; **~y trick** n juego sucio.

disability [dɪsə'bɪlɪtɪ] n incapacidad f; **disabled** [dɪs'eɪbld] a disminuido, minusválido.

disadvantage [dɪsəd'vɑːntɪdʒ] n desventaja, inconveniente m.

disagree [dɪsə'griː] vi (*differ*) discrepar; (*be against, think otherwise*): **to ~ (with)** no estar de acuerdo (con); **~able** a desagradable; **~ment** n (*gen*) desacuerdo; (*quarrel*) riña.

disallow ['dɪsə'lau] vt (*goal*) anular.

disappear [dɪsə'pɪə*] vi desaparecer; **~ance** n desaparición f.

disappoint [dɪsə'pɔɪnt] vt decepcionar; (*hopes*) defraudar; **~ing** a decepcionante; **~ment** n decepción f.

disapproval [dɪsə'pruːvəl] n desaprobación f.

disapprove [dɪsə'pruːv] vi: **to ~ of** desaprobar.

disarm [dɪs'ɑːm] vt desarmar; **~ament** n desarme m; **~ing** a encantador(a).

disaster [dɪ'zɑːstə*] n desastre m; **disastrous** a desastroso.

disband [dɪs'bænd] vt disolver // vi desbandarse.

disbelief [dɪsbə'liːf] n incredulidad f.

disc [dɪsk] n disco.

discard [dɪs'kɑːd] vt (*old things*) tirar; (*fig*) descartar.

discern [dɪ'sɜːn] vt percibir, discernir; **~ing** a perspicaz.

discharge [dɪs'tʃɑːdʒ] vt (*duties*) cumplir, desempeñar; (*ship etc*) descargar; (*patient*) dar de alta; (*employee*) despedir; (*soldier*) licenciar; (*defendant*) poner en libertad // n ['dɪstʃɑːdʒ] (ELEC) descarga; (*dismissal*) despedida; (*of duty*) desempeño; (*of debt*) pago, descargo.

disciple [dɪ'saɪpl] n discípulo.

discipline ['dɪsɪplɪn] n disciplina // vt disciplinar.

disclaim [dɪs'kleɪm] vt negar.

disclose [dɪs'kləuz] vt revelar; **disclosure** [-'kləuʒə*] n revelación f.

disco ['dɪskəu] n abbr of **discothèque.**

discoloured [dɪs'kʌləd] a descolorado.

discomfort [dɪs'kʌmfət] n incomodidad f; (*unease*) inquietud f; (*physical*) malestar m.

disconcert [dɪskən'sɜːt] vt desconcertar.

disconnect [dɪskə'nekt] vt (*gen*) separar; (ELEC *etc*) desconectar.

discontent [dɪskən'tent] n descontento; **~ed** a descontento.

discontinue [dɪskən'tɪnjuː] vt interrumpir; (*payments*) suspender.

discord ['dɪskɔːd] n discordia; (MUS) disonancia; **~ant** [dɪs'kɔːdənt] a disonante.

discothèque ['dɪskəutek] n discoteca.

discount ['dɪskaunt] n descuento // vt [dɪs-'kaunt] descontar.

discourage [dɪs'kʌrɪdʒ] vt desalentar; (*oppose*) oponerse a; **discouraging** a desalentador(a).

discourteous [dɪs'kɜːtɪəs] a descortés.

discover [dɪs'kʌvə*] vt descubrir; **~y** n descubrimiento.

discredit [dɪs'kredɪt] vt desacreditar.

discreet [dɪ'skriːt] a (*tactful*) discreto; (*careful*) circunspecto, prudente; **~ly** ad discretamente.

discrepancy [dɪ'skrepənsɪ] n (*difference*) diferencia; (*disagreement*) discrepancia.

discretion [dɪ'skreʃən] n (*tact*) discreción f; (*care*) prudencia, circunspección f.

discriminate [dɪ'skrɪmɪneɪt] vi: to ~ between distinguir entre; to ~ against discriminar contra; **discriminating** a perspicaz; **discrimination** [-'neɪʃən] n (discernment) perspicacia; (bias) discriminación f.

discuss [dɪ'skʌs] vt (gen) discutir; (a theme) tratar; ~**ion** [dɪ'skʌʃən] n discusión f.

disdain [dɪs'deɪn] n desdén m // vt desdeñar.

disease [dɪ'ziːz] n enfermedad f.

disembark [dɪsɪm'bɑːk] vt, vi desembarcar.

disengage [dɪsɪn'geɪdʒ] vt soltar; (clutch) desembragar.

disentangle [dɪsɪn'tæŋgl] vt desenredar.

disfigure [dɪs'fɪgə*] vt desfigurar.

disgrace [dɪs'greɪs] n ignominia; (downfall) caída; (shame) vergüenza, escándalo // vt deshonrar; ~**ful** a vergonzoso; (behaviour) escandaloso.

disgruntled [dɪs'grʌntld] a disgustado, malhumorado.

disguise [dɪs'gaɪz] n disfraz m // vt disfrazar; **in** ~ disfrazado.

disgust [dɪs'gʌst] n repugnancia // vt repugnar, dar asco a; ~**ing** a repugnante, asqueroso.

dish [dɪʃ] n (gen) plato; to do or wash the ~**es** fregar los platos; to ~ up vt servir; to ~ out vt repartir; ~**cloth** n paño de cocina, bayeta.

dishearten [dɪs'hɑːtn] vt desalentar.

dishevelled [dɪ'ʃevəld] a despeinado, desmelenado.

dishonest [dɪs'ɔnɪst] a (person) poco honrado, tramposo; (means) fraudulento; ~**y** n falta de honradez.

dishonour [dɪs'ɔnə*] n deshonra; ~**able** a deshonroso.

dishwasher ['dɪʃwɔʃə*] n lavaplatos m inv; (person) friegaplatos m/f inv.

disillusion [dɪsɪ'luːʒən] vt desilusionar.

disinfect [dɪsɪn'fekt] vt desinfectar; ~**ant** n desinfectante m.

disintegrate [dɪs'ɪntɪgreɪt] vi disgregarse, desintegrarse.

disinterested [dɪs'ɪntrəstɪd] a desinteresado.

disjointed [dɪs'dʒɔɪntɪd] a inconexo.

disk [dɪsk] n = **disc.**

dislike [dɪs'laɪk] n antipatía, aversión f // vt tener antipatía a.

dislocate ['dɪsləkeɪt] vt dislocar.

dislodge [dɪs'lɔdʒ] vt sacar; (enemy) desalojar.

disloyal [dɪs'lɔɪəl] a desleal.

dismal ['dɪzml] a (dark) sombrío; (depressing) triste; (depressed) abatido; (very bad) fatal.

dismantle [dɪs'mæntl] vt desmontar, desarmar.

dismay [dɪs'meɪ] n consternación f // vt consternar.

dismiss [dɪs'mɪs] vt (worker) despedir;

(official) destituir; (idea, LAW) rechazar; (possibility) descartar // vi (MIL) romper filas; ~**al** n despedida; destitución f.

dismount [dɪs'maunt] vi apearse.

disobedience [dɪsə'biːdɪəns] n desobediencia; **disobedient** [-ənt] a desobediente.

disobey [dɪsə'beɪ] vt desobedecer.

disorder [dɪs'ɔːdə*] n desorden m; (rioting) disturbio; (MED) trastorno; (disease) enfermedad f; ~**ly** a (untidy) desordenado; (meeting) alborotado; (conduct) escandaloso.

disorganized [dɪs'ɔːgənaɪzd] a desorganizado.

disorientated [dɪs'ɔːrɪənteɪtəd] a desorientado.

disown [dɪs'əun] vt desconocer.

disparaging [dɪs'pærɪdʒɪŋ] a despreciativo.

disparity [dɪs'pærɪtɪ] n disparidad f.

dispatch [dɪs'pætʃ] vt enviar; (kill) despachar // n (sending) envío; (speed) prontitud f; (PRESS) informe m; (MIL) parte m.

dispel [dɪs'pel] vt disipar, dispersar.

dispensary [dɪs'pensərɪ] n dispensario, farmacia.

dispense [dɪs'pens] vt dispensar, repartir; to ~ with fus prescindir de; **dispenser** n (container) distribuidor m automático; **dispensing chemist** n farmacéutico.

dispersal [dɪs'pəːsl] n dispersión f; **disperse** [-'pəːs] vt dispersar // vi dispersarse.

displace [dɪs'pleɪs] vt (shift) sacar de su sitio; ~**d person** n (POL) desplazado/a; ~**ment** n cambio de sitio.

display [dɪs'pleɪ] n (exhibition) exposición f; (MIL) alarde m; (of feeling) manifestación f; (pej) aparato, pompa // vt exponer; manifestar; (ostentatiously) lucir.

displease [dɪs'pliːz] vt (offend) ofender; (annoy) enojar, enfadar; (be unpleasant to) desagradar; ~**d with** disgustado con; **displeasure** [-'pleʒə*] n disgusto.

disposable [dɪs'pəuzəbl] a para (usar y) tirar.

disposal [dɪs'pəuzl] n (sale) venta; (of house) traspaso; (arrangement) colocación f; (of rubbish) destrucción f; **at one's** ~ a disposición de uno

dispose [dɪs'pəuz] vt: to ~ of (time, money) disponer de; (unwanted goods) deshacerse de; (throw away) tirar; ~**d a**: ~**d to do** dispuesto a hacer; **disposition** [-'zɪʃən] n disposición f.

disproportionate [dɪsprə'pɔːʃənət] a desproporcionado.

disprove [dɪs'pruːv] vt refutar.

dispute [dɪs'pjuːt] n disputa; (verbal) discusión f; (also: industrial ~) conflicto (laboral) // vt (argue) disputar; (question) cuestionar.

disqualification [dɪskwɔlɪfɪ'keɪʃən] n

inhabilitación f; (SPORT, from driving) descalificación f.

disqualify [dɪs'kwɒlɪfaɪ] _t (SPORT) descalificar; **to ~ sb for sth/from doing sth** inhabilitar a alguien para algo/hacer algo.

disregard [dɪsrɪ'gɑːd] vt desatender; (ignore) no hacer caso de.

disrepair [dɪsrɪ'pɛə*] n: **to fall into ~** desmoronarse.

disreputable [dɪs'rɛpjutəbl] a (person) de mala fama; (behaviour) vergonzoso.

disrespectful [dɪsrɪ'spɛktful] a irrespetuoso.

disrupt [dɪs'rʌpt] vt (plans) desbaratar; (conversation) interrumpir; **~ion** [-'rʌpʃən] n trastorno; desbaratamiento; interrupción f.

dissatisfaction [dɪssætɪs'fækʃən] n disgusto, descontento; **dissatisfied** [-'sætɪsfaɪd] a insatisfecho.

dissect [dɪ'sɛkt] vt disecar.

dissent [dɪ'sɛnt] n disensión f.

disservice [dɪs'səːvɪs] n: **to do sb a ~** perjudicar a alguien.

dissident ['dɪsɪdnt] a, n disidente m/f.

dissipate ['dɪsɪpeɪt] vt disipar; (waste) desperdiciar.

dissociate [dɪ'səufɪeɪt] vt disociar.

dissolute ['dɪsəluːt] a disoluto.

dissolve [dɪ'zɒlv] vt disolver // vi disolverse.

dissuade [dɪ'sweɪd] vt: **to ~ sb (from)** disuadir a alguien (de).

distance ['dɪstns] n distancia; **in the ~** a lo lejos.

distant ['dɪstnt] a lejano; (manner) reservado, frío.

distaste [dɪs'teɪst] n repugnancia; **~ful** a repugnante, desagradable.

distil [dɪs'tɪl] vt destilar; **~lery** a destilería.

distinct [dɪs'tɪŋkt] a (different) distinto (clear) claro; (unmistakeable) inequívoco; **as ~ from** a diferencia de; **~ion** [dɪs-'tɪŋkʃən] n distinción f; (in exam) sobresaliente m; **~ive** a distintivo; **~ly** ad claramente.

distinguish [dɪs'tɪŋgwɪʃ] vt distinguir; **~ed** a (eminent) distinguido; **~ing** a (feature) distintivo.

distort [dɪs'tɔːt] vt torcer, retorcer; **~ion** [dɪs'tɔːʃən] n deformación f; (of sound) distorsión f.

distract [dɪs'trækt] vt distraer; (attention) apartar; (bewilder) aturdir; **~ed** a distraído; **~ion** [dɪs'trækʃən] n distracción f; (confusion) aturdimiento; (amusement) diversión f.

distraught [dɪs'trɔːt] a turbado, enloquecido.

distress [dɪs'trɛs] n (anguish) angustia; (misfortune) desgracia; (want) miseria; (pain) dolor m; (danger) peligro // vt (cause anguish) apenar, afligir; (pain) doler; **~ing** a doloroso; **~ signal** n señal f de socorro.

distribute [dɪs'trɪbjuːt] vt (gen) distribuir; (share out) repartir; **distribution** [-'bjuːʃən] a distribución f; **distributor** n (AUT) distribuidor m; (COMM) distribuidora.

district ['dɪstrɪkt] n (of country) zona, región f; (of town) barrio; (ADMIN) distrito; **~ attorney** n (US) fiscal m/f; **~ nurse** n (Brit) enfermera que asiste a domicilio.

distrust [dɪs'trʌst] n desconfianza // vt desconfiar de.

disturb [dɪs'təːb] vt (gen) perturbar; (bother) molestar; (interrupt) interrumpir; (upset) trastornar; (disorganize) desordenar; **~ance** n (gen) perturbación f; (political etc) disturbio; (violence) alboroto; (of mind) trastorno; **~ing** a inquietante, perturbador(a).

disuse [dɪs'juːs] n: **to fall into ~** caer en desuso.

disused [dɪs'juːzd] a abandonado.

ditch [dɪtʃ] a zanja; (irrigation ~) acequia // vt (col) deshacerse de.

dither ['dɪðə*] vi vacilar.

ditto ['dɪtəu] ad idem, lo mismo.

divan [dɪ'væn] n diván m.

dive [daɪv] n (from board) salto; (underwater) buceo; (of submarine) sumersión f (AVIAT) picada // vi saltar; bucear; sumergirse; picar; **diver** n (SPORT) saltador/a m/f; (underwater) buzo.

diverge [daɪ'vəːdʒ] vi divergir.

diverse [daɪ'vəːs] a diversos(as), varios(as).

diversify [daɪ'vəːsɪfaɪ] vt diversificar.

diversion [daɪ'vəːʃən] n (AUT) desviación f; (distraction, MIL) diversión f.

diversity [daɪ'vəːsɪtɪ] n diversidad f.

divert [daɪ'vəːt] vt (turn aside) desviar; (amuse) divertir.

divest [daɪ'vɛst] vt: **to ~ sb of sth** despojar a alguien de algo.

divide [dɪ'vaɪd] vt dividir; (separate) separar // vi dividirse; (road) bifurcarse.

dividend ['dɪvɪdɛnd] a dividendo; (fig) beneficio.

divine [dɪ'vaɪn] a divino.

diving ['daɪvɪŋ] n (SPORT) salto; (underwater) buceo; **~ board** n trampolín m; **~ suit** a escafandra.

divinity [dɪ'vɪnɪtɪ] n divinidad f, (SCOL) teología.

division [dɪ'vɪʒən] a división f; (sharing out) repartimiento; (disagreement) discordia; (POL) votación f.

divorce [dɪ'vɔːs] n divorcio // vt divorciarse de; **~d** a divorciado; **divorcee** [-'siː] n divorciado/a.

divulge [daɪ'vʌldʒ] vt divulgar, revelar.

D.I.Y. a, n abbr of **do-it-yourself.**

dizziness ['dɪzɪnɪs] n vértigo.

dizzy ['dɪzɪ] a (person) mareado; (height) vertiginoso; **to feel ~** marearse, estar mareado.

DJ n abbr of **disc jockey.**

do [duː] pt **did**, pp **done** vt, vi (gen) hacer; (speed) ir a; (THEATRE) representar // n (*col*) fiesta; **he didn't laugh** no se rió; **she swims better than I ~** nada mejor que yo; **he laughed, didn't he?** se rió ¿no?; **that will ~!** ¡basta!; **to make ~ with** contentarse con; **~ you agree?** ¿está Usted de acuerdo?; **to ~ one's hair** (*comb*) peinarse; (*style*) arreglarse el pelo; **will it ~?** ¿sirve?, ¿conviene?; **to ~ well** prosperar, tener éxito; **to ~ without sth** prescindir de algo; **to ~ away with** *vt fus* (*kill*) exterminar; (*suppress*) suprimir; **to ~ up** *vt* (*laces*) liar, atar; (*room*) renovar.

docile ['dəʊsaɪl] *a* dócil.

dock [dɔk] *n* (*NAUT*) muelle *m*; (*LAW*) banquillo (de los acusados); **~s** *npl* muelles *mpl*, puerto // *vi* (*arrive*) llegar; (*enter ~*) atracar el muelle; (*pay etc*) rebajar; **~er** *n* trabajador *m* portuario, estibador *m*; **~yard** *n* astillero.

doctor ['dɔktə*] *n* médico; (*Ph.D. etc*) doctor/a *m/f* // *vt* (*fig*) arreglar, falsificar; (*drink etc*) adulterar.

doctrine ['dɔktrɪn] *n* doctrina.

document ['dɔkjumənt] *n* documento; **~ary** [-'mɛntərɪ] *a* documental // *n* documental *m*; **~ation** [-'teɪʃən] *n* documentación *f*.

dodge [dɔdʒ] *n* (*of body*) regate *m*; (*fig*) truco // *vt* (*gen*) evadir; (*blow*) esquivar.

dodgems ['dɔdʒəmz] *npl* coches *mpl* de choque.

dog [dɔg] *n* perro // *vt* seguir los pasos de; **~ biscuits** *npl* galletas *fpl* de perro; **~ collar** *n* collar *m* de perro; (*fig*) cuello de cura.

dogged ['dɔgɪd] *a* tenaz, obstinado.

dogma ['dɔgmə] *n* dogma *m*; **~tic** [-'mætɪk] *a* dogmático.

doings ['duːɪŋz] *npl* (*events*) sucesos *mpl*; (*acts*) hechos *mpl*.

do-it-yourself [duːɪtjɔː'sɛlf] *n* bricolaje *m*.

doldrums ['dɔldrəmz] *npl*: **to be in the ~** (*person*) estar abatido; (*business*) estar encalmado.

dole [dəʊl] *n* (*Brit*) (*payment*) subsidio de paro; **on the ~** parado; **to ~ out** *vt* repartir.

doleful ['dəʊlful] *a* triste, lúgubre.

doll [dɔl] *n* muñeca; **to ~ o.s. up** ataviarse.

dollar ['dɔlə*] *n* dólar *m*.

dolphin ['dɔlfɪn] *n* delfín *m*.

domain [də'meɪn] *n* campo, competencia; (*empire*) dominio.

dome [dəʊm] *n* (*ARCH*) cúpula; (*shape*) bóveda.

domestic [də'mɛstɪk] *a* (*gen*) doméstico; (*national*) nacional; (*home-loving*) hogareño; (*internal*: *trade*) interior; (: *strife*) interno; **~ated** *a* domesticado; (*home-loving*) casero, hogareño.

dominant ['dɔmɪnənt] *a* dominante.

dominate ['dɔmɪneɪt] *vt* dominar; **domination** [-'neɪʃən] *n* dominación *f*.

domineering [dɔmɪ'nɪərɪŋ] *a* dominante.

dominion [də'mɪnɪən] *n* dominio.

domino ['dɔmɪnəʊ], *pl* **~es** *n* ficha de dominó; **~es** *n* (*game*) dominó.

donate [də'neɪt] *vt* donar; **donation** [də'neɪʃən] *n* donativo.

done [dʌn] *pp of* **do**.

donkey ['dɔŋkɪ] *n* burro.

donor ['dəʊnə*] *n* donante *m/f*.

don't [dəʊnt] = **do not**.

doom [duːm] *n* (*fate*) suerte *f*; (*death*) muerte *f* // *vt*: **to be ~ed to failure** ser condenado al fracaso.

door [dɔː*] *n* puerta; (*entry*) entrada; **next ~** en la casa de al lado; **~bell** *n* timbre *m*; **~ handle** *n* tirador *m*; (*of car*) manija; **~ knocker** *n* aldaba; **~man** *n* (*in hotel*) portero; **~mat** *n* felpudo, estera; **~step** *n* peldaño.

dope [dəʊp] *n* (*col*: *person*) imbécil *m/f* // *vt* (*horse etc*) drogar.

dopey ['dəʊpɪ] *a* (*dizzy*) mareado.

dormant ['dɔːmənt] *a* inactivo; (*latent*) latente.

dormitory ['dɔːmɪtrɪ] *n* dormitorio.

dormouse ['dɔːmaʊs], *pl* **-mice** [-maɪs] *n* lirón *m*.

dosage ['dəʊsɪdʒ] *n* dósis *f inv*.

dose [dəʊs] *n* dósis *f inv* // *vt*: **to ~ o.s.** medicinarse.

doss house ['dɔs-] *n* pensión *f* de mala muerte.

dot [dɔt] *n* punto; **~ted with** salpicado de; **on the ~** en punto.

dote [dəʊt]: **to ~ on** *vt fus* adorar, idolatrar.

double ['dʌbl] *a* doble // *ad* (*twice*): **to cost ~** costar el doble // *n* (*gen*) doble *m* // *vt* doblar; (*efforts*) redoblar // *vi* doblarse; **at the ~** corriendo; **~s** *n* (*TENNIS*) juego de dobles; **~ bass** *n* contrabajo; **~ bed** *n* cama matrimonial; **~ bend** *n* doble curva; **~-breasted** *a* cruzado; **~-cross** *vt* (*trick*) engañar; (*betray*) traicionar; **~-decker** *n* autobús *m* de dos pisos; **~ room** *n* cuarto para dos; **doubly** *ad* doblemente.

doubt [daʊt] *n* duda // *vt* dudar; (*suspect*) dudar de; **to ~ that** dudar que; **there is no ~ that** no cabe duda de que; **~ful** *a* dudoso; (*person*) sospechoso; **~less** *ad* sin duda.

dough [dəʊ] *n* masa, pasta; **~nut** *n* buñuelo.

dove [dʌv] *n* paloma; **~tail** *vi* (*fig*) encajar.

dowdy ['daʊdɪ] *a* desaliñado; (*inelegant*) poco elegante.

down [daʊn] *n* (*fluff*) pelusa; (*feathers*) plumón *m*, flojel *m* // *ad* (~ *wards*) abajo, hacia abajo; (*on the ground*) por/en tierra // *prep* abajo // *vt* (*col*: *drink*) beberse; (: *food*) devorar; **the D~s** zona de colinas del sur de Inglaterra; **~ with X!** ¡abajo X!; **~-at-heel** *a* desaliñado; **~cast** *a* abatido; **~fall** *n* caída, ruina; **~hearted** *a* desanimado; **~hill** *ad*: **to go ~hill** ir cuesta abajo; **~ payment** *n* enganche *m*, pago al contado; ~**pour** n aguacero; ~**right** a (clear) manifiesto; (out-and-out) terminante, definitivo; ~**stairs** ad (below) (en la casa) de abajo; (~wards) escaleras abajo; ~**stream** ad aguas o río abajo; ~**-to-earth** a práctico; ~**town** ad en el centro de la ciudad; ~**ward** a, ad, ~**wards** ad hacia abajo.

dowry ['dauri] n dote f.

doz. abbr of **dozen.**

doze [dəuz] vi dormitar; **to** ~ **off** vi quedarse medio dormido.

dozen ['dʌzn] n docena.

Dr. abbr of **doctor; drive.**

drab [dræb] a gris, monótono.

draft [drɑːft] n (first copy) borrador m; (COMM) giro; (US: call-up) quinta f; vt (plan) redactar; (send) mandar; (conscript) quintar; (write roughly) hacer un borrador de; see also **draught.**

drag [dræg] vt arrastrar; (river) dragar // vi arrastrarse por el suelo // n (col) lata; **to** ~ **on** vi ser interminable.

dragonfly ['drægənflai] n libélula.

drain [drein] n desaguadero; (in street) sumidero; (source of loss) desagüe m; (loss) pérdida; (on resources) sumidero // vt (land, marshes) desaguar; (MED) drenar; (reservoir) desecar; (fig) agotar // vi escurrirse; ~**age** n (act) desagüe m; (MED, AGR) drenaje m; (sewage) alcantarillado; ~**ing board**, ~**board** (US) n escurridera, escurridor m; ~**pipe** n tubo de desagüe.

dram [dræm] n (drink) trago.

drama ['drɑːmə] n (art) teatro; (play) drama m; ~**tic** [drə'mætik] a dramático; ~**tist** ['dræmətist] n dramaturgo.

drank [dræŋk] pt of **drink.**

drape [dreip] vt cubrir; ~**s** npl (US) cortinas fpl; **draper** n pañero.

drastic ['dræstik] a (measure) severo; (change) radical; (forceful) enérgico.

draught [drɑːft] n (of air) corriente f; (drink) trago; (NAUT) calado; ~**s** n juego de damas; **on** ~ (beer) de barril; ~**board** n tablero de damas.

draughtsman ['drɑːftsmən] n proyectista m, delineante m.

draw [drɔː] pt **drew**, pp **drawn** vt (pull) tirar; (take out) sacar; (attract) atraer; (picture) dibujar; (money) retirar // vi (SPORT) empatar // n (SPORT) empate m; (lottery) sorteo; (attraction) atracción f; **to** ~ **near** vi acercarse; **to** ~ **out** vi (lengthen) alargar; **to** ~ **up** vi (stop) pararse // vt (document) redactar; ~**back** n inconveniente m, desventaja; ~**bridge** n puente m levadizo.

drawer [drɔː] n cajón m.

drawing ['drɔːiŋ] n dibujo; ~ **board** n tablero de (dibujante); ~ **pin** n chinche m; ~ **room** n salón m.

drawl [drɔːl] n habla lenta y cansina.

drawn [drɔːn] pp of **draw.**

dread [dred] n pavor m, terror m // vt

temer, tener miedo o pavor a; ~**ful** a espantoso.

dream [driːm] n sueño // vt, vi, pt, pp **dreamed** or **dreamt** [dremt] soñar; ~**er** n soñador/a m/f; ~**y** a (distracted) soñador(a), distraído; (music) de sueño.

dreary ['driəri] a monótono, aburrido.

dredge [dredʒ] vt dragar; **dredger** n (ship) draga; (also: **sugar dredger**) espolvoreador m.

dregs [dregz] npl heces fpl.

drench [drentʃ] vt empapar; **to get** ~**ed** mojarse hasta los huesos.

dress [dres] n vestido; (clothing) ropa // vt vestir; (wound) vendar; (CULIN) aliñar // vi vestirse; **to** ~ **up** vi vestirse de etiqueta; (in fancy dress) disfrazarse; ~ **circle** n principal m; ~**er** a (furniture) aparador m; (: US) cómoda con espejo; ~**ing** n (MED) vendaje m; (CULIN) aliño; ~**ing gown** n bata; ~**ing room** n (THEATRE) camarín m; (SPORT) vestidor m; ~**ing table** n tocador m; ~**maker** n modista, costurera; ~**making** n costura; ~ **rehearsal** n ensayo general; ~ **shirt** n camisa de frac.

drew [druː] pt of **draw.**

dribble ['dribl] vi gotear, caer gota a gota; (baby) babear // vt (ball) regatear.

dried [draid] a (gea) seco; (fruit) paso; (milk) en polvo.

drift [drift] n (of current etc) velocidad f; (of sand etc) montón m; (distance off course) deriva; (meaning) significado // vi (boat) ir a la deriva; (sand, snow) amontonarse; ~**wood** n madera de deriva.

drill [dril] n taladro; (bit) broca; (of dentist) fresa; (for mining etc) perforadora, barrena; (MIL) instrucción f // vt perforar, taladrar // vi (for oil) perforar.

drink [driŋk] n bebida // vt, vi, pt **drank**, pp **drunk** beber, tomar; ~**er** n bebedor/a m/f; ~**ing water** n agua potable.

drip [drip] n (act) goteo; (one ~) gota; (MED) gota a gota m // vi gotear, caer gota a gota; ~**-dry** a (shirt) de lava y pon; ~**ping** n pringue m; ~**ping wet** a calado.

drive [draiv] n paseo (en coche); (journey) viaje m; (also: ~**way**) entrada; (energy) energía, vigor m, (PSYCH) impulso; (SPORT) ataque m // vt, pt **drove**, pp **driven** ['drivn] vt (car) conducir; (urge) hacer trabajar; (by power) mover; (nail) clavar; (push) empujar; (TECH, motor) impulsar // vi (AUT: al controls) conducir; (: travel) pasearse en coche; **left-/right-hand** ~ conducción f a la izquierda/derecha.

driver ['draivə*] n conductor m; (of taxi, bus) chofer m; ~**'s license** n (US) permiso de conducir.

driving ['draiviŋ] n el conducir, automovilismo; ~ **instructor** n instructor m de conducción; ~ **lesson** n clase f de conducción; ~ **licence** n (Brit) permiso

drizzle ['drɪzl] *n* llovizna // *vi* lloviznar.

drone [drəun] *n* zumbido; (*male bee*) zángano.

drool [dru:l] *vi* babear; **to ~ over sth** extasiarse ante algo.

droop [dru:p] *vi* colgar; (*fig*) decaer, desanimarse.

drop [drɔp] *n* (*of water*) gota; (*lessening*) baja; (*fall*) caída; (*of cliff*) pendiente *m*, declive *m* // *vt* (*allow to fall*) dejar caer; (*voice, eyes, price*) bajar; (*set down from car*) dejar; (*omit*) omitir // *vi* caer; (*price, temperature*) bajar; (*wind*) amainar; **~ off** *vi* (*sleep*) dormirse // *vt* (*passenger*) bajar; **to ~ out** *vi* (*withdraw*) retirarse; **~-out** *n* marginado; **~per** *n* cuentagotas *m inv*; **~pings** *npl* excremento *sg* (de animal).

drought [draut] *n* sequía.

drove [drəuv] *pt of* **drive**.

drown [draun] *vt* ahogar // *vi* ahogarse.

drowsy ['drauzɪ] *a* soñoliento; **to be ~** tener sueño.

drudgery ['drʌdʒərɪ] *n* trabajo monótono.

drug [drʌg] *n* medicamento; (*narcotic*) droga // *vt* drogar; **~ addict** *n* drogadicto/a; **~gist** *n* (*US*) farmacéutico; **~store** *n* (*US*) farmacia.

drum [drʌm] *n* tambor *m*; (*large*) bombo; (*for oil, petrol*) bidón *m*; **~s** *npl* batería *sg* // *vi* tocar el tambor; (*with fingers*) tamborilear; **~mer** *n* tambor *m*; **~stick** *n* (*MUS*) palillo; (*of chicken*) muslo.

drunk [drʌŋk] *pp of* **drink** // *a* borracho // *n* (*also*: **~ard**) borracho/a; **~en** *a* borracho; **~enness** *n* embriaguez *f*.

dry [draɪ] *a* seco; (*day*) sin lluvia; (*climate*) árido, seco // *vt* secar; (*tears*) enjugarse // *vi* secarse; **to ~ up** *vi* agotarse; (*in speech*) atascarse; **~-cleaner's** *n* tintorería; **~-cleaning** *n* lavado en seco; **~er** *n* lavadora; **~ness** *n* sequedad *f*; **~ rot** *n* putrefacción *f* fungoide.

dual ['djuəl] *a* doble; **~-control** *a* de doble mando; **~ nationality** *n* doble nacionalidad *f*; **~-purpose** *a* de doble uso.

dubbed [dʌbd] *a* (*CINEMA*) doblado.

dubious ['dju:bɪəs] *a* dudoso; (*reputation, company*) sospechoso.

duchess ['dʌtʃɪs] *n* duquesa.

duck [dʌk] *n* pato // *vi* agacharse; **~ling** *n* patito.

duct [dʌkt] *n* conducto, canal *m*.

dud [dʌd] *n* (*shell*) obús *m* que no estalla; (*object, tool*): **it's a ~** es una filfa // *a*: **~ cheque** cheque *m* sin fondos.

due [dju:] *a* (*proper*) debido; (*expected*) esperado; (*fitting*) conveniente, oportuno // *n* (*debt*) deuda; (*desert*) lo que merece uno // *ad*: **~ north** derecho al norte; **~s** *npl* (*for club, union*) cuota *sg*; (*in harbour*) derechos *mpl*; **in ~ course** a su debido tiempo; **~ to** debido a.

duel ['djuəl] *n* duelo.

duet [dju:'ɛt] *n* dúo.

dug [dʌg] *pt, pp of* **dig**.

duke [dju:k] *n* duque *m*.

dull [dʌl] *a* (*light*) apagado; (*slow*) torpe; (*boring*) pesado; (*sound, pain*) sordo; (*weather, day*) gris // *vt* (*pain, grief*) aliviar; (*mind, senses*) entorpecer.

duly ['dju:lɪ] *ad* debidamente; (*on time*) a su debido tiempo.

dumb [dʌm] *a* mudo; (*stupid*) estúpido; **~founded** [dʌm'faundɪd] *a* pasmado.

dummy ['dʌmɪ] *n* (*tailor's model*) maniquí *m*; (*for baby*) chupete // *a* falso, postizo.

dump [dʌmp] *n* (*heap*) montón *m*; (*place*) basurero, vaciadero; (*col*) casucha; (*MIL*) depósito // *vt* (*put down*) verter, vaciar; (*get rid of*) deshacerse de; (*goods*) inundar el mercado con; **~ing** *n* (*ECON*) dumping *m*; (*of rubbish*): **'no ~ing'** 'prohibido verter basura'.

dumpling ['dʌmplɪŋ] *n* bola de masa hervida.

dunce [dʌns] *n* zopenco.

dune [dju:n] *n* duna.

dung [dʌŋ] *n* estiércol *m*.

dungarees [dʌŋgə'ri:z] *npl* mono *sg*.

dungeon ['dʌndʒən] *n* calabozo.

dupe [dju:p] *n* (*victim*) víctima // *vt* engañar.

duplicate ['dju:plɪkət] *n* duplicado // *vt* ['dju:plɪkeɪt] duplicar; (*on machine*) multicopiar; **in ~** por duplicado; **duplicator** *n* multicopista *m*.

durable ['djuərəbl] *a* duradero.

duration [djuə'reɪʃən] *n* duración *f*.

duress [djuə'rɛs] *n*: **under ~** por compulsión.

during ['djuərɪŋ] *prep* durante.

dusk [dʌsk] *n* crepúsculo, anochecer *m*.

dust [dʌst] *n* polvo // *vt* (*furniture*) desempolvorar; (*cake etc*): **to ~ with** espolvorear de; **~bin** *n* (*Brit*) cubo de la basura; **~er** *n* paño, trapo, bayeta; (*feather ~*) plumero; **~ jacket** *n* sobrecubierta; **~man** *n* (*Brit*) basurero; **~y** *a* polvoriento.

Dutch [dʌtʃ] *a* holandés(esa) // *n* (*LING*) holandés *m*; **~man/woman** *n* holandés/esa *m/f*.

duty ['dju:tɪ] *n* deber *m*; (*tax*) derechos *mpl* de aduana; **on ~** de servicio; (*at night etc*) de guardia; **off ~** libre (de servicio); **~-free** *a* libre de derechos de aduana.

dwarf [dwɔ:f] *pl* **dwarves** [dwɔ:vz] *n* enano // *vt* empequeñecer.

dwell [dwɛl], *pt, pp* **dwelt** [dwɛlt] *vi* morar; **to ~ on** *vt fus* explayarse en; **~ing** *n* vivienda.

dwindle ['dwɪndl] *vi* menguar, disminuir.

dye [daɪ] *n* tinte *m* // *vt* teñir.

dying ['daɪɪŋ] *a* moribundo, agonizante; (*moments*) final; (*words*) último.

dynamic [daɪ'næmɪk] *a* dinámico; **~s** *n*, *np* dinámica *sg*.

dynamite ['daɪnəmaɪt] *n* dinamita.

dynamo ['daɪnəməu] n dinamo f.
dynasty ['dɪnəstɪ] n dinastía.

E

each [iːtʃ] det cada inv // pron cada uno; ~ **other** el uno al otro; **they hate** ~ **other** se odian (entre ellos o mutuamente); **they have 2 books** ~ tiene 2 libros por persona.

eager ['iːgə*] a (gen) impaciente; (zeopleul) ilusionado; (ambitious) ambicioso; **te be** ~ **to do sth** ansiar hacer algo, impacientarse por hacer algo; **to ɔe** ~ **for** ansiar, anhelar.

eagle ['iːgl] n águila.

ear [iə*] n oreja; (MUS) oído; (of corn) espiga; ~**ache** n dolor m de oídos; ~**drum** n tímpano.

earl [əːl] n conde m.

early ['əːlɪ] ad (gen) temprano; (before time) con tiempo, con anticipación // a (gen) temprano; (reply) pronto; (first) primero; (work) juvenil; **have an** ~ **night** acuéstate temprano; **in the** ~ **or** ~ **in the spring/19th century** a principios de primavera/del siglo diez y nueve; **as** ~ **as possible** cuánto antes, lo más pronto posible.

earmark ['iəmɑːk] vt reservar (for para), destinar (for a).

earn [əːn] vt (gen) ganar; (salary) percibir; (interest) devengar; (praise) merecerse.

earnest ['əːnɪst] a serio, formal; **in** ~ ad en serio.

earnings ['əːnɪŋz] npl (personal) sueldo, ingresos mpl; (company) ganancias fpl.

ear: ~**phones** npl auriculares mpl; ~**ring** n pendiente m, arete m; ~**shot** n: **within** ~**shot** al alcance del oído.

earth [əːθ] n (gen) tierra; (ELEC) cable m de toma de tierra // vt (ELEC) conectar a tierra; ~**enware** n loza de barro; ~**quake** n terremoto; ~**y** a (fig: vulgar) grosero; (: sensual) sensual.

earwig ['iəwɪg] n tijereta.

ease [iːz] n (gen) facilidad f; (relief) alivio; (calm) tranquilidad f; (relaxed state) comodidad f // vt facilitar, aliviar; (loosen) soltar; (relieve: pressure) aflojar; (help pass): **to** ~ **sth in/out** meter/sacar con cuidado; **at** ~! descanso!; **to** ~ **off** or **up** vi (gen) suavizarse; (at work) dejar de trabajar tanto; (wind) amainar; (rain) moderarse.

easel ['iːzl] n caballete m.

east [iːst] n este m, oriente m // a del este, oriental // ad al este, hacia el este; **the E** ~ el Oriente.

Easter ['iːstə*] n Pascua (de Resurrección).

easterly ['iːstəlɪ] a (to the east) al este; (from the east) del este.

eastern ['iːstən] a del este, oriental.

East Germany n Alemania Oriental.

eastward(s) ['iːstwəd(z)] ad hacia el este.

easy ['iːzɪ] a (gen) fácil; (simple) sencillo; (slow) lento, pausado; (comfortable) holgado, cómodo; (relaxed) natural, llano // ad: **to take it** or **things** ~ (not worry) tomarlo con calma; (go slowly) ir despacio; (rest) descansar; ~ **chair** n sillón m; ~**going** a acomodadizo.

eat [iːt] pt **ate**, pp **eaten** ['iːtn] vt (gen) comer; (supper) cenar; **to** ~ **into, to** ~ **away at** v fus corroer; ~**able** a comestible.

eau de Cologne [əudəkə'ləun] n (agua de) Colonia.

eaves [iːvz] npl alero sg.

eavesdrop ['iːvzdrɔp] vi escuchar a escondidas (on sb a uno).

ebb [eb] n reflujo // vi bajar; (fig: also: ~ **away**) decaer; ~ **tide** n marea menguante.

ebony ['ebənɪ] n ébano.

eccentric [ɪk'sentrɪk] a, n excéntrico/a.

ecclesiastical [ɪkliːzɪ'æstɪkəl] a eclesiástico.

echo ['ekəu] pl ~**es** n eco m // vt (sound) repetir // vi resonar, hacer eco.

eclipse [ɪ'klɪps] n eclipse m // vt eclipsar.

ecology [ɪ'kɔlədʒɪ] n ecología.

economic [iːkə'nɔmɪk] a económico; (business etc) rentable; ~**al** a económico; ~**s** n (la) economía; **economist** [ɪ'kɔnəmɪst] n economista m/f.

economize [ɪ'kɔnəmaɪz] vi economizar, ahorrar.

economy [ɪ'kɔnəmɪ] a economía.

ecstasy ['ekstəsɪ] n éxtasis m; **ecstatic** [-'tætɪk] a extático.

ecumenical [iːkjuˈmenɪkl] a ecuménico.

eczema ['eksɪmə] n eczema m

edge [edʒ] n (of knife etc) filo; (of object) borde m; (of lake etc) orilla // vt (SEWING) ribetear; **on** ~ (fig) = **edgy**; **to** ~ **away from** alejarse poco a poco; ~**ways** ad: **he couldn't get a word in** ~**ways** no pudo meter baza; **edging** n (SEWING) ribete m; (of path) borde m.

edgy ['edʒɪ] a nervioso, inquieto.

edible ['edɪbl] a comestible.

edict ['iːdɪkt] n edicto.

edifice ['edɪfɪs] n edificio.

edit ['edɪt] vt (be editor of) dirigir (cut) cortar; ~**ion** [ɪ'dɪʃən] n (gen) edición f; (number printed) tirada; ~**or** n (of newspaper) director m, (of book) autor m de la edición; ~**orial** ['tɔːrɪəl] a editorial, de la dirección // n editorial m.

educate ['edjukeɪt] vt (gen) educar; (instruct) instruir.

education [edju'keɪʃən] n educación f; (schooling) enseñanza; (scol) pedagogía; ~**al** a (policy etc) educacional; (teaching) docente; (instructive) educativo.

EEC n abbr of **European Economic Community** CEE (Comunidad Económica Europea)

eel [iːl] n anguila.

eerie ['ɪərɪ] a (strange) extraño; (mysterious) misterioso.

effect [ɪ'fɛkt] n efecto // vt efectuar, llevar a cabo; ~s npl efectos mpl; **to take ~** (drug) surtir efecto; **in ~** en realidad; ~**ive** a (gen) eficaz; (striking) impresionante; (real) efectivo; **to become ~ive** entrar en vigor; ~**iveness** n eficacia.

effeminate [ɪ'fɛmɪnɪt] a afeminado.

effervescent [ɛfə'vɛsnt] a efervescente.

efficiency [ɪ'fɪʃənsɪ] n (gen) eficiencia; (of machine) rendimiento.

efficient [ɪ'fɪʃənt] a eficiente.

effigy [ˈɛfɪdʒɪ] n efigie f.

effort [ˈɛfət] n esfuerzo; **to make an ~ to** esforzarse por; ~**less** a sin esfuerzo (alguno).

effrontery [ɪ'frʌntərɪ] n descaro.

effusive [ɪ'fjuːsɪv] a efusivo.

e.g. ad abbr of exempli gratia p. ej. (por ejemplo).

egg [ɛg] n huevo; **hard-boiled/poached/soft-boiled ~** huevo duro/escalfado/pasado por agua; **scrambled ~s** huevos revueltos; **to ~ on** vt incitar; ~**cup** n huevera; ~**shell** n cáscara de huevo.

ego [ˈiːgəu] n ego; ~**ism** n egoísmo; ~**ist** n egoísta m/f.

Egypt [ˈiːdʒɪpt] n Egipto; ~**ian** [ɪ'dʒɪpʃən] a, n egipcio/a.

eiderdown [ˈaɪdədaun] n edredón m.

eight [eɪt] num ocho; **eighteen** num diez y ocho, dieciocho; **eighth** a, n octavo; ~**y** num ochenta.

Eire [ˈɛərə] n Eire m.

either [ˈaɪðə*] det cualquier ... de los dos; (both, each) uno u otro; **on ~ side** en ambos lados // pron: ~ **(of them)** cualquiera (de los dos); **I don't like ~** no me gusta ni uno ni otro // ad tampoco; **no, I don't ~** no, yo tampoco // conj: ~ **yes or no** o sí o no.

eject [ɪ'dʒɛkt] vt echar; (tenant) desahuciar; ~**or seat** n asiento proyectable.

eke [iːk]: **to ~ out** vt (make last) escatimar; (add to) suplir las deficiencias de.

elaborate [ɪ'læbərɪt] a complicado; (decorated) rebuscado // (vb: [ɪ'læbəreɪt]) vt elaborar // vi explicarse con muchos detalles.

elapse [ɪ'læps] vi transcurrir.

elastic [ɪ'læstɪk] a, n elástico; ~ **band** n gomita.

elated [ɪ'leɪtɪd] a: **to be ~** regocijarse; **elation** [ɪ'leɪʃən] n regocijo.

elbow [ˈɛlbəu] n codo.

elder [ˈɛldə*] a mayor // n (tree) saúco; (person) mayor; (of tribe) anciano; ~**ly** a de edad, mayor // n: **the ~ly** la gente mayor.

eldest [ˈɛldɪst] a, n el/la mayor.

elect [ɪ'lɛkt] vt elegir; **to ~ to do** optar por hacer // a: **the president ~** el presidente electo; ~**ion** [ɪ'lɛkʃən] n elección f; ~**ioneering** [ɪlɛkʃə'nɪərɪŋ] n campaña electoral; ~**or** n elector/a m/f;

~**oral** a electoral; ~**orate** n electorado.

electric [ɪ'lɛktrɪk] a eléctrico; ~**al** a eléctrico; ~ **blanket** n manta eléctrica; ~ **chair** n silla eléctrica; ~ **cooker** n cocina eléctrica; ~ **fire** n estufa eléctrica.

electrician [ɪlɛk'trɪʃən] n electricista m/f.

electricity [ɪlɛk'trɪsɪtɪ] n electricidad f.

electrify [ɪ'lɛktrɪfaɪ] vt (RAIL) electrificar; (audience) electrizar.

electro... [ɪlɛktrəu] pref: ~**cute** [-kjuːt] vt electrocutar; **electrode** [ɪ'lɛktrəud] n electrodo; ~**magnetic** a electromagnético.

electron [ɪ'lɛktrɔn] n electrón m.

electronic [ɪlɛk'trɔnɪk] a electrónico; ~**s** n electrónica.

elegance [ˈɛlɪgəns] n elegancia; **elegant** [ˈɛlɪgənt] a elegante.

element [ˈɛlɪmənt] n (gen) elemento; **to brave the ~s** salir a la intemperie; ~**ary** [-ˈmɛntərɪ] a (gen) elemental; (primitive) rudimentario; (school, education) de primera enseñanza.

elephant [ˈɛlɪfənt] n elefante m.

elevate [ˈɛlɪveɪt] vt (gen) elevar; (in rank) ascender.

elevation [ɛlɪ'veɪʃən] n elevación f; (rank) ascenso; (height) altura.

elevator [ˈɛlɪveɪtə*] n (US) ascensor m.

eleven [ɪ'lɛvn] num once; ~**ses** npl las once; ~**th** a undécimo.

elf [ɛlf], pl **elves** [ɛlvz] n duende m.

elicit [ɪ'lɪsɪt] vt: **to ~ (from)** sacar (de).

eligible [ˈɛlɪdʒəbl] a elegible; **to be ~ for sth** llenar los requisitos para algo.

eliminate [ɪ'lɪmɪneɪt] vt eliminar; (strike out) suprimir; (suspect) descartar; **elimination** [-'neɪʃən] n eliminación f; supresión f.

élite [eɪ'liːt] n élite f.

elm [ɛlm] n olmo.

elocution [ɛlə'kjuːʃən] n elocución f.

elongated [ˈiːlɔŋgeɪtɪd] a alargado, estirado.

elope [ɪ'ləup] vi fugarse con su amante; ~**ment** n fuga.

eloquence [ˈɛləkwəns] n elocuencia; **eloquent** [-wənt] a elocuente.

else [ɛls] ad lo(s) demás; **something ~** otra cosa; **somewhere ~** en otra parte; **everywhere ~** en todas partes (menos aquí); **where ~?** ¿dónde más?, ¿en qué otra parte?; **there was little ~ to do** apenas quedaba otra cosa que hacer; **nobody ~ spoke** no habló nadie más; ~**where** ad (be) en otra parte; (go) a otra parte.

elucidate [ɪ'luːsɪdeɪt] vt aclarar, elucidar.

elude [ɪ'luːd] vt (gen) eludir; (blow) esquivar; (pursuer) escaparse de, zafarse de.

elusive [ɪ'luːsɪv] a esquivo; (answer) difícil de encontrar.

emaciated [ɪ'meɪsɪeɪtɪd] a demacrado.

emanate [ˈɛməneɪt] vi emanar, proceder.

emancipate [ɪ'mænsɪpeɪt] vt emancipar;
~d a liberado; **emancipatioc** [-'peɪʃən] n
emancipación f, liberación f.

embalm [ɪm'bɑːm] vt embalsamar.

embankment [ɪm'bæŋkmənt] n terraplén
m; (riverside) dique m.

embargo [ɪm'bɑːgəʊ], pl ~es n
prohibición f.

embark [ɪm'bɑːk] vi embarcarse // vt
embarcar; **to ~ on** (fig) emprender,
lanzarse a; ~**ation** [embɑː'keɪʃən] n
(people) embarco; (goods) embarque m.

embarrass [ɪm'bærəs] vt desconcertar,
azorar; (financially etc) poner en un
aprieto; ~**ing** a embarazoso; ~**ment** n
desconcierto, azoramiento; (financial)
apuros mpl.

embassy ['embəsɪ] n embajada.

embed [ɪm'bed] vt (gen) empotrar; (teeth
etc) clavar.

embellish [ɪm'belɪʃ] vt embellecer; (fig.
adornar.

embers ['embəz] npl rescoldo sg, ascua sg.

embezzle [ɪm'bezl] vt desfalcar,
malversar; ~**ment** n desfalco,
malversación f.

embitter [ɪm'bɪtə*] vt amargar; (fig)
envenenar; ~**ed** a resentido, amargado.

emblem ['embləm] n emblema m.

embody [ɪm'bɒdɪ] vt (features) encarnar;
(ideas) expresar.

embossed [ɪm'bɒst] a realzado; ~ **with**
con grabado en relieve.

embrace [ɪm'breɪs] vt abrazar, dar un
abrazo a; (include) abarcar; (adopt: idea)
adherirse a // vi abrazarse // n abrazo.

embroider [ɪm'brɔɪdə*] vt bordar; (fig:
story) adornar, embellecer; ~**y** n
bordado.

embryo ['embrɪəʊ] n (also fig) embrión m.

emerald ['emərəld] n esmeralda.

emerge [ɪ'mɜːdʒ] vi (gen) salir, aparecer;
(arise) surgir; **emergence** n salida,
aparición f; surgimiento.

emergency [ɪ'mɜːdʒənsɪ] n (event)
emergencia; (crisis) crisis f; (need)
necesidad f urgente; **in an** ~ en caso de
urgencia; **state of** ~ estado de
emergencia; ~ **exit** n salida de
emergencia; ~ **landing** n aterrizaje m
forzoso; ~ **meeting** n reunión f
extraordinaria.

emery ['emərɪ]: ~ **board** n lima de uñas;
~ **paper** n papel m de esmeril.

emetic [ɪ'metɪk] n emético.

emigrant ['emɪgrənt] n emigrante m/f.

emigrate ['emɪgreɪt] vi emigrarse;
emigration [-'greɪʃən] n emigración f.

eminence ['emɪnəns] n eminencia;
eminent [-ənt] a eminente.

emission [ɪ'mɪʃən] n emisión f.

emit [ɪ'mɪt] vt (gen) emitir; (smoke)
arrojar; (smell) despedir; (sound) producir.

emotion [ɪ'məʊʃən] n emoción f; ~**al** a
(person) sentimental; (scene)
conmovedor(a), emocionante; ~**ally** ad
con emoción.

emotive [ɪ'məʊtɪv] a emotivo.

emperor ['empərə*] n emperador m.

emphasis ['emfəsɪs], pl ~**ses** [-siːz] n
énfasis m in

emphasize ['emfəsaɪz] vt (word, point)
subrayar, recalcar; (feature) hacer
resaltar.

emphatic [em'fætɪk] a (strong) enérgico;
(unambiguous, clear) enfático; ~**ally** ad
con énfasis.

empire ['empaɪə*] n imperio.

empirical [em'pɪrɪkl] a empírico.

employ [ɪm'plɔɪ] vt emplear; ~**ee** [-'iː] n
empleado/a; ~**er** n patrón/ona m/f,
empresario; ~**ment** n (gen) empleo;
(work) trabajo; **full** ~**ment** pleno
empleo; ~**ment agency** n agencia de
colocaciones; ~**ment exchange** n bolsa
de trabajo.

empower [ɪm'paʊə*] vt: **to** ~ **sb to do**
sth autorizar a uno a hacer algo.

empress ['empris] n emperatriz f.

emptiness ['emptinɪs] n (gen) vacío; (of
life etc) vaciedad f.

empty ['emptɪ] a vacío; (place) desierto;
(house) desocupado; (threat) vano // n
(bottle) envase m // vt vaciar; (place)
dejar vacío // vi vaciarse; (house) quedar
desocupado; (place) quedar desierto;
~**-handed** a con las manos vacías.

emulate ['emjʊleɪt] vt emular.

emulsion [ɪ'mʌlʃən] n emulsión f.

enable ['neɪbl] vt: **to** ~ **sb to do sth**
(allow) permitir a uno hacer algo;
(prepare) capacitar a uno para hacer algo.

enact [ɪn'ækt] vt (law) promulgar; (play)
representar (role) hacer.

enamel [ɪ'næməl] n esmalte m.

enamoured [ɪ'næməd] a: **to be** ~ **of**
(person) estar enamorado de; (activity etc)
tener gran afición a; (idea) aferrarse a.

encased [ɪn'keɪst] a: ~ **in** (enclosed)
encerrado en; (covered) revestido de.

enchant [ɪn'tʃɑːnt] vt encantar; ~**ing** a
encantador(a).

encircle [ɪn'sɜːkl] vt (gen) rodear; (waist)
ceñir.

encl. abbr of **enclosed** adj. (adjunto).

enclose [ɪn'kləʊz] vt (land) cercar; (with
letter etc) adjuntar; (in receptacle)
encerrar; **please find** ~**d** le adjunto.

enclosure [ɪn'kləʊʒə*] n cercado, recinto;
(comm) carta adjunta.

encore [ɔŋ'kɔː*] excl ¡otra!, ¡bis! // n bis m

encounter [ɪn'kaʊntə*] n encuentro // vt
encontrar, encontrarse con; (difficulty)
tropezar con.

encourage [ɪn'kʌrɪdʒ] vt alentar, animar;
(growth) estimular; ~**ment** n estímulo; (of
industry) fomento.

encroach [ɪn'krəʊtʃ] vi: **to** ~ (**up**)**on**
(gen) invadir; (time) ocupar.

encrusted [ɪn'krʌstəd] a: ~ **with**
incrustado de.

encumber [ɪn'kʌmbə*] vt: **to be** ~**ed**
with (carry) tener que cargar con; (debts)
estar gravado de.

encyclop(a)edia [ɛnsaɪkləu'piːdɪə] n enciclopedia.

end [end] n (gen, also aim) fin m; (of table) extremo; (of street) final m; (SPORT) lado // vt terminar, acabar; (also: **bring to an ~, put an ~ to**) acabar con // vi terminar, acabar; **in the ~** al fin, por fin, finalmente; **on ~** (object) de punta, de cabeza; **to stand on ~** (hair) erizarse; **for hours on ~** horas seguidas; **to ~ up** vi: **to ~ up in** terminar en; (place) ir a parar en.

endanger [ɪn'deɪndʒə*] vt poner en peligro.

endear [ɪn'dɪə*] vr: **to ~ o.s. to** hacerse querer de; **~ing** a simpático, atractivo; **~ment** n cariño, palabra cariñosa.

endeavour [ɪn'devə*] n esfuerzo; (attempt) tentativa; (striving) empeño // vi: **to ~ to do** esforzarse por hacer; (try) procurar hacer.

ending ['endɪŋ] n fin m, conclusión f; (of book) desenlace m; (LING) terminación f.

endless ['endlɪs] a interminable, inacabable.

endorse [ɪn'dɔːs] vt (cheque) endosar; (approve) aprobar; **~ment** n (on driving licence) nota de inhabilitación.

endow [ɪn'dau] vt (provide with money) dotar; (: institution) fundar; **to be ~ed with** estar dotado de.

endurance [ɪn'djuərəns] n resistencia; **endure** vt (bear) aguantar, soportar; (resist) resistir // vi (last) durar; (resist) resistir.

enemy ['enəmɪ] a, n enemigo/a.

energetic [enə'dʒetɪk] a enérgico.

energy ['enədʒɪ] n energía.

enforce [ɪn'fɔːs] vt (LAW) hacer cumplir; **~d** a forzoso, forzado.

engage [ɪn'geɪdʒ] vt (attention) llamar; (in conversation) abordar; (worker) contratar; (taxi) alquilar; (clutch) embragar // vi (TECH) engranar con; **to ~ in** dedicarse a, ocuparse en; **~d** a (busy, in use) ocupado; (betrothed) prometido; **to get ~d** prometerse; **he is ~d in research** se dedica a la investigación; **~d tone** n señal f de comunicando; **~ment** n (appointment) compromiso, cita; (battle) combate m; (to marry) compromiso; (period) noviazgo; **~ment ring** n alianza, anillo de prometida.

engaging [ɪn'geɪdʒɪŋ] a atractivo, simpático.

engender [ɪn'dʒendə*] vt engendrar.

engine ['endʒɪn] n (AUT) motor m; (RAIL) locomotora; **~ driver** n maquinista m.

engineer [endʒɪ'nɪə*] n ingeniero; (US: RAIL) maquinista m; **~ing** n ingeniería.

England ['ɪŋglənd] n Inglaterra.

English ['ɪŋglɪʃ] a inglés(esa) // n (LING) el inglés; **the ~** los ingleses; **~man/woman** n inglés/esa m/f.

engrave [ɪn'greɪv] vt grabar; **engraving** n grabado.

engrossed [ɪn'grəust] a: **~ in** absorto en.

engulf [ɪn'gʌlf] vt sumergir, hundir.

enhance [ɪn'hɑːns] vt (gen) intensificar, aumentar; (beauty) realzar.

enigma [ɪ'nɪgmə] n enigma m; **~tic** [enɪg-'mætɪk] a enigmático.

enjoy [ɪn'dʒɔɪ] vt (possess) poseer; (have: health, fortune) disfrutar de, gozar de; (food) comer con gusto; **to ~ o.s.** divertirse, pasarlo bien; **~able** a (pleasant) agradable; (amusing) divertido; **~ment** n (use) disfrute m; (joy) placer m.

enlarge [ɪn'lɑːdʒ] vt aumentar; (broaden) extender; (PHOT) ampliar // vi: **to ~ on** (subject) tratar con más detalles; **~ment** n (PHOT) ampliación f.

enlighten [ɪn'laɪtn] vt (inform) informar, instruir; **~ed** a (cultured) culto; (knowledgeable) bien informado; (tolerant) comprensivo; **~ment** n (HISTORY): **the E~ment** la Ilustración, el Siglo de las Luces.

enlist [ɪn'lɪst] vt alistar; (support) conseguir // vi alistarse.

enmity ['enmɪtɪ] n enemistad f.

enormity [ɪ'nɔːmɪtɪ] n enormidad f; **enormous [-məs]** a enorme.

enough [ɪ'nʌf] a: **~ time/books** bastante tiempo/bastantes libros // n: **have you got ~?** ¿tiene Usted bastante? // ad: **big ~** bastante grande; **he has not worked ~** no ha trabajado bastante; **~! ¡basta ya!; that's ~, thanks** con eso basta, gracias; **I've had ~ of him** estoy harto de él; **... which, funnily ~ ...** ... lo que, por extraño que parezca... .

enquire [ɪn'kwaɪə*] vt, vi = **inquire.**

enrage [ɪn'reɪdʒ] vt enfurecer, hacer rabiar.

enrich [ɪn'rɪtʃ] vt enriquecer.

enrol [ɪn'rəul] vt inscribir; (SCOL) matricular // vi inscribirse; matricularse; **~ment** n inscripción f; matriculación f.

en route [ɒn'ruːt] ad (on the way to) camino de; (on the way) en camino.

ensign ['ensaɪn] n (flag) bandera; (MIL) alférez m.

enslave [ɪn'sleɪv] vt esclavizar.

ensue [ɪn'sjuː] vi seguirse; (result) resultar; (happen) sobrevenir.

ensure [ɪn'ʃuə*] vt asegurar.

entail [ɪn'teɪl] vt (imply) suponer; (result in) acarrear.

entangle [ɪn'tæŋgl] vt enredar, enmarañar; **~ment** n enredo.

enter ['entə*] vt (room) entrar en; (club) hacerse socio de; (army) alistarse en; (sb for a competition) inscribir; (write down) anotar, apuntar // vi entrar; **to ~ for** vt fus presentarse para; **to ~ into** vt fus (relations) establecer; (plans) formar parte de; (debate) tomar parte en; (agreement) llegar a, firmar; **to ~ (up)on** vt fus (career) emprender.

enteritis [entə'raɪtɪs] n enteritis f.

enterprise ['entəpraɪz] n empresa; (spirit) iniciativa; **free ~** la libre empresa; **private ~** la iniciativa privada;

enterprising a emprendedor(a)

entertain [cntə'tein] vt (amuse) divertir; (receive: guest) recibir (en casa); (idea) abrigar; (plan) estudiar; ~**er** n artista m/f; ~**ing** a divertido, entretenido; ~**ment** n (amusement) diversión f, (show) espectáculo; (party) fiesta.

enthralled [in'θrɔːld] a encantado, cautivado.

enthusiasm [in'θuːziæzəm] n entusiasmo.

enthusiast [in'θuːziæst] n entusiasta m/f, ~**ic** [-'æstik] a entusiasta inv; to be ~**ic** about entusiasmarse por.

entice [in'tais] vt tentar; (seduce) seducir; **enticing** a atractivo, tentador(a).

entire [in'taiə*] a entero, completo; (in total) total, todo; ~**ly** ad totalmente; ~**ty** [in'taiərəti] n: **in its** ~ en su totalidad.

entitle [in'taitl] vt: **to** ~ **sb to sth** dar a uno derecho a algo; ~**d** a (book) que se titula; **to be** ~**d to do** tener derecho a hacer.

entourage [ɔntu'raːʒ] n séquito.

entrails ['entreilz] npl entrañas fpl.

entrance n ['entrəns] n entrada // vt [in-'trɑːns] encantar, hechizar; **to gain** ~ **to** (university etc) ingresar en; ~ **examination** n examen m de ingreso; ~ **fee** n cuota.

entrant ['entrənt] n participante m/f.

entreat [en'triːt] vt rogar, suplicar; ~**y** n ruego, súplica.

entrée ['ɔntrei] n (CULIN) entrada.

entrenched [en'trentʃd] a atrincherado.

entrepreneur [ɔntrəprə'nɔː] n empresario; (of works) contratista m/f.

entrust [in'trʌst] vt: **to** ~ **sth to sb** confiar algo a uno.

entry ['entri] n entrada; (permission to enter) acceso; (in register) apunte m; (in account) partida; ~ **form** n boleto de inscripción; **no** ~ prohibido el paso; (AUT) dirección prohibida.

enumerate [i'njuːməreit] vt enumerar.

enunciate [i'nʌnsieit] vt pronunciar; (principle etc) enunciar.

envelop [in'veləp] vt envolver.

envelope ['envələup] n sobre m.

envious ['enviəs] a envidioso; (look) de envidia.

environment [in'vaiərnmənt] n medio ambiente; ~**al** [-'mentl] a ambiental.

envisage [in'vizidʒ] vt (foresee) prever; (imagine) concebir, representarse.

envoy ['envɔi] n enviado.

envy ['envi] n envidia // vt tener envidia a; **to** ~ **sb sth** envidiar algo a uno.

enzyme ['enzaim] n enzima.

ephemeral [i'femərl] a efímero.

epic ['epik] n épica // a épico.

epidemic [epi'demik] n epidemia.

epilepsy ['epilepsi] n epilepsia; **epileptic** [-'leptik] a, n epiléptico/a.

episode ['episəud] n episodio.

epistle [i'pisl] n epístola.

epitaph ['epitaːf] n epitafio.

epitome [i'pitəmi] n epítome m; **epitomize** vt epitomar, resumir.

epoch ['iːpɔk] n época.

equable ['ekwəbl] a uniforme, igual; (character) tranquilo, afable.

equal ['iːkwl] a (gen) igual; (treatment) equitativo // n igual m/f // vt ser igual a; **to be** ~ **to** (task) estar a la altura de; ~**ity** [iː'kwɔliti] n igualdad f; ~**ize** vt, vi igualar; (SPORT) lograr el empate; ~**izer** n igualada; ~**ly** ad igualmente; (share etc) por igual.

equanimity [ekwə'nimiti] n ecuanimidad f.

equate [i'kweit] vt: **to** ~ **sth with** considerar algo equivalente a; **equation** [i'kweiʃən] n (MATH) ecuación f.

equator [i'kweitə*] n ecuador m; ~**ial** [ekwə'tɔːriəl] a ecuatorial.

equilibrium [iːkwi'libriəm] n equilibrio.

equinox ['iːkwinɔks] n equinoccio.

equip [i'kwip] vt (gen) equipar; (person) proveer; **to be well** ~**ped** estar bien dotado; ~**ment** n equipo; (tools) avíos mpl.

equitable ['ekwitəbl] a equitativo.

equivalent [i'kwivələnt] a equivalente; **to be** ~ **to** equivaler a // n equivalente m.

equivocal [i'kwivəkl] a equívoco; (open to suspicion) ambiguo.

era ['iərə] n era, época.

eradicate [i'rædikeit] vt erradicar, extirpar.

erase [i'reiz] vt borrar; **eraser** n goma de borrar.

erect [i'rekt] a erguido // vt erigir, levantar; (assemble) montar.

erection [i'rekʃən] n construcción f; (assembly) montaje m; (structure) edificio; (MED) erección f.

ermine ['ɔːmin] n armiño.

erode [i'rəud] vt (GEO) erosionar; (metal) corroer, desgastar; **erosion** [i'rəuʒən] n erosión f, desgaste m.

erotic [i'rɔtik] a erótico; ~**ism** [i'rɔtisizm] n erotismo.

err [əː*] vi errar, equivocarse; (REL) pecar.

errand ['erənd] n recado, mandado; ~ **boy** n recadero.

erratic [i'rætik] a irregular; (uneven) desigual, poco uniforme.

erroneous [i'rəuniəs] a erróneo.

error ['erə*] n error m, equivocación f.

erupt [i'rʌpt] vi estar en erupción; (MED) hacer erupción; (fig) estallar; ~**ion** [i'rʌpʃən] n erupción f; (fig) explosión f.

escalate ['eskəleit] vi extenderse, intensificarse; **escalation** [-'leiʃən] n escalamiento, intensificación f.

escalator ['eskəleitə*] n escalera móvil.

escapade [eskə'peid] n travesura.

escape [i'skeip] n (gen) fuga; (from duties) escapatoria; (from chase) fuga, evasión f // vi (gen) escaparse; (flee) huir, evadirse; (leak) fugarse // vt evitar, eludir; (consequences) escapar a; **to** ~ **from**

(*place*) escaparse de; (*person*) escaparse a; (*clutches*) librarse de; **escapism** *n* escapismo.

escort ['eskɔːt] *n* acompañante *m/f*; (*MIL*) escolta; (*NAUT*) convoy *m* // *vt* [ɪ'skɔːt] acompañar; (*MIL, NAUT*) escoltar.

Eskimo ['eskɪməu] *n* esquimal *m/f*.

especially [ɪ'speʃlɪ] *ad* (*gen*) especialmente; (*above all*) sobre todo; (*particularly*) en particular.

espionage ['espɪɔnɑːʒ] *n* espionaje *m*.

esplanade [esplɔ'neɪd] *n* (*by sea*) paseo marítimo.

espouse [ɪ'spauz] *vt* adherirse a.

Esquire [ɪ'skwaɪɔ] *n* (*abbr* **Esq.**): **J. Brown, ~** Sr. Don J. Brown.

essay ['eseɪ] *n* (*SCOL*) ensayo.

essence ['esns] *n* esencia.

essential [ɪ'senʃl] *a* (*necessary*) imprescindible; (*basic*) esencial; **~ly** *ad* esencialmente.

establish [ɪ'stæblɪʃ] *vt* establecer; (*facts*) verificar; (*proof*) demostrar; (*relations*) entablar; **~ed** *a* (*business*) de buena reputación; (*staff*) de plantilla; **~ment** *n* establecimiento; **the E~ment** la clase dirigente.

estate [ɪ'steɪt] *n* (*land*) finca, hacienda; (*property*) propiedad *f*; (*inheritance*) herencia; (*POL*) estado; **housing ~** urbanización *f*; **industrial ~** polígono industrial; **~ agent** *n* agente *m/f* inmobiliario; **~ car** *n* (*Brit*) furgoneta.

esteem [ɪ'stiːm] *n*: **to hold sb in high ~** estimar en mucho a uno // *vt* estimar.

estimate ['estɪmət] *n* estimación *f*, apreciación *f*; (*assessment*) tasa, cálculo; (*COMM*) presupuesto // *vt* [-meɪt] estimar; tasar, calcular; **estimation** [-'meɪʃən] *n* opinión *f*, juicio; (*esteem*) aprecio.

estrange [ɪ'streɪndʒ] *vt* enajenar.

estuary ['estjuərɪ] *n* estuario, ría.

etching ['etʃɪŋ] *n* aguafuerte *f*.

eternal [ɪ'tɜːnl] *a* eterno.

eternity [ɪ'tɜːnɪtɪ] *n* eternidad *f*.

ether ['iːθɔ] *n* éter *m*.

ethical ['eθɪkl] *a* ético; (*honest*) honrado; **ethics** ['eθɪks] *n* ética // *npl* moralidad *f*.

ethnic ['eθnɪk] *a* étnico.

etiquette ['etɪket] *n* etiqueta.

eucalyptus [juːkɔ'lɪptɔs] *n* eucalipto.

euphemism ['juːfəmɪzm] *n* eufemismo.

euphoria [juː'fɔːrɪə] *n* euforia.

Europe ['juɔrɔp] *n* Europa; **European** [-'piːɔn] *a*, *n* europeo/a.

euthanasia [juːθɔ'neɪzɪə] *n* eutanasia.

evacuate [ɪ'vækjueɪt] *vt* desocupar; **evacuation** [-'eɪʃən] *n* evacuación *f*.

evade [ɪ'veɪd] *vt* evadir, eludir.

evaluate [ɪ'væljueɪt] *vt* evaluar; (*value*) tasar; (*evidence*) interpretar.

evangelist [ɪ'vændʒɔlɪst] *n* evangelizador *m*, evangelista *m/f*.

evaporate [ɪ'væpɔreɪt] *vi* evaporarse, desvanecerse // *vt* evaporar; **~d milk** *n*

leche *f* evaporada; **evaporation** [-'reɪʃən] *n* evaporación *f*.

evasion [ɪ'veɪʒən] *n* evasiva, evasión *f*; **evasive** [-sɪv] *a* evasivo.

eve [iːv] *n*: **on the ~ of** en vísperas de.

even ['iːvn] *a* (*level*) llano; (*smooth*) liso; (*speed, temperature*) uniforme; (*number*) par; (*nature*) ecuánime; (*SPORT*) igual(es) // *ad* hasta, aun, siquiera; **~ more** aun más; **~ so** aun así; **not ~** ni siquiera; **~ he was there** hasta él estuvo allí; **~ on Sundays** incluso los domingos; **to ~ out** *vi* nivelarse; **to get ~ with sb** ajustar cuentas con uno.

evening ['iːvnɪŋ] *n* tarde *f*; (*dusk*) atardecer *m*; (*night*) noche *f*; (*event*) velada; **in the ~** por la tarde; **~ class** *n* clase *f* nocturna; **~ dress** *n* (*man's*) traje *m* de etiqueta; (*woman's*) traje *m* de noche.

event [ɪ'vent] *n* suceso, acontecimiento; (*SPORT*) prueba; **in the ~ of** en caso de (que); **~ful** *a* accidentado; (*game etc*) lleno de emoción.

eventual [ɪ'ventʃuəl] *a* (*last*) final; (*resulting*) consiguiente; **~ity** [-'ælɪtɪ] *n* eventualidad *f*; **~ly** *ad* (*finally*) finalmente, al fin y al cabo; (*in time*) a la larga.

ever ['evɔ] *ad* nunca, jamás; (*at all times*) alguna vez; **the best ~** el/la mejor que se ha visto jamás; **have you ~ seen it?** ¿lo ha visto Usted jamás?; **better than ~** mejor que nunca; **~ since** *ad* desde entonces // *conj* después de que; **~green** *n* árbol *m* de hoja perenne; **~lasting** *a* eterno, perpetuo.

every ['evrɪ] *det* (*each*) cada; (*all*) todo; **~ day** cada día; **~ other car** cada dos coches; **~ now and then** de vez en cuando; **~body** *pron* todos *pl*, todo el mundo; **~day** *a* (*daily*) diario, cotidiano; (*usual*) corriente; (*common*) vulgar; (*routine*) rutinario; **~one = ~body**; **~thing** *pron* todo; **~where** *ad* (*be*) en todas partes; (*go*) a o por todas partes.

evict [ɪ'vɪkt] *vt* desahuciar; **~ion** [ɪ'vɪkʃən] *n* desahucio.

evidence ['evɪdɔns] *n* (*proof*) prueba; (*of witness*) testimonio; (*facts*) datos *mpl*, hechos *mpl*; **to give ~** prestar declaración, dar testimonio.

evident ['evɪdɔnt] *a* evidente, manifiesto; **~ly** *ad* naturalmente.

evil ['iːvl] *a* malo; (*influence*) funesto; (*smell*) horrible // *n* mal *m*, maldad *f*; **~doer** *n* malhechor/a *m/f*.

evocative [ɪ'vɔkətɪv] *a* sugestivo, evocador(a).

evoke [ɪ'vɔuk] *vt* evocar.

evolution [iːvɔ'luːʃən] *n* evolución *f*, desarrollo.

evolve [ɪ'vɔlv] *vt* desarrollar // *vi* evolucionar, desarrollarse.

ewe [juː] *n* oveja.

ex-... [eks] *pref* ex.

exact [ɪg'zækt] *a* exacto // *vt*: **to ~ sth**

(from) exigir algo (de); ~**ing** a exigente; (*conditions*) arduo; ~**itude** n exactitud f; ~**ly** ad exactamente; (*time*) en punto.

exaggerate [ɪg'zædʒəreɪt] vt, vi exagerar; **exaggeration** [-'reɪʃən] a exageración f.

exalted [ɪg'zɔːltɪd] a exaltado, elevado.

exam [ɪg'zæm] n abbr of **examination**.

examination [ɪgzæmɪ'neɪʃən] f (*gen*) examen m; (*LAW*) interrogación f; (*inquiry*) investigación f.

examine [ɪg'zæmɪn] vt (*gen*) examinar; (*inspect*) inspeccionar, escudriñar (*SCOL, LAW: person*) interrogar; (*at customs: luggage*) registrar; **examiner** n inspector m.

example [ɪg'zɑːmpl] n ejemplo; (*copy*) ejemplar m; **for** ~ por ejemplo.

exasperate [ɪg'zɑːspəreɪt] vt exasperar, irritar; **exasperating** a irritante.

excavate ['ekskəveɪt] vt excavar, **excavation** [-'veɪʃən] n excavación f.

exceed [ɪk'siːd] vt exceder; (*number*) pasar de; (*speed limit*) sobrepasar; (*limits*) rebasar; (*hopes*) superar; ~**ingly** ad sumamente, sobremanera.

excel [ɪk'sel] vi sobresalir.

excellence ['eksələns] n excelencia.

Excellency ['eksələnsɪ] n: His ~ Su Excelencia.

excellent ['eksələnt] a excelente.

except [ɪk'sept] prep (*also*: ~ **for**, ~**ing**) excepto, salvo, con excepción de // vt exceptuar, excluir; ~ **if/when** excepto si/cuando; ~ **that** salvo que; ~**ion** [ɪk'sepʃən] n excepción f; **to take** ~**ion to** ofenderse por; ~**ional** [ɪk'sepʃənl] a excepcional.

excerpt ['eksɜːpt] n extracto.

excess [ɪk'ses] n exceso; (*COMM*) excedente m; ~ **baggage** n exceso de equipaje; ~**fare** n suplemento; ~**ive** a excesivo.

exchange [ɪks'tʃeɪndʒ] n cambio; (*of goods*) canje m; (*of ideas*) intercambio; (*also*: **telephone** ~) central f (telefónica) // vt cambiar; canjear.

exchequer [ɪks'tʃekə*] n hacienda.

excise ['eksaɪz] n impuestos mpl sobre el comercio exterior // [ɪk'saɪz] suprimir.

excite [ɪk'saɪt] vt (*stimulate*) excitar; (*awaken*) despertar; (*move*) entusiasmar; **to get** ~**d** emocionarse; ~**ment** n emoción f; (*anticipation*) ilusión f; (*agitation*) agitación f; **exciting** a emocionante.

exclaim [ɪk'skleɪm] vi exclamar; **exclamation** [eksklə'meɪʃən] n exclamación f; **exclamation mark** n punto de admiración f.

exclude [ɪk'skluːd] vt excluir; (*except*) exceptuar; **exclusion** [ɪk'skluːʒən] n exclusión f.

exclusive [ɪk'skluːsɪv] a exclusivo; (*club, district*) selecto; ~ **of tax** excluyendo impuestos; ~**ly** ad únicamente.

excommunicate [ekskə'mjuːnɪkeɪt] vt excomulgar.

excrement ['ekskrəmənt] n excremento.

excrete [ɪk'skriːt] vi excretar.

excruciating [ɪk'skruːʃɪeɪtɪŋ] a agudísimo, atroz.

excursion [ɪk'skɔːʃən] n excursión f.

excusable [ɪk'skjuːzəbl] a perdonable.

excuse [ɪk'skjuːs] n disculpa, excusa; (*evasion*) pretexto // vt [ɪk'skjuːz] disculpar, perdonar; **to** ~ **sb from doing sth** dispensar a uno de hacer algo; ~ **me!** ¡perdón!; **if you will** ~ **me** con su permiso.

execute ['eksɪkjuːt] vt (*plan*) realizar; (*order*) cumplir; (*person*) ajusticiar, ejecutar; **execution** n realización f; cumplimiento; ejecución f; **executioner** n verdugo.

executive [ɪg'zekjutɪv] n (*COMM, POL*) ejecutivo // a ejecutivo.

executor [ɪg'zekjutə*] n albacea m, testamentario.

exemplary [ɪg'zemplərɪ] a ejemplar.

exemplify [ɪg'zemplɪfaɪ] vt ejemplificar.

exempt [ɪg'zempt] a: ~ **from** exento de // vt: **to** ~ **sb from** eximir a uno de; ~**ion** [ɪg'zempʃən] n exención f; (*immunity*) inmunidad f.

exercise ['eksəsaɪz] n ejercicio // vt ejercer; (*right*) valerse de; (*dog*) llevar de paseo // vi hacer ejercicio(s); ~ **book** n cuaderno.

exert [ɪg'zɜːt] vt ejercer; **to** ~ **o.s.** esforzarse, afanarse; (*overdo things*) trabajar demasiado; ~**ion** n esfuerzo.

exhaust [ɪg'zɔːst] n (*pipe*) escape m; (*fumes*) gases mpl de escape // vt agotar; ~**ion** [ɪg'zɔːstʃən] n agotamiento; **nervous** ~**ion** postración f nerviosa; ~**ive** a exhaustivo.

exhibit [ɪg'zɪbɪt] n (*ART*) obra expuesta; (*LAW*) objeto expuesto // vt (*show*) manifestar; (*emotion*) acusar; (*film*) presentar; (*paintings*) exponer; ~**ion** [eksɪ'bɪʃən] n exposición f; ~**ionist** [eksɪ'bɪʃənɪst] n exhibicionista m/f.

exhilarating [ɪg'zɪləreɪtɪŋ] a estimulante, tónico.

exhort [ɪg'zɔːt] vt exhortar.

exile ['eksaɪl] n exilio; (*person*) exiliado/a // vt desterrar, exiliar.

exist [ɪg'zɪst] vi existir; (*live*) vivir; ~**ence** n existencia; (*life*) vida; ~**ing** a existente, actual.

exit ['eksɪt] n salida.

exonerate [ɪg'zɔnəreɪt] vt: **to** ~ **from** exculpar de.

exorcize ['eksɔːsaɪz] vt exorcizar.

exotic [ɪg'zɔtɪk] a exótico.

expand [ɪk'spænd] vt (*widen*) ensanchar; (*number*) aumentar // vi (*trade etc*) expandirse; (*gas, metal*) dilatarse.

expanse [ɪk'spæns] n extensión f; (*of wings*) envergadura.

expansion [ɪk'spænʃən] n (*of town*) ensanche m; (*of trade*) expansión f.

expatriate [eks'pætrɪət] n expatriado/a.

expect [ɪk'spekt] vt (*gen*) esperar; (*count*

on) contar con; (*suppose*) suponer // *vi*: to be ~ing estar encinta; ~ant mother *n* mujer *f* encinta; ~ation [ɛkspɛk'teɪʃən] *n* esperanza, expectativa.

expedience [ɛk'spiːdɪəns], expediency [ɛk'spiːdɪənsɪ] *n* conveniencia; expedient *a* conveniente, oportuno // *n* recurso, expediente *m*.

expedition [ɛkspə'dɪʃən] *n* expedición *f*.

expel [ɪk'spɛl] *vt* arrojar; (*SCOL*) expulsar.

expend [ɪk'spɛnd] *vt* gastar; (*use up*) consumir; ~able *a* prescindible; ~iture *n* gastos *mpl*, desembolso.

expense [ɪk'spɛns] *n* gasto, gastos *mpl*; (*high cost*) costa; ~s *npl* (*COMM*) gastos *mpl*; at the ~ of a costa *o* expensas de; ~ account *n* cuenta de gastos.

expensive [ɪk'spɛnsɪv] *a* caro, costoso.

experience [ɪk'spɪərɪəns] *n* experiencia // *vt* experimentar; (*suffer*) sufrir; ~d *a* experimentado.

experiment [ɪk'spɛrɪmənt] *n* experimento // *vi* hacer experimentos; ~al [-'mɛntl] *a* experimental.

expert ['ɛkspəːt] *a* experto, perito // *n* experto, perito; (*specialist*) especialista *m/f*; ~ise [-'tiːz] *n* pericia.

expire [ɪk'spaɪə*] *vi* (*gen*) expirar; (*end*) terminar; (*run out*) caducar, vencerse; expiry *n* expiración *f*; terminación *f*; vencimiento.

explain [ɪk'spleɪn] *vt* explicar; (*clarify*) aclarar; (*demonstrate*) exponer; explanation [ɛksplə'neɪʃən] *n* explicación *f*; aclaración *f*; explanatory [ɪk'splænətrɪ] *a* explicativo; aclaratorio.

explicit [ɪk'splɪsɪt] *a* explícito.

explode [ɪk'spləud] *vi* estallar, explotar; (*with anger*) reventar // *vt* volar, explotar.

exploit ['ɛksplɔɪt] *n* hazaña // [ɪk'splɔɪt] explotar; ~ation [-'teɪʃən] *n* explotación *f*.

exploration [ɛksplə'reɪʃən] *n* exploración *f*; exploratory [ɪk'splɔrətrɪ] *a* (*fig*: *talks*) exploratorio, de sondaje.

explore [ɪk'splɔː*] *vt* explorar; (*fig*) examinar, sondar; explorer *n* explorador *m*.

explosion [ɪk'spləuʒən] *n* explosión *f*; explosive [-sɪv] *a*, *n* explosivo.

exponent [ɪk'spəunənt] *n* exponente *m/f*, intérprete *m/f*.

export [ɛk'spɔːt] *vt* exportar // *n* ['ɛkspɔːt] exportación *f* // *cpd* de exportación; ~ation [-'teɪʃən] *n* exportación *f*; ~er *n* exportador *m*.

expose [ɪk'spəuz] *vt* exponer; (*unmask*) desenmascarar; ~d *a* expuesto; (*position*) desabrigado.

exposure [ɪk'spəuʒə*] *n* exposición *f*; (*PHOT*) revelación *f*; (: *shot*) fotografía; to die from ~ (*MED*) morir de frío; ~ meter *n* fotómetro.

expound [ɪk'spaund] *vt* exponer, explicar.

express [ɪk'sprɛs] *a* (*definite*) expreso, explícito; (*letter etc*) urgente // *n* (*train*) rápido // *ad* (*send*) por carta urgente // *vt* expresar; (*squeeze*) exprimir; ~ion [ɪk-

'sprɛʃən] *n* expresión *f*; ~ive *a* expresivo; ~ly *ad* expresamente.

expulsion [ɪk'spʌlʃən] *n* expulsión *f*.

exquisite [ɛk'skwɪzɪt] *a* exquisito.

extend [ɪk'stɛnd] *vt* (*visit, street*) prolongar; (*building*) ensanchar; (*offer*) ofrecer // *vi* (*land*) extenderse.

extension [ɪk'stɛnʃən] *n* extensión *f*; (*building*) ampliación *f*; (*TEL*: *line*) línea derivada; (: *telephone*) extensión *f*; (*of deadline*) prórroga.

extensive [ɪk'stɛnsɪv] *a* (*gen*) extenso; (*broad*) vasto, ancho; (*frequent*) general, común; he's travelled ~ly ha viajado por muchos países.

extent [ɪk'stɛnt] *n* (*breadth*) extensión *f*; (*scope*) alcance *m*; to some ~ hasta cierto punto; to the ~ of... hasta el punto de...; to such an ~ that... hasta tal punto que...; to what ~? ¿hasta qué punto?

exterior [ɛk'stɪərɪə*] *a* exterior, externo // *n* exterior *m*; (*appearance*) aspecto.

exterminate [ɪk'stəːmɪneɪt] *vt* exterminar; extermination [-'neɪʃən] *n* exterminación *f*.

external [ɛk'stəːnl] *a* externo, exterior; ~ly *ad* por fuera.

extinct [ɪk'stɪŋkt] *a* extinto; ~ion [ɪk-'stɪŋkʃən] *n* extinción *f*.

extinguish [ɪk'stɪŋgwɪʃ] *vt* extinguir, apagar; ~er *n* extintor *m*.

extort [ɪk'stɔːt] *vt* sacar a la fuerza (*from sb* de uno); ~ion [ɪk'stɔːʃən] *n* exacción *f*; ~ionate [ɪk'stɔːʃnət] *a* excesivo, exorbitante.

extra ['ɛkstrə] *a* adicional; (*excessive*) de más, de sobra; (*bonus*: *payment*) extraordinario // *ad* (*in addition*) especialmente // *n* (*addition*) extra *m*, suplemento; (*THEATRE*) extra *m/f*, comparsa *m/f*; (*newspaper*) edición *f* extraordinaria.

extra... [ɛkstrə] *pref* extra... .

extract [ɪk'strækt] *vt* sacar, extraer; (*confession*) arrancar, obtener // *n* ['ɛkstrækt] extracto.

extradite ['ɛkstrədaɪt] *vt* (*from country*) conceder la extradición de; (*to country*) obtener la extradición de; extradition [-'dɪʃən] *n* extradición *f*.

extramarital [ɛkstrə'mærɪtl] *a* extra-matrimonial.

extramural [ɛkstrə'mjuərl] *a* de extramuros.

extraordinary [ɪk'strɔːdnrɪ] *a* extra-ordinario; (*odd*) raro.

extravagant [ɪk'strævəgənt] *a* (*lavish*) pródigo; (*wasteful*) derrochador(a); (*price*) exorbitante; (*praise*) excesivo; (*odd*) raro.

extreme [ɪk'striːm] *a* extremo; (*poverty etc*) extremado; (*case*) excepcional // *n* extremo, extremidad *f*; ~ly *ad* sumamente, extremadamente; extremist *a*, *n* extremista *m/f*.

extremity [ɪk'strɛmɪtɪ] *n* extremidad *f*, punta; (*need*) apuro, necesidad *f*.

extricate ['ɛkstrɪkeɪt] *vt* librar.

extrovert ['ɛkstrəvəːt] n extrovertido/a.

exuberant [ɪg'zjuːbərnt] a (person) eufórico; (style) exuberante.

exude [ɪg'zjuːd] vt rezumar, sudar.

exult [ɪg'zʌlt] vi regocijarse.

eye [aɪ] n ojo // vt mirar de soslayo, ojear; **to keep an ~ on** vigilar, estar pendiente de; **~ball** n globo del ojo; **~bath** n ojera; **~brow** n ceja; **~brow pencil** n lápiz m de cejas; **~-catching** a llamativo; **~drops** npl gotas fpl para los ojos, **~lash** n pestaña; **~lid** n párpado; **~opener** n revelación f, gran sorpresa; **~shadow** n sombreador m de ojos; **~sight** n vista; **~sore** n monstruosidad f; **~wash** n (fig) disparates mpl, tonterías fpl; **~ witness** n testigo m/f presencial.

eyrie ['ɪərɪ] n aguilera.

F

F. abbr of **Fahrenheit.**

fable ['feɪbl] n fábula.

fabric ['fæbrɪk] n tejido, tela.

fabrication [fæbrɪ'keɪʃən] n invención f.

fabulous ['fæbjuləs] a fabuloso.

façade [fə'sɑːd] n fachada.

face [feɪs] n cara; (ANAT) cara, rostro; (of clock) esfera; (side, surface) superficie f // vt (person) encararse con; (building) dar a; **to lose ~** desprestigiarse; **in the ~ of** (difficulties etc) en vista de; **on the ~ of it** a primera vista; **~ to ~** cara a cara; **to ~ up to** vt fus hacer frente a, arrostrar; **~ cloth** n paño; **~ cream** n crema (de belleza); **~ lift** n cirugía estética; **~ powder** n polvos mpl; **~-saving** a para salvar las apariencias.

facet ['fæsɪt] n faceta.

facetious [fə'siːʃəs] a chistoso.

face value ['feɪs'væljuː] n (of stamp) valor m nominal; **to take sth at ~** (fig) tomar algo en sentido literal, aceptar las apariencias de algo.

facial ['feɪʃəl] a de la cara.

facile ['fæsaɪl] a superficial, ligero.

facilitate [fə'sɪlɪteɪt] vt facilitar.

facilities [fə'sɪlɪtɪz] npl facilidades fpl.

facing ['feɪsɪŋ] prep frente a // a de enfrente.

fact [fækt] n hecho; **in ~** en realidad.

faction ['fækʃən] n facción f.

factor ['fæktə*] n factor m.

factory ['fæktərɪ] n fábrica.

factual ['fæktjuəl] a objetivo.

faculty ['fækəltɪ] n facultad f; (US: teaching staff) profesorado.

fade [feɪd] vi desteñirse; (sound, hope) desvanecerse; (light) apagarse; (flower) marchitarse.

fag [fæg] n (col: cigarette) pitillo; **~ end** n colilla; **~ged out** a (col) agotado.

fail [feɪl] vt (candidate) suspender; (exam) no aprobar // vi acabarse; (engine) fallar; (voice) desfallecer; (patient) debilitarse; **to ~ to do sth** (neglect) dejar de hacer algo;

(be unable) no poder hacer algo; **without ~** sin falta; **~ing** n falta, defecto // prep a falta de; **~ure** ['feɪljə*] n fracaso; (person) fracasado/a; (mechanical etc) fallo.

faint [feɪnt] a débil; (recollection) vago; (mark) apenas visible // n desmayo // vi desmayarse; **to feel ~** estar mareado, marearse; **~hearted** a pusilánime; **~ly** ad débilmente, vagamente; **~ness** n debilidad f.

fair [fɛə*] a justo; (colour) rubio; (weather) bueno; (good enough) suficiente; (sizeable) considerable // ad (play) limpio // n feria; (fuafair) parque m de atracciones; **~ly** ad (justly) con justicia; (equally) equitativamente; (quite) bastante; **~ness** n justicia; (impartiality) imparcialidad f.

fairy ['fɛərɪ] n hada; **~ tale** n cuento de hadas.

faith [feɪθ] n fe f; (trust) confianza; (sect) religión f; **~ful** a fiel; **~fully** ad fielmente; **yours ~fully** le saluda atentamente.

fake [feɪk] n (painting etc) falsificación f; (person) impostor m // a falso // vt fingir; (painting etc) falsificar; **his illness is a ~** su enfermedad es una invención.

falcon ['fɔːlkən] n halcón m.

fall [fɔːl] n caída; (US: autumn) otoño // vi, pt **fell**, pp **fallen** ['fɔːlən] caer, caerse; (price) bajar; **~s** npl (waterfall) cascada, salto de agua; **to ~ flat** vi (on one's face) caerse (boca abajo); (plan) fracasar; **to ~ back** vi retroceder; **to ~ back on** vt fus (remedy etc) recurrir a; **to ~ backwards** vi caer de espaldas; **to ~ behind** vi quedarse atrás; **to ~ down** vi (person) caerse; (building, hopes) derrumbarse; **to ~ for** vt fus (trick) dejarse engañar por; (person) enamorarse de; **to ~ in** vi (roof) hundirse; (MIL) alinearse; **to ~ off** vi caerse; (diminish) disminuir; **to ~ out** vi (friends etc) reñir; (MIL) romper filas; **to ~ through** vi (plan, project) fracasar.

fallacy ['fæləsɪ] n (error) error m; (lie) mentira.

fallible ['fæləbl] a falible.

fallout ['fɔːlaut] n lluvia radioactiva; **~ shelter** n refugio contra ataques nucleares.

false [fɔːls] a (gen) falso; (hair, teeth etc) postizo; (disloyal) desleal, traidor(a); **under ~ pretences** con engaños; **~hood** n (lie) mentira; (falseness) falsedad f; **~ly** ad (accuse) falsamente; **~ teeth** npl dentadura postiza sg.

falter ['fɔːltə*] vi vacilar.

fame [feɪm] n fama.

familiar [fə'mɪlɪə*] a familiar; (well-known) conocido; (subject) estar enterado de; **to be ~ with** (subject) estar enterado de; **~ity** [fəmɪlɪ'ærɪtɪ] n familiaridad f; **~ize** [fə'mɪlɪəraɪz] vt: **to ~ize o.s. with** familiarizarse con.

family ['fæmɪlɪ] n familia; **~ business** n

negocio familiar; ~ **doctor** n médico de cabecera.

famine ['fæmɪn] n hambre f.

famished ['fæmɪʃt] a hambriento.

famous ['feɪməs] a famoso, célebre; ~**ly** ad (get on) estupendamente.

fan [fæn] n abanico; (ELEC) ventilador m; (person) aficionado/a // vt abanicar; (fire, quarrel) atizar; **to** ~ **out** vi desparramarse.

fanatic [fə'nætɪk] n fanático/a; ~**al** a fanático.

fan belt ['fænbɛlt] n correa de ventilador.

fanciful ['fænsɪful] a (gen) fantástico; (imaginary) imaginario.

fancy ['fænsɪ] n (whim) capricho, antojo; (taste) afición f, gusto; (imagination) imaginación f; (delusion) quimera // a (decorative) hermoso; (luxury) de lujo; (as decoration) de adorno // vt (feel like, want) tener ganas de; (imagine) imaginarse; (think) creer; **to take a** ~ **to** encapricharse por, tomar afición a; **it took** or **caught my** ~ me cayó en gracia; **to** ~ **that...** imaginarse que...; **he fancies her** le gusta (ella); ~ **dress** n disfraz m; ~**-dress ball** n baile m de disfraces.

fang [fæŋ] n colmillo.

fantastic [fæn'tæstɪk] a fantástico.

fantasy ['fæntəzɪ] n fantasía.

far [fɑː*] a (distant) lejano // ad lejos; ~ **away**, ~ **off** (a lo) lejos; ~ **better** mucho mejor; ~ **from** lejos de; **by** ~ con mucho; **go as** ~ **as the farm** vaya hasta la granja; **as** ~ **as I know** que yo sepa; **how** ~? ¿hasta dónde?; (fig) ¿hasta qué punto?; **the F** ~ **East** el Extremo Oriente; ~**away** a remoto.

farce [fɑːs] n farsa; **farcical** a absurdo.

fare [fɛə*] n (on trains, buses) precio (del billete); (in taxi: cost) tarifa; (: passenger) pasajero; (food) comida.

farewell [fɛə'wɛl] excl. n adiós m.

farm [fɑːm] n granja, finca, estancia (AM) // vt cultivar; ~**er** n granjero, estanciero (AM); ~**hand** n peón m; ~**house** n casa de labranza; ~**ing** n (gen) agricultura; (tilling) cultivo; ~**land** n tierra de cultivo; ~ **worker** n = ~**hand**; ~**yard** n corral m.

far-sighted ['fɑː'saɪtɪd] a previsor(a).

fart [fɑːt] (col!) n pedo // vi tirarse un pedo.

farther ['fɑːðə*] ad más lejos, más allá.

farthest ['fɑːðɪst] superlative of **far.**

fascinate ['fæsɪneɪt] vt fascinar; **fascination** [-'neɪʃən] n fascinación f.

fascism ['fæʃɪzəm] n fascismo; **fascist** [-ɪst] a, n fascista m/f.

fashion ['fæʃən] n moda; (manner) manera // vt formar; **in** ~ a la moda; **out of** ~ pasado de moda; ~**able** a de moda; ~ **show** n desfile m de modelos.

fast [fɑːst] a rápido; (dye, colour) sólido; (clock): **to be** ~ estar adelantado // ad rápidamente, de prisa; (stuck, held) firmemente // n ayuno // vi ayunar; ~

asleep profundamente dormido.

fasten ['fɑːsn] vt asegurar, sujetar; (coat, belt) abrochar // vi cerrarse; ~**er**, ~**ing** n (gen) cierre m; (of door etc) cerrojo; **zip** ~**er** cremallera.

fastidious [fæs'tɪdɪəs] a (fussy) delicado; (demanding) exigente.

fat [fæt] a gordo; (meat) con mucha grasa; (greasy) grasiento // n grasa; (on person) carnes fpl; (lard) manteca.

fatal ['feɪtl] a (gen) fatal; (injury) mortal; (consequence) funesto; ~**ism** n fatalismo; ~**ity** [fə'tælɪtɪ] n (road death etc) víctima m/f; ~**ly** ad: ~**ly injured** herido a muerte.

fate [feɪt] n destino; (of person) suerte f; ~**ful** a fatídico.

father ['fɑːðə*] n padre m; ~**hood** n paternidad f; ~**-in-law** r suegro; ~**ly** a paternal.

fathom ['fæðəm] n braza // vt (NAUT) sondear; (unravel) desentrañar; (understand) lograr comprender.

fatigue [fə'tiːg] n fatiga, cansancio.

fatten ['fætn] vt, vi engordar.

fatty ['fætɪ] a (food) graso // n (fam) gordito/a, gordinflón/ona m/f.

faucet ['fɔːsɪt] n (US) grifo.

fault [fɔːlt] n (error) falta; (blame) culpa; (defect: in character) defecto; (in manufacture) desperfecto; (GEO) falla // vt tachar; **it's my** ~ es culpa mía; **to find** ~ **with** criticar, poner peros a; **at** ~ culpable; ~**less** a (action) intachable; (person) sin defectos; ~**y** a defectuoso.

fauna ['fɔːnə] n fauna.

faux pas ['fəu'pɑː] n paso en falso; (gaffe) plancha.

favour, favor (US) ['feɪvə*] n favor m; (support) apoyo; (approval) aprobación f // vt (proposition) estar a favor de, aprobar; (person etc) favorecer; (assist) ser propicio a; **to ask a** ~ **of** pedir un favor a; **to do sb a** ~ hacer un favor a uno; **to find** ~ **with** caer en gracia de; **in** ~ **of** a favor de; ~**able** a favorable; ~**ite** [-rɪt] a, n favorito, preferido; ~**itism** n favoritismo.

fawn [fɔːn] n cervato // a (also: ~-coloured) color de cervato, leonado.

fear [fɪə*] n miedo, temor m // vt tener miedo a o de, temer; **for** ~ **of** por temor a; ~**ful** a temeroso, miedoso; (cowardly) tímido; (awful) terrible; ~**less** a (gen) sin miedo o temor; (bold) audaz.

feasible ['fiːzəbl] a factible.

feast [fiːst] n banquete m; (REL: also: ~ **day**) fiesta // vt, vi banquetear.

feat [fiːt] n hazaña.

feather ['fɛðə*] n pluma; ~-**weight** n (BOXING) peso pluma.

feature ['fiːtʃə*] n (gen) característica; (ANAT) rasgo; (article) crónica // vt (subj: film) presentar // vi figurar; ~**s** npl (of face) facciones fpl; ~ **film** n película (de largo metraje).

February ['fɛbruərɪ] n febrero.

fed [fɛd] *pt, pp* of **feed**.

federal ['fɛdərəl] *a* federal; **federation** [-'reɪʃən] *n* federación *f.*

fed-up [fɛd'ʌp] *a*: **to be ~** estar harto.

fee [fi:] *n* derechos *mpl*, honorarios *mpl*; (*of school*) matrícula; (*of club*) cuota.

feeble ['fi:bl] *a* débil; **~-minded** *a* imbécil.

feed [fi:d] *n* (*gen*) comida; (*of baby*) alimento infantil; (*of animal*) pienso // *vt, pt, pp* fed (*gen*) alimentar; (*baby: breastfeed*) dar el pecho a; (*animal*) dar de comer a; (*data, information*): **to ~ into** suministrar a; **to ~ on** *vt fus* alimentarse de; **~ing bottle** *n* biberón *m.*

feel [fi:l] *n* (*sensation*) sensación *f*; (*sense of touch*) tacto // *vt, pt, pp* felt tocar, palpar; (*cold, pain etc*) sentir; (*think, believe*) creer; **to ~ hungry/cold** tener hambre/frío; **to ~ lonely/better** sentirse solo/mejor; **it ~s soft** es suave al tacto; **to ~ like** (*want*) tener ganas de; **to ~ about** *or* **around** tantear; **~er** *n* (*of insect*) antena; **to put out ~ers** (*fig*) sondear; **~ing** *n* (*gen*) sensación *f*; (*foreboding*) presentimiento; (*opinion*) opinión *f*; (*emotion*) sentimiento.

feet [fi:t] *pl* of **foot**.

feign [feɪn] *vt* fingir.

feline ['fi:laɪn] *a* felino.

fell [fɛl] *pt* of **fall** // *vt* (*tree*) talar.

fellow ['fɛləu] *n* (*gen*) tipo; (*fam*) tío; (*of learned society*) socio; **~ student** *n* compañeros *mpl* de curso, condiscípulos *mpl*; **~ citizen** *n* conciudadano; **~ countryman** *n* compatriota *m/f*; **~ men** *npl* semejantes *mpl*; **~ship** *n* compañerismo; (*grant*) beca.

felony ['fɛlənɪ] *n* crimen *m.*

felt [fɛlt] *pt, pp* of **feel** // *n* fieltro; **~-tip pen** *n* rotulador *m.*

female ['fi:meɪl] *n* (*woman*) mujer *f*; (*ZOOL*) hembra // *a* femenino.

feminine ['fɛmɪnɪn] *a* femenino.

feminist ['fɛmɪnɪst] *n* feminista.

fence [fɛns] *n* valla, cerca // *vt* (*also: ~ in*) cercar // *vi* hacer esgrima; **fencing** *n* esgrima.

fend [fɛnd] *vi*: **to ~ for o.s.** arreglárselas por su cuenta.

fender ['fɛndə*] *n* guardafuego; (*US: AUT*) parachoques *m inv*; (: *RAIL*) trompa.

ferment [fə'mɛnt] *vi* fermentar // *n* ['fə:mɛnt] (*fig*) agitación *f*; **~ation** [-'teɪʃən] *n* fermentación *f.*

fern [fə:n] *n* helecho.

ferocious [fə'rəuʃəs] *a* feroz; **ferocity** [-'rɔsɪtɪ] *n* ferocidad *f.*

ferret ['fɛrɪt] *n* hurón *m* // *vt*: **to ~ out** descubrir.

ferry ['fɛrɪ] *n* (*small*) barca (de pasaje), balsa; (*large: also:* **~boat**) transbordador *m* // *vt* transportar.

fertile ['fə:taɪl] *a* fértil; (*BIOL*) fecundo; **fertility** [fə'tɪlɪtɪ] *n* fertilidad *f*; fecundidad *f*; **fertilize** ['fə:tɪlaɪz] *vt* fertilizar;

fecundar; (*AGR*) abonar; **fertilizer** *n* fertilizante *m.*

fervent ['fə:vənt] *a* ardiente, apasionado.

fester ['fɛstə*] *vi* ulcerarse.

festival ['fɛstɪvəl] *n* (*REL*) fiesta; (*ART, MUS*) festival *m.*

festive ['fɛstɪv] *a* festivo; **the ~ season** (*Christmas*) las Navidades.

festivities [fɛs'tɪvɪtɪz] *npl* fiestas *fpl.*

fetch [fɛtʃ] *vt* ir a buscar; (*sell for*) venderse por.

fetching ['fɛtʃɪŋ] *a* atractivo.

fête [feɪt] *n* fiesta.

fetish ['fɛtɪʃ] *n* fetiche *m.*

fetters ['fɛtəz] *npl* grillos *mpl.*

feud [fju:d] *n* (*hostility*) enemistad *f*; (*quarrel*) disputa.

feudal ['fju:dl] *a* feudal; **~ism** *n* feudalismo.

fever ['fi:və*] *n* fiebre *f*; **~ish** *a* febril.

few [fju:] *a* (*not many*) pocos; (*some*) algunos, unos; **a ~** a unos pocos // *pron* algunos; **~er** *a* menos; **~est** a los/las menos.

fiancé [fɪ'ɑ:ŋseɪ] *n* novio, prometido; **~e** *n* novia, prometida.

fiasco [fɪ'æskəu] *n* fiasco.

fibre, fiber (*US*) ['faɪbə*] *n* fibra; **~-glass** *n* fibra de vidrio.

fickle ['fɪkl] *a* inconstante.

fiction ['fɪkʃən] *n* (*gen*) ficción *f*; **~al** *a* novelesco; **fictitious** [fɪk'tɪʃəs] *a* ficticio.

fiddle ['fɪdl] *n* (*MUS*) violín *m*; (*cheating*) trampa; (*swindle*) estafa // *vt* (*accounts*) falsificar; **to ~ with** *vt fus* jugar con; **fiddler** *n* violinista *m/f.*

fidelity [fɪ'dɛlɪtɪ] *n* fidelidad *f.*

fidget ['fɪdʒɪt] *vi* moverse nerviosamente; **~y** *a* nervioso.

field [fi:ld] *n* campo; (*ELEC*) prado; (*fig*) esfera, especialidad *f*; (*competitors*) competidores *mpl*; (*entrants*) concurrentes *mpl*; **~ glasses** *npl* gemelos *mpl*; **~ marshal** *n* mariscal *m*; **~work** *n* trabajo de campo.

fiend [fi:nd] *n* demonio; **~ish** *a* diabólico.

fierce [fɪəs] *a* feroz; (*wind, attack*) violento; (*heat*) intenso; (*fighting, enemy*) encarnizado.

fiery ['faɪərɪ] *a* (*burning*) ardiente; (*temperament*) apasionado.

fifteen [fɪf'ti:n] *num* quince.

fifth [fɪfθ] *a, n* quinto.

fiftieth ['fɪftɪɪθ] *a* quincuagésimo.

fifty ['fɪftɪ] *num* cincuenta.

fig [fɪg] *n* higo.

fight [faɪt] *n* (*gen*) pelea; (*MIL*) combate *m*; (*struggle*) lucha // *(vb: pt, pp* fought) *vt* luchar contra; (*cancer, alcoholism*) combatir // *vi* pelear, luchar; **~er** *n* combatiente *m/f*; (*fig*) luchador/a *m/f*; (*plane*) caza; **~ing** *n* (*gen*) el luchar; (*battle*) combate *m.*

figment ['fɪgmənt] *n*: **a ~ of the imagination** una quimera.

figurative ['fɪgjurətɪv] *a* figurado.

figure 260 **fit**

figure ['fɪgə*] n (DRAWING, GEOM) figura, dibujo; (number, cipher) cifra; (body, outline) talle m, tipo // vt (esp US) imaginar // vi (appear) figurar; **to ~ out** vt (understand) comprender; **~head** n mascarón m de proa; **~ skating** n patinaje m de figuras.

file [faɪl] n (tool) lima; (dossier) expediente m; (folder) carpeta; (row) fila // vt limar; (papers) clasificar; (LAW: claim) presentar; (store) archivar; **to ~ in/out** vi entrar/salir en fila; **to ~ past** vt fus desfilar ante; **filing** n el archivar; **filing cabinet** n fichero, archivo.

fill [fɪl] vt llenar // n: **to eat one's ~** llenarse; **to ~ in** vt rellenar; **to ~ up** vt llenar (hasta el borde) // vi (AUT) poner gasolina.

fillet ['fɪlɪt] n filete m.

filling ['fɪlɪŋ] n (CULIN) relleno; (for tooth) empaste m; **~ station** n estación f de servicio.

film [fɪlm] n película // vt (scene) filmar // vi rodar (una película); **~ star** n astro, estrella de cine; **~strip** n tira de película.

filter ['fɪltə*] n filtro // vt filtrar; **~ tip** n boquilla.

filth [fɪlθ] n suciedad f; **~y** a sucio; (language) obsceno.

fin [fɪn] n (gen) aleta.

final ['faɪnl] a (last) final, último; (definitive) definitivo, terminante // n (SPORT) final f; **~s** npl (SCOL) exámenes mpl finales.

finale [fɪ'nɑːlɪ] n final m.

final: ~ist n (SPORT) finalista m/f; **~ize** vt concluir, completar; **~ly** ad (lastly) por último, finalmente; (eventually) por fin; (irrevocably) de modo definitivo.

finance [faɪ'næns] n (money) fondos mpl; **~s** npl finanzas fpl // vt financiar; **financial** [-'nænʃəl] a financiero; (economic) económico; **financier** n (gen) financiero; (investor) inversionista m/f.

find [faɪnd] pt, pp **found** vt (gen) encontrar, hallar; (come upon) descubrir // n hallazgo; descubrimiento; **to ~ sb guilty** (LAW) declarar culpable a uno; **to ~ out** vt averiguar; (truth, secret) descubrir; **to ~ out about** (by chance) enterarse de; **~ings** npl (LAW) veredicto sg, fallo sg; (of report) recomendaciones fpl.

fine [faɪn] a (delicate) fino; (good) bueno; (beautiful) bonito // ad (well) bien; (small) delgado // n (LAW) multa // vt (LAW) multar; **to be ~** (weather) hacer buen tiempo; **~ arts** npl bellas artes fpl.

finery ['faɪnərɪ] n adornos mpl.

finesse [fɪ'nɛs] n sutileza.

finger ['fɪŋgə*] n dedo // vt (touch) manosear; (MUS) tocar (distraídamente); **little/index ~** dedo meñique/índice; **~nail** n uña; **~print** n huella dactilar; **~tip** n yema del dedo.

finicky ['fɪnɪkɪ] a (fussy) delicado.

finish ['fɪnɪʃ] n (end) fin m; (goal) meta; (polish etc) acabado // vt, vi terminar; **to ~ off** vt acabar, terminar; (kill) acabar con; **to ~ third** llegar el tercero; **~ing line** n línea de llegada o meta.

finite ['faɪnaɪt] a finito.

Finland ['fɪnlənd] n Finlandia.

Finn [fɪn] n finlandés/esa m/f; **~ish** a finlandés(esa) // n (LING) finlandés m.

fiord [fjɔːd] n fiordo.

fir [fəː*] n abeto.

fire ['faɪə*] n (gen) fuego; (accidental) incendio // vt (gun) disparar; (set fire to) incendiar; (excite) exaltar; (interest) despertar; (dismiss) despedir // vi encenderse; **on ~** ardiendo, en llamas; **~ alarm** n alarma de incendios; **~arm** n arma de fuego; **~ brigade** n (cuerpo de) bomberos mpl; **~ engine** n coche m de bomberos; **~ escape** n escalera de incendios; **~ extinguisher** n extintor m (de fuego); **~man** n bombero; **~place** n chimenea; **~proof** a a prueba de fuego; **~side** n hogar m; **~ station** n parque m de bomberos; **~wood** n leña; **~works** npl fuegos mpl artificiales.

firing ['faɪərɪŋ] n (MIL) disparos mpl, tiroteo; **~ squad** n pelotón m de ejecución.

firm [fəːm] a firme // n firma; **~ly** ad firmemente; **~ness** n firmeza.

first [fəːst] a primero // ad (before others) primero; (when listing reasons etc) en primer lugar, primeramente // n (person: in race) primero; (AUT) primera; **at ~** al principio; **~ of all** ante todo; **~-aid kit** n botiquín m; **~-class** a de primera clase; **~-hand** a de primera mano; **~ly** ad en primer lugar; **~ name** n nombre m de pila; **~-rate** a de primera clase.

fir tree n abeto.

fiscal ['fɪskəl] a fiscal.

fish [fɪʃ] n, pl inv pez m; (food) pescado // vt, vi pescar; **to go ~ing** ir de pesca; **~erman** n pescador m; **~ery** n pesquería; **~ fingers** npl dedos mpl de pescado; **~ing boat** n barca de pesca; **~ing line** n sedal m; **~ing rod** n caña (de pescar); **~ing tackle** n aparejo (de pescar); **~ market** n mercado de pescado; **~monger** n pescadero; **~monger's (shop)** n pescadería; **~y** a (fig) sospechoso.

fission ['fɪʃən] n fisión f.

fissure ['fɪʃə*] n fisura.

fist [fɪst] n puño.

fit [fɪt] a (MED, SPORT) en (buena) forma; (proper) adecuado, apropiado // vt (clothes) sentar bien a; (try on: clothes) probar; (facts) cuadrar o corresponder con; (accommodate) ajustar, adaptar; (correspond exactly) encajar en // vi (clothes) entallar; (in space, gap) caber; (correspond) corresponder // n (MED) ataque m; **~ to** apto para; **~ for** apropiado para; **this dress is a good ~** este vestido me sienta bien; **to ~ in** vi (gen) encajarse; (fig: person) llevarse bien (con todos); **to ~ out** (also ~ **up**) vt equipar; **~ful** a espasmódico, intermitente; **~ment** n mueble m; **~ness** n (MED) salud f; (of remark) conveniencia; **~ter** n ajustador m; **~ting** a apropiado // n (of dress) prueba; **~tings** npl instalaciones fpl.

five [faiv] num cinco; **fiver** n (Brit: col) billete m de cinco libras.

fix [fiks] vt (secure) fijar, asegurar; (mend) arreglar // n: **to be in a ~** estar en un aprieto; **~ed** [fikst] a (prices etc) fijo; **~ture** ['fikstʃə*] n cosa fija; (furniture) mueble m fijo; (SPORT) partido.

fizz [fiz] vi hacer efervescencia.

fizzle ['fizl]: **~ out** vi apagarse.

fizzy ['fizi] a (drink) gaseoso; (gen) efervescente.

fjord [fjɔːd] = **fiord**.

flabbergasted ['flæbəgɑːstid] a pasmado.

flabby ['flæbi] a flojo; (fat) gordo.

flag [flæg] n bandera; (stone) losa // vi acabarse, decaer; **to ~ sb down** hacer signos a uno para que se detenga; **~pole** n asta de bandera.

flagrant ['fleigrənt] a flagrante.

flair [fleə*] n aptitud f especial.

flake [fleik] n (of rust, paint) escama; (of snow, soap powder) copo // vi (also: ~ **off**) desprenderse en escamas.

flamboyant [flæm'bɔiənt] a (dress) vistoso; (person) extravagante.

flame [fleim] n llama.

flamingo [flə'miŋgəu] n flamenco.

flammable ['flæməbl] a inflamable.

flan [flæn] n tarta.

flank [flæŋk] n flanco; (of person) costado // vt flanquear.

flannel ['flænl] n (also: **face ~**) paño; (fabric) franela; (col) coba; **~s** npl pantalones mpl de franela.

flap [flæp] n (of pocket) cartera; (of envelope) solapa; (of table) hoja (plegadiza); (wing movement) aletazo // vt (wings) aletear // vi (sail, flag) ondear.

flare [fleə*] n llamarada; (MIL) bengala; (in skirt etc) vuelo; **to ~ up** vi encenderse; (fig: person) encolerizarse; (: revolt) estallar.

flash [flæʃ] n relámpago; (also: **news ~**) noticias fpl de última hora; (PHOT) flash m // vt (light, headlights) encender y apagar (la luz); (torch) encender // vi brillar, relampaguear; **in a ~** en un instante; he **~ed by** or **past** pasó como un rayo; **~back** n flashback m; **~ bulb** n bombilla fusible; **~er** n (AUT) intermitente m.

flashy ['flæʃi] a (pej) ostentoso.

flask [flɑːsk] n frasco; (also: **vacuum ~**) termo.

flat [flæt] a llano; (smooth) liso; (tyre) desinflado; (beer) muerto; (MUS) desafinado // n (apartment) piso, apartamento; (MUS) bemol m; (AUT) pinchazo; **~ly** ad terminantemente, de plano; **~ness** n (of land) llanura, lo llano; **~ten** vt (also: **~ten out**) allanar;

(smooth out) alisar; (demolish) aplastar.

flatter ['flætə*] vt adular, halagar; **~er** n adulador/a m/f; **~ing** a halagüeño; **~y** n adulación f.

flatulence ['flætjuləns] n flatulencia.

flaunt [flɔːnt] vt ostentar, lucir.

flavour, flavor (US) ['fleivə*] n sabor m, gusto // vt sazonar, condimentar; **~ed with** con sabor a; **~ing** n condimento.

flaw [flɔː] n defecto; **~less** a intachable.

flax [flæks] n lino; **~en** a rubio.

flea [fliː] n pulga; **~pit** n cine m de baja categoría.

flee [fliː], pt, pp **fled** [fled] vi huir de, abandonar // vi huir, fugarse.

fleece [fliːs] n vellón m; (wool) lana // vt (col) pelar.

fleet [fliːt] n (gen) flota; (of lorries etc) escuadra.

fleeting ['fliːtiŋ] a fugaz.

Flemish ['flemiʃ] a flamenco.

flesh [fleʃ] n carne f; (of fruit) pulpa; **of ~ and blood** de carne y hueso.

flew [fluː] pt of **fly**.

flex [fleks] n cordón m // vt (muscles) tensar; **~ibility** [-i'biliti] n flexibilidad f; **~ible** a flexible.

flick [flik] n golpecito; (with finger) capirotazo; (with whip) chasquido // vt dar un golpecito a; **to ~ through** vt fus hojear.

flicker ['flikə*] vi (light) parpadear; (flame) vacilar // n parpadeo.

flier ['flaiə*] n aviador/a m/f.

flight [flait] n vuelo; (escape) huida, fuga; (also: ~ **of steps**) tramo (de escaleras); **to take ~** huir, darse a la fuga; **to put to ~** ahuyentar; **~ deck** n (AVIAT) cabina.

flimsy ['flimzi] a (thin) muy ligero; (weak) débil.

flinch [flintʃ] vi acobardarse.

fling [fliŋ], pt, pp **flung** vt arrojar.

flint [flint] n pedernal m; (in lighter) piedra.

flip [flip] vt dar la vuelta a; (coin) echar a cara o cruz.

flippant ['flipənt] a poco serio.

flirt [flɜːt] vi coquetear, flirtear // n coqueta m/f; **~ation** [-'teiʃən] n coqueteo, flirteo.

flit [flit] vi revolotear.

float [fləut] n flotador m; (in procession) carroza // vi flotar; (swimmer) hacer la plancha // vt (gen) hacer flotar; (company) lanzar.

flock [flɔk] n (of sheep) rebaño; (of birds) bandada; (of people) multitud f.

flog [flɔg] vt azotar; (col) vender.

flood [flʌd] n inundación f; (of words, tears etc) torrente m // vt inundar; **~ing** n inundación f; **~light** n foco.

floor [flɔː*] n suelo; (storey) piso; (of sea) fondo; (dance ~) pista // vt (fig) dejar sin respuesta; **ground ~** (Brit), **first ~** (US) planta baja; **first ~** (Brit), **second ~**

(US) primer piso; ~**board** n tabla; ~ **show** n cabaret m.

flop [flɔp] n fracaso // vi (fail) fracasar.

floppy ['flɔpi] a flojo.

flora ['flɔːrə] n flora; **floral** ['flɔːrl] a floral.

florid ['flɔrid] a (style) florido.

florist ['flɔrist] n florista m/f; ~'s (shop) n florería.

flounce [flauns] n volante m; to ~ out vi salir enfadado.

flounder ['flaundə*] vi tropezar.

flour ['flauə*] n harina.

flourish ['flʌriʃ] vi florecer; ~**ing** a floreciente.

flout [flaut] vt burlarse de.

flow [fləu] n (movement) flujo; (direction) curso; (tide) corriente f // vi correr, fluir; (blood) derramarse.

flower ['flauə*] n flor f // vi florecer; ~**bed** n macizo; ~**pot** n tiesto; ~**y** a florido.

flown [fləun] pp of **fly**.

flu [fluː] n gripe f.

fluctuate ['flʌktjueit] vi fluctuar; **fluctuation** [-'eiʃən] n fluctuación f.

fluent ['fluːənt] a (speech) elocuente; he **speaks** ~ **French**, he's ~ **in French** domina el francés; ~**ly** ad con fluidez.

fluff [flʌf] n pelusa; ~**y** a velloso.

fluid ['fluːid] a, n fluido, líquido.

fluke [fluːk] n (col) chiripa.

flung [flʌŋ] pt, pp of **fling**.

fluorescent [fluə'resnt] a fluorescente.

fluoride ['fluəraid] n fluoruro.

flurry ['flʌri] n (of snow) ráfago; (haste) agitación f; ~ **of activity** frenesí m de actividad.

flush [flʌʃ] n (on face) rubor m; (plenty) plenitud f, abundancia // vt limpiar con agua // vi ruborizarse // a: ~ **with** a ras de; to ~ **the toilet** hacer funcionar el WC; ~**ed** a ruborizado.

flustered ['flʌstəd] a aturdido.

flute [fluːt] n flauta.

flutter ['flʌtə*] n emoción f; (of wings) revoloteo, aleteo; (fam: bet) apuesta // vi revolotear.

flux [flʌks] n flujo; **in a state of** ~ cambiando continuamente.

fly [flai] n (insect) mosca; (on trousers: also: **flies**) bragueta // (vb: pt **flew**, pp **flown**) vt (gen) hacer volar; (plane) pilot(e)ar; (cargo) transportar (en avión); (distances) recorrer (en avión) // vi volar; (passengers) ir o subir en avión; (escape) evadirse; (flag) ondear; **to let** ~ desahogarse; ~**ing** n (activity) (el) volar // a: ~**ing visit** visita relámpago; **with** ~**ing colours** con lucimiento; ~**ing saucer** n platillo volante; ~**over** n (Brit: bridge) paso a desnivel o superior; ~**past** n desfile m aéreo; ~**sheet** n (for tent) doble techo.

foal [fəul] n potro.

foam [fəum] n espuma // vi echar espuma; ~ **rubber** n espuma de caucho.

fob [fɔb] vt: **to** ~ **sb off** deshacerse de alguien con excusas.

focal ['fəukəl] a focal.

focus ['fəukəs], pl ~**es** n foco // vt (field glasses etc) enfocar; **to** ~ **on** enfocar a; **in/out of** ~ enfocado/desenfocado.

fodder ['fɔdə*] n pienso.

foe [fəu] n enemigo.

foetus ['fiːtəs] n feto.

fog [fɔg] n niebla; ~**gy** a: **it's** ~**gy** hay niebla, está brumoso.

foil [fɔil] vt frustrar // n hoja; (also: **kitchen** ~) papel m (de) aluminio; (FENCING) florete m.

fold [fəuld] n (bend, crease) pliegue m; (of skin) arruga; (AGR) redil m // vt doblar; **to** ~ **up** vi (map etc) plegarse, doblarse; (business) quebrar // vt (map etc) plegar; ~**er** n (for papers) carpeta; (brochure) folleto; ~**ing** a (chair, bed) plegable.

foliage ['fəuliidʒ] n follaje m.

folk [fəuk] npl gente f // a popular, folklórico; ~**s** npl familia, parientes mpl; ~**lore** ['fəuklɔː*] n folklore m; ~**song** n canción f popular o folklórica.

follow ['fɔləu] vt seguir // vi seguir; (result) resultar; he ~**ed suit** hizo lo mismo; **to** ~ **up** (letter, offer) responder a; (case) investigar; ~**er** n seguidor/a m/f; (POL) partidario/a; ~**ing** a siguiente // n afición f, partidarios mpl.

folly ['fɔli] n locura.

fond [fɔnd] a (loving) cariñoso; **to be** ~ **of** tener cariño a.

fondle ['fɔndl] vt acariciar.

fondness ['fɔndnis] n (for things) gusto; (for people) cariño.

font [fɔnt] n pila bautismal.

food [fuːd] n comida; ~ **mixer** n batidora; ~ **poisoning** n botulismo; ~**stuffs** npl comestibles mpl.

fool [fuːl] n tonto/a; (CULIN) puré m de frutas con nata // vt engañar // vi (gen: ~ **around**) bromear; (waste time) perder el tiempo; ~**hardy** a temerario; ~**ish** a tonto; (stupid) estúpido; (careless) imprudente; ~**proof** a (plan etc) infalible.

foot [fut], pl **feet** n pie m; (measure) pie m (= 304 mm); (of animal) pata // vt (bill) pagar; **on** ~ a pie; ~**ball** n balón m; (game) fútbol m; ~**baller** n futbolista m; ~**brake** n freno de pie; ~**bridge** n puente m para peatones; ~**hills** npl estribaciones fpl; ~**hold** n pie m firme; ~**ing** n (fig) posición f; **to lose one's** ~**ing** perder el pie; **on an equal** ~**ing** en pie de igualdad; ~**lights** npl candilejas fpl; ~**man** n lacayo; ~**note** n nota de pie; ~**path** n sendero; (pavement) acera; ~**sore** a con los pies adoloridos; ~**step** n paso; ~**wear** n calzado.

for [fɔː*] prep (gen) para; (as, in exchange for, because of) por; (during) durante; (in spite of) a pesar de // conj pues, ya que; **it was sold** ~ **100 pesetas** se vendió por 100 pesetas; **what** ~? ¿para qué?; **what's it** ~? ¿para qué sirve?; **he was away** ~

2 years estuvo fuera 2 años; he went ~ the paper fue a buscar el periódico; ~ sale se vende.

forage ['fɔrɪdʒ] n forraje m.

foray ['fɔreɪ] n incursión f.

forbid [fə'bɪd], pt **forbad(e)** [fə'bæd], pp **forbidden** [fə'bɪdn] vt prohibir; ~ding a (gloomy) lúgubre; (severe) severo.

force [fɔːs] n fuerza // vt forzar; **to** ~ **o.s.** to hacer un esfuerzo por; **the F~s** npl las Fuerzas Armadas; **in** ~ en vigor; ~d [fɔːst] a forzado; ~ful a enérgico.

forceps ['fɔːseps] npl fórceps m inv.

forcibly ['fɔːsəblɪ] ad a la fuerza.

ford [fɔːd] n vado // vt vadear.

forearm ['fɔːrɑːm] n antebrazo.

foreboding [fɔː'bəudɪŋ] n presagio.

forecast ['fɔːkɑːst] n pronóstico // vt (irg: like cast) pronosticar.

forefathers ['fɔːfɑːðəz] npl antepasados mpl.

forefinger ['fɔːfɪŋgə*] n (dedo) índice m.

forego = **forgo**.

foregone ['fɔːgɔn] a: **it's a** ~ **conclusion** es una conclusión inevitable.

foreground ['fɔːgraund] n primer plano.

forehead ['fɔrɪd] n frente f.

foreign ['fɔrɪn] a extranjero; (trade) exterior; ~er n extranjero; ~ exchange n divisas fpl; F~ Minister n Ministro de Asuntos Exteriores; F~ Office n Ministerio de Asuntos Exteriores.

foreleg ['fɔːlɛg] n pata delantera.

foreman ['fɔːmən] n capataz m; (in construction) maestro de obras.

foremost ['fɔːməust] a principal.

forensic [fə'rɛnsɪk] a forense.

forerunner ['fɔːrʌnə*] n precursor/a m/f.

foresee [fɔː'siː] (irg: like see) vt prever; ~able a previsible.

foresight ['fɔːsaɪt] n previsión f.

forest ['fɔrɪst] n bosque m.

forestall [fɔː'stɔːl] vt prevenir.

forestry ['fɔrɪstrɪ] n silvicultura.

foretaste ['fɔːteɪst] n (gen) anticipo; (sample) muestra.

foretell [fɔː'tɛl] (irg: like tell) vt predecir, pronosticar.

forever [fə'rɛvə*] ad para siempre.

foreword ['fɔːwəːd] n prefacio.

forfeit ['fɔːfɪt] n pérdida; (fine) multa // vt perder (derecho a).

forgave [fə'geɪv] pt of **forgive**.

forge [fɔːdʒ] n fragua; (smithy) herrería // vt (signature, money) falsificar; (metal) forjar; **to** ~ **ahead** vi avanzar constantemente; **forger** n falsificador/a m/f; ~ry n falsificación f.

forget [fə'gɛt], pt **forgot**, pp **forgotten** vt olvidar // vi olvidarse; ~ful a olvidadizo; ~fulness n (gen) olvido; (thoughtlessness) descuido; (oblivion) falta de memoria.

forgive [fə'gɪv], pt **forgave**, pp **forgiven** vt perdonar; **to** ~ **sb for sth** perdonar algo a uno; ~ness n perdón m.

forgo [fɔː'gəu] (irg: like go) vt (give up)

renunciar a; (go without) privarse de.

forgot [fə'gɔt] pt of **forget**.

forgotten [fə'gɔtn] pp of **forget**.

fork [fɔːk] n (for eating) tenedor m; (for gardening) horca; (of roads) bifurcación f; (in tree) horcadura // vi (road) bifurcarse; **to** ~ **out** vt (col: pay) desembolsar; ~ed [fɔːkt] a (lightning) en zigzag; ~-lift truck n elevadora-transportadora de horquilla.

form [fɔːm] n forma; (scol) clase f; (questionnaire) formulario // vt formar; **in top** ~ en plena forma.

formal ['fɔːməl] a (offer, receipt) oficial; (person etc) ceremonioso; (occasion, dinner) oficial, protocolario; (dress) de etiqueta; ~ity [-'mælɪtɪ] n ceremonia; ~ities npl formalidades fpl; ~ly ad oficialmente.

format ['fɔːmæt] n formato.

formation [fɔː'meɪʃən] n formación f.

formative ['fɔːmətɪv] a (years) formativo.

former ['fɔːmə*] a anterior; (earlier) antiguo; (ex) ex; **the** ~ ... **the latter** ... aquél ... éste ...; ~ly ad antiguamente.

formidable ['fɔːmɪdəbl] a formidable.

formula ['fɔːmjulə] n fórmula.

formulate ['fɔːmjuleɪt] vt formular.

forsake [fə'seɪk], pt **forsook** [fə'suk], pp **forsaken** [fə'seɪkən] vt (gen) abandonar; (plan) renunciar a.

fort [fɔːt] n fuerte m.

forte ['fɔːtɪ] n fuerte m.

forth [fɔːθ] ad en adelante; **back and** ~ de acá para allá; **and so** ~ y así sucesivamente; ~coming a próximo, venidero; (character) comunicativo; ~right a franco.

fortieth ['fɔːtɪɪθ] a cuadragésimo.

fortification [fɔːtɪfɪ'keɪʃən] n fortificación f; **fortify** ['fɔːtɪfaɪ] vt fortalecer.

fertitude ['fɔːtɪtjuːd] n fortaleza.

fortnight ['fɔːtnaɪt] n quincena; ~ly a quincenal // ad quincenalmente.

fortress ['fɔːtrɪs] n fortaleza.

fortuitous [fɔː'tjuːɪtəs] a fortuito.

fortunate ['fɔːtʃnɪt] a: **to be** ~ tener suerte; **it is** ~ **that** ... es afortunado que...; ~ly ad afortunadamente.

fortune ['fɔːtʃən] n suerte f, (wealth) fortuna; ~-teller n adivina.

forty ['fɔːtɪ] num cuarenta.

forum ['fɔːrəm] n foro.

forward ['fɔːwəd] a (movement, position) avanzado; (front) delantero; (not shy) atrevido // n (sport) delantero // vt (letter) remitir; (career) progresar; **to move** ~ avanzar; ~(s) ad (hacia) adelante.

fossil ['fɔsl] n fósil m.

foster ['fɔstə*] vt fomentar; ~ **brother** n hermano de leche; ~ **child** n hijo adoptivo; ~ **mother** n madre f adoptiva.

fought [fɔːt] pt, pp of **fight**.

foul [faul] a (gen) sucio, puerco; (weather) horrible; (smell etc) asqueroso // n (football) falta (en contra) // vt (dirty) ensuciar; (*block*) atascar; (*football player*) cometer una falta contra; ~ **play** n (*SPORT*) mala jugada; (*LAW*) muerte f violenta.

found [faund] *pt, pp of* **find** // *vt* (*establish*) fundar; ~**ation** [-'deɪʃən] n (*act*) fundación f; (*basis*) base f; (*also*: ~**ation cream**) crema base; ~**ations** npl (*of building*) cimientos mpl.

founder ['faundə*] n fundador/a m/f // vi hundirse.

foundry ['faundrɪ] n fundición f.

fountain ['fauntɪn] n fuente f; ~ **pen** n pluma-fuente f.

four [fɔ:*] num cuatro; **on all** ~**s** a gatas; ~**-poster** n cama a columnas; ~**some** ['fɔ:səm] n grupo de cuatro personas; ~**teen** num catorce; ~**teenth** a décimocuarto; ~**th** a cuarto.

fowl [faul] n ave f (de corral).

fox [fɔks] n zorro // vt confundir; ~**trot** n fox m.

foyer ['fɔɪeɪ] n vestíbulo.

fracas ['fræka:] n gresca, riña.

fraction ['frækʃən] n fracción f.

fracture ['fræktʃə*] n fractura // vt fracturar.

fragile ['frædʒaɪl] a frágil.

fragment ['frægmənt] n fragmento; ~**ary** a fragmentario.

fragrance ['freɪgrəns] n fragancia; **fragrant** [-ənt] a fragante, oloroso.

frail [freɪl] a (*fragile*) frágil, quebradizo; (*weak*) delicado.

frame [freɪm] n (*gen*) estructura; (*body*) talle m; (*TECH*) armazón m; (*of picture, door etc*) marco; (*of spectacles*: *also*: ~**s**) montura // vt encuadrar; (*reply*) formular; (*fam*) incriminar; ~ **of mind** n estado de ánimo; ~**work** n marco.

France [fra:ns] n Francia.

franchise ['fræntʃaɪz] n (*POL*) derecho de votar, sufragio.

frank [fræŋk] a franco // vt (*letter*) franquear; ~**ly** ad francamente; ~**ness** n franqueza.

frantic ['fræntɪk] a frenético.

fraternal [frə'tə:nl] a fraterno; **fraternity** [-nɪtɪ] n (*club*) fraternidad f; (*US*) club m de estudiantes; (*guild*) cofradía; **fraternize** ['frætənaɪz] vi confraternizar.

fraud [frɔ:d] n fraude m; (*person*) impostor m; ~**ulent** a fraudulento.

fraught [frɔ:t] a: ~ **with** cargado de.

fray [freɪ] n combate m, lucha // vi deshilacharse; **tempers were** ~**ed** tenían los nervios a punto.

freak [fri:k] n (*person*) fenómeno; (*event*) suceso anormal; (*thing*) cosa insólita.

freckle ['frekl] n peca.

free [fri:] a (*gen*) libre; (*not fixed*) suelto; (*gratis*) gratuito; (*unoccupied*) desocupado; (*liberal*) generoso // vt (*prisoner etc*) poner en libertad; (*jammed object*) soltar; ~ **(of charge)** ad gratis; ~**dom** ['fri:dəm] n libertad f; ~**-for-all** n riña general; ~ **kick** n tiro libre; ~**lance** a

independiente; ~**ly** ad libremente; generosamente; ~**mason** n francmasón m; ~ **trade** n libre comercio; ~**way** n (*US*) autopista; ~**wheel** vi ir en punto muerto; ~ **will** n libre albedrío; **of one's own** ~ **will** por su propia voluntad.

freeze [fri:z], *pt* **froze**, *pp* **frozen** vi helarse, congelarse // vt helar; (*prices, food, salaries*) congelar // n helada; congelación f; **freezer** n congelador m.

freezing ['fri:zɪŋ] a helado; ~ **point** n punto de congelación; **3 degrees below** ~ tres grados bajo cero.

freight [freɪt] n (*goods*) carga; (*money charged*) flete m; ~ **car** n (*US*) vagón m de mercancías.

French [frentʃ] a francés(esa) // n (*LING*) francés m; **the** ~ los franceses; ~ **fried (potatoes)** npl patatas fpl fritas; ~**man/woman** n francés/esa m/f; ~ **window** n puertaventana.

frenzy ['frenzɪ] n frenesí m.

frequency ['fri:kwənsɪ] n frecuencia; **frequent** [-ənt] a frecuente // vt [frɪ'kwent] frecuentar; **frequently** [-əntlɪ] ad frecuentemente, a menudo.

fresco ['freskəu] n fresco.

fresh [freʃ] a (*gen*) fresco; (*new*) nuevo; (*water*) dulce; ~**en** vi (*wind, air*) soplar más recio; **to** ~**en up** vi (*person*) lavarse, arreglarse; ~**ly** ad (*newly*) nuevamente; (*recently*) recientemente; ~**ness** n frescura.

fret [fret] vi inquietarse.

friar ['fraɪə*] n fraile m; (*before name*) fray.

friction ['frɪkʃən] n fricción f.

Friday ['fraɪdɪ] n viernes m.

fridge [frɪdʒ] n nevera.

friend [frend] n amigo/a; ~**liness** n simpatía; ~**ly** a simpático; ~**ship** n amistad f.

frieze [fri:z] n friso.

frigate ['frɪgɪt] n fragata.

fright [fraɪt] n susto; **to take** ~ asustarse; ~**en** vt asustar; ~**ening** a espantoso; ~**ful** a espantoso, horrible; ~**fully** ad terriblemente.

frigid ['frɪdʒɪd] a (*MED*) frígido, frío; ~**ity** [frɪ'dʒɪdɪtɪ] n frialdad f; (*MED*) frigidez f.

frill [frɪl] n volante m.

fringe [frɪndʒ] n flequillo; (*edge*: *of forest etc*) borde m, margen m; ~ **benefits** npl ventajas fpl supletorias.

frisky ['frɪskɪ] a juguetón(ona), fogoso.

fritter ['frɪtə*] n buñuelo; **to** ~ **away** vt desperdiciar.

frivolous ['frɪvələs] a frívolo.

frizzy ['frɪzɪ] a rizado.

fro [frəu] *see* **to**.

frock [frɔk] n vestido.

frog [frɔg] n rana; ~**man** n hombre-rana m.

frolic ['frɔlɪk] vi juguetear.

from [frɔm] *prep* de; ~ **January (on)** a partir de enero; ~ **what he says** por lo que dice.

front [frʌnt] n (foremost part) parte f
delantera; (of house) fachada; promenade:
also: sea ~) paseo marítimo; (MIL, POL,
METEOROLOGY) frente m; (fig: appearances)
apariencias fpl // a delantero, primero; in
~ (of) delante (de); ~al a frontal; ~
door n puerta principal; ~ier ['frʌntiə*] n
frontera; ~ page n primera plana; ~
room n (Brit) salón m, sala; ~-wheel
drive n tracción f delantera.

frost [frɔst] n (gen) helada; ~visible)
escarcha; ~bite n congelación f; ~ed a
(glass) deslustrado; ~y a (window)
cubierto de escarcha; (welcome) glacial.

froth [frɔθ] n espuma.

frown [fraun] n ceño // vi fruncir el ceño.

froze [frəuz] pt of **freeze**.

frozen ['frəuzn] pp of **freeze**.

frugal ['fruːgəl] a frugal.

fruit [fruːt] n, pl inv fruta; ~erer n frutero;
~erer's (shop) n frutería; ~ful a
provechoso; ~ion [fruːˈɪʃən] n: to come
to ~ion realizarse; ~ machine n
máquina tragaperras.

frustrate [frʌsˈtreɪt] vt frustrar; ~d a
frustrado; **frustration** [-ˈtreɪʃən] a
frustración f.

fry [fraɪ], pt, pp **fried** vt freír; **small** ~
gente f menuda; ~ing pan n sartén f.

ft. abbr of **foot, feet**.

fuchsia ['fjuːʃə] n fucsia.

fudge [fʌdʒ] n (CULIN) dulce m de azúcar,
manjar m.

fuel [fjuəl] n (for heating) combustible m;
(coal) carbón m; (wood) leña; (for propelling) carburante m; ~ oil n aceite m
combustible; ~ tank n depósito de
combustible.

fugitive ['fjuːdʒɪtɪv] n fugitivo.

fulfil [fulˈfɪl] vt (function) cumplir con;
(condition) satisfacer; (wish, desire)
realizar; ~ment n satisfacción f,
realización f.

full [ful] a lleno; (fig) pleno; (complete)
completo; (information) detallado // ad: ~
well perfectamente; I'm ~ estoy lleno;
~ employment pleno empleo; ~ fare
pasaje m completo; a ~ two hours dos
horas completas; at ~ speed a máxima
velocidad; in ~ (reproduce, quote)
íntegramente; ~-length a (portrait) de
cuerpo entero; ~ moon n luna llena;
~-sized a (portrait etc) de tamaño
natural; ~ stop n punto; ~-time a
(work) de tiempo completo // n (SPORT)
final m; ~y ad completamente; ~y-
fledged a (teacher, barrister) diplomado.

fumble ['fʌmbl]: to ~ with vt fus
revolver, manosear.

fume [fjuːm] vi humear, echar humo; ~s
npl humo sg, gases mpl.

fumigate ['fjuːmɪgeɪt] vt fumigar.

fun [fʌn] n (amusement) diversión f; (joy)
alegría; to have ~ divertirse; for ~ en
broma; to make ~ of vt fus burlarse de.

function ['fʌŋkʃən] n función f // vi
funcionar; ~al a funcional.

fund [fʌnd] n fondo; (source, store) fuente f;
~s npl fondos mpl.

fundamental [fʌndəˈmɛntl] a
fundamental.

funeral ['fjuːnərəl] n (burial) entierro;
(ceremony) funerales mpl; ~ service n
misa de difuntos.

funfair ['fʌnfɛə*] n parque m de
atracciones.

fungus ['fʌŋgəs], pl -gi [-gaɪ] n hongo.

funnel ['fʌnl] n embudo; (of ship)
chimenea.

funnily ['fʌnɪlɪ] ad de modo divertido.

funny ['fʌnɪ] a gracioso, divertido;
(strange) curioso, raro.

fur [fəː*] n piel f; (in kettle etc) sarro; ~
coat n abrigo de pieles.

furious ['fjuərɪəs] a furioso; (effort)
violento; ~ly ad con furia.

furlong ['fəːlɔŋ] n octava parte de una milla.

furlough ['fəːləu] n (US) licencia.

furnace ['fəːnɪs] n horno.

furnish ['fəːnɪʃ] vt amueblar; (supply)
suministrar; ~ings npl muebles mpl.

furniture ['fəːnɪtʃə*] n muebles mpl; **piece
of** ~ mueble m; ~ polish n cera de
lustrar.

furrier ['fʌrɪə*] n peletero.

furrow ['fʌrəu] n surco.

furry ['fəːrɪ] a peludo.

further ['fəːðə*] a (new) nuevo, adicional;
(place) más lejano // ad más lejos; (more)
más; (moreover) además // vt promover,
adelantar; ~ education n educación f
superior; ~more [fəːðəˈmɔː*] ad además.

furthest ['fəːðɪst] superlative of **far**.

furtive ['fəːtɪv] a furtivo.

fury ['fjuərɪ] n furia.

fuse, fuze (US) [fjuːz] n fusible m; (for
bomb etc) mecha // vt (metal) fundir; (fig)
fusionar // vi fundirse; (ELEC): **to** ~ **the
lights** fundir los plomos; ~ box n
caja de fusibles.

fuselage ['fjuːzəlɑːʒ] n fuselaje m.

fusion ['fjuːʒən] n fusión f.

fuss [fʌs] n (noise) bulla; (dispute) lío;
(complaining) protesta; (ceremony)
ceremonias fpl; **to make a** ~ armar un
lío o jaleo; ~y a (person) exigente.

futile ['fjuːtaɪl] a vano; **futility** [-ˈtɪlɪtɪ] n
inutilidad f.

future ['fjuːtʃə*] a (gen) futuro; (coming)
venidero // n futuro; **futuristic** [-ˈrɪstɪk] a
futurístico.

fuzzy ['fʌzɪ] a (PHOT) borroso; (hair) muy
rizado.

G

gabble ['gæbl] vi hablar atropelladamente;
(gossip) cotorrear.

gable ['geɪbl] n aguilón m.

gadget ['gædʒɪt] n aparato.

Gaelic ['geɪlɪk] n (LING) gaélico.

gag [gæg] n (joke) chiste m // vt
amordazar.

gaiety ['geııtı] n alegría.

gaily ['geılı] ad alegremente.

gain [geın] n ganancia // vt ganar // vi (watch) adelantarse; **to ~ by sth** sacar provecho de algo; **to ~ on sb** ir ganando terreno a uno.

gait [geıt] n modo de andar.

gala ['gɑ:lə] n fiesta.

galaxy ['gæləksı] n galaxia.

gale [geıl] n (wind) vendaval m.

gallant ['gælənt] a valiente; (towards ladies) atento; **~ry** n valentía; (courtesy) cortesía.

gall-bladder ['gɔ:lblædə*] n vesícula biliar.

gallery ['gælərı] n galería; (also: **art ~**) museo.

galley ['gælı] n (ship's kitchen) cocina; (ship) galera.

gallon ['gæln] n galón m (4.543 litros).

gallop ['gæləp] n galope m // vi galopar.

gallows ['gæləuz] n horca.

gallstone ['gɔ:lstəun] n cálculo biliario.

gamble ['gæmbl] n (risk) riesgo; (bet) apuesta // vt: **to ~ on** apostar a; (fig) confiar en que // vi jugar; (COMM) especular; **gambler** n jugador/a m/f; **gambling** n el juego.

game [geım] n (gen) juego; (match) partido; (of cards) partida; (HUNTING) caza // a valiente; (ready): **to be ~ for anything** atreverse a todo; **~ bird** n ave f de caza; **~keeper** n guardabosques m inv.

gammon ['gæmən] n (bacon) tocino ahumado; (ham) jamón m ahumado.

gang [gæŋ] n pandilla; (of workmen) brigada // vi: **to ~ up on sb** conspirar contra uno.

gangrene ['gæŋgri:n] n gangrena.

gangster ['gæŋstə*] n gángster m.

gangway ['gæŋweı] n (in theatre etc) pasillo; (on ship) pasarela; (on dock) pasadera.

gaol [dʒeıl] = **jail.**

gap [gæp] n vacío, hueco; (in trees, traffic) claro; (in time) intervalo.

gape [geıp] vi estar o quedarse boquiabierto; **gaping** a (hole) muy abierto.

garage ['gærɑ:ʒ] n garaje m.

garbage ['gɑ:bıdʒ] n basura; **~ can** n (US) cubo de la basura.

garbled ['gɑ:bld] a (distorted) falsificado, amañado.

garden ['gɑ:dn] n jardín m; **~er** n jardinero; **~ing** n jardinería.

gargle ['gɑ:gl] vi hacer gárgaras.

gargoyle ['gɑ:gɔıl] n gárgola.

garish ['gɛərıʃ] a chillón(ona).

garland ['gɑ:lənd] n guirnalda.

garlic ['gɑ:lık] n ajo.

garment ['gɑ:mənt] n prenda (de vestir).

garnish ['gɑ:nıʃ] vt adornar; (CULIN) aderezar.

garrison ['gærısn] n guarnición f // vt guarnecer.

garrulous ['gærjuləs] a gárrulo.

garter ['gɑ:tə*] n liga; **~ belt** portaligas m inv.

gas [gæs] n gas m; (US: gasoline) gasolina // vt asfixiar con gas; **~ cooker** n cocina de gas; **~ cylinder** n bombona de gas; **~ fire** n estufa de gas.

gash [gæʃ] n raja; (on face) cuchillada // vt (gen) rajar; (with knife) acuchillar.

gasket ['gæskıt] n (AUT) junta.

gas: ~mask n careta antigás; **~ meter** n contador m de gas.

gasoline ['gæsəli:n] n (US) gasolina.

gasp [gɑ:sp] n grito sofocado // vi (pant) jadear; **to ~ out** vt (say) decir con voz entrecortada.

gas: ~ ring n hornillo de gas; **~ stove** n cocina de gas; **~sy** a gaseoso; **~ tap** n llave f del gas.

gastric ['gæstrık] a gástrico; **~ ulcer** n úlcera gástrica.

gate [geıt] n puerta; (RAIL) barrera; **~crash** vt colarse de gorra en; **~way** n puerta.

gather ['gæðə*] vt (flowers, fruit) coger; (assemble) reunir; (pick up) recoger; (SEWING) fruncir; (understand) entender // vi (assemble) reunirse; **~ing** n reunión f, asamblea.

gauche [gəuʃ] a torpe.

gaudy ['gɔ:dı] a chillón(ona).

gauge [geıdʒ] n medida; (RAIL) entrevía; (instrument) indicador m // vt medir.

gaunt [gɔ:nt] a descarnado; (grim, desolate) desolado.

gauntlet ['gɔ:ntlıt] n (fig): **to run the ~** correr baquetas; **to throw down the ~** arrojar el guante.

gauze [gɔ:z] n gasa.

gave [geıv] pt of **give.**

gay [geı] a (person) alegre; (colour) vistoso, vivo; (homosexual) gay.

gaze [geız] n mirada fija; **to ~ at sth** mirar algo con fijeza.

gazelle [gə'zɛl] n gacela.

gazetteer [gæzə'tıə*] n diccionario geográfico.

G.B. abbr of **Great Britain.**

G.C.E. n abbr of **General Certificate of Education.**

gear [gıə*] n equipo, herramientas fpl; (TECH) engranaje m; (AUT) velocidad f, marcha; **top/low ~** tercera (o cuarta)/primera velocidad; **in ~** en marcha; **~ box** n caja de cambios; **~ lever, ~ shift** (US) n palanca de velocidades; **~ wheel** n rueda dentada.

geese [gi:s] pl of **goose.**

gelatin(e) ['dʒɛləti:n] n gelatina.

gelignite ['dʒɛlıgnaıt] n gelignita.

gem [dʒɛm] n joya.

Gemini ['dʒɛmınaı] n Géminis m, Gemelos mpl.

gender ['dʒɛndə*] n género.

general ['dʒɛnərl] n general m // a
general; **in** ~ en general; ~ **election** n
elecciones fpl generales; ~**ization**
[-aɪ'zeɪʃən] n generalización f; ~**ize** vt
generalizar; ~**ly** ad generalmente, en
general; ~ **practitioner (G.P.)** n médico
general.

generate ['dʒɛnəreɪt] vt (ELEC) generar;
(fig) producir.

generation [dʒɛnə'reɪʃən] n generación f.

generator ['dʒɛnəreɪtə*] n generador m.

generosity [dʒɛnə'rɔsɪtɪ] n generosidad f;
generous ['dʒɛnərəs] a generoso; (helping
etc) abundante.

genetics [dʒɪ'nɛtɪks] n genética.

Geneva [dʒɪ'niːvə] n Ginebra.

genial ['dʒiːnɪəl] a afable, simpático.

genitals ['dʒɛnɪtlz] npl órganos npl
genitales.

genius ['dʒiːnɪəs] n genio.

genocide ['dʒɛnəʊsaɪd] n genocidio.

gent [dʒɛnt] n abbr of **gentleman.**

genteel [dʒɛn'tiːl] a fino, elegante.

gentle ['dʒɛntl] a (sweet) amable, dulce;
(touch etc) ligero, suave; (animal) manso.

gentleman ['dʒɛntlmən] n señor m; (well-
bred man) caballero.

gentleness ['dʒɛntlnɪs] n dulzura; (of
touch) suavidad f; (of animal)
mansedumbre f.

gently ['dʒɛntlɪ] ad suavemente.

gentry ['dʒɛntrɪ] n alta burguesía.

gents [dʒɛnts] n (aseos de) caballeros mpl.

genuine ['dʒɛnjuɪn] a auténtico; (person)
sincero.

geographic(al) [dʒɪə'græfɪk(l)] a
geográfico; **geography** [dʒɪ'ɔgrəfɪ] n
geografía.

geological [dʒɪə'lɔdʒɪkl] a geológico;
geologist [dʒɪ'ɔlədʒɪst] n geólogo;
geology [dʒɪ'ɔlədʒɪ] n geología.

geometric(al) [dʒɪə'mɛtrɪk(l)] a
geométrico; **geometry** [dʒɪ'ɔmətrɪ] n
geometría.

geranium [dʒɪ'reɪnjəm] n geranio.

germ [dʒəːm] n (gen) microbio, bacteria;
(BIO, fig) germen m.

German ['dʒəːmən] a alemán(ana) // n
alemán/ana m/f; (LING) alemán m; ~
measles n rubéola.

Germany ['dʒəːmənɪ] n Alemania.

germination [dʒəːmɪ'neɪʃən] n ger-
minación f.

gesticulate [dʒɛs'tɪkjuleɪt] vi gesticular.

gesture ['dʒɛstjə*] n gesto.

get [gɛt], pt, pp **got**, pp **gotten** (US) vt
(obtain) obtener; (receive) recibir;
(achieve) conseguir; (find) encontrar;
(catch) coger; (fetch) traer, ir a buscar;
(understand) entender // vi (become)
hacerse, volverse; to ~ **old** hacerse viejo,
envejecer; to ~ **to** (place) llegar a; **he
got under the fence** pasó por debajo de
la barrera; to ~ **ready/washed**
prepararse/lavarse; to ~ **sb to do sth**
hacer que alguien haga algo; to ~ **sth**

out of sth sacar algo de algo; to ~ **about**
vi salir mucho, viajar mucho; (news)
divulgarse; to ~ **along** vi (agree)
entenderse; (depart) marcharse, (manage)
= **to get by;** to ~ **at** vt fus (attack)
atacar; (reach) llegar a; (the truth)
descubrir; to ~ **away** vi marcharse; (on
holiday) irse de vacaciones; (escape)
escaparse; to ~ **away with** vt fus hacer
impunemente; to ~ **back** vi (return)
volver // vt recobrar; to ~ **by** vi (pass)
lograr pasar; (manage) arreglárselas; to
~ **down** vi bajarse // vt (object) bajar;
(depress) deprimir; to ~ **down to** vt fus
(work) ponerse a (hacer); to ~ **in** vi
(train) llegar; (arrive home) volver a casa,
regresar; to ~ **off** vi (from train etc)
bajar; (depart: person, car) marcharse //
vt fus (train, bus) bajar de; to ~ **on** vi (at
exam etc) tener éxito; (agree) entenderse
// vt (horse) subir; to ~ **out** vi salir; (of
vehicle) bajar; (news) saberse // vt (take
out) sacar; to ~ **out of** vt fus (duty etc)
escaparse de; to ~ **over** vt (illness)
recobrarse de; (put across) hacer
comprender; to ~ **round** vt fus rodear;
(fig: person) engatusar a; to ~ **through**
to vt fus (TEL) comunicar con; to ~
together vi reunirse; to ~ **up** vi (rise)
levantarse // vt fus levantar; to ~ **up to**
vt fus (reach) llegar a; (prank etc) hacer;
~**away** n fuga, escape m.

geyser ['giːzə*] n calentador m de agua;
(GEO) géiser m.

Ghana ['gɑːnə] n Ghana.

ghastly ['gɑːstlɪ] a horrible; (pale) pálido.

gherkin ['gəːkɪn] n pepinillo.

ghetto ['gɛtəʊ] n ghetto.

ghost [gəʊst] n fantasma m; ~**ly** a
fantasmal.

giant ['dʒaɪənt] n gigante m // a
gigantesco, gigante.

gibberish ['dʒɪbərɪʃ] n galimatías m.

gibe [dʒaɪb] n pulla.

giblets ['dʒɪblɪts] npl menudillos mpl.

giddiness ['gɪdɪnɪs] n vértigo; **giddy** a
(dizzy) mareado; (speed) vertiginoso;
(frivolous) atolondrado; **it makes me
giddy** me marea.

gift [gɪft] n (gen) regalo; (offering)
obsequio; (ability) talento; ~**ed** a dotado.

gigantic [dʒaɪ'gæntɪk] a gigantesco.

giggle ['gɪgl] vi reírse con risa tonta // n
risilla tonta.

gill [dʒɪl] n (measure) = 0.14 l // n [gɪl] (of
fish) agalla, branquia.

gilt [gɪlt] a, n dorado; ~**-edged** a (COMM)
del Estado.

gimmick ['gɪmɪk] n truco.

gin [dʒɪn] n (liquor) ginebra.

ginger ['dʒɪndʒə*] n jengibre m; ~ **ale** n
cerveza de jengibre; ~**bread** n pan m de
jengibre; ~**haired** a pelirrojo.

gingerly ['dʒɪndʒəlɪ] ad con pies de plomo.

gipsy ['dʒɪpsɪ] n gitano/a.

giraffe [dʒɪ'rɑːf] n jirafa.

girder ['gəːdə*] n viga.

girdle ['gɔːdl] n (corset) faja // vt ceñir.

girl [gɜːl] n (small) niña; (young woman) chica, joven f, muchacha; **an English ~** una (chica) inglesa; **~friend** n (of girl) amiga; (of boy) novia; **~ish** a de niña.

girth [gɜːθ] n circunferencia; (stoutness) gordura.

gist [dʒɪst] n lo esencial.

give [gɪv], pt **gave**, pp **given** vt (gen) dar; (deliver) entregar; (as gift) regalar // vi (break) romperse; (stretch: fabric) dar de sí; **to ~ sb sth, ~ sth to sb** dar algo a uno; **to ~ away** vt (give free) regalar; (betray) traicionar; (disclose) revelar; **to ~ back** vt devolver; **to ~ in** vi ceder // vt entregar; **to ~ off** vt despedir; **to ~ out** vt distribuir; **to ~ up** vi renunciar, darse por vencido // vt renunciar a; **to ~ up smoking** dejar de fumar; **to ~ way** vi ceder; (AUT) ceder el paso.

glacier ['glæsɪə*] n glaciar m.

glad [glæd] a contento; **~den** vt alegrar.

gladioli [glædɪ'əʊlaɪ] npl gladíolos mpl.

gladly ['glædlɪ] ad con mucho gusto.

glamorous ['glæmərəs] a encantador(a), atractivo; **glamour** n encanto, atractivo.

glance [glɑːns] n ojeada, mirada // vi: **to ~ at** echar una ojeada a; **to ~ off** (bullet) rebotar; **glancing** a (blow) oblicuo.

gland [glænd] n glándula.

glare [glɛə*] n luz f deslumbradora, brillo // vi deslumbrar; **to ~ at** mirar ferozmente a; **glaring** a (mistake) notorio.

glass [glɑːs] n vidrio, cristal m; (for drinking) vaso; (: with stem) copa; (also: **looking ~**) espejo; **~es** npl gafas fpl; **~house** n invernadero; **~ware** n cristalería; **~y** a (eyes) vidrioso.

glaze [gleɪz] vt (door) poner cristal a; (pottery) barnizar // n barniz m; **~d** a (eye) vidrioso; (pottery) barnizado.

glazier ['gleɪzɪə*] n vidriero.

gleam [gliːm] n destello // vi brillar; **~ing** a reluciente.

glee [gliː] n alegría, regocijo.

glen [glɛn] n cañada, valle m estrecho.

glib [glɪb] a de mucha labia; **~ness** n labia.

glide [glaɪd] vi deslizarse; (AVIAT, birds) planear // n deslizamiento; (AVIAT) vuelo sin motor; **glider** n (AVIAT) planeador m; **gliding** n (AVIAT) vuelo sin motor.

glimmer ['glɪmə*] n luz f trémula.

glimpse [glɪmps] n vista momentánea, vislumbre m /// vt vislumbrar, entrever.

glint [glɪnt] n destello; (in the eye) chispa // vi centellear.

glisten ['glɪsn] vi relucir, brillar.

glitter ['glɪtə*] vi relucir, brillar // n brillo.

gloat [gləʊt] vi: **to ~ (over)** recrearse en, saborear.

global ['gləʊbl] a mundial; (sum) global.

globe [gləʊb] n globo, esfera.

gloom [gluːm] n tinieblas fpl, oscuridad f; (sadness) tristeza, melancolía; **~y** a

(dark) oscuro; (sad) triste; (pessimistic) pesimista.

glorify ['glɔːrɪfaɪ] vt glorificar; (praise) alabar.

glorious ['glɔːrɪəs] a glorioso; **glory** n gloria.

gloss [glɔs] n (shine) brillo; (paint) pintura brillante o esmalte; **to ~ over** vt fus encubrir.

glossary ['glɔsərɪ] n glosario.

glossy ['glɔsɪ] a lustroso.

glove [glʌv] n guante m; **~ compartment** n (AUT) guantera.

glow [gləʊ] vi (shine) brillar; (fire) arder // n brillo.

glower ['glauə*] vi: **to ~ at** mirar con ceño.

glucose ['gluːkəus] n glucosa.

glue [gluː] n goma (de pegar) // vt pegar.

glum [glʌm] a (mood) abatido; (person, tone) melancólico.

glut [glʌt] n superabundancia.

glutton ['glʌtn] n glotón/ona m/f; **a ~ for work** un trabajador incansable; **~y** n gula, glotonería.

glycerin(e) ['glɪsəriːn] n glicerina.

gnarled [nɑːld] a nudoso.

gnat [næt] n mosquito.

gnaw [nɔː] vt roer.

gnome [nəum] n gnomo.

go [gəʊ], pt **went**, pp **gone** vi ir; (travel) viajar; (depart) irse, marcharse; (work) funcionar, marchar; (be sold) venderse; (time) pasar; (fit, suit): **to ~ with** hacer juego con; (become) ponerse; (break etc) estropearse, romperse // n, pl **~es**: **to have a ~ (at)** probar suerte (con); **to be on the ~** moverse, estar trabajando; **whose ~ is it?** ¿a quién le toca?; **he's going to do it** va a hacerlo; **to ~ for a walk** ir de paseo; **to ~ dancing** ir a bailar; **how did it ~?** ¿qué tal salió o resultó?, ¿cómo ha ido?; **to ~ about** vi (rumour) propagarse // vt fus: **how do I ~ about this?** ¿cómo me las arreglo para hacer esto?; **to ~ ahead** vi (make progress) avanzar; (get going) seguir; **to ~ along** vi ir // vt fus bordear; **to ~ along with** estar de acuerdo con; **to ~ away** vi irse, marcharse; **to ~ back** vi volver; (fall back) retroceder; **to ~ back on** vt fus (promise) faltar a; **to ~ by** vi (years, time) pasar // vt fus guiarse por; **to ~ down** vi bajar; (ship) hundirse; (sun) ponerse // vt fus bajar por; **to ~ for** vt fus (fetch) ir por; (like) gustar; (attack) atacar; **to ~ in** vi entrar; **to ~ in for** vt fus (competition) presentarse a; **to ~ into** vt fus entrar en; (investigate) investigar; (embark on) embarcarse en; **to ~ off** vi irse, marcharse; (food) pasarse; (explode) estallar; (event) realizarse // vt fus dejar de gustar; **to ~ on** vi seguir, continuar; (happen) pasar, ocurrir; **to ~ on doing sth** seguir haciendo algo; **to ~ out** vi salir; (fire, light) apagarse; **to ~ over** vi (ship) zozobrar // vt fus (check) revisar; **to**

~ **through** vt fus (town etc) atravesar; to
~ **up** vi subir; **to** ~ **without** vt fus
pasarse sin.

goad [gəud] vt aguijonear.

go-ahead ['gəuəhed] a emprendedor(a) //
n luz f verde.

goal [gəul] n meta; (score) gol m;
~**keeper** n portero; ~-**post** n poste m de
la portería.

goat [gəut] n cabrío, cabra m/f.

gobble ['gɔbl] vt (also: ~ **down**, ~ **up**)
engullirse (ávidamente).

goblet ['gɔblit] n copa.

goblin ['gɔblin] n duende m.

go-cart ['gəukɑ:t] n go-cart m.

god [gɔd] n dios m; G~ n Dios m; ~**child**
n ahijado/a; ~**dess** n diosa; ~**father** n
padrino; ~-**forsaken** a dejado de la mano
de Dios; ~**mother** n madrina; ~**send** n
don m del cielo; ~**son** n ahijado.

goggles ['gɔglz] npl gafas fpl submarinas.

going ['gəuiŋ] n (conditions) estado del
terreno // a: **the** ~ **rate** la tarifa
corriente o en vigor.

gold [gəuld] n oro // a de oro; ~**en** a
(made of ~) de oro; (~ in colour) dorado;
~**fish** n pez m de colores; ~**mine** n mina
de oro.

golf [gɔlf] n golf m; ~ **club** n club m de
golf; (stick) palo (de golf); ~ **course** n
campo de golf; ~**er** n jugador/a m/f de
golf.

gondola ['gɔndələ] n góndola.

gone [gɔn] pp de go.

gong [gɔŋ] n gong m.

gonorrhea [gɔnə'rɪə] n gonorrea.

good [gud] a (gen) bueno; (kind) bueno,
amable; (well-behaved) educado; (useful)
útil // n bien m, provecho; ~**s** npl bienes
mpl; (COMM) mercancías fpl; **to be** ~ **at**
tener aptitud para; **to be** ~ **for** servir
para; **it's** ~ to te hace bien; **would
you be** ~ **enough to...?** ¿podría hacerme
el favor de...?, ¿sería tan amable de...?; **a**
~ **deal (of)** mucho; **a** ~ **many** muchos;
to make ~ reparar; **for** ~ para siempre,
definitivamente; ~ **morning/afternoon!**
¡buenos días/buenas tardes!; ~ **evening!**
¡buenas noches!; ~ **night!** ¡buenas
noches!; ~**bye!** ¡adiós!; **to say** ~**bye**
despedirse; G~ **Friday** n Viernes m
Santo; ~-**looking** a guapo; ~**ness** n (of
person) bondad f; **for** ~**ness sake!** ¡Por
Dios!; ~**ness gracious!** ¡Dios mío!;
~ **will** n buena voluntad f.

goose [gu:s], pl **geese** n ganso, oca.

gooseberry ['guzbəri] n grosella espinosa.

gooseflesh ['gu:sfleʃ] n, **goose pimples**
npl carne f de gallina.

gore [gɔ:*] vt cornear // n sangre f.

gorge [gɔːdʒ] n barranco // vr: **to** ~ **o.s.**
(on) atracarse (de).

gorgeous ['gɔːdʒəs] a magnífico,
maravilloso.

gorilla [gə'rilə] n gorila m.

gorse [gɔːs] n aulaga.

gory ['gɔːri] a sangriento.

go-slow ['gəu'sləu] n huelga de trabajo
lento.

gospel ['gɔspl] n evangelio.

gossip ['gɔsip] n (scandal) chismorreo,
chismes mpl; (chat) charla;
(scandalmonger) chismoso/a; (talker)
hablador/a m/f // vi cotillear.

got [gɔt] pt, pp of get; ~**ten** (US) pp of get.

gout [gaut] n gota.

govern ['gʌvən] vt (gen) gobernar;
(dominate) dominar.

governess ['gʌvənis] n institutriz f.

government ['gʌvnmənt] n gobierno;
~**al** [-'mentl] a gubernamental.

governor ['gʌvənə*] n gobernador m; (of
jail) director/a m/f.

gown [gaun] n traje m; (of teacher, judge)
toga.

G.P. n abbr of **general practitioner.**

GPO n abbr of **General Post Office.**

grab [græb] vt coger, arrebatar.

grace [greis] n (REL) gracia; (gracefulness)
elegancia, finura // vt (favour) honrar;
(adorn) adornar; **5 days'** ~ un plazo de 5
días; **to say** ~ bendecir la mesa; ~**ful** a
elegante, gracioso; **gracious** ['greiʃəs] a
amable.

grade [greid] n (quality) clase f, calidad f;
(degree) grado; (US SCOL) clase f // vt
clasificar.

gradient ['greidiənt] n pendiente f.

gradual ['grædjuəl] a paulatino; ~**ly** ad
paulatinamente.

graduate ['grædjuit] n graduado,
licenciado // vi ['grædjueit] graduarse,
licenciarse; **graduation** [-'eiʃən] n
graduación f.

graft [grɑːft] n (AGR, MED) injerto; (bribery)
corrupción f // vt injertar.

grain [grein] n grano; (corn) granos mpl,
cereales mpl; (in wood) fibra.

gram [græm] n gramo.

grammar ['græmə*] n gramática;
grammatical [grə'mætikl] a gramatical.

gramme [græm] n = **gram.**

gramophone ['græməfəun] n tocadiscos
m inv.

granary ['grænəri] n granero, troj f.

grand [grænd] a magnífico, imponente;
~**children** npl nietos mpl; ~**dad** n yayo,
abuelito; ~**daughter** n nieta; ~**eur**
['grændə*] n magnificencia, lo grandioso;
~**father** n abuelo; ~**iose** ['grændiəuz] a
grandioso; (pej) pomposo; ~**ma** n yaya,
abuelita; ~**mother** n abuela; ~**pa** n =
~**dad**; ~**piano** a piano de cola; ~**son** n
nieto; ~**stand** n (SPORT) tribuna.

granite ['grænit] n granito.

granny ['græni] n abuelita, yaya.

grant [grɑːnt] vt (concede) conceder;
(admit) asentir // n (SCOL) beca; **to take**
sth for ~**ed** dar algo por sentado.

granulated sugar ['grænjuleitid-] n
azúcar m granulado.

granule ['grænju:l] n gránulo.

grape [greip] n uva; **sour ~s** (fig) envidia.

grapefruit ['greipfru:t] n pomelo, toronja (AM).

graph [grɑːf] n gráfica; **~ic** a gráfico.

grapple ['græpl] vi: **to ~ with sth** esforzarse por resolver algo.

grasp [grɑːsp] vt agarrar, asir; (understand) comprender // n (grip) asimiento; (reach) alcance m; (understanding) comprensión f; **~ing** a avaro.

grass [grɑːs] n hierba; (lawn) césped m; **~hopper** n saltamontes m inv; **~land** n pradera; **~roots** a popular; **~ snake** n culebra; **~y** a cubierto de hierba.

grate [greit] n (fireplace) chimenea; (of iron) parrilla // vi rechinar // vt (CULIN) rallar.

grateful ['greitful] a agradecido.

grater ['greitə*] n rallador m.

gratify ['grætifai] vt complacer; (whim) satisfacer; **~ing** a grato.

grating ['greitiŋ] n (iron bars) rejilla // a (noise) áspero.

gratitude ['grætitju:d] n agradecimiento.

gratuity [grə'tju:iti] n gratificación f.

grave [greiv] n tumba // a serio, grave; **~digger** n sepulturero.

gravel ['grævl] n grava.

grave: **~stone** n lápida; **~yard** n cementerio, camposanto.

gravity ['græviti] n gravedad f; (seriousness) seriedad f.

gravy ['greivi] n salsa.

gray [grei] a = **grey.**

graze [greiz] vi pacer // vt (touch lightly) rozar; (scrape) raspar // n (MED) rasguño.

grease [gri:s] n (fat) grasa; (lubricant) lubricante m // vt engrasar; **~proof** a a prueba de grasa; (paper) apergaminado; **greasy** a grasiento.

great [greit] a grande; (col) magnífico, estupendo; **G~ Britain** n Gran Bretaña; **~grandfather/mother** n bisabuelo/a; **~ly** ad sumamente, mucho, muy; **~ness** n grandeza.

Greece [gri:s] n Grecia.

greed [gri:d] n (also: **~iness**) codicia, avaricia; (for food) gula; **~ily** ad con avidez; **~y** a avaro; (for food) glotón(ona).

Greek [gri:k] a griego // n griego/a; (LING) griego.

green [gri:n] a verde; (inexperienced) novato // n verde m; (stretch of grass) césped m; **~s** npl verduras fpl; **~gage** n claudia; **~grocer** n verdulero; **~house** n invernadero; **~ish** a verdoso.

Greenland ['gri:nlənd] n Groenlandia.

greet [gri:t] vt saludar; (welcome) dar la bienvenida a; **~ing** n (gen) saludo; (welcome) bienvenida.

gregarious [grə'gɛəriəs] a gregario.

grenade [grə'neid] n granada.

grew [gru:] pt of **grow.**

grey [grei] a gris; **~-haired** a canoso; **~hound** n galgo.

grid [grid] n reja; (ELEC) red f.

grief [gri:f] n dolor m, pena.

grievance ['gri:vəns] n motivo de queja, agravio.

grieve [gri:v] vi afligirse, acongojarse // vt dar pena a; **to ~ for** llorar por.

grievous ['gri:vəs] a penoso.

grill [gril] n (on cooker) parrilla // vt asar a la parrilla; (question) interrogar duramente.

grille [gril] n reja; (AUT) rejilla.

grim [grim] a siniestro; (fam) horrible.

grimace [gri'meis] n mueca // vi hacer muecas.

grime [graim] n mugre f; **grimy** a mugriento.

grin [grin] n sonrisa abierta // vi sonreír abiertamente.

grind [graind] pt, pp **ground** vt (coffee, pepper etc) moler; (make sharp) afilar // n (work) trabajo pesado y aburrido; **to ~ one's teeth** rechinar los dientes.

grip [grip] n (hold) asimiento; (of hands) apretón m; (handle) asidero; (of racquet etc) mango; (holdall) maletín m; (understanding) comprensión f // vt agarrar; **to come to ~s with** luchar a brazo partido con; **~ping** a absorbente.

grisly ['grizli] a horripilante, horrible.

gristle ['grisl] n cartílago.

grit [grit] n gravilla; (courage) valor m // vt (road) poner gravilla en; **to ~ one's teeth** apretar los dientes.

groan [grəun] n gemido, quejido // vi gemir, quejarse.

grocer ['grəusə*] n tendero de ultramarinos; **~ies** npl comestibles mpl; **~'s (shop)** n tienda de ultramarinos.

groggy ['grɔgi] a aturdido; (BOXING) grogui.

groin [grɔin] n ingle f.

groom [grum] n mozo de caballos; (also: **bride~**) novio // vt (horse) cuidar; **well-~ed** acicalado.

groove [gru:v] n ranura, surco.

grope [grəup] vi ir a tientas; **to ~ for** vt fus buscar a tientas.

gross [grəus] a grueso; (COMM) bruto; **~ly** ad (greatly) enormemente.

grotesque [grə'tɛsk] a grotesco.

grotto ['grɔtəu] n gruta.

ground [graund] pt, pp of **grind** // n suelo, tierra; (SPORT) campo, terreno; (reason: gen pl) causa, razón f // vt (plane) mantener en tierra; (US. ELEC) conectar con tierra // vi (ship) varar, encallar; **~s** npl (of coffee etc) poso sg; (gardens etc) jardines mpl, parque m; **on the ~** en el suelo; **to the ~** al suelo; **~ floor** n planta baja; **~ing** n (in education) conocimientos mpl básicos; **~less** a infundado; **~sheet** n tela impermeable; **~ staff** n personal m de tierra; **~work** n preparación f.

group [gru:p] n grupo; (musical) conjunto

// (*vb*: *also*: ~ **together**) *vt* agrupar *// vi* agruparse.

grouse [graus] *n*, *pl inv* (*bird*) urogallo *// vi* (*complain*) quejarse.

grove [grəuv] *n* arboleda.

grovel ['grɔvl] *vi* (*fig*) humillarse.

grow [grəu], *pt* **grew**, *pp* **grown** *vi* (*gen*) crecer; (*plants*) cultivarse; (*increase*) aumentarse; (*spread*) extenderse, desarrollarse; (*become*) volverse; **to** ~ **rich/weak** enriquecerse/debilitarse *// vt* cultivar, dejar crecer; **to** ~ **up** *vi* crecer, hacerse hombre/mujer; ~**er** *n* cultivador/a *m/f*, productor/a *m/f*; ~**ing** *a* creciente.

growl [graul] *vi* gruñir.

grown [grəun] *pp of* grow; ~-**up** *n* adulto, persona mayor.

growth [grəuθ] *n* crecimiento, desarrollo; (*what has grown*) brote *m*; (MED) acceso, tumor *m*.

grub [grʌb] *n* gusano; (*col: food*) comida.

grubby ['grʌbɪ] *a* sucio, mugriento.

grudge [grʌdʒ] *n* motivo de rencor *// vt* **to** ~ **sb sth** dar algo a uno de mala gana, escatimar algo a uno; **to bear sb a** ~ guardar rencor a uno; **he** ~**s** (**giving**) **the money** da el dinero de mala gana.

gruelling ['gruəlɪŋ] *a* penoso, duro.

gruesome ['gru:səm] *a* horrible.

gruff [grʌf] *a* (*voice*) bronco; (*manner*) brusco.

grumble ['grʌmbl] *vi* refunfuñar, quejarse.

grumpy ['grʌmpɪ] *a* gruñón(ona).

grunt [grʌnt] *vi* gruñir *// n* gruñido.

guarantee [gærən'ti:] *n* garantía *// vt* garantizar.

guarantor [gærən'tɔ:*] *n* garante *m/f*, fiador/a *m/f*.

guard [gɑ:d] *n* guardia; (RAIL) jefe *m* de tren *// vt* guardar; ~**ed** *a* (*fig*) cauteloso; ~**ian** *n* guardián/ana *m/f*; (*of minor*) tutor/a *m/f*; ~'**s van** *n* (RAIL) furgón *m*.

guerrilla [gə'rɪlə] *n* guerrillero; ~ **warfare** *n* guerra de guerrillas.

guess [ges] *vi*, *vt* (*gen*) adivinar; (*suppose*) suponer *// n* suposición *f*, conjetura; **to take** *or* **have a** ~ tratar de adivinar; ~ **work** *n* conjeturas *fpl*.

guest [gest] *n* invitado/a; (*in hotel*) huésped/a *m/f*; ~-**house** *n* casa de huéspedes, pensión *f*; ~ **room** *n* cuarto de huéspedes.

guffaw [gʌ'fɔ:] *n* carcajada *// vi* reírse a carcajadas.

guidance ['gaɪdəns] *n* (*gen*) dirección *f*; (*advice*) consejos *mpl*.

guide [gaɪd] *n* (*person*) guía *m/f*; (*book*, *fig*) guía *f // vt* guiar; (**girl**) ~ *n* exploradora; ~-**book** *n* guía; ~ **dog** *n* perro guía; ~**lines** *npl* (*fig*) principios *mpl* generales.

guild [gɪld] *n* gremio; ~**hall** *n* (*Brit*) ayuntamiento.

guile [gaɪl] *n* astucia; ~**less** *a* cándido.

guillotine ['gɪlətiːn] *n* guillotina.

guilt [gɪlt] *n* culpabilidad *f*; ~**y** *a* culpable.

guinea pig ['gɪnɪpɪg] *n* conejillo de Indias.

guise [gaɪz] *n*: **in** *or* **under the** ~ **of** so capa de.

guitar [gɪ'tɑ:*] *n* guitarra; ~**ist** *n* guitarrista *m/f*.

gulf [gʌlf] *n* golfo; (*abyss*) abismo.

gull [gʌl] *n* gaviota.

gullet ['gʌlɪt] *n* esófago; (*fam*) garganta.

gullible ['gʌlɪbl] *a* crédulo.

gully ['gʌlɪ] *n* barranco.

gulp [gʌlp] *vi* tragar saliva *// vt* (*also*: ~ **down**) tragarse *// n*: **at one** ~ de un trago.

gum [gʌm] *n* (ANAT) encía; (*glue*) goma; (*sweet*) caramelo de goma; (*also*: chewing-~) chicle *m // vt* engomar, pegar con goma; ~**boots** *npl* botas *fpl* de goma.

gun [gʌn] *n* (*gen*) arma de fuego; (*small*) pistola; (*shotgun*) escopeta; (*rifle*) fusil *m*; (*cannon*) cañón *m*; ~**boat** *n* cañonero; ~**fire** *n* fuego, disparos *mpl*; ~**man** *n* pistolero; ~**ner** *n* artillero; **at** ~**point** bajo la amenaza de un arma; ~**powder** *n* pólvora; ~**shot** *n* escopetazo, cañonazo; ~**smith** *n* armero.

gurgle ['gɜ:gl] *vi* gorgotear.

gush [gʌʃ] *vi* chorrear; (*fig*) deshacerse en efusiones.

gusset [gʌsɪt] *n* escudete *m*.

gust [gʌst] *n* (*of wind*) ráfaga.

gusto ['gʌstəu] *n* entusiasmo.

gut [gʌt] *n* intestino, tripa; (MUS etc) cuerda de tripa, ~**s** *npl* (*courage*) valor *m*.

gutter ['gʌtə*] *n* (*of roof*) canalón *m*; (*in street*) arroyo.

guttural ['gʌtərl] *a* gutural.

guy [gaɪ] *n* (*also*: ~**rope**) cuerda; (*col: man*) tío, tipo.

guzzle ['gʌzl] *vi* tragar *// vt* engullir.

gym [dʒɪm] *n* (*also*: **gymnasium**) gimnasio; (*also*: **gymnastics**) gimnasia; ~**nast** *n* gimnasta *m/f*; ~**nastics** *n* gimnasia; ~ **shoes** *npl* zapatillas *fpl* de gimnasia; ~ **slip** *n* túnica de colegiala.

gynaecologist, gynecologist (US) [gaɪnɪ'kɔlədʒɪst] *n* ginecólogo; **gynaecology, gynecology** (US) [-nə'kɔlədʒɪ] *n* ginecología.

gypsy ['dʒɪpsɪ] *n* = **gipsy**.

gyrate [dʒaɪ'reɪt] *vi* girar.

H

haberdashery [hæbə'dæʃərɪ] *n* mercería.

habit ['hæbɪt] *n* hábito, costumbre *f*; (*costume*) hábito.

habitable ['hæbɪtəbl] *a* habitable.

habitual [hə'bɪtjuəl] *a* acostumbrado, habitual; (*drinker, liar*) empedernido; ~**ly** *ad* por costumbre.

hack [hæk] *vt* (*cut*) cortar; (*slice*) tajar *// n* corte *m*; (*axe blow*) hachazo.

hackneyed ['hæknɪd] *a* trillado, gastado.

had [hæd] *pt*, *pp of* **have**.

haddock ['hædək], pl ~ or ~s n especie de merluza.

hadn't ['hædnt] = had not.

haemorrhage, hemorrhage (US) ['hemərıdʒ] n hemorragia.

haemorrhoids, hemorrhoids (US) ['hemərɔıdz] npl hemorroides fpl.

haggard ['hægəd] a ojeroso.

haggle ['hægl] vi (argue) discutir; (bargain) regatear.

Hague [heig] n: The ~ La Haya.

hail [heıl] n (weather) granizo // vt saludar; (call) llamar a // vi granizar; ~**stone** n (piedra de) granizo.

hair [hɛə*] n (gen) pelo, cabellos mpl; (one ~) pelo, cabello; (head of ~) cabellera; (on legs) vello; **grey** ~ canas fpl; ~**brush** n cepillo (del pelo); ~**cut** n corte m de pelo; ~**do** n peinado; ~**dresser** n peluquero; ~**dresser's** n peluquería; ~**-drier** n secador m de pelo; ~**net** n redecilla; ~**piece** n trenza postiza; ~**pin** n horquilla; ~**pin bend** n curva de horquilla; ~**raising** a espeluznante; ~ **remover** n depilador m; (cream) crema depilatoria; ~ **spray** n laca; ~**style** n peinado; ~**y** a peludo; velludo.

half [hɑ:f], pl **halves** n mitad f // a medio // ad medio, a medias; ~**-an-hour** media hora; **two and a** ~ dos y media; ~ **a pound** media libra; **to cut sth in** ~ cortar algo por la mitad; ~ **asleep** medio dormido; ~**-price** a mitad de precio; ~**-back** n (SPORT) medio; ~**-breed, ~-caste** n mestizo; ~**-hearted** a indiferente, poco entusiasta; ~**-hour** n media hora; ~**-penny** ['heıpnı] n medio penique; ~**-time** n medio tiempo; ~**way** ad a medio camino.

halibut ['hælıbət] n, pl inv halibut m.

hall [hɔ:l] n (for concerts) sala; (entrance way) hall m, vestíbulo; **town** ~ palacio municipal; ~ **of residence** n residencia (universitaria).

hallmark ['hɔ:lmɑ:k] n (mark) marca; (seal) sello.

hallo [hə'ləu] excl = **hello**.

hallucination [həlu:sı'neıʃən] n alucinación f.

halo ['heıləu] n (of saint) aureola.

halt [hɔ:lt] n (stop) alto, parada; (RAIL) apeadero // vt parar // vi pararse; (process) interrumpirse.

halve [hɑ:v] vt partir por la mitad.

halves [hɑ:vz] pl of **half**.

ham [hæm] n jamón m (cocido); (actor) comicastro.

hamburger ['hæmbə:gə*] n hamburguesa.

hamlet ['hæmlıt] n aldea.

hammer ['hæmə*] n martillo // vt amartillar // vi (on door) golpear.

hammock ['hæmək] n hamaca.

hamper ['hæmpə*] vt estorbar // n cesto.

hand [hænd] n mano f; (of clock) manecilla; (writing) letra; (applause) aplausos mpl; (worker) obrero; (measure) palmo // vt

(give) dar, pasar; (deliver) entregar; **to give sb a** ~ dar una mano a uno, ayudar a uno; **at** ~ a la mano; **in** ~ entre manos; **on the one** ~ ..., **on the other** ~ ... por una parte ... por otra (parte) ..; **to** ~ **in** vt entregar; **to** ~ **out** vt distribuir; **to** ~ **over** vt (deliver) entregar; (surrender) ceder; ~**bag** n bolso; ~**basin** n lavabo; ~**book** n manual m; ~**brake** n freno de mano; ~**cuffs** npl esposas fpl; ~**ful** n puñado.

handicap ['hændıkæp] n handicap m, desventaja // vt estorbar; **mentally/physically** ~**ped** incapacitado mentalmente/físicamente.

handicraft ['hændıkrɑ:ft] n artesanía.

handkerchief ['hæŋkətʃıf] n pañuelo.

handle ['hændl] n (of door etc) tirador m, manija; (of cup etc) asa; (of knife etc) mango; (for winding) manivela; (fam: name) título // vt (touch) tocar; (deal with) encargarse de; (treat: people) manejar; '~ **with care**' 'tratar con cuidado'; **to fly off the** ~ perder los estribos; ~**bar(s)** n(pl) manillar m.

hand-luggage ['hændlʌgıdʒ] n equipaje m de mano.

handmade ['hændmeıd] a hecho a mano.

handout ['hændaut] n (distribution) repartición f; (charity) limosna; (leaflet) folleto.

handshake ['hændʃeık] n apretón m de manos.

handsome ['hænsəm] a guapo.

handwriting ['hændraıtıŋ] n letra.

handy ['hændı] a (close at hand) a mano; (convenient) práctico; (skilful) hábil, diestro; ~**man** n (hombre) mañoso.

hang [hæŋ], pt, pp **hung** vt colgar; (criminal: pt, pp **hanged**) ahorcar; (head) bajar // vi colgar; **to** ~ **about** vi haraganear; **to** ~ **on** vi (wait) esperar; **to** ~ **up** vi (TEL) colgar.

hangar ['hæŋə*] n hangar m.

hanger ['hæŋə*] n percha; ~**-on** n parásito.

hangover ['hæŋəuvə*] n (after drinking) resaca.

hang-up ['hæŋʌp] n complejo.

hanker ['hæŋkə*] vi: **to** ~ **after** (miss) echar de menos; (long for) añorar.

hankie, hanky ['hæŋkı] n abbr of **handkerchief**.

haphazard [hæp'hæzəd] a fortuito.

happen ['hæpən] vi suceder, ocurrir; (take place) tener lugar, realizarse; **to** ~ **upon** tropezar con; ~**ing** n suceso, acontecimiento.

happily ['hæpılı] ad (luckily) afortunadamente; (cheerfully) alegremente.

happiness ['hæpınıs] n (gen) felicidad f; (joy) alegría.

happy ['hæpı] a feliz, alegre; **to be** ~ (with) estar contento (con); **to be** ~ ser feliz.

harass ['hærəs] vt acosar, hostigar;

~**ment** n persecución f; (worry) preocupación f.

harbour, harbor (US) ['haːbə*] n puerto // vt (hope etc) abrigar; (hide) esconder.

hard [haːd] a (gen) duro; (difficult) difícil; (work) arduo; (person) severo // ad (work) mucho, duro, duramente; (think, try) seriamente; **to look** ~ mirar fijo o fijamente; **no** ~ **feelings!** sin rencor; **to be** ~ **of hearing** ser duro de oído; **to be** ~ **done by** ser tratado injustamente; ~**back** n libro encuadernado; ~**board** n chapa de madera; ~**en** vt endurecer; (fig) curtir // vi endurecerse; ~**headed** a poco sentimental, práctico; ~ **labour** n trabajos mpl forzados.

hardly ['haːdlɪ] ad (scarcely) apenas; that can ~ be true difícilmente puede ser cierto; ~ **ever** casi nunca.

hardness ['haːdnɪs] n dureza.

hardship ['haːdʃɪp] n (troubles) penas fpl; (financial) apuro.

hard-up [haːd'ʌp] a (col) pelado.

hardware ['haːdwɛə*] n ferretería, (COMPUTERS) material m; ~ **shop** n ferretería.

hard-wearing [haːd'wɛərɪŋ] a resistente, duradero.

hard-working [haːd'wəːkɪŋ] a trabajador(a).

hardy ['haːdɪ] a fuerte; (plant) resistente.

hare [hɛə*] n liebre f; ~-**brained** a casquivano.

harem [haː'riːm] n harén m.

haricot (bean) ['hærɪkəu] n alubia.

harm [haːm] n daño, mal m // vt (person) hacer daño a, perjudicar; (thing) dañar; **out of** ~'s **way** a salvo; ~**ful** a perjudicial; (pest) dañino; ~**less** a inofensivo.

harmonica [haː'mɔnɪkə] n armónica.

harmonious [haː'məunɪəs] a armonioso; **harmonize** ['haːmənaɪz] vt, vi armonizar; **harmony** ['haːmənɪ] n armonía.

harness ['haːnɪs] n arreos mpl // vt (horse) enjaezar; (resources) aprovechar.

harp [haːp] n arpa // vi: **to** ~ **on about** hablar constantemente de; ~**ist** n arpista m/f.

harpoon [haː'puːn] n arpón m.

harrowing ['hærəuɪŋ] a horroroso.

harsh [haːʃ] a (hard) duro, cruel; (severe) severo; (unpleasant) desagradable; (: colour) chillón(ona); (contrast) violento; ~**ness** n dureza.

harvest ['haːvɪst] n cosecha; (of grapes) vendimia // vt, vi cosechar; ~**er** n (machine) cosechadora.

has [hæz] vb see **have**.

hash [hæʃ] n (CULIN) picadillo; (fig: mess) lío.

hashish ['hæʃɪʃ] n hachís m, hachich m.

hasn't ['hæznt] = **has not**.

hassle ['hæsl] n pelea // vt molestar a.

haste [heɪst] n prisa; **hasten** ['heɪsn] vt acelerar // vi darse prisa; **hastily** ad de prisa; **hasty** a apresurado.

hat [hæt] n sombrero.

hatch [hætʃ] n (NAUT: also: ~**way**) escotilla // vi salir del cascarón // vt incubar; (plot) tramar.

hatchback ['hætʃbæk] n (AUT) coche m con puerta trasera.

hatchet ['hætʃɪt] n hacha.

hate [heɪt] vt odiar, aborrecer // n odio; ~**ful** a odioso; **hatred** n odio.

hat trick ['hættrɪk] n (SPORT, also fig) tres triunfos seguidos.

haughty ['hɔːtɪ] a altanero, arrogante.

haul [hɔːl] vt tirar; (by lorry) transportar // n (of fish) redada; (of stolen goods etc) botín m; ~**age** n transporte m; (costs) gastos mpl de transporte; ~**ier** n contratista m de transportes.

haunch [hɔːntʃ] n anca; (of meat) pierna.

haunt [hɔːnt] vt (subj: ghost) aparecer en; (frequent) frecuentar; (obsess) obsesionar // n guarida; ~**ed house** casa de fantasmas.

have [hæv], pt, pp **had** vt (gen) tener; (possess) poseer; (meal, shower) tomar; **to** ~ **sth done** hacer hacer algo; **she has to do it** tiene que hacerlo; **I had better leave** más vale que me marche; **I won't** ~ **it** no lo tolero; **he has gone** se ha ido; **to** ~ **it out with sb** ajustar cuentas con alguien; **to** ~ **a baby** parir, dar a luz.

haven ['heɪvn] n puerto; (fig) refugio.

haven't ['hævnt] = **have not**.

haversack ['hævəsæk] n mochila.

havoc ['hævək] n estragos mpl.

hawk [hɔːk] n halcón m.

hay [heɪ] n heno; ~ **fever** n fiebre f del heno; ~**stack** n almiar m.

haywire ['heɪwaɪə*] a (col): **to go** ~ (person) volverse loco; (plan) embarullarse.

hazard ['hæzəd] n riesgo // vt aventurar; ~**ous** a (dangerous) peligroso; (risky) arriesgado.

haze [heɪz] n neblina.

hazelnut ['heɪzlnʌt] n avellana.

hazy ['heɪzɪ] a brumoso; (idea) vago.

he [hiː] pron él; ~ **who...** él que..., quien...; ~-**man** n macho.

head [hed] n cabeza; (leader) jefe/a m/f // vt (list) encabezar; (group) capitanear; ~**s or tails** cara (o cruz); ~ **first** de cabeza, ~ **over heels** patas arriba; **to** ~ **the ball** cabecear (la pelota); **to** ~ **for** vt fus dirigirse a; ~**ache** n dolor m de cabeza; ~**ing** n título; ~**lamp** n faro; ~**land** n promontorio; ~**light** = ~**lamp**; ~**line** n titular m; ~**long** ad (fall) de cabeza; (rush) precipitadamente; ~**master/ mistress** n director/a m/f (de escuela); ~ **office** n oficina central, central // ~-**on** a (collision) de frente; ~**phones** npl auriculares mpl; ~**quarters (HQ)** npl sede f central; (MIL) cuartel m general; ~**rest** n reposacabezas m inv; ~-**room** n (in car) espacio para la cabeza; (under bridge) luz f; ~**scarf** n pañuelo (de cabeza); ~**stone** n

lápida mortuoria; **~strong** *a*
voluntarioso; **~ waiter** *n* jefe *m* de
camareros; **~way** *n* progreso; **to make
~way** avanzar; **~wind** *n* viento
contrario.

heal [hi:l] *vt* curar // *vi* cicatrizarse.

health [hɛlθ] *n* salud *f*; **good ~!** ¡salud y
pesetas!; **~ food** *n* comida natural; **H~
Service** *n* Seguro de Enfermedad; **~y** *a*
(*gen*) sano.

heap [hi:p] *n* montón *m* // *vt* amontonar;
(*plate*) colmar.

hear [hɪə*], *pt*, *pp* **heard** [hə:d] *vt* oír;
(*perceive*) sentir; (*listen to*) escuchar;
(*lecture*) asistir a // *vi* oír; **to ~ about** oír
hablar de; **to ~ from sb** tener noticias de
alguien; **~ing** *n* (*sense*) oído; (*LAW*) vista;
~ing aid *n* audífono; **~say** *n* rumores
mpl, hablillas *fpl*.

hearse [hə:s] *n* coche *m* fúnebre.

heart [hɑ:t] *n* corazón *m*; **~s** *npl* (*CARDS*)
corazones *mpl*; **at ~** en el fondo; **by ~**
(*learn, know*) de memoria; **~ attack** *n*
ataque *m* cardíaco; **~beat** *n* latido (del
corazón); **~breaking** *a* desgarrador(a);
to be ~broken estar angustiado; **~burn**
n acedía; **~ failure** *n* fallo cardíaco;
~felt *a* (*cordial*) cordial; (*deeply felt*) más
sentido.

hearth [hɑ:θ] *n* (*gen*) hogar *m*; (*fireplace*)
chimenea.

heartily ['hɑ:tɪlɪ] *ad* sinceramente,
cordialmente; (*laugh*) a carcajadas; (*eat*)
con buen apetito.

heartless ['hɑ:tlɪs] *a* cruel.

hearty ['hɑ:tɪ] *a* cordial.

heat [hi:t] *n* (*gen*) calor *m*; (*ardour*) ardor
m; (*SPORT. also:* **qualifying ~**) prueba
eliminatoria // *vt* calentar; (*fig*) acalorar;
to ~ up *vi* (*gen*) calentarse; **~ed** *a*
caliente; (*fig*) acalorado; **~er** *n*
calentador *m*.

heath [hi:θ] *n* (*Brit*) brezal *m*.

heathen ['hi:ðn] *a*, *n* pagano/a.

heather ['hɛðə*] *n* brezo.

heating ['hi:tɪŋ] *n* calefacción *f*.

heatstroke ['hi:tstrəuk] *n* insolación *f*.

heatwave ['hi:tweɪv] *n* ola de calor.

heave [hi:v] *vt* (*pull*) tirar de; (*push*)
empujar con esfuerzo; (*lift*) levantar (con
esfuerzo) // *vi* (*water*) agitarse // *n* tirón
m; empujón *m*; (*effort*) esfuerzo; (*throw*)
echada.

heaven ['hɛvn] *n* cielo; (*REL*) paraíso; **~ly**
a celestial; (*REL*) divino.

heavily ['hɛvɪlɪ] *ad* pesadamente; (*drink,
smoke*) con exceso; (*sleep, sigh*)
profundamente.

heavy ['hɛvɪ] *a* pesado; (*work*) duro; (*sea,
rain, meal*) fuerte; (*drinker, smoker*) gran;
(*eater*) comilón(ona); **~weight** *n* (*SPORT*)
peso pesado.

Hebrew ['hi:bru:] *a* hebreo.

heckle ['hɛkl] *vt* interrumpir.

hectic ['hɛktɪk] *a* febril, agitado.

he'd [hi:d] = **he would; he had.**

hedge [hɛdʒ] *n* seto // *vt* cercar (con un

seto) // *vi* contestar con evasivas; **to ~
one's bets** (*fig*) cubrirse.

hedgehog ['hɛdʒhɔg] *n* erizo.

heed [hi:d] *vt* (*also:* **take ~ of**) (*attend to*)
hacer caso de; (*bear in mind*) tener en
cuenta; **~less** *a* desatento.

heel [hi:l] *n* talón *m* // *vt* (*shoe*) poner
tacón a.

hefty ['hɛftɪ] *a* (*person*) fornido; (*piece*)
grande; (*price*) gordo.

heifer ['hɛfə*] *n* novilla, ternera.

height [haɪt] *n* (*of person*) talle *m*; (*of
building*) altura; (*high ground*) cerro;
(*altitude*) altitud *f*; **~en** *vt* elevar; (*fig*)
aumentar.

heir [ɛə*] *n* heredero; **~ess** *n* heredera;
~loom *n* reliquia de familia.

held [hɛld] *pt*, *pp* of **hold.**

helicopter ['hɛlɪkɔptə*] *n* helicóptero.

hell [hɛl] *n* infierno; **~!** ¡demonios!

he'll [hi:l] = **he will, he shall.**

hellish ['hɛlɪʃ] *a* infernal; (*fam*) horrible.

hello [hə'ləu] *excl* ¡hola!; (*surprise*)
¡caramba!

helm [hɛlm] *n* (*NAUT*) timón *m*.

helmet ['hɛlmɪt] *n* casco.

help [hɛlp] *n* ayuda; (*charwoman*) criada,
asistenta; (*assistant etc*) empleado // *vt*
ayudar; **~!** ¡socorro!; **~ yourself** sírvete;
he can't ~ it no es culpa suya; **~er** *n*
ayudante *m/f*; **~ful** *a* útil, servicial;
~ing *n* ración *f*; **~less** *a* (*incapable*)
incapaz; (*defenceless*) indefenso.

hem [hɛm] *n* dobladillo; **to ~ in** *vt* cercar.

hemisphere ['hɛmɪsfɪə*] *n* hemisferio.

hen [hɛn] *n* gallina.

hence [hɛns] *ad* (*therefore*) por lo tanto; **2
years ~** de aquí a 2 años; **~forth** *ad* de
hoy en adelante.

henchman ['hɛntʃmən] *n* (*pej*) secuaz *m*.

henpecked ['hɛnpɛkt] *a* dominado por su
mujer.

her [hə:*] *pron* (*direct*) la; (*indirect*) le;
(*stressed, after prep*) ella // *a* su.

herald ['hɛrəld] *n* (*forerunner*)
precursor/a *m/f* // *vt* anunciar.

heraldry ['hɛrəldrɪ] *n* heráldica.

herb [hə:b] *n* hierba.

herd [hə:d] *n* rebaño.

here [hɪə*] *ad* aquí; **~!** (*present*) presente!;
~ she is aquí está; **~after** *ad* en el
futuro // *n*: **the ~after** (la vida de)
ultratumba; **~by** *ad* (*in letter*) por la
presente.

hereditary [hɪ'rɛdɪtrɪ] *a* hereditario;
heredity [-tɪ] *n* herencia.

heresy ['hɛrəsɪ] *n* herejía.

heretic ['hɛrətɪk] *n* hereje *m/f*; **~al**
[hɪ'rɛtɪkl] *a* herético.

heritage ['hɛrɪtɪdʒ] *n* (*gen*) herencia; (*fig*)
patrimonio.

hermit ['hə:mɪt] *n* ermitaño.

hernia ['hə:nɪə] *n* hernia.

hero ['hɪərəu], *pl* **~es** *n* héroe *m*; (*in book,
film*) protagonista *m*; **~ic** [hɪ'rəuɪk] *a*
heroico.

heroin ['herəuin] n heroína.
heroine ['herəuin] n heroína (in book, film) protagonista.
heroism ['herəuizm] n heroísmo.
heron ['herən] n garza.
herring ['heriŋ] n arenque m.
hers [hə:z] pron (el) suyo/(la) suya etc.
herself [hə:'self] pron (reflexive) se; (emphatic) ella misma; (after prep) sí (misma).
he's [hi:z] = he is; he has.
hesitant ['hezitənt] a vacilante, dudoso.
hesitate ['heziteit] vi dudar, vacilar; **hesitation** [-'teiʃən] n indecisión f.
hew [hju:] vt cortar con hacha.
hexagon ['heksəgən] n hexágono; **~al** [-'sægənl] a hexagonal.
hi [hai] excl ¡oye!, ¡hola!
hibernate ['haibəneit] vi invernar.
hiccough, hiccup ['hikʌp] vi hipar; **~s** npl hipo sg.
hid [hid] pt of hide.
hidden ['hidn] pp of hide.
hide [haid] n (skin) piel f // (vb: pt hid, pp hidden) vt esconder, ocultar // vi: to ~ (from sb) esconderse o ocultarse (de alguien); **~-and-seek** n escondite m; **~away** n escondite m.
hideous ['hidiəs] a horrible.
hiding ['haidiŋ] n (beating) paliza; **to be in ~** (concealed) estar escondido; **~ place** n escondrijo.
hierarchy ['haiəra:ki] a jerarquía.
high [hai] a (gen) alto; (speed, number) grande; (price) elevado; (wind) fuerte; (voice) agudo // ad alto, a gran altura; **it is 20 m ~** tiene 20 m de altura; **~ in the air** en las alturas; **~brow** a culto; **~chair** n silla alta; **~-handed** a despótico; **~-heeled** a de tacón alto; **~jack = hijack**; **~ jump** n (SPORT) salto de altura; **~light** n (fig: of event) punto culminante // vt subrayar; **~ly** ad sumamente; **~ly strung** a hipertenso; **H~ Mass** n misa mayor; **~ness** n altura; **Her H~ness** Su Alteza; **~-pitched** a agudo; **~-rise block** n torre f de pisos; **~ school** n colegio de segunda enseñanza, Instituto; **~ street** n calle f mayor; **~way** n carretera.
hijack ['haidʒæk] vt secuestrar; **~er** n secuestrador a m/f.
hike [haik] vi (go walking) ir de excursión; (tramp) caminar // n caminata; **hiker** n excursionista m/f.
hilarious [hi'leəriəs] a (behaviour, event) regocijante.
hill [hil] n colina; (high) montaña; (slope) cuesta; **~side** n ladera; **~y** a montañoso; (uneven) accidentado.
hilt [hilt] n (of sword) empuñadura; **to the ~** completamente.
him [him] pron (direct) le, lo; (indirect) le; (stressed, after prep) él; **~self** pron (reflexive) se; (emphatic) él mismo; (after prep) sí (mismo).
hind [haind] a posterior // n cierva.

hinder ['hində*] vt estorbar, impedir; **hindrance** ['hindrəns] a estorbo, obstáculo.
Hindu ['hindu:] n hindú m/f.
hinge [hindʒ] n bisagra, gozne m // vi (fig): **to ~ on** depender de.
hint [hint] n indirecta; (advice) consejo // vi: **to ~ that** insinuar que // vi soltar indirectas; **to ~ at** hacer una alusión a.
hip [hip] n cadera; **~ pocket** n bolsillo de atrás.
hippopotamus [hipə'potəməs], pl **~es** or **-mi** [-mai] n hipopótamo.
hire ['haiə*] vt (car, equipment) alquilar; (worker) contratar // n alquiler m; (of person) salario; **for ~** se alquila; (taxi) libre; **~ purchase (H.P.)** n compra a plazos.
his [hiz] pron (el) suyo/(la) suya etc // a su.
Hispanic [his'pænik] a hispánico.
hiss [his] vi silbar, sisear // n silbido, siseo.
historian [hi'stɔ:riən] n historiador/a m/f.
historic(al) [hi'stɔrik(l)] a histórico.
history ['histəri] n historia.
hit [hit], pt, pp **hit** vt (strike) golpear, pegar; (reach: target) alcanzar; (collide with: car) chocar contra // n golpe m; (success) éxito, sensación f; **to ~ it off with sb** hacer buenas migas con alguien.
hitch [hitʃ] vt (fasten) atar, amarrar; (also: ~ up) alzar // n (difficulty) dificultad f; **to ~ a lift** hacer autostop.
hitch-hike ['hitʃhaik] vi hacer autostop; **hitch-hiker** n autostopista m/f.
hive [haiv] n colmena.
hoard [hɔ:d] n acumulación f // vt acumular; **~ing** n acumulación f; (for posters) cartelera.
hoarfrost ['hɔ:frɔst] n escarcha.
hoarse [hɔ:s] a ronco.
hoax [həuks] n trampa.
hobble ['hɔbl] vi cojear // vt (horse) manear.
hobby ['hɔbi] a pasatiempo, afición f; **~-horse** n (fig) tema, manía.
hobo ['həubəu] n (US) vagabundo.
hockey ['hɔki] n hockey m.
hoe [həu] n azadón m // vi azadonar.
hog [hɔg] n cerdo, puerco // vt (fig) acaparar; **to go the whole ~** liarse la manta a la cabeza.
hoist [hɔist] n (lift) montacargas m inv; (crane) grúa.
hold [həuld], pt, pp **held** vt tener; (contain) contener; (keep back) retener; (believe) sostener; (take - of) coger; (take weight) soportar; (meeting) celebrar // vi (withstand pressure) resistir; (be valid) valer; (stick) pegarse // n (handle) asidero; (grasp) asimiento; (fig) dominio; (WRESTLING) presa; (NAUT) bodega; **~ the line!** (TEL) no cuelgue, **to ~ one's own** (fig) defenderse; **to catch or get (a) ~ of** agarrarse, asirse de; **to ~ back** vt retener; (secret) guardarse; **to ~ down** vt (person) sujetar; (job) conservar; **to ~ off** vt (enemy) rechazar; **to ~ on** vi

agarrarse bien; (*wait*) esperar; ~ on!
(*TEL*) no cuelgue; **to ~ on to** *vt fus*
agarrarse a; (*keep*) guardar; **to ~ out** *vt*
alargar // *vi* (*resist*) resistir; **to ~ up** *vt*
(*raise*) levantar; (*support*) apoyar; (*delay*)
atrasar; (*rob*) asaltar; **~all** *n* funda,
neceser *m*; **~er** *n* (*of ticket, record*)
poseedor/a *m/f*; (*of office, title etc*) titular
m/f; **~ing** *n* (*share*) interés *m*; **~up** *n*
(*robbery*) atraco; (*delay*) parada; (*in
traffic*) embotellamiento.

hole [həul] *n* agujero // *vt* agujerear.

holiday ['hɔlədɪ] *n* vacaciones *fpl*; (*day off*)
(día de fiesta, feriado; **~-maker** *n*
veraneante *m/f*; **~ resort** *n* punto de
veraneo.

holiness ['həulɪnɪs] *n* santidad *f*.

Holland ['hɔlənd] *n* Holanda.

hollow ['hɔləu] *a* hueco, vacío; (*eyes*)
hundido; (*sound*) sordo; (*doctrine*) falso //
n (*gen*) hueco; (*in ground*) hoyo // *vt*: **to
~ out** ahuecar.

holly ['hɔlɪ] *n* acebo; **~hock** *n* malva loca.

holster ['həulstə*] *n* pistolera.

holy ['həulɪ] *a* (*gen*) santo, sagrado;
(*water*) bendito; **H~ Ghost** or **Spirit** *n*
Espíritu *m* Santo.

homage ['hɔmɪdʒ] *n* homenaje *m*; **to pay
~ to** rendir homenaje a.

home [həum] *n* casa; (*country*) patria;
(*institution*) asilo // *a* (*domestic*) casero, de
casa; (*ECON, POL*) nacional // *ad* (*direction*)
a casa; **at ~** en casa; **to go/come ~**
ir/volver a casa; **make yourself at ~**
¡estás en tu casa!; **~ address** *n* señas *fpl*;
~land *n* tierra natal; **~less** *a* sin hogar,
sin casa; **~ly** *a* (*domestic*) casero;
(*simple*) sencillo; **~-made** *a* hecho en
casa; **~ rule** *n* autonomía; **H~
Secretary** *n* (*Brit*) Ministro del Interior;
~sick *a*: **to be ~sick** tener morriña,
tener nostalgia; **~ town** *n* ciudad *f* natal;
~ward ['həumwəd] *a* (*journey*) hacia
casa; **~work** *n* tarea.

homicide ['hɔmɪsaɪd] *n* (*US*) homicidio.

homosexual [hɔməu'sɛksjuəl] *a*, *n*
homosexual *m*.

honest ['ɔnɪst] *a* honrado; (*sincere*) franco,
sincero; **~ly** *ad* honradamente;
francamente; **~y** *n* honradez *f*.

honey ['hʌnɪ] *n* miel *f*; **~comb** *n* panal *m*;
(*pattern*) nido de abejas; **~moon** *n* luna
de miel; (*trip*) viaje *m* de novios.

honk [hɔŋk] *vi* (*AUT*) tocar la bocina.

honorary ['ɔnərərɪ] *a* no remunerado;
(*duty, title*) honorario.

honour, honor (*US*) ['ɔnə*] *vt* honrar // *n*
honor *m*, honra; **~able** *a* honorable; **~s
degree** *n* (*SCOL*) título universitario.

hood [hud] *n* capucha; (*Brit: AUT*) capota;
(*US: AUT*) capó *m*.

hoodlum ['hu:dləm] *n* matón *m*.

hoof [hu:f], *pl* **hooves** *n* pezuña.

hook [huk] *n* gancho; (*on dress*) corchete
m, broche *m*; (*for fishing*) anzuelo // *vt*
enganchar.

hooligan ['hu:lɪgən] *n* gamberro.

hoop [hu:p] *n* aro.

hoot [hu:t] *vi* (*AUT*) tocar la bocina; (*siren*)
tocar la sirena // *n* bocinazo; toque *m* de
sirena; **to ~ with laughter** morirse de
risa; **~er** *n* (*AUT*) bocina; (*NAUT*) sirena.

hooves [hu:vz] *pl of* **hoof**.

hop [hɔp] *vi* saltar, brincar; (*on one foot*)
saltar con un pie // *n* salto, brinco.

hope [həup] *vt*, *vi* esperar // *n* esperanza; **I
~ so/not** espero que sí/no; **~ful** *a*
(*person*) optimista, lleno de esperanzas;
(*situation*) prometedor(a); **~fully** *ad* con
optimismo, con esperanza; **~less** *a*
desesperado.

hops [hɔps] *npl* lúpulo *sg*.

horde [hɔ:d] *n* horda.

horizon [hə'raɪzn] *n* horizonte *m*; **~tal**
[hɔrɪ'zɔntl] *a* horizontal.

hormone ['hɔ:məun] *n* hormona.

horn [hɔ:n] *n* cuerno; (*MUS*) trompa; (*AUT*)
bocina; **~-rimmed** de concha; **~ed** *a*
(*animal*) con cuernos.

hornet ['hɔ:nɪt] *n* avispón *m*.

horny ['hɔ:nɪ] *a* (*material*) córneo; (*hands*)
calloso.

horoscope ['hɔrəskəup] *n* horóscopo.

horrible ['hɔrɪbl] *a* horrible.

horrid ['hɔrɪd] *a* horrible, horroroso.

horrify ['hɔrɪfaɪ] *vt* horrorizar.

horror ['hɔrə*] *n* horror *m*; **~ film** *n*
película de horror.

hors d'œuvre [ɔ:'də:vrə] *n* entremeses
mpl.

horse [hɔ:s] *n* caballo; **on ~back** a
caballo; **~man/woman** *n* jinete
m/amazona; **~power (h.p.)** *n* caballo (de
fuerza); **~racing** *n* carreras *fpl* de
caballos; **~radish** *n* rábano picante;
~shoe *n* herradura.

horticulture ['hɔ:tɪkʌltʃə*] *n* horticultura.

hose [həuz] *n* (*also: ~pipe*) manga.

hosiery ['həuzɪər*] *n* calcetería.

hospitable ['hɔspɪtəbl] *a* hospitalario.

hospital ['hɔspɪtl] *n* hospital *m*.

hospitality [hɔspɪ'tælɪtɪ] *n* hospitalidad *f*.

host [həust] *n* anfitrión *m*; (*in hotel etc*)
huésped *m*; (*large number*): **a ~ of**
multitud de; (*REL*) hostia.

hostage ['hɔstɪdʒ] *n* rehén *m*.

hostel ['hɔstl] *n* hostal *m*; **youth ~** *n*
albergue *m* de juventud.

hostess ['həustɪs] *n* anfitriona; (*air ~*)
azafata; (*in night-club*) cabaretera.

hostile ['hɔstaɪl] *a* hostil; **hostility** [-'stɪlɪtɪ]
n hostilidad *f*.

hot [hɔt] *a* caliente; (*weather*) caluroso, de
calor; (*as opposed to only warm*) muy
caliente; (*spicy*) picante; (*fig*) ardiente,
acalorado; **~ dog** *n* perro caliente.

hotel [həu'tɛl] *n* hotel *m*; **~ier** *n* hotelero.

hot: **~headed** *a* exaltado; **~house** *n*
invernadero; **~ly** *ad* con pasión,
apasionadamente; **~-water bottle** *n*
bolsa de agua caliente.

hound [haund] *vt* acosar // *n* perro de
caza.

hour ['auə*] *n* hora; ~**ly** *ad* cada hora.

house [haus, *pl:* 'hauzız] *n* (*also: firm*) casa; (*POL*) cámara; (*THEATRE*) sala // *vt* [hauz] (*person*) alojar; **on the** ~ (*fig*) la casa invita; ~ **arrest** *n* arresto domiciliario; ~**boat** *n* casa flotante; ~**breaking** *n* robo (en una casa); ~**coat** *n* bata; ~**hold** *n* familia; ~**keeper** *n* ama de llaves; ~**keeping** *n* (*work*) trabajos domésticos *mpl*; ~**keeping (money)** dinero para gastos domésticos; ~**warming party** *n* fiesta de estreno de casa; ~**wife** *n* ama de casa; ~**work** *n* faenas *fpl* (de la casa).

housing ['hauzıŋ] *n* (*act*) alojamiento; (*houses*) viviendas *fpl*; ~ **estate** *n* bloque *m* de viviendas.

hovel ['hɔvl] *n* pocilga.

hover ['hɔvə*] *vi* flotar (en el aire); ~**craft** *n* hidroala *m*, aerodeslizador *m*.

how [hau] *ad* cómo; ~ **are you?** ¿cómo está Vd?, ¿cómo estás?; ~ **long have you been here?** ¿cuánto tiempo hace que estás aquí?; ~ **lovely!** ¡qué bonito!; ~ **many/much?** ¿cuántos/cuánto?; ~ **old are you?** ¿cuántos años tienes?; ~**ever** *ad* de cualquier manera; (+ *adjective*) por muy ... que; (*in questions*) cómo // *conj* sin embargo, no obstante.

howl [haul] *n* aullido // *vi* aullar.

h.p., H.P. *abbr of* **hire purchase; horse power.**

HQ *abbr of* **headquarters.**

hub [hʌb] *n* (*of wheel*) centro.

hubbub ['hʌbʌb] *n* barahúnda, barullo.

hubcap ['hʌbkæp] *n* tapacubo.

huddle ['hʌdl] *vi:* **to ~ together** amontonarse.

hue [hju:] *n* color *m*, matiz *m*; ~ **and cry** *n* alarma.

huff [hʌf] *n*: **in a ~** con rabieta.

hug [hʌg] *vt* abrazar // *n* abrazo.

huge [hju:dʒ] *a* enorme.

hulk [hʌlk] *n* (*wreck*) barco viejo; (*hull*) casco.

hull [hʌl] *n* (*of ship*) casco.

hullo [hə'ləu] *excl* = **hello.**

hum [hʌm] *vt* tararear, canturrear // *vi* tararear, canturrear; (*insect*) zumbar // *n* zumbido.

human ['hju:mən] *a, n* humano.

humane [hju:'meın] *a* humano, humanitario.

humanity [hju:'mænıtı] *n* humanidad *f.*

humble ['hʌmbl] *a* humilde // *vt* humillar; **humbly** *ad* humildemente.

humbug ['hʌmbʌg] *n* embustes *mpl*; (*sweet*) caramelo de menta.

humdrum ['hʌmdrʌm] *a* (*boring*) monótono, aburrido; (*routine*) rutinario.

humid ['hju:mıd] *a* húmedo; ~**ity** [-'mıdıtı] *n* humedad *f.*

humiliate [hju:'mılıeıt] *vt* humillar; **humiliation** [-'eıʃən] *n* humillación *f.*

humility [hju:'mılıtı] *n* humildad *f.*

humorist ['hju:mərıst] *n* humorista *m/f.*

humorous ['hju:mərəs] *a* gracioso, divertido.

humour, humor (*US*) ['hju:mə*] *n* humorismo; sentido del humor; (*mood*) humor *m* // *vt* (*person*) complacer.

hump [hʌmp] *n* (*in ground*) montículo; (*camel's*) giba.

hunch [hʌntʃ] *n* (*premonition*) presentimiento; ~**back** *n* joroba; ~**ed** *a* jorobado.

hundred ['hʌndrəd] *num* ciento; (*before n*) cien; ~**weight** *n* (*Brit*) = 50.8 kg; 112 lb; (*US*) = 45.3 kg, 100 lb.

hung [hʌŋ] *pt, pp, of* **hang.**

Hungarian [hʌŋ'gεərıən] *a, n* húngaro/a.

Hungary ['hʌŋgərı] *n* Hungría.

hunger ['hʌŋgə*] *n* hambre *f* // *vi:* **to ~ for** (*gen*) tener hambre de; (*desire*) anhelar // **strike** *n* huelga de hambre; **hungrily** [-grəlı] *ad* ávidamente, con ganas; **hungry** [-grı] *a* hambriento; **to be hungry** tener hambre.

hunt [hʌnt] *vt* (*seek*) buscar; (*SPORT*) cazar // *vi* cazar // *n* caza, cacería; ~**er** *n* cazador *m*; ~**ing** *n* caza.

hurdle ['hə:dl] *n* (*SPORT*) valla; (*fig*) obstáculo.

hurl [hə:l] *vt* lanzar, arrojar.

hurrah [hu'ra:], **hurray** [hu'reı] *n* ¡viva!, ¡vítor!

hurricane ['hʌrıkən] *n* huracán *m.*

hurried ['hʌrıd] *a* (*fast*) apresurado; (*rushed*) hecho de prisa; ~**ly** *ad* con prisa, apresuradamente.

hurry ['hʌrı] *n* prisa // *vi* apresurarse, darse prisa // *vt* (*person*) dar prisa a; (*work*) apresurar; **to be in a ~** tener prisa.

hurt [hə:t], *pt, pp* **hurt** *vt* hacer daño a // *vi* doler // *a* lastimado; ~**ful** *a* (*gen*) dañoso; (*remark*) hiriente.

hurtle ['hə:tl] *vi:* **to ~ past** pasar como un rayo; **to ~ down** caer con violencia.

husband ['hʌzbənd] *n* marido.

hush [hʌʃ] *n* silencio // *vt* hacer callar; (*cover up*) encubrir; ~**!** ¡chitón!, ¡cállate!

husk [hʌsk] *n* (*of wheat*) cáscara.

husky ['hʌskı] *a* ronco; (*burly*) fornido // *n* perro esquimal.

hustle ['hʌsl] *vt* (*push*) empujar; (*hurry*) dar prisa a // *n* bullicio, actividad febril; ~ **and bustle** *n* vaivén *m.*

hut [hʌt] *n* cabaña, (*shed*) cobertizo.

hutch [hʌtʃ] *n* conejera.

hyacinth ['haıəsınθ] *n* jacinto.

hybrid ['haıbrıd] *a, n* híbrido.

hydrant ['haıdrənt] *n* (*also: fire ~*) boca de incendios.

hydraulic [haı'drɔ:lık] *a* hidráulico.

hydroelectric [haıdrəu'lεktrık] *a* hidroeléctrico.

hydrogen ['haıdrədʒən] *n* hidrógeno.

hyena [haı'i:nə] *n* hiena.

hygiene ['haıdʒi:n] *n* higiene *f*; **hygienic** [-'dʒi:nık] *a* higiénico.

hymn [hım] *n* himno.

hyphen ['haɪfn] n guión m.
hypnosis [hɪp'nəʊsɪs] n hipnosis f;
hypnotic [-'nɔtɪk] a hipnótico; **hypnotism**
['hɪpnətɪzm] n hipnotismo; **hypnotist**
['hɪpnətɪst] n hipnotista m/f; **hypnotize**
['hɪpnətaɪz] vt hipnotizar.
hypocrisy [hɪ'pɔkrɪsɪ] n hypocresía;
hypocrite ['hɪpəkrɪt] n hipócrita m/f;
hypocritical [hɪpə'krɪtɪkl] a hipócrita.
hypothesis [haɪ'pɔθɪsɪs], pl **-ses** [-siːz] n
hipótesis f; **hypothetic(al)** [-pəʊ'θetɪk(l)] a
hipotético.
hysteria [hɪ'stɪərɪə] n histeria; **hysterical**
[-'sterɪkl] a histérico; **hysterics** [-'sterɪks]
npl histeria sg, histerismo sg.

I

I [aɪ] pron yo.
ice [aɪs] n hielo // vt (cake) alcorzar;
(drink) helar // vi (also: ~ over, ~ up)
helarse; ~ **age** n período glacial; ~ **axe**
n piolet m; ~**berg** n iceberg m; ~**box** n
(US) nevera; ~-**cold** a helado; ~ **cream**
n helado; ~ **cube** n cubito de hielo; ~
hockey n hockey m sobre hielo.
Iceland ['aɪslənd] n Islandia; ~**er** n
islandés/esa m/f; ~**ic** [-'lændɪk] a
islandés(esa).
ice: ~ **rink** n pista de hielo; ~ **skating** n
patinaje m sobre hielo.
icicle ['aɪsɪkl] n carámbano.
icing ['aɪsɪŋ] n (CULIN) alcorza, garapiña;
(AVIAT etc) formación f de hielo; ~ **sugar**
n azúcar m de alcorza.
icon ['aɪkɔn] n ícono.
icy ['aɪsɪ] a (road) helado; (fig) glacial.
I'd [aɪd] = **I would; I had.**
idea [aɪ'dɪə] n idea.
ideal [aɪ'dɪəl] n ideal m // a ideal; ~**ist** n
idealista m/f.
identical [aɪ'dentɪkl] a idéntico.
identification [aɪdentɪfɪ'keɪʃən] n
identificación f; **means of** ~ documentos
mpl personales.
identify [aɪ'dentɪfaɪ] vt identificar.
identikit picture [aɪ'dentɪkɪt-] n retrato-
robot m.
identity [aɪ'dentɪtɪ] n identidad f.
ideological [aɪdɪə'lɔdʒɪkəl] a ideológico;
ideology [-dɪ'ɔlədʒɪ] n ideología.
idiocy ['ɪdɪəsɪ] n idiotez f; (stupid act)
estupidez f.
idiom ['ɪdɪəm] n modismo; (style of
speaking) lenguaje m.
idiosyncrasy [ɪdɪəʊ'sɪŋkrəsɪ] n
idiosincrasia.
idiot ['ɪdɪət] n (gen) idiota m/f; (fool)
tonto/a; ~**ic** [-'ɔtɪk] a idiota; tonto.
idle ['aɪdl] a (gen) ocioso; (lazy)
holgazán(ana); (unemployed) desocupado;
(pointless) inútil // vi (machine) marchar
en vacío // vt: **to ~ away the time**
malgastar el tiempo; ~**ness** n ociosidad f;
holgazanería; desocupación f.
idol ['aɪdl] n ídolo; ~**ize** vt idolatrar.

if [ɪf] conj si.
igloo ['ɪgluː] n iglú m.
ignite [ɪg'naɪt] vt encender; (set fire to)
incendiar // vi encenderse.
ignition [ɪg'nɪʃən] n (AUT) encendido; **to
switch on/off the** ~ encender/apagar
el motor; ~ **key** n (AUT) llave f de
contacto.
ignorance ['ɪgnərəns] n ignorancia;
ignorant [-ənt] a ignorante; **to be
ignorant of** ignorar.
ignore [ɪg'nɔː'] vt (person) no hacer caso
de; (fact) pasar por alto.
I'll [aɪl] = **I will; I shall.**
ill [ɪl] a enfermo, malo; (bad) malo // n mal
m; (fig) infortunio // ad mal; **to take** or **be
taken** ~ ponerse enfermo, enfermar;
~-**advised** a poco recomendable;
(misled) mal aconsejado; ~-**at-ease** a
incómodo.
illegal [ɪ'liːgl] a ilegal.
illegible [ɪ'ledʒɪbl] a ilegible.
illegitimate [ɪlɪ'dʒɪtɪmət] a ilegítimo.
ill: ~-**fated** a malogrado; ~ **feeling** n
rencor m.
illicit [ɪ'lɪsɪt] a ilícito.
illiterate [ɪ'lɪtərət] a analfabeto.
ill-mannered [ɪl'mænəd] a mal educado.
illness ['ɪlnɪs] n enfermedad f.
illogical [ɪ'lɔdʒɪkl] a ilógico.
ill-treat [ɪl'triːt] vt maltratar.
illuminate [ɪ'luːmɪneɪt] vt (room, street)
iluminar, alumbrar; (subject) aclarar;
illumination [-'neɪʃən] n alumbrado;
illuminations npl luminarias fpl.
illusion [ɪ'luːʒən] n ilusión f; **to be under
the** ~ **that...** estar bajo la ilusión de
que...; **illusory** [-sərɪ] a ilusorio.
illustrate ['ɪləstreɪt] vt (gen) ilustrar;
(subject) aclarar; (point) poner ejemplos a;
illustration [-'streɪʃən] n (example)
ejemplo; (explanation) aclaración f; (in
book) lámina.
illustrious [ɪ'lʌstrɪəs] a ilustre.
ill will [ɪl'wɪl] n rencor m.
I'm [aɪm] = **I am.**
image ['ɪmɪdʒ] n imagen f.
imaginary [ɪ'mædʒɪnərɪ] a imaginario;
imagination [-'neɪʃən] n imaginación f;
(inventiveness) inventiva; (illusion)
fantasía; **imaginative** [-nətɪv] a
imaginativo; **imagine** vt imaginarse;
(delude o.s.) hacerse la ilusión de (que).
imbalance [ɪm'bæləns] n (gen)
desequilibrio; (inequality) falta de
correspondencia.
imbecile ['ɪmbəsiːl] n imbécil m/f.
imbue [ɪm'bjuː] vt: **to ~ sth with** imbuir
algo de.
imitate ['ɪmɪteɪt] vt imitar; **imitation**
[-'teɪʃən] n imitación f; (copy) copia;
(mimicry) mímica.
immaculate [ɪ'mækjulət] a perfecta-
tamente limpio; (REL) inmaculado.
immaterial [ɪmə'tɪərɪəl] a incorpóreo; **it
is** ~ **whether...** no importa si... .

immature [ɪmə'tjuə*] a (person) poco maduro; (of one's youth) juvenil.

immediate [ɪ'miːdɪət] a inmediato; (pressing) urgente, apremiante; ~**ly** ad (at once) en seguida; ~**ly nex** to muy junto a.

immense [ɪ'mens] a inmenso, enorme.

immerse [ɪ'mɜːs] vt (submerge) sumergir; (sink) hundir; **to be ~d in** (fig) estar absorto en.

immersion heater [ɪ'mɔːʃ-] n calentador m de inmersión.

immigrant ['ɪmɪgrənt] n inmigrante m/f; **immigrate** [-greɪt] vi inmigrar; **immigration** [-'greɪʃən] n inmigración f.

imminent ['ɪmɪnənt] a inminente.

immobile [ɪ'məubaɪl] a inmóvil; **immobilize** [-bɪlaɪz] vt inmovilizar.

immoral [ɪ'mɒrl] a inmoral; ~**ity** [-'rælɪtɪ] n inmoralidad f.

immortal [ɪ'mɔːtl] a inmortal; ~**ize** vt inmortalizar.

immune [ɪ'mjuːn] a: ~ **(to)** inmune (contra); **immunity** n (MED) inmunidad f; (COMM) exención f.

immunization [ɪmjunaɪ'zeɪʃən] n inmunización f; **immunize** ['ɪmjunaɪz] vt inmunizar.

imp [ɪmp] n diablillo.

impact ['ɪmpækt] n (gen) impacto.

impair [ɪm'peə*] vt perjudicar.

impale [ɪm'peɪl] vt atravesar.

impart [ɪm'pɑːt] vt comunicar.

impartial [ɪm'pɑːʃl] a imparcial; ~**ity** [ɪmpɑːʃɪ'ælɪtɪ] n imparcialidad f.

impassable [ɪm'pɑːsəbl] a (barrier) infranqueable; (river) invadeable; (road) intransitable.

impatience [ɪm'peɪʃəns] n impaciencia; **impatient** [-ənt] a impaciente; **to get** or **grow impatient** impacientarse.

impeccable [ɪm'pekəbl] a impecable.

impede [ɪm'piːd] vt estorbar, dificultar.

impediment [ɪm'pedɪmənt] n obstáculo, estorbo; (also: **speech** ~) defecto (del habla).

impending [ɪm'pendɪŋ] a (near) próximo.

impenetrable [ɪm'penɪtrəbl] a (gen) impenetrable; (unfathomable) insondable.

imperative [ɪm'perətɪv] a (tone) imperioso; (necessary) indispensable; (pressing) urgente // n (LING) imperativo.

imperceptible [ɪmpə'septɪbl] a imperceptible, insensible.

imperfect [ɪm'pɜːfɪkt] a imperfecto; (goods etc) defectuoso; ~**ion** [-'fekʃən] n (biemish) desperfecto; (state) imperfección f.

imperial [ɪm'pɪərɪəl] a imperial; ~**ism** n imperialismo.

imperil [ɪm'perɪl] vt arriesgar, poner en peligro.

impersonal [ɪm'pɜːsənl] a impersonal.

impersonate [ɪm'pɜːsəneɪt] vt hacerse pasar por; (THEATRE) imitar.

impertinent [ɪm'pɜːtɪnənt] a impertinente, insolente.

impervious [ɪm'pɜːvɪəs] a impermeable; (fig): ~ to insensible a.

impetuous [ɪm'petjuəs] a impetuoso, irreflexivo.

impetus ['ɪmpətəs] n ímpetu m; (fig) impulso.

impinge [ɪm'pɪndʒ]: **to ~ on** vt fus invadir, abusar de; (affect) afectar a.

implausible [ɪm'plɔːzɪbl] a inverosímil.

implement ['ɪmplɪmənt] n instrumento, herramienta f // vt ['ɪmplɪmənt] hacer efectivo; (carry out) realizar.

implicate ['ɪmplɪkeɪt] vt (compromise) comprometer; (involve) enredar; **implication** [-'keɪʃən] n consecuencia, implicancia (AM).

implicit [ɪm'plɪsɪt] a (gen) implícito; (complete) absoluto.

implore [ɪm'plɔː*] vt (person) suplicar.

imply [ɪm'plaɪ] vt (involve) implicar; (mean) significar; (hint) dar a entender que; **it is implied** se sobreentiende.

impolite [ɪmpə'laɪt] a mal educado.

import [ɪm'pɔːt] vt importar // n ['ɪmpɔːt] (COMM) importación f; (: article) artículo importado; (meaning) significado, sentido.

importance [ɪm'pɔːtəns] n importancia; **important** [-ənt] a importante; **it's not important** no importa, no tiene importancia.

importer [ɪm'pɔːtə*] n importador/a m/f.

impose [ɪm'pəuz] vt imponer // vi: **to ~ on sb** abusar de uno; **imposing** a imponente, impresionante.

impossible [ɪm'pɒsɪbl] a imposible; (person) insoportable.

impostor [ɪm'pɒstə*] n impostor/a m/f.

impotence ['ɪmpətəns] n impotencia; **impotent** [-ənt] a impotente.

impound [ɪm'paund] vt embargar.

impoverished [ɪm'pɒvərɪʃt] a necesitado, (land) agotado.

impracticable [ɪm'præktɪkəbl] a no factible, irrealizable.

impractical [ɪm'præktɪkl] a (person) poco práctico.

imprecise [ɪmprɪ'saɪs] a impreciso.

impregnable [ɪm'pregnəbl] a invulnerable; (castle) inexpugnable.

impregnate ['ɪmpregneɪt] vt (gen) impregnar; (soak) empapar; (fertilize) fecundar.

impresario [ɪmprɪ'sɑːrɪəu] n empresario.

impress [ɪm'pres] vt impresionar; (mark) estampar // vi hacer buena impresión; **to ~ sth on sb** convencer a uno de algo; **it ~ed itself on me** se me grabó (en la memoria).

impression [ɪm'preʃən] n impresión f; (footprint etc) huella; (print run) edición f; **to be under the ~ that** tener la impresión de que, ~**able** a influenciable; (sensitive) sensible; ~**ist** n impresionista m/f.

impressive [ɪm'presɪv] a impresionante.

imprint ['ɪmprɪnt] n impresión f, huella.
imprison [ɪm'prɪzn] vt encarcelar; ~ment n encarcelamiento, cárcel f.
improbable [ɪm'prɔbəbl] a improbable, inverosímil.
impromptu [ɪm'prɔmptju:] a improvisado // ad de improviso.
improper [ɪm'prɔpə*] a (incorrect) impropio; (unseemly) indecoroso; (indecent) indecente.
impropriety [ɪmprə'praɪətɪ] n falta de decoro; (indecency) indecencia; (of language) impropiedad f.
improve [ɪm'pru:v] vt mejorar // vi mejorarse; (become perfect) perfeccionarse; (pupils) hacer progresos; ~ment n mejoramiento, perfección f; progreso.
improvise ['ɪmprəvaɪz] vt, vi improvisar.
imprudent [ɪm'pru:dnt] a imprudente.
impudent ['ɪmpjudnt] a descarado, insolente.
impulse ['ɪmpʌls] n impulso; **to act on** ~ obrar sin reflexión; **impulsive** [-'pʌlsɪv] a irreflexivo.
impunity [ɪm'pju:nɪtɪ] n: **with** ~ impunemente.
impure [ɪm'pjuə*] a (adulterated) adulterado; (not pure) impuro; **impurity** n (gen) impureza.
in [ɪn] prep en; (within) dentro de; (with time: during, within): ~ **2 days** en 2 días; (: after): ~ **2 weeks** dentro de 2 semanas; (with town, country): **it's** ~ **France** está en Francia // ad dentro, adentro; (fashionable) de moda; **is he** ~? ¿está en casa?; ~ **the country** en el campo; ~ **the distance** a lo lejos; ~ **town** en el centro (de la ciudad); ~ **the sun** al sol, bajo el sol; ~ **the rain** bajo la lluvia; ~ **French** en francés; **1** ~ **10** uno sobre 10, uno de cada 10; ~ **hundreds** por centenares; **the best pupil** ~ **the class** el mejor alumno de la clase; **written** ~ **pencil** escrito con lápiz; ~ **saying this** al decir esto; **their party is** ~ su partido ha llegado al poder; **to ask sb** ~ invitar a uno a entrar; **to run/limp** ~ entrar corriendo/cojeando; **the** ~**s and outs** los recovecos.
in., ins abbr of **inch(es)**.
inability [ɪnə'bɪlɪtɪ] n incapacidad f.
inaccessible [ɪnək'sɛsɪbl] a inaccesible.
inaccuracy [ɪn'ækjurəsɪ] n inexactitud f; **inaccurate** [-rət] a inexacto, incorrecto.
inactivity [ɪnæk'tɪvɪtɪ] n inactividad f.
inadequate [ɪn'ædɪkwət] a (insufficient) insuficiente; (unsuitable) inadecuado; (person) incapaz.
inadvertently [ɪnəd'və:tntlɪ] ad por equivocación o descuido.
inadvisable [ɪnəd'vaɪzəbl] a no aconsejable.
inane [ɪ'neɪn] a necio, fatuo.
inanimate [ɪn'ænɪmət] a inanimado.
inapplicable [ɪn'æplɪkəbl] a inaplicable.
inappropriate [ɪnə'prəuprɪət] a

inoportuno, inconveniente; (word, expression) impropio.
inapt [ɪn'æpt] a impropio; ~**itude** n incapacidad f.
inarticulate [ɪnɑ:'tɪkjulət] a (person) incapaz de expresarse; (speech) inarticulado.
inasmuch as [ɪnəz'mʌtʃæz] ad (given that) puesto que; (since) ya que.
inattentive [ɪnə'tɛntɪv] a distraído.
inaudible [ɪn'ɔːdɪbl] a inaudible.
inaugural [ɪ'nɔːgjurəl] a (speech) de apertura; **inaugurate** [-reɪt] vt inaugurar; **inauguration** [-'reɪʃən] n ceremonia de apertura.
in-between [ɪnbɪ'twiːn] a intermedio, de entre medio.
inborn [ɪn'bɔːn] a (feeling) innato.
inbred [ɪn'brɛd] a innato; (family) engendrado por endogamia.
incalculable [ɪn'kælkjuləbl] a incalculable.
incapable [ɪn'keɪpəbl] a incapaz.
incapacitate [ɪnkə'pæsɪteɪt] vt: **to** ~ **sb** incapacitar a uno.
incapacity [ɪnkə'pæsɪtɪ] n (inability) incapacidad f.
incarcerate [ɪn'kɑːsəreɪt] vt encarcelar.
incarnate [ɪn'kɑːnɪt] a en persona // vt ['ɪnkɑːneɪt] encarnar; **incarnation** [-'neɪʃən] n encarnación f.
incendiary [ɪn'sɛndɪərɪ] a incendiario.
incense ['ɪnsɛns] n incienso // vt [ɪn'sɛns] (anger) indignar, encolerizar.
incentive [ɪn'sɛntɪv] n incentivo, estímulo.
incessant [ɪn'sɛsnt] a incesante, contínuo; ~**ly** ad constantemente.
incest ['ɪnsɛst] n incesto.
inch [ɪntʃ] n pulgada; **to be within an** ~ **of** estar a dos dedos de; **he didn't give an** ~ no dio concesión alguna; **to** ~ **forward** avanzar palmo a palmo.
incidence ['ɪnsɪdns] n (of crime, disease) frecuencia.
incident ['ɪnsɪdnt] n incidente m, suceso; (in book) episodio.
incidental [ɪnsɪ'dɛntl] a no esencial, accesorio; (unplanned) fortuito; ~ **to** al margen de; ~**ly** [-'dɛntəlɪ] ad (by the way) a propósito.
incinerator [ɪn'sɪnəreɪtə*] n incinerador m.
incipient [ɪn'sɪpɪənt] a incipiente.
incision [ɪn'sɪʒən] n corte m.
incisive [ɪn'saɪsɪv] a (mind) penetrante; (tone) mordaz; (remark etc) tajante.
incite [ɪn'saɪt] vt provocar.
inclination [ɪnklɪ'neɪʃən] n (tendency) tendencia, inclinación f.
incline ['ɪnklaɪn] n pendiente m, cuesta // (vb: [ɪn'klaɪn]) vt (slope) inclinar; (head) poner de lado // vi inclinarse; **to be** ~**d to** (tend) ser propenso a; (be willing) estar dispuesto a.
include [ɪn'kluːd] vt incluir, comprender;

(*in letter*) adjuntar; **including** *prep* incluso, inclusive.

inclusion [ɪn'kluːʒən] *n* inclusión *f*; **inclusive** [-sɪv] *a* inclusivo // *ad* inclusive.

incognito [ɪnkəg'niːtəu] *ad de* incógnito.

incoherent [ɪnkəu'hɪərənt] *a* incoherente.

income ['ɪŋkʌm] *n* (*personal*) ingresos *mpl*; (*from property etc*) renta, (*profit*) rédito; ~ **tax** *n* impuesto sobre la renta; ~ **tax inspector** *n* inspector/a *m/f* fiscal; ~ **tax return** *n* registro fiscal.

incoming ['ɪnkʌmɪŋ] *a*: ~ **flight** vuelo entrante.

incomparable [ɪn'kɒmpərəbl] *a* incomparable, sin par.

incompatible [ɪnkəm'pætɪbl] *a* incompatible.

incompetence [ɪn'kɒmpɪtəns] *n* incompetencia; **incompetent** [-ənt] *a* incompetente.

incomplete [ɪnkəm'pliːt] *a* incompleto; (*unfinished*) sin terminar.

incomprehensible [ɪnkɒmprɪ'hensɪbl] *a* incomprensible.

inconceivable [ɪnkən'siːvəbl] *a* inconcebible.

inconclusive [ɪnkən'kluːsɪv] *a* sin resultado (definitivo); (*argument*) poco convincente.

incongruous [ɪn'kɒŋgruəs] *a* (*foolish*) absurdo, estrafalario; (*remark, act*) disonante, nada lógico.

inconsiderate [ɪnkən'sɪdərət] *a* desconsiderado; **how ~ of him!** ¡qué falta de consideración (de su parte)!

inconsistent [ɪnkən'sɪstnt] *a* inconsecuente; ~ **with** (**que**) no concuerda con.

inconspicuous [ɪnkən'spɪkjuəs] *a* poco llamativo, modesto; **to make o.s.** ~ no llamar la atención.

inconstant [ɪn'kɒnstnt] *a* inconstante.

incontinent [ɪn'kɒntɪnənt] *a* incontinente.

inconvenience [ɪnkən'viːnjəns] *n* (*gen*) inconvenientes *mpl*; (*trouble*) molestia, incomodidad *f* // *vt* incomodar; **inconvenient** [-ənt] *a* incómodo, poco práctico; (*time, place*) inoportuno.

incorporate [ɪn'kɔːpəreɪt] *vt* incorporar; (*contain*) comprender; (*add*) agregar; ~**d** *a*: ~**d company** (*US: abbr* **Inc.**) Sociedad Anónima (S.A.).

incorrect [ɪnkə'rekt] *a* incorrecto.

incorruptible [ɪnkə'rʌptɪbl] *a* (*gen*) incorruptible; (*not open to bribes*) insobornable.

increase ['ɪnkriːs] *n* aumento // *vi* [ɪn'kriːs] aumentarse; (*grow*) crecer; (*price*) subir; **increasing** *a* (*number*) creciente, en aumento; **increasingly** *ad* de más en más, cada vez más.

incredible [ɪn'kredɪbl] *a* increíble.

incredulous [ɪn'kredjuləs] *a* incrédulo.

increment ['ɪnkrɪmənt] *n* aumento, incremento.

incriminate [ɪn'krɪmɪneɪt] *vt* incriminar.

incubation [ɪnkju'beɪʃən] *n* incubación *f*;

incubator ['ɪnkjubeɪtə*] *n* incubadora.

incumbent [ɪn'kʌmbənt] *n* ocupante *m/f* // *a*: **it is** ~ **on him to... le incumbe...**.

incur [ɪn'kɜː*] *vt* (*expenses*) contraer; (*gen*) incurrir en.

incurable [ɪn'kjuərəbl] *a* incurable; (*fig*) irremediable.

incursion [ɪn'kɜːʃən] *n* incursión *f*.

indebted [ɪn'detɪd] *a*: **to be ~ to sb** estar en deuda con uno.

indecent [ɪn'diːsnt] *a* indecente; ~ **assault** *n* atentado contra el pudor; ~ **exposure** *n* exhibicionismo.

indecisive [ɪndɪ'saɪsɪv] *a* indeciso; (*discussion*) no resuelto, inconcluyente.

indeed [ɪn'diːd] *ad* de hecho, realmente; **yes ~!** claro que sí.

indefinite [ɪn'defɪnɪt] *a* indefinido; (*uncertain*) incierto; ~**ly** *ad* (*wait*) indefinidamente.

indelible [ɪn'delɪbl] *a* imborrable.

indemnify [ɪn'demnɪfaɪ] *vt* indemnizar, resarcir.

indentation [ɪnden'teɪʃən] *n* mella; (*TYP*) sangría.

independence [ɪndɪ'pendns] *n* independencia; **independent** [-ənt] *a* independiente; **to become independent** independizarse.

index ['ɪndeks] *n* (*pl* ~**es: in book**) índice *m*; (: *in library etc*) catálogo; (*pl*: **indices** ['ɪndɪsiːz]: *ratio, sign*) exponente *m*; ~ **card** *n* ficha; ~ **finger** *n* índice *m*; ~**-linked** *a* vinculado al índice del coste de la vida.

India ['ɪndɪə] *n* la India; ~**n** *a, n* indio/a; **Red ~n** piel roja *m/f*.

indicate ['ɪndɪkeɪt] *vt* indicar; **indication** [-'keɪʃən] *n* indicio, señal *f*; **indicator** *n* (*gen*) indicador *m*.

indices ['ɪndɪsiːz] *pl of* **index**.

indict [ɪn'daɪt] *vt* acusar; ~**ment** *n* acusación *f*.

indifference [ɪn'dɪfrəns] *n* indiferencia; **indifferent** [-ənt] *a* indiferente; (*poor*) regular.

indigenous [ɪn'dɪdʒɪnəs] *a* indígena *inv*.

indigestion [ɪndɪ'dʒestʃən] *n* indigestión *f*, empacho.

indignant [ɪn'dɪgnənt] *a*: **to be ~ about** **sth** indignarse por algo; **indignation** [-'neɪʃən] *n* indignación *f*.

indignity [ɪn'dɪgnɪtɪ] *n* indignidad *f*; (*insult*) ultraje *m*, afrenta.

indigo ['ɪndɪgəu] *a* color de añil // *n* añil *m*.

indirect [ɪndɪ'rekt] *a* indirecto; ~**ly** *ad* indirectamente.

indiscreet [ɪndɪ'skriːt] *a* indiscreto; (*rash*) imprudente; **indiscretion** [-'skreʃən] *n* indiscreción *f*; imprudencia.

indiscriminate [ɪndɪ'skrɪmɪnət] *a* indistinto.

indispensable [ɪndɪ'spensəbl] *a* indispensable, imprescindible.

indisposed [ɪndɪ'spəuzd] *a* (*unwell*) indispuesto.

indisputable [ɪndɪ'spjuːtəbl] *a* incontestable.

indistinct [ɪndɪ'stɪŋkt] *a* indistinto; (*memory, noise*) confuso.

individual [ɪndɪ'vɪdjuəl] *n* individuo // *a* individual; (*personal*) personal; (*for/of one only*) particular; ~ist *n* individualista *m/f*; ~ity [-'ælɪtɪ] *n* individualidad *f*; ~ly *ad* individualmente; particularmente.

indoctrinate [ɪn'dɔktrɪneɪt] *vt* adoctrinar; **indoctrination** [-'neɪʃən] *n* adoctrinamiento.

indolent ['ɪndələnt] *a* indolente, perezoso.

indoor ['ɪndɔː*] *a* (*inner*) interior; (*household*) de casa; (*inside*) de puertas adentro; (*swimming-pool*) cubierto; (*games*) de salón; (*sport*) bajo cubierta; ~s [ɪn'dɔːz] *ad* dentro; (*at home*) en casa.

induce [ɪn'djuːs] *vt* inducir; (*bring about*) producir; (*provoke*) provocar; ~ment *n* (*incentive*) incentivo, aliciente *m*.

induction [ɪn'dʌkʃən] *n* (*MED: of birth*) inducción *f*; ~ **course** *n* curso de inducción.

indulge [ɪn'dʌldʒ] *vt* (*desire*) dar rienda suelta a; (*whim*) condescender con; (*person*) complacer; (*child*) consentir // *vi*: **to** ~ **in** darse el lujo de; **indulgence** *n* (*of desire*) gratificación *f*; (*leniency*) complacencia; **indulgent** *a* indulgente.

industrial [ɪn'dʌstrɪəl] *a* industrial; ~ **action** *n* huelga; ~ **estate** *n* zona industrial; ~ist *n* industrial *m/f*; ~ize *vt* industrializar.

industrious [ɪn'dʌstrɪəs] *a* (*gen*) trabajador(a); (*student*) aplicado.

industry ['ɪndəstrɪ] *n* industria; (*diligence*) aplicación *f*.

inebriated [ɪ'niːbrɪeɪtɪd] *a* borracho.

inedible [ɪn'edɪbl] *a* incomible; (*plant etc*) no comestible.

ineffective [ɪnɪ'fɛktɪv] *a* ineficaz, inútil.

inefficiency [ɪnɪ'fɪʃənsɪ] *n* ineficacia; **inefficient** [-ənt] *a* ineficaz, ineficiente.

ineligible [ɪn'elɪdʒɪbl] *a* (*candidate*) inelegible; **to be** ~ **for sth** no tener derecho a algo.

inept [ɪ'nept] *a* incompetente, incapaz.

inequality [ɪnɪ'kwɔlɪtɪ] *n* desigualdad *f*.

inert [ɪ'nɜːt] *a* inerte, inactivo; (*immobile*) inmóvil; ~**ia** [ɪ'nɜːʃə] *n* inercia; (*laziness*) pereza.

inescapable [ɪnɪ'skeɪpəbl] *a* ineludible.

inestimable [ɪn'estɪməbl] *a* inestimable.

inevitable [ɪn'evɪtəbl] *a* inevitable; (*necessary*) forzoso.

inexcusable [ɪnɪks'kjuːzəbl] *a* imperdonable.

inexhaustible [ɪnɪg'zɔːstɪbl] *a* inagotable.

inexorable [ɪn'eksərəbl] *a* inexorable, implacable.

inexpensive [ɪnɪk'spensɪv] *a* económico.

inexperience [ɪnɪk'spɪərɪəns] *n* falta de experiencia; ~**d** *a* inexperto.

inexplicable [ɪnɪk'splɪkəbl] *a* inexplicable.

inextricable [ɪnɪk'strɪkəbl] *a* inextricable.

infallible [ɪn'fælɪbl] *a* infalible.

infamous ['ɪnfəməs] *a* infame, **infamy** [-mɪ] *n* infamia.

infancy ['ɪnfənsɪ] *n* infancia.

infant ['ɪnfənt] *n* (*baby*) criatura; (*young child*) niño/a; ~**ile** *a* infantil; (*pej*) aniñado; ~ **school** *n* escuela de párvulos.

infantry ['ɪnfəntrɪ] *n* infantería; ~**man** *n* soldado (de infantería).

infatuated [ɪn'fætjueɪtɪd] *a*: ~ **with** (*gen*) encaprichado por; (*in love*) enamorado de; **infatuation** [-'eɪʃən] *n* encaprichamiento; enamoramiento.

infect [ɪn'fekt] *vt* (*wound*) infectar; (*person*) contagiar; (*fig: pej*) corromper; ~**ed with** (*illness*) contagiado de; ~**ion** [ɪn'fekʃən] *n* infección *f*; (*fig*) contagio; ~**ious** [ɪn'fekʃəs] *a* contagioso; (*also: fig*) infeccioso.

infer [ɪn'fɜː*] *vt* deducir, inferir; ~**ence** ['ɪnfərəns] *n* deducción *f*, inferencia.

inferior [ɪn'fɪərɪə*] *a, n* inferior *m/f*; ~**ity** [-rɪ'ɔrɪtɪ] *n* inferioridad *f*; ~**ity complex** *n* complejo de inferioridad.

infernal [ɪn'fɜːnl] *a* infernal.

inferno [ɪn'fɜːnəu] *n* infierno; (*fig*) hoguera.

infertile [ɪn'fɜːtaɪl] *a* estéril, infecundo; **infertility** [-'tɪlɪtɪ] *n* esterilidad *f*, infecundidad *f*.

infested [ɪn'festɪd] *a*: ~ (**with**) plagado (de).

infidelity [ɪnfɪ'delɪtɪ] *n* infidelidad *f*.

in-fighting ['ɪnfaɪtɪŋ] *n* (*fig*) luchas *fpl* internas.

infiltrate ['ɪnfɪltreɪt] *vt* (*troops etc*) infiltrarse en // *vi* infiltrarse.

infinite ['ɪnfɪnɪt] *a* infinito.

infinitive [ɪn'fɪnɪtɪv] *n* infinitivo.

infinity [ɪn'fɪnɪtɪ] *n* (*also MATH*) infinito; (*an* ~) infinidad *f*.

infirm [ɪn'fɜːm] *a* enfermo, débil; ~**ary** *n* hospital *m*; ~**ity** *n* debilidad *f*; (*illness*) enfermedad *f*, achaque *m*.

inflame [ɪn'fleɪm] *vt* inflamar.

inflammable [ɪn'flæməbl] *a* inflamable; (*explosive*) explosivo.

inflammation [ɪnflə'meɪʃən] *n* inflamación *f*.

inflate [ɪn'fleɪt] *vt* (*tyre, balloon*) inflar; (*fig*) hinchar; ~**d** *a* (*style*) exagerado; (*value*) excesivo; **inflation** [ɪn'fleɪʃən] *n* (*ECON*) inflación *f*; **inflationary** [ɪn-'fleɪʃnərɪ] *a* inflacionario.

inflexible [ɪn'fleksɪbl] *a* inflexible.

inflict [ɪn'flɪkt] *vt*: **to** ~ **on** infligir en; (*tax etc*) imponer a; ~**ion** [ɪn'flɪkʃən] *n* imposición *f*.

inflow ['ɪnfləu] *n* afluencia.

influence ['ɪnfluəns] *n* influencia // *vt* influir en, influenciar; (*persuade*) sugestionar; **under the** ~ **of alcohol** en estado de embriaguez; **influential** [-'enʃl] *a* influyente.

influenza [ɪnflu'enzə] *n* gripe *f*.

influx ['ɪnflʌks] *n* afluencia.

inform [ɪnˈfɔːm] *vt*: to ~ sb of sth informar a uno sobre o de algo; (*warn*) avisar a uno de algo; (*communicate*) comunicar algo a uno // *vi* soplar; to ~ on sb delatar a uno.

informal [ɪnˈfɔːml] *a* (*person, manner*) desenvuelto; (*tone*) familiar; (*visit, discussion*) extraoficial; (*intimate*) de confianza; ~ity [-ˈmælɪtɪ] *n* falta de ceremonia; (*intimacy*) intimidad *f*; (*familiarity*) familiaridad *f* (*ease*) afabilidad *f*.

information [ɪnfəˈmeɪʃən] *n* información *f*, informes *mpl*; (*news*) noticias *fpl*; (*knowledge*) conocimientos *mpl*; (*LAW*) delatación *f*; a piece of ~ un dato.

informative [ɪnˈfɔːmətɪv] *a* informativo.

informer [ɪnˈfɔːməʳ] *n* delator/a *m/f*; (*also: police* ~) soplón/ona *m/f*.

infra-red [ɪnfrəˈred] *a* infrarrojo.

infrequent [ɪnˈfriːkwənt] *a* infrecuente.

infringe [ɪnˈfrɪndʒ] *vt* infringir, violar // *vi*: to ~ on invadir, abusar de; ~ment *n* infracción *f*; (*of rights*) invasión *f*; (*SPORT*) falta.

infuriate [ɪnˈfjʊərɪeɪt] *vt* enfurecer; **infuriating** *a* enloquecedor(a).

ingenious [ɪnˈdʒiːnjəs] *a* ingenioso; **ingenuity** [-dʒɪˈnjuːɪtɪ] *n* ingeniosidad *f*.

ingenuous [ɪnˈdʒenjuəs] *a* ingenuo.

ingot [ˈɪŋgət] *n* lingote *m*, barra.

ingrained [ɪnˈgreɪnd] *a* arraigado.

ingratiate [ɪnˈgreɪʃɪeɪt] *vt*: to ~ o.s. with congraciarse con.

ingratitude [ɪnˈgrætɪtjuːd] *n* ingratitud *f*.

ingredient [ɪnˈgriːdɪənt] *n* ingrediente *m*.

inhabit [ɪnˈhæbɪt] *vt* habitar, vivir en; (*occupy*) ocupar; ~ant *n* habitante *m/f*.

inhale [ɪnˈheɪl] *vt* inhalar // *vi* (*in smoking*) aspirar.

inherent [ɪnˈhɪərənt] *a*: ~ in or to inherente a.

inherit [ɪnˈherɪt] *vt* heredar; ~ance *n* herencia; (*fig*) patrimonio.

inhibit [ɪnˈhɪbɪt] *vt* inhibir, impedir; to ~ sb from doing sth impedir a uno hacer algo; ~ion [-ˈbɪʃən] *n* inhibición *f*.

inhospitable [ɪnhɔsˈpɪtəbl] *a* (*person*) inhospitalario; (*place*) inhóspito.

inhuman [ɪnˈhjuːmən] *a* inhumano.

inimitable [ɪˈnɪmɪtəbl] *a* inimitable.

iniquity [ɪˈnɪkwɪtɪ] *n* inicuidad *f*, (*injustice*) injusticia.

initial [ɪˈnɪʃl] *a* inicial; (*first*) primero // *n* inicial *f* // *vt* firmar con las iniciales; ~s *npl* iniciales *fpl*; (*abbreviation*) siglas *fpl*; ~ly *ad* al principio, en primer lugar.

initiate [ɪˈnɪʃɪeɪt] *vt* (*start*) iniciar, dar comienzo a; to ~ sb into a secret iniciar a uno en un secreto; to ~ proceedings against sb (*LAW*) entablar proceso contra uno; **initiation** [-ˈeɪʃən] *n* (*into secret etc*) iniciación *f*; (*beginning*) comienzo.

initiative [ɪˈnɪʃətɪv] *n* iniciativa.

inject [ɪnˈdʒekt] *vt* (*liquid*) inyectar; (*fig*) injertar; ~ion [ɪnˈdʒekʃən] *n* inyección *f*.

injunction [ɪnˈdʒʌŋkʃən] *n* interdicto.

injure [ˈɪndʒəʳ] *vt* herir, lastimar; (*fig*) perjudicar; (*offend*) ofender; **injury** *n* herida, lesión *f*; (*wrong*) perjuicio, daño; **injury time** *n* (*SPORT*) descuento.

injustice [ɪnˈdʒʌstɪs] *n* injusticia.

ink [ɪŋk] *n* tinta.

inkling [ˈɪŋklɪŋ] *n* sospecha; (*idea*) idea, atisbo.

inlaid [ˈɪnleɪd] *a* taraceado, entarimado.

inland [ˈɪnlənd] *a* interior, del interior // *ad* [ɪnˈlænd] tierra adentro; I~ Revenue *n* (*Brit*) el fisco.

in-laws [ˈɪnlɔːz] *npl* parientes *mpl* políticos.

inlet [ˈɪnlɛt] *a* (*GEO*) ensenada, cala; (*TECH*) admisión *f*, entrada.

inmate [ˈɪnmeɪt] *n* (*in prison*) presidiario; (*in asylum*) internado/a.

inn [ɪn] *n* posada, mesón *m*.

innate [ɪˈneɪt] *a* innato.

inner [ˈɪnəʳ] *a* interior, interno; ~ city *n* centro de la ciudad; ~ tube *n* (*of tyre*) cámara.

innocence [ˈɪnəsns] *n* inocencia; **innocent** [-nt] *a* inocente.

innocuous [ɪˈnɔkjuəs] *a* innocuo.

innovation [ɪnəˈveɪʃən] *n* novedad *f*.

innuendo [ɪnjuˈɛndəu], *pl* ~es *n* indirecta.

innumerable [ɪˈnjuːmrəbl] *a* innumerable.

inoculation [ɪnɔkjuˈleɪʃən] *n* inoculación *f*.

inopportune [ɪnˈɔpətjuːn] *a* inoportuno.

inordinately [ɪˈnɔːdɪnətlɪ] *ad* desmesuradamente.

inorganic [ɪnɔːˈgænɪk] *a* inorgánico.

in-patient [ˈɪnpeɪʃənt] *n* paciente *m/f* interno/a.

input [ˈɪnput] *n* (*ELEC*) entrada; (*COMM*) inversión *f*.

inquest [ˈɪnkwest] *n* pesquisa judicial; (*coroner's*) encuesta judicial.

inquire [ɪnˈkwaɪəʳ] *vi* pedir informes // *vt* (*ask*) preguntar; (*seek information about*) pedir informes sobre; to ~ about *vt fus* (*person*) preguntar por; (*fact*) informarse de; to ~ into *vt fus* investigar, indagar; **inquiring** *a* (*mind*) penetrante; (*look*) interrogativo; **inquiry** *n* pregunta; (*LAW*) investigación *f*, pesquisa; (*commission*) comisión *f* investigadora; **inquiry office** *n* oficina de informaciones.

inquisitive [ɪnˈkwɪzɪtɪv] *a* (*curious*) activo, inquiridor(a); (*prying*) preguntón(ona), fisgón(ona).

inroad [ˈɪnrəud] *n* incursión *f*; (*fig*) invasión *f*.

insane [ɪnˈseɪn] *a* loco; (*MED*) demente.

insanitary [ɪnˈsænɪtərɪ] *a* insalubre.

insanity [ɪnˈsænɪtɪ] *n* demencia, locura.

insatiable [ɪnˈseɪʃəbl] *a* insaciable.

inscribe [ɪnˈskraɪb] *vt* inscribir; (*book etc*): to ~ (*to sb*) dedicar (a uno).

inscription [ɪnˈskrɪpʃən] *n* (*gen*) inscripción *f*; (*in book*) dedicatoria.

inscrutable [ɪnˈskruːtəbl] *a* inescrutable, insondable.

insect ['ɪnsɛkt] n insecto; ~**icide** [ɪn-'sɛktɪsaɪd] n insecticida m.

insecure [ɪnsɪ'kjuə*] a inseguro; **insecurity** n inseguridad f.

insensible [ɪn'sɛnsɪbl] a impasible, insensible; (unconscious) inconsciente.

insensitive [ɪn'sɛnsɪtɪv] a insensible.

inseparable [ɪn'sɛprəbl] a inseparable; **they were ~ friends** les unía una estrecha amistad.

insert [ɪn'səːt] vt (between things) intercalar; (into sth) introducir; (in paper) publicar; (: advert) poner // n ['ɪnsəːt] hoja suelta (intercalada); ~**ion** [ɪn'səːʃən] n inserción f; (publication) publicación f; (of pages) materia añadida.

inshore [ɪn'ʃɔː*] a cercano a la orilla o costa // ad (be) cerca de la orilla; (move) hacia la orilla.

inside ['ɪn'saɪd] n interior m; (lining) forro // a interior, interno; (secret) secreto // ad (within) (por) dentro; (with movement) hacia dentro; (fam: in prison) en la cárcel // prep dentro de; (of time): ~ **10 minutes** en menos de 10 minutos; ~**s** npl (col) tripas fpl; ~ **forward** n (SPORT) delantero interior; ~ **lane** n (AUT: in Britain) el lado o carril izquierdo; ~ **out** ad (turn) al revés; (know) a fondo.

insidious [ɪn'sɪdɪəs] a insidioso; (underground) clandestino.

insight ['ɪnsaɪt] n perspicacia.

insignificant [ɪnsɪg'nɪfɪknt] a insignificante.

insincere [ɪnsɪn'sɪə*] a poco sincero; **insincerity** [-'sɛrɪtɪ] n falta de sinceridad, doblez f.

insinuate [ɪn'sɪnjueɪt] vt insinuar; **insinuation** [-'eɪʃən] n insinuación f; (hint) indirecta.

insipid [ɪn'sɪpɪd] a soso, insulso.

insist [ɪn'sɪst] vi insistir; **to ~ on doing** empeñarse en hacer; **to ~ that** insistir en que; (claim) exigir que; ~**ence** n insistencia; (stubbornness) empeño; ~**ent** a insistente; empeñado.

insole ['ɪnsəul] n plantilla.

insolence ['ɪnsələns] n insolencia, descaro; **insolent** [-ənt] a insolente, descarado.

insoluble [ɪn'sɔljubl] a insoluble.

insolvent [ɪn'sɔlvənt] a insolvente.

insomnia [ɪn'sɔmnɪə] n insomnio.

inspect [ɪn'spɛkt] vt inspeccionar, examinar; (troops) pasar revista a; ~**ion** [ɪn'spɛkʃən] n inspección f, examen m; ~**or** n inspector/a m/f; (RAIL) revisor m.

inspiration [ɪnspə'reɪʃən] n inspiración f; **inspire** [ɪn'spaɪə*] vt inspirar.

instability [ɪnstə'bɪlɪtɪ] n inestabilidad f.

install [ɪn'stɔːl] vt instalar; ~**ation** [ɪnstə'leɪʃən] n instalación f.

instalment, (US) **installment** [ɪn-'stɔːlmənt] n plazo; (of story) entrega; (of TV serial etc) episodio.

instance ['ɪnstəns] n ejemplo, caso; **for ~** por ejemplo; **in the first ~** en primer lugar.

instant ['ɪnstənt] n instante m, momento // a instantáneo, inmediato; (coffee) en polvo; ~**ly** ad en seguida.

instead [ɪn'stɛd] ad en cambio; ~ **of** en lugar de, en vez de.

instep ['ɪnstɛp] n empeine m.

instigation [ɪnstɪ'geɪʃən] n instigación f.

instil [ɪn'stɪl] vt: **to ~ into** infundir a, inculcar en.

instinct ['ɪnstɪŋkt] n instinto; ~**ive** [-'stɪŋktɪv] a instintivo; ~**ively** [-'stɪŋktɪvlɪ] ad por instinto.

institute ['ɪnstɪtjuːt] n instituto; (professional body) colegio // vt (inquiry) iniciar, empezar; (proceedings) entablar.

institution [ɪnstɪ'tjuːʃən] n (gen) institución f; (beginning) iniciación f; (organization) instituto; (MED: home) asilo; (asylum) manicomio; (custom) costumbre f.

instruct [ɪn'strʌkt] vt: **to ~ sb in sth** instruir a uno en o sobre algo; **to ~ sb to do sth** dar instrucciones a uno de hacer algo; ~**ion** [ɪn'strʌkʃən] n (teaching) instrucción f; ~**ions** npl órdenes fpl; ~**ions (for use)** modo de empleo; ~**ive** a aleccionador(a); ~**or** n instructor/a m/f.

instrument ['ɪnstrumənt] n instrumento; ~**al** [-'mɛntl] a (MUS) instrumental; **to be ~al in** contribuir materialmente a; ~ **panel** n tablero (de instrumentos).

insubordinate [ɪnsə'bɔːdənɪt] a insubordinado; **insubordination** [-'neɪʃən] n insubordinación f; (disobedience) desobediencia.

insufferable [ɪn'sʌfrəbl] a insufrible.

insufficient [ɪnsə'fɪʃənt] a insuficiente.

insular ['ɪnsjulə*] a insular; (outlook) de miras estrechas.

insulate ['ɪnsjuleɪt] vt aislar; **insulating tape** n cinta aislante; **insulation** [-'leɪʃən] n aislamiento.

insulin ['ɪnsjulɪn] n insulina.

insult ['ɪnsʌlt] n insulto; (offence) ofensa // vt [ɪn'sʌlt] insultar, injuriar; ofender; ~**ing** a insultante; ofensivo.

insuperable [ɪn'sjuːprəbl] a insuperable.

insurance [ɪn'ʃuərəns] n seguro; **fire/life ~** seguro sobre la vida/contra incendios; ~ **agent** n agente m/f de seguros; ~ **policy** n póliza (de seguros).

insure [ɪn'ʃuə*] vt asegurar.

insurrection [ɪnsə'rɛkʃən] n insurrección f.

intact [ɪn'tækt] a íntegro; (unharmed) ileso, sano.

intake ['ɪnteɪk] n (TECH) entrada, toma; (: pipe) tubo de admisión; (of food) cantidad admitida; (SCOL): **an ~ of 200 a year** 200 matriculados al año.

intangible [ɪn'tændʒɪbl] a intangible.

integral ['ɪntɪgrəl] a (whole) íntegro; (part) integrante.

integrate ['ıntıgreıt] vt integrar /; vi integrarse.

integrity [ın'tegrıtı] n honradez f, rectitud f.

intellect ['ıntəlekt] n intelecto; ~ual [-'lektjuəl] a, n intelectual m/f.

intelligence [ın'telıdʒəns] n inteligencia; (MIL etc) informes mpl; I~ Service n Servicio de Inteligencia; **intelligent** [-ənt] a inteligente.

intelligible [ın'telıdʒıbl] a inteligible, comprensible.

intend [ın'tend] vt (gift etc): to ~ sth for destinar algo a; to ~ to do sth tener intención de o proponerse hacer algo; ~ed a (effect) deseado // n prometido/a.

intense [ın'tens] a intenso; (person) nervioso; ~ly ad intensamente; (very) sumamente.

intensify [ın'tensıfaı] vt intensificar; (increase) aumentar.

intensity [ın'tensıtı] n intensidad f; (strength) fuerza.

intensive [ın'tensıv] a intensivo; ~ care unit n centro de cuidados intensivos.

intent [ın'tent] n propósito // a (absorbed) absorto; (attentive) atento; to all ~s and purposes prácticamente; to be ~ on doing sth estar resuelto a hacer algo.

intention [ın'tenʃən] n intento, propósito; (plan) proyecto; ~al a intencional, deliberado; ~ally ad a propósito.

intently [ın'tentlı] ad atentamente, fijamente.

inter [ın'tə:*] vt enterrar.

interact [ıntər'ækt] vi influirse mutuamente; ~ion [-'ækʃən] n influencia mútua, acción f recíproca.

intercede [ıntə'si:d] vi: to ~ (with) interceder (con).

intercept [ıntə'sept] vt interceptar; (stop) detener; ~ion [-'sepʃən] n intercepción f; detención f.

interchange ['ıntətʃeındʒ] n intercambio; (exchange) canje m; (on motorway) paso a desnivel // vt [ıntə'tʃeındʒ] intercambiar; canjear; ~able a intercambiable.

intercom ['ıntəkɔm] n sistema m de intercomunicación.

interconnect [ıntəkə'nekt] vi (rooms) conectarse.

intercourse ['ıntəkɔːs] n (sexual) relaciones fpl; (social) trato.

interest ['ıntrıst] n (also COMM) interés m; (profit) ventaja, provecho // vt interesar; to be ~ed in interesarse por; ~ing a interesante.

interfere [ıntə'fıə*] vi: to ~ in (quarrel, other people's business) entrometerse o mezclarse en; to ~ with (hinder) estorbar; (damage) estropear; (radio) interferir con.

interference [ıntə'fıərəns] n (gen) intromisión f; (RADIO, TV) interferencia.

interim ['ıntərım] n: in the ~ entretanto, en el interino.

interior [ın'tıərıə*] n interior m // a interior.

interject [ıntə'dʒekt] vt interponerse; ~ion [-'dʒekʃən] n interyección f.

interlock [ıntə'lɔk] vi entrelazarse; (wheels etc) endentarse.

interloper ['ıntələupə*] n intruso.

interlude ['ıntəlu:d] n intérvalo; (rest) descanso; (THEATRE) intermedio.

intermarry [ıntə'mærı] vi casarse (parientes).

intermediary [ıntə'mi:dıərı] n intermediario.

intermediate [ıntə'mi:dıət] a intermedio, medio.

intermission [ıntə'mıʃən] n (THEATRE) descanso.

intermittent [ıntə'mıtnt] a intermitente.

intern [ın'tə:n] vt internar; (enclose) encerrar // a ['ıntə:n] (US) interno.

internal [ın'tə:nl] a interno, interior; ~ly ad interiormente; 'not to be taken ~ly' 'uso externo'; ~ revenue n (US) rentas fpl públicas.

international [ıntə'næʃənl] a internacional; ~ game partido internacional; ~ player jugador/a m/f internacional.

interplay ['ıntəpleı] n interacción f.

interpret [ın'tə:prıt] vt interpretar; (translate) traducir; (understand) entender // vi hacer de intérprete; ~ation [-'teıʃən] n interpretación f; traducción f; entendimiento; ~er n intérprete m/f.

interrelated [ıntərı'leıtıd] a interrelacionado.

interrogate [ın'terəugeıt] vt interrogar; **interrogation** [-'geıʃən] n interrogatorio; **interrogative** [ıntə'rogatıv] a interrogativo.

interrupt [ıntə'rʌpt] vt, vi interrumpir; ~ion [-'rʌpʃən] n interrupción f.

intersect [ıntə'sekt] vt cruzar // vi (roads) cruzarse; ~ion [-'sekʃən] n intersección f; (of roads) cruce m.

intersperse [ıntə'spə:s] vt esparcir, entremezclar.

intertwine [ıntə'twaın] vt entrelazar // vi entrelazarse.

interval ['ıntəvl] n intérvalo; (scoL) recreo; (THEATRE, SPORT) descanso; at ~s a ratos, de vez en cuando.

intervene [ıntə'vi:n] vi (gen) intervenir; (take part) participar; (occur) sobrevenir; **intervention** [-'venʃən] n intervención f.

interview ['ıntəvju:] n (RADIO, TV etc) entrevista // vt entrevistarse con; ~ee [-'i:] n entrevistado/a; ~er n entrevistador/a m/f.

intestine [ın'testın] n: large/small ~ intestino grueso/delgado.

intimacy ['ıntıməsı] n intimidad f; (relations) relaciones fpl íntimas.

intimate ['ıntımıt] a íntimo; (friendship) estrecho; (knowledge) profundo // vt ['ıntımeıt] (announce) dar a entender.

intimidate [ın'tımıdeıt] vt intimidar,

amedrentar; **intimidation** [-'deɪʃən] n intimidación f.

into ['ɪntu] prep (gen) en; (towards) a; (inside) hacia el interior de; ~ **3 pieces/French** en 3 pedazos/ francés.

intolerable [ɪn'tɔlərəbl] a intolerable, insufrible; **intolerance** [-rəns] n intolerancia; **intolerant** [-rənt] a: **intolerant of** intolerante con o para.

intonation [ɪntəu'neɪʃən] n entonación f.

intoxicate [ɪn'tɔksɪkeɪt] vt embriagar; ~d a embriagado; **intoxication** [-'keɪʃən] n embriaguez f.

intractable [ɪn'træktəbl] a (child) intratable; (material) difícil de trabajar; (problem) espinoso.

intransigent [ɪn'trænsɪdʒənt] a intransigente.

intransitive [ɪn'trænsɪtɪv] a intransitivo.

intravenous [ɪntrə'viːnəs] a intravenoso.

intrepid [ɪn'trepɪd] a intrépido.

intricate ['ɪntrɪkət] a intrincado; (complex) complejo.

intrigue [ɪn'triːg] n intriga // vt interesar, fascinar // vi andar en intrigas; **intriguing** a intrigante.

intrinsic [ɪn'trɪnsɪk] a intrínseco.

introduce [ɪntrə'djuːs] vt introducir, meter; **to ~ sb (to sb)** presentar uno (a otro); **to ~ sb to** (pastime, technique) introducir a uno a; **introduction** [-'dʌkʃən] n introducción f; (of person) presentación f; **introductory** [-'dʌktərɪ] a preliminar.

introspective [ɪntrəu'spektɪv] a introspectivo.

introvert ['ɪntrəuvɜːt] a, n introvertido/a.

intrude [ɪn'truːd] vi (person) entrometerse; **to ~ on or into** estorbar; **intruder** n intruso/a; **intrusion** [-ʒən] n invasión f; **intrusive** [-sɪv] a intruso.

intuition [ɪntjuː'ɪʃən] n intuición f; **intuitive** [-'tjuːɪtɪv] a intuitivo.

inundate ['ɪnʌndeɪt] vt: **to ~ with** inundar de.

invade [ɪn'veɪd] vt invadir; **invader** n invasor/a m/f.

invalid [ɪn'vælɪd] n inválido/a // a [ɪn'vælɪd] (not valid) inválido, nulo; ~ate [ɪn'vælɪdeɪt] vt invalidar, anular.

invaluable [ɪn'væljuəbl] a inestimable.

invariable [ɪn'veərɪəbl] a invariable.

invasion [ɪn'veɪʒən] n invasión f.

invent [ɪn'vent] vt inventar; ~**ion** [ɪn'venʃən] n invento; (inventiveness) inventiva; (lie) ficción f, mentira; ~**ive** a ingenioso; ~**iveness** n ingenio, inventiva; ~**or** n inventor/a m/f.

inventory ['ɪnvəntrɪ] n inventario f.

inverse [ɪn'vɜːs] a, n inverso; ~**ly** ad a la inversa.

invert [ɪn'vɜːt] vt invertir, volver al revés; ~**ed commas** npl comillas fpl.

invertebrate [ɪn'vɜːtɪbrət] n invertebrado.

invest [ɪn'vest] vt, vi invertir.

investigate [ɪn'vestɪgeɪt] vt investigar; (study) estudiar, examinar; **investigation**

[-'geɪʃən] n investigación f, pesquisa; examen m; **investigator** n investigador/a m/f.

investiture [ɪn'vestɪtʃə*] n investidura.

investment [ɪn'vestmənt] n inversión f.

investor [ɪn'vestə*] n inversionista m/f.

inveterate [ɪn'vetərət] a empedernido.

invigorating [ɪn'vɪgəreɪtɪŋ] a vigorizante.

invincible [ɪn'vɪnsɪbl] a invencible.

inviolate [ɪn'vaɪələt] a inviolado.

invisible [ɪn'vɪzɪbl] a invisible; ~ **ink** n tinta simpática.

invitation [ɪnvɪ'teɪʃən] n invitación f.

invite [ɪn'vaɪt] vt (gen) invitar; (to drink, food) convidar; (opinions etc) solicitar, pedir; (trouble) buscarse; **inviting** a atractivo; (look) incitante; (food) apetitoso.

invoice ['ɪnvɔɪs] n factura // vt facturar.

invoke [ɪn'vəuk] vt invocar; (aid) implorar; (law) recurrir a.

involuntary [ɪn'vɔləntrɪ] a involuntario.

involve [ɪn'vɔlv] vt (entail) suponer, implicar; **to ~ sb (in)** comprometer a uno (con); ~**d** a complicado; ~**ment** n (gen) enredo; (obligation) compromiso; (difficulty) apuro.

invulnerable [ɪn'vʌlnərəbl] a invulnerable.

inward ['ɪnwəd] a (movement) interior, interno; (thought, feeling) íntimo; ~**ly** ad (feel, think etc) para sí, para dentro; ~**(s)** ad hacia dentro.

iodine ['aɪoudiːn] n yodo.

iota [aɪ'əutə] n (fig) jota, ápice m.

IOU n abbr of **I owe you** pagaré m.

IQ n abbr of **intelligence quotient** cociente m intelectual.

Iran [ɪ'rɑːn] n Irán m; ~**ian** [ɪ'reɪnɪən] a, n iraní m/f.

Iraq [ɪ'rɑːk] n El Irak; ~**i** a, n iraki m/f.

irascible [ɪ'ræsɪbl] a irascible.

irate [aɪ'reɪt] a enojado, indignado.

Ireland ['aɪələnd] n Irlanda.

iris ['aɪrɪs], pl ~**es** n (ANAT) iris m; (BOT) lirio.

Irish ['aɪrɪʃ] a irlandés(esa) // npl: **the ~** los irlandeses; ~**man/ woman** n irlandés/esa m/f.

irk [ɜːk] vt fastidiar; ~**some** a fastidioso.

iron ['aɪən] n hierro; (for clothes) plancha // a de hierro // vt (clothes) planchar; ~**s** npl (chains) grillos mpl: **to ~ out** vt (crease) quitar; (fig) allanar.

ironic(al) [aɪ'rɔnɪk(l)] a irónico.

ironing ['aɪənɪŋ] n (act) planchado; (ironed clothes) ropa planchada; (to be ironed) ropa por planchar; ~ **board** n tabla de planchar.

ironmonger ['aɪənmʌŋgə*] n ferretero; ~**'s (shop)** n ferretería, quincallería.

iron ore ['aɪən'ɔː*] n mineral m de hierro.

irony ['aɪrənɪ] n ironía; **the ~ of it is that...** lo irónico es que...

irrational [ɪ'ræʃənl] a irracional.

irreconcilable [ɪrekən'saɪləbl] a

inconciliable, irreconciliable.

irrefutable [ırı'fju:təbl] a irrefutable.

irregular [ı'regjulə*] a irregular (surface) desigual; (illegal) ilegal; ~**ity** [-'lærıtı] n irregularidad f; desigualdad f.

irrelevant [ı'reləvənt] a fuera de lugar, inoportuno.

irreparable [ı'repröbl] a irreparable.

irreplaceable [ırı'pleısəbl] a irremplazable.

irrepressible [ırı'presəbl] a irrefrenable.

irreproachable [ırı'prəutfəb] a irreprochable.

irresistible [ırı'zıstıbl] a irresistible.

irresolute [ı'rezəlu:t] a indeciso.

irrespective [ırı'spektıv]: ~ **of** prep sin tener en cuenta, no importa.

irresponsible [ırı'sponsıbl] a (act) irresponsable; (person) poco serio.

irreverent [ı'revərnt] a irreverente, irrespetuoso.

irrevocable [ı'revəkəbl] a irrevocable.

irrigate ['ırıgeıt] vt regar; **irrigation** [-'geıʃən] n riego.

irritable ['ırıtəbl] a irritable; (moor) de mal humor.

irritate ['ırıteıt] vt irritar; (MED) picar; **irritation** [-'teıʃən] n irritación f, enojo; picazón m, picor m.

is [ız] vb see **be.**

Islam ['ızla:m] n Islam m.

island ['aılənd] n isla; (also: **traffic** ~) refugio; ~**er** n isleño/a.

isle [aıl] n isla.

isn't ['ıznt] = **is not.**

isolate ['aısəleıt] vt aislar; ~**d** a aislado; **isolation** ['aısə'leıʃən] n aislamiento.

isotope ['aısəutəup] n isótopo.

Israel ['ızreıl] n Israel m; ~**i** [ız'reılı] a, n israelí m/f.

issue ['ısju:] n cuestión f, asunto; (outcome) resultado; (of banknotes etc) emisión f; (of newspaper etc) número; (offspring) sucesión f, descendencia // vt (rations, equipment) distribuir, repartir; (orders) dar; (certificate) expedir; (decree) promulgar; (book) publicar; (cheques) extender; (banknotes, stamps) emitir.

isthmus ['ısməs] n istmo.

it [ıt] pron (subject) él/ella; (direct object) lo/la; (indirect object) le; (impersonal) ello; (after prep) él/ella/ello; ~**'s raining** llueve, está lloviendo; **where is** ~? ¿dónde está?; **he's proud of** ~ le enorgullece; **he agreed to** ~ está de acuerdo (con ello).

Italian [ı'tæljən] a italiano // n italiano/a; (LING) el italiano.

italic [ı'tælık] a cursivo; ~**s** npl cursiva sg.

Italy ['ıtəlı] n Italia.

itch [ıtʃ] n comezón m; (fig) prurito // vi (person) sentir o tener comezón; (part of body) picar; **I'm** ~**ing to do sth** rabio por hacer algo; ~**ing** n comezón m; ~**y** a: **to be** ~**y** picar.

it'd ['ıtd] = **it would; it had.**

item ['aıtəm] n (gen) artículo; (detail) detalle m; (on agenda) asunto a tratar; (in programme) número; (also: **news** ~) noticia, ~**ize** vt detallar.

itinerant [ı'tınərənt] a ambulante.

itinerary [aı'tınərərı] n itinerario.

it'll ['ıtl] = **it will, it shall.**

its [ıts] a su // pron (el) suyo/(la) suya.

it's [ıts] = **it is; it has.**

itself [ıt'self] pron (reflexive) sí mismo/a; (emphatic) él mismo/ella misma.

ITV n abbr of **Independent Television.**

I.U.D. n abbr of **intra-uterine device** DIU.

I've [aıv] = **I have.**

ivory ['aıvərı] n marfil m; ~ **tower** n (fig) torre f de marfil.

ivy ['aıvı] n hiedra.

J

jab [dʒæb] vt (elbow) dar un codazo a; (punch) dar un golpe rápido a; **to** ~ **sth into sth** clavar algo en algo // n codazo; golpe m (rápido); (MED: col) pinchazo.

jabber ['dʒæbə*] vt, vi farfullar.

jack [dʒæk] n (AUT) gato; (BOWLS) boliche m; (CARDS) sota; **to** ~ **up** vt (AUT) alzar con gato.

jackdaw ['dʒækdɔ:] n grajilla.

jacket ['dʒækıt] n chaqueta, americana; (of boiler etc) camisa; (of book) sobrecubierta; **potatoes in their** ~**s** patatas con su piel.

jack-knife ['dʒæknaıf] n navaja.

jackpot ['dʒækpɔt] n premio gordo.

jade [dʒeıd] n (stone) jade m.

jaded ['dʒeıdıd] a (tired) cansado; (fed-up) hastiado.

jagged ['dʒægıd] a dentado.

jail [dʒeıl] n cárcel f; ~**break** n fuga o evasión f (de la cárcel); ~**er** n carcelero.

jam [dʒæm] n mermelada; (also: **traffic** ~) embotellamiento; (difficulty) apuro // vt (passage etc) obstruir, cerrar; (mechanism, drawer etc) atascar; (RADIO) interferir // vi atascarse, trabarse; **to** ~ **sth into sth** meter algo por la fuerza en algo.

Jamaica [dʒə'meıkə] n Jamaica.

jangle ['dʒæŋgl] vi sonar (de manera) discordante.

janitor ['dʒænıtə*] n (caretaker) portero, conserje m.

January ['dʒænjuərı] n enero.

Japan [dʒə'pæn] n (el) Japón; ~**ese** [dʒæpə'ni:z] a japonés(esa) // n, pl inv japonés/esa m/f; (LING) japonés m.

jar [dʒɑ:*] n (glass: large) jarra; (: small) tarro // vi (sound) chirriar; (colours) desentonar.

jargon ['dʒɑ:gən] n jerga.

jasmin(e) ['dʒæzmın] n jazmín m.

jaundice ['dʒɔ:ndıs] n ictericia; ~**d** a (fig: embittered) amargado; (: disillusioned) desilusionado.

jaunt [dʒɔ:nt] n excursión f; ~y a alegre.
javelin ['dʒævlɪn] n jabalina.
jaw [dʒɔ:] n mandíbula.
jaywalker ['dʒeɪwɔ:kə*] n peatón m imprudente.
jazz [dʒæz] n jazz m; **to ~ up** vt (liven up) animar, avivar; ~**y** a de colores llamativos.
jealous ['dʒɛləs] a (gen) celoso; (envious) envidioso; **to be ~** tener celos; ~**y** n celos mpl; envidia.
jeans [dʒi:nz] npl (pantalones) vaqueros o tejanos mpl.
jeep [dʒi:p] n jeep m.
jeer [dʒɪə*] vi: **to ~ (at)** (boo) abuchear; (mock) mofarse (de).
jelly ['dʒɛlɪ] n jalea, gelatina; ~**fish** n medusa.
jeopardize ['dʒɛpədaɪz] vt arriesgar, poner en peligro; **jeopardy** [-dɪ] n: **to be in jeopardy** estar en peligro o a riesgo.
jerk [dʒɔ:k] n (jolt) sacudida; (wrench) tirón m // vt dar una sacudida a // vi (vehicle) traquetear.
jerkin ['dʒɔ:kɪn] n cazadora.
jerky ['dʒɔ:kɪ] a espasmódico.
jersey ['dʒɔ:zɪ] n jersey m.
jest [dʒɛst] n broma.
jet [dʒɛt] n (of gas, liquid) chorro; (AVIAT) avión m a reacción; ~**-black** a de azabache; ~ **engine** n motor m a reacción.
jettison ['dʒɛtɪsn] vt desechar.
jetty ['dʒɛtɪ] n muelle m, embarcadero.
Jew [dʒu:] n judío; ~**ess** n judía.
jewel ['dʒu:əl] n joya; (in watch) rubí m; ~**ler** n joyero; ~**ler's (shop)** n joyería; ~**lery** n joyas fpl, alhajas fpl.
Jewish ['dʒu:ɪʃ] a judío.
jibe [dʒaɪb] n pulla.
jiffy ['dʒɪfɪ] n (col): **in a ~** en un instante.
jig [dʒɪg] n jiga.
jigsaw ['dʒɪgsɔ:] n (also: ~ **puzzle**) rompecabezas m inv.
jilt [dʒɪlt] vt dar calabazas a.
jingle ['dʒɪŋgl] n (advert) estribillo // vi tintinear.
jinx [dʒɪŋks] n (col) gafe m, maldición f.
jitters ['dʒɪtəz] npl (col): **to get the ~** ponerse nervioso.
job [dʒɔb] n (gen) trabajo; (task) tarea; (duty) deber m; (post) empleo; (fam: difficulty) dificultad f; **it's a good ~ that...** menos mal que...; **just the ~!** ¡estupendo!; ~**less** a sin trabajo.
jockey ['dʒɔkɪ] n jockey m // vi: **to ~ for position** maniobrar para conseguir una posición.
jocular ['dʒɔkjulə*] a (humorous) jocoso; (merry) alegre.
jog [dʒɔg] vt empujar (ligeramente) // vi (run) hacer footing; **to ~ along** ir tirando; **to ~ sb's memory** refrescar la memoria a uno; ~**ging** n footing m.
join [dʒɔɪn] vt (things) juntar, unir; (become member of) inscribirse en, afiliarse a;

(meet: people) reunirse o encontrarse con // vi (roads, rivers) confluir // n juntura; **to ~ up** vi unirse; (MIL) alistarse.
joiner ['dʒɔɪnə*] n carpintero; ~**y** n carpintería.
joint [dʒɔɪnt] n (TECH) junta, unión f; (wood) ensambladura; (ANAT) articulación f; (CULIN) asado; (col: place) garito // a (common) común; (combined) combinado; (committee) mixto; **by ~ agreement** por común acuerdo; ~**ly** ad (gen) mutuamente, en común; (collectively) colectivamente; (together) conjuntamente.
joke [dʒəuk] n chiste m; (also: **practical ~**) broma // vi bromear; **to play a ~ on** gastar una broma a; **joker** n chistoso/a, bromista m/f; (CARDS) comodín m.
jolly ['dʒɔlɪ] a (merry) alegre; (enjoyable) divertido // ad (col) muy, terriblemente.
jolt [dʒəult] n (shake) sacudida; (blow) golpe m; (shock) susto // vt sacudir; asustar.
Jordan ['dʒɔ:dən] n Jordania.
jostle ['dʒɔsl] vt dar empellones a, codear.
jot [dʒɔt] n: **not one ~** ni jota, ni pizca; **to ~ down** vt apuntar; ~**ter** n bloc m; (SCOL) cuaderno.
journal ['dʒɔ:nl] n (paper) periódico; (magazine) revista; (diary) diario; ~**ese** [-'li:z] n (pej) lenguaje m periodístico; ~**ism** n periodismo; ~**ist** n periodista m/f.
journey ['dʒɔ:nɪ] n viaje m; (distance covered) trayecto // vi viajar; **return ~** viaje de regreso.
joy [dʒɔɪ] n alegría; ~**ful**, ~**ous** a alegre; ~ **ride** n paseo en coche; (illegal) paseo en coche robado.
J.P. n abbr of **Justice of the Peace.**
Jr, Jun., Junr abbr of **junior.**
jubilant ['dʒu:bɪlnt] a jubiloso; **jubilation** [-'leɪʃən] n júbilo.
jubilee ['dʒu:bɪli:] n aniversario.
judge [dʒʌdʒ] n juez m // vt (gen) juzgar; (estimate) considerar; **judg(e)ment** n juicio; (punishment) sentencia, fallo.
judicial [dʒu:'dɪʃl] a judicial.
judicious [dʒu:'dɪʃəs] a juicioso.
judo ['dʒu:dəu] n judo.
jug [dʒʌg] n jarro.
juggernaut ['dʒʌgənɔ:t] n (huge truck) mastodonte m.
juggle ['dʒʌgl] vi hacer juegos malabares; **juggler** n malabarista m/f.
Jugoslav ['ju:gəu'slɑ:v] a, n = **Yugoslav.**
juice [dʒu:s] n zumo, jugo; **juicy** a jugoso.
jukebox ['dʒu:kbɔks] n rocola.
July [dʒu:'laɪ] n julio.
jumble ['dʒʌmbl] n revoltijo // vt (also: ~ **up**: mix up) revolver; (: disarrange) mezclar; ~ **sale** n (Brit) venta de objetos usados.
jumbo (jet) ['dʒʌmbəu] n jumbo-jet m.
jump [dʒʌmp] vi saltar, dar saltos; (start) asustarse, sobresaltarse; (increase) aumentar // vt saltar // n salto; aumento; **to ~ the queue** colarse.

jumper ['dʒʌmpə*] n suéter m, jersey m.
jumpy ['dʒʌmpɪ] a nervioso.
junction ['dʒʌŋkʃən] n (of roads) cruce m; (RAIL) empalme m.
juncture ['dʒʌŋktʃə*] n: **at this ~** en este momento, en esta coyuntura.
June [dʒuːn] n junio.
jungle ['dʒʌŋgl] n selva, jungla.
junior ['dʒuːnɪə*] a (in age) menor, más joven; (competition) juvenil; (position) subalterno // n menor m/f, joven m/f; **~ school** n escuela primaria.
junk [dʒʌŋk] n (cheap goods) baratijas fpl, (lumber) trastos viejos mpl; (rubbish) basura; (ship) junco; **~shop** n tienda de objetos usados.
jurisdiction [dʒuərɪs'dɪkʃən] n jurisdicción f.
jurisprudence [dʒuərɪs'pruːdəns] n jurisprudencia.
jury ['dʒuərɪ] n jurado.
just [dʒʌst] a justo // ad (exactly) exactamente; (only) sólo, solamente; **he's ~ done it/left** acaba de hacerlo/irse; **~ right** perfecto, perfectamente; **~ two o'clock** las dos en punto; **~ as well that...** menos mal que...; **~ as he was leaving** en el momento en que se marchaba; **~ before/enough** justo antes/lo suficiente; **~ here** aquí mismo; **he ~ missed** ha fallado por poco; **~ listen** escucha (solamente).
justice ['dʒʌstɪs] n justicia; **J~ of the Peace (J.P.)** n juez m de paz.
justifiable [dʒʌstɪ'faɪəbl] a justificable; **justifiably** ad justificadamente.
justification [dʒʌstɪfɪ'keɪʃən] n justificación f; **justify** ['dʒʌstɪfaɪ] vt justificar.
justly ['dʒʌstlɪ] ad (gen) justamente; (with reason) con razón.
justness ['dʒʌstnɪs] n justicia.
jut [dʒʌt] vi (also: **~ out**) sobresalir.
juvenile ['dʒuːvənaɪl] a juvenil; (court) de menores; (books) para jóvenes // n joven m/f, menor m/f de edad.
juxtapose ['dʒʌkstəpəuz] vt yuxtaponer.

K

kaleidoscope [kə'laɪdəskəup] n calidoscopio.
kangaroo [kæŋgə'ruː] n canguro.
keel [kiːl] n quilla; **on an even ~** (fig) en equilibrio.
keen [kiːn] a (interest, desire) grande, vivo; (eye, intelligence) agudo; (competition) intenso; (edge) afilado; (eager) entusiasta inv; **to be ~ to do** or **on doing sth** tener muchas ganas de hacer algo; **to be ~ on sth/sb** interesarse por algo/alguien; **~ness** n (eagerness) entusiasmo, interés m.
keep [kiːp], pt, pp **kept** vt (retain, preserve) guardar; (hold back) quedarse con; (shop, diary) llevar; (feed: family etc) mantener; (promise) cumplir; (chickens, bees etc)

criar // vi (food) conservarse; (remain) seguir, continuar // n (of castle) torreón m; (food etc) comida, subsistencia; **to ~ doing sth** seguir haciendo algo; **to ~ sb from doing sth** impedir a alguien hacer algo; **to ~ sth from happening** impedir que algo ocurra; **to ~ sb happy** hacer a alguien feliz; **to ~ a place tidy** mantener un lugar limpio; **to ~ sth to o.s.** guardar algo para sí mismo; **to ~ sth (back) from sb** ocultar algo a alguien; **to ~ time** (clock) mantener la hora exacta; **to ~ on** vi seguir, continuar; **to ~ out** vi (stay out) permanecer fuera; **'~ out'** prohibida la entrada; **to ~ up** vt mantener, conservar // vi no retrasarse; **to ~ up with** (pace) ir al paso de; (level) mantenerse a la altura de; **~er** n guardián m; **~ing** n (care) cuidado; **in ~ing with** de acuerdo con; **~sake** n recuerdo.
keg [keg] n barrilete m, barril m.
kennel ['kenl] n perrera; **~s** npl criadero sg de perros.
Kenya ['kenjə] n Kenia.
kept [kept] pt, pp de **keep**.
kerb [kəːb] n bordillo.
kernel ['kəːnl] n almendra.
kerosene ['kerəsiːn] n keroseno.
ketchup ['ketʃəp] n salsa de tomate, catsup m.
kettle ['ketl] n hervidor m, olla.
key [kiː] n (gen) llave f; (MUS) tono; (of piano, typewriter) tecla; **~board** n teclado; **~hole** n ojo (de la cerradura); **~note** n (MUS) tónica; **~ring** n llavero; **~stone** n piedra clave.
khaki ['kɑːkɪ] n caqui.
kick [kɪk] vt (person) dar una patada a; (ball) dar un puntapié a // vi (horse) dar coces // n patada; puntapié m; (of rifle) culatazo; (thrill): **he does it for ~s** lo hace para divertirse; **to ~ off** vi (SPORT) hacer el saque inicial; **~-off** n (SPORT) saque m inicial.
kid [kɪd] n (child) chiquillo; (animal) cabrito; (leather) cabritilla // vi (col) bromear.
kidnap ['kɪdnæp] vt secuestrar; **~per** n secuestrador/a m/f; **~ping** n secuestro.
kidney ['kɪdnɪ] n riñón m.
kill [kɪl] vt (gen) matar; (murder) asesinar; (destroy) destruir; (finish off) acabar con // n acto de matar; **~er** n asesino; **~ing** n (one) asesinato; (several) matanza // a (funny) divertido.
kiln [kɪln] n horno.
kilo ['kiːləu] n kilo; **~gram(me)** ['kɪləugræm] n kilo, kilogramo; **~metre, ~meter** (US) ['kɪləmiːtə*] n kilómetro; **~watt** ['kɪləuwɒt] n kilovatio.
kilt [kɪlt] n falda escocesa.
kimono [kɪ'məunəu] n quimono.
kin [kɪn] n parientes mpl.
kind [kaɪnd] a (generous) bondadoso; (good) bueno, amable // n clase f, especie f; (species) género; **in ~** (COMM) en

especie; a ~ of una especie de; two of a ~ dos de la misma especie.

kindergarten ['kɪndəgɑːtn] n jardín m de infancia.

kind-hearted [kaɪnd'hɑːtɪd] a bondadoso, de buen corazón.

kindle ['kɪndl] vt encender.

kindly ['kaɪndlɪ] a (gen) bondadoso; (good) bueno; (gentle) cariñoso // ad bondadosamente, amablemente; **will you ~**... sea Usted tan amable de... .

kindness ['kaɪndnɪs] n bondad f, amabilidad f.

kindred ['kɪndrɪd] n familia, parientes mpl // a: ~ **spirit** espíritu m afín.

king [kɪŋ] n rey m; ~**dom** n reino; ~**fisher** n martín m pescador; ~**-size** a de tamaño extra.

kink [kɪŋk] n (of rope) enroscadura.

kinky ['kɪŋkɪ] a (odd) excéntrico; (pej) pervertido.

kiosk ['kiːɔsk] n quiosco; (TEL) cabina.

kipper ['kɪpə*] n arenque m ahumado.

kiss [kɪs] n beso // vt besar; **to ~ (each other)** besarse.

kit [kɪt] n (gen) avíos mpl; (equipment) equipo; (set of tools etc) (caja de) herramientas fpl; (for assembly) mecano.

kitchen ['kɪtʃɪn] n cocina; ~ **garden** n huerto; ~ **sink** n fregadero; ~**ware** n batería de cocina.

kite [kaɪt] n (toy) cometa.

kitten ['kɪtn] n gatito.

kitty ['kɪtɪ] n (pool of money) fondo común; (CARDS) polla.

kleptomaniac [klɛptəu'meɪnɪæk] n cleptómano/a.

knack [næk] n: **to have the ~ of doing sth** tener el don de hacer algo.

knapsack ['næpsæk] n mochila.

knead [niːd] vt amasar.

knee [niː] n rodilla; ~**cap** n rótula.

kneel [niːl], pt, pp **knelt** vi arrodillarse.

knell [nɛl] n toque m de difuntos.

knelt [nɛlt] pt, pp of **kneel**.

knew [njuː] pt of **know**.

knickers ['nɪkəz] npl bragas fpl.

knife [naɪf], pl **knives** n cuchillo // vt acuchillar.

knight [naɪt] n caballero; (CHESS) caballo; ~**hood** n caballería; (title): **to get a ~hood** recibir el título de sir.

knit [nɪt] vt hacer a punto; (brows) fruncir // vi hacer punto; (bones) soldarse; **to ~ together** (fig) unir, juntar; ~**ting** n labor f de punto; ~**ting machine** n máquina de tricotar; ~**ting needle** n aguja de hacer punto; ~**wear** n géneros mpl de punto.

knives [naɪvz] pl of **knife**.

knob [nɔb] n (of door) tirador m; (of stick) puño; (lump) bulto; (fig): **a ~ of butter** una porción de mantequilla.

knock [nɔk] vt (strike) golpear; (bump into) chocar contra; (fig: col) denigrar // n golpe m; (on door) llamada; **to ~ at or on the door** llamar a la puerta; **to ~ down**

vt atropellar; **to ~ off** vi (col: finish) despachar // vt (col: steal) biriar; **to ~ out** vt dejar sin sentido; (BOXING) poner fuera de combate, dejar K.O.; ~**er** n (on door) aldaba; ~**-kneed** a patizambo; ~**out** n (BOXING) K.O. m, knockout m.

knot [nɔt] n (gen) nudo // vt anudar; ~**ty** a (fig) complicado.

know [nəu], pt **knew**, pp **known** vt (gen) saber; (person, author, place) conocer; **to ~ that**... saber que...; **to ~ how to swim** saber nadar; ~**-all** n sabelotodo m/f; ~**-how** n habilidad f; ~**ing** a (of complicity) de complicidad (: spiteful) malicioso; ~**ingly** ad (purposely) adrede; (spitefully) maliciosamente.

knowledge ['nɔlɪdʒ] n (gen) conocimiento; (range of learning) saber m, conocimientos mpl; (learning) erudición f, ciencia; ~**able** a entendido, erudito.

known [nəun] pp of **know**.

knuckle ['nʌkl] n nudillo.

K.O. n abbr of **knockout**.

Koran [kɔ'rɑːn] n Corán m.

L

l. abbr of **litre**.

lab [læb] n abbr of **laboratory**.

label ['leɪbl] n etiqueta; (brand: of record) marca // vt poner etiqueta a.

laboratory [lə'bɔrətɔrɪ] n laboratorio.

laborious [lə'bɔːrɪəs] a penoso.

labour, labor (US) ['leɪbə*] n (task) trabajo; (~ force) mano f de obra; (workers) trabajadores mpl; (MED) (dolores mpl del) parto // vi: **to ~ (at)** trabajar (en) // vt insistir en; **in ~** (MED) de parto; **L~, the L~** party el partido laborista; **hard ~** trabajos mpl forzados; ~**ed** a (movement) penoso; (style) pesado; ~**er** n peón m; (on farm) peón m, bracero; (day ~er) jornalero.

labyrinth ['læbɪrɪnθ] n laberinto.

lace [leɪs] n encaje m; (of shoe etc) cordón m // vt (shoe) atar.

lack [læk] n (absence) falta; (scarcity) escasez f // vt no tener, carecer de; **through or for ~** of por falta de; **to be ~ing** faltar, no haber.

lackadaisical [lækə'deɪzɪkl] a (careless) descuidado; (indifferent) indiferente.

laconic [lə'kɔnɪk] a lacónico.

lacquer ['lækə*] n laca.

lad [læd] n muchacho, chico; (in stable etc) mozo.

ladder ['lædə*] n escalera (de mano); (in tights) carrera // vt (tights) hacer una carrera en.

laden ['leɪdn] a: ~ (with) cargado (de).

ladle ['leɪdl] n cucharón m.

lady ['leɪdɪ] n señora; (distinguished, noble) dama; **young ~** señorita; **'ladies' (toilets)** 'señoras'; ~**-bird**, ~**bug** (US) n mariquita; ~**-in-waiting** n dama de honor; ~**like** a fino.

lag [læg] vi (also: ~ **behind**) retrasarse,

quedarse atrás // vt (pipes) calorifugar

lager ['lɑːgəˀ] n cerveza (rubia).

lagging ['lægɪŋ] n revestimiento.

lagoon [lə'guːn] n laguna.

laid [leɪd] pt, pp of **lay.**

lain [leɪn] pp of **lie.**

lair [lɛəˀ] n guarida.

lake [leɪk] n lago.

lamb [læm] n cordero; (meat) carne f de cordero; ~ **chop** n chuleta de cordero; **lambswool** n lana de cordero.

lame [leɪm] a cojo; (weak) débil, poco convincente.

lament [lə'mɛnt] n lamento // vt lamentarse de; ~**able** ['læməntəbl] a lamentable.

laminated ['læmɪneɪtɪd] a laminado.

lamp [læmp] n lámpara.

lampoon [læm'puːn] vt satirizar.

lamp: ~**post** n farol m; ~**shade** n pantalla.

lance [lɑːns] n lanza // vt (MED) abrir con lanzeta; ~ **corporal** n soldado de primera clase.

lancet ['lɑːnsɪt] n lanceta.

land [lænd] n (gen) tierra; (country) país m; (piece of ~) terreno; (estate) tierras fpl, finca; (AGR) campo // vi (from ship) desembarcar; (AVIAT) aterrizar; (fig: fall) caer, terminar // vt (obtain) conseguir; (passengers, goods) desembarcar; **to** ~ **up in/at** ir a parar a/en; ~**ing** n desembarco; aterrizaje m; (of staircase) rellano; ~**ing craft** n barca de desembarco; ~**ing gear** n tren m de aterrizaje; ~**ing stage** n desembarcadero; ~**ing strip** n pista de aterrizaje; ~**lady** n (of boarding house) patrona; (owner) dueña; ~**locked** a cercado de tierra; ~**lord** n propietario; (of pub etc) patrón m; ~**lubber** n hombre m de tierra; ~**mark** n lugar m conocido; **to be a** ~**mark** (fig) hacer época; ~**owner** n terrateniente m/f.

landscape ['lænskeɪp] n paisaje m; ~**d** a reformado artísticamente.

landslide ['lændsleɪd] n (GEO) corrimiento de tierras; (fig: POL) victoria arrolladora.

lane [leɪn] n (in country) vereda; (in town) callejón m; (AUT) carril m; (in race) calle f; (for air or sea traffic) ruta.

language ['læŋgwɪdʒ] n lenguaje m; (national tongue) idioma m, lengua; **bad** ~ lenguaje indecente.

languid ['læŋgwɪd] a lánguido.

languish ['læŋgwɪʃ] vi languidecer.

lank [læŋk] a (hair) lacio.

lanky ['læŋkɪ] a larguirucho.

lantern ['læntn] n linterna; (NAUT) farol m.

lap [læp] n (of track) vuelta; (of body): **to sit on sb's** ~ sentarse en las rodillas de uno // vt (also: ~ **up**) lamer // vi (waves) chapotear; ~**dog** n perro faldero.

lapel [lə'pɛl] n solapa.

Lapland ['læplænd] n Laponia; **Lapp** [læp] a, n lapón/ona m/f.

lapse [læps] n error m, equivocación f;

(moral) desliz m // vi (expire) caducar; (LAW) equivocarse; (morally) caer en un desliz; (time) pasar, transcurrir; **to** ~ **into bad habits** volver a las andadas; ~ **of time** lapso, período.

larceny ['lɑːsənɪ] n latrocinio; **petty** ~ robo de menor cuantía.

lard [lɑːd] n manteca (de cerdo).

larder ['lɑːdəˀ] n despensa.

large [lɑːdʒ] a (gen) grande; (fat) gordo; **at** ~ (free) en libertad; (generally) en general; ~**ly** ad en gran parte; ~-**scale** a (map) en gran escala; (fig) importante.

lark [lɑːk] n (bird) alondra; (joke) travesura, broma; **to** ~ **about** vi bromear, divertirse tontamente.

larva ['lɑːvə] pl -**vae** [-viː] n larva.

laryngitis [lærɪn'dʒaɪtɪs] n laringitis f.

larynx ['lærɪŋks] n laringe f.

lascivious [lə'sɪvɪəs] a lascivo.

laser ['leɪzəˀ] n láser m.

lash [læʃ] n latigazo; (punishment) azote m; (gen: eyelash) pestaña // vt azotar; (tie) atar; **to** ~ **out** vi: **to** ~ **out at or against sb** atacar violentamente a alguien; **to** ~ **out** (col: spend) gastar generosamente.

lass [læs] n chica.

lasso [læ'suː] n lazo // vt coger con lazo.

last [lɑːst] a (gen) último; (final) último, final // ad por último // vi (endure) durar; (continue) continuar, seguir; ~ **week** la semana pasada; ~ **night** anoche; **at** ~ por fin; ~ **but one** penúltimo; ~**ing** a duradero; ~-**minute** a de última hora.

latch [lætʃ] n picaporte m, pestillo; ~**key** n llavín m.

late [leɪt] a (not on time) tarde, atrasado; (far on in day etc) tardío; (hour) avanzado; (recent) reciente; (former) antiguo, ex; (deed) tardío // ad tarde; (behind time, schedule) con retraso; **of** ~ últimamente; **in** ~ **May** hacia fines de mayo; **the** ~ **Mr X** el difunto Sr X; ~**comer** n recién llegado; ~**ly** ad últimamente; ~**ness** n (of person) retraso; (of event) lo tardío.

later ['leɪtəˀ] a (date etc) posterior; (version etc) más reciente // ad más tarde, después.

lateral ['lætərl] a lateral.

latest ['leɪtɪst] a último; **at the** ~ a más tardar.

lathe [leɪð] n torno.

lather ['lɑːðəˀ] n espuma (de jabón) // vt enjabonar // vi hacer espuma.

Latin ['lætɪn] n latín m // a latino; ~ **America** n América latina; ~-**American** a latinoamericano.

latitude ['lætɪtjuːd] n latitud f.

latrine [lə'triːn] n letrina.

latter ['lætəˀ] a (date etc) segundo // n: **the** ~ el último, éste; ~**ly** ad últimamente.

lattice ['lætɪs] n enrejado; (on window) reja.

laudable ['lɔːdəbl] a loable.

laugh [lɑːf] n risa; (loud) carcajada // vi

reírse, reír; reírse a carcajadas; **to ~ at** vt fus reírse de; **to ~ off** vt tomar algo a risa; **~able** a risible, ridículo; **to be the ~ing stock of the town** ser el hazmerreír de la ciudad; **~ter** n risa.

launch [lɔ:ntʃ] n (boat) lancha; see also **~ing** // vt (ship, rocket, plan) lanzar; **~ing** n (of rocket etc) lanzamiento; (inauguration) estreno; **~(ing) pad** n plataforma de lanzamiento.

launder ['lɔ:ndə*] vt lavar.

launderette [lɔ:n'drɛt] n lavandería (automática).

laundry ['lɔ:ndrɪ] n lavandería; (clothes) ropa sucia; **to do the ~** hacer la colada.

laureate ['lɔ:rɪət] a see **poet.**

laurel ['lɔrl] n laurel m.

lava ['lɑ:və] n lava.

lavatory ['lævətərɪ] n lavabo; **lavatories** npl servicios mpl, aseos mpl.

lavender ['lævəndə*] n lavanda.

lavish ['lævɪʃ] a abundante; (giving freely): **~ with** pródigo en // vt: **to ~ sth on sb** colmar a uno de algo.

law [lɔ:] n ley f; (study) derecho; (of game) regla; **~-abiding** a que cumple la ley; **~ and order** n órden m público; **~breaker** n infractor m (de la ley); **~ court** n tribunal m (de justicia); **~ful** a legítimo, lícito; **~fully** ad legalmente; **~less** a (act) ilegal; (person) rebelde; (country) desordenado.

lawn [lɔ:n] n césped m; **~mower** n cortacésped m; **~ tennis** [-'tɛnɪs] n tenis m.

law: ~ school n facultad f de derecho; **~ student** n estudiante m/f de derecho.

lawsuit ['lɔ:su:t] n pleito.

lawyer ['lɔjə*] n abogado; (for sales, wills etc) notario.

lax [læks] a flojo; (negligent) negligente.

laxative ['læksətɪv] n laxante m.

laxity ['læksɪtɪ] n flojedad f; (moral) relajamiento; (negligence) negligencia.

lay [leɪ] pt of **lie** // a laico; (not expert) profano // vt, pt, pp **laid** (place) colocar; (eggs, table) poner; (trap) tender; **to ~ aside** or **by** vt dejar a un lado; **to ~ down** vt (pen etc) dejar; (~ flat) acostar; (arms) rendir; (policy) asentar; **to ~ down the law** imponer la ley; **to ~ off** vt (workers) despedir, poner en paro; **to ~ on** vt (water, gas) instalar; (provide) proveer; **to ~ out** vt (design) diseñar; (display) disponer; (spend) gastar; **to ~ up** vt (store) guardar; (ship) desarmar; (subj: illness) obligar a guardar cama; **~about** n vago/a; **~-by** n apartadero.

layer ['leɪə*] n capa.

layette [leɪ'ɛt] n canastilla, ajuar m (de niño).

layman ['leɪmən] n persona no experta; (REL) lego.

layout ['leɪaut] n (design) plan m, trazado; (disposition) disposición f; (PRESS) composición f.

laze [leɪz] vi no hacer nada; (pej)

holgazanear; **laziness** n pereza; **lazy** a perezoso, vago.

lb. abbr of **pound** (weight).

lead [li:d] n (front position) delantera; (SPORT) liderato; (distance, time ahead) ventaja; (clue) pista; (ELEC) cable m; (for dog) correa; (THEATRE) papel m principal // n [lɛd] plomo; (in pencil) mina // (vb: pt, pp **led**) vt conducir; (induce) llevar; (be leader of) dirigir; (SPORT) ir en cabeza de // vi ir primero; **to ~ to** llevar a, salir a; **to ~ astray** vt llevar por mal camino; **to ~ away** vt llevar; **to ~ back** vt hacer volver; **to ~ on** vt (tease) coquetear con; **to ~ on to** vt (induce) incitar a; **to ~ up to** conducir a.

leader ['li:də*] n (gen) jefe m, líder m; (of union etc) dirigente m/f; (of gang) cabecilla m; (guide) guía m/f; (of newspaper) artículo de fondo; **~ship** n dirección f; (quality) dotes fpl de mando.

leading ['li:dɪŋ] a (main) principal; (outstanding) destacado; (first) primero; (front) delantero; **~ lady** n (THEATRE) primera actriz f; **~ light** n (person) figura principal.

leaf [li:f], pl **leaves** n hoja // vi: **to ~ through** hojear; **to turn over a new ~** reformarse.

leaflet ['li:flɪt] n folleto.

league [li:g] n sociedad f; (FOOTBALL) liga; **to be in ~ with** estar de manga con.

leak [li:k] n (of liquid, gas) escape m, fuga; (hole) agujero; (in roof) gotera; (of money) filtración f // vi (shoes, container) hacer agua; (pipe) tener (un) escape; (roof) gotear; (container) salirse; (gas) escaparse; (fig: news) filtrarse // vt (gen) dejar escapar; (exude) rezumar; **the information was ~ed to the enemy** las informaciones se pasaron al enemigo; **the news ~ed out** trascendió la noticia.

lean [li:n] a (thin) flaco; (meat) magro // (vb: pt, pp **leaned** or **leant** [lɛnt]) vt: **to ~ sth on** apoyar algo en // vi (slope) inclinarse; (rest): **to ~ against** apoyarse contra; **to ~ on** apoyarse en; (fig: rely on) contar con (el apoyo de); **to ~ back/forward** vi inclinarse hacia atrás/hacia adelante; **to ~ over** vi ladearse; **~ing** a inclinado // n: **~ing (towards)** inclinación f (hacia); **~-to** n colgadizo.

leap [li:p] n salto // vi, pt, pp **leaped** or **leapt** [lɛpt] saltar; **~frog** n pídola; **~ year** n año bisiesto.

learn [lɜ:n], pt, pp **learned** or **learnt** vt (gen) aprender; (come to know of) enterarse de // vi aprender; **to ~ how to do sth** aprender a hacer algo; **~ed** ['lɜ:nɪd] a erudito; **~er** n principiante m/f; **~ing** n el saber m, conocimientos mpl.

lease [li:s] n arriendo // vt arrendar.

leash [li:ʃ] n cuerda.

least [li:st] a (slightest) menor; (smallest) más pequeño; (smallest amount of) mínimo // ad menos // n: **the ~** lo menos; **the ~**

possible effort el mínimo de esfuerzo posible; at ~ por lo menos, a menos; not in the ~ en absoluto.

leather ['leðə*] n cuero.

leave [li:v], pt, pp **left** vt dejar; (go away from) abandonar // vi irse; (train) salir // n permiso; to be left quedar, sobrar; there's some milk left over sobra o queda algo de leche; on ~ de permiso; to take one's ~ of despedirse de; to ~ out vt omitir.

leaves [li:vz] pl of **leaf.**

Lebanon ['lebənən] n Líbano.

lecherous ['letʃərəs] a lascivo.

lecture ['lektʃə*] n conferencia; (SCOL) clase f // vi dar una clase // vt (scold) sermonear; **to give a ~ on** dar una conferencia sobre; **lecturer** n conferenciante m/f; (at university) profesor adjunto/profesora adjunta m/f.

led [led] pt, pp of **lead.**

ledge [ledʒ] n (of window, on wall) repisa, reborde m; (of mountain) plataforma.

ledger ['ledʒə*] n libro mayor.

lee [li:] n sotavento.

leek [li:k] n puerro.

leer [lɪə*] vi: **to ~ at sb** mirar impúdicamente a alguien.

leeway ['li:weɪ] n (fig): **to have some ~** tener cierta libertad de acción.

left [left] pt, pp of **leave** // a izquierdo (POL) de izquierda // n izquierda // ad a la izquierda; the L~ (POL) la izquierda; **~-handed** a zurdo; the **~-hand side** n la izquierda; **~-luggage (office)** n consigna; **~-overs** npl sobras fpl; **~-wing** a (POL) de izquierdas, izquierdista.

leg [leg] n pierna; (of animal) pata; (of chair) pie m; (CULIN: of meat) pierna; (of journey) etapa; lst/2nd ~ (SPORT) partido de ida/de vuelta; **to pull sb's ~** bromear con uno.

legacy ['legəsɪ] n legado.

legal ['li:gl] a (gen) lícito; (of law) legal, (enquiry etc) jurídico; **~ize** vt legalizar; **~ly** ad legalmente; **~ tender** n moneda corriente.

legend ['ledʒənd] n leyenda; **~ary** a legendario.

legible ['ledʒəbl] a legible.

legion ['li:dʒən] n legión f.

legislate ['ledʒɪsleɪt] vi legislar; **legislation** [-'leɪʃən] n legislación f; **legislative** [-'lətɪv] a legislativo; **legislature** [-lətʃə*] n cuerpo legislativo.

legitimacy [lɪ'dʒɪtɪməsɪ] n legitimidad f; **legitimate** [-mət] a legítimo.

leg-room ['legru:m] n espacio para las piernas.

leisure ['leʒə*] n ocio, tiempo libre; at ~ con tranquilidad; **~ centre** n centro de diversiones; **~ly** a pausado, lento.

lemon ['lemən] n limón m; **~ade** [-'neɪd] n (fruit juice) limonada; (fizzy) gaseosa.

lend [lend], pt, pp **lent** vt: **to ~ sth to sb** prestar algo a alguien; **~er** n prestador/a

m/f; **~ing library** n biblioteca circulante.

length [leŋθ] n largo, longitud f; (section: of road, pipe etc) tramo; at ~ (at last) por fin, finalmente; (lengthily) largamente; **~en** vt alargar // vi alargarse; **~ways** ad de largo; **~y** a largo, extenso; (meeting) prolongado.

leniency ['li:nɪənsɪ] n indulgencia; **lenient** [-ənt] a indulgente.

lens [lenz] n (of spectacles) lente f; (of camera) objetivo.

lent [lent] pt, pp of **lend.**

Lent [lent] n Cuaresma.

lentil ['lentl] n lenteja.

Leo ['li:əu] n Leo.

leopard ['lepəd] n leopardo.

leotard ['li:əta:d] n leotardo.

leper ['lepə*] n leproso/a; **leprosy** [-prəsɪ] n lepra.

lesbian ['lezbɪən] n lesbiana.

less [les] det a (in size, degree etc) menor; (in quantity) menos // pron, ad menos; ~ **than half** menos de la mitad; ~ **than ever** cada vez menos; the ~ he works... cuanto menos trabaja...

lessen ['lesn] vi disminuir, menguar // vt disminuir, reducir.

lesson ['lesn] n lección f; **a maths ~** una clase o una lección de matemáticas.

lest [lest] conj: ~ **it happen** para que no pase.

let [let], pt, pp **let** vt (allow) dejar, permitir; (lease) alquilar; ~'s go ¡vamos!; ~ **him come** que venga; 'to ~' 'se alquila'; **to ~ down** vt (lower) bajar; (dress) alargar; (tyre) desinflar; (hair) soltar; (disappoint) defraudar; **to ~ go** vi soltar; (fig) dejarse ir // vt abandonar; **to ~ in** vt dejar entrar; (visitor etc) hacer pasar; **to ~ off** vt dejar libre; (firework etc) disparar; (smell etc) despedir; **to ~ on** vt (col) divulgar (that que); **to ~ out** vt dejar salir; (dress) ensanchar; **to ~ up** vi amainar, disminuir.

lethal ['li:θl] a mortífero; (wound) mortal.

lethargic [le'θa:dʒɪk] a letárgico; **lethargy** ['leθədʒɪ] n letargo.

letter ['letə*] n (of alphabet) letra; (correspondence) carta; ~ **bomb** n carta con bomba explosiva; **~ box** n buzón m; **~ing** n letras fpl.

lettuce ['letɪs] n lechuga.

let-up ['letʌp] n descanso, tregua.

leukaemia, leukemia (US) [lu:'ki:mɪə] n leucemia.

level ['levl] a (flat) llano; (flattened) nivelado; (uniform) igual // ad a nivel // n nivel m; (flat place) llano // vt nivelar, allanar; **to be ~ with** estar a nivel de; 'A' ~s npl Bachillerato Superior, B.U.P.; 'O' ~s npl bachillerato elemental, octavo de básica; **on the ~** (fig: honest) en serio; **to ~ off o out** vi (prices etc) estabilizarse; ~ **crossing** n paso a nivel; **~-headed** a sensato.

lever ['li:və*] n palanca // vt: **to ~ up**

alzar con palanca; ~**age** n (fig: influence) influencia.

levity ['lɛvɪtɪ] n frivolidad f, informalidad f.

levy ['lɛvɪ] n impuesto // vt exigir, recaudar.

lewd [lu:d] a impúdico, obsceno.

liability [laɪə'bɪlɪtɪ] n responsabilidad f; (handicap) desventaja; (risk) riesgo; **liabilities** npl obligaciones fpl; (COMM) deudas fpl, pasivo sg.

liable ['laɪəbl] a (subject): ~ **to** sujeto a; **to be ~ for** ser responsable de; **to be ~ to** (likely) tener tendencia a.

liaison [li:'eɪzɔn] n (coordination) enlace m; (affair) relaciones fpl amorosas.

liar ['laɪə*] n mentiroso/a.

libel ['laɪbl] n calumnia // vt calumniar.

liberal ['lɪbərl] a (gen) liberal; (generous): ~ **with** generoso con.

liberate ['lɪbəreɪt] vt liberar; **liberation** [-'reɪʃən] n liberación f.

liberty ['lɪbətɪ] n libertad f; **to be at ~ to** tener permiso para; **to take the ~ of doing sth** tomarse la libertad de hacer algo.

Libra ['li:brə] n Libra.

librarian [laɪ'brɛərɪən] n bibliotecario/a; **library** ['laɪbrərɪ] n biblioteca.

libretto [lɪ'brɛtəʊ] n libreto.

Libya ['lɪbɪə] n Libia; ~**n** a, n libio/a.

lice [laɪs] pl of **louse**.

licence, license (US) ['laɪsns] n (gen) licencia; (permit) permiso; (also: **driving ~**) carnet m de conducir; (excessive freedom) libertinaje m; ~ **number** n matrícula; ~ **plate** n placa (de matrícula).

license ['laɪsns] n (US) = **licence** // vt autorizar, licenciar; ~**d** a (for alcohol) autorizado para la venta de bebidas alcohólicas.

licensee [laɪsn'si:] n (in a pub) patrón/ona m/f.

licentious [laɪ'sɛnʃəs] a licencioso.

lichen ['laɪkən] n líquen m.

lick [lɪk] vt lamer // n lamedura; **a ~ of paint** una mano de pintura.

licorice ['lɪkərɪs] n = **liquorice**.

lid [lɪd] n (of box, case) tapa; (of pan) cobertera.

lido ['laɪdəʊ] n piscina.

lie [laɪ] n mentira // vi mentir // vi, pt **lay**, pp **lain** (act) echarse; (state) estar echado, estar acostado; (of object: be situated) estar, encontrarse; **to ~ low** (fig) esconderse; **to ~ about** vi (things) estar en desorden; (people) gandulear; **to have a ~-down** echarse (una siesta); **to have a ~-in** quedarse pegado a las sábanas.

lieu [lu:]: **in ~ of** prep en lugar de.

lieutenant [lɛf'tɛnənt] n lugarteniente m; (MIL) teniente m.

life [laɪf], pl **lives** n (gen) vida; (way of ~) modo de vivir; (of licence etc) vigencia; ~ **assurance** n seguro de vida; ~**belt** n cinturón m salvavidas; ~**boat** n bote m salvavidas; ~**guard** n vigilante m; ~

jacket n chaleco salvavidas; ~**less** a sin vida; (dull) soso; ~**like** a natural; ~**line** n cuerda salvavidas; ~**long** a de toda la vida; ~**-saver** n bañero, socorrista m/f; ~ **sentence** n condena perpetua; ~**-sized** a de tamaño natural; ~ **span** n vida; ~ **support system** n (MED) respirador m artificial; ~**time** n: **in his ~time** durante su vida; **once in a ~time** una vez en la vida.

lift [lɪft] vt levantar; (steal) robar // vi (fog) levantarse, disiparse // n (elevator) ascensor m; **to give sb a ~** llevar a uno en el coche; ~**-off** n despegue m.

ligament ['lɪgəmənt] n ligamento.

light [laɪt] n (gen) luz f; (flame) lumbre f; (lamp) luz f, lámpara; (daylight) luz del día; (headlight) faro; (rear ~) luz trasera; (for cigarette etc): **have you got a ~?** ¿tiene fuego? // vt, pt, pp **lighted** or **lit** (candle, cigarette, fire) encender; (room) alumbrar // a (colour) claro; (not heavy, also fig) ligero; (room) alumbrado; **to ~ up** vi (smoke) encender un cigarrillo; (face) iluminarse // vt (illuminate) iluminar, alumbrar; ~ **bulb** n bombilla; ~**en** vi (grow ~) clarear // vt (give light to) iluminar; (make lighter) aclarar; (make less heavy) aligerar; ~**er** n (also: **cigarette ~er**) encendedor m, mechero; ~**-headed** a (dizzy) mareado; (excited) exaltado; (by nature) casquivano; ~**-hearted** a alegre; ~**house** n faro; ~**ing** n (act) iluminación f; (system) alumbrado; ~**ly** ad (touch) ligeramente; (thoughtlessly) a la ligera; (slightly) levemente; (not seriously) con poca seriedad; **to get off ~ly** ser castigado con poca severidad; ~ **meter** n (PHOT) fotómetro; ~**ness** n claridad f; (in weight) ligereza.

lightning ['laɪtnɪŋ] n relámpago, rayo; ~ **conductor** n pararrayos m inv.

light: ~weight a (suit) ligero // n (BOXING) peso ligero; ~ **year** n año luz.

like [laɪk] vt (person) querer, tener cariño a; (things) gustarle a uno // prep como // a parecido, semejante // n: **the ~** semejante m/f; **his ~s and dislikes** sus gustos y aversiones; **I would ~, I'd ~** me gustaría; (for purchase) quisiera; **would you ~ a coffee?** ¿te apetece un café?; **to be** or **look ~ sb/sth** parecerse a alguien/algo; **that's just ~ him** es muy de él, es característico de él; **it is nothing ~...** no tiene parecido alguno con...; ~**able** a simpático, agradable.

likelihood ['laɪklɪhʊd] n probabilidad f; **likely** [-lɪ] a probable; **he's likely to leave** es probable que se vaya.

like-minded [laɪk'maɪndɪd] a de la misma opinión.

liken ['laɪkən] vt: **to ~ sth to sth** comparar algo con algo.

likewise ['laɪkwaɪz] ad igualmente.

liking ['laɪkɪŋ] n: **to his ~** para su gusto.

lilac ['laɪlək] n lila // a (colour) de color lila.

lily ['lɪlɪ] n lirio, azucena; ~ **of the valley** n lirio de los valles.

limb [lɪm] n miembro.

limber ['lɪmbə*]: **to** ~ **up** vi (fig) entrenarse; (SPORT) desentumecerse

limbo ['lɪmbəu] n: **to be in** ~ (fig) caer en el olvido.

lime [laɪm] n (tree) limero; (fruit) lima; (GEO) cal f.

limelight ['laɪmlaɪt] n: **to be in the** ~ (fig) ser el centro de atención.

limerick ['lɪmərɪk] n quintilla humorística.

limestone ['laɪmstəun] n piedra caliza.

limit ['lɪmɪt] n límite m // vt limitar; ~**ation** [-'teɪʃən] n limitación f; ~**ed** a limitado; **to be** ~ **ed to** limitarse a; ~**ed (liability) company (Ltd)** n sociedad f anónima; ~**less** a sin límites.

limousine ['lɪməziːn] n limusina.

limp [lɪmp] n: **to have a** ~ tener cojera // vi cojear // a flojo.

limpet ['lɪmpɪt] n lapa.

limpid ['lɪmpɪd] a límpido, cristalino.

line [laɪn] n (gen) línea; (straight ~) raya; (rope) cuerda; (for fishing) sedal m; (wire) hilo; (row, series) fila, hilera; (of writing) renglón m; (on face) arruga; (specialty) rama // vt (SEWING) forrar (with de); **to** ~ **the streets** ocupar las aceras; **in** ~ **with** de acuerdo con; **to** ~ **up** vi hacer cola // vt alinear, poner en fila; ~**d** a (face) arrugado; (paper) rayado.

linear ['lɪnɪə*] a lineal.

linen ['lɪnɪn] n ropa blanca; (cloth) lino.

liner ['laɪnə*] n vapor m de línea, transatlántico.

linesman ['laɪnzmən] n (SPORT) juez m de línea.

line-up ['laɪnʌp] n alineación f.

linger ['lɪŋɡə*] vi retrasarse, tardar en marcharse; (smell, tradition) persistir.

lingerie ['lænʒəriː] n ropa interior (de mujer).

lingering ['lɪŋɡərɪŋ] a persistente; (death) lento.

lingo ['lɪŋɡəu], pl ~**es** n (pej) jerga.

linguist ['lɪŋɡwɪst] n lingüista m/f; ~**ic** a lingüístico; ~**ics** n lingüística.

lining ['laɪnɪŋ] n forro.

link [lɪŋk] n (of a chain) eslabón f; (connection) conexión f; (bond) vínculo, lazo // vt vincular, unir; ~**s** npl campo sg de golf; **to** ~ **up** vt acoplar // vi unirse; ~-**up** n (gen) unión f; (in space) acoplamiento.

lino ['laɪnəu], **linoleum** [lɪ'nəulɪəm] n linóleo.

lintel ['lɪntl] n dintel m.

lion ['laɪən] n león m; ~**ess** n leona.

lip [lɪp] n labio; (of jug) pico; (of cup etc) borde m; ~-**read** vi leer los labios; ~ **service** n: **to pay** ~ **service to sth** alabar algo pero sin hacer nada; ~**stick**
n lápiz m labial, barra de labios.

liquefy ['lɪkwɪfaɪ] vt liquidar.

liqueur [lɪ'kjuə*] n licor m.

liquid ['lɪkwɪd] a, n líquido.

liquidate ['lɪkwɪdeɪt] vt liquidar; **liquidation** [-'deɪʃən] n liquidación f; **liquidator** n liquidador/a m/f.

liquidize ['lɪkwɪdaɪz] vt (CULIN) licuar.

liquor ['lɪkə*] n licor m, bebidas alcohólicas fpl.

liquorice ['lɪkərɪs] n regaliz m.

lisp [lɪsp] n ceceo

list [lɪst] n lista; (of ship) inclinación f // vt (write down) hacer una lista de; (enumerate) catalogar // vi (ship) inclinarse.

listen ['lɪsn] vi escuchar, oír; (pay attention) atender; ~**er** n oyente m/f.

listless ['lɪstlɪs] a apático, indiferente.

lit [lɪt] pt, pp of **light**.

litany ['lɪtənɪ] n letanía.

literacy ['lɪtərəsɪ] a capacidad f de leer y escribir; ~ **campaign** campaña de alfabetización.

literal ['lɪtərl] a literal; ~**ly** ad literalmente.

literary ['lɪtərərɪ] a literario.

literate ['lɪtərət] a que sabe leer y escribir; (fig) culto.

literature ['lɪtərɪtʃə*] n literatura; (brochures etc) folletos mpl.

lithe [laɪð] a ágil.

litigation [lɪtɪ'ɡeɪʃən] a litigio.

litre, liter (US) ['liːtə*] n litro.

litter ['lɪtə*] n (rubbish) basura; (paper) papel m tirado; (young animals) camada, cría; (stretcher) camilla; ~ **bin** n papelera; ~**ed** a: ~**ed with** (scattered) esparcido con; (covered with) lleno de.

little ['lɪtl] a (small) pequeño; (not much) poco; often translated by suffix: eg ~ **house** casita // ad poco; **a** ~ un poco (de); ~ **by** ~ poco a poco.

liturgy ['lɪtədʒɪ] n liturgia

live [laɪv] vi vivir // vt (a life) llevar; (experience) vivir // a (laɪv) (animal) vivo; (wire) conectado; (broadcast) en directo; (shell) cargado; **to** ~ **down** vt hacer olvidar; **to** ~ **on** vt fus (food) vivirse de, alimentarse de; **to** ~ **up to** vt fus (fulfil) cumplir con; (justify) justificar.

livelihood ['laɪvlɪhud] n sustento.

lively ['laɪvlɪ] a (gen) vivo; (talk) animado; (pace) rápido; (party, tune) alegre.

liver ['lɪvə*] n (ANAT) hígado; ~**ish** a (fig) rezongón (ona).

livery ['lɪvərɪ] n librea.

lives [laɪvz] pl of **life**.

livestock ['laɪvstɔk] n ganado.

livid ['lɪvɪd] a lívido; (furious) furioso.

living ['lɪvɪŋ] a (alive) vivo // n: **to earn** or **make a** ~ ganarse la vida; ~ **conditions** npl condiciones f de vida; ~ **room** n sala (de estar); ~ **standards** npl nivel m de vida; ~ **wage** n sueldo suficiente para vivir.

lizard ['lɪzəd] n lagartija.

llama ['lɑːmə] n llama.

load [ləud] n (gen) carga; (weight) peso // vt: to ~ (with) cargar (con); (fig) colmar (de); a ~ of, ~s of (fig) (gran) cantidad de, montones de; ~ed a (dice) cargado; (question, word) intencionado; (col: rich) forrado (de dinero); (: drunk) trompa.

loaf [ləuf], pl **loaves** n (barra de) pan m // vi (also: ~ about, ~ around) holgazanear.

loan [ləun] n préstamo; (COMM) empréstito // vt prestar; **on** ~ prestado.

loath [ləuθ] a: **to be** ~ **to do sth** estar poco dispuesto a hacer algo.

loathe [ləuð] vt aborrecer; (person) odiar; **loathing** n aversión f; odio; **it fills me with loathing** me da asco.

loaves [ləuvz] pl of **loaf.**

lobby ['lɔbɪ] n vestíbulo, sala de espera; (POL: pressure group) grupo de presión // vt presionar.

lobe [ləub] n lóbulo.

lobster ['lɔbstə*] n langosta; (large) bogavante m.

local ['ləukl] a local // n (pub) bar m; **the** ~**s** npl los vecinos, los del lugar; ~**ity** [-'kælɪtɪ] n localidad f; ~**ly** [-kəlɪ] ad en la vecindad.

locate [ləu'keɪt] vt (find) localizar; (situate) colocar.

location [ləu'keɪʃən] n situación f; **on** ~ (CINEMA) en exteriores, fuera del estudio.

loch [lɔx] n lago.

lock [lɔk] n (of door, box) cerradura; (of canal) esclusa; (stop) tope m; (of hair) mechón m // vt (with key) cerrar con llave; (immobilize) inmovilizar // vi (door etc) cerrarse con llave; (wheels) bloquearse, trabarse.

locker ['lɔkə*] n casillero.

locket ['lɔkɪt] n medallón m.

lockout ['lɔkaut] n paro patronal, lockout m.

locomotive [ləukə'məutɪv] n locomotora.

locum ['ləukəm] n (MED) (médico) interino.

locust ['ləukəst] n langosta.

lodge [lɔdʒ] n casa del guarda; (porter's) portería; (FREEMASONRY) logia // vi (person): **to** ~ **(with)** alojarse (en casa de) // vt (complaint) presentar; **lodger** n huésped/a m/f.

lodgings ['lɔdʒɪŋz] npl alojamiento sg; (house) casa sg de huéspedes.

loft [lɔft] n desván m.

lofty ['lɔftɪ] a alto; (haughty) orgulloso.

log [lɔg] n (of wood) leño, tronco; (book) = **logbook.**

logarithm ['lɔgərɪðəm] n logaritmo.

logbook ['lɔgbuk] n (NAUT) diario de a bordo; (AVIAT) libro de vuelo; (of car) documentación f (del coche).

loggerheads ['lɔgəhɛdz] npl: **at** ~ **(with)** de pique (con).

logic ['lɔdʒɪk] n lógica; ~**al** a lógico.

logistics [lɔ'dʒɪstɪks] n logística.

loin [lɔɪn] n (CULIN) lomo, solomillo; ~**s** npl lomos mpl; ~ **cloth** n taparrabo.

loiter ['lɔɪtə*] vi perder el tiempo; (pej) merodear.

loll [lɔl] vi (also: ~ **about**) repantigarse.

lollipop ['lɔlɪpɔp] n piruli m; (iced) polo; ~ **man/lady** n persona encargada de ayudar a los niños a cruzar la calle.

London ['lʌndən] n Londres; ~**er** n londinense m/f.

lone [ləun] a solitario.

loneliness ['ləunlɪnɪs] n soledad f, aislamiento; **lonely** [-lɪ] a solitario, solo.

loner ['ləunə*] n solitario.

long [lɔŋ] a largo // ad mucho tiempo, largamente // vi: **to** ~ **for** sth anhelar o suspirar por algo; **in the** ~ **run** a la larga; **so** or **as** ~ **as** mientras, con tal que; **don't be** ~! ¡no tardes!, ¡vuelve pronto!; **how** ~ **is the street?** ¿cuánto tiene la calle de largo?; **how** ~ **is the lesson?** ¿cuánto dura la lección?; **6 metres** ~ que mide 6 metros, de 6 metros de largo; **6 months** ~ que dura 6 meses, de 6 meses de duración; **all night** ~ toda la noche; ~ **before** mucho antes; **before** ~ (+ future) dentro de poco; (+ past) poco tiempo después; **at** ~ **last** al fin, por fin; ~**-distance** a (race) de larga distancia; (call) interurbano; ~**-haired** a de pelo largo; ~**hand** n escritura (corriente); ~**ing** n anhelo, ansia; (nostalgia) nostalgia // a anhelante.

longitude ['lɔŋgɪtjuːd] n longitud f.

long: ~ **jump** n salto de longitud; ~**-lost** a desaparecido hace mucho tiempo; ~**-playing record** (L.P.) n elepé m, disco de larga duración; ~**-range** a de gran alcance; ~**-sighted** a (fig) previsor(a); ~**-standing** a de mucho tiempo; ~**-suffering** a sufrido; ~**-term** a largo plazo; ~ **wave** a de onda larga; ~**-winded** a prolijo.

loo [luː] n (col) wáter m.

loofah ['luːfə] n esponja de lufa.

look [luk] vi mirar; (seem) parecer; (building etc): **to** ~ **south/on to the sea** dar al sur/al mar // n mirada; (glance) vistazo; (appearance) aire m, aspecto; ~**s** npl físico, apariencia; **to** ~ **like sb** parecerse a alguien; **to** ~ **after** vt fus cuidar a; **to** ~ **at** vt fus mirar; (consider) considerar; **to** ~ **back** vi mirar hacia atrás; **to** ~ **down on** vt fus (fig) despreciar, mirar con desprecio; **to** ~ **for** vt fus buscar; **to** ~ **forward to** vt fus esperar con ilusión; **to** ~ **into** vt investigar; **to** ~ **on** vi mirar (como espectador); **to** ~ **out** vi (beware): **to** ~ **out (for)** tener cuidado (de); **to** ~ **out for** vt fus (seek) buscar; (await) esperar; **to** ~ **round** vi volver la cabeza; **to** ~ **to** vt fus ocuparse de; (rely on) contar con; **to** ~ **up** vi mirar hacia arriba; (improve) mejorar // vt (word) buscar; (friend) visitar; **to** ~ **up to** vt fus admirar; ~**-out**

n (*tower etc*) puesto de observación;
(*person*) vigía m; **to be on the ~-out for**
sth estar al acecho de algo.
loom [lu:m] n telar m // vi asomarse;
(*threaten*) amenazar.
loony ['lu:nı] n (*col*) loco/a; **~ bin** n (*col*)
manicomio.
loop [lu:p] n lazo; (*bend*) vuelta, recodo;
(*contraceptive*) espiral f; **~hole** n
escapatoria.
loose [lu:s] a (*gen*) suelto; (*not tight*) flojo;
(*wobbly etc*) movedizo; (*clothes*) ancho;
(*morals, discipline*) relajado; **to be at a ~**
end no saber qué hacer; **~ly** ad
libremente, aproximadamente; **loosen** vt
(*free*) soltar; (*untie*) desatar; (*slacken*)
aflojar.
loot [lu:t] n botín m // vt saquear; **~ing** n
pillaje m.
lop [lɔp]: **to ~ off** vt cortar; (*branches*)
podar.
lop-sided ['lɔp'saıdıd] a desequilibrado.
lord [lɔ:d] n señor m; **L~ Smith** Lord
Smith; **the L~** el Señor; **the (House of)**
L~s la Cámara de los Lores; **~ship** n:
your L~ship su señoría; (*arrogant*) arrogante; **~ship** n:
your L~ship su señoría.
lore [lɔ:*] n saber m popular, tradiciones
fpl.
lorry ['lɔrı] n camión m; **~ driver** n
camionero.
lose [lu:z] pt, pp **lost** vt perder // vi perder,
ser vencido; **to ~ (time)** (*clock*)
atrasarse; **loser** n perdedor/a m/f.
loss [lɔs] n pérdida; **to be at a ~** no saber
qué hacer; **to be a dead ~** ser
completamente inútil.
lost [lɔst] pt, pp of **lose** // a perdido; **~**
property n objetos mpl perdidos.
lot [lɔt] n (*at auctions*) lote m; (*destiny*)
suerte f; **the ~** el todo, todos; **a ~**
mucho, bastante; **a ~ of, ~s of** mucho(s)
(pl); **to draw ~s (for sth)** echar suertes
(para decidir algo); **I read a ~** leo
bastante.
lotion ['ləuʃən] n loción f.
lottery ['lɔtərı] n lotería.
loud [laud] a (*voice*) alto; (*shout*) fuerte;
(*noisy*) estrepitoso; (*gaudy*) chillón(ona) //
ad (*speak etc*) en alta voz; **~hailer** n
megáfono; **~ly** ad (*noisily*) ruidosamente;
(*aloud*) en alta voz; **~speaker** n altavoz
m.
lounge [laundʒ] n salón m, sala (de estar)
// vi reposar, holgazanear; **~ suit** n traje
m de calle.
louse [laus], pl **lice** n piojo.
lousy ['lauzı] a (*fig*) vil, asqueroso.
lout [laut] n gamberro.
lovable ['lʌvəbl] a amable, simpático.
love [lʌv] n amor m // vt amar, querer; **to**
~ to do gustar(le a uno) mucho hacer; **to**
be in ~ with estar enamorado de; **to**
make ~ hacer el amor; **for the ~ of** por
amor de; **'15 ~'** (*TENNIS*) 15 a cero; **I ~**
paella me gusta mucho la paella, **'with**
~' con cariño; **~ affair** n aventura

sentimental; **~ letter** n carta de amor; **~**
life n vida sentimental.
lovely ['lʌvlı] a (*delightful*) precioso,
encantador(a); (*beautiful*) hermoso.
lover ['lʌvə*] n amante m/f; (*amateur*): **a**
~ of un aficionado a o un amante de.
lovesong ['lʌvsɔŋ] n canción f de amor.
loving ['lʌvıŋ] a amoroso, cariñoso.
low [ləu] a, ad bajo // n (*METEOROLOGY*)
área de baja presión // vi (*cow*) mugir; **to**
feel ~ sentirse deprimido; **to turn**
(down) ~ vt bajar; **~-cut** a (*dress*)
escotado.
lower ['ləuə*] vt bajar; (*reduce*) reducir //
vr: **to ~ o.s. to** (*fig*) rebajarse a.
low: **~-grade** a de baja calidad; **~ly** a
humilde; **~-lying** a de bajo nivel.
loyal ['lɔıəl] a leal; **~ty** n lealtad f.
lozenge ['lɔzındʒ] n (*MED*) pastilla.
L.P. n abbr of **long-playing record.**
L-plates ['elpleıts] npl placa de aprendiz
de conductor.
Ltd abbr of **limited company** S.A.
lubricant ['lu:brıkənt] n lubricante m;
lubricate [-keıt] vt lubricar, engrasar.
lucid ['lu:sıd] a lúcido; **~ity** [-'sıdıtı] n
lucidez f.
luck [lʌk] n suerte f; **bad ~** mala suerte;
good ~! ¡que tengas suerte!, ¡suerte!;
~ily ad afortunadamente; **~y** a
afortunado.
lucrative ['lu:krətıv] a lucrativo.
ludicrous ['lu:dıkrəs] a absurdo.
ludo ['lu:dəu] n parchís m.
lug [lʌg] vt (*drag*) arrastrar; (*pull*) tirar de.
luggage ['lʌgıdʒ] n equipaje m; **~ rack** n
(*in train*) rejilla, redecilla; (*on car*) vaca,
portaequipajes m inv.
lukewarm ['lu:kwɔ:m] a tibio, templado.
lull [lʌl] a tregua // vt (*child*) acunar;
(*person, fear*) calmar.
lullaby ['lʌləbaı] n canción f de cuna.
lumbago [lʌm'beıgəu] n lumbago.
lumber ['lʌmbə*] n (*junk*) trastos viejos
mpl; (*wood*) maderos mpl; **~jack** n
maderero.
luminous ['lu:mınəs] a luminoso.
lump [lʌmp] n terrón m; (*fragment*) trozo;
(*in sauce*) grumo; (*in throat*) nudo;
(*swelling*) bulto // vt (*also*: **~ together**)
amontonar; **a ~ sum** suma global; **~y** a
(*sauce*) lleno de grumos.
lunacy ['lu:nəsı] n locura.
lunar ['lu:nə*] a lunar.
lunatic ['lu:nətık] a, n loco/a; **~ asylum** n
manicomio.
lunch [lʌntʃ] n almuerzo, comida // vi
almorzar; **~ time** n hora del almuerzo o
de comer.
luncheon ['lʌntʃən] n almuerzo; **~ meat** n
pastel m de carne.
lung [lʌŋ] n pulmón m; **~ cancer** n cáncer
m de pulmón.
lunge [lʌndʒ] vi (*also*: **~ forward**)
abalanzarse; **to ~ at** arremeter contra.
lurch [lə:tʃ] vi dar sacudidas // n sacudida;

to leave sb in the ~ dejar a uno plantado.
lure [luə*] n (bait) cebo; (decoy) señuelo // vt atraer, seducir.
lurid ['luərɪd] a (light) misterioso; (dress) chillón(ona); (account) sensacional; (detail) horrible.
lurk [lə:k] vi (hide) esconderse; (wait) estar al acecho.
luscious ['lʌʃəs] a delicioso.
lush [lʌʃ] a exuberante.
lust [lʌst] n lujuria; (greed) codicia; to ~ after vt fus codiciar; ~ful a lascivo, lujurioso.
lustre, luster (US) ['lʌstə*] n lustre m, brillo.
lusty ['lʌstɪ] a robusto, fuerte.
lute [lu:t] n laúd m.
Luxembourg ['lʌksəmbə:g] n Luxemburgo.
luxuriant [lʌg'zjuərɪənt] a exuberante.
luxurious [lʌg'zjuərɪəs] a lujoso; **luxury** ['lʌkʃərɪ] n lujo // cpd de lujo.
lying ['laɪɪŋ] n mentiras fpl // a mentiroso.
lynch [lɪntʃ] vt linchar; ~ing n linchamiento.
lynx [lɪnks] n lince m.
lyre ['laɪə*] n lira.
lyric ['lɪrɪk] a lírico; ~s npl (of song) letra sg; ~al a lírico.

M

m. abbr of **metre; mile; million.**
M.A. abbr of **Master of Arts** licenciado en letras.
mac [mæk] n impermeable m.
macaroni [mækə'rəunɪ] n macarrones mpl.
mace [meɪs] n (BOT) macis f.
machine [mə'ʃi:n] n máquina // vt (dress etc) coser a máquina; ~ gun n ametralladora; ~ry n maquinaria; (fig) mecanismo; **machinist** n operario (de máquina).
mackerel ['mækrl] n, pl inv caballa.
mackintosh ['mækɪntəʃ] n impermeable m.
mad [mæd] a (gen) loco; (crazed) demente; (angry) furioso.
madam ['mædəm] n señora.
madden ['mædn] vt volver loco.
made [meɪd] pt, pp of **make; ~-to-measure** a hecho a la medida.
madly ['mædlɪ] ad locamente.
madman ['mædmən] n loco.
madness ['mædnɪs] n locura.
magazine [mægə'zi:n] n revista; (MIL: store) almacén m; (of firearm) recámara.
maggot ['mægət] n gusano.
magic ['mædʒɪk] n magia // a mágico; ~al a mágico; ~ian [mə'dʒɪʃən] n mago; (conjurer) prestidigitador m.
magistrate ['mædʒɪstreɪt] n juez m/f (municipal).

magnanimous [mæg'nænɪməs] a magnánimo.
magnate ['mægneɪt] n magnate m.
magnet ['mægnɪt] n imán m; ~ic [-'netɪk] a magnético; ~ism n magnetismo.
magnification [mægnɪfɪ'keɪʃən] n aumento.
magnificence [mæg'nɪfɪsns] n magnificencia; **magnificent** [-nt] a magnífico.
magnify ['mægnɪfaɪ] vt aumentar; (fig) exagerar; ~ing glass n lupa.
magnitude ['mægnɪtju:d] n magnitud f.
magnolia [mæg'nəulɪə] n magnolia.
magpie ['mægpaɪ] n urraca.
mahogany [mə'hɔgənɪ] n caoba // cpd de caoba.
maid [meɪd] n criada; old ~ (pej) solterona.
maiden ['meɪdn] n doncella // a (aunt etc) solterona; (speech, voyage) inaugural; ~ name n nombre m de soltera.
mail [meɪl] n correo; (letters) cartas fpl // vt (post) echar al correo; (send) mandar por correo; ~box n (US) buzón m; ~-order n pedido postal; (business) venta por correo.
maim [meɪm] vt mutilar, lisiar.
main [meɪn] a principal, mayor // n (pipe) cañería maestra; the ~s (ELEC) la red eléctrica; in the ~ en general; ~land n continente m; ~stay n (fig) pilar m; ~stream n corriente f principal.
maintain [meɪn'teɪn] vt mantener; (keep up) conservar (en buen estado); (affirm) sostener; **maintenance** ['meɪntənəns] n mantenimiento.
maisonette [meɪzə'net] n apartamento de dos pisos.
maize [meɪz] n maíz m.
majestic [mə'dʒestɪk] a majestuoso; **majesty** ['mædʒɪstɪ] n majestad f.
major ['meɪdʒə*] n (MIL) comandante m // a principal; (MUS) mayor.
Majorca [mə'jɔ:kə] n Mallorca.
majority [mə'dʒɔrɪtɪ] n mayoría.
make [meɪk] pt, pp **made** vt hacer; (manufacture) hacer, fabricar; (cause to be): to ~ sb sad hacer o poner triste a alguien; (force): to ~ sb do sth obligar a uno a hacer algo; (equal): 2 and 2 ~ 4 2 y 2 son 4 / n marca; to ~ do with contentarse con; to ~ for vt fus (place) dirigirse a; to ~ out vt (decipher) descifrar; (understand) entender; (see) distinguir; to ~ up vt (invent) inventar; (parcel) envolver // vi reconciliarse; (with cosmetics) maquillarse; to ~ up for vt fus compensar; ~-believe a fingido; **maker** n fabricante m/f; ~shift a improvisado; ~-up a maquillaje m.
making ['meɪkɪŋ] n (fig): in the ~ en vías de formación.
malaise [mæ'leɪz] n malestar m.
malaria [mə'lɛərɪə] n malaria.
Malay [mə'leɪ] a, n malayo/a.
Malaysia [mə'leɪzɪə] n Malaysia.

male [meɪl] n (BIOL, ELEC) macho // a (sex, attitude) masculino; (child etc) varón.

malevolent [mə'levələnt] a malévolo.

malfunction [mæl'fʌŋkʃən] n funcionamiento defectuoso.

malice ['mælɪs] n (ill will) malevolencia; (rancour) rencor m; **malicious** [mə'lɪʃəs] a malévolo; rencoroso.

malign [mə'laɪn] vt difamar, calumniar // a maligno.

malignant [mə'lɪgnənt] a (MED) maligno.

malingerer [mə'lɪŋgərə*] n enfermo fingido.

malleable ['mælɪəbl] a maleable.

mallet ['mælɪt] n mazo.

malnutrition [mælnju:'trɪʃən] n desnutrición f.

malpractice [mæl'præktɪs] n falta profesional.

malt [mɔːlt] n malta.

Malta ['mɔːltə] n Malta; **Maltese** [-'tiːz] a, n, pl inv maltés/esa m/f.

maltreat [mæl'triːt] vt maltratar.

mammal ['mæml] n mamífero.

mammoth ['mæməθ] n mamut m // a gigantesco.

man [mæn], pl **men** n hombre m; (CHESS) pieza // vt (NAUT) tripular; (MIL) guarnecer; **an old ~** un viejo; **~ and wife** marido y mujer.

manacle ['mænəkl] a manilla; **~s** npl grillos mpl.

manage ['mænɪdʒ] vi arreglárselas, ir tirando // vt (be in charge of) dirigir; (person etc) manejar; **~able** a manejable; **~ment** n dirección f, administración f; **manager/ess** n director/a m/f; (SPORT) entrenador/a m/f; **managerial** [-ə'dʒɪərɪəl] a directivo; **managing director** n director m general.

mandarin ['mændərɪn] n (also: ~ orange) mandarina; (person) mandarín m.

mandate ['mændeɪt] n mandato.

mandatory ['mændətərɪ] a obligatorio.

mandolin(e) ['mændəlɪn] n mandolina.

mane [meɪn] n (of horse) crin f, (of lion) melena.

manfully ['mænfəlɪ] ad violentamente.

mangle ['mæŋgl] vt mutilar, magullar // n rodillo.

mango ['mæŋgəu], pl **~es** n mango.

mangy ['meɪndʒɪ] a roñoso, sarnoso.

manhandle ['mænhændl] vt maltratar.

manhole ['mænhəul] n pozo de visita.

manhood ['mænhud] n edad f viril.

man-hour ['mæn'auə*] n hora-hombre f.

manhunt ['mænhʌnt] n caza de hombre.

mania ['meɪnɪə] n manía; **maniac** [ˈmeɪnɪæk] n maníaco; (fig) maniático.

manicure ['mænɪkjuə*] n manicura // vt (person) hacer la manicura a; **~ set** n estuche m de manicura.

manifest ['mænɪfest] vt manifestar, mostrar // a manifiesto; **~ation** [-'teɪʃən] n manifestación f.

manifesto [mænɪ'festəu] n manifiesto.

manipulate [mə'nɪpjuleɪt] vt manipular, manejar.

mankind [mæn'kaɪnd] n la humanidad, el género humano.

manly ['mænlɪ] a varonil.

man-made ['mæn'meɪd] a artificial.

manner ['mænə*] n manera, modo; (behaviour) conducta, manera de ser; (type) clase f; **~s** npl modales mpl, educación f; **bad ~s** mala educación; **~ism** n hábito, peculiaridad f.

manoeuvre, maneuver (US) [mə'nuːvə*] vt, vi maniobrar // n maniobra.

manor ['mænə*] a (also: ~ house) casa solariega.

manpower ['mænpauə*] n mano f de obra.

mansion ['mænʃən] n palacio, casa grande.

manslaughter ['mænslɔːtə*] n homicidio no premeditado.

mantelpiece ['mæntlpiːs] n repisa, chimenea.

mantle ['mæntl] n manto (fig) capa.

manual ['mænjuəl] a manual // n manual m; (MUS) teclado.

manufacture [mænju'fæktʃə*] vt fabricar // n fabricación f, **manufacturer** n fabricante m/f.

manure [mə'njuə*] n estiércol m, abono.

manuscript ['mænjuskrɪpt] n manuscrito.

Manx [mæŋks] a de la Isla de Man.

many ['menɪ] det mucho(-as) // pron muchos/as; **a great ~** muchísimos, buen número de; **~ a time** muchas veces.

map [mæp] n mapa m // vt trazar el mapa de; **to ~ out** vt proyectar.

maple ['meɪpl] n arce m.

mar [mɑː*] vt estropear.

marathon ['mærəθən] n maratón m.

marauder [mə'rɔːdə*] n merodeador m; (intruder) intruso.

marble ['mɑːbl] n mármol m; (toy) canica.

March [mɑːtʃ] n marzo.

march [mɑːtʃ], vi (MIL) marchar; (fig) caminar con resolución // n marcha; (demonstration) manifestación f, marcha; **~past** n desfile m.

mare [meə*] n yegua.

margarine [mɑːdʒə'riːn] n margarina.

margin ['mɑːdʒɪn] n margen m; **~al** a marginal.

marigold ['mærɪgəuld] n caléndula.

marijuana [mærɪ'wɑːnə] n marijuana.

marina [mə'riːnə] n marina.

marine [mə'riːn] a marino // n soldado de marina.

marital ['mærɪtl] a matrimonial; **~ status** estado civil.

maritime ['mærɪtaɪm] a marítimo.

marjoram ['mɑːdʒərəm] n orégano.

mark [mɑːk] n marca, señal f; (imprint) huella; (stain) mancha; (SCOL) puntuación f, nota; (currency) marco // vt marcar;

manchar; (SCOL) calificar; **to ~ time**
marcar el paso; **to ~ out** vt trazar; **~ed**
a marcado, acusado; **~er** n (sign)
marcador m; (bookmark) registro.

market ['mɑːkɪt] n mercado // vt (COMM)
vender; **black ~** mercado negro;
Common M~ Mercado Común; **~ day** n
día de mercado; **~ garden** n (Brit)
huerto; **~ing** n márketing m,
mercadotecnia; **~-place** n mercado; **~
research** n análisis m inv de mercados.

marksman ['mɑːksmən] n tirador m;
~ship n puntería.

marmalade ['mɑːməleɪd] n mermelada
(de naranjas).

maroon [mə'ruːn] vt (fig): **to be ~ed**
(shipwrecked) naufragarse; (fig) quedar
abandonado // a marrón.

marquee [mɑː'kiː] n entoldado.

marquess, marquis ['mɑːkwɪs] n
marqués m.

marriage ['mærɪdʒ] n (state) matrimonio;
(wedding) boda; (act) casamiento; **~
bureau** n agencia matrimonial; **~
certificate** n partida de casamiento.

married ['mærɪd] a casado; (life, love)
conyugal.

marrow ['mærəu] n médula; (vegetable)
calabacín m.

marry ['mærɪ] vt casarse con; (subj: father,
priest etc) casar // vi (also: **get married**)
casarse.

marsh [mɑːʃ] n pantano; (salt ~) marisma.

marshal ['mɑːʃl] n (MIL) mariscal m; (at
sports meeting etc) oficial m // vt (facts)
ordenar; (soldiers) formar.

marshmallow [mɑːʃ'mæləu] n
malvavisco.

marshy ['mɑːʃɪ] a pantanoso.

martial ['mɑːʃl] a marcial; **~ law** n ley f
marcial.

martyr ['mɑːtə*] n mártir m/f // vt
martirizar; **~dom** n martirio.

marvel ['mɑːvl] n maravilla, prodigio //
vi: **to ~ (at)** maravillarse (de); **~lous,
~ous** (US) a maravilloso.

Marxism ['mɑːksɪzəm] n marxismo;
Marxist [-sɪst] a, n marxista m/f.

marzipan ['mɑːzɪpæn] n mazapán m.

mascara [mæs'kɑːrə] n rímel m.

mascot ['mæskət] n mascota.

masculine ['mæskjulɪn] a masculino;
masculinity [-'lɪnɪtɪ] n masculinidad f.

mash [mæʃ] n (mix) mezcla; (pulp)
amasijo; **~ed potatoes** puré m de
patatas.

mask [mɑːsk] n máscara // vt enmascarar.

masochist ['mæsəukɪst] n masoquista m/f.

mason ['meɪsn] n (also: **stone~**) albañil
m; (also: **free~**) masón m; **~ic**
[mə'sɔnɪk] a masónico; **~ry** n masonería;
(building) mampostería.

masquerade [mæskə'reɪd] n baile m de
máscaras; (fig) farsa // vi: **to ~ as**
disfrazarse de, hacerse pasar por.

mass [mæs] n (people) muchedumbre f;
(PHYSICS) masa; (REL) misa; (great quantity)

montón m // vi reunirse; (MIL)
concentrarse; **the ~es** las masas.

massacre ['mæsəkə*] n masacre f // vt
masacrar.

massage ['mæsɑːʒ] n masaje m // vt dar
masaje a.

masseur [mæ'sɔː*] n masajista m;
masseuse [-'sɔːz] n masajista f.

massive ['mæsɪv] a (solid) sólido; (head
etc) grande; (support, intervention) masivo.

mass media ['mæs'miːdɪə] npl medios mpl
de comunicación masiva.

mass-production ['mæsprə'dʌkʃən] n
fabricación f en serie.

mast [mɑːst] n (NAUT) mástil m; (RADIO etc)
torre f.

master ['mɑːstə*] n maestro; (landowner)
señor m, amo; (in secondary school)
profesor m; (title for boys): **M~ X**
Señorito X // vt dominar; (learn) aprender
a fondo; **~ key** n llave f maestra; (go well)
magistral; **~mind** n inteligencia superior
// vt dirigir, planear; **M~ of Arts** n
Licenciado en Letras; **~piece** n obra
maestra; **~ plan** n plan m rector; **~
stroke** n golpe m maestro; **~y** n
maestría.

masturbate ['mæstəbeɪt] vi masturbarse;
masturbation [-'beɪʃən] n masturbación f.

mat [mæt] n estera; (also: **door~**) felpudo
// a = **matt**.

match [mætʃ] n cerilla; (game) partido;
(fig) igual m/f // vt emparejar; (go well
with) hacer juego con; (equal) igualar, ser
igual a // vi hacer juego; **to be a good ~**
hacer una buena pareja; **~box** n caja de
cerillas; **~ing** a que hace juego; **~less** a
sin par, incomparable.

mate [meɪt] n compañero; (assistant)
ayudante m/f; (CHESS) mate m; (in
merchant navy) segundo de a bordo // vi
acoplarse, parearse // vt acoplar, parear.

material [mə'tɪərɪəl] n (substance)
materia; (equipment) material m; (cloth)
tela, tejido; (data) datos mpl // a material;
(important) importante; **~s** npl materiales
mpl; **~istic** [-ə'lɪstɪk] a materialista;
~ize vi materializarse.

maternal [mə'tɜːnl] a maternal.

maternity [mə'tɜːnɪtɪ] n maternidad f; **~
dress** vestido premamá; **~ hospital** n
hospital m de maternidad.

mathematical [mæθə'mætɪkl] a
matemático; **mathematician** [-mə'tɪʃən] n
matemático; **mathematics** [-tɪks], **maths**
[mæθs] n matemáticas fpl.

matinée ['mætɪneɪ] n función f de tarde.

mating ['meɪtɪŋ] n aparejamiento; **~ call**
n llamada del macho; **~ season** n época
de celo.

matriarchal [meɪtrɪ'ɑːkl] a matriarcal.

matrices ['meɪtrɪsiːz] pl of **matrix**.

matrimonial [mætrɪ'məunɪəl] a
matrimonial.

matrimony ['mætrɪmənɪ] n matrimonio.

matrix ['meɪtrɪks] pl **matrices** n matriz
f.

matron ['meɪtrən] n (in hospital) enfermera jefe; (in school) ama de llaves; ~ly a de matrona; (fig: figure) ●orpulento.

matt [mæt] a mate.

matted ['mætɪd] a enmarañado.

matter ['mætə*] n cuestión f, asunto; (PHYSICS) sustancia, materia; (content) contenido; (MED: pus) pus m // vi importar; it doesn't ~ no importa; what's the ~? ¿qué pasa?; no ~ what pase lo que pase; as a ~ of course por rutina; as a ~ of fact de hecho; ~-of-fact a prosaico, práctico.

mattress ['mætrɪs] n colchón m.

mature [mə'tjuə*] a maduro // vi madurar; **maturity** n madurez f.

maudlin ['mɔːdlɪn] a llorón(ona).

maul [mɔːl] vt magullar.

mausoleum [mɔːsə'lɪəm] n mausoleo.

mauve [məuv] a de color malva.

maxim ['mæksɪm] n máxima.

maxima ['mæksɪmə] pl of **maximum**.

maximum ['mæksɪməm] a máximo // n, pl **maxima** máximo.

May [meɪ] n mayo.

may [meɪ] vi (conditional: might) (indicating possibility): he ~ come puede que venga; (be allowed to): ~ I smoke? ¿puedo fumar?; (wishes): ~ God bless you! que Dios le bendiga.

maybe ['meɪbiː] ad quizá(s).

mayday ['meɪdeɪ] n S.O.S. m (llamada de socorro internacional).

mayhem ['meɪhɛm] n mutilación f criminal.

mayonnaise [meɪə'neɪz] n mayonesa.

mayor [mɛə*] n alcalde m; ~ess n alcaldesa.

maypole ['meɪpəul] n mayo.

maze [meɪz] n laberinto.

M.D. abbr of **Doctor of Medicine**.

me [miː] pron me; (stressed, after prep) mí; with ~ conmigo; it's ~ soy yo.

meadow ['mɛdəu] n prado, pradera.

meagre, meager (US) ['miːgə*] a escaso, pobre.

meal [miːl] n comida; (flour) harina; ~time n hora de comer.

mean [miːn] a (with money) tacaño; (unkind) mezquino, malo; (shabby) humilde, vil; (of poor quality) inferior; (average) medio // vt, pt, pp **meant** (signify) querer decir, significar; (intend): to ~ to do sth pensar o pretender hacer algo // n medio, término medio; ~s npl medio sg, manera sg; (resource) recursos mpl, medios mpl; by ~s of mediante, por medio de; by all ~s! ¡naturalmente!; ¡claro que sí!; do you ~ it? ¿lo dices en serio?; what do you ~? ¿qué quiere decir?

meander [mɪ'ændə*] vi (river) serpentear; (person) vagar.

meaning ['miːnɪŋ] n significado, sentido; ~ful a significativo; ~less a sin sentido.

meanness ['miːnnɪs] n (with money)

tacañería; (shabbiness) vileza, bajeza; (unkindness) maldad f, mezquindad f.

meant [mɛnt] pt, pp of **mean**.

meantime ['miːntaɪm], **meanwhile** ['miːnwaɪl] ad (also: in the ~) mientras tanto.

measles ['miːzlz] n sarampión m; German ~ rubéola.

measly ['miːzlɪ] a (col) miserable.

measure ['mɛʒə*] vt medir; (for clothes etc) tomar las medidas a; (consider) pesar // vi medir // n medida; (ruler) regla; ~d a moderado; (tone) mesurado; ~ments npl medidas fpl.

meat [miːt] n carne f; cold ~ fiambre m; ~ball n albóndiga; ~ pie n pastel m de carne; ~y a carnoso (fig) sustancioso.

mechanic [mɪ'kænɪk] n mecánico; ~s n mecánica // npl mecanismo sg; ~al a mecánico.

mechanism ['mɛkənɪzm] n mecanismo.

mechanization [mɛkənaɪ'zeɪʃən] n mecanización f.

medal ['mɛdl] n medalla; ~lion [mɪ'dælɪən] n medallón m; ~list, ~ist (US) n (SPORT) ganador/a m/f.

meddle ['mɛdl] vi: to ~ in entrometerse en; to ~ with sth manosear algo; ~some a entrometido.

media ['miːdɪə] npl medios mpl de comunicación.

mediaeval [mɛdɪ'iːvl] a = **medieval**.

mediate ['miːdɪeɪt] vi mediar; **mediation** [-'eɪʃən] n mediación f; **mediator** n intermediario, mediador/a m/f.

medical ['mɛdɪkl] a médico // n reconocimiento médico.

medicated ['mɛdɪkeɪtɪd] a medicinal.

medicinal [mɛ'dɪsɪnl] a medicinal.

medicine ['mɛdsɪn] n medicina; (drug) medicamento; ~ chest n botiquín m.

medieval [mɛdɪ'iːvl] a medieval.

mediocre [miːdɪ'əukə*] a mediocre; **mediocrity** [-'ɔkrɪtɪ] n mediocridad f.

meditate ['mɛdɪteɪt] vi meditar; **meditation** [-'teɪʃən] n meditación f.

Mediterranean [mɛdɪtə'reɪnɪən] a mediterráneo; the ~ (Sea) el (Mar) Mediterráneo.

medium ['miːdɪəm] a mediano, regular // n (pl **media**: means) medio; (pl **mediums**: person) médium m/f.

medley ['mɛdlɪ] n mezcla; (MUS) popurrí m.

meek [miːk] a manso, dócil.

meet [miːt] pt, pp **met** vt (gen) encontrar; (accidentally) encontrarse con, tropezar con; (by arrangement) reunirse con; (for the first time) conocer; (go and fetch) ir a buscar; (opponent) enfrentarse con; (obligations) cumplir // vi encontrarse; (in session) reunirse; (join: objects) unirse; (get to know) conocerse; to ~ with vt fus reunirse con; (face: difficulty) tropezar con; ~ing n encuentro; (session: of club etc) reunión f; (interview) entrevista; (COMM) junta, sesión f; (POL) mitin m.

megalomaniac [mɛgəlou'meɪnɪæk] a, n megalómano/a.

megaphone ['mɛgəfoun] n megáfono.

melancholy ['mɛlənkəlɪ] n melancolía // a melancólico.

melee ['mɛleɪ] n refriega.

mellow ['mɛləu] a (sound) dulce; (colour) suave; (fruit) maduro // vi (person) madurar.

melodious [mɪ'ləudɪəs] a melodioso.

melodrama ['mɛləudrɑːmə] n melodrama m.

melody ['mɛlədɪ] n melodía.

melon ['mɛlən] n melón m.

melt [mɛlt] vi (metal) fundirse; (snow) derretirse; (fig) ablandarse // vt (also: ~ down) fundir; to ~ away vi desvanecerse; ~ing point n punto de fusión; ~ing pot n (fig) crisol m.

member ['mɛmbə*] n (gen) miembro; (of club) socio; M~ of Parliament (M.P.) diputado; ~ship n (members) número de miembros; to seek ~ship of pedir el ingreso a; ~ship card carnet m de socio.

membrane ['mɛmbreɪn] n membrana.

memento [mə'mɛntəu] n recuerdo.

memo ['mɛməu] n apunte m, nota.

memoirs ['mɛmwɑːz] npl memorias fpl.

memorable ['mɛmərəbl] a memorable.

memorandum [mɛmə'rændəm], pl -da [-də] n apunte m, nota; (POL) memorándum m.

memorial [mɪ'mɔːrɪəl] n monumento conmemorativo // a conmemorativo.

memorize ['mɛməraɪz] vt aprender de memoria.

memory ['mɛmərɪ] n memoria; (recollection) recuerdo.

men [mɛn] pl of **man**.

menace ['mɛnəs] n amenaza // vt amenazar; **menacing** a amenazador(a).

menagerie [mɪ'nædʒərɪ] n casa de fieras.

mend [mɛnd] vt reparar, arreglar; (darn) zurcir // vi reponerse // n (gen) remiendo; (darn) zurcido; to be on the ~ ir mejorando; ~ing n reparación f; (clothes) ropa por remendar.

menial ['miːnɪəl] a doméstico; (pej) bajo // n criado.

meningitis [mɛnɪn'dʒaɪtɪs] n meningitis f.

menopause ['mɛnəupɔːz] n menopausia.

menstruate ['mɛnstrueɪt] vi menstruar; **menstruation** [-'eɪʃən] n menstruación f.

mental ['mɛntl] a mental; ~ity [-'tælɪtɪ] n mentalidad f.

mention ['mɛnʃən] n mención f // vt mencionar; (speak of) hablar de; don't ~ it! ¡de nada!

menu ['mɛnjuː] n (set ~) menú m; (printed) carta.

mercenary ['məːsɪnərɪ] a, n mercenario.

merchandise ['məːtʃəndaɪz] n mercancías fpl.

merchant ['məːtʃənt] n comerciante m/f; ~ bank n banco comercial; ~ navy n marina mercante.

merciful ['məːsɪful] a compasivo; (fortunate) afortunado.

merciless ['məːsɪlɪs] a despiadado.

mercury ['məːkjurɪ] n mercurio.

mercy ['məːsɪ] n compasión f; (REL) misericordia; at the ~ of a la merced de.

mere [mɪə*] a simple, mero; ~ly ad simplemente, sólo.

merge [məːdʒ] vt (join) unir; (mix) mezclar; (fuse) fundir // vi unirse; (COMM) fusionarse; **merger** n (COMM) fusión f.

meridian [mə'rɪdɪən] n meridiano.

meringue [mə'ræŋ] n merengue m.

merit ['mɛrɪt] n mérito // vt merecer.

mermaid ['məːmeɪd] n sirena.

merriment ['mɛrɪmənt] n alegría.

merry ['mɛrɪ]38 a alegre; ~-go-round n tiovivo.

mesh [mɛʃ] n malla; (TECH) engranaje m // vi (gears) engranar.

mesmerize ['mɛzməraɪz] vt hipnotizar.

mess [mɛs] n (gen) confusión f; (of objects) revoltijo; (tangle) lío; (MIL) comedor m; to ~ about vi (col) perder el tiempo; (pass the time) entretenerse; to ~ about with vt fus (col) (play with) divertirse con; (handle) manosear; to ~ up vt (disarrange) desordenar; (spoil) estropear; (dirty) ensuciar.

message ['mɛsɪdʒ] n recado, mensaje m.

messenger ['mɛsɪndʒə*] n mensajero/a.

messy ['mɛsɪ] a (dirty) sucio; (untidy) desordenado.

met [mɛt] pt, pp of **meet**.

metabolism [mɛ'tæbəlɪzəm] n metabolismo.

metal ['mɛtl] n metal m; ~lic [-'tælɪk] a metálico; ~lurgy [-'tælədʒɪ] n metalurgia.

metamorphosis [mɛtə'mɔːfəsɪs], pl -ses [-siːz] n metamorfosis f inv.

metaphor ['mɛtəfə*] n metáfora.

metaphysics [mɛtə'fɪzɪks] n metafísica.

mete [miːt]: to ~ out vt fus (gen) repartir; (punishment) imponer.

meteor ['miːtɪə*] n meteoro.

meteorological [miːtɪərə'lɔdʒɪkl] a meteorológico; **meteorology** [-'rɔlədʒɪ] n meteorología.

meter ['miːtə*] n (instrument) contador m; (US) = **metre**.

method ['mɛθəd] n método; ~ical [mɪ'θɔdɪkl] a metódico.

Methodist ['mɛθədɪst] a, n metodista m/f.

meths [mɛθs], **methylated spirit** ['mɛθɪleɪtɪd-] n alcohol m metilado o desnaturalizado.

meticulous [mɛ'tɪkjuləs] a meticuloso.

metre, meter (US) ['miːtə*] n metro.

metric ['mɛtrɪk] a métrico.

metronome ['mɛtrənəum] n metrónomo.

metropolis [mɪ'trɔpəlɪs] n metrópoli f.

mettle ['mɛtl] n (spirit) valor m, ánimo; (tone) temple m.

mew [mjuː] vi (cat) maullar.

mews [mjuːz] n: ~ cottage casa

acondicionada en antiguos establos o cocheras.

Mexican ['mɛksɪkən] *a, n* mejicano/a, mexicano/a (*AM*).

Mexico ['mɛksɪkəu] *n* Méjico, México (*AM*).

mezzanine ['mɛtsəniːn] *n* entresuelo.

miaow [miːˈau] *vi* maullar.

mice [maɪs] *pl of* mouse.

microbe ['maɪkrəub] *n* microbio.

micro... [maɪkrəu] *pref* micro...; **~film** *n* microfilm *m*; **~phone** *n* micrófono; **~processor** *n* microprocesador *m*; **~scope** *n* microscopio; **~scopic** [-'skɔpɪk] *a* microscópico; **~wave** *a* de microonda.

mid [mɪd] *a*: **in ~ May** a mediados de mayo; **in ~ afternoon** a media tarde; **in ~ air** en el aire; **~day** *n* mediodía *m*.

middle ['mɪdl] *n* medio, centro; (*haif*) mitad *f*; (*waist*) cintura // *a* medio; (*quantity, size*) mediano; **~-aged** *a* de mediana edad; **the M~ Ages** *npl* la Edad Media; **~-class** *a* de clase media; **M~ East** *n* Oriente *m* Medio; **~man** *n* intermediario; **~ name** *n* segundo nombre.

middling ['mɪdlɪŋ] *a* mediano.

midge [mɪdʒ] *n* mosca.

midget ['mɪdʒɪt] *n* enano // *a* minúsculo.

Midlands ['mɪdləndz] *npl* la región central de Inglaterra.

midnight ['mɪdnaɪt] *n* medianoche *f*.

midriff ['mɪdrɪf] *n* diafragma *m*.

midst [mɪdst] *n*: **in the ~ of** entre, en medio de.

midsummer [mɪd'sʌmə*] *n*: **a ~ day** un día de pleno verano.

midway [mɪd'weɪ] *a, ad*: **~ (between)** a mitad de camino, a medio camino (entre).

midweek [mɪd'wiːk] *ad* entre semana.

midwife ['mɪdwaɪf], *pl* **-wives** [-waɪvz] *n* comadrona, partera; **~ry** [-wɪfərɪ] *n* partería.

midwinter [mɪd'wɪntə*] *n*: **in ~** en pleno invierno.

might [maɪt] *vb*: **he ~ be there** podría estar allí, puede que está allí; **I ~ as well go** más vale que vaya; **you ~ like to try** podría intentar // *n* fuerza, poder *m*; **~y** *a* fuerte, poderoso.

migraine ['miːgreɪn] *n* jaqueca.

migrant ['maɪgrənt] *n* (*bird*) ave *f* migratoria; (*person*) emigrante *m/f*; (*fig*) nómada *m/f* // *a* migratorio; (*worker*) emigrante.

migrate [maɪ'greɪt] *vi* emigrar; **migration** [-'greɪʃən] *n* emigración *f*.

mike [maɪk] *n abbr of* **microphone** micro.

mild [maɪld] *a* (*character*) pacífico; (*climate*) templado; (*slight*) ligero; (*taste*) suave; (*illness*) benigno, leve.

mildew ['mɪldjuː] *n* moho.

mildness ['maɪldnɪs] *n* (*softness*) suavidad *f*; (*gentleness*) dulzura; (*quiet character*) apacibilidad *f*.

mile [maɪl] *n* milla; **~age** *n* número de

millas; (*AUT*) kilometraje *m*; **~stone** *n* mojón *m*.

milieu ['miːljə] *n* medio, medio ambiente.

militant ['mɪlɪtnt] *a, n* militante *m/f*.

military ['mɪlɪtərɪ] *a* militar.

militate ['mɪlɪteɪt] *vi*: **to ~ against** militar contra.

militia [mɪ'lɪʃə] *n* milicia.

milk [mɪlk] *n* leche *f* // *vt* (*cow*) ordeñar; (*fig*) chupar; **~man** *n* lechero; **~ shake** *n* batido de leche; **~y** *a* lechoso; **M~y Way** *n* Vía Láctea.

mill [mɪl] *n* (*windmill etc*) molino; (*coffee ~*) molinillo; (*factory*) fábrica; (*spinning ~*) hilandería // *vt* moler // *vi* (*also*: **~ about**) moverse por todas partes, apiñarse.

millennium [mɪ'lɛnɪəm], *pl* **~s** *or* **-ia** [-nɪə] *n* milenio, milenario.

miller ['mɪlə*] *n* molinero.

millet ['mɪlɪt] *n* mijo.

milli... ['mɪlɪ] *pref*: **~gram(me)** *n* miligramo; **~litre** *n* mililitro; **~metre** *n* milímetro.

milliner ['mɪlɪnə*] *n* modista de sombreros; **~y** *n* sombrerería.

million ['mɪljən] *n* millón *m*; **a ~ times** un millón de veces; **~aire** *n* millonario.

millstone ['mɪlstəun] *n* piedra de molino.

milometer [maɪ'lɒmɪtə*] *n* cuenta-kilómetros *m inv*.

mime [maɪm] *n* mímica; (*actor*) mimo // *vt* remedar // *vi* actuar de mimo.

mimic ['mɪmɪk] *n* imitador/a *m/f* // *a* mímico // *vt* remedar, imitar; **~ry** *n* imitación *f*.

min. *abbr of* **minute(s)**; **minimum**.

minaret [mɪnə'rɛt] *n* alminar *m*.

mince [mɪns] *vt* picar // *vi* (*in walking*) andar con pasos menudos // *n* (*CULIN*) carne *f* picada, picadillo; **~meat** *n* conserva de fruta picada; **~ pie** *n* empanadilla rellena de fruta picada; **mincer** *n* máquina de picar carne.

mind [maɪnd] *n* (*gen*) mente *f*; (*intellect*) inteligencia; (*contrasted with matter*) espíritu // *vt* (*attend to, look after*) ocuparse de, cuidar; (*be careful of*) tener cuidado con; (*object to*). **I don't ~ the noise** no me importa el ruido; **it is on my ~** me preocupa; **to my ~** en mi opinión; **to be out of one's ~** estar fuera de juicio; **never ~!** ¡es igual! ¡no importa!; (*don't worry*) ¡no se preocupe!; **to bear sth in ~** tomar o tener algo en cuenta; **to make up one's ~** decidirse; **'~ the step'** cuidado con el escalón; **~ful** *a*: **~ful of** consciente de; **~less** *a* estúpido.

mine [maɪn] *pron* (*el*) mío/(*la*) mía *etc* // *a*: **this book is ~** este libro es mío // *n* mina // *vt* (*coal*) extraer, explotar; (*ship, beach*) minar; **~field** *n* campo de minas; **miner** *n* minero.

mineral ['mɪnərəl] *a* mineral // *n* mineral *m*; **~s** *apl* (*soft drinks*) aguas *fpl* minerales, gaseosa *sg*.

minesweeper ['maɪnswiːpə*] n dragaminas m inv.

mingle ['mɪŋgl] vi: **to ~ with** mezclarse con.

mingy ['mɪndʒɪ] a (col) tacaño.

miniature ['mɪnətʃə*] a (en) miniatura // n miniatura.

minibus ['mɪnɪbʌs] n microbús m.

minicab ['mɪnɪkæb] n microtaxi m.

minim ['mɪnɪm] n (MUS) blanca.

minimal ['mɪnɪml] a mínimo.

minimize ['mɪnɪmaɪz] vt minimizar.

minimum ['mɪnɪməm] n, pl **minima** ['mɪnɪmə] mínimo // a mínimo.

mining ['maɪnɪŋ] n explotación f minera // a minero.

miniskirt ['mɪnɪskɜːt] n minifalda.

minister ['mɪnɪstə*] n (POL) ministro; (REL) pastor m // vi atender; **~ial** [-'tɪərɪəl] a (POL) ministerial.

ministry ['mɪnɪstrɪ] n ministerio.

mink [mɪŋk] n visón m; **~ coat** n abrigo de visón.

minnow ['mɪnəu] n pececillo (de agua dulce).

minor ['maɪnə*] a menor; (unimportant) sin importancia; (inferior) secundario; (MUS) menor // a (LAW) menor m/f de edad.

minority [maɪ'nɔrɪtɪ] n minoría; (age) minoridad f.

minster ['mɪnstə*] n catedral f.

minstrel ['mɪnstrəl] n juglar m.

mint [mɪnt] n (plant) menta, herbabuena; (sweet) caramelo de menta // vt (coins) acuñar; **the (Royal) M~** la (Real) Casa de la Moneda; **in ~ condition** en perfecto estado.

minuet [mɪnju'et] n minué m.

minus ['maɪnəs] n (also: **~ sign**) signo de menos // prep menos.

minute ['mɪnɪt] n minuto; (fig) momento; **~s** npl actas fpl // a [maɪ'njuːt] diminuto; (search) minucioso; **at the last ~** a última hora.

miracle ['mɪrəkl] n milagro; **miraculous** [mɪ'rækjuləs] a milagroso.

mirage ['mɪrɑːʒ] n espejismo.

mirror ['mɪrə*] n espejo; (in car) retrovisor m // vt reflejar.

mirth [mɜːθ] n alegría; (laughter) risa, risas fpl.

misadventure [mɪsəd'ventʃə*] n desgracia, accidente m.

misanthropist [mɪ'zænθrəpɪst] n misántropo.

misapprehension ['mɪsæprɪ'henʃən] n equivocación f.

misbehave [mɪsbɪ'heɪv] vi portarse mal; **misbehaviour** n mala conducta.

miscalculate [mɪs'kælkjuleɪt] vt calcular mal; **miscalculation** [-'leɪʃən] n error m (de cálculo).

miscarriage ['mɪskærɪdʒ] n (MED) aborto; (failure) fracaso; **~ of justice** error m judicial.

miscellaneous [mɪsɪ'leɪnɪəs] a vario(s), diverso(s).

mischance [mɪs'tʃɑːns] n desgracia, mala suerte f.

mischief ['mɪstʃɪf] n (naughtiness) travesura; (harm) mal m, daño; (maliciousness) malicia; **mischievous** [-ʃɪvəs] a travieso; dañoso; (playful) malicioso.

misconception ['mɪskən'sepʃən] n concepto erróneo, equivocación f.

misconduct [mɪs'kɔndʌkt] n mala conducta; **professional ~** falta profesional.

miscount [mɪs'kaunt] vt, vi contar mal.

misdeed [mɪs'diːd] n delito.

misdemeanour, misdemeanor (US) [mɪsdɪ'miːnə*] n delito, ofensa.

misdirect [mɪsdɪ'rekt] vt (person) informar mal; (letter) poner señas incorrectas en.

miser ['maɪzə*] n avaro/a.

miserable ['mɪzərəbl] a (unhappy) triste, desgraciado; (wretched) miserable; (despicable) despreciable.

miserly ['maɪzəlɪ] a avariento, tacaño.

misery ['mɪzərɪ] n (unhappiness) tristeza, sufrimiento; (wretchedness) miseria, desdicha.

misfire [mɪs'faɪə*] vi fallar.

misfit ['mɪsfɪt] n (person) inadaptado/a, desplazado/a.

misfortune [mɪs'fɔːtʃən] n desgracia.

misgiving(s) [mɪs'gɪvɪŋ(z)] n(pl) (mistrust) recelo; (apprehension) presentimiento.

misguided [mɪs'gaɪdɪd] a equivocado.

mishandle [mɪs'hændl] vt (treat roughly) maltratar; (mismanage) manejar mal.

mishap ['mɪshæp] n desgracia, contratiempo.

mishear [mɪs'hɪə*] (irg: like hear) vt oír mal.

misinform [mɪsɪn'fɔːm] vt informar mal.

misinterpret [mɪsɪn'tɜːprɪt] vt interpretar mal.

misjudge [mɪs'dʒʌdʒ] vt juzgar mal.

mislay [mɪs'leɪ] (irg: like lay) vt extraviar, perder.

mislead [mɪs'liːd] (irg: like lead) vt llevar a conclusiones erróneas; **~ing** a engañoso, erróneo.

mismanage [mɪs'mænɪdʒ] vt administrar mal; **~ment** n mala administración f.

misnomer [mɪs'nəumə*] n nombre m inapropiado o equivocado.

misogynist [mɪ'sɔdʒɪnɪst] n misógino.

misplace [mɪs'pleɪs] vt (lose) extraviar, perder.

misprint ['mɪsprɪnt] n errata, error m de imprenta.

mispronounce [mɪsprə'nauns] vt pronunciar mal.

misread [mɪs'riːd] (irg: like read) vt leer mal.

misrepresent [mɪsreprɪ'zent] *vt* falsificar.

miss [mɪs] *vt* (train etc) perder; (fail to hit) errar, fallar; (regret the absence of): I ~ him (yo) le echo de menos o a faltar // *vi* fallar // *n* (shot) tiro fallido o perdido; (fig): that was a near ~ (near accident) faltó poco para que chocáramos; to ~ out *vt* omitir.

Miss [mɪs] *n* Señorita.

missal ['mɪsl] *n* misal *m*.

misshapen [mɪs'ʃeɪpən] *a* deforme.

missile ['mɪsaɪl] *n* (AVIAT) mísil *m*; (object thrown) proyectil *m*.

missing ['mɪsɪŋ] *a* (pupil) ausente; (thing) perdido; (MIL) desaparecido; to go ~ desaparecer.

mission ['mɪʃən] *n* misión *f*; ~ary *n* misionero.

misspent ['mɪs'spent] *a*: his ~ youth su juventud disipada.

mist [mɪst] *n* (light) neblina; (heavy) niebla; (at sea) bruma // *vi* (also: ~ over, ~ up) empañarse.

mistake [mɪs'teɪk] *n* error *m* // *vt* (irg: like take) entender mal, equivocarse sobre; to ~ A for B confundir A con B; **mistaken** *a* (idea etc) equivocado; to be mistaken equivocarse, engañarse.

mister ['mɪstə*] *n* (col) señor *m*; see **Mr.**

mistletoe ['mɪsltəu] *n* muérdago.

mistook [mɪs'tuk] *pt of* **mistake**.

mistreat [mɪs'triːt] *vt* maltratar; ~ment *n* maltrato.

mistress ['mɪstrɪs] *n* (lover) amante *f*; (of house) señora (de la casa); (in primary school) maestra; (in secondary school) profesora; see **Mrs.**

mistrust [mɪs'trʌst] *vt* desconfiar de, dudar de.

misty ['mɪstɪ] *a* nebuloso, brumoso; (day) de niebla; (glasses) empañado.

misunderstand [mɪsʌndə'stænd] (irg: like understand) *vt, vi* entender mal; ~ing *n* malentendido.

misuse [mɪs'juːs] *n* mal uso; (of power) abuso // *vt* [mɪs'juːz] abusar de; (funds) malversar.

mitigate ['mɪtɪgeɪt] *vt* mitigar.

mitre, miter (US) ['maɪtə*] *n* mitra; (CARPENTRY) inglete *m*.

mitt(en) ['mɪt(n)] *n* mitón *m*.

mix [mɪks] *vt* (gen) mezclar; (combine) unir // *vi* mezclarse; (people) llevarse bien // n mezcla; to ~ up *vt* mezclar; (confuse) confundir; ~ed *a* (assorted) variado, surtido; (school etc) mixto; ~ed-up a (confused) confuso, revuelto; ~er *n* (for food) licuadora; (person) persona sociable; ~ture *n* mezcla; ~-up *n* confusión *f*.

moan [məun] *n* gemido // *vi* gemir; (col: complain): to ~ (about) quejarse (de).

moat [məut] *n* foso.

mob [mɔb] *n* multitud *f*; (pej): the ~ el populacho // *vt* acosar.

mobile ['məubaɪl] *a* móvil // *n* móvil *m*; ~ home *n* caravana.

mobility [məu'bɪlɪtɪ] *n* movilidad *f*.

mobilize ['məubɪlaɪz] *vt* movilizar.

moccasin ['mɔkəsɪn] *n* mocasín *m*.

mock [mɔk] *vt* (make ridiculous) ridiculizar; (laugh at) burlarse de // *a* fingido; ~ery *n* burla; ~ing a burlón(ona); ~-up *n* maqueta.

mode [məud] *n* modo; (fashion) moda.

model ['mɔdl] *n* (gen) modelo; (ARCH) maqueta; (person: for fashion, ART) modelo *m/f* // *a* model // *vt* modelar // *vi* servir de modelo; ~ railway ferrocarril *m* de juguete; to ~ clothes pasar modelos, ser modelo.

moderate ['mɔdərət] *a, n* moderado/a // (vb: [-reit]) *vi* moderarse, calmarse // *vt* moderar; **moderation** [-'reɪʃən] *n* moderación *f*.

modern ['mɔdən] *a* moderno; ~ize *vt* modernizar.

modest ['mɔdɪst] *a* modesto; ~y *n* modestia.

modicum ['mɔdɪkəm] *n*: a ~ of un mínimo de.

modification [mɔdɪfɪ'keɪʃən] *n* modificación *f*; **modify** ['mɔdɪfaɪ] *vt* modificar.

modulation [mɔdjʊ'leɪʃən] *n* modulación *f*.

mohair ['məuhɛə*] *n* moer *m*.

moist [mɔɪst] *a* húmedo; ~en ['mɔɪsn] *vt* humedecer; ~ure ['mɔɪstʃə*] *n* humedad *f*; ~urizer ['mɔɪstʃəraɪzə*] *n* crema hidratante.

molar ['məulə*] *n* muela.

molasses [məu'læsɪz] *n* melaza.

mole [məul] *n* (animal) topo; (spot) lunar *m*.

molecule ['mɔlɪkjuːl] *n* molécula.

molehill ['məulhɪl] *n* topera.

molest [məu'lest] *vt* importunar.

mollusc ['mɔləsk] *n* molusco.

mollycoddle ['mɔlɪkɔdl] *vt* mimar.

molten ['məultən] *a* fundido; (lava) líquido.

moment ['məumənt] *n* momento; ~ary *a* momentáneo; ~ous [-'mentəs] *a* trascendental, importante.

momentum [məu'mentəm] *n* momento; (fig) ímpetu *m*; to gather ~ cobrar velocidad.

monarch ['mɔnək] *n* monarca *m/f*; ~y *n* monarquía.

monastery ['mɔnəstərɪ] *n* monasterio.

monastic [mə'næstɪk] *a* monástico.

Monday ['mʌndɪ] *n* lunes *m*.

monetary ['mʌnɪtərɪ] *a* monetario.

money ['mʌnɪ] *n* dinero; to make ~ ganar dinero; ~lender *n* prestamista *m/f*; ~ order *n* giro.

mongol ['mɔŋgəl] *a, n* (MED) mongólico.

mongrel ['mʌŋgrəl] *n* (dog) perro cruzado.

monitor ['mɔnɪtə*] *n* (SCOL) monitor *m*; (also: television ~) receptor *m* de control // *vt* controlar.

monk [mʌŋk] *n* monje *m*.

monkey ['mʌŋkɪ] *n* mono; ~ nut *n*

cacahuete *m*; ~ **wrench** *n* llave *f* inglesa.

mono... [mɔnəu] *pref*: ~**chrome** *a* monocromo.

monocle ['mɔnəkl] *n* monóculo.

monogram ['mɔnəgræm] *n* monograma *m*.

monologue ['mɔnɔlɔg] *n* monólogo.

monopoly [mə'nɔpəli] *n* monopolio.

monorail ['mɔnəureil] *n* monorriel *m*.

monosyllabic [mɔnəusı'læbık] *a* monosilábico.

monotone ['mɔnətəun] *n* monotonía; **to speak in a** ~ hablar en un solo tono.

monotonous [mə'nɔtənəs] *a* monótono; **monotony** [-nı] *n* monotonía.

monsoon [mɔn'suːn] *n* monzón *m/f*.

monster ['mɔnstə*] *n* monstruo.

monstrosity [mɔns'trɔsıtı] *n* monstruosidad *f*.

monstrous ['mɔnstrəs] *a* (*huge*) enorme; (*atrocious*) monstruoso.

montage [mɔn'tɑːʒ] *n* montaje *m*.

month [mʌnθ] *n* mes *m*; ~**ly** *a* mensual // *ad* mensualmente // *n* (*magazine*) revista mensual.

monument ['mɔnjumənt] *n* monumento; ~**al** [-'mentl] *a* monumental.

moo [muː] *vi* mugir.

mood [muːd] *n* humor *m*; **to be in a good/bad** ~ estar de buen/mal humor; ~**y** *a* (*variable*) de humor variable; (*sullen*) melancólico.

moon [muːn] *n* luna; ~**beam** *n* rayo de luna; ~**light** *n* luz *f* de la luna; ~**lit** *a*: a ~**lit night** una noche de luna.

moor [muə*] *n* páramo // *vt* (*ship*) amarrar // *vi* echar las amarras.

Moor [muə*] *n* moro/a.

moorings ['muərıŋz] *npl* (*chains*) amarras *fpl*; (*place*) amarradero *sg*.

Moorish ['muərıʃ] *a* moro; (*architecture*) árabe, morisco.

moorland ['muələnd] *n* páramo, brezal *m*.

moose [muːs] *n*, *pl inv* alce *m*.

mop [mɔp] *n* fregona; (*of hair*) greña, melena // *vt* fregar; **to** ~ **up** *vt* limpiar.

mope [məup] *vi* estar *o* andar deprimido.

moped ['məupɛd] *n* (*Brit*) ciclomotor *m*.

moral ['mɔrl] *a* moral // *n* moraleja; ~**s** *npl* moralidad *f*, moral *f*.

morale [mɔ'rɑːl] *n* moral *f*.

morality [mɔ'rælıtı] *n* moralidad *f*.

morass [mə'ræs] *n* pantano.

morbid ['mɔːbıd] *a* (*depressed*) melancólico; (*MED*) mórbido; **don't be** ~! ¡no seas morboso!

more [mɔː*] *det*, *ad* más; **once** ~ otra vez, una vez más; **I want** ~ quiero más; ~ **dangerous** than más peligroso que; ~ **or less** más o menos; ~ **than ever** más que nunca.

moreover [mɔː'rəuvə*] *ad* además, por otra parte.

morgue [mɔːg] *n* depósito de cadáveres.

moribund ['mɔrıbʌnd] *a* moribundo.

Mormon ['mɔːmən] *n* mormón/ona *m/f*.

morning ['mɔːnıŋ] *n* (*gen*) mañana; (*early* ~) madrugada; **good** ~ buenas días; **in the** ~ por la mañana; **7 o'clock in the** ~ las 7 de la mañana; **tomorrow** ~ mañana por la mañana.

Moroccan [mə'rɔkən] *a*, *n* marroquí *m/f*.

Morocco [mə'rɔkəu] *n* Marruecos *m*.

moron ['mɔːrɔn] *n* imbécil *m/f*; ~**ic** [mə'rɔnık] *a* imbécil.

morose [mə'rəus] *a* hosco, malhumorado.

morphine ['mɔːfiːn] *n* morfina.

Morse [mɔːs] *n* (*also*: ~ **code**) (alfabeto *m*) morse.

morsel ['mɔːsl] *n* (*of food*) bocado.

mortal ['mɔːtl] *a*, *n* mortal *m/f*; ~**ity** [-'tælıtı] *n* mortalidad *f*.

mortar ['mɔːtə*] *n* argamasa; (*dish*) mortero.

mortgage ['mɔːgıdʒ] *n* hipoteca // *vt* hipotecar.

mortify ['mɔːtıfaı] *vt* mortificar, humillar.

mortuary ['mɔːtjuərı] *n* depósito de cadáveres.

mosaic [məu'zeıık] *n* mosaico.

Moscow ['mɔskəu] *n* Moscú *m*.

Moslem ['mɔzləm] *a*, *n* = **Muslim**.

mosque [mɔsk] *n* mezquita.

mosquito [mɔs'kiːtəu] *pl* ~**es** *n* mosquito.

moss [mɔs] *n* musgo.

most [məust] *det* la mayor parte de, la mayoría de // *pron* la mayor parte, la mayoría // *ad* el más (*very*) muy; **the** ~ (*also*: + *adjective*) el más; ~ **of them** la mayor parte de ellos; **I saw the** ~ yo vi el que más; **at the** (*very*) ~ a lo sumo, todo lo más; **to make the** ~ **of** aprovechar (al máximo); ~**ly** *ad* en su mayor parte, principalmente; **a** ~ **interesting book** un libro interesantísimo.

MOT *n abbr of* **Ministry of Transport: the** ~ (*test*) inspección (anual) obligatoria de coches y camiones.

motel [məu'tɛl] *n* motel *m*.

moth [mɔθ] *n* mariposa nocturna; (*clothes* ~) polilla; ~**ball** *n* bola de naftalina; ~**-eaten** *a* apolillado.

mother ['mʌðə*] *n* madre *f* // *a* materno // *vt* (*care for*) cuidar (como a una madre); ~**hood** *n* maternidad *f*; ~**-in-law** *n* suegra; ~**ly** *a* maternal; ~**-of-pearl** *n* nácar *m*; ~**-to-be** *n* futura madre; ~ **tongue** *n* lengua materna.

motif [məu'tiːf] *n* motivo; (*theme*) tema *m*.

motion ['məuʃən] *n* movimiento; (*gesture*) ademán *m*, señal *f*; (*at meeting*) moción *f* // *vt*, *vi*: **to** ~ (**to**) **sb to do sth** hacer señas a uno para que haga algo; ~**less** *a* inmóvil; ~ **picture** *n* película.

motivated ['məutıveıtıd] *a* motivado; **motivation** [-'veıʃən] *n* motivación *f*.

motive ['məutıv] *n* motivo // *a* motor (*f*: motora, motriz).

motley ['mɔtlı] *a* variado.

motor ['məutə*] *n* motor *m*; (*col*: *vehicle*) coche *m*, automóvil *m* // *a* motor (*f*:

motora, motriz); ~**bike** n moto f; ~**boat**
n lancha motora; ~**car** r. coche m,
automóvil m; ~**cycle** n motocicleta;
~**cyclist** n motorista m/f; ~**ing** n automovilismo; ~**ist** n conductor/a m/f,
automovilista m/f; ~ **oil** n aceite m de
coche; ~ **racing** n carreras fpl de coches,
automovilismo; ~ **scooter** n moto f; ~
vehicle n automóvil m; ~**way** n (Brit)
autopista.

mottled ['mɔtld] a abigarrado, multicolor.

motto ['mɔtəu] pl ~**es** n lema m
(watchword) consigna.

mould, mold (US) [məuld] n molde m;
(mildew) moho // vt moldear; (fig) formar;
~**er** vi (decay) decaer; ~**ing** n moldura;
~**y** a enmohecido.

moult, molt (US) [məult] vi mudar (la
piel/la pluma).

mound [maund] n montón m, montículo.

mount [maunt] n monte m; (horse)
montura; (for jewel etc) engaste m; (for
picture) marco // vt montar, subir a // vi
(also: ~ up) subirse, montarse.

mountain ['mauntin] n montaña //cpd de
montaña; ~**eer** [-'niə*] n alpinista m/f,
montañero/a; ~**eering** [-'niəriŋ] n
alpinismo, montañismo; **to go** ~**eering**
hacer alpinismo; ~**ous** a montañoso;
~**side** n ladera de la montaña.

mourn [mɔːn] vt llorar, lamentar // vt to
~ **for** llorar la muerte de, lamentarse
por; ~**er** n pariente m/f/amigo del
difunto; ~**ful** a triste, lúgubre; ~**ing** n
luto // cpd (dress) de luto; **in** ~**ing** de
luto.

mouse [maus], pl **mice** n ratón m; ~**trap**
n ratonera.

moustache [məs'tɑːʃ] n bigote m.

mousy ['mausi] a (person) tímido; (hair)
pardusco.

mouth [mauθ], pl ~**s** [-ðz] n boca; (of river)
desembocadura; ~**ful** n bocado; ~
organ n armónica; ~**piece** n (of musical
instrument) boquilla; (spokesman) portavoz
m; ~**wash** n enjuague m; ~**watering** a
apetitoso.

movable ['muːvəbl] a movible.

move [muːv] n (movement) movimiento;
(in game) jugada; (: turn to play) turno;
(change of house) mudanza // vt mover;
(emotionally) conmover; (POL: resolution
etc) proponer // vi (gen) moverse;
(traffic) circular; (also: ~ **house**)
trasladarse, mudarse; **to** ~ **sb to do sth**
mover a uno a hacer algo; **to get a** ~ **on**
darse prisa; **to** ~ **about** vi ir de acá para
allá; (travel) viajar; **to** ~ **along** vi
avanzar, adelantarse; **to** ~ **away** vi
alejarse; **to** ~ **back** vi retroceder; **to** ~
forward vi avanzar // vt adelantar; **to** ~
in vi (to a house) instalarse (en una casa);
to ~ **on** vi ponerse en camino; **to** ~ **out**
vi (of house) abandonar (una casa); **to** ~
up vi subir; (employee) ser ascendido.

movement ['muːvmənt] n movimiento;
(TECH) mecanismo.

movie ['muːvi] n película; **to go to the** ~**s**
ir al cine; ~ **camera** n cámara
cinematográfica.

moving ['muːviŋ] a (emotional)
conmovedor(a); (that moves) móvil.

mow [məu], pt **mowed** or **mown** or
mown vt (grass) cortar; (corn: also: ~
down) segar; ~**er** n segadora; (for lawn)
cortacéspedes m inv.

M.P. n abbr of **Member of Parliament.**

m.p.h. abbr of **miles per hour.**

Mr ['mistə*] n: ~ **Smith** (el) Sr. Smith.

Mrs ['misiz] n: ~ **Smith** (la) Sra. Smith.

Ms [miz] n = **Miss** or **Mrs**: ~ **Smith** (la)
Sa. Smith.

M.Sc. abbr of **Master of Science.**

much [mʌtʃ] det mucho // ad, a or pron
mucho; (before pp) muy; **how** ~ **is it?**
¿cuánto es?, ¿cuánto cuesta?; **too** ~
demasiado; **it's not** ~ no es mucho; **as** ~
as tanto como; **however** ~ **he tries** por
mucho que se esfuerce.

muck [mʌk] n (dirt) suciedad f; (fig)
porquería; **to** ~ **about** vi (col) perder el
tiempo; (enjoy o.s.) entretenerse; **to** ~ **up**
vt (col: ruin) arruinar, estropear; ~**y** a
(dirty) sucio.

mucus ['mjuːkəs] n moco.

mud [mʌd] n barro, lodo.

muddle ['mʌdl] n desorden m, confusión f;
(mix-up) embrollo, lío // vt (also: ~ **up**)
embrollar, confundir; **to** ~ **through** vi
salir del paso sin saber cómo.

mud: ~**dy** a fangoso, cubierto de lodo;
~**guard** n guardabarros m inv; ~**pack** n
mascarilla (de belleza); ~**slinging** n
injurias fpl, difamación f.

muff [mʌf] n manguito // vt (chance)
desperdiciar; (lines) estropear.

muffin ['mʌfin] n mollete m.

muffle ['mʌfl] vt (sound) amortiguar;
(against cold) embozar; ~**d** a sordo,
apagado.

mufti ['mʌfti] n: **in** ~ vestido de paisano.

mug [mʌg] n (cup) taza (alta, sin platillo);
(: for beer) jarra; (col: face) jeta; (: fool)
bobo // vt (assault) asaltar; ~**ging** n
asalto.

muggy ['mʌgi] a bochornoso.

mule [mjuːl] n mula.

mull [mʌl]: **to** ~ **over** vt meditar sobre.

mulled [mʌld] a: ~ **wine** vino calentado y
con especias.

multi... [mʌlti] pref multi...; ~**coloured,**
~**colored** (US) a multicolor.

multifarious [mʌlti'fεəriəs] a múltiple.

multiple ['mʌltipl] a, n múltiplo; ~
sclerosis n esclerosis f múltiple; ~ **store**
n (cadena de) grandes almacenes.

multiplication [mʌltipli'keiʃən] n
multiplicación f; **multiply** ['mʌltiplai] vt
multiplicar // vi multiplicarse.

multitude ['mʌltitjuːd] n multitud f.

mum [mʌm] n mamá // a: **to keep** ~
callarse.

mumble ['mʌmbl] vt, vi hablar entre dientes, refunfuñar.

mummy ['mʌmi] n (mother) mamá; (embalmed) momia.

mumps [mʌmps] n paperas fpl.

munch [mʌntʃ] vt, vi mascar.

mundane [mʌn'deɪn] a mundano.

municipal [mju:'nɪsɪpl] a municipal; ~ity [-'pælɪtɪ] n municipio.

munitions [mju:'nɪʃənz] npl municiones fpl.

mural ['mjuərl] n (pintura) mural m.

murder ['mɜ:də*] n asesinato; (in law) homicidio // vt asesinar, matar; (spoil) estropear; ~er n asesino; ~ess n asesina; ~ous a homicida.

murky ['mɜ:kɪ] a oscuro; (fig) tenebroso.

murmur ['mɜ:mə*] n murmullo // vt, vi murmurar.

muscle ['mʌsl] n músculo; (fig: strength) fuerza (muscular); to ~ in vi introducirse por fuerza; **muscular** ['muskjulə*] a muscular; (person) musculoso.

muse [mju:z] vi meditar // n musa.

museum [mju:'zɪəm] n museo.

mushroom ['mʌʃrum] n (gen) seta, hongo; (food) champiñón m // vi (fig) crecer de la noche a la mañana.

mushy ['mʌʃɪ] a triturado; (pej) sensiblero.

music ['mju:zɪk] n música; ~al a melodioso; (person) musical // n (show) (comedia) musical; ~al instrument n instrumento musical; ~ hall n teatro de variedades; ~ian [-'zɪʃən] n músico/a.

musket ['mʌskɪt] n mosquete m.

Muslim ['mʌzlɪm] a, n musulmán/ana m/f.

muslin ['mʌzlɪn] n muselina.

mussel ['mʌsl] n mejillón m.

must [mʌst] auxiliary vb (obligation): I ~ do it debo hacerlo, tengo que hacerlo; (probability): he ~ be there by now ya debe estar allí // n necesidad f; it's a ~ es imprescindible.

mustard ['mʌstəd] n mostaza.

muster ['mʌstə*] vt juntar, reunir.

mustn't ['mʌsnt] = **must not.**

musty ['mʌstɪ] a mohoso, que huele a humedad.

mute [mju:t] a, n mudo/a.

muted ['mju:tɪd] a callado; (MUS) apagado.

mutilate ['mju:tɪleɪt] vt mutilar; **mutilation** [-'leɪʃən] n mutilación f.

mutinous ['mju:tɪnəs] a (troops) amotinado; (attitude) rebelde.

mutiny ['mju:tɪnɪ] n motín m // vi amotinarse.

mutter ['mʌtə*] vt, vi murmurar, hablar entre dientes.

mutton ['mʌtn] n carne f de cordero.

mutual ['mju:tʃuəl] a mutuo; (gen: shared) común; ~ly ad mutuamente.

muzzle ['mʌzl] n hocico; (protective device) bozal m; (of gun) boca // vt amordazar; (dog) poner un bozal a.

my [maɪ] a mi // interj: ~! ¡caramba!

mynah bird ['maɪnə*] n mainat m.

myopic [maɪ'ɒpɪk] a miope.

myself [maɪ'sɛlf] pron (reflexive) me; (emphatic) yo mismo; (after prep) mí (mismo).

mysterious [mɪs'tɪərɪəs] a misterioso; **mystery** ['mɪstərɪ] n misterio.

mystic ['mɪstɪk] a, n místico/a; ~al a místico.

mystify ['mɪstɪfaɪ] vt (perplex) dejar perplejo; (disconcert) desconcertar.

myth [mɪθ] n mito; ~ical a mítico; ~ological [mɪθə'lɒdʒɪkl] a mitológico; ~ology [mɪ'θɒlədʒɪ] n mitología.

N

nab [næb] vt (col: grab) coger; (: catch out) pillar.

nag [næg] n (pej: horse) rocín m // vt (scold) regañar; (annoy) fastidiar; ~ging a (doubt) persistente; (pain) continuo // n quejas fpl.

nail [neɪl] n (human) uña; (metal) clavo // vt clavar; (fig: catch) coger, pillar; to ~ sb down to doing sth comprometer a uno a que haga algo; ~brush n cepillo para las uñas; ~file n lima para las uñas; ~ polish n esmalte m o laca para las uñas; ~ scissors npl tijeras fpl para las uñas.

naïve [naɪ'i:v] a ingenuo; (simple) sencillo.

naked ['neɪkɪd] a (nude) desnudo; (fig) inerme, indefenso; (flame) expuesto al aire; ~ness n desnudez f.

name [neɪm] n (gen) nombre m; (surname) apellido; (reputation) fama, renombre m // vt (child) poner nombre a; (criminal) dar el nombre de; (appoint) nombrar; by ~ de nombre; **maiden** ~ nombre de soltera; in the ~ of en nombre de; what's your ~? ¿cómo se llama?; to give one's ~ and address dar las señas; ~less a anónimo, sin nombre; ~ly ad a saber; ~sake n tocayo/a.

nanny ['nænɪ] n niñera; ~ goat n cabra.

nap [næp] n (sleep) sueñecito, siesta.

napalm ['neɪpɑ:m] n napalm m.

nape [neɪp] n: the ~ of the neck la nuca, el cogote.

napkin ['næpkɪn] n (also: table ~) servilleta; (Brit: for baby) pañal m.

nappy ['næpɪ] n pañal m; ~ liner n gasa; ~ rash n prurito.

narcissus [nɑ:'sɪsəs], pl -si [-saɪ] n narciso.

narcotic [nɑ:'kɒtɪk] a, n narcótico.

narrate [nə'reɪt] vt narrar, contar; **narrative** ['nærətɪv] n narrativa // a narrativo; **narrator** n narrador/a m/f.

narrow ['nærəu] a estrecho, angosto; (fig) de miras estrechas, intolerante // vi estrecharse, angostarse; (diminish) reducirse; to ~ down the possibilities to reducir las posibilidades a; ~ly ad (miss) por poco; ~-minded a de miras estrechas.

nasal ['neɪzl] a nasal.

nastiness ['nɑ:stɪnɪs] n (malice)

malevolencia; (*rudeness*) grosería.

nasty ['nɑːstɪ] a (*unpleasant: remark*) feo, horrible; (: *person*) antipático (*malicious*) rencoroso; (*rude*) grosero; (*revolting: taste, smell*) asqueroso, repugnante; (*wound, disease etc*) peligroso, grave.

nation ['neɪʃən] n nación f.

national ['næʃənl] a, n nacional m/f; ~**ism** n nacionalismo; ~**ist** a, n nacionalista m/f; ~**ity** [-'nælɪtɪ] a nacionalidad f; ~**ization** [-aɪ'zeɪʃən] n nacionalización f; ~**ize** vt nacionalizar; ~**ly** ad (*nationwide*) en escala nacional; (*as a nation*) nacionalmente, como nación.

nationwide ['neɪʃənwaɪd] a en escala o a nivel nacional.

native ['neɪtɪv] n (*local inhabitant*) natural m/f, nacional m/f; (*in colonies*) indígena m/f; nativo/a // a (*indigenous*) indígena; (*of one's birth*) natal; (*innate*) natural, innato.

NATO ['neɪtəu] n abbr of **North Atlantic Treaty Organization** OTAN (Organización del Tratado del Atlántico del Norte).

natter ['nætə*] vi charlar.

natural ['nætʃrəl] a natural; (*unaffected: manner*) inafectada, sin afectación; ~**ist** n naturalista m/f; ~**ize** vt: **to become** ~**ized** (*person*) naturalizarse; (*plant*) aclimatarse; ~**ly** ad naturalmente, (*of course*) desde luego, por supuesto; (*instinctively*) por instinto, por naturaleza; ~**ness** n naturalidad f.

nature ['neɪtʃə*] n naturaleza; (*group, sort*) género, clase f; (*character*) carácter m, genio; **by** ~ por o de naturaleza.

naughty ['nɔːtɪ] a (*child*) travieso; (*story, film*) verde, escabroso.

nausea ['nɔːsɪə] n náusea; **nauseate** [-sieɪt] vt dar náuseas a; (*fig*) dar asco a **nauseating** [-sieɪtɪŋ] a nauseabundo; (*fig*) asqueroso.

nautical ['nɔːtɪkl] a náutico, marítimo; (*mile*) marino.

naval ['neɪvl] a naval, de marina; ~ **officer** n oficial m/f de marina.

nave [neɪv] n nave f.

navel ['neɪvl] n ombligo.

navigable ['nævɪgəbl] a navegable.

navigate ['nævɪgeɪt] vt (*guide*) gobernar; (*sail along*) navegar por; (*fig*) guiar // vi navegar; **navigation** [-'geɪʃən] n (*action*) navegación f; (*science*) náutica; **navigator** n navegador/a m/f, navegante m/f.

navvy ['nævɪ] n peón m caminero.

navy ['neɪvɪ] n marina de guerra; (*ships*) armada, flota; ~(-**blue**) a azul marino.

Nazi ['nɑːtsɪ] n nazi m/f; **nazism** n nazismo.

neap tide [niːp] n marea muerta.

near [nɪə*] a (*place*) cercano, vecino; (*time*) próximo; (*relation*) estrecho, íntimo // ad cerca // prep (also: ~ **to**) (*space*) cerca de, junto a; (*time*) cerca de, casi // vt acercarse a, aproximarse a; ~**by** [nɪə'baɪ] a cercano, próximo // ad cerca; N~ **East** n Cercano Oriente m; ~**ly** ad casi, por poco; **I** ~**ly fell** por poco me caigo; ~ **miss** n tiro cercano; ~**ness** n proximidad f, cercanía; (*relationship*) intimidad f ~**side** n (AUT. *in Britain*) lado izquierdo; (: *in Spain*) lado derecho; ~**sighted** a miope, corto de vista.

neat [niːt] a (*place*) bien arreglado o cuidado; (*person*) pulcro, esmerado; (*skilful*) diestro; (: *plan*) hábil, ingenioso; (*spirits*) solo.

nebulous ['nebjuləs] a nebuloso; (*fig*) vago, confuso.

necessarily ['nesɪsrɪlɪ] ad necesariamente.

necessary ['nesɪsrɪ] a necesario, preciso; **he did all that was** ~ hizo todo lo necesario.

necessitate [nɪ'sesɪteɪt] vt necesitar, exigir.

necessity [nɪ'sesɪtɪ] n (*thing needed*) necesidad f, requisito; (*compelling circumstances*) la necesidad; **necessities** npl artículos mpl de primera necesidad.

neck [nek] n (ANAT) cuello; (*of animal*) pescuezo // vi besuquearse, abrazarse; ~ **and** ~ parejos; **to stick one's** ~ **out** arriesgarse.

necklace ['neklɪs] n collar m.

neckline ['neklaɪ] n escote m.

necktie ['nektaɪ] n corbata.

née [neɪ] a: ~ **Scott** de soltera Scott.

need [niːd] n (*lack*) escasez f, falta; (*necessity*) necesidad f; (*thing needed*) requisito, necesidad f // vt (*require*) necesitar; **I** ~ **to do it** tengo que o debo hacerlo, hay que hacerlo; **you don't** ~ **to go** no hace falta que vayas.

needle ['niːdl] n aguja // vt (*fig: fam*) picar, fastidiar.

needless ['niːdlɪs] a innecesario, inútil; ~ **to say** huelga decir que.

needlework ['niːdlwəːk] n (*activity*) costura, labor f de aguja.

needy ['niːdɪ] a necesitado.

negation [nɪ'geɪʃən] n negación f.

negative ['negətɪv] n (PHOT) negativo; (*answer*) negativa // a negativo.

neglect [nɪ'glekt] vt (*one's duty*) faltar a, no cumplir con; (*child*) descuidar, desatender // n (*gen*) negligencia, abandono; (*personal*) dejadez f; (*of duty*) incumplimiento.

negligee ['neglɪʒeɪ] n (*nightdress*) salto de cama; (*housecoat*) bata.

negligence ['neglɪdʒəns] n negligencia, descuido; **negligent** [-ənt] a (*careless*) descuidado, negligente; (*forgetful*) olvidadizo.

negligible ['neglɪdʒɪbl] a insignificante, despreciable.

negotiable [nɪ'gəuʃəbl] a (*cheque*) negociable; (*road*) transitable.

negotiate [nɪ'gəuʃɪeɪt] vi negociar // vt (*treaty*) negociar; (*transaction*) gestionar, tramitar; (*obstacle*) franquear;

negotiation [-'eɪʃən] n negociación f, gestión f; **negotiator** n negociador/a m/f.

Negress ['niːgrɪs] n negra.

Negro ['niːgrəu] a, n negro.

neigh [neɪ] n relincho // vi relinchar.

neighbour, neighbor (US) ['neɪbə*] n vecino/a; **~hood** n (place) vecindad f, barrio; (people) vecindario; **~ing** a vecino; **~ly** a amistoso, de buen vecino.

neither ['naɪðə*] a ni // conj: **I didn't move and ~ did John** no me he movido, ni Juan tampoco // pron ninguno // ad: **~ good nor bad** ni bueno ni malo.

neo... [niːəu] pref neo-.

neon ['niːɔn] n neón m; **~ light** n lámpara de neón.

nephew ['nevjuː] n sobrino.

nerve [nɜːv] n (ANAT) nervio; (courage) valor m; (impudence) descaro, frescura; **~-racking** a que crispa los nervios; **~s** npl . (fig: anxiety) nerviosidad f, nerviosismo.

nervous ['nɜːvəs] a (anxious, ANAT) nervioso; (timid) tímido, miedoso; **~ breakdown** n crisis f nerviosa; **~ly** ad nerviosamente; tímidamente; **~ness** n nerviosidad f, nerviosismo; timidez f.

nest [nest] n (of bird) nido; (of wasp) avispero // vi anidar.

nestle ['nesl] vi: **to ~ up to sb** arrimarse a uno.

net [net] n (gen) red f; (fig) trampa // a (COMM) neto, líquido // vt coger con red; (SPORT) marcar; **~ball** n básquet m.

Netherlands ['neðələndz] npl: **the ~** los Países Bajos.

nett [net] a = **net**.

netting ['netɪŋ] n red f, redes fpl.

nettle ['netl] n ortiga.

network ['netwɜːk] n red f.

neurosis [njuə'rəusɪs] pl **-ses** [-siːz] n neurosis f; **neurotic** [-'rɔtɪk] a, n neurótico/a.

neuter ['njuːtə*] a (sexless) castrado, sin sexo; (LING) neutro // vt castrar, capar.

neutral ['njuːtrəl] a (person) neutral; (colour etc, ELEC) neutro // n (AUT) punto muerto; **~ity** [-'trælɪtɪ] n neutralidad f.

neutron ['njuːtrɔn] n neutrón m; **~ bomb** n bomba de neutrones.

never ['nevə*] ad nunca, jamás; **I ~ went** no fui nunca; **~ in my life** jamás en la vida; **~-ending** a interminable, sin fin; **~theless** [nevəðə'les] ad sin embargo, no obstante.

new [njuː] a (brand ~) nuevo; (recent) reciente; (different) nuevo, distinto; (inexperienced) tierno, nuevo; **~-born** a recién nacido; **~-comer** ['njuːkʌmə*] n recién venido o llegado; **~ly** ad nuevamente, recién; **~ moon** n luna nueva; **~ness** n novedad f; (fig) inexperiencia.

news [njuːz] n noticias fpl; **a piece of ~** una noticia; **the ~** (RADIO, TV) las noticias fpl, telediario; **~ agency** n agencia de noticias; **~agent** n vendedor/a m/f de periódicos; **~caster** n presentador/a m/f de noticias; **~ flash** n noticia de última hora; **~ letter** n hoja informativa, boletín m; **~paper** n periódico, diario; **~reel** n noticiario; **~ stand** n quiosco o puesto de periódicos.

New Year ['njuː'jɪə*] n Año Nuevo; **~'s Day** n Día m de Año Nuevo; **~'s Eve** n Nochevieja.

New York ['njuː'jɔːk] n Nueva York.

New Zealand [njuː'ziːlənd] n Nueva Zelanda.

next [nekst] a (in space) próximo, vecino; (in time) próximo, siguiente // ad (place) después; (time) después, luego; **~ time** la próxima vez; **~ year** el año próximo o que viene; **~ door** ad en la casa de al lado // a vecino, de al lado; **~-of-kin** n pariente(s) m(pl) cercano(s); **~ to** prep junto a, al lado de.

N.H.S. n abbr of **National Health Service**.

nib [nɪb] n plumilla.

nibble ['nɪbl] vt mordisquear, mordiscar; (ZOOL) roer.

nice [naɪs] a (likeable) simpático, majo; (kind) amable; (pleasant) agradable; (attractive) bonito, mono; (subtle) fino, preciso; **~-looking** a atractivo, guapo; **~ly** ad amablemente, bien.

niche [niːʃ] n nicho.

nick [nɪk] n (wound) rasguño; (cut, indentation) mella, muesca // vt (col) birlar, robar; **in the ~ of time** a última hora.

nickel ['nɪkl] n níquel m.

nickname ['nɪkneɪm] n apodo, mote m // vt apodar.

nicotine ['nɪkətiːn] n nicotina.

niece [niːs] n sobrina.

Nigeria [naɪ'dʒɪərɪə] n Nigeria; **~n** a, n nigeriano/a.

niggardly ['nɪgədlɪ] a (person) avaro, tacaño; (amount) miserable.

niggling ['nɪglɪŋ] a (trifling) nimio, insignificante; (annoying) molesto.

night [naɪt] n (gen) noche f; (evening) tarde f; **last ~** anoche; **the ~ before last** anteanoche; **good ~!** ¡buenas noches!; **at** o **by ~** de noche, por la noche; **~cap** n (drink) resopón m; **~ club** n cabaret m; **~dress** n camisón m; **~fall** n anochecer m; **~ie** ['naɪtɪ] n camisón m.

nightingale ['naɪtɪŋgeɪl] n ruiseñor m.

nightly ['naɪtlɪ] a de noche, nocturno // ad todas las noches, cada noche.

night: ~mare n pesadilla; **~ school** n clase(s) f(pl) nocturna(s); **~ shift** n turno nocturno o de noche; **~-time** n noche f, **~ watchman** n sereno.

nil [nɪl] n cero, nada.

nimble ['nɪmbl] a (agile) ágil, ligero; (skilful) diestro.

nine [naɪn] num nueve; **~teen** num diecinueve, diez y nueve; **~ty** num noventa.

ninth [naɪnθ] a noveno.

nip [nɪp] *vt* (*pinch*) pellizcar; (*bite*) morder // *n* (*drink*) trago, gota.

nipple ['nɪpl] *n* (ANAT) pezón *m*; (*of bottle*) tetilla; (TECH) boquilla, manguito.

nippy ['nɪpɪ] *a* (*person*) ágil, rápido; (*taste*) picante.

nitrate ['naɪtreɪt] *n* nitrato.

nitrogen ['naɪtrədʒən] *n* nitrógeno.

no [nəu] *ad* no // a ninguno, no ... alguno // *n* no.

nobility [nəu'bɪlɪtɪ] *n* nobleza.

noble ['nəubl] *a* (*person*) noble; (*title*) de nobleza; (*generous*) noble; **~man** *n* noble *m*, aristócrata *m*.

nobody ['nəubədɪ] *pron* nadie.

nod [nɔd] *vi* saludar con la cabeza; (*in agreement*) decir que sí con la cabeza; (*doze*) cabecear // *vt* inclinar // *n* inclinación *f* de cabeza; to ~ **off** *vi* cabecear.

noise [nɔɪz] *n* ruido; (*din*) escándalo, estrépito; **noisily** *ad* ruidosamente; **noisy** *a* (*gen*) ruidoso; (*child*) escandaloso.

nomad ['nəumæd] *n* nómada *m/f*; **~ic** [-'mædɪk] *a* nómada.

nominal ['nɔmɪnl] *a* nominal.

nominate ['nɔmɪneɪt] *vt* (*propose*) proponer; (*appoint*) nombrar; **nomination** [-'neɪʃən] *n* propuesta; nombramiento.

nominee [nɔmɪ'niː] *n* candidato/a.

non... [nɔn] *pref* no, des..., in...; **~alcoholic** *a* no alcohólico; **~aligned** *a* no alineado; **~committal** ['nɔnkə'mɪtl] *a* (*reserved*) reservado; (*uncommitted*) evasivo; **~conformist** *a* no conformista; **~descript** ['nɔndɪskrɪpt] *a* indeterminado; (*pej*) mediocre.

none [nʌn] *pron* (*person*) nadie; (*thing*) ninguno, nada // *ad* de ninguna manera.

nonentity [nɔ'nentɪtɪ] *n* cero a la izquierda, nulidad *f*.

nonetheless [nʌnðə'les] *ad* sin embargo, no obstante.

non: **~fiction** *n* literatura no novelesca; **~plussed** *a* perplejo.

nonsense ['nɔnsəns] *n* tonterías *fpl*, disparates *fpl*.

non-stop ['nɔn'stɔp] *a* continuo; (RAIL) directo // *ad* sin parar.

noodles ['nuːdlz] *npl* tallarines *mpl*.

nook [nuk] *n* rincón *m*; **~s and crannies** escondrijos *mpl*.

noon [nuːn] *n* mediodía *m*.

no-one ['nəuwʌn] *pron* = **nobody**.

noose [nuːs] *n* lazo corredizo; (*hangman's*) dogal *m*.

nor [nɔː*] *conj* = **neither** // *ad* see **neither.**

norm [nɔːm] *n* norma.

normal ['nɔːml] *a* (*usual*) normal; (*ordinary*) corriente, regular; **~ly** *ad* normalmente.

north [nɔːθ] *n* norte *m* // *a* del norte, norteño // *ad* al *o* hacia el norte; **N~ America** *n* América del Norte; **~east** *n* nor(d)este *m*; **~ern** ['nɔːðən] *a* norteño,

del norte; **N~ern Ireland** *n* Irlanda del Norte; **N~ Pole** *n* Polo Norte; **N~ Sea** *n* Mar *m* del Norte; **~ward(s)** ['nɔːθwəd(z)] *ad* hacia el norte, **~west** *n* nor(d)oeste *m*.

Norway ['nɔːweɪ] *a* Noruega; **Norwegian** [-'wiːdʒən] *a*, *n* noruego/a.

nose [nəuz] *n* (ANAT) nariz *f*; (ZOOL) hocico; (*sense of smell*) olfato // *vi*: to ~ **about** curiosear; **~bleed** *n* hemorragia nasal; **~dive** *n* (*deliberate*) picado vertical; (*involuntary*) caída de narices; **~y** *a* curioso, fisgón(ona).

nostalgia [nɔs'tældʒɪə] *n* nostalgia; **nostalgic** *a* nostálgico.

nostril ['nɔstrɪl] *n* ventana de la nariz; **~s** *npl* narices *fpl*.

nosy ['nəuzɪ] *a* = **nosey.**

not [nɔt] *ad* no; ~ **at all** no ... en absoluto; ~ **that...** no es que...; ~ **yet** todavía no; ~ **now** ahora no **why** ~? ¿por qué no?

notable ['nəutəbl] *a* notable.

notary ['nəutərɪ] *n* notario.

notch [nɔtʃ] *n* muesca, corte *m*.

note [nəut] *n* (MUS) nota; (*banknote*) billete *m*; (*letter*) nota, carta; (*record*) nota, apunte *m*; (*fame*) importancia, renombre *m*; (*tone*) tono // *vt* (*observe*) notar, observar; (*write down*) apuntar, anotar; **~book** *n* libreta, cuaderno; **~case** *n* cartera, billetero; **~d** ['nəutɪd] *a* célebre, conocido; **~paper** *n* papel *m* para cartas.

nothing ['nʌθɪŋ] *n* nada; (*zero*) cero; for ~ (*free*) gratis, sin pago; (*in vain*) en balde.

notice ['nəutɪs] *n* (*announcement*) anuncio; (*attention*) atención *f*, interés *m*; (*warning*) aviso; (*dismissal*) despido; (*resignation*) dimisión *f*; (*period of time*) plazo // *vt* (*observe*) notar, observar; to **take** ~ **of** tomar nota de, prestar atención a; **at short** ~ a corto plazo, con poca anticipación; **until further** ~ hasta nuevo aviso; **~able** *a* evidente, obvio; **~board** *n* (*Brit*) tablón *m* de anuncios.

notification [nəutɪfɪ'keɪʃən] *n* aviso; **notify** ['nəutɪfaɪ] *vt* avisar notificar.

notion ['nəuʃən] *n* noción *f*, concepto; (*opinion*) opinión *f*.

notorious [nəu'tɔːrɪəs] *a* notorio, célebre.

notwithstanding [nɔtwɪθ'stændɪŋ] *ad* no obstante, sin embargo; ~ **this** a pesar de esto.

nougat ['nuːgaː] *n* turrón *m*.

nought [nɔːt] *n* cero.

noun [naun] *n* nombre *m*, sustantivo.

nourish ['nʌrɪʃ] *vt* nutrir, alimentar; (*fig*) fomentar, nutrir; **~ing** *a* nutritivo, rico; **~ment** *n* alimento, sustento.

novel ['nɔvl] *n* novela // *a* (*new*) nuevo, original; (*unexpected*) insólito; **~ist** *n* novelista *m/f*; **~ty** *n* novedad *f*.

November [nəu'vembə*] *n* noviembre *m*.

novice ['nɔvɪs] *n* principiante *m/f*, novato/a; (REL) novicio/a.

now [nau] *ad* (*at the present time*) ahora; (*these days*) actualmente, hoy día; **right**

~ ahora mismo; ~ **and then,** ~ **and again** de vez en cuando; **from** ~ **on** de ahora en adelante; ~**adays** ['nauədeiz] *ad* hoy (en) día, actualmente.

nowhere ['nəuwɛə*] *ad* (*direction*) a ninguna parte; (*location*) en ninguna parte.

nozzle ['nɔzl] *n* (*gen*) boquilla; (*TECH*) tobera, inyector *m*.

nuance ['nju:ɑ:ns] *n* matiz *m*.

nuclear ['nju:klɪə*] *a* nuclear.

nucleus ['nju:klɪəs], *pl* -**lei** [-lɪaɪ] *n* núcleo.

nude [nju:d] *a, n* desnudo/a; **in the** ~ desnudo.

nudge [nʌdʒ] *vt* dar un codazo a.

nudist ['nju:dɪst] *n* nudista *m/f.*

nudity ['nju:dɪtɪ] *n* desnudez *f.*

nuisance ['nju:sns] *n* molestia, fastidio; (*person*) pesado, latoso; **what a** ~! ¡qué lata!

null [nʌl] *a:* ~ **and void** nulo y sin efecto; ~**ify** ['nʌlɪfaɪ] *vt* anular, invalidar.

numb [nʌm] *a* entumecido; (*fig*) insensible // *vt* entumecer, entorpecer.

number ['nʌmbə*] *n* número; (*numeral*) número, cifra // *vt* (*pages etc*) numerar, poner número a; (*amount to*) sumar, ascender a; **to be** ~**ed among** figurar entre; **a** ~ **of** varios, algunos; **they were ten in** ~ eran diez; ~ **plate** *n* placa de matrícula.

numbness ['nʌmnɪs] *n* entumecimiento; (*fig*) insensibilidad *f.*

numeral ['nju:mərəl] *n* número, cifra.

numerical ['nju:'mɛrɪkl] *a* numérico.

numerous ['nju:mərəs] *a* numeroso, muchos.

nun [nʌn] *n* monja, religiosa.

nurse [nɔ:s] *n* enfermero/a; (*nanny*) niñera // *vt* (*patient*) cuidar, atender; (*baby*) criar, amamantar; (*fig*) guardar; **wet** ~ nodriza.

nursery ['nɔ:sərɪ] *n* (*institution*) guardería infantil; (*room*) cuarto de los niños; (*for plants*) criadero, semillero; ~ **rhyme** *n* canción *f* infantil; ~ **school** *n* parvulario, escuela de párvulos; ~ **slope** *n* (*SKI*) cuesta para principiantes.

nursing ['nɔ:sɪŋ] *n* (*profession*) profesión *f* de enfermera; (*care*) asistencia, cuidado; ~ **home** *n* clínica de reposo.

nut [nʌt] *n* (*TECH*) tuerca; (*BOT*) nuez *f*; ~**s** *a* (*col*) loco; ~**case** *n* (*col*) loco/a, chalado/a; ~**crackers** *npl* cascanueces *m inv*; ~**meg** ['nʌtmɛg] *n* nuez *f* moscada.

nutrient ['nju:trɪənt] *n* nutrimento.

nutrition [nju:'trɪʃən] *n* nutrición *f*, alimentación *f*; **nutritious** [-ʃəs] *a* nutritivo, rico.

nutshell ['nʌtʃɛl] *n* cáscara de nuez; **in a** ~ en resumidas cuentas.

nylon ['naɪlɔn] *n* nilón *m* // *a* de nilón; ~**s** *npl* medias *fpl* (de nilón).

nymph [nɪmf] *n* ninfa.

O

oaf [əuf] *n* zoquete *m.*

oak [əuk] *n* roble *m* // *a* de roble

O.A.P. *abbr of* **old-age pensioner.**

oar [ɔ:*] *n* remo; **oarsman** *n* remero.

oasis [əu'eɪsɪs], *pl* -**ses** [-si:z] *n* oasis *m.*

oath [əuθ] *n* juramento; (*swear word*) palabrota; **on** ~ bajo juramento.

oatmeal ['əutmi:l] *n* harina de avena.

oats [əuts] *n* avena.

obedience [ə'bi:dɪəns] *n* obediencia; **in** ~ **to** de acuerdo con; **obedient** [-ənt] *a* obediente.

obesity [əu'bi:sɪtɪ] *n* obesidad *f.*

obey [ə'beɪ] *vt* obedecer; (*instructions, regulations*) cumplir.

obituary [ə'bɪtjuərɪ] *n* necrología.

object ['ɔbdʒɪkt] *n* (*gen*) objeto; (*purpose*) objeto, propósito; (*LING*) complemento // *vi* [əb'dʒɛkt]: **to** ~ **to** (*attitude*) protestar contra; (*proposal*) oponerse a; **I** ~! ¡yo protesto!; ~**ion** [əb'dʒɛkʃən] *n* protesta, **I have no** ~**ion to...** no tengo inconveniente en que...; ~**ionable** [əb'dʒɛkʃənəbl] *a* (*gen*) desagradable; (*conduct*) censurable; ~**ive** *a*, *n* objetivo; ~**ivity** [ɔbdʒɪk'tɪvɪtɪ] *n* objetividad *f*; ~**or** *n* objetor/a *m/f.*

obligation [ɔblɪ'geɪʃən] *n* obligación *f*; (*debt*) deber *m*; **without** ~ sin compromiso.

obligatory [ə'blɪgətərɪ] *a* obligatorio.

oblige [ə'blaɪdʒ] *vt* (*force*): **to** ~ **sb to do sth** forzar *o* obligar a uno a hacer algo; (*do a favour for*) complacer, hacer un favor a; **I should be** ~**d if...** le agradecería que...; **obliging** *a* servicial, atento.

oblique [ə'bli:k] *a* oblicuo; (*allusion*) indirecto.

obliterate [ə'blɪtəreɪt] *vt* borrar.

oblivion [ə'blɪvɪən] *n* olvido; **oblivious** [-ɪəs] *a*: **oblivious of** inconsciente de.

oblong ['ɔblɔŋ] *a* rectangular // *n* rectángulo.

obnoxious [əb'nɔkʃəs] *a* odioso, detestable; (*smell*) nauseabundo.

oboe ['əubəu] *n* oboe *m.*

obscene [əb'si:n] *a* obsceno; **obscenity** [-'sɛnɪtɪ] *n* obscenidad *f.*

obscure [əb'skjuə*] *a* oscuro // *vt* oscurecer; (*hide: sun*) esconder; **obscurity** *n* oscuridad *f.*

obsequious [əb'si:kwɪəs] *a* obsequioso.

observance [əb'zə:vns] *n* observancia, cumplimiento; (*ritual*) práctica.

observant [əb'zə:vnt] *a* observador(a).

observation [ɔbzə'veɪʃən] *n* observación *f*; (*by police etc*) vigilancia; (*MED*) examen *m.*

observatory [əb'zə:vətrɪ] *n* observatorio.

observe [əb'zə:v] *vt* (*gen*) observar; (*rule*) cumplir; **observer** *n* observador/a *m/f.*

obsess [əb'sɛs] *vt* obsesionar; ~**ion** [əb-

'seʃən] n obsesión f, idea fija; ~ive a
obsesivo, obsesionante.

obsolescence [ɔbsə'lɛsns] n caída en
desuso; **obsolete** ['ɔbsəli:t] a (que está en)
desuso.

obstacle ['ɔbstəkl] n obstáculo; (nuisance)
estorbo; ~ **race** n carrera de obstáculos.

obstetrician [ɔbstə'trɪʃən] n obstétrico;
obstetrics [-'stɛtrɪks] n obstetricia.

obstinate ['ɔbstɪnɪt] a terco, porfiado;
(determined) tenaz.

obstruct [əb'strʌkt] vt (block) obstruir;
(hinder) estorbar, obstaculizar; ~ **ion** [əb-
'strʌkʃən] n obstrucción f; estorbo,
obstáculo.

obtain [əb'teɪn] vt (get) obtener; (achieve)
conseguir; ~**able** a asequible.

obtrusive [əb'tru:sɪv] a (person)
importuno, entrometido; (building etc)
demasiado visible.

obvious ['ɔbvɪəs] a (clear) obvio, evidente;
(unsubtle) poco sutil; ~**ly** ad
evidentemente, naturalmente.

occasion [ə'keɪʒən] n (gen) oportunidad f,
ocasión f; (reason) motivo; (time) ocasión
f, vez f; (event) acontecimiento // vt
ocasionar, causar; ~**ally** ad de vez en
cuando.

occult [ɔ'kʌlt] a (gen) oculto.

occupant ['ɔkjupənt] n (of house)
inquilino/a; (of car) ocupante m/f.

occupation [ɔkju'peɪʃən] n (of house)
tenencia; (job) trabajo (: calling) oficio;
unfit for ~ (house) inhabitable; ~**al
hazard** n riesgo profesional.

occupier ['ɔkjupaɪə*] n inquilino/a.

occupy ['ɔkjupaɪ] vt (gen) ocupar; (house)
habitar, vivir en; (time) emplear, pasar;
(attention) entretener; **to ~ o.s. with** or
by doing (as job) dedicarse a hacer; (to
pass time) pasar el tiempo haciendo.

occur [ə'kə:*] vi pasar, suceder; **to ~ to
sb** ocurrírsele a uno; **it ~s to me that...**
se me ocurre que...; ~**rence** n (event)
acontecimiento; (existence) existencia.

ocean ['əuʃən] n océano; ~**-going** a de
alta mar; ~ **liner** n transatlántico.

o'clock [ə'klɔk] ad: **it is 5** ~ son las 5.

octagonal [ɔk'tægənl] a octagonal.

octane ['ɔkteɪn] n octano.

octave ['ɔktɪv] n octava.

October [ɔk'təubə*] n octubre m.

octopus ['ɔktəpəs] n pulpo.

odd [ɔd] a (strange) extraño, raro; (number) impar; (left over) sobrante, suelto;
60~ 60 y pico; **at ~ times** de vez en
cuando; **to be the ~ one out** estar de
más; ~**ity** n rareza; (person) excéntrico;
~**-job man** n hombre m que hace de
todo; ~ **jobs** npl bricolaje m; ~**ly** ad
curiosamente, extrañamente; ~**ments**
npl (COMM) retales mpl; ~**s** npl (in betting)
puntos mpl de ventaja; **it makes no ~s**
no importa, lo mismo da; **at ~s**
reñidos(as).

ode [əud] n oda.

odious ['əudɪəs] a odioso.

odour, odor (US) ['əudə*] n olor m;
(perfume) perfume m; ~**less** a inodoro.

of [ɔv, əv] prep de; **a friend ~ ours** un
amigo nuestro; **3 ~ them** 3 de ellos; **the
5th ~ July** el 5 de julio; **a boy ~ 10** un
niño de 10 años; **made ~ wood** hecho de
madera.

off [ɔf] a, ad (engine) desconectado; (light)
apagado; (tap) cerrado; (food: bad)
pasado, malo; (milk) cortado; (cancelled)
anulado // prep de; **to be** ~ (to leave)
irse, marcharse; **to be 5 km** ~ estar a 5
kilómetros; **a day** ~ un día libre o sin
trabajar; **to have an** ~ **day** tener un día
malo; **he had his coat** ~ se había
quitado el abrigo, **10%** ~ (COMM) (con el)
10% de descuento; **5 km** ~ **(the road)** a 5
km (de la carretera); **on the ~ coast** frente
a la costa; **on the ~ chance** por si acaso.

offal ['ɔfl] n (CULIN) menudencias fpl.

off-colour ['ɔf'kʌlə*] a (ill) indispuesto.

offence, offense (US) [ə'fɛns] n (crime)
delito; (insult) ofensa; **to take** ~ **at**
ofenderse por.

offend [ə'fɛnd] vt (person) ofender; ~**er** n
delincuente m/f; (against regulations)
infractor/a m/f.

offensive [ə'fɛnsɪv] a ofensivo (smell etc)
repugnante // n (MIL) ofensiva.

offer ['ɔfə*] n (gen) oferta, ofrecimiento;
(proposal) propuesta // vt ofrecer;
(opportunity) facilitar; **'on** ~' (COMM) 'en
oferta'; ~**ing** n ofrenda; ~**tory** n (REL)
ofertorio.

offhand [ɔf'hænd] a informal // ad de
improviso.

office ['ɔfɪs] n (place) oficina; (room)
despacho; (position) carga, oficio; **to take**
~ entrar en funciones; ~ **block** n bloque
m de oficinas; ~ **boy** n mozo (de oficina);
officer n (MIL etc) oficial m; (of organization) director m; (also: **police officer**)
agente m/f de policía; ~ **worker** n
oficinista m/f.

official [ə'fɪʃl] a (authorized) oficial,
autorizado // n funcionario, oficial m;
~**dom** n burocracia.

officious [ə'fɪʃəs] a oficioso.

offing ['ɔfɪŋ] n: **in the** ~ (fig) en
perspectiva.

off: ~**-licence** n (Brit: shop) bodega,
tienda de vinos y bebidas alcohólicas;
~**-peak** a de temporada de poca
actividad; ~**-putting** a que desanima;
~**-season** a, ad fuera de temporada.

offset ['ɔfsɛt] (irg: like set) vt (counteract)
contrarrestar, compensar // n (also: ~
printing) offset m.

offshore [ɔf'ʃɔ:*] a (que está) cerca de la
costa.

offside ['ɔf'saɪd] a (SPORT) fuera de juego.

offspring ['ɔfsprɪŋ] n descendencia,
descendientes mpl or fpl.

off: ~**-stage** ad entre bastidores; ~**-the-
peg** ad confeccionado; ~**-white** a blanco
grisáceo.

often ['ɔfn] ad a menudo, con frecuencia.

ogle ['ougl] vt echar miradas a.

oil [ɔɪl] n aceite m; (petroleum) petróleo // vt (machine) engrasar; ~can n lata de aceite; ~field n campo petrolífero; ~-fired a que quema aceite combustible; ~ painting n pintura de óleo; ~ refinery n refinería de petróleo; ~ rig n torre f de perforación; ~skins npl impermeables mpl de hule, chubasquero sg; ~ tanker n petrolero; ~ well n pozo (de petróleo); ~y a aceitoso; (food) grasiento.

ointment ['ɔɪntmənt] n ungüento.

O.K., okay ['əu'keɪ] excl O.K., ¡está bien!, ¡vale! // a bien // vt dar el visto bueno a.

old [əuld] a viejo; (former) antiguo; how ~ are you? ¿cuántos años tienes?, ¿qué edad tienes?; he's 10 years ~ tiene 10 años; ~er brother hermano mayor; ~ age n la vejez; ~-age pensioner (O.A.P.) n jubilado/a; ~-fashioned a anticuado, pasado de moda.

olive ['ɔlɪv] n (fruit) aceituna; (tree) olivo // a (also: ~-green) verde oliva; ~ oil n aceite m de oliva.

Olympic [əu'lɪmpɪk] a olímpico; the ~ Games, the ~s los Juegos Olímpicos.

omelet(te) ['ɔmlɪt] n tortilla (de huevo).

omen ['əumən] n presagio.

ominous ['ɔmɪnəs] a de mal agüero, amenazador(a).

omission [əu'mɪʃən] n omisión f; (error) descuido.

omit [əu'mɪt] vt omitir; (by mistake) olvidar, descuidar.

on [ɔn] prep en, sobre // ad (machine) conectado, en; (light, radio) encendido; (tap) abierto; **is the meeting still** ~? ¿todavía hay reunión?; **when is this film** ~? ¿cuándo van a poner esta película?; ~ **the wall** en la pared, colgado de la pared; ~ **television** en la televisión; ~ **horseback** a caballo; ~ **seeing this** al ver esto; ~ **arrival** al llegar; ~ **the left** a la izquierda; ~ **Friday** el viernes; **a week** ~ **Friday** el viernes en ocho días; **to have one's coat** ~ tener el abrigo puesto; **to go** ~ seguir adelante; **it's not** ~! ¡eso no se hace!

once [wʌns] ad una vez; (formerly) antiguamente // conj una vez que; **at** ~ en seguida, inmediatamente; (simultaneously) a la vez; ~ **a week** una vez por semana; ~ **more** otra vez; ~ **and for all** de una vez por todas; ~ **upon a time** érase una vez.

oncoming ['ɔnkʌmɪŋ] a (traffic) que viene de frente.

one [wʌn] det, num un, uno, una // pron uno; (impersonal) se // a (sole) único; (same) mismo; **this** ~ éste/a; **that** ~ ése/a, aquél/aquella; ~ **by** ~ uno por uno; ~ **never knows** nunca se sabe; ~ **another** el uno al otro; ~-**man** a (business) individual; ~-**man band** n un hombre-orquesta; ~**self** pron uno mismo; (after

prep, also emphatic) sí (mismo/a); '~-**way**' 'dirección única'.

ongoing ['ɔngəuɪŋ] a continuo.

onion ['ʌnjən] n cebolla.

onlooker ['ɔnlukə*] n espectador/a m/f.

only ['əunlɪ] ad solamente, sólo // a único, solo // conj solamente que, pero; **an** ~ **child** un hijo único; **not** ~ ... **but also...** no sólo ... sino también... .

onset ['ɔnsɛt] n (beginning) comienzo; (attack) ataque m.

onslaught ['ɔnslɔ:t] n ataque m, embestida.

onto ['ɔntu] prep = **on to**.

onus ['əunəs] n responsabilidad f.

onward(s) ['ɔnwəd(z)] ad (move) (hacia) adelante; **from this time** ~ de ahora en adelante.

onyx ['ɔnɪks] n ónice m, onyx m.

ooze [u:z] vi rezumar.

opal ['əupl] n ópalo.

opaque [əu'peɪk] a opaco.

open ['əupn] a abierto; (car) descubierto; (road, view) despejado; (meeting) público; (admiration) manifiesto // vt abrir // vi (flower, eyes, door, debate) abrirse; (book etc: commence) comenzar; **to** ~ **out** vt fus (subj: room, road) dar a; **to** ~ **up** vt abrir; (blocked road) despejar // vi abrirse, empezar; **in the** ~ (**air**) al aire libre; ~**ing** n abertura, comienzo; (opportunity) oportunidad f; (job) puesto vacante, vacante f; ~**ly** ad abiertamente; ~-**minded** a imparcial; ~-**necked** a sin corbata.

opera ['ɔpərə] n ópera; ~ **glasses** npl gemelos mpl; ~ **house** n teatro de la ópera.

operate ['ɔpəreɪt] vt (machine) hacer funcionar; (company) dirigir // vi funcionar; (drug) hacer efecto; **to** ~ **on sb** (MED) operar a alguien.

operatic [ɔpə'rætɪk] a de ópera.

operating ['ɔpəreɪtɪŋ]: ~ **table** n mesa de operaciones; ~ **theatre** n sala de operaciones.

operation [ɔpə'reɪʃən] n (gen) operación f; (of machine) funcionamiento; **to be in** ~ estar en funcionamiento o funcionando; ~**al** a operacional, en buen estado.

operative ['ɔpərətɪv] a (measure) en vigor.

operator ['ɔpəreɪtə*] n (of machine) maquinista m/f, operario; (TEL) operador/a m/f, telefonista m/f.

operetta [ɔpə'rɛtə] n opereta; (in Spain) zarzuela.

ophthalmic [ɔf'θælmɪk] a oftálmico.

opinion [ə'pɪnɪən] n (gen) opinión f; (point of view) parecer m, juicio; ~**ated** a testarudo; ~ **poll** n encuesta, sondeo.

opium ['əupɪəm] n opio.

opponent [ə'pəunənt] n adversario/a, contrincante m/f.

opportune ['ɔpətju:n] a oportuno; **opportunist** [-'tju:nɪst] n oportunista m/f.

opportunity [ɔpə'tju:nɪtɪ] n oportunidad f.

oppose [ə'pəuz] vt oponerse a; to be ~d to sth oponerse a algo, resistirse a aceptar algo; **opposing** a (side) opuesto, contrario.

opposite ['ɔpəzit] a opuesto; (house etc) de enfrente // ad en frente // prep en frente de, frente a // n lo contrario.

opposition [ɔpə'zifən] n oposición f.

oppress [ə'pres] vt oprimir; ~ion [ə'prefən] n opresión f; ~ive a opresivo.

opt [ɔpt] vi: to ~ for elegir; to ~ to do optar por hacer; to ~ out of optar por no hacer.

optical ['ɔptikl] a óptico.

optician [ɔp'tifən] n óptico.

optimism ['ɔptimizəm] n optimismo.

optimist ['ɔptimist] n optimista m/f; ~ic [-'mistik] a optimista.

optimum ['ɔptiməm] a óptimo.

option ['ɔpfən] n opción f; to keep one's ~s open (fig) mantener las opciones abiertas; ~al a facultativo, discrecional.

opulent ['ɔpjulənt] a opulento.

or [ɔ*] conj o; (before o, ho) u; (with negative): he hasn't seen ~ heard anything no ha visto ni oído nada; ~ else si no.

oracle ['ɔrəkl] n oráculo.

oral ['ɔrəl] a oral // n examen m oral.

orange ['ɔrindʒ] n (fruit) naranja // a color naranja.

oration [ɔ:'reifən] n oración f; **orator** ['ɔrətə*] n orador/a m/f.

orbit ['ɔːbit] n órbita // vt, vi orbitar.

orchard ['ɔːtfəd] n huerto.

orchestra ['ɔːkistrə] n orquesta; **orchestral** [-'kestrəl] a orquestral.

orchid ['ɔːkid] n orquídea.

ordain [ɔ:'dein] vt (REL) ordenar, decretar; (decide) mandar.

ordeal [ɔ:'diːl] n experiencia penosa.

order ['ɔːdə*] n orden m; (command) orden f; (type, kind) clase f; (state) estado; (COMM) pedido, encargo // vt (also: put in ~) arreglar, poner en orden; (COMM) encargar, pedir; (command) mandar, ordenar; in ~ (of document) en regla; in ~ to do para hacer; to ~ sb to do sth mandar a uno hacer algo; ~ly n (MIL) ordenanza m; (MED) enfermero (auxiliar) // a (room) en orden, ordenado; (person) ordenado.

ordinary ['ɔːdnri] a corriente, normal; (pej) ordinario, vulgar; **out of the** ~ fuera de lo común.

ordnance ['ɔːdnəns] n (MIL: unit) artillería; **O~ Survey** n servicio oficial de topografía y cartografía.

ore [ɔ:*] n mineral m.

organ ['ɔːgən] n órgano; ~ic [ɔː'gænik] a orgánico.

organism ['ɔːgənizəm] n organismo.

organist ['ɔːgənist] n organista m/f.

organization [ɔːgənai'zeifən] n organización f; **organize** ['ɔːgənaiz] vt

organizar; **organizer** ['ɔːgənaizə*] n organizador/a m/f.

orgasm ['ɔːgæzəm] n orgasmo.

orgy ['ɔːdʒi] n orgía.

Orient ['ɔːriənt] n Oriente m; **oriental** [-entl] a oriental.

orientate ['ɔːrienteit] vt orientar.

origin ['ɔridʒin] n origen m; (point of departure) procedencia.

original [ə'ridʒinl] a original; (first) primero, (earlier) primitivo // n original m; ~ity [-'næliti] n originalidad f; ~ly ad (at first) al principio, (with originality) con originalidad.

originate [ə'ridʒineit] vi: to ~ from or in surgir de, tener su origen en.

ornament ['ɔːnəmənt] n adorno; (trinket) chuchería; ~al [-'mentl] a decorativo, de adorno.

ornate [ɔː'neit] a muy ornado, vistoso.

ornithologist [ɔːni'θɔlədʒist] n ornitólogo; **ornithology** [-dʒi] n ornitología.

orphan ['ɔːfn] n huérfano // vt: to be ~ed quedar huérfano; ~age n orfelinato.

orthodox ['ɔːθədɔks] a ortodoxo; ~y n ortodoxia.

orthopaedic, orthopedic (US) [ɔːθə'piːdik] a ortopédico; ~s n ortopedia.

oscillate ['ɔsileit] vi oscilar; (person) vacilar.

ostensibly [ɔs'tensibli] ad aparentemente.

ostentatious [ɔsten'teifəs] a pretencioso, aparatoso; (person) ostentativo.

osteopath ['ɔstiəpæθ] n osteópata m/f.

ostracize ['ɔstrəsaiz] vt condenar al ostracismo.

ostrich ['ɔstritf] n avestruz m.

other ['ʌðə*] a otro; ~ than (another way) de otra manera que; (apart from) aparte de; ~wise ad, conj de otra manera; (if not) si no.

otter ['ɔtə*] n nutria.

ought [ɔːt] pt ought auxiliary vb: I ~ to do it debería hacerlo; this ~ to have been corrected esto debiera de haberse corregido; he ~ to win (probability) debe o debiera ganar.

ounce [auns] n onza (28.35g).

our ['auə*] a nuestro; ~s pron (el) nuestro/(a) nuestra etc; ~selves pron pl (reflexive, after prep) nosotros; (emphatic) nosotros mismos.

oust [aust] vt desalojar.

out [aut] ad fuera, afuera; (not at home) fuera (de casa); (light, fire) apagado; ~ there allí, allí fuera; he's ~ (absent) no está, ha salido; to be ~ in one's calculations equivocarse (en sus cálculos), to run ~ salir corriendo; ~ loud en alta voz; ~ of (outside) fuera de; (because of: anger etc) por; ~ of petrol sin gasolina; "~ of order" "no funciona"; ~-of-the-way (fig) insólito.

outback ['autbæk] n interior m.

outboard ['autbɔːd] a: ~ motor motor m de fuera de borda.

outbreak ['autbreik] n (of war) comienzo;

(*of disease*) epidemia; (*of violence etc*) arranque *m*.

outburst ['autbə:st] *n* explosión *f*, arranque *m*.

outcast ['autkɑ:st] *n* paria *m/f*.

outcome ['autkʌm] *n* resultado.

outcry ['autkraɪ] *n* protesta ruidosa.

outdated [aut'deɪtɪd] *a* anticuado, fuera de moda.

outdo [aut'du:] (*irg: like do*) *vt* exceder.

outdoor [aut'dɔ:*]*a*, **~s** *ad* al aire libre.

outer ['autə*] *a* exterior, externo; **~ space** *n* el espacio.

outfit ['autfɪt] *n* equipo; (*clothes*) traje *m*; **~ter's** *n* camisería.

outgoing ['autgəuɪŋ] *a* (*character*) extrovertido; **~s** *npl* gastos *mpl*.

outgrow [aut'grəu] (*irg: like grow*) *vt*: **he has ~n his clothes** su ropa le queda pequeña ya.

outing ['autɪŋ] *n* excursión *f*, paseo.

outlandish [aut'lændɪʃ] *a* estrafalario.

outlaw ['autlɔ:] *n* proscrito // *vt* (*person*) declarar fuera de la ley; (*practice*) declarar ilegal.

outlay ['autleɪ] *n* inversión *f*.

outlet ['autlɛt] *n* salida; (*of pipe*) desagüe *m*; (*for emotion*) desahogo; (*also:* **retail ~**) lugar *m* de venta.

outline ['autlaɪn] *n* (*shape*) contorno, perfil *m*; (*of plan*) trazado; (*sketch*) esbozo, idea general.

outlive [aut'lɪv] *vt* sobrevivir.

outlook ['autluk] *n* perspectiva; (*opinion*) punto de vista.

outlying ['autlaɪɪŋ] *a* remoto, aislado.

outmoded [aut'məudɪd] *a* anticuado, pasado de moda.

outnumber [aut'nʌmbə*] *vt* exceder en número.

outpatient ['autpeɪʃənt] *n* paciente *m/f* de consulta externa.

outpost ['autpəust] *n* puesto avanzado.

output ['autput] *n* (*volumen m de*) producción *f*, rendimiento.

outrage ['autreɪdʒ] *n* (*scandal*) escándalo; (*atrocity*) atrocidad *f* // *vt* ultrajar; **~ous** ['reɪdʒəs] *a* monstruoso.

outright [aut'raɪt] *ad* completamente // *a* ['autraɪt] completo.

outset ['autsɛt] *n* principio.

outside [aut'saɪd] *n* exterior *m*; (*surface*) superficie *f*; (*aspect*) aspecto // *a* exterior, externo // *ad* fuera // *prep* fuera de; (*beyond*) más allá de; **at the ~** (*fig*) a lo sumo; **~ lane** *n* (*AUT. in Britain*) carril *m* de la derecha; **~-left** *n* (*FOOTBALL*) extremo izquierdo; **outsider** *n* (*stranger*) extraño, forastero.

outsize ['autsaɪz] *a* (*clothes*) de talla grande.

outskirts ['autskə:ts] *npl* alrededores *mpl*, afueras *fpl*.

outspoken [aut'spəukən] *a* muy franco.

outstanding [aut'stændɪŋ] *a* excepcional, destacado; (*unfinished*) pendiente.

outstay [aut'steɪ] *vt*: **to ~ one's welcome** quedarse más tiempo de lo indicado.

outstretched [aut'strɛtʃt] *a* (*hand*) extendido.

outward ['autwəd] *a* (*sign, appearances*) externo; (*journey*) de ida; **~ly** *ad* por fuera.

outweigh [aut'weɪ] *vt* pesar más que.

outwit [aut'wɪt] *vt* ser más listo que, burlar.

oval ['əuvl] *a* ovalado // *n* óvalo.

ovary ['əuvərɪ] *n* ovario.

ovation [əu'veɪʃən] *n* ovación *f*.

oven ['ʌvn] *n* horno; **~proof** *a* refractario.

over ['əuvə*] *ad* encima, por encima // *a* (*or ad*) (*finished*) terminado // *prep* (por) encima de; (*above*) sobre; (*on the other side of*) al otro lado de; (*more than*) más de; (*during*) durante; **~ here** (por) aquí; **~ there** (por) allí *o* allá; **all ~** (*everywhere*) por todas partes; **~ and ~** (*again*) una y otra vez; **~ and above** más de; **to ask sb ~** invitar a uno; **to bend ~** inclinarse.

over... ['əuvə*] *pref* sobre..., super...; **~abundant** *a* superabundante.

overall ['əuvərɔ:l] *a* (*length*) total; (*study*) de conjunto // *a* [əuvər'ɔ:l] en conjunto; **~s** *npl* mono *sg o* bata *sg* (de trabajo).

overbalance [əuvə'bæləns] *vi* perder el equilibrio.

overbearing [əuvə'bɛərɪŋ] *a* autoritario, imperioso.

overboard ['əuvəbɔ:d] *ad* (*NAUT*) por la borda; **man ~!** ¡hombre al agua!

overcast ['əuvəkɑ:st] *a* encapotado.

overcharge [əuvə'tʃɑ:dʒ] *vt*: **to ~ sb** cobrar un precio excesivo a uno.

overcoat ['əuvəkəut] *n* abrigo, sobretodo.

overcome [əuvə'kʌm] (*irg: like come*) *vt* (*gen*) vencer; (*difficulty*) superar.

overcrowded [əuvə'kraudid] *a* atestado de gente, (*country*) superpoblado.

overdo [əuvə'du:] (*irg: like do*) *vt* exagerar; (*overcook*) cocer demasiado.

overdose ['əuvədəus] *n* dosis *f* excesiva.

overdraft ['əuvədrɑ:ft] *n* saldo deudor.

overdrawn [əuvə'drɔ:n] *a* (*account*) en descubierto.

overdue [əuvə'dju:] *a* retrasado; (*recognition*) tardío.

overestimate [əuvər'ɛstɪmeɪt] *vt* sobreestimar.

overexcited [əuvərɪk'saɪtɪd] *a* sobreexcitado.

overexpose [əuvərɪk'spəuz] *vt* (*PHOT*) sobreexponer.

overflow [əuvə'fləu] *vi* desbordarse // *n* ['əuvəfləu] (*excess*) exceso; (*of river*) desbordamiento; (*also:* **~ pipe**) cañería de) desagüe *m*.

overgrown [əuvə'grəun] *a* (*garden*) cubierto de hierba.

overhaul [əuvə'hɔ:l] *vt* revisar, repasar // *n* ['əuvəhɔ:l] revisión *f*.

overhead [əuvə'hɛd] *ad* por lo alto // *a*

['ɔuvəhɛd] de arriba; (*railway*) elevado, aéreo; ~s *npl* gastos *mpl* generales.

overhear [ɔuvə'hɛə*] (*irg: like* hear) *vt* oír por casualidad.

overjoyed [ɔuvə'dʒɔid] *a* encantado, lleno de alegría.

overland ['ɔuvəlænd] *a, ad* por tierra.

overlap [ɔuvə'læp] *vi* traslaparse // *n* ['ɔuvəlæp] traslapo.

overleaf [ɔuvə'li:f] *ad* al dorso.

overload [ɔuvə'loud] *vt* sobrecargar.

overlook [ɔuvə'luk] *vt* (*have view on*) dar a, tener vistas a; (*miss: by mistake*) pasar por alto; (: *deliberately*) no hacerse caso de; (*forgive*) perdonar.

overnight [ɔuvə'nait] *ad* durante la noche; (*fig*) de la noche a la mañana // *a* de noche; **to stay** ~ pasar la noche.

overpass ['ɔuvəpɑːs] *n* paso superior.

overpower [ɔuvə'pauə*] *vt* dominar; ~ing *a* (*heat, stench*) abrumador(a).

overrate [ɔuvə'reit] *vt* sobreestimar.

override [ɔuvə'raid] (*irg: like* ride) *vt* (*order, objection*) no hacer caso de; **overriding** *a* predominante.

overrule [ɔuvə'ruːl] *vt* (*decision*) anular; (*claim*) denegar.

overseas [ɔuvə'siːz] *ad* en ultramar; (*abroad*) en el extranjero // *a* (*trade*) exterior; (*visitor*) extranjero.

overseer ['ɔuvəsiə*] *n* (*in factory*) superintendente *m/f*; (*foreman*) capataz *m*.

overshadow [ɔuvə'fædou] *vt* (*fig*) eclipsar.

overshoot [ɔuvə'fuːt] (*irg: like* shoot) *vt* excederse.

oversight ['ɔuvəsait] *n* descuido.

oversleep [ɔuvə'sliːp] (*irg: like* sleep) *vi* despertarse (muy) tarde.

overspend [ɔuvə'spend] (*irg: like* spend) *vi* gastar demasiado.

overspill ['ɔuvəspil] *n* exceso de población.

overstate [ɔuvə'steit] *vt* exagerar; ~ment *n* exageración *f*.

overt [əu'vəːt] *a* abierto.

overtake [ɔuvə'teik] (*irg: like* take) *vt* sobrepasar; (*AUT*) adelantar; **overtaking** *n* (*AUT*) adelantamiento.

overthrow [ɔuvə'θrou] (*irg: like* throw) *vt* (*government*) derrocar.

overtime ['ɔuvətaim] *n* horas *fpl* extraordinarias.

overtone ['ɔuvətoun] *n* (*fig*) sugestión *f*, alusión *f*.

overture ['ɔuvətʃuə*] *n* (*MUS*) obertura; (*fig*) propuesta.

overturn [ɔuvə'təːn] *vt, vi* volcar.

overweight [ɔuvə'weit] *a* demasiado gordo o pesado.

overwhelm [ɔuvə'wɛlm] *vt* aplastar; ~ing *a* (*victory, defeat*) arrollador(a); (*desire*) irresistible.

overwork [ɔuvə'wɔːk] *n* trabajo excesivo // *vt* hacer trabajar demasiado // *vi* trabajar demasiado.

overwrought [ɔuvə'rɔːt] *a* sobreexcitado.

owe [əu] *vt* deber; **to** ~ **sb sth, to** ~ **sth to sb** deber algo a uno; **owing to** *prep* debido a, por causa de.

owl [aul] *n* búho, lechuza.

own [əun] *vt* tener, poseer // *a* propio; **a room of my** ~ una habitación propia; **to get one's** ~ **back** tomar revancha; **on one's** ~ solo, a solas; **to** ~ **up** *vi* confesar; ~er *n* dueño; ~ership *n* posesión *f*.

ox [ɔks], *pl* ~en ['ɔksn] *n* buey *m*.

oxide ['ɔksaid] *n* óxido.

oxtail ['ɔksteil] *a*: ~ **soup** sopa de rabo de buey.

oxygen ['ɔksidʒən] *n* oxígeno; ~ **mask/tent** máscara/tienda de oxígeno.

oyster ['ɔistə*] *n* ostra.

oz. *abbr of* **ounce(s)**.

ozone ['əuzoun] *n* ozono.

P

p [piː] *abbr of* **penny, pence**.

p.a. *abbr of* **per annum**.

pa [pɑː] *n* (*col*) papá *m*.

pace [peis] *n* paso; (*rhythm*) ritmo // *vi*: **to** ~ **up and down** pasarse de un lado a otro; **to keep** ~ **with** llevar el mismo paso que; (*events*) mantenerse a la altura de *o* al corriente de; ~**maker** *n* (*MED*) regulador *m* cardíaco, marcapasos *m inv*.

pacific [pə'sifik] *a* pacífico // *n*: **the P**~ (*Ocean*) el (Océano) Pacífico.

pacifist ['pæsifist] *a* pacifista *m/f*.

pacify ['pæsifai] *vt* (*soothe*) apaciguar; (*country*) pacificar.

pack [pæk] *n* (*gen*) paquete *m*; (*of hounds*) jauría; (*of thieves etc*) manada, bando; (*of cards*) baraja; (*bundle*) fardo; (*back* ~) mochila // *vt* (*wrap*) empaquetar; (*fill*) llenar; (*in suitcase etc*) meter *o* poner (en maleta); (*cram*) llenar atestar; (*fig: meeting etc*) llenar de partidarios; **to** ~ **sb off** despachar a uno; ~ **it in!** (*col*) ¡déjalo!; **to** ~ **one's case** hacerse la maleta.

package ['pækidʒ] *n* paquete *m*; (*bulky*) bulto; (*also:* ~ **deal**) acuerdo global; ~ **tour** *n* viaje *m* todo incluido.

packet ['pækit] *n* paquete *m*; (*NAUT*) paquebote *m*.

packing ['pækiŋ] *n* embalaje *m*; (*external*) envase *m*; (*internal*) relleno ~ **case** *n* cajón *m* de embalaje.

pact [pækt] *n* pacto.

pad [pæd] *n* (*of paper*) bloc *m*; (*cushion*) cojinete *m*; (*launching* ~) plataforma (de lanzamiento); (*foot*) pata; (*col: flat*) casa // *vi* andar (sin hacer ruido) ~**ding** *n* relleno; (*fig*) paja.

paddle ['pædl] *n* (*oar*) canalete *m* // *vt* impulsar con canalete // *vi* (*with feet*) chapotear; ~ **steamer** *n* vapor *m* de ruedas; **paddling pool** *n* estanque *m* de juegos.

paddock ['pædək] *n* corral *m*

paddy field ['pædɪ-] n arrozal m.
padlock ['pædlɔk] n candado // vt cerrar con candado.
padre ['pɑːdrɪ] n capellán m.
paediatrics, pediatrics (US) [piːdɪ'ætrɪks] n pediatría.
pagan ['peɪgən] a, n pagano/a.
page [peɪdʒ] n (of book) página; (of newspaper) plana; (also: ~ boy) paje m // vt (in hotel etc) buscar (a uno) llamando su nombre.
pageant ['pædʒənt] n (procession) desfile m; (show) espectáculo; ~ry n pompa.
pagoda [pə'gəudə] n pagoda.
paid [peɪd] pt, pp of **pay** // a (work) remunerado; (official) asalariado; **to put ~ to** acabar con.
pail [peɪl] n cubo, balde m.
pain [peɪn] n dolor m; **to be in ~** sufrir; **on ~ of death** so pena de muerte; **to take ~s to do sth** tomarse trabajo en hacer algo; **~ed** a (expression) afligido; **~ful** a doloroso; (difficult) penoso; (disagreeable) desagradable; **~killer** n calmante m; **~less** a que no causa dolor; **painstaking** ['peɪnzteɪkɪŋ] a (person) concienzudo, esmerado.
paint [peɪnt] n pintura // vt pintar; **to ~ one's face** pintarse (la cara); **to ~ the door blue** pintar la puerta de azul; **~brush** n (artist's) pincel m; (decorator's) brocha; **~er** n pintor/a m/f; **~ing** n pintura.
pair [pɛə*] n (of shoes, gloves etc) par m; (of people) pareja; **a ~ of scissors** unas tijeras; **a ~ of trousers** unos pantalones, un pantalón.
pajamas [pɪ'dʒɑːməz] npl (US) pijama m.
Pakistan [pɑːkɪ'stɑːn] n Paquistán m; **~i** a, n paquistaní.
pal [pæl] n (col) compinche m/f, compañero/a.
palace ['pæləs] n palacio.
palatable ['pælɪtəbl] a sabroso; (acceptable) aceptable.
palate ['pælɪt] n paladar m.
palaver [pə'lɑːvə*] n (fuss) lío; (hindrances) molestias fpl.
pale [peɪl] a (gen) pálido; (colour) claro; **to grow ~** palidecer; **to be beyond the ~** estar excluido; **~ness** n palidez f.
Palestine ['pælɪstaɪn] n Palestina; **Palestinian** [-'tɪnɪən] a, n palestino/a.
palette ['pælɪt] n paleta.
paling ['peɪlɪŋ] n (stake) estaca; (fence) valla.
palisade [pælɪ'seɪd] n palizada.
pall [pɔːl] n (of smoke) capa (de humo) // vi perder el sabor.
pallid ['pælɪd] a pálido.
palm [pɑːm] n (gen) palma; (also: ~ tree) palmera, palma // vt: **to ~ sth off on sb** (col) encajar algo a uno; **~ist** n quiromántico/a; **P~ Sunday** n Domingo de Ramos.
palpable ['pælpəbl] a palpable.

palpitation [pælpɪ'teɪʃən] n palpitación f; **to have ~s** tener vahídos.
paltry ['pɔːltrɪ] a (insignificant) baladí; (miserable) vil.
pamper ['pæmpə*] vt mimar.
pamphlet ['pæmflət] n folleto.
pan [pæn] n (also: **sauce~**) cacerola, cazuela; (also: **frying ~**) sartén m; (of lavatory) taza // vi (CINEMA) tomar una vista panorámica.
panacea [pænə'sɪə] n panacea.
Panama ['pænəmɑː] n Panamá m.
pancake ['pænkeɪk] n canapé m.
panda ['pændə] n panda m/f; **~ car** n coche m de la policía.
pandemonium [pændɪ'məunɪəm] n (noise) estruendo; (mess) caos m.
pander ['pændə*] vi: **to ~** complacer a.
pane [peɪn] n cristal m.
panel ['pænl] n (of wood) panel m; (of cloth) paño; (RADIO, TV) tablero; **~ling, ~ing** (US) n paneles mpl, entrepaños mpl.
pang [pæŋ] n: **~s of conscience** remordimiento sg; **~s of hunger** dolores mpl del hambre.
panic ['pænɪk] n (terror) pánico // vi aterrarse; **~ky** a (person) asustadizo; **~-stricken** a preso de pánico.
pannier ['pænɪə*] n (on bicycle) cartera; (on mule etc) alforja.
panorama [pænə'rɑːmə] n panorama m.
pansy ['pænzɪ] n (BOT) pensamiento; (col) maricón m.
pant [pænt] vi jadear.
panther ['pænθə*] n pantera.
panties ['pæntɪz] npl bragas fpl, pantis mpl.
pantomime ['pæntəmaɪm] n revista musical representada en Navidad, basada en cuentos de hadas.
pantry ['pæntrɪ] n despensa.
pants [pænts] n (woman's) bragas fpl; (man's) calzoncillos mpl; (US: trousers) pantalones mpl.
papal ['peɪpəl] a papal.
paper ['peɪpə*] n papel m; (also: **news~**) periódico, diario; (study, article) artículo; (exam) examen m // a de papel // vt empapelar; (identity) **~s** npl papeles mpl, documentos mpl; **~back** n libro de bolsillo; **~ bag** n saco de papel; **~ clip** n grapa; **~ hankie** n pañuelo de papel; **~ money** n papel moneda; **~weight** n pisapapeles m inv; **~work** n trabajo administrativo; (pej) papeleo.
papier-mâché ['pæpɪeɪ'mæʃeɪ] n cartón m piedra.
paprika ['pæprɪkə] n pimienta húngara o roja.
par [pɑː*] n par f; (GOLF) par m; **to be on a ~ with** correr parejas con.
parable ['pærəbl] n parábola.
parachute ['pærəʃuːt] n paracaídas m inv // vi lanzarse en paracaídas; **~ jump** n salto en paracaídas.
parade [pə'reɪd] n desfile m // vt (gen)

recorrer, desfilar por; (*show off*) hacer alarde de // *vi* desfilar; (*MIL*) pasar revista.

paradise ['pærədaɪs] *n* paraíso.

paradox ['pærədɔks] *n* paradoja; ~**ical** [-'dɔksɪkl] *a* paradójico.

paraffin ['pærəfɪn] *n*: ~ (**oil**) petróleo.

paragraph ['pærəgrɑːf] *n* párrafo.

parallel ['pærəlɛl] *a* en paralelo; (*fig*) semejante // *n* (*line*) paralela; (*fig*, *GEO*) paralelo.

paralysis [pə'rælɪsɪs] *n* parálisis *f*; **paralyze** ['pærəlaɪz] *vt* paralizar.

paramount ['pærəmaunt] *a*: **of** ~ **importance** de la mayor importancia, primordial.

paranoia [pærə'nɔɪə] *n* paranoia; **paranoiac** *a* paranoico.

paraphernalia [pærəfə'neɪlɪə] *n* (*gear*) avíos *mpl*.

paraplegic [pærə'pliːdʒɪk] *n* parapléjico.

parasite ['pærəsaɪt] *n* parásito.

parasol [pærə'sɔl] *n* sombrilla, quitasol *m*.

paratrooper ['pærətruːpə*] *n* paracaidista *m/f*.

parcel ['pɑːsl] *n* paquete *m* // *vt* (*also*: ~ **up**) empaquetar, embalar.

parch [pɑːtʃ] *vt* secar, resecar; ~**ed** *a* (*person*) muerto de sed.

parchment ['pɑːtʃmənt] *n* pergamino.

pardon ['pɑːdn] *n* perdón *m*; (*LAW*) indulto // *vt* perdonar; indultar; ~**!** ¡perdone!; ~ **me!**, **I beg your** ~**!** ¡perdone Usted!; (**I beg your**) ~? ¿cómo?

parent ['pɛərənt] *n* padre *m*/madre *f*; ~**s** *npl* padres *mpl*; ~**al** [pə'rɛntl] *a* paternal/maternal.

parenthesis [pə'rɛnθɪsɪs], *pl* ~**theses** [-θɪsiːz] *n* paréntesis *m inv*.

Paris ['pærɪs] *n* París.

parish ['pærɪʃ] *n* parroquia; ~**ioner** [pə'rɪʃənə*] *n* feligrés/esa *m/f*.

Parisian [pə'rɪzɪən] *a*, *n* parisino/a, parisiense *m/f*.

parity ['pærɪtɪ] *n* paridad *f*, igualdad *f*.

park [pɑːk] *n* parque *m* // *vt* estacionar // *vi* aparcar, estacionarse; ~**ing** *n* aparcamiento, estacionamiento; **'no** ~**ing'** 'prohibido estacionarse'; ~**ing lot** *n* (*US*) parking *m*; ~**ing meter** *n* parquímetro.

parliament ['pɑːləmənt] *n* parlamento; (*Spanish*) Cortes *mpl*; ~**ary** [-'mɛntərɪ] *a* parlamentario.

parlour, **parlor** (*US*) ['pɑːlə*] *n* sala de recibo, salón *m*.

parochial [pə'rəukɪəl] *a* parroquial; (*pej*) de miras estrechas.

parody ['pærədɪ] *n* parodia // *vt* parodiar.

parole [pə'rəul] *n*: **on** ~ libre bajo palabra.

parquet ['pɑːkeɪ] *n*: ~ **floor(ing)** parquet *m*.

parrot ['pærət] *n* loro, papagayo; ~ **fashion** *ad* mecánicamente.

parry ['pærɪ] *vt* parar.

parsimonious [pɑːsɪ'məunɪəs] *a* parco.

parsley ['pɑːslɪ] *n* perejil *m*.

parsnip ['pɑːsnɪp] *n* chirivía.

parson ['pɑːsn] *n* (*parish*) párroco; (*gen*) cura *m*.

part [pɑːt] *n* (*gen*, *MUS*) parte *f*; (*bit*) trozo; (*of machine*) pieza; (*THEATRE etc*) papel *m*; (*of serial*) entrega // *ad* = **partly** // *vt* dividir; (*break*) partir // *vi* (*people*) separarse; (*roads*) bifurcarse; (*crowd*) apartarse; (*break*) romperse; **to take** ~ **in** participar *e* tomar parte en; **to take sth in good** ~ tomar algo en buena parte; **to take so's** ~ defender a uno; **for my** ~ por mi parte; **for the most** ~ en la mayor parte; **to** ~ **with** *vt fus* ceder, entregar; (*money*) pagar; (*get rid of*) deshacerse de; **in** ~ **exchange** como parte del pago; **spare** ~ pieza de recambio.

partial ['pɑːʃl] *a* parcial; **to be** ~ **to** ser aficionado a; ~**ly** *ad* en parte.

participant [pɑː'tɪsɪpənt] *n* (*in competition*) concursante *m/f*; **participate** [-peɪt] *vi*: **to participate in** participar en; **participation** [-'peɪʃən] *n* participación *f*.

participle ['pɑːtɪsɪpl] *n* participio.

particle ['pɑːtɪkl] *n* partícula; (*of dust*) grano; (*fig*) pizca.

particular [pə'tɪkjʊlə*] *a* (*special*) particular; (*concrete*) concreto; (*given*) determinado; (*detailed*) detallado, minucioso; (*fussy*) quisquilloso, exigente; ~**s** *npl* (*information*) datos *mpl*, detalles *mpl*; (*details*) pormenores *mpl*; ~**ly** *ad* especialmente, en particular.

parting ['pɑːtɪŋ] *n* (*act of*) separación *f*; (*farewell*) despedida; (*in hair*) raya // *a* de despedida.

partisan [pɑːtɪ'zæn] *a*, *n* partidario/a.

partition [pɑː'tɪʃən] *n* (*POL*) división *f*; (*wall*) tabique *m* // *vt* dividir; dividir con tabique.

partly ['pɑːtlɪ] *ad* en parte.

partner ['pɑːtnə*] *n* (*COMM*) socio/a; (*SPORT*, *at dance*) pareja; (*spouse*) cónyuge *m/f*; (*friend etc*) compañero/a // *vt* acompañar; ~**ship** *n* (*gen*) asociación *f*; (*COMM*) sociedad *f*.

partridge ['pɑːtrɪdʒ] *n* perdiz *f*.

part-time ['pɑːt'taɪm] *a*, *ad* de medio tiempo *o* media jornada.

party ['pɑːtɪ] *n* (*POL*) partido (*celebration*) fiesta; (*group*) grupo; (*LAW*) parte *f*, interesado // *a* (*POL*) de partido; (*dress etc*) de fiesta, de gala.

pass [pɑːs] *vt* (*time*, *object*) pasar; (*place*) pasar por; (*exam*) aprobar; (*overtake*, *surpass*) rebasar; (*approve*) aprobar // *vi* pasar; (*SCOL*) aprobar, ser aprobado // *n* (*permit*) permiso, (*membership card*) carnet *m*; (*in mountains*) puerto, desfiladero; (*SPORT*) pase *m*; (*SCOL*: *also*: ~ **mark**): **to get a** ~ **in** aprobar en; **to** ~ **sth through sth** pasar algo por algo; **to** ~ **away** *vi* fallecer; **to** ~ **by** *v* pasar //

vt (*ignore*) pasar por alto; **to ~ for** pasar por; **to ~ out** *vi* desmayarse; **to ~ up** *vt* renunciar a; **~able** *a* (*road*) transitable; (*work*) pasable.

passage ['pæsɪdʒ] *n* (*also*: **~way**) pasillo; (*act of passing*) tránsito; (*fare, in book*) pasaje *m*; (*by boat*) travesía; (*MECH, MED*) tubo.

passenger ['pæsɪndʒə*] *n* pasajero, viajero.

passer-by [pɑːsə'baɪ] *n* transeúnte *m/f*.

passing ['pɑːsɪŋ] *a* (*fleeting*) pasajero; **in ~** de paso.

passion ['pæʃən] *n* pasión *f*; (*anger*) cólera; **~ate** *a* apasionado; colérico.

passive ['pæsɪv] *a* (*also* LING) pasivo.

Passover ['pɑːsəuvə*] *n* Pascua (de los judíos).

passport ['pɑːspɔːt] *n* pasaporte *m*.

password ['pɑːswɜːd] *n* santo y seña.

past [pɑːst] *prep* (*further than*) más allá de; (*later than*) después de // *a* pasado; (*president etc*) antiguo // *n* el pasado; (*antecedents*) antecedentes *mpl*; **he's ~ forty** tiene más de cuarenta años; **for the ~ few/3 days** durante los últimos/3 días; **to run ~** pasar a la carrera por.

pasta ['pæstə] *n* pastas *fpl*.

paste [peɪst] *n* (*gen*) pasta; (*glue*) engrudo // *vt* (*stick*) pegar; (*glue*) engomar.

pastel ['pæstl] *a* pastel; (*painting*) al pastel.

pasteurized ['pæstəraɪzd] *a* pasteurizado.

pastille ['pæstl] *n* pastilla.

pastime ['pɑːstaɪm] *n* pasatiempo.

pastor ['pɑːstə*] *n* pastor *m*.

pastoral ['pɑːstərl] *a* pastoral.

pastry ['peɪstrɪ] *n* pasta; (*cakes*) pastas *fpl*, pasteles *mpl*.

pasture ['pɑːstʃə*] *n* (*grass*) pasto; (*land*) prado, pasto.

pasty ['pæstɪ] *n* empanada // *a* ['peɪstɪ] pastoso; (*complexion*) pálido.

pat [pæt] *vt* dar una palmadita a; (*dog etc*) acariciar // *n* (*of butter*) pastelillo; **to give sb a ~ on the back** felicitar a uno.

patch [pætʃ] *n* (*of material*) parche *m*; (*piece*) pedazo; (*mend*) remiendo; (*of land*) terreno // *vt* (*clothes*) remendar; **to ~ up** *vt* (*mend temporarily*) componer de modo provisional; (*quarrel*) hacer las paces con; **~work** *n* labor *m* de retazos; **~y** *a* desigual.

pâté ['pæteɪ] *n* pastel *m* de carne.

patent ['peɪtnt] *n* patente *f* // *vt* patentar // *a* patente, evidente; **~ leather** *n* charol *m*.

paternal [pə'tɜːnl] *a* paternal; (*relation*) paterno; **paternity** [-nɪtɪ] *n* paternidad *f*.

path [pɑːθ] *n* senda, sendero; (*trail, track*) pista; (*of missile*) trayectoria.

pathetic [pə'θetɪk] *a* (*pitiful*) patético, lastimoso; (*very bad*) malísimo; (*moving*) conmovedor(a).

pathologist [pə'θɔlədʒɪst] *n* patólogo; **pathology** [-dʒɪ] *n* patología.

pathos ['peɪθɔs] *n* patetismo, lo patético.

pathway ['pɑːθweɪ] *n* sendero, vereda.

patience ['peɪʃns] *n* paciencia; (*CARDS*) solitario.

patient ['peɪʃnt] *n* paciente *m/f* // *a* paciente, sufrido.

patio ['pætɪəu] *n* patio.

patriot ['peɪtrɪət] *n* patriota *m/f*; **~ic** [pætrɪ'ɔtɪk] *a* patriótico.

patrol [pə'trəul] *n* patrulla /. *vt* patrullar por; **~ car** *n* coche *m* patrulla; **~man** *n* (*US*) policía *m*.

patron ['peɪtrən] *n* (*in shop*) cliente *m/f*; (*of charity*) patrocinador/a *m/f*; **~ of the arts** mecenas *m*; **~age** ['pætrənɪdʒ] *n* mecenazgo, protección *f*; **~ize** ['pætrənaɪz] *vt* (*shop*) ser cliente de; (*business*) patrocinar; (*look down on*) tratar con condescendencia; **~ saint** *n* patrono.

patter ['pætə*] *n* golpeteo; (*of feet*) pasos *mpl* ligeros; (*sales talk*) jerga // *vi* andar con pasos ligeros; (*rain*) tamborilear.

pattern ['pætən] *n* modelo; (*SEWING*) patrón *m*; (*design*) dibujo; (*sample*) muestra.

paunch [pɔːntʃ] *n* panza, barriga.

pauper ['pɔːpə*] *n* pobre *m/f*.

pause [pɔːz] *n* pausa; (*interval*) intérvalo // *vi* hacer una pausa.

pave [peɪv] *vt* pavimentar; **to ~ the way for** preparar el terreno para.

pavement ['peɪvmənt] *n* (*Brit*) acera.

pavilion [pə'vɪlɪən] *n* pabellón *m*; (*for band etc*) quiosco; (*SPORT*) caseta.

paving ['peɪvɪŋ] *n* pavimento, enlosado; **~ stone** *n* losa.

paw [pɔː] *n* pata; (*of cat*) garra // *vt* tocar con la pata; (*touch*) tocar, manosear; (*amorously*) sobar.

pawn [pɔːn] *n* (*CHESS*) peón *m*; (*fig*) instrumento // *vt* empeñar; **~broker** *n* prestamista *m/f*; **~shop** *n* monte *m* de piedad.

pay [peɪ] *n* paga; (*wage etc*) sueldo // (*vb*: *pt, pp* **paid**) *vt* pagar; (*debt*) liquidar; (*visit*) hacer; (*respect*) ofrecer // *vi* pagar; (*be profitable*) rendir; **to ~ attention (to)** prestar atención (a); **to ~ back** *vt* (*money*) devolver; (*person*) pagar; **to ~ for** *vt* pagar por; **to ~ in** *vt* ingresar; **to ~ off** *vt* liquidar; **to ~ up** *vt* pagar (de mala gana); **~able** *a* pagadero; **~ day** *n* día *m* de paga; **~ee** *n* portador/a *m/f*; **~ing** *a* provechoso; **~ment** *n* pago; **~ advance** *n* anticipo; **monthly ~ment** mensualidad *f*; **~ packet** *n* sobre *m* de paga; **~roll** *n* nómina; **~ slip** *n* hoja de paga.

p.c. *abbr of* **per cent.**

pea [piː] *n* guisante *m*; **sweet ~** guisante de olor.

peace [piːs] *n* paz *f*; (*calm*) paz *f*, tranquilidad *f*; **~able** *a* pacífico; **~ful** *a* (*gentle*) pacífico; (*calm*) tranquilo, sosegado; **~-keeping** *n* pacificación *f*; **~ offering** *n* prenda de paz.

peach [piːtʃ] *n* melocotón *m*, durazno (*AM*).

peacock ['piːkɔk] *n* pavo real.

peak [piːk] n (of mountain: top) cumbre f, cima; (: point) pico; (of cap) visera; (fig) cumbre f; ~ **hours** npl horas fpl punta.

peal [piːl] n (of bells) repique m, toque m de campanas; ~ **of laughter** carcajada.

peanut ['piːnʌt] n cacahuete m, maní m (AM); ~ **butter** n manteca de cacahuete.

pear [pɛə*] n pera; ~ **tree** n peral m.

pearl [pɜːl] n perla; **mother-of-~** n nácar m.

peasant ['pɛznt] n campesino/a.

peat [piːt] n turba.

pebble ['pɛbl] n guijarro.

peck [pɛk] vt (also: ~ at) picotear; (food) comer sin ganas // n picotazo; (kiss) beso ligero; ~**ing order** n orden m de jerarquía; ~**ish** a (col) con hambre.

peculiar [pɪ'kjuːlɪə*] a (odd) extraño, raro; (typical) propio, característico; (marked) especial; ~ **to** propio de; ~**ity** [pɪkjuːlɪ'ærɪtɪ] n peculiaridad f; (feature) característica; (oddity) rareza, singularidad f.

pedal ['pɛdl] n pedal m // vi pedalear.

pedantic [pɪ'dæntɪk] a pedante.

peddle ['pɛdl] vt vender (de puerta en puerta); **peddler** n vendedor/a m/f ambulante.

pedestal ['pɛdəstl] n pedestal m.

pedestrian [pɪ'dɛstrɪən] n peatón m // a pedestre; ~ **crossing** n paso de peatones.

pedigree ['pɛdɪgriː] n genealogía; (of animal) raza // cpd (animal) de raza, de casta.

peek [piːk] vi mirar a hurtadillas.

peel [piːl] n piel f; (of orange, lemon) peladuras fpl // vt pelar // vi (paint etc) desconcharse; (wallpaper) despegarse, desprenderse.

peep [piːp] n (look) mirada furtiva; (sound) pío // vi piar; **to ~ out** vi asomar la cabeza; ~**hole** n mirilla.

peer [pɪə*] vi: **to ~ at** mirar con ojos de miope // n (noble) par m; (equal) igual m; ~**age** n nobleza; ~**less** a sin par.

peeved [piːvd] a enojado.

peevish ['piːvɪʃ] a malhumorado.

peg [pɛg] n clavija; (for coat etc) gancho, colgador; (also: **clothes ~**) pinza; (tent ~) estaca // vt (prices) fijar; **off the ~** ad de confección.

pejorative [pɪ'dʒɔrətɪv] a peyorativo.

pekingese [piːkɪ'niːz] n pequinés/esa m/f.

pelican ['pɛlɪkən] n pelícano.

pellet ['pɛlɪt] n bolita; (bullet) perdigón m.

pelmet ['pɛlmɪt] n galería.

pelt [pɛlt] vt: **to ~ sb with sth** tirar algo a uno // vi (rain) llover a cántaros // n pellejo.

pelvis ['pɛlvɪs] n pelvis f.

pen [pɛn] n pluma; (for sheep) redil m; ~ **play** ~ parque m de niño; ~ **name** n seudónimo.

penal ['piːnl] a penal; ~**ize** vt penar; (SPORT) castigar.

penalty ['pɛnltɪ] n (gen) pena; (fine)

multa; (SPORT) castigo; ~ **(kick)** n (FOOTBALL) penalty m.

penance ['pɛnəns] n penitencia.

pence [pɛns] pl of **penny.**

pencil ['pɛnsl] n lápiz m; (for eyebrows) lapiz de cejas; **propelling** ~ lapicero; ~ **sharpener** n sacapuntas m inv.

pendant ['pɛndnt] a pendiente m.

pending ['pɛndɪŋ] prep antes de // a pendiente.

pendulum ['pɛndjuləm] n péndulo.

penetrate ['pɛnɪtreɪt] vt penetrar; **penetrating** a penetrante; **penetration** [-'treɪʃən] n penetración f.

penfriend ['pɛnfrɛnd] n amigo/a por correspondencia.

penguin ['pɛŋgwɪn] n pingüino.

penicillin [pɛnɪ'sɪlɪn] n penicilina.

peninsula [pə'nɪnsjulə] n península.

penis ['piːnɪs] n pene m.

penitence ['pɛnɪtns] n penitencia; **penitent** [-nt] a (gen) arrepentido; (REL) penitente.

penitentiary [pɛnɪ'tɛnʃərɪ] n (US) cárcel f, presidio.

penknife ['pɛnnaɪf] n navaja.

pennant ['pɛnənt] n banderola.

penniless ['pɛnɪlɪs] a sin dinero.

penny ['pɛnɪ], pl **pennies** ['pɛnɪz] or **pence** [pɛns] n penique m.

pension ['pɛnʃən] n (gen) pensión f; (old-age) jubilación f, (MIL) retiro; ~**er** n jubilado; ~ **fund** n caja de jubilaciones.

pensive ['pɛnsɪv] a pensativo; (withdrawn) preocupado.

pentagon ['pɛntəgən] n pentágono.

Pentecost ['pɛntɪkɔst] n Pentecostés m.

penthouse ['pɛnthaus] n ático.

pent-up ['pɛntʌp] a (feelings) reprimido.

penultimate [pɛ'nʌltɪmət] a penúltimo.

people ['piːpl] npl gente f; (citizens) pueblo sg, ciudadanos mpl // n (nation, race) pueblo, nación f // vt poblar; **several** ~ **came** vinieron varias personas; ~ **say that...** dice la gente que...

pep [pɛp] n (col) energía; **to ~ up** vt animar.

pepper ['pɛpə*] n pimienta; (vegetable) pimiento // vt (fig) salpicar; ~**mint** n menta; (sweet) pastilla de menta.

peptalk ['pɛptɔːk] n (col) palabras fpl para levantar los ánimos.

per [pɜː*] prep por; ~ **day/person** por día/persona; ~ **cent** por ciento; ~ **annum** al año.

perceive [pə'siːv] vt percibir; (realize) darse cuenta de.

percentage [pə'sɛntɪdʒ] n porcentaje m.

perception [pə'sɛpʃən] n percepción f; (insight) perspicacia; **perceptive** [-'sɛptɪv] a perspicaz.

perch [pɜːtʃ] n (fish) perca; (for bird) percha // vi posarse.

percolator ['pɜːkəleɪtə*] n cafetera filtradora.

percussion [pə'kʌʃən] n percusión f.

peremptory [pə'rɛmptəri] a perentorio; (*person: imperious*) imperioso.
perennial [pə'rɛnɪəl] a perenne.
perfect ['pə:fɪkt] a perfecto // n (*also*: ~ **tense**) perfecto // vt [pə'fɛkt] perfeccionar; ~**ion** [-'fɛkʃən] n perfección f; ~**ionist** n perfeccionista m/f.
perforate ['pə:fəreɪt] vt perforar; ~**d** a (*stamp*) dentado; **perforation** [-'reɪʃən] n perforación f.
perform [pə'fɔ:m] vt (*carry out*) realizar, cumplir; (*concert etc*) representar; (*piece of music*) interpretar // vi (*animal*) hacer trucos; (*THEATRE*) actuar; (*TECH*) funcionar; ~**ance** n (*of task*) cumplimiento, realización f; (*of an artist*) representación f; (*of player etc*) actuación f; (*of car, engine*) funcionamiento; (*of function*) desempeño; ~**er** n (*actor*) actor/actriz m/f; (*MUS*) interprete m/f; ~**ing** a (*animal*) amaestrado.
perfume ['pə:fju:m] n perfume m // vt perfumar.
perhaps [pə'hæps] ad quizá(s), tal vez.
peril ['pɛrɪl] n peligro, riesgo.
perimeter [pə'rɪmɪtə*] n perímetro.
period ['pɪərɪəd] n período; (*HISTORY*) época; (*time limit*) plazo; (*SCOL*) clase f; (*full stop*) punto; (*MED*) regla, reglas fpl // a (*costume, furniture*) de época; ~**ic** [-'ɔdɪk] a periódico; ~**ical** [-'ɔdɪkl] n periódico; ~**ically** [-'ɔdɪklɪ] ad de vez en cuando, cada cierto tiempo.
peripheral [pə'rɪfərəl] a periférico; **periphery** [-rɪ] n periferia.
periscope ['pɛrɪskəup] n periscopio.
perish ['pɛrɪʃ] vi perecer; (*decay*) echarse a perder, deteriorar(se); ~**able** a perecedero; ~**ing** a (*col: cold*) helado, glacial.
perjure ['pə:dʒə*] vt: to ~ **o.s.** perjurarse; **perjury** n (*LAW*) perjurio.
perk [pə:k] n pago encima del sueldo; to ~ **up** vi (*cheer up*) animarse; (*in health*) sentirse mejor; ~**y** a (*cheerful*) alegre, despabilado.
perm [pə:m] n permanente f.
permanent ['pə:mənənt] a permanente.
permissible [pə'mɪsɪbl] a permisible, lícito.
permission [pə'mɪʃən] n permiso; (*authorization*) licencia.
permissive [pə'mɪsɪv] a permisivo.
permit ['pə:mɪt] n permiso, licencia // vt [pə'mɪt] permitir; (*authorize*) autorizar; (*accept*) tolerar.
permutation [pə:mju'teɪʃən] n permutación f.
pernicious [pə:'nɪʃəs] a nocivo; (*MED*) pernicioso.
perpendicular [pə:pən'dɪkjulə*] a perpendicular.
perpetrate ['pə:pɪtreɪt] vt cometer.
perpetual [pə'pɛtjuəl] a perpetuo.
perpetuate [pə'pɛtjueɪt] vt perpetuar.
perplex [pə'plɛks] vt dejar perplejo.
persecute ['pə:sɪkju:t] vt (*pursue*)

perseguir; (*harass*) acosar; **persecution** [-'kju:ʃən] n persecución f.
persevere [pə:sɪ'vɪə*] vi persistir.
Persian ['pə:ʃən] a, n persa m/f.
persist [pə'sɪst] vi: to ~ (**in doing sth**) persistir (en hacer algo); ~**ence** n empeño; (*of disease*) pertinacia; ~**ent** a persistente; (*determined*) porfiado; (*disease*) pertinaz.
person ['pə:sn] n persona; ~**able** a atractivo; ~**al** a personal; (*private*) particular; (*visit*) en persona; (*TEL*) persona a persona; (*column*) de anuncios personales; ~**ality** [-'nælɪtɪ] n personalidad f; ~**ally** ad personalmente; ~**ify** [-'sɔnɪfaɪ] vt encarnar.
personnel [pə:sə'nɛl] n personal m.
perspective [pə'spɛktɪv] n perspectiva.
perspex ['pə:spɛks] n plexiglás m.
perspiration [pə:spɪ'reɪʃən] n transpiración f, sudor m; **perspire** [-'spaɪə*] vi transpirar, sudar.
persuade [pə'sweɪd] vt persuadir; **persuasion** [-'sweɪʒən] n persuasión f; (*persuasiveness*) persuasiva; (*creed*) creencia; **persuasive** [-'sweɪsɪv] a persuasivo.
pert [pə:t] a impertinente, fresco.
pertaining [pə:'teɪnɪŋ]: ~ **to** prep relacionado con.
pertinent ['pə:tɪnənt] a pertinente, a propósito.
perturb [pə'tə:b] vt perturbar.
Peru [pə'ru:] n el Perú.
peruse [pə'ru:z] vt leer con detención, examinar.
Peruvian [pə'ru:vjən] a, n peruano/a.
pervade [pə'veɪd] vt impregnar, saturar.
perverse [pə'və:s] a perverso; (*stubborn*) terco; (*wayward*) travieso; **perversion** [-'və:ʃən] n perversión f.
pervert ['pə:və:t] n pervertido/a // vt [pə'və:t] pervertir.
pessary ['pɛsərɪ] n pesario.
pessimism ['pɛsɪmɪzəm] n pesimismo; **pessimist** [-mɪst] n pesimista m/f; **pessimistic** [-'mɪstɪk] a pesimista.
pest [pɛst] n plaga; (*insect*) insecto nocivo; (*fig*) lata, molestia.
pester ['pɛstə*] vt molestar, acosar.
pesticide ['pɛstɪsaɪd] n pesticida m.
pet [pɛt] n animal doméstico; (*favourite*) favorito // vt acariciar // vi (*col*) besuquearse, sobarse.
petal ['pɛtl] n pétalo.
peter ['pi:tə*]: to ~ **out** vi agotarse, acabarse.
petite [pə'ti:t] a chiquita.
petition [pə'tɪʃən] n petición f.
petrified ['pɛtrɪfaɪd] a (*fig*) pasmado, horrorizado; **petrify** vt petrificar; (*frighten*) pasmar.
petrol ['pɛtrəl] n (*Brit*) gasolina; (*for lighter*) bencina.
petroleum [pə'trəulɪəm] n petróleo.
petrol: ~ **pump** n (*in car*) bomba de

gasolina; (in garage) surtidor m de gasolina; ~ station n gasolinera; ~ tank n depósito de gasolina.

petticoat ['petɪkəut] n enagua; (slip) combinación f.

pettiness ['petɪnɪs] n mezquindad f.

petty ['petɪ] a (mean) mezquino; (unimportant) nimio; ~ cash n dinero suelto; ~ officer n contramaestre m.

petulant ['petjulənt] a malhumorado.

pew [pju:] n banco.

pewter ['pju:tə*] n peltre m.

phallic ['fælɪk] a fálico.

phantom ['fæntəm] n fantasma m.

Pharaoh ['fɛərəu] n Faraón m.

pharmacist ['fɑ:məsɪst] n farmacéutico; **pharmacy** [-sɪ] n farmacia.

phase [feɪz] n fase f // vt: to ~ sth in/out introducir/reducir algo por etapas.

Ph.D. abbr of **Doctor of Philosophy**.

pheasant ['feznt] n faisán m.

phenomenon [fə'nɔmɪnən], pl **-mena** [-mɪnə] n fenómeno.

phial ['faɪəl] n ampolla.

philanthropist [fɪ'lænθrəpɪst] n filántropo/a.

philately [fɪ'lætəlɪ] n filatelia.

Philippines ['fɪlɪpi:nz] npl (also: **Philippine Islands**) Filipinas fpl.

philosopher [fɪ'lɔsəfə*] n filósofo; **philosophical** [fɪlə'sɔfɪkl] a filosófico; **philosophy** [-fɪ] n filosofía.

phlegm [flem] n flema; ~atic [fleg-'mætɪk] a flemático.

phobia ['fəubjə] n fobia.

phone [fəun] n teléfono // vt telefonear, llamar (por teléfono); **to be on the ~** tener teléfono; (be calling) estar llamando; **to ~ back** vt, vi devolver la llamada.

phonetics [fə'netɪks] n fonética.

phoney ['fəunɪ] a falso; (person) insincero // n (person) farsante m/f.

phosphate ['fɔsfeɪt] n fosfato.

phosphorus ['fɔsfərəs] n fósforo.

photo ['fəutəu] n fotografía.

photo... ['fəutəu] pref: ~**copier** n fotocopiador m; ~**copy** n fotocopia // vt fotocopiar; ~**genic** [-'dʒenɪk] a fotogénico; ~**graph** n fotografía // vt fotografiar; ~**grapher** [fə'tɔgrəfə*] n fotógrafo; ~**graphic** [-'græfɪk] a fotográfico; ~**graphy** [fə'tɔgrəfɪ] n fotografía; ~**stat** ['fəutəustæt] n fotóstato.

phrase [freɪz] n frase f // vt expresar; ~**book** n libro de frases.

physical ['fɪzɪkl] a físico.

physician [fɪ'zɪʃən] n médico.

physicist ['fɪzɪsɪst] n físico.

physics ['fɪzɪks] n física.

physiology [fɪzɪ'ɔlədʒɪ] n fisiología.

physiotherapy [fɪzɪəu'θerəpɪ] n fisioterapia.

physique [fɪ'zi:k] n físico.

pianist ['pi:ənɪst] n pianista m/f.

piano [pɪ'ænəu] n piano; **grand ~** piano de cola.

pick [pɪk] n (tool: also: ~-**axe**) pico, piqueta // vt (select) elegir, escoger; (gather) recoger; (lock) forzar; **take your ~** escoja lo que quiera; **the ~** of lo mejor de; **to ~** one's teeth limpiarse los dientes; **to ~** pockets ratear, ser carterista; **to ~** off vt (kill) matar de un tiro; **to ~** on vt fus (person) meterse con; **to ~** out vt escoger; (distinguish) lograr ver; **to ~** up vi (improve) reponerse // vt (from floor) recoger; (telephone) descolgar; (buy) comprar; (find) encontrar; (learn) aprender; **to ~** up speed acelerarse; **to ~** o.s. up levantarse.

picket ['pɪkɪt] n (in strike) guardia, piquete m // vt piquetear; ~ **line** n línea de huelgistas.

pickle ['pɪkl] n (also: ~s: as condiment) escabeche m; (fig: mess) apuro // vt encurtir; (in vinegar) conservar en vinagre.

pickpocket ['pɪkpɔkɪt] n carterista m/f.

pickup 'pɪkʌp] n (on record player) pickup m; (small truck) furgoneta.

picnic ['pɪknɪk] n picnic m, merienda de campo f, vi merendar en el campo.

pictorial [pɪk'tɔ:rɪəl] a pictórico; (magazine etc) ilustrado.

picture ['pɪktʃə*] n cuadro; (painting) pintura; (photograph) fotografía; (film) película // vt pintar; **the ~s** el cine; ~**book** n libro de imágenes.

picturesque [pɪktʃə'resk] a pintoresco.

pidgin ['pɪdʒɪn] a: ~ **English** el inglés macarrónico.

pie [paɪ] n pastel m; (open) tarta; (of meat) empanada.

piebald ['paɪbɔ:ld] a pío.

piece [pi:s] n pedazo, trozo; (of land) terreno, (of cake) porción f, (item): **a ~** of furniture/advice un mueble/un consejo // vt: **to ~** together juntar; (TECH) montar; **to take to ~s** desmontar; ~**meal** ad poco a poco; ~**work** n trabajo a destajo.

pier [pɪə*] n muelle m; (jetty) embarcadero, malecón m.

pierce [pɪəs] v penetrar, atravesar; (puncture) pinchar.

piercing [pɪəsɪŋ] a (cry) penetrante.

piety ['paɪətɪ] n piedad f.

pig [pɪg] n cerdo, puerco; (fig) cochino.

pigeon ['pɪdʒən] n paloma; (as food) pichón m; ~**hole** n casilla.

piggy bank ['pɪgɪbæŋk] n hucha en forma de cerdito.

pigheaded ['pɪg'hedɪd] a terco, testarudo.

pigment ['pɪgmənt] n pigmento; ~**ation** [-'teɪʃən] n pigmentación f.

pigmy ['pɪgmɪ] a = pygmy.

pigsty ['pɪgstaɪ] n pocilga.

pigtail ['pɪgteɪl] n (girl's) trenza; (Chinese) coleta.

pike [paɪk] n (spear) pica; (fish) lucio.

pilchard ['pɪltʃəd] n sardina arenque.

pile [paɪl] n (heap) montón m; (of carpet)

pelo; (of cloth) pelillo // (vb: also: ~ up) vt amontonar; (fig) acumular // vi amontonarse.

piles [paɪlz] npl (MED) almorranas fpl, hemorroides mpl.

pile-up ['paɪlʌp] n (AUT) accidente m múltiple.

pilfer ['pɪlfə*] vt ratear; ~**ing** n ratería.

pilgrim ['pɪlgrɪm] n peregrino/a; ~**age** n peregrinaje m, romería.

pill [pɪl] n píldora; the ~ la píldora.

pillage ['pɪlɪdʒ] n saqueo, pillaje m.

pillar ['pɪlə*] n (gen) pilar m; (concrete) columna; ~ **box** n (Brit) buzón m.

pillion ['pɪljən] n (of motor cycle) asiento de atrás.

pillory ['pɪlərɪ] vt poner en ridículo.

pillow ['pɪləʊ] n almohada; ~**case** n funda.

pilot ['paɪlət] n piloto // a (scheme etc) piloto // vt pilotar; (fig) guiar, conducir; ~ **light** n piloto.

pimp [pɪmp] n alcahuete m, chulo.

pimple ['pɪmpl] n grano.

pin [pɪn] n alfiler m; (TECH) perno; (: wooden) clavija // vt prender (con alfiler); sujetar con perno; ~**s and needles** hormigueo sg; **rolling/ safety** ~ rodillo/imperdible m; **to** ~ **sb down** (fig) hacer que uno concrete; **to** ~ **sth on sb** (fig) acusar (falsamente) a uno de algo.

pinafore ['pɪnəfɔ:*] n delantal m; ~ **dress** n mandil m.

pinball ['pɪnbɔ:l] n billar m automático.

pincers ['pɪnsəz] npl pinzas fpl, tenazas fpl.

pinch [pɪntʃ] n pellizco; (of salt etc) pizca // vt pellizcar; (col: steal) birlar; (: arrest) coger, pescar // vi (shoe) apretar; **to feel the** ~ pasar apuros.

pincushion ['pɪnkʊʃən] n acerico.

pine [paɪn] n (also: ~ **tree**) pino // vi: **to** ~ **for** suspirar por; **to** ~ **away** languidecer.

pineapple ['paɪnæpl] n piña, ananás m.

ping [pɪŋ] n (noise) tintineo; (of bullet through air) subido; ~-**pong** n pingpong m.

pink [pɪŋk] a rosado, color de rosa // n (colour) color m de rosa; (BOT) clavel m, clavellina.

pinnacle ['pɪnəkl] n cumbre f.

pinpoint ['pɪnpɔɪnt] vt poner el dedo en.

pint [paɪnt] n pinta (0.57 litros); **to go for a** ~ ir a tomar una cerveza.

pin-up ['pɪnʌp] n fotografía de mujer bonita.

pioneer [paɪə'nɪə*] n pionero.

pious ['paɪəs] a piadoso, devoto.

pip [pɪp] n (seed) pepita; (time signal on radio) señal f.

pipe [paɪp] n tubo, caño; (for smoking) pipa // vi conducir en cañerías; ~**s** npl (gen) cañería sg; (also: bag~**s**) gaita sg; **to** ~ **down** vi (col) callarse; ~ **dream** n sueño imposible; ~**line** n tubería, cañería; (for oil) oleoducto; (for gas) gasoducto; **piper** n

(gen) flautista m/f; (with bagpipes) gaitero.

piping ['paɪpɪŋ] ad: ~ **hot** bien caliente.

piquant ['pi:kənt] a picante.

pique [pi:k] n pique m, resentimiento.

pirate ['paɪərət] n pirata m; ~ **radio** n emisora ilegal.

pirouette [pɪru'ɛt] n pirueta // vi piruetear.

Pisces ['paɪsi:z] n Piscis m.

piss [pɪs] vi (col) mear; ~**ed** a (col: drunk) trompa.

pistol ['pɪstl] n pistola.

piston ['pɪstən] n pistón m, émbolo.

pit [pɪt] n hoyo; (also: **coal** ~); (in garage) foso de inspección; (also: **orchestra** ~) platea; (quarry) cantera // vt: **to** ~ **A against B** oponer A a B; ~**s** npl (AUT) box m.

pitch [pɪtʃ] n (throw) lanzamiento; (MUS) tono; (SPORT) campo, terreno; (tar) brea; (in market etc) puesto // vt (throw) arrojar, lanzar // vi (fall) caer(se); (NAUT) cabecear; **to** ~ **a tent** armar una tienda (de campaña); ~-**black** a negro como boca de lobo; ~**ed battle** n batalla campal.

pitcher ['pɪtʃə*] n cántaro, jarro.

pitchfork ['pɪtʃfɔːk] n horca.

piteous ['pɪtɪəs] a lastimoso.

pitfall ['pɪtfɔːl] n escollo, peligro.

pith [pɪθ] n (of orange) médula; (fig) meollo.

pithy ['pɪθɪ] a jugoso.

pitiable ['pɪtɪəbl] a lastimoso.

pitiful ['pɪtɪful] a (touching) lastimoso, conmovedor(a); (contemptible) lamentable, miserable.

pitiless ['pɪtɪlɪs] a despiadado.

pittance ['pɪtns] n miseria.

pity ['pɪtɪ] n (compassion) compasión f, piedad f; (shame) lástima // vt tener lástima a, compadecer(se de); **what a** ~**!** ¡qué lástima!

pivot ['pɪvət] n eje m // vi: **to** ~ **on** girar sobre; (fig) depender de.

pixie ['pɪksɪ] n duende m.

placard ['plækɑːd] n (sign) letrero; (in march etc) pancarta.

placate [plə'keɪt] vt apaciguar.

place [pleɪs] n lugar m, sitio; (rank) rango; (seat) plaza, asiento; (post) puesto; (home): **at/to his** ~ en/a su casa // vt (object) poner, colocar; (identify) reconocer, ubicar; (find a post for) dar un puesto a, colocar; **to take** ~ tener lugar; **to be** ~**d** (in race, exam) colocarse; **out of** ~ (not suitable) fuera de lugar; **in the first** ~ en primer lugar; **to change** ~**s with sb** trocarse con uno.

placid ['plæsɪd] a apacible.

plagiarism ['pleɪdʒjərɪzm] n plagio.

plague [pleɪg] n plaga; (MED) peste f // vt (fig) acosar, atormentar; **to** ~ **sb** fastidiar a uno.

plaice [pleɪs] n, pl inv platija.

plaid [plæd] n (material) tela a cuadros; (pattern) plaid m.

plain [pleɪn] a (clear) claro, evidente; (simple) sencillo, llano; (frank) franco, abierto; (not handsome) sin atractivo; (pure) natural, puro // ad claro, claramente // n llano, llanura in // ~clothes (police) de paisano; ~ly ad claramente, evidentemente; (frankly) francamente, con franqueza; ~ness n claridad f; sencillez f; franqueza.

plaintiff ['pleɪntɪf] n demandante m/f.

plait [plæt] n trenza // vt trenzar.

plan [plæn] n (drawing) plano; (scheme) plan m, proyecto; (schedule) programa m // vt (think in advance) proyectar; (prepare) planear, planificar // vi hacer proyectos; to ~ to do proponerse hacer.

plane [pleɪn] n (AVIAT) avión m; (tree) plátano; (tool) cepillo; (MATH) plano.

planet ['plænɪt] n planeta m; ~arium [-'tɛərɪəm] n planetario.

plank [plæŋk] n tabla; (POL) punto.

planner ['plænə*] n planificador/a m/f.

planning ['plænɪŋ] n planificación f; **family** ~ planificación familiar.

plant [plɑːnt] n planta; (machinery) maquinaria; (factory) fábrica // vt plantar; (field) sembrar; (bomb) colocar; (fam) colocar a escondidas.

plantation [plæn'teɪʃən] n plantación; (estate) hacienda.

plaque [plæk] n placa.

plasma ['plæzmə] n plasma m.

plaster ['plɑːstə*] n (for walls) yeso; (also: sticking ~) curitas m inv, parche m // vt enyesar; (cover): to ~ with llenar o cubrir de; ~ed (col) trompa; ~er n yesero.

plastic ['plæstɪk] n plástico // a de plástico.

plasticine ['plæstɪsiːn] n plasticina.

plastic surgery ['plæstɪk'sɜːdʒərɪ] n cirujía plástica.

plate [pleɪt] n (dish) plato; (metal, in book) lámina; (PHOT, dental) placa.

plateau ['plætəu], pl ~s or ~x [-z] n meseta, altiplanicie f.

plateful ['pleɪtful] n plato.

plate glass [pleɪt'glɑːs] n vidrio cilindrado.

platform ['plætfɔːm] n (RAIL) andén m; (stage) plataforma; (at meeting) tribuna; (POL) programa m electoral; ~ ticket n billete m de andén.

platinum ['plætɪnəm] n platino.

platitude ['plætɪtjuːd] n lugar m común, tópico.

platoon [plə'tuːn] n pelotón m.

platter ['plætə*] n fuente f, platón m.

plausible ['plɔːzɪbl] a verosímil, admisible; (person) convincente.

play [pleɪ] n (gen) juego; (also: ~time) recreo; (THEATRE) obra, comedia // vt (game) jugar; (instrument) tocar; (THEATRE) representar; (: part) hacer (el papel de); (fig) desempeñar // vi jugar;

(amuse o.s.) divertirse; (frolic) juguetear; to ~ down vt quitar importancia a; to ~ up vt (cause trouble to) fastidiar a; ~acting n teatro; ~er n jugador/a m/f; (THEATRE) actor/actriz m/f; (MUS) músico/a; ~ful a juguetón(ona); ~ground n (in park) parque m de juegos; (in school) patio de recreo; ~group n jardín m de niños; ~ing card n naipe m, carta; ~ing field n campo de deportes; ~mate n compañero de juego; ~-off n (SPORT) partido de desempate; ~pen n corral m; ~thing n juguete m; ~wright n dramaturgo.

plea [pliː] n (request) súplica, petición f; (excuse) pretexto, disculpa; (LAW) alegato, defensa.

plead [pliːd] vt (LAW) interceder; (give as excuse) poner como pretexto // vi (LAW) declarar; (beg): to ~ with sb suplicar o rogar a uno.

pleasant ['plɛznt] a agradable; (surprise) grato; (person) simpático; ~ness n (of person) simpatía, amabilidad f; (of place) lo agradable; ~ries npl (polite remarks) cortesías fpl.

please [pliːz] vt (give pleasure to) dar gusto a, agradar; (get on well with) caer en gracia a // vi (think fit): do as you ~ haga lo que quiera o lo que le da la gana; ~! ¡por favor!; ~ yourself! ¡como Usted guste!, ¡como quiera!; ~d a (happy) alegre, contento; ~d (with) satisfecho (de); **pleasing** a (gen) agradable; (surprise) grato; (flattering) halagüeño.

pleasure ['plɛʒə*] n placer m, gusto; (will) voluntad f // cpd de recreo; 'it's a ~' el gusto es mío; **it's a** ~ **to see him** da gusto verle.

pleat [pliːt] n pliegue m.

plebs [plɛbz] npl (pej) la plebe.

plectrum ['plɛktrəm] n plectro.

pledge [plɛdʒ] n (object) prenda; (promise) promesa, voto // vt (pawn) empeñar; (promise) prometer.

plentiful ['plɛntɪful] a copioso, abundante.

plenty ['plɛntɪ] n abundancia; ~ of (enough) bastante; (many) muchos.

pleurisy ['pluərɪsɪ] n pleuresía.

pliable ['plaɪəbl] a flexible; (fig) manejable.

pliers ['plaɪəz] npl alicates mpl, tenazas fpl.

plight [plaɪt] n condición f, situación f difícil.

plimsolls ['plɪmsəlz] npl zapatos mpl de tenis.

plod [plɔd] vi caminar penosamente; (fig) trabajar laboriosamente; ~der n empollón/ona m/f; ~ding a laborioso.

plonk [plɔŋk] (col) n (wine) vino corriente // vt: to ~ sth down dejar caer algo (pesadamente).

plot [plɔt] n (scheme) complot m, conjura; (of story, play) argumento; (of land) terreno // vt (mark out) trazar; (conspire) tramar, urdir // vi conspirar; ~ter n conspirador/a m/f.

plough, plow (*US*) [plau] *n* arado // *vt* (*earth*) arar; **to ~ back** *vt* (*COMM*) reinvertir; **to ~ through** *vt fus* (*crowd*) abrirse paso por la fuerza.

ploy [plɔɪ] *n* truco, estratagema.

pluck [plʌk] *vt* (*fruit*) coger; (*musical instrument*) puntear; (*bird*) desplumar // *n* valor *m*, ánimo; **to ~ up courage** hacer de tripas corazón; **~y** *a* valiente, valeroso.

plug [plʌg] *n* tapón *m*; (*ELEC*) enchufe *m*, clavija; (*AUT: also:* **sparking ~**) bujía // *vt* (*hole*) tapar; (*col: advertise*) dar publicidad a.

plum [plʌm] *n* (*fruit*) ciruela // *a* (*col: job*) breva, chollo.

plumage ['plu:mɪdʒ] *n* plumaje *m*.

plumb [plʌm] *ad* (*exactly*) exactamente, en punto // *vt* sondar, sondear.

plumber ['plʌmə*] *n* fontanero; **plumbing** [-mɪŋ] *n* (*trade*) fontanería; (*piping*) instalación *f* de cañerías.

plume [plu:m] *n* (*gen*) pluma; (*on helmet*) penacho.

plummet ['plʌmɪt] *vi*: **to ~ (down)** caer a plomo.

plump [plʌmp] *a* rechoncho, rollizo // *vt*: **to ~ sth (down) on** dejar caer algo en; **to ~ for** (*col: choose*) optar por.

plunder ['plʌndə*] *n* pillaje *m*; (*loot*) botín *m* // *vt* pillar, saquear; (*tomb*) robar.

plunge [plʌndʒ] *n* (*dive*) salto; (*submersion*) zambullida; (*bath*) baño // *vt* sumergir, hundir // *vi* (*fall*) caer; (*dive*) saltar; (*person*) arrojarse; (*sink*) hundirse; **to take the ~** resolverse; **plunger** *n* émbolo; **plunging** *a* (*neckline*) escotado.

pluperfect [plu:'pɔ:fɪkt] *n* pluscuamperfecto.

plural ['pluərl] *n* plural *m*.

plus [plʌs] *n* (*also:* **~ sign**) signo más // *prep* más, y, además de; **ten/twenty ~** diez/veinte y pico.

plush [plʌʃ] *a* de felpa.

ply [plaɪ] *vt* (*a trade*) ejercer // *vi* (*ship*) ir y venir; (*for hire*) ofrecerse (para alquilar); **three ~** (*wool*) de tres cordones; **to ~ sb with drink** ofrecer bebidas a alguien muchas veces; **~wood** *n* madera contrachapada.

P.M. *abbr of* **Prime Minister.**

p.m. *ad abbr of* **post meridiem** de la tarde *o* noche.

pneumatic [nju:'mætɪk] *a* neumático.

pneumonia [nju:'məunɪə] *n* pulmonía.

poach [pəutʃ] *vt* (*cook*) escalfar; (*steal*) cazar en vedado // *vi* cazar/pescar en finca ajena; **~ed** *a* (*egg*) escalfado; **~er** *n* cazador *m* furtivo; **~ing** *n* caza/pesca furtiva.

pocket ['pɔkɪt] *n* bolsillo; (*of air, GEO, fig*) bolsa; (*BILLIARDS*) tronera // *vt* meter en el bolsillo; (*steal*) embolsar; (*BILLIARDS*) entronerar; **to be out of ~** salir perdiendo; **~book** *n* (*US. wallet*) cartera; **~ knife** *n* navaja; **~ money** *n* dinero para gastos personales.

pod [pɔd] *n* vaina.

podgy ['pɔdʒɪ] *a* gordinflón(ona).

poem ['pəuɪm] *n* poema *m*.

poet ['pəuɪt] *n* poeta *m/f*; **~ess** *n* poetisa; **~ic** [-'etɪk] *a* poético; **~ laureate** *n* poeta laureado; **~ry** *n* poesía.

poignant ['pɔɪnjənt] *a* conmovedor(a); (*sharp*) agudo.

point [pɔɪnt] *n* (*gen*) punto; (*tip*) punta; (*purpose*) fin *m*, finalidad *f*; (*use*) utilidad *f*, (*significant part*) lo significativo; (*characteristic*) rasgo; (*also:* **decimal ~**): **2 ~ 3 (2.3**) dos punto tres // *vt* (*show*) subrayar; (*gun etc*): **to ~ sth at sb** apuntar algo a uno // *vi* señalar con el dedo; **~s** *npl* (*AUT*) contactos *mpl*; (*RAIL*) agujas *fpl*; **to make a ~ of** no dejar de; **to get the ~** comprender; **to come to the ~** ir al grano; **there's no ~ (in doing)** no hay para qué (hacer); **to ~ out** *vt* señalar; **to ~ to** indicar con el dedo; (*fig*) indicar, señalar; **~-blank** *ad* (*also:* **at ~-blank range**) a quemarropa; **~ed** *a* (*shape*) puntiagudo, afilado; (*remark*) directo, enfático; **~edly** *ad* directamente, con énfasis; **~er** *n* (*stick*) puntero; (*needle*) aguja, indicador *m*; **~less** *a* (*useless*) inútil; (*senseless*) sin sentido; (*motiveless*) sin motivo; **~ of view** *n* punto de vista.

poise [pɔɪz] *n* (*balance*) equilibrio; (*of head, body*) aire *m*, porte *m*; (*calmness*) confianza.

poison ['pɔɪzn] *n* veneno // *vt* envenenar; **~ing** *n* envenenamiento; **~ous** *a* venenoso; (*fumes etc*) tóxico; (*fig*) pernicioso.

poke [pəuk] *vt* (*fire*) hurgar, atizar; (*jab with finger, stick etc*) empujar; (*put*): **to ~ sth in(to)** introducir algo en // *n* (*to fire*) hurgonada; (*push*) empujón *m*; (*with elbow*) codazo; **to ~ about** *vi* fisgar.

poker ['pəukə*] *n* badila, atizador *m*; (*CARDS*) póker *m*; **~-faced** *a* de cara impasible.

poky ['pəukɪ] *a* estrecho.

Poland ['pəulənd] *n* Polonia.

polar ['pəulə*] *a* polar; **~ bear** *n* oso polar.

polarize ['pəuləraɪz] *vt* polarizar.

pole [pəul] *n* palo; (*GEO*) polo; (*TEL*) poste *m*; (*flag~*) asta; (*tent ~*) mástil *m*.

Pole [pəul] *n* polaco/a.

pole vault ['pəulvɔ:lt] *n* salto con pértiga.

police [pə'li:s] *n* policía // *vt* mantener el orden en; **~ car** *n* coche-patrulla *m*; **~man** *n* policía *m*, guardia *m*; **~ state** *n* estado policiaco; **~ station** *n* comisaría; **~woman** *n* mujer *f* policía.

policy ['pɔlɪsɪ] *n* política; (*also:* **insurance ~**) póliza.

polio ['pəulɪəu] *n* polio *f*.

Polish ['pəulɪʃ] *a*, *n* polaco.

polish ['pɔlɪʃ] *n* (*for shoes*) betún *m*; (*for floor*) cera (de lustrar); (*for nails*) esmalte *m*; (*shine*) brillo, lustre *m*; (*fig: refinement*) cultura, urbanidad *f* // *vt* (*shoes*) limpiar;

(*make shiny*) pulir, sacar brillo a; (*fig: improve*) refinar, repasar; **to ~ off** *vt* (*work*) terminar; (*food*) despachar **~ed** *a* (*fig: person*) culto; (: *manners*) fino.

polite [pə'laɪt] *a* cortés, atento; (*formal*) correcto; **~ness** *n* cortesía.

politic ['pɒlɪtɪk] *a* prudente; **~al** [pə'lɪtɪkl] *a* político; **~ian** [-'tɪʃən] *n* político; **~s** *npl* política *sg*.

polka ['pɒlkə] *n* polca; **~ dot** *n* punto.

poll [pəʊl] *n* (*votes*) votación *f*, votos *mpl*; (*also: opinion ~*) sondeo, encuesta *f*; *vt* (*votes*) recibir, obtener.

pollen ['pɒlən] *n* polen m.

pollination [pɒlɪ'neɪʃən] *n* polinización *f.*

polling ['pəʊlɪŋ]: **~ booth** *n* cabina de votar; **~ day** *n* día *m* de elecciones; **~ station** *n* centro electoral.

pollute [pə'luːt] *vt* contaminar; **pollution** [-'luːʃən] *n* polución *f*, contaminación *f.*

polo ['pəʊləʊ] *n* (*sport*) polo; **~-neck** *a* de cuello vuelto.

polyester [pɒlɪ'estə*] *n* poliéster *m.*

polygamy [pə'lɪgəmɪ] *n* poligamia.

Polynesia [pɒlɪ'niːzɪə] *n* Polinesia.

polytechnic [pɒlɪ'teknɪk] *n* politécnico, escuela de formación profesional.

polythene ['pɒlɪθiːn] *n* politeno.

pomegranate ['pɒmɪgrænɪt] *n* granada.

pommel ['pɒmɪ] *n* pomo *// vt* dar de puñetazos.

pomp [pɒmp] *n* pompa.

pompous ['pɒmpəs] *a* pomposo.

pond [pɒnd] *n* (*natural*) charca; (*artificial*) estanque *m.*

ponder ['pɒndə*] *vt* meditar; **~ous** *a* pesado.

pontiff ['pɒntɪf] *n* pontífice *m.*

pontificate [pɒn'tɪfɪkeɪt] *vi* (*fig*): **to ~** (*about*) pontificar (sobre).

pontoon [pɒn'tuːn] *n* pontón *m*; (*card game*) veintiuna.

pony ['pəʊnɪ] *n* poney *m*, jaca; **~tail** *n* cola de caballo; **~ trekking** *n* excursión *f* a caballo.

poodle ['puːdl] *n* perro de lanas.

pool [puːl] *n* (*of rain*) charca; (*pond*) estanque *m*; (*also: swimming ~*) piscina; (*billiards*) trucos *mpl // vt* juntar; (*football*) **~s** quinielas *fpl.*

poor [puə*] *a* pobre; (*bad*) de baja calidad *// npl:* **the ~** los pobres; **~ly** *a* mal, enfermo.

pop [pɒp] *n* ¡pum!; (*sound*) ruido seco; (*MUS*) pop *m*; (*US: col: father*) papá *m*; (*lemonade*) gaseosa *// vt* (*put*) poner *// vi* reventar; (*cork*) saltar; **to ~ in** *vi* entrar de sopetón; **to ~ out** *vi* salir un momento; **to ~ up** *vi* aparecer inesperadamente; **~ concert** *n* concierto pop; **~corn** *n* palomitas *fpl.*

pope [pəʊp] *n* papa *m.*

poplar ['pɒplə*] *n* álamo.

poplin ['pɒplɪn] *n* popelina.

poppy ['pɒpɪ] *n* amapola.

populace ['pɒpjʊləs] *n* pueblo, plebe *f.*

popular ['pɒpjʊlə*] *a* popular; (*fashionable*) de moda; **~ity** [-'lærɪtɪ] *n* popularidad *f*; **~ize** *vt* popularizar; (*disseminate*) vulgarizar.

populate ['pɒpjʊleɪt] *vt* poblar; **population** [-'leɪʃən] *n* población *f.*

populous ['pɒpjʊləs] *a* populoso.

porcelain ['pɔːslɪn] *n* porcelana.

porch [pɔːtʃ] *n* pórtico, entrada.

porcupine ['pɔːkjʊpaɪn] *n* puerco espín.

pore [pɔː*] *n* poro *// vi:* **to ~ over** estar absorto en.

pork [pɔːk] *n* carne *f* de cerdo.

pornographic [pɔːnə'græfɪk] *a* pornográfico; **pornography** [-'nɒgrəfɪ] *n* pornografía.

porous ['pɔːrəs] *a* poroso.

porpoise ['pɔːpəs] *n* marsopa.

porridge ['pɒrɪdʒ] *n* avena.

port [pɔːt] *n* (*harbour*) puerto; (*NAUT: left side*) babor *m*; (*wine*) (vino de) oporto.

portable ['pɔːtəbl] *a* portátil.

portend [pɔː'tend] *vt* presagiar, anunciar; **portent** ['pɔːtent] *n* presagio, augurio.

porter ['pɔːtə*] *n* (*for luggage*) mozo; (*doorkeeper*) portero, conserje *m.*

porthole ['pɔːthəʊl] *n* portilla.

portion ['pɔːʃən] *n* porción *f*; (*helping*) ración *f.*

portly ['pɔːtlɪ] *a* corpulento.

portrait ['pɔːtreɪt] *n* retrato.

portray [pɔː'treɪ] *vt* retratar; (*in writing*) describir, representar; **~al** *n* representación *f.*

Portugal ['pɔːtjʊgl] *n* Portugal *m.*

Portuguese [pɔːtjʊ'giːz] *a* portugués(esa) *// n, pl inv* portugués-esa *m/f*; (*LING*) portugués *m.*

pose [pəʊz] *n* postura, actitud *f*; (*pej*) afectación *f*, pose *f // vi* posar; (*pretend*): **to ~ as** darse tono de *// vt* (*question*) plantear.

posh [pɒʃ] *a* (*col*) elegante, de lujo.

position [pə'zɪʃən] *n* posición *f*; (*job*) puesto *// vi* colocar.

positive ['pɒzɪtɪv] *a* positivo (*certain*) seguro; (*definite*) definitivo.

posse ['pɒsɪ] *n* (*US*) pelotón *m.*

possess [pə'zes] *vt* poseer; **~ion** [pə'zeʃən] *n* posesión *f*; **~ive** *a* posesivo.

possibility [pɒsɪ'bɪlɪtɪ] *n* posibilidad *f*; **possible** ['pɒsɪbl] *a* posible; **as big as possible** lo más grande posible; **possibly** ['pɒsɪblɪ] *ad* (*perhaps*) posiblemente, tal vez; **I cannot possibly come me** es imposible venir.

post [pəʊst] *n* (*letters, delivery*) correo; (*job, situation*) puesto; (*pole*) poste *m // vt* (*send by post*) echar al correo; (*MIL*) apostar; (*bills*) fijar, pegar; (*appoint*): **to ~ to** enviar a; **~age** *n* porte *m*, franqueo; **~al** *a* postal, de correos; **~al order** *n* giro postal; **~box** *n* buzón *m*; **~card** *n* tarjeta postal.

postdate [pəʊst'deɪt] *vt* (*cheque*) poner fecha adelantada a.

poster ['pəustə*] n cartel m.
posterior [pɔs'tɪərɪə*] n (col) culo, trasero.
posterity [pɔs'tɛrɪtɪ] n posteridad f.
postgraduate ['pəust'grædjuət] n postgraduado.
posthumous ['pɔstjuməs] a póstumo.
post: ~**man** n cartero; ~**mark** n matasellos m inv; ~**master** n administrador/a m/f de correos.
post-mortem [pəust'mɔːtəm] n autopsia.
post office ['pəustɔfɪs] n (building) correos f; (organization) Administración General de Correos; ~ **box (P.O. box)** n apartado postal.
postpone [pɔs'pəun] vt aplazar; ~**ment** n aplazamiento.
postscript ['pəustskrɪpt] n posdata.
postulate ['pɔstjuleɪt] vt postular.
posture ['pɔstʃə*] n postura, actitud f.
postwar ['pəust'wɔː*] a de posguerra.
posy ['pəuzi] n ramillete m (de flores).
pot [pɔt] n (for cooking) olla; (for flowers) maceta; (for jam) tarro, pote m; (col: marijuana) mota // vt (plant) poner en tiesto; (conserve) conservar.
potato [pə'teɪtəu], pl ~**es** n patata, papa (AM).
potent ['pəutnt] a potente, poderoso; (drink) fuerte.
potential [pə'tɛnʃl] a potencial, en potencial // n potencial m, potencialidad f.
pothole ['pɔthəul] n (in road) bache m; (underground) caverna; **potholer** n espeleólogo; **potholing** n: **to go potholing** dedicarse a la espeleología.
potion ['pəuʃən] n poción f, pócima.
potluck [pɔt'lʌk] n: **to take** ~ contentarse con lo que haya.
potshot ['pɔtʃɔt] n: **to take a** ~ **at sth** tirar a algo sin apuntar.
potted ['pɔtɪd] a (food) en conserva; (plant) en tiesto o maceta.
potter ['pɔtə*] n (artistic) ceramista m/f; (artisan) alfarero // vi: **to** ~ **around,** ~ **about** ocuparse en fruslerías; ~**y** n cerámica; alfarería.
potty ['pɔtɪ] a (col: mad) chiflado // n orinal m de niño.
pouch [pautʃ] n (ZOOL) bolsa; (for tobacco) petaca.
pouf(fe) [puːf] n pouf m.
poultice ['pəultɪs] n cataplasma, emplasto.
poultry ['pəultrɪ] n aves fpl de corral; (dead) pollos mpl; ~ **farm** n granja avícola.
pounce [pauns] vi: **to** ~ **on** precipitarse sobre // n salto, ataque m.
pound [paund] n (gen) libra; (for dogs) corral m; (for cars) depósito // vt (beat) golpear; (crush) machacar // vi (beat) dar golpes; ~ **sterling** n (libra) esterlina.
pour [pɔː*] vt echar; (tea) servir // vi correr, fluir; (rain) llover a cántaros; **to** ~ **away or off** vt vaciar, verter; **to** ~ **in** vi (people) entrar en tropel; **to** ~ **out** vi (people) salir en tropel // vt (drink) echar, servir; ~**ing** a: ~**ing rain** lluvia torrencial.
pout [paut] vi hacer pucheros.
poverty ['pɔvətɪ] n pobreza, miseria; (fig) falta, escasez f; ~**stricken** a necesitado.
powder ['paudə*] n polvo; (face ~) polvos mpl; (gun~) pólvora // vt polvorear; **to** ~ **one's face** empolvarse; ~ **compact** n polvera; ~ **room** n aseos mpl; ~**y** a polvoriento.
power ['pauə*] n (gen) poder m; (strength) fuerza; (nation) potencia; (ability, POL: of party, leader) poder m, poderío; (drive) empuje m; (TECH) potencia; (ELEC) fuerza, energía // vt impulsar; ~ **cut** n apagón m; ~**ed** a: ~**ed by** impulsado por; ~**ful** a poderoso; (engine) potente; (build) fuerte; (emotion) intenso; ~**less** a impotente, ineficaz; ~ **line** n línea de conducción eléctrica; ~ **point** n enchufe m; ~ **station** n central f eléctrica.
p.p. abbr of per procurationem: ~ **J. Smith** p.p. (por poder de) J. Smith.
practicable ['præktɪkəbl] a (scheme) factible.
practical ['præktɪkl] a práctico; ~ **joke** n broma pesada; ~**ly** ad (almost) prácticamente.
practice ['præktɪs] n (habit) costumbre f; (exercise) práctica, ejercicio; (training) adiestramiento; (MED) clientela // vt, vi (US) = **practise; in** ~ (in reality) en la práctica; **out of** ~ desentrenado.
practise, practice (US) ['præktɪs] vt (carry out) practicar; (be in the habit of) tener por costumbre; (profession) ejercer; (train at) hacer ejercicios de // vi (train) entrenar, adiestrarse; **practising** a (Christian etc) practicante; (lawyer) que ejerce.
practitioner [præk'tɪʃənə*] n practicante m/f; (MED) médico/a.
pragmatic [præg'mætɪk] a pragmático.
prairie ['prɛərɪ] n pradera, pampa.
praise [preɪz] n alabanza, elogio, alabanzas fpl, elogios mpl; ~**worthy** a loable, digno de elogios.
pram [præm] n cochecito de niño.
prance [prɑːns] vi (horse) hacer cabriolas.
prank [præŋk] n travesura.
prattle ['prætl] vi parlotear; (child) balbucear.
prawn [prɔːn] n gamba; (small) quisquilla.
pray [preɪ] vi rezar; ~**er** n oración f, rezo; (entreaty) ruego, súplica; ~**er book** n devocionario, misal m.
preach [priːtʃ] vi predicar; ~**er** n predicador/a m/f; (US) pastor m.
preamble [prɪ'æmbl] n preámbulo.
prearranged [priːə'reɪndʒd] a arreglado de antemano.
precarious [prɪ'kɛərɪəs] a precario.
precaution [prɪ'kɔːʃən] n precaución f.
precede [prɪ'siːd] vt, vi preceder.
precedence ['prɛsɪdəns] n precedencia;

(*priority*) prioridad *f*; **precedent** [-ant] *n* precedente *m*.

preceding [pri'si:dɪŋ] *a* precedente.

precept ['pri:sept] *n* precepto.

precinct ['pri:sɪŋkt] *n* recinto ~**s** *npl* contornos *mpl*; **pedestrian** ~ zona reservada para peatones; **shopping** ~ zona comercial.

precious ['prefəs] *a* precioso; *stylized*) afectado.

precipice ['presɪpɪs] *n* precipicio, despeñadero.

precipitate [pri'sɪpɪtɪt] *a* ('*hasty*) precipitado, apresurado // *vt* [pri'sɪpɪteɪt] (*hasten*) acelerar; (*bring about*) causar; **precipitation** [-'teɪʃən] *n* precipitación *f*.

precipitous [pri'sɪpɪtəs] *a* (*steep*) escarpado.

precise [pri'saɪs] *a* preciso, exacto; (*person*) escrupuloso; ~**ly** *ad* exactamente, precisamente; **precision** [-'sɪʒən] *n* precisión *f*.

preclude [pri'klu:d] *vt* excluir.

precocious [pri'kəufəs] *a* precoz.

preconceived [pri:kən'si:vd] *a* (*idea*) preconcebido.

precursor [pri:'kə:sə*] *n* precursor/a *m/f*.

predator ['predətə*] *n* animal *m* de rapiña; ~**y** *a* rapaz, de rapiña.

predecessor ['pri:dɪsesə*] *n* antecesor/a *m/f*.

predestination [pri:destɪ'neɪʃən] *n* predestinación *f*.

predetermine [pri:dɪ'tə:mɪn] *vt* predeterminar.

predicament [pri'dɪkəmənt] *n* apuro.

predict [pri'dɪkt] *vt* pronosticar; ~**ion** [-'dɪkʃən] *n* pronóstico.

predominant [pri'dɒmɪnənt] *a* predominante; **predominate** [-neɪt] *vi* predominar.

pre-eminent [pri:'emɪnənt] *a* preeminente.

pre-empt [pri:'emt] *vt* apropiarse de antemano.

preen [pri:n] *vt*: **to** ~ **itself** (*bird*) limpiarse (las plumas); **to** ~ **o.s.** pavonearse.

prefab ['pri:fæb] *n* casa prefabricada.

prefabricated [pri:'fæbrɪkeɪtɪd] *a* prefabricado.

preface ['prefəs] *n* prefacio.

prefect ['pri:fekt] *n* (*Brit: in school*) tutor *m*, monitor *m*.

prefer [pri'fə:*] *vt* preferir; ~**able** ['prefrəbl] *a* preferible; ~**ably** ['prefrəbli] *ad* de preferencia; ~**ence** ['prefrəns] *n* preferencia, prioridad *f*; ~**ential** [prefə'renʃəl] *a* preferente.

prefix ['pri:fɪks] *n* prefijo.

pregnancy ['pregnənsi] *n* embarazo; **pregnant** [-ənt] *a* embarazada; **to be pregnant** estar encinta; **pregnant with** preñado de.

prehistoric ['pri:hɪs'tɔrɪk] *a* prehistórico.

prejudge [pri:'dʒʌdʒ] *vt* prejuzgar.

prejudice ['predʒudɪs] *n* (*bias*) prejuicio; (*harm*) perjuicio // *vt* (*predispose*) predisponer; (*harm*) perjudicar; ~**d** *a* (*person*) predispuesto, con prejuicios; (*view*) parcial, interesado.

prelate ['prelət] *n* prelado.

preliminary [pri'lɪmɪnəri] *a* preliminar.

prelude ['prelju:d] *n* preludio.

premarital ['pri:'mærɪtl] *a* premarital.

premature ['premətjuə*] *a* prematuro.

premeditated [pri:'medɪteɪtɪd] *a* premeditado.

premier ['premɪə*] *a* primero, principal // *n* (*POL*) primer ministro.

première ['premɪeə*] *n* estreno.

premise ['premɪs] *n* premisa; ~**s** *npl* local *m*; (*house*) casa *sg*; (*shop*) tienda *sg*; **on the** ~**s** en el local.

premium ['pri:mɪəm] *n* premio; (*COMM*) prima; **to be at a** ~ ser muy solicitado.

premonition [premə'nɪʃən] *n* presentimiento.

preoccupation [pri:ɔkju'peɪʃən] *n* preocupación *f*; **preoccupied** [-'ɔkjupaɪd] *a* (*worried*) preocupado; (*absorbed*) absorto.

prep [prep] *n* (*SCOL: study*) deberes *mpl*; ~ **school** *n* = **preparatory school**.

prepaid [pri:'peɪd] *a* con porte pagado.

preparation [prepə'reɪʃən] *n* preparación *f*; ~**s** *npl* preparativos *mpl*.

preparatory [prə'pærətəri] *a* preparatorio, preliminar; ~ **to con** miras a; ~ **school** *n* escuela preparatoria.

prepare [pri'peə*] *vt* preparar, disponer // *vi*: **to** ~ **for** prepararse o disponerse para; (*make preparations*) hacer preparativos para; ~**d to** dispuesto a.

preponderance [pri'pɔndərns] *n* preponderancia, predominio.

preposition [prepə'zɪʃən] *n* preposición *f*.

preposterous [pri'pɔstərəs] *a* absurdo, ridículo.

prerequisite [pri:'rekwɪzɪt] *n* requisito (previo).

prerogative [pri'rɔgətɪv] *n* prerrogativa.

presbyterian [prezbɪ'tɪərɪən] *a*, *n* presbiteriano/a.

preschool ['pri:'sku:l] *a* preescolar.

prescribe [pri'skraɪb] *vt* prescribir; (*MED*) recetar.

prescription [pri'skrɪpʃən] *n* prescripción *f*; (*MED*) receta.

presence ['prezns] *n* presencia; (*attendance*) asistencia; ~ **of mind** presencia de ánimo.

present ['preznt] *a* (*in attendance*) presente; (*current*) actual // *n* (*gift*) regalo; (*actuality*) actualidad *f*, presente *m* // *vt* [pri'zent] (*introduce*) presentar; (*expound*) exponer; (*give*) presentar, dar, ofrecer; (*THEATRE*) representar; **at** ~ actualmente; ~**able** [pri'zentəbl] *a* presentable; ~**ation** [-'teɪʃən] *n* presentación *f*; (*gift*) obsequio; (*of case*) exposición *f*; (*THEATRE*) representación *f*;

~**-day** a actual; ~**ly** ad (*soon*) dentro de poco.

preservation [prɛzə'veɪʃən] n conservación f.

preservative [prɪ'zɜːvətɪv] n preservativo.

preserve [prɪ'zɜːv] vt (*keep safe*) preservar, proteger; (*maintain*) conservar; (*food*) hacer una conserva de; (*in salt*) salar // n (*for game*) coto, vedado; (*often pl: jam*) conserva, confitura.

preside [prɪ'zaɪd] vi presidir.

presidency ['prɛzɪdənsɪ] n presidencia; **president** [-ənt] n presidente m/f; **presidential** [-'dɛnʃl] a presidencial.

press [prɛs] n (*tool, machine, newspapers*) prensa; (*printer's*) imprenta; (*crowd*) apiñamiento, agolpamiento; (*of hand*) apretón m // vt (*push*) empujar; (*squeeze*) apretar; (*clothes: iron*) planchar; (*TECH*) prensar; (*harry*) acosar; (*insist*): **to ~ sth on sb** insistir en que uno acepte algo // vi (*squeeze*) apretar; (*pressurize*) ejercer presión; **we are ~ed for time** tenemos poco tiempo; **to ~ on** vi avanzar; (*hurry*) apretar el paso; ~ **agency** n agencia de prensa; ~ **conference** n conferencia de prensa; ~ **cutting** n recorte m (de periódico); ~**ing** a apremiante; ~ **stud** n botón m de presión.

pressure ['prɛʃə*] n presión f; (*urgency*) apremio, urgencia; (*influence*) influencia; (*MED*) tensión f nerviosa; ~ **cooker** n olla a presión; ~ **gauge** n manómetro; ~ **group** n grupo de presión; **pressurized** a a presión.

prestige [prɛs'tiːʒ] n prestigio; **prestigious** [-'tɪdʒəs] a prestigioso.

presumably [prɪ'zjuːməblɪ] ad se supone que, cabe presumir que.

presume [prɪ'zjuːm] vt presumir, suponer; **to ~ to do** (*dare*) atreverse a; (*set out to*) pretender.

presumption [prɪ'zʌmpʃən] n suposición f; (*pretension*) pretensión f; (*boldness*) atrevimiento.

presuppose [priːsə'pəʊz] vt presuponer.

pretence, pretense (*US*) [prɪ'tɛns] n (*claim*) pretensión f; (*display*) ostentación f; (*pretext*) pretexto; (*make-believe*) fingimiento; **on the ~ of** so pretexto de.

pretend [prɪ'tɛnd] vt (*feign*) fingir // vi (*feign*) fingir; (*claim*): **to ~ to sth** pretender a algo.

pretension [prɪ'tɛnʃən] n (*presumption*) presunción f; (*claim*) pretensión f.

pretentious [prɪ'tɛnʃəs] a presumido; (*ostentacious*) ostentoso, aparatoso.

pretext ['priːtɛkst] n pretexto.

pretty ['prɪtɪ] a (*gen*) hermoso; (*person*) guapo; (*dress*) bonito; (*sum*) importante // ad (*quite*) bastante; (*nearly*) casi.

prevail [prɪ'veɪl] vi (*win*) imponerse; (*be current*) imperar; (*be in fashion*) estar de moda; (*be usual*) prevalecer; (*persuade*): **to ~ (up)on sb to do sth** persuadir a uno a hacer algo; ~**ing** a (*dominant*)

imperante; (*usual*) corriente.

prevalent ['prɛvələnt] a (*dominant*) predominante; (*usual*) corriente; (*fashionable*) en boga; (*present-day*) actual.

prevent [prɪ'vɛnt] vt: **to ~ (sb) from doing sth** impedir (a uno) hacer algo; ~**able** a evitable; ~**ative** a preventivo; ~**ion** [-'vɛnʃən] n prevención f; ~**ive** a preventivo.

preview ['priːvjuː] n (*of film*) preestreno; (*fig*) anticipo.

previous ['priːvɪəs] a previo, anterior; (*hasty*) prematuro; ~**ly** ad previamente, con anticipación; (*in earlier times*) antes.

prewar [priː'wɔː*] a de preguerra, prebélico.

prey [preɪ] n presa // vi: **to ~ on** vivir a costa de; (*feed on*) alimentarse de; (*plunder*) robar, pillar; **it was ~ing on his mind** le agobiaba, le preocupaba.

price [praɪs] n precio // vt (*goods*) fijar el precio de; ~**less** a inapreciable.

prick [prɪk] n pinchazo; (*with pin*) alfilerazo; (*sting*) picadura // vt pinchar; picar; **to ~ up one's ears** aguzar el oído.

prickle ['prɪkl] n (*sensation*) escozor m; (*BOT*) espina; (*ZOOL*) púa; **prickly** a espinoso; (*fig: person*) malhumorado; (: *touchy*) quisquilloso.

pride [praɪd] n orgullo; (*pej*) soberbia // vt: **to ~ o.s. on** enorgullecerse de, ufanarse de.

priest [priːst] n sacerdote m; ~**ess** n sacerdotisa; ~**hood** n (*practice*) sacerdocio; (*priests*) clero.

prig [prɪg] n presumido/a, pedante m/f.

prim [prɪm] a (*formal*) estirado; (*affected*) remilgado; (*prudish*) gazmoño.

primarily ['praɪmərɪlɪ] ad (*above all*) ante todo; (*firstly*) en primer lugar.

primary ['praɪmərɪ] a primario; (*first in importance*) principal; ~ **school** n escuela primaria.

primate ['praɪmɪt] n (*REL*) primado // a ['praɪmeɪt] (*ZOOL*) primate m.

prime [praɪm] a primero, principal; (*basic*) fundamental; (*excellent*) selecto, de primera clase // vt (*gun, pump*) cebar; (*fig*) preparar, aprestar; **in the ~ of life** en la flor de la vida; ~ **minister** n primer ministro; **primer** n (*book*) libro de texto; (*paint*) pintura de base.

primitive ['prɪmɪtɪv] a primitivo; (*crude*) rudimentario; (*uncivilized*) inculto.

primrose ['prɪmrəʊz] n primavera, prímula.

primus (stove) ['praɪməs] n hornillo de campaña a presión.

prince [prɪns] n príncipe m.

princess [prɪn'sɛs] n princesa.

principal ['prɪnsɪpl] a principal // n director/a m/f.

principality [prɪnsɪ'pælɪtɪ] n principado.

principle ['prɪnsɪpl] n principio.

print [prɪnt] n (*impression*) marca, impresión f; (*letters*) letra de molde; (*fabric*) estampado; (*ART*) estampa,

grabado; (PHOT) positiva // vt (gen)
imprimir; (on mind) grabar; "write in
capitals) escribir en letras de molde; **out
of** ~ agotado; **~ed matter** n impresos
mpl; **~er** n impresor/a m/f; **~ing** n (art)
imprenta; (act) impresión f; (quantity)
tirada; **~ing press** n (prensa de)
imprenta.

prior ['praɪə*] a anterior, previo // a **prior**
m; ~ **to doing** antes de o hasta hacer.

priority [praɪ'ɔrɪtɪ] n prioridad f.

prise [praɪz] vt: **to ~ open** abrir con
palanca.

prism ['prɪzəm] n prisma m.

prison ['prɪzn] n cárcel f, prisión f ; / a
carcelario; **~er** n (in prison) preso; (under
arrest) detenido; (in dock) acusado.

privacy ['prɪvəsɪ] n (seclusion)
aislamiento, soledad f; (intimacy)
intimidad f.

private ['praɪvɪt] a (personal) particular;
(confidential) secreto, reservado;
(intimate) privado, íntimo; (sitting etc) a
puertas cerradas '; n soldado raso; '~'
(on envelope) 'privado'; (on door) 'uso
particular o privado'; **in ~** en privado; ~
enterprise n la empresa privada; **~ eye**
n detective m privado; **~ly** ad en privado;
(in o.s.) en el fondo.

privet ['prɪvɪt] n alheña.

privilege ['prɪvɪlɪdʒ] n privilegio;
(prerogative) prerrogativa; **~d** a
privilegiado.

privy ['prɪvɪ] a: **to be ~ to** estar enterado
de; **P ~ Council** n Consejo Privado.

prize [praɪz] n premio // a premiado; (first
class) de primera clase // vt apreciar,
estimar; **~-giving** n distribución f de
premios; **~winner** n premiado/a.

pro [prəu] n (SPORT) profesional m/f; **the
~s and cons** los pros y los contras.

probability [prɔbə'bɪlɪtɪ] n probabilidad f;

probable ['prɔbəbl] a probable; (plausible)
verosímil; **probably** ['prɔbəblɪ] ad proba-
blemente.

probation [prə'beɪʃən] n: **on ~**
(employee) de prueba; (LAW) en libertad
condicional.

probe [prəub] n (MED, SPACE) sonda;
(enquiry) encuesta, sondeo // vt sondar;
(investigate) indagar.

problem ['prɔbləm] n problema m; **~atic**
[-'mætɪk] a problemático.

procedure [prə'siːdʒə*] n (ADMIN, LAW)
procedimiento; (method) proceder m;
(bureaucratic) trámites mpl.

proceed [prə'siːd] vi proceder; (continue):
to ~ (with) continuar o seguir (con);
~ings npl acto sg, actos mpl; (LAW)
medidas fpl; (meeting) función f; (records)
actas fpl; **~s** ['prəusiːdz] npl ganancias fpl,
ingresos mpl.

process ['prəuses] n proceso; (method)
método, sistema m; (proceeding)
procedimiento // vt tratar, elaborar; **in ~**
en curso; **~ing** n elaboración f.

procession [prə'seʃən] n desfile m;
funeral ~ cortejo fúnebre.

proclaim [prə'kleɪm] vt proclamar;
(announce) anunciar; **proclamation**
[prɔklə'meɪʃən] n proclamación f; (written)
proclama.

procreation [prəukrɪ'eɪʃən] n procreación
f.

procure [prə'kjuə*] vt conseguir, obtener.

prod [prɔd] vt (push) empujar; (with elbow)
dar un codazo a; (jab) pinchar // n empuje
m; codazo; pinchazo.

prodigal ['prɔdɪgl] a pródigo.

prodigious [prə'dɪdʒəs] a prodigioso.

prodigy ['prɔdɪdʒɪ] n prodigio.

produce ['prɔdjuːs] n (AGR) productos mpl
agrícolas // vt [prə'djuːs] (gen) producir;
(profit) rendir; (show) presentar, mostrar;
(THEATRE) presentar, poner en escena;
(offspring) dar a luz; **producer** n
(THEATRE) director/a m/f; (AGR, CINEMA)
productor/a m/f.

product ['prɔdʌkt] n (thing) producto;
(result) fruto, resultado.

production [prə'dʌkʃən] n (act)
producción f; (thing) producto; (THEATRE)
representación f, obra; **~ line** n línea o
cadena de montaje.

productive [prə'dʌktɪv] a productivo;
productivity [prɔdʌk'tɪvɪtɪ] n
productividad f.

profane [prə'feɪn] a profano; (language
etc) fuerte.

profess [prə'fes] vt profesar; (regret)
manifestar.

profession [prə'feʃən] n profesión f; **~al**
n profesional m/f; (expert) perito // a
profesional; perito, experto; (by profession)
de oficio.

professor [prə'fesə*] n catedrático/a.

proficiency [prə'fɪʃənsɪ] n pericia,
habilidad f; **proficient** [-ənt] a perito,
hábil.

profile ['prəufaɪl] n perfil m.

profit ['prɔfɪt] n (COMM) ganancia; (fig)
provecho // vi: **to ~ by or from**
aprovechar o sacar provecho de;
~ability [-ə'bɪlɪtɪ] n rentabilidad f;
~able a (ECON) rentable; (useful)
provechoso; **~eering** [-'tɪərɪŋ] n (pej)
ganancias fpl excesivas.

profound [prə'faund] a profundo.

profuse [prə'fjuːs] a profuso, pródigo; **~ly**
ad profusamente, pródigamente;
profusion [-'fjuːʒən] n profusión f,
abundancia.

progeny ['prɔdʒɪnɪ] n progenie f, prole f.

programme, program (US)
['prəugræm] n programa m // vt
programar; **programming, programing**
(US) n programación f.

progress ['prəugres] n progreso;
(development) desarrollo // vi [prə'gres]
progresar, avanzar; **in ~** en curso o
en marcha; **~ion** [-'greʃən] n progresión f;
~ive [-'gresɪv] a progresivo; (person)
progresista m/f.

prohibit [prə'hɪbɪt] vt prohibir; **to ~ sb from doing sth** prohibir a uno hacer algo; **~ion** [prəʊɪ'bɪʃən] n (US) prohibicionismo; **~ive** a (price etc) excesivo.

project ['prɔdʒekt] n proyecto // (vb: [prə'dʒekt]) vt proyectar // vi (stick out) salir, sobresalir.

projectile [prə'dʒektaɪl] n proyectil m.

projection [prə'dʒekʃən] n proyección f; (overhang) saliente m.

projector [prə'dʒektə*] n proyector m.

proletarian [prəʊlɪ'tɛərɪən] a, n proletario/a; **proletariat** [-rɪət] n proletariado.

proliferate [prə'lɪfəreɪt] vi proliferar, multiplicarse; **proliferation** [-'reɪʃən] n proliferación f.

prolific [prə'lɪfɪk] a prolífico.

prologue ['prəʊlɔg] n prólogo.

prolong [prə'lɔŋ] vt prolongar, extender.

prom [prɔm] n abbr of **promenade** baile m de gala.

promenade [prɔmə'nɑːd] n (by sea) paseo marítimo; **~ concert** n concierto (en que parte del público permanece de pie).

prominence ['prɔmɪnəns] n (fig) eminencia, importancia; **prominent** [-ənt] a (standing out) saliente; (important) eminente, importante.

promiscuous [prə'mɪskjuəs] a (sexually) libertino.

promise ['prɔmɪs] n prómesa // vt, vi prometer; **promising** a prometedor(a).

promontory ['prɔməntrɪ] n promontorio.

promote [prə'məʊt] vt (gen) promover; (new product) hacer propaganda por; (MIL) ascender; **promoter** n (of sporting event) promotor/a m/f; **promotion** [-'məʊʃən] n (gen) promoción f; (MIL) ascenso.

prompt [prɔmpt] a pronto // ad (punctually) puntualmente // vt (urge) mover, incitar; (THEATRE) apuntar; **to ~ sb to do sth** mover a uno a hacer algo; **~er** n (THEATRE) apuntador/a m/f; **~ly** ad (punctually) puntualmente; (rapidly) rápidamente; **~ness** n puntualidad f; rapidez f.

prone [prəʊn] a (lying) postrado; **~ to** propenso a.

prong [prɔŋ] n diente m, púa.

pronoun ['prəʊnaʊn] n pronombre m.

pronounce [prə'naʊns] vt pronunciar; (declare) declarar // vi: **to ~ (up)on** pronunciarse sobre; **~d** a (marked) marcado; **~ment** n declaración f.

pronunciation [prənʌnsɪ'eɪʃən] n pronunciación f.

proof [pruːf] n prueba; (of alcohol) graduación f normal // a: **~ against** a prueba de; **~reader** n corrector/a m/f de pruebas.

prop [prɔp] n apoyo, (fig) sostén m // vt (also: **~ up**) apoyar; (lean): **to ~ sth against** apoyar algo contra.

propaganda [prɔpə'gændə] n propaganda.

propagate ['prɔpəgeɪt] vt propagar.

propel [prə'pel] vt impulsar, propulsar; **~ler** n hélice f; **~ling pencil** n lapicero.

proper ['prɔpə*] a (suited, right) propio; (exact) justo; (apt) apropiado, conveniente; (timely) oportuno; (seemly) correcto, decente; (authentic) verdadero; (col: real) auténtico.

property ['prɔpətɪ] n (gen) propiedad f; (goods) bienes mpl; (estate) hacienda; **it's their ~** es suyo, les pertenece.

prophecy ['prɔfɪsɪ] n profecía; **prophesy** [-saɪ] vt profetizar; (fig) predecir.

prophet ['prɔfɪt] n profeta m/f; **~ic** [prə'fetɪk] a profético.

proportion [prə'pɔːʃən] n proporción f; (share) parte f, porción f; **~al** a proporcional; **~ate** a proporcionado.

proposal [prə'pəʊzl] n propuesta; (offer) oferta; (plan) proyecto; (of marriage) declaración f; (suggestion) sugerencia.

propose [prə'pəʊz] vt proponer; (offer) ofrecer // vi declararse; **to ~ to do** proponerse hacer.

proposition [prɔpə'zɪʃən] n propuesta, proposición f.

proprietor [prə'praɪətə*] n propietario, dueño.

propulsion [prə'pʌlʃən] n propulsión f.

pro rata [prəʊ'rɑːtə] ad a prorrateo.

prosaic [prəʊ'zeɪɪk] a prosaico.

prose [prəʊz] n prosa.

prosecute ['prɔsɪkjuːt] vt (LAW) procesar; **prosecution** [-'kjuːʃən] n procesa, causa; (accusing side) parte f actora; **prosecutor** n acusador/a m/f; (also: **public prosecutor**) fiscal m.

prospect ['prɔspekt] n (view) vista; (chance) posibilidad f; (outlook) perspectiva; (hope) esperanza f // (vb: [prə'spekt]) vt explorar // vi buscar; **~s** npl (for work etc) perspectivas fpl; **~ing** n prospección f; **~ive** a (possible) probable, esperado; (certain) futuro; (heir) presunto; (legislation) en perspectiva; **~or** n explorador/a m/f.

prospectus [prə'spektəs] n prospecto.

prosper ['prɔspə*] vi prosperar; **~ity** [-'sperɪtɪ] n prosperidad f; **~ous** a próspero.

prostitute ['prɔstɪtjuːt] n prostituta.

prostrate ['prɔstreɪt] a postrado; (fig) abatido.

protagonist [prə'tægənɪst] n protagonista m/f.

protect [prə'tekt] vt proteger; **~ion** n protección f; **~ive** a protector(a); **~or** n protector/a m/f.

protégé ['prəʊteʒeɪ] n protegido.

protein ['prəʊtiːn] n proteína.

protest ['prəʊtest] n protesta // (vb: [prə'test]) vi protestar // vt (affirm) afirmar, declarar.

Protestant ['prɔtɪstənt] a, n protestante m/f.

protocol ['prəʊtəkɔl] n protocolo.

prototype ['prəʊtətaɪp] n prototipo.

protracted [prə'træktɪd] a prolongado.

protrude [prə'tru:d] *vi* salir fuera, sobresalir.

proud [praud] *a* orgulloso; (*pej*) soberbio, altanero; (*imposing*) imponente.

prove [pru:v] *vt* probar; (*verify*) comprobar; (*show*) demostrar // *vi*: **to ~ correct** resultar correcto; **to ~ o.s.** ponerse a prueba.

proverb ['prɔvə:b] *n* refrán *m*, **~ial** [prə'və:biəl] *a* proverbial.

provide [prə'vaid] *vt* proporcionar, dar; **to ~ sb with sth** proveer a uno de algo; **to ~ for** *vt* (*person*) mantener a; (*emergency*) prevenir; **~d (that)** *conj* con tal que, siempre que.

providing [prə'vaidiŋ] *conj* a condición de que, siempre que.

province ['prɔvins] *n* provincia; (*fig*) esfera; **provincial** [prə'vinʃəl] *a* de provincia; (*pej*) provinciano.

provision [prə'viʒən] *n* (*gen*) provisión *f*; (*supply*) suministro; (*supplying*) abastecimiento; **~s** *npl* (*food*) comestibles *mpl*; **~al** *a* provisional; (*temporary*) interino.

proviso [prə'vaizəu] *n* condición *f*, estipulación *f*.

provocation [prɔvə'keiʃən] *n* provocación *f*.

provocative [prə'vɔkətiv] *a* provocativo; (*stimulating*) sugestivo.

provoke [prə'vəuk] *vt* (*arouse*) provocar, incitar; (*cause*) causar, producir; (*anger*) irritar.

prow [prau] *n* proa.

prowess ['prauis] *n* (*skill*) destreza, habilidad *f*; (*courage*) valor *m*.

prowl [praul] *vi* (*also*: **~ about, ~ around**) rondar // *n*: **on the ~** de ronda; **~er** *n* rondador/a *m/f*; (*thief*) ladrón/ona *m/f*.

proximity [prɔk'simiti] *n* proximidad *f*.

proxy ['prɔksi] *n* poder *m*; (*person*) apoderado/a; **by ~** por poder *o* poderes.

prudence ['pru:dns] *n* prudencia; **prudent** [-ənt] *a* prudente.

prudish ['pru:diʃ] *a* gazmoño.

prune [pru:n] *n* ciruela pasa // *vt* podar.

pry [prai] *vi*: **to ~ into** entrometerse en.

psalm [sɑ:m] *n* salmo.

pseudo- [sju:dəu] *pref* seudo...; **~nym** *n* seudónimo.

psychiatric [saiki'ætrik] *a* psiquiátrico; **psychiatrist** [-'kaiətrist] *n* psiquiatra *m/f*; **psychiatry** ['kaiətri] *n* psiquiatría.

psychic ['saikik] *a* (*also*: **~al**) psíquico // *n* medium *m/f*.

psychoanalyse [saikəu'ænəlaiz] *vt* psicoanalizar; **psychoanalysis** [-kəuə'nælisis] *n* psicoanálisis *m inv*; **psychoanalyst** [-'ænəlist] *n* psicoanalista *m/f*.

psychological [saikə'lɔdʒikl] *a* psicológico.

psychologist [sai'kɔlədʒist] *n* psicólogo; **psychology** [-dʒi] *n* psicología.

psychopath ['saikəupæθ] *n* psicópata *m/f*.

psychosomatic ['saikəusə'mætik] *a* psicosomático.

psychotic [sai'kɔtik] *a, n* psicótico.

pub [pʌb] *n abbr of* **public house** *pub m*, taberna.

puberty ['pju:bəti] *n* pubertad *f*.

public ['pʌblik] *a, n* público.

publican ['pʌblikən] *n* tabernero.

publication [pʌbli'keiʃən] *n* publicación *f*.

public: ~ convenience *n* aseos *mpl* públicos; **~ house** *n* bar *m*, pub *m*.

publicity [pʌb'lisiti] *n* publicidad *f*.

publicly ['pʌblikli] *ad* públicamente, en público.

public: ~ opinion *n* opinión *f* pública; **~ relations** *n* relaciones *fpl* públicas; **~ school** *n* (*Brit*) escuela privada; **~-spirited** *a* de buen ciudadano.

publish ['pʌbliʃ] *vt* publicar; **~er** *n* editor/a *m/f*; **~ing** *n* (*industry*) la industria editorial.

puce [pju:s] *a* de color pardo rojizo.

pucker ['pʌkə*] *vt* (*pleat*) arrugar; (*brow etc*) fruncir.

pudding ['pudiŋ] *n* pudín *m*; (*sweet*) postre *m*; **black ~** morcilla.

puddle ['pʌdl] *n* charco.

puff [pʌf] *n* soplo; (*from mouth*) bocanada; (*sound*) resoplido; (*also*: **powder ~**) borla // *vt*: **to ~ one's pipe** chupar la pipa // *vi* (*gen*) soplar; (*pant*) jadear; **to ~ out smoke** echar humo; **to ~ up** *vi* hinchar, inflar; **~ed** *a* (*col*: *out of breath*) sin aliento.

puffin ['pʌfin] *n* frailecillo.

puffy ['pʌfi] *a* hinchado.

pull [pul] *n* (*tug*): **to give sth a ~** dar un tirón a algo; (*fig*: *advantage*) ventaja; (: *influence*) influencia // *vt* tirar de; (*tug*) jalar; (*muscle*) torcerse; (*haul*) tirar, arrastrar // *vi* tirar, dar un tirón; **to ~ a face** hacer muecas; **to ~ to pieces** hacer pedazos; **to ~ one's punches** no emplear toda la fuerza; **to ~ one's weight** hacer su parte // **to ~ o.s. together** serenarse; **to ~ sb's leg** tomarle el pelo a uno; **to ~ apart** *vt* (*break*) romper (en dos); **to ~ down** *vt* (*house*) derribar; **to ~ in** *vi* (*AUT*: *at the kerb*) parar (junto a la acera); (*RAIL*) llegar (al andén); **to ~ off** *vt* (*deal etc*) cerrar, concluir con éxito; **to ~ out** *vi* irse, marcharse; (*AUT*: *from kerb*) salir // *vt* sacar, arrancar; **to ~ through** *vi* salir (de un apuro); (*MED*) recobrar la salud; **to ~ up** *vi* (*stop*) parar // *vt* (*uproot*) arrancar, desarraigar; (*stop*) parar.

pulley ['puli] *n* polea.

pullover ['puləuvə*] *n* jersey *m*.

pulp [pʌlp] *n* (*of fruit*) pulpa; (*for paper*) pasta.

pulpit ['pulpit] *n* púlpito.

pulsate [pʌl'seit] *vi* pulsar, latir.

pulse [pʌls] *n* (*ANAT*) pulso; (*of music, engine*) pulsación *f*; (*BOT*) legumbre *f*.

pulverize ['pʌlvəraiz] *vt* pulverizar; (*fig*) hacer polvo.

puma ['pju:mə] n puma.

pummel ['pʌml] vt dar de puñetazos.

pump [pʌmp] n bomba; (shoe) zapato de tenis // vt sacar con una bomba; (fig: col) sonsacar; **to ~ up** vt inflar.

pumpkin ['pʌmpkɪn] n calabaza.

pun [pʌn] n juego de palabras.

punch [pʌntʃ] n (blow) golpe m, puñetazo; (tool) punzón m; (for tickets) taladro; (drink) ponche m // vt (hit): **to ~ sb/sth** dar un puñetazo o golpear a uno/algo; (make a hole in) punzar; **~card** n tarjeta perforada; **~line** n palabras que rematan un chiste; **~up** n (col) riña.

punctual ['pʌŋktjuəl] a puntual; **~ity** [-'ælɪtɪ] n puntualidad f.

punctuate ['pʌŋktjueɪt] vt interrumpir; **punctuation** [-'eɪʃən] n puntuación f.

puncture ['pʌŋktʃə*] n pinchazo // vt pinchar.

pundit ['pʌndɪt] n sabio.

pungent ['pʌndʒənt] a acre.

punish ['pʌnɪʃ] vt castigar; **~ment** n castigo.

punt [pʌnt] n (boat) batea.

punter ['pʌntə*] n (gambler) jugador/a m/f.

puny ['pju:nɪ] a débil.

pup [pʌp] n cachorro.

pupil ['pju:pl] n alumno/a.

puppet ['pʌpɪt] n títere m.

puppy ['pʌpɪ] n cachorro, perrito.

purchase ['pə:tʃɪs] n compra; (grip) pie m firme // vt comprar; **purchaser** n comprador/a m/f.

pure [pjuə*] a puro.

purée ['pjuəreɪ] n puré m.

purge [pə:dʒ] n (MED) purgante m; (POL) purga // vt purgar.

purification [pjuərɪfɪ'keɪʃən] n purificación f, depuración f; **purify** ['pjuərɪfaɪ] vt purificar, depurar.

purist ['pjuərɪst] n purista m/f.

puritan ['pjuərɪtən] n puritano/a; **~ical** [-'tænɪkl] a puritano.

purity ['pjuərɪtɪ] n pureza.

purl [pə:l] n punto del revés.

purple ['pə:pl] a purpúreo, (bruise) morado.

purport [pə:'pɔ:t] vi: **to ~ to be/do** dar a entender que es/hace.

purpose ['pə:pəs] n propósito; **on ~** a propósito, adrede; **~ful** a resuelto, determinado.

purr [pə:*] n ronroneo // vi ronronear.

purse [pə:s] n monedero; (bag) bolsa // vt fruncir.

purser ['pə:sə*] n (NAUT) contador m de navío.

pursue [pə'sju:] vt seguir, perseguir; (profession) ejercer; **pursuer** n perseguidor/a m/f.

pursuit [pə'sju:t] n (chase) caza; (persecution) persecución f; (occupation) carrera; (pastime) pasatiempo.

purveyor [pə'veɪə*] n proveedor/a m/f.

pus [pʌs] n pus m.

push [puʃ] n (gen) empuje m; (shove) empujón m; (attack) ataque m; (advance) avance m // vt empujar; (button) apretar; (promote) promover; (thrust): **to ~ sth (into)** meter algo a la fuerza (en) // vi empujar; (fig) hacer esfuerzos; **to ~ aside** vt apartar con la mano; **to ~ off** vi (col) largarse; **to ~ on** vi (continue) seguir adelante; **to ~ through** vt (measure) despachar; **to ~ up** vt (total, prices) hacer subir; **~chair** n sillita de ruedas; **~ing** a emprendedor(a), enérgico; **~over** n (col): **it's a ~over** está tirado; **~y a** (pej) agresivo.

puss [pus], **pussy(-cat)** ['pusɪ(kæt)] n minino.

put [put], pt, pp **put** vt (place) poner, colocar; (~ into) meter; (say) declarar, expresar; (a question) hacer; (estimate) calcular; **to ~ about** vi (NAUT) virar // vt (rumour) diseminar; **to ~ across** vt (ideas etc) comunicar; **to ~ away** vt (store) guardar; **to ~ back** vt (replace) devolver a su lugar; (postpone) posponer; **to ~ by** vt (money) guardar; **to ~ down** vt (on ground) poner en el suelo; (animal) sacrificar; (in writing) apuntar; (suppress: revolt etc) sofocar; (attribute) atribuir; **to ~ forward** vt (ideas) presentar, proponer; (date) adelantar; **to ~ in** vt (application, complaint) presentar; **to ~ off** vt (postpone) aplazar; (discourage) desanimar; **to ~ on** vt (clothes, lipstick etc) ponerse; (light etc) encender; (play etc) presentar; (weight) ganar; (brake) echar; (attitude) adoptar postura de; **to ~ out** vt (fire, light) apagar; (one's hand) alargar; (news, rumour) sacar a luz, diseminar; (tongue etc) sacar; (person: inconvenience) molestar, fastidiar; **to ~ up** vt (raise) levantar, alzar; (hang) colgar; (build) construir; (increase) aumentar; (accommodate) alojar; **to ~ up with** vt fus aguantar.

putrid ['pju:trɪd] a podrido.

putt [pʌt] vt golpear con poca fuerza // n put m, golpe m corto; **~er** n (GOLF) putter m; **~ing green** n campo de golf en miniatura.

putty ['pʌtɪ] n masilla.

puzzle ['pʌzl] n (riddle) acertijo; (jigsaw) rompecabezas m inv; (crossword) crucigrama m; (mystery) misterio, problema m // vt dejar perplejo, confundir // vi devanarse los sesos; **puzzling** a misterioso, enigmático.

pygmy ['pɪgmɪ] n pigmeo.

pyjamas [pɪ'dʒa:məz] npl pijama m.

pylon ['paɪlən] n pilón m, poste m.

pyramid ['pɪrəmɪd] n pirámide m.

python ['paɪθən] n pitón m.

Q

quack [kwæk] n (of duck) graznido; (pej: doctor) curandero // vi graznar.

quad [kwɔd] abbr of **quadrangle; quadruplet.**

quadrangle ['kwɔdræŋgl] n (courtyard: abbr: quad) patio.

quadruple [kwɔ'drupl] a cuádruple // n cuádruplo // vt, vi cuadruplicar.

quadruplets [kwɔ'dru:plɪts] npl cuatrillizos mpl.

quagmire ['kwægmaɪə*] n lodazal m, cenegal m.

quail [kweɪl] n (bird) codorniz f // vi amedrentarse.

quaint [kweɪnt] a curioso; (picturesque) pintoresco.

quake [kweɪk] vi temblar // n abbr of **earthquake.**

Quaker ['kweɪkə*] n cuáquero/a.

qualification [kwɔlɪfɪ'keɪʃən] n (reservation) reserva; (modification) modificación f; (act) calificación f; (degree) título; **qualified** ['kwɔlɪfaɪd] a (trained) cualificado; (fit) apto, competente; (limited) limitado; (professionally) con título.

qualify ['kwɔlɪfaɪ] vt calificar; (capacitate) capacitar; (modify) modificar; (limit) moderar // vi (SPORT) clasificarse; **to ~ (as)** calificarse (de), graduarse (en); **to ~ (for)** reunir los requisitos (para).

quality ['kwɔlɪtɪ] n calidad f; (moral) cualidad f.

qualm [kwɑ:m] n escrúpulo.

quandary ['kwɔndrɪ] n: **to be in a ~** estar en un dilema.

quantity ['kwɔntɪtɪ] n cantidad f.

quarantine ['kwɔrntiːn] n cuarentena.

quarrel ['kwɔrl] n (argument) riña; (fight) pelea // vi reñir; pelearse; **~some** a pendenciero.

quarry ['kwɔrɪ] n (for stone) cantera; (animal) presa.

quart [kwɔːt] n cuarto de galón = 1.136 litros.

quarter ['kwɔːtə*] n cuarto, cuarta parte f; (of year) trimestre m; (district) barrio // vt dividir en cuartos; (MIL: lodge) alojar; **~s** npl (barracks) cuartel m; (living ~s) alojamiento sg; **a ~ of an hour** un cuarto de hora; **~ final** n cuarto de final; **~ly** a trimestral // ad cada 3 meses, trimestralmente; **~master** n (MIL) comisario, intendente m militar.

quartet(te) [kwɔː'tet] n cuarteto.

quartz [kwɔːts] n cuarzo.

quash [kwɔʃ] vt (verdict) anular.

quasi- ['kweɪzaɪ] pref cuasi.

quaver ['kweɪvə*] n (MUS) corchea // vi temblar.

quay [kiː] n (also: ~side) muelle m.

queasy ['kwiːzɪ] a (sickly) delicado.

queen [kwiːn] n (gen) reina; (CARDS etc)

dama; **~ mother** n reina madre.

queer [kwɪə*] a (odd) raro, extraño; (suspect) sospechoso // n (col) maricón m.

quell [kwel] vt calmar; (put down) sofocar.

quench [kwentʃ] vt apagar.

query ['kwɪərɪ] n (question) pregunta; (doubt) duda; (fig) interrogante f // vt preguntar; poner en duda.

quest [kwest] n busca, búsqueda.

question ['kwestʃən] n pregunta; (matter) asunto, cuestión f // vt (gen) preguntar; (doubt) dudar de; (interrogate) interrogar, hacer preguntas a; **beyond ~** fuera de toda duda; **out of the ~** imposible, ni hablar; **~able** a discutible; (doubtful) dudoso; **~ mark** n punto de interrogación; **~naire** [-'nɛə*] n cuestionario.

queue [kjuː] n cola // vi hacer cola.

quibble ['kwɪbl] vi sutilizar.

quick [kwɪk] a rápido; (temper) vivo; (agile) ágil; (mind) listo; (eye) agudo; (ear) fino; **be ~!** ¡date prisa!; **~en** vt apresurar // vi apresurarse, darse prisa; **~ly** ad rápidamente, de prisa; **~ness** n rapidez f; agilidad f; (liveliness) viveza; **~sand** n arenas fpl movedizas; **~step** n (dance) fox-trot m, quickstep m; **~-witted** a perspicaz.

quid [kwɪd] n, pl inv (Brit: col) libra.

quiet ['kwaɪət] a tranquilo; (silent) callado; (ceremony) discreto // n silencio, tranquilidad f; **keep ~!** ¡cállate!, ¡silencio!; **~en** (also: **~en down**) vi (grow calm) calmarse; (grow silent) callarse // vt calmar; hacer callar; **~ly** ad tranquilamente; (silently) silenciosamente; **~ness** n (silence) silencio; (calm) tranquilidad f.

quilt [kwɪlt] n edredón m; (continental) **~** n edredón m.

quin [kwɪn] abbr of **quintuplet.**

quinine [kwɪ'niːn] n quinina.

quintet(te) [kwɪn'tet] n quinteto.

quintuplets [kwɪn'tjuːplɪts] npl quintillizos mpl.

quip [kwɪp] n pulla.

quirk [kwɜːk] n peculiaridad f.

quit [kwɪt], pt, pp **quit** or **quitted** vt dejar, abandonar; (premises) desocupar // vi (give up) retirarse; (go away) irse; (resign) dimitir; (stop work) abandonar (una empresa).

quite [kwaɪt] ad (rather) bastante; (entirely) completamente; **~ a few of them** un buen número de ellos; **~ (so)!** ¡así es!, ¡exactamente!

quits [kwɪts] a: **~ (with)** en paz (con).

quiver ['kwɪvə*] vi estremecerse // n (for arrows) carcaj m.

quiz [kwɪz] n (game) concurso; (questioning) interrogatorio // vt interrogar; **~zical** a burlón(ona).

quoits [kwɔɪts] npl juego de aros.

quorum ['kwɔːrəm] n quórum m.

quota ['kwəʊtə] n cuota.

quotation [kwəʊ'teɪʃən] n cita; (estimate)

presupuesto; ~ **marks** *npl* comillas *fpl*.
quote [kwəut] *n* cita // *vt* (*sentence*) citar; (*price*) fijar // *vi*: **to ~ from** citar de.
quotient ['kwəuʃənt] *n* cociente *m*.

R

rabbi ['ræbaɪ] *n* rabino.
rabbit ['ræbɪt] *n* conejo; ~ **hole** *n* hura (de conejos); ~ **hutch** *n* conejera.
rabble ['ræbl] *n* (*pej*) chusma, populacho.
rabies ['reɪbiːz] *n* rabia.
RAC *n abbr of* **Royal Automobile Club**.
raccoon [rə'kuːn] *n* mapache *m*.
race [reɪs] *n* (*gen*) carrera; (*species*) raza, estirpe *f* // *vt* (*horse*) presentar (en carrera); (*engine*) acelerar // *vi* (*compete*) competir; (*run*) correr; (*pulse*) latir a ritmo acelerado; ~ **course** *n* hipódromo; ~ **horse** *n* caballo de carreras; ~ **track** *n* hipódromo; (*for cars*) autódromo.
racial ['reɪʃl] *a* racial; ~ **ism** *n* racismo; ~ **ist** *a*, *n* racista *m/f*.
racing ['reɪsɪŋ] *n* carreras *fpl*; ~ **car** *n* coche *m* de carreras; ~ **driver** *n* corredor/a *m/f* de coches.
racist ['reɪsɪst] *a*, *n* (*pej*) racista *m/f*.
rack [ræk] *n* (*also*: **luggage ~**) rejilla; (*shelf*) estante *m*; (*also*: **roof ~**) baca, portaequipajes *m inv*; (*clothes ~*) percha // *vt* (*cause pain to*) atormentar.
racket ['rækɪt] *n* (*for tennis*) raqueta; (*noise*) ruido, estrépito; (*swindle*) estafa, timo.
racoon [rə'kuːn] *n* = **raccoon**.
racquet ['rækɪt] *n* raqueta.
racy ['reɪsɪ] *a* picante, salado.
radar ['reɪdɑ:*] *n* radar *m*.
radiance ['reɪdɪəns] *n* brillantez *f*, resplandor *m*; **radiant** [-ənt] *a* brillante, resplandeciente.
radiate ['reɪdɪeɪt] *vt* (*heat*) radiar, irradiar // *vi* (*lines*) extenderse.
radiation [reɪdɪ'eɪʃən] *n* radiación *f*.
radiator ['reɪdɪeɪtə*] *n* radiador *m*; ~ **cap** *n* tapón *m* de radiador.
radical ['rædɪkl] *a* radical.
radio ['reɪdɪəu] *n* radio *f*; **on the ~** por radio; ~ **station** *n* emisora.
radio... [reɪdɪəu] *pref*: ~ **active** *a* radioactivo; ~ **activity** *n* radioactividad *f*; ~ **controlled** *a* teledirigido; ~ **graphy** [-'ɔgrəfɪ] *n* radiografía; ~ **logy** [-'ɔlədʒɪ] *n* radiología; ~ **telephone** *n* radioteléfono; ~ **therapy** *n* radioterapia.
radish ['rædɪʃ] *n* rábano.
radius ['reɪdɪəs], *pl* **radii** [-ɪaɪ] *n* radio.
raffia ['ræfɪə] *n* rafia.
raffle ['ræfl] *n* rifa, sorteo // *vt* rifar.
raft [rɑ:ft] *n* (*also*: **life ~**) balsa.
rafter ['rɑ:ftə*] *n* viga.
rag [ræg] *n* (*piece of cloth*) trapo; (*torn cloth*) harapo; (*pej*: *newspaper*) periodicucho; (*for charity*) actividades estudiantiles benéficas // *vt* tomar el pelo a; ~ **s** *npl* harapos *mpl*; ~ **-and-bone man**

n trapero; ~ **doll** *n* muñeca de trapo.
rage [reɪdʒ] *n* (*fury*) rabia, furor *m*; (*fashion*) boga // *vi* (*person*) rabiar, estar furioso; (*storm*) bramar.
ragged ['rægɪd] *a* (*edge*) desigual, mellado; (*cuff*) roto; (*appearance*) andrajoso, harapiento; (*coastline*) accidentado.
raid [reɪd] *n* (*MIL*) incursión *f*; (*criminal*) asalto; (*attack*) ataque *m*; (*by police*) redada // *vt* invadir, atacar; asaltar; ~ **er** *n* invasor/a *m/f*; (*criminal*) asaltante *m/f*.
rail [reɪl] *n* (*on stair*) barandilla, pasamanos *m inv*; (*on bridge, balcony*) pretil *m*; (*of ship*) borda; (*for train*) riel *m*, carril *m*; ~ **s** *npl* vía *sg*; **by ~** por ferrocarril; ~ **ing(s)** *n(pl)* verja *sg*, enrejado *sg*; ~ **road** (*US*), ~ **way** *n* ferrocarril *m*, vía férrea; ~ **wayman** *n* ferroviario; ~ **way station** *n* estación *f* de ferrocarril.
rain [reɪn] *n* lluvia // *vi* llover; **in the ~** bajo la lluvia; **it's ~ ing** llueve, está lloviendo; ~ **bow** *n* arco iris; ~ **coat** *n* impermeable *m*; ~ **drop** *n* gota de lluvia; ~ **fall** *n* lluvia; ~ **y** *a* lluvioso.
raise [reɪz] *n* aumento // *vt* (*lift*) levantar; (*build*) erigir, edificar; (*increase*) aumentar; (*doubts*) suscitar; (*a question*) plantear; (*cattle, family*) criar; (*crop*) cultivar; (*army*) reclutar; (*funds*) reunir; (*loan*) obtener; **to ~ one's voice** alzar la voz.
raisin ['reɪzn] *n* paso de Corinto.
rake [reɪk] *n* (*tool*) rastrillo; (*person*) libertino // *vt* (*garden*) rastrillar; (*fire*) hurgar; (*with machine gun*) barrer.
rakish ['reɪkɪʃ] *a* (*suave*) gallardo; **at a ~ angle** echado al lado.
rally ['rælɪ] *n* (*POL etc*) reunión *f*, mitin *m*; (*AUT*) rallye *m*; (*TENNIS*) peloteo // *vt* reunir; (*encourage*) reanimar // *vi* reunirse; (*sick person, Stock Exchange*) recuperarse; **to ~ round** *vt fus* (*fig*) dar apoyo a.
ram [ræm] *n* carnero; (*TECH*) pisón *m* // *vt* (*crash into*) dar contra, chocar con; (*tread down*) apisonar.
ramble ['ræmbl] *n* caminata, excursión *f* en el campo // *vi* (*pej*: *also*: ~ **on**) divagar; **rambler** *n* excursionista *m/f*; (*BOT*) trepadora; **rambling** *a* (*speech*) divagador(a); (*BOT*) trepador(a) // *n* excursionismo.
ramp [ræmp] *n* rampa.
rampage [ræm'peɪdʒ] *n*: **to be on the ~** desbocarse // *vi*: **they went rampaging through the town** corrieron como locos por la ciudad.
rampant ['ræmpənt] *a* (*disease etc*) violento.
rampart ['ræmpɑ:t] *n* terraplén *m*; (*wall*) muralla.
ramshackle ['ræmʃækl] *a* destartalado.
ran [ræn] *pt of* **run**.
ranch [rɑ:ntʃ] *n* hacienda, estancia; ~ **er** *n* ganadero.

rancid ['rænsɪd] a rancio.

rancour, rancor (US) ['ræŋkə*] n rencor m.

random ['rændəm] a fortuito, sin orden // n: **at** ~ al azar.

randy ['rændɪ] a (col) cachondo.

rang [ræŋ] pt of **ring**.

range [reɪndʒ] n (of mountains) cadena, cordillera; (of missile) alcance m; (of voice) extensión f; (series) serie f; (of products) surtido; (MIL: also: **shooting** ~) campo de tiro; (also: **kitchen** ~) fogón m // vt (place) colocar; (arrange) arreglar // vi: **to** ~ **over** (wander) recorrer; (extend) extenderse por; **to** ~ **from ... to...** oscilar entre ... y...; **ranger** n guardabosques m inv.

rank [ræŋk] n (row) fila; (MIL) rango; (status) categoría; (also: **taxi** ~) parada // vi: **to** ~ **among** figurar entre // a (stinking) fétido, rancio; **the** ~ **and file** (fig) la base.

rankle ['ræŋkl] vi (insult) doler.

ransack ['rænsæk] vt (search) registrar, (plunder) saquear.

ransom ['rænsəm] n rescate m; **to hold sb to** ~ (fig) poner a uno entre la espada y la pared.

rant [rænt] vi divagar, desvariar; ~**ing** n lenguaje m declamatorio.

rap [ræp] n golpecito, golpe m seco // vt tocar, dar un golpecito en.

rape [reɪp] n violación f // vt violar.

rapid ['ræpɪd] a rápido; ~**s** npl (GEO) rápidos mpl; ~**ity** [rə'pɪdɪtɪ] n rapidez f.

rapist ['reɪpɪst] n violador m.

rapport [ræ'pɔː*] n armonía, relación amistosa.

rapture ['ræptʃə*] n éxtasis m, rapto; **rapturous** a extático; (applause) entusiasta.

rare [rɛə*] a raro, poco común; (CULIN: steak) poco hecho.

rarely ['rɛəlɪ] ad rara vez.

rarity ['rɛərɪtɪ] n rareza.

rascal ['rɑːskl] n pillo, pícaro.

rash [ræʃ] a imprudente, precipitado // n (MED) salpullido, erupción f (cutánea).

rasher ['ræʃə*] n lonja.

rasp [rɑːsp] n (tool) escofina.

raspberry ['rɑːzbərɪ] n frambuesa; ~ **bush** n frambueso.

rasping ['rɑːspɪŋ] a: **a** ~ **noise** un ruido áspero.

rat [ræt] n rata.

ratchet ['rætʃɪt] n (TECH) trinquete m.

rate [reɪt] n (ratio) razón f; (percentage) tanto por ciento; (price) precio; (: of hotel) tarifa; (of interest) tipo; (speed) velocidad f // vt (value) tasar; (estimate) estimar: **to** ~ **as** ser considerado como; ~**s** npl (Brit) impuesto sg municipal; (fees) tarifa sg; ~**able value** n valor m impuesto; ~**payer** n contribuyente m/f.

rather ['rɑːðə*] ad antes, más bien; (in speech) mejor dicho; **it's** ~ **expensive** es algo caro; (too much) es demasiado caro;

there's ~ **a lot** hay bastante; **I would** or **I'd** ~ **go** preferiría ir.

ratify ['rætɪfaɪ] vt ratificar.

rating ['reɪtɪŋ] n (valuation) tasación f; (value) valor m; (standing) posición f; (NAUT: category) clase f; (: sailor) marinero.

ratio ['reɪʃɪəʊ] n razón f; **in the** ~ **of 100 to 1** a razón de 100 a 1.

ration ['ræʃən] n ración f; ~**s** npl víveres mpl // vt racionar.

rational ['ræʃənl] a racional; (solution, reasoning) lógico, razonable; (person) cuerdo, sensato; **rationale** [-'nɑːl] n razón f fundamental; ~**ise** vt organizar lógicamente, racionalizar; ~**ly** ad racionalmente; (logically) lógicamente.

rationing ['ræʃənɪŋ] n racionamiento.

rattle ['rætl] n golpeteo; (of train etc) traqueteo; (of hail) tamborileo; (object: of baby) sonaja, sonajera; (: of sports fan) matraca; (of snake) cascabel m // vi sonar, golpear; traquetear; tamborilear; (small objects) castañetear // vt agitar, sacudir; ~**snake** n serpiente f de cascabel.

raucous ['rɔːkəs] a estridente, ronco.

ravage ['rævɪdʒ] vt hacer estragos, destrozar; ~**s** npl estragos mpl.

rave [reɪv] vi (in anger) encolerizarse; (with enthusiasm) entusiasmarse; (MED) delirar, desvariar.

raven ['reɪvən] n cuervo.

ravenous ['rævənəs] a hambriento, famélico.

ravine [rə'vɪn] n barranco.

raving ['reɪvɪŋ] a: ~ **lunatic** loco de atar.

ravioli [rævɪ'əʊlɪ] n raviolis mpl.

ravish ['rævɪʃ] vt encantar; ~**ing** a encantador(a).

raw [rɔː] a (uncooked) crudo; (not processed) bruto; (sore) vivo; (inexperienced) novato, inexperto; ~ **material** n materia prima.

ray [reɪ] n rayo; ~ **of hope** (rayo de) esperanza.

rayon ['reɪən] n rayón m.

raze [reɪz] vt arrasar.

razor ['reɪzə*] n (open) navaja (safety ~) máquina de afeitar; ~ **blade** n hoja de afeitar.

Rd abbr of **road**.

re [riː] prep con referencia a.

reach [riːtʃ] n alcance m; (BOXING) envergadura; (of river etc) extensión f entre dos recodos // vt alcanzar, llegar a; (achieve) lograr; (stretch out) alargar, extender // vi alcanzar, extenderse; **within** ~ (object) al alcance (de la mano); **out of** ~ fuera del alcance; **to** ~ **out for sth** alargar o tender la mano para tomar algo.

react [riː'ækt] vi reaccionar; ~**ion** [-'ækʃən] n reacción f; ~**ionary** [-'ækʃənrɪ] a, n reaccionario/a.

reactor [riː'æktə*] n reactor m.

read [riːd], pt, pp **read** [rɛd] vi leer // vt

leer; (*understand*) entender; (*study*) estudiar; **to ~ out** *vt* leer en alta voz; **~able** *a* (*writing*) legible; (*book*) que merece leerse; **~er** *n* lector/a *m/f*; (*book*) libro de lecturas; (*at university*) profesor/a *m/f*; **~ership** *n* (*of paper etc*) número de lectores.

readily ['redili] *ad* (*willingly*) de buena gana; (*easily*) fácilmente; (*quickly*) en seguida.

readiness ['redinis] *n* buena voluntad; (*preparedness*) preparación *f*; **in ~** (*prepared*) listo, preparado.

reading ['ri:diŋ] *n* lectura; (*understanding*) comprensión *f*; (*on instrument*) indicación *f*.

readjust [ri:ə'dʒʌst] *vt* reajustar // *vi* (*person*): **to ~ to** reorientarse a.

ready ['redi] *a* listo, preparado; (*willing*) dispuesto; (*available*) disponible // *ad*: **~-cooked** listo para comer // *n*: **at the ~** (*MIL*) listo para tirar; **~-made** *a* confeccionado; **~ reckoner** *n* libro de cálculos hechos.

reaffirm [ri:ə'fə:m] *vt* reafirmar.

real [riəl] *a* verdadero, auténtico; **in ~ terms** en términos reales; **~ estate** *n* bienes *mpl* raíces; **~ism** *n* (*also ART*) realismo; **~ist** *n* realista *m/f*; **~istic** [-'listik] *a* realista.

reality [ri:'æliti] *n* realidad *f*; **in ~** en realidad.

realization [riəlai'zeiʃən] *n* comprensión *f*; (*COMM*) realización *f*.

realize ['riəlaiz] *vt* (*understand*) darse cuenta de; (*a project, COMM: asset*) realizar.

really ['riəli] *ad* verdaderamente, realmente; **~?** ¿de veras?

realm [relm] *n* reino; (*fig*) esfera.

reap [ri:p] *vt* segar; (*fig*) cosechar, recoger; **~er** *n* segadora.

reappear [ri:ə'piə*] *vi* reaparecer; **~ance** *n* reaparición *f*.

reapply [ri:ə'plai] *vi*: **to ~ for** aplicar de nuevo.

rear [riə*] *a* trasero // *n* parte *f* trasera // *vt* (*cattle, family*) criar // *vi* (*also*: **~ up**) (*animal*) encabritarse; **~-engined** *a* (*AUT*) con motor trasero; **~guard** *n* retaguardia.

rearm [ri:'a:m] *vt, vi* rearmar; **~ament** *n* rearme *m*.

rearrange [ri:ə'reindʒ] *vt* ordenar o arreglar de nuevo.

rear-view ['riəvju:] *a*: **~ mirror** (*AUT*) espejo retrovisor.

reason ['ri:zn] *n* (*gen*) razón *f*; (*cause*) motivo, causa; (*sense*) sensatez *f* // *vi*: **to ~ with sb** alegar razones para convencer a uno; **it stands to ~ that** es lógico que; **~able** *a* razonable; (*sensible*) sensato; **~ably** *ad* razonablemente; **~ed** *a* (*argument*) razonado; **~ing** *n* razonamiento, argumentos *mpl*.

reassemble [ri:ə'sembl] *vt* (*machine*) montar de nuevo // *vi* reunirse de nuevo.

reassure [ri:ə'ʃuə*] *vt* tranquilizar,

alentar; **to ~ sb of** tranquilizar a uno diciendo que; **reassuring** *a* alentador(a).

rebate ['ri:beit] *n* (*on product*) rebaja; (*on tax etc*) descuento.

rebel ['rebl] *n* rebelde *m/f* // *vi* [ri'bel] rebelarse, sublevarse; **~lion** *n* rebelión *f*, sublevación *f*; **~lious** *a* rebelde; (*child*) revoltoso.

rebirth [ri:'bə:θ] *n* renacimiento.

rebound [ri'baund] *vi* (*ball*) rebotar // *n* ['ri:baund] rebote *m*.

rebuff [ri'bʌf] *n* desaire *m*, rechazo // *vt* rechazar.

rebuild [ri:'bild] (*irg: like* **build**) *vt* reconstruir.

rebuke [ri'bju:k] *n* reprimenda // *vt* reprender.

recalcitrant [ri'kælsitrənt] *a* reacio.

recall [ri'kɔ:l] *vt* (*remember*) recordar; (*ambassador etc*) retirar // *n* aviso, llamada.

recant [ri'kænt] *vi* retractarse.

recap ['ri:kæp] *vt, vi* recapitular.

recapture [ri:'kæptʃə*] *vt* (*town*) reconquistar; (*atmosphere*) hacer revivir.

recede [ri'si:d] *vi* retroceder; **receding** *a* (*forehead, chin*) huidizo.

receipt [ri'si:t] *n* (*document*) recibo; (*act of receiving*) recepción *f*; **~s** *npl* (*COMM*) ingresos *mpl*.

receive [ri'si:v] *vt* recibir; (*guest*) acoger; (*wound*) sufrir; **receiver** *n* (*TEL*) auricular *m*; (*of stolen goods*) receptador/a *m/f*; (*COMM*) recibidor/a *m/f*.

recent ['ri:snt] *a* reciente; **~ly** *ad* recién, recientemente.

receptacle [ri'septikl] *n* receptáculo.

reception [ri'sepʃən] *n* (*gen*) recepción *f*; (*welcome*) acogida; **~ desk** *n* recepción *f*; **~ist** *n* recepcionista *m/f*.

receptive [ri'septiv] *a* receptivo.

recess [ri'ses] *n* (*in room*) hueco; (*for bed*) nicho; (*secret place*) escondrijo; (*POL etc: holiday*) vacaciones *fpl*; **~ion** *n* recesión *f*.

recharge [ri:'tʃa:dʒ] *vt* (*battery*) recargar.

recipe ['resipi] *n* receta.

recipient [ri'sipiənt] *n* recibidor/a *m/f*; (*of letter*) destinatario/a.

reciprocal [ri'siprəkl] *a* recíproco.

recital [ri'saitl] *n* recital *m*.

recite [ri'sait] *vt* (*poem*) recitar; (*complaints etc*) enumerar.

reckless ['rekləs] *a* temerario, imprudente; (*speed*) excesivo, peligroso; **~ly** *ad* imprudentemente; de modo peligroso.

reckon ['rekən] *vt* (*count*) contar; (*consider*) considerar; (*think*): **I ~ that... me** parece que...; **~ing** *n* (*calculation*) cálculo; **the day of ~ing** el día del juicio (final).

reclaim [ri'kleim] *vt* (*land*) recuperar; (*from sea*) rescatar; (*demand back*) reclamar; **reclamation** [reklə'meiʃən] *n* recuperación *f*, rescate *m*.

recline [ri'klain] *vi* reclinarse; (*lean*) apoyarse; **reclining** *a* (*seat*) reclinable.

recluse [rɪ'kluːs] n recluso.

recognition [rekəg'nɪʃən] a reconocimiento; **transformed beyond** ~ tan transformado que resulta irreconocible.

recognizable ['rekəgnaɪzəbl] a: ~ (by) reconocible (por).

recognize ['rekəgnaɪz] vt reconocer, conocer; **to** ~ **by/as** reconocer de/por.

recoil [rɪ'kɔɪl] vi (gun) retroceder; (person): **to** ~ **from doing** sth sentir repugnancia por hacer algo.

recollect [rekə'lekt] vt recordar, acordarse de; ~**ion** [-'lekʃən] n recuerdo.

recommend [rekə'mend] vt recomendar; ~**ation** [-'deɪʃən] n recomendación f.

recompense ['rekəmpens] vt recompensar // n recompensa.

reconcile ['rekənsaɪl] vt (two people) reconciliar; (two facts) conciliar; **to** ~ **o.s. to sth** resignarse a algo, conformarse a algo; **reconciliation** [-sɪlɪ'eɪʃən] n reconciliación f.

reconnaissance [rɪ'kɒnɪsns] n (MIL) reconocimiento.

reconnoitre, reconnoiter (US) [rekə'nɔɪtə*] vt, vi (MIL) reconocer.

reconsider [riːkən'sɪdə*] vt repensar.

reconstitute [riː'kɒnstɪtjuːt] vt reconstituir.

reconstruct [riːkən'strʌkt] vt reconstruir; ~**ion** [-kʃən] n reconstrucción f.

record ['rekɔːd] n (MUS) disco; (of meeting etc) relación f; (register) registro, partida; (file) archivo; (also: **police** ~) antecedentes mpl; (written) expediente m; (SPORT) récord m // vt [rɪ'kɔːd] (set down) registrar; (relate) hacer constar; (MUS song etc) grabar; **in** ~ **time** en un tiempo récord; **off the** ~ a no oficial // ad confidencialmente; ~ **card** n (in file) ficha; ~**er** n (MUS) flauta de pico; (TECH) contador m; ~ **holder** n (SPORT) recordman m; ~**ing** n (MUS) grabación f; ~ **player** n tocadiscos m inv.

recount [rɪ'kaunt] vt contar.

re-count ['riːkaunt] n (POL: of votes) segundo escrutinio // n [riː'kaunt] volver a contar.

recoup [rɪ'kuːp] vt: **to** ~ **one's losses** recuperar las pérdidas.

recourse [rɪ'kɔːs] n recurso; **to have** ~ **to** recurrir a.

recover [rɪ'kʌvə*] vt recobrar, recuperar; (rescue) rescatar // vi (from illness) reponerse; (from shock) sobreponerse; ~**y** n recuperación f; rescate m; (MED) mejora.

recreate [riːkrɪ'eɪt] vt recrear.

recreation [rekrɪ'eɪʃən] n recreación f; (play) recreo; ~**al** a de recreo.

recrimination [rɪkrɪmɪ'neɪʃən] n recriminación f.

recruit [rɪ'kruːt] n recluta m/f // vt reclutar; ~**ment** n reclutamiento.

rectangle ['rektæŋgl] n rectángulo; **rectangular** [-'tæŋgjulə*] a rectangular.

rectify ['rektɪfaɪ] vt rectificar.

rector ['rektə*] n (REL) párroco; (SCOL) rector/a m/f; ~**y** n casa del párroco.

recuperate [rɪ'kuːpəreɪt] vi reponerse, restablecerse.

recur [rɪ'kɜː*] vi repetirse; (opportunity) producirse de nuevo; ~**rence** n repetición f; ~**rent** a repetido.

red [red] n rojo // a rojo; **to be in the** ~ deber dinero; **R** ~ **Cross** Cruz f Roja; ~**currant** n grosella; ~**den** vt enrojecer // vi enrojecerse; ~**dish** a (hair) rojizo.

redecorate [riː'dekəreɪt] vt decorar de nuevo; **redecoration** [-reɪʃən] n renovación f.

redeem [rɪ'diːm] vt (gen) redimir; (sth in pawn) desempeñar; (fig, also REL) rescatar; ~**ing** a: ~**ing feature** rasgo bueno o favorable.

redeploy [riːdɪ'plɔɪ] vt (resources) disponer de nuevo.

red: ~**-haired** a pelirrojo; ~**-handed** a: **to be caught** ~**-handed** cogerse con las manos en la masa; ~**head** n pelirrojo/a; ~**-hot** a candente.

redirect [riːdaɪ'rekt] vt (mail) reexpedir.

redness ['rednɪs] n lo rojo; (of hair) rojez f.

redo [riː'duː] (irg: like do) vt rehacer.

redouble [riː'dʌbl] vt: **to** ~ **one's efforts** intensificar los esfuerzos.

redress [rɪ'dres] n reparación f // vt reajustar.

red tape n (fig) trámites mpl, papeleo.

reduce [rɪ'djuːs] vt reducir; (lower) rebajar; '~ **speed now'** (AUT) 'reduzca la velocidad'; **at a** ~**d price** (of goods) a precio rebajado; **reduction** [rɪ'dʌkʃən] n reducción f; (of price) rebaja; (discount) descuento.

redundancy [rɪ'dʌndənsɪ] n desempleo.

redundant [rɪ'dʌndnt] a (worker) parado, sin trabajo; (detail, object) superfluo; **to be made** ~ quedarse sin trabajo.

reed [riːd] n (BOT) junco, caña; (MUS of clarinet etc) lengüeta.

reef [riːf] n (at sea) arrecife m.

reek [riːk] vi: **to** ~ (of) oler o heder a.

reel [riːl] n (gen) carrete m, bobina; (of film) rollo, película // vt (TECH) devanar; (also: ~ **in**) cobrar // vi (sway) tambalear.

re-election [riːɪ'lekʃən] n reelección f.

re-enter [riː'entə*] vt reingresar en; **re-entry** n reingreso.

ref [ref] n (col) abbr of **referee**.

refectory [rɪ'fektərɪ] n refectorio, comedor m.

refer [rɪ'fɜː*] vt (send) remitir; (ascribe) referir a, relacionar con // vi: **to** ~ **to** (allude to) referirse a, aludir a; (apply to) relacionarse con; (consult) remitirse a.

referee [refə'riː] n árbitro; (for job application letter) persona que recomienda a otro // vt arbitrar.

reference ['refrəns] n (mention) referencia; (sending) remisión f; (relevance) relación f; (for job application letter) referencia, carta de recomendación; **with ~ to** con referencia a; (*COMM: in letter*) me remito a; **~ book** *n* libro de consulta.

referendum [rɛfə'rɛndəm], *pl* **-da** [-də] *n* referéndum *m*.

refill [ri:'fɪl] *vt* rellenar // *n* ['ri:fɪl] repuesto, recambio.

refine [rɪ'faɪn] *vt* (*sugar, oil*) refinar; **~d** *a* (*person, taste*) refinado, culto; **~ment** *n* (*of person*) cultura, educación *f*; **~ry** *n* refinería.

reflect [rɪ'flɛkt] *vt* (*light, image*) reflejar // *vi* (*think*) reflexionar, pensar; **it ~s badly/well on him** le perjudica/le hace honor; **~ion** [-'flɛkʃən] *n* (*act*) reflexión *f*; (*image*) reflejo; (*criticism*) reproche *m*, crítica; **on ~ion** pensándolo bien; **~or** *n* (*also AUT*) captafaros *m inv*, reflector *m*.

reflex ['ri:flɛks] *a*, *n* reflejo; **~ive** [rɪ'flɛksɪv] *a* (*LING*) reflexivo.

reform [rɪ'fɔ:m] *n* reforma // *vt* reformar; **the R~ation** [rɛfə'meɪʃən] *n* la Reforma; **~er** *n* reformador/a *m/f*; **~ist** *n* reformista *m/f*.

refrain [rɪ'freɪn] *vi*: **to ~ from doing** abstenerse de hacer // *n* estribillo.

refresh [rɪ'frɛʃ] *vt* refrescar; **~er course** *n* curso de repaso; **~ments** *npl* (*drinks*) refrescos *mpl*.

refrigeration [rɪfrɪdʒə'reɪʃən] *n* refrigeración *f*; **refrigerator** [-'frɪdʒəreɪtə*] *n* refrigeradora, nevera.

refuel [ri:'fjuəl] *vi* repostar combustible.

refuge ['rɛfju:dʒ] *n* refugio, asilo; **to take ~ in** refugiarse en.

refugee [rɛfju'dʒi:] *n* refugiado/a.

refund ['ri:fʌnd] *n* reembolso // *vt* [rɪ'fʌnd] devolver, reembolsar.

refurbish [ri:'fɔ:bɪʃ] *vt* restaurar, renovar.

refusal [rɪ'fju:zəl] *n* negativa; **first ~** primera opción.

refuse ['rɛfju:s] *n* basura // (*vb*: [rɪ'fju:z]) *vt* (*reject*) rehusar; (*say no to*) negarse a // *vi* negarse; (*horse*) rehusar; **~ bin** *n* cubo de la basura; **~ tip** *n* vertedero.

refute [rɪ'fju:t] *vt* refutar, rebatir.

regain [rɪ'geɪn] *vt* recobrar, recuperar.

regal ['ri:gl] *a* regio, real.

regalia [rɪ'geɪlɪə] *n*, *npl* insignias *fpl* reales.

regard [rɪ'gɑːd] *n* (*gaze*) mirada; (*aspect*) respecto; (*attention*) atención *f*; (*esteem*) respeto, consideración *f* // *vt* (*consider*) considerar; (*look at*) mirar; **'with kindest ~s'** con muchos recuerdos; **~ing, as ~s, with ~ to** con respecto a, en cuanto a; **~less** *ad* a pesar de todo.

regatta [rɪ'gætə] *n* regata.

regent ['ri:dʒənt] *n* regente *m/f*.

régime [reɪ'ʒi:m] *n* régimen *m*.

regiment ['rɛdʒɪmənt] *n* regimiento // *vt* reglamentar; **~al** [-'mɛntl] *a* militar; **~ation** [-'teɪʃən] *n* reglamentación *f*.

region ['ri:dʒən] *n* región *f*; **in the ~ of** (*fig*) alrededor de; **~al** *a* regional.

register ['rɛdʒɪstə*] *n* (*gen*) registro; (*list*) lista // *vt* registrar; (*birth*) declarar; (*letter*) certificar; (*subj: instrument*)

marcar, indicar // *vi* (*at hotel*) registrarse; (*sign on*) inscribirse; (*make impression*) producir impresión; **~ed** *a* (*design*) registrado; (*letter*) certificado.

registrar ['rɛdʒɪstrɑ:*] *n* secretario (del registro civil).

registration [rɛdʒɪs'treɪʃən] *n* (*act*) inscripción *f*; (*AUT: also*: **~ number**) matrícula.

registry ['rɛdʒɪstrɪ] *n* registro, archivo; **~ office** *n* registro civil; **to get married in a ~ office** casarse por lo civil.

regret [rɪ'grɛt] *n* sentimiento, pesar *m*; (*remorse*) remordimiento // *vt* sentir, lamentar; (*repent of*) arrepentirse de; **~fully** *ad* con pesar, sentidamente; **~table** *a* lamentable; (*loss*) sensible.

regroup [ri:'gru:p] *vt* reagrupar // *vi* reagruparse.

regular ['rɛgjulə*] *a* (*gen*) regular; (*usual*) corriente, normal; (*soldier*) de línea; (*intensive*) verdadero // *n* (*client etc*) cliente *m/f* habitual; **~ity** [-'lærɪtɪ] *n* regularidad *f*; **~ly** *ad* con regularidad.

regulate ['rɛgjuleɪt] *vt* regular; (*TECH*) arreglar, ajustar; **regulation** [-'leɪʃən] *n* (*rule*) regla, reglamento; (*adjustment*) ajuste *m*.

rehabilitation ['ri:həbɪlɪ'teɪʃən] *n* rehabilitación *f*.

rehearsal [rɪ'hɔ:səl] *n* ensayo; **rehearse** *vt* ensayar.

reign [reɪn] *n* reinado; (*fig*) dominio // *vi* reinar; (*fig*) imperar; **~ing** *a* (*monarch*) reinante, actual; (*predominant*) imperante.

reimburse [ri:ɪm'bɔ:s] *vt* reembolsar; **~ment** *n* reembolso.

rein [reɪn] *n* (*for horse*) rienda; **to give ~** dar rienda suelta a.

reincarnation [ri:ɪnkɑ:'neɪʃən] *n* reencarnación *f*.

reindeer ['reɪndɪə*] *n*, *pl inv* reno.

reinforce [ri:ɪn'fɔ:s] *vt* reforzar; **~d** *a* (*concrete*) armado; **~ment** *n* (*action*) reforzamiento; **~ments** *npl* (*MIL*) refuerzos *mpl*.

reinstate [ri:ɪn'steɪt] *vt* (*worker*) reintegrar a su puesto.

reiterate [ri:'ɪtəreɪt] *vt* reiterar, repetir.

reject ['ri:dʒɛkt] *n* (*COMM*) artículo defectuoso // *vt* [rɪ'dʒɛkt] rechazar; (*plan*) desechar; (*solution*) descartar; **~ion** [rɪ'dʒɛkʃən] *n* rechazo.

rejoice [rɪ'dʒɔɪs] *vi*: **to ~ at** *or* **over** regocijarse *o* alegrarse de.

rejuvenate [rɪ'dʒu:vəneɪt] *vt* rejuvenecer.

rekindle [ri:'kɪndl] *vt* reencender; (*fig*) despertar.

relapse [rɪ'læps] *n* (*MED*) recaída; (*into crime*) reincidencia.

relate [rɪ'leɪt] *vt* (*tell*) contar, relatar; (*connect*) relacionar // *vi* relacionarse; **~d** *a* afín, conexo; (*person*) emparentado; **~d to** con referencia a, relacionado con; **relating to** *prep* acerca de.

relation [rɪ'leɪʃən] *n* (*person*) pariente *m/f*; (*link*) relación *f*; **~ship** *n* relación *f*;

(*personal ties*) relaciones *fpl*; (*also:* family ~ship) parentesco.

relative ['relətiv] *n* pariente *m/f*, familiar *m/f* // *a* relativo.

relax [rɪ'læks] *vi* descansar; (*person: unwind*) relajarse // *vt* relajar (*mind, person*) descansar; ~**ation** [riːlæk'seɪʃən] *n* (*rest*) descanso; (*ease*) relajación *f*, relax *m*; (*amusement*) recreo; (*entertainment*) diversión *f*; ~**ed** *a* relajado (*tranquil*) tranquilo; ~**ing** a enervante.

relay ['riːleɪ] *n* (*race*) carrera de relevos // *vt* (*message*) retransmitir.

release [rɪ'liːs] *n* (*from prison, obligation*) liberación *f*, libertad *f*; (*of shot*) disparo; (*of gas etc*) escape *m*; (*of film etc*) estreno // *vt* (*prisoner*) poner en libertad; (*book, film*) estrenar; (*report, news*) publicar; (*gas etc*) despedir, arrojar; (*free: from wreckage etc*) soltar; (*TECH: catch, spring etc*) desenganchar; (*let go*) soltar, aflojar.

relegate ['relɪgeɪt] *vt* relegar; (*SPORT*): **to be ~d** descender.

relent [rɪ'lent] *vi* ablandarse, ceder; ~**less** a implacable.

relevance ['reləvəns] *n* relación *f*; **relevant** [-ənt] *a* relacionado; (*fact*) pertinente; (*apt*) oportuno.

reliable [rɪ'laɪəbl] *a* (*person, firm*) de confianza, de fiar; (*method, machine*) seguro; (*news*) fidedigno; **reliably** *ad*: **to be reliably informed that...** saber de fuente fidedigna que... .

reliance [rɪ'laɪəns] *n*: ~ (**on**) dependencia (de).

relic ['relɪk] *n* (*REL*) reliquia; (*of the past*) vestigio.

relief [rɪ'liːf] *n* (*from pain, anxiety*) alivio, desahogo; (*help, supplies*) socorro, ayuda; (*ART, GEO*) relieve *m*.

relieve [rɪ'liːv] *vt* (*pain, patient*) aliviar; (*bring help to*) ayudar, socorrer; (*burden*) aligerar; (*take over from: gen*) sustituir a; (: *guard*) relevar; **to ~ sb of sth** quitar algo a uno; **to ~ o.s.** hacer sus necesidades.

religion [rɪ'lɪdʒən] *n* religión *f*; **religious** a religioso.

relinquish [rɪ'lɪŋkwɪʃ] *vt* abandonar; (*plan, habit*) renunciar a.

relish ['relɪʃ] *n* (*CULIN*) salsa, condimento; (*enjoyment*) entusiasmo; (*flavour*) sabor *m*, gusto // *vt* (*food etc*) saborear; **to ~ doing** gustar de hacer.

reload [riː'ləud] *vt* recargar.

reluctance [rɪ'lʌktəns] *n* renuencia; **reluctant** [-ənt] *a* renuente; **reluctantly** [-əntlɪ] *ad* con renuencia.

rely [rɪ'laɪ]: **to ~ on** *vt fus* confiar en, fiarse de; (*be dependent on*) depender de.

remain [rɪ'meɪn] *vi* (*survive*) quedar; (*be left*) sobrar; (*continue*) quedar(se), permanecer; ~**der** *n* resto; ~**ing** a sobrante; ~**s** *npl* restos *mpl*; (*leftovers*) desperdicios *mpl*.

remand [rɪ'mɑːnd] *n*: **on** ~ detenido (en espera del juicio) // *vt*: **to ~ in custody**

reencarcelar, mantener bajo custodia; ~ **home** *n* reformatorio.

remark [rɪ'mɑːk] *n* comentario // *vt* comentar; (*notice*) observar, notar; ~**able** *a* notable; (*outstanding*) extraordinario.

remarry [riː'mærɪ] *vi* casarse por segunda vez.

remedial [rɪ'miːdɪəl] *a* (*tuition, classes*) de niños atrasados.

remedy ['remədɪ] *n* remedio // *vt* remediar, curar.

remember [rɪ'membə*] *vt* recordar, acordarse de; (*bear in mind*) tener presente; **remembrance** *n* (*memory*) memoria; (*souvenir*) recuerdo.

remind [rɪ'maɪnd] *vt*: **to ~ sb to do sth** recordar a uno que haga algo; **to ~ sb of sth** recordar algo a uno; **she ~s me of her mother** me recuerda a su madre; ~**er** *n* advertencia; (*souvenir*) recuerdo.

reminisce [remɪ'nɪs] *vi* recordar viejas historias; **reminiscent** *a*: **to be reminiscent of sth** recordar algo.

remiss [rɪ'mɪs] *a* descuidado; **it was ~ of him** fue un descuido suyo.

remission [rɪ'mɪʃən] *n* remisión *f*; (*of debt, sentence*) perdón *m*.

remit [rɪ'mɪt] *vt* (*send: money*) remitir, enviar; ~**tance** *n* remesa, envío.

remnant ['remnənt] *n* resto; (*of cloth*) retazo.

remorse [rɪ'mɔːs] *n* remordimientos *mpl*; ~**ful** *a* arrepentido; ~**less** a (*fig*) implacable, despiadado.

remote [rɪ'məut] *a* (*distant*) lejano; (*person*) distante; ~ **control** *n* telecontrol *m*; ~**ly** *ad* remotamente; (*slightly*) levemente; ~**ness** *n* alejamiento; distancia.

remould [riː'məuld] *vt* (*tyre*) recauchutar.

removable [rɪ'muːvəbl] *a* (*detachable*) amovible, separable.

removal [rɪ'muːvəl] *n* (*taking away*) el quitar; (*from house*) mudanza; (*from office: sacking*) destitución *f*; (*MED*) extirpación *f*; ~ **van** *n* camión *m* de mudanzas.

remove [rɪ'muːv] *vt* quitar; (*employee*) destituir; (*name: from list*) tachar, borrar; (*doubt, abuse*) disipar; (*TECH*) retirar, separar; (*MED*) extirpar; **removers** *npl* (*company*) agencia de mudanzas.

remuneration [rɪmjuːnə'reɪʃən] *n* remuneración *f*.

rend [rend], *pt, pp* **rent** *vt* rasgar, desgarrar.

render ['rendə*] *vt* (*give*) dar, prestar; (*hand over*) entregar; (*reproduce*) reproducir; (*make*) hacer, volver; (*return*) devolver; ~**ing** *n* (*MUS etc*) interpretación *f*.

rendez-vous ['rɒndɪvuː] *n* cita.

renegade ['renɪgeɪd] *n* renegado.

renew [rɪ'njuː] *vt* renovar; (*resume*) reanudar; (*loan etc*) prorrogar; (*negotiations*) volver a; (*acquaintance*) entablar de nuevo; ~al n renovación f; reanudación f; prórroga.

renounce [rɪˈnauns] vt renunciar a; (*disown*) renunciar.

renovate [ˈrenəveɪt] vt renovar; **renovation** [-ˈveɪʃən] n renovación f.

renown [rɪˈnaun] n renombre m; ~ed a renombrado.

rent [rent] pt, pp of **rend** // n alquiler m, arriendo // vt alquilar; ~al n (*for television, car*) alquiler m.

renunciation [rɪnʌnsɪˈeɪʃən] n renuncia.

reorganize [riːˈɔːgənaɪz] vt reorganizar.

rep [rep] n abbr of **representative; repertory.**

repair [rɪˈpeə*] n reparación f, compostura; (*patch*) remiendo // vt reparar, componer; (*shoes*) remendar; **in good/bad** ~ en buen/mal estado; ~ **kit** n caja de herramientas para reparaciones.

repartee [repɑːˈtiː] n dimes y diretes.

repay [riːˈpeɪ] vt (*pay: like* **pay**) (*money*) devolver, reembolsar; (*person*) pagar; (*debt*) liquidar; (*sb's efforts*) devolver, corresponder a; ~**ment** n reembolso, devolución f; (*of debt*) pago.

repeal [rɪˈpiːl] n (*of law*) abrogación f; (*of sentence*) anulación f // vt abrogar, revocar.

repeat [rɪˈpiːt] n (RADIO, TV) retransmisión f // vt repetir // vi repetirse; ~**edly** ad repetidas veces.

repel [rɪˈpel] vt (*lit, fig*) repugnar; ~**lent** a repugnante // n: **insect** ~**lent** crema/loción f anti-insectos.

repent [rɪˈpent] vi: to ~ (of) arrepentirse (de); ~**ance** n arrepentimiento.

repercussion [riːpəˈkʌʃən] n (*consequence*) repercusión f; **to have** ~**s** repercutir.

repertoire [ˈrepətwɑː*] n repertorio.

repertory [ˈrepətərɪ] n (*also:* ~ **theatre**) teatro de repertorio.

repetition [repɪˈtɪʃən] n repetición f.

repetitive [rɪˈpetɪtɪv] a (*movement, work*) reiterativo; (*speech*) lleno de repeticiones.

replace [rɪˈpleɪs] vt (*put back*) devolver a su sitio; (*take the place of*) reemplazar, sustituir; ~**ment** n (*gen*) reemplazo; (*act*) reposición f; (*person*) suplente m/f.

replenish [rɪˈplenɪʃ] vt (*glass*) rellenar; (*stock etc*) reponer; (*with fuel*) repostar.

replete [rɪˈpliːt] a repleto; (*well-fed*) lleno.

replica [ˈreplɪkə] n copia, reproducción f.

reply [rɪˈplaɪ] n respuesta, contestación f // vi contestar, responder.

report [rɪˈpɔːt] n informe m; (PRESS etc) reportaje m; (*also:* **school** ~) nota; (*of gun*) estallido // vt informar sobre; (PRESS etc) hacer un reportaje sobre; (*bring to notice: occurrence*) dar cuenta de // vi (*make a report*) presentar un informe; (*present o.s.*): **to** ~ (**to sb**) presentarse (ante uno); ~**er** n periodista m/f.

reprehensible [reprɪˈhensɪbl] a reprensible, censurable.

represent [reprɪˈzent] vt representar; (*fig*) hablar en nombre de; (COMM) ser agente de; ~**ation** [-ˈteɪʃən] n representación f; (*petition*) petición f; ~**ations** npl (*protest*) quejas fpl; ~**ative** n representante m/f // a representativo.

repress [rɪˈpres] vt reprimir; ~**ion** [-ˈpreʃən] n represión f; ~**ive** a represivo.

reprieve [rɪˈpriːv] n (LAW) indulto; (*fig*) alivio // vt indultar, suspender la pena de.

reprimand [ˈreprɪmɑːnd] n reprimenda // vt reprender.

reprint [ˈriːprɪnt] n reimpresión f // vt [riːˈprɪnt] reimprimir.

reprisal [rɪˈpraɪzl] n represalia.

reproach [rɪˈprəutʃ] n reproche m // vt: **to** ~ **sb with sth** reprochar algo a uno; **beyond** ~ intachable; ~**ful** a lleno de reproches.

reproduce [riːprəˈdjuːs] vt reproducir // vi reproducirse; **reproduction** [-ˈdʌkʃən] n reproducción f; **reproductive** [-ˈdʌktɪv] a reproductor(a).

reprove [rɪˈpruːv] vt: **to** ~ **sb for sth** reprender algo a uno.

reptile [ˈreptaɪl] n reptil m.

republic [rɪˈpʌblɪk] n república; ~**an** a, n republicano/a.

repudiate [rɪˈpjuːdɪeɪt] vt (*accusation*) rechazar; (*friend*) repudiar; (*obligation*) desconocer.

repugnant [rɪˈpʌgnənt] a repugnante.

repulse [rɪˈpʌls] vt rechazar, repulsar; **repulsive** a repulsivo.

reputable [ˈrepjutəbl] a (*make etc*) de toda confianza; (*person*) formal.

reputation [repjuˈteɪʃən] n reputación f.

repute [rɪˈpjuːt] n reputación f, fama; ~**d** a supuesto; ~**dly** ad según dicen o se dice.

request [rɪˈkwest] n petición f; (*formal*) solicitud f // vt: **to** ~ **sth of or from sb** pedir algo a uno; (*formally*) solicitar algo a uno.

requiem [ˈrekwɪəm] n réquiem m.

require [rɪˈkwaɪə*] vt (*need: subj: person*) necesitar, tener necesidad de; (: *thing, situation*) exigir; (*want*) pedir; (*order*) insistir en que; ~**ment** n requisito; (*need*) necesidad f.

requisite [ˈrekwɪzɪt] n requisito // a preciso, imprescindible; **toilet** ~**s** artículos mpl de aseo personal.

requisition [rekwɪˈzɪʃən] n: ~ (**for**) solicitud f (de) // vt (MIL) requisar.

reroute [riːˈruːt] vt (*train etc*) desviar.

resale [ˈriːˈseɪl] n reventa.

rescue [ˈreskjuː] n rescate m // vt rescatar; **to** ~ **from** librar de; ~ **party** n expedición f de salvamento; **rescuer** n salvador/a m/f.

research [rɪˈsəːtʃ] n investigaciones fpl // vt investigar; ~**er** n investigador/a m/f; ~ **work** n investigación f.

resell [riːˈsel] vt revender.

resemblance [rɪˈzembləns] n parecido; **to**

bear a ~ to parecerse a; **resemble** vt parecerse a.

resent [rɪ'zɛnt] vt resentirse de, **~ful** a resentido; **~ment** n resentimiento.

reservation [rɛzə'veɪʃən] n (gen) reserva; (on road: also: **central ~**) faja intermedia.

reserve [rɪ'zɜːv] n reserva; (SPORT) suplente m/f; (game ~) coto // vt (seats etc) reservar; **~s** npl (MIL) reserva sg; **in ~ de reserva; ~d** a reservado.

reservoir ['rɛzəvwɑː*] n (large) embalse m; (small) depósito.

reshape [riː'ʃeɪp] vt (policy) reformar, rehacer.

reshuffle [riː'ʃʌfl] n: **Cabinet ~** (POL) reconstrucción f del gabinete.

reside [rɪ'zaɪd] vi residir, vivir.

residence ['rɛzɪdəns] n residencia; (formal: home) domicilio; (length of stay) permanencia; **resident** [-ənt] n vecino, (in hotel) huésped/a m/f // a (population) permanente; (doctor) interno; **residential** [-'dɛnʃəl] a residencial.

residue ['rɛzɪdjuː] n resto, residuo; (COMM) saldo.

resign [rɪ'zaɪn] vt (one's post) renunciar a // vi dimitir; **to ~ o.s. to** (endure) resignarse a; **~ation** [rɛzɪg'neɪʃən] n renuncia; (state of mind) resignación f; **~ed** a resignado.

resilience [rɪ'zɪlɪəns] n (of material) elasticidad f; (of person) resistencia; **resilient** [-ənt] a (person) resistente.

resin ['rɛzɪn] n resina.

resist [rɪ'zɪst] vt resistir, oponerse a; **~ance** n resistencia.

resolute ['rɛzəluːt] a resuelto.

resolution [rɛzə'luːʃən] n (gen) resolución f; (purpose) propósito.

resolve [rɪ'zɔlv] n resolución f; (purpose) propósito // vt resolver // vi resolverse; **to ~ to do** resolver hacer; **~d** a resuelto.

resonant ['rɛzənənt] a resonante.

resort [rɪ'zɔːt] n (town) centro de turismo; (recourse) recurso // vi: **to ~ to** recurrir a; **in the last ~** en último caso.

resound [rɪ'zaund] vi resonar, retumbar; **the room ~ed with shouts** los gritos resonaron en el cuarto; **~ing** a sonoro; (fig) clamoroso.

resource [rɪ'sɔːs] n recurso; **~s** npl recursos mpl; **~ful** a inventivo, ingenioso.

respect [rɪs'pɛkt] n (consideration) respeto; (relation) respecto; **~s** npl recuerdos mpl, saludos mpl // vt respetar; **with ~ to** con respecto a; **in this ~** en cuanto a eso; **~ability** [-ə'bɪlɪtɪ] a respetabilidad f; **~able** a respetable; (large) apreciable; (passable) tolerable; **~ful** a respetuoso.

respective [rɪs'pɛktɪv] a respectivo; **~ly** ad respectivamente.

respiration [rɛspɪ'reɪʃən] n respiración f.

respiratory [rɛs'pɪrətərɪ] a respiratorio.

respite ['rɛspaɪt] n respiro; (LAW) prórroga.

resplendent [rɪs'plɛndənt] a resplandeciente.

respond [rɪs'pɔnd] vi responder; (react) reaccionar, **response** [-'pɔns] n respuesta; reacción f.

responsibility [rɪspɔnsɪ'bɪlɪtɪ] n responsabilidad f.

responsible [rɪs'pɔnsɪbl] a (liable): **~ (for)** responsable (de); (character) serio, formal; (job) de confianza.

responsive [rɪs'pɔnsɪv] a sensible.

rest [rɛst] n descanso, reposo; (MUS) pausa, silencio; (support) apoyo; (remainder) resto // vi descansar; (be supported): **to ~ on** posar(se) en // vt (lean): **to ~ sth on/against** apoyar algo en o sobre/contra.

restart [riː'stɑːt] vt (engine) volver a arrancar; (work) volver a empezar.

restaurant ['rɛstərɔŋ] n restorán m, restaurante m; **~ car** n coche-comedor m.

restful ['rɛstful] a descansado, reposado.

rest home n residencia para jubilados.

restitution [rɛstɪ'tjuːʃən] n: **to make ~ to sb for sth** indemnizar a uno por algo.

restive ['rɛstɪv] a inquieto; (horse) rebelón(ona).

restless ['rɛstlɪs] a inquieto; **~ly** ad inquietamente.

restoration [rɛstə'reɪʃən] n restauración f; **restore** [rɪ'stɔː*] vt (building) restaurar; (sth stolen) devolver; (health) restablecer.

restrain [rɪs'treɪn] vt (feeling) contener, refrenar; (person): **to ~ (from doing)** disuadir (de hacer); **~ed** a (style) moderado; **~t** n (restriction) freno, control m; (moderation) moderación f; (of style) reserva.

restrict [rɪs'trɪkt] vt restringir, limitar; **~ion** [-kʃən] n restricción f, limitación f; **~ive** a restrictivo.

rest room n (US) aseos npl.

result [rɪ'zʌlt] n resultado // vi: **to ~ in** terminar en, dar por resultado; **as a ~ of** a consecuencia de.

resume [rɪ'zjuːm] vt, vi (work, journey) reanudar.

résumé ['reɪzjuːmeɪ] n resumen m.

resumption [rɪ'zʌmpʃən] n reanudación f.

resurgence [rɪ'sɜːdʒəns] n resurgimiento.

resurrection [rɛzə'rɛkʃən] n resurrección f.

resuscitate [rɪ'sʌsɪteɪt] vt (MED) resucitar; **resuscitation** [-'teɪʃn] n resucitación f.

retail ['riːteɪl] n venta al por menor // cpd al por menor // vt vender al por menor o al detalle; **~er** n detallista m/f.

retain [rɪ'teɪn] vt (keep) retener, conservar; (employ) contratar; **~er** n (servant) criado; (fee) anticipo.

retaliate [rɪ'tælɪeɪt] vi: **to ~ (against)** tomar represalias (contra), **retaliation** [-'eɪʃən] n represalias fpl.

retarded [rɪ'tɑːdɪd] a retrasado.

retch [rɛtʃ] vi dar arcadas.

retentive [rɪ'tentɪv] a (*memory*) retentivo.
reticent ['retɪsnt] a reservado.
retina ['retɪnə] n retina.
retinue ['retɪnjuː] n séquito, comitiva.
retire [rɪ'taɪə*] vi (*give up work*) jubilarse; (*withdraw*) retirarse; (*go to bed*) (ir a) acostarse; **~d** a (*person*) jubilado; **~ment** n (*state*) retiro; (*act*) jubilación f; **retiring** a (*leaving*) saliente; (*shy*) retraído.
retort [rɪ'tɔːt] n (*reply*) réplica // vi contestar.
retrace [riː'treɪs] vt: **to ~ one's steps** volver sobre sus pasos, desandar lo andado.
retract [rɪ'trækt] vt (*statement*) retirar; (*claws*) retraer; (*undercarriage, aerial*) replegar // vi retractarse; **~able** a replegable.
retrain [riː'treɪn] vt reeducar; **~ing** n readaptación f profesional.
retreat [rɪ'triːt] n (*place*) retiro; (*act*) retraimiento; (*MIL*) retirada // vi retirarse; (*flood*) bajar.
retribution [retrɪ'bjuːʃən] n desquite m.
retrieve [rɪ'triːv] vt (*gen*) recobrar; (*situation, honour*) salvar; (*error, loss*) recuperar; **retriever** n perro cobrador, perdiguero.
retrospect ['retrəspekt] n: **in ~** retrospectivamente, mirando hacia atrás; **~ive** [-'spektɪv] a (*law*) retroactivo.
return [rɪ'tɜːn] n (*going or coming back*) vuelta, regreso; (*of sth stolen etc*) devolución f; (*recompense*) recompensa; (*FINANCE: from land, shares*) ganancia, ingresos mpl; (*report*) informe m // cpd (*journey*) de regreso; (*ticket*) de ida y vuelta; (*match*) de vuelta // vi (*person etc: come or go back*) volver, regresar; (*symptoms etc*) reaparecer // vt devolver; (*favour, love etc*) corresponder a; (*verdict*) declarar; (*POL: candidate*) elegir; **~s** npl (*COMM*) ingresos mpl; **in ~** en cambio; **many happy ~s (of the day)!** ¡muchas felicidades!, ¡feliz cumpleaños!
reunion [riː'juːnɪən] n reunión f.
reunite [riːjuː'naɪt] vt reunir; (*reconcile*) reconciliar.
rev [rev] n abbr of **revolution** (*AUT*) // (vb: also: **~ up**) vt girar (el motor de) // vi acelerarse.
reveal [rɪ'viːl] vt (*make known*) revelar; **~ing** a revelador(a).
reveille [rɪ'vælɪ] n (*MIL*) diana.
revel ['revl] vi: **to ~ in sth/in doing sth** deleitarse en algo/en hacer algo.
revelation [revə'leɪʃən] n revelación f.
reveller ['revlə*] n jaranero, juergista m/f; **revelry** [-rɪ] n jarana, juerga.
revenge [rɪ'vendʒ] n venganza; (*in sport*) revancha; **to take ~ on** vengarse de.
revenue ['revənjuː] n ingresos mpl, renta; (*on investment*) rédito; (*profit*) ganancia.
reverberate [rɪ'vɜːbəreɪt] vi (*sound*) resonar, retumbar; **reverberation** [-'reɪʃən] n retumbo, eco.
revere [rɪ'vɪə*] vt reverenciar, venerar;

reverence ['revərəns] n reverencia; **reverent** ['revərənt] a reverente.
reverie ['revərɪ] n ensueño.
reversal [rɪ'vɜːsl] n (*of order*) inversión f; (*of direction*) cambio completo; (*of decision*) revocación f.
reverse [rɪ'vɜːs] n (*opposite*) contrario; (*back: of cloth*) revés m; (: *of coin*) reverso, (: *of paper*) dorso; (*AUT: also: ~ gear*) marcha atrás, contramarcha // a (*order*) inverso; (*direction*) contrario // vt (*turn over*) volver al revés; (*invert*) invertir; (*change: opinion*) cambiar (completamente) de // vi (*AUT*) poner en marcha atrás.
revert [rɪ'vɜːt] vi: **to ~ to** volver a.
review [rɪ'vjuː] n (*magazine, MIL*) revista; (*of book, film*) reseña; (*examination*) repaso, examen m // vt repasar, examinar; (*MIL*) pasar revista a; (*book, film*) reseñar; **~er** n crítico/a.
revile [rɪ'vaɪl] vt injuriar, vilipendiar.
revise [rɪ'vaɪz] vt (*manuscript*) corregir; (*opinion*) modificar; (*study: subject*) repasar; (*look over*) revisar; **revision** [rɪ'vɪʒən] n corrección f; modificación f; repaso; revisión f.
revitalize [riː'vaɪtəlaɪz] vt revivificar.
revival [rɪ'vaɪvl] n (*recovery*) restablecimiento; (*of interest*) renacimiento; (*THEATRE*) reestreno; (*of faith*) despertar m.
revive [rɪ'vaɪv] vt (*gen*) resucitar; (*custom*) restablecer; (*hope, courage*) reanimar; (*play*) reestrenar // vi (*person*) volver en sí, restablecerse; (*from faint*) revivir; (*activity*) recobrarse.
revoke [rɪ'vəʊk] vt revocar.
revolt [rɪ'vəʊlt] n rebelión f, sublevación f // vi rebelarse, sublevarse // vt dar asco a, repugnar; **~ing** a asqueroso, repugnante.
revolution [revə'luːʃən] n revolución f; **~ary** a, n revolucionario/a; **~ize** vt revolucionar.
revolve [rɪ'vɒlv] vi dar vueltas, girar.
revolver [rɪ'vɒlvə*] n revólver m.
revolving [rɪ'vɒlvɪŋ] a (*chair etc*) giratorio; **~ door** n puerta giratoria.
revue [rɪ'vjuː] n (*THEATRE*) revista.
revulsion [rɪ'vʌlʃən] n asco, repugnancia.
reward [rɪ'wɔːd] n premio, recompensa // vt: **to ~ (for)** recompensar o premiar (por); **~ing** a (*fig*) provechoso, valioso.
rewire [riː'waɪə*] vt (*house*) renovar el alambrado de.
reword [riː'wɜːd] vt expresar en otras palabras.
rewrite [riː'raɪt] (*irg: like* **write**) vt volver a escribir o redactar.
rhapsody ['ræpsədɪ] n (*MUS*) rapsodia; (*fig*) transporte m (de admiración).
rhetoric [retərɪk] n retórica; **~al** [rɪ'tɒrɪkl] a retórico.
rheumatic [ruː'mætɪk] a reumático; **rheumatism** ['ruːmətɪzəm] n reumatismo, reúma.

Rhine [raɪn] n: the ~ el (río) Rin.

rhinoceros [raɪ'nɔsərəs] n rinoceronte m.

rhododendron [rəudə'dendrn] n rododendro.

Rhone [rəun] n: the ~ el (río) Ródano.

rhubarb ['ru:bɑ:b] n ruibarbo.

rhyme [raɪm] n rima; (verse) poesía.

rhythm ['rɪðm] n ritmo; ~ method método de Ojino; ~ic(al) a rítmico.

rib [rɪb] n (ANAT) costilla // vt (mock) tomar el pelo a.

ribald ['rɪbəld] a escabroso.

ribbon ['rɪbən] n cinta; in ~s (torn) hecho trizas.

rice [raɪs] n arroz m; ~field n arrozal m; ~ pudding n arroz m con leche.

rich [rɪtʃ] a rico; (banquet) suntuoso; (soil) fértil; (food) fuerte; (: sweet) empalagoso; the ~ los ricos; ~es npl riqueza sg; ~ness n riqueza; suntuosidad f; fertilidad f.

rickets ['rɪkɪts] n raquitismo.

rickety ['rɪkɪtɪ] a desvencijado; (shaky) tambaleante.

rickshaw ['rɪkʃɔ:] n rikisha.

ricochet ['rɪkəʃeɪ] n rebote m // vi rebotar.

rid [rɪd], pt, pp rid vt: to ~ sb of sth librar a uno de algo; to get ~ of deshacerse o desembarazarse de.

ridden ['rɪdn] pp of ride.

riddle ['rɪdl] n (conundrum) acertijo; (mystery) enigma m, misterio; (sieve) criba // vt: to be ~d with ser lleno o plagado de.

ride [raɪd] n (gen) paseo; (on horse) cabalgata; (distance covered) viaje m, recorrido // (vb: pt rode, pp ridden) vi (as sport) montar; (go somewhere: on horse, bicycle) dar un paseo, pasearse; (journey: on bicycle, motor cycle, bus) viajar // vt (a horse) montar a; (distance) viajar; to ~ a bicycle ir en bicicleta; to ~ at anchor (NAUT) estar al ancla; to take sb for a ~ (fig) engañar a uno; **rider** n (on horse) jinete m; (on bicycle) ciclista m/f; (on motorcycle) motociclista m/f.

ridge [rɪdʒ] n (of hill) cresta; (of roof) caballete m; (wrinkle) arruga.

ridicule ['rɪdɪkju:l] n irrisión f, mofa // vt poner en ridículo, mofarse de; **ridiculous** [-'dɪkjuləs] a ridículo.

riding ['raɪdɪŋ] n montar m a caballo; ~ school n escuela de equitación.

rife [raɪf] a: to be ~ ser muy común; to be ~ with abundar en.

riffraff ['rɪfræf] n gentuza.

rifle ['raɪfl] n rifle m, fusil m // vt saquear; ~ range n campo de tiro; (at fair) tiro al blanco.

rift [rɪft] n (fig: disagreement: between friends) desavenencia; (: in party) escisión f.

rig [rɪg] n (also: oil ~) torre f de perforación // vt (election etc) falsificar los resultados de; to ~ out vt ataviar de;

to ~ up vt armar; ~ging n (NAUT) aparejo.

right [raɪt] a (true, correct) correcto, exacto; (suitable) indicado, debido; (proper) apropiado, propio; (just) justo; (morally good) bueno; (not left) derecho // a (title, claim) derecho; (not left) derecha // ad (correctly) bien, correctamente; (straight) derecho, directamente; (not on the left) a la derecha; (to the ~) hacia la derecha // vt enderezar // excl ¡bueno!, ¡está bien!; to be ~ (person) tener razón; all ~! ¡está bien!; (enough) ¡basta!; ~ now ahora mismo; ~ in the middle justo en medio, en pleno centro; ~ away en seguida; by ~s en justicia; on the ~ a la derecha; ~ angle n ángulo recto; ~eous ['raɪtʃəs] a justado, honrado; (anger) justificado; ~eousness ['raɪtʃəsnɪs] n justicia; ~ful a (heir) legítimo; ~hand a por la derecha; ~handed a (person) que usa la mano derecha ~ly ad correctamente, debidamente; (with reason) con razón; ~wing a (POL) derechista.

rigid ['rɪdʒɪd] a rígido; (principle) inflexible; ~ity [rɪ'dʒɪdɪt] n rigidez f, inflexibilidad f.

rigmarole ['rɪgmərəul] n galimatías m.

rigorous ['rɪgərəs] a riguroso.

rigour, rigor (US) ['rɪgə] n rigor m, severidad f.

rig-out ['rɪgaut] n (col) atuendo.

rile [raɪl] vt irritar.

rim [rɪm] n borde m; (of spectacles) aro; (of wheel) aro, llanta.

rind [raɪnd] n (of bacon) piel f (of lemon etc) cáscara; (of cheese) costra.

ring [rɪŋ] n (of metal) aro; (on finger) anillo; (of people, objects) círculo, grupo; (of spies) camarilla; (for boxing) cuadrilátero; (of circus) pista; (bull~) ruedo, plaza; (sound of bell) toque m; (telephone call) llamada // (vb: pt rang, pp rung) vi (on telephone) llamar por teléfono; (large bell) repicar; (also: ~ out: voice, words) sonar; (ears) zumbar // vt (TEL: also: ~ up) llamar; (bell etc) hacer sonar; (doorbell) tocar; to ~ back vt, vi (TEL) devolver la llamada; to ~ off vi (TEL) colgar, cortar la comunicación; ~ing a (of large bell) repique m; (in ears) zumbido; ~leader n (of gang) cabecilla m/f.

ringlets ['rɪŋlts] npl rizos mpl, tirabuzones mpl.

ring road n carretera periférica o de circunvalación.

rink [rɪŋk] n (also: ice ~) pista.

rinse [rɪns] n (of dishes) enjuague m; (of hair) reflejo // vt enjuagar; dar reflejos a.

riot ['raɪət] n motín m, disturbio // vi amotinarse; to run ~ desmandarse; ~er n amotinado/a; ~ous a (gen) alborotado; (party) bullicioso; (uncontrolled) desenfrenado.

rip [rɪp] n rasgón m, rasgadura // vt

rasgar, desgarrar // vi correr; ~cord n cabo de desgarre.

ripe [raɪp] a (fruit) maduro; (ready) listo; ~n vt madurar // vi madurarse; ~ness n madurez f.

ripple ['rɪpl] n onda, rizo; (sound) murmullo // vi rizarse // vt rizar.

rise [raɪz] n (slope) cuesta, pendiente m; (hill) altura; (increase: in wages) aumento; (: in prices, temperature) subida, alza; (fig: to power etc) ascenso // vi, pt rose, pp risen ['rɪzn] (gen) elevarse; (prices) subir; (waters) crecer; (river) nacer; (sun) salir; (person: from bed etc) levantarse; (also: ~ up: rebel) sublevarse; (in rank) ascender; to give ~ to dar lugar o origen a; to ~ to the occasion ponerse a la altura de las circunstancias.

risk [rɪsk] n riesgo, peligro // vt (gen) arriesgar; (dare) atreverse a; to take or run the ~ of doing correr el riesgo de hacer; at ~ en peligro; at one's own ~ bajo su propia responsabilidad; ~y a arriesgado, peligroso.

risqué ['riːskeɪ] a (joke) subido de color.

rissole ['rɪsəʊl] n croqueta.

rite [raɪt] n rito; funeral ~s exequias fpl.

ritual ['rɪtjʊəl] a ritual // n ritual m, rito.

rival ['raɪvl] n rival m/f; (in business) competidor/a m/f o a rival, opuesto // vt competir con; ~ry n rivalidad f, competencia.

river ['rɪvə*] n río; up/down ~ río arriba/abajo; ~bank n orilla del río; ~bed n lecho, cauce m; ~side n ribera, orilla // cpd (port, traffic) de río, del río.

rivet ['rɪvɪt] n roblón m, remache m // vt remachar; (fig) clavar.

Riviera [rɪvɪ'ɛərə] n: the (French) ~ la Costa Azul (Francesa).

road [rəʊd] n (gen) camino; (motorway etc) carretera; (in town) calle f; ~block n barricada; ~hog n loco del volante; ~map n mapa m de carreteras; ~side n borde m (del camino) // cpd al lado de la carretera; ~sign n señal f (de carretera o calle); ~ user n usuario de la vía pública; ~way n calzada; ~worthy a (car) listo para conducir.

roam [rəʊm] vi vagar // vt vagar por.

roar [rɔː*] n (of animal) rugido, bramido; (of crowd) rugido; (of vehicle, storm) estruendo; (of laughter) carcajada // vi rugir, bramar; hacer estruendo; to ~ with laughter reírse a carcajadas; to do a ~ing trade hacer buen negocio.

roast [rəʊst] n carne f asada, asado // vt (meat) asar; (coffee) tostar.

rob [rɔb] vt robar; to ~ sb of sth robar algo a uno; (fig: deprive) quitarle algo a uno; ~ber n ladrón/ona m/f; ~bery n robo.

robe [rəʊb] n (for ceremony etc) toga; (also: bath ~) bata.

robin ['rɔbɪn] n petirrojo.

robot ['rəʊbɔt] n robot m.

robust [rəʊ'bʌst] a robusto, fuerte.

rock [rɔk] n (gen) roca; (boulder) peña, peñasco; (sweet) pirulí // vt (swing gently: cradle) balancear, mecer; (: child) arrullar; (shake) sacudir // vi mecerse, balancearse; sacudirse; on the ~s (drink) sobre las rocas; (marriage etc) en ruinas; to ~ the boat (fig) causar perturbaciones; ~ and roll n rocanrol m; ~-bottom a (fig) por los suelos; ~ery n cuadro alpino.

rocket ['rɔkɪt] n cohete m.

rocking ['rɔkɪŋ]: ~ chair n mecedora; ~ horse n caballo de balancín.

rocky ['rɔkɪ] a (gen) rocoso; (unsteady: table) débil.

rod [rɔd] n vara, varilla; (TECH) barra; (also: fishing ~) caña.

rode [rəʊd] pt of ride.

rodent ['rəʊdnt] n roedor m.

rodeo ['rəʊdɪəʊ] n rodeo.

roe [rəʊ] n (species: also: ~ deer) corzo; (of fish): hard/soft ~ hueva/lecha.

rogue [rəʊg] n pícaro, pillo; **roguish** a pícaro.

role [rəʊl] n papel m, rol m.

roll [rəʊl] n rollo; (of banknotes) fajo; (also: bread ~) panecillo, bollo; (register) lista, nómina; (sound: of drums etc) redoble m; (movement: of ship) balanceo // vt hacer rodar; (also: ~ up: string) enrollar; (: sleeves) arremangar; (cigarettes) liar; (also: ~ out: pastry) aplanar // vi (gen) rodar; (drum) redoblar; (in walking) bambolearse; (ship) balancearse; to ~ by vi (time) pasar; to ~ in vi (mail, cash) entrar a raudales; to ~ over vi dar una vuelta; to ~ up vi (col: arrive) presentarse, aparecer // vt (carpet) arrollar; ~ call n acto de pasar lista; ~er n rodillo; (wheel) rueda; ~er skates npl patines mpl de rueda.

rollicking ['rɔlɪkɪŋ] a alegre, divertido.

rolling ['rəʊlɪŋ] a (landscape) ondulado; ~ pin n rodillo (de cocina); ~ stock n (RAIL) material m rodante.

Roman ['rəʊmən] a, n romano/a; ~ Catholic a, n católico (romano).

romance [rə'mæns] n (love affair) amoríos mpl, aventura sentimental; (charm) lo romántico.

Romanesque [rəʊmə'nɛsk] a románico.

Romania [rəʊ'meɪnɪə] n = **Rumania**.

romantic [rə'mæntɪk] a romántico; **romanticism** [-tɪsɪzəm] n romanticismo.

romp [rɔmp] n retozo, juego // vi (also: ~ about) jugar, brincar.

rompers ['rɔmpəz] npl pelele m.

roof [ruːf] pl ~s n (gen) techo; (of house) techo, tejado; (of car) baca // vt techar, poner techo a; the ~ of the mouth el paladar, el cielo de la boca; ~ing n techumbre f; ~ rack n (AUT) baca, portaequipajes m inv.

rook [ruk] n (bird) graja; (CHESS) torre f.

room [ruːm] n (in house) cuarto, habitación f, pieza; (also: bed~) dormitorio; (in school etc) sala; (space) sitio, cabida; ~s *npl* (*lodging*) alojamiento *sg*; '~s to let' 'se alquilan pisos *o* cuartos'; **single/double** ~ habitación individual/doble *o* para dos personas; ~**mate** *n* compañero/a de cuarto; ~ **service** *n* servicio de habitaciones; ~**y** *a* espacioso.

roost [ru:st] *n* percha *f*; *vi* pasar la noche.

rooster ['ru:stə*] *n* gallo.

root [ru:t] *n* (*BOT, MATH*) raíz *f*; *vi* (*plant, belief*) arriesgarse; **to** ~ **about** *vi* (*fig*) andar buscando; **to** ~ **for** *vt fus* apoyar a; **to** ~ **out** *vt* desarraigar.

rope [rəup] *n* cuerda; (*NAUT*) cable *m*; *vt* (*box*) atar *o* amarrar con (una) cuerda; (*climbers: also:* ~ **together**) encordarse; **to** ~ **sb in** (*fig*) persuadir a uno a tomar parte; **to know the** ~**s** (*fig*) conocer un negocio a fondo; ~ **ladder** *n* escala de cuerda.

rosary ['rəuzəri] *n* rosario.

rose [rəuz] *pt of* **rise** // *n* rosa; (*also:* ~**bush**) rosal *m*; (*on watering can*) roseta // *a* color de rosa.

rosé ['rəuzei] *n* vino rosado, clarete *m*.

rose: ~**bed** *n* rosaleda; ~**bud** *n* capullo de rosa; ~**bush** *n* rosal *m*.

rosemary ['rəuzməri] *n* romero.

rosette [rəu'zet] *n* rosetón *m*.

roster ['rɔstə*] *n*: **duty** ~ lista de deberes.

rostrum ['rɔstrəm] *n* tribuna.

rosy ['rəuzi] *a* rosado, sonrosado; **a** ~ **future** un futuro prometedor.

rot [rɔt] *n* (*decay*) putrefacción *f*, podredumbre *f*; (*fig: pej*) decadencia // *vt, vi* pudrirse, corromperse.

rota ['rəutə] *n* lista (de tandas).

rotary ['rəutəri] *a* rotativo.

rotate [rəu'teit] *vt* (*revolve*) hacer girar, dar vueltas a; (*change round: crops*) cultivar en rotación; (: *jobs*) alternar // *vi* (*revolve*) girar, dar vueltas; **rotating** *a* (*movement*) rotativo; **rotation** [-'teiʃən] *n* rotación *f*; **in rotation** por turno.

rotor ['rəutə*] *n* rotor *m*.

rotten ['rɔtn] *a* (*decayed*) podrido; (: *wood*) carcomido; (*fig*) corrompido; (*col: bad*) vil, miserable; **to feel** ~ (*ill*) sentirse muy mal.

rotting ['rɔtiŋ] *a* podrido.

rotund [rəu'tʌnd] *a* rotundo.

rouble, ruble (*US*) ['ru:bl] *n* rublo.

rouge [ru:ʒ] *n* colorete *m*.

rough [rʌf] *a* (*skin, surface*) áspero; (*terrain*) quebrado; (*road*) desigual; (*voice*) bronco; (*person, manner: coarse*) tosco, grosero; (*weather*) borrascoso; (*treatment*) brutal; (*sea*) bravo; (*cloth*) basto; (*plan*) preliminar; (*guess*) aproximado; (*violent*) violento // *n* (*person*) matón *m*; (*GOLF*): **in the** ~ en las hierbas altas; **to** ~ **it** vivir sin comodidades; **to sleep** ~ pasar la noche al raso; ~**-and-ready** *a* improvisado; ~**en** *vt* (*a surface*) poner áspero; ~**ly** *ad* (*handle*) torpemente; (*make*) toscamente; (*approximately*)

aproximadamente; ~**ness** *n* aspereza; tosquedad *f*; brutalidad *f*.

roulette [ru:'let] *n* ruleta.

Roumania [ru:'meiniə] *n* = **Rumania.**

round [raund] *a* redondo // *a* círculo; (*of toast*) rodaja; (*of policeman*) ronda; (*of milkman*) recorrido; (*of doctor*) visitas *fpl*; (*game: of cards, in competition*) partida; (*of ammunition*) cartucho; (*BOXING*) asalto; (*of talks*) ronda // *vt* (*corner*) doblar // *prep* alrededor de // *ad*: **all** ~ por todos lados; **the long way** ~ el camino menos directo; **all the year** ~ durante todo el año; **it's just** ~ **the corner** (*fig*) está a la vuelta de la esquina; **to go** ~ **to sb's** (*house*) ir a casa de uno; **to go** ~ **the back** pasar por atrás; **to go** ~ **a house** visitar una casa; **to go the** ~**s** (*story*) divulgarse; **to** ~ **off** *vt* (*speech etc*) acabar, poner término a; **to** ~ **up** *vt* (*cattle*) acorralar; (*people*) reunir; (*prices*) redondear; ~**about** *n* (*AUT*) glorieta, redondel *m*; (*at fair*) tiovivo // *a* (*route, means*) indirecto; **a** ~ **of applause** una salva de aplausos; **a** ~ **of drinks** una ronda de bebidas; ~**ed** *a* redondeado; (*style*) expresivo; ~**ly** *ad* (*fig*) rotundamente; ~**shouldered** *a* cargado de espaldas; ~ **trip** *n* viaje *m* de ida y vuelta; ~**up** *n* rodeo; (*of criminals*) redada.

rouse [rauz] *vt* (*wake up*) despertar; (*stir up*) suscitar; **rousing** *a* emocionado, entusiasta.

rout [raut] *n* (*MIL*) derrota; (*flight*) fuga // *vt* derrotar.

route [ru:t] *n* ruta, camino; (*of bus*) recorrido; (*of shipping*) rumba, derrota; ~ **map** *n* (*for journey*) mapa *m* de carreteras.

routine [ru:'ti:n] *a* (*work*) rutinario // *n* rutina; (*THEATRE*) número.

roving ['rəuviŋ] *a* (*wandering*) errante; (*salesman*) ambulante.

row [rəu] *n* (*line*) fila, hilera; (*KNITTING*) pasada // *n* [rau] (*noise*) estrépito, estruendo; (*racket*) escándalo; (*dispute*) bronca, pelea; (*fuss*) jaleo, follón *m*; (*scolding*) regaño // *vi* (*in boat*) remar // *vi* [rau] reñir(se) // *vt* (*boat*) conducir remando.

rowdy ['raudi] *a* (*person: noisy*) ruidoso; (: *quarrelsome*) pendenciero; (*occasion*) alborotado // *n* pendenciero.

rowing ['rəuiŋ] *n* remo; ~ **boat** *n* bote *m* de remos.

royal ['rɔiəl] *a* real; ~**ist** *a, n* monárquico/a; ~**ty** *n* (~ *persons*) familia real; (*payment to author*) derechos *mpl* de autor.

R.S.V.P. *abbr of* **répondez s'il vous plaît** SRC (Se Ruega Contestación).

rub [rʌb] *vt* (*gen*) frotar; (*hard*) restregar; (*polish*) sacar brillo a // *n* (*gen*) frotamiento; (*touch*) roce *m*; **to** ~ **sb up the wrong way** coger a uno a contrapelo;

to ~ **off** vi borrarse; **to ~ off on** influir en; **to ~ out** vt borrar.

rubber ['rʌbə*] n caucho, goma; (Brit: eraser) goma de borrar; ~ **band** n goma, gomita; ~ **plant** n árbol m del caucho, gomero; ~ y a elástico.

rubbish ['rʌbɪʃ] n (from household) basura; (waste) desperdicios mpl; (fig: pej) tonterías fpl; (trash) pacotilla; ~ **bin** n cubo de la basura; ~ **dump** n (in town) vertedero, basurero.

rubble ['rʌbl] n escombros mpl.

ruby ['ru:bɪ] n rubí m.

rucksack ['rʌksæk] n mochila.

ructions ['rʌkʃənz] npl lío sg, jaleo sg.

rudder ['rʌdə*] n timón m.

ruddy ['rʌdɪ] a (face) rubicundo, frescote; (col: damned) condenado.

rude [ru:d] a (impolite: person) grosero; (: word, manners) rudo, grosero; (sudden) repentino; (shocking) verde, indecente; ~**ly** ad groseramente, toscamente; repentinamente; ~**ness** n grosería, tosquedad f.

rudiment ['ru:dɪmənt] n rudimento; ~**ary** [-'mentərɪ] a rudimentario.

rue [ru:] vt arrepentirse de; ~**ful** a arrepentido.

ruffian ['rʌfɪən] n matón m, criminal m.

ruffle ['rʌfl] vt (hair) despeinar; (clothes) arrugar; (fig: person) agitar.

rug [rʌg] n alfombra; (for knees) manta.

rugby ['rʌgbɪ] n (also: ~ **football**) rugby m.

rugged ['rʌgɪd] a (landscape) accidentado; (features, character) fuerte.

rugger ['rʌgə*] n (col) rugby m.

ruin ['ru:ɪn] n ruina // vt arruinar; (spoil) estropear; ~**s** npl ruinas fpl, restos mpl; ~**ous** a ruinoso.

rule [ru:l] n (norm) norma, costumbre f; (regulation) regla; (government) dominio; (ruler) metro // vt (country, person) gobernar; (decide) disponer; (draw: lines) trazar // vi regir; (LAW) fallar; **to ~ out** excluir; **as a ~** por regla general; ~**d** a (paper) rayado; **ruler** n (sovereign) soberano; (for measuring) regla; **ruling** n (of a party) gobernante; (class) dirigente // n (LAW) fallo, decisión f.

rum [rʌm] n ron m.

Rumania [ru:'meɪnɪə] n Rumanía; ~**n** a, n rumano/a.

rumble ['rʌmbl] n retumbo, ruido sordo; (of thunder) redoble m // vi retumbar, hacer un ruido sordo; (stomach, pipe) sonar.

rummage ['rʌmɪdʒ] vi revolverlo todo.

rumour, rumor (US) ['ru:mə*] n rumor m // vt: **it is ~ed that...** se rumorea que... .

rump [rʌmp] n (of animal) ancas fpl, grupa; ~ **steak** n filete m de lomo.

rumpus ['rʌmpəs] n (col) lío, jaleo; (quarrel) pelea, riña.

run [rʌn] n carrera; (outing) paseo, excursión f; (distance travelled) trayecto; (series) serie f; (THEATRE) temporada; (SKI) pista // (vb: pt **ran,** pp **run**) vt

(operate: business) dirigir; (: competition, course) organizar; (: hotel, house) administrar, llevar; (to pass: hand) pasar; (water, bath) abrir el grifo (del baño) // vi (gen) correr; (work: machine) funcionar, marchar; (bus, train: operate) circular, ir; (: travel) ir; (continue: play) seguir; (: contract) ser válido; (flow: river, bath) fluir; (colours, washing) desteñirse; (in election) ser candidato; **there was a ~ on** (meat, tickets) hubo mucha demanda de; **in the long ~** a la larga, a largo plazo; **on the ~** en fuga; **I'll ~ you to the station** te llevaré a la estación en coche; **to ~ a risk** correr un riesgo; **to ~ about** vi (children) correr por todos lados; **to ~ across** vt fus (find) dar con, toparse con; **to ~ away** vi huir; **to ~ down** vi (clock) parar // vt (AUT) atropellar; (criticize) criticar; **to be ~ down** estar debilitado; **to ~ off** vt (water) dejar correr // vi huir corriendo; **to ~ out** vi (person) salir corriendo; (liquid) irse; (lease) caducar, vencer; (money) acabarse; **to ~ out of** vt fus quedar sin; **to ~ over** vt sep (AUT) atropellar // vt fus (revise) repasar; **to ~ through** vt fus (instructions) repasar; **to ~ up** vt (debt) incurrir en, **to ~ up against** (difficulties) tropezar con; ~**away** a (horse) desbocado; (truck) sin frenos; (person) fugitivo.

rung [rʌŋ] pp of **ring** // n (of ladder) escalón m, peldaño.

runner ['rʌnə*] n (in race: person) corredor/a m/f; (: horse) caballo; (on sledge) patín m; (on curtain) anillo; (wheel) ruedecilla; ~ **bean** n (BOT) judía escarlata; ~**up** n subcampeón/ona m/f.

running ['rʌnɪŋ] n (sport) atletismo; (race) carrera // a (water) corriente; (commentary) continuo; **6 days ~** 6 días seguidos; ~ **board** n estribo.

runny ['rʌnɪ] a derretido.

run-of-the-mill ['rʌnəvðə'mɪl] a común y corriente.

runt [rʌnt] n (also: pej) redrojo, enano.

runway ['rʌnweɪ] n (AVIAT) pista de aterrizaje.

rupee [ru:'pi:] n rupia.

rupture ['rʌptʃə*] n (MED) hernia // vt: **to ~ o.s.** causarse una hernia, quebrarse.

rural ['ruərl] a rural.

ruse [ru:z] n ardid m.

rush [rʌʃ] n ímpetu m; (hurry) prisa; (COMM) demanda repentina; (BOT) junco; (current) corriente f fuerte, ráfaga // vt apresurar; (work) hacer de prisa; (attack: town etc) asaltar // vi correr, precipitarse; ~ **hour** n horas fpl punta.

rusk [rʌsk] n bizcocho tostado.

Russia ['rʌʃə] n Rusia; ~**n** a, n ruso/a.

rust [rʌst] n herrumbre f, moho // vi oxidarse.

rustic ['rʌstɪk] a rústico.

rustle ['rʌsl] vi susurrar // vt (paper) hacer crujir; (US: cattle) hurtar, robar.

rustproof ['rʌstpruːf] *a* inoxidable, a prueba de herrumbre.

rusty ['rʌstɪ] *a* oxidado, mohoso.

rut [rʌt] *n* rodera, carril *m*; (*ZOOL*) celo; **to be in a ~** ir encarrilado.

ruthless ['ruːθlɪs] *a* despiadado, ~**ness** *n* crueldad *f*, implacabilidad *f*.

rye [raɪ] *n* centeno; ~ **bread** *n* pan de centeno.

S

sabbath ['sæbəθ] *n* domingo; (*Jewish*) sábado.

sabbatical [sə'bætɪkl] *a*: ~ **year** año de licencia.

sabotage ['sæbɔtɑːʒ] *n* sabotaje *m* // *vt* sabotear.

saccharin(e) ['sækərɪn] *n* sacarina.

sack [sæk] *n* (*bag*) saco, costal *m* // *vt* (*dismiss*) despedir; (*plunder*) saquear; **to get the ~** ser despedido; ~**ing** *n* (*material*) harpillera.

sacrament ['sækrəmənt] *n* sacramento.

sacred ['seɪkrɪd] *a* sagrado, santo.

sacrifice ['sækrɪfaɪs] *n* sacrificio // *vt* sacrificar.

sacrilege ['sækrɪlɪdʒ] *n* sacrilegio.

sacrosanct ['sækrəʊsæŋkt] *a* sacrosanto.

sad [sæd] *a* (*unhappy*) triste; (*deplorable*) lamentable; ~**den** *vt* entristecer.

saddle ['sædl] *n* silla (de montar); (*of cycle*) sillín *m* // *vt* (*horse*) ensillar; **to be ~d with sth** (*col*) quedar cargado con algo; ~**bag** *n* alforja.

sadism ['seɪdɪzm] *n* sadismo; **sadist** *n* sadista *m/f*; **sadistic** [sə'dɪstɪk] *a* sádico.

sadly ['sædlɪ] *ad* tristemente; ~ **lacking (in)** muy deficiente (en).

sadness ['sædnɪs] *n* tristeza.

safari [sə'fɑːrɪ] *n* safari *m*.

safe [seɪf] *a* (*out of danger*) fuera de peligro; (*not dangerous, sure*) seguro; (*unharmed*) a salvo, ileso; (*trustworthy*) digno de confianza // *n* caja de caudales, caja fuerte; ~ **and sound** sano y salvo; (*just*) **to be on the ~ side** por mayor seguridad; ~**guard** *n* protección *f*, garantía // *vt* proteger, defender; ~**keeping** *n* custodia; ~**ly** *ad* seguramente, con seguridad; (*without mishap*) sin peligro.

safety ['seɪftɪ] *n* seguridad *f* // *a* de seguridad; ~ **first!** ¡precaución!; ~ **belt** *n* cinturón *m* de seguridad; ~ **pin** *n* imperdible *m*.

saffron ['sæfrən] *n* azafrán *m*.

sag [sæg] *vi* aflojarse.

sage [seɪdʒ] *n* (*herb*) salvia; (*man*) sabio.

Sagittarius [sædʒɪ'teərɪəs] *n* Sagitario.

sago ['seɪgəʊ] *n* sagú *m*.

said [sed] *pt, pp of* **say**.

sail [seɪl] *n* (*on boat*) vela; (*trip*): **to go for a ~** tomar un paseo en barco // *vt* (*boat*) gobernar // *vi* (*travel: ship*) navegar; (: *passenger*) pasear en barco; (*set off*)

zarpar; they ~**ed into Copenhagen** llegaron a Copenhague; **to ~ through** *vi, vt fus* (*fig*) hacer con facilidad; ~**boat** *n* (*US*) velero, barco de vela; ~**ing** *n* (*SPORT*) balandrismo; **to go ~ing** salir en balandro; ~**ing ship** *n* barco de vela; ~**or** *n* marinero, marino.

saint [seɪnt] *n* santo; **S~ John** San Juan; ~**ly** *a* santo.

sake [seɪk] *n*: **for the ~ of** por (motivo de).

salad ['sæləd] *n* ensalada; ~ **bowl** *n* ensaladera; ~ **cream** *n* mayonesa; ~ **dressing** *n* aliño; ~ **oil** *n* aceite *m* para ensaladas.

salami [sə'lɑːmɪ] *n* salami *m*.

salary ['sælərɪ] *n* sueldo.

sale [seɪl] *n* venta; (*at reduced prices*) liquidación *f*, saldo; "**grand ~**" grandes rebajas; "**for ~**" "se vende"; **on ~** en venta; ~**room** *n* sala de subastas; **salesman/woman** *n* vendedor/a *m/f*; (*in shop*) dependiente/a *m/f*; (*representative*) viajante *m/f*; **salesmanship** *n* arte *m* de vender.

saliva [sə'laɪvə] *n* saliva.

sallow ['sæləʊ] *a* cetrino.

salmon ['sæmən] *n, pl inv* salmón *m*.

saloon [sə'luːn] *n* (*US*) bar *m*, taberna; (*AUT*) (coche *m* de) turismo; (*ship's lounge*) cámara, salón *m*.

salt [sɔlt] *n* sal *f* // *vt* salar; (*put ~ on*) poner sal en; ~ **cellar** *n* salero; ~**water** *a* de agua salada; ~**y** *a* salado.

salutary ['sæljutəri] *a* saludable.

salute [sə'luːt] *n* saludo; (*of guns*) salva // *vt* saludar.

salvage ['sælvɪdʒ] *n* (*saving*) salvamento, recuperación *f*; (*things saved*) objetos *mpl* salvados // *vt* salvar.

salvation [sæl'veɪʃən] *n* salvación *f*; **S~ Army** *n* Ejército de Salvación.

salve [sælv] *n* (*cream etc*) ungüento, bálsamo.

salver ['sælvəˀ] *n* bandeja.

same [seɪm] *a* mismo // *ad* de la misma forma, igual // *pron*: **the ~** el mismo/la misma; **the ~ book as** el mismo libro que; **all** *or* **just the ~** sin embargo, aun así; **to do the ~ (as sb)** hacer lo mismo (que otro); **the ~ to you!** ¡igualmente!

sample ['sɑːmpl] *n* muestra // *vt* (*food, wine*) probar.

sanatorium [sænə'tɔːrɪəm], *pl* -**ria** [-rɪə] *n* sanatorio.

sanctify ['sæŋktɪfaɪ] *vt* santificar.

sanctimonious [sæŋktɪ'məʊnɪəs] *a* santurrón(ona).

sanction ['sæŋkʃən] *n* sanción *f* // *vt* sancionar.

sanctity ['sæŋktɪtɪ] *n* (*gen*) santidad *f*; (*inviolability*) inviolabilidad *f*.

sanctuary ['sæŋktjʊərɪ] *n* (*gen*) santuario; (*refuge*) asilo, refugio.

sand [sænd] *n* arena; (*beach*) playa // *vt* enarenar.

sandal ['sændl] *n* sandalia; (*wood*) sándalo.

sand: ~**bag** n saco de arena; ~**bank** n banco de arena; ~**castle** n castillo de arena; ~ **dune** n duna; ~**paper** n papel m de lija; ~**pit** n (for children) cajón m de arena; ~ **stone** n piedra arenisca.

sandwich ['sændwɪtʃ] n bocadillo, sándwich m // vt (also: ~ **in**) intercalar; ~**ed between** apretujado entre; **cheese/ham** ~ sándwich de queso/jamón; ~ **board** n cartelón m; ~ **course** n curso de medio tiempo.

sandy ['sændɪ] a arenoso; (colour) rojizo.

sane [seɪn] a cuerdo, sensato; (sensible) prudente.

sang [sæŋ] pt of **sing.**

sanitarium [sænɪ'tɛərɪəm] (US) = **sanatorium.**

sanitary ['sænɪtərɪ] a (system, arrangements) sanitario; (clean) higiénico; ~ **towel**, ~ **napkin** (US) n paño higiénico, compresa higiénica.

sanitation [sænɪ'teɪʃən] n (in house) saneamiento; (in town) sanidad f, higiene f.

sanity ['sænɪtɪ] a cordura; (common sense) juicio, sentido común.

sank [sæŋk] pt of **sink.**

Santa Claus [sæntə'klɔːz] n San Nicolás, Papá Noel.

sap [sæp] n (of plants) savia // vt (strength) minar, agotar.

sapling ['sæplɪŋ] n árbol nuevo o joven.

sapphire ['sæfaɪə*] n zafiro.

sarcasm ['sɑːkæzm] n sarcasmo; **sarcastic** [-'kæstɪk] a sarcástico.

sardine [sɑː'diːn] n sardina.

Sardinia [sɑː'dɪnɪə] n Cerdeña.

sari ['sɑːrɪ] n sari m.

sash [sæʃ] n faja.

sat [sæt] pt, pp of **sit.**

Satan ['seɪtn] n Satanás m.

satchel ['sætʃl] n bolsa; (child's) cartera.

satellite ['sætəlaɪt] n satélite m.

satin ['sætɪn] n raso // a de raso.

satire ['sætaɪə*] n sátira; **satirical** [sə'tɪrɪkl] a satírico; **satirize** ['sætɪraɪz] vt satirizar.

satisfaction [sætɪs'fækʃən] n satisfacción f; (of debt) liquidación f; **satisfactory** [-'fæktərɪ] a satisfactorio.

satisfy ['sætɪsfaɪ] vt satisfacer; (pay) liquidar; (convince) convencer; ~**ing** a satisfactorio.

saturate ['sætʃəreɪt] vt: **to** ~ **(with)** empapar o saturar (de); **saturation** [-'reɪʃən] n saturación f.

Saturday ['sætədɪ] n sábado.

sauce [sɔːs] n salsa; (sweet) crema; (fig: cheek) frescura; ~**pan** n perola.

saucer ['sɔːsə*] n platillo.

saucy ['sɔːsɪ] a fresco, descarado; (flirtatious) coqueta.

sauna ['sɔːnə] n sauna.

saunter ['sɔːntə*] vi deambular.

sausage ['sɒsɪdʒ] n salchicha; (cold meat) embutido; ~ **roll** n empanadita.

sauté ['sɔːteɪ] a salteado.

savage ['sævɪdʒ] a (cruel, fierce) feroz, furioso; (primitive) salvaje // n salvaje m/f // vt (attack) embestir; ~**ry** n ferocidad f; salvajismo.

save [seɪv] vt (rescue) salvar, rescatar; (money, time) ahorrar; (put by) guardar; (avoid: trouble) evitar // vi (also: ~ **up**) ahorrar // n (SPORT) parada // prep salvo, excepto.

saving ['seɪvɪŋ] n (on price etc) economía // a: **the** ~ **grace** of el único mérito de; ~**s** npl ahorros mpl; ~**s bank** n caja de ahorros.

saviour ['seɪvjə*] n salvador/a m/f.

savour, savor (US) ['seɪvə*] n sabor m, gusto // vt saborear; ~**y** a sabroso; (dish: not sweet) no dulce; (: salted) salado.

saw [sɔː] pt of **see** // n (tool) sierra // vt, pt **sawed**, pp **sawed** or **sawn** serrar; ~**dust** n (a)serrín m; ~**mill** n aserradero.

saxophone ['sæksəfəun] n saxófono.

say [seɪ] n: **to have one's** ~ expresar su opinión; **to have a** or **some** ~ **in** sth tener voz o tener que ver en algo // vt, pt, pp **said** decir; **to** ~ **yes/no** decir que sí/no; **that is to** ~ es decir; **that goes without** ~**ing** eso va sin decir; ~**ing** n dicho, refrán m.

scab [skæb] n costra; (pej) esquirol/a m/f; ~**by** a costroso, lleno de costras.

scaffold ['skæfəuld] n (for execution) cadalso, patíbulo; ~**ing** n andamios mpl, andamiaje m.

scald [skɔːld] n escaldadura // vt escaldar; ~**ing** a (hot) hirviendo.

scale [skeɪl] n (gen, MUS) escala; (of fish) escama; (of salaries, fees etc) escalafón m; (of map, also size, extent) escala // vt (mountain) escalar; (tree) trepar; ~**s** npl (small) balanza sg; (large) báscula sg; **on a large** ~ a gran escala; ~ **of charges** tarifa, lista de precios; **social** ~ escala social; ~ **drawing** n dibujo a escala; ~ **model** n modelo a escala.

scallop ['skɒləp] n (ZOOL) venera; (SEWING) festón m.

scalp [skælp] n cabellera // vt escalpar.

scalpel ['skælpl] n escalpelo.

scamp [skæmp] n diablillo, travieso.

scamper ['skæmpə*] vi: **to** ~ **away**, ~ **off** irse corriendo.

scan [skæn] vt (examine) escudriñar; (glance at quickly) dar un vistazo a; (TV, RADAR) explorar, registrar.

scandal ['skændl] n escándalo; (gossip) chismes mpl; ~**ize** vt escandalizar; ~**ous** a escandaloso; (libellous) calumnioso.

Scandinavia [skændɪ'neɪvɪə] n Escandinavia; ~**n** a escandinavo.

scant [skænt] a escaso; ~**y** a escaso.

scapegoat ['skeɪpgəut] n cabeza de turco, chivo expiatorio.

scar [skɑː] n cicatriz f // vt marcar con una cicatriz // vi cicatrizarse.

scarce [skɛəs] a escaso; ~**ly** ad apenas; **scarcity** n escasez f; (shortage) carestía.

scare [skɛə*] n susto, sobresalto; (panic)

pánico // vt asustar, espantar; **to ~ sb stiff** dejar muerto de miedo a uno; **bomb ~** amenaza de bomba; **~crow** n espantapájaros m inv; **~d** a: **to be ~d** asustárse, estar asustado.

scarf [skɑːf], pl **scarves** n (long) bufanda; (square) pañuelo.

scarlet ['skɑːlit] a escarlata; **~ fever** n escarlatina.

scarves [skɑːvz] pl of **scarf**.

scary ['skɛəri] a (col) de miedo.

scathing ['skeiðiŋ] a mordaz.

scatter ['skætə*] vt (spread) esparcir, desparramar; (put to flight) dispersar // vi desparramarse; dispersarse; **~brained** a ligero de cascos; (forgetful) olvidadizo.

scavenger ['skævəndʒə*] n (refuse collector) basurero; (ZOOL) animal m que se alimenta de la carroña.

scene [siːn] n (THEATRE, fig etc) escena; (of crime, accident) escenario; (sight, view) vista, perspectiva; (fuss) escándalo; **~ry** n (THEATRE) decorado; (landscape) paisaje m; **scenic** a (picturesque) pintoresco.

scent [sɛnt] n perfume m, olor m; (fig: track) rastro, pista; (sense of smell) olfato // vt perfumar; (smell) oler; (sniff out) husmear; (suspect) sospechar.

sceptic, skeptic (US) ['skɛptik] a escéptico/a; **~al** a escéptico; **~ism** ['skɛptisizm] n escepticismo.

sceptre, scepter (US) ['sɛptə*] n cetro.

schedule ['ʃɛdjuːl] n (of trains) horario; (of events) programa m; (plan) plan m; (list) lista // vt (timetable) establecer el horario de; (list) catalogar; (visit) fijar la hora de; **on ~** a la hora, sin retraso; **to be ahead of/behind ~** estar adelantado/en retraso.

scheme [skiːm] n (plan) plan m, proyecto; (method) esquema m; (plot) intriga; (trick) ardid m; (arrangement) disposición f // vi proyectar // vi (plan) hacer proyectos; (intrigue) intrigar; **scheming** a intrigante.

schism ['skizəm] n cisma m.

schizophrenia [skitsəu'friːniə] n esquizofrenia; **schizophrenic** [-sə'frɛnik] a esquizofrénico.

scholar ['skɔlə*] n (pupil) alumno/a, estudiante m/f; (learned person) sabio, erudito; **~ly** a erudito; **~ship** n erudición f; (grant) beca.

school [skuːl] n (gen) escuela, colegio; (in university) facultad f // vt (animal) amaestrar; **~ age** n edad f escolar; **~book** n libro de texto; **~boy** n alumno; **~days** npl años mpl del colegio; **~girl** n alumna; **~ing** n enseñanza; **~master/mistress** n (primary) maestro/a; (secondary) profesor/a m/f; **~room** n clase f; **~teacher** n maestro/a.

schooner ['skuːnə*] n (ship) goleta; (glass) jarra.

sciatica [sai'ætikə] n ciática.

science ['saiəns] n ciencia; **~ fiction** n ciencia-ficción f; **scientific** [-'tifik] a

científico; **scientist** n científico.

scimitar ['simitə*] n cimitarra.

scintillating ['sintileitiŋ] a brillante, ingenioso.

scissors ['sizəz] npl tijeras fpl; **a pair of ~** unas tijeras.

scoff [skɔf] vt (col: eat) engullir // vi: **to ~ (at)** (mock) mofarse (de).

scold [skəuld] vt regañar.

scone [skɔn] n panecillo.

scoop [skuːp] n cucharón m; (for flour etc) pala; (PRESS) exclusiva; **to ~ out** vt excavar; **to ~ up** vt recoger.

scooter ['skuːtə*] n (motor cycle) moto f; (toy) patinete m.

scope [skəup] n (of plan, undertaking) ámbito; (reach) alcance m; (of person) competencia; (opportunity) campo (de acción).

scorch [skɔːtʃ] vt (clothes) chamuscar; (earth, grass) quemar, secar; **~er** n (col: hot day) día m abrasador; **~ing** a abrasador(a).

score [skɔː*] n (points etc) puntuación f; (MUS) partitura; (reckoning) cuenta; (twenty) veinte m, veintena // vt (goal, point) ganar; (mark) rayar // vi marcar un tanto; (FOOTBALL) marcar (un) gol; (keep score) llevar el tanteo; **on that ~** en lo que se refiere a eso; **to ~ 6 out of 10** obtener una puntuación de 6 sobre 10; **~board** n marcador m; **~card** n (SPORT) tanteador m; **scorer** n marcador m; (keeping score) tanteador m.

scorn [skɔːn] n desprecio // vt despreciar; **~ful** a desdeñoso, despreciativo.

Scorpio ['skɔːpiəu] n Escorpión m.

scorpion ['skɔːpiən] n escorpión m.

Scot [skɔt] n escocés/esa m/f.

scotch [skɔtʃ] vt (rumour) desmentir; (plan) abandonar; **S~** n whisky m escocés.

Scotland ['skɔtlənd] n Escocia.

Scots [skɔts] a escocés(esa); **~man/woman** n escocés/esa m/f; **Scottish** ['skɔtiʃ] a escocés(esa).

scoundrel ['skaundrl] n canalla m/f, sinvergüenza m/f.

scour ['skauə*] vt (clean) fregar, estregar; (search) recorrer, registrar; **~er** n estropajo.

scourge [skɔːdʒ] n azote m.

scout [skaut] n (MIL, also: **boy ~**) explorador m; **to ~ around** reconocer el terreno.

scowl [skaul] vi fruncir el ceño; **to ~ at sb** mirar con ceño a uno.

scraggy ['skrægi] a flaco, descarnado.

scram [skræm] vi (col) largarse.

scramble ['skræmbl] n (climb) subida (difícil); (struggle) pelea // vi: **to ~ out/through** salir/abrirse paso con dificultad; **to ~ for** pelear por; **~d eggs** npl huevos mpl revueltos.

scrap [skræp] n (bit) pedacito; (fig: pizca; (fight) riña, bronca; (also: **~ iron**) chatarra, hierro viejo // vt reducir a chatarra; (*discard*) desechar, descartar // *vi* reñir, armar (una) bronca; ~s *npl* (*waste*) sobras *fpl*, desperdicios *mpl*; ~**book** *n* álbum *m* de recortes.

scrape [skreɪp] *n* (*fig*) lío, apuro // *vt* raspar; (*skin etc*) rasguñar; (~ *against*) rozar // *vi*: **to** ~ **through** pasar con dificultad; **scraper** *n* raspador *m*.

scrap: ~ **heap** *n* (*fig*): **on the** ~ **heap** desperdiciado; ~ **merchant** *n* chatarrero; ~ **paper** *n* pedazos *mpl* de papel; ~**py** *a* (*poor*) pobre; (*speech*) inconexo; (*bitty*) fragmentario.

scratch [skrætʃ] *n* rasguño; (*from claw*) arañazo // *a*: ~ **team** equipo improvisado // *vt* (*record*) rayar; (*with claw, nail*) rasguñar, arañar // *vi* rascarse; **to start from** ~ partir de cero, empezar desde el principio; **to be up to** ~ estar a la altura (de las circunstancias).

scrawl [skrɔːl] *n* garabatos *mpl* // *vi* hacer garabatos.

scream [skriːm] *n* chillido // *vi* chillar.

screech [skriːtʃ] *vi* chirriar.

screen [skriːn] *n* (CINEMA, TV) pantalla; (*movable*) biombo; (*wall*) tabique *m*; (*also*: **wind**~) parabrisas *m inv*; (*fig*) cortina // *vt* (*conceal*) tapar; (*from the wind etc*) proteger; (*film*) proyectar; (*candidates etc*) investigar a; ~**ing** *n* (MED) investigación *f* médica; ~ **test** *n* prueba de pantalla.

screw [skruː] *n* tornillo; (*propeller*) hélice *f* // *vt* atornillar; (*also*: ~ **in**) apretar; ~**driver** *n* destornillador *m*; ~**y** *a* (*col*) chiflado.

scribble [ˈskrɪbl] *n* garabatos *mpl* // *vt* escribir con prisa.

script [skrɪpt] *n* (CINEMA *etc*) guión *m*; (*writing*) escritura, letra.

Scripture [ˈskrɪptʃə*] *n* Sagrada Escritura.

scriptwriter [ˈskrɪptraɪtə*] *n* guionista *m/f*.

scroll [skrəul] *n* rollo.

scrounge [skraundʒ] *vt* (*col*): **to** ~ **sth off** *or* **from sb** obtener algo de otro por gorronería // *vi*: **to** ~ **on sb** vivir a costa de uno; **scrounger** *n* gorrón/ona *m/f*.

scrub [skrʌb] *n* (*clean*) fregado; (*land*) maleza // *vt* fregar, restregar; (*reject*) cancelar, anular.

scruff [skrʌf] *n*: **by the** ~ **of the neck** por el pescuezo.

scruffy [ˈskrʌfɪ] *a* desaliñado, piojoso.

scruple [ˈskruːpl] *n* escrúpulo; **scrupulous** *a* escrupuloso.

scrutinize [ˈskruːtɪnaɪz] *vt* escudriñar; (*votes*) escrutar; **scrutiny** [-nɪ] *n* escrutinio, examen *m*.

scuff [skʌf] *vt* desgastar, restregar.

scuffle [ˈskʌfl] *n* refriega.

scullery [ˈskʌlərɪ] *n* fregadero, trascocina.

sculptor [ˈskʌlptə*] *n* escultor *m*; **sculpture** [-tʃə*] *n* escultura.

scum [skʌm] *n* (*on liquid*) nata; (*pej*: *people*) canalla; (*fig*) heces *fpl*.

scurry [ˈskʌrɪ] *vi*: **to** ~ **off** escabullirse.

scurvy [ˈskɔːvɪ] *n* escorbuto.

scuttle [ˈskʌtl] *n* (*also*: **coal** ~) cubo, carbonera // *vt* (*ship*) barrenar // *vi* (*scamper*): **to** ~ **away**, ~ **off** escabullirse.

scythe [saɪð] *n* guadaña.

sea [siː] *n* mar *m or f*; **on the** ~ (*boat*) en el mar; (*town*) junto al mar; **to be all at** ~ (*fig*) estar despistado; **out** *o* or **at** ~ en alta mar; ~ **bird** *n* ave *f* marina; ~**board** *n* litoral *m*; ~ **breeze** *n* brisa de mar; ~**farer** *n* marinero; ~**food** *n* mariscos *mpl*; ~ **front** *n* (*beach*) playa; (*prom*) paseo marítimo; ~**going** *a* (*ship*) de alta mar; ~**gull** *n* gaviota.

seal [siːl] *n* (*animal*) foca; (*stamp*) sello // *vt* (*close*) cerrar; (: *with* ~) sellar; **to** ~ **off** obturar; **it** ~**ed his fate** decidió su destino.

sea level [ˈsiːlɛvl] *n* nivel *m* del mar.

sealing wax [ˈsiːlɪŋwæks] *n* lacre *m*.

sea lion [ˈsiːlaɪən] *n* león *m* marino.

seam [siːm] *n* costura; (*of metal*) juntura; (*of coal*) veta, filón *m*.

seaman [ˈsiːmən] *n* marinero.

seamless [ˈsiːmlɪs] *a* sin costura.

seamstress [ˈsɛmstrɪs] *n* costurera.

seance [ˈseɪɔns] *n* sesión *f* de espiritismo.

sea: ~**plane** *n* hidroavión *m*; ~**port** *n* puerto de mar.

search [sɔːtʃ] *n* (*for person, thing*) busca, búsqueda; (*of drawer, pockets*) registro; (*inspection*) reconocimiento // *vt* (*look in*) buscar en; (*examine*) examinar; (*person, place*) registrar // *vi*: **to** ~ **for** buscar; **to** ~ **through** *vt fus* registrar; **in** ~ **of** en busca de; ~**ing** *a* penetrante; ~**light** *n* reflector *m*; ~ **party** *n* pelotón *m* de salvamento; ~ **warrant** *n* mandamiento (judicial).

sea: ~**shore** *n* playa, orilla del mar; ~**sick** *a* mareado; ~**side** *n* playa, orilla del mar; ~**side resort** *n* playa.

season [ˈsiːzn] *n* (*of year*) estación *f*; (*sporting etc*) temporada; (*gen*) época, período // *vt* (*food*) sazonar; ~**al** *a* estacional; ~**ing** *n* condimento, aderezo; ~ **ticket** *n* billete *m* de abono.

seat [siːt] *n* (*in bus, train: place*) asiento; (*chair*) silla; (PARLIAMENT) escaño; (*buttocks*) culo, trasero; (*of government*) sede *f* // *vt* sentar; (*have room for*) tener asientos para; **to be** ~**ed** sentarse; ~ **belt** *n* cinturón *m* de seguridad.

sea: ~ **water** *n* agua *m* del mar; ~**weed** *n* alga marina; ~**worthy** *a* marinero, en condiciones de navegar.

sec. *abbr of* **second(s)**.

secede [sɪˈsiːd] *vi* separarse.

secluded [sɪˈkluːdɪd] *a* retirado; **seclusion** [-ˈkluːʒən] *n* retiro.

second [ˈsɛkənd] *a* segundo // *ad* (*in race etc*) en segundo lugar // *n* (*gen*) segundo; (AUT. *also*: ~ **gear**) segunda; (COMM) artículo con algún desperfecto // *vt* (*motion*) apoyar; ~**ary** *a* secundario; ~**ary school** *n* escuela secundaria; ~**class** *a* de segunda clase; ~**hand** *a* de segunda

mano, usado; ~ **hand** n (on clock)
segundero; ~**ly** ad en segundo lugar;
~**ment** [sɪ'kɔndmənt]   n   traslado
temporal; ~-**rate** a de segunda categoría.
secrecy ['si:krəsɪ] n secreto; **secret** [-krɪt]
a, n secreto.
secretarial   [sɛkrɪ'tɛərɪəl]   a   de
secretario/a.
secretariat [sɛkrɪ'tɛərɪət] n secretaría.
secretary ['sɛkrətərɪ] n secretario/a; **S~**
of State (Brit: POL) Ministro (con cartera).
secretive ['si:krətɪv] a reservado, sigiloso.
sect [sɛkt] n secta; ~**arian** [-'tɛərɪən] a
sectario.
section ['sɛkʃən] n sección f; (part) parte f;
(of document) artículo; (of opinion) sector
m; ~**al** (a drawing) en corte.
sector ['sɛktə*] n sector m.
secular ['sɛkjulə*] a secular, seglar.
secure [sɪ'kjuə*] a (free from anxiety)
seguro; (firmly fixed) firme, fijo // vt (fix)
asegurar, afianzar; (get) conseguir.
security [sɪ'kjuərɪtɪ] n seguridad f; (for
loan) fianza; (: object) prenda.
sedate [sɪ'deɪt] a (calm) tranquilo;
(formal) serio, formal // vt tratar con
calmantes.
sedation [sɪ'deɪʃən] n (MED) sedación f;
sedative ['sɛdɪtɪv] n sedante m, sedativo.
sedentary ['sɛdntrɪ] a sedentario.
sediment ['sɛdɪmənt] n sedimento.
seduce [sɪ'dju:s] vt (gen) seducir;
seduction [-'dʌkʃən] n seducción f;
seductive [-'dʌktɪv] a seductor(a).
see [si:], pt **saw**, pp **seen** vt (gen) ver;
(accompany): **to ~ sb to the door**
acompañar a uno a la puerta; (understand)
ver, comprender; (look at) mirar // vi ver,
// n sede f; **to ~ that** (ensure) asegurar
que; **to ~ about** vt atender a, encargarse
de; **to ~ off** vt despedirse de; **to ~**
through vt penetrar (con la vista) // vt fus
llevar a cabo; **to ~ to** vt fus atender a,
encargarse de.
seed [si:d] n semilla; (in fruit) pepita;
(sperm) semen m, simiente f; (fig) germen
m; (TENNIS) preseleccionado/a; ~**ling** n
planta de semillero; ~**y** a (shabby) desaseado, raído.
seeing ['si:ɪŋ] conj: ~ (**that**) visto que, en
vista de que.
seek [si:k], pt, pp **sought** vt (gen) buscar;
(post) solicitar.
seem [si:m] vi parecer; ~**ingly** ad
aparentemente, según parece.
seen [si:n] pp of **see**.
seep [si:p] vi filtrarse.
seesaw ['si:sɔ:] n balancín m, columpio.
seethe [si:ð] vi hervir; **to ~ with anger**
enfurecerse.
segment ['sɛgmənt] n segmento.
segregate ['sɛgrɪgeɪt]   vt   segregar;
segregation [-'geɪʃən] n segregación f.
seismic ['saɪzmɪk] a sísmico.
seize [si:z] vt (grasp) agarrar, asir; (take
possession of) secuestrar; (: territory)
apoderarse de; (opportunity) aprovecharse

de; **to ~ (up)on** vt fus valerse de; **to ~**
up vi (TECH) agarrotarse.
seizure ['si:ʒə*] n (MED) ataque m; (LAW)
incautación f.
seldom ['sɛldəm] ad rara vez.
select [sɪ'lɛkt] a selecto, escogido // vt
escoger, elegir; (SPORT) seleccionar; ~**ion**
[-'lɛkʃən] n selección f, elección f; (COMM)
surtido; ~**ive** a selectivo; ~**or** n (person)
seleccionado/a m/f.
self [sɛlf] pron se; (after prep) sí mismo //
n, pl **selves** uno mismo; **him~/her~** él
mismo/ella misma; **the ~** el yo.
self... pref auto...; ~-**appointed** a
autonombrado; ~-**assured** a seguro de sí
mismo; ~-**catering** a sin pensión;
~-**centred** a egocéntrico; ~-**coloured** a
de color natural; (of one colour) de un
color; ~-**confidence** n confianza en sí
mismo;   ~-**conscious**   a   cohibido;
~-**contained** a (ger) independiente;
(flat) con entrada particular; ~-**control** n
autodominio; ~-**defence** n defensa
propia; ~-**discipline** n autodisciplina;
~-**employed** a que trabaja por cuenta
propia;   ~-**evident**   a   patente;
~-**governing** a autónomo; ~-**important**
a presumido; ~-**indulgent** a inmoderado;
~-**interest** n egoísmo; ~-**ish** a egoísta;
~-**ishness** n egoísmo; ~-**lessly** ad
desinteresadamente;   ~-**pity**   n
autocompasión   f;   ~-**portrait**   n
autorretrato; ~-**possessed** a sereno,
dueño de sí mismo; ~-**preservation** n
propia conservación f; ~-**reliant** a
independiente, seguro de sí mismo;
~-**respect**   n   amor   n   propio;
~-**righteous**   a   santurrón(ona);
~-**sacrifice** n abnegación f; ~-**satisfied**
a satisfecho de sí mismo; ~-**service** a de
autoservicio;   ~-**sufficient**   a   auto-
suficiente; ~-**taught** a autodidacta.
sell [sɛl], pt, pp **sold** vt vender // vi
venderse; **to ~ at** or **for £10** vender a 10
libros; **to ~ off** vt liquidar; **to ~ out** vi
transigir, transar (AM); ~**er** n vendedor/a
m/f, ~**ing price** n precio de venta.
sellotape ['sɛləuteɪp] n celo ®
sellout ['sɛlaut] n traición f; (of tickets): **it**
was a ~ fue un éxito de taquilla.
selves [sɛlvz] pl of **self**.
semaphore ['sɛməfɔ:*] n semáforo.
semen ['si:mən] n semen m.
semi... [sɛmɪ] pref semi... medio...;
~**circle** n semicírculo; ~**colon** n punto y
coma;   ~**conscious** a semiconsciente;
~**detached**   (**house**)   n   (casa)
semiseparada; ~-**final** n semi-final m
seminar ['sɛmɪnɑ:*] n seminario
semitone ['sɛmɪtəun] n (MUS) semitono.
semolina [sɛmə'li:nə] n sémola.
senate ['sɛnɪt] n senado; **senator** n
senador/a m/f.
send [sɛnd], pt, pp **sent** vt mandar, enviar;
(dispatch) despachar; (telegram) poner; **to**
~ **away** vt (letter, goods) despachar; **to**
~ **away for** vt fus despachar por, **to ~**

back *vt* devolver; **to ~ for** *vt fus* mandar traer; **to ~ off** *vt* (*goods*) despachar; (*SPORT: player*) expulsar; **to ~ out** *vt* (*invitation*) mandar; (*signal*) emitir; **to ~ up** *vt* (*person, price*) hacer subir; (*parody*) parodiar; **~er** *n* remitente *m/f*; **~-off** *n*: **a good ~-off** una buena despedida.

senile ['si:naɪl] *a* senil; **senility** [sɪ'nɪlɪtɪ] *n* senilidad *f.*

senior ['si:nɪə*] *a* (*older*) mayor, más viejo; (: *on staff*) más antiguo; (*of higher rank*) superior // *n* mayor *m*; (*in service*) miembro más antiguo; **~ity** [-'ɔrɪtɪ] *n* antigüedad *f.*

sensation [sɛn'seɪʃən] *n* sensación *f*; **~al** *a* sensacional; **~alism** *n* sensacionalismo.

sense [sɛns] *n* sentido; (*feeling*) sensación *f*; (*good ~*) sentido común, juicio; (*sentiment*) opinión *f* // *vt* sentir, percibir; **it makes ~** tiene sentido; **~less** *a* estúpido, insensato; (*unconscious*) sin-sentido.

sensibility [sɛnsɪ'bɪlɪtɪ] *n* sensibilidad *f*; **sensibilities** *npl* delicadeza *sg.*

sensible ['sɛnsɪbl] *a* sensato, juicio; (*cautious*) prudente; (*reasonable*) razonable, lógico; (*perceptible*) apreciable.

sensitive ['sɛnsɪtɪv] *a* sensible; (*touchy*) susceptible; **sensitivity** [-'tɪvɪtɪ] *n* sensibilidad *f*; susceptibilidad *f.*

sensual ['sɛnsjuəl] *a* sensual.

sensuous ['sɛnsjuəs] *a* sensual.

sent [sɛnt] *pt, pp of* **send.**

sentence ['sɛntns] *n* (*LING*) frase *f*, oración *f*; (*LAW*) sentencia, fallo *m* // *vt*: **to ~ sb to death/to 5 years** condenar a uno a muerte/a 5 años de cárcel.

sentiment ['sɛntɪmənt] *n* sentimiento; (*opinion*) opinión *f*; **~al** [-'mɛntl] *a* sentimental; **~ality** [-'tælɪtɪ] *n* sentimentalismo.

sentry ['sɛntrɪ] *n* centinela *m.*

separate ['sɛprɪt] *a* separado; (*distinct*) distinto // (*vb*: ['sɛpəreɪt]) *vt* separar; (*part*) dividir // *vi* separarse; **~ly** *ad* por separado; **~s** *npl* (*clothes*) coordinados *mpl*; **separation** [-'reɪʃən] *n* separación *f.*

September [sɛp'tɛmbə*] *n* se(p)tiembre *m.*

septic ['sɛptɪk] *a* séptico.

sequel ['si:kwl] *n* consecuencia, resultado; (*of story*) continuación *f.*

sequence ['si:kwəns] *n* sucesión *f*, serie *f*; (*CINEMA*) secuencia.

sequin ['si:kwɪn] *n* lentejuela.

serenade [sɛrə'neɪd] *n* serenata // *vt* dar serenata a.

serene [sɪ'ri:n] *a* sereno, tranquilo; **serenity** [sə'rɛnɪtɪ] *n* serenidad *f*, tranquilidad *f.*

sergeant ['sɑ:dʒənt] *n* sargento.

serial ['sɪərɪəl] *n* novela por entregas; **~ize** *vt* publicar por entregas; **~ number** *n* número de serie.

series ['sɪərɪ:s] *n* serie *f.*

serious ['sɪərɪəs] *a* serio; (*grave*) grave;

~ly *ad* en serio; gravemente; **~ness** *n* seriedad *f*; gravedad *f.*

sermon ['sɜ:mən] *n* sermón *m.*

serrated [sɪ'reɪtɪd] *a* serrado, dentellado.

serum ['sɪərəm] *n* suero.

servant ['sɜ:vənt] *n* (*gen*) servidor/a *m/f*; (*house ~*) criado/a; **civil ~** funcionario.

serve [sɜ:v] *vt* (*gen*) servir; (*in shop: goods*) servir, despachar; (: *customer*) atender; (*subj: train*) pasar por; (*treat*) tratar; (*apprenticeship*) hacer; (*prison term*) cumplir // *vi* (*also TENNIS*) sacar; (*be useful*): **to ~ as/for/to do** servir de/para/para hacer // *n* (*TENNIS*) saque *m*; **to ~ out, ~ up** *vt* (*food*) servir.

service ['sɜ:vɪs] *n* (*gen*) servicio; (*REL*) misa; (*AUT*) mantenimiento; (*of dishes*) vajilla, juego // *vt* (*car, washing machine*) mantener; (: *repair*) reparar; **the S~s** las fuerzas armadas; **to be of ~ to sb** ser útil a uno; **~able** *a* servible, utilizable; **~ area** *n* (*on motorway*) servicios *mpl*; **~man** *n* militar *m*; **~ station** *n* estación *f* de servicio.

serviette [sɜ:vɪ'ɛt] *n* servilleta.

servile ['sɜ:vaɪl] *a* servil.

session ['sɛʃən] *n* (*sitting*) sesión *f*; **to be in ~** estar celebrando sesión.

set [sɛt] *n* juego; (*RADIO*) aparato; (*TV*) televisor *m*; (*of utensils*) batería (*of cutlery*) cubierto; (*of books*) colección *f*; (*TENNIS*) set *m*; (*group of people*) grupo; (*CINEMA*) plató *m*; (*THEATRE*) decorado; (*HAIRDRESSING*) marcado // *a* (*fixed*) fijo; (*ready*) listo; (*resolved*) resuelto, decidido // (*vb*: *pt, pp* **set**) *vt* (*place*) poner, colocar; (*fix*) fijar; (: *a time*) señalar; (*adjust*) ajustar, arreglar; (*decide: rules etc*) establecer, decidir // *vi* (*sun*) ponerse; (*jam, jelly*) cuajarse; (*concrete*) fraguar; **to be ~ on doing sth** estar empeñado en hacer algo; **to ~ to music** poner música a; **to ~ on fire** incendiar, poner fuego a; **to ~ free** poner en libertad; **to ~ sth going** poner algo en marcha; **to ~ sail** zarpar, hacerse a la vela; **to ~ about** *vt fus* (*task*) ponerse a; **to ~ aside** *vt* poner aparte, dejar de lado; **to ~ back** *vt* (*in time*): **to ~ back (by)** retrasar (por); **to ~ off** *vi* partir // *vt* (*bomb*) hacer estallar; (*cause to start*) poner en marcha; (*show up well*) hacer resaltar; **to ~ out** *vi*: **to ~ out to do sth** ponerse a hacer algo // *vt* (*arrange*) disponer; (*state*) exponer; **to ~ up** *vt* (*organization, record*) establecer; **to ~ up shop** (*fig*) establecerse; **~back** *n* (*hitch*) revés *m*, contratiempo.

settee [sɛ'ti:] *n* sofá *m.*

setting ['sɛtɪŋ] *n* (*frame*) marco; (*placing*) colocación *f*; (*of sun*) puesta; (*of jewel*) engaste *m*, montadura.

settle ['sɛtl] *vt* (*argument, matter*) componer; (*accounts*) ajustar, liquidar; (*land*) colonizar; (*MED: calm*) calmar, sosegar // *vi* (*dust etc*) depositarse; (*weather*) serenarse; (*also*: **~ down**)

instalarse, establecerse; **to ~ for sth**
convenir en aceptar algo; **to ~ in** vi
instalarse; **to ~ on sth** quedar en algo; **to
~ up with sb** ajustar cuentas con uno;
~ment n (payment) liquidación f; (agreement) acuerdo, convenio; (village etc)
pueblo; **settler** n colono/a, colonizador/a
m/f.

setup ['sɛtʌp] n (arrangement) plan m;
(situation) situación f.

seven ['sɛvn] num siete; **~teen** num diez y
siete, diecisiete; **~th** a séptimo; **~ty** num
setenta.

sever ['sɛvə*] vt cortar; (relations) romper.

several ['sɛvrəl] a, pron varios mpl,
algunos mpl; **~ of us** varios de nosotros.

severance ['sɛvərəns] n (of relations)
ruptura; **~ pay** n pago de despedida.

severe [sɪ'vɪə*] a severo; (serious) grave;
(hard) duro; (pain) intenso; **severity**
[sɪ'vɛrɪtɪ] n severidad f; gravedad f;
intensidad f.

sew [səu], pt **sewed**, pp **sewn** vt, vi coser;
to ~ up vt coser, zurcir.

sewage ['su:ɪdʒ] n (effluence) aguas fpl
residuales; (system) alcantarillado.

sewer ['su:ə*] n alcantarilla, cloaca.

sewing ['səuɪŋ] n costura; **~ machine** n
máquina de coser.

sewn [səun] pp of **sew**.

sex [sɛks] n sexo; **to have ~ with sb**
tener sexo con alguien; **~ act** n acto
sexual.

sextet [sɛks'tɛt] n sexteto.

sexual ['sɛksjuəl] a sexual.

sexy ['sɛksɪ] a sexy.

shabby ['ʃæbɪ] a (person) desharrapado,
(clothes) raído, gastado.

shack [ʃæk] n choza, chabola.

shackles ['ʃæklz] npl grillos mpl, grilletes
mpl.

shade [ʃeɪd] n sombra; (for lamp) pantalla;
(for eyes) visera; (of colour) matiz m,
tonalidad f // vt dar sombra a; **in the ~**
en la sombra.

shadow ['ʃædəu] n sombra // vt (follow)
seguir y vigilar; **~ cabinet** n (POL)
gabinete paralelo formado por el partido de
oposición; **~y** a oscuro; (dim) indistinto.

shady ['ʃeɪdɪ] a sombreado; (fig: dishonest)
sospechoso; (: deal) turbio.

shaft [ʃɑ:ft] n (of arrow, spear) astil m; (AUT,
TECH) eje m, árbol m; (of mine) pozo; (of
lift) hueco, caja; (of light) rayo.

shaggy ['ʃægɪ] a peludo.

shake [ʃeɪk], pt **shook**, pp **shaken** vt
sacudir; (building) hacer temblar;
(perturb) inquietar, perturbar; (weaken)
debilitar; (surprise) sorprender, pasmar //
vi estremecerse; (tremble) temblar // a
(movement) sacudida; **to ~ hands with
sb** estrechar la mano con uno; **to ~ off** vt
sacudirse; (fig) deshacerse de; **to ~ up** vt
agitar; **shaky** a (hand, voice) trémulo;
(building) inestable.

shall [ʃæl] auxiliary vb: **I ~ go** iré.

shallot [ʃə'lɔt] n chalote m.

shallow ['ʃæləu] a poco profundo; (fig)
superficial.

sham [ʃæm] n fraude m, engaño // a falso,
fingido // vt fingir, simular.

shambles ['ʃæmblz] n confusión f.

shame [ʃeɪm] n vergüenza; (pity) lástima
// vt avergonzar; **it is a ~ that/to do es**
una lástima que/hacer; **what a ~!** ¡qué
lástima!; **~faced** a avergonzado; **~ful** a
vergonzoso; **~less** a descarado;
(immodest) impúdico.

shampoo [ʃæm'pu:] n champú m // vt
lavar el pelo (con champú).

shamrock ['ʃæmrɔk] n trébol m.

shandy ['ʃændɪ] n mezcla de cerveza con
gaseosa.

shan't [ʃɑ:nt] = **shall not**.

shanty town ['ʃæntɪ-] n barrio de
chabolas.

shape [ʃeɪp] n forma // vt formar, dar
forma a; (sb's ideas) formar; (sb's life)
determinar // vi (also: **~ up**) (events)
desarrollarse; (person) formarse; **to take
~** tomar forma; **-shaped** suff: **heart-
shaped** en forma de corazón; **~less** a
informe, sin forma definida; **~ly** a bien
formado o proporcionado.

share [ʃɛə*] n (part) parte f, porción f;
(contribution) cuota; (COMM) acción f // vt
dividir; (have in common) compartir; **to ~
out** (among or between) repartir
(entre); **~holder** n accionista m/f.

shark [ʃɑ:k] n tiburón m.

sharp [ʃɑ:p] a (razor, knife) afilado; (point)
puntiagudo; (outline) definido; (pain)
intenso; (MUS) desafinado; (contrast)
marcado; (voice) agudo; (person: quick-
witted) astuto; (dishonest) poco
escrupuloso // n (MUS) sostenido // ad: **at
2 o'clock ~** a las 2 en punto; **~en** vt
afilar; (pencil) sacar punta a; (fig)
agudizar; **~ener** n (also: **pencil ~ener**)
afilador m; **~-eyed** a de vista aguda;
~-witted a listo, perspicaz.

shatter ['ʃætə*] vt hacer añicos o pedazos;
(fig: ruin) destruir, acabar con // vi
hacerse añicos.

shave [ʃeɪv] vt afeitar, rasurar // vi
afeitarse // n: **to have a ~** afeitarse;
shaver n (also: **electric shaver**)
máquina de afeitar (eléctrica).

shaving ['ʃeɪvɪŋ] n (action) el afeitarse,
rasurado; **~s** npl (of wood etc) virutas fpl;
~ brush n brocha (de afeitar); **~ cream**
n crema (de afeitar).

shawl [ʃɔ:l] n chai m.

she [ʃi:] pron ella; **~-cat** n gata; **NB: for
ships, countries follow the gender of your
translation.**

sheaf [ʃi:f], pl **sheaves** n (of corn) gavilla;
(of arrows) haz m; (of papers) fajo.

shear [ʃɪə*], pt **sheared**, pp **sheared** or
shorn vt (sheep) esquilar, trasquilar; **to
~ off** vt cercenar; **~s** npl (for hedge)
tijeras fpl de jardín.

sheath [ʃi:θ] n vaina; (contraceptive)
preservativo.

sheaves [ʃiːvz] *pl of* **sheaf**.

shed [ʃed] *n* cobertizo // *vt, pt, pp* **shed** (*gen*) desprenderse de; (*skin*) mudar; (*tears*) derramar.

she'd [ʃiːd] = **she had; she would**.

sheep [ʃiːp] *n, pl inv* oveja; ~**dog** *n* perro pastor; ~**ish** *a* tímido, vergonzoso; ~**skin** *n* piel *f* de carnero.

sheer [ʃiə*] *a* (*utter*) puro, completo; (*steep*) escarpado; (*almost transparent*) diáfano // *ad* verticalmente.

sheet [ʃiːt] *n* (*on bed*) sábana; (*of paper*) hoja; (*of glass, metal*) lámina.

sheik(h) [ʃeɪk] *n* jeque *m*.

shelf [ʃelf], *pl* **shelves** *n* estante *m*.

shell [ʃel] *n* (*on beach*) concha; (*of egg, nut etc*) cáscara; (*explosive*) proyectil *m*, obús *m*; (*of building*) armazón *m* // *vt* (*peas*) desenvainar; (*MIL*) bombardear.

she'll [ʃiːl] = **she will; she shall**.

shellfish [ˈʃelfɪʃ] *n, pl inv* crustáceo; (*pl: as food*) mariscos *mpl*.

shelter [ˈʃeltə*] *n* abrigo, refugio // *vt* (*aid*) amparar, proteger; (*give lodging to*) abrigar; (*hide*) esconder // *vi* abrigarse, refugiarse; ~**ed** *a* (*life*) protegido; (*spot*) abrigado.

shelve [ʃelv] *vt* (*fig*) aplazar; ~**s** *pl of* **shelf**.

shepherd [ˈʃepəd] *n* pastor *m* // *vt* (*guide*) guiar, conducir; ~**ess** *n* pastora *f*; ~**'s pie** *n* pastel *m* de carne y patatas.

sheriff [ˈʃerɪf] *n* sheriff *m*.

sherry [ˈʃerɪ] *n* jerez *m*.

she's [ʃiːz] = **she is; she has**.

shield [ʃiːld] *n* escudo; (*TECH*) blindaje *m* // *vt*: **to ~ (from)** proteger (contra).

shift [ʃɪft] *n* (*change*) cambio; (*of place*) traslado; (*of workers*) turno // *vt* trasladar; (*remove*) quitar // *vi* moverse; (*change place*) cambiar de sitio; ~ **work** *n* trabajo por turnos; ~**y** *a* tramposo; (*eyes*) furtivo.

shilling [ˈʃɪlɪŋ] *n* chelín *m*.

shimmer [ˈʃɪmə*] *n* reflejo trémulo // *vi* relucir.

shin [ʃɪn] *n* espinilla.

shine [ʃaɪn] *n* brillo, lustre // (*vb: pt, pp* **shone**) *vi* brillar, relucir // *vt* (*shoes*) lustrar, sacar brillo a; **to ~ a torch on sth** dirigir una linterna hacia algo.

shingle [ˈʃɪŋgl] *n* (*on beach*) guijarras *fpl*; ~**s** *n* (*MED*) herpes *mpl* or *fpl*.

shiny [ˈʃaɪnɪ] *a* brillante, lustroso.

ship [ʃɪp] *n* buque *m*, barco // *vt* (*goods*) embarcar; (*oars*) desarmar; (*send*) transportar *o* enviar (por vía marítima); ~**building** *n* construcción *f* de barcos; ~**ment** *n* (*act*) embarque *m*; (*goods*) envío; ~**per** *n* exportador *a m/f*; ~**ping** *n* (*act*) embarque *m*; (*traffic*) buques *mpl*; ~**shape** *a* en regla; ~**wreck** *n* naufragio; ~**yard** *n* astillero.

shire [ʃaɪə*] *n* condado.

shirk [ʃəːk] *vt* eludir, esquivar; (*obligations*) faltar a.

shirt [ʃəːt] *n* camisa; **in ~ sleeves** en mangas de camisa.

shiver [ˈʃɪvə*] *n* temblor *m*, estremecimiento // *vi* temblar, estremecerse.

shoal [ʃəul] *n* (*of fish*) banco.

shock [ʃɔk] *n* (*impact*) choque *m*; (*ELEC*) descarga (eléctrica); (*emotional*) conmoción *f*; (*start*) sobresalto, susto; (*MED*) postración *f* nerviosa // *vt* dar un susto a; (*offend*) escandalizar; ~ **absorber** *n* amortiguador *m*; ~**ing** *a* (*awful*) espantoso; (*improper*) escandaloso; ~**proof** *a* a prueba de choques.

shod [ʃɔd] *pt, pp of* **shoe** // *a* calzado.

shoddy [ˈʃɔdɪ] *a* de pacotilla, de bajísima calidad.

shoe [ʃuː] *n* zapato; (*for horse*) herradura; (*brake ~*) zapata // *vt, pt, pp* **shod** (*horse*) herrar; ~**brush** *n* cepillo para zapatos; ~**horn** *n* calzador *m*; ~**lace** *n* cordón *m*; ~**maker** *n* zapatero; ~ **polish** *n* betún *m*; ~**shop** *n* zapatería.

shone [ʃɔn] *pt, pp of* **shine**.

shook [ʃuk] *pt of* **shake**.

shoot [ʃuːt] *n* (*on branch, seedling*) retoño, vástago // (*vb: pt, pp* **shot**) *vt* disparar; (*kill*) matar (con arma de fuego); (*wound*) herir (con arma de fuego); (*execute*) fusilar; (*film*) rodar, filmar // *vi* (*with gun, bow*): **to ~ (at)** tirar (a); (*FOOTBALL*) chutar; **to ~ down** *vt* (*plane*) derribar; **to ~ in/out** *vi* entrar corriendo/salir disparado; **to ~ up** *vi* (*fig*) subir (vertiginosamente); ~**ing** *n* (*shots*) tiros *mpl*; (*HUNTING*) caza con escopeta; ~**ing star** *n* estrella fugaz.

shop [ʃɔp] *n* tienda; (*workshop*) taller *m* // *vi* (*also*: **go ~ping**) ir de compras; ~ **assistant** *n* dependiente/a *m/f*; ~ **floor** *n* (*fig*) de la base; ~**keeper** *n* tendero/a; ~**lifter** *n* mechero/a; ~**lifting** *n* mechería; ~**per** *n* comprador/a *m/f*; ~**ping** *n* (*goods*) compras *fpl*; ~**ping bag** *n* bolsa (de compras); ~**ping centre**, ~**ping center** (*US*) *n* zona comercial *o* de tiendas; ~**-soiled** *a* usado; ~ **steward** *n* (*INDUSTRY*) enlace *m/f*; ~ **window** *n* escaparate *m*.

shore [ʃɔː*] *n* (*of sea, lake*) orilla // *vt*: **to ~ (up)** reforzar.

shorn [ʃɔːn] *pp of* **shear**.

short [ʃɔːt] *a* (*not long*) corto; (*in time*) breve, de corta duración; (*person*) bajo; (*curt*) brusco, seco; (*insufficient*) insuficiente // *vi* (*ELEC*) ponerse en cortocircuito // *n* (*also*: ~ **film**) cortometraje *m*; (*a pair of*) ~**s** (*unos*) pantalones *mpl* cortos; **to be ~ of sth** estar falto de algo; **in ~** en pocas palabras; **it is ~ for** es la forma abreviada de; **to cut ~** (*speech, visit*) interrumpir, terminar inesperadamente; **to fall ~ of** resultar (ser) insuficiente; **to stop ~** parar en seco; **to stop ~ of** detenerse antes de; ~**age** *n* escasez *f*, falta; ~**bread** *n* torta seca y quebradiza; ~**circuit** *n* cortocircuito // *vt* poner en cortocircuito // *vi* ponerse en cortocircuito; **~coming** n defecto, deficiencia; **~(crust) pastry** n pasta quebradiza; **~cut** a atajo; **~en** vt acortar; (visit) interrumpir; **~hand** n taquigrafía; **~hand typist** n taquimecanógrafo/a; **~ list** r (for job) lista de candidatos escogidos; **~-lived** a efímero; **~ly** ad en breve, dentro de poco; **~ness** n (of distance) cortedad f (of time) brevedad f; (manner) brusquedad f; **~-sighted** a corto de vista, miope; (fig) imprudente; **~ story** n cuento; **~-tempered** a enojadizo; **~erm** a (effect) a corto plazo; **~ wave** n (RADIO) onda corta.

shot [ʃɔt] pt, pp of **shoot** // n (sound) tiro, disparo; (person) tirador/a m/f; (try) tentativa; (injection) inyección f; (PHOT) toma, fotografía; **~gun** n escopeta.

should [ʃud] auxiliary vb: **I ~ go now** debo irme ahora; **he ~ be there now** debe de haber llegado (ya); **I ~ go if I were you** yo en tu lugar me iría; **I ~ like to** me gustaría.

shoulder ['ʃəuldə*] n hombro; (of road): **hard ~** andén m // vt (fig) cargar con; **~ blade** n omóplato.

shouldn't ['ʃudnt] = **should not**.

shout [ʃaut] n grito // vt gritar // vi gritar, dar voces; **to ~ down** vt hundir a gritos; **~ing** n gritería.

shove [ʃʌv] n empujón m // vt empujar; (col: put): **to ~ sth in** meter algo; **to ~ off** vi (NAUT) alejarse del muelle; (fig: col) largarse.

shovel ['ʃʌvl] n pala; (mechanical) excavadora // vt mover con pala.

show [ʃəu] n (of emotion) demostración f; (semblance) apariencia; (exhibition) exposición f; (THEATRE) función f, espectáculo // (vb: pt **showed**, pp **shown**) vt mostrar, enseñar; (courage etc) mostrar, manifestar; (exhibit) exponer; (film) proyectar // vi mostrarse; (appear) aparecer; **to ~ sb in** hacer pasar a uno; **to ~ off** vi (pej) presumir // vt (display) lucir; (pej) hacer gala de; **to ~ sb out** acompañar a uno a la puerta; **to ~ up** vi (stand out) destacar; (col: turn up) presentarse // vt descubrir; (unmask) desenmascarar; **~ business** n el mundo del espectáculo; **~down** n crisis f, momento decisivo.

shower ['ʃauə*] n (rain) chaparrón m, chubasco; (of stones etc) lluvia; (also: **~bath**) ducha // vi llover // vt: **to ~ sb with sth** colmar a uno de algo; **~proof** a impermeable; **~y** a (weather) lluvioso.

showing ['ʃəuiŋ] n (of film) proyección f.

show jumping ['ʃəudʒʌmpiŋ] n hipismo.

shown [ʃəun] pp of **show**.

show: **~-off** n (col: person) presumido; **~piece** n (of exhibition etc) obra más importante o central; **~room** n sala de muestras.

shrank [ʃræŋk] pt of **shrink**.

shrapnel ['ʃræpnl] n metralla.

shred [ʃred] n (gen pl) triza, jirón m // vt hacer trizas (CULIN) desmenuzar.

shrewd [ʃruːd] a astuto; **~ness** n astucia.

shriek [ʃriːk] n chillido // vt, vi chillar.

shrill [ʃril] a agudo, estridente.

shrimp [ʃrimp] n camarón m.

shrine [ʃrain] n santuario, sepulcro.

shrink [ʃriŋk] pt **shrank**, pp **shrunk** vi encogerse; (be reduced) reducirse // vt encoger; **to ~ from doing sth** no atreverse a hacer algo; **~age** n encogimiento, reducción f.

shrivel ['ʃrivl] (also: **~ up**) vt (dry) secar; (crease) arrugar // vi secarse, arrugarse.

shroud [ʃraud] n sudario // vt: **~ed in mystery** envuelto en el misterio.

Shrove Tuesday ['ʃrəuv'tjuːzdi] a martes m de carnaval.

shrub [ʃrʌb] n arbusto; **~bery** n arbustos mpl.

shrug [ʃrʌg] n encogimiento de hombros // vt, vi: **to ~ (one's shoulders)** encogerse de hombros; **to ~ off** vt negar importancia a.

shrunk [ʃrʌŋk] pp of **shrink**.

shudder ['ʃʌdə*] n estremecimiento, escalofrío // vi estremecerse.

shuffle ['ʃʌfl] vt (cards) barajar; **to ~ (one's feet)** arrastrar los pies.

shun [ʃʌn] vt rehuir, esquivar.

shunt [ʃʌnt] vt (RAIL) maniobrar // vi: **to ~ to and fro** mancar de aquí para allá.

shut [ʃʌt], pt, pp **shut** vt cerrar // vi cerrarse, **to ~ down** vt, vi cerrarse, parar; **to ~ off** vt (supply etc) interrumpir, cortar; **to ~ up** vi (col: keep quiet) callarse // vt (close) cerrar; (silence) callar; **~ter** n contraventana; (PHOT) obturador m.

shuttle ['ʃʌtl] n lanzadera; (also: **~ service**) servicio de transporte entre dos estaciones.

shuttlecock ['ʃʌtlkɔk] n volante m.

shy [ʃai] a tímido; (reserved) reservado, cohibido; (unsociable) huraño; **~ness** n timidez f; reserva; lo huraño.

Siamese [saiə'miːz] a: **~ cat** gato siamés.

Sicily [ˈsisili] n Sicilia.

sick [sik] a (ill) enfermo; (nauseated) mareado; (humour) negro (vomiting): **to be ~** vomitar; **to feel ~** estar mareado; **to be ~ of** (fig) estar harto de; **~ bay** n enfermería; **~en** vt dar asco a // vi enfermar; **~ening** a (fig) asqueroso.

sickle ['sikl] n hoz f.

sick: **~ leave** n baja por enfermedad; **~ly** a enfermizo; (causing nausea) nauseabundo; **~ness** n enfermedad f, mal m; (vomiting) náuseas fpl; **~ pay** n subsidio de enfermedad.

side [said] n (gen) lado; (of body) costado; (of lake) orilla; (aspect) aspecto; (team) equipo, (of hill) ladera // a (door, entrance) accesorio // vi: **to ~ with so** tomar el partido de uno; **by the ~ of** al lado de; **~ by ~** juntos(as), lado a lado; **from all ~s** de todos lados; **to take ~ (with)**

siding 358 sit-in

tomar partido (con); **~board** n aparador
m; **~boards, ~burns** npl patillas fpl; **~
effect** n efecto secundario; **~light** n
(AUT) luz f lateral; **~line** n (SPORT) línea
lateral; (fig) empleo suplementario;
~long a de soslayo; **~ road** n calle f
lateral; **~saddle** ad a mujeriegas, a la
inglesa; **~ show** n (stall) caseta; (fig)
atracción f secundaria; **~step** vt (fig)
esquivar; **~track** vt (fig) desviar (de su
propósito); **~walk** n (US) acera; **~ways**
ad de lado.

siding ['saɪdɪŋ] n (RAIL) apartadero, vía
muerta.

sidle ['saɪdl] vi: **to ~ up (to)** acercarse
furtivamente (a).

siege [siːdʒ] n cerco, sitio.

sieve [sɪv] n coladera // vt cribar.

sift [sɪft] vt cribar; (fig: information)
escudriñar.

sigh [saɪ] n suspiro // vi suspirar.

sight [saɪt] n (faculty) vista, visión f;
(spectacle) espectáculo; (on gun) mira,
alza // vt ver, divisar; **in ~** a la vista; **out
of ~** fuera de (la) vista; **~seeing** n
excursionismo, turismo; **to go ~seeing**
visitar monumentos.

sign [saɪn] n (with hand) señal f, seña;
(indication) indicio; (trace) huella, rastro;
(notice) letrero; (written) signo // vt
firmar; **to ~ sth over to sb** firmar el
traspaso de algo a uno; **to ~ up** vi (MIL)
alistarse // vt (contract) contratar.

signal ['sɪgnl] n señal f // vi (AUT)
señalizar // vt (person) hacer señas a uno;
(message) transmitir.

signature ['sɪgnətʃə*] n firma.

signet ring ['sɪgnətrɪŋ] n anillo de sello.

significance [sɪg'nɪfɪkəns] n significado;
(importance) trascendencia; **significant**
[-ənt] a significativo; trascendente.

signify ['sɪgnɪfaɪ] vt significar.

sign: ~ language n la mímica, lenguaje
m por señas o de señas; **~post** n
indicador m.

silence ['saɪlns] n silencio // vt hacer
callar; (guns) reducir al silencio; **silencer**
n (on gun, AUT) silenciador m.

silent ['saɪlnt] a (gen) silencioso; (not
speaking) callado; (film) mudo; **to remain
~** guardar silencio.

silhouette [sɪluː'et] n silueta; **~d against**
destacado sobre o contra.

silicon chip ['sɪlɪkən'tʃɪp] n plata de
silicio, astilla de silicona.

silk [sɪlk] n seda // a de seda; **~y** a sedoso.

silly ['sɪlɪ] a (person) tonto; (idea) absurdo.

silt [sɪlt] n sedimento.

silver ['sɪlvə*] n plata; (money) moneda
suelta // a de plata, plateado; **~ paper** n
papel m de plata; **~-plated** a plateado;
~smith n platero; **~y** a plateado.

similar ['sɪmɪlə*] a: **~ to** parecido o
semejante a; **~ity** [-'lærɪtɪ] n parecido,
semejanza; **~ly** ad del mismo modo.

simmer ['sɪmə*] vi hervir a fuego lento.

simpering ['sɪmpərɪŋ] a afectado;
(foolish) bobo.

simple ['sɪmpl] a (easy) sencillo (foolish,
COMM) simple; **~ton** n inocentón ona m/f;
simplicity [-'plɪsɪtɪ] n sencillez f;
(foolishness) ingenuidad f; **simplify**
['sɪmplɪfaɪ] vt simplificar.

simulate ['sɪmjuleɪt] vt simular;
simulation [-'leɪʃən] n simulacion f.

simultaneous [sɪməl'teɪnɪəs] a
simultáneo; **~ly** ad simultáneamente.

sin [sɪn] n pecado // vi pecar.

since [sɪns] ad desde entonces, después //
prep desde // conj (time) desde que;
(because) ya que, puesto que; **~ then**
desde entonces.

sincere [sɪn'sɪə*] a sincero; **yours ~ly** le
saluda (afectuosamente); **sincerity**
[-'serɪtɪ] n sinceridad f.

sinful ['sɪnful] a (thought) pecaminoso;
(person) pecador(a).

sing [sɪŋ], pt **sang**, pp **sung** vt cantar // vi
(gen) cantar; (bird) trinar; (ears) zumbar.

singe [sɪndʒ] vt chamuscar.

singer ['sɪŋə*] n cantante m/f.

singing ['sɪŋɪŋ] n (gen) canto; (songs)
canciones fpl; (in the ears) zumbido.

single ['sɪŋgl] a único, solo; (unmarried)
soltero; (not double) simple, sencillo; (bed,
room) individual // n (also: **~ ticket**)
billete m sencillo; (record) single m; **~s**
npl (TENNIS) individual m; **to ~ out** vt
(choose) escoger; (point out) singularizar;
~ bed n cama individual; **in ~ file** en
fila de uno; **~-handed** ad sin ayuda;
~-minded a resuelto, firme; **~ room** n
cuarto individual.

singular ['sɪŋgjulə*] a (odd) raro, extraño;
(LING) singular // n (LING) singular m.

sinister ['sɪnɪstə*] a siniestro.

sink [sɪŋk] n fregadero // (vb: pt **sank**, pp
sunk) vt (ship) hundir, echar a pique;
(foundations) excavar; (piles etc) to: **to ~ sth
into** fijar algo bajo tierra // vi (gen) hundirse;
to ~ in vi (fig) penetrar, calar; **a ~ing
feeling** un sentimiento de que toda se
acaba.

sinner ['sɪnə*] n pecador/a m/f.

sinus ['saɪnəs] n (ANAT) seno.

sip [sɪp] n sorbo // vt sorber, beber a
sorbitos.

siphon ['saɪfən] n sifón m; **to ~ off** vt
quitar poco a poco.

sir [sə*] n señor m; **S~ John Smith** el
Señor John Smith; **yes ~** sí, señor.

siren ['saɪərn] n sirena.

sirloin ['səːlɔɪn] n solomillo.

sister ['sɪstə*] n hermana; (nurse)
enfermera jefe; **~-in-law** n cuñada.

sit [sɪt], pt, pp **sat** vi sentarse; (be sitting)
estar sentado; (assembly) reunirse // vt
(exam) presentarse a; **to ~ down** vi
sentarse; **to ~ in on** asistir a; **to ~ up** vi
incorporarse; (not go to bed) velar.

site [saɪt] n sitio; (also: **building ~**) solar
m // vt situar.

sit-in ['sɪtɪn] n (demonstration)

manifestación f de brazos caídos.

sitting ['sɪtɪŋ] n (of assembly etc) sesión f; (in canteen) turno; ~ **room** n sala de estar.

situated ['sɪtjueɪtɪd] a situado.

situation [sɪtju'eɪʃɔn] n situación f.

six [sɪks] num seis; ~ **teen** num diez y seis, dieciséis; ~ **th** a sexto; ~ **ty** num sesenta.

size [saɪz] n (gen) tamaño; (extent) extensión f; (of clothing) talla; (of shoes) número; (glue) cola, apresto; **to** ~ **up** vt formarse una idea de; ~ **able** a importante, considerable.

sizzle ['sɪzl] vi crepitar.

skate [skeɪt] n patín m; (fish: pl inv) raya // vi patinar; ~ **board** n skateboard m; **skater** n patinador/a m/f; **skating** n patinaje m; **skating rink** n pista de patinaje.

skeleton ['skɛlɪtn] n esqueleto; (TECH) armazón m; (outline) esquema m; ~ **key** n llave f maestra; ~ **staff** n personal m reducido.

sketch [skɛtʃ] n (drawing) dibujo; (outline) esbozo, bosquejo; (THEATRE) pieza corta // vt dibujar; esbozar; ~ **book** n libro de dibujos; ~ **pad** n bloc m de dibujo; ~ **y** a incompleto.

skewer ['skju:ə*] n broqueta.

ski [ski:] n esquí m // vi esquiar; ~ **boot** n bota de esquí.

skid [skɪd] n patinazo // vi patinar; ~ **mark** n huella de patinazo.

ski: ~ **er** n esquiador/a m/f; ~ **ing** n esquí m; ~ **jump** n pista para salto de esquí.

skilful ['skɪlful] a diestro, experto.

ski lift n telesilla.

skill [skɪl] n destreza, pericia; ~ **ed** a hábil, diestro; (worker) cualificado.

skim [skɪm] vt (milk) desnatar; (glide over) rozar, rasar // vi: **to** ~ **through** (book) hojear.

skimp [skɪmp] vt (work) chapucear; (cloth etc) escatimar; ~ **y** a (meagre) escaso; (skirt) muy corto.

skin [skɪn] n (gen) piel f; (complexion) cutis m // vt (fruit etc) pelar; (animal) despellejar; ~ **-deep** a superficial; ~ **diving** n natación f submarina; ~ **ny** a flaco, magro; ~ **tight** a (dress etc) muy ajustado.

skip [skɪp] n brinco, salto; (container) cuba // vi brincar; (with rope) saltar a la comba // vt (pass over) omitir, saltar.

ski pants npl pantalones mpl de esquí.

skipper ['skɪpə*] n (NAUT, SPORT) capitán m.

skipping rope ['skɪpɪŋ-] n cuerda (de saltar).

skirmish ['skə:mɪʃ] n escaramuza.

skirt [skə:t] n falda // vt (surround) ceñir, rodear; (go round) ladear; ~ **ing board** n rodapié m.

skit [skɪt] n sátira, parodia.

skittle ['skɪtl] n bolo; ~ **s** n (game) boliche m.

skive [skaɪv] vi (Brit: col) gandulear.

skull [skʌl] n calavera; (ANAT) cráneo.

skunk [skʌŋk] n mofeta; (fig: person) canalla m/f.

sky [skaɪ] n cielo; ~ **-blue** a azul celeste; ~ **light** n tragaluz m, claraboya; ~ **scraper** n rascacielos m inv.

slab [slæb] n (stone) bloque m; (flat) losa; (of cake) porción f gruesa.

slack [slæk] a (loose) flojo; (slow) de poca actividad; (careless) descuidado; ~ **s** npl pantalones mpl; ~ **en** (also: ~ **en off**) vi aflojarse // vt aflojar; (speed) disminuir.

slag [slæg] n escoria, escombros mpl; ~ **heap** n escorial m, escombrera.

slalom ['slɑ:ləm] n slalom m.

slam [slæm] vt (door) cerrar de golpe; (throw) arrojar violentamente; (criticize) hablar mal de // vi cerrarse de golpe.

slander ['slɑ:ndə*] n calumnia, difamación f // vt calumniar, difamar; ~ **ous** a calumnioso, difamatorio.

slang [slæŋ] n argot m; (jargon) jerga; (private language) caló.

slant [slɑ:nt] n sesgo, inclinación f; (fig) punto de vista; ~ **ed**, ~ **ing** a inclinado.

slap [slæp] n palmada; (in face) bofetada; (fig) palmetazo // vt dar una palmada/bofetada a // ad (directly) exactamente, directamente; ~ **dash** a descuidado; ~ **stick** n (comedy) payasadas fpl.

slash [slæʃ] vt acuchillar; (fig: prices) quemar.

slate [sleɪt] n pizarra // vt (fig: criticize) criticar duramente.

slaughter ['slɔ:tə*] n (of animals) matanza; (of people) carnicería // vt matar; ~ **house** n matadero.

Slav [slɑ:v] a eslavo.

slave [sleɪv] n esclavo // vi (also: ~ **away**) sudar tinta; ~ **ry** n esclavitud f; **slavish** a servil.

Slavonic [slə'vɔnɪk] a eslavo.

slay [sleɪ] vt matar.

sleazy ['sli:zɪ] a (fig: place) de mala fama.

sledge [slɛdʒ] n trineo; ~ **hammer** n mazo.

sleek [sli:k] a (gen) lustroso; (neat) pulcro.

sleep [sli:p] n sueño // vi, pt, pp **slept** dormir; **to go to** ~ dormirse; **to** ~ **in** vi (oversleep) dormir tarde; ~ **er** n (person) durmiente m/f; (RAIL: on track) traviesa; (: train) coche-cama m; ~ **ily** ad soñolientamente; ~ **ing bag** n saco de dormir; ~ **ing car** n coche-cama m; ~ **ing pill** n somnífero; ~ **lessness** n insomnio; ~ **walker** n sonámbulo/a; ~ **y** a soñoliento.

sleet [sli:t] n nevisca.

sleeve [sli:v] n manga; (TECH) manguito; ~ **less** a (garment) sin mangas.

sleigh [sleɪ] n trineo.

sleight [slaɪt] n: ~ **of hand** escamoteo.

slender ['slɛndə*] a delgado; (means) escaso.

slept [slɛpt] pt, pp of **sleep.**

slice [slaɪs] n (of meat) tajada; (of bread)

rebanada; (*of lemon*) rodaja; (*utensil*) pala // *vt* cortar, tajar; rebanar.

slick [slɪk] *a* (*skilful*) hábil, diestro; (*quick*) rápido; (*astute*) astuto // *n* (*also*: **oil ~**) masa flotante.

slid [slɪd] *pt, pp of* **slide.**

slide [slaɪd] *n* (*in playground*) tobogán *m*; (*PHOT*) diapositiva; (*also*: **hair ~**) pasador *m* // (*vb*: *pt, pp* **slid**) *vt* correr, deslizar // *vi* (*slip*) resbalarse; (*glide*) deslizarse; **sliding** *a* (*door*) corredizo.

slight [slaɪt] *a* (*slim*) delgado; (*frail*) delicado; (*pain etc*) leve; (*trifling*) sin importancia; (*small*) pequeño // *n* desaire *m* // *vt* (*offend*) ofender, desairar; **not in the ~est** (ni) en lo más mínimo, en absoluto; **~ly** *ad* ligeramente, un poco.

slim [slɪm] *a* delgado, esbelto // *vi* adelgazar.

slime [slaɪm] *n* limo, cieno; **slimy** *a* limoso.

slimming ['slɪmɪŋ] *n* adelgazamiento; **a ~ diet** un régimen.

sling [slɪŋ] *n* (*MED*) cabestrillo; (*weapon*) honda // *vt, pt, pp* **slung** tirar, arrojar.

slip [slɪp] *n* (*slide*) resbalón *m*; (*fall*) tropezón *m*; (*mistake*) descuido; (*underskirt*) combinación *f*; (*of paper*) trozo // *vt* (*slide*) deslizar // *vi* (*slide*) deslizarse; (*stumble*) resbalar(se); (*decline*) decaer; **to give sb the ~** eludir *o* escaparse de uno; **to ~ away** escabullirse; **to ~ in** *vt* meter // *vi* meterse; **to ~ out** *vi* (*go out*) salir (un momento).

slipper ['slɪpə*] *n* zapatilla.

slippery ['slɪpərɪ] *a* resbaladizo.

slip: ~ road *n* carretera de acceso; **~shod** *a* descuidado; **~-up** *n* (*error*) equivocación *f*; (*by neglect*) descuido; **~way** *n* grada, gradas *fpl*.

slit [slɪt] *n* raja; (*cut*) corte *m* // *vt, pt, pp* **slit** rajar, cortar.

slither ['slɪðə*] *vi* deslizarse.

slob [slɔb] *n* (*col*) patán *m*.

slog [slɔg] *vi* sudar tinta; **it was a ~** costó trabajo (hacerlo).

slogan ['sləugən] *n* slogan *m*, lema *m*.

slop [slɔp] *vi* (*also*: **~ over**) derramarse, desbordarse // *vt* derramar, verter.

slope [sləup] *n* (*up*) cuesta, pendiente *m*; (*down*) declive *m*; (*side of mountain*) falda, vertiente *m* // *vi*: **to ~ down** estar en declive; **to ~ up** inclinarse; **sloping** *a* en pendiente; en declive.

sloppy ['slɔpɪ] *a* (*work*) descuidado; (*appearance*) desaliñado.

slot [slɔt] *n* ranura // *vt*: **to ~ into** encajar en; **~ machine** *n* máquina tragaperras.

slouch [slautʃ] *vi*: **to ~ about** (*laze*) gandulear.

slovenly ['slʌvənlɪ] *a* (*dirty*) desaliñado, desaseado; (*careless*) descuidado.

slow [sləu] *a* lento; (*watch*): **to be ~** atrasarse // *ad* lentamente, despacio // *vt, vi* (*also*: **~ down, ~ up**) retardar; '**~**' (*road sign*) 'disminuir velocidad'; **~ly** *ad*

lentamente, despacio; in ~ motion a cámara lenta; **~ness** *n* lentitud *f*.

sludge [slʌdʒ] *n* lodo, fango.

slug [slʌg] *n* babosa; (*bullet*) posta; **~gish** *a* (*slow*) lento; (*lazy*) perezoso.

sluice [slu:s] *n* (*gate*) esclusa; (*channel*) canal *m*.

slum [slʌm] *n* (*area*) tugurios *mpl*; (*house*) casucha.

slumber ['slʌmbə*] *n* sueño.

slump [slʌmp] *n* (*economic*) depresión *f* // *vi* hundirse.

slung [slʌŋ] *pt, pp of* **sling.**

slur [slɔ:*] *n* calumnia // *vt* calumniar, difamar; (*word*) pronunciar indistintamente.

slush [slʌʃ] *n* nieve *f* a medio derretir; **~y** *a* (*snow*) a medio derretir; (*street*) fangoso; (*fig*) sentimental, sensiblero.

slut [slʌt] *n* marrana.

sly [slaɪ] *a* (*clever*) astuto; (*nasty*) malicioso.

smack [smæk] *n* (*slap*) manotada; (*blow*) golpe *m* // *vt* dar una manotada a, golpear con la mano // *vi*: **to ~ of** saber a, oler a.

small [smɔ:l] *a* pequeño; **~holder** *n* granjero, parcelero; **~ish** *a* más bien pequeño; **~pox** *n* viruela; **~ talk** *n* cháchara.

smart [smɑ:t] *a* elegante; (*clever*) listo, inteligente; (*quick*) rápido, vivo // *vi* escocer, picar; **to ~en up** *vi* arreglarse // *vt* arreglar.

smash [smæʃ] *n* (*also*: **~-up**) choque *m* // *vt* (*break*) hacer pedazos; (*car etc*) estrellar; (*SPORT: record*) romper // *vi* (*collide*) chocar; (*against wall etc*) estrellarse; **~ing** *a* (*col*) cojonudo.

smattering ['smætərɪŋ] *n*: **a ~ of** ligeros conocimientos *mpl* de.

smear [smɪə*] *n* mancha; (*MED*) citología // *vt* untar; (*fig*) calumniar, difamar.

smell [smɛl] *n* olor *m*; (*sense*) olfato // (*vb*: *pt, pp* **smelt** *or* **smelled**) *vt, vi* oler; **it ~s good/of garlic** huele bien/a ajo; **~y** *a* que huele mal.

smile [smaɪl] *n* sonrisa // *vi* sonreír; **smiling** *a* sonriente.

smirk [smɔ:k] *n* sonrisa falsa *o* afectada.

smith [smɪθ] *n* herrero; **~y** ['smɪðɪ] *n* herrería.

smock [smɔk] *n* blusa; (*children's*) delantal *m*.

smoke [sməuk] *n* humo // *vi* fumar; (*chimney*) echar humo // *vt* (*cigarettes*) fumar; **~d** *a* (*bacon, glass*) ahumado; **smoker** *n* (*person*) fumador/a *m/f*; (*RAIL*) coche *m* fumador; **~ screen** *n* cortina de humo; **smoking** *n*: '**no smoking**' (*sign*) 'prohibido fumar'; **smoky** *a* (*gen*) humeante; (*room*) lleno de humo.

smooth [smu:ð] *a* (*gen*) liso; (*sea*) tranquilo; (*flat*) llano; (*flavour, movement*) suave; (*person*) culto, refinado; (: *pej*) meloso // *vt* alisar; (*also*: **~ out**) (*creases, difficulties*) allanar.

smother ['smʌðə*] vt sofocar; (repress) ahogar.

smoulder ['smouldə*] vi arder sin llama.

smudge [smʌdʒ] n mancha // vt manchar.

smug [smʌg] a presumido.

smuggle ['smʌgl] vt pasar de contrabando; **smuggler** n contrabandista m/f; **smuggling** n contrabando.

smutty ['smʌtı] a (fig) verde, obsceno.

snack [snæk] n bocado; ~ **bar** n cafetería.

snag [snæg] n dificultad f, pero.

snail [sneıl] n caracol m.

snake [sneık] n (gen) serpiente f; (harmless) culebra; (poisonous) víbora.

snap [snæp] n (sound) castañetazo; (of whip) chasquido; (click) golpe m seco; (photograph) foto f // a repentino // vi (fingers etc) castañetear; (whip) chasquear; (break) quebrar; (photograph) tomar una foto de // vi (break) quebrarse; (fig: person) contestar bruscamente; (sound) hacer un ruido seco; **to ~ shut** cerrarse de golpe; **to ~ at** vt fus (subj: dog) intentar morder; **to ~ off** vi (break) romperse (y separarse); **to ~ up** vt aprovecharse de, agarrar; ~**shot** n foto f (instantánea).

snare [snɛə*] n trampa // vt cazar con trampa; (fig) engañar.

snarl [snɑ:l] n gruñido // vi gruñir.

snatch [snætʃ] n (fig) robo; (small amount): ~**es** de trocitos mpl de // vt (~ away) arrebatar; (grasp) coger, agarrar.

sneak [sni:k] vi: **to ~ in/out** entrar/salir a hurtadillas // n (fam) soplón/ona m/f; ~**y** a furtivo.

sneer [snıə*] n sonrisa de desprecio // vi sonreír con desprecio; (mock) mofarse.

sneeze [sni:z] n estornudo // vi estornudar.

sniff [snıf] n (of dog) husmeo; (of person) sorbo (por las narices) // vi sorber (por la nariz) // vt husmear, oler.

snigger ['snıgə*] n risa disimulada // vi reírse con disimulo.

snip [snıp] n tijeretazo; (piece) recorte m; (bargain) ganga // vt tijeretear.

sniper ['snaıpə*] n francotirador/a m/f.

snippet ['snıpıt] n retazo.

snivelling ['snıvlıŋ] a (whimpering) llorón(ona).

snob [snɔb] n snob m/f; ~**bery** n snobismo; ~**bish** a snob.

snooker ['snu:kə*] n especie de billar.

snoop [snu:p] vi: **to ~ about** fisgonear; ~**er** n fisgón/ona m/f.

snooty ['snu:tı] a presumido.

snooze [snu:z] n siesta // vi echar una siesta.

snore [snɔ:*] vi roncar // n ronquido.

snorkel ['snɔ:kl] n tubo snorkel.

snort [snɔ:t] n bufido // vi bufar.

snout [snaut] n hocico, morro.

snow [snəu] n nieve f // vi nevar; ~**ball** n bola de nieve // vi acumularse; ~**bound** a bloqueado por la nieve; ~**drift** n ventisquero; ~**drop** n campanilla; ~**fall**

n nevada; ~**flake** n copo de nieve; ~**man** n figura de nieve; ~**plough**, ~**plow** (US) n quitanieves m inv; ~**storm** n nevada, nevasca; S~ **White** n Blanca Nieves.

snub [snʌb] vt rechazar con desdén // n desaire m, repulsa.

snuff [snʌf] n rapé m.

snug [snʌg] a (sheltered) abrigado; (fitted) ajustado.

snuggle ['snʌgl] vi: **to ~ up to sb** arrimarse a uno.

so [səu] ad (degree) tan; (manner: thus) así, de este modo // conj así que, por tanto; ~ **that** (purpose) para que, a fin de que; ~ (result) de modo que; ~ **do I** y yo también; **if ~** de ser así, si es así; **I hope** ~ espero que sí; **10 or ~** 10 más o menos; ~ **far** hasta aquí; ~ **long!** ¡hasta luego!; ~ **many** tantos(as); ~ **much** ad, det tanto; ~ **and** ~ n Fulano.

soak [səuk] vt (drench) empapar; (put in water) remojar // vi remojarse, estar a remojo; **to ~ in** vi penetrar; **to ~ up** vt absorber.

soap [səup] n jabón m; ~**flakes** npl escamas fpl de jabón; ~ **powder** n jabón en polvo; ~**y** a jabonoso.

soar [sɔ:*] vi (on wings) remontarse; (building etc) elevarse

sob [sɔb] n sollozo // vi sollozar.

sober ['səubə*] a (serious) serio; (sensible) sensato; (moderate) moderado; (not drunk) sobrio; (colour, style) discreto; **to ~ up** vi pasársele a uno la borrachera.

Soc. abbr of **society**.

so-called ['səu'kɔ:ld] a llamado.

soccer ['sɔkə*] n fútbol m.

sociable ['səuʃəbl] a sociable.

social ['səuʃl] a (gen) social; (sociable) sociable // n velada, fiesta; ~ **climber** n arribista m/f; ~ **club** n club m; ~**ism** n socialismo; ~**ist** a, n socialista m/f; ~**ly** ad socialmente; ~ **science** n ciencias fpl sociales; ~ **security** n seguridad f social; ~ **work** n asistencia social; ~ **worker** n asistente/a m/f social.

society [sə'saıətı] n sociedad f; (club) asociación f; (also: **high** ~) buena sociedad.

sociologist [səusı'ɔlədʒıst] n sociólogo; **sociology** [-dʒı] n sociología.

sock [sɔk] n calcetín m.

socket [sɔkıt] n (ELEC) enchufe m.

sod [sɔd] n (of earth) césped m; (col!) cabrón/ona m/f.

soda ['səudə] n (CHEM) sosa; (also: ~ **water**) sifón m.

sodden ['sɔdn] a empapado.

sodium ['səudıəm] n sodio.

sofa ['səufə] n sofá m.

soft [sɔft] a (gen) blando; (gentle, not loud) suave; (kind) tierno, compasivo; (weak) débil; (stupid) tonto; ~ **drink** n bebida no alcohólica; ~**en** ['sɔfn] vt ablandar; suavizar, debilitar // vi ablandarse; suavizarse; debilitarse; ~~**hearted** a

compasivo, bondadoso; ~**ly** *ad*
suavemente; (*gently*) delicadamente, con
delicadeza; ~**ness** *n* blandura; suavidad *f*;
(*sweetness*) dulzura; (*tenderness*) ternura.

soggy ['sɔgɪ] *a* empapado.

soil [sɔɪl] *n* (*earth*) tierra, suelo // *vt*
ensuciar; ~**ed** *a* sucio.

solace ['sɔlɪs] *n* consuelo.

solar ['səulə*] *a* solar.

sold [səuld] *pt, pp of* **sell**; ~ **out** (*COMM*)
agotado.

solder ['sɔuldə*] *vt* soldar // *n* soldadura.

soldier ['səuldʒə*] *n* (*gen*) soldado; (*army
man*) militar *m*.

sole [səul] *n* (*of foot*) planta; (*of shoe*) suela;
(*fish: pl inv*) lenguado // *a* único; ~**ly** *ad*
únicamente, solo, solamente.

solemn ['sɔləm] *a* solemne.

solicitor [sə'lɪsɪtə*] *n* (*for wills etc*)
notario; (*in court*) abogado.

solid ['sɔlɪd] *a* (*not hollow*) sólido; (*gold etc*)
macizo; (*person*) serio // *n* sólido.

solidarity [sɔlɪ'dærɪtɪ] *n* solidaridad *f*.

solidify [sə'lɪdɪfaɪ] *vi* solidificarse.

solitaire [sɔlɪ'tɛə*] *n* (*game, gem*)
solitario.

solitary ['sɔlɪtərɪ] *a* solitario, solo;
(*isolated*) apartado, aislado; (*only*) único;
~ **confinement** *n* incomunicación *f*.

solitude ['sɔlɪtjuːd] *n* soledad *f*.

solo ['səuləu] *n* solo; ~**ist** *n* solista *m/f*.

soluble ['sɔljubl] *a* soluble.

solution [sə'luːʃən] *n* solución *f*.

solve [sɔlv] *vt* resolver, solucionar.

solvent ['sɔlvənt] *a* (*COMM*) solvente // *n*
(*CHEM*) solvente *m*.

sombre, somber (*US*) ['sɔmbə*] *a*
sombrío.

some [sʌm] *det* (*a few*) algunos(as);
(*certain*) algún/una; (*a certain number or
amount*) *see phrases below*; (*unspecified*)
algo de // *pron* algunos/as; (*a bit*) algo //
ad: ~ **10 people** unas 10 personas; ~
children came vinieron algunos niños;
have ~ **tea** tome té; **there's** ~ **milk in
the fridge** hay leche en la refrigeradora;
~ **was left** quedaba algo; **I've got** ~
(*books etc*) tengo algunos; (*milk, money
etc*) tengo algo; ~**body** *pron* alguien; ~
day *ad* algún día; ~**how** *ad* de alguna
manera; (*for some reason*) por una u otra
razón; ~**one** *pron* = ~**body**.

somersault ['sʌməsɔːlt] *n* (*deliberate*)
salto mortal; (*accidental*) vuelco // *vi* dar
un salto mortal; dar vuelcos.

something ['sʌmθɪŋ] *pron* algo.

sometime ['sʌmtaɪm] *ad* (*in future*) algún
día, en algún momento; (*in past*): ~ **last
month** durante el mes pasado.

sometimes ['sʌmtaɪmz] *ad* a veces.

somewhat ['sʌmwɔt] *ad* algo.

somewhere ['sʌmwɛə*] *ad* (*be*) en alguna
parte; (*go*) a alguna parte; ~ **else** (*be*) en
otra parte; (*go*) a otra parte.

son [sʌn] *n* hijo.

song [sɔŋ] *n* canción *f*; ~**writer** *n*

compositor/a *m/f* de canciones.

sonic ['sɔnɪk] *a* (*boom*) sónico.

son-in-law ['sʌnɪnlɔː] *n* yerno.

sonnet ['sɔnɪt] *n* soneto.

soon [suːn] *ad* pronto, dentro de poco;
(*early*) temprano; ~ **afterwards** poco
después; *see also* **as**; ~**er** *ad* (*time*) antes,
más temprano; (*preference*): **I would**
~**er do that** preferiría hacer eso; ~**er
or later** tarde o temprano.

soot [sut] *n* hollín *m*.

soothe [suːð] *vt* tranquilizar; (*pain*) aliviar.

sophisticated [sə'fɪstɪkeɪtɪd] *a* sofisticado.

soporific [sɔpə'rɪfɪk] *a* soporífero.

sopping ['sɔpɪŋ] *a*: ~ **wet** totalmente
empapado.

soppy ['sɔpɪ] *a* (*pej*) bobo, tonto.

soprano [sə'prɑːnəu] *n* soprano *f*.

sorcerer ['sɔːsərə*] *n* hechicero.

sordid ['sɔːdɪd] *a* (*dirty*) sucio, asqueroso;
(*wretched*) miserable.

sore [sɔː*] *a* (*painful*) doloroso, que duele;
(*offended*) resentido // *n* llaga; ~**ly** *ad*: **I
am** ~**ly tempted** casi estoy por.

sorrow ['sɔrəu] *n* pena, dolor *m*; ~**ful** *a*
afligido, triste.

sorry ['sɔrɪ] *a* (*regretful*) arrepentido;
(*condition, excuse*) lastimoso; ~**!** ¡lo
siento!, ¡perdón!, ¡perdone!; **to feel** ~ **for
sb** sentir lástima por uno; **I feel** ~ **for
him** me da lástima.

sort [sɔːt] *n* clase *f*, género, tipo // *vt* (*also*:
~ **out**: *papers*) clasificar; (: *problems*)
arreglar, solucionar; ~**ing office** *n*
oficina de distribución de correos.

SOS *n abbr of* **save our souls**.

so-so ['səusəu] *ad* regular, así-así.

soufflé ['suːfleɪ] *n* suflé *m*.

sought [sɔːt] *pt, pp of* **seek**.

soul [səul] *n* alma *m*; ~**-destroying** *a*
embrutecedor(a); ~**ful** *a* lleno de
sentimiento; ~**less** *a* desalmado.

sound [saund] *a* (*healthy*) sano; (*safe, not
damaged*) firme, sólido; (*secure*) seguro;
(*reliable, not superficial*) formal, digno de
confianza; (*sensible*) sensato, razonable //
ad: ~ **asleep** profundamente dormido //
n (*noise*) sonido, ruido; (*GEO*) estrecho //
vt (*alarm*) sonar; (*also*: ~ **out**: *opinions*)
consultar, sondear // *vi* sonar, resonar;
(*fig: seem*) parecer; **to** ~ **like** sonar a; ~
barrier *n* barrera del sonido; ~ **effects**
npl efectos *mpl* sonoros; ~**ing** *n* (*NAUT etc*)
sondeo; ~**ly** *ad* (*sleep*) profundamente;
(*beat*) completamente; ~**proof** *a* a
prueba de sonidos; ~**track** *n* (*of film*)
banda sonora.

soup [suːp] *n* (*thick*) sopa; (*thin*) caldo; **in
the** ~ (*fig*) en apuros; ~**spoon** *n* cuchara
sopera.

sour ['sauə*] *a* agrio; (*milk*) cortado; (*fig*)
desabrido, acre.

source [sɔːs] *n* fuente *f*.

south [sauθ] *n* sur *m* // *a* del sur // *ad* al
sur, hacia el sur; **S~ Africa** *n* África del
Sur; **S~ African** *a, n* sudafricano/a; **S~
America** *n* América (del Sur); **S~**

American a, n sudamericano/a; ~-**east** n sudeste m; ~**erly** ['sʌðəlɪ a sur; (from the ~) del sur; ~**ern** ['sʌðən] a del sur, meridional; **S~ Pole** n Polo Sur; ~**ward(s)** ad hacia el sur; ~-**west** n suroeste m.

souvenir [su:və'nɪə*] n recuerdo.

sovereign ['sɔvrɪn] a, n soberano; ~**ty** n soberanía.

soviet ['sɔuvɪət] a soviético; **the S~ Union** la Unión Soviética.

sow [sau] n cerda, puerca // vt [səu], pt **sowed**, pp **sown** [səun] (gen) sembrar; (spread) esparcir.

soy [sɔɪ] n: ~ **sauce** salsa de soja.

soya bean ['sɔɪbiːn] n semilla de soja.

spa [spɑː] n (spring) baños mpl térmicos; (town) balneario.

space [speɪs] n (gen) espacio; (room) sitio // vt (also: ~ **out**) espaciar; ~**craft** n nave f espacial; ~**man/woman** n astronauta m/f, cosmonauta m/f; **spacing** n espaciamiento.

spacious ['speɪʃəs] a amplio.

spade [speɪd] n (tool) pala, laya; ~**s** npl (CARDS: British) picos mpl; (: Spanish) espadas fpl.

spaghetti [spə'gɛtɪ] n espaguetis mpl, fideos mpl.

Spain [speɪn] n España.

span [spæn] n (of bird, plane) envergadura; (of hand) palmo; (of arch) luz f; (in time) lapso // vt extenderse sobre, cruzar; (fig) abarcar.

Spaniard ['spænjəd] n español/a m/f.

spaniel ['spænjəl] n perro de aguas.

Spanish ['spænɪʃ] a español(a) // n (LING) español m, castellano.

spank [spæŋk] vt zurrar.

spanner ['spænə*] n llave f (inglesa).

spar [spɑː*] n palo, verga // vi (BOXING) entrenarse.

spare [spɛə*] a (free) desocupado; (surplus) sobrante, de más; (available) disponible // n (part) pieza de repuesto // vt (do without) pasarse sin; (afford to give) tener de sobra; (refrain from hurting) perdonar; (be grudging with) escatimar; ~ **part** n pieza de repuesto; ~ **time** n ratos mpl de ocio, tiempo libre.

sparing ['spɛərɪŋ] a: to be ~ **with** ser parco en; ~**ly** ad escasamente.

spark [spɑːk] n chispa; (fig) chispazo; ~(**ing**) **plug** n bujía.

sparkle ['spɑːkl] n centelleo, destello // vi centellear; (shine) relucir, brillar; **sparkling** a centelleante; (wine) espumoso.

sparrow ['spærəu] n gorrión m.

sparse [spɑːs] a esparcido, escaso.

spasm ['spæzəm] n (MED) espasmo; (fig) arranque m, acceso; ~**odic** [-'mɔdɪk] a espasmódico.

spastic ['spæstɪk] n espástico/a.

spat [spæt] pt, pp of **spit**.

spate [speɪt] n (fig): ~ **of** torrente m de; **in** ~ (river) crecido.

spatter [spætə*] vt salpicar, rociar.

spatula [spætjulə] n espátula.

spawn [spɔːn] vi desovar, frezar // n huevas fpl.

speak [spiːk], pt **spoke**, pp **spoken** vt (language) hablar; (truth) decir // vi hablar; (make a speech) intervenir; **to** ~ **to sb/of or about sth** hablar con uno/de o sobre algo; ~ **up!** ¡habla fuerte!; ~**er** n (in public) orador/a m/f; (also: **loud~er**) altavoz m, parlante m; (POL): **the S~er** el Presidente del Congreso.

spear [spɪə*] n lanza; (for fishing) arpón m // vt alancear; arponear; ~**head** n punta de lanza.

special ['spɛʃl] a especial; (edition etc) extraordinario; (delivery) urgente; **take** ~ **care** ponga un cuidado especial; ~**ist** n especialista m/f; ~**ity** [spɛʃɪ'ælɪtɪ] n especialidad f; ~**ize** vi: **to** ~**ize (in)** especializarse en; ~**ly** ad sobre todo, en particular.

species ['spiːʃiːz] n especie f.

specific [spə'sɪfɪk] a específico; ~**ally** ad específicamente.

specification [spɛsɪfɪ'keɪʃən] n especificación f; ~**s** npl presupuesto; **specify** ['spɛsɪfaɪ] vt, vi especificar, precisar.

specimen ['spɛsɪmən] n ejemplar m, espécimen m.

speck [spɛk] n grano, mota.

speckled ['spɛkld] a moteado.

specs [spɛks] npl (col) gafas fpl.

spectacle ['spɛktəkl] n espectáculo; ~**s** npl gafas fpl, anteojos mpl; **spectacular** [-'tækjulə*] a espectacular; (success) impresionante.

spectator [spɛk'teɪtə*] n espectador/a m/f.

spectre, specter (US) ['spɛktə*] n espectro, fantasma m.

spectrum ['spɛktrəm], pl **-tra** [-trə] n espectro.

speculate ['spɛkjuleɪt] vi especular; (try to guess): **to** ~ **about** especular sobre; **speculation** [-'leɪʃən] n especulación f.

speech [spiːtʃ] n (faculty) habla, palabra; (formal talk) discurso; (talk) palabras fpl; (language) idioma m, lenguaje m; ~**less** a mudo, estupefacto.

speed [spiːd] n velocidad f, rapidez f; (haste) prisa; (promptness) prontitud f, at **full** or **top** ~ a máxima velocidad; **to** ~ **up** vi acelerarse // vt acelerar; ~**boat** n lancha motora; ~**ily** ad rápido, rápidamente; ~**ing** n (AUT) exceso de velocidad, velocidad f máxima; ~**ometer** [spɪ'dɔmɪtə*] n velocímetro; ~**way** n (SPORT) carreras fpl de moto; ~**y** a (fast) veloz, rápido, (prompt) pronto.

spell [spɛl] n (also: **magic** ~) encanto, hechizo; (period of time) rato, período; (turn) turno // vt, pt, pp **spelt** or **spelled** (also: ~ **out**) deletrear; (fig) anunciar, presagiar; **to cast a** ~ **on sb** hechizar a uno; **he can't** ~ no sabe escribir bien, sabe poco de ortografía; ~**bound** *a* embelesado, hechizado; ~**ing** *n* ortografía.

spend [spɛnd], *pt, pp* **spent** [spɛnt] *vt* (*money*) gastar; (*time*) pasar; (*life*) dedicar; ~**thrift** *n* derrochador/a *m/f*, pródigo/a.

sperm [spɔ:m] *n* esperma; ~ **whale** *n* cachalote *m*.

spew [spju:] *vt* vomitar, arrojar.

sphere [sfɪə*] *n* esfera; **spherical** ['sfɛrɪkl] *a* esférico.

sphinx [sfɪŋks] *n* esfinge *f*.

spice [spaɪs] *n* especia // *vt* especiar; **spicy** *a* especiado; (*fig*) picante.

spider ['spaɪdə*] *n* araña.

spike [spaɪk] *n* (*point*) punta; (*ZOOL*) pincho, púa; (*BOT*) espiga.

spill [spɪl], *pt, pp* **spilt** *or* **spilled** *vt* derramar, verter // *vi* derramarse; **to** ~ **over** desbordarse.

spin [spɪn] *n* (*revolution of wheel*) vuelta, revolución *f*; (*AVIAT*) barrena; (*trip in car*) paseo (en coche) // (*vb: pt, pp* **spun**) *vt* (*wool etc*) hilar; (*wheel*) girar // *vi* girar, dar vueltas; **to** ~ **out** *vt* alargar, prolongar.

spinach ['spɪnɪtʃ] *n* espinaca; (*as food*) espinacas *fpl*.

spinal ['spaɪnl] *a* espinal; ~ **cord** *n* columna vertebral.

spindly ['spɪndlɪ] *a* zanquivano.

spin-drier [spɪn'draɪə*] *n* secador *m* centrífugo.

spine [spaɪn] *n* espinazo, columna vertebral; (*thorn*) espina; ~**less** *a* (*fig*) débil, flojo.

spinning ['spɪnɪŋ] *n* (*of thread*) hilado; (*art*) hilandería; ~ **top** *n* peonza; ~ **wheel** *n* rueca, torno de hilar.

spinster ['spɪnstə*] *n* soltera; (*pej*) solterona.

spiral ['spaɪərl] *n* espiral *m* // *a* en espiral; ~ **staircase** *n* escalera de caracol.

spire [spaɪə*] *n* aguja, chapitel *m*.

spirit ['spɪrɪt] *n* (*gen*) espíritu *m*; (*soul*) alma *m*; (*ghost*) fantasma *m*; (*humour*) humor *m*; (*courage*) valor *m*, ánimo; ~**s** *npl* (*drink*) alcohol *m*, bebidas *fpl* alcohólicas; **in good** ~**s** alegre, de buen ánimo; ~**ed** *a* enérgico, vigoroso; ~ **level** *n* nivel *m* de aire.

spiritual ['spɪrɪtjuəl] *a* espiritual // *n* (*also*: **Negro** ~) canción *f* religiosa, espiritual *m*; ~**ism** *n* espiritualismo.

spit [spɪt] *n* (*for roasting*) asador *m*, espetón *m* // *vi*, *pt, pp* **spat** escupir; (*sound*) chisporrotear.

spite [spaɪt] *n* rencor *m*, ojeriza // *vt* causar pena a, mortificar; **in** ~ **of** a pesar de, pese a; ~**ful** *a* rencoroso, malévolo.

spittle ['spɪtl] *n* saliva, baba.

splash [splæʃ] *n* (*sound*) chapoteo; (*of colour*) mancha // *vt* salpicar de // *vi* (*also*: ~ **about**) chapotear.

spleen [spli:n] *n* (*ANAT*) bazo.

splendid ['splɛndɪd] *a* espléndido; **splendour, splendor** (*US*) [-də*] *n* esplendor *m*; (*of achievement*) brillo, gloria.

splint [splɪnt] *n* tablilla.

splinter ['splɪntə*] *n* (*of wood*) astilla; (*in finger*) espigón *m* // *vi* astillarse, hacer astillas.

split [splɪt] *n* hendedura, raja; (*fig*) división *f*; (*POL*) escisión *f* // (*vb: pt, pp* **split**) *vt* partir, rajar; (*party*) dividir; (*work, profits*) repartir // *vi* (*divide*) dividirse, escindirse; **to** ~ **up** *vi* (*couple*) separarse; (*meeting*) acabarse.

splutter ['splʌtə*] *vi* chisporrotear; (*person*) balbucear.

spoil [spɔɪl], *pt, pp* **spoilt** *or* **spoiled** *vt* (*damage*) dañar; (*mar*) estropear, echar a perder; (*child*) mimar, consentir; ~**s** *npl* despojo *sg*, botín *m*; ~**sport** *n* aguafiestas *m inv*.

spoke [spəuk] *pt of* **speak** // *n* rayo, radio.

spoken ['spəukn] *pp of* **speak.**

spokesman ['spəuksmən] *n* vocero, portavoz *m*.

sponge [spʌndʒ] *n* esponja; (*cake*) pastel *m* // *vt* (*wash*) lavar con esponja // *vi*: **to** ~ **on sb** vivir a costa de uno; ~ **bag** *n* esponjera; ~ **cake** *n* bizcocho, pastel *m*; **spongy** *a* esponjoso.

sponsor ['spɔnsə*] *n* (*RADIO, TV*) patrocinador/a *m/f*; (*for membership*) padrino; (*COMM*) fiador/a *m/f* // *vt* patrocinar; apadrinar; (*idea etc*) presentar, promover; ~**ship** *n* patrocinio.

spontaneous [spɔn'teɪnɪəs] *a* espontáneo.

spool [spu:l] *n* carrete *m*; (*of sewing machine*) canilla.

spoon [spu:n] *n* cuchara; ~**feed** *vt* dar de comer con cuchara; (*fig*) tratar como un niño; ~**ful** *n* cucharada.

sporadic [spə'rædɪk] *a* esporádico.

sport [spɔ:t] *n* deporte *m*; (*person*) buen perdedor *m*; ~**ing** *a* deportivo; ~**s car** *n* coche *m* sport; ~**s jacket** *n* chaqueta sport; **sportsman** *n* deportista *m*; **sportsmanship** *n* deportividad *f*; **sportswear** *n* trajes *mpl* de deporte *o* sport; **sportswoman** *n* deportista; ~**y** *a* deportivo.

spot [spɔt] *n* sitio, lugar *m*; (*dot: on pattern*) punto, mancha; (*pimple*) grano; (*freckle*) peca; (*small amount*): **a** ~ **of** un poquito de // *vt* (*notice*) notar, observar; **on the** ~ en el acto, acto seguido; (*in difficulty*) en un aprieto; ~ **check** *n* reconocimiento rápido; ~**less** *a* nítido, perfectamente limpio; ~**light** *n* foco, reflector *m*; ~**ted** *a* (*pattern*) de puntos; ~**ty** *a* (*face*) con granos.

spouse [spauz] *n* cónyuge *m/f*.

spout [spaut] *n* (*of jug*) pico; (*pipe*) caño // *vi* chorrear.

sprain [spreɪn] *n* torcedura // *vt*: **to** ~ **one's ankle** torcerse el tobillo.

sprang [spræŋ] *pt of* **spring.**

sprawl [sprɔːl] vi tumbarse.

spray [spreɪ] n rociada; (of sea) espuma; (container) atomizador m; (of paint) pistola rociadora; (of flowers) ramita // vt rociar; (crops) regar.

spread [spred] n extensión f; (distribution) diseminación f, propagación f; (col: food) comilona // (vb: pt, pp **spread**) vt extender; diseminar; (butter) untar; (wings, sails) desplegar; (scatter) esparcir // vi extenderse; diseminarse, untarse; desplegarse; esparcirse.

spree [spriː] n: **to go on a** ~ ir de juerga.

sprightly ['spraɪtlɪ] a vivo, enérgico.

spring [sprɪŋ] n (leap) salto, brinco; (coiled metal) resorte m; (season) primavera; (of water) fuente f, manantial f // vi, pt **sprang**, pp **sprung** (arise) brotar, nacer; (leap) saltar, brincar; **to** ~ **up** vi nacer de repente, aparecer repentinamente; ~**board** n trampolín m; ~-**clean** n (also: ~-**cleaning**) limpieza general; ~**time** n primavera; ~**y** a elástico; (grass) mueIle.

sprinkle ['sprɪŋkl] vt (pour) rociar; **to** ~ **water on**, ~ **with water** rociar o salpicar de agua; ~**d with** (fig) sembrado o salpicado de.

sprint [sprɪnt] n sprint m // vi (gen) correr a toda velocidad; (SPORT) sprintar; ~**er** n sprinter m/f, corredor/a m/f.

sprite [spraɪt] n duende m.

sprout [spraut] vi brotar, retoñar; (Brussels) ~**s** npl coIecillos mpl de Bruselas.

spruce [spruːs] n (BOT) pícea // a aseado, pulcro.

sprung [sprʌŋ] pp of **spring**.

spry [spraɪ] a ágil, activo.

spun [spʌn] pt, pp of **spin**.

spur [spəː*] n espuela; (fig) estímulo, aguijón m // vt (also: ~ **on**) estimular, incitar; **on the** ~ **of the moment** de improviso.

spurn [spəːn] vt desdeñar, rechazar.

spurt [spəːt] n esfuerzo supremo; (of energy) arrebato // vi hacer un esfuerzo supremo.

spy [spaɪ] n espía m/f // vi: **to** ~ **on** espiar a // vt (see) divisar, lograr ver; ~**ing** n espionaje m.

sq. abbr of **square**.

squabble ['skwɔbl] n riña, pelea // vi reñir, pelear.

squad [skwɔd] n (MIL, POLICE) pelotón m, escuadra.

squadron ['skwɔdrn] n (MIL) escuadrón m; (AVIAT, NAUT) escuadra.

squalid ['skwɔlɪd] a vil, miserable, escuálido.

squall [skwɔːl] n (storm) chubasco; (wind) ráfaga.

squalor ['skwɔlə*] n miseria.

squander ['skwɔndə*] vt (money) derrochar, despilfarrar; (chances) desperdiciar.

square [skwɛə*] n cuadro; (in town) plaza // a cuadrado; (col: ideas, tastes) pasota //

vt (arrange) arreglar; (MATH) cuadrar; all ~ igual(es); a ~ **meal** una comida abundante; **2 metres** ~ 2 metros en cuadro; **1** ~ **metre** un metro cuadrado; ~**ly** ad en cuadro; (fully) de lleno.

squash [skwɔʃ] n (drink): **lemon/orange** ~ zumo de limón/naranja; (SPORT) squash m, frontenis m // vt aplastar; **to** ~ **together** apiñar.

squat [skwɔt] a achaparrado // vi agacharse, sentarse en cuclillas; ~**ter** n persona que ocupa ilegalmente una casa.

squawk [skwɔːk] vi graznar.

squeak [skwiːk] n chirrido, rechinamiento; (of shoe) crujido; (of mouse) chillido // vi chirriar, rechinar; crujir; chillar.

squeal [skwiːl] vi chillar, dar gritos agudos.

squeamish ['skwiːmɪʃ] a delicado, remilgado.

squeeze [skwiːz] n (gen) estrujón m; (of hand) apretón m; (in bus etc) apiñamiento // vt estrujar, apretar; (hand, arm) apretar; **to** ~ **out** vt exprimir; (fig) excluir; **to** ~ **through** abrirse paso con esfuerzos.

squelch [skweltʃ] vi aplastar, despachurrar.

squid [skwɪd] n calamar m.

squint [skwɪnt] vi bizquear, ser bizco // n (MED) estrabismo; **to** ~ **at sth** mirar algo de soslayo.

squirm [skwəːm] vi retorcerse, revolverse.

squirrel ['skwɪrəl] n ardilla.

squirt [skwəːt] vi salir a chorros.

Sr abbr of **senior**.

St abbr of **saint**; **street**.

stab [stæb] n (with knife etc) puñalada; (of pain) pinchazo; (col: try): **to have a** ~ **at** (**doing**) **sth** intentar (hacer) algo // vt apuñalar.

stability [stə'bɪlɪtɪ] n estabilidad f; **stabilize** ['steɪbəlaɪz] vt estabilizar // vi estabilizarse; **stable** ['steɪbl] a estable // n cuadra, caballeriza.

stack [stæk] n montón m, pila // vt amontonar, apilar.

stadium ['steɪdɪəm] n estadio.

staff [staːf] n (work force) personal m, plantilla; (stick) bastón m // vt proveer de personal.

stag [stæg] n ciervo, venado.

stage [steɪdʒ] n escena; (profession): **the** ~ el escenario, el teatro; (point) etapa; (platform) plataforma // vt (play) poner en escena, representar; (demonstration) montar, organizar; (fig: perform: recovery etc) llevar a cabo; ~**coach** n diligencia; ~ **door** n entrada de artistas; ~ **manager** n director/a m/f de escena.

stagger ['stægə*] vi tambalear // vt (amaze) asombrar; (hours, holidays) escalonar; ~**ing** a (amazing) asombroso, pasmoso.

stagnant ['stægnənt] a estancado; **stagnate** ['stægneɪt] vi estancarse.

stag party n fiesta de solteros.

...d] a serio, formal.

...tein] n mancha; (*colouring*) tintura ...nanchar; (*wood*) teñir; **~ed glass** ...ow n vidriera de colores; **~less** a ...l) inoxidable.

...r [steɔ*] n (*step*) peldaño, escalón m; ...s npl escaleras fpl; **~case, ~way** n ...scalera.

...ake [steɪk] n estaca, poste m; (*BETTING*) apuesta // vt apostar; **to be at ~** estar en juego.

stalactite ['stæləktaɪt] n estalactita.

stalagmite ['stæləgmaɪt] n estalagmita.

stale [steɪl] a (*bread*) duro; (*food*) no fresco, pasado.

stalemate ['steɪlmeɪt] n tablas fpl (por ahogado); (*fig*) estancamiento.

stalk [stɔːk] n tallo, caña // vt acechar, cazar al acecho; **to ~ off** irse con paso airado.

stall [stɔːl] n (*in market*) puesto; (*in stable*) casilla (de establo) // vt (*AUT*) parar // vi (*AUT*) pararse; (*fig*) buscar evasivas; **~s** npl (*in cinema, theatre*) butacas fpl.

stallion ['stæliən] n caballo padre, semental m.

stalwart ['stɔːlwət] n (*in build*) fornido; (*in spirit*) valiente.

stamina ['stæminə] n resistencia.

stammer ['stæmə*] n tartamudeo, balbuceo // vi tartamudear, balbucir.

stamp [stæmp] n sello, estampilla; (*mark, also fig*) marca, huella; (*on document*) timbre m // vi patear // vt patear, golpear con el pie; (*in dance*) zapatear; (*letter*) poner sellos en; (*with rubber ~*) marcar con estampilla; **~ album** n álbum m para sellos; **~ collecting** n filatelia.

stampede [stæm'piːd] n estampida.

stance [stæns] n postura.

stand [stænd] n (*position*) posición f, postura; (*for taxis*) parada; (*hall ~*) perchero; (*music ~*) atril m; (*SPORT*) tribuna; (*news ~*) quiosco // (*vb*: pt, pp **stood**) vi (*be*) estar, encontrarse; (*be on foot*) estar de pie; (*rise*) levantarse; (*remain*) quedar en pie // vt (*place*) poner, colocar; (*tolerate, withstand*) aguantar, soportar; (*cost*) pagar; (*invite*) invitar; **to make a ~** resistir; (*fig*) aferrarse a un principio; **to ~ for parliament** presentarse como candidato al parlamento; **to ~ by** vi (*be ready*) estar listo // vt fus (*opinion*) aferrarse a; **to ~ for** vt fus (*defend*) apoyar; (*signify*) significar; (*tolerate*) aguantar, permitir; **to ~ in for** vt fus suplir a; **to ~ out** vi (*be prominent*) destacarse; **to ~ up** vi (*rise*) levantarse, ponerse de pie; **to ~ up for** vt fus defender; **to ~ up to** vt fus hacer frente a.

standard ['stændəd] n patrón m, norma; (*flag*) estandarte m; (*degree*) grado // a (*size etc*) normal, corriente, stándard; **~s** npl (*morals*) valores mpl morales; **~ize** vt estandarizar; **~ lamp** n lámpara de pie; **~ of living** n nivel m de vida.

stand-by ['stændbaɪ] n (*alert*) alerta, aviso; **to be on ~** estar sobre aviso; **~ ticket** n (*AVIAT*) billete m standby.

stand-in ['stændɪn] n suplente m/f; (*CINEMA*) doble m/f.

standing ['stændɪŋ] a (*upright*) derecho; (*on foot*) de pie, en pie // n reputación f; **of many years'** que lleva muchos años; **~ order** n (*at bank*) giro bancario; **~ orders** npl (*MIL*) reglamento sg general; **~ room** n sitio para estar de pie.

stand: **~-offish** a reservado, poco afable; **~point** n punto de vista; **~still** n: **at a ~still** paralizado, en paro; **to come to a ~still** pararse, quedar paralizado.

stank [stæŋk] pt of **stink**.

staple ['steɪpl] n (*for papers*) grapa // a (*food etc*) corriente // vt unir con grapa, engrapar; **stapler** n grapadora.

star [stɑː*] n estrella; (*celebrity*) estrella, astro // vi: **to ~ in** ser la estrella o el astro de.

starboard ['stɑːbəd] n estribor m.

starch [stɑːtʃ] n almidón m; **~ed** a (*collar*) almidonado; **~y** a feculento.

stardom ['stɑːdəm] n estrellato, calidad f de estrella.

stare [steə*] n mirada fija // vt: **to ~ at** mirar fijo.

starfish ['stɑːfɪʃ] n estrella de mar.

stark [stɑːk] a (*bleak*) severo, escueto // ad: **~ naked** en cueros, en pelota.

starlight ['stɑːlaɪt] n: **by ~** a la luz de las estrellas.

starling ['stɑːlɪŋ] n estornino.

starry ['stɑːrɪ] a estrellado; **~-eyed** a (*innocent*) inocentón(ona), ingenuo.

start [stɑːt] n (*beginning*) principio, comienzo; (*departure*) salida; (*sudden movement*) salto, sobresalto; (*advantage*) ventaja // vt empezar, comenzar; (*cause*) causar; (*found*) fundar; (*engine*) poner en marcha // vi (*begin*) comenzar, empezar; (*with fright*) asustarse, sobresaltarse; (*train etc*) salir; **to ~ off** vi empezar, comenzar; (*leave*) salir, ponerse en camino; **to ~ up** vi comenzar; (*car*) ponerse en marcha // vt comenzar; (*car*) poner en marcha; **~er** n (*AUT*) botón m de arranque; (*SPORT: official*) juez m/f de salida; (: *runner*) corredor/a m/f; (*CULIN*) entrada; **~ing point** n punto de partida.

startle ['stɑːtl] vt asustar, sobrecoger; **startling** a alarmante.

starvation [stɑː'veɪʃən] n hambre f; (*MED*) inanición f; **starve** vi pasar hambre; (*to death*) morir de hambre // vt hacer pasar hambre; (*fig*) privar; **I'm starving** estoy muerto de hambre.

state [steɪt] n estado // vt (*say, declare*) afirmar; (*a case*) presentar, exponer; **the S~s** los Estados Unidos; **to be in a ~** estar agitado; **~ly** a majestuoso, imponente; **~ment** n afirmación f; (*LAW*) declaración f; **statesman** n estadista m.

static ['stætɪk] n (*RADIO*) parásitos mpl // a estático; **~ electricity** n estática.

station ['steɪʃən] n (gen) estación f; (place) puesto, sitio; (RADIO) emisora; (rank) posición f social // vt colocar, situar; (MIL) apostar.

stationary ['steɪʃnərɪ] a estacionario, fijo.

stationer's (shop) ['steɪʃənəz] n papelería; **stationery** [-nərɪ] n papel m de escribir.

station master n (RAIL) jefe m de estación.

station wagon n (US) break m.

statistic [stə'tɪstɪk] n estadística; ~s npl (science) estadística sg; ~al a estadístico.

statue ['stætjuː] n estatua.

stature ['stætʃə*] n estatura; (fig) talla.

status ['steɪtəs] n condición f, estado; (reputation) reputación f, status m: the ~ quo el statu quo; ~ symbol n símbolo de prestigio.

statute ['stætjuːt] n estatuto, ley f; **statutory** a estatutario.

staunch [stɔːntʃ] a firme, incondicional.

stave [steɪv] vt: to ~ off (attack) rechazar; (threat) evitar.

stay [steɪ] n (period of time) estancia // vi (remain) quedar, quedarse; (as guest) hospedarse; (spend some time) pasar (un) tiempo; to ~ put seguir en el mismo sitio; to ~ the night pasar la noche; to ~ behind vi quedar atrás; to ~ in vi (at home) quedarse en casa; to ~ on vi quedarse; to ~ out vi (of house) no volver a casa; to ~ up vi (at night) velar, no acostarse; ~ing power n resistencia.

steadfast ['stedfɑːst] a firme, resuelto.

steadily ['stedɪlɪ] ad (firmly) firmemente; (unceasingly) sin parar; (fixedly) fijamente; (walk) normalmente; (drive) a velocidad constante.

steady ['stedɪ] a (constant) constante, fijo; (unswerving) firme; (regular) regular; (person, character) sensato, juicioso; (diligent) trabajador; (calm) sereno // vt (hold) mantener firme; (stabilize) estabilizar; (nerves) calmar; to ~ o.s. on or against sth afirmarse en algo.

steak [steɪk] n (gen) filete m; (beef) bistec m.

steal [stiːl], pt **stole**, pp **stolen** vt, vi robar.

stealth [stelθ] n: by ~ a escondidas, sigilosamente; ~y a cauteloso, sigiloso.

steam [stiːm] n vapor m; (mist) vaho, humo // vt empañar; (CULIN) cocer al vapor // vi echar vapor; (ship): to ~ along avanzar, ir avanzando; ~ engine n máquina de vapor; ~er n vapor m; ~roller n apisonadora; ~y a vaporoso; (room) lleno de vapor; (window) empañado.

steel [stiːl] n acero // a de acero; ~works n (fábrica) siderúrgica.

steep [stiːp] a escarpado, abrupto; (stair) empinado; (price) exorbitante, excesivo // vt empapar, remojar.

steeple ['stiːpl] n aguja, campanario; ~chase n carrera de obstáculos; ~jack

---

n reparador m de chimeneas.

steer [stɪə*] vt conducir, dirigir // vi conducir; ~ing n (AUT) dirección f; ~ing wheel n volante m.

stellar ['stelə*] a estelar.

stem [stem] n (of plant) tallo; (of glass) pie m; (of pipe) cañón m // vt detener; (blood) restañar; to ~ from vt fus proceder de.

stench [stentʃ] n hedor m.

stencil ['stensl] n (typed) cliché m, clisé m; (lettering) plantilla // vt hacer un cliché de.

step [step] n paso; (sound) paso, pisada; (stair) peldaño, escalón m // vi: to ~ forward dar un paso adelante; ~s npl = ~ladder; to ~ down vi (fig) retirarse; to ~ off vt fus bajar de; to ~ on vt fus pisar; to ~ over vt fus pasar por encima de; to ~ up vt (increase) aumentar; ~brother n hermanastro; ~daughter n hijastra; ~father n padrastro; ~ladder n escalera de tijera o doble; ~mother n madrastra; ~ping stone n pasadera; ~sister n hermanastra; ~son n hijastro.

stereo ['stɪərɪəu] n estéreo // a (also: ~phonic) estereofónico.

stereotype ['stɪərɪətaɪp] n estereotipo // vt estereotipar.

sterile ['steraɪl] a estéril; **sterility** [-'rɪlɪtɪ] n esterilidad f; **sterilization** [-zeɪʃən] n esterilización f; **sterilize** ['sterɪlaɪz] vt esterilizar.

sterling ['stɜːlɪŋ] a esterlina; (silver) de ley; (fig) auténtico.

stern [stɜːn] a severo, austero // n (NAUT) popa.

stethoscope ['steθəskəup] n estetoscopio.

stew [stjuː] n cocido, estofado; (fig: mess) apuro // vt, vi estofar, guisar; (fruit) cocer.

steward ['stjuːəd] n (gen) camarero; ~ess n azafata.

stick [stɪk] n palo; (as weapon) porra; (walking ~) bastón m // (vb: pt, pp **stuck**) vt (glue) pegar; (thrust): to ~ sth into clavar o hincar algo en; (col: put) meter; (col: tolerate) aguantar, soportar // vi pegar, pegarse; (come to a stop) quedarse parado; (in mind etc) atascarse; (pin etc) clavarse; to ~ out, ~ up vi sobresalir; to ~ up for vt fus defender; ~er n etiqueta engomada.

stickler ['stɪklə*] n: to be a ~ for dar mucha importancia a.

stick-up ['stɪkʌp] n asalto, atraco.

sticky ['stɪkɪ] a pegajoso; (label) engomado; (fig) difícil.

stiff [stɪf] a rígido, tieso; (hard) duro; (difficult) difícil; (person) inflexible; (price) exorbitante; ~en vt hacer más rígido; (limb) entumecer // vi endurecerse; (grow stronger) fortalecerse; ~ness n rigidez f, tiesura; dificultad f; (character) frialdad f.

stifle ['staɪfl] vt ahogar, sofocar; **stifling** a (heat) sofocante, bochornoso.

stigma ['stɪgmə], pl (BOT, MED, REL) ~ta [tə], (fig) ~s n estigma m.

stile [staɪl] *n* escalera para pasar una cerca.

stiletto [stɪ'letəu] *n* (*also*: ~ **heel**) tacón *m* de aguja.

still [stɪl] *a* inmóvil, quieto // *ad* (*up to this time*) todavía; (*even*) aún; (*nonetheless*) sin embargo, aun así; **~born** *a* nacido muerto; ~ **life** *n* naturaleza muerta.

stilt [stɪlt] *n* zanco; (*pile*) pilar *m*, soporte *m*.

stilted ['stɪltɪd] *a* afectado.

stimulant ['stɪmjulənt] *n* estimulante *m*.

stimulate ['stɪmjuleɪt] *vt* estimular; **stimulating** *a* estimulante; **stimulation** [-'leɪʃən] *n* estímulo.

stimulus ['stɪmjuləs], *pl* **-li** [-laɪ] *n* estímulo, incentivo.

sting [stɪŋ] *n* (*wound*) picadura; (*pain*) escozor *m*, picazón *m*; (*organ*) aguijón *m* // (*vb*: *pt*, *pp* **stung**) *vt* picar // *vi* picar, escocer.

stingy ['stɪndʒɪ] *a* tacaño.

stink [stɪŋk] *n* hedor *m*, tufo // *vi*, *pt* **stank**, *pp* **stunk** heder, apestar; **~ing** *a* hediondo, fétido.

stint [stɪnt] *n* tarea, destajo; **to do one's** ~ hacer su parte // *vi*: **to** ~ **on** escatimar.

stipend ['staɪpend] *n* (*of vicar etc*) estipendio, sueldo.

stipulate ['stɪpjuleɪt] *vt* estipular, poner como condición; **stipulation** [-'leɪʃən] *n* estipulación *f*, condición *f*.

stir [stə:*] *n* (*fig*: *agitation*) conmoción *f* // *vt* (*tea etc*) remover; (*fire*) atizar; (*move*) mover; (*fig*: *emotions*) conmover // *vi* moverse, menearse; **to** ~ **up** *vt* excitar; (*trouble*) fomentar; **~ring** *a* conmovedor(a).

stirrup ['stɪrəp] *n* estribo.

stitch [stɪtʃ] *n* (*SEWING*) puntada; (*KNITTING*) punto; (*MED*) punto (de sutura); (*pain*) punzada // *vt* coser; (*MED*) suturar.

stoat [stəut] *n* armiño.

stock [stɔk] *n* (*COMM*: *reserves*) existencias *fpl*, stock *m*; (: *selection*) surtido; (*AGR*) ganado, ganadería; (*CULIN*) caldo; (*fig*: *lineage*) estirpe *f*; (*FINANCE*) capital *m*; (: *shares*) acciones *fpl* // *a* (*fig*: *reply etc*) clásico, acostumbrado // *vt* (*have in* ~) tener (en existencia o almacén); (*supply*) proveer, abastecer; **to take** ~ **of** (*fig*) asesorar, examinar; **to** ~ **up with** *vt* abastecerse de; **~s** *npl* cepo *sg*; **~s and shares** acciones y valores.

stockade [stɔ'keɪd] *n* estacada.

stockbroker ['stɔkbrəukə*] *n* agente *m/f* o corredor/a *m/f* de bolsa.

stock exchange *n* bolsa.

stocking ['stɔkɪŋ] *n* media.

stock market *n* bolsa (de valores).

stockpile ['stɔkpaɪl] *n* reserva // *vt* acumular, almacenar.

stocktaking ['stɔkteɪkɪŋ] *n* (*COMM*) inventario, balance *m*.

stocky ['stɔkɪ] *a* (*strong*) robusto; (*short*) achaparrado.

stodgy ['stɔdʒɪ] *a* indigesto, pesado.

stoical ['stəuɪkəl] *a* estoico.

stoke [stəuk] *vt* cargar, cebar.

stole [stəul] *pt of* **steal** // *n* estola.

stolen ['stəuln] *pp of* **steal**.

stomach ['stʌmək] *n* (*ANAT*) estómago; (*belly*) vientre *m*; (*appetite*) apetito // *vt* tragar, aguantar; ~ **ache** *n* dolor *m* de estómago.

stone [stəun] *n* piedra; (*in fruit*) hueso; (*weight*) medida de peso (6.348kg) // *a* de piedra // *vt* apedrear; **~-cold** *a* helado; **~-deaf** *a* totalmente sordo; **~work** *n* (*art*) cantería; (*stones*) piedras *fpl*; **stony** *a* pedregoso; (*glance*) glacial.

stood [stud] *pt*, *pp of* **stand**.

stool [stu:l] *n* taburete *m*.

stoop [stu:p] *vi* (*also*: **have a** ~) ser cargado de espaldas; (*bend*) inclinarse, encorvarse.

stop [stɔp] *n* parada, alto; (*in punctuation*) punto // *vt* parar, detener; (*break off*) suspender; (*block*) tapar, cerrar; (*also*: **put a** ~ **to**) terminar, poner término a // *vi* pararse, detenerse; (*end*) acabarse; **to** ~ **doing sth** dejar de hacer algo; **to** ~ **dead** *vi* pararse en seco; **to** ~ **off** *vi* interrumpir el viaje; **to** ~ **up** *vt* (*hole*) tapar; **~gap** *n* recurso (temporal); **~lights** *npl* (*AUT*) luces *fpl* de detención; **~over** *n* parada intermedia.

stoppage ['stɔpɪdʒ] *n* (*strike*) paro; (*temporary stop*) interrupción *f*; (*of pay*) suspensión *f*; (*blockage*) obstrucción *f*.

stopper ['stɔpə*] *n* tapón *m*.

stopwatch ['stɔpwɔtʃ] *n* cronómetro.

storage ['stɔ:rɪdʒ] *n* almacenaje *m*.

store [stɔ:*] *n* (*stock*) provisión *f*; (*depot*, *large shop*) almacén *m*; (*reserve*) reserva, repuesto; **~s** *npl* víveres *mpl* // *vt* almacenar; (*keep*) guardar; **to** ~ **up** *vt* acumular; **~room** *n* despensa.

storey, story (*US*) ['stɔ:rɪ] *n* piso.

stork [stɔ:k] *n* cigüeña.

storm [stɔ:m] *n* tormenta; (*wind*) vendaval *m*; (*fig*) tempestad *f* // *vi* (*fig*) rabiar // *vt* tomar por asalto, asaltar; **~ cloud** *n* nubarrón *m*; **~y** *a* tempestuoso.

story ['stɔ:rɪ] *n* historia, relato; (*joke*) cuento, chiste *m*; (*plot*) argumento; (*lie*) cuento, embuste *m*; (*US*) = **storey**; **~book** *n* libro de cuentos; **~teller** *n* cuentista *m/f*.

stout [staut] *a* (*strong*) sólido, macizo; (*fat*) gordo, corpulento // *n* cerveza negra.

stove [stəuv] *n* (*for cooking*) cocina; (*for heating*) estufa.

stow [stəu] *vt* meter, poner; (*NAUT*) estibar; **~away** *n* polizón /ona *m/f*.

straddle ['strædl] *vt* montar a horcajadas.

straggle ['strægl] *vi* (*wander*) vagar en desorden; (*lag behind*) rezagarse; **straggler** *n* rezagado; **straggling**, **straggly** *a* (*hair*) desordenado.

straight [streɪt] *a* recto, derecho; (*honest*) honrado; (*frank*) franco, directo; (*simple*) sencillo; (*in order*) en orden // *ad* derecho, directamente; (*drink*) sin mezcla; **to put**

or **get** sth ~ dejar algo en claro; ~ **away**, ~ **off** (*at once*) en seguida; ~en *vi* (*also*: ~**en out**) enderezar, poner derecho; ~**-faced** a solemne, sin expresión; ~**forward** a (*simple*) sencillo; (*honest*) honrado, franco.

strain [streɪn] *n* (*gen*) tensión *f*; (*TECH*) esfuerzo; (*MED*) torcedura; (*breed*) raza *f*; *vt* (*back etc*) torcerse; (*tire*) cansar; (*stretch*) estirar; (*filter*) filtrar // *vi* esforzarse; ~**s** *npl* (*MUS*) son *m*; ~**ed** a (*muscle*) torcido; (*laugh*) forzado; (*relations*) tenso; ~**er** *n* colador *m*.

strait [streɪt] *n* (*GEO*) estrecho; ~**-jacket** *n* camisa de fuerza; ~**-laced** a mojigato, gazmoño.

strand [strænd] *n* (*of thread*) hebra, (*of hair*) trenza; (*of rope*) ramal *m*; ~**ed** a abandonado (sin recursos), desamparado.

strange [streɪndʒ] a (*not known*) desconocido; (*odd*) extraño, raro; **stranger** *n* desconocido/a; (*from another area*) forastero/a.

strangle ['stræŋgl] *vt* estrangular; (*sobs etc*) ahogar; ~**hold** *n* (*fig*) dominio completo; **strangulation** [-'leɪʃən] *n* estrangulación *f*.

strap [stræp] *n* correa; (*of slip, dress*) tirante *m* // *vt* atar con correa; (*punish*) azotar.

strapping ['stræpɪŋ] a robusto, fornido.

strata ['strɑːtə] *pl of* **stratum**.

stratagem ['strætɪdʒəm] *n* estratagema.

strategic [strə'tiːdʒɪk] a estratégico.

strategy ['strætɪdʒɪ] *n* estrategia.

stratum ['strɑːtəm], *pl* **-ta** *n* estrato.

straw [strɔː] *n* paja; (*drinking* ~) caña, pajita.

strawberry ['strɔːbərɪ] *n* fresa.

stray [streɪ] a (*animal*) extraviado; (*bullet*) perdido; (*scattered*) disperso // *vi* extraviarse, perderse.

streak [striːk] *n* raya; (*fig: of madness etc*) vena // *vt* rayar // *vi*: **to** ~ **past** pasar como un rayo; ~**y** a rayado.

stream [striːm] *n* riachuelo, arroyo; (*jet*) chorro; (*current*) corriente *f*; (*of people*) oleada // *vt* (*SCOL*) dividir en grupos por habilidad // *vi* correr, fluir; **to** ~ **in/out** (*people*) entrar/salir en tropel.

streamer ['striːmə*] *n* serpentina.

streamlined ['striːmlaɪnd] a aerodinámico.

street [striːt] *n* calle *f* // a callejero; ~**car** *n* (*US*) tranvía; ~ **lamp** *n* farol *m*.

strength [strɛŋθ] *n* fuerza; (*of girder, knot etc*) resistencia; ~**en** *vt* fortalecer, reforzar.

strenuous ['strɛnjuəs] a (*tough*) arduo; (*energetic*) enérgico; (*determined*) tenaz.

stress [strɛs] *n* (*force, pressure*) presión *f*; (*mental strain*) tensión *f*; (*accent*) énfasis *m*, acento; (*TECH*) tensión *f*, carga // *vt* subrayar, recalcar.

stretch [strɛtʃ] *n* (*of sand etc*) trecho, tramo // *vi* estirarse; (*extend*): **to** ~ **to** *or* **as far as** extenderse hasta // *vt* extender,

estirar; (*make demands of*) exigir el máximo esfuerzo a; **to** ~ **out** *vi* tenderse // *vt* (*arm etc*) extender; (*spread*) estirar.

stretcher ['strɛtʃə*] *n* camilla.

strewn [struːn] a: ~ **with** cubierto *o* sembrado de.

stricken ['strɪkən] a (*wounded*) herido; (*ill*) enfermo.

strict [strɪkt] a (*person*) severo, riguroso; (*precise*) estricto, exacto; ~**ly** ad (*exactly*) estrictamente; (*totally*) terminantemente; (*severely*) rigurosamente; ~**ness** *n* exactitud *f*; rigor *m*, severidad *f*.

stride [straɪd] *n* zancada, tranco // *vi*, *pt* **strode**, *pp* **stridden** ['strɪdn] dar zancadas, andar a trancos.

strident ['straɪdnt] a estridente; (*colour*) chillón(ona).

strife [straɪf] *n* lucha.

strike [straɪk] *n* huelga; (*of oil etc*) descubrimiento; (*attack*) ataque *m*; (*SPORT*) golpe *m* // (*vb*: *pt*, *pp* **struck**) *vt* golpear, pegar; (*oil etc*) descubrir; (*obstacle*) topar con // *vi* declarar la huelga; (*attack*) atacar; (*clock*) dar la hora; **to** ~ **a match** encender un fósforo; **to** ~ **down** *vt* derribar; **to** ~ **out** *vt* borrar, tachar; **to** ~ **up** (*MUS*) empezar a tocar; (*conversation*) entablar; (*friendship*) trabar; ~**breaker** *n* rompehuelgas *m/f inv*; **striker** *n* huelgista *m/f*; (*SPORT*) delantero; **striking** a impresionante; (*nasty*) chocante; (*colour*) llamativo.

string [strɪŋ] *n* (*gen*) cuerda; (*row*) hilera // *vt*, *pt*, *pp* **strung**: **to** ~ **together** ensartar // *vi*: **to** ~ **out** extenderse; **the** ~**s** *npl* (*MUS*) los instrumentos de cuerda; **to pull** ~**s** (*fig*) mover palancas; ~ **bean** *n* judía verde, habichuela; ~**(ed) instrument** *n* (*MUS*) instrumento de cuerda.

stringent ['strɪndʒənt] a riguroso, severo.

strip [strɪp] *n* tira; (*of land*) franja; (*of metal*) cinta, lámina // *vt* desnudar; (*also*: ~ **down**: *machine*) desmontar // *vi* desnudarse; ~ **cartoon** *n* tira cómica.

stripe [straɪp] *n* raya; (*MIL*) galón *m*; ~**d** a a rayas, rayado.

stripper ['strɪpə*] *n* artista de striptease.

striptease ['strɪptiːz] *n* striptease *m*.

strive [straɪv], *pt* **strove**, *pp* **striven** ['strɪvn] *vi*: **to** ~ **to do** sth esforzarse *o* luchar por hacer algo.

strode [strəud] *pt of* **stride**.

stroke [strəuk] *n* (*blow*) golpe *m*; (*MED*) ataque *m* fulminante; (*caress*) caricia; (*of pen*) trazo // *vt* acariciar, frotar suavemente; **at a** ~ de golpe.

stroll [strəul] *n* paseo, vuelta // *vi* dar un paseo *o* una vuelta.

strong [strɔŋ] a fuerte; **they are 50** ~ son 50; ~**box** *n* caja fuerte; ~**hold** *n* fortaleza; (*fig*) baluarte *m*; ~**ly** ad fuertemente, con fuerza; (*believe*)

firmemente; **~room** n cámara
acorazada.

strove [strəuv] pt of **strive.**

struck [strʌk] pt, pp of **strike.**

structural ['strʌktʃərəl] a estructural;
structure n estructura; (building)
construcción f.

struggle ['strʌgl] n lucha // vi luchar.

strum [strʌm] vt (guitar) rasguear.

strung [strʌŋ] pt, pp of **string.**

strut [strʌt] n puntal m // vi pavonearse.

stub [stʌb] n (of ticket etc) talón m; (of
cigarette) colilla; to **~ out** vt apagar; to
~ one's toe dar con el dedo contra algo.

stubble ['stʌbl] n rastrojo; (on chin) barba
(de pocos días).

stubborn ['stʌbən] a terco, testarudo.

stuck [stʌk] pt, pp of **stick** // a (jammed)
atascado; **~-up** a engreído, presumido.

stud [stʌd] n (shirt ~) botón m; (of boot)
taco; (of horses) caballeriza; (also: ~
horse) caballo padre o semental // vt
(fig): **~ded with** sembrado de.

student ['stju:dənt] n estudiante m/f // a
estudiantil.

studio ['stju:dıəu] n estudio; (sculptor's)
taller m.

studious ['stju:dıəs] a aplicado; (studied)
calculado; **~ly** ad (carefully) con esmero.

study ['stʌdı] n (gen) estudio // vt estudiar;
(examine) examinar, escudriñar // vi
estudiar.

stuff [stʌf] n materia; (cloth) tela;
(substance) material m, sustancia // vt
llenar; (CULIN) rellenar; (animals) disecar;
~ing n relleno; **~y** a (room) mal
ventilado; (person) de miras estrechas.

stumble ['stʌmbl] vi tropezar, dar un
traspié; to **~ across** (fig) tropezar con;
stumbling block n tropiezo, obstáculo.

stump [stʌmp] n (of tree) tocón m; (of
limb) muñón m // vt: to be **~ed** quedar
perplejo.

stun [stʌn] vt dejar sin sentido.

stung [stʌŋ] pt, pp of **sting.**

stunk [stʌŋk] pp of **stink.**

stunning ['stʌnıŋ] a (fig) pasmoso.

stunt [stʌnt] n proeza excepcional; (AVIAT)
vuelo acrobático; (publicity ~) truco
publicitario; **~ed** a enano, achaparrado;
~ man n doble m.

stupefy ['stju:pıfaı] vt dejar estupefacto.

stupendous [stju:'pɛndəs] a estupendo,
asombroso.

stupid ['stju:pıd] a estúpido, tonto; **~ity**
[-'pıdıtı] n estupidez f; **~ly** ad
estúpidamente.

stupor ['stju:pə°] n estupor m.

sturdy ['stə:dı] a robusto, fuerte.

stutter ['stʌtə°] n tartamudeo // vi
tartamudear.

sty [staı] n (for pigs) pocilga.

stye [staı] n (MED) orzuelo.

style [staıl] n estilo; **stylish** a elegante, a
la moda.

stylus ['staıləs] n (of record player) aguja.

suave [swɑ:v] a cortés, fino.

sub... [sʌb] pref sub...; **~conscious** a
subconsciente // n subconsciente m;
~divide vt subdividir; **~division** n
subdivisión f.

subdue [səb'dju:] vt sojuzgar; (passions)
dominar; **~d** a (light) tenue; (person)
sumiso, manso.

subject ['sʌbdʒıkt] n súbdito; (SCOL) tema
m, materia // vt [səb'dʒɛkt]: to **~** sb to
sth someter a uno a algo; **to be ~ to**
(law) estar sujeto a; **~ion** [-'dʒɛkʃən] n
sometimiento, sujeción f; **~ive** a
subjetivo; **~ matter** n materia; (content)
contenido.

subjugate ['sʌbdʒugeıt] vt subyugar.

sublet [sʌb'lɛt] vt subarrendar.

sublime [sə'blaım] a sublime.

submachine gun ['sʌbmə'ʃi:n-] n
metralleta.

submarine [sʌbmə'ri:n] n submarino.

submerge [səb'mə:dʒ] vt sumergir; (flood)
inundar // vi sumergirse.

submission [səb'mıʃən] n sumisión f;
submissive [-'mısıv] a sumiso.

submit [səb'mıt] vt someter // vi
someterse.

subnormal [sʌb'nɔ:məl] a anormal;
(backward) retrasado.

subordinate [sə'bɔ:dınət] a, n
subordinado.

subpoena [səb'pi:nə] (LAW) n comparendo,
citación f // vt mandar comparecer.

subscribe [səb'skraıb] vi suscribir; to **~
to** (opinion, fund) suscribir, aprobar;
(newspaper) suscribirse a; **subscriber** n
(to periodical, telephone) abonado/a.

subscription [səb'skrıpʃən] n abono,
suscripción f.

subsequent ['sʌbsıkwənt] a subsiguiente,
posterior; **~ly** ad después, más tarde.

subside [səb'saıd] vi hundirse; (flood)
bajar; (wind) amainar; **subsidence**
[-'saıdns] n hundimiento; (in road) socavón
m.

subsidiary [səb'sıdıərı] n sucursal f, filial
f.

subsidize ['sʌbsıdaız] vt subvencionar;
subsidy [-dı] n subvención f.

subsistence [səb'sıstəns] n subsistencia;
(allowance) dietas fpl.

substance ['sʌbstəns] n sustancia; (fig)
esencia.

substandard [sʌb'stændəd] a inferior.

substantial [səb'stænʃl] a sustancial,
sustancioso; (fig) importante; **~ly** ad sus-
tancialmente.

substantiate [səb'stænʃıeıt] vt
comprobar.

substitute ['sʌbstıtju:t] n (person)
suplente m/f; (thing) sustituto // vt: to **~
A for B** sustituir B por A, reemplazar A
por B; **substitution** [-'tju:ʃən] n sustitución
f, reemplazo.

subterfuge ['sʌbtəfju:dʒ] n subterfugio.

subterranean [sʌbtə'reınıən] a
subterráneo.

subtitle ['sʌbtaɪtl] n subtítulo.
subtle ['sʌtl] a sutil; ~**ty** n sutileza.
subtract [səb'trækt] vt sustraer, restar; ~**ion** [-'trækʃən] n sustracción f, resta.
suburb ['sʌbəːb] n arrabal m, suburbio; ~**an** [sə'bəːbən] a suburbano; (train etc) de cercanías.
subversive [səb'vəːsɪv] a subversivo.
subway ['sʌbweɪ] n (Brit) paso subterráneo o inferior; (US) metro.
succeed [sək'siːd] vi (person) tener éxito; (plan) salir bien // vt suceder a; **to ~ in doing** lograr hacer; ~**ing** a (following) sucesivo, seguido.
success [sək'sɛs] n éxito; (gain) triunfo; ~**ful** a (venture) de éxito; **to be ~ful** (in doing) lograr (hacer); ~**fully** ad con éxito.
succession [sək'sɛʃən] n (series) sucesión f, serie f; (descendants) descendencia; **successive** [-'sɛsɪv] a sucesivo, consecutivo; **successor** [-'sɛsə*] n sucesor/a m/f.
succinct [sək'sɪŋkt] a sucinto.
succulent ['sʌkjulənt] a suculento.
succumb [sə'kʌm] vi sucumbir.
such [sʌtʃ] a, det tal, semejante; ~of that kind): ~ **a book** un libro parecido; ~ **books** tales libros; (so much): ~ **courage** tanto valor; ~ **a long trip** un viaje tan largo; ~ **a lot of** tanto; ~ **as** (like) tal como; **a noise** ~ **as to** un ruido tal que; **as** ~ ad como tal // pron los/las que; ~**-and-** det tal o cual; **until** ~ **time as** hasta que.
suck [sʌk] vt chupar; (bottle) sorber; (breast) mamar; ~**er** n (ZOOL) ventosa; (col) bobo, primo.
suckle ['sʌkl] vt amamantar.
suction ['sʌkʃən] n succión f.
sudden ['sʌdn] a (rapid) repentino, súbito; (unexpected) imprevisto; **all of a** ~, ~**ly** ad de repente; (unexpectedly) inesperadamente.
suds [sʌdz] npl jabonaduras fpl.
sue [suː] vt demandar.
suede [sweɪd] n ante m.
suet ['suɪt] n sebo.
suffer ['sʌfə*] vt sufrir, padecer; (bear) aguantar; (allow) permitir, tolerar // vi sufrir, padecer; ~**er** n víctima m/f; (MED) enfermo; ~**ing** n sufrimiento, padecimiento; (pain) dolor m.
suffice [sə'faɪs] vi bastar, ser suficiente.
sufficient [sə'fɪʃənt] a suficiente, bastante.
suffix ['sʌfɪks] n sufijo.
suffocate ['sʌfəkeɪt] vi ahogarse, asfixiarse; **suffocation** [-'keɪʃən] n sofocación f, asfixia.
suffrage ['sʌfrɪdʒ] n sufragio; (vote) derecho de votar.
sugar ['ʃugə*] n azúcar m // vt echar azúcar a; ~ **beet** n remolacha; ~ **cane** n caña de azúcar; ~**y** a azucarado.
suggest [sə'dʒɛst] vt sugerir; (advise) aconsejar; ~**ion** [-'dʒɛstʃən] n sugerencia;

(hypnosis) sugestión f; ~**ive** a sugestivo; (pej) indecente.
suicidal [suɪ'saɪdl] a suicida; **suicide** ['suɪsaɪd] n suicidio; (person) suicida m/f.
suit [suːt] n (man's) traje m; (woman's) conjunto; (LAW) litigio, pleito; (CARDS) palo // vt (gen) convenir; (clothes) sentar a, ir bien a; (adapt): **to** ~ **sth to** adaptar o ajustar algo a; ~**able** a conveniente; (apt) indicado; ~**ably** ad convenientemente, en forma debida.
suitcase ['suːtkeɪs] n maleta.
suite [swiːt] n (of rooms) grupo de habitaciones; (MUS) suite f; (furniture): **bedroom/dining room** ~ (juego de) dormitorio/comedor m.
suitor ['suːtə*] n pretendiente m.
sulk [sʌlk] vi tener mohíno; ~**y** a con mohíno.
sullen ['sʌlən] a hosco, malhumorado.
sulphur, sulfur (US) ['sʌlfə*] n azufre m.
sultan ['sʌltən] n sultán m.
sultana [sʌl'tɑːnə] n (fruit) pasa de Esmirna.
sultry ['sʌltrɪ] a (weather) bochornoso; (seductive) seductor(a).
sum [sʌm] n (gen) suma; (total) total m; **to** ~ **up** vt recapitular // vi hacer un resumen.
summarize ['sʌməraɪz] vt resumir.
summary ['sʌmərɪ] n resumen m // a (justice) sumario.
summer ['sʌmə*] n verano // a de verano; ~**house** n (in garden) cenador m, glorieta; ~**time** n (season) verano; ~ **time** n (by clock) hora de verano.
summit ['sʌmɪt] n cima, cumbre f; ~ (**conference**) n conferencia cumbre.
summon ['sʌmən] vt (person) llamar; (meeting) convocar; (LAW) citar; **to** ~ **up** vt cobrar; ~**s** n llamamiento, llamada // vt citar, emplazar.
sump [sʌmp] n (AUT) cárter m.
sumptuous ['sʌmptjuəs] a suntuoso.
sun [sʌn] n sol m; ~**bathe** vi tomar el sol; ~**burn** n (painful) quemadura; (tan) bronceado; ~**burnt** a (tanned) bronceado; (painfull-) quemado por el sol.
Sunday ['sʌndɪ] n domingo.
sundial ['sʌndaɪəl] n reloj m de sol.
sundry ['sʌndrɪ] a varios, diversos; **all and** ~ todos y cada uno; **sundries** npl géneros mpl diversos.
sunflower ['sʌnflauə*] n girasol m.
sung [sʌŋ] pp of sing.
sunglasses ['sʌnglɑːsɪz] npl gafas fpl de sol.
sunk [sʌŋk] pp of sink.
sun: ~**light** n luz f del sol; ~**lit** a iluminado por el sol; ~**ny** a soleado; (day) de sol; (fig) alegre; ~**rise** n salida del sol; ~**set** n puesta del sol; ~**shade** n (over table) sombrilla; ~**shine** n sol m; ~**spot** n mancha solar; ~**stroke** n insolación f; ~**tan** n bronceado, ~**tan oil** n bronceador m, crema bronceadora.
super ['suːpə*] a (col) bárbaro.

superannuation [su:pərænju'eıʃən] n jubilación f.

superb [su:'pə:b] a magnífico, espléndido.

supercilious [su:pə'sılıəs] a (disdainful) desdeñoso; (haughty) altanero.

superficial [su:pə'fıʃəl] a superficial.

superfluous [su'pə:fluəs] a superfluo, de sobra.

superhuman [su:pə'hju:mən] a sobrehumano.

superimpose ['su:pərım'pəuz] vt sobreponer.

superintendent [su:pərın'tendənt] n superintendente m/f; (POLICE) subjefe m.

superior [su'pıərıə] a superior; (smug) desdeñoso // n superior m; ~ity [-'ɔrıtı] n superioridad f; desdén m.

superlative [su'pə:lətıv] a, n superlativo.

superman ['su:pəmæn] n superhombre m.

supermarket ['su:pəma:kıt] n supermercado.

supernatural [su:pə'nætʃərəl] a sobrenatural.

superpower ['su:pəpauə*] n (POL) superpotencia.

supersede [su:pə'si:d] vt suplantar.

supersonic ['su:pə'sɔnık] a supersónico.

superstition [su:pə'stıʃən] n superstición f; **superstitious** [-ʃəs] a supersticioso.

supertanker ['su:pətæŋkə*] n superpetrolero.

supervise ['su:pəvaız] vt supervisar; **supervision** [-'vıʒən] n supervisión f; **supervisor** n supervisor/a m/f.

supper ['sʌpə*] n cena; **to have** ~ cenar.

supple ['sʌpl] a flexible.

supplement ['sʌplımənt] n suplemento // vt [sʌplı'ment] suplir; ~**ary** [-'mentərı] a suplementario.

supplier [sə'plaıə*] n suministrador/a m/f; (COMM) distribuidor/a m/f.

supply [sə'plaı] vt (provide) suministrar, facilitar; (equip): **to** ~ **(with)** abastecer (de) // n suministro, provisión f; (supplying) abastecimiento // a (teacher etc) suplente; **supplies** npl (food) víveres mpl; (MIL) pertrechos mpl; ~ **and demand** la oferta y la demanda.

support [sə'pɔ:t] n (moral, financial etc) apoyo; (TECH) soporte m // vt apoyar; (financially) mantener; (uphold) sostener; ~**er** n (POL etc) partidario; (SPORT) aficionado.

suppose [sə'pəuz] vt, vi (gen) suponer; (imagine) imaginarse; **to be** ~**d to do sth** deber hacer algo; ~**dly** [sə'pəuzıdlı] ad que se supone, según cabe suponer; **supposing** conj en caso de que; **supposition** [sʌpə'zıʃən] n suposición f.

suppository [sə'pɔzıtərı] n supositorio.

suppress [sə'pres] vt suprimir; (yawn) ahogar; ~**ion** [sə'preʃən] n represión f.

supremacy [su'preməsı] n supremacia; **supreme** [-'pri:m] a supremo.

surcharge ['sə:tʃa:dʒ] n sobrecarga; (extra tax) recargo.

sure [ʃuə*] a (gen) seguro; (definite, convinced) cierto; (aim) certero; ~**!** (of course) ¡claro!, ¡por supuesto!; ~**-footed** a de pie firme; ~**ly** ad (certainly) seguramente.

surety ['ʃuərətı] n garantía, fianza; (person) fiador/a m/f.

surf [sə:f] n olas fpl.

surface ['sə:fıs] n superficie f // vt (road) revestir // vi salir a la superficie.

surfboard ['sə:fbɔ:d] n plancha (de surfing), acuaplano.

surfeit ['sə:fıt] n: a ~ of exceso de.

surfing ['sə:fıŋ] n surfing m.

surge [sə:dʒ] n oleada, oleaje m // vi avanzar a tropel.

surgeon ['sə:dʒən] n cirujano; **dental** ~ odontólogo.

surgery ['sə:dʒərı] n cirugía; (room) consultorio; **to undergo** ~ operarse; ~ **hours** npl horas fpl de consulta.

surgical ['sə:dʒıkl] a quirúrgico; ~ **spirit** n alcohol m.

surly ['sə:lı] a hosco, malhumorado.

surmount [sə:'maunt] vt superar, sobreponerse a.

surname ['sə:neım] n apellido.

surpass [sə:'pa:s] vt superar, exceder.

surplus ['sə:pləs] n (gen) excedente m; (COMM) superávit m // a excedente, sobrante.

surprise [sə'praız] n (gen) sorpresa; (astonishment) asombro // vt sorprender; asombrar; **surprising** a sorprendente; asombroso.

surrealist [sə'rıəlıst] a surrealista.

surrender [sə'rendə*] n rendición f, entrega // vi rendirse, entregarse.

surreptitious [sʌrəp'tıʃəs] a subrepticio.

surround [sə'raund] vt rodear, circundar; (MIL etc) cercar; ~**ing** a circundante; ~**ings** npl alrededores mpl, cercanías fpl.

surveillance [sə:'veıləns] n vigilancia.

survey ['sə:veı] n inspección f, examen m; (inquiry) encuesta // vt [sə:'veı] (gen) examinar, inspeccionar (look at) mirar, contemplar; (make inquiries about) hacer una encuesta sobre; ~**or** n agrimensor m.

survival [sə'vaıvl] n supervivencia; **survive** vi sobrevivir; (custom etc) perdurar // vt sobrevivir a; **survivor** n superviviente m/f.

susceptible [sə'septəbl] a: ~ **(to)** susceptible o sensible (a).

suspect ['sʌspekt] a, n sospechoso // vt [səs'pekt] sospechar.

suspend [səs'pend] vt suspender; ~**er belt** n portaligas m inv; ~**ers** npl ligas fpl; (US) tirantes mpl.

suspense [səs'pens] n incertidumbre f, duda; (in film etc) suspense m.

suspension [səs'penʃən] n (gen, AUT) suspensión f; (of driving licence) privación f; ~ **bridge** n puente m colgante.

suspicion [səs'pıʃən] n (gen) sospecha; (distrust) recelo; (trace) traza; **suspicious**

[-ʃəs] a (*suspecting*) receloso; (*causing* ~) sospechoso.

sustain [səs'teɪn] vt sostener, apoyar; (*suffer*) sufrir, padecer; ~**ed** a (*effort*) sostenido.

sustenance ['sʌstɪnəns] n sustento.

swab [swɔb] n (MED) algodón n, orunda

swagger ['swægə*] vi pavonearse.

swallow ['swɔləʊ] n (*bird*) golondrina; (*of food etc*) trago // vt tragar; to ~ **up** vt (*savings etc*) consumir

swam [swæm] pt of **swim.**

swamp [swɔmp] n pantano, ciénaga // vt abrumar, agobiar; ~**y** a pantanoso.

swan [swɔn] n cisne m.

swap [swɔp] n canje m, intercambio // vt: **to ~ (for)** canjear (por).

swarm [swɔːm] n (*of bees*) enjambre m; (*gen*) multitud f // vi hormiguear, pulular.

swarthy ['swɔːðɪ] a moreno.

swastika ['swɔstɪkə] n suástika, cruz f gamada.

swat [swɔt] vt aplastar.

sway [sweɪ] vi mecerse, balancearse // vt (*influence*) mover, influir en.

swear [swɛə*], pt **swore**, pp **sworn** vi jurar; **to ~ to sth** declarar algo bajo juramento; ~**word** n taco, palabrota.

sweat [swɛt] vt sudor m // vi sudar.

sweater ['swɛtə*] n suéter m.

sweaty ['swɛtɪ] a sudoroso.

swede [swiːd] n nabo.

Swede [swiːd] n sueco/a; **Sweden** n Suecia; **Swedish** a, n (LING) sueco.

sweep [swiːp] n (*act*) barredura; (*of sum*) golpe m; (*range*) extensión f, alcance m; (*also*: **chimney** ~) deshollinador m // (*vb*: pt, pp **swept**) vt barrer; (*mines*) rastrear // vi barrer; **to ~ away** vt barrer; (*rub out*) borrar; **to ~ past** vi pasar rápidamente; (*brush by*) rozar; **to ~ up** vi recoger la basura; ~**ing** a (*gesture*) dramático; (*generalized*) generalizado.

sweet [swiːt] n (*candy*) dulce m, caramelo; (*pudding*) postre m // a dulce; (*sugary*) azucarado; (*fresh*) fresco, nuevo; (*fig*) dulce, amable; ~**corn** n maíz m; ~**en** vt endulzar; (*add sugar to*) poner azúcar a; ~**heart** n novio/a; (*in speech*) amor; ~**ly** ad dulcemente; (*gently*) suavemente; ~**ness** n (*gen*) dulzura; (*amount of sugar*) lo dulce, lo azucarado; ~ **pea** n guisante m de olor.

swell [swɛl] n (*of sea*) marejada, oleaje m // a (*col*: *excellent*) estupendo, excelente // (*vb*: pt **swelled**, pp **swollen** or **swelled**) vt hinchar, inflar // vi hincharse, inflarse; ~**ing** n (MED) hinchazón m.

sweltering ['swɛltərɪŋ] a sofocante, de mucho calor.

swept [swɛpt] pt, pp of **sweep.**

swerve [swɜːv] vi desviarse bruscamente.

swift [swɪft] n (*bird*) vencejo // a rápido, veloz; ~**ness** n rapidez f, velocidad f.

swig [swɪg] n (*col*: *drink*) trago.

swill [swɪl] n bazofia // vt (*also*: ~ **out**, ~

down) lavar, limpiar con agua.

swim [swɪm] n: **to go for a ~** ir a nadar // (*vb*: pt **swam**, pp **swum**) vi nadar; (*head*, *room*) dar vueltas // vt pasar a nado; ~**mer** n nadador/a m/f; ~**ming** n natación f; ~**ming baths** npl piscina sg; ~**ming cap** n gorro de baño; ~**ming costume** n bañador m, traje m de baño; ~**ming pool** n piscina; ~**suit** n bañador m, traje m de baño.

swindle ['swɪndl] n estafa // vt estafar; **swindler** n estafador/a m/f.

swine [swaɪn] n, pl inv cerdos mpl, puercos mpl; (*col!*) canalla sg.

swing [swɪŋ] n (*in playground*) columpio; (*movement*) balanceo, vaivén m; (*change of direction*) viraje m; (*rhythm*) ritmo // (*vb*: pt, pp **swung**) vt balancear; (*on a ~*) columpiar; (*also*: ~ **round**) voltear bruscamente // vi balancearse, columpiarse; (*also*: ~ **round**) volver bruscamente; **to be in full ~** estar en plena marcha; ~ **door** n puerta giratoria.

swipe [swaɪp] n golpe m fuerte // vt (*hit*) golpear fuerte; (*col*: *steal*) guindar.

swirl [swɜːl] vi arremolinarse.

Swiss [swɪs] a, n, pl inv suizo/a.

switch [swɪtʃ] n (*for light*, *radio etc*) interruptor m; (*change*) cambio; (*of hair*) trenza postiza // vt (*change*) cambiar de; **to ~ off** vt apagar; (*engine*) parar; **to ~ on** vt encender, prender; (*engine*, *machine*) arrancar; ~**board** n (TEL) central f de teléfonos.

Switzerland ['swɪtsələnd] n Suiza.

swivel ['swɪvl] vi (*also*: ~ **round**) girar.

swollen ['swəʊlən] pp of **swell.**

swoon [swuːn] vi desmayarse, desvanecerse.

swoop [swuːp] n (*by police etc*) redada // vi (*also*: ~ **down**) calarse, precipitarse

swop [swɔp] = **swap.**

sword [sɔːd] n espada; ~**fish** n pez m espada

swore [swɔː*] pt of **swear.**

sworn [swɔːn] pp of **swear.**

swot [swɔt] vt, vi empollar.

swum [swʌm] pp of **swim.**

swung [swʌŋ] pt, pp of **swing.**

sycamore ['sɪkəmɔː*] n sicomoro.

syllable ['sɪləbl] n sílaba.

syllabus ['sɪləbəs] n programa m de estudios.

symbol ['sɪmbl] n símbolo; ~**ic(al)** [-'bɔlɪk(l)] a simbólico; ~**ism** n simbolismo; ~**ize** vt simbolizar.

symmetrical [sɪ'metrɪkl] a simétrico; **symmetry** ['sɪmɪtrɪ] n simetría.

sympathetic [sɪmpə'θetɪk] a compasivo; (*pleasant*) simpático; ~**ally** ad con compasión.

sympathize ['sɪmpəθaɪz] vi: **to ~ with** sb compadecerse de uno; **sympathizer** n (POL) simpatizante m/f.

sympathy ['sɪmpəθɪ] n (*pity*) compasión f; (*liking*) simpatía; **with our deepest ~**

nuestro más sentido pésame; ~ **strike** *n* huelga por solidaridad.

symphony ['sɪmfənɪ] *n* sinfonía; ~ **orchestra** *n* orquesta sinfónica.

symposium [sɪm'pəuzɪəm] *n* simposio.

symptom ['sɪmptəm] *n* síntoma *m*, indicio; ~**atic** [-'mætɪk] *a* sintomático.

synagogue ['sɪnəgɔg] *n* sinagoga.

synchronize ['sɪŋkrənaɪz] *vt* sincronizar // *vi*: **to ~ with** sincronizarse con.

syndicate ['sɪndɪkɪt] *n* (*gen*) sindicato; (*of newspapers*) cadena.

syndrome ['sɪndrəum] *n* síndrome *m*.

synonym ['sɪnənɪm] *n* sinónimo; ~**ous** [sɪ'nɔnɪməs] *a*: ~**ous** (**with**) sinónimo (con).

synopsis [sɪ'nɔpsɪs], *pl* **-ses** [-siːz] *n* sinopsis *f inv*.

syntax ['sɪntæks] *n* sintáxis *f*.

synthesis ['sɪnθəsɪs], *pl* **-ses** [-siːz] *n* síntesis *f inv*.

synthetic [sɪn'θetɪk] *a* sintético.

syphilis ['sɪfɪlɪs] *n* sífilis *f*.

syphon ['saɪfən] = **siphon**.

Syria ['sɪrɪə] *n* Siria; ~**n** *a*, *n* sirio/a.

syringe [sɪ'rɪndʒ] *n* jeringa.

syrup ['sɪrəp] *n* jarabe *m*, almíbar *m*.

system ['sɪstəm] *n* (*gen*) sistema; (*method*) método; (ANAT) organismo; ~**atic** [-'mætɪk] *a* sistemático; metódico; ~**s analyst** *n* analista *m/f* de sistemas.

T

ta [tɑ:] *excl* (*Brit*: *col*) gracias.

tab [tæb] *n* (*gen*) lengüeta; (*label*) etiqueta; **to keep ~s on** (*fig*) vigilar.

tabby ['tæbɪ] *n* (*also*: ~ **cat**) gato atigrado.

table ['teɪbl] *n* mesa; (*of statistics etc*) cuadro, tabla // *vt* (*motion etc*) presentar; **to lay** *or* **set the ~** poner la mesa; ~**cloth** *n* mantel *m*; ~ **d'hôte** [tɑ:bl'dəut] *n* menú *m*; ~**mat** *n* mantel *m* individual; ~**spoon** *n* cuchara grande; (*also*: ~**spoonful**: *as measurement*) cucharada.

tablet ['tæblɪt] *n* (MED) tableta, pastilla; (*for writing*) bloc *m*; (*of stone*) lápida.

table: ~ **tennis** *n* ping-pong *m*, tenis *m* de mesa; ~ **wine** *n* vino de mesa.

taboo [tə'bu:] *n* tabú *m* // *a* tabú.

tacit ['tæsɪt] *a* tácito.

taciturn ['tæsɪtɜːn] *a* taciturno.

tack [tæk] *n* (*nail*) tachuela, chincheta; (*stitch*) hilván *m*; (NAUT) bordada // *vt* (*nail*) clavar con chinchetas; (*stitch*) hilvanar // *vi* virar.

tackle ['tækl] *n* (*gear*) equipo; (*also*: **fishing** ~) aparejo; (*for lifting*) polea; (RUGBY) atajo // *vt* (*difficulty*) enfrentar; (*grapple with*) agarrar; (RUGBY) atajar.

tacky ['tækɪ] *a* pegajoso.

tact [tækt] *n* tacto, discreción *f*; ~**ful** *a* discreto, diplomático; ~**fully** *ad* discretamente.

tactical ['tæktɪkl] *a* táctico; **tactics** [-tɪks] *n*, *npl* táctica *sg*.

tactless ['tæktlɪs] *a* indiscreto, falto de tacto; ~**ly** *ad* indiscretamente.

tadpole ['tædpəul] *n* renacuajo.

tag [tæg] *n* (*label*) etiqueta; (*loose end*) cabo; **to ~ along with sb** acompañar a uno.

tail [teɪl] *n* (*gen*) cola; (ZOOL) rabo (*of shirt*, *coat*) faldón *m* // *vt* (*follow*) seguir los talones a; **to ~ away**, ~ **off** *vi* (*in size*, *quality etc*) ir disminuyendo; ~ **coat** *n* frac *m*; ~ **end** *n* cola, parte *f* final; ~**gate** *n* puerta trasera.

tailor ['teɪlə*] *n* sastre *m*; ~**ing** *n* (*cut*) corte *m*; (*craft*) sastrería; ~**-made** *a* hecho a la medida; (*fig*) especial.

tailwind ['teɪlwɪnd] *n* viento de cola.

tainted ['teɪntɪd] *a* (*food*) pasado; (*water*, *air*) contaminado; (*fig*) manchado.

take [teɪk], *pt* **took**, *pp* **taken** *vt* (*gen*) tomar; (*grab*) coger; (*gain*: *prize*) ganar; (*require*: *effort*, *courage*) exigir, hacer falta; (*tolerate*) aguantar; (*hold*: *passengers etc*) tener cabida para; (*accompany*, *bring*, *carry*) llevar; (*exam*) presentarse a; **to ~ sth from** (*drawer etc*) sacar algo de; (*person*) coger algo a; **I ~ it that...** supongo que...; **to ~ after** *vt fus* parecerse a; **to ~ apart** *vt* desmontar; **to ~ away** *vt* (*remove*) quitar; (*carry off*) llevar; **to ~ back** *vt* (*return*) devolver; (*one's words*) retractar; **to ~ down** *vt* (*building*) demoler; (*letter etc*) poner por escrito; **to ~ in** *vt* (*deceive*) engañar; (*understand*) entender; (*include*) abarcar; (*lodger*) acoger, recibir; **to ~ off** *vi* (AVIAT) despegar // *vt* (*remove*) quitar; (*imitate*) imitar; **to ~ on** *vt* (*work*) emprender; (*employee*) contratar; (*opponent*) desafiar; **to ~ out** *vt* sacar; (*remove*) quitar; **to ~ over** *vt* (*business*) tomar posesión de // *vi*: **to ~ over from sb** relevar a uno; **to ~ to** *vt fus* (*person*) coger simpatía a; (*activity*) aficionarse a; **to ~ up** *vt* (*a dress*) acortar; (*occupy*: *time*, *space*) ocupar; (*engage in*: *hobby etc*) dedicarse a; ~**away** *a* (*food*) para llevar; ~**-home pay** *n* salario neto; ~**off** *n* (AVIAT) despegue *m*; ~**over** *n* (COMM) absorción *f*; ~**over bid** *n* oferta de compra.

takings ['teɪkɪŋz] *npl* (COMM) ingresos *mpl*.

talc [tælk] *n* (*also*: ~**um powder**) talco.

tale [teɪl] *n* (*story*) cuento; (*account*) relación *f*; **to tell ~s** (*fig*: *lie*) chismear.

talent ['tælnt] *n* talento; ~**ed** *a* talentoso, de talento.

talk [tɔ:k] *n* (*gen*) charla; (*gossip*) habladurías *fpl*, chismes *mpl*; (*conversation*) conversación *f* // *vi* (*speak*) hablar; (*chatter*) charlar; **to ~ about** hablar de; **to ~ sb into doing sth** convencer a uno de que debe hacer algo; **to ~ sb out of doing sth** disuadir a uno de algo; **to ~ shop** hablar de asuntos profesionales; **to ~ over** vt hablar de; **~ative** a hablador(a).

tall [tɔːl] a (gen) alto; (tree) grande; **to be 6 feet ~** medir 6 pies, tener 6 pies de alto; **~boy** n cómoda alta; **~ness** n altura; **~story** n historia inverosímil.

tally ['tælɪ] n cuenta // vi: **to ~ (with)** corresponder (con).

talon ['tælən] n garra.

tambourine [tæmbə'riːn] n pandereta.

tame [teɪm] a (mild) manso; (tamed) domesticado; (fig: story, style) soso.

tamper ['tæmpə*] vi: **to ~ with** entrometerse en.

tampon ['tæmpən] n tampón m.

tan [tæn] n (also: **sun~**) bronceado // vi broncear // vt ponerse moreno // a (colour) marrón.

tandem ['tændəm] n tándem m.

tang [tæŋ] n sabor m fuerte.

tangerine [tændʒə'riːn] n mandarina.

tangible ['tændʒəbl] a tangible.

tangle ['tæŋgl] n enredo; **to get in(to) a ~** enredarse.

tango ['tæŋgou] n tango.

tank [tæŋk] n (water ~) depósito, tanque m; (for fish) acuario; (MIL) tanque m.

tanker ['tæŋkə*] n (ship) petrolero; (truck) camión m cisterna o tanque.

tanned [tænd] a (skin) moreno, bronceado.

tantalizing ['tæntəlaɪzɪŋ] a tentador(a).

tantamount ['tæntəmaunt] a: **~ to** equivalente a.

tantrum ['tæntrəm] n rabieta.

tap [tæp] n (on sink etc) grifo; (gentle blow) golpecito; (gas ~) llave f // vt dar golpecitos; (resources) utilizar, explotar; **~-dancing** n zapateado.

tape [teɪp] n cinta; (also: **magnetic ~**) cinta magnética; (sticky ~) cinta adhesiva // vt (record) grabar (en cinta); **~ measure** n cinta métrica, metro.

taper ['teɪpə*] n cirio // vi afilarse.

tape recorder ['teɪprɪkɔːdə*] n grabadora.

tapered ['teɪpəd], **tapering** ['teɪpərɪŋ] a afilado.

tapestry ['tæpɪstrɪ] n (object) tapiz m; (art) tapicería.

tapioca [tæpɪ'ouka] n tapioca.

tar [tɑː] n alquitrán m, brea.

tarantula [tə'ræntjulə] n tarántula.

target ['tɑːgɪt] n (gen) blanco; **~ practice** tiro al blanco.

tariff ['tærɪf] n tarifa.

tarmac ['tɑːmæk] n (on road) alquitranado; (AVIAT) pista de aterrizaje.

tarnish ['tɑːnɪʃ] vt quitar el brillo a.

tarpaulin [tɑː'pɔːlɪn] n alquitranado.

tarragon ['tærəgən] n estragón m.

tart [tɑːt] n (CULIN) tarta; (col: pej: woman) fulana // a (flavour) agrio, ácido.

tartan ['tɑːtn] n tartán m, escocés m // a de tartán.

tartar ['tɑːtə*] n (on teeth) sarro; **~(e) sauce** n salsa tártara.

task [tɑːsk] n tarea; **to take to ~** reprender; **~ force** n (MIL, POLICE) destacamento especial.

tassel ['tæsl] n borla.

taste [teɪst] n sabor m, gusto; (also: **after~**) dejo; (sip) sorbo; (fig: glimpse, idea) muestra, idea // vt probar // vi: **to ~ of or like** (fish etc) saber a; **you can ~ the garlic (in it)** se nota el sabor a ajo; **can I have a ~ of this wine?** ¿puedo probar el vino?; **to have a ~ for sth** ser aficionado a algo; **in good/bad ~** de buen/mal gusto; **~ful** a de buen gusto; **~fully** ad con buen gusto; **~less** a (food) insípido; (remark) de mal gusto; **tasty** a sabroso, rico.

tattered ['tætəd] a see **tatters.**

tatters ['tætəz] npl: **in ~** (also: **tattered**) hecho jirones.

tattoo [tə'tuː] n tatuaje m; (spectacle) espectáculo militar // vt tatuar.

tatty ['tætɪ] a (col) raído.

taught [tɔːt] pt, pp of **teach.**

taunt [tɔːnt] n burla // vt burlarse de.

Taurus ['tɔːrəs] n Tauro.

taut [tɔːt] a tirante, tenso.

tawdry ['tɔːdrɪ] a cursi, de mal gusto.

tawny ['tɔːnɪ] a leonado.

tax [tæks] n impuesto // vt gravar (con un impuesto); (fig: test) abrumar; (: patience) agotar; **direct ~** contribución directa; **~ation** [-'seɪʃən] n impuestos mpl; **~ collector** n recaudador/a m/f; **~-free** a libre de impuestos.

taxi ['tæksɪ] n taxi m // vi (AVIAT) rodar de suelo.

taxidermist ['tæksɪdɜːmɪst] n taxidermista m/f.

taxi: ~ driver n taxista m/f; **~ rank, ~ stand** n parada de taxis.

tax: ~ payer n contribuyente m/f; **~ return** n declaración f de ingresos.

TB abbr of **tuberculosis.**

tea [tiː] n té m; (snack) merienda; **high ~** merienda-cena; **~ bag** n bolsa de té; **~ break** n descanso para el té; **~ cake** n bollo.

teach [tiːtʃ], pt, pp **taught** vt: **to ~ sb sth, ~ sth to sb** enseñar algo a uno // vi enseñar; (be a teacher) ser profesor/a; **~er** n (in secondary school) profesor/a m/f, (in primary school) maestro/a; **~ing** n enseñanza.

tea: ~ cosy n cubretetera; **~cup** n taza para té.

teak [tiːk] n (madera de) teca.

tea leaves npl hojas fpl de té.

team [tiːm] n equipo; (of animals) pareja; **~ work** n trabajo de equipo.

teapot ['tiːpɔt] n tetera.

tear [tɛə*] n rasgón m, desgarrón m // n [tɪə*] lágrima // (vb: pt **tore**, pp **torn**) vt romper, rasgar // vi rasgarse; **in ~s** llorando; **to burst into ~s** deshacerse en lágrimas; **to ~ along** vi (rush) precipitarse; **~ful** a lloroso; **~ gas** n gas m lacrimógeno.

tearoom ['ti:ru:m] n salón m de té, cafetería.

tease [ti:z] n bromista m/f // vt bromear, tomar el pelo a.

tea: ~ **set** n juego de té; ~**spoon** n cucharilla; (also: ~**spoonful:** as measurement) cucharadita.

teat [ti:t] n (of bottle) tetina.

tea: ~**time** n hora del té; ~ **towel** n trapo de cocina.

technical ['tɛknɪkl] a técnico; ~**ity** [-'kælɪtɪ] n detalle m técnico; ~**ly** ad técnicamente.

technician [tɛk'nɪʃn] n técnico.

technique [tɛk'ni:k] n técnica.

technological [tɛknə'lɔdʒɪkl] a tecnológico; **technology** [-'nɔlədʒɪ] n tecnología.

teddy (bear) ['tɛdɪ] n osito de felpa.

tedious ['ti:dɪəs] a pesado, aburrido.

tee [ti:] n (GOLF) tee m.

teem [ti:m] vi abundar, pulular; to ~ **with** rebosar de; it is ~**ing (with rain)** llueve a mares.

teenage ['ti:neɪdʒ] a (fashions etc) de o para los jóvenes; **teenager** n joven m/f (de 13 a 19 años).

teens [ti:nz] npl: to be in one's ~ ser un adolescente, no haber cumplido los 20.

tee-shirt ['ti:ʃɔ:t] n = **T-shirt.**

teeter ['ti:tə*] vi balancearse.

teeth [ti:θ] pl of **tooth.**

teethe [ti:ð] vi echar los dientes.

teething ['ti:ðɪŋ]: ~ **ring** n mordedor m; ~ **troubles** npl (fig) dificultades fpl iniciales.

teetotal ['ti:'təutl] a (person) abstemio.

telecommunications ['tɛlɪkəmju:nɪ'keɪʃənz] n telecomunicaciones fpl.

telegram ['tɛlɪgræm] n telegrama m.

telegraph ['tɛlɪgrɑ:f] n telégrafo; ~**ic** [-'græfɪk] a telegráfico; ~ **pole** n poste m de telégrafos.

telepathic [tɛlɪ'pæθɪk] a telepático; **telepathy** [tə'lɛpəθɪ] n telepatía.

telephone ['tɛlɪfəun] n teléfono // vt (person) llamar por teléfono; (message) telefonear; ~ **booth,** ~ **box** n cabina telefónica; ~ **call** n llamada (telefónica); ~ **directory** n guía (telefónica); ~ **exchange** n central f telefónica; ~ **number** n número de teléfono; **telephonist** [tə'lɛfənɪst] n telefonista m/f.

telephoto ['tɛlɪ'fəutəu] a: ~ **lens** teleobjetivo.

teleprinter ['tɛlɪprɪntə*] n teletipo.

telescope ['tɛlɪskəup] n telescopio; **telescopic** [-'skɔpɪk] a telescópico.

televise ['tɛlɪvaɪz] vt televisar.

television ['tɛlɪvɪʒən] n televisión f; ~ **set** n televisor m.

telex ['tɛlɛks] n telex m.

tell [tɛl], pt, pp **told** vt decir; (relate: story) contar; (distinguish): to ~ **sth from** distinguir algo de // vi (have effect) tener efecto; to ~ **sb to do sth** mandar a uno que haga algo; to ~ **sb off** reñir o regañar a uno; ~**er** n (in bank) cajero; ~**ing** a (remark, detail) revelador(a); ~**tale** a (sign) indicador(a).

telly ['tɛlɪ] n (col) abbr of **television.**

temerity [tə'mɛrɪtɪ] n temeridad f.

temper ['tɛmpə*] n (nature) carácter m; (mood) humor m; (bad ~) genio, mal genio; (fit of anger) cólera; (of child) rabieta // vt (moderate) moderar; to be in a ~ estar de mal humor; to lose one's ~ perder la paciencia.

temperament ['tɛmprəmənt] n (nature) temperamento; ~**al** [-'mɛntl] a temperamental.

temperance ['tɛmpərns] n moderación f; (in drinking) sobriedad f.

temperate ['tɛmprət] a moderado; (climate) templado.

temperature ['tɛmprəʃə*] n temperatura; to have or run a ~ tener fiebre.

tempered ['tɛmpəd] a (steel) templado.

tempest ['tɛmpɪst] n tempestad f.

temple ['tɛmpl] n (building) templo; (ANAT) sien f.

tempo ['tɛmpəu], pl ~**s** or **tempi** [-pi:] n tempo; (fig: of life etc) ritmo.

temporal ['tɛmpərl] a temporal.

temporarily ['tɛmpərərɪlɪ] ad temporalmente.

temporary ['tɛmpərərɪ] a provisional, temporal; (passing) transitorio; (worker) temporero.

tempt [tɛmpt] vt tentar; to ~ **sb into doing sth** tentar o inducir a uno a hacer algo; ~**ation** [-'teɪʃən] n tentación f; ~**ing** a tentador(a).

ten [tɛn] num diez.

tenable ['tɛnəbl] a sostenible.

tenacious [tə'neɪʃəs] a tenaz; **tenacity** [-'næsɪtɪ] n tenacidad f.

tenancy ['tɛnənsɪ] n alquiler m; (of house) inquilinato; **tenant** n (rent-payer) inquilino; (occupant) habitante m/f.

tend [tɛnd] vt cuidar / vi: to ~ **to do sth** tener tendencia a hacer algo.

tendency ['tɛndənsɪ] n tendencia.

tender ['tɛndə*] a tierno, blando; (delicate) delicado; (sore) sensible, dolorido; (affectionate) tierno, cariñoso // n (COMM: offer) oferta; (money): **legal** ~ moneda de curso legal // vt ofrecer; ~**ize** vt (CULIN) ablandar; ~**ness** n ternura; (of meat) blandura.

tendon ['tɛndən] n tendón m.

tenement ['tɛnəmənt] n casa de pisos.

tennis ['tɛnɪs] n tenis m; ~ **ball** n pelota de tenis; ~ **court** n pista de tenis; ~ **racket** n raqueta de tenis.

tenor ['tɛnə*] n (MUS) tenor m.

tenpin bowling ['tɛnpɪn-] n los bolos mpl.

tense [tɛns] a tenso; (stretched) tirante; (stiff) rígido, tieso // n (LING) tiempo; ~**ness** n tensión f.

tension ['tɛnʃən] n tensión f.

tent [tɛnt] n tienda (de campaña).

tentacle ['tɛntəkl] n tentáculo

tentative ['tɛntətɪv] a experimental; (conclusion) provisional.

tenterhooks ['tɛntəhuks] npl: **on ~** sobre ascuas.

tenth [tɛnθ] a décimo.

tent: ~ **peg** n clavija, estaquilla; ~ **pole** n mástil m.

tenuous ['tɛnjuəs] a tenue.

tenure ['tɛnjuə*] n posesión f, tenencia.

tepid ['tɛpɪd] a tibio.

term [tɜːm] n (limit) límite m; (COMM) plazo; (word) término; (period) período; (SCOL) trimestre m // vt llamar; ~s npl (conditions) condiciones fpl; (COMM) precio, tarifa; **in the short/long** ~ a corto/largo plazo; **to be on good ~s with sb** levarse bien con uno; **to come to ~s with** (person) llegar a un acuerdo con; (problem) adaptarse a.

terminal ['tɜːmɪnl] a terminal; (disease) mortal // n (ELEC) borne m; (also: air ~) terminal f; (also: **coach** ~) estación f terminal.

terminate ['tɜːmɪneɪt] vt terminar // vi: **to** ~ **in** acabar por; **termination** [-'neɪʃən] n terminación f; (of contract) conclusión f.

terminology [tɜːmɪ'nɔlədʒɪ] n terminología.

terminus ['tɜːmɪnəs], pl **-mini** [-mɪnaɪ] n término, estación f terminal.

termite ['tɜːmaɪt] n termita.

terrace ['tɛrəs] n terraza; (row of houses) hilera de casas adosadas; **the** ~**s** (SPORT) gradas fpl; ~**ed** a (garden) escalonado; (house) adosado.

terrain [tɛ'reɪn] n terreno.

terrible ['tɛrɪbl] a terrible, horrible; (fam) malísimo; **terribly** ad terriblemente; (very badly) malísimamente.

terrier ['tɛrɪə*] n terrier m.

terrific [tə'rɪfɪk] a fantástico, fenomenal, (wonderful) maravilloso.

terrify ['tɛrɪfaɪ] vt aterrorizar.

territorial [tɛrɪ'tɔːrɪəl] a territorial.

territory ['tɛrɪtərɪ] n territorio.

terror ['tɛrə*] n terror m; ~**ism** n terrorismo; ~**ist** n terrorista m/f; ~**ize** vt aterrorizar.

terse [tɜːs] a (style) conciso; (reply) brusco.

test [tɛst] n (trial, check) prueba, ensayo; (: of goods in factory) control m; (of courage etc, CHEM) prueba; (MED) examen m; (exam) examen m, test m; (also: driving ~) examen m de conducir // vt probar, poner a prueba.

testament ['tɛstəmənt] n testamento; **the Old/New T~** el Antiguo/Nuevo Testamento.

testicle ['tɛstɪkl] n testículo.

testify ['tɛstɪfaɪ] vi (LAW) prestar declaración; **to** ~ **to sth** atestiguar algo.

testimonial [tɛstɪ'məunɪəl] n (reference) recomendación f; (gift) obsequio.

testimony ['tɛstɪmənɪ] n (LAW) testimonio, declaración f.

test: ~ **match** n (CRICKET, RUGBY) partido internacional; ~ **pilot** n piloto de pruebas; ~ **tube** n probeta.

testy ['tɛstɪ] a irritable.

tetanus ['tɛtənəs] n tétano.

tether ['tɛðə*] vt atar (con una cuerda) // n: **at the end of one's** ~ a punto de perder la paciencia.

text [tɛkst] n texto; ~**book** n libro de texto.

textiles ['tɛkstaɪlz] npl textiles mpl, tejidos mpl.

texture ['tɛkstʃə*] n textura.

Thai [taɪ] a, n tailandés/esa m/f; ~**land** n Tailandia.

Thames [tɛmz] n: **the** ~ el (río) Támesis.

than [ðæn, ðən] conj que; (with numerals): **more** ~ **10/once** más de 10/una vez; **I have more/less** ~ **you** tengo más/menos que tú.

thank [θæŋk] vt dar las gracias a, agradecer; ~ **you (very much)** muchas gracias; ~**s** npl gracias fpl; ~**s to** prep gracias a; ~**ful** a: ~**ful (for)** agradecido por; ~**less** a ingrato; **Thanksgiving (Day)** n día m de acción de gracias.

that [ðæt, ðət] conj que // det ese/esa; (more remote) aquel/aquella // pron ése/ésa; aquél/aquélla; (neuter) eso; aquello; (relative: subject) que; (: object) que, el cual/la cual etc; (with time): **on the day** ~ **he came** el día que vino // ad: ~ **high** tan alto, así de alto; **it's about** ~ **high** es más o menos así de alto; ~ **one** ése/ésa; aquél/aquélla; **what's** ~? ¿qué es eso?; **who's** ~? ¿quién es?; **is** ~ **you?** ¿eres tú?; (formal) ¿es Usted?; ~**'s what he said** eso es lo que dijo; **all** ~ todo eso; **I can't work** ~ **much** no puedo trabajar tanto.

thatched [θætʃt] a (roof) de paja; ~ **cottage** casita con tejado de paja.

thaw [θɔː] n deshielo // vi (ice) derretirse; (food) descongelarse // vt (food) descongelar.

the [ðiː, ðə] def art el/la; (pl) los/las; (neuter) lo; ~ **sooner** ~ **better** cuanto antes mejor.

theatre, theater (US) ['θɪətə*] n teatro; ~**-goer** n aficionado al teatro.

theatrical [θɪ'ætrɪkl] a teatral.

theft [θɛft] n robo.

their [ðɛə*] a su; ~**s** pron (el) suyo/(la) suya etc; **a friend of** ~**s** un amigo suyo.

them [ðɛm, ðəm] pron (direct) los/las; (indirect) les; (stressed, after prep) ellos/ellas; **I see** ~ los veo; **give** ~ **the book** dales el libro.

theme [θiːm] n tema m; ~ **song** tema (musical).

themselves [ðəm'sɛlvz] pl pron (subject) ellos mismos/ellas mismas; (complement) se; (after prep) sí (mismos/as).

then [ðɛn] ad (at that time) entonces; (next) pues; (later) luego, después; (and also) además // *conj* (*therefore*) en ese caso, entonces // *a*: **the ~ president** el entonces presidente; **from ~ on** desde entonces.

theological [θɪə'lɒdʒɪkl] *a* teológico; **theology** [θɪ'ɒlədʒɪ] *n* teología.

theorem ['θɪərəm] *n* teorema *m*.

theoretical [θɪə'rɛtɪkl] *a* teórico; **theorize** ['θɪəraɪz] *vi* elaborar una teoría; **theory** ['θɪərɪ] *n* teoría.

therapeutic(al) [θɛrə'pju:tɪk(l)] *a* terapéutico.

therapist ['θɛrəpɪst] *n* terapeuta *m/f*; **therapy** *n* terapia.

there [ðɛə*] *ad* allí, allá, ahí; ~, ~! ¡cálmate!; **it's ~** está ahí; ~ **is**, ~ **are** hay; ~ **he is** ahí está; **on/in ~** allí encima/dentro; ~**abouts** *ad* por ahí; ~**after** *ad* después; ~**fore** *ad* por lo tanto; ~**'s** = ~ **is**; ~ **has**.

thermal ['θə:ml] *a* termal.

thermometer [θə'mɒmɪtə*] *n* termómetro.

Thermos ['θə:məs] *n* termo.

thermostat ['θə:məustæt] *n* termostato.

thesaurus [θɪ'sɔ:rəs] *n* tesoro.

these [ði:z] *pl det* estos/as // *pl pron* éstos/as.

thesis ['θi:sɪs], *pl* **-ses** [-si:z] *n* tesis *f*.

they [ðeɪ] *pl pron* ellos/ellas; (*stressed*) ellos (mismos)/ellas (mismas); ~ **say that...** (*it is said that*) se dice que...; ~**'d** = **they had; they would;** ~**'ll** = **they shall, they will;** ~**'re** = **they are;** ~**'ve** = **they have.**

thick [θɪk] *a* espeso; (*fat*) grueso; (*dense*) denso, espeso; (*stupid*) torpe // *n*: **in the ~ of the battle** en plena batalla; **it's 20 cm ~** tiene 20 cm de espesor; ~**en** *vi* espesarse // *vt* (*sauce etc*) espesar; ~**ness** *n* espesor *m*, grueso; ~**set** *a* rechoncho; ~**skinned** *a* (*fig*) insensible.

thief [θi:f], *pl* **thieves** [θi:vz] *n* ladrón/ona *m/f*.

thieving ['θi:vɪŋ] *n* robo.

thigh [θaɪ] *n* muslo.

thimble ['θɪmbl] *n* dedal *m*.

thin [θɪn] *a* (*gen*) delgado; (*watery*) aguado; (*light*) tenue; (*hair, crowd*) escaso; (*fog*) poco denso // *vt*: **to ~ (down)** (*sauce, paint*) diluir.

thing [θɪŋ] *n* (*gen*) cosa; (*object*) objeto, artículo; (*matter*) asunto; (*mania*) manía; ~**s** *npl* (*belongings*) efectos *mpl* (personales); **the best ~ would be to...** lo mejor sería...; **how are ~s?** ¿qué tal?

think [θɪŋk], *pt, pp* **thought** *vi* pensar // *vt* pensar, creer; (*imagine*) imaginar; **what did you ~ of them?** ¿qué te parecieron?; **to ~ about sth/sb** pensar en algo/alguien; **I'll ~ about it** lo pensaré; **to ~ of doing sth** pensar en hacer algo; **I ~ so/not** creo que sí/no; **to ~ well of sb** tener buen concepto de alguien; **to ~ over** *vt* reflexionar sobre, meditar; **to ~ up** *vt* imaginar; ~**ing** *a* pensante.

thinly ['θɪnlɪ] *ad* (*cut*) en lonchas finas; (*spread*) con una capa fina.

thinness ['θɪnnɪs] *n* delgadez *f*.

third [θə:d] *a* tercer(a) // *n* tercero; (*fraction*) tercio; (*scol: degree*) de tercera clase; ~**ly** *ad* en tercer lugar; ~ **party insurance** *n* seguro contra terceras personas; ~**-rate** *a* (de calidad) mediocre; **the T~ World** *n* el Tercer Mundo.

thirst [θə:st] *n* sed *f*; ~**y** *a* (*person*) sediento; **to be** ~**y** tener sed.

thirteen ['θə:'ti:n] *num* trece.

thirty ['θə:tɪ] *num* treinta.

this [ðɪs] *det* este/esta // *pron* éste/ésta; (*neuter*) esto; ~ **is what he said** esto es lo que dijo; ~ **high** así de alto.

thistle ['θɪsl] *n* cardo.

thong [θɒŋ] *n* correa.

thorn [θɔ:n] *n* espina; ~**y** *a* espinoso.

thorough ['θʌrə] *a* (*search*) minucioso; (*knowledge, research*) profundo; ~**bred** *a* (*horse*) de pura sangre; ~**fare** *n* calle *f*; **'no ~fare'** "prohibido el paso"; ~**ly** *ad* minuciosamente; profundamente, a fondo.

those [ðəuz] *pl pron* esos/esas; (*more remote*) aquellos/as // *pl det* ésos/ésas; aquéllos/as.

though [ðəu] *conj* aunque // *ad* sin embargo.

thought [θɔ:t] *pt, pp of* **think** // *n* pensamiento; (*opinion*) opinión *f*; (*intention*) intención *f*; ~**ful** *a* pensativo; (*considerate*) considerado; ~**less** *a* desconsiderado.

thousand ['θauzənd] *num* mil; **two ~** dos mil; ~**s of** miles de; ~**th** *a* milésimo.

thrash [θræʃ] *vt* apalear; (*defeat*) derrotar; **to ~ about** *vi* revolcarse; **to ~ out** *vt* discutir largamente.

thread [θrɛd] *n* hilo; (*of screw*) rosca // *vt* (*needle*) enhebrar; ~**bare** *a* raído.

threat [θrɛt] *n* amenaza; ~**en** *vi* amenazar // *vt*: **to ~en sb with sth/to do** amenazar a uno con algo/ con hacer.

three [θri:] *num* tres; ~**-dimensional** *a* tridimensional; ~**fold** *ad*: **to increase** ~**fold** triplicar; ~**-piece suit** *n* traje *m* de tres piezas; ~**-piece suite** *n* tresillo; ~**-ply** *a* (*wool*) triple; ~**-wheeler** *n* (*car*) coche *m* de tres ruedas.

thresh [θrɛʃ] *vt* (*AGR*) trillar.

threshold ['θrɛʃhəuld] *n* umbral *m*.

threw [θru:] *pt of* **throw**.

thrift [θrɪft] *n* economía; ~**y** *a* económico.

thrill [θrɪl] *n* (*excitement*) emoción *f*; (*shudder*) estremecimiento // *vt* emocionar; estremecer; **to be** ~**ed** (*with gift etc*) estar encantado; ~**er** *n* película/novela de suspense.

thrive [θraɪv], *pt* **thrived** *or* **throve** [θrəuv], *pp* **thrived** *or* **thriven** ['θrɪvn] *vi* (*grow*) crecer; (*do well*) prosperar; **thriving** *a* próspero.

throat [θrəut] *n* garganta; **to have a sore ~** tener dolor de garganta.

throb [θrɒb] *n* (*of heart*) latido; (*of engine*)

vibración *f* // *vi* latir; vibrar; (*pain*) dar punzadas.

throes [θrəʊz] *npl*: **in the ~ of** en medio de.

thrombosis [θrɔm'bəʊsɪs] *n* trombosis *f*.

throne [θrəʊn] *n* trono.

throttle ['θrɔtl] *n* (*AUT*) acelerador *m* // *vt* ahogar.

through [θruː] *prep* por, a través de; (*time*) durante; (*by means of*) por medio de, mediante; (*owing to*) gracias a // *a* (*ticket, train*) directo // *ad* completamente, de parte a parte; **to put sb ~ to sb** (*TEL*) poner a alguien (en comunicación) con alguien; **to be ~** (*TEL*) tener comunicación; (*have finished*) haber terminado; **"no ~ way"** "calle sin salida"; **~out** *prep* (*place*) por todas partes de, por todo; (*time*) durante todo, en todo // *ad* por o en todas partes.

throw [θrəʊ] *n* tirada, tiro; (*SPORT*) lanzamiento // *vt, pt* **threw**, *pp* **thrown** tirar, echar; (*SPORT*) lanzar; (*rider*) derribar; (*fig*) desconcertar; **to ~ a party** dar una fiesta; **to ~ away** *vt* tirar; **to ~ off** *vt* deshacerse de; **to ~ out** *vt* tirar; **to ~ up** *vi* vomitar; **~away** *a* para tirar, desechable; **~-in** *n* (*SPORT*) saque *m*.

thru [θruː] (*US*) = **through**.

thrush [θrʌʃ] *n* zorzal *m*, tordo.

thrust [θrʌst] *n* (*TECH*) empuje *m* // *vt, pt, pp* **thrust** empujar; (*push in*) introducir.

thud [θʌd] *n* golpe *m* sordo.

thug [θʌg] *n* (*criminal*) criminal *m/f*; (*pej*) bruto.

thumb [θʌm] *n* (*ANAT*) pulgar *m*, dedo gordo (*col*) // *vt* (*book*) hojear; **to ~ a lift** hacer dedo o autostop; **~tack** *n* (*US*) chinche *m*.

thump [θʌmp] *n* golpe *m*; (*sound*) porrazo // *vt, vi* golpear.

thunder ['θʌndə*] *n* (*gen*) trueno; (*sudden noise*) tronido; (*of applause etc*) estruendo // *vi* tronar; (*train etc*): **to ~ past** pasar como un trueno; **~bolt** *n* rayo; **~clap** *a* trueno; **~storm** *n* tormenta; **~struck** *a* pasmado; **~y** *a* tormentoso.

Thursday ['θɜːzdɪ] *n* jueves *m*.

thus [ðʌs] *ad* así, de este modo.

thwart [θwɔːt] *vt* frustrar.

thyme [taɪm] *n* tomillo.

thyroid ['θaɪrɔɪd] *n* tiroides *m*.

tiara [tɪ'ɑːrə] *n* tiara, diadema.

tic [tɪk] *n* tic *m*.

tick [tɪk] *n* (*sound: of clock*) tictac *m*; (*mark*) palomita; (*ZOOL*) garrapata; (*col*): **in a ~** en un instante // *vi* hacer tictac // *vt* marcar; **to ~ off** *vt* marcar; (*person*) poner como un trapo.

ticket ['tɪkɪt] *n* billete *m*, tíquet *m*; (*for cinema*) entrada; (*in shop: on goods*) etiqueta; (*for library*) tarjeta; **~ collector** *n* revisor *m*; **~ office** *n* taquilla.

tickle ['tɪkl] *n* cosquillas *fpl* // *vt* hacer cosquillas a; **ticklish** *a* que tiene cosquillas.

tidal ['taɪdl] *a* de marea; **~ wave** *n* maremoto.

tiddlywinks ['tɪdlɪwɪŋks] *n* juego de la pulga.

tide [taɪd] *n* marea; (*fig: of events*) curso, marcha.

tidiness ['taɪdɪnəs] *n* (*good order*) buen orden *m*; (*neatness*) limpieza, aseo.

tidy ['taɪdɪ] *a* (*room*) ordenado; (*dress, work*) limpio; (*person*) (bien) arreglado // *vt* (*also:* **~ up**) poner en orden.

tie [taɪ] *n* (*string etc*) atadura; (*also:* **neck~**) corbata; (*fig: link*) vínculo, lazo; (*SPORT: draw*) empate *m* // *vt* (*gen*) atar // *vi* (*SPORT*) empatar; **to ~ in a bow** hacer un lazo; **to ~ a knot in sth** hacer un nudo a algo; **to ~ down** *vt* atar; (*fig*): **to ~ sb down to** obligar a uno a; **to ~ up** *vt* (*parcel*) envolver; (*dog*) atar; (*boat*) amarrar; (*arrangements*) concluir, despachar; **to be ~d up** (*busy*) estar ocupado.

tier [tɪə*] *n* grada; (*of cake*) piso.

tiger ['taɪgə*] *n* tigre *m/f*.

tight [taɪt] *a* (*rope*) tirante; (*money*) escaso; (*clothes*) ajustado; (*budget, programme*) apretado; (*col: drunk*) borracho // *a* (*squeeze*) muy fuerte; (*shut*) herméticamente; **~s** *npl* pantimedias *fpl*; (*for gym*) malla *sg*; **~en** *vt* (*rope*) estirar; (*screw*) apretar // *vi* apretarse, estirarse; **~fisted** *a* tacaño; **~ly** *ad* (*grasp*) muy fuerte; **~-rope** *n* cuerda floja.

tile [taɪl] *n* (*on roof*) teja; (*on floor*) baldosa; (*on wall*) azulejo, baldosín *m*; **~d** *a* embaldosado.

till [tɪl] *n* caja (registradora) // *vt* (*land*) cultivar // *prep, conj* = **until**.

tiller ['tɪlə*] *n* (*NAUT*) caña del timón.

tilt [tɪlt] *vt* inclinar // *vi* inclinarse.

timber ['tɪmbə*] *n* (*material*) madera; (*trees*) árboles *mpl*.

time [taɪm] *n* tiempo; (*epoch: often pl*) época; (*by clock*) hora; (*moment*) momento; (*occasion*) vez *f*; (*MUS*) compás *m* // *vt* (*gen*) calcular o medir el tiempo de; (*race*) cronometrar; (*remark etc*) elegir el momento para; **a long ~** mucho tiempo; **for the ~ being** de momento, por ahora; **from ~ to ~** de vez en cuando; **in ~** (*soon enough*) a tiempo; (*after some time*) con el tiempo; (*MUS*) al compás; **in a week's ~** dentro de una semana; **on ~** a la hora; **5 ~s 5** 5 por 5; **what ~ is it?** ¿qué hora es? **to have a good ~** pasarlo bien, divertirse; **~ bomb** *n* bomba de efecto retardado; **~keeper** *n* (*SPORT*) cronómetro; **~less** *a* eterno; **~ limit** *n* (*gen*) limitación *f* de tiempo; (*COMM*) plazo; **~ly** *a* oportuno; **~ off** *n* tiempo libre; **timer** *n* (*in kitchen*) reloj *m* programador; **~ switch** *n* interruptor *m*; **~table** *n* horario; **~ zone** *n* huso horario.

timid ['tɪmɪd] *a* tímido.

timing ['taɪmɪŋ] *n* (*SPORT*) cronometraje

m; (*gen*) elección *f* del momento; **the ~ of his resignation** el momento que eligió para dimitir.

timpani ['tɪmpənɪ] *npl* tímpanos *mpl*.

tin [tɪn] *n* estaño; (*also*: ~ **plate**) hojalata; (*can*) lata; ~ **foil** *n* papel *m* de estaño.

tinge [tɪndʒ] *n* matiz *m* // *vt*: ~**d with** teñido de.

tingle ['tɪŋgl] *n* picotazo // *vi* sentir picazón.

tinker ['tɪŋkə*] *n* calderero; (*gipsy*) gitano; **to ~ with** *vt* manosear.

tinkle ['tɪŋkl] *vi* tintinear // *n* (*col*): **to give sb a ~** dar un telefonazo a alguien.

tinned [tɪnd] *a* (*food*) en lata, en conserva.

tin opener ['tɪnəupnə*] *n* abrelatas *m inv*.

tinsel ['tɪnsl] *n* oropel *m*.

tint [tɪnt] *n* matiz *m*; (*for hair*) tinte *m*.

tiny ['taɪnɪ] *a* minúsculo, pequeñito.

tip [tɪp] *n* (*end*) punta; (*gratuity*) propina; (*for rubbish*) basurero; (*advice*) aviso // *vt* (*waiter*) dar una propina a; (*tilt*) inclinar; (*overturn*: *also*: ~ **over**) dar la vuelta a, volcar; (*empty*: *also*: ~ **out**) vaciar, echar; ~**-off** *n* (*hint*) aviso, advertencia; ~**ped** *a* (*cigarette*) con filtro.

tipsy ['tɪpsɪ] *a* algo borracho, mareado.

tiptoe ['tɪptəu] *n*: **on ~** de puntillas.

tiptop ['tɪp'tɔp] *a*: **in ~ condition** en perfectas condiciones.

tire ['taɪə*] *n* (*US*) = **tyre** // *vt* cansar // *vi* (*gen*) cansarse; (*become bored*) aburrirse; ~**d** *a* cansado; **to be ~d of sth** estar cansado o harto de algo; **tiredness** *n* cansancio; ~**less** *a* incansable; ~**some** *a* aburrido; **tiring** *a* cansado.

tissue ['tɪʃuː] *n* tejido; (*paper handkerchief*) pañuelo de papel, kleenex *m*; ~ **paper** *n* papel *m* de seda.

tit [tɪt] *n* (*bird*) herrerillo común; **to give ~ for tat** dar ojo por ojo.

titbit ['tɪtbɪt] *n* (*food*) golosina; (*news*) suceso.

titillate ['tɪtɪleɪt] *vt* estimular, excitar.

titivate ['tɪtɪveɪt] *vt* emperejilar.

title ['taɪtl] *n* título; ~ **deed** *n* (*LAW*) título de propiedad; ~ **role** *n* papel *m* principal.

titter ['tɪtə*] *vi* reírse entre dientes.

titular ['tɪtjulə*] *a* (*in name only*) nominal.

to [tuː, tə] *prep* a; (*towards*) hacia; (*of time*) a, hasta; (*of*) de; **give it ~ me** dámelo; **the key ~ the front door** la llave de la puerta; **the main thing is ~...** lo importante es...; **to go ~ France/school** ir a Francia/al colegio; **a quarter ~ 5** las 5 menos cuarto; **pull/push the door ~** tirar/empujar la puerta; **to go ~ and fro** ir y venir.

toad [təud] *n* sapo; ~**stool** *n* hongo venenoso.

toast [təust] *n* (*CULIN*: *also*: **piece of ~**) tostada; (*drink, speech*) brindis *m* // *vt* (*CULIN*) tostar; (*drink to*) brindar; ~**er** *n* tostador *m*.

tobacco [tə'bækəu] *n* tabaco; ~**nist** *n* estanquero; ~**nist's** (**shop**) *n* estanco.

toboggan [tə'bɔgən] *n* tobogán *m*.

today [tə'deɪ] *ad, n* (*also fig*) hoy *m*.

toddler ['tɔdlə*] *n* niño que empieza a andar.

toddy ['tɔdɪ] *n* ponche *m*.

toe [təu] *n* dedo (del pie); (*of shoe*) punta; **to ~ the line** (*fig*) obedecer, conformarse; ~**nail** *n* uña del pie.

toffee ['tɔfɪ] *n* caramelo; ~ **apple** *n* pirulí *m*.

toga ['təugə] *n* toga.

together [tə'geðə*] *ad* juntos; (*at same time*) al mismo tiempo, a la vez; ~ **with** *prep* junto con; ~**ness** *n* compañerismo.

toil [tɔɪl] *n* trabajo duro, labor *f* // *vi* esforzarse.

toilet ['tɔɪlət] *n* (*lavatory*) servicios *mpl*, wáter *m* // *cpd* (*bag, soap etc*) de aseo; ~ **bowl** *n* palangana; ~ **paper** *n* papel *m* higiénico; ~**ries** *npl* artículos *mpl* de aseo; (*make-up etc*) artículos *mpl* de tocador; ~ **roll** *n* rollo de papel higiénico; ~ **water** *n* agua de tocador.

token ['təukən] *n* (*sign*) señal *f*, muestra; (*souvenir*) recuerdo; (*voucher*) cupón *m*; **book/record ~** vale *m* para comprar libros/discos.

told [təuld] *pt, pp* of **tell**.

tolerable ['tɔlərəbl] *a* (*bearable*) soportable; (*fairly good*) pasable.

tolerance ['tɔlərns] *n* (*also*: *TECH*) tolerancia; **tolerant** *a*: **tolerant of** tolerante con.

tolerate ['tɔləreɪt] *vt* tolerar; **toleration** [-'reɪʃən] *n* tolerancia.

toll [təul] *n* (*of casualties*) número de víctimas; (*tax, charge*) peaje *m* // *vi* (*bell*) doblar; ~**bridge** *n* puente *m* de peaje.

tomato [tə'mɑːtəu] *n, pl* ~**es** *n* tomate *m*.

tomb [tuːm] *n* tumba.

tombola [tɔm'bəulə] *n* tómbola.

tomboy ['tɔmbɔɪ] *n* marimacho.

tombstone ['tuːmstəun] *n* lápida.

tomcat ['tɔmkæt] *n* gato.

tomorrow [tə'mɔrəu] *ad, n* (*also fig*) mañana; **the day after ~** pasado mañana; ~ **morning** mañana por la mañana.

ton [tʌn] *n* tonelada; ~**s of** (*col*) montones *mpl* de.

tone [təun] *n* tono / *vi* armonizar; **to ~ down** *vt* (*colour criticism*) suavizar; (*sound*) bajar; (*MUS*) entonar; **to ~ up** *vt* (*muscles*) tonificar; ~**-deaf** *a* que no tiene oído.

tongs [tɔŋz] *npl* (*for coal*) tenazas *fpl*; (*for hair*) tenacillas *fpl*.

tongue [tʌŋ] *n* lengua; ~ **in cheek** *ad* irónicamente; ~**-tied** *a* (*fig*) mudo; ~**-twister** *n* trabalenguas *m inv*.

tonic ['tɔnɪk] *n* (*MED*) tónico; (*MUS*) tónica; (*also*: ~ **water**) (agua) tónica.

tonight [tə'naɪt] *ad, n* esta noche.

tonnage ['tʌnɪdʒ] *n* (*NAUT*) tonelaje *m*.

tonsil ['tɔnsl] *n* amígdala, anginas *fpl* (*col*); ~**litis** [-'laɪtɪs] *n* amigdalitis *f*, (inflamación *f* de las) anginas.

too [tu:] ad (excessively) demasiado; (very) muy; (also) también; ~ **much** ad demasiado; ~ **many** det demasiados/as.

took [tuk] pt of **take**.

tool [tu:l] n herramienta; ~ **box** n caja de herramientas.

toot [tu:t] n (of horn) bocinazo; (of whistle) silbido // vi (with car-horn) tocar la bocina.

tooth [tu:θ], pl **teeth** n (ANAT, TECH) diente m; (molar) muela; ~**ache** n dolor m de muelas; ~**brush** n cepillo de dientes; ~**paste** n pasta de dientes; ~**pick** n palillo.

top [tɔp] n (of mountain) cumbre f, cima; (of head) coronilla; (of ladder) lo alto; (of cupboard, table) superficie f; (fig: of box jar) tapa, tapadera; (: of bottle) tapón m; (of list etc) cabeza; (toy) peonza // a más alto; (in rank) principal, primero; (best) mejor // vt (exceed) exceder; (be first in) ir a la cabeza de; **on** ~ **of** sobre, encima de; **from** ~ **to toe** de pies a cabeza; **to** ~ **up** vt llenar; ~**coat** n sobretodo; ~ **hat** n sombrero de copa; ~**heavy** a (object) desequilibrado.

topic ['tɔpɪk] n tema m, tópico; ~**al** a actual.

top: ~**less** a (bather etc) con el pecho al descubierto, topless; ~**level** a (talks) al más alto nivel; ~**most** a más alto.

topple ['tɔpl] vt volcar, derribar // vi caerse.

topsy-turvy ['tɔpsɪ'tɔːvɪ] a, ad patas arriba.

torch [tɔːtʃ] n antorcha; (electric) linterna.

tore [tɔː*] pt of **tear**.

torment ['tɔːmɛnt] n tormento // vt [tɔː'mɛnt] atormentar; (fig: annoy) fastidiar.

torn [tɔːn] pp of **tear**.

tornado [tɔː'neɪdəu], pl ~**es** n tornado.

torpedo [tɔː'piːdəu], pl ~**es** n torpedo.

torrent ['tɔrnt] n torrente m; ~**ial** [-'rɛnʃl] a torrencial.

torso ['tɔːsəu] n torso.

tortoise ['tɔːtəs] n tortuga; ~**shell** ['tɔːtəʃɛl] a de carey.

tortuous ['tɔːtjuəs] a tortuoso.

torture ['tɔːtʃə*] n tortura // vt torturar; (fig) atormentar.

Tory ['tɔːrɪ] a, n conservador/a m/f.

toss [tɔs] vt tirar, echar; (head) sacudir (la cabeza); **to** ~ **a coin** echar a cara o cruz; **to** ~ **up for sth** jugar a cara o cruz algo; **to** ~ **and turn in bed** dar vueltas en la cama.

tot [tɔt] n (drink) copita; (child) nene/a m/f.

total ['təutl] a total, entero // n total m, suma // vt (add up) sumar; (amount to) ascender a.

totalitarian [təutælɪ'tɛərɪən] a totalitario.

totem pole ['təutəm-] n poste m totémico.

totter ['tɔtə*] vi tambalearse.

touch [tʌtʃ] n (gen) tacto; (contact) contacto; (FOOTBALL) fuera de juego // vt (gen) tocar; (emotionally) conmover; **a** ~ **of** (fig) una pizca o un poquito de; **to get**

in ~ **with sb** ponerse en contacto con uno; **to lose** ~ (friends) perder contacto; **to** ~ **on** vt fus (topic) aludir (brevemente) a; **to** ~ **up** vt (paint) retocar; ~**and-go** a arriesgado; ~**down** n aterrizaje m; (on sea) amerizaje m; ~**ed** a conmovido; (col) chiflado; ~**ing** a conmovedor(a); ~**line** n (SPORT) línea de banda; ~**y** a (person) susceptible.

tough [tʌf] a (gen) duro; (difficult) difícil; (resistant) resistente; (person) fuerte; (: pej) bruto // n (gangster etc) gorila m; ~**en** vt endurecer; ~**ness** n dureza; dificultad f; resistencia; fuerza.

toupee ['tuːpeɪ] n peluca.

tour ['tuə*] n viaje m, vuelta; (also: **package** ~) viaje m organizado; (of town, museum) visita // vt viajar por; ~**ing** n viajes mpl turísticos turismo.

tourism ['tuərɪzm] n turismo.

tourist ['tuərɪst] n turista m/f // cpd turístico; ~ **office** n oficina de turismo.

tournament ['tuənəmənt] n torneo.

tousled ['tauzld] a (hair) despeinado.

tout [taut] vi: **to** ~ **for** solicitar clientes para // n: **ticket** ~ revendedor/a m/f.

tow [təu] vt remolcar; **'on** ~' (AUT) "a remolque".

toward(s) [tə'wɔːd(z)] prep hacia; (of attitude) respecto a, con; (of purpose) para.

towel ['tauəl] n toalla; ~**ling** n (fabric) felpa; ~ **rail** n toallero.

tower ['tauə*] n torre f; ~ **block** n rascacielos m inv; ~**ing** a muy alto, imponente.

town [taun] n ciudad f; **to go to** ~ ir a la ciudad; (fig) hacer con entusiasmo; ~ **clerk** n secretario del Ayuntamiento; ~ **council** n consejo municipal; ~ **hall** n ayuntamiento; ~ **planning** n urbanismo.

towrope ['təurəup] n cable m de remolque.

toxic ['tɔksɪk] a tóxico.

toy [tɔɪ] n juguete m; **to** ~ **with** vt fus jugar con; (idea) acariciar; ~**shop** n juguetería.

trace [treɪs] n rastro // vt (draw) trazar, delinear; (follow) seguir la pista de; (locate) encontrar.

track [træk] n (mark) huella, pista; (path: gen) camino, senda; (: of bullet etc) trayectoria; (: of suspect, animal) pista, rastro; (RAIL) vía; (on tape, SPORT) pista // vt seguir la pista de; **to keep** ~ **of** mantenerse al tanto de, seguir; **to** ~ **down** vt (prey) averiguar el paradero de; (sth lost) buscar y encontrar; ~ **suit** n chándal m.

tract [trækt] n (GEO) región f; (pamphlet) folleto.

tractor ['træktə*] n tractor m.

trade [treɪd] n comercio, negocio; (skill, job) oficio, empleo // vi negociar, comerciar; **to** ~ **in** vt (old car etc) ofrecer como parte del pago; ~**in price** n valor m de un objeto usado que se descuenta del precio de otro nuevo; ~**mark** n marca de fábrica; ~ **name** n marca registrada;

trader n comerciante m/f; **tradesman** n (shopkeeper) tendero; ~ **union** n sindicato; ~ **unionism** n sindicalismo; **trading** n comercio; **trading estate** n zona comercial.

tradition [trə'dɪʃən] n tradición f; ~**al** a tradicional.

traffic ['træfɪk] n (gen, AUT) tráfico, circulación f; (air ~ etc) tránsito // vi: to ~ **in** (pej: liquor, drugs) traficar en; ~ **circle** n (US) cruce m giratorio; ~ **jam** n embotellamiento; ~ **lights** npl semáforo sg; ~ **warden** n guardia m/f de tráfico.

tragedy ['trædʒədɪ] n tragedia.

tragic ['trædʒɪk] a trágico.

trail [treɪl] n (tracks) rastro, pista; (path) camino, sendero; (wake) estela // vt (drag) arrastrar; (follow) seguir la pista de; (follow closely) vigilar // vi arrastrarse; to ~ **behind** vi quedar a la zaga; ~**er** n (AUT) remolque m; (US) caravana; (CINEMA) trailer m, ávance m.

train [treɪn] n tren m; (of dress) cola; (series) serie f; (followers) séquito // vt (educate) formar; (sportsman) entrenar; (dog) amaestrar; (point: gun etc): to ~ **on** apuntar a // vi (SPORT) entrenarse; (be educated) recibir una formación; ~**ed** a (worker) cualificado, adiestrado; (teacher) diplomado; (animal) amaestrado; ~**ee** [treɪ'niː] n persona que está aprendiendo; (in trade) aprendiz/a m/f; ~**er** n (SPORT) entrenador/a m/f; (of animals) domador/a m/f; ~**ing** n formación f; adiestramiento; entrenamiento; **in** ~ **ing** (SPORT) en forma; ~**ing college** n (for teachers) escuela normal; (gen) colegio de formación profesional.

traipse [treɪps] vi andar con desgana.

trait [treɪt] n rasgo.

traitor ['treɪtə*] n traidor/a m/f.

tram [træm] n (also: ~**car**) tranvía m.

tramp [træmp] n (person) vagabundo // vi andar con pasos pesados.

trample ['træmpl] vt: to ~ (**underfoot**) pisotear.

trampoline ['træmpəliːn] n trampolín m.

trance [trɑːns] n trance m; (MED) catalepsia.

tranquil ['træŋkwɪl] a tranquilo; ~**lity** n tranquilidad f; ~**lizer** n (MED) tranquilizante m.

transact [træn'zækt] vt (business) tramitar; ~**ion** [-'zækʃən] n transacción f, negocio.

transatlantic ['trænzət'læntɪk] a transatlántico.

transcend [træn'sɛnd] vt trascender.

transcript ['trænskrɪpt] n copia; ~**ion** [-'skrɪpʃən] n transcripción f.

transept ['trænsɛpt] n crucero.

transfer ['trænsfə*] n (gen) transferencia; (SPORT) traspaso; (picture, design) calcomanía // vt [træns'fəː*] trasladar, pasar; to ~ **the charges** (TEL) llamar a cobro revertido; ~**able** [-'fəːrəbl] a trans-

ferible; '**not** ~**able**' "intransferible".

transform [træns'fɔːm] vt transformar; ~**ation** [-'meɪʃən] n transformación f; ~**er** n (ELEC) transformador m.

transfusion [træns'fjuːʒən] n transfusión f.

transient ['trænzɪənt] a transitorio.

transistor [træn'zɪstə*] n (ELEC) transistor m; ~ **radio** n radio f a transistores.

transit ['trænzɪt] n: **in** ~ de tránsito, de paso.

transition [træn'zɪʃən] n transición f; ~**al** a transitorio.

transitive ['trænzɪtɪv] a (LING) transitivo.

transitory ['trænzɪtərɪ] a transitorio.

translate [trænz'leɪt] vt traducir; **translation** [-'leɪʃən] n traducción f; **translator** n traductor/a m/f.

transmission [trænz'mɪʃən] n transmisión f.

transmit [trænz'mɪt] vt transmitir; ~**ter** n transmisor m; (station) emisora.

transparency [træns'pɛərnsɪ] n (PHOT) diapositiva.

transparent [træns'pærnt] a transparente.

transplant [træns'plɑːnt] vt transplantar // n ['trænsplɑːnt] (MED) transplante m.

transport ['trænspɔːt] n (gen) transporte m; (also: **road/rail** ~) transportes mpl // vt [-'pɔːt] transportar; (carry) acarrear; ~**ation** [-'teɪʃən] n transporte m; ~ **café** n cafetería de carretera.

transverse ['trænzvəːs] a transversal.

transvestite [trænz'vɛstaɪt] n travesti m/f.

trap [træp] n (snare, trick) trampa; (carriage) cabriolé m // vt coger en una trampa; (immobilize) bloquear; (jam) atascar; ~ **door** n escotilla.

trapeze [trə'piːz] n trapecio.

trappings ['træpɪŋz] npl adornos mpl.

trash [træʃ] n (pej: goods) pacotilla; (: nonsense) basura; ~ **can** n (US) cubo de la basura.

trauma ['trɔːmə] n trauma m; ~**tic** [-'mætɪk] a traumático.

travel ['trævl] n viaje m // vi viajar // vt (distance) recorrer; ~ **agency** n agencia de viajes; ~**ler**, ~**er** (US) n viajero/a; ~**ler's cheque** n cheque m de viajero; ~**ling**, ~**ing** (US) n los viajes mpl, el viajar; ~ **sickness** n mareo.

traverse ['trævəs] vt atravesar, cruzar.

travesty ['trævəstɪ] n parodia.

trawler ['trɔːlə*] n barco rastreador o de rastra.

tray [treɪ] n (for carrying) bandeja; (on desk) cajón m.

treacherous ['trɛtʃərəs] a traidor(a); **treachery** n traición f.

treacle ['triːkl] n melaza.

tread [trɛd] n (step) paso, pisada; (sound) ruido de pasos; (of tyre) banda de rodadura // vi, pt **trod**, pp **trodden** pisar; to ~ **on** vt fus pisar sobre.

treason ['triːzn] n traición f.

treasure ['treʒə*] n tesoro // vt (value) apreciar, valorar; ~ **hunt** n caza del tesoro.

treasurer ['treʒərə*] n tesorero.

treasury ['treʒəri] n: the ~ (POL) el Ministerio de Hacienda.

treat [tri:t] n (present) regalo; (pleasure) placer m // vt tratar: to ~ sb to sth invitar a uno a algo.

treatise ['tri:tiz] n tratado.

treatment ['tri:tmənt] n tratamiento.

treaty ['tri:ti] n tratado.

treble ['trebl] a triple // n (MUS) triple m // vt triplicar // vi triplicarse.

tree [tri:] n árbol m; ~ **trunk** n tronco de árbol.

trek [trek] n (long journey) viaje m largo y peligroso; (tiring walk) caminata; (as holiday) excursión f.

trellis ['trelis] n enrejado.

tremble ['trembl] vi temblar; **trembling** n temblor m // a tembloroso.

tremendous [tri'mendəs] a tremendo; (enormous) enorme; (excellent) estupendo.

tremor ['tremə*] n temblor m; (also: earth ~) temblor m de tierra.

trench [trentʃ] n trinchera.

trend [trend] n (tendency) tendencia; (of events) curso; (fashion) moda; ~y a (idea) según las tendencias actuales; (clothes) a la última moda.

trepidation [trepi'deiʃən] n agitación f; (fear) ansia.

trespass ['trespəs] vi: to ~ on entrar sin permiso en; "no ~ing" "prohibido el paso".

tress [tres] n trenza.

trestle ['tresl] n caballete m; ~ **table** n mesa de caballete.

trial ['traiəl] n (LAW) juicio, proceso (test: of machine etc) prueba; (hardship) desgracia; by ~ **and error** por tanteo.

triangle ['traiæŋgl] n (MATH, MUS) triángulo; **triangular** [-'æŋgjulə*] a triangular.

tribal ['traibəl] a tribal.

tribe [traib] n tribu f; **tribesman** n miembro de una tribu.

tribulation [tribju'leiʃən] n tribulación f, sufrimiento.

tribunal [trai'bju:nl] n tribunal m.

tributary ['tribjutəri] n (river) afluente m.

tribute ['tribju:t] n homenaje m; (payment) tributo; to pay ~ to rendir homenaje a.

trice [trais] n: in a ~ en un santiamén.

trick [trik] n trampa; (deceit) truco; (joke) broma; (CARDS) baza // vt engañar; to play a ~ on sb gastar una broma a uno; ~ery n astucia.

trickle ['trikl] n (of water etc) hililo // vi gotear.

tricky ['triki] a difícil, delicado.

tricycle ['traisikl] n triciclo.

trifle ['traifl] n bagatela; (CULIN) dulce m

de bizcocho, fruta y natillas // ad: a ~ **long** un poquito largo; **trifling** a insignificante.

trigger ['trigə*] n (of gun) gatillo; to ~ **off** vt desencadenar.

trigonometry [trigə'nɔmətri] n trigonometría.

trill [tril] n (of bird) trino.

trim [trim] a (elegant) aseado; (house, garden) en buen estado; (figure) con buen tipo // n (haircut etc) recorte m; (on car) tapicería // vt arreglar; (cut) recortar; (decorate) adornar; (NAUT: a sail) orientar; ~**mings** npl decoraciones fpl; (cuttings) recortes mpl.

Trinity ['triniti] n: the ~ la Trinidad.

trinket ['triŋkit] n chuchería; (piece of jewellery) baratija.

trio ['tri:əu] n trío.

trip [trip] n viaje m; (excursion) excursión f; (stumble) traspié m // vi (also: ~ **up**) tropezar; (go lightly) andar a paso ligero // vt poner la zancadilla a.

tripe [traip] n (CULIN) callos mpl; (pej: rubbish) bobadas fpl.

triple ['tripl] a triple.

triplets ['triplits] npl trillizos/as m/fpl.

triplicate ['triplikət] n: in ~ por triplicado.

tripod ['traipɔd] n trípode m.

trite [trait] a gastado, trillado.

triumph ['traiʌmf] n triunfo // vi: to ~ (over) vencer; ~**ant** [-'ʌmfənt] a triunfante.

trivia ['triviə] npl trivialidades fpl.

trivial ['triviəl] a insignificante; (commonplace) trivial; ~**ity** [-'æliti] n trivialidad f.

trod [trɔd], **trodden** ['trɔdn] pt, pp of **tread**.

trolley ['trɔli] n carrito; ~ **bus** n trolebús m.

trombone [trɔm'bəun] n trombón m.

troop [tru:p] n grupo, banda; ~s npl (MIL) tropas fpl; to ~ **in/out** vi entrar/salir en grupo; ~**er** n (MIL) soldado de caballería.

trophy ['trəufi] n trofeo.

tropic ['trɔpik] n trópico; ~**al** a tropical.

trot [trɔt] n trote m // vi trotar; on the ~ (fig: col) de corrido.

trouble ['trʌbl] n problema m, dificultad f; (worry) preocupación f; (bother, effort) molestia, esfuerzo; (unrest) inquietud f; (MED): **stomach** ~ problemas mpl gástricos // vt molestar; (worry) preocupar, inquietar // vi: to ~ to do sth molestarse en hacer algo; ~s npl (POL etc) conflictos mpl; to be in ~ estar en un apuro; to go to the ~ of doing sth tomarse la molestia de hacer algo; what's the ~? ¿qué pasa?; ~d a (person) preocupado; (epoch, life) agitado; ~**maker** n elemento perturbador; (child) niño alborotado; ~**shooter** n (in conflict) conciliador m; ~**some** a molesto, inoportuno.

trough [trɔf] n (also: **drinking** ~)

abrevadero; (*also*: **feeding** ~) comedero; (*channel*) canal *m*.

troupe [tru:p] *n* grupo.

trousers ['trauzəz] *npl* pantalones *mpl*. ~

trousseau ['tru:səu], *pl* ~x *or* ~s [-z] *n* ajuar *m*.

trout [traut] *n*, *pl inv* trucha.

trowel ['trauəl] *n* paleta.

truant ['truənt] *n*: **to play** ~ hacer novillos.

truce [tru:s] *n* tregua.

truck [trʌk] *n* camión *m*; (*RAIL*) vagón *m*; ~ **driver** *n* camionero; ~ **farm** *n* (*US*) huerto de hortalizas.

truculent ['trʌkjulənt] *a* agresivo.

trudge [trʌdʒ] *vi* andar con dificultad *o* pesadamente.

true [tru:] *a* verdadero; (*accurate*) exacto; (*genuine*) auténtico; (*faithful*) fiel.

truffle ['trʌfl] *n* trufa.

truly ['tru:lɪ] *ad* auténticamente; (*truthfully*) verdaderamente; (*faithfully*) fielmente; **yours** ~ (*in letter*) (le saluda) atentamente.

trump [trʌmp] *n* triunfo; ~**ed-up** *a* inventado.

trumpet ['trʌmpɪt] *n* trompeta.

truncheon ['trʌntʃən] *n* porra.

trundle ['trʌndl] *vt*, *vi*: **to** ~ **along** rodar haciendo ruido.

trunk [trʌŋk] *n* (*of tree, person*) tronco; (*of elephant*) trompa; (*case*) baúl *m*; ~s *npl* (*also*: **swimming** ~s) bañador *m*; ~ **call** *n* (*TEL*) llamada interurbana.

truss [trʌs] *n* (*MED*) braguero; **to** ~ (**up**) *vt* atar.

trust [trʌst] *n* confianza; (*COMM*) trust *m*, cartel *m*; (*obligation*) responsabilidad *f*; (*LAW*) fideicomiso // *vt* (*rely on*) tener confianza en; (*entrust*): **to** ~ **sth to sb** confiar algo a uno; ~**ed** *a* de confianza; ~**ee** [trʌs'ti:] *n* (*LAW*) depositario, fideicomisario; (*of school etc*) administrador/a *m/f*; ~**ful**, ~**ing** *a* confiado; ~**worthy** *a* digno de confianza; ~**y** *a* fiel.

truth [tru:θ], *pl* ~s [tru:ðz] *n* verdad *f*; ~**ful** *a* (*person*) que dice la verdad; ~**fully** *ad* sinceramente; ~**fulness** *n* veracidad *f*.

try [traɪ] *n* tentativa, intento; (*RUGBY*) ensayo // *vt* (*LAW*) juzgar, procesar; (*test*: *sth new*) probar, someter a prueba; (*attempt*) intentar; (*strain*) hacer sufrir // *vi* probar; **to** ~ **to do sth** intentar hacer algo; **to** ~ **on** *vt* (*clothes*) probarse; **to** ~ **out** *vt* probar, poner a prueba; ~**ing** *a* penoso, cansado.

tsar [zɑ:*] *n* zar *m*.

T-shirt ['ti:ʃə:t] *n* camiseta.

tub [tʌb] *n* cubo; (*bath*) tina, bañera.

tuba ['tju:bə] *n* tuba.

tubby ['tʌbɪ] *a* regordete.

tube [tju:b] *n* tubo; (*underground*) metro; (*for tyre*) cámara de aire; ~**less** *a* sin cámara.

tuberculosis [tjubɔ:kju'ləusɪs] *n* tuberculosis *f*.

tube station *n* estación *f* de metro.

tubing ['tju:bɪŋ] *n* tubería; **a piece of** ~ un trozo de tubo.

tubular ['tju:bjulə*] *a* tubular; (*furniture*) de tubo.

TUC *n abbr of* **Trades Union Congress**.

tuck [tʌk] *n* (*SEWING*) pliegue *m* // *vt* (*put*) poner; **to** ~ **away** *vt* esconder; **to** ~ **in** *vt* meter; (*child*) arropar // *vi* (*eat*) comer con mucho apetito; **to** ~ **up** *vt* (*child*) arropar; ~ **shop** *n* tienda de golosinas.

Tuesday ['tju:zdɪ] *n* martes *m*.

tuft [tʌft] *n* mechón *m*; (*of grass etc*) manojo.

tug [tʌg] *n* (*ship*) remolcador *m* // *vt* remolcar; ~**-of-war** *n* lucha de la cuerda.

tuition [tju:'ɪʃən] *n* enseñanza; (*private* ~) clases *fpl* particulares.

tulip ['tju:lɪp] *n* tulipán *m*.

tumble ['tʌmbl] *n* (*fall*) caída // *vi* caerse, tropezar // *vt* tirar; ~**down** *a* destartalado; ~ **dryer** *n* secador *m* de ropa automático.

tumbler ['tʌmblə*] *n* vaso.

tummy ['tʌmɪ] *n* (*col*: *belly*) barriga; (: *stomach*) vientre *m*.

tumour ['tju:mə*] *n* tumor *m*.

tumult ['tju:mʌlt] *n* tumulto; ~**uous** [-'mʌltjuəs] *a* tumultuoso.

tuna ['tju:nə] *n*, *pl inv* (*also*: ~ **fish**) atún *m*.

tune [tju:n] *n* (*melody*) melodía // *vt* (*MUS*) afinar; (*RADIO, TV, AUT*) sintonizar; **to be in/out of** ~ (*instrument*) estar afinado/ desafinado; (*singer*) cantar bien/mal; **to be in/out of** ~ **with** (*fig*) armonizar/desentonar con; **to** ~ **up** *vi* (*musician*) afinar (su instrumento); ~**ful** *a* melodioso; **tuner** *n* (*radio set*) sintonizador *m*; **piano tuner** afinador *m* de pianos.

tunic ['tju:nɪk] *n* túnica.

tuning ['tju:nɪŋ] *n* sintonización *f*; (*MUS*) afinación *f*; ~ **fork** *n* diapasón *m*.

Tunisia [tju:'nɪzɪə] *n* Túnez *m*.

tunnel ['tʌnl] *n* túnel *m*; (*in mine*) galería // *vi* construir un túnel/una galería.

tunny ['tʌnɪ] *n* atún *m*.

turban ['tə:bən] *n* turbante *m*.

turbine ['tə:baɪn] *n* turbina.

turbulence ['tə:bjuləns] *n* (*AVIAT*) turbulencia; **turbulent** *a* turbulento.

tureen [tə'ri:n] *n* sopera.

turf [tə:f] *n* turba; (*clod*) césped *m* // *vt* poner césped; **to** ~ **out** *vt* (*col*) echar a la calle.

turgid ['tə:dʒɪd] *a* (*speech*) pesado.

Turk [tə:k] *n* turco/a.

turkey ['tə:kɪ] *n* pavo.

Turkey ['tə:kɪ] *n* Turquía; **Turkish** *a*, *n* turco; **Turkish bath** *n* baño turco.

turmoil ['tə:mɔɪl] *n* desorden *m*, alboroto.

turn [tə:n] *n* turno; (*in road*) curva; (*tendency*: *of mind, events*) disposición *f*, propensión f; (THEATRE) número; (MED) desmayo // vt girar, volver; (collar, steak) dar la vuelta a; (change): **to ~ sth into** convertir algo en // vi volver; (person: look back) volverse; (reverse direction) dar la vuelta; (milk) cortarse; (change) cambiar; (become) convertirse en; **a good ~** un favor; **it gave me quite a ~** me dio un susto (bastante grande); **'no left ~'** (AUT) 'prohibido girar a la izquierda'; **it's your ~** te toca a ti; **in ~** por turnos; **to take ~s** turnarse; **to ~ about** vi dar una vuelta completa; **to ~ away** vi volver la cabeza; **to ~ back** vi volverse atrás; **to ~ down** vt (refuse) rechazar; (reduce) bajar; (fold) doblar (hacia abajo); **to ~ in** vi (col: go to bed) acostarse // vt (fold) doblar hacia dentro; **to ~ off** vi (from road) desviarse // vt (light, radio etc) apagar; (engine) parar; **to ~ on** vt (light, radio etc) encender; (engine) poner en marcha; **to ~ out** vt (light, gas) apagar // vi: **to ~ out to be...** resultar ser...; **to ~ up** vi (person) llegar, presentarse; (lost object) aparecer // vt (gen) subir; **~ing in** (in road) vuelta; **~ing point** n (fig) momento decisivo.

turnip ['tə:nɪp] n nabo.

turnout ['tə:naut] n asistencia, número de asistentes.

turnover ['tə:nəuvə*] n (COMM: amount of money) cifra de negocios; (: of goods) movimiento.

turnpike ['tə:npaɪk] n (US) autopista de peaje.

turnstile ['tə:nstaɪl] n torniquete m.

turntable ['tə:nteɪbl] n (on record player) plato.

turn-up ['tə:nʌp] n (on trousers) vuelta.

turpentine ['tə:pəntaɪn] n (also: turps) trementina.

turquoise ['tə:kwɔɪz] n (stone) turquesa // a color turquesa.

turret ['tʌrɪt] n torrecilla.

turtle ['tə:tl] n tortuga marina.

tusk [tʌsk] n colmillo.

tussle ['tʌsl] n (fight) lucha; (scuffle) pelea.

tutor ['tju:tə*] n (gen) profesor/a m/f; **~ial** [-'tɔ:rɪəl] n (SCOL) seminario.

T.V. [ti:'vi:] n abbr of **television**.

twaddle ['twɔdl] n tonterías fpl, bobadas fpl.

twang [twæŋ] n (of instrument) punteado; (of voice) timbre m nasal // vi vibrar // vt (guitar) puntear.

tweed [twi:d] n tweed m.

tweezers ['twi:zəz] npl pinzas fpl de depilar.

twelfth [twelfθ] a duodécimo; **T~ Night** n Día de Reyes.

twelve [twelv] num doce.

twentieth ['twentɪθ] a vigésimo.

twenty ['twentɪ] num veinte.

twerp [twə:p] n (col) imbécil m/f.

twice [twaɪs] ad dos veces; **~ as much** dos veces más.

twig [twɪg] n ramita // vi (col) caer en la cuenta.

twilight ['twaɪlaɪt] n crepúsculo, ocaso.

twin [twɪn] a, n gemelo/a // vt tener como gemelo.

twine [twaɪn] n bramante m // vi (plant) enroscarse.

twinge [twɪndʒ] n (of pain) punzada; (of conscience) remordimiento.

twinkle ['twɪŋkl] n centelleo // vi centellear; (eyes) parpadear.

twirl [twə:l] n giro // vt dar vueltas a // vi girar rápidamente.

twist [twɪst] n (action) torsión f; (in road, coil) vuelta; (in wire, flex) enroscadura; (in story) cambio imprevisto // vt torcer, retorcer; (weave) entrelazar; (roll around) enrollar; (fig) deformar // vi serpentear.

twit [twɪt] n (col) tonto.

twitch [twɪtʃ] n sacudida; (nervous) tic m nervioso // vi moverse nerviosamente.

two [tu:] num dos; **to put ~ and ~ together** (fig) atar cabos; **~-door** a (AUT) de dos puertas; **~-faced** a (pej: person) falso; **~-fold** ad: **to increase ~-fold** duplicar; **~-piece (suit)** n traje m de dos piezas; **~-piece (swimsuit)** n dos piezas m inv, bikini m; **~-seater** n (plane) avión m biplaza; (car) coche m de dos plazas; **~some** n (people) pareja; **~-way** a: **~-way traffic** circulación f en ambas direcciones.

tycoon [taɪ'ku:n] n: (business) **~** magnate m.

type [taɪp] n (category) tipo, género; (model) modelo; (TYP) tipo, letra // vt (letter etc) escribir a máquina; **~cast** a (actor) encasillado; **~script** n texto mecanografiado; **~writer** n máquina de escribir; **~written** a mecanografiado.

typhoid ['taɪfɔɪd] n tifoidea.

typhoon [taɪ'fu:n] n tifón m.

typhus ['taɪfəs] n tifus m.

typical ['tɪpɪkl] a típico; **typify** [-faɪ] vt ser típico de.

typing ['taɪpɪŋ] n mecanografía; **typist** n mecanógrafa.

tyranny ['tɪrənɪ] n tiranía.

tyrant ['taɪərnt] n tirano/a.

tyre, tire (US) ['taɪə*] n neumático, llanta.

tzar [zɑ:*] n = **tsar**.

U

U-bend ['ju:bend] n (in pipe) recodo.

ubiquitous [ju:'bɪkwɪtəs] a ubicuo, omnipresente.

udder ['ʌdə*] n ubre f.

UFO ['ju:fəu] n abbr of **unidentified flying object** OVNI m (objeto volante no identificado).

ugliness ['ʌglɪnɪs] n fealdad f; **ugly** a feo; (dangerous) peligroso.

U.K. n abbr of **United Kingdom**.

ulcer ['ʌlsə*] n úlcera.

Ulster ['ʌlstə*] n Úlster m, Irlanda del Norte.

ulterior [ʌl'tɪərɪə*] a ulterior; ~ **motive** motivo oculto.

ultimate ['ʌltɪmət] a último, final; (authority) supremo; ~**ly** ad (in the end) por último, al final; (fundamentally) en el fondo.

ultimatum [ʌltɪ'meɪtəm] n ultimátum m.

ultraviolet ['ʌltrə'vaɪəlɪt] a ultravioleta.

umbilical cord [ʌmbɪ'laɪkl-] n cordón m umbilical.

umbrella [ʌm'brɛlə] n paraguas m inv.

umpire ['ʌmpaɪə*] n árbitro // vt arbitrar.

umpteen [ʌmp'tiːn] a tantísimos; **for the** ~**th time** por enésima vez.

UN, UNO abbr of **United Nations (Organization).**

unable [ʌn'eɪbl] a: **to be** ~ **to do sth** ser incapaz o no poder hacer algo.

unabridged [ʌnə'brɪdʒd] a íntegro.

unaccompanied [ʌnə'kʌmpənɪd] a no acompañado.

unaccountably [ʌnə'kauntəblɪ] ad inexplicablemente.

unaccustomed [ʌnə'kʌstəmd] a: **to be** ~ **to** no tener costumbre de.

unaided [ʌn'eɪdɪd] a sin ayuda, por sí solo.

unanimous [juː'nænɪməs] a unánime; ~**ly** ad unánimemente.

unarmed [ʌn'ɑːmd] a (without a weapon) desarmado; (defenceless) inerme.

unassuming [ʌnə'sjuːmɪŋ] a modesto, sin pretensiones.

unattached [ʌnə'tætʃt] a (person) libre; (part etc) suelto, separable.

unattended [ʌnə'tɛndɪd] a (car, luggage) sin vigilancia.

unattractive [ʌnə'træktɪv] a poco atractivo.

unauthorized [ʌn'ɔːθəraɪzd] a desautorizado.

unavoidable [ʌnə'vɔɪdəbl] a inevitable.

unaware [ʌnə'wɛə*] a: **to be** ~ **of** ignorar, no darse cuenta de; ~**s** ad de improviso.

unbalanced [ʌn'bælənst] a desequilibrado; (mentally) trastornado.

unbearable [ʌn'bɛərəbl] a insoportable.

unbeatable [ʌn'biːtəbl] a (team) imbatible; (price) inmejorable.

unbeaten [ʌn'biːtn] a imbatido.

unbeknown(st) [ʌnbɪ'nəun(st)] ad: ~ **to me** sin saberlo (yo).

unbelievable [ʌnbɪ'liːvəbl] a increíble.

unbend [ʌn'bɛnd] (irg: like **bend**) vi suavizarse // vt (wire) enderezar.

unblock [ʌn'blɔk] vt (pipe) desatascar.

unborn [ʌn'bɔːn] a sin nacer.

unbounded [ʌn'baundɪd] a ilimitado, sin límite.

unbreakable [ʌn'breɪkəbl] a irrompible.

unbridled [ʌn'braɪdld] a (fig) desenfrenado.

unbroken [ʌn'brəukən] a (seal) intacto;

(series) continuo; (record) imbatido; (spirit) indómito.

unburden [ʌn'bɜːdn] vr: **to** ~ **o.s.** desahogarse.

unbutton [ʌn'bʌtn] vt desabrochar.

uncalled-for [ʌn'kɔːldfɔː*] a gratuito, inmerecido.

uncanny [ʌn'kænɪ] a extraño, extraordinario.

unceasing [ʌn'siːsɪŋ] a incesante.

uncertain [ʌn'sɜːtn] a incierto; (character) indeciso; ~**ty** n incertidumbre f.

unchanged [ʌn'tʃeɪndʒd] a sin cambiar o alterar.

uncharitable [ʌn'tʃærɪtəbl] a poco caritativo.

uncharted [ʌn'tʃɑːtɪd] a inexplorado.

unchecked [ʌn'tʃɛkt] a desenfrenado.

uncivil [ʌn'sɪvɪl] a grosero.

uncle ['ʌŋkl] n tío.

uncomfortable [ʌn'kʌmfətəbl] a incómodo; (uneasy) molesto.

uncommon [ʌn'kɔmən] a poco común, raro.

unconcerned [ʌnkən'sɜːnd] a indiferente, despreocupado.

unconditional [ʌnkən'dɪʃənl] a incondicional.

unconscious [ʌn'kɔnʃəs] a sin sentido; (unaware) inconsciente // n: **the** ~ **el** inconsciente; ~**ly** ad inconscientemente.

uncontrollable [ʌnkən'trəuləbl] a (temper) ingobernable; (laughter) incontenible.

uncouth [ʌn'kuːθ] a grosero, inculto.

uncover [ʌn'kʌvə*] vt (gen) descubrir; (take lid off) destapar.

undecided [ʌndɪ'saɪdɪd] a (character) indeciso; (question) no resuelto, pendiente.

undeniable [ʌndɪ'naɪəbl] a innegable.

under ['ʌndə*] prep debajo de; (less than) menos de; (according to) según, de acuerdo con // ad debajo, abajo; ~ **there** allí abajo; ~ **repair** en reparación.

under... [ʌndə*] pref sub; ~**age** a menor de edad; ~**carriage** n tren m de aterrizaje; ~**clothes** npl ropa sg interior; ~**coat** n (paint) primera mano; ~**cover** a clandestino; ~**current** n corriente f submarina; (fig) tendencia oculta; ~**cut** vt irg rebajar los precios para competir con; ~**developed** a subdesarrollado; ~**dog** n desvalido; ~**done** a (CULIN) poco hecho; ~**estimate** v: subestimar; ~**exposed** a (PHOT) subexpuesto; ~**fed** a subalimentado; ~**foot** ad bajo los pies; ~**go** vt irg sufrir; (treatment) recibir; ~**graduate** n estudiante m/f; ~**ground** n (railway) metro; (POL) movimiento clandestino // a subterráneo; ~**growth** n maleza; ~**hand(ed)** a (fig) turbio; ~**lie** vt irg estar debajo de; (fig) ser la razón fundamental de; ~**line** vt subrayar; ~**ling** ['ʌndəlɪŋ] n (pej) subalterno; ~**mine** vt socavar, minar; ~**neath** [ʌndə'niːθ] ad debajo // prep debajo de, bajo; ~**paid** a mal pagado; ~**pants** npl

(*Brit*) calzoncillos *mpl*; ~**pass** *n* paso subterráneo; ~**price** *vt* vender demasiado barato; ~**privileged** *a* desamparado; ~**rate** *vt* menospreciar, subestimar; ~**side** *n* parte *f* inferior, revés *m*; ~**skirt** *n* enaguas *fpl*.

understand [ʌndə'stænd] (*irg: like* **stand**) *vt, vi* entender, comprender; (*assume*) sobreentender; ~**able** *a* comprensible; ~**ing** *a* comprensivo // *n* comprensión *f*, entendimiento; (*agreement*) acuerdo.

understatement [ʌndə'steitmənt] *n* descripción *f* insuficiente; (*quality*) modestia (excesiva).

understood [ʌndə'stud] *pt, pp of* **understand** // *a* entendido; (*implied*) sobreentendido.

understudy ['ʌndəstʌdi] *n* suplente *m/f*.

undertake [ʌndə'teik] (*irg: like* **take**) *vt* acometer; **to** ~ **to do sth** comprometerse a hacer algo.

undertaker ['ʌndəteikə*] *n* director *m* de pompas fúnebres, sepulturero.

undertaking [ʌndə'teikiŋ] *n* empresa; (*promise*) promesa.

underwater [ʌndə'wɔːtə*] *ad* bajo el agua // *a* submarino.

underwear ['ʌndəwɛə*] *n* ropa interior.

underweight [ʌndə'weit] *a* de peso insuficiente; (*person*) demasiado delgado.

underworld ['ʌndəwəːld] *n* (*of crime*) hampa, inframundo.

underwriter ['ʌndəraitə*] *n* (*INSURANCE*) (re)asegurador/a *m/f*.

undesirable [ʌndi'zaiərəbl] *a* indeseable.

undies ['ʌndiz] *npl* (*col*) paños *mpl* menores.

undignified [ʌn'dignifaid] *a* indecoroso.

undisputed [ʌndi'spjuːtid] *a* incontestable.

undo [ʌn'duː] (*irg: like* **do**) *vt* deshacer; ~**ing** *n* ruina, perdición *f*.

undoubted [ʌn'dautid] *a* indudable; ~**ly** *ad* indudablemente, sin duda.

undress [ʌn'dres] *vi* desnudarse.

undue [ʌn'djuː] *a* indebido, excesivo.

undulating ['ʌndjuleitiŋ] *a* ondulante.

unduly [ʌn'djuːli] *ad* excesivamente, demasiado.

unearth [ʌn'əːθ] *vt* desenterrar.

unearthly [ʌn'əːθli] *a* (*hour*) inverosímil.

uneasy [ʌn'iːzi] *a* intranquilo; (*worried*) preocupado.

uneconomic(al) ['ʌniːkə'nɔmik(l)] *a* antieconómico.

uneducated [ʌn'edjukeitid] *a* sin educación, inculto.

unemployed [ʌnim'plɔid] *a* parado, sin trabajo // *n*: **the** ~ los parados; **unemployment** [-'plɔimənt] *n* paro, desempleo.

unending [ʌn'endiŋ] *a* interminable.

unenthusiastic [ʌninθuːzi'æstik] *a* poco entusiasta.

unerring [ʌn'əːriŋ] *a* infalible.

uneven [ʌn'iːvn] *a* desigual; (*road etc*) quebrado, accidentado.

unexpected [ʌnik'spektid] *a* inesperado.

unfair [ʌn'fɛə*] *a*: ~ **(to)** injusto (con); ~**ly** *ad* injustamente.

unfaithful [ʌn'feiθful] *a* infiel.

unfamiliar [ʌnfə'miliə*] *a* nuevo, desconocido.

unfashionable [ʌn'fæʃnəbl] *a* pasado *o* fuera de moda.

unfasten [ʌn'fɑːsn] *vt* desatar.

unfavourable, unfavorable (*US*) [ʌn'feivərəbl] *a* desfavorable.

unfeeling [ʌn'fiːliŋ] *a* insensible.

unfinished [ʌn'finiʃt] *a* incompleto, sin terminar.

unfit [ʌn'fit] *a* con mala salud, enfermo; (*incompetent*) incompetente, incapaz; ~ **for work** no apto para trabajar.

unflagging [ʌn'flægiŋ] *a* incansable.

unfold [ʌn'fəuld] *vt* desdoblar; (*fig*) revelar // *vi* abrirse, revelarse.

unforeseen ['ʌnfɔː'siːn] *a* imprevisto.

unforgettable [ʌnfə'getəbl] *a* inolvidable.

unforgivable [ʌnfə'givəbl] *a* imperdonable.

unfortunate [ʌn'fɔːtʃnət] *a* desgraciado; (*event, remark*) inoportuno; ~**ly** *ad* desgraciadamente.

unfounded [ʌn'faundid] *a* infundado.

unfriendly [ʌn'frendli] *a* antipático.

unfurnished [ʌn'fəːniʃt] *a* desamueblado.

ungainly [ʌn'geinli] *a* desgarbado.

unhappiness [ʌn'hæpinəs] *n* tristeza; **unhappy** *a* (*sad*) triste; (*unfortunate*) desgraciado; (*childhood*) infeliz; **unhappy with** (*arrangements etc*) poco contento con, descontento de.

unharmed [ʌn'hɑːmd] *a* ileso; (*col*) sano y salvo.

unhealthy [ʌn'helθi] *a* (*gen*) malsano; (*person*) enfermizo, con poca salud.

unheard-of [ʌn'həːdɔv] *a* inaudito, sin precedente.

unhook [ʌn'huk] *vt* desenganchar; (*from wall*) descolgar; (*dress*) desabrochar.

unhurt [ʌn'həːt] *a* ileso.

unidentified [ʌnai'dentifaid] *a* no identificado.

uniform ['juːnifɔːm] *n* uniforme *m* // *a* uniforme; ~**ity** [-'fɔːmiti] *n* uniformidad *f*.

unify [juːnifai] *vt* unificar, unir.

unilateral [juːni'lætərəl] *a* unilateral.

unintentional [ʌnin'tenʃənl] *a* involuntario.

union [juːnjən] *n* unión *f*; (*also:* **trade** ~) sindicato // *a* sindical; **U**~ **Jack** *n* bandera del Reino Unido.

unique [juː'niːk] *a* único.

unison ['juːnisn] *n*: **in** ~ en armonía.

unit ['juːnit] *n* unidad *f*; (*team, squad*) grupo; **kitchen** ~ mueble *m* de cocina.

unite [juː'nait] *vt* unir // *vi* unirse; ~**d** *a* unido; **U**~**d Kingdom (U.K.)** *n* Reino Unido; **U**~**d Nations (Organization) (UN, UNO)** *n* (Las) Naciones Unidas *fpl* (O.N.U.); **U**~**d States (of America)**

(US, USA) *n* (Los) Estados Unidos *mpl* (EE.UU.).

unity [ˈjuːnɪtɪ] *n* unidad *f*.

universal [juːnɪˈvɜːsl] *a* universal.

universe [ˈjuːnɪvɜːs] *n* universo.

university [juːnɪˈvɜːsɪtɪ] *n* universidad *f*.

unjust [ʌnˈdʒʌst] *a* injusto.

unkempt [ʌnˈkɛmpt] *a* descuidado; (*hair*) despeinado.

unkind [ʌnˈkaɪnd] *a* poco amable; (*comment etc*) cruel.

unknown [ʌnˈnəʊn] *a* desconocido.

unladen [ʌnˈleɪdn] *a* (*ship, weight*) vacío.

unleash [ʌnˈliːʃ] *vt* soltar; (*fig*) desencadenar.

unless [ʌnˈlɛs] *conj* a menos que, a no ser que; ~ **he comes** a menos que venga; ~ **otherwise stated** salvo indicación contraria.

unlike [ʌnˈlaɪk] *a* distinto // *prep* a diferencia de.

unlikely [ʌnˈlaɪklɪ] *a* improbable.

unlimited [ʌnˈlɪmɪtɪd] *a* ilimitado.

unload [ʌnˈləʊd] *vt* descargar.

unlock [ʌnˈlɒk] *vt* abrir (con llave).

unlucky [ʌnˈlʌkɪ] *a* desgraciado; (*object, number*) que da mala suerte; **to be** ~ tener mala suerte.

unmarried [ʌnˈmærɪd] *a* soltero.

unmask [ʌnˈmɑːsk] *vt* desenmascarar.

unmistakable [ʌnmɪsˈteɪkəbl] *a* inconfundible.

unmitigated [ʌnˈmɪtɪɡeɪtɪd] *a* no mitigado, absoluto.

unnatural [ʌnˈnætʃrəl] *a* (*gen*) antinatural; (*manner*) afectado; (*habit*) perverso.

unnecessary [ʌnˈnɛsəsərɪ] *a* innecesario, inútil.

unnoticed [ʌnˈnəʊtɪst] *a*: **to go** ~ pasar desapercibido.

unobtainable [ʌnəbˈteɪnəbl] *a* inconseguible.

unoccupied [ʌnˈɒkjupaɪd] *a* (*seat etc*) libre.

unofficial [ʌnəˈfɪʃl] *a* no oficial; (*strike*) espontáneo, sin la aprobación de la central.

unorthodox [ʌnˈɔːθədɒks] *a* poco ortodoxo.

unpack [ʌnˈpæk] *vi* deshacer las maletas.

unpalatable [ʌnˈpælətəbl] *a* (*truth*) desagradable.

unparalleled [ʌnˈpærəleld] *a* (*unequalled*) sin par; (*unique*) sin precedentes.

unpleasant [ʌnˈplɛznt] *a* (*disagreeable*) desagradable; (*person, manner*) antipático.

unplug [ʌnˈplʌg] *vt* desenchufar, desconectar.

unpopular [ʌnˈpɒpjulə*] *a* poco popular.

unprecedented [ʌnˈprɛsɪdəntɪd] *a* sin precedentes.

unpredictable [ʌnprɪˈdɪktəbl] *a* imprevisible.

unproductive [ʌnprəˈdʌktɪv] *a* improductivo.

unqualified [ʌnˈkwɒlɪfaɪd] *a* (*teacher*) sin

título, no cualificado; (*success*) total, incondicional.

unravel [ʌnˈrævl] *vt* desenmarañar.

unreal [ʌnˈrɪəl] *a* irreal.

unrealistic [ʌnrɪəˈlɪstɪk] *a* poco realista.

unreasonable [ʌnˈriːznəbl] *a* poco razonable; (*demand*) excesivo.

unrelated [ʌnrɪˈleɪtɪd] *a* sin relación; (*family*) sin parentesco.

unrelenting [ʌnrɪˈlɛntɪŋ] *a* implacable.

unreliable [ʌnrɪˈlaɪəbl] *a* (*person*) informal; (*machine*) de poca confianza.

unrelieved [ʌnrɪˈliːvd] *a* (*monotony*) monótono.

unrepeatable [ʌnrɪˈpiːtəbl] *a* (*offer*) irrepetible.

unrepresentative [ʌnrɛprɪˈzɛntətɪv] *a* poco representativo o característico.

unrest [ʌnˈrɛst] *n* inquietud *f*, malestar *m*; (*POL*) disturbios *mpl*.

unroll [ʌnˈrəʊl] *vt* desenrollar.

unruly [ʌnˈruːlɪ] *a* indisciplinado.

unsafe [ʌnˈseɪf] *a* (*journey*) peligroso; (*car etc*) inseguro.

unsaid [ʌnˈsɛd] *a*: **to leave sth** ~ dejar algo sin decir.

unsatisfactory [ˈʌnsætɪsˈfækəərɪ] *a* insatisfactorio.

unsavoury, unsavory (*US*) [ʌn'seɪvərɪ] *a* (*fig*) repugnante.

unscathed [ʌnˈskeɪðd] *a* ileso.

unscrew [ʌnˈskruː] *vt* destornillar.

unscrupulous [ʌnˈskruːpjuləs] *a* sin escrúpulos.

unsettled [ʌnˈsɛtld] *a* inquieto, inestable; (*weather*) variable.

unshaven [ʌnˈʃeɪvn] *a* sin afeitar.

unsightly [ʌnˈsaɪtlɪ] *a* feo.

unskilled [ʌnˈskɪld] *a*: ~ **worker** obrero no cualificado.

unspeakable [ʌnˈspiːkəbl] *a* indecible; (*bad*) horrible.

unsteady [ʌnˈstɛdɪ] *a* inestable

unstuck [ʌnˈstʌk] *a*: **to come** ~ despegarse; (*fig*) fracasar.

unsuccessful [ʌnsəkˈsɛsful] *a* (*attempt*) infructuoso; (*writer, proposal*) sin éxito; **to be** ~ (*in attempting sth*) no tener éxito, fracasar; ~**ly** *ad* en vano, sin éxito.

unsuitable [ʌnˈsuːtəbl] *a* inconveniente, inapropiado.

unsure [ʌnˈʃuə*] *a* inseguro, poco seguro.

unsuspecting [ʌnsəˈspɛktɪŋ] *a* confiado.

unswerving [ʌnˈswɜːvɪŋ] *a* inquebrantable.

untangle [ʌnˈtæŋgl] *vt* desenredar.

untapped [ʌnˈtæpt] *a* (*resources*) sin explotar.

unthinkable [ʌnˈθɪŋkəbl] *a* inconcebible, impensable.

untidy [ʌnˈtaɪdɪ] *a* (*room*) desordenado, en desorden; (*appearance*) descuidado.

untie [ʌnˈtaɪ] *vt* desatar.

until [ənˈtɪl] *prep* hasta // *conj* hasta que; ~ **he comes** hasta que venga; ~ **then** hasta entonces.

untimely [ʌn'taɪmlɪ] a inoportuno; (death) prematuro.

untold [ʌn'təuld] a (story) inédito; (suffering) indecible; (wealth) incalculable.

untoward [ʌntə'wɔːd] a desfavorable.

unused [ʌn'juːzd] a sin usar, nuevo.

unusual [ʌn'juːʒuəl] a insólito, poco común.

unveil [ʌn'veɪl] vt descubrir.

unwavering [ʌn'weɪvərɪŋ] a inquebrantable.

unwelcome [ʌn'welkəm] a (at a bad time) inoportuno; (unpleasant) desagradable.

unwell [ʌn'wel] a: to feel ~ estar indispuesto; to be ~ estar enfermo.

unwieldy [ʌn'wiːldɪ] a difícil de manejar.

unwilling [ʌn'wɪlɪŋ] a: to be ~ to do sth estar poco dispuesto a hacer algo. ~ly ad de mala gana.

unwind [ʌn'waɪnd] (irg: like wind) vt desenvolver // vi (relax) relajarse.

unwitting [ʌn'wɪtɪŋ] a inconsciente.

unworthy [ʌn'wɜːðɪ] a indigno.

unwrap [ʌn'ræp] vt desenvolver.

up [ʌp] prep: to go/be ~ sth subir/estar encima de algo // ad hacia arriba, arriba; ~ there allí arriba; ~ above encima, allí arriba; to be ~ (out of bed) estar levantado; it is ~ to you Ud decide; tú decides; what is he ~ to? ¿qué es lo que quiere?, ¿qué está tramando?; he is not ~ to it no es capaz de hacerlo; ~-and-coming a prometedor(a); ~s and downs npl (fig) altibajos mpl.

upbringing ['ʌpbrɪŋɪŋ] n educación f.

update [ʌp'deɪt] vt poner al día, modernizar; (contract etc) actualizar.

upgrade [ʌp'greɪd] vt ascender; (job) revalorizar.

upheaval [ʌp'hiːvl] n trastorno, conmoción f.

uphill [ʌp'hɪl] a cuesta arriba; (fig: task) penoso, difícil // ad: to go ~ ir cuesta arriba.

uphold [ʌp'həuld] (irg: like hold) vt sostener.

upholstery [ʌp'həulstərɪ] n tapicería.

upkeep ['ʌpkiːp] n mantenimiento.

upon [ə'pɔn] prep sobre.

upper ['ʌpə*] a superior, de arriba // n (of shoe) pala; ~-class a de clase alta; ~most a el más alto; what was ~most in my mind lo que me preocupaba más.

upright ['ʌpraɪt] a vertical; (fig) honrado.

uprising ['ʌpraɪzɪŋ] n sublevación f.

uproar ['ʌprɔː*] n tumulto, escándalo.

uproot [ʌp'ruːt] vt desarraigar.

upset ['ʌpsɛt] n (to plan etc) revés m, contratiempo; (MED) trastorno // vt [ʌp'sɛt] (irg: like set) (glass etc) volcar; (spill) derramar; (plan) alterar; (person) molestar, perturbar // a [ʌp'set] preocupado, perturbado; (stomach) trastornado.

upshot ['ʌpʃɔt] n resultado.

upside-down ['ʌpsaɪddaun] ad al revés.

upstairs [ʌp'stɛəz] ad arriba // a (room) de arriba // n el piso superior.

upstart ['ʌpstɑːt] n advenedizo.

upstream [ʌp'striːm] ad río arriba.

uptake ['ʌpteɪk] n: he is quick/slow on the ~ es muy listo/ algo torpe.

up-to-date ['ʌptə'deɪt] a moderno, actual.

upturn ['ʌptəːn] n (in luck) mejora.

upward ['ʌpwəd] a ascendente; ~(s) ad hacia arriba.

uranium [juə'reɪnɪəm] n uranio.

urban ['əːbən] a urbano.

urbane [əː'beɪn] a cortés.

urchin ['əːtʃɪn] a pilluelo, golfillo.

urge [əːdʒ] n (force) impulso; (desire) deseo // vt: to ~ sb to do sth incitar a uno a hacer algo.

urgency ['əːdʒənsɪ] n urgencia; (of tone) insistencia; **urgent** a urgente.

urinal ['juərɪnl]n urinario.

urinate ['juərɪneɪt] vi orinar; **urine** n orina, orines mpl.

urn [əːn] n urna; also: tea ~) tetera.

us [ʌs] pron nos; (after prep) nosotros/as.

US, USA n abbr of **United States (of America)**.

usage ['juːzɪdʒ] n uso, costumbre f.

use [juːs] n uso, empleo; (usefulness) utilidad f // vt [juːz] usar, emplear; she ~d to do it (ella) solía hacerlo; in ~ en uso; out of ~ anticuado, que ya no se usa; to be of ~ servir; it's no ~ (pointless) es inútil; (not useful) no sirve; to be ~d to estar acostumbrado a; to ~ up vt agotar, consumir; ~d (a car) usado; ~ful a útil; to be ~ful servir; ~less a inútil; user n usuario/a.

usher ['ʌʃə*] n ujier m, portero; ~ette [-'ret] n (in cinema) acomodadora.

USSR n: the ~ la U.R.S.S.

usual ['juːʒuəl] a normal, corriente; ~ly ad normalmente.

usurp [juː'zəːp] vt usurpar.

utensil [juː'tensl] n utensilio; **kitchen ~s** batería sg de cocina.

uterus ['juːtərəs] n útero.

utilitarian [juːtɪlɪ'teərɪən] a utilitario.

utility [juː'tɪlɪtɪ] n utilidad f; ~ room n trascocina.

utilize ['juːtɪlaɪz] vt utilizar.

utmost ['ʌtməust] a mayor // n: to do one's ~ hacer todo lo posible.

utter ['ʌtə*] a total, completo // vt pronunciar, proferir; ~ance n palabras fpl, declaración f; ~ly ad completamente, totalmente.

U-turn ['juː'təːn] n viraje m en U.

V

v. abbr of **verse; versus; volt; vide** véase.

vacancy ['veɪkənsɪ] n (job) vacante f; (room) cuarto libre; **vacant** a desocupado, libre; (expression) distraído; **vacate**

[vɔ'keɪt] vt (house) desocupar; (job) salir de; (throne) renunciar a.
vacation [vɔ'keɪʃɔn] n vacaciones fpl.
vaccinate ['væksɪneɪt] vt vacunar; **vaccination** [-'neɪʃɔn] n vacunación f.
vaccine ['væksiːn] n vacuna.
vacuum ['vækjum] n vacío; ~ **cleaner** n aspiradora; ~ **flask** n termo.
vagabond ['vægɔbɔnd] n vagabundo.
vagina [vɔ'dʒaɪnɔ] n vagina.
vagrant ['veɪgrnt] n vagabundo.
vague [veɪg] a vago; (blurred: memory) borroso; (uncertain) incierto, impreciso; (person) distraído; ~**ly** ad vagamente.
vain [veɪn] a (conceited) vanidoso; (useless) vano, inútil; **in** ~ en vano.
vale [veɪl] n valle m.
valentine ['vælɔntaɪn] n: **V~'s Day** Día m de los Enamorados.
valid ['vælɪd] a válido; (ticket) valedero; (law) vigente; ~**ity** [-'lɪdɪtɪ] n validez f; vigencia.
valley ['vælɪ] n valle m.
valour, valor (US) ['vælɔ*] n valor m, valentía.
valuable ['væljuɔbl] a (jewel) de valor; (time) valioso; ~**s** npl objetos mpl de valor.
valuation [vælju'eɪʃɔn] n tasación f, valuación f.
value ['væljuː] n valor m; (importance) importancia // vt (fix price of) tasar, valorar; (esteem) apreciar; (cherish) tener en mucho; ~ **added tax (VAT)** n tasa al valor añadido o agregado; ~**d** a (appreciated) apreciado.
valve [vælv] n (gen) válvula; (MED) valva.
vampire ['væmpaɪɔ*] n vampiro/vampiresa.
van [væn] n (AUT) furgoneta; (RAIL) furgón m (de equipajes).
vandal ['vændl] n vándalo; ~**ism** n vandalismo; ~**ize** vt dañar, destruir.
vanilla [vɔ'nɪlɔ] n vainilla.
vanish ['vænɪʃ] vi desvanecerse, esfumarse.
vanity ['vænɪtɪ] n vanidad f; ~ **case** n neceser m.
vantage point ['vɑːntɪdʒ-] n posición f ventajosa.
vapour, vapor (US) ['veɪpɔ*] n vapor m; (steam) vaho.
variable ['vɛɔrɪɔbl] a variable.
variance ['vɛɔrɪɔns] n: **to be at** ~ **(with)** desentonar (con), estar en desacuerdo (con).
variation [vɛɔrɪ'eɪʃɔn] n variedad f; (in opinion) variación f.
varicose ['værɪkɔus] a: ~ **veins** varices fpl.
varied ['vɛɔrɪd] a variado.
variety [vɔ'raɪɔtɪ] n variedad f, diversidad f; (quantity) surtido; ~ **show** n variedades fpl.
various ['vɛɔrɪɔs] a varios(as), diversos(as).

varnish ['vɑːnɪʃ] n (gen) barniz m; (nail ~) esmalte m // vt (gen) barnizar; (nails) pintar (con esmalte).
vary ['vɛɔrɪ] vt variar; (change) cambiar // vi variar; (disagree) discrepar; (deviate) desviarse; ~**ing** a diversos(as).
vase [vɑːz] n florero.
vaseline ['væsɪliːn] n vaselina.
vast [vɑːst] a enorme; (success) abrumador(a); ~**ness** n inmensidad f.
vat [væt] n tina, tinaja.
VAT [væt] n abbr of **Value Added Tax.**
Vatican ['vætɪkɔn] n: **the** ~ el Vaticano.
vault [vɔːlt] n (of roof) bóveda; (tomb) tumba; (in bank) sótano // vt (also: ~ **over**) saltar (por encima de).
veal [viːl] n ternera.
veer [vɪɔ*] vi virar.
vegetable ['vɛdʒtɔbl] n (BOT) vegetal m; (edible plant) legumbre f, hortaliza; ~**s** npl (cooked) verduras fpl // a vegetal; ~ **garden** n huerto.
vegetarian [vɛdʒɪ'tɛɔrɪɔn] a, n vegetariano/a.
vegetate ['vɛdʒteɪt] vi vegetar.
vegetation [vɛdʒɪ'teɪʃɔn] n vegetación f.
vehement ['viːɪmɔnt] a vehemente; (impassioned) apasionado.
vehicle ['viːɪkl] n vehículo.
veil [veɪl] n velo // vt velar.
vein [veɪn] n vena; (of ore etc) veta.
velocity [vɪ'lɔsɪtɪ] n velocidad f.
velvet ['vɛlvɪt] n terciopelo // a aterciopelado.
vendetta [vɛn'dɛtɔ] n vendetta.
vending machine ['vɛndɪŋ-] n distribuidor m automático.
vendor ['vɛndɔ*] n vendedor/a m/f.
veneer [vɔ'nɪɔ*] n chapa, enchapado; (fig) barniz m, apariencia.
venereal [vɪ'nɪɔrɪɔl] a: ~ **disease (VD)** enfermedad f venérea.
Venetian blind [vɪ'niːʃɔn-] n persiana.
Venezuela [vɛnɛ'zweɪlɔ] n Venezuela; ~**n** a, n venezolano/a.
vengeance ['vɛndʒɔns] n venganza; **with a** ~ (fig) con creces.
venison ['vɛnɪsn] n carne f de venado.
venom ['vɛnɔm] n veneno; ~**ous** a venenoso.
vent [vɛnt] n (opening) abertura; (air-hole) respiradero; (in wall) rejilla (de ventilación) // vt (fig: feelings) desahogar.
ventilate ['vɛntɪleɪt] vt ventilar; **ventilation** [-'leɪʃɔn] n ventilación f; **ventilator** n ventilador m.
ventriloquist [vɛn'trɪlɔkwɪst] n ventrílocuo.
venture ['vɛntʃɔ*] n empresa // vt aventurar; (opinion) ofrecer // vi arriesgarse, lanzarse.
venue ['vɛnjuː] n lugar m; (meeting place) lugar m de reunión.
veranda(h) [vɔ'rændɔ] n terraza; (with glass) galería.
verb [vɔːb] n verbo; ~**al** a verbal.

verbatim [vɔː'beɪtɪm] a, ad palabra por palabra.

verbose [vɔː'bəus] a prolijo.

verdict ['vɜːdɪkt] n veredicto, fallo; (fig) opinión f, juicio.

verge [vɜːdʒ] n borde m, margen m; **to be on the ~ of doing sth** estar a punto de hacer algo; **to ~ on** vt fus rayar en.

verify ['verɪfaɪ] vt comprobar, verificar.

vermin ['vɜːmɪn] npl (animals) bichos mpl; (insects, fig) sabandijas fpl.

vermouth ['vɜːməθ] n vermut m.

vernacular [və'nækjulə*] n vernáculo.

versatile ['vɜːsətaɪl] a (person) de talentos variados; (machine, tool etc) que tiene muchos usos; (mind) ágil, flexible.

verse [vɜːs] n versos mpl, poesía; (stanza) estrofa; (in bible) versículo.

versed [vɜːst] a: **(well-) ~ in** versado en, conocedor de.

version ['vɜːʃən] n versión f.

versus ['vɜːsəs] prep contra.

vertebra ['vɜːtɪbrə], pl **~e** [-briː] n vértebra; **vertebrate** [-brɪt] n vertebrado.

vertical ['vɜːtɪkl] a vertical.

vertigo ['vɜːtɪgəu] n vértigo.

very ['verɪ] ad muy // a: **the ~ book which** el mismo libro que; **the ~ last** el último (de todos); **at the ~ least** al menos; **~ much** muchísimo.

vespers ['vespəz] npl vísperas fpl.

vessel ['vesl] n (ANAT, NAUT) vaso; (container) vasija.

vest [vest] n camiseta; (US: waistcoat) chaleco; **~ed interests** npl (COMM) intereses mpl creados.

vestibule ['vestɪbjuːl] n vestíbulo.

vestige ['vestɪdʒ] n vestigio, rastro.

vestry ['vestrɪ] n sacristía.

vet [vet] n abbr of **veterinary surgeon** // vt repasar, revisar.

veteran ['vetərn] n veterano; **~ car** n coche m antiguo.

veterinary ['vetrɪnərɪ] a veterinario; **~ surgeon** n veterinario.

veto ['viːtəu] pl **~es** n veto // vt vetar, vedar.

vex [veks] vt (irritate) fastidiar; (make impatient) impacientar; **~ed** a (question) batallón(ona), controvertido.

via ['vaɪə] prep por, por vía de.

viable ['vaɪəbl] a viable.

viaduct ['vaɪədʌkt] n viaducto.

vibrate [vaɪ'breɪt] vi vibrar; **~ion** [-'breɪʃən] n vibración f.

vicar ['vɪkə*] n párroco; **~age** n parroquia.

vice [vaɪs] n (evil) vicio; (TECH) torno de banco.

vice- [vaɪs] pref vice-; **~chairman** n vicepresidente m.

vice versa ['vaɪsɪ'vɜːsə] ad viceversa.

vicinity [vɪ'sɪnɪtɪ] n (area) vecindad f; (nearness) proximidad f.

vicious ['vɪʃəs] a (violent) violento; (depraved) depravado; (cruel) cruel;

(bitter) rencoroso; **~ness** n violencia; depravación f; crueldad f; rencor m.

victim ['vɪktɪm] n víctima m/f; **~ization** [-'zeɪʃən] n (gen) persecución f; (in strike) represalias fpl; **~ize** vt (strikers etc) tomar represalias contra.

victor ['vɪktə*] n vencedor/a m/f.

Victorian [vɪk'tɔːrɪən] a victoriano.

victorious [vɪk'tɔːrɪəs] a vencedor(a).

victory ['vɪktərɪ] n victoria.

video ['vɪdɪəu] cpd vídeo; **~(-tape) recorder** n video-grabadora.

vie [vaɪ] vi: **to ~ with** competir con.

Vienna [vɪ'enə] n Viena.

view [vjuː] n vista, perspectiva; (landscape) paisaje m; (opinion) opinión f, criterio // vt (look at) mirar; (examine) examinar; **on ~** (in museum etc) expuesto; **in full ~ (of)** en plena vista (de); **in ~ of the fact that** en vista del hecho de que; **~er** n (small projector) visionadora; (TV) televidente m/f; **~finder** n visor m de imagen; **~point** n punto de vista.

vigil ['vɪdʒɪl] n vigilia; **to keep ~** velar; **~ance** n vigilancia; **~ant** a vigilante.

vigorous ['vɪgərəs] a enérgico, vigoroso; **vigour, vigor** (us) n energía, vigor m.

vile [vaɪl] a (action) vil, infame; (smell) asqueroso.

vilify ['vɪlɪfaɪ] vt vilipendiar.

villa ['vɪlə] n (country house) casa de campo; (suburban house) chalet m.

village ['vɪlɪdʒ] n aldea; **villager** n aldeano/a.

villain ['vɪlən] n (scoundrel) malvado; (criminal) maleante m/f.

vindicate ['vɪndɪkeɪt] vt vindicar, justificar.

vindictive [vɪn'dɪktɪv] a vengativo.

vine [vaɪn] n vid f.

vinegar ['vɪnɪgə*] n vinagre m.

vineyard ['vɪnjɑːd] n viña, viñedo.

vintage ['vɪntɪdʒ] n (year) vendimia, cosecha; **~ wine** n vino añejo.

vinyl ['vaɪnl] n vinilo.

violate ['vaɪəleɪt] vt violar; **violation** [-'leɪʃən] n violación f.

violence ['vaɪələns] n violencia; **violent** a (gen) violento; (intense) intenso.

violet ['vaɪələt] a violado, violeta // n (plant) violeta.

violin [vaɪə'lɪn] n violín m; **~ist** n violinista m/f.

VIP n abbr of **very important person.**

viper ['vaɪpə*] n víbora.

virgin ['vɜːdʒɪn] n virgen m/f // a virgen; **the Blessed V~** la Santísima Virgen; **~ity** [-'dʒɪnɪtɪ] n virginidad f.

Virgo ['vɜːgəu] n Virgo.

virile ['vɪraɪl] a viril; **virility** [vɪ'rɪlɪtɪ] n virilidad f; (fig) machismo.

virtually ['vɜːtjuəlɪ] ad (almost) virtualmente.

virtue ['vɜːtjuː] n virtud f; **by ~ of** en virtud de.

virtuoso [vɜːtju'əuzəu] n virtuoso.

virtuous ['vəːtjuəs] a virtuoso.
virulent ['virulənt] a virulento.
virus ['vaiərəs] n virus m.
visa ['viːzə] n visado, visa (AM).
vis-à-vis [viːzə'viː] prep respecto de.
visibility [vizi'biliti] n visibilidad f.
visible ['vizəbl] a visible; **visibly** ad visiblemente.
vision ['viʒən] n (sight) vista; (foresight, in dream) visión f; ~ary n visionario.
visit ['vizit] n visita // vt (person) visitar, hacer una visita a; (place) ir a, (ira) conocer; ~or n (gen) visitante m/f; (to one's house) visita; (tourist) turista m/f; (tripper) excursionista m/f; ~ors' book n libro de visitas.
visor ['vaizə*] n visera.
vista ['vistə] n vista, panorama.
visual ['vizjuəl] a visual; ~ize vt imaginarse; (foresee) prever.
vital ['vaitl] a (essential) esencial, imprescindible; (important) de suma importancia; (crucial) crítico; (person) enérgico, vivo; (of life) vital; ~ity [-'tæliti] n energía, vitalidad f; ~ly ad: ~ly important de primera importancia.
vitamin ['vitəmin] n vitamina.
vivacious [vi'veiʃəs] a vivaz, alegre.
vivid ['vivid] a (account) gráfico; (light) intenso; (imagination) vivo.
vivisection [vivi'sekʃən] n vivisección f.
V-neck [viːnek] n cuello de pico.
vocabulary [vəu'kæbjuləri] n vocabulario.
vocal ['vəukl] a vocal; (noisy) ruidoso; ~ chords npl cuerdas fpl vocales; ~ist n cantante m/f.
vocation [vəu'keiʃən] n vocación f; ~al a vocacional.
vociferous [və'sifərəs] a vinglero.
vodka ['vodkə] n vodka.
vogue [vəug] n boga, moda.
voice [vois] n voz f // vt (opinion) expresar.
void [void] n vacío; (hole) hueco // a (gen) vacío; (vacant) vacante; (null) nulo, inválido.
volatile ['vɔlətail] a volátil.
volcanic [vɔl'kænik] a volcánico; **volcano** [-'keinəu], pl -es n volcán m.
volley ['vɔli] n (of gunfire) descarga; (of stones etc) lluvia; (TENNIS etc) voleo; ~ball n balonvolea, vol(e)ibol m (AM).
volt [vəult] n voltio; ~age n voltaje m.
voluble ['vɔljubl] a locuaz, hablador(a).
volume ['vɔljuːm] n (gen) volumen m; (book) tomo.
voluntarily ['vɔləntrili] ad libremente, de su propia voluntad.
voluntary ['vɔləntəri] a voluntario, espontáneo; (unpaid) (CLID) gratuito.
volunteer [vɔlən'tiə*] n voluntario // vi ofrecerse (de voluntario).
voluptuous [və'lʌptjuəs] a voluptuoso.
vomit ['vɔmit] n vómito //, vt, vi vomitar.
vote [vəut] n voto; (votes cast) votación f; (right to ~) derecho de votar; (franchise) sufragio // vt (chairman) elegir // vi votar,

ir a votar; **voter** n votante m/f; **voting** n votación f.
vouch [vautʃ]: **to ~ for** vt garantizar, responder de.
voucher ['vautʃə*] n (for meal, petrol) vale m.
vow [vau] n voto // vi hacer voto.
vowel ['vauəl] n vocal f.
voyage ['voidʒ] n (journey) viaje m; (crossing) travesía.
vulgar ['vʌlgə*] a (rude) ordinario, grosero; (in bad taste) de mal gusto; ~ity [-'gæriti] n grosería; mal gusto.
vulnerable ['vʌlnərəbl] a vulnerable.
vulture ['vʌltʃə*] n buitre m.

W

wad [wɔd] n (of cotton wool, paper) bolita; (of banknotes etc) fajo.
waddle ['wɔdl] vi anadear.
wade [weid] vi: **to ~ through** caminar por el agua; (fig: a book) leer con dificultad.
wafer ['weifə*] n (biscuit) galleta, barquillo; (REL) oblea.
waffle ['wɔfl] n (CULIN) buñuelo, panqueque m // vi meter paja.
waft [wɔft] vt hacer flotar // vi flotar.
wag [wæg] vt menear, agitar // vi moverse, menearse.
wage [weidʒ] n (also: ~s) sueldo, salario // vt: **to ~ war** hacer la guerra; ~ claim n demanda de aumento de sueldo; ~ earner n asalariado/a; ~ freeze n congelación f de salarios.
wager ['weidʒə*] n apuesta // vt apostar.
waggle ['wægl] vt menear, mover.
wag(g)on ['wægən] n (horse-drawn) carro; (truck) camión m; (RAIL) vagón m.
wail [weil] n gemido // vi gemir.
waist [weist] n cintura, talle m; ~coat n chaleco; ~line n talle m.
wait [weit] n espera; (interval) pausa // vi esperar; **to lie in ~ for** acechar a; I can't ~ to (fig) estoy deseando lo ~ for esperar (a); **to ~ on** vt fus servir a; 'no ~ing' (AUT) 'prohibido aparcar'; ~er n camarero; ~ing list n lista de espera; ~ing room n sala de espera; ~ress n camarera.
waive [weiv] vt renunciar a.
wake [weik], pt **woke** or **waked**, pp **woken** or **waked** vt (also: ~ up) despertar // vi (also: ~ up) despertarse // n (for dead person) vela, velatorio; (NAUT) estela; **waken** vt, vi = **wake**.
Wales [weilz] n País m de Gales.
walk [wɔːk] n paseo; (hike) excursión f a pie, caminata; (gait) paso, andar m; (in park etc) paseo, alameda // vi andar; (for pleasure, exercise) pasearse // vt (distance) recorrer a pie, pasear; (dog) sacar de paseo, pasear; **10 minutes'** ~ **from here** desde aquí hay 10 minutos a pie; **people from all** ~**s of** life gente de todas las esferas; ~**er** n (person)

paseante m/f, caminante m/f; ~ie-talkie ['wɔːkɪ'tɔːkɪ] n walkie-talkie m, transmisor-receptor m (portátil); ~ing n el andar; ~ing shoes npl zapatos mpl para andar; ~ing stick n bastón m; ~out n (of workers) huelga sorpresa; ~over n (col) triunfo fácil; ~way n paseo.

wall [wɔːl] n pared f; (exterior) muro; (city ~ etc) muralla; ~ed a (city) amurallado; (garden) con tapia.

wallet ['wɔlɪt] n cartera.

wallflower ['wɔːlflauə*] n alhelí m; to be a ~ (fig) comer pavo.

wallop ['wɔləp] vt (col) zurrar.

wallow ['wɔləu] vi revolcarse.

wallpaper ['wɔːlpeɪpə*] n papel m pintado.

walnut ['wɔːlnʌt] n nuez f; (tree) nogal m.

walrus ['wɔːlrəs], pl ~ or ~es n morsa.

waltz [wɔːlts] n vals m // vi bailar el vals.

wand [wɔnd] n (also: magic ~) varita (mágica).

wander ['wɔndə*] vi (person) vagar, deambular; (thoughts) divagar // vt recorrer, vagar por; ~er n vagabundo; ~ing a errante; (thoughts) distraído.

wane [weɪn] vi menguar.

wangle ['wæŋgl] vt (col): to ~ sth agenciarse algo.

want [wɔnt] vt (wish for) querer, desear; (demand) exigir; (need) necesitar; (lack) carecer de // n: for ~ of por falta de; ~s npl (needs) necesidades fpl; to ~ to do querer hacer; to ~ sb to do sth querer que uno haga algo; ~ing a falto, deficiente; to be found ~ing no estar a la altura de las circunstancias.

wanton ['wɔntn] a (playful) juguetón(ona); (licentious) lascivo.

war [wɔː*] n guerra; to make ~ hacer la guerra.

ward [wɔːd] n (in hospital) sala; (POL) distrito electoral; (LAW: child) pupilo; to ~ off vt desviar, parar; (attack) rechazar.

warden ['wɔːdn] n (of institution) director m; (of park, game reserve) guardián m; (also: traffic ~) guardia m/f.

warder ['wɔːdə*] n guardián m, carcelero.

wardrobe ['wɔːdrəub] n (cupboard) armario; (clothes) guardarropa.

warehouse ['wɛəhaus] n almacén m, depósito.

wares [wɛəz] npl mercancías fpl.

war: ~fare n guerra; ~head n cabeza armada.

warily ['wɛərɪlɪ] ad con cautela, cautelosamente.

warlike ['wɔːlaɪk] a guerrero.

warm [wɔːm] a caliente; (thanks) efusivo; (clothes etc) cálido; (welcome, day) caluroso; it's ~ hace calor; I'm ~ tengo calor; to ~ up vi (person, room) calentarse; (athlete) hacer ejercicios de calentamiento; (discussion) acalorarse // vt calentar; ~-hearted a afectuoso; ~ly ad afectuosamente; ~th n calor m.

warn [wɔːn] vt avisar, prevenir; ~ing n aviso, advertencia; ~ing light n luz f de advertencia.

warp [wɔːp] vi deformarse.

warrant ['wɔrnt] n (guarantee) garantía; (LAW) mandato judicial.

warranty ['wɔrəntɪ] n garantía.

warren ['wɔrən] n (of rabbits) madriguera; (house) conejera.

warrior ['wɔrɪə*] n guerrero.

warship ['wɔːʃɪp] n buque m o barco de guerra.

wart [wɔːt] n verruga.

wartime ['wɔːtaɪm] n: in ~ en tiempos de guerra, en la guerra.

wary ['wɛərɪ] a cauteloso, cauto.

was [wɔz] pt of be.

wash [wɔʃ] vt lavar // vi lavarse // n (clothes etc) lavado; (bath) baño; (of ship) estela; to have a ~ lavarse; to ~ away vt (stain) quitar lavando; (subj: river etc) llevarse; to ~ off vt quitar lavando; to ~ up vi fregar los platos; ~able a lavable; ~basin n lavabo; ~er n (TECH) arandela; ~ing n (dirty) ropa sucia; (clean) colada; ~ing machine n lavadora; ~ing powder n jabón m en polvo; ~ing-up n fregado, platos mpl (para fregar); ~-out n (col) fracaso; ~room n servicios mpl.

wasn't ['wɔznt] = was not.

wasp [wɔsp] n avispa.

wastage ['weɪstɪdʒ] n desgaste m; (loss) pérdida; natural ~ desgaste natural.

waste [weɪst] n derroche m, despilfarro; (wastage) desgaste m; (of time) pérdida; (food) sobras fpl; (rubbish) basura, desperdicios mpl // a (material) de desecho; (left over) sobrante; (land) baldío // vt (squander) malgastar, derrochar; (time) perder; (opportunity) desperdiciar; (use up) consumir; to ~ away vi consumirse; ~bin n cubo de la basura; ~ disposal unit n triturador m de basura; ~ful a derrochador(a); (process) antieconómico; ~ ground n terreno baldío; ~paper basket n papelera; ~ pipe n tubo de desagüe.

watch [wɔtʃ] n reloj m; (act of watching) vigilia; (vigilance) vigilancia; (guard: MIL) centinela m; (NAUT: spell of duty) guardia // vt (look at) mirar, observar; (: match, programme) ver; (spy on, guard) vigilar; (be careful of) cuidarse de, tener cuidado de // vi ver, mirar; (keep guard) montar guardia; to ~ out vi cuidarse, tener cuidado; ~dog n perro guardián; ~ful a vigilante, observador(a); ~maker n relojero; ~man n guardián m; (also: night ~man) sereno; (in factory) vigilante m nocturno; ~ strap n pulsera (de reloj); ~word n lema m.

water ['wɔːtə*] n agua // vt (plant) regar; to ~ down vt (milk) aguar; ~ closet n wáter m; ~colour n acuarela; ~cress n berro; ~fall n cascada, salto de agua; ~ hole n charco; ~ing can n regadera; ~

level n nivel m del agua; ~ **lily** n nenúfar m; ~**line** n (NAUT) línea de flotación; ~**logged** a empapado; ~ **main** n cañería del agua; ~**mark** n (on paper) filigrana; ~**melon** n sandía; ~ **polo** n polo acuático; ~**proof** a impermeable; ~**shed** n (GEO) cuenca; (fig) momento crítico; ~-**skiing** n esquí m acuático; ~ **tank** n depósito de agua; ~**tight** a hermético; ~**works** npl central f depuradora; ~**y** a (colour) desvaído; (coffee) aguado; (eyes) lloroso.

watt [wɔt] n vatio.

wave [weiv] n ola; (of hand) ademán m, señal f; (RADIO) onda; (in hair) ondulación f; (fig) oleada // vi agitar la mano; (flag) ondear // vt (handkerchief) agitar; (weapon) blandir; (hair) ondular; ~**length** n longitud f de onda.

waver ['weivə*] vi oscilar; (person) vacilar.

wavy ['weivi] a ondulado.

wax [wæks] n cera // vt encerar // vi (moon) crecer; ~**works** npl museo sg de cera.

way [wei] n (gen) camino; (distance) trayecto, recorrido; (direction) dirección f, sentido; (manner) modo, manera; (habit) costumbre f; (condition) estado; **which** ~? ¿por dónde?, ¿en qué dirección?; to be in one's ~ estar en camino; to be in the ~ bloquear el camino; to go out of one's ~ to do sth desvivirse por hacer algo; to lose one's ~ extraviarse; in a ~ en cierto modo o sentido; by the ~ a propósito; '~ out' 'salida'; the ~ back el camino de vuelta; 'give ~' (AUT) 'ceda el paso'.

waylay [wei'lei] (irg: like **lay**) vt acechar.

wayward ['weiwəd] a (wilful) voluntarioso; (capricious) caprichoso; (naughty) travieso.

W.C. ['dʌblju'si:] n wáter m.

we [wi:] pl pron nosotros/as.

weak [wi:k] a (gen) débil, flojo; (tea) claro; ~**en** vi debilitarse; (give way) ceder // vt debilitar; (lessen) disminuir; ~**ling** n persona débil o delicada; ~**ness** n debilidad f; (fault) punto débil.

wealth [wɛlθ] n (money, resources) riqueza; (of details) abundancia; ~**y** a rico.

wean [wi:n] vt destetar.

weapon ['wɛpɔn] n arma.

wear [wɛə*] n (use) uso; (deterioration through use) desgaste m; (clothing): sports/baby~ ropa de deportes/para niños // (vb: pt **wore**, pp **worn**) vt (clothes) llevar; (shoes) calzar; (put on) ponerse; (damage: through use) gastar, usar // vi (last) durar; (rub through etc) desgastarse; ~ **and tear** n desgaste m; to ~ **away** vt gastar // vi desgastarse; to ~ **down** vt gastar; (strength) agotar; to ~ **off** vi (pain etc) pasar, desaparecer; to ~ **out** vt desgastar; (person, strength) agotar.

weariness ['wiərinis] n cansancio; (boredom) aburrimiento, hastío.

weary ['wiəri] a (tired) cansado; (dispirited) abatido // vt cansar // vi: to ~ of cansarse de, aburrirse de.

weasel ['wi:zl] n (ZOOL) comadreja.

weather ['wɛðə*] n tiempo // vt (storm, crisis) hacer frente a; ~-**beaten** a curtido; ~ **cock** n veleta; ~ **forecast** n boletín m meteorológico; ~ **vane** r = ~ **cock**.

weave [wi:v] pt **wove**, pp **woven** vt (cloth) tejer; (fig) entretejer; **weaver** n tejedor/a m/f; **weaving** n tejeduría.

web [wɛb] n (of spider) telaraña; (cn foot) membrana; (network) red f; ~**bed** a (foot) palmeado; ~**bing** n (on chair) cinchas fpl.

wed [wɛd] pt, pp **wedded** vt casar // vi casarse // n: **the newly-~s** los recién casados.

we'd [wi:d] = **we had**; **we would**.

wedded ['wɛdid] pt, pp of **wed**.

wedding ['wɛdiŋ] n boda, casamiento; **silver/golden** ~ bodas fpl de plata/de oro; ~ **day** n día m de la boda; ~ **dress** n traje m de novia; ~ **present** n regalo de boda; ~ **ring** n anillo de boda.

wedge [wɛdʒ] n (of wood etc) cuña; (of cake) porción f // vt acuñar; (pack tightly) apretar.

wedlock ['wɛdlɔk] n matrimonio.

Wednesday ['wɛdnzdi] n miércoles m.

wee [wi:] a (Scottish) pequeñito.

weed [wi:d] n mala hierba, maleza // vt escardar, desherbar; ~-**killer** n herbicida m.

week [wi:k] n semana; ~ **day** n día m laborable; ~**end** n fin m de semana; ~**ly** ad semanalmente, cada semana // a semanal // n semanario.

weep [wi:p] pt, pp **wept** vi, vt llorar; ~**ing willow** n sauce m llorón.

weigh [wei] vt, vi pesar; to ~ **down** vt sobrecargar; (fig: with worry) agobiar; to ~ **up** vt pesar; ~**bridge** n báscula-puente f.

weight [weit] n peso; (on scale) pesa; to lose/put on ~ adelgazarse/engordarse; ~**lessness** n ingravidez f; ~ **lifter** n levantador m de pesos; ~**y** a pesado.

weir [wiə*] n presa.

weird [wiəd] a raro, extraño.

welcome ['wɛlkəm] a bienvenido // n bienvenida // vt dar la bienvenida a; (be glad of) alegrarse de; **welcoming** a acogedor(a); (speech) de bienvenida.

weld [wɛld] n soldadura // vt soldar; ~**er** n (person) soldador m; ~**ing** n soldadura.

welfare ['wɛlfeə*] n bienestar m; (social aid) asistencia social; ~ **state** n estado de bienestar

well [wɛl] n fuente f, pozo // ad bien // a: **to be** ~ estar bien (de salud) // excl ¡vaya!, ¡bueno!; **as** ~ también; **as** ~ **as** igual que; ~ **done!** ¡bien hecho!; **get** ~ **soon!** ¡que te mejores pronto!; **to do** ~ ir o salir bien; **to** ~ **up** vi brotar.

we'll [wi:l] = **we will**, **we shall**.

well: ~-**behaved** a bien educado, formal; ~-**being** n bienestar m; ~-**built** a (person) fornido; ~-**deserved** a merecido; ~-**developed** a bien desarrollado; ~-**dressed** a bien vestido; ~-**heeled** a (col: wealthy) rico; ~-**informed** a enterado.

wellingtons ['welıntənz] n (alsc: **wellington boots**) botas fpl de goma.

well: ~-**known** a (person) conocido; ~-**mannered** a educado; ~-**meaning** a bienintencionado; ~-**off** a pudiente, con dinero; ~-**read** a culto; ~-**to-do** a acomodado; ~-**wisher** n admirador/a m/f, amigo.

Welsh [welʃ] a galés(esa) // n (LING) galés m; ~ **man/woman** n galés/esa m/f.

went [went] pt of **go**.

wept [wept] pt, pp of **weep**.

were [wə:*] pt of **be**.

we're [wıə*] = **we are**.

weren't [wə:nt] = **were not**.

west [west] n oeste m // a oeste del oeste // ad hacia el o al oeste; t**he W~** n el Oeste, el Occidente; the **W~ Country** n el suroeste de Inglaterra; ~**erly** a (situation) oeste; (wind) del oeste; ~**ern** a occidental // n (CINEMA) película del oeste; **W~ Germany** n Alemania Occidental; **W~ Indies** npl Antillas fpl; ~**ward(s)** ad hacia el oeste.

wet [wet] a (damp) húmedo; (~ through) mojado; (rainy) lluvioso; to **get** ~ mojarse; '~ **paint**' 'recién pintado'; to be a ~ **blanket** (fig) ser un/una aguafiestas; ~**ness** n humedad f; ~ **suit** n traje m de buzo.

we've [wi:v] = **we have**.

whack [wæk] vt dar un buen golpe a; ~**ed** a (col: tired) reventado.

whale [weıl] n (ZOOL) ballena.

wharf [wɔ:f], pl **wharves** [wɔ:vz] n muelle m.

what [wɔt] excl ¡qué!, ¡cómo! // det que // pron (interrogative) ¿qué?, ¿cómo? (relative, indirect: object) lo que; (: subject) el/la que; ~ **are you doing**? ¿qué haces?; **I saw** ~ **you did** he visto lo que hiciste; ~ **a mess**! ¡que lío!; ~ **is it called**? ¿cómo se llama?; ~ **about me**? ¿y yo?; ~**ever** det: ~**ever book you choose** cualquier libro que elija // pron: do ~**ever** is necessary haga lo que sea necesario; no **reason** ~**ever** or ~**soever** ninguna razón sea la que sea; **nothing** ~**ever** nada en absoluto.

wheat [wi:t] n trigo.

wheel [wi:l] n rueda; (AUT: also: steering ~) volante m; (NAUT) timón m // vt (pram etc) empujar // vi (also: ~ **round**) dar la vuelta, girar; ~**barrow** n carretilla; ~**chair** n silla de ruedas; ~**house** n timonera.

wheeze [wi:z] n respiración f ruidosa // vi resollar.

when [wen] ad cuándo // conj cuando; (whereas) mientras; **on the day** ~ **I met**

him el día que le conocí; ~**ever** conj cuando, todas las veces que; (every time that) siempre que.

where [wɛə*] ad dónde // conj dónde; **this is** ~ **aquí es** donde; ~**abouts** ad ¿dónde? // n: **nobody knows his** ~**abouts** nadie conoce su paradero; ~**as** conj visto que, mientras; **wherever** [-'ɛvə*] ad dondequiera que; (interrogative) ¿dónde?; ~**withal** n recursos mpl.

whet [wet] vt estimular.

whether ['weðə*] conj si; **I don't know** ~ **to accept or not** no sé si aceptar o no; ~ **you go or not** vayas o no vayas.

which [wıtʃ] det (interrogative) ¿qué?, ¿cuál?; ~ **one of you**? ¿cuál de vosotros?; ~ **picture do you want**? ¿qué cuadro quieres? // pron (interrogative) ¿cuál?; (relative: subject) que, lo que; (: object) el cual etc, el cual etc, lo cual; **I don't mind** ~ no me importa cuál; **the apple** ~ **is on the table** la manzana que está sobre la mesa; **the chair on** ~ **you are sitting** la silla sobre la que estás sentado; **he said he knew**, ~ **is true** el dijo que sabía, lo cual es cierto; **in** ~ **case** en cuyo caso; ~**ever** det: **take** ~**ever book you prefer** coja el libro que prefiera; ~**ever book you take** cualquier libro que coja.

whiff [wıf] n bocanada.

while [waıl] n rato, momento // conj durante; (as long as) mientras; (although) aunque; **for a** ~ durante algún tiempo.

whim [wım] n capricho.

whimper ['wımpə*] n (weeping) lloriqueo; (moan) quejido // vi lloriquear; quejarse.

whimsical ['wımzıkl] a (person) caprichoso; (look) extraño.

whine [waın] n (of pain) gemido; (of engine) zumbido // vi gemir; zumbar.

whip [wıp] n látigo; (for riding) fusta; (Brit: POL) oficial disciplinario del partido // vt azotar; (snatch) arrebatar; ~**ped cream** n crema batida; ~-**round** n colecta.

whirl [wə:l] n remolino // vt hacer girar, dar vueltas a // vi girar, dar vueltas; (leaves, water etc) arremolinarse; ~**pool** n remolino; ~**wind** n torbellino.

whirr [wə:*] vi rechinar, zumbar.

whisk [wısk] n (CULIN) batidor m // vt batir; to ~ **sth away from sb** arrebatarle algo a uno; to ~ **sb away** or **off** llevar rápidamente a uno.

whisker ['wıskə*] n: ~s (of animal) bigotes mpl; (of man) patillas fpl.

whisk(e)y ['wıskı] n whisky m.

whisper ['wıspə*] n cuchicheo; (rumour) rumor m; (of leaves) susurro, murmullo // vi cuchichear, hablar bajo; (fig) susurrar.

whist [wıst] n whist m.

whistle ['wısl] n (sound) silbido; (object) silbato // vi silbar.

white [waıt] a blanco; (pale) pálido // n blanco; (of egg) clara; ~-**collar worker** n oficinista m/f; ~ **elephant** n (fig) maula; ~ **lie** n mentira piadosa; ~**ness** n blancura; ~ **paper** n (POL) libro rojo; ~**wash** n (paint) jalbegue m, cal f // vt enjalbegar; (fig) encubrir.

whiting ['waɪtɪŋ] n, pl inv (fish) pescadilla.

Whitsun ['wɪtsn] n pentecostés m.

whittle ['wɪtl] vt: to ~ **away**, ~ **down** reducir poco a poco.

whizz [wɪz] vi: to ~ **past** or **by** pasar a toda velocidad; ~ **kid** n (col) prodigio, portento.

who [hu:] pron (relative) que, el que etc, quien; (interrogative) ¿quién?; (pl) ¿quiénes?; ~**ever** pron: ~**ever finds it** cualquiera o quienquiera que lo encuentre; **ask** ~**ever you like** pregunta a quien quieras; ~**ever be marries** no importa con quién se case.

whole [həʊl] a (complete) todo, entero; (not broken) intacto // n (total) total m; (sum) conjunto; **the** ~ **of the town** toda la ciudad, la ciudad entera; **on the** ~, **as a** ~ en general; ~**hearted** a sincero, cordial; ~**sale** n venta al por mayor // a al por mayor; (destruction) sistemático; ~**saler** n mayorista m/f; ~**some** a sano; **wholly** ad totalmente, enteramente.

whom [hu:m] pron que, a quien; (interrogative) ¿a quién?

whooping cough ['hu:pɪŋkɔf] n tos f ferina.

whopper ['wɔpə*] n cosa muy grande; (lie) bola; **whopping** a (col: big) enorme.

whore [hɔ:*] n (col: pej) puta.

whose [hu:z] det: ~ **book is this?** ¿de quién es este libro?; **the man** ~ **son you rescued** el hombre cuyo hijo salvaste; **the girl** ~ **sister you were speaking to** la chica con cuya hermana estabas hablando // pron: ~ **is this?** ¿de quién es esto?; **I know** ~ **it is** yo sé de quien es.

why [waɪ] ad por qué; (interrogative) ¿por qué?, ¿para qué? // excl ¡toma!, ¡cómo!; **tell me** ~ dime por qué, dime la razón; ~**ever** ad por qué.

wick [wɪk] n mecha.

wicked ['wɪkɪd] a malvado, cruel.

wicker ['wɪkə*] n (also: ~**work**) artículos mpl de mimbre.

wicket ['wɪkɪt] n (CRICKET) palos mpl.

wide [waɪd] a ancho; (region, knowledge) vasto, grande; (choice) grande // ad: **to open** ~ abrir de par en par; **to shoot** ~ errar el tiro; ~**awake** a bien despierto; (fig) despabilado; ~**ly** ad (different) muy; **it is** ~**ly believed that...** hay una convicción general de que...; **widen** vt ensanchar; ~**ness** n anchura; ~ **open** a abierto de par en par; ~**spread** a (belief etc) extendido, general.

widow ['wɪdəʊ] n viuda; ~**ed** a viudo; ~**er** n viudo.

width [wɪdθ] n anchura; (of cloth) ancho.

wield [wi:ld] vt (sword) manejar; (power) ejercer.

wife [waɪf], pl **wives** [waɪvz] n mujer f, esposa.

wig [wɪg] n peluca.

wiggle ['wɪgl] vt menear (rápidamente) // vi menearse.

wild [waɪld] a (animal) salvaje; (plant) silvestre; (rough) furioso, violento; (idea) disparatado, descabellado; (person) loco; ~**s** npl regiones fpl salvajes, tierras fpl vírgenes; ~**erness** ['wɪldənɪs] n desierto; ~**life** n fauna; ~**ly** ad (roughly) violentamente; (foolishly) locamente; (rashly) descabelladamente.

wilful ['wɪlful] a (person) voluntarioso; (action) deliberado; (obstinate) testarudo; (child) travieso.

will [wɪl] auxiliary vb: **he** ~ **come** vendrá // vt, pt, pp **willed**: **to** ~ **sb to do sth** desear que alguien haga algo; **he** ~**ed himself to go on** con gran fuerza de voluntad, continuó // n voluntad f; (testament) testamento; ~**ing** a (with goodwill) de buena voluntad; (submissive) complaciente; ~**ingly** ad con mucho gusto; ~**ingness** n buena voluntad.

willow ['wɪləʊ] n sauce m.

will power n fuerza de voluntad.

wilt [wɪlt] vi marchitarse.

wily ['waɪlɪ] a astuto.

win [wɪn] n (in sports etc) victoria, triunfo // (vb: pt, pp **won**) vt ganar; (obtain) conseguir, lograr // vi ganar, tener éxito; **to** ~ **over**, ~ **round** vt atraerse.

wince [wɪns] vi estremecerse.

winch [wɪntʃ] n torno.

wind [wɪnd] n viento; (MED) flatulencia; (breath) aliento // (vb: [waɪnd], pt, pp **wound**) vt enrollar; (wrap) envolver; (clock, toy) dar cuerda a // vi (road, river) serpentear // vt [waɪnd] (take breath away from) dejar sin aliento a; **to** ~ **up** vt (clock) dar cuerda a; (debate) concluir, terminar; ~**break** n abrigaca; ~**fall** n golpe m de suerte; ~**ing** a (road) tortuoso; ~ **instrument** n (MUS) instrumento de viento; ~**mill** n molino de viento.

window ['wɪndəʊ] n ventana; (in car, train) ventanilla; (in shop etc) escaparate m; ~ **box** n jardinera (de ventana); ~ **cleaner** n (person) limpiacristales m inv; ~ **ledge** n alféizar m; ~ **pane** n cristal m; ~ **sill** n alféizar m.

windpipe ['wɪndpaɪp] n tráquea.

windscreen ['wɪndskri:n], **windshield** ['wɪndʃi:ld] (US) n parabrisas m inv; ~ **washer** n lavaparabrisas m inv; ~ **wiper** n limpiaparabrisas m inv.

windswept ['wɪndswɛpt] a azotado por el viento.

windy ['wɪndɪ] a de mucho viento; **it's** ~ hace viento.

wine [waɪn] n vino; ~ **cellar** n bodega; ~ **glass** n copa (para vino); ~ **list** n lista de vinos; ~ **merchant** n vinatero; ~ **tasting** n degustación f de vinos.

wing [wɪŋ] n (gen) ala; (AUT) aleta, guardabarros m inv; ~**s** npl (THEATRE) bastidores mpl; ~**er** n (SPORT) extremo.

wink [wɪŋk] n guiño, pestañec // vi guiñar,

pestañear; (light etc) parpadear.

winner ['wɪnə*] n ganador/a rf.

winning ['wɪnɪŋ] a (team) ganador(a); (goal) decisivo; ~s npl ganancias fpl; ~ **post** n meta.

winter ['wɪntə*] n invierno // vi invernar; ~ **sports** npl deportes mpl de invierno.

wintry ['wɪntrɪ] a invernal.

wipe [waɪp] n: **to give sth a** ~ pasar un trapo sobre algo // vt limpiar; **to** ~ **off** vt limpiar con un trapo; **to** ~ **out** vt (debt) liquidar; (memory) borrar; (destroy) destruir.

wire [waɪə*] n alambre m; (ELEC) cable m (eléctrico); (TEL) telegrama m // vt (house) instalar el alambrado de; (also: ~ up) conectar // vi poner un telegrama.

wireless ['waɪəlɪs] n radio f.

wiring ['waɪərɪŋ] n instalación eléctrica, alambrado.

wiry ['waɪərɪ] a nervioso, nervudo.

wisdom ['wɪzdəm] n sabiduría, saber m; (good sense) cordura; (care) prudencia; ~ **tooth** n muela del juicio.

wise [waɪz] a sabio; (sensible) cuerdo; (careful) prudente.

...wise [waɪz] suff: **time** ~ en cuanto a o respecto al tiempo.

wisecrack ['waɪzkræk] n broma.

wish [wɪʃ] n (desire) deseo // vt desear; (want) querer; **best** ~**es** (on birthday etc) felicidades fpl; **with best** ~**es** (in letter) saludos mpl, recuerdos mpl; **to** ~ **sb goodbye** despedirse de uno; **he** ~**ed me well** me deseó mucha suerte; **to** ~ **to do/sb to do sth** querer hacer/que alguien haga algo; **to** ~ **for** desear; **it's** ~**ful thinking** es un espejismo.

wisp [wɪsp] n mechón m; (of smoke) voluta.

wistful ['wɪstful] a pensativo.

wit [wɪt] n (wittiness) ingenio, gracia; (intelligence) entendimiento; (person) chistoso/a.

witch [wɪtʃ] n bruja; ~**craft** n brujería.

with [wɪð, wɪθ] prep con; **red** ~ **anger** rojo de cólera; **the man** ~ **the grey hat** el hombre del sombrero gris; **to be** ~ **it** (fig) estar al tanto o a la moda; **I am** ~ **you** (I understand) te entiendo.

withdraw [wɪð'drɔː] (irg: like **draw**) vt retirar, sacar // vi retirarse; (go back on promise) retractarse; **to** ~ **money (from the bank)** retirar fondos (del banco); ~**al** n retirada; ~**n** a (person) reservado, introvertido.

wither ['wɪðə*] vi marchitarse; ~**ed** a marchito.

withhold [wɪθ'həuld] (irg: like **hold**) vt (money) retener; (decision) aplazar; (permission) negar; (information) ocultar.

within [wɪð'ɪn] prep dentro de // ad dentro; ~ **reach** al alcance de la mano; ~ **sight of** a la vista de; ~ **the week** antes de acabar la semana.

without [wɪð'aut] prep sin.

withstand [wɪθ'stænd] (irg: like **stand**) vt resistir a.

witness ['wɪtnɪs] n (person) testigo; (evidence) testimonio // vt (event) presenciar; (document) atestiguar la veracidad de; ~ **box**, ~ **stand** (US) n tribuna de los testigos.

witticism ['wɪtɪsɪzm] n dicho ingenioso.

witty ['wɪtɪ] a ingenioso, salado.

wives [waɪvz] pl of **wife**.

wizard ['wɪzəd] n hechicero.

wk abbr of **week**.

wobble ['wɔbl] vi tambalearse; (chair) ser poco firme.

woe [wəu] n desgracia.

woke [wəuk], **woken** ['wəukən] pt, pp of **wake**.

wolf [wulf], pl **wolves** [wulvz] n lobo.

woman ['wumən], pl **women** n mujer f; ~**ly** a femenino.

womb [wuːm] n (ANAT) matriz f, útero.

women ['wɪmɪn] pl of **woman**.

won [wʌn] pt, pp of **win**.

wonder ['wʌndə*] n maravilla, prodigio; (feeling) asombro // vi: **to** ~ **whether** preguntarse si; **to** ~ **at** asombrarse de; **to** ~ **about** pensar sobre o en; **it's no** ~ **that** no es de extrañarse que; ~**ful** a maravilloso; ~**fully** ad maravillosamente, estupendamente.

won't [wəunt] = **will not**.

woo [wuː] vt (woman) cortejar.

wood [wud] n (timber) madera; (forest) bosque m; ~ **carving** n escultura de madera; ~**ed** a arbolado; ~**en** a de madera; (fig) inexpresivo; ~**pecker** n pájaro carpintero; ~**wind** n (MUS) instrumentos mpl de viento de madera; ~**work** n carpintería; ~**worm** n carcoma.

wool [wul] n lana; **to pull the** ~ **over sb's eyes** (fig) dar a uno gato por liebre; ~**len**, ~**en** (US) a de lana; ~**lens** npl géneros mpl de lana; ~**ly**, ~**y** (US) a lanudo, de lana; (fig: ideas) confuso.

word [wəːd] n palabra; (news) noticia; (message) aviso // vt redactar; **in other** ~**s** en otras palabras; **to break/keep one's** ~ faltar a la palabra/cumplir la promesa; ~**ing** n redacción f.

wore [wɔː*] pt of **wear**.

work [wəːk] n (gen) trabajo; (job) empleo, trabajo; (ART, LITERATURE) obra // vi trabajar; (mechanism) funcionar, marchar; (medicine) ser eficaz, surtir efecto // vt (clay, wood etc) tallar; (mine etc) explotar; (machine) manejar, hacer funcionar; (cause) producir; **to be out of** ~ estar parado, no tener trabajo; ~**s** n (factory) fábrica // npl (of clock, machine) mecanismo sg; **to** ~ **loose** vi (part) desprenderse; (knot) aflojarse; **to** ~ **on** vt fus trabajar en, dedicarse a; (principle) basarse en; **to** ~ **out** vi (plans etc) salir bien, funcionar // vt (problem) resolver; (plan) elaborar; **does it** ~ **out?** ¿da resultado?; **it** ~**s out at £100** suma 100 libras; **to get** ~**ed up** exaltarse; ~**able** a (solution) práctico, factible; ~**er** n trabajador/a, obrero; ~**ing class** n clase

f obrera; ~**ing-class** a de clase obrera;
in ~**ing order** en funcionamiento;
~**man** n obrero; ~**manship** n (art)
hechura, arte m; (skill) habilidad f,
trabajo; ~**shop** n taller m; ~-**to-rule** n
huelga de celo.

world [wɔːld] n mundo // cpd (champion)
del mundo; (power, war) mundial; **to think
the** ~ **of sb** (fig) tener un concepto muy
alto de uno; ~**ly** a mundano; ~-**wide** a
mundial, universal.

worm [wɔːm] n gusano; (earth~) lombriz f.

worn [wɔːn] pp of **wear** // a usado; ~-**out**
a (object) gastado; (person) rendido,
agotado.

worried ['wʌrɪd] a preocupado.

worry ['wʌrɪ] n preocupación f // vt
preocupar, inquietar // vi preocuparse;
~**ing** a inquietante.

worse [wɔːs] a, ad peor, inferior // n el
peor, lo peor; **a change for the** ~ un
empeoramiento; **worsen** vt, vi empeorar;
~ **off** a (fig): **you'll be** ~ **off this way**
de esta forma estarás peor que nunca.

worship ['wɔːʃɪp] n culto; (act) adoración f
// vt adorar; **Your W**~ (to mayor) señor
alcalde; (to judge) señor juez; ~**per** n
devoto/a.

worst [wɔːst] a (el/la) peor // ad peor // n
lo peor; **at** ~ en lo peor de los casos.

worth [wɔːθ] n valor m // a: **to be** ~
valer; **it's** ~ **it** vale o merece la pena;
~**less** a sin valor; (useless) inútil;
~**while** a (activity) que merece la pena;
(cause) loable.

worthy [wɔːðɪ] a (person) respetable;
(motive) honesto; ~ **of** digno de.

would [wud] auxiliary vb: **she** ~ **come**
ella vendría; **he** ~ **have come** él hubiera
venido; ~ **you like a biscuit?** ¿quieres
una galleta?; **he** ~ **go on Mondays** solía
ir los lunes; ~-**be** a (pej) presunto,
aspirante.

wound [waund] pt, pp of **wind** // n [wuːnd]
herida // vt [wuːnd] herir.

wove [wəuv], **woven** ['wəuvən] pt, pp of
weave.

wrangle ['ræŋgl] n riña // vi reñir.

wrap [ræp] n (stole) chal m; (cape) capa //
vt (also: ~ **up**) envolver; ~**per** n (of
book) cubierta, tapa; ~**ping paper** n
papel m de envolver.

wrath [rɔθ] n cólera.

wreath [riːθ], pl ~**s** [riːðz] n (funeral ~)
corona; (of flowers) guirnalda.

wreathe [riːð] vt ceñir.

wreck [rɛk] n naufragio; (ship) restos mpl
del barco; (pej: person) ruina // vt
destruir, hundir; (fig) arruinar; ~**age** n
restos mpl; (of building) escombros mpl.

wren [rɛn] n (zool) reyezuelo.

wrench [rɛntʃ] n (TECH) llave f inglesa;
(tug) tirón m // vt arrancar; **to** ~ **sth
from sb** arrebatar algo violentamente a
uno.

wrestle ['rɛsl] vi: **to** ~ **(with sb)** luchar
(con o contra uno); **wrestler** n luchador n
(de lucha libre); **wrestling** n lucha libre;
wrestling match n partido de lucha
libre.

wretched ['rɛtʃɪd] a miserable.

wriggle ['rɪgl] n (gen) culebreo / vi (gen)
serpentear.

wring [rɪŋ], pt, pp **wrung** vt torcer,
retorcer; (wet clothes) escurrir; (fig): **to** ~
sth out of sb sacar algo por la fuerza a
uno.

wrinkle ['rɪŋkl] n arruga // vt arrugar //
vi arrugarse.

wrist [rɪst] n muñeca; ~ **watch** n reloj m
de pulsera.

writ [rɪt] n mandato judicial; **to issue a** ~
against sb demandar a uno (en juicio).

write [raɪt], pt wrote, pp **written** vt, vi
escribir; **to** ~ **down** vt escribir; (note)
apuntar; **to** ~ **off** vt (debt) borrar (como
incobrable); (depreciate) depreciar; **to** ~
out vt escribir; **to** ~ **up** vt redactar;
~-**off** n pérdida total; **the car is a** ~-**off**
el coche es pura chatarra; **writer** n
escritor/a m/f.

writhe [raɪð] vi retorcerse.

writing ['raɪtɪŋ] n escritura; (hand-~)
letra; (of author) obra; **in** ~ por escrito;
~ **paper** n papel m de escribir.

written ['rɪtn] pp of **write**.

wrong [rɔŋ] a (bad) malo; (unfair) injusto;
(incorrect) equivocado, incorrecto; (not
suitable) inoportuno, inconveniente // ad
mal; equivocadamente // n mal m; (injustice) injusticia // vt ser injusto con;
(hurt) agraviar; **you are** ~ **to do it** estás
equivocado en hacerlo, cometes un error
al hacerlo; **you are** ~ **about that,
you've got it** ~ en eso, estás equivocado;
to be in the ~ no tener razón, tener la
culpa; **what's** ~? ¿qué pasa?; **to go** ~
(person) equivocarse; (plan) salir mal;
(machine) tener una avería; ~**ful** a
injusto; ~**ly** ad injustamente.

wrote [rəut] pt of **write**.

wrought [rɔːt] a: ~ **iron** hierro forjado.

wrung [rʌŋ] pt, pp of **wring**.

wry [raɪ] a irónico.

wt. abbr of **weight**.

X

Xmas ['ɛksməs] n abbr of **Christmas**.

X-ray [ɛks'reɪ] n radiografía; ~**s** npl rayos
mpl X // vt hacer una radiografía a.

xylophone ['zaɪləfəun] n xilófono.

Y

yacht [jɔt] n yate m; ~**ing** n (sport)
balandrismo; **yachtsman** n balandrista m.

Yank [jæŋk] n (pej) yanqui m/f.

yap [jæp] vi (dog) aullar.

yard [jɑːd] n patio; (measure) yarda;
~**stick** n (fig) criterio, norma.

yarn [jɑːn] n hilo; (tale) cuento, historia.

yawn [jɔːn] n bostezo // vi bostezar.

yd. *abbr of* **yard(s).**

year [jiɔ*] *n* año; **to be 8 ~s old** tener 8 años; **~ly** *a* anual // *ad* anualmente, cada año.

yearn [jəːn] *vi:* **to ~ for** sth añorar o suspirar por algo; **~ing** *n* ansia, añoranza.

yeast [jiːst] *n* levadura.

yell [jɛl] *n* grito, alarido // *vi* gritar.

yellow ['jɛləu] *a*, *n* amarillo.

yelp [jɛlp] *n* aullido // *vi* aullar.

yeoman ['jəumən] *n*: **Y~ of the Guard** alabardero de la Casa Real.

yes [jɛs] *ad*, *n* sí *m*.

yesterday ['jɛstədi] *ad*, *n* ayer *m*.

yet [jɛt] *ad* todavía // *conj* sin embargo, a pesar de todo; **it is not finished ~** todavía no está acabado; **the best ~** el mejor hasta ahora; **as ~** hasta ahora, todavía.

yew [juː] *n* tejo.

Yiddish ['jidiʃ] *n* judío.

yield [jiːld] *n* producción *f*; (AGR) cosecha; (COMM) rendimiento // *vt* (gen) producir; (profit) rendir // *vi* rendirse, ceder.

yoga ['jəugə] *n* yoga.

yog(h)ourt, yog(h)urt ['jəugət] *n* yogur *m*.

yoke [jəuk] *n* (of oxen) yunta; (on shoulders) balancín *m*; (fig) yugo // *vt* acoplar.

yolk [jəuk] *n* yema (de huevo).

yonder ['jɔndə*] *ad* allá (a lo lejos).

you [juː] *pron* tú; (pl) vosotros; (polite form) usted; (: pl) ustedes; (complement) te; (: pl) os; (after prep) tí; (: pl) vosotros; (: formal) le/la; (: pl) les; (after prep) usted; (: pl) ustedes; (one): **~ never know** uno nunca sabe; (impersonal): **~ can't do that** eso no se hace.

you'd [juːd] = **you had; you would.**

you'll [juːl] = **you will, you shall.**

young [jʌŋ] *a* joven // *npl* (of animals) la cría *sg*; (people): **the ~** los jóvenes, la juventud *sg*; **~er** *a* (brother etc) menor; **~ish** *a* bastante joven; **~ster** *n* joven *m/f*.

your [jɔ:*] *a* tu; (pl) vuestro; (formal) su.

you're [juə*] = **you are.**

yours [jɔːz] *pron* tuyo; (: pl) vuestro; (formal) suyo; **is it ~?** ¿es tuyo etc?; **~ sincerely** or **faithfully** le saluda atentamente.

yourself [jɔː'sɛlf] *pron* (reflexive) tú mismo; (complement) te; (after prep) tí (mismo); (formal) usted mismo; (: complement) se; (: after prep) sí (mismo); **yourselves** pl *pron* vosotros mismos; (after prep) vosotros (mismos); (formal) ustedes (mismos); (: complement) se; (: after prep) sí mismos.

youth [juːθ] *n* juventud *f*; (young man: pl ~s [juːðz]) joven *m*; **~ful** *a* juvenil; **~ hostel** *n* albergue *m* de juventud.

you've [juːv] = **you have.**

Yugoslav ['juːgəu'slaːv] *a*, *n* yugoeslavo/a; **~ia** *n* Yugoeslavia.

Yuletide ['juːlaid] *n* Navidad *f*.

Z

zany ['zeini] *a* tonto.

zeal [ziːl] *n* celo, entusiasmo; **~ous** ['zɛləs] *a* celoso, entusiasta.

zebra ['ziːbrə] *a* cebra; **~ crossing** *n* paso de peatones.

zenith ['zɛniθ] *n* cénit *m*.

zero ['ziərəu] *n* cero.

zest [zɛst] *n* ánimo, vivacidad *f*.

zigzag ['zigzæg] *n* zigzag *m* // *vi* zigzaguear.

zinc [ziŋk] *n* cinc *m*, zinc *m*.

Zionism ['zaiənizm] *n* sionismo; **Zionist** *n* sionista *m/f*.

zip [zip] *n* (also: **~ fastener, ~per**) cremallera // *vt* (also: **~ up**) cerrar la cremallera de.

zodiac ['zəudiæk] *n* zodíaco.

zombie ['zɔmbi] *n* (fig): **like a ~** como un sonámbulo.

zone [zəun] *n* zona.

zoo [zuː] *n* (jardín *m*) zoológico.

zoological [zuː'lɔdʒikl] *a* zoológico.

zoologist [zuː'ɔdʒist] *n* zoólogo.

zoology [zuː'ɔlədʒi] *n* zoología.

zoom [zuːm] *vi:* **to ~ past** pasar zumbando; **~ lens** *n* zoom *m*.

SPANISH VERB TABLES

1 Gerund. *2* Imperative. *3* Present. *4* Preterite. *5* Future. *6* Present subjunctive.
7 Imperfect subjunctive. *8* Past participle. *9* Imperfect.
Etc indicates that the irregular root is used for all persons of the tense, e.g. **oír**: 6 oiga, oigas, oigamos, oigáis, oigan.

acertar *2* acierta *3* acierto, aciertas, acierta, aciertan *6* acierte, aciertes, acierte, acierten

acordar *2* acuerda *3* acuerdo, acuerdas, acuerda, acuerdan *6* acuerde, acuerdes, acuerde, acuerden

advertir *1* advirtiendo *2* advierte *3* advierto, adviertes, advierte, advierten *4* advirtió, advirtieron *6* advierta, adviertas, advierta, advirtamos, advirtáis, adviertan *7* advirtiera *etc*

agradecer *3* agradezco *6* agradezca *etc*

aparecer *3* aparezco *6* aparezca *etc*

aprobar *2* aprueba *3* apruebo, apruebas, aprueba, aprueban *6* apruebe, apruebes, apruebe, aprueben

atravesar *2* atraviesa *3* atravieso, atraviesas, atraviesa, atraviesan *6* atraviese, atravieses, atraviese, atraviesen

caber *3* quepo *4* cupe, cupiste, cupo, cupimos, cupisteis, cupieron *5* cabré *etc* 6 quepa *etc* 7 cupiera *etc*

caer *1* cayendo *3* caigo *4* cayó, cayeron *6* caiga *etc* 7 cayera *etc*

calentar *2* calienta *3* caliento, calientas, calienta, calientan *6* caliente, calientes, caliente, calienten

cerrar *2* cierra *3* cierro, cierras, cierra, cierran *6* cierre, cierres, cierre, cierren

COMER *1* comiendo *2* come, comed *3* como, comes, come, comemos, coméis, comen *4* comí, comiste, comió, comimos, comisteis, comieron *5* comeré, comerás, comerá, comeremos, comeréis, comerán *6* coma, comas, coma, comamos, comáis, coman *7* comiera, comieras, comiera, comiéramos, comierais, comieran *8*

comido *9* comía, comías, comía, comíamos, comíais, comían

conocer *3* conozco *6* conozca *etc*

contar *2* cuenta *3* cuento, cuentas, cuenta, cuentan *6* cuente, cuentes, cuente, cuenten

costar *2* cuesta *3* cuesto, cuestas, cuesta, cuestan *6* cueste, cuestes, cueste, cuesten

dar *3* doy *4* di, diste, dio, dimos, disteis, dieron *7* diera *etc*

decir *2* di *3* digo *4* dije, dijiste, dijo, dijimos, dijisteis, dijeron *5* diré *etc* 6 diga *etc* 7 dijera *etc* 8 dicho

despertar *2* despierta *3* despierto, despiertas, despierta, despiertan *6* despierte, despiertes, despierte, despierten

divertir *1* divirtiendo *2* divierte *3* divierto, diviertes, divierte, divierten *4* divirtió, divirtieron *6* divierta, diviertas, divierta, divirtamos, divirtáis, diviertan *7* divirtiera *etc*

dormir *1* durmiendo *2* duerme *3* duermo, duermes, duerme, duermen *4* durmió, durmieron *6* duerma, duermas, duerma, durmamos, durmáis, duerman *7* durmiera *etc*

empezar *2* empieza *3* empiezo, empiezas, empieza, empiezan *4* empecé *6* empiece, empieces, empiece, empecemos, empecéis, empiecen

entender *2* entiende *3* entiendo, entiendes, entiende, entienden *6* entienda, entiendas, entienda, entiendan

ESTAR *2* está *3* estoy, estás, está, están *4* estuve, estuviste, estuvo, estuvimos, estuvisteis, estuvieron *6* esté, estés, esté, estén *7* estuviera *etc*

HABER *3* he, has, ha, hemos, han *4* hube, hubiste, hubo, hubimos,

hubisteis, hubieron *5* habré *etc 6*
haya *etc 7* hubiera *etc*

HABLAR *1* hablando *2* habla,
hablad *3* hablo, hablas, habla,
hablamos, habláis, hablan *4* hablé
hablaste, habló, hablamos,
hablasteis, hablaron *5* hablaré,
hablarás, hablará, hablaremos,
hablaréis, hablarán *6* hable, hables,
hable, hablemos, habléis, hablen *7*
hablara, hablaras, hablara,
habláramos, hablarais, hablaran *8*
hablado *9* hablaba, hablabas,
hablaba, hablábamos, hablabais,
hablaban

hacer *2* haz *3* hago *4* hice, hiciste,
hizo, hicimos, hicisteis, hicieron *5*
haré *etc 6* haga *etc 7* hiciera *etc 8*
hecho

instruir *1* instruyendo *2* instruye *3*
instruyo, instruyes, instruye,
instruyen *4* instruyó, instruyeron *6*
instruya *etc 7* instruyera *etc*

ir *1* yendo *2* ve *3* voy, vas, va, vamos,
vais, van *4* fui, fuiste, fue, fuimos,
fuisteis, fueron *6* vaya, vayas, vaya,
vayamos, vayáis, vayan *7* fuera *etc*
8 iba, ibas, iba, íbamos, ibais, iban

jugar *2* juega *3* juego, juegas, juega,
juegan *4* jugué *6* juegue *etc*

leer *1* leyendo *4* leyó, leyeron *7* leyera
etc

morir *1* muriendo *2* muere *3* muero,
mueres, muere, mueren *4* murió,
murieron *6* muera, mueras, muera,
muramos, muráis, mueran *7*
muriera *etc 8* muerto

mostrar *2* muestra *3* muestro,
muestras, muestra, muestran *6*
muestre, muestres, muestre,
muestren

mover *2* mueve *3* muevo, mueves,
mueve, mueven *6* mueva, muevas,
mueva, muevan

negar *2* niega *3* niego, niegas, niega,
niegan *4* negué *6* niegue, niegues,
niegue, neguemos, neguéis,
nieguen

ofrecer *3* ofrezco *6* ofrezca *etc*

oír *1* oyendo *2* oye *3* oigo, oyes, oye,
oyen *4* oyó, oyeron *6* oiga *etc 7*
oyera *etc*

oler *2* huele *3* huelo, hueles, huele,

huelen *6* huela, huelas, huela,
huelan

parecer *3* parezco *6* parezca *etc*

pedir *1* pidiendo *2* pide *3* pido,
pides, pide, piden *4* pidió, pidieron
6 pida *etc 7* pidiera *etc*

pensar *2* piensa *3* pienso, piensas,
piensa, piensan *6* piense, pienses,
piense, piensen

perder *2* pierde *3* pierdo, pierdes,
pierde, pierden *6* pierda, pierdas,
pierda, pierdan

poder *1* pudiendo *2* puede *3* puedo,
puedes, puede, pueden *4* pude,
pudiste, pudo, pudimos, pudisteis,
pudieron *5* podré *etc 6* pueda,
puedas, pueda, puedan *7* pudiera
etc

poner *2* pon *3* pongo *4* puse, pusiste,
puso, pusimos, pusisteis, pusieron
5 pondré *etc 6* ponga *etc 7* pusiera
etc 8 puesto

preferir *1* prefiriendo *2* prefiere *3*
prefiero, prefieres, prefiere,
prefieren *4* prefirió, prefirieron *6*
prefiera, prefieras, prefiera,
prefiramos, prefiráis, prefieran *7*
prefiriera *etc*

querer *2* quiero *3* quiero, quieres,
quiere, quieren *4* quise, quisiste,
quiso, quisimos, quisisteis,
quisieron *5* querré *etc 6* quiera,
quieras, quiera, quieran *7* quisiera
etc

reír *2* ríe *3* río, ríes, ríe, ríen *4* rio,
rieron *6* ría, rías, ría, riamos, riáis,
rían *7* riera *etc*

repetir *1* repitiendo *2* repite *3* repito,
repites, repite, repiten *4* repitió,
repitieron *6* repita *etc 7* repitiera *etc*

rogar *2* ruega *3* ruego, ruegas, ruega,
ruegan *4* rogué *6* ruegue, ruegues,
ruegue, roguemos, roguéis,
rueguen

saber *3* sé *4* supe, supiste, supo,
supimos, supisteis, supieron *5*
sabré *etc 6* sepa *etc 7* supiera *etc*

salir *2* sal *3* salgo *5* saldré *etc 6* salga
etc

seguir *1* siguiendo *2* sigue *3* sigo,
sigues, sigue, siguen *4* siguió,
siguieron *6* siga *etc 7* siguiera *etc*

sentar *2* sienta *3* siento, sientas,

sienta, sientan *6* siente, sientes,
siente, sienten

sentir *1* sintiendo *2* siente *3* siento,
sientes, siente, sienten *4* sintió,
sintieron *6* sienta, sientas, sienta,
sintamos, sintáis, sientan *7* sintiera
etc

SER *2* sé *3* soy, eres, es, somos, sois,
son *4* fui, fuiste, fue, fuimos,
fuisteis, fueron *6* sea *etc* *7* fuera *etc*
9 era, eras, era, éramos, erais, eran

servir *1* sirviendo *2* sirve *3* sirvo,
sirves, sirve, sirven *4* sirvió,
sirvieron *6* sirva *etc* *7* sirviera *etc*

soñar *2* sueña *3* sueño, sueñas,
sueña, sueñan *6* sueñe, sueñes,
sueñe, sueñen

tener *2* ten *3* tengo, tienes, tiene,
tienen *4* tuve, tuviste, tuvo,
tuvimos, tuvisteis, tuvieron *5* tendré
etc *6* tenga *etc* *7* tuviera *etc*

traer *1* trayendo *3* traigo *4* traje,
trajiste, trajo, trajimos, trajisteis,
trajeron *6* traiga *etc* *7* trajera *etc*

valer *2* val *3* valgo *5* valdré *etc* *6*
valga *etc*

venir *2* ven *3* vengo, vienes, viene,
vienen *4* vine, viniste, vino,
vinimos, vinisteis, vinieron *5*
vendré *etc* *6* venga *etc* *7* viniera *etc*

ver *3* veo *6* vea *etc* *8* visto *9* veía *etc*

vestir *1* vistiendo *2* viste *3* visto,
vistes, viste, visten *4* vistió, vistieron
6 vista *etc* *7* vistiera *etc*

VIVIR *1* viviendo *2* vive, vivid *3*
vivo, vives, vive, vivimos, vivís,
viven *4* viví, viviste, vivió, vivimos,
vivisteis, vivieron *5* viviré, vivirás,
vivirá, viviremos, viviréis, vivirán *6*
viva, vivas, viva, vivamos, viváis,
vivan *7* viviera, vivieras, viviera,
viviéramos, vivierais, vivieran *8*
vivido *9* vivía, vivías, vivía,
vivíamos, vivíais, vivían

volver *2* vuelve *3* vuelvo, vuelves,
vuelve, vuelven *6* vuelva, vuelvas,
vuela, vuelvan *8* vuelto.

VERBOS IRREGULARES EN INGLÉS

present	pt	pp	present	pt	pp
arise	arose	arisen	eat	ate	eaten
awake	awoke	awaked	fall	fell	fallen
be (am,	was,	been	feed	fed	fed
is, are;	were		feel	felt	felt
being)			fight	fought	fought
bear	bore	born(e)	find	found	found
beat	beat	beaten	flee	fled	fled
become	became	become	fling	flung	flung
befall	befell	befallen	fly	flew	flown
begin	began	begun	forbid	forbade	forbidden
behold	beheld	beheld	forecast	forecast	forecast
bend	bent	bent	forget	forgot	forgotten
beset	beset	beset	forgive	forgave	forgiven
bet	bet,	bet,	forsake	forsook	forsaken
	betted	betted	freeze	froze	frozen
bid	bid	bid	get	got	got, (US)
bind	bound	bound			gotten
bite	bit	bitten	give	gave	given
bleed	bled	bled	go	went	gone
blow	blew	blown	(goes)		
break	broke	broken	grind	ground	ground
breed	bred	bred	grow	grew	grown
bring	brought	brought	hang	hung,	hung,
build	built	built		hanged	hanged
burn	burnt,	burnt,	have	had	had
	burned	burned	hear	heard	heard
burst	burst	burst	hide	hid	hidden
buy	bought	bought	hit	hit	hit
can	could	(been able)	hold	held	held
cast	cast	cast	hurt	hurt	hurt
catch	caught	caught	keep	kept	kept
choose	chose	chosen	kneel	knelt,	knelt,
cling	clung	clung		kneeled	kneeled
come	came	come	know	knew	known
cost	cost	cost	lay	laid	laid
creep	crept	crept	lead	led	led
cut	cut	cut	lean	leant,	leant,
deal	dealt	dealt		leaned	leaned
dig	dug	dug	leap	leapt,	leapt,
do (3rd	did	done		leaped	leaped
person;			learn	learnt,	learnt,
he/she/				learned	learned
it/does)			leave	left	left
draw	drew	drawn	lend	lent	lent
dream	dreamed,	dreamed,	let	let	let
	dreamt	dreamt	lie	lay	lain
drink	drank	drunk	(lying)		
drive	drove	driven	light	lit,	lit,
dwell	dwelt	dwelt		lighted	lighted

present	pt	pp	present	pt	pp
lose	lost	lost	speed	sped, speeded	sped, speeded
make	made	made			
may	might	—	spell	spelt, spelled	spelt, spelled
mean	meant	meant			
meet	met	met	spend	spent	spent
mistake	mistook	mistaken	spill	spilt, spilled	spilt, spilled
mow	mowed	mown, mowed			
			spin	spun	spun
must	(had to)	(had to)	spit	spat	spat
pay	paid	paid	split	split	split
put	put	put	spoil	spoiled, spoilt	spoiled, spoilt
quit	quit, quitted	quit, quitted			
			spread	spread	spread
read	read	read	spring	sprang	sprung
rend	rent	rent	stand	stood	stood
rid	rid	rid	steal	stole	stolen
ride	rode	ridden	stick	stuck	stuck
ring	rang	rung	sting	stung	stung
rise	rose	risen	stink	stank	stunk
run	ran	run	stride	strode	strode
saw	sawed	sawn	strike	struck	struck, stricken
say	said	said			
see	saw	seen	strive	strove	striven
seek	sought	sought	swear	swore	sworn
sell	sold	sold	sweep	swept	swept
send	sent	sent	swell	swelled	swollen, swelled
set	set	set			
shake	shook	shaken	swim	swam	swum
shall	should	—	swing	swung	swung
shear	sheared	shorn, sheared	take	took	taken
			teach	taught	taught
shed	shed	shed			
shine	shone	shone	tear	tore	torn
shoot	shot	shot	tell	told	told
show	showed	shown	think	thought	thought
shrink	shrank	shrunk	throw	threw	thrown
shut	shut	shut	thrust	thrust	thrust
sing	sang	sung	tread	trod	trodden
sink	sank	sunk	wake	woke, waked	woken, waked
sit	sat	sat			
slay	slew	slain	wear	wore	worn
sleep	slept	slept	weave	wove, weaved	woven, weaved
slide	slid	slid			
sling	slung	slung	wed	wedded, wed	wedded, wed
slit	slit	slit			
smell	smelt, smelled	smelt, smelled	weep	wept	wept
			win	won	won
sow	sowed	sown, sowed	wind	wound	wound
			wring	wrung	wrung
	poke	spoken	write	wrote	written

404

LOS NÚMEROS

un, uno(a)/primer, primero(a)	1
dos/segundo(a)	2
tres/tercer, tercero(a)	3
cuatro/cuarto(a)	4
cinco/quinto(a)	5
seis/sexto(a)	6
siete/séptimo(a)	7
ocho/octavo(a)	8
nueve/noveno(a)	9
diez/décimo(a)	10
once/undécimo(a)	11
doce/duodécimo(a)	12
trece/decimotercio(a)	13
catorce/decimocuarto(a)	14
quince/decimoquinto(a)	15
dieciséis/decimosexto(a)	16
diecisiete/decimoséptimo(a)	17
dieciocho/decimooctavo(a)	18
diecinueve/decimonoveno(a)	19
veinte/vigésimo(a)	20
veintiuno	21
veintidós	22
treinta	30
treinta y uno(a)	31
treinta y dos	32
cuarenta	40
cuarenta y uno(a)	41
cincuenta	50
cincuenta y uno(a)	51
sesenta	60
sesenta y uno(a)	61
setenta	70
setenta y uno(a)	71
setenta y dos	72
ochenta	80
ochenta y uno(a)	81
noventa	90
noventa y uno(a)	91
cien, ciento/centésimo(a)	100
ciento uno(a)	101
doscientos(as)	200
doscientos(as) uno(a)	201
trescientos(as)	300
trescientos(as) uno(a)	301
quatrocientos(as)	400
quinientos(as)	500
seiscientos(as)	600
setecientos(as)	700
ochocientos(as)	800
novecientos(as)	900

NUMBERS

one/first	
two/second	
three/third	
four/fourth	
five/fifth	
six/sixth	
seven/seventh	
eight/eighth	
nine/ninth	
ten/tenth	
eleven/eleventh	
twelve/twelfth	
thirteen/thirteenth	
fourteen/fourteenth	
fifteen/fifteenth	
sixteen/sixteenth	
seventeen/seventeenth	
eighteen/eighteenth	
nineteen/nineteenth	
twenty/twentieth	
twenty-one	
twenty-two	
thirty	
thirty-one	
thirty-two	
forty	
forty-one	
fifty	
fifty-one	
sixty	
sixty-one	
seventy	
seventy-one	
seventy-two	
eighty	
eighty-one	
ninety	
ninety-one	
a hundred, one hundred/hundredth	
a hundred and one	
two hundred	
two hundred and one	
three hundred	
three hundred and one	
four hundred	
five hundred	
six hundred	
seven hundred	
eight hundred	
nine hundred	

...simo(a)	1000	a thousand, one thousand/thousandth
...dos	1002	a thousand and two
cinco mil	5000	five thousand
un millón	1,000,000	a million, one million

Ejemplos	Examples
va a llegar el 7 (de mayo)	he's arriving on the 7th (of May)
vive en el número 7	he lives at number 7
el capítulo/la página 7	chapter/page 7
llegó séptimo	he came in 7th
1º (1ª), 2º (2ª), 3º (3ª), 4º (4ª), 5º (5ª)	1st, 2nd, 3rd, 4th, 5th

N.B. In Spanish the ordinal numbers from 1 to 10 are commonly used; from 11 to 20 rather less; above 21 they are rarely written and almost never heard in speech. The custom is to replace the forms for 21 and above by the cardinal number.

LA HORA

THE TIME

¿qué hora es?	*what time is it?*
es/son	*it's o it is*
¿a qué hora?	*(at) what time?*
a	*at*
medianoche, las doce (de la noche)	midnight
la una (de la madrugada)	one (o'clock) (a.m. *o* in the morning), 1 a.m.
la una y diez	ten past one
la una y cuarto *or* quince	a quarter past one, one fifteen
la una y media *or* treinta	half past one, one thirty
las dos menos cuarto, la una cuarenta y cinco	a quarter to two, one forty-five
la dos menos diez, la una cincuenta	ten to two, one fifty
mediodía, las doce (de la tarde)	twelve (o'clock), midday, noon
la una (de la tarde), las trece (horas)	one (o'clock) (p.m. *o* in the afternoon)
las siete (de la tarde), las diecinueve (horas)	seven (o'clock) (p.m. *o* at night)
...nueve y media (de la noche), ...intiuna (horas) y media	nine thirty (p.m. *o* at night)

406